Lawrence H. Hammer
Oklahoma State University

William K. Carter
University of Virginia

Milton F. Usry
University of West Florida

Cost Accounting

11TH EDITION

COLLEGE DIVISION South-Western Publishing Co.
Cincinnati Ohio

Sponsoring Editor: David L. Shaut
Developmental Editor: Mary H. Draper
Production Editor: Peggy A. Williams
Production House: Gex, Inc.
Cover Designer: Michael Lindsay/Hulefeld Assoc., Inc.
Cover Photographer: Michael Wilson
Interior Designer: Lesiak/Crampton Design
Marketing Manager: Sharon C. Oblinger

AE88KA

Library of Congress Cataloging-in-Publication Data

Hammer, Lawrence H.
Cost accounting / Lawrence H. Hammer, William K. Carter, Milton F. Usry. — 11th ed.
p. cm.
Usry's name appears first in the earlier edition.
Includes bibliographical references and index.
ISBN 0-538-82807-2
1. Cost accounting. I. Carter, William K. II. Usry, Milton F. III. Title.
HF5686.C8M344 1993
657'.42—dc20 93-11101
CIP

1 2 3 4 5 6 7 8 9 K 1 0 9 8 7 6 5 4 3

Printed in the United States of America

I(T)P

International Thomson Publishing
South-Western Publishing Co. is an ITP Company. The ITP trademark is used under license.

This book is printed on acid-free paper that meets Environmental Protection Agency standards for recycled paper.

Preface

In the past decade, globalization of business, increased competition, and new manufacturing technologies forced many companies to reevaluate their business practices. This process led to changes in management philosophy and to alterations in business systems, which in turn made it necessary for accountants to reevaluate the usefulness of information provided to management by the accounting system. Accounting systems created primarily to provide information for external reporting or created at a time when manufacturing technologies and systems were essentially labor driven do not provide the information necessary to plan and control these new business systems. In some cases the information provided by obsolete accounting systems is useless; in others it is dangerously misleading.

To provide the kind of information needed by management, accountants began to redesign accounting systems. Different kinds of data are needed for different kinds of decisions, and different kinds of business systems require different kinds of accounting systems to provide that data. As business systems change over time, accounting systems must be reevaluated. Depending on the nature and magnitude of changes in the business systems, accounting systems may need to be changed. Recognition of these relationships leads to the development and implementation of new measurement systems, such as quality costing, activity based costing, and backflush costing, as well as to increased reporting of nonfinancial performance measures.

The eleventh edition of *Cost Accounting* emphasizes the belief that accounting information should be useful in planning and controlling the company's business systems. To be effective in this mission, the accounting system must be tailored to the unique nature of the business systems employed by the company. Since the nature of the goods and services produced by different companies vary substantially, the business systems required to produce and market such a variety vary as well. Because of these differences, there is no one accounting system or alternative that is superior to all others in all situations. The most economical and efficient accounting system or alternative depends on the business system and the information needs of management. To adequately prepare the student, this textbook not only demonstrates the mechanics of alternative accounting systems and techniques but also explains the logic behind the different alternatives. The objective is to help the student learn to look at the business system first and then to design an accounting system that can collect and generate the kind of information that is needed.

This textbook is designed to provide the necessary background for those who prepare accounting information and for those who use such information. Not only is the system of collecting, organizing, processing, and reporting economic data presented, but the use of accounting information in decision making is presented as well. This dual emphasis stems from a belief that (1) the accountant must understand how the user will use the information in order to design an accounting system that will collect and report the kind of information needed and (2) the user of accounting information must understand how the accounting system works in order to most efficiently use the information reported by it.

Highlights of Changes in the Eleventh Edition

The textbook has undergone significant reorganization and expansion to incorporate and expand on new concepts and practices in cost/managerial accounting. As with the preceding edition, considerable effort has been made to enhance clarity and thoroughness of the coverage throughout. The most noticeable changes from the tenth edition follow:

1. The discussion of spoilage and rework has been removed from the job order and process costing chapters (new Chapters 5 and 6). Production losses in both kinds of costing systems are now presented in a separate chapter (new Chapter 7) that discusses such production losses in light of total quality management (TQM) and the need for continuous improvement. This change was made for two reasons. First, removing spoilage and rework from the job order and process cost chapters simplifies the presentation. This makes it possible for the student to concentrate on understanding and mastering the fundamentals of these two costing systems without the distraction of learning how to handle the cost of spoilage and rework at the same time. Second, pooling the accounting treatment of spoilage and rework in the same chapter provides an ideal opportunity to introduce the concept of TQM and emphasize the importance of measuring the cost of quality.
2. The materials chapters have been substantially reorganized and revised. Accounting for materials procurement and planning materials requirements are now presented in the first materials chapter (new Chapter 9). The second materials chapter presents an expanded discussion of just-in-time inventory (JIT) and backflush costing (new Chapter 10). Although this topic was discussed in the 10th edition, it has been expanded to a full chapter in the 11th edition because of the increasing importance and use of JIT in manufacturing.
3. A new chapter has been added that discusses activity based costing (ABC) and activity based management (ABM) in depth (new Chapter 14). As was the case with the new chapter on JIT, the coverage has expanded to a full chapter in the 11th edition because of the increasing importance, interest, and use of ABC in manufacturing.
4. The chapter covering cost behavior analysis (Chapter 12 in the tenth edition) is now Chapter 3. This material was moved to the beginning of the book because a firm understanding of how costs are affected when business activity changes is required in order to effectively cost products or services, to plan costs, and to control costs.
5. Responsibility accounting and reporting is now presented along with flexible budgeting in a completely rewritten chapter that follows the budgeting chapters and precedes the standard cost chapters (new Chapter 17). Chapter 17 discusses the traditional view of responsibility accounting and reporting, including the preparation of flexible budgets and variance reports, and then presents an analysis of dysfunctional behavior

attributable to the misuse of such systems and to limitations on the usefulness of control data reported to managers by such systems.

6. The discussion of capital budgeting (Chapter 22 in the tenth edition) is presented in two chapters in the eleventh edition (new Chapters 22 and 23). New Chapter 22 discusses planning and controlling capital expenditures, with an expanded discussion and illustration of the process of estimating cash flows. New Chapter 23 presents the techniques used to evaluate the economic viability of capital projects.

Organization of the Book

The organization of the materials presented is designed to provide maximum flexibility in meeting different course objectives. Part One presents material that forms a foundation for understanding the basic concepts and objectives of cost/managerial accounting systems. It thoroughly discusses the cost concept, cost objects, classifications of cost, and cost behavior. Part Two then discusses and illustrates the flow of cost in manufacturing and services businesses. It begins with a general explanation of the flow of costs through the accounts and then expands into an in-depth discussion of the two basic costing systems: job order costing and process costing. Part Two includes the cost of quality, accounting for production losses, and joint- and by-product costing. Part Three focuses on an in-depth understanding of the elements of cost, materials, labor and overhead, from both the planning and control perspectives.

Part Four elaborates on the heart of planning and control: static and flexible budgeting, responsibility accounting and reporting, and standard costing. And Part Five, the final section, covers the entire spectrum of analysis of costs and profits, including direct costing, cost-volume-profit analysis, differential cost analysis, capital expenditure planning and analysis, decision making under uncertainty, marketing cost and profitability analysis, profit performance measurements, and transfer pricing.

Organization for Instruction

The presentation of the fundamental theoretical and practical aspects of cost accounting provides wide flexibility for classroom usage. In addition to its applicability to the traditional two-semester course sequence, this textbook may be used in a variety of one-semester courses. For these alternative courses, a suggested outline, by chapter numbers, follows:

Course Description	Textbook Chapters
Cost Accounting (two-semester course)	Chapters 1-14 (first semester) Chapters 15-26 (second semester)
Cost Accounting (one-semester course)	Chapters 1-14 and 17
Cost Control (one-semester course)	Chapters 1-4, 9-14, and 17-19
Budgetary Control (one-semester course)	Chapters 1-4, 15-19, and 22-23
Cost Analysis (one-semester course)	Chapters 14-26

End of Chapter Materials

Many of the end-of-chapter materials are new or revised and include discussion question, exercises, problems, and cases. For each topic, these materials afford coverage of relevant concepts and techniques at progressive levels in the learning process, thereby providing a significant student-learning benefit. Selected exercises and problems with which the template diskette may be used are designated by symbols in the margin. The end-of-chapter materials include numerous items from the examinations administered by the America Institute of Certified Public Accountants (AICPA adapted), the Institute of Management Accounting (ICMA adapted), the Institute of Internal Auditors (CIA adapted), the Canadian Institute of Chartered Accountants (CICA adapted), the Certified General Accountants' Association of Canada (CGA-Canada Adapted), and the Society of Management Accountants of Canada (SMAC adapted).

Learning and Teaching Aids that Accompany the Book

For the Instructor

Solutions Manual. This manual contains detailed solutions to the end-of-chapter materials, including the discussion questions, exercises, problems, and cases. Items with which the template diskette may be used are designated by symbols in the margin. In addition, a listing of items coded for use with the template diskette is provided.

Instructor's Manual. The manual contains a Summary section, which gives an abbreviated restatement of the contents of each chapter; and a Discussion section, which gives additional material for use in responding to students' questions and in clarifying some of the more difficult points in a chapter. In addition, a schedule of concepts covered by the exercises and problems, and a schedule of estimated time requirements for solving problems are included. Also included in the Instructor's Manual are transparency masters of selected illustrations from the textbook.

Solutions Transparencies. Transparencies of solutions to all exercises, problems, and cases are available to the instructor.

Test Bank, prepared by Edward J. VanDerbeck of Xavier University, Cincinnati. A test bank of multiple choice questions and examination problems accompanied by solutions is available in both printed and microcomputer (MicroExam 4.0) versions. The Test Bank is designed to save time in preparing and grading periodic and final examinations.

Spreadsheet Applications. These template diskettes are used with Lotus 1-2-3®[1] for solving selected end-of-chapter exercises and problems identified in the textbook with the symbol in the margin. The diskettes, which also provide a Lotus 1-2-3 tutorial, are provided free of charge to instructors at educational institutions who adopt this text.

Decision Tools. The Decision Tools software is a set of programs, for use with MS-DOS computers, which assist the student in solving dozens of problems from the text. The purpose of this software is to aid the instructor in changing the focus of text problems and cases from computation to "what if" analysis. The software helps the student analyze the solution (graphically with some of the tools) and easily change the problem parameters in order to see the effect of changes.

[1] Lotus and 1-2-3 are registered trademarks of the Lotus Development Corporation. Any reference to Lotus or 1-2-3 refers to this footnote.

Decision Tools software also contains a "pop-up" word processor and calculator for writing up cases, as well as context-sensitive help screens and mouse support.

For the Student

Study Guide, prepared by Edward J. VanDerbeck. This study guide contains a brief summary of each chapter, as well as questions and exercises with answers, thus providing students with immediate feedback on their comprehension of material.

Practice Cases, prepared by William K. Carter. Four cases—a job order case, a process cost case, a standard cost analysis case, and a budgeting case—are available. Each case acquaints students with basic procedural and analytical characteristics without involving time-consuming details. Notes and solutions for the four cases are provided for the instructor.

Electronic Spreadsheet Applications for Cost Accounting, third edition, by Gaylord N. Smith of Albion College. This supplemental text-workbook with template diskettes includes accounting applications and a Lotus 1-2-3® tutorial. It requires approximately 20-25 hours for completion and is available in IBM and Macintosh[2] (Excel) versions.

Acknowledgements

The authors wish to express appreciation to the many users of the previous editions who offered helpful suggestions. Thanks are given to the students and teachers of the University of West Florida, Oklahoma State University, and the University of Virginia who class-tested new materials and made suggestions for improvements. We wish to also thank the following accounting educators who served as reviewers and provided many helpful suggestions and insights:

John A. Beegle
Western Carolina University

Dale A. Davis
University of Michigan — Flint

Margaret L. Gagne
University of Colorado at Colorado Springs

Mark J. Madan
The College of Staten Island

Otto B. Martinson
Old Dominion University

Gail Pastoria
Youngstown State University

Donald J. Rouk
Georgia College

[2] Macintosh is a trademark of Macintosh Laboratory, Inc., and is used by Apple Computer, Inc., with its express permission. Any reference to Macintosh refers to this footnote.

John L. Stancil
Cumberland College

Helen M. Traugh
University of Alabama at Birmingham

We would also like to thank Ellen Mills, Katherine Longbotham, Pamela Anglin, Navarro College; and Dale Davis, University of Michigan—Flint, for their reviews of the answers in the solutions manual, test bank, and practice cases.

Finally, we wish to express our appreciation to our wives, Jane Nickelson Hammer, Imelda Smith Carter, and Dona White Usry for their patience, assistance, and encouragement in the preparation and completion of this as well as earlier editions.

Lawrence H. Hammer
William K. Carter
Milton F. Usry

About the Authors

Lawrence H. Hammer teachers primarily in the areas of cost accounting and income taxation at Oklahoma State University. He earned his BS from Sam Houston State University, MBA from North Texas State University, and DBA from Indiana University, and he is a CPA.

Dr. Hammer is widely published in the tax literature, and he has served on the editorial review boards of *The Accounting Review* and *The Journal of Accounting Education.* He is a member of the American Accounting Association Management Accounting Section, the American Taxation Association, the American Institute of CPAs, and the National Association of Accountants.

William K. Carter teaches cost accounting and managerial accounting at the graduate and undergraduate levels in the McIntire School of Commerce, University of Virginia. He earned BS and MS degrees in accounting from the University of Southern Mississippi and a PhD from Oklahoma State University, and he is a CPA. He has written articles on accounting, accounting education, marketing, and finance, which have appeared in a variety of journals including *The Accounting Review* and the *Journal of Accountancy.* He has published cases on cost accounting and on business policy.

Dr. Carter has served on committees of the American Assembly of Collegiate Schools of Business and the American Accounting Association, and on the editorial boards of *The Journal of Accounting Education* and the Education Section of *The Accounting Review.* He has testified as an expert witness in litigation involving accounting matters and has conducted consulting engagements and executive development programs for clients that include IBM, Babcock & Wilcox, the Institute of Chartered Financial Analysts, the Consumer Bankers Association, and the Administrators of Accounting Programs Group of the American Accounting Association.

Dr. Carter is a member of the National Association of Accountants, the American Institute of CPAs, and the American Accounting Association Management Accounting Section.

Milton F. Usry is the Mary Ball Washington Professor of Accountancy at the University of West Florida after previously serving on the Oklahoma State University faculty (1961-1986). He earned his BBA from Baylor University, MBA from the University of Houston, PhD from the University of Texas at Austin, and is a CPA. He has written numerous articles, especially in the areas of cost accounting and accounting education, and has served on the editorial boards of several national professional journals.

Dr. Usry received the Oklahoma State University College of Business Administration Outstanding Teacher Award on three occasions. He has served in numerous professional organizations, including the American Accounting Association, the American Institute of CPAs, and the Institute of Management Accountants.

In the area of professional certification, Dr. Usry has been a member of the AICPA Board of Examiners and the Institute of Certified Management Accountants Board of Regents. In the field government service, he has served on the National Board of the Fund for the Improvement of Postsecondary Education of the U.S. Department of Education. In the private sector, he currently serves as chairman of the Baptist Health Care Board of Directors, Pensacola, Florida.

Contents in Brief

Contents

Part 1 Costs: Concepts and Objectives 1

PART 1

Costs: Concepts and Objectives

CHAPTER 1

Management, the Controller, and Cost Accounting

Learning Objectives

After studying this chapter, you will be able to:

1. Model the management process as three interrelated activities: planning, organizing, and control.
2. Identify and distinguish three kinds of plans: short-range, long-range, and strategic.
3. Identify and differentiate the tasks in which management is aided by information about costs and benefits.
4. Identify which of the management accountant's ethical responsibilities apply to a particular ethical issue.
5. State the role of the pronouncements of the Cost Accounting Standards Board.

This chapter describes the environment of cost accounting from internal and external perspectives. Within the organization, cost accounting is presented as part of the management function, and the roles of the controller and cost department are discussed. In the external environment, the certification movement, ethical expectations, and other private and governmental influences on cost accounting are examined.

Management

Management is composed of three groups: (1) operating management, consisting of supervisors; (2) middle management, represented by department heads, division managers, and branch managers; and (3) executive management, consisting of the president, executive vice-presidents, and executives in charge of marketing, purchasing, engineering, manufacturing, finance, and accounting.

Management consists of many activities, including making decisions, giving orders, establishing policies, providing work and rewards, and hiring people to carry out policies. Management sets objectives to be achieved by integrating its knowledge and skills with the abilities of the employees. To be successful, management must effectively perform the basic functions of planning, organizing, and control. All three functions require participation by all management levels.

Planning and control are divided for theoretical purposes, just as time frames are divided into discrete operating periods. However, these divisions are artificially designed for the convenience of analysis and do not reflect the dynamic way in which an entity evolves. In reality, planning and control are simultaneous, inseparable, and interwoven processes. Time frames such as short- and long-range periods are not clearly distinguishable. Control of an activity takes place simultaneously with the planning for the next cycle of that same activity, and simultaneously with the planning and control of other activities. Plans are made for the immediate future and for the long term, controlled action takes place, feedback from operations is obtained, and plans are adjusted, all in a continuum.[1]

Planning

Planning, the construction of a detailed operating program, is the process of sensing external opportunities and threats, determining desirable objectives, and employing resources to accomplish these objectives. Planning investigates the nature of the company's business, its major policies, and the timing of major action steps. Effective planning is based on analyses of facts and requires reflective thinking, imagination, and foresight.

An example of routine planning is the estimation of daily cash balances for a 30-day period, with plans made to buy or sell short-term investments on certain days so that the organization's cash balance stays within a desired range. This kind of planning is so routine that the personnel involved are not likely to see that their work involves decisions of any kind; the decisions are all "programmed." Examples of nonroutine planning include executive management's responses to the sudden appearance of a new competitor, a new or proposed government regulation of the industry, or a significant change in customer tastes. This kind of planning involves so many unique, complex decisions that it defies any attempt to reduce all the relevant variables and the relationships among them into a "programmable" task.

Effective planning requires participation and coordination of the engineering, manufacturing, marketing, research, finance, and accounting functions. No group should plan or act independently from others. Failure to recognize this fundamental principle can cause unnecessary planning difficulties and even financial disaster for the organization.

Planning includes determining company objectives, which are measurable targets or results. In stating the objectives of a business, many people first think of profit. Although profit is indispensable in a successful business, it is a limited concept and cannot be the sole objective. The companies best able to maximize profits are those that produce goods or services at an excellent level of quality and value, in a volume, at a time, at a cost, and at a price that will win the cooperation of employees, gain the goodwill of customers, and meet social responsibilities.

Three kinds of plans are identifiable in business entities. **Strategic plans** are formulated at the highest levels of management, take the broadest view of the company and its environment, are the least quantifiable, and are formulated at irregular intervals by an essentially unsystematic process that begins with identifying an external threat or opportunity. Strategic planning decisions determine the future nature of the firm, its products, and its customers, and they have the potential to alter the external environment.

Short-range plans, often called budgets, are sufficiently detailed to permit preparation of budgeted financial statements for the entity as of a future date (typically the end of the budget period). These plans are prepared through a systematized process, are highly quantified, are expressed in financial terms, focus mainly on the organization itself by taking the external environment as a given, and usually are prepared for periods of a month, quarter, or year.

[1] *Management Accounting Guidelines, No. 3*, "Framework for Internal Control (exposure draft)" (Hamilton, Ontario: Society of Management Accountants of Canada, 1984).

In addition to these two kinds of plans are the long-range plans prepared by some entities. **Long-range plans**, or long-range budgets, typically extend three to five years into the future. In terms of their degree of detail and quantifiability, long-range plans are an intermediate step between short-range plans and strategic plans. For example, a long-range plan may culminate in a highly summarized set of financial statements or other quantified objectives such as targeted financial ratios (e.g., earnings per share) as of a date five years in the future. As a long-range plan is revised and refined during the early portions of the planning period, it serves as a starting point for successive sets of short-range plans.

Organizing

Organizing is the establishment of the framework within which activities are to be performed. The terms *organize* and *organization* refer to the systematization of interdependent parts into one unit. Organizing requires bringing the many functional units of an enterprise into a coordinated structure and assigning authority and responsibility to individuals. Organizing efforts include motivating people to work together for the good of the company. Because of the different attitudes and ambitions of people, organizational structure is developed through instruction, experimentation, and patience.

Organization involves the establishment of functional divisions, departments, sections, or branches. These units are created to permit specialization of labor. A manufacturing firm, for example, usually consists of three fundamental units: manufacturing, marketing, and administration. Within these units, departments are formed according to the nature, location, and amount of work, the degree of specialization, and the number of employees.

Management assigns work to each organizational unit created. An effective division of work among employees is vital in attaining company objectives. Also important are the relationships among managers and between superiors and subordinates.

Control

Control is management's systematic effort to achieve objectives by comparing performance to plans and taking appropriate action to correct important differences. Activities are continually monitored to see that results stay within desired boundaries. Actual results of each activity are compared with plans, and if significant differences are noted, remedial actions may be taken. Figure 1-1 illustrates the control process.

The concept of control in business differs from that used in engineering, where controls are designed to work continuously, to use physical measures as their information inputs, and to work largely independently of human decision making. Thermostats and fuses are simple examples of engineering controls. In contrast, the control process in business always includes a human decision maker. In addition, the information on which control actions are based includes financial information, and the control activity is periodic rather than continuous.

The concept of control in business also differs from that used in military and police work, in which the need for coercive force is always possible, although undesirable, in achieving control. In business, control is achieved through others' actions only with their cooperation.

FIGURE 1-1 *Control Diagram*

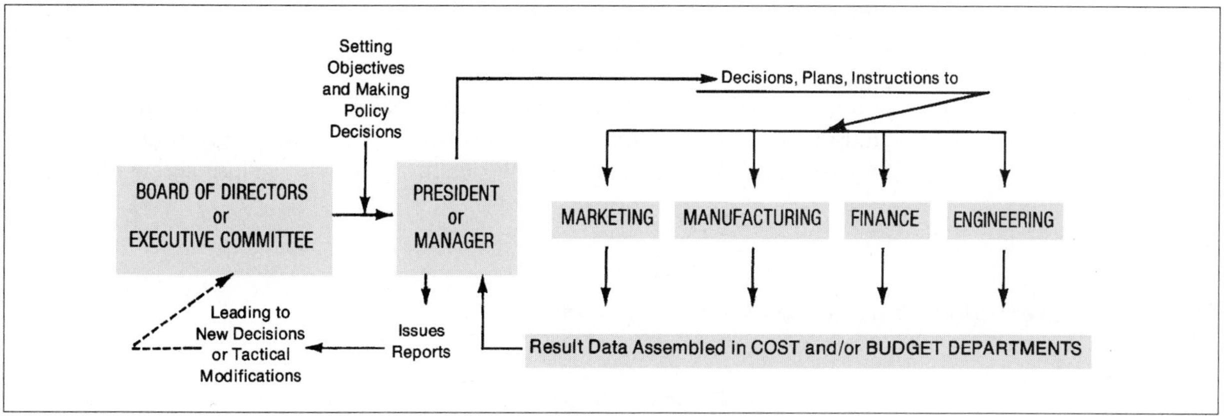

Authority, Responsibility, and Accountability

In a small firm, planning and control are performed by a single person, usually the owner or general manager intimately familiar with the firm's products, processes, financing, and customers. In a large company with many organizational units and a variety of products or services, planning and control are larger tasks. Large firms assign planning and control functions to many people, so that reports and corrective actions will not be too far removed from the activity being controlled.

Authority is the power to direct others to perform or not perform activities. Authority is the key to the managerial job and the basis for responsibility. It is the force that binds the organization together.

Authority originates with executive management, which delegates it to lower levels. Delegation is essential to organizational structure. Through delegation, the chief executive's area of influence is extended, but the chief executive remains responsible for delegated functions because delegation does not mean release from responsibility.

Responsibility, or obligation, is closely related to authority. It originates principally in the superior–subordinate relationship in that the superior has the authority to require specific work from others. If subordinates accept the obligation to perform, they create their own responsibility. The superior still is ultimately responsible for subordinates' performance.

Another facet of responsibility is **accountability**—reporting results to higher authority. Reporting is important because it enables measurement of the extent to which objectives are reached.

Usually accountability is imposed on an individual rather than a group. This principle of individual accountability is well established in both profit and nonprofit organizations. If the organizational structure permits pooling of judgment, responsibility is diffused and accountability nullified.

The Organization Chart

An **organization chart** shows an entity's principal management positions, helps to define authority, responsibility, and accountability, and is essential in developing a cost accounting system capable of reporting the responsibilities of individuals. The coordinated development of a company's organization with the cost and budgetary system leads to an approach to accounting and reporting called **responsibility accounting**.

Most organization charts are based on the line-staff concept. The assumption of this concept is that all positions or functional units can be categorized into two groups: the line, which makes decisions, and the staff, which gives advice and performs technical functions. A line-staff organization chart is illustrated in Figure 1-2.

FIGURE 1-2 ***Organization Chart Based on Line-Staff Concept***

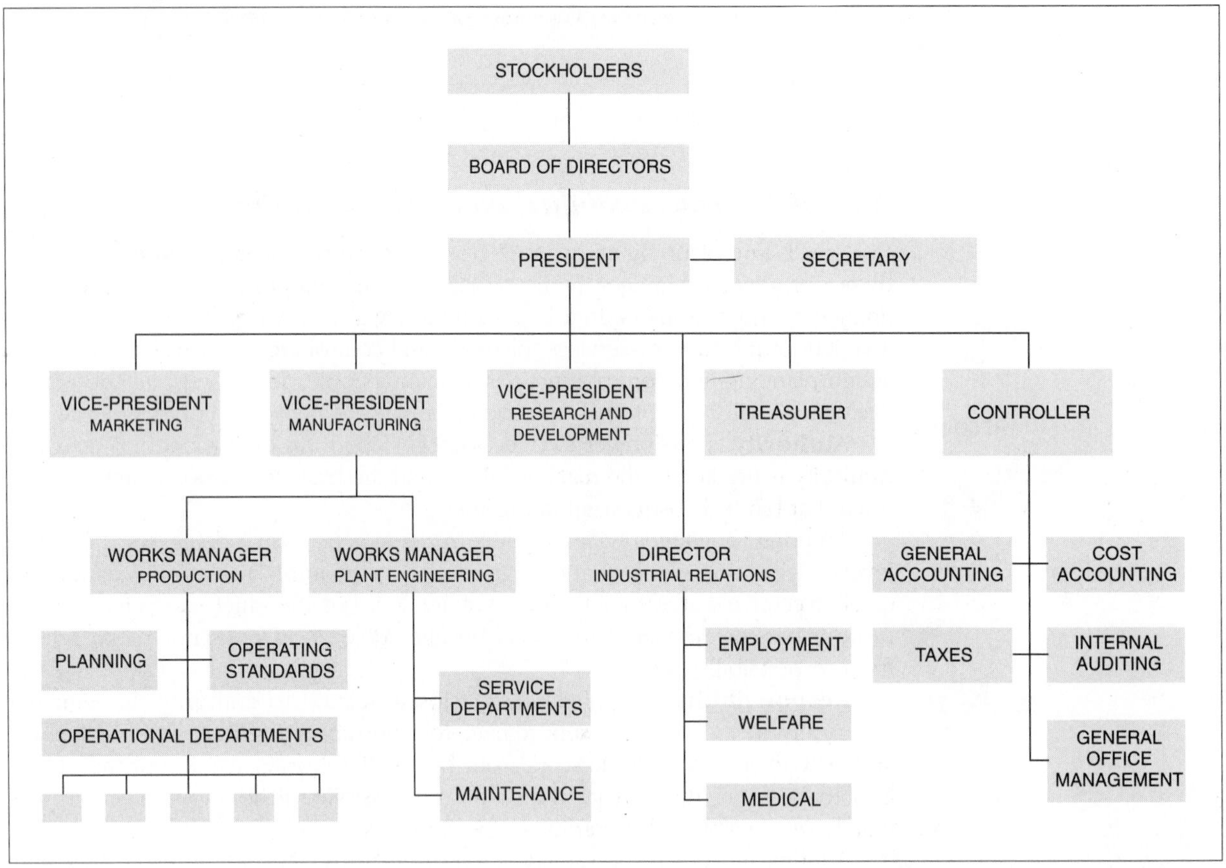

Another type of organization chart is based on the functional-teamwork concept of management, which emphasizes the most important functions of an enterprise: resources, processes, and human interrelations. The resources function involves the acquisition, disposal, and prudent management of a wide variety of resources—tangible and intangible, human and physical. The processes function deals with activities such as product design, research and development, purchasing, manufacturing, advertising, marketing, and billing. The human interrelations function directs the company's efforts concerning the behavior of people inside and outside the company. A functional-teamwork organization chart is illustrated in Figure 1-3.

FIGURE 1-3 *Organization Chart Based on Functional-Teamwork Concept*

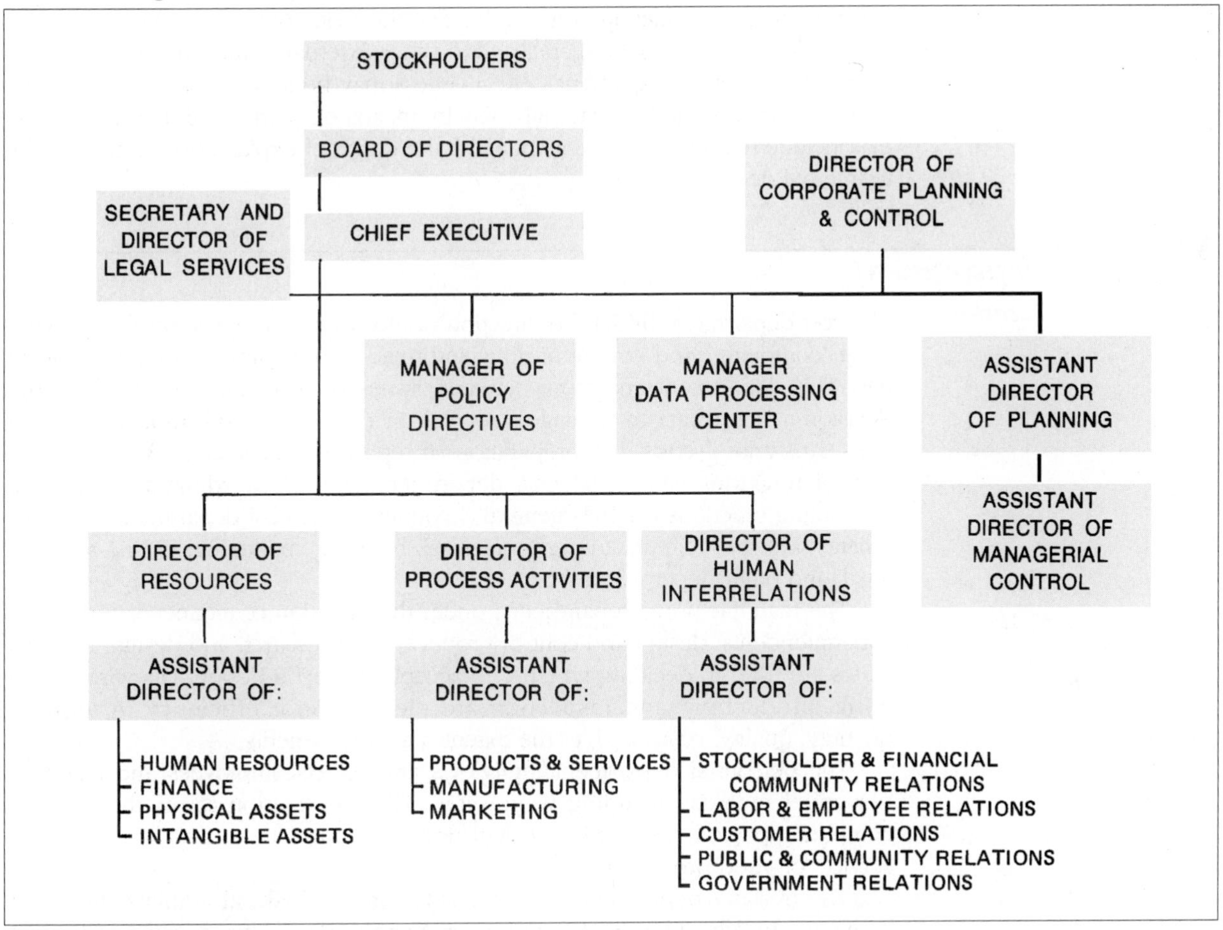

The Controller's Participation in Planning and Control

The **controller** is the executive manager responsible for the accounting function. The controller coordinates management's participation in planning and controlling the attainment of objectives, in determining the effectiveness of policies, and in creating organizational structures and processes. The controller also is responsible for observing methods of planning and control throughout the enterprise and for proposing improvements in them.

Effective control depends on communicating information to management. By issuing performance reports, the controller advises other managers of activities requiring corrective action. These reports emphasize deviations from a predetermined plan, following the principle of management by exception.[2]

Using the accounting system and other systems, the controller provides information for planning a company's future and for controlling its activities. This informa-

[2] The principle of management by exception is a belief that managers should be provided with information that directs their attention to activities that require corrective action. The concept is premised on the belief that managers do not have enough time to review every action of every subordinate nor to consult with each subordinate prior to each action.

tion includes the basic financial statements. The controller also gathers, compiles, and communicates much information beyond the scope of financial statements.

Investors, government agencies, and other external parties also receive information by which management's effectiveness may be judged. This information is usually communicated to external users by means of quarterly and annual reports that include financial statements but lack the depth of explanatory detail available to internal decision makers.

The Cost Department

The cost department, under the direction of the controller, is responsible for gathering, compiling, and communicating information regarding a company's activities. This department analyzes costs and issues performance reports and other decision-making data to managers for use in controlling and improving operations. Analysis of costs and preparation of reports are facilitated by proper division of functions within the cost department and by coordination with other accounting functions, such as general accounting. The cost department also coordinates with the manufacturing, personnel, treasury, marketing, public relations, legal, and other departments.

The manufacturing departments, under the direction of engineers and factory superintendents, design and control production. In research and design, cost estimates are used in deciding whether to accept or reject a design. Likewise, scheduling, production, and inspection are measured for efficiency in terms of quantity, quality, costs, and, to the extent practical, benefits.

The personnel department interviews and selects employees and maintains personnel records, including wage rates. This information forms the basis for computing payroll costs and for calculating the labor-related costs of any activity, service, or good produced.

The treasury department is responsible for the financial administration of a company. In scheduling cash requirements and expectations, it relies on budgets and related reports from the cost department.

The marketing department needs a quality product at a competitive price in order to attract customers. Although prices should not be set merely by adding a predetermined percentage to cost, costs cannot be ignored. Marketing managers use cost data to determine which products are most profitable and to determine sales policies.

The public relations department has the function of maintaining good relations between the company and its public, especially its customers and stockholders. Points of friction are likely to include prices, wages, profits, and dividends. The cost department provides information for public releases concerning these areas.

The legal department uses cost information as an aid in maintaining compliance with contracts and laws, including the Equal Pay Act, union contracts, the Robinson-Patman Act, the Employee Retirement Security Act of 1974, and the income tax, social security, and unemployment compensation laws, all of which can affect costs.

The Role of Cost Accounting

In the past, cost accounting was widely regarded as the calculation of the inventory cost presented in the balance sheet and cost of goods sold figure in the income statement. This view limits the broad range of information that managers need for decision making to nothing more than the product cost data that satisfy external reporting rules (tax regulations and generally accepted accounting principles). Such a restrictive definition is inappropriate today and is certainly an inaccurate description of the uses of cost accounting information. Cost accounting furnishes management with necessary tools for planning and controlling activities, improving quality and efficiency, and making both routine and strategic decisions. The collection, presentation, and analysis of information regarding costs and benefits helps management accomplish the following tasks:

1. Creating and executing plans and budgets for operating under expected competitive and economic conditions. An important aspect of plans is their potential for motivating people to perform in a way consistent with company goals.
2. Establishing costing methods that permit control of activities, reductions of costs, and improvements of quality.
3. Controlling physical quantities of inventory, and determining the cost of each product or service produced for the purpose of pricing and for evaluating the performance of a product, department, or division.
4. Determining company costs and profit for an annual accounting period or a shorter period. This includes determining the cost of inventory and cost of goods sold according to external reporting rules.
5. Choosing among two or more short-run or long-run alternatives that might alter revenues or costs.

Notice the distinction between determining the cost of a product in task 3 and the costing of inventory for external reporting in task 4. The distinction is that the cost of a product (task 3) can be calculated for many purposes, including predicting costs and making decisions, while inventory costing for external reporting (task 4) deals with satisfying generally accepted accounting principles and tax regulations.[3] In very simple production settings, the two are often the same. For example, if all units produced in a facility are alike, any reasonable way of dividing the total cost equally among the units will suffice for both external reporting and for many decision-making purposes. Although the costs incurred in such a setting may be large and complex, the product line is extremely simple—all units are identical—and so the costing of each unit of the product is simple, too. This is the model of manufacturing that is generally assumed in economic theory.

Many actual manufacturing settings are much more complicated than the economist's model. A firm can produce a diverse product line in a single facility, where the same resources are used very differently in producing different products. In addition to a diverse product line, some settings exhibit complex cost structures, and the combination of the two makes it difficult to predict or identify the costs of producing one unit of one product. In these settings, the challenge to cost accounting is to measure the cost of all the things consumed in making a unit or lot of a product. When precision is needed in such a calculation (for example, in quoting a fiercely competitive price to a customer who needs a million units or batches), then the level of detail needed in calculating cost goes far beyond anything required by external reporting rules.

---

[3] Service businesses provide excellent examples of this distinction. Consider a walk-in medical clinic, auto oil change and lubrication shop, or hairdresser, in which all jobs are of such short duration that there are no fully or partially completed jobs on hand at the end of a business day. In such a setting, the inventory costing role in external reporting (task 4) simply does not exist, but product costs (task 3) still must be known by management to permit decisions such as which services to provide and what prices to charge.

In sum, the information needs of managers range from simple to complex, and depend on the nature of products and processes, the particular decision to be made, the competitive environment, and other factors. In contrast, the nature of inventory costing required in external reporting is constant through time unless an external reporting rule is changed. In addition, inventory costing must satisfy only the following: (1) it must be based on actual historical costs, verifiable through documented transactions; (2) it must be consistent from period to period; and (3) it must include all manufacturing costs in the cost calculated for each unit of output.

The simplest cost accounting systems can generate product cost data that satisfy external reporting rules (task 4). There is a dangerous tendency among some executives to support only the amount of cost accounting effort needed for external reporting, ignoring managers' potentially much greater needs for detailed, reliable product cost information (task 3).

Budgeting

The **budget** is the quantified, written expression of management's plans. All levels of management should be involved in creating it. A workable budget promotes coordination of personnel, clarification of policies, and crystallization of plans. It also creates greater internal harmony and unanimity of purpose among managers and workers.

In recent years, considerable attention has been given to the behavioral implications of providing managers with data required for planning and control. Budgeting plays an important role in influencing individual and group behavior at all stages of the management process, including (1) setting goals, (2) informing individuals about what they should contribute to the accomplishment of the goals, (3) motivating desirable performance, (4) evaluating performance, and (5) suggesting when corrective action should be taken. In short, accountants cannot ignore the behavioral sciences (psychology, social psychology, and sociology) because the decision-making function of accounting is essentially a behavioral function.

Managers' attitudes toward the budget depend a great deal on relationships within the management group. Guided by the company plan, with opportunities for increased compensation, greater satisfaction, and eventually promotion, the middle and lower strata of a management group can potentially achieve remarkable results. A discordant management group, unwilling to accept the budget's underlying assumptions, might perform unacceptably.

The following elements have been suggested as means for motivating personnel to aim for goals set forth in a budget.[4]

1. A compensation system that builds and maintains a clearly understood relationship between results and rewards.
2. A system for performance appraisal that employees understand with regard to their individual effectiveness and key results, their tasks and their responsibilities, their degree and span of influence in decision making, as well as the time allowed to judge their results.
3. A system of communication that allows employees to query their superiors with trust and honest communication.

[4] Paul E. Sussman, "Motivating Financial Personnel," *The Journal of Accountancy,* Vol. 141, No. 2, p. 80.

4. A system of promotion that generates and sustains employee faith in its validity and judgment.
5. A system of employee support through coaching, counseling, and career planning.
6. A system that considers not only company objectives, but also employees' skills and capacities.
7. A system that does not settle for mediocrity, but reaches for realistic and attainable standards, stressing improvement and providing an environment in which the concept of excellence can grow.

Empirical research in this field contributes to a useful understanding of the interrelationships of budgeting and human behavior. Numerous research projects have been undertaken and more are needed. Illustrating the insights that such studies provide, one research project indicated that budgetary participation and budget goal clarity had significant positive effects on managers' attitudes and performance, while excessively high goals had adverse effects. The study also found that budgetary evaluation and feedback exerted only weak effects on managers' attitudes and performance.[5] Budgeting is examined in depth in Chapters 15, 16, and 17.

Controlling Costs

The responsibility for cost control should be assigned to specific individuals who are also accountable for budgeting the costs under their control. Each manager's responsibilities should be limited to the costs that are controllable by the manager, and performance should be measured by comparing actual costs with budgeted costs. The responsibility for sales revenues and profits should be assigned to those managers as well. Systems designed to achieve these goals are called **responsibility accounting systems**.

To aid in controlling costs, the cost accountant may use predetermined cost amounts called **standard costs**. Standard costs also can be the foundation for budgets and cost reports. Standard costs are examined in Chapters 18 and 19.

One aspect of cost control that is receiving increased attention is the identification of the costs of different activities rather than the costs of different departments and products. In a complex production setting, it is often found that only a small fraction of total activity actually adds value to the final output. Other activities, called **non-value-added activities**, generally are a result of the embedded complexity of production settings and are not specific to the production of any particular good or service. Examples of non-value-added activities in a factory are retrieving, handling, and moving materials; expediting; holding inventories; and reworking defective units. Reporting the costs of non-value-added activities is a first step toward their reduction or elimination.

Pricing

Management's pricing policy ideally should assure long-run recovery of all costs and a profit, even under adverse conditions. Although supply and demand usually are determining factors in pricing, the establishment of a profitable sales price requires consideration of costs. Competitively bidding on a proposed job is

[5] Izzettin Kenis, "Effects of Budgetary Goal Characteristics on Managerial Attitudes and Performance," *The Accounting Review*, Vol. LIV, No. 4, pp. 707-721.

a difficult pricing decision if there is little or no past experience with the kind of good or service involved.

Determining Profits

Cost accounting is used to calculate the cost of the output sold during a period; this and other costs are matched with revenues to calculate profits. Costs and profits may be reported for segments of the firm or for the entire firm, depending on management's needs and external reporting requirements.

The matching process involves identifying short-run and long-run costs and variable and fixed (capacity) costs. Variable manufacturing costs are assigned first to the units manufactured and then matched with revenue when these units are sold. (Nonmanufacturing costs, both fixed and variable, typically are matched with revenues of the period.) Fixed manufacturing costs are matched with revenues by one of the following alternatives:

1. Matching total fixed costs assigned to a period with revenues of that period; this alternative is called **direct costing** or **variable costing.**
2. Matching some or all of the fixed manufacturing costs with units of product; these are then expensed as part of the income statement's cost of goods sold figure when the related units are sold. This alternative is called **absorption costing** and is required for external (tax and financial) reporting.

These alternatives give the same reported results in the long run but yield a different profit for individual short periods such as years. They are examined in more detail in Chapter 20.

Choosing Among Alternatives

Cost accounting provides information concerning the different revenues and costs that might result from alternative actions. Based on this information, management makes both short-range and long-range decisions concerning entering new markets, developing new products, discontinuing individual products or whole product lines, buying versus making a necessary component of a product, and buying versus leasing equipment. In the decisions to add new products and discontinue existing products, reliable cost information is especially crucial to the competitive success of the firm. Misstated costs create the possibility that undesirable business might be initiated or continued and desirable business rejected.

Cost Accounting and Manufacturing Technology

Factory automation, which has spread rapidly, results in capital-intensive processes, often with computerized systems that use robot-controlled machinery. Automation is expensive, however, and is not a cure-all for an obsolete production process. Many problems are rooted in systems and attitudes, and by focusing on those areas first, the firm can reap even greater gains from automation. In automating a process, employee involvement and motivation are the first step, and simplification of the existing process is second. Only then should a large investment in automation be considered. Innovative and experimental applications, including changes in systems and attitudes, now permeate business from product design to production scheduling, the manufacturing process, inventory management, quality control, and strategic decision making.

Changes in manufacturing technology have spawned a long list of new terminology, including computer-aided design (CAD), computer-aided engineering (CAE), computer-aided manufacturing (CAM), just-in-time production (JIT), computer numerical control machinery (CNC), optimized production technology (OPT), flexible manufacturing systems (FMS), and computer-integrated manufacturing (CIM). These innovations are discussed in appropriate places throughout this text.

Technology is changing the nature of costs, producing, for example, lower inventory levels, less use of labor, and increasing levels of fixed costs. In this new environment, cost accounting systems are being challenged to evolve and take on increased relevance. Reliable cost accounting information has become a competitive weapon.

Certification and Ethics

Persons engaged in cost accounting or other accounting functions within an organization are referred to as "management accountants" or "internal accountants." They may also be referred to by their professional certification, **Certified Management Accountant (CMA)**, which is a formal recognition of professional competence and educational achievement in the field.

Requirements for the CMA certificate include passing a demanding examination offered by the Institute of Certified Management Accountants and completing two years of professional experience in management accounting within seven years of passing the examination.

In 1983, the National Association of Accountants[6] (NAA) issued a code of ethics for management accountants, both CMAs and others. Although individuals practicing as independent certified public accountants have been subject to a code of conduct for many decades, these standards are the first ever issued for management accountants and may serve to increase public faith in the integrity of the business community. This code of ethics, *Standards of Ethical Conduct for Management Accountants*, is presented in Exhibit 1-1. Among codes of ethics, this one is distinct in prescribing the steps to be followed in resolving an ethical conflict.

Influence of Private and Governmental Organizations

Occasionally the research and pronouncements of professional organizations contribute to the development of cost accounting. These organizations include the Financial Accounting Standards Board (FASB), the Governmental Accounting Standards Board (GASB), the American Institute of Certified Public Accountants (AICPA), the Institute of Management Accountants (IMA), the American Accounting Association (AAA), and the Financial Executives Institute (FEI). In addition, cost accounting is influenced by university research, individuals, and private companies.

[6] Now named the Institute of Management Accountants (IMA).

EXHIBIT 1-1 ***Standards of Ethical Conduct for Management Accountants***[7]

Management accountants have an obligation to the organizations they serve, their profession, the public, and themselves to maintain the highest standards of ethical conduct. In recognition of this obligation, the National Association of Accountants has promulgated the following standards of ethical conduct for management accountants. Adherence to these standards is integral to achieving the *Objectives of Management Accounting.* Management accountants shall not commit acts contrary to these standards nor shall they condone the commission of such acts by others within their organizations.

Competence

Management accountants have a responsibility to:

- Maintain an appropriate level of professional competence by ongoing development of their knowledge and skills.
- Perform their professional duties in accordance with relevant laws, regulations, and technical standards.
- Prepare complete and clear reports and recommendations after appropriate analyses of relevant and reliable information.

Confidentiality

Management accountants have a responsibility to:

- Refrain from disclosing confidential information acquired in the course of their work except when authorized, unless legally obligated to do so.
- Inform subordinates as appropriate regarding the confidentiality of information acquired in the course of their work and monitor their activities to assure the maintenance of that confidentiality.
- Refrain from using or appearing to use confidential information acquired in the course of their work for unethical or illegal advantage either personally or through third parties.

Integrity

Management accountants have a responsibility to:

- Avoid actual or apparent conflicts of interest and advise all appropriate parties of any potential conflict.
- Refrain from engaging in any activity that would prejudice their ability to carry out their duties ethically.
- Refuse any gift, favor, or hospitality that would influence or would appear to influence their actions.
- Refrain from either actively or passively subverting the attainment of the organization's legitimate and ethical objectives.
- Recognize and communicate professional limitations or other constraints that would preclude responsible judgment or successful performance of an activity.
- Communicate unfavorable as well as favorable information and professional judgments or opinions.
- Refrain from engaging in or supporting any activity that would discredit the profession.

Objectivity

Management accountants have a responsibility to:

- Communicate information fairly and objectively.
- Disclose fully all relevant information that could reasonably be expected to influence an intended user's understanding of the reports, comments, and recommendations presented.

Resolution of Ethical Conflict

In applying the standards of ethical conduct, management accountants may encounter problems in identifying unethical behavior or in resolving an ethical conflict. When faced with significant ethical issues, management accountants should follow the established policies of the organization bearing on the resolution of such conflict. If these policies do not resolve the ethical conflict, management accountants should consider the following courses of action:

- Discuss such problems with the immediate superior except when it appears that the superior is involved, in which case the problem should be presented initially to the next higher managerial level. If satisfactory resolution cannot be achieved when the problem is initially presented, submit the issues to the next higher managerial level.

  If the immediate superior is the chief executive officer, or equivalent, the acceptable reviewing authority may be a group such as the audit committee, executive committee, board of directors, board of trustees, or owners. Contact with levels above the immediate superior should be initiated only with the superior's knowledge, assuming the superior is not involved.
- Clarify relevant concepts by confidential discussion with an objective advisor to obtain an understanding of possible courses of action.
- If the ethical conflict still exists after exhausting all levels of internal review, the management accountant may have no other recourse on significant matters than to resign from the organization and to submit an informative memorandum to an appropriate representative of the organization.

Except where legally prescribed, communication of such problems to authorities or individuals not employed or engaged by the organization is not considered appropriate.

The rapid growth of international business has led several international organizations to become involved in accounting, including cost accounting. These organizations include the International Accounting Standards Committee (IASC) and the Organization for Economic Cooperation and Development (OECD).

In the public sector, there are federal, state, and local government regulations embodied in many accounting systems. At the national level, the Internal

[7] "Standards of Ethical Conduct for Management Accountants" (New York: Institute of Management Accountants, 1989). Copyright June 1, 1983, Institute of Management Accountants (formerly National Association of Accountants). All rights reserved. Reprinted with permission.

Revenue Service (IRS) and the Cost Accounting Standards Board (CASB) have a significant influence on cost accounting.

Taxation

Federal income tax liability is determined in accordance with the Internal Revenue Code[8] as enacted and amended by Congress. The Treasury Department, acting under authority granted by Congress, issues regulations[9] which interpret the tax statutes enacted by Congress. The Internal Revenue Service, a branch of the Treasury Department, collects taxes and issues rulings and procedures as guidance to taxpayers.[10] The influence of these statutes, regulations, rulings, and procedures cannot be ignored. Similar considerations apply for state and local income taxation. Management's planning and decision making must consider tax consequences at all these levels.

Cost Accounting Standards Board

The Cost Accounting Standards Board, established by Congress in 1970, sets cost accounting standards for domestic companies that are awarded large federal contracts or subcontracts, whether civilian or defense related. In 1980 the CASB was dissolved because Congress believed the board's purpose had been accomplished; however, the board's standards became part of all major federal procurement regulations and remained in effect. Congress reestablished the board in 1988.

The CASB issues Cost Accounting Standards (CASs) that address all aspects of cost allocation that affect the cost of federal contracts, including methods of allocation, definition and measurement of costs which may be allocated, and determination of the accounting period to which costs are assignable. Full allocation of all costs of a period, including administrative expenses and all other indirect costs, is the basis for determining the cost of a contract.

Although specific CASs are discussed where appropriate in subsequent chapters, it should be noted here that four of the standards—numbers 409, 414, 416, and 417—have a potential impact far beyond the government contracting area. CAS 409 requires contractors to depreciate their assets for contract-costing purposes over lives that are based on documented historical usefulness, irrespective of the lives used for financial and tax reporting. CASs 414 and 417 recognize as a contract cost the imputed cost of capital committed to facilities, thereby overturning the government's long-standing practice of disallowing interest and other financing-type costs. CAS 416, in contrast to financial reporting and income tax rules, recognizes a cost for self-insurance; under this standard, a long-term average loss is assigned to each period regardless of the timing of actual losses.

As a condition of contracting, contractors can be required to disclose their cost accounting practices. Disclosures include the major elements of direct costs, methods used to charge materials costs (fifo, lifo, standard cost, etc.), methods of charging direct labor (actual rates, average rates, standard rates, etc.), and the allocation bases used for charging indirect costs to contracts.

---

[8] *Title 26 of the United States Code.*

[9] *Title 26 of the Code of Federal Regulations.*

[10] Revenue Rulings and Revenue Procedures are published weekly in the *Internal Revenue Bulletin* and semiannually in the *Cumulative Bulletin.*

Summary

Management can be viewed as encompassing the processes of planning, organizing, and control. The management team includes the controller, who coordinates planning and control for the firm. The cost department coordinates with other departments and plays a central role in budgeting, cost control, pricing, reporting, and choosing among alternatives.

Both professional certification and a code of ethics now exist for management accountants. These and other external constraints, including pronouncements of the Cost Accounting Standards Board, exert significant influence on cost accounting.

Key Terms

planning *(3)*
strategic plans *(3)*
short-range plans *(3)*
long-range plans *(4)*
organizing *(4)*
control *(4)*
authority *(5)*
responsibility *(5)*
accountability *(5)*
organization chart *(5)*
responsibility accounting *(6)*
controller *(7)*
budget *(10)*
responsibility accounting systems *(11)*
standard costs *(11)*
non-value-added activities *(11)*
direct costing *(12)*
variable costing *(12)*
absorption costing *(12)*
Certified Management Accountant (CMA) *(13)*

Discussion Questions

Q1-1 Define the concepts of planning and control and discuss how they relate to each other and contribute to progress toward achieving objectives.

Q1-2 Distinguish between short-range and long-range plans.

Q1-3 Distinguish between long-range plans and strategic plans.

Q1-4 Is responsibility accounting identical with the concept of accountability? Explain.

Q1-5 In what manner does the controller exercise control over the activities of other members of management?

Q1-6 Discuss the functions of the cost department.

Q1-7 Numerous nonaccounting departments require cost data and must also provide data to the cost department. Discuss.

Q1-8 Why must the controller be aware of developments in the field of communications?

Q1-9 Why is the budget an essential tool in cost planning?

Q1-10 Will the Standards of Ethical Conduct for Management Accountants prevent management fraud? Explain.

Q1-11 How are CASB standards defined and what degree of authority do they have?

Exercises

E1-1 Planning and Control. In practice, planning and control are inseparable. One example of their inseparability is the fact that the results of control activities serve as inputs for the next planning cycle. That is, a control effort or investigation may point to a flaw in planning, and the flaw is then corrected in formulating the next period's plans.

Required: Give at least two other examples showing how planning and control are inseparable.

E1-2 Planning. Identify each of the following numbered items as an example of one of the three kinds of planning by writing for each item the appropriate letter identified below:

A = an example of a short-range plan
B = an example of a long-range plan
C = an example of a strategic plan

(1) A forecast made in 1995 of total sales expected in the years 1996, 1997, and 1998
(2) The number of units of product expected to be sold in the next year
(3) A plan for discontinuing one of the two divisions of the company
(4) Estimates of quarterly net income for the remaining three quarters of the current year
(5) A plan to be the first company to establish a biomedical research lab on an orbiting space station
(6) A 1996 sinking-fund agreement calling for annual cash deposits sufficient to retire outstanding bonds that will mature in the year 2005

E1-3 Control. Each of the following paragraphs describes a kind of control:

(a) It is desired to keep water in a tank at a level of one to two inches below the brim. A water pressure line is installed in the tank with a valve to start and stop the flow, an arm attached to the valve, and a hollow plastic float on the end of the arm. Whenever the water level is two inches or more below the brim, the float drops low enough to open the valve. When the water level is one inch from the brim, the float raises the arm which closes the valve.
(b) A student desires to earn a grade average of at least 90% in a cost accounting course. On the first quiz, the student receives a grade of 80%. Upon learning of this grade, the student decides to study more earnestly and to do more homework problems before each of the remaining quizzes.
(c) A home owner has worked hard to make a lawn free of weeds and wants to keep it that way during an upcoming two-year absence. Before leaving, the home owner contracts with the local franchise of WeedChem Company for five lawn treatments per year for two years. The treatments are guaranteed to control weeds.
(d) After suffering heavy casualties in a three-day battle, friendly forces gained control of Hill 334 and captured the enemy communications post at that location.

Required:
(1) Determine which one of the four paragraphs describes a kind of control that comes closest to what control means in managing a business. Explain.
(2) Take each one of the other three paragraphs, in turn, and explain why it lacks some essential attribute or attributes of management control.

Cases

CI-1 Ethics. Adam Williams was recently hired as assistant controller of GroChem Inc., which processes chemicals for use in fertilizers. Williams was selected for this position because of his past experience in the chemical-processing field. In his first month on the job, Williams made a point of getting to know the people responsible for the plant operations and learning how things are done at GroChem.

During a conversation with the plant supervisor, Williams asked about the company procedures for handling toxic waste materials. The plant supervisor replied that he was not involved with the disposal of wastes and suggested that Williams might be wise to ignore this issue. This response strengthened Williams' determination to probe this area further, to be sure that the company was not vulnerable to litigation.

On further investigation, Williams discovered evidence that GroChem uses a nearby residential landfill to dump toxic wastes. It appears that some members of GroChem's management team are aware of this situation and may have been involved in arranging for this dumping, but Williams was unable to determine whether his superior, the controller, is involved.

GroChem does not have an established policy on how to resolve issues such as this. Uncertain how he should proceed, Williams began to consider his options by outlining the following three alternative courses of action:

(a) Seek the advice of his superior, the controller.
(b) Anonymously release the information to the local newspaper.
(c) Discuss the situation with an outside member of the Board of Directors with whom he is acquainted.

Required:
(1) In light of the fact that Williams had been hired only recently and that his job is not involved in the dumping of wastes, does he have an ethical responsibility to take

some action? Cite the Standards of Ethical Conduct for Management Accountants to support your answer.

(2) Which of the 15 responsibilities in Standards of Ethical Conduct for Management Accountants apply to Williams' situation?

(3) For each of the three alternate courses of action that Williams has outlined, explain whether or not the action is appropriate.

(4) Without prejudice to your answer to requirement 3, assume that Williams seeks the advice of his superior, the controller, and discovers that the controller is involved in dumping the toxic wastes. Identify the steps that Williams should take to resolve this situation.

(ICMA adapted)

CI-2 Ethics. The Alert Company is a closely held investment-services group that has been very successful over the past five years, consistently providing most members of the top management group with 50% bonuses. In addition, both the chief financial officer and the chief executive officer have received 100% bonuses. Alert expects this trend to continue.

Recently the top management group of Alert, which holds 35% of the outstanding common stock, learned that a major corporation is interested in acquiring Alert. Alert's management is concerned that this corporation may make an attractive offer to the other stockholders and that management will be unable to prevent the takeover. If the acquisition occurs, this executive group is uncertain about continued employment in the new corporate structure. As a consequence, the management group is considering changes to several accounting policies and practices which, while not in accordance with generally accepted accounting principles, would make the company a less attractive acquisition. The chief financial officer has told Roger Deerling, Alert's controller, to implement some of these changes. Deerling has also been informed by the chief financial officer that Alert's management does not intend to disclose these changes immediately to anyone outside the immediate top management group.

Required:

(1) Which of the 15 responsibilities in Standards of Ethical Conduct for Management Accountants apply to the chief financial officer's behavior?

(2) Which of the 15 responsibilities in Standards of Ethical Conduct for Management Accountants apply to Deerling's situation?

(3) Identify the steps Deerling should take to resolve this situation.

(4) What social and ethical responsibilities should Alert's management consider before mounting the takeover defense described above?

(ICMA adapted)

CI-3 Ethics. Allstar Brands, headquartered in Cincinnati, is a large, diversified manufacturer with plants located throughout North and South America and the Pacific Rim. The company has a strong commitment to equal opportunity employment and emphasizes this commitment in frequent communications with management and supervisory personnel. In several locations, Allstar has training programs directed at improving the skill levels of minority groups. In addition, to ensure that the corporate policy is implemented, all supervisory personnel must attend seminars on nondiscriminatory personnel practices.

Allstar's Manufacturing Accounting Department (MAD) is located at the Cincinnati headquarters. MAD not only performs the traditional functions of manufacturing accounting, but also designs nonfinancial performance measurement systems and other tools and programs to support Allstar's total quality management (TQM) philosophy. Employment in MAD is considered a management accounting career choice and can also serve as a step to a higher position in another department. Roger Dixon, MAD director, has the authority to hire all department personnel. Dixon delegates the initial screening of all job applications and some preliminary interviews to one of his senior management accountants, Peter Foxworth. Foxworth then recommends candidates to Dixon for further consideration. This arrangement has been in place for two years. Foxworth is concerned that during this time, Dixon has not hired any minority applicants, despite the fact that many were qualified. Several minority candidates recommended by Foxworth were not even interviewed by Dixon. When asked about these conditions, Dixon told Foxworth to pay attention to his own responsibilities.

Foxworth believes Dixon has intentionally discriminated against minority applicants and that Dixon's behavior must be corrected. Foxworth is uncertain how he should proceed because Allstar Brands does not have an established policy on how to resolve such issues. Foxworth is considering taking one of the three following alternative courses of action:

(a) Discuss Dixon's behavior with the director of Personnel, who is a management peer of Dixon.

(b) Informally discuss Dixon's behavior and ways to change it with a group of MAD senior management accountants.

(c) Discuss Dixon's behavior privately with the chief financial officer, Dixon's supervisor.

Required:

(1) Which of the 15 responsibilities in Standards of Ethical Conduct for Management Accountants apply to Dixon's behavior?

(2) Which of the 15 responsibilities in Standards of Ethical Conduct for Management Accountants apply to Foxworth's situation?

(3) For each of the three alternative courses of action Foxworth is considering, explain whether or not the action is appropriate.
(4) Identify the steps that Foxworth should take in attempting to resolve this situation.

(ICMA adapted)

C1-4 Ethics. Joseph Rodriquez is the controller of the Ceramics Division (CD) of Northeastern Company. Rodriquez reports directly to the CD general manager, Susan Czeisla. One of Rodriquez's responsibilities is obtaining data from all CD department managers to prepare annual budgets. The current year's budget reflects a CD sales increase of 8% over last year, compared with the usual 4% to 6% annual sales increases experienced in the past. The CD sales manager has assured Rodriquez that the 8% increase is attainable, and the CD production manager has pointed out that the plant operated at only 75% of capacity last year, so ample production capacity is available to sustain the planned sales increase.

At the end of the first quarter of the current year, CD sales were 1% below budget. Rodriquez was then instructed by Czeisla to revise the budget to reflect a 12% sales increase over last year. Rodriquez expressed surprise at this request but was assured by Czeisla that, "our salespeople can produce a 12% increase over last year, and the budget should show it that way. . . . The budget must show it that way to help us convince the bank that we'll be able to repay the loan we'll be applying for in the second quarter." With this assurance, Rodriquez revised the budget to reflect the 12% increase.

At the end of the second quarter, CD sales were 3% below the revised budget. Czeisla instructed Rodriquez to revise the budget again, this time to reflect a 14% sales increase over last year. "In preparing our application for the bank loan, we found the figures weren't coming out quite right for the loan amount we need. We'll be applying at a different bank now, and the 14% sales increase will take care of the problem with the figures. I've been assured by our salespeople that if a 14% increase is what the company needs, then they can give me 14%, so that's what we're going to do. They're team players, Joseph, and I know you'll be a team player, too."

Required:

(1) Which of the 15 responsibilities in the Standards of Ethical Conduct for Management Accountants apply to Rodriquez's situation?
(2) What might Rodriquez have done differently to avoid or mitigate this problem?
(3) In addition to his ethical responsibilities to CD, what other ethical responsibilities does Rodriquez need to consider?

C1-5 Ethics. Mary Jones is controller of the Non-Ferrous Metals Division of Southeast Manufacturing Incorporated (SMI) in Tuscaloosa, Alabama. Last year, she served as her division's representative on an SMI corporate-level task force charged with developing specific objectives and performance specifications for a new computer system that is to be purchased this year. Due to her pivotal role on that task force, she has just been named to a new SMI corporate-level committee charged with reviewing, evaluating, and ranking the 10 to 20 proposals that SMI expects to receive from computer vendors now that SMI has put the proposed system out for bids.

A single parent, Jones expects to incur over $400,000 in medical expenses resulting from treatments for her youngest child, who has contracted a potentially fatal disease. Approximately $150,000 of that amount will not be covered by insurance. Due to this personal financial situation, Jones has investigated some career opportunities that would involve higher salary and more generous insurance benefits, but no position has been offered to her. Her most recent interview was for the controller position at Crimson Systems, a supplier of large-scale computer hardware and custom-designed software.

Crimson Systems' vice-president for finance declined to offer Jones the controller position, but instead said, "We're offering you a temporary consulting engagement—Sunday afternoons for the next four months—helping us write our proposal for the SMI job; your fee will be $500 per hour."

Required:

(1) Which of the 15 responsibilities in the Standards of Ethical Conduct for Management Accountants apply to Jones' situation?
(2) What might Jones have done in her interview with Crimson Systems to precipitate this problem?
(3) What might Jones have done differently to avoid or mitigate this problem?
(4) In addition to her ethical responsibilities to SMI, what other ethical responsibilities does Jones have to consider?

CHAPTER 2

Cost Concepts and the Cost Accounting Information System

Learning Objectives

After studying this chapter, you will be able to:

1. Define the term *cost object* and give examples of cost objects relevant to different types of decisions.
2. Describe several degrees of cost traceability implied by the terms *direct cost* and *indirect cost.*
3. State the considerations involved in creating a cost accounting information system.
4. Explain why increased attention is being given to nonfinancial performance measures.
5. Name and describe the ways costs are classified.

Cost accounting was once considered to apply only to manufacturing. Today, however, every type and size of organization benefits from the use of cost accounting. For example, cost accounting is used by financial institutions, transportation companies, professional service firms, hospitals, churches, schools, colleges, universities, and governmental units, as well as the marketing and administrative activities of manufacturing firms.

Chapter 1 introduced cost accounting as part of the management function and described influences on cost accounting from internal and external environments. This chapter presents the fundamental concepts of cost accounting and introduces cost accounting as an information system.

The Cost Concept

Cost concepts have developed according to the needs of accountants, economists, and engineers. Accountants have defined cost as "an exchange price, a forgoing, a sacrifice made to secure benefit. In financial accounting, the forgoing or sacrifice at date of acquisition is represented by a current or future diminution in cash or other assets."[1]

Frequently the term *cost* is used synonymously with *expense.* However, an expense may be defined as a measured outflow of goods or services, which is matched with revenue to determine income, or as:

> . . . the decrease in net assets as a result of the use of economic services in the creation of revenues or of the imposition of taxes by governmental

[1] Robert T. Sprouse and Maurice Moonitz, *Accounting Research Study No. 3,* "A Tentative Set of Broad Accounting Principles for Business Enterprises," (New York: American Institute of Certified Public Accountants, 1962), p. 25.

> units. Expense is measured by the amount of the decrease in assets or the increase in liabilities related to the production and delivery of goods and the rendering of services . . . expense in its broadest sense includes all expired costs which are deductible from revenues.[2]

To contrast cost and expense, consider a purchase of raw materials for cash. Because net assets are unaffected, there is no expense. The firm's resources are simply converted from cash to materials. The materials are acquired at some cost, but they are not yet an expense. When the firm later sells the output into which the raw materials have been incorporated, the cost of the materials is written off among expenses on the income statement. Every expense is a cost, but not every cost is an expense; assets are costs, for example, but they are not (yet) expenses.

The term *cost* is made specific when it is modified by such descriptions as direct, prime, conversion, indirect, fixed, variable, controllable, product, period, joint, estimated, standard, sunk, or out of pocket. Each modification implies a certain attribute that is important in measuring cost. Each of these costs is recorded and accumulated when management assigns costs to inventories, prepares financial statements, plans and controls costs, makes strategic plans and decisions, chooses among alternatives, motivates personnel, and evaluates performance. The accountant involved in planning and decision making must also work with future, replacement, imputed, differential, and opportunity costs, none of which is recorded and reported in external financial statements.

Cost Objects

A **cost object**, or cost objective, is defined as any item or activity in which costs are accumulated and measured. The following items and activities can be considered cost objects:

Product	Process
Batch of like units	Department
Customer order	Division
Contract	Project
Product line	Strategic goal

The concept of a cost object is one of the most pervasive ideas in cost accounting. The selection of a cost object provides the answer to the most fundamental question about cost: The cost of what?

Because of the multiple needs in cost finding, planning, and control, cost accounting systems are multidimensional. For example, it is necessary to assign costs to each product unit, but also necessary to plan and control costs for which individual managers are assigned responsibility, on a departmental, geographical or functional basis. The design of cost accounting systems and their implementation must address these multiple requirements.

Traceability of Costs to Cost Objects

Once the cost object is selected, measurement of costs depends heavily on the **traceability** of costs to the cost object. The traceability of costs determines how objective, reliable, and meaningful the resulting cost measure will be, and there-

[2] *Ibid.*, p. 49.

fore how confident a decision maker can be in understanding and relying on the cost measure as a basis for prediction and decision making.

The traceability of costs to a cost object varies by degree. A common way of characterizing costs is to label them as either direct or indirect costs of a particular cost object, as if there were only two degrees of traceability. In fact, degrees of traceability exist along a continuum.

To illustrate the different degrees of traceability on the continuum, the cost object is defined here as a product unit. This is the most commonly used definition; for example, when the terms *direct cost* and *indirect cost* are used without a specified cost object, it is customary to assume that a single unit of product is the cost object.

At the extreme of directly traceable costs are those items that can be physically or contractually identified as components of the finished unit of product. For example, the unit can be examined, weighed, and measured to find the type and quantity of each raw material and component part incorporated in it, or royalty or patent license agreements can be read to find what fee is owed to a patent holder for permission to manufacture the unit.

Near that extreme are the costs that can be empirically traced to the unit's production by observing the production process. These include: the labor expended to convert raw materials into finished product and some material-handling labor; paper patterns and other materials that are consumed in the production of each unit but are not physically incorporated into it; and some energy costs. Of course, not all items that are physically or empirically traceable to a unit will be important enough to justify the effort required to trace and record them. Whether tracing is justified depends on how precise a measure of direct costs is needed and how difficult or costly the tracing will be. For that reason, cost accounting systems generally treat as direct costs only some of the cost items that could conceivably be traced directly to the product unit.

Beyond those cost items that are physically, contractually, or empirically traceable, some degree of arbitrariness enters any attempt to identify additional costs for a product unit. For example, the traceable material and labor costs of a small number of defective units that may be produced along with the good units could be included logically as part of the cost of the good units. But exactly how much should be included is subject to debate. Is it the average actual amount of the cost of defective units? Is it the actual amount that occurs on the next production run? Or is it the amount that would occur under ideal conditions (which may be zero)? Even when the purpose of the ultimate cost measure is known in advance, the answer to this question is not always clear.

Moving from this extreme toward the middle of the continuum, we find costs traceable to a batch or lot of like units of the product, such as setup cost (the cost of adjusting machinery before the batch can be produced). Setup cost can be identified with a single product unit in the batch only by means of an allocation: the setup costs can be divided by the actual number of units produced in a batch, or by the normal number, or by the ideal number. Again, an essentially arbitrary choice is required if these costs are to be allocated to each unit of product. Notice that if the batch is defined as the cost object, setup costs can be classified as directly traceable.

Further along on the continuum are costs traceable to all the units of a particular product ever produced. These include the costs of initial product design, development, testing, process engineering, and worker training. To identify these with a single product unit requires allocation over the total number of units of the product to be produced in the entire product life cycle. That number of units is generally difficult to predict, and even the most experienced manager in the industry would estimate it with considerable forecasting error.

Following the pattern of the continuum, the next costs are those traceable to the process used in making the product, then the costs traceable to the department in which the process is carried out, then the costs traceable to the building or plant location in which the department is located, and so on. In each of these steps, a sufficiently broad redefinition of the cost object causes the costs to be reclassified as directly traceable costs.

At the far extreme of the continuum are those costs that can be identified with a unit of product only by the most arbitrary and indefensible allocations. An example is the allocation of a small fraction of general corporate-level costs, such as income taxes and bond interest, to each unit of product produced by each department, of each plant, of each division of the corporation. The number of arithmetic steps involved in such an allocation, and the very arbitrary choices of methods used and quantities estimated at each step, make the results questionable for practically any purpose related to prediction or decision making.

Among those manufacturers who have come to view cost accounting information as a competitive weapon, and who have begun thoroughly to examine and restructure their cost accounting systems, there is a trend toward relying on traceability as the most important basis for classifying and understanding costs.

Cost Traceability in Service Industries

The traceability of costs is as important for decision making in service businesses as in manufacturing. For routine pricing decisions, bidding on jobs, and dropping or adding a service, knowing the costs of different services is of paramount importance in any competitive environment, and the traceability of costs is as fundamental in calculating the cost of a service as it is in calculating the cost of a manufactured good.

A simple and common example is found in the hotel business. Room service menus commonly include a statement such as "A $2 delivery charge will be added to each order." Why not adjust the listed prices of all items on the menu by just enough to recover delivery costs, rather than apply a separate delivery charge? The reason is that an arbitrary allocation would be required to calculate the amount of delivery cost that should be added to each item. Should it be the same for a $1 item as for a $30 item? Should it be large enough to justify delivering a single-item order? The obvious answer is that the price necessary to justify the costs of delivering an order should be applied to each order, rather than applying some fraction of it to each item.

Notice the explicit use of multiple cost objects in the room-service example. The room service menu lists each item with a separate price. In determining that price, management treats an individual unit of each item as the cost object. In determining the delivery charge to be added to each order, the order is treated as the cost object. This is a reasonable pattern of pricing because the cost of a delivery is not traceable to an item, but to the delivery of an order.[3]

[3] Do not be confused by the trivial case in which an order consists of a single item. The delivery cost of a single-item order is traceable to the item only because the item and the order are identical in that instance. In general, it is the order, of any size, that causes the delivery cost to be incurred.

The Cost Accounting Information System

Systematic, comparative cost information and analytical cost and profit data are needed so that managers can set profit goals, establish departmental targets for middle and operating management, evaluate the effectiveness of plans, pinpoint specific successes or failures, and decide on adjustments and improvements in the organization. An integrated and coordinated information system provides the information needed by managers and communicates it promptly, in a form understandable to the user. Opportunities can be missed because of poor communication.

Accounting data are accumulated in many forms, methods, and systems due to the varying types and sizes of businesses. A successful information system should be tailored to give the most efficient blend of sophistication and simplicity. Designing a cost accounting information system requires an understanding of both the organizational structure and the type of information required. The system may enhance or thwart the achievement of desired results, depending on the extent to which sound behavioral judgment is applied in developing, administering, and improving the system and in educating employees to fulfill the system's requirements.

The cost accounting information system must reflect the division of authority so that individual managers can be held accountable. The system should be designed to promote the concept of management by exception. That is, it should provide management with information that facilitates prompt identification of activities that require attention. Although the accounting records will not provide all the necessary information for effective management, the accountant who designs the system must know how employees are paid, how inventories are controlled, how equipment is costed, machine capacities, and other operating information.

The information system should focus management's attention. Some significant aspects of performance may be difficult to measure, while some easily measured but less significant factors may cause the firm to pursue or overemphasize the wrong activities. Managers should be informed of appropriate, intended uses and limitations of information.

Some requirements for record keeping and reporting are imposed on an organization by external forces. These legal, regulatory, and contractual requirements must be met by a cost-effective system. Any sophistication in a system beyond these requirements is justified solely by its value to management.

Chart of Accounts

Every profit and nonprofit organization, irrespective of its size and complexity, must maintain some type of general ledger accounting system. For such a system to function, data are collected, identified, and coded for recording in journals and posting to ledger accounts. The prerequisite for efficiently accomplishing these tasks is a well-designed **chart of accounts** for classifying costs and expenses.

In a chart of accounts, the accounts should be arranged and designated to give maximum information with a minimum of supplementary analysis. They should provide detail sufficient for costs to be identified with the responsible manager and, ideally, with the activity causing the costs.

A typical chart of accounts is divided into two parts: balance sheet accounts for assets, liabilities, and capital; and income statement accounts for sales, cost of goods sold, factory overhead, marketing expenses, administrative expenses, and other expenses and income. Account numbers are commonly used to avoid the confusion created by different spellings and abbreviations of the same account title. The use of numbers to represent accounts is the simplest form of symbolizing and is essential when electronic data processing equipment is used. A condensed chart of accounts is illustrated as follows, using simple three-digit account numbers:

BALANCE SHEET ACCOUNTS (100-299)
Current Assets (100-129)
Property, Plant, and Equipment (130-159)
Intangible Assets (170-179)
Current Liabilities (200-219)
Long-Term Liabilities (220-229)
Capital (250-299)

INCOME STATEMENT ACCOUNTS (300-899)
Sales (300-349)
Cost of Goods Sold (350-399)
Factory Overhead (400-499)
Marketing Expenses (500-599)
Administrative Expenses (600-699)
Other Expenses (700-749)
Other Income (800-849)
Income Taxes (890-899)

Electronic Data Processing

Successful management is a process of continual decision making. The decision making is more complex when a company has more than one plant, located throughout one or more countries; when product lines contain a wide array of product variations; when many reports are required by taxing authorities, regulatory agencies, employees, and stockholders; and when policies and objectives must be communicated from executive management to several levels of middle and operating management. The information system aids decision making by collecting, classifying, analyzing, and reporting data. These activities are called **data processing**, and the procedures, forms, and equipment used in the process are called the **data processing system**. Any accounting system, even a cash register in a supermarket, is a data processing system designed to provide pertinent, timely information to management.

The speed and flexibility of computers have led many businesses to convert data processing to electronic systems, replacing paper documents and ledgers with magnetic recording media. These systems can handle large amounts of routine data easily, verify their accuracy, provide summaries; automatically write checks, reports, and other documents; and maintain general and subsidiary records.

An electronic data processing system can be programmed to recognize and report any circumstances that deviate from prescribed boundaries, so that the concept of management by exception is applied. The system also greatly expands the ability of management to use mathematical models or simulations to plan operations. For example, managers can use a computer to simulate a complete operating budget and manipulate product mix, price, cost factors, and the marketing program. By studying alternative combinations of the variables, managers reduce the uncertainty in making decisions.

When electronic data processing is used, accounting procedures must be carefully programmed for the system. The programming process includes analyzing each procedure, preparing flowcharts that reduce the procedure to a logical design, and writing the detailed code of instructions for the system to follow. One inherent advantage of the extensive analysis required in programming an electronic data processing system is that possibly vague accounting procedures may become more concise and better understood in the process. The use of electronic data processing systems enables controllers and their staffs to become the nerve centers of large corporations.

Sensitivity to Changing Methods

Cost accounting systems should reflect the production methods used. Consider the examples of automation and just-in-time production. Highly automated, robotics-oriented manufacturing processes may employ little if any labor directly traceable to each unit of output; this minimizes the focus of planning and controlling direct labor and calls for methods of cost allocation that are not based on labor. The just-in-time (JIT) philosophy seeks to reduce dramatically investment in inventories, which alters accounting's traditional focus on tracking large stocks of work in process.

Management accountants have always been called on to identify, measure, accumulate, report, and interpret a wide range of useful information. The cost accounting information system has never been restricted to information that is exclusively financial (measured in dollars). For example, cost accounting reports routinely include physical measures of output produced each period and the percentage of total output that is defective, neither of which necessarily requires measurement in dollars before it is meaningful for use in planning, control, performance evaluation, and decision making. Now automation, JIT, intensified competition, and other changes in the manufacturing environment have created a need to modify and further broaden the range of information with which management accountants deal, whether such information is integrated into the accounting journals and ledgers or not. This has prompted an increase in attention to nonfinancial performance measures by many organizations.

Nonfinancial Performance Measures

Many managers have found that the usefulness of nonfinancial performance measures is not limited to performance evaluation. The reasons for the increased attention being given to these measures include:

1. Dissatisfaction with financial measures. Comprehensive financial performance measures, such as total cost or income for a product line or a division, are not always regarded as serving any particular decision-making purpose. This limited usefulness is a result of these financial measures being produced by an accounting system that serves many purposes simultaneously, including external reporting, routine planning and control of operations, planning and control of unusual or nonrecurring events and decisions, strategic planning, and the evaluation of managers, departments, products, and product lines.
2. Growing recognition that traditional financial measures are affected by phenomena that are not necessarily relevant to the purpose at hand. Examples of these phenomena are the essentially arbitrary choices of

accounting methods, such as first-in, first-out versus weighted-average costing, and straight-line versus declining-balance depreciation.

3. Dissatisfaction with the slow pace at which a company's accounting and data processing departments can add, delete, or modify traditional financial measures when the need arises. Financial data typically are processed by large, highly systematized data processing systems. In such systems, any proposal for change is examined for its auditability, its compliance with law, regulation, and reporting rules, and its vulnerability to misstatement, unauthorized access, and misuse. Often the result is a considerable delay in responding to users' requests for modifications of performance measures.
4. Dissatisfaction with financial measures of plant utilization. These measures are easily misinterpreted as encouraging inappropriate overuse of available capacity merely to improve the reported utilization measure. Examples of these utilization measures are fixed overhead volume and idle capacity variances, which are examined in Chapters 18 and 19.
5. Dissatisfaction with financial measures of processing efficiency. In practice, many cost systems fail to take full advantage of the flexibility and power of control measures, producing reports that are criticized as being too late, too aggregated, too difficult to interpret, or simply misleading.

Nonfinancial performance measures respond to these problems by using simple physical data rather than allocated accounting data, by being unconnected to the general financial accounting system, by being selected to measure only one specific aspect of performance rather than to be "all things for all purposes," or by a combination of these factors. Some nonfinancial performance measures are simple counts or percentages of desirable or undesirable events and are intended to measure the efficiency or effectiveness of a production process. Examples of this kind of nonfinancial performance measures include: the number of defective units produced, number of good units produced, good units as a percentage of total units, hours of machine downtime, unscheduled downtime as a percentage of total downtime, number of days operating on schedule, days operating on schedule as a percentage of total days operating, weight of scrap material produced, and scrap weight as a percentage of shipped weight.

Other nonfinancial performance measures turn up in JIT environments. These provide signals of overall processing efficiency by measuring the extent to which the factory has achieved the JIT ideal of minimum inventories or its corollary, maximum material velocity. Examples of such measures include the average number of units in process, the maximum number of units in process during a period, total lead time between receipt of a customer order and shipment, and processing time as a fraction of the total time a unit is in the factory.[4]

A third type of nonfinancial performance measure indicates success in simplifying a process. Simplification is an important step in improving the management of costs and is a precondition for successful automation of a process. Examples of nonfinancial measures that are relevant to planning and controlling a simplification

---

[4] Processing time as a fraction of total time, called *manufacturing cycle efficiency*, is calculated as:

$$\frac{\text{Processing Time}}{\text{Processing Time} + \text{Waiting Time} + \text{Moving Time} + \text{Inspection Time}}$$

Only processing time adds any value to the product, so it is desirable for processing time to be as large a fraction of total time as possible. Unfortunately, cycle efficiencies are generally less than .1, and levels as low as .01 are not unheard of.

effort include: the number of times a unit is handled in the factory, the number of times a unit is retrieved from and returned to storage, the number of times a unit is moved between any two locations, and the total distance a unit is moved within the factory before shipment. (The three types of measures presented thus far are not mutually exclusive; for example, gradual implementation of JIT is a popular way of achieving simplification, so many of the JIT-related measures can also be measures of simplification, and vice versa.)

All three types of nonfinancial measures mentioned thus far can serve as tools for planning and controlling production processes and for evaluating the performance of a department, a team of workers and managers, a product, or a plant. A very different use of the measures mentioned as well as other nonfinancial performance measures is in planning and controlling the firm's progress toward attaining strategic objectives or "critical success factors." For example, nonfinancial performance measures that would be useful in pursuing an objective of providing excellent customer service and satisfaction include the percentage of on-time deliveries and the number of units or orders returned by customers. Nonfinancial performance measures that would be useful in pursuing the objective of world-class employee involvement and motivation include the average number of written suggestions made by each employee per year (typically between one and six, but now approaching 100 in some firms).

The increased interest in nonfinancial performance measures originated outside the operations of cost accounting systems, and in part it is a response to perceived problems with traditional accounting measures. It would be counter-productive, though, to view this development as a threat to the management accountant's role. Rather, the essential skills of the management accountant can be applied to the identification, measurement, verification, reporting, and interpretation of any performance measure, whether it is stated in dollars or not.

For example, if a firm's production engineers or salespeople begin ignoring financial measures (because they are viewed as being too late, too aggregated, or too unresponsive to changing needs), they may develop their own measures—including the ones already mentioned—of each department's performance. If engineers and salespeople regard the new measures as more timely or more relevant, then management is likely to request the same information. The management accountant would then be required, after the fact, to verify the information and estimate or explain its financial impact. It is more efficient for the management accountant to become involved early in the process to help establish efficient and verifiable data-gathering and -reporting systems.

Rather than being a threat to management accountants' position as the firm's internal information consultants, nonfinancial performance measures can be a signal that management accounting is more important than ever. The essential challenge to management accountants and to accounting systems is clear and simple: their roles must be defined broadly enough to involve many kinds of measurement, regardless of whether the measures are tied to the financial accounting system.

Classifications of Costs

Cost classifications are essential for meaningful summarization of cost data. The most commonly used classifications are based on the relationship of costs to the following:

1. The product (a single lot, batch, or unit of a good or service)
2. The volume of production

3. The manufacturing departments, processes, cost centers, or other subdivisions
4. The accounting period
5. A decision, action, or evaluation

Costs in Relation to the Product

The process of classifying costs and expenses can begin by relating costs to the different phases in the operation of a business. In a manufacturing concern, total operating cost consists of two elements: manufacturing cost and commercial expenses. Figure 2-1 illustrates this division of total operating cost and identifies some of the elements included in each division.

FIGURE 2-1 ***Classification of Costs in Relation to the Product***

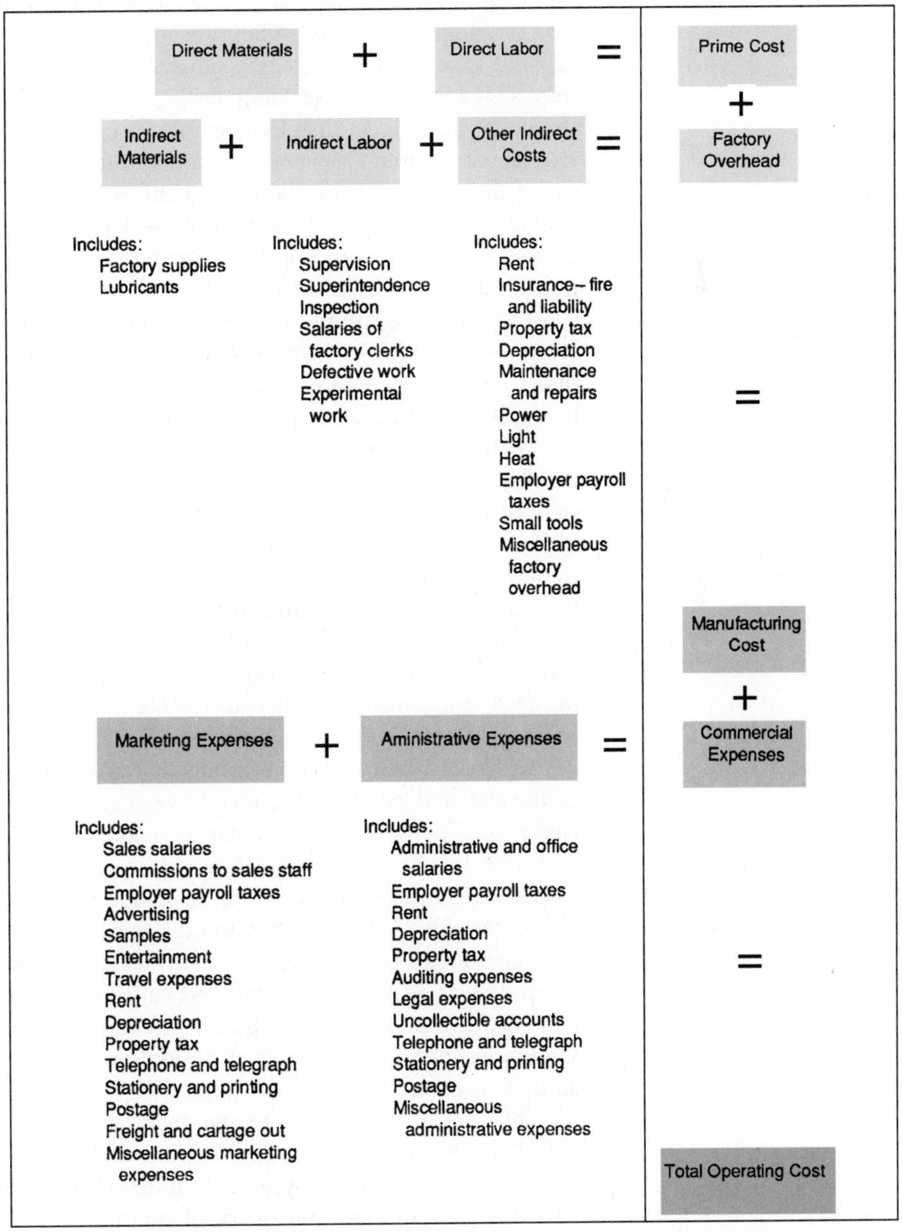

Manufacturing Costs. **Manufacturing cost**—also called production cost or factory cost—is usually defined as the sum of three cost elements: direct materials, direct labor, and factory overhead. Direct materials and direct labor together are called **prime cost**. Direct labor and factory overhead together are called **conversion cost**.

Direct materials are all materials that form an integral part of the finished product and that are included explicitly in calculating the cost of the product. Examples of direct materials are the lumber to make furniture and the crude oil to make gasoline. The ease with which the materials items can be traced to the final product is a major consideration in classifying items as direct materials. For example, the tacks in furniture form part of the finished product, but because the cost of the tacks required for each piece of furniture is trivial, they are classified as indirect materials.

Direct labor is labor that converts direct materials into the finished product and can be assigned feasibly to a specific product. In highly automated factories, two problems often arise when an attempt is made to identify direct labor as a separate cost element. First, the same workers perform many kinds of tasks. They may shift between direct labor tasks and indirect labor tasks so quickly and so frequently that direct and indirect labor costs are difficult or impossible to separate. Second, direct labor may be a trivial fraction of total production costs, making it difficult to justify identifying direct labor as a separate cost element. In settings in which one or both of these circumstances exist, a single conversion cost classification is appropriate, leaving direct material as the only cost element traced directly to the product.

Factory overhead—also called manufacturing overhead, manufacturing expenses, or factory burden—consists of all manufacturing costs not traced directly to specific output. Simply stated, factory overhead includes all manufacturing costs except direct materials and direct labor.

Indirect materials are those materials needed for the completion of a product but are not classified as direct materials because they do not become part of the product. Examples include sandpaper, paper patterns, and flux. Indirect materials also include materials that normally would be classified as direct material. When the consumption of such materials is so minimal, or the tracing so complex, treating them as direct materials becomes futile or uneconomical. Examples include nails, screws, glue, and staples. Factory supplies, a form of indirect materials, consist of such items as lubricating oils, grease, cleaning rags, and brushes needed to maintain the working area and machinery in a usable and safe condition.

Indirect labor is labor not directly traced to the construction or composition of the finished product. Indirect labor includes the wages of supervisors, shop clerks, general helpers, maintenance workers, and, usually, material handlers. In a service business, indirect labor cost can include the wages of receptionists, switchboard operators, file clerks, and supply clerks.

While only direct materials and direct labor are traced to a single unit of product, other levels of traceability are also useful in understanding the nature of production costs. These were illustrated earlier in the discussion of the cost concept and cost objects: setup costs are directly traceable to a batch, but are indirect to a single unit in the batch; product design costs are directly traceable to the sum of all units ever produced of that particular product, but are indirect to a single unit or batch; and so on. This suggests one of the fundamental tenets of cost accounting: different costs are meaningful and useful for different purposes.

Most cost accounting systems include in factory overhead all costs that are not traceable to a specific unit or lot of output. In such systems, the manufacturing costs directly traceable to a batch, a customer order, an entire production facility, a new product or product variation, or a strategic goal are combined in a single overhead classification, because none of these costs is viewed as being directly traceable to the product.

For any careful analysis of what causes costs or how to manage costs better, disaggregation of overhead into different categories is an important but often difficult step. Without careful disaggregation, for example, the difference in the cost of running a large number of small batches of many different products, rather than a few large batches of a few products, is not discernable. A manufacturer may be so inefficient in managing some part of overhead costs that a competitive disadvantage can result, but the mismanaged cost item may not be reported to any responsible manager. Instead, the mismanaged cost may be just one of many components of a large and growing total of overhead costs, representing some of the indirect labor, some of the indirect materials, some energy costs, and so on. In the future, **computer-integrated manufacturing** (CIM), employing database management technology on a company wide scale may remedy the shortcomings of today's information systems.

Commercial Expenses. **Commercial expenses** fall into two large classifications: marketing expenses and administrative expenses (also called general and administrative expenses). **Marketing expenses** begin at the point at which the factory costs end. That is, when manufacturing has been completed and the product is in salable condition. They include the expenses of promotion, selling, and delivery. **Administrative expenses** include expenses incurred in directing and controlling the organization. Not all such expenses are allocated as administrative expenses. The salary of a vice-president in charge of manufacturing can be treated as a manufacturing cost, and the salary of a vice-president in charge of marketing can be treated as a marketing expense.

Costs in Relation to the Volume of Production

Some costs vary in proportion to changes in the volume of production or output, while others remain relatively constant in amount. The tendency of costs to vary with output must be considered by management if it desires to plan and control costs successfully.

Variable Costs. The total amounts of **variable costs** change in proportion to changes in activity within a relevant range. Stated differently, variable costs show a relatively constant amount *per unit* as activity changes within a relevant range. They usually are assignable to operating departments with reasonable ease and accuracy and are controllable by supervisor of a specific operating level. Variable costs generally include direct materials and direct labor. The following list identifies overhead costs usually classified as variable costs.

Supplies
Fuel
Small tools
Spoilage, salvage, and reclamation expenses
Receiving costs
Royalties
Communication costs
Overtime premium
Materials handling

Fixed Costs. **Fixed costs** are constant in total amount within a relevant range of activity. Stated differently, fixed costs *per unit* decrease as activity increases within a relevant range. Control responsibility for fixed costs usually rests with middle or executive management rather than operating supervisors. The following factory overhead costs usually are classified as fixed costs.

Salaries of production executives
Depreciation
Property tax
Patent amortization
Supervisory salaries
Insurance—property and liability
Wages of security guards and janitors
Maintenance and repairs of buildings and grounds
Rent

Fixed costs may be thought of as the costs of being in business, while variable costs are the costs of doing business. In some cases, management actions may determine whether a cost is classified as fixed or variable. For example, if a truck is rented at a rate per mile, the cost is variable. If the truck is purchased and subsequently depreciated by the straight-line method, the cost is fixed. The same is true regardless of whether the truck is used in production, marketing, or administration. Marketing and administration provide many examples of variable and fixed expenses, including close counterparts to many of the variable and fixed factory overhead examples listed. For example, factory supplies are part of variable factory overhead, while office supplies used in sales offices are part of variable marketing expenses.

Semivariable Costs. Some costs contain both fixed and variable elements; these are called **semivariable costs**. For example, the cost of electricity is usually semivariable. Electricity used for lighting tends to be a fixed cost because lights are needed regardless of the level of activity, while electricity used as power to operate equipment will vary depending on the usage of the equipment. The following are other examples of semivariable overhead costs:

Inspection
Cost-department services
Payroll-department services
Personnel-department services
Factory office services
Materials and inventory services
Water and sewage
Maintenance and repairs of plant machinery
Compensation insurance
Health and accident insurance
Payroll taxes
Industrial relations expenses
Heat, light, and power

Because each manufacturing and nonmanufacturing cost usually is classified as either fixed or variable for analytical purposes, a semivariable cost must be divided into its fixed and variable components. Methods of accomplishing this division are discussed in Chapter 3.

Costs in Relation to Manufacturing Departments or Other Segments

A business can be divided into segments having any of a variety of names. The division of a factory into departments, processes, work cells, cost centers, or cost pools also serves as the basis for classifying and accumulating costs and assigning responsibility for cost control. As a product passes through a department or cost center, it is charged with directly traceable costs (typically direct materials and direct labor) and a share of indirect costs (factory overhead).

To achieve the greatest degree of control, department managers should participate in the development of budgets for their respective departments or cost centers. Such budgets should clearly identify those costs about which the manager can make decisions and for which the manager accepts responsibility. At the end of a reporting period, the efficiency of a department and the manager's success in controlling costs can be measured by comparing actual costs with the budget.

Producing and Service Departments. The departments of a factory generally fall into two categories: producing departments and service departments. In a **producing department**, manual and machine operations such as forming and assembling are performed directly on the product or its parts. If two or more different types of machines perform operations on a product within the same department, it is possible to increase the accuracy of product costs by dividing the department into two or more cost centers.

In a **service department**, service is rendered for the benefit of other departments. In some instances, these services benefit other service departments as well as the producing departments. Although a service department does not directly engage in production, its costs are part of factory overhead and are a cost of the product. Service departments that are common to many industrial concerns include maintenance, payroll, cost accounting, data processing, and food services.[5]

In connection with materials and labor, the term *direct* refers to costs that are traced directly to a unit of output; factory overhead is indirect with regard to specific units or lots of output; in this classification system, specific output is the cost object. The terms *direct* and *indirect* can also be used in connection with charging overhead costs to departments of any organization. If a cost is traceable to the department in which it originates, it is referred to as a **direct departmental cost**; the salary of the departmental supervisor is an example. If a cost is shared by several departments that benefit from its incurrence, it is referred to as an **indirect departmental cost**; building rent and building depreciation are examples of indirect departmental costs. In this cost classification system, the department is the cost object.[6]

---

[5] Do not confuse service businesses with the concept of service departments in manufacturing. Service businesses do not produce a tangible good as their output. Within a service business, however, there are producing departments and service departments. In a large law firm, for example, there may be departments for tax, real estate, and probate work; these are the producing departments—the departments that come into direct contact with the client. The library of the law firm would be an example of a service department.

[6] Similarly, when costs of a multidivision conglomerate company are allocated among its various divisions, the division serves as the cost object. When the amounts expended to improve product quality, customer service, and employee involvement are reported, strategic goals are the cost objects.

Service department costs also constitute indirect costs for other departments. When all service department costs have been allocated, each producing department's overhead will consist of its own direct and indirect departmental cost and the apportioned charges from service departments.

Common Costs and Joint Costs. Common costs and joint costs are types of indirect costs. *Common costs* are costs of facilities or services employed by two or more operations. Common costs are particularly prevalent in organizations with many departments or segments. The degree of segmentation increases the tendency for more costs to be common. For example, the salary of the marketing vice-president is usually not a common cost shared with the human resources department. If the marketing department provides its service to several segments of the entire firm, however, it can be considered a common cost shared by those segments.

Joint costs occur when the production of one product makes it inevitable that one or more other products are also produced. The meat-packing, oil and gas, and liquor industries are good examples of production that involves joint costs. In such industries, joint costs can be allocated to joint products only by arbitrary calculations. Data resulting from joint cost allocation must therefore be very carefully treated in some decisions, as explained in Chapter 8.

Costs in Relation to an Accounting Period

Costs can be classified as capital expenditures or as revenue expenditures. A **capital expenditure** is intended to benefit future periods and is reported as an asset. A **revenue expenditure** benefits the current period and is reported as an expense. Assets ultimately flow into the expense stream as they are consumed or lose usefulness.

Distinguishing between capital and revenue expenditures is essential for matching costs with revenues in measuring periodic income. However, a precise distinction between the two classifications is not always feasible. In many cases, the initial classification depends on management's attitude toward such expenditures and on the nature of the company's operations. The amount of the expenditure and the number of detailed records it requires are also factors that influence the distinction between these two classifications. For example, trash barrels purchased for $10 each may be recorded as expenses, although technically they are assets because they will be used for many years.

Costs in Relation to a Decision, Action, or Evaluation

When a choice must be made among possible actions or alternatives, it is important to identify the costs (and the revenues, cost reductions, and savings) that are relevant to the choice. Consideration of irrelevant items is a waste of time and can divert attention from relevant items; more importantly, an irrelevant factor may be misinterpreted as relevant.

Differential cost is one name for a cost that is relevant to a choice among alternatives. Differential cost is sometimes called marginal cost or incremental cost. If a differential cost will be incurred only if one particular alternative is followed, then that cost can also be called an out-of-pocket cost associated with that alternative. An amount of revenue or other benefit that will be missed or lost if a particular alternative is followed is called an opportunity cost of that alternative. A cost that has already been incurred and is, therefore, irrelevant to a decision is referred to as a sunk cost. In a decision to discontinue a product or division, some of the product's or division's costs may be unaffected by the decision; these are called unavoidable costs. The avoidable costs, in contrast, are relevant to the decision. These decision-making concepts are discussed in Chapter 21.

When the performance of a manager is evaluated, an important step involves classifying costs that are controllable by that manager. Costs that are uncontrollable by the manager generally are irrelevant to evaluations of the manager's performance, and the manager should not be held responsible for them. These aspects of responsibility accounting are discussed in Chapter 17.

Summary

The concepts of cost object and cost traceability are fundamental to the study of cost accounting. The different degrees of traceability and the wide variety of important cost objects create a large number of categories into which costs are classified.

The chart of accounts is the skeleton of the cost accounting information system. The system's output includes much of the information managers use in planning and control. Outside the basic accounting system, but still important in managing, are the nonfinancial performance measures now receiving increased attention.

Key Terms

cost object *(21)*
traceability *(21)*
chart of accounts *(24)*
data processing *(25)*
data processing system *(25)*
manufacturing cost *(30)*
prime cost *(30)*
conversion cost *(30)*
direct materials *(30)*
direct labor *(30)*
factory overhead *(30)*
indirect materials *(30)*
indirect labor *(30)*
computer-integrated manufacturing *(31)*
commercial expenses *(31)*
marketing expenses *(31)*
administrative expenses *(31)*
variable costs *(31)*
fixed costs *(32)*
semivariable costs *(32)*
producing department *(33)*
service department *(33)*
direct departmental costs *(33)*
indirect departmental costs *(33)*
capital expenditure *(34)*
revenue expenditure *(34)*

Discussion Questions

Q2-1 (a) Explain the terms *cost* and *expense* as they are used for financial reporting. The explanation should indicate distinguishing characteristics of the terms, their similarities, and interrelationships.

(b) Classify each of the following items as a cost, expense, or other category. Explain how the classification of each item can change.

(1) cost of goods sold

(2) uncollectible accounts expense

(3) depreciation expense for plant machinery

(4) organization costs

(5) spoiled goods

Q2-2 What are cost objects and why are they important?

Q2-3 (a) Why is the particular choice of a cost object important in classifying costs as direct or indirect?

(b) Give an example of how the choice of a different cost object changes the direct or indirect classification of a single item of cost.

Q2-4 (a) When all manufacturing costs are divided into three elements—direct material, direct labor, and overhead—what is the cost object?

(b) For what purpose would a disaggregation of overhead be useful?

(c) Identify some cost objects that may require disaggregating the total overhead cost.

Q2-5 Define a cost system.

Q2-6 Enumerate the requirements of a good information system.

Q2-7 What is the purpose of a chart of accounts?

Q2-8 What are the advantages of an electronic data processing system?

Q2-9 Increased interest in nonfinancial performance measures is partly a response to perceived weaknesses of traditional financial measures. What are these perceived weaknesses?

Q2-10 In addition to being measured in nonmonetary terms, what are the other attributes of nonfinancial performance measures that distinguish them from financial measures?

Q2-11 Identify four examples of nonfinancial performance measures and explain what four different aspects of performance they might be used to monitor.

Q2-12 What challenge to cost accountants and cost systems is posed by the increased interest in nonfinancial performance measures?

Q2-13 Enumerate the most commonly used classifications of costs.

Q2-14 Describe indirect materials and give an appropriate example.

Q2-15 Describe indirect labor and give an appropriate example.

Q2-16 (a) What is a service department? Name several examples.

(b) How do producing departments classify their apportioned share of service-department expenses?

Q2-17 Expenditures can be divided into two general categories, capital expenditures and revenue expenditures.

(a) Distinguish between these two categories and their treatment in the accounts.

(b) Discuss the impact on both present and future balance sheets and income statements of improperly distinguishing between capital and revenue expenditures.

(c) What criteria do firms generally use in establishing a policy for classifying expenditures under these two general categories?

Exercises

E2-1 Manufacturing Costs. For each bicycle produced, Matheson Company incurs direct material cost of $6, direct labor of $3, and variable factory overhead of $1. Matheson's fixed factory overhead totals $1,000 per month.

Required:

(1) Identify the prime cost per unit.

(2) Identify the variable conversion cost per unit.

(3) Identify the variable manufacturing cost per unit.

(4) Calculate total manufacturing costs that should be incurred in a month in which 500 bicycles are produced.

E2-2 Manufacturing Costs. The estimated unit costs for CNR Inc., when it is operating at a production and sales level of 12,000 units, are as follows:

Cost Item	Estimated Unit Cost
Direct materials	$32
Direct labor	10
Variable factory overhead	15
Fixed factory overhead	6
Variable marketing	3
Fixed marketing	4

Required:

(1) Identify the estimated conversion cost per unit.

(2) Identify the estimated prime cost per unit.

(3) Determine the estimated total variable cost per unit.

(4) Compute the total cost that would be incurred during a month with a production level of 12,000 units and a sales level of 8,000 units.

(ICMA adapted)

E2-3 Fixed and Variable Costs. In the year 19A, the Titanic Company had sales of $19,950,000, with $11,571,000 variable and $7,623,000 fixed costs. 19B sales are expected to decrease 15%, and the cost relationship is expected to remain constant (the fixed costs will not change).

Required: Determine Titanic Company's expected operating income or loss for the year 19B.

E2-4 Nonfinancial Performance Measures.

Required: Match each of the nonfinancial performance measures in the first column with the most closely related goal, objective, or other aspect of performance in the second column.

(1) Absenteeism	(a) Product innovation
(2) Number of warranty repairs	(b) Product quality
(3) Rejects, as a percentage of units inspected	(c) Product simplification
(4) Patents applied for	(d) Employee motivation
(5) On-time deliveries, as a percentage of all deliveries	(e) Process simplification
(6) Number of times each unit handled during production	(f) Customer service
(7) Number of unique parts kept in inventory	
(8) Number of customer complaints	

E2-5 Manufacturing Costs. Randall Company manufactures mainframe computers. The prime cost of producing a computer is $300,000 and the conversion cost is $400,000, but the total manufacturing cost is only $600,000.

Required: Determine the cost of direct labor per computer.

E2-6 Manufacturing Costs. Sunshine Company manufactures diamond-tipped cutting blades. The total manufacturing cost of one blade is $1,000, of which $400 is the conversion cost. The direct labor cost of a blade is one-sixth as large as the direct material cost.

Required: Determine the amount of factory overhead cost per blade.

E2-7 Manufacturing Costs. Chianti Company manufactures airbrake systems for long-haul trucks. The prime cost to produce one system is $800, the conversion cost is $400, and the total manufacturing cost is $1,000.

Required: Determine the cost of direct labor per system.

E2-8 Manufacturing Costs. Smithson Inc. manufactures wave soldering machines. The total manufacturing cost of one machine is $3,000, of which $2,000 is the conversion cost. The direct labor cost of a machine is half as large as the direct material cost.

Required: Determine the amount of factory overhead cost per machine.

E2-9 Cost Objects, Traceability, and Pricing. Some retail stores that accept bank credit cards will give the customer a discount if a purchase is paid for in cash. The logic behind this practice is that the banks that process credit-card transactions charge the merchant a service fee, usually between 1% and 5% of the amount of credit card transactions each month. If a customer pays the merchant in cash rather than by credit card, the merchant avoids incurring that extra cost.

Required: Answer the following questions:

(1) In establishing a price structure in which both cash and bank credit-card purchases are common, what are the relevant cost objects?

(2) What does this imply about prices in a store in which credit cards are accepted but no discount is given for cash purchases?

(3) What are the competitive implications for a store like the one described in requirement 2?

(4) Instead of offering a discount on cash transactions, why not reduce all the prices in the store and then levy a small additional charge on customers that use credit cards, to cover the banks' processing fees?

E2-10 Cost Objects, Traceability, and Pricing. When Johnson Tractor Repair Shop (JTRS) repairs a lawn tractor or small garden tractor for a customer, the tractor is picked up and delivered at no extra charge. When JTRS started business, about half of its customers transported their own tractors, rather than waiting for JTRS to schedule a pickup.

Over the years, the local market for lawn-tractor repair services has become increasingly competitive. JTRS has encountered difficulty in matching the prices offered by competitors and in maintaining market share. A further problem is that the cost of pickups and deliveries has become a financial problem in JTRS's cost structure, because nearly all of JTRS's remaining customers now request the free pickup and delivery. Most of JTRS's original customers who were willing and able to transport their tractors for service now take their tractor repair business to JTRS's competitors. JTRS competitors all charge extra for pickup and delivery of tractors.

Required: Answer the following questions:

(1) What cost objects are relevant to JTRS's pricing structure?

(2) If you are a lawn-tractor owner who also owns a small truck, why might you find that JTRS's prices for repair services are not competitive?

E2-11 Manufacturing Costs. When Bahalia Bookcase Company operates at a production and sales level of 2,000 units, the estimated unit costs are as follows:

Cost Item	Estimated Unit Cost
Lumber	$12
Direct labor	2
Variable factory overhead	5
Fixed factory overhead	4
Variable marketing	1
Fixed marketing	3

Required:

(1) Calculate the estimated conversion cost per unit.

(2) Calculate the estimated prime cost per unit.

(3) Calculate the estimated variable manufacturing cost per unit.

(4) Calculate the estimated total variable cost per unit.

(5) Calculate the total cost that would be incurred during a month with a production level of 2,000 units and a sales level of 1,900 units.

(6) Give some examples of items that would be accounted for as indirect materials by Bahalia.

(7) In the list of cost items and estimated amounts provided, which entry includes an estimate of the costs referred to in the answer to requirement 6?

(ICMA adapted)

E2-12 Manufacturing Costs. Ingerson Manufacturing produces self-propelled rock-drilling machines for use in mining, road building, and excavation. The direct materials cost of one machine is $12,000, and the total manufacturing cost is $20,000. The overhead cost of one machine is one-third as large as its prime cost.

Required: Determine the direct labor cost of one machine.

Cases

C2-1 Cost Objects, Traceability, and Pricing. The food-service manager of Too-Simple Hotel is planning a new price structure for room service. It has been determined that the hotel's cost of a glass of orange juice is 20 cents. To provide the normal 75% profit margin on sales, 80 cents would need to be charged. Profit would then be 80 – 20 or 60 cents, which is 75% of the 80-cent sales price.

For menu items delivered by room service, a higher price will be charged to cover the cost of delivery to a guest's room. The cost of a delivery is 60 cents (not counting the cost of whatever menu items are delivered). To earn a normal profit, additional revenues averaging $2.40 must be earned on a delivery. The profit would then be $2.40 – $.60, or $1.80, which is 75% of the $2.40 delivery revenue.

The food-service manager estimates that an average delivery involves two items, so $1.20, or one-half the necessary $2.40 delivery revenue, will be added to the menu price of every room-service item. That brings the room-service price of a glass of orange juice to $.80 + $1.20, or $2.00.

Required: Answer the following questions:

(1) What percentage of profit margin on sales will be earned on a room-service order consisting of four glasses of orange juice?

(Requirements continued.)

(2) What percentage of profit margin on sales will be earned on a room-service order consisting of one glass of orange juice?
(3) What is the food-service manager treating as the cost object in setting room service prices?
(4) What refinement of the definition of cost objects would produce the desired 75% profit margin on sales?
(5) Using the refinement devised in requirement 4, recalculate the percentage of profit margin for requirements 1 and 2.
(6) What are the competitive implications of the food-service manager's planned price structure, compared with those resulting from the refined price structure?

C2-2 Cost Objects and Traceability. CCN Company produces more than 100 different variations of its basic product and has expended $250,000 in perfecting its newest variation, Zeggo, to the point of starting production. This amount includes the cost of routine design improvement efforts, testing, assembly-line modifications, and training.

Zeggo's production will share an assembly line with several of CCN's other product variations, but only one variation can be produced on the line at one time. Each variation requires a different setup of the machinery on the line. To begin a batch of Zeggo, the machines on the line must first be set up, at a cost of $1,000.

Each unit of Zeggo that is produced results in $5 of cost that the CCN cost accounting system traces directly to the product unit, plus another $1 of cost that could be traced, but only with great difficulty. The CCN system classifies the $1 as indirect cost.

CCN's cost accounting system allocates a share of factory overhead to each unit produced; this factory overhead amount includes an allocation of all the manufacturing costs that are not directly traced to the product. Each unit of Zeggo will be allocated $10 of factory overhead.

Required:

(1) Name every cost object for which some amount of cost is identified in the information given and determine the amount of cost for each cost object.
(2) In addition to the cost objects named in your answer to requirement 1, name other items that are mentioned in the case that could serve as cost objects for some purpose. For each one, describe a purpose for which it could serve as the cost object.
(3) Calculate the total cost expected to result from producing the first batch of Zeggo, which will be a batch of 300 units.
(4) CCN plans to produce one more unit of Zeggo. No setup will be required, because the assembly line has just finished a Zeggo production run. Determine the amount of cost that would be expected to result from producing the one additional unit.
(5) Determine the total cost that the CCN cost accounting system will report for the batch of 300 units referred to in requirement 3. (Your answer should be larger than the answer to requirement 3.)
(6) Determine the cost that the CCN cost accounting system will report for the one additional unit referred to in requirement 4. (Your answer should be larger than the answer to requirement 4.)
(7) Explain why the results of requirements 5 and 6 are larger than those of requirements 3 and 4. Specifically: (a) What types of activities have costs that are included in the amounts reported by the cost accounting system but that do not result from producing a batch or a unit of Zeggo? Give examples of these activities. (b) Other than the costs of activities, what kinds of costs account for the difference? Give examples.

CHAPTER 3

Cost Behavior Analysis

Learning Objectives

After studying this chapter, you will be able to:

1. Classify an expenditure as fixed, variable, or semivariable.
2. List reasons for separating fixed and variable costs.
3. Compute the fixed and variable components of costs by three methods.
4. Define, compute, and explain the use of the coefficient of determination.
5. Define, compute, and explain the use of the standard error of the estimate.
6. Compute an estimate of cost using the equation developed by the method of least squares and then compute a confidence interval for that estimate.
7. (Appendix) Develop the regression and correlation equations.

Some costs vary in total directly with changes in activity, while others remain relatively unaffected. Because of the dynamic nature of business, companies often are faced with the need to make changes in the level and mix of their business activities. In order for management to plan a company's activities intelligently and control its costs effectively, the relationship between cost incurrence and changes in activity must be thoroughly understood. This chapter discusses the effect of changes in business activity on costs and classifies costs as fixed, variable, or semivariable with respect to activity. In addition, techniques used to segregate the fixed and variable components of costs are illustrated. Although the discussion centers on production costs and activities, the concepts and techniques are equally applicable to marketing and administrative activities.

Classifying Cost

Success in planning and controlling cost depends on a thorough understanding of the relationship between the incurrence of cost and business activity. Careful study and analysis of the effect of business activities on costs generally will result in the classification of each type of expenditure as a fixed, variable, or semivariable cost.

Fixed Cost

A **fixed cost** is defined as one that does not change in total as business activity increases or decreases. Although some kinds of costs may have the appearance of being fixed, all costs are variable in the long run. If all business activity decreases to zero and there is no prospect for an increase, a firm will liquidate and avoid all costs. If activity is expected to increase beyond the capacity of current facilities, fixed costs must be increased to handle the expected increase in volume. For example, factory overhead includes items such as supervision, depreciation, rent, property insurance, and property taxes—all generally considered to be fixed costs. If management expects demand for the company's products to increase beyond present capacity, it must acquire additional plant, equipment, indirect labor, and possibly supervisors in order to produce the level of output necessary to meet demand. Such additions result in an incremental increase in the level of expenditure for each of these items of factory overhead.

For this reason, a particular kind of expenditure should be classified as a fixed cost only within a limited range of activity. This limited range of activity is referred to as the **relevant range**. Total fixed cost will change outside the relevant range of activity. Figure 3-1 depicts changes in fixed cost at different levels of activity and the relevant range.

Some expenditures are fixed as a result of management policy. For example, the level of advertising expenditure and the amount of charitable contribution are determined by management and are not directly related to sales or production activity. Such expenditures are sometimes referred to as **discretionary fixed costs** or **programmed fixed costs**. Expenditures that require a series of payments over a long-term period of time are often called **committed fixed costs**. Examples include interest on long-term debt and long-term lease rentals.

FIGURE 3-1 *Fixed Cost*

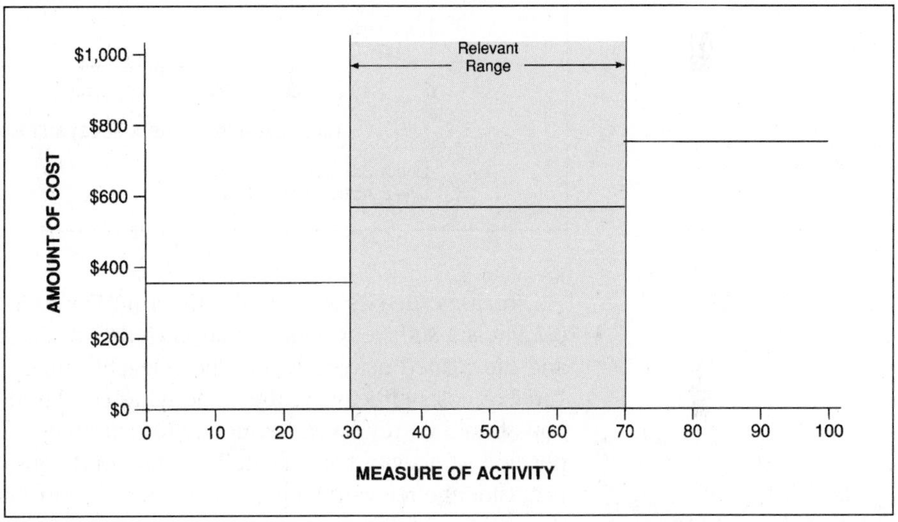

Variable Cost

A **variable cost** is defined as one that increases in total proportionately with an increase in activity and decreases proportionately with a decrease in activity. Variable costs include the cost of direct materials, direct labor, some supplies, some indirect labor, small tools, rework, and normal spoilage. Variable costs usually can be directly identified with the activity that causes the cost.

In practice, the relationship between a business activity and the related variable cost usually is treated as if it were linear; that is, total variable cost is assumed to increase by a constant amount for each unit increase in activity. However, the actual relationship is rarely perfectly linear over the entire range of possible activity. Productive efficiency usually changes when the work load is very light or very heavy. When the volume of activity increases to a certain level, management may add newer, more efficient machinery or replace existing machinery with more productive machinery. As a result of these factors, the cost per unit of activity usually is different at widely varied levels of activity. Nevertheless, within a limited range of activity, the relationship between an activity and the related cost may closely approximate linearity. This relationship is illustrated in Figure 3-2. The solid line (line B) represents actual variable costs at all levels of activity, and the dashed line (line A) represents the calculated variable cost at all levels of activity as determined from observations within the relevant range of activity.

FIGURE 3-2 *Variable Cost*

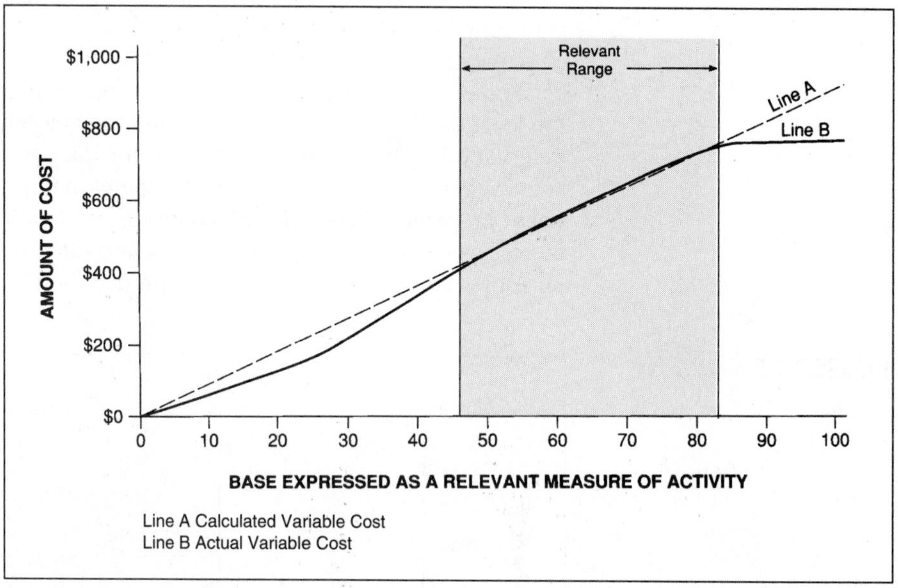

In cases such as the one illustrated in Figure 3-2, a constant variable-cost rate usually is a sufficient approximation of the relationship between the variable cost and the related activity within the relevant range. However, to plan and control variable costs effectively, the underlying conditions that cause the incurrence of cost should be reviewed frequently to determine whether or not the variable cost per unit of activity has changed. When conditions change or the level of activity is outside the relevant range, a new variable-cost rate should be computed.

Semivariable Cost

A **semivariable cost** is defined as one that displays both fixed and variable characteristics. Examples include the cost of electricity, water, gas, fuel oil, coal, some supplies, maintenance, some indirect labor, employee group-term life insurance, pension cost, payroll taxes, and travel and entertainment.

Three reasons for the semivariable characteristic of some types of expenditures are:

1. A minimum of organization may be needed, or a minimum quantity of supplies or services may need to be consumed, in order to maintain readiness to operate. Beyond this minimum level of cost, which is essentially fixed, additional cost varies with volume.
2. Accounting classifications, based on the object of expenditure or function, commonly group fixed and variable items together. For example, the cost

of steam used for heating, which is dependent on the weather, and the cost of steam used for manufacturing, which is dependent upon the volume of production, may be charged to the same account, resulting in a mixture of fixed and variable costs in the same account.[1]

A semivariable cost is illustrated in the graph in Figure 3-3. The solid line in Figure 3-3 represents actual costs at all levels of activity. In this illustration, the actual-cost line (line C) is nonlinear. This situation could occur because of the use of different production techniques or equipment and/or because of different degrees of capacity utilization at different levels of activity. The dashed lines are linear and represent calculated fixed-cost and total-cost components (line A and line B, respectively) at all levels of activity, as determined from observations within the relevant range. Estimated total variable cost is the difference between the points on line B and line A. Where line B and line C coincide, the linear assumption closely approximates the actual relationship. This area of coincidence is the relevant range. The use of the calculated fixed cost and the variable cost rate to estimate cost at any level of activity outside of the relevant range would result in unreliable estimates.

FIGURE 3-3 *Semivariable Cost*

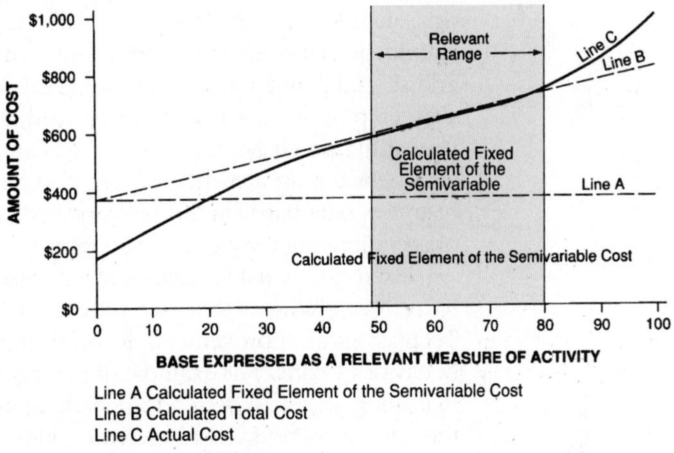

Separating Fixed and Variable Costs

In order to plan, analyze, control, measure, or evaluate costs at different levels of activity, fixed and variable costs must be separated. Those costs that are entirely fixed or entirely variable within the range of activity anticipated must be identified, and the fixed and variable components of semivariable costs must be estimated. As discussed in later chapters, the separation of fixed and variable costs is necessary for the following purposes:

1. Predetermined factory overhead rate computation and variance analysis.
2. Flexible budget preparation and variance analysis.
3. Direct costing and contribution margin analysis.
4. Break-even and cost-volume-profit analysis.
5. Differential and comparative cost analysis.

[1] *NA(C)A Bulletin*, Vol.30, No. 20, pp. 1224–1225.

6. Short-run profit maximization and cost minimization analysis.
7. Capital budgeting analysis.
8. Marketing profitability analysis by territories, products, and customers.

In practice, managerial judgment often is used to classify costs as fixed or variable.[2] In such cases, classification is based on the personal experience of management. Although such an approach is expedient, it often results in unreliable estimates of cost. The behavior of a particular type of cost is not always readily apparent from casual observation. Furthermore, managers often attempt to simplify the process by classifying all costs as either entirely fixed or entirely variable, thereby ignoring the fact that some costs are semivariable. Generally, more reliable classifications and cost estimates are obtained by using one of the following computational methods, all of which are illustrated in this section: (1) the high and low points method, (2) the scattergraph method, or (3) the method of least squares. These methods are used not only to estimate the fixed and variable components of semivariable costs, but also to determine whether a cost is entirely fixed or entirely variable within the relevant range of activity.

Although the use of a computational method typically results in a more reliable analysis of cost behavior than the simple use of managerial judgment, the analyst should keep in mind that the results obtained are dependent on historical data. If abnormal or unusual conditions occurred during one or more of the periods included in the data base, the observations reflecting such abnormalities should be removed from the sample. In this respect, managerial judgment can and should play an important role in cost behavior analysis. For example, training new employees, a labor strike or work slowdown, a temporary equipment failure, or the purchase of a batch of substandard materials could distort the relationship between an activity and a related cost. To enhance prediction accuracy, the historical data base should be inspected by experienced managers, and abnormal observations should be removed from the sample.

Fixed and variable cost estimates based on historical data should be adjusted to reflect changes that are expected to occur during the forecast period. Technological improvements in production techniques or facilities can affect the behavior of costs. For example, if management acquires (or plans to acquire) new machinery that is expected to operate more efficiently than machinery used during the sample period, cost-behavior estimates based on historical data should be adjusted to reflect the expected improvement in efficiency. Product design changes, as well as changes in production technology, may affect cost-behavior. For example, changes in the kinds of materials used in a product may make it necessary to operate machinery at a different speed than that required during the sample period. This, in turn, may affect the machinery's rate of energy or fuel consumption and possibly the amount of preventive maintenance required. To the extent these changes are anticipated, cost-behavior estimates should be adjusted.

If the historical data base includes observations from several different years, the analyst should consider the potential distorting effects of inflation. If the rate of inflation was substantial during one or more of the periods in the sample, fixed and variable cost estimates are likely to be unreliable. One way to compensate for this problem would be first to restate the cost for each period in the sample to current dollars, and then to perform the analysis on the inflation-adjusted costs.

To illustrate the three computational methods of determining the fixed and variable elements of cost, assume that the data presented in Exhibit 3-1 are taken from Barker Company's records for the preceding year.

---

[2] Maryanne M. Mowen, *Accounting for Costs as Fixed and Variable* (Montvale, N.J.: Institute of Management Accountants (formerly National Association of Accountants), 1986), pp. 19–20.

EXHIBIT 3-1

Barker Company
Electricity Cost and Labor Hour Data

Month	Electricity Cost	Direct Labor Hours
January	$ 640	34,000
February	620	30,000
March	620	34,000
April	590	39,000
May	500	42,000
June	530	32,000
July	500	26,000
August	500	26,000
September	530	31,000
October	550	35,000
November	580	43,000
December	680	48,000
Total	$6,840	420,000
Monthly average	$ 570	35,000

High and Low Points Method

In the **high and low points method**, the fixed and variable elements of a cost are computed from two data points. The data points (periods) selected from the historical data are the periods of highest and lowest activity. These periods usually, but not always, have the highest and lowest figures for the cost being analyzed. If the periods of highest or lowest activity levels are not the same as those having the highest or lowest level of cost, the activity level should govern the selection, because activity is presumed to drive cost. The high and low periods are selected because they represent conditions for the two activity levels that are the farthest apart. However, care must be taken not to select data points distorted by abnormal conditions.

With the data provided in Exhibit 3-1 for Barker Company, the fixed and variable elements are determined as follows:

	Cost	Activity Level
High	$680	48,000 hours
Low	–500	–26,000 hours
Difference	$180	22,000 hours

Variable rate: $180 ÷ 22,000 hours = $.00818 per direct labor hour

	High	Low
Total cost	$680	$500
Variable cost* (rounded)	–393	–213
Fixed cost	$287	$287

* Direct labor hours × $.00818

The high and low activity levels differ by 22,000 direct labor hours, with a cost difference of $180. The assumption is that the difference in the costs at the two levels of activity occurred because of differences in the activity being measured and, therefore, is pure variable cost. The variable rate is determined by dividing the difference in expense ($180) by the difference in activity (22,000 direct labor hours). In this example, the variable rate is determined to be $.00818 per direct labor hour. The total variable cost at either the high or low level of activity can be determined by multiplying the variable rate times the activity level. This results in a total variable cost at the high level of $393 ($.00818 × 48,000 hours) and at the low level, \$213 (\$.00818 × 26,000 hours). At either the high or low level of activity, the difference between the total cost and the total variable cost is the fixed cost, which in this example is determined to be \$287. The fixed cost is the same, whether computed from the high or low data.[3] With variable and fixed elements established, the cost totals for various levels of activity can be calculated.

The high and low points method is simple, but it has the disadvantage of using only two data points to determine cost behavior, and it is based on the assumption that the other data points lie on a straight line between the high and low points. Because it uses only two data points, it may result in estimates of fixed and variable costs that are biased. As a result, estimates of total cost based on fixed and variable costs computed with the high and low points method often are more inaccurate than estimates derived by other methods that consider a larger number of data points.

Scattergraph Method

The **scattergraph method** can be used to analyze cost behavior. In this method, the cost being analyzed (the dependent variable) is plotted on a vertical line (the y-axis) and the associated activity (the independent variable,—for example, direct labor dollars, direct labor hours, machine hours, units of output, or percentage of capacity) is plotted along a horizontal line (the x-axis).

The data for Barker Company (Exhibit 3-1) are plotted on the graph in Figure 3-4. Each point in Figure 3-4 represents the electricity cost for a particular month. For instance, the point labeled *Nov.* represents the electricity cost for November, when 43,000 direct labor hours were worked. The x-axis shows the direct labor hours, and the y-axis shows the electricity cost. Line B is plotted by visual inspection. This line represents the trend shown by the majority of data points. Generally, there should be as many data points above as below the line. Another line (line A) is drawn parallel to the base line from the point at which line B intersects the y-axis, which is read from the scattergraph as approximately \$440. This line represents the fixed element of the electricity cost for all activity levels within the relevant range.

The area bounded by lines A and B shows the increase in electricity cost as direct labor hours increase. This increase is computed as follows:

Average monthly cost	−	Fixed element	=	Average monthly variable element of cost
\$570	−	\$440	=	\$130

$$\frac{\text{Average monthly variable element of cost}}{\text{Average monthly direct labor hours}} = \text{Variable cost per direct labor hour}$$

$$\frac{\$130}{35{,}000\text{ hours}} = \$.0037 \text{ per direct labor hour}$$

Thus the electricity cost consists of \$440 fixed cost per month and of a variable factor of \$.0037 per direct labor hour.

[3] The high and low points method is equivalent to solving two simultaneous equations, based on the assumption that both points fall on the true variable cost line. With the sample figures, equations could be set up and solved as follows:

$$\begin{array}{rl} F + 48{,}000\,V = & \$\ 680 \\ -F - 26{,}000\,V = & -500 \\ \hline 22{,}000\,V = & \$\ 180 \end{array}$$

$V = \$180 \div 22{,}000 = \$.00818$ per direct labor hour

In the scattergraph in Figure 3-4, line B is drawn as a straight line, even though the points do not follow a perfect linear pattern. In most analyses, a straight line is adequate, because it is a reasonable approximation of cost behavior within the relevant range.

FIGURE 3-4 *Scattergraph Representing the Fixed and Variable Elements for Electricity Cost*

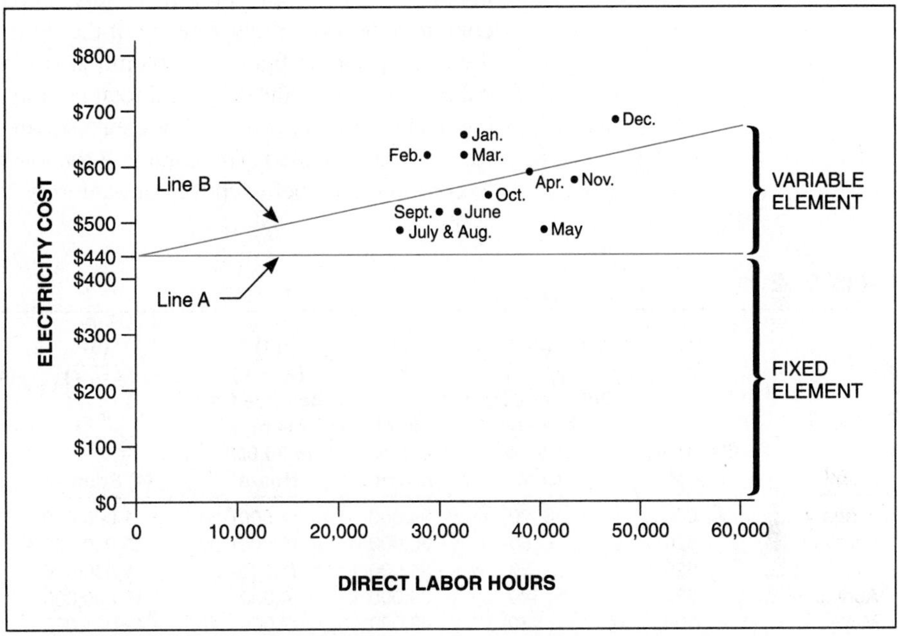

The scattergraph method is an improvement over the high and low points method because it utilizes all available data, not just two data points. In addition, the method makes it possible to inspect the data visually to determine whether or not the cost appears to be related to the activity and whether or not such a relationship is approximately linear. Visual inspection also facilitates detection of abnormal data points (sometimes referred to as outliers). Nevertheless, a cost behavior analysis using the scattergraph method is still likely to be biased because the cost line drawn through the data plot is based on visual interpretation.

Method of Least Squares

The **method of least squares** (sometimes called **regression analysis**) determines mathematically a line of best fit or a linear regression line through a set of plotted points, so that the sum of the squared deviations of each actual plotted point from the point directly above or below it on the regression line is at a minimum.[4] Exhibit 3-2 illustrates this method using Barker Company data from Exhibit 3-1.

Preparing the table in Exhibit 3-2 requires the following steps:

1. First, determine the average electricity cost, $\bar{y}$, and the average direct labor hours, $\bar{x}$. Add the observations in columns 1 and 3, and then divide by the number of observations. The average for electricity cost, $\bar{y}$, is $570 ($6,840 total electricity cost ÷ 12 months). The average for direct labor hours, $\bar{x}$, is 35,000 (420,000 total direct labor hours ÷ 12 months).

[4] The regression equation is developed in the appendix to this chapter.

2. Next, compute the differences between actual monthly figures for electricity cost, y_i, and direct labor hours, x_i, and their respective monthly averages, $\bar{y}$ and $\bar{x}$ computed in step 1. These differences are entered in columns 2 and 4 and should sum to zero, unless there is some rounding error.
3. Next, two multiplications must be made. First, square each of the figures in column 4, $(x_i - \bar{x})$; enter the results in column 5, $(x_i - \bar{x})^2$; and total column 5. Second, multiply each of the figures in column 4, $(x_i - \bar{x})$, by the corresponding figures in column 2, $(y_i - \bar{y})$; enter the products in column 6, $(x_i - \bar{x})(y_i - \bar{y})$; and total column 6. (Also, notice that the figures in column 2, $(y_i - \bar{y})$, are also squared, entered in column 7, $(y_i - \bar{y})^2$, and totaled. The column 7 total will be used in the next section to compute the coefficient of correlation.)

EXHIBIT 3-2

Month	(1) y_i Electricity Cost	(2) $(y_i - \bar{y})$ Difference from Average of \$570 Cost	(3) x_i Direct Labor Hours	(4) $(x_i - \bar{x})$ Difference from Average of 35,000 Hours	(5) $(x_i - \bar{x})^2$ (4) Squared	(6) $(x_i - \bar{x})(y_i - \bar{y})$ (4) × (2)	(7) $(y_i - \bar{y})^2$ (2) Squared
January........	$ 640	$ 70	34,000	(1,000)	1,000,000	(70,000)	4,900
February	620	50	30,000	(5,000)	25,000,000	(250,000)	2,500
March...........	620	50	34,000	(1,000)	1,000,000	(50,000)	2,500
April	590	20	39,000	4,000	16,000,000	80,000	400
May..............	500	(70)	42,000	7,000	49,000,000	(490,000)	4,900
June.............	530	(40)	32,000	(3,000)	9,000,000	120,000	1,600
July	500	(70)	26,000	(9,000)	81,000,000	630,000	4,900
August	500	(70)	26,000	(9,000)	81,000,000	630,000	4,900
September...	530	(40)	31,000	(4,000)	16,000,000	160,000	1,600
October........	550	(20)	35,000	0	0	0	400
November....	580	10	43,000	8,000	64,000,000	80,000	100
December....	680	$110	48,000	13,000	169,000,000	1,430,000	12,100
Total..........	$6,840	0	420,000	0	512,000,000	2,270,000	40,800

The variable rate for electricity cost, b, is computed as follows:

$$b = \frac{\Sigma(x_i - \bar{x})(y_i - \bar{y})}{\Sigma(x_i - \bar{x})^2} = \frac{\text{Column 6 total}}{\text{Column 5 total}} = \frac{\$2{,}270{,}000}{512{,}000{,}000} = \$.0044 \text{ per direct labor hour}$$

The fixed cost, a, can be computed using the formula for a straight line as follows:

$$\bar{y} = a + b\bar{x}$$
$$\$570 = a + (\$.0044)(35{,}000)$$
$$\$570 = a + \$154$$
$$a = \$416 \text{ fixed element of electricity cost per month}$$

These results differ from those determined by the scattergraph method because fitting a line visually through the data points is not as accurate as fitting a line mathematically. The mathematical preciseness of the method of least squares injects a high degree of objectivity into the analysis. However, it is still useful to plot the data in order to verify visually the existence of a linear relationship between the dependent variable and the independent variable. Plotting the data makes it easier to spot abnormal data which can distort the least-squares estimates. If abnormal data are found, they should be removed from the sample data set before using the least-squares formulas. In this illustration, the sample size was small in order to simplify the computations. In practice, the sample size should be sufficiently large to represent normal operating conditions.

Correlation Analysis. The use of the scattergraph method makes it possible visually to determine whether or not there is a reasonable degree of correlation between the cost and the activity being analyzed. In a statistical sense, **correlation** is a measure of the covariation between two variables—the independent variable (x, or direct labor hours in the illustration) and the dependent variable (y, or electricity cost in the illustration). In addition to computing the fixed cost and the variable rate for semivariable expenses or the variable rate for entirely variable expenses, the correlation between the independent variable and the dependent variable should be assessed. If all plotted points fall on the regression line, perfect correlation exists. If correlation is high and the past relationship between the two variables continues in the future, the activity chosen will be useful for predicting future levels of the cost being analyzed.

Mathematical measurements can be used to quantify correlation. In statistical theory, the **coefficient of correlation**, denoted r, is a measure of the extent to which two variables are related linearly. When $r = 0$, there is no correlation; and when $r = \pm 1$, the correlation is perfect. If the sign of r is positive, the relationship between the dependent variable, y, and the independent variable, x, is positive, which means that the value of y increases as the value of x increases, and the regression line slopes upward to the right. If the sign of r is negative, the relationship between the dependent variable, y, and the independent variable, x, is negative or inverse, which means that the value of y decreases as the value of x increases, and the regression line slopes downward to the right.

The **coefficient of determination** is found by squaring the coefficient of correlation and is denoted as r^2. The coefficient of determination is considered easier to interpret than the coefficient of correlation because it represents the percentage of variance in the dependent variable explained by the independent variable. The word *explained* means that the variations in the dependent variable are related to, but not necessarily caused by, the variations in the independent variable. Although the coefficient of correlation and the coefficient of determination are mathematical measures of covariation, they do not establish a cause-and-effect relationship between the dependent variable and the independent variable. Such a relationship must be theoretically developed or physically observed.

The formula for calculating the coefficient of correlation[5] is:

$$r = \frac{\Sigma(x_i - \bar{x})(y_i - \bar{y})}{\sqrt{\Sigma(x_i - \bar{x})^2 \, \Sigma(y_i - \bar{y})^2}}$$

where $(x_i - \bar{x})$ is the difference between each observation of the independent variable (direct labor hours in the Barker Company illustration) and its average; and $(y_i - \bar{y})$ is the difference between each observation of the dependent variable (electricity cost) and its average. The coefficient of correlation, r, and the coefficient of determination, r^2, for the data in Exhibit 3-2 are calculated as follows:

[5] The equations for the coefficient of determination and the coefficient of correlation are developed in the appendix to this chapter.

$$r = \frac{\Sigma(x_i - \bar{x})(y_i - \bar{y})}{\sqrt{\Sigma(x_i - \bar{x})^2 \, \Sigma(y_i - \bar{y})^2}} = \frac{\text{Column 6 total}}{\sqrt{(\text{Column 5 total})(\text{Column 7 total})}}$$

$$= \frac{2{,}270{,}000}{\sqrt{(512{,}000{,}000)(40{,}800)}} = .49666$$

$$r^2 = .24667$$

A coefficient of determination that is less than .25 means that less than 25 percent of the change in electricity cost is related to the change in direct labor hours. Apparently, the cost in this case is related not only to direct labor hours but to other factors as well, such as the time of day or the season of the year. Furthermore, some other activity, such as machine hours, may be more closely correlated with electricity cost, thereby providing a better basis for predicting electricity cost.

To illustrate a case in which a high degree of correlation exists, the cost of electricity listed in Exhibit 3-1 is slightly altered in Exhibit 3-3, with direct labor hours remaining unchanged.

EXHIBIT 3-3

Month	(1) y_i Electricity Cost	(2) $(y_i - \bar{y})$ Difference from Average of $655 Cost	(3) x_i Direct Labor Hours	(4) $(x_i - \bar{x})$ Difference from Average of 35,000 Hours	(5) $(x_i - \bar{x})^2$ (4) Squared	(6) $(x_i - \bar{x})(y_i - \bar{y})$ (4) × (2)	(7) $(y_i - \bar{y})^2$ (2) Squared
January........	$ 660	$ 5	34,000	(1,000)	1,000,000	(5,000)	25
February	590	(65)	30,000	(5,000)	25,000,000	325,000	4,225
March...........	660	5	34,000	(1,000)	1,000,000	(5,000)	25
April..............	680	25	39,000	4,000	16,000,000	100,000	625
May	740	85	42,000	7,000	49,000,000	595,000	7,225
June	610	(45)	32,000	(3,000)	9,000,000	135,000	2,025
July	580	(75)	26,000	(9,000)	81,000,000	675,000	5,625
August..........	550	(105)	26,000	(9,000)	81,000,000	945,000	11,025
September ...	630	(25)	31,000	(4,000)	16,000,000	100,000	625
October........	640	(15)	35,000	0	0	0	225
November	750	95	43,000	8,000	64,000,000	760,000	9,025
December	770	115	48,000	13,000	169,000,000	1,495,000	13,225
Total..........	$7,860	0	420,000	0	512,000,000	5,120,000	53,900

Based on these altered data, the following solution indicates a very high correlation between the two variables, which means that this relationship could be accepted as the basis for calculating electricity cost for planning and control.

$$r = \frac{\Sigma(x_i - \bar{x})(y_i - \bar{y})}{\sqrt{\Sigma(x_i - \bar{x})^2 \, \Sigma(y_i - \bar{y})^2}} = \frac{\text{Column 6 total}}{\sqrt{(\text{Column 5 total})(\text{Column 7 total})}}$$

$$= \frac{5{,}120{,}000}{\sqrt{(512{,}000{,}000)(53{,}900)}} = .97463$$

$$r^2 = .94991$$

Standard Error of the Estimate. The regression equation, which in the Barker Company illustration is $y_i' = \$416 + \$.0044x_i$, can be used to predict cost at any level of activity within the relevant range. However, since the regression equation is determined from a limited sample and since variables that are not included in the regression equation may have some influence on the cost being predicted, the estimated cost will usually be different from the actual cost at the same level of activity. The visual scatter around the regression line portrayed in Figure 3-4 illustrates that the actual electricity cost will likely vary from what might be estimated using the calculated fixed cost and the variable cost rate. Because some variation can be expected, management should determine an acceptable range of tolerance for use in exercising control over expenses. Costs within the limits of variation can be accepted. Costs beyond the limits should be investigated, and any necessary corrective action should be taken.

The **standard error of the estimate** is defined as the standard deviation about the regression line. A small value for the standard error of the estimate indicates a good fit. When r^2 equals one, the standard error equals zero. Management can use this concept to develop a confidence interval which, in turn, can be used to decide whether a given level of cost variance is likely to require management action. To illustrate, the table in Exhibit 3-4 can be prepared from the data in Exhibit 3-1.

EXHIBIT 3-4

Month	(1) x_i Direct Labor Hours	(2) y_i Actual Electricity Cost	(3) $(y_i' = a + bx_i)$ Predicted Electricity Cost*	(4) $(y_i - y_i')$ Prediction Error (2) – (3)	(5) $(y_i - y_i')^2$ Prediction Error Squared (4) Squared
January	34,000	$ 640	$ 566	$ 74	$ 5,476
February.......	30,000	620	548	72	5,184
March	34,000	620	566	54	2,916
April..............	39,000	590	588	2	4
May	42,000	500	601	(101)	10,201
June	32,000	530	557	(27)	729
July...............	26,000	500	530	(30)	900
August..........	26,000	500	530	(30)	900
September ...	31,000	530	552	(22)	484
October	35,000	550	570	(20)	400
November	43,000	580	605	(25)	625
December	48,000	680	627	53	2,809
Total	420,000	$6,840	$6,840	0**	$30,628

* Calculated regression line, y_i', values, (direct labor hours × $.0044) + $416, are rounded to the nearest dollar.

** The sum of column (4) is always zero, except for rounding error.

Based on the computations in Exhibit 3-4, the standard error of the estimate is then calculated as follows:

$$s' = \sqrt{\frac{\Sigma(y_i - y_i')^2}{n - 2}} = \sqrt{\frac{\text{Column 5 total}}{12 - 2}} = \sqrt{\frac{\$30{,}628}{10}} = \$55.34$$

The prediction errors are usually assumed to follow a normal distribution. However, for small samples, the Student's *t* distribution is a more appropriate assumption. A table of selected *t* values (based on the assumption that two tails of the distribution are of concern, i.e., that managers are concerned about both favorable and unfavorable variances) is provided in Exhibit 3-5.

EXHIBIT 3-5

Table of Selected Values of Student's *t* Distribution

Degrees of Freedom	**Desired Confidence Level**			
	90%	**95%**	**99%**	**99.8%**
1	6.314	12.706	63.657	318.310
2	2.920	4.303	9.925	22.326
3	2.353	3.182	5.841	10.213
4	2.132	2.776	4.604	7.173
5	2.015	2.571	4.032	5.893
6	1.943	2.447	3.707	5.208
7	1.895	2.365	3.499	4.785
8	1.860	2.306	3.355	4.501
9	1.833	2.262	3.250	4.297
10	1.812	2.228	3.169	4.144
11	1.796	2.201	3.106	4.025
12	1.782	2.179	3.055	3.930
13	1.771	2.160	3.012	3.852
14	1.761	2.145	2.977	3.787
15	1.753	2.131	2.947	3.733
20	1.725	2.086	2.845	3.552
25	1.708	2.060	2.787	3.450
30	1.697	2.042	2.750	3.385
40	1.684	2.021	2.704	3.307
60	1.671	2.000	2.660	3.232
120	1.658	1.980	2.617	3.160
∞	1.645	1.960	2.576	3.090

The acceptable range of actual cost around the predicted cost would be computed for a sample of size n by multiplying the standard error of the estimate by the t value for $n - 2$ degrees of freedom[6] at the desired confidence level, t_p, and by a correction factor for small samples as follows:

$$y'_i \pm t_p s' \sqrt{1 + \frac{1}{n} + \frac{(x_i - \bar{x})^2}{\Sigma(x_i - \bar{x})^2}}$$

where all variables are as previously defined.

To illustrate the computation and use of the confidence interval, assume that the actual level of activity for a period is 40,000 direct labor hours. The electricity cost computed for the budget from the regression equation determined in the previous example is \$592 [\$416 + (\$.0044 × 40,000)]. Assume further that management wants to be 95 percent confident that the actual electricity cost is within acceptable tolerance limits. Based on the table factor of 2.228 for t at the 95-percent confidence level, with $df = 12 - 2$, and on the standard error of the estimate computed above ($s' = \$55.34$), the confidence interval would be:

[6] Degrees of freedom (df) refers to the number of values that are free to vary after certain restrictions have been placed on the data. In general, if a regression equation involves p unknown parameters, then $df = n - p$. In linear bivariate regression there are two unknown parameters, a and b; thus, $df = n - 2$.

$$y_i' \pm t_{95\%} s' \sqrt{1 + \frac{1}{n} + \frac{(x_i - \bar{x})^2}{\Sigma(x_i - \bar{x})^2}}$$

$$\$592.00 \pm (2.228)(\$55.34) \sqrt{1 + \frac{1}{12} + \frac{(40{,}000 - 35{,}000)^2}{512{,}000{,}000}}$$

$$\$592.00 \pm (2.228)(\$55.34)(1.064)$$

$$\$592.00 \pm \$131.19$$

Management can expect the actual electricity cost to be between \$460.81 (\$592.00 − \$131.19) and \$723.19 (\$592.00 + \$131.19) about 95 percent of the time. Electricity cost outside of these limits will occur because of random chance only 5 percent of the time. If the actual electricity cost is less than \$460.81 or greater than \$723.19, management should investigate the cause and take any necessary corrective action.

For large samples, the Student's *t* distribution approaches the normal distribution and the correction factor for small samples (the square-root term) approaches one. For large samples, therefore, the computation of the acceptable range of actual cost around the predicted cost may be simplified by omitting the correction factor and using the appropriate *z* value for the normal distribution.[7] If the sample size used in computing the regression equation and the standard error of the estimate in the illustration were large, the 95-percent confidence interval for electricity cost at 40,000 direct labor hours would be:

$$\$592.00 \pm (1.960)(\$55.34)$$
$$\$592.00 \pm \$108.47$$

After the fixed and variable components of cost have been computed using the method of least squares, it is useful to plot the regression line against the sample data, so that the pattern of deviations of the actual observations from the corresponding estimates on the regression line can be inspected. Normally, the distribution of observations around the regression line should be uniform for all values of the independent variable (referred to as **homoscedastic**) and randomly distributed around the regression line as depicted in Figure 3-5. However, if the variance differs at different points on the regression line (referred to as **heteroscedastic**), as depicted in Figure 3-6, or if the observations around the regression line appear to be correlated with one another (referred to as **serial correlation** or **autocorrelation**), as depicted in Figure 3-7, the standard error of the estimate and the confidence intervals based on the standard error are unreliable measures.[8]

[7] The *t* values presented in Exhibit 3-5 for $df = \infty$ are equal to the *z* values for the normal distribution.

[8] For a comprehensive discussion, see chapter 19, "Multiple Regression and Correlation," by Michael J. Brennan and Thomas M. Carroll, *Preface to Quantitative Economics and Econometrics* (Cincinnati: South-Western Publishing Co., 1987).

FIGURE 3-5
Homoscedasticity (Random Error Term)

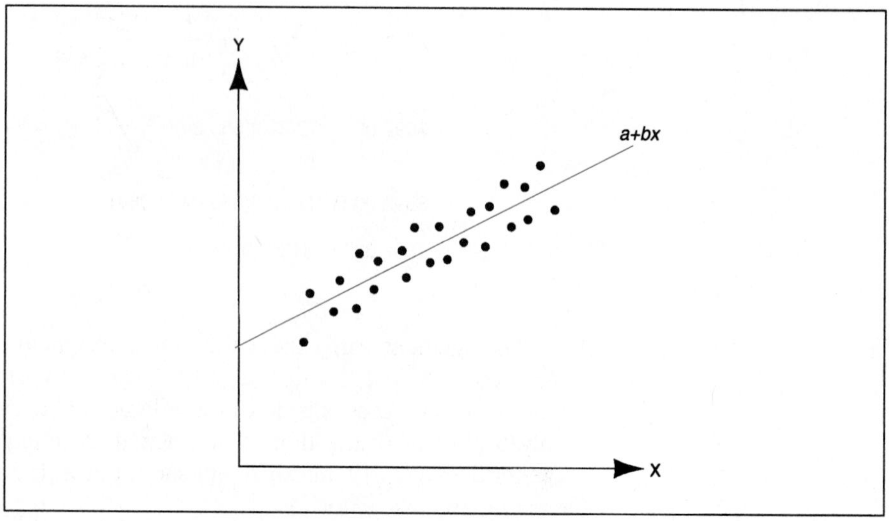

FIGURE 3-6
Heteroscedasticity

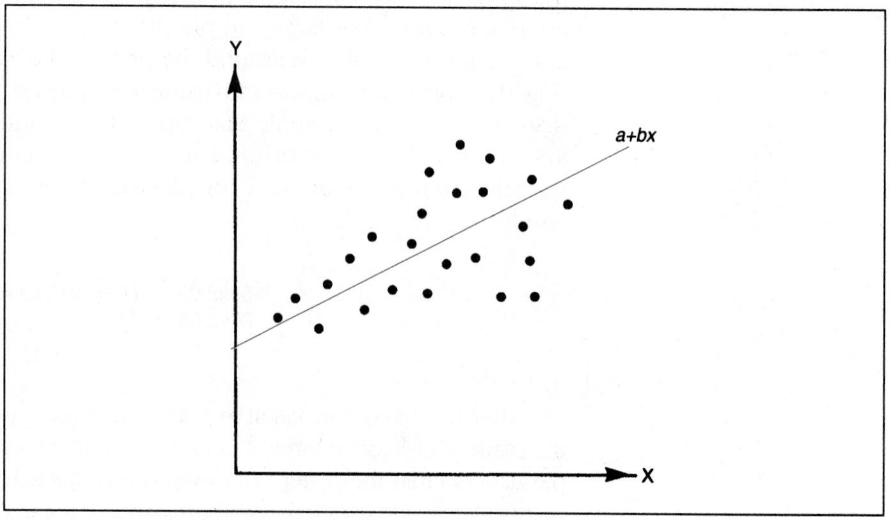

FIGURE 3-7 *Serial Correlation*

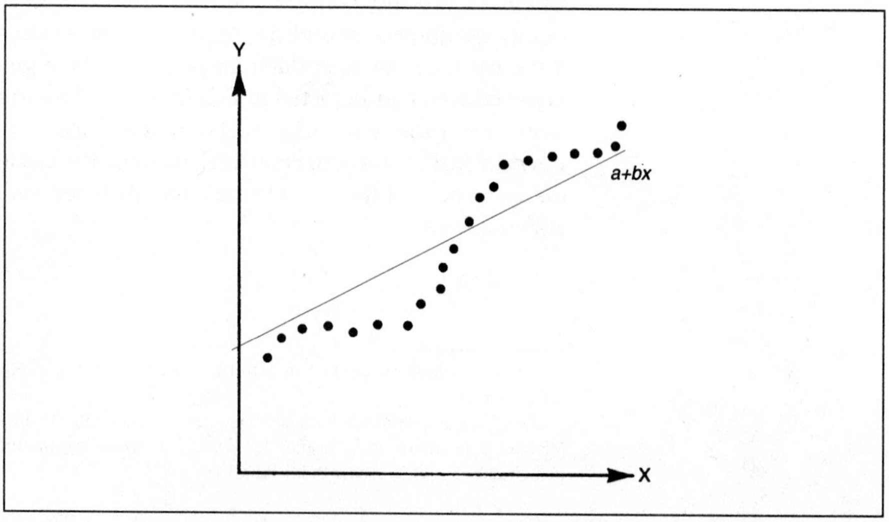

Method of Least Squares for Multiple Independent Variables

Typically, cost behavior is shown as dependent on a single measure of volume or on some other independent variable. In the preceding discussion, for example, the behavior of the dependent variable, electricity cost, was described by the independent variable, direct labor hours. However, a cost can vary because of more than one factor.

Multiple Regression Analysis is a further application and expansion of the method of least squares, permitting consideration of more than one independent variable. In multiple regression analysis, the least squares equation for a straight line, $y_i = a + bx_i + e_i$, is expanded to include more than one independent variable. For example, in the equation $y_i = a + bx_i + cz_i + e_i$, c is the variable rate for an additional independent variable z. Although the cost relationship can no longer be shown on a two-dimensional graph and the arithmetical computations become more complex, the widespread availability of computer programs makes the use of multiple regression analysis feasible.

The least-squares concept is fundamentally the same when there are two or more independent variables as when there is only one. The assumption of normality still applies. In the case of multiple regression, however, it is the joint probability distribution of the variables that is assumed to be normally distributed (sometimes referred to as multivariate normal). One additional assumption is that the independent variables are not correlated with one another. When the independent variables are correlated with one another, they are said to be collinear, a condition referred to as **multicollinearity**. When the degree of multicollinearity is high, the relationship between one or more of the independent variables and the dependent variable may be obscured.[9] The presence of multicollinearity would not affect the estimate of cost unless one or more important independent variables—activity measures—were omitted from the regression model because of an apparent lack of relationship to the dependent variable—cost. Omitting important variables from the multiple-regression model is referred to as **specification error** and is more of a problem in analyzing the sources of cost incurrence than in estimating cost.

If the cost behavior of a group of expenditures in one or more ledger accounts is being described, an alternate to multiple variables (and hence to the considerations necessitated by multiple variables when applying the least squares method) may be possible. That is, expenses may be grouped and classified in sufficient detail so that expenses in a particular group are all largely related to only one independent variable. This would allow the use of the method of least squares as earlier illustrated, that is, simple regression analysis. If this approach is not feasible, as when more than one independent variable is still required to describe the cost behavior, then multiple regression analysis should be employed.[10]

Summary

Because of the dynamic nature of business, companies often are faced with the need to make changes in the level and mix of their business activities. For management to plan a company's activities intelligently and control its costs effectively, the relationship of cost incurrence to changes in activity must be understood thoroughly. This chapter discussed the effect of changes in business

[9] *Ibid.*
[10] *Ibid.*

activity on costs and classified costs as fixed, variable, or semivariable with respect to activity. Three techniques for segregating the fixed and variable components of costs were illustrated: the high and low points method, the scattergraph method, and the method of least squares. The most accurate method is the method of least-squares; however, the reliability of least-squares cost estimates depends on the correlation between the activity and the cost being analyzed. The coefficient of correlation should be used to find the most accurate predictor. In addition, the standard error of the estimate can be computed on the basis of least-squares estimates and used to develop a confidence interval for cost control. Although the discussion centered on production costs and activities, the concepts and techniques are equally applicable to marketing and administrative activities.

Appendix Development of the Regression and Correlation Equations

The formula for a straight line is $y = a + bx$; consequently, the regression equation is:

$$y_i = a + bx_i + e_i$$

where y_i = dependent variable (cost) at period i
x_i = independent variable (activity) at period i
a = intercept (estimate of fixed cost)
b = slope (estimate of variable cost per unit of activity)
e_i = prediction error, i.e., the difference between y_i (an actual observation) and $a + bx_i$ (an estimate of y_i)

Since the regression line exactly splits the plotted sample y_is, so that the sum of the values of the e_is above the line exactly equals the sum of the values of the e_is below the line, the sum of the e_is equals zero. Therefore, the e_is values are squared before being summed to produce a value that can be worked with. This sum of the squared error terms, SSE, is expressed as follows:

$$\text{SSE} = \Sigma(y_i - a - bx_i)^2 = \Sigma y_i^2 - 2b\Sigma x_i y_i + 2ab\Sigma x_i + b^2\Sigma x_i^2 + na^2 - 2a\Sigma y_i$$

where y, a, b, and x are as previously defined and n is the sample size. (For ease of presentation, the subscripts for x and y have been omitted in the remainder of the appendix.) To find the minimum value of SSE, take partial derivatives with respect to the two unknowns, a and b, and then set the partial derivatives equal to zero as follows:

$$\frac{\delta \text{SSE}}{\delta a} = 2b\Sigma x + 2na - 2\Sigma y = 0$$

$$\frac{\delta \text{SSE}}{\delta b} = -2\Sigma xy + 2a\Sigma x + 2b\Sigma x^2 = 0$$

Rearranging terms and dividing through by 2 yields the so-called normal equations:

$$\Sigma y = na + b\Sigma x$$
$$\Sigma xy = a\Sigma x + b\Sigma x^2$$

The two normal equations each contain two unknowns. However, since the two equations are not linear transformations of one another, they can be solved. One way is to multiply both sides of the first equation by $\Sigma x/n$ and then to subtract the first equation from the second in order to eliminate one of the unknowns (a in this case):

$$\begin{aligned} \Sigma xy &= a\Sigma x + b\Sigma x^2 \\ -\frac{\Sigma x \Sigma y}{n} &= -a\Sigma x - \frac{b\Sigma x \Sigma x}{n} \\ \hline \Sigma xy - \frac{\Sigma x \Sigma y}{n} &= b\Sigma x^2 - \frac{b\Sigma x \Sigma x}{n} \quad \text{or} \quad n\Sigma xy - \Sigma x\Sigma y = nb\Sigma x^2 - b\Sigma x\Sigma x \end{aligned}$$

Solving for b yields:

$$b = \frac{n\Sigma xy - \Sigma x\Sigma y}{n\Sigma x^2 - \Sigma x\Sigma x} = \frac{\Sigma(x - \bar{x})(y - \bar{y})}{\Sigma(x - \bar{x})^2}$$

where $\bar{x} = \Sigma x/n$ and $\bar{y} = \Sigma y/n$. Since $y = a + bx$, then the remaining unknown, a, is computed as follows:

$$a = \bar{y} - b\bar{x}$$

The coefficient of correlation, r, is a measure of the relationship between the independent and the dependent variables, which is captured by the regression coefficient, b. Since the coefficient of determination, r^2, is the portion of the total variation in the dependent variable that is explained by covariation in the independent variable, it is computed by multiplying the sum of the squared deviations of the independent variable about its mean, $\Sigma(x - \bar{x})^2$, by b^2 and then dividing the product by the sum of the dependent variable's deviations about its mean, $\Sigma(y - \bar{y})^2$, as follows:

$$r^2 = b^2\left[\frac{\Sigma(x - \bar{x})^2}{\Sigma(y - \bar{y})^2}\right]$$

$$r^2 = \left[\frac{\Sigma(x - \bar{x})(y - \bar{y})}{\Sigma(x - \bar{x})^2}\right]^2 \left[\frac{\Sigma(x - \bar{x})^2}{\Sigma(y - \bar{y})^2}\right]$$

$$r^2 = \left[\frac{\Sigma(x - \bar{x})(y - \bar{y})}{\Sigma(x - \bar{x})^2}\right] \left[\frac{\Sigma(x - \bar{x})(y - \bar{y})}{\cancel{\Sigma(x - \bar{x})^2}}\right] \left[\frac{\cancel{\Sigma(x - \bar{x})^2}}{\Sigma(y - \bar{y})^2}\right]$$

$$r^2 = \frac{[\Sigma(x - \bar{x})(y - \bar{y})]^2}{\Sigma(x - \bar{x})^2\,\Sigma(y - \bar{y})^2}$$

The coefficient of correlation, r, is computed by taking the square root of both sides of the last equation.

$$r = \frac{\Sigma(x - \bar{x})(y - \bar{y})}{\sqrt{\Sigma(x - \bar{x})^2\,\Sigma(y - \bar{y})^2}}$$

Key Terms

fixed cost *(40)*
relevant range *(41)*
discretionary fixed costs or programmed fixed costs *(41)*
committed fixed costs *(41)*
variable cost *(41)*
semivariable cost *(42)*
high and low points method *(45)*
scattergraph method *(46)*
method of least squares or regression analysis *(47)*
correlation *(49)*

coefficient of correlation *(49)*
coefficient of determination *(49)*
standard error of the estimate *(51)*
homoscedastic *(53)*
heteroscedastic *(53)*
serial correlation or autocorrelation *(53)*
multiple regression analysis *(55)*
multicollinearity *(55)*
specification error *(55)*

Discussion Questions

Q3-1 Explain the difference between fixed, variable, and semivariable costs.

Q3-2 What is meant by the term *relevant range*?

Q3-3 Why should semivariable costs be segregated into their fixed and variable components?

Q3-4 Discuss the advantage and the disadvantage of using managerial judgment to separate fixed and variable costs.

Q3-5 What computational methods are available for separating the fixed and variable components of semivariable costs?

Q3-6 What are the advantages and disadvantages of each of the three different methods of separating fixed and variable components of costs?

Q3-7 Explain the meaning of the \$200 and the \$4 in the regression equation, $y_i = \$200 + \$4x_i$, where y_i denotes the total monthly cost of indirect supplies and x_i is machine hours per month.
(ICMA adapted)

Q3-8 Define and explain the difference between the coefficient of correlation and the coefficient of determination.

Q3-9 What is the standard error of the estimate?

Q3-10 With respect to the method of least squares, what is meant by the term *heteroscedasticity*, and what problem is likely to occur if it is present?

Q3-11 Define and explain the significance of the term *serial correlation*.

Q3-12 What is meant by the term *multicollinearity* as it is applied in multiple regression analysis?

Exercises

E3-1 High and Low Points Method. Edd Company wants to segregate the fixed and variable portions of maintenance cost, believed to be a semivariable cost, as measured against machine hours. The following information has been provided for the first six months of the current year:

Month	Machine Hours	Maintenance Cost
January	2,500	\$1,250
February	2,200	1,150
March	2,100	1,100
April	2,600	1,300
May	2,300	1,180
June	2,400	1,200

Required: Using the high and low points method, compute the variable cost rate and the fixed cost for maintenance cost.

E3-2 Statistical Scattergraph. Keefer Company production management is interested in determining the fixed and variable components of supplies cost, a semivariable cost, as measured against direct labor hours. Data for the first ten months of the current year follow:

Month	Labor Hours	Supplies Cost
January	450	\$600
February	475	700
March	500	750
April	550	650

Month	Labor Hours	Supplies Cost
May	725	$900
June	750	800
July	675	825
August	525	725
September	600	775
October	625	850

Required: Graph the data provided and determine the fixed and variable components of supplies cost.

E3-3 Method of Least Squares. Tiptop Company management is interested in predicting travel and entertainment expense based on the number of expected sales calls on customers. Over the past 50 weeks, the company's Sales Department reported that its sales force made 6,250 calls on customers, an average of 125 calls per week. Travel and entertainment expenses over the same period totaled $500,000, an average of $10,000 per week. The travel and entertainment expense deviations from its average multiplied by the sales call deviations from its average and summed $[\Sigma(x_i - \bar{x})(y_i - \bar{y})]$ is 87,000, and the sales call deviations from its average squared and summed $[\Sigma(x_i - \bar{x})^2]$ is 1,450.

Required: Using the method of least squares, estimate the total cost of travel and entertainment for a week in which the company's sales personnel make 200 sales calls.

E3-4 Method of Least Squares. The following data were collected for the most recent twelve-month period by the cost accountant in one of Axelrod Company's manufacturing plants.

Month	Electricity Cost	Machine Hours
January	$1,600	2,790
February	1,510	2,680
March	1,500	2,600
April	1,450	2,500
May	1,460	2,510
June	1,520	2,610
July	1,570	2,750
August	1,530	2,700
September	1,480	2,530
October	1,470	2,520
November	1,450	2,490
December	1,460	2,520

Required: Using the method of least squares, compute the fixed cost and the variable cost rate for electricity cost. Round estimates to the nearest cent.

E3-5 Correlation Analysis. The controller of Berry Electronics Company would like to know how closely the incurrence of factory overhead in the company's Semiconductor Manufacturing Department correlates with machine hours. Total factory overhead over the past 12 months is $108,000, and 5,760 machine hours were logged in for the same period. The sum of the machine hour differences from average $[\Sigma(x_i - \bar{x})^2]$ is 850, and the sum of the factory overhead cost differences from average $[\Sigma(y_i - \bar{y})^2]$ is $3,400. The machine hour differences from average multiplied by the factory overhead cost differences from average and summed $[\Sigma(x_i - \bar{x})(y_i - \bar{y})]$ is 1,564.

Required: Compute the coefficient of correlation, r, and the coefficient of determination, r^2, for factory overhead and machine hours in the Semiconductor Manufacturing Department.

E3-6 Correlation Analysis. The management of Hidalgo Inc. collected the following data over the most recent 12 months:

Month	Shipping Expense	Sales Revenue
January	$560	$26,500
February	600	30,000

Month	Shipping Expense	Sales Revenue
March	$600	$29,000
April	580	28,000
May	570	27,000
June	550	25,500
July	590	30,000
August	610	33,000
September	650	35,000
October	620	32,000
November	630	30,500
December	640	33,500

Required: Compute the coefficient of correlation, r, and the coefficient of determination, r^2, for shipping expense and sales revenue.

E3-7 Cost Behavior and Correlation Analysis. Cyclops Company's total maintenance cost for the past 10 months is $50,000. Some of the maintenance activity appears related to the operation of machinery, and the accountant wants to determine whether machine hours should be used as a basis upon which to estimate maintenance cost at various levels of capacity. Machine hours for the same period totaled 40,000 hours. The machine hour differences from average multiplied by the maintenance cost differences from its average and summed $[\Sigma(x_i - \bar{x})(y_i - \bar{y})]$ is 2,400. The machine hour differences from average squared and summed $[\Sigma(x_i - \bar{x})^2]$ is 6,250, and the maintenance cost differences from average squared and summed $[\Sigma(y_i - \bar{y})^2]$ is 1,000.

Required:

(1) Compute the coefficient of correlation, r, and the coefficient of determination, r^2, for maintenance cost and machine hours.

(2) Compute the variable maintenance cost per machine hour, using the method of least squares.

(3) Compute the fixed maintenance cost, using the method of least squares.

E3-8 Choosing Appropriate Activity Measure and Separating Fixed and Variable Costs. Total electricity cost for the past 20 months is $42,000. An activity measure on which to base estimates of electricity cost is needed. The two activity measures being considered are direct labor hours and machine hours. Direct labor hours for the period totaled 180,000, and machine hours totaled 120,000. The direct labor hour differences from average multiplied by the electricity cost differences from its average and summed $[\Sigma(x_i - \bar{x})(y_i - \bar{y})]$ is 5,700. The direct labor hour differences from average squared and summed $[\Sigma(x_i - \bar{x})^2]$ is 28,500. The electricity cost differences from average squared and summed $[\Sigma(y_i - \bar{y})^2]$ is 1,264. The machine hour differences from average multiplied by the electricity cost differences from its average and summed $[\Sigma(x_i - \bar{x})(y_i - \bar{y})]$ is 7,000. The machine hour differences from average squared and summed $[\Sigma(x_i - \bar{x})^2]$ is 50,000.

Required:

(1) Compute the coefficient of correlation, r, and the coefficient of determination, r^2, for direct labor hours and electricity cost.

(2) Compute the coefficient of correlation, r, and the coefficient of determination, r^2, for machine hours and electricity cost.

(3) Which activity measure should be used for the estimation of fixed and variable electricity cost? Explain.

(4) Compute the variable electricity cost rate and the fixed cost, using the method of least squares.

E3-9 Standard Error of the Estimate. The controller of Fratiani Company used the method of least squares to compute the fixed and variable components of utility cost from the following data:

Month	Utility Cost	Labor Hours
January	$3,600	2,650
February	4,000	3,000
March	4,000	2,900
April	3,800	2,800
May	3,700	2,700
June	3,500	2,550

Month	Utility Cost	Labor Hours
July	$3,900	3,000
August	4,100	3,300
September	4,500	3,500
October	4,200	3,200
November	4,300	3,050
December	4,400	3,350

Required: Assuming that the least squares estimate of fixed cost is $1,000 and the variable rate is $1.00, compute the standard error of the estimate to three decimal places.

E3-10 Standard Error of the Estimate and Confidence Interval Estimation. The production supervisor of Pylex Inc. would like to know the range of maintenance cost that should be expected about 90% of the time at the 1,500-machine-hour level of activity. The least squares estimate of maintenance cost at that level of activity is $500. The least squares parameter estimates,—that is, the estimates of fixed cost and the variable cost rate—were derived from a sample of data for a recent 15-month period. The machine hour average for the sample period is 1,300, and the machine hour deviations from its average squared and summed [$\Sigma(x_i - \bar{x})^2$] is 150,000. The prediction error squared [$\Sigma(y_i - y_i')^2$] over the same sample period is $49,972.

Required: Compute the standard error of the estimate and the 90% confidence interval estimate for maintenance cost at the 1,500-machine-hour level of activity.

Problems

P3-1 Correlation Analysis. The Cost Department of Quick Supply Company attempts to establish a budget to assist in the control of marketing expenses. An examination of individual expenses shows:

Item	Fixed Portion	Variable Portion
Sales staff:		
Salaries	$1,200	none
Retainers	2,000	none
Commissions	none	4% of sales
Advertising	5,000	none
Travel expense	?	?

Statistical analysis is needed to split the travel expense satisfactorily into its fixed and variable portions. Before such an analysis is begun, it is thought that the variable portion of the travel expense might vary in accordance either with the number of calls made on customers each month or the value of orders received each month. Records reveal the following details over the past twelve months:

Month	Calls Made	Orders Received	Travel Expense
January	410	$53,000	$3,000
February	420	65,000	3,200
March	380	48,000	2,800
April	460	73,000	3,400
May	430	62,000	3,100
June	450	67,000	3,200
July	390	60,000	2,900
August	470	76,000	3,300
September	480	82,000	3,500
October	490	62,000	3,400
November	440	64,000	3,200
December	460	80,000	3,400

Required:

(1) Compute the coefficient of correlation, r, and coefficient of determination, r^2, between (a) the travel expense and the number of calls made and (b) the travel expense and orders received. (Round to four decimal places.)

(2) Compare the answers obtained in requirements 1a and 1b.

P3-2 Choosing Appropriate Activity Measure; Cost Behavior Analysis. The controller of Pitzky Corporation has asked for help in the selection of the appropriate activity measure to be used in estimating variable supplies cost for the company's budget. The following information about past expenses and two potential activity measures has been supplied:

Month	Supplies Cost	Labor Hours	Machine Hours
January	$ 1,505	5,000	2,000
February	1,395	4,600	1,990
March	1,565	5,160	2,140
April	1,515	5,100	2,080
May	1,445	4,830	1,960
June	1,415	4,750	1,940
July	1,465	4,900	2,020
August	1,505	5,080	1,990
September	1,575	5,200	2,140
October	1,535	5,130	2,050
November	1,500	4,950	2,030
December	1,580	5,300	2,260
Total	$18,000	60,000	24,600

Required:

(1) Compute the coefficient of correlation, r, and the coefficient of determination, r^2, between supplies cost and each of the two activity measures.

(2) Identify which of the two activity measures should be used as a basis upon which to estimate the allowable supplies cost.

(3) Using the activity measure selected in requirement 2 above, determine the fixed cost and the variable cost rate by the method of least squares.

P3-3 Choosing Appropriate Activity Measure; Cost Behavior Analysis. The management of the KXR Corporation has asked for help in the selection of the appropriate activity measure to be used in estimating electricity cost in one of its manufacturing plants. The following information about past expenses and two potential activity measures has been supplied:

Month	Electricity Cost	Labor Hours	Machine Hours
January	$ 1,600	4,200	2,300
February	1,570	4,000	2,150
March	1,610	4,360	2,400
April	1,550	4,000	2,250
May	1,530	4,050	2,160
June	1,540	4,100	2,240
July	1,520	4,150	2,180
August	1,530	4,250	2,170
September	1,580	4,150	2,260
October	1,650	4,500	2,500
November	1,660	4,600	2,540
December	1,620	4,400	2,450
Total	$18,960	50,760	27,600

Required:

(1) Compute the coefficient of correlation, r, and the coefficient of determination, r^2, between the cost of electricity and each of the two activity measures.

(2) Identify which of the two activity measures should be used as a basis on which to estimate the allowable cost of electricity.

(3) Using the activity measure selected in requirement 2, compute an estimate of fixed electricity cost and the variable electricity rate by the method of least squares.

P3-4 Cost Behavior Analysis; Correlation Analysis; Standard Error of the Estimate. The following data have been collected by the controller of Lynpax Corporation over the past 12 months:

Month	Maintenance Cost	Machine Hours
January	$ 2,200	2,500
February	2,130	2,350
March	2,000	2,000
April	2,170	2,400
May	2,050	2,100
June	2,220	2,600
July	2,150	2,450
August	2,250	2,550
September	2,290	2,700
October	2,150	2,450
November	2,210	2,400
December	2,100	2,300
Total	$25,920	28,800

Required:

(1) Using the high and low points method, determine the average amount of fixed maintenance cost per month and the variable maintenance rate per machine hour.

(2) Determine the fixed cost and the variable cost rate, using the method of least squares.

(3) Compute the coefficient of correlation, r, and the coefficient of determination, r^2, between the machine hours and the maintenance cost.

(4) Compute the standard error of the estimate.

(5) Determine the 95% confidence interval for maintenance cost at the 2,500-machine-hour level of activity.

P3-5 Three Methods of Cost Behavior Analysis; Correlation Analysis; Standard Error of the Estimate. The management of the Rest-Time Hotel is interested in an analysis of the fixed and variable costs in the electricity used relative to hotel occupancy. The following data have been gathered from records for the year:

Month	Guest Days	Electricity Cost
January	1,000	$ 400
February	1,500	500
March	2,500	500
April	3,000	700
May	2,500	600
June	4,500	800
July	6,500	1,000
August	6,000	900
September	5,500	900
October	3,000	700
November	2,500	600
December	3,500	800
Total	42,000	$8,400

Required:

(1) Determine the fixed and variable elements of the electricity cost (round the variable rate to four decimal places), using each of the following methods:
  (a) the method of least squares
  (b) the high and low points method
  (c) a scattergraph with trend line fitted by inspection
(2) Compute the coefficient of correlation, r, and the coefficient of determination, r^2, for guest days and electricity cost.
(3) Compute the standard error of the estimate.
(4) Compute the 90% confidence interval for electricity cost at the 2,000-guest-days capacity.

P3-6 Three Methods of Cost Behavior Analysis; Correlation Analysis; Standard Error of the Estimate. A company making tubing from aluminum billets uses a process in which the billets are heated by induction to a very high temperature before being put through an extruding machine that shapes the tubing from the heated billets. The inducer, a very large coil into which the billet is placed, must sustain a great flow of electric current to heat the billets to the necessary temperature. Regardless of the number of billets to be processed, the coil is kept on during the entire operating day because of the time involved in starting it up. The Cost Accounting Department wants to charge the variable electricity cost to each billet and the fixed electricity cost to factory overhead. The following data have been assembled:

Month	Number of Billets	Cost of Electricity
January	2,000	$ 455
February	1,800	450
March	1,900	435
April	2,200	485
May	2,100	470
June	2,000	475
July	1,400	400
August	1,900	450
September	1,800	435
October	2,400	500
November	2,300	495
December	2,200	470
Total	24,000	$5,520

Required:

(1) Determine the fixed and variable elements of the electricity cost, using each of the following methods:
  (a) the high and low points method
  (b) a scattergraph with trend line fitted by inspection
  (c) the method of least squares
(2) Compute the coefficient of correlation, r, and the coefficient of determination, r^2.
(3) Compute the standard error of the estimate, and the 95% confidence interval for electricity cost at the 2,200-billets level of activity.

P3-7 Cost Behavior Analysis; Correlation Analysis; Standard Error of the Estimate. Randal Company manufactures a wide range of electrical products at several different plant locations. Due to fluctuations, its Franklin plant has been experiencing difficulties in estimating the level of monthly overhead.

Management needs more accurate estimates to plan its operational and financial needs. A trade association publication indicates that for companies like Randal, overhead tends to vary with direct labor hours. Based on this information, one member of the accounting staff proposes that the overhead cost behavior pattern be determined in order to calculate the overhead cost in relation to budgeted direct labor hours. Another member of the accounting staff suggests that a good starting place for determining the cost behavior pattern of the overhead cost would be an analysis of historical data to provide a basis for estimating future overhead costs.

Direct labor hours and the respective factory overhead costs for the past three years are as follows:

	19A		19B		19C	
Month	**Direct Labor Hours**	**Factory Overhead Costs**	**Direct Labor Hours**	**Factory Overhead Costs**	**Direct Labor Hours**	**Factory Overhead Costs**
January	2,000	$8,500	2,100	$8,700	2,000	$8,600
February	2,400	9,900	2,300	9,300	2,300	9,300
March	2,200	8,950	2,200	9,300	2,300	9,400
April	2,300	9,000	2,200	8,700	2,200	8,700
May	2,000	8,150	2,000	8,000	2,000	8,100
June	1,900	7,550	1,800	7,650	1,800	7,600
July	1,400	7,050	1,200	6,750	1,300	7,000
August	1,000	6,450	1,300	7,100	1,200	6,900
September	1,200	6,900	1,500	7,350	1,300	7,100
October	1,700	7,500	1,700	7,250	1,800	7,500
November	1,600	7,150	1,500	7,100	1,500	7,000
December	1,900	7,800	1,800	7,500	1,900	7,600

Required:

(1) Compute the amount of fixed factory overhead and the variable cost rate, using the method of least squares. (Round fixed factory overhead to the nearest dollar and the variable cost rate to the nearest cent.)

(2) Compute the coefficient of correlation, r, and the coefficient of determination, r^2, for factory overhead costs and direct labor hours. (Round to four decimal places.)

(3) Compute the standard error of the estimate. (Round to the nearest dollar.)

(4) Compute the 95% confidence interval for factory overhead costs at the 2,200-direct-labor-hour level of activity. (Assume that the sample size is sufficiently large that the normal probability distribution can be assumed and that the correction factor for small samples can be omitted. Round to the nearest dollar.)

P3-8 Choosing Appropriate Activity Measure; Cost Behavior Analysis; Standard Error of the Estimate. Based on observation and knowledge of the production process, the controller of Whirlwind Company believes that the bulk of variable maintenance cost is driven by either labor hours or machine hours. Data gathered for the past 24 months follows:

Months	**Maintenance Cost**	**Labor Hours**	**Machine Hours**
January, 19A	$ 1,195	950	809
February, 19A	1,116	1,024	744
March, 19A	1,390	1,109	987
April, 19A	1,449	1,148	987
May, 19A	1,618	1,313	1,186
June, 19A	1,525	1,261	1,154
July, 19A	1,687	1,552	1,291
August, 19A	1,650	1,372	1,238
September, 19A	1,595	1,366	1,186
October, 19A	1,675	1,455	1,246
November, 19A	1,405	1,221	997
December, 19A	1,251	1,150	841
January, 19B	950	999	502
February, 19B	1,175	1,022	733
March, 19B	1,425	1,220	1,090
April, 19B	1,506	1,283	1,135
May, 19B	1,608	1,339	1,174
June, 19B	1,653	1,250	1,246
July, 19B	1,675	1,440	1,264
August, 19B	1,724	1,290	1,323
September, 19B	1,626	1,335	1,230
October, 19B	1,575	1,164	1,165
November, 19B	1,653	1,373	1,237
December, 19B	1,418	1,124	1,035

Required:

(1) Compute the correlation coefficient, r, and the coefficient of determination, r^2, for maintenance cost with each of the two activity measures suggested by the controller.
(2) Using the method of least squares and the activity measure most highly correlated with maintenance cost, compute the variable maintenance cost rate and the estimated fixed maintenance cost.
(3) Compute the standard error of the estimate using the variable rate and estimated fixed cost computed in requirement 2.
(4) Compute the 95% confidence interval estimate at the 1,100-hour level of activity. Student's t value at the 95% level of confidence for a two-tail test is 2.074 for 22 degrees of freedom, 2.069 for 23 degrees of freedom, and 2.064 for 24 degrees of freedom.

Cases

C3-1 Cost Behavior Analysis Using Method of Least Squares. Elisko Inc. is a major book distributor that ships books throughout the United States. Elisko's Shipping Department consists of a manager plus 10 other permanent positions—four supervisors and six loaders. The four supervisors and six loaders provide the minimum staff and frequently must be supplemented by additional workers during weeks when the volume of shipments is heavy. Thus the number of persons shipping the orders frequently averages over 30 per week—10 permanent plus 20 temporary workers. The temporary workers are hired through a local agency.

Elisko must use temporary workers to maintain a minimum daily shipment rate of 95% of orders presented for shipping. The loss of efficiency from using temporary workers is minimal, and the $10.00-per-hour cost of temporary workers is less than the $15.00 per hour paid for the loaders and $22.50 per hour paid for the supervisors on Elisko's permanent staff. The agency requires Elisko to utilize each temporary worker for at least four hours each day.

Jim Locter, shipping manager, schedules temporary help based on forecasted orders for the coming week. Supervisors serve as loaders until temporary help is needed. A supervisor stops loading when the ratio of loaders to supervisors reaches 7 to 1. Locter knows that he will need temporary help when the forecasted average daily orders exceed 300. Locter frequently requested from two to four extra temporary workers per day to guard against unexpected rush orders. If there is not enough work, he dismisses the extra people at noon after four hours of work. The agency is not pleased with Locter's practice of overhiring and notified Elisko that it is changing its policy. From now on, if a worker is dismissed before an eight-hour assignment is completed, Elisko will still be charged for an eight-hour day plus mileage back to the agency for reassignment. This policy is to go into effect the following week.

Paula Brand, general manager, called Jim Locter to her office when she received the notice from the agency. She told Locter, "Your staffing levels have to be better. This penalty could cost us up to $500 per week in labor cost for which we receive no benefit. Why can't you schedule more accurately?"

Locter replied, "I agree that the staffing should be better, but I can't do it accurately when there are rush orders. By being able to lay off people at noon, I have been able to adjust for the uncertain order schedule without cost to the company. Of course, the agency's new policy changes this."

Locter and Brand contacted Elisko's controller, Mitch Berg, regarding the problem of how to estimate the number of workers needed each week. Berg realized that Locter needs a quick solution until he can study the work flow. Berg suggested a regression analysis using the number of orders shipped as the independent variable and the number of workers (permanent plus temporary) as the dependent variable. Berg indicated that data for the past year are available and that the analysis could be done quickly on the Accounting Department's microcomputer.

Berg completed the two regression analyses that follow. The first regression is based on the data for the entire year. The second regression excludes the weeks when only the 10 permanent staff persons worked; these weeks were unusual and appear to be out of the relevant range.

Regression Equation

$W = a + bS$

where: W = total workers (permanent plus temporary)
S = orders shipped

	Regression 1 (Daily Data for 52 Weeks)	Regression 2 (Daily Data for 38 Weeks)
a	5.062	.489
b	.023	.028
Standard error (s) of the estimate	2.012	.432
Coefficient of determination (r^2)	.962	.998

Locter is not familiar with regression analysis and is, therefore, unsure how to implement this technique. He wonders which regression data he should employ; that is, which data are better. When Loctor recognized that the regression is based on actual orders shipped by week, Berg told him he can use the forecasted shipments for the week to determine the number of workers needed.

Required:

(1) Using Regression 1 based on data from a full year, calculate the number of temporary workers who should be hired for a forecast of 1,200 shipments.
(2) Which one of the two regressions appears to be better? Explain.
(3) Explain the circumstances under which this regression should be used in planning for temporary workers.
(4) Explain how the regression might be improved.

(ICMA adapted)

C3-2 Regression and Correlation Analysis-Utility and Implementation. Ned McCarty, controller of Arkansas Distribution Company, is responsible for development and administration of the company's internal information system as well as the coordination of the company's budget preparation.

At a meeting with Donna Tuma, the vice-president, McCarty proposed that the company employ regression analysis (the least squares method) and correlation analysis as a standard part of its internal information system relating to sales and expenses. He feels that such analyses, including projections, would be significant decision-making aids.

Tuma admitted that she had forgotten the exact mechanics of regression and correlation analysis. However, she made two points.

First, that regression and correlation calculations for weekly or monthly amounts would involve enormous numbers of calculations, because the company's budget and control system uses weekly amounts for sales and some expenses and monthly amounts for other expenses.

Second, a great deal of caution must be exercised when relying on predictions calculated by regression analysis techniques.

McCarty agreed that a large number of calculations would be required, but feels that this problem might be overcome by computerizing the analysis. The computerized analysis would have to suit the company's budget and control system and cover all significant sales and cost accounts, of which there are about 100.

The company's microcomputer is not large and operates only with a flexible-diskette data-storage device. No standard computer programs are available for this kind of analysis. Therefore, a program must be specially written, its accompanying data gathered, and the processing problems solved.

To pursue his idea, McCarty decided to obtain sample data regarding sales and related selling expenses for the past five years. Using regression analysis, he predicts sales of $30,500,000 for the coming year and calculates a coefficient of correlation of .4 between sales and the selling expenses.

Required:

(1) Explain both the advantages and the limitations of using regression and correlation analysis according to McCarty.
(2) Identify matters that should be considered before the regression analysis is made, based on the sample data collected.

(CICA adapted)

C3-3 Cost Behavior Analysis; Correlation Analysis; Standard Error of the Estimate. A company's Cost Department has compiled weekly records of production volume (in units), electric power used, and direct labor hours employed. The range of output for which the following statistics were computed is from 500 to 2,000 units per week:

Electric power:

$y = 1{,}000 + .4x$, where y is electric power and x is units of production
Standard error of the estimate: 100
Coefficient of correlation: .45

Direct labor:

$y = 100 + 1.2x$, where y is direct labor hours and x is units of production
Standard error of the estimate: 300
Coefficient of correlation: .70

Required:

(1) Compute the best estimate of the additional number of required direct labor hours, if production for the next period is 500 units greater than production in this period.
(2) Comment on the reliability of the above equations for estimating electric power and direct labor requirements, together with the necessary assumptions if the estimating equations are to be used to predict future requirements. An interpretation of the coefficient of correlation and the standard error of the estimate should be included.

CGA-Canada (adapted). Reprint with permission.

C3-4 Cost Behavior Analysis; Alternative Models. Motorco Corporation plans to acquire several retail automotive parts stores as part of its expansion program. Motorco carries out extensive review of possible acquisitions prior to making any decision to approach a specific company. Projections of future financial performance are one of the aspects of such a review. One form of projection relies heavily on using past performance (normally 10 prior years) to estimate future performance.

Currently, Motorco is conducting a preacquisition review of Alpha Auto Parts, a regional chain of retail automotive parts stores. Among the financial data to be projected for Alpha are the future rental costs for its stores. The following schedule presents the rent and revenues (in millions of dollars) for the past 10 years:

Year	Revenues	Annual Rent Expense
19A..................	$22	$1.00
19B..................	24	1.15
19C..................	36	1.40
19D..................	27	1.10
19E..................	43	1.55
19F..................	33	1.25
19G..................	45	1.65
19H..................	48	1.60
19I..................	61	1.80
19J..................	60	1.95

The following three alternative methods of estimating future rental expense are being considered:

Alternative A: A linear regression was performed using time as the independent variable. The resulting formula is as follows:

$$\text{Rental expense} = .93 + .0936y$$
$$r = .895$$
$$\text{Standard error of the estimate} = .150$$

where y is equal to (actual year − 19A), e.g., 19J = 10.

Alternative B: The annual rental expense was related to annual revenues through linear regression. The formula for predicting rental expense in this case is as follows:

$$\text{Rental expense} = .5597 + .02219y$$
$$r = .978$$
$$\text{Standard error of the estimate} = .070$$

where y is equal to (Revenues ÷ 1,000,000), e.g., y for 19J is 60.

Alternative C: The third alternative is to calculate rental expense as a percent of revenues using the arithmetical average for the 10-year period of 19A-19J inclusive. The formula for predicting rental expense in this case is as follows:

$$\text{Rental expense} = (\Sigma E \div \Sigma R)y = (14.45 \div 399)y = .0362y$$

where ΣE is equal to the sum of the rental expenses for the 10-year period, ΣR is equal to the sum of the revenues for the 10-year period, and y is equal to revenue in the prediction year, e.g., y for 19J is 60.

Required:

(1) Discuss the advantages and disadvantages of each of the three alternative methods for estimating the rental expense for Alpha Auto Parts.

(2) Identify one method from alternatives A, B, or C that Motorco should use to estimate rental expense and explain why that alternative is preferred.

(3) Explain whether a statistical technique is an appropriate method in this situation for estimating rental expense. (ICMA adapted)

C3-5 Multiple Regression Analysis. Multiple regression is a procedure used to measure the relationship of one variable with two or more other variables. Regression provides a relational statement rather than a causal statement with regard to the relationship. The basic formula for a multiple regression equation is:

$$y_i' = a + bx_i + cz_i + e_i$$

For a regression equation to provide meaningful information, it should comply with the basic criteria of goodness of fit and specification analysis. Specification analysis is determined by examining the data and the relationships of the variables for (a) linearity within a relevant range, (b) constant variance of error terms (homoscedasticity), (c) independence of observations (serial correlation), (d) normality, and (e) multicollinearity.

Required:

(1) Explain what is meant by the following: "Regression provides a relational statement rather than a causal statement."

(2) Explain the meaning of each of the symbols that appear in the basic formula of the multiple regression equation just stated.

(3) Identify the statistical factors used to test a regression equation for goodness of fit and, for each item identified, indicate whether a high or low value describes a "good" fit.

(4) Explain what each of the following terms means with respect to regression analysis:
   (a) Linearity within a relevant range
   (b) Constant variance (homoscedasticity)
   (c) Serial correlation
   (d) Normality
   (e) Multicollinearity (ICMA adapted)

C3-6 Multiple Regression and Correlation Analysis. John Wood, a financial analyst for a major automobile corporation, has been monitoring the funds used in advertising campaigns and the funds used for automobile factory rebates. Financial data have been accumulated for the last 24 months along with customer sales, that is, automobiles sold. Wood contends that there may be a relationship between the level of automobile sales and funds expended on advertising and/or factory rebates. If such a relationship can be determined, the company may be able to estimate sales demand based on various levels of funding commitments for one or both types of expenditures.

Regression equations and supporting statistical values developed for the various relationships between variables are as follows:

	Equation	Coefficient of Determination r^2	Standard Error of the Estimate s
Equation 1	D = 2.455 + .188A	.4140	1.325
Equation 2	D = 2.491 + .44R	.3140	1.434
Equation 3	R = 6.052 + .005A	.0002	2.202
Equation 4	D = -.184 + .186A + .437R	.7030	.922

where the notations used in the equations are as follows:

A = advertising funds in $100,000
R = funds for factory rebates in $1,000,000
D = customer sales demand (automobiles sold) in 10,000 units

The appropriate t values for use in determining confidence intervals are as follows:

50% confidence	.69
95% confidence	2.07

Required:

(1) Assuming the corporation is projecting advertising expenditures amounting to $1,500,000 and factory rebate expenditures amounting to $12,000,000 for the next time period, calculate expected customer demand in units using:
   (a) Equation 1
   (b) Equation 2

(2) Assume that equation 4 is employed to estimate a total customer demand of 104,160 automobiles for a time period. Using a 50% confidence level, determine the range of automobile sales that could occur during the time period.

(3) Select the regression equation that would be most advantageous to predict customer sales demand and explain why it is the best.

(4) Explain the significance of equation 3 and how it may be used in evaluating equation 4.

(ICMA adapted)

PART 2

Cost Accumulation

CHAPTER 4

Cost Systems and Cost Accumulation

Learning Objectives

After studying this chapter, you will be able to:

1. Present the flow of manufacturing costs using general journal entries and T accounts.
2. Prepare a statement of cost of goods sold for a manufacturer.
3. Prepare financial statements for a manufacturer.
4. Name different kinds of cost systems, state how each system measures costs, and tell which cost elements are included in product costs under each system.
5. Distinguish between job order and process costing, and give examples of businesses in which each is used.

Chapter 2 introduced fundamental cost concepts, including cost behavior, and Chapter 3 discussed cost behavior in depth. Chapter 2 also introduced cost accounting as an information system, and this chapter builds on that discussion. Many varieties of cost accounting systems are used, and several will be introduced in this chapter.

One of the fundamental roles of any cost system is cost accumulation, which consists of identifying, measuring, and recording cost information in relevant categories or classifications. Several different cost accumulation methods are used in practice, and this chapter will introduce and compare the most common ones. Before the cost accumulation methods and varieties of cost systems are presented, the logical pattern by which costs flow through an accounting system will be examined.

Flow of Costs in a Manufacturing Enterprise

Cost accounting neither adds new steps to the familiar accounting cycle nor discards the principles studied in financial accounting. Cost accounting is concerned with recording and measuring cost elements as the related resources flow through the productive process. The flow of costs parallels the flow of resources and is illustrated in Figure 4-1. In Figure 4-1, all manufacturing costs, regardless of their fixed or variable behavior, flow through the work in process and finished goods inventory accounts. This reflects the full absorption cost assumption that was mentioned in Chapter 2.

The manufacturing process, the physical arrangement of the factory, and the decision-making needs of managers constitute the basis for determining how costs will be accumulated. Typically, the general ledger accounts for manufacturing costs are Materials, Payroll, Factory Overhead Control, Work in Process, Finished Goods, and Cost of Goods Sold. These accounts are used to recognize and measure the flow of costs, from the acquisition of materials, through factory

FIGURE 4-1 *Flow of Manufacturing Costs*

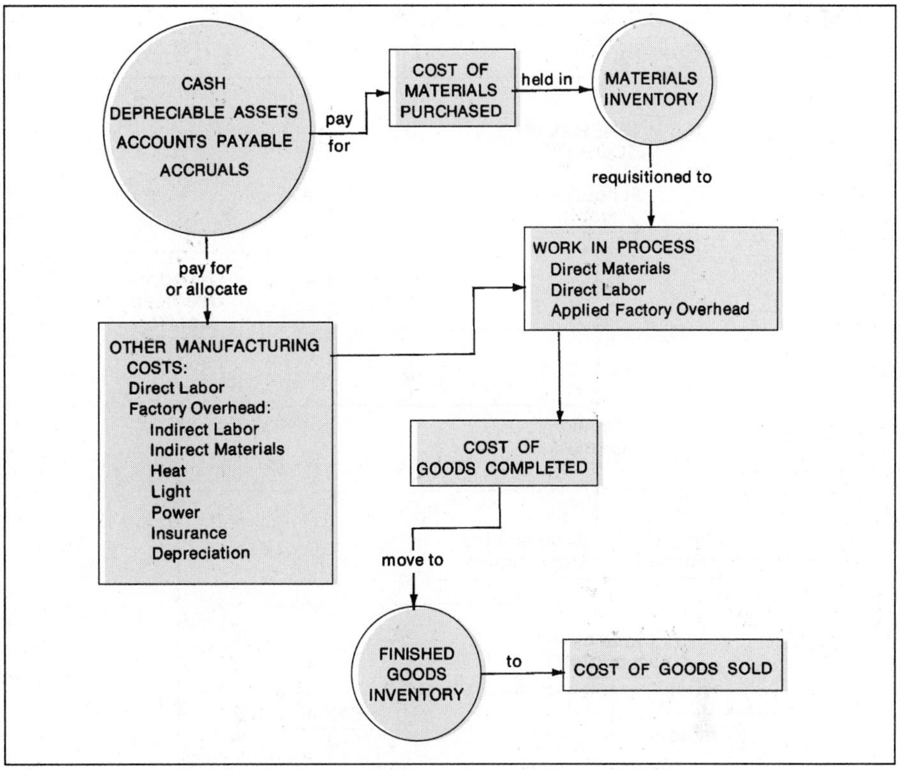

operations, to the cost of products sold. Cost accounts are expansions of general accounts and are related to general accounts, as shown in Figure 4-2.

From left to right in Figure 4-2, the manufacturing portions of costs are shown flowing through the cost accounts and through some of the general accounts. The nonmanufacturing portions of all costs, such as the marketing and administrative portions of depreciation and payroll, are not depicted here. This diagram, like the preceding one, reflects full absorption costing because all manufacturing costs, whether fixed or variable, flow through the work in process and finished goods inventory accounts.

Not only do the arrows in the diagram depict the flow of costs through the accounting system, but each individual arrow also represents a specific type of accounting entry. The left-hand point of each arrow represents the credit portion of an entry, and the right-hand point represents the debit portion of the same entry. The arrows are labeled with the letters (a) through (r) as follows:

a Payments on account
b Expenses paid in advance
c Purchases and improvements of long-lived manufacturing assets
d Various payments for resources
e Payments of wages and salaries
f Purchases of raw materials and factory supplies on credit
g Recording payroll[1]

[1] Figure 4-2 shows the entire payroll amount being credited to the liability account titled Accrued Payroll; this simplified approach will be used throughout this chapter. In practice, there are a number of liabilities involved, such as the amounts of employees' state and federal income taxes that the employer must withhold and pay to government agencies. All such liabilities are recorded, and the remainder of the total payroll is due to employees. These and other details of payroll accounting are discussed in Chapter 11. Do not confuse the liability account Accrued Payroll with the temporary clearing account entitled Payroll, which merely facilitates calculating payroll costs and distributing them to the cost accounts on different dates.

FIGURE 4-2 *Relationship Between General Accounts and Cost Accounts (Under Full Absorption Costing)*

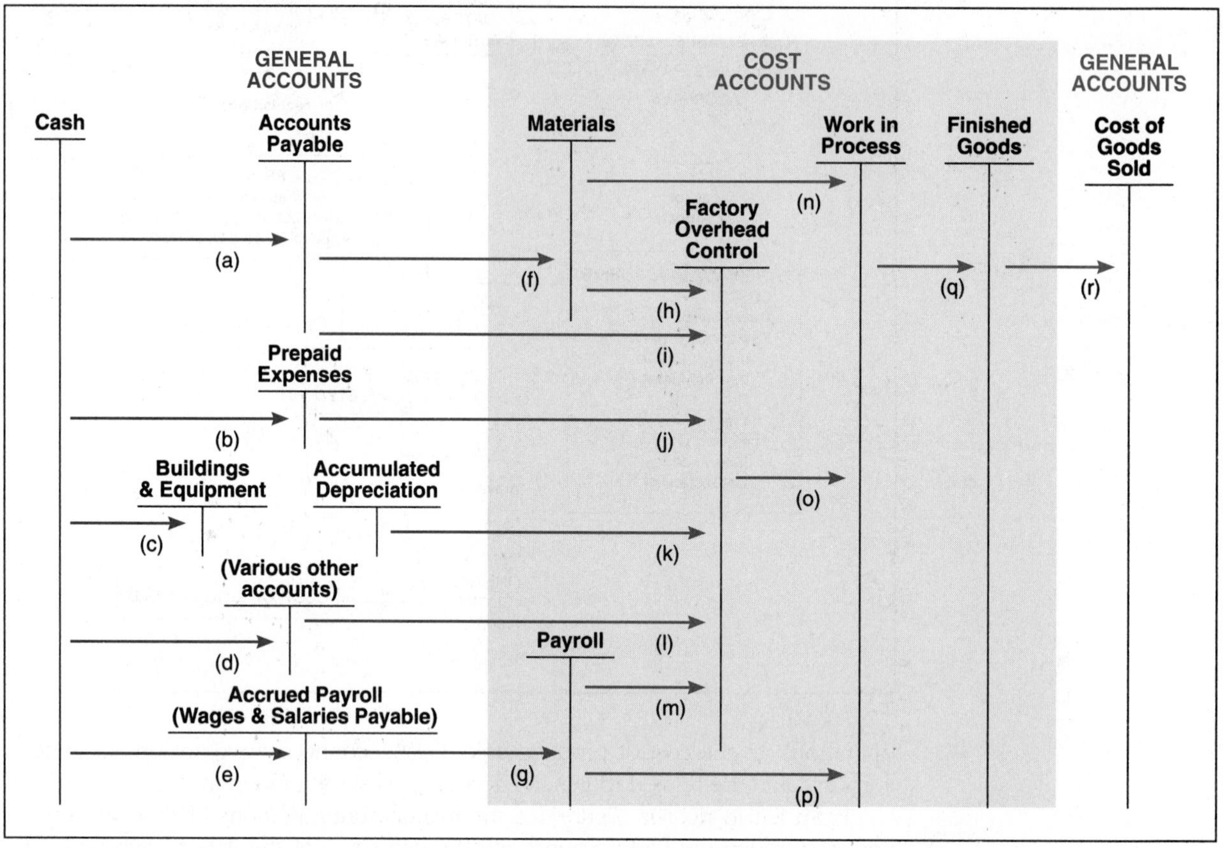

h Issuing factory supplies (indirect materials) to production
i Incurring various indirect manufacturing costs on credit
j Manufacturing portion of any prepayments that have expired
k Manufacturing portion of depreciation
l Manufacturing portion of various other resources used
m Charging all types of indirect labor cost to production
n Issuing direct materials to production
o Charging manufacturing overhead costs to production
p Charging direct labor cost to production
q Charging cost of completed units to the finished goods account
r Charging cost of sold units to the cost of goods sold account

Cost accounting makes extensive use of a control account–subsidiary record format when detailed information about general ledger accounts is needed. Hundreds of different materials items, for example, may be included in one materials account in the general ledger. The general ledger's factory overhead account may include indirect labor, supplies, rent, insurance, taxes, repairs, and many other costs. Each such general ledger account, called a **controlling account**, is supported by a number of **subsidiary accounts** or **subsidiary records**. A separate materials subsidiary account is used for each type of material, and a separate overhead subsidiary account is used for each item of overhead cost. Many kinds of subsidiary accounts are described and illustrated in later chapters.

Controlling accounts supported by subsidiary records are also used in the general accounts. For example, although Figure 4-2 shows only a single account entitled Accounts Payable, it would be supported by individual accounts payable, one for each creditor, or by individual vouchers payable, one for each bill to be paid.

The flow of costs to ledger accounts is based on information in source documents, which is journalized and posted. These documents, whether paper or electronic, are the fundamental evidence of an economic event. The following table lists typical source documents involving manufacturing costs:

Cost	Source Document Examples
Materials	Purchase invoices, materials requisitions
Labor	Time tickets or time sheets, clock cards
Factory overhead	Vendors' invoices, utility bills, depreciation schedules

To illustrate the flow of costs in a manufacturing enterprise, assume that New Hope Manufacturing Company begins a new fiscal year with the financial position as shown in the balance sheet in Exhibit 4-1.

EXHIBIT 4-1

New Hope Manufacturing Company
Balance Sheet
January 1, 19—

Assets			
Current assets:			
Cash		$ 183,000	
Marketable securities		76,000	
Accounts receivable		313,100	
Inventories:			
Finished goods	$ 68,700		
Work in process	234,300		
Materials	135,300	438,300	
Prepaid expenses		15,800	
Total current assets			$ 1,026,200
Property, plant, and equipment:			
Land		$ 41,500	
Buildings	$ 580,600		
Machinery and equipment	1,643,000		
	$2,223,600		
Less accumulated depreciation	1,010,700	1,212,900	
Total property, plant, and equipment			1,254,400
Total assets			$ 2,280,600
Liabilities			
Current liabilities:			
Accounts payable		$ 553,000	
Estimated income tax payable		35,700	
Due on long-term debt		20,000	
Total current liabilities			$ 608,700
Long-term debt			204,400
Total liabilities			$ 813,100
Stockholders' Equity			
Common stock		$ 528,000	
Retained earnings		939,500	
Total stockholders' equity			1,467,500
Total liabilities and stockholders' equity			$ 2,280,600

During January, New Hope completed transactions that are journalized in summary form below and posted to ledger accounts as shown on the next page. The revenue and expense accounts are not closed at the end of January, because in practice a formal closing usually is done only at year-end.

New Hope Manufacturing Company

Transactions		Journal Entries		
(a) Materials purchased and received on account	$100,000	Materials	100,000	
		Accounts Payable		100,000
		This is a summary entry. The materials account is an inventory control account; subsidiary records will indicate the details of the materials received.		
(b) Materials requisitioned during the month:		Work in Process	80,000	
For production	$ 80,000	Factory Overhead Control	12,000	
For indirect factory use	12,000	Materials		92,000
		The indirect factory materials are kept in the inventory control account as well as in subsidiary records to control their purchase and usage.		
(c) Total gross payroll	$160,000	Payroll	160,000	
Payroll was accrued and paid.		Accrued Payroll		160,000
		Accrued Payroll	160,000	
		Cash		160,000
		The accrued payroll account is used to establish a record until the payroll department has prepared the paychecks to be distributed to the employees.		
(d) The distribution of the payroll was:		Work in Process	104,000	
Direct labor	65%	Factory Overhead Control	24,000	
Indirect factory labor	15	Marketing Expenses Control	20,800	
Marketing salaries	13	Administrative Expenses Control	11,200	
Administrative salaries	7	Payroll		160,000
(e) Factory overhead consisting of:		Factory Overhead Control	22,500	
Depreciation	$ 21,300	Accumulated Depreciation		21,300
Prepaid insurance	1,200	Prepaid Expenses		1,200
(f) General factory overhead costs (not itemized)	$ 26,340	Factory Overhead Control	26,340	
70% were paid in cash; the balance was credited to Accounts Payable.		Cash		18,438
		Accounts Payable		7,902
(g) Amount received from customers in payment of their accounts	$205,000	Cash	205,000	
		Accounts Receivable		205,000
(h) The following liabilities were paid:		Accounts Payable	227,000	
Accounts payable	$227,000	Estimated Income Tax Payable	35,700	
Estimated income tax	35,700	Cash		262,700
(i) Factory overhead accumulated in the factory overhead control account was charged to the work in process account.		Work in Process	84,840	
		Factory Overhead Control		84,840
(j) Work completed and transferred to finished goods	$320,000	Finished Goods	320,000	
		Work in Process		320,000
(k) Sales	$384,000	Cash	153,600	
40% was paid in cash; the balance was charged to Accounts Receivable. The cost of goods sold was 75% of sales.		Accounts Receivable	230,400	
		Sales		384,000
		Cost of Goods Sold	288,000	
		Finished Goods		288,000
(l) Provision for income tax	$ 26,000	Provision for Income Tax	26,000	
		Estimated Income Tax Payable		26,000

Cash

1/1	183,000	(c)	160,000
(g)	205,000	(f)	18,438
(k)	153,600	(h)	262,700
	541,600		*441,138*
100,462			

Marketable Securities

1/1	76,000		

Accounts Receivable

1/1	313,100	(g)	205,000
(k)	230,400		
	543,500		
338,500			

Finished Goods

1/1	68,700	(k)	288,000
(j)	320,000		
	388,700		
100,700			

Work in Process

1/1	234,300	(j)	320,000
(b)	80,000		
(d)	104,000		
(i)	84,840		
	503,140		
183,140			

Materials

1/1	135,300	(b)	92,000
(a)	100,000		
	235,300		
143,300			

Prepaid Expenses

1/1	15,800	(e)	1,200
14,600			

Land

1/1	41,500		

Buildings

1/1	580,600		

Machinery and Equipment

1/1	1,643,000		

Accumulated Depreciation

		1/1	1,010,700
		(e)	21,300
			1,032,000

Accrued Payroll

(c)	160,000	(c)	160,000

Accounts Payable

(h)	227,000	1/1	553,000
		(a)	100,000
		(f)	7,902
			660,902
		433,902	

Estimated Income Tax Payable

(h)	35,700	1/1	35,700
		(l)	26,000
			61,700
		26,000	

Due on Long-Term Debt

		1/1	20,000

Long-Term Debt

		1/1	204,400

Common Stock

		1/1	528,000

Retained Earnings

		1/1	939,500

Sales

		(k)	384,000

Cost of Goods Sold

(k)	288,000		

Factory Overhead Control

(b)	12,000	(i)	84,840
(d)	24,000		
(e)	22,500		
(f)	26,340		
	84,840		

Payroll

(c)	160,000	(d)	160,000

Marketing Expenses Control

(d)	20,800		

Administrative Expenses Control

(d)	11,200		

Provision for Income Tax

(l)	26,000		

Reporting the Results of Operations

The results of operations of a manufacturing enterprise are reported in the conventional financial statements just as they are for any other form of business. These statements summarize the period's operations and show financial position at the end of the period.

Income Statement

Exhibit 4-2 shows the income statement of New Hope Manufacturing Company for the month of January, based on the transactions listed on page 76:

EXHIBIT 4-2

New Hope Manufacturing Company Income Statement For Month Ended January 31, 19—		
Sales		$384,000
Less cost of goods sold (Schedule 1)		288,000
Gross profit		$ 96,000
Less commercial expenses:		
Marketing expense	$ 20,800	
Administrative expense	11,200	32,000
Income from operations		$ 64,000
Less provision for income tax		26,000
Net income		$ 38,000

In the income statement, the cost of goods sold is shown as a single figure. Although this practice is followed in published reports, additional information is necessary for internal purposes. Therefore, a supporting schedule of the cost of goods sold is usually produced, as illustrated for New Hope in Exhibit 4-3.

Balance Sheet

The balance sheet complements the income statement. Either statement alone is an incomplete financial picture of the status and progress of a company. The balance sheet in Exhibit 4-4 shows the financial position of New Hope Manufacturing Company at the end of January.

Statement of Cash Flows

Whenever the income statement and balance sheet are reported externally, generally accepted accounting principles require that they be accompanied by the statement of cash flows. For a period as short as one month, as in the New Hope Manufacturing Company example, external reporting is very rare, so a statement of cash flows is not illustrated here. Introductory and intermediate financial accounting textbooks can be consulted for an illustration of how a statement of cash flows is prepared.

EXHIBIT 4-3

New Hope Manufacturing Company
Schedule 1
Cost of Goods Sold Statement
For Month Ended January 31, 19—

① Direct materials:			
Materials inventory, January 1, 19—		$135,300	
Purchases		100,000	
Materials available for use		$235,300	
Less: Indirect materials used	$ 12,000		
Materials inventory, January 31	143,300	155,300	
Direct materials consumed			$ 80,000
② Direct labor			104,000
③ Factory overhead:			
Indirect materials		$ 12,000	
Indirect labor		24,000	
Depreciation		21,300	
Insurance		1,200	
General factory overhead		26,340	84,840
Total manufacturing cost			$268,840
④ Add work in process inventory, January 1			234,300
			$503,140
Less work in process inventory, January 31			183,140
Cost of goods manufactured			$320,000
⑤ Add finished goods inventory, January 1			68,700
Cost of goods available for sale			$388,700
Less finished goods inventory, January 31			100,700
Cost of goods sold			$288,000

① The direct materials section is made up of the beginning materials inventory, purchases, and the ending inventory of materials, with an adjustment for the indirect materials that were added to factory overhead.

② The direct labor section indicates the cost of labor that can be identified directly with the products manufactured.

③ Factory overhead includes all costs that are indirectly involved in manufacturing the products. (Note: Chapter 5 and the factory overhead chapters 12 and 13, will introduce and demonstrate the use of a predetermined factory overhead rate.)

④ The total manufacturing costs incurred during the period are adjusted for the work in process inventories at the beginning and end of the period.

⑤ The cost of goods manufactured during the period is adjusted for the finished goods inventory at the beginning and end of the period.

EXHIBIT 4-4

New Hope Manufacturing Company
Balance Sheet
January 31, 19—

Assets			
Current assets:			
Cash		$ 100,462	
Marketable securities		76,000	
Accounts receivable		338,500	
Inventories:			
Finished goods	$ 100,700		
Work in process	183,140		
Materials	143,300	427,140	
Prepaid expenses		14,600	
Total current assets			$ 956,702
Property, plant, and equipment:			
Land		$ 41,500	
Buildings	$ 580,600		
Machinery and equipment	1,643,000		
	$2,223,600		
Less accumulated depreciation	1,032,000	1,191,600	
Total property, plant, and equipment			1,233,100
Total assets			$2,189,802
Liabilities			
Current liabilities:			
Accounts payable		$ 433,902	
Estimated income tax payable		26,000	
Due on long-term debt		20,000	
Total current liabilities			$ 479,902
Long-term debt			204,400
Total liabilities			$ 684,302
Stockholders' Equity			
Common stock		$ 528,000	
Retained earnings			
Balance, January 1	$ 939,500		
January net income	38,000	977,500	
Total stockholders' equity			1,505,500
Total liabilities and stockholders' equity			$2,189,802

Cost Systems

The previous section presented an overall view of the flow of costs. The remainder of this chapter discusses refinements in accounting for the flow of costs by distinguishing among different cost systems and among different methods of cost accumulation.

Costs that are allocated to units of production may be actual costs or standard costs. In an **actual cost system** or **historical cost system**, cost information is collected as cost is incurred, but the presentation of results is delayed until all manufacturing operations of the accounting period have been performed or, in a service business, until the period's services have been rendered. In a **standard cost system**, products, operations, and processes are costed based on predetermined quantities of resources to be used and predetermined prices of those resources. Actual costs are also recorded, and variances or differences between actual costs and standard costs are collected in separate accounts. The presentation in this and subsequent chapters is in the context of cost systems that measure costs primarily at actual amounts. The discussion of standard cost systems is deferred to Chapters 18 and 19.

As stated in Chapter 2, the costs allocated to units of production may include all manufacturing costs (called **full absorption costing**) or only the variable manufacturing costs (called **direct costing** or **variable costing**). The presentation in this and subsequent chapters assumes full absorption costing. Direct costing is deferred to Chapter 20.

Four possible cost systems can be constructed by recognizing that costs can be measured at either actual or standard amounts, in either direct costing or full absorption costing. Actually, a classification of costing systems includes many more possibilities, all based on the cost accounting terminology introduced in Chapter 2. On the question of which cost elements are allocated to production, there are three possibilities: prime costing, direct (variable) costing, and full absorption costing. On the question of how the cost elements are measured, two possibilities have been mentioned already—all costs may be measured at historical (actual) amounts, or all at predetermined (standard) amounts. A third possibility is to use a hybrid of historical and predetermined measures—direct materials and direct labor at historical amounts, and overhead at a predetermined rate. This hybrid system is encountered often in practice and is discussed in Chapters 12 and 13. It also is assumed in Chapters 5, 6, 7, and 8 except where otherwise stated. Figure 4-3 summarizes the possible accounting systems mentioned thus far.

FIGURE 4-3
A Classification of Cost Systems

	MANUFACTURING COST ELEMENTS ALLOCATED TO PRODUCTION		
COSTS MEASURED AT:	Direct Material, Direct Labor	Direct Material, Direct Labor, Variable Overhead	Direct Material, Direct Labor, Variable Overhead, Fixed Overhead
Historical Amounts	(1) Actual Prime Costing	(4) Actual Direct Costing	(7) Actual Full Absorption Costing
Historical Amounts for Direct Material & Direct Labor, Predetermined Amount for Overhead	(2) Actual Prime Costing	(5) A Hybrid Direct Costing	(8) A Hybrid Full Absorption Costing
Predetermined Amounts	(3) Standard Prime Costing	(6) Standard Direct Costing	(9) Standard Full Absorption Costing

Although the authoritative literature in financial accounting is not entirely clear on this point, most financial accountants agree that generally accepted accounting principles require actual full absorption costing, which is represented by cell 7 in the matrix (see Figure 4-3). Many manufacturing firms use other systems but are able to meet external reporting requirements by adjusting their account balances at the end of each reporting period. For tax reporting, the Tax Reform Act of 1986 requires certain purchasing and storage costs to be allocated to inventory, which represents a step beyond the full absorption of manufacturing costs. This tax requirement is known as **super absorption** or **super-full absorption**.

One survey[2] indicated that in defense-related industries, where cost-plus contracting is the dominant form of business, actual cost is the measure most commonly used in cost accounting systems, and full absorption costing is more common than direct costing. Outside the defense-related industries, many more respondents to the survey reported using standard costing than actual costing, and about three times as many reported using full absorption costing as reported using direct costing.

Cost Accumulation

Any of the previously mentioned cost systems can be used with job order costing, with process costing, or with other cost accumulation methods. Job order costing and process costing will be introduced briefly in this section. None of the discussion thus far in this text has specified the cost accumulation method used. All illustrations have been general; for example, the journal entries illustrated in this chapter for New Hope Company are consistent with both job order and process costing. Details of the differences between the two methods are discussed in Chapters 5 and 6.

Job order and process costing are the two most widely used cost accumulation methods, and they have several aspects in common. Although the ultimate cost object in both of these methods is the unit of product, the two methods differ fundamentally in their approach to cost tracing. In job order costing, cost is traced to an individual batch, lot, or contract. In process costing, cost is traced to a department, operation, or some other subdivision within the factory. A third method, backflush costing, differs markedly from job order and process costing; it will be introduced briefly in this chapter and discussed in detail in Chapter 10.

Job Order Costing

In **job order costing**, costs are accumulated for each batch, lot, or customer order. This method, which will be discussed in detail in Chapter 5, is used when the products manufactured within a department or cost center are heterogeneous. Further, it presupposes the possibility of physically identifying the jobs produced and of charging each job with its own cost. The detailed records showing the costs of each job constitute a subsidiary ledger supporting the general ledger's work in process account.

[2] Robert A. Howell, James D. Brown, Stephen R. Soucy, and Allen H. Seed, *Management Accounting in the New Manufacturing Environment*, (Montvale, N.J.: Institute of Management Accountants (formerly the National Association of Accountants), 1987), pp. 36, 96.

Job order costing is applicable to made-to-order work in factories, workshops, and repair shops; to work by builders, construction engineers, and printers; and to service businesses such as medical, legal, architectural, accounting, and consulting firms.

When a job produces a specific quantity for inventory, job order costing permits the computation of a unit cost for product costing purposes. When jobs are performed on the basis of customer specifications, job order costing permits the computation of a profit or loss on each order. Since costs are accumulated as an order goes through production, these costs may be compared with estimates that were made when an order was taken. Job order costing thereby provides opportunities for controlling costs and for evaluating the profitability of a contract, product, or product line.

Many modern manufacturing processes are becoming highly automated. Increasingly, labor-intensive production processes such as assembly lines are being automated through robotics. In such systems, manufacturing changes can be made more efficiently than they can be in labor-intensive systems because the learning period required by humans is eliminated. In a robotics production process, the first unit of product is produced as efficiently as the last unit. As a consequence, robotics systems can enhance the likelihood of manufacturing many different products and using job order costing to accumulate some or all manufacturing costs, provided the costs are traceable to individual jobs in a reasonably accurate, practical manner. However, if traceability of costs to individual jobs is not feasible or practical, then process costing may be required.

Process Costing

Process costing accumulates costs by production process or by department.[3] This method, which will be discussed in detail in Chapter 6, is used when all units worked on within a department or other work area are homogeneous, or when there is no need to distinguish among units, or when it is not practical to do so. Process costing accumulates all the costs of operating a process for a period of time and then divides the costs by the number of units of product that passed through that process during the period; the result is a unit cost. If the product of one process becomes the material of the next, a unit cost is computed for each process. The process cost method is applicable to industries such as flour mills, breweries, chemical plants, and textile factories where large quantities of one product or a few products are produced. It is also applicable to assembly and testing operations involving large numbers of similar items such as power tools, electrical parts, or small appliances.

Most firms using process costing maintain continuous high-volume production, and unless the just-in-time philosophy is applied, a considerable amount of partially processed inventory typically is on hand in each department at the end of each accounting period. A partially processed unit obviously should not be assigned a full amount of cost; therefore, some adjustment of the basic unit cost is needed. The calculations necessary to account for partially completed inventory represent one of the fundamental characteristics of the process cost method. These calculations are discussed in Chapter 6.

In an actual (historical) cost system that uses process costing, the presence of partially completed inventory at the end of an accounting period results in a sec-

[3] While departments may exist in either job order or process costing, the department is the focus for cost tracing in process costing.

ond accounting problem: the treatment of the cost of that inventory in the next accounting period. The solution is to select a cost flow assumption like those used in accounting for nonmanufacturing inventories. In practice, the most common cost flow assumption for process costing is the weighted-average cost method, which averages or blends the costs of the incomplete beginning inventory with all the costs incurred in the current period; this method is discussed in detail in Chapter 6. Professional licensing examinations for accountants also require familiarity with the first-in, first-out cost flow assumption, which is discussed in the appendix to Chapter 6.

Aspects Common to Both Job Order and Process Costing

Although the textbook discussion of job order and process costing emphasizes manufacturing activity, both job order and process costing are also used by service organizations. For example, an automobile repair shop uses job order costing to accumulate the costs associated with work performed on each automobile. Process costing may be used by an airline to accumulate costs per passenger mile, or by a hospital to accumulate costs per patient day.

In both job order and process costing, considerable attention is devoted to detailed calculations of the cost of work in process. In job order costing, the general ledger's work in process account is supported by subsidiary records of jobs' costs, with a separate record showing detailed costs of each job currently in production. In process costing, the general ledger's work in process account may be supported by subsidiary records of departments' costs, with one record for each department.[4] The detailed tracking of work in process distinguishes these two cost accumulation methods from a third method, called backflushing or backflush costing, in which little or no separate accounting is done for the work in process inventory.

Many companies use both the job order and the process cost methods. For example, a company manufacturing a railway car to the customer's specifications uses job order costing to accumulate the cost per railway car. However, the multiple small metal stampings required for the job are manufactured in a department that uses fast and repetitive stamping machines. The cost of these stampings is accumulated by process costing. Although the company is using both job order and process costing in this example, there is no real blending of the two methods because they are employed in separate operations. Other systems exist in which a real blending of job order and process costing does occur.

Blended Methods

In some manufacturing, different units have significantly different direct materials costs, but all units undergo identical conversion in large quantities. In these cases, direct materials costs are accumulated using job order costing, and conversion costs are accumulated using process costing.

An example is a simple assembly operation in which inexpensive brass-plated lamps and expensive solid brass lamps are assembled in large numbers. Identical labor steps are performed on all units and identical wiring and

---

[4] Alternatively, if the number of departments is small, a separate general ledger work in process account may be maintained for each department instead of a single work in process controlling account; the journal entries, illustrated previously, for New Hope Manufacturing Company assume that a single work in process controlling account is used.

switches (direct materials) are installed. A high-quality cloth shade is attached to the solid brass bases, and a low-cost cloth or plastic shade is attached to the brass-plated bases. The cost differences for bases and shades are significant, while all other costs are identical for all units. A workable solution is to trace the direct material cost to the specific batch or lot by using job order cost accumulation for direct materials, and to use process cost accumulation for labor and overhead costs.

A more general example of the need for a blended costing method is provided by some **flexible manufacturing systems (FMS)**. Increasing numbers of factories are moving from manufacturing processes involving manual and/or fixed automated systems toward FMS. An FMS consists of an integrated collection of automated production processes, automated materials movement, and computerized system controls to manufacture efficiently a highly flexible variety of products. The extent of product variety is constrained by the need for the products to share certain broad characteristics that allow grouping within a particular family of products while maintaining considerable flexibility. For example, at the General Electric plant in Erie, Pennsylvania, diesel engines of substantially different sizes can be manufactured on the same automated production line, without significant retooling and setups.

Flexible manufacturing systems affect many of the factors that management should consider when it evaluates a system. The effect of each system—manual, fixed automation, and flexible manufacturing—on these factors is summarized in Exhibit 4-5.

EXHIBIT 4-5

Three Manufacturing Systems Compared

Factor	Manual Systems	Fixed Automation Systems	Flexible Manufacturing Systems
Numbers of kinds of products	Many	Only one	Several
Viable production volumes	Low	High range	Middle
Product quality	Varies	Tightly constrained	Consistent
Setup times	High (learning curve)	Very high	Short
Learning curve effect	Substantial	Depends on degree of automation	None
Lead times (per unit) to supply customer demands	Usually high	Moderate	Moderate/low
Direct labor cost (per unit)	High	Low	Very low
Direct labor cost (in total)	High	High	Very low
Inventories: Materials*	High	High	High
Work in process*	High	High	Low
Machine utilization	Low	High	High
Space required	Extensive	Extensive	Moderate
Capital cost	Low	High	High
Sensitivity to effects of breakdowns of single machine or group of machines	Low	High	Low
Responsiveness to changes in demand	High	Low	High

* Use of a Just-in Time inventory system will cause inventories to be low.

David M. Dilts and Grant W. Russell, "Accounting for the Factory of the Future," *Management Accounting*, Vol. 66, No. 9, pp. 34–40.

A comparison of these factors makes the flexible manufacturing system attractive. However, the substantial capital cost and the scarcity of expert knowledge in the field must be weighted against it. Nevertheless, the adoption of this and other modernized processes is expected to accelerate.

In an FMS, a group of related machines is coordinated by computer. Each manufacturing step in the production of any one of a variety of products is capable of being performed by one or more of the machines in the group. The computer's software includes detailed instructions for each machine's work in the production of each product. If all units of all products are to pass through the FMS at the same speed, then all units are responsible for the same amount of conversion cost, because the time spent in the FMS is generally the best measure of conversion effort. If speeds differ, conversion costs are charged to units on the basis of processing time.

For example, suppose the function of the last machine in the FMS is to test all electronic components in every unit of product. The simplest product made by the FMS may have only three electronic components to be tested, while the most elaborate product made by the same FMS may have 20. If the testing machine takes three seconds to perform all the tests needed by a unit, regardless of the number of components to be tested, then each unit of any product consumes the same amount of testing resources. The same is true of a multipoint soldering robot that takes five seconds to solder any number of connections on a unit. In such a setting, all units of all products can be treated identically with respect to conversion costs, making process costing appropriate for accumulating conversion costs. But because the amount and cost of materials and parts vary significantly from one product to another, job order costing is appropriate for accumulating material costs.

Backflush Costing

In recent years, some manufacturing facilities and parts of facilities have increased their processing speeds so much that their average elapsed time between receipt of raw materials and production of finished work has been reduced from a matter of weeks or months to a matter of hours. Not surprisingly, these developments question the usefulness of job order or process costing because of the detailed tracking of the costs of work in process that both of those methods entail.

Backflush costing is a workable way to accumulate manufacturing costs in a factory or part of a factory in which processing speeds are extremely fast. It is workable because it bypasses the routine cost accounting entries that are required in subsidiary records for job order and process cost accumulation, thus saving considerable data processing time. Where there is insufficient time and insufficient incentive to track the detailed costs of work in process, backflushing provides a method of cost accumulation by working backward through the available accounting information after production is completed; that is, at the end of each accounting period. Backflush costing is discussed and illustrated in Chapter 10. Exhibit 4-6 gives a summary comparison of cost accumulation methods, including backflush costing.

EXHIBIT 4-6

Comparison of Cost Accumulation Methods

Aspects of Typical System	METHODS: Job Order	Blended	Process	Backflush
Cost object to which costs are physically traced	A specific job batch, lot, or contract	Material, to a specific job; conversion, to a process or department	A process or department of a production facility	A production facility
Amount of output produced before processing may change	One job, batch, lot, or contract	Material may change for each job	Thousands or hundreds of thousands of units of output	Unlimited
Cost elements that differ from one output to another	All cost elements may differ	Material may differ dramatically; conversion, by small degrees	All cost elements may differ by small degree	Only material cost differs
Amount of detailed accounting done for work in process	High	High	Moderate (summarized for each department or process)	None
Source of information used to control processing	Financial and physical data recorded	Financial and physical data recorded	Financial and physical data recorded	Visual observation

Summary

The general ledger of a manufacturing concern contains the same accounts found in any general ledger plus a small number of cost accounts. As transactions are recorded, manufacturing costs flow through the accounts in a way that largely parallels the flow of resources through production.

Cost accounting systems differ as to which cost elements are included in product cost and as to how those cost elements are measured. External reporting rules require actual full absorption cost. In most cost accounting systems, costs are accumulated by the job order method, the process method, or by a blend of the two.

Key Terms

controlling account *(74)*
subsidiary accounts, subsidiary records *(74)*
actual cost system, historical cost system *(80)*
standard cost system *(81)*
full absorption costing *(81)*
direct costing, variable costing *(81)*
super absorption, super-full absorption *(82)*
job order costing *(82)*
process costing *(83)*
flexible manufacturing system (FMS) *(85)*
backflush costing *(86)*

Discussion Questions

Q4-1 Enumerate the five parts of the cost of goods sold section of the income statement.

Q4-2 Discuss the complementary relationship between the balance sheet and the income statement.

Q4-3 A corporation's annual financial statements and reports are criticized because it is claimed that the income statement does not by any means give a clear picture of annual earning power, and the balance sheet does not disclose the true value of the plant assets. Considering the criticism made, offer an explanation of the nature and purpose of the income statement and of the balance sheet, together with comments on their limitations.

Q4-4 If a company uses actual full absorption process costing, what attribute of the cost accounting system is described by each of the three terms—actual, full absorption, and process?

Q4-5 Distinguish among prime, direct, and absorption costing systems.

Q4-6 What is the difference between actual costing and standard costing?

Q4-7 Distinguish among the process, job order, and backflush cost accumulation methods.

Q4-8 In defense-related industries, in which cost-plus contracting is the dominant form of business, what cost accounting systems are dominant?

Q4-9 What is meant by super-full absorption?

Q4-10 Name some industries in which job order costing is common.

Q4-11 Name some industries in which process costing is common.

Q4-12 What are some important aspects common to both job order and process costing?

Q4-13 What is meant by a blended costing method?

Q4-14 What characterizes flexible manufacturing systems?

Q4-15 What are the advantages of a flexible manufacturing system over other manufacturing systems?

Q4-16 How does the initial cost of creating a flexible manufacturing system compare with that of other manufacturing systems?

Q4-17 What distinguishes the kind of manufacturing setting suited for backflush costing from those suited for job order or process costing?

Exercises

E4-1 Cost of Goods Sold. Brief Manufacturing incurred manufacturing costs totaling $110,000 in July. Inventories were as follows (in thousands):

	June 30	July 31
Finished Goods	$150	$120
Work in Process	80	90

Required: Calculate cost of goods sold for July.

E4-2 Cost of Goods Sold. Mulcahey Company has gathered the following data concerning its May operations (in thousands):

Work in process inventory, beginning	$250
Direct materials used	90
Finished goods inventory, ending	300
Direct labor	60
Work in process inventory, ending	210
Factory overhead	80
Finished goods inventory, beginning	340

Required: Calculate cost of goods sold for May.

E4-3 Cost of Goods Manufactured; Cost of Goods Sold. Aspen Company incurred the following costs during the month: direct labor, $120,000; factory overhead, $108,000; and direct materials purchases, $160,000. Inventories were costed as follows:

	Beginning	Ending
Finished Goods	$27,000	$30,000
Work in Process	61,500	57,500
Direct Materials	37,500	43,500

Required: Calculate (1) the cost of goods manufactured and (2) the cost of goods sold.

E4-4 Manufacturing Costs; Cost of Goods Manufactured; Inventories. Cost data on the activities of Sinbad Manufacturing for May are as follows:

	April 30	May 31
(a) Account balances:		
Finished Goods	$45,602	$?
Work in Process	60,420	52,800
Direct Material	10,250	12,700
Indirect Material	5,600	5,180

(b) Transactions in May:	
Supplies purchased	$ 16,500
Cost of goods sold	280,000
Raw materials purchased	105,000
Indirect labor	22,000
Factory heat, light, and power	11,220
Factory rent	18,500
Factory insurance	2,000
Sales commissions	48,000
Administrative expenses	25,000
Production supervisor's salary	5,000

(c) 4,250 direct labor hours were worked in May. Laborers work a 40-hour week and are paid $22 per hour for the regular shift and time-and-a-half for each hour of overtime. Of the 4,250 hours, 250 hours were worked in overtime in May. Sinbad treats the overtime premium as a part of overhead.

Required:
(1) Calculate the factory overhead incurred in May.
(2) Determine the cost of goods manufactured in May.
(3) Determine the ending balance in finished goods at May 31. (SMAC adapted)

E4-5 Journal Entries for the Cost Accounting Cycle. Dunnington Company had the following transactions in March:
(a) Materials were purchased on account, $40,000.
(b) Materials were requisitioned: $33,000 for production and $2,000 for indirect factory use.
(c) Total payroll of $40,000 was recorded.
(d) The payroll was paid.
(e) Of the total payroll, $32,000 was direct labor and $8,000 was indirect factory labor.
(f) Various factory overhead costs totaling $4,000 were paid in cash.
(g) Various factory overhead costs totaling $18,000 were incurred on account.
(h) Other factory overhead consisted of $2,100 depreciation, $780 expired insurance, and $1,250 accrued property taxes.
(i) Total factory overhead was charged to the work in process account.
(j) Cost of completed production transferred to storage, $92,000.
(k) Sales on account were $80,000, half of which was collected. The cost of goods sold was 75% of the sales price.

Required: Prepare journal entries for these transactions.

E4-6 Journal Entries for the Cost Accounting Cycle. The general ledger of the Pacific Bearings Company contained the following accounts, among others, on January 1: Finished Goods, $15,000; Work in Process, $30,000; Materials, $25,000. During January the following transactions were completed:
(a) Materials were purchased on account at a cost of $13,500.
(b) Steel in the amount of $17,500 was issued from stores.
(c) Requisitions for indirect materials and supplies amounted to $1,800.
(d) The total payroll for January amounted to $27,000, including marketing salaries of $5,000 and administrative salaries of $3,000. Labor time tickets show that $17,000 of the labor cost was direct labor. A payroll clearing account is used.
(e) Various indirect manufacturing costs totaling $2,508 were paid in cash.
(f) Various indirect manufacturing costs totaling $8,500 were incurred on account.
(g) Total factory overhead is charged to Work in Process.
(h) Cost of production completed in January totaled $60,100, and finished goods on January 31 totaled $15,100.
(i) Customers to whom shipments were made during the month were billed for $75,000.

Required: Prepare journal entries for these transactions.

E4-7 Cost of Goods Manufactured Statement. Wallace Industries, a maker of steel cable for use in bridges, closes its books and prepares financial statements at the end of each month. The preclosing trial balance as of May 31, 19A, (in thousands) is as follows:

	Debit	Credit
Cash and Marketable Securities	$ 54	
Accounts and Notes Receivable	210	
Finished Goods (4/30/19A)	247	
Work in Process (4/30/19A)	150	
Direct Materials (4/30/19A)	28	
Property, Plant, and Equipment (net)	1,140	
Accounts, Notes, and Taxes Payable		$ 70
Bonds Payable		600
Paid-in Capital		100
Retained Earnings		930
Sales		1,488
Sales Discounts	20	
Interest Revenue		2

	Debit	Credit
Purchases of Direct Materials	$ 510	
Direct Labor	260	
Indirect Factory Labor	90	
Office Salaries	122	
Sales Salaries	42	
Utilities	135	
Rent	9	
Property Tax	60	
Insurance	20	
Depreciation	54	
Interest Expense	6	
Freight In	15	
Freight Out	18	
	$3,190	$3,190

Additional information is as follows:

(a) 80% of the utilities cost is related to manufacturing cable; the remaining 20% is related to the sales and administrative functions in the office building.
(b) All of the rent was for the office building.
(c) The property taxes were assessed on the manufacturing plant.
(d) 60% of the insurance cost is related to manufacturing cable; the remaining 40% is related to the sales and administrative functions.
(e) Depreciation for the month was:

Manufacturing plant	$20,000
Manufacturing equipment	30,000
Office equipment	4,000
	$54,000

(f) May 31, 19A inventory balances were:

Finished Goods	$175,000
Work in Process	130,000
Direct Materials	23,000

Required: Prepare a cost of goods manufactured statement for Wallace Industries for May, 19A.

(ICMA adapted)

E4-8 Cost of Goods Sold Statement. Cinnabar Company has provided the following data concerning its operations for the year ended December 31, 19A:

123

Raw materials on hand, December 31	$ 24,000
Work in process, December 31	30,000
Finished goods, December 31	40,000
Factory supplies on hand, December 31	14,000
Sales	1,100,000
Factory maintenance	38,400
Administrative salaries	108,000
Discounts on raw materials purchases	4,200
Delivery expenses	16,000
Interest income	1,000
Factory supplies used	22,400
Common stock ($10 par value)	2,000,000
Retained earnings	525,000
Trade accounts payable	273,500
Accumulated depreciation—factory building and equipment	47,500

Building and equipment	500,000
Trade accounts receivable	450,000
Cash	170,000
Finished goods, January 1, 19A	37,500
Direct labor	180,000
Bad debt expense	2,500
Factory power and heat	19,400
Advertising	8,400
Insurance expired—factory building and equipment	4,800
Work in process, January 1, 19A	84,000
Depreciation—factory building and equipment	17,500
Factory superintendence	100,000
Interest expense	1,500
Raw materials purchased	400,000
Indirect factory labor	20,000
Sales returns	2,200
Sales discounts	1,300

Required: Prepare the cost of goods sold statement. CGA-Canada (adapted). Reprint with permission.

Problems

P4-1 Cost of Goods Manufactured and Sold. For July, Bridgewell Company had cost of goods manufactured equal to $50,000; direct materials used, $16,000; cost of goods sold, $60,000; direct labor, $24,000; purchases of materials, $25,000; cost of goods available for sale, $70,000; and total factory labor, $29,000. Work in process was $15,000 on July 1 and $25,000 on July 31. The company uses a single materials account for direct and indirect materials.

Required: Prepare the following:

(1) A cost of goods sold statement. For brevity, show single line items for factory overhead and direct materials used.

(2) Summary general journal entries to record:
  (a) purchase of materials on account
  (b) use of materials, including indirect materials of $2,000
  (c) accrual of the factory payroll, including indirect labor of $5,000 (use a payroll clearing account)
  (d) distribution of factory labor cost
  (e) transfer of completed work to finished goods
  (f) sales on account, at a markup equal to 75% of production cost

P4-2 Cost of Goods Manufactured and Sold. For June, Scottsburg Company had cost of goods manufactured equal to $120,000; materials purchases, $33,000; depreciation of manufacturing assets, $17,000; cost of goods sold, $140,000; expired insurance on manufacturing assets, $2,000; cost of goods available for sale, $190,000; and total factory labor, $49,000. Inventories were as follows:

	June 1	June 30
Materials	$15,000	$19,000
Work in Process	40,000	30,000
Finished Goods	?	?

General factory overhead of $13,000 was incurred in June; this figure includes all factory overhead except indirect labor, indirect materials, depreciation, and insurance. Direct labor cost for the month was six times larger than indirect labor cost. The cost of indirect materials used was $1,000. The company uses a single materials account for direct and indirect materials.

Required: Prepare the following:
(1) A cost of goods sold statement
(2) Summary general journal entries to record:
  (a) purchase of materials on account
  (b) use of materials
  (c) accrual of the factory payroll, using a payroll clearing account
  (d) distribution of factory labor cost
  (e) transfer of completed work to finished goods
  (f) sales, at a markup equal to 50% of production cost

P4-3 Cost of Goods Manufactured; Prime and Conversion Costs. Madeira Company's purchases of materials during March totaled $110,000, and the cost of goods sold for March was $345,000. Factory overhead was 50% of direct labor cost. Other information pertaining to Madeira Company's inventories and production for March is as follows:

	Beginning	Ending
Inventories:		
Finished Goods	$102,000	$105,000
Work in Process	40,000	36,000
Materials	20,000	26,000

Required:
(1) Prepare a schedule of cost of goods manufactured.
(2) Compute the prime cost charged to Work in Process.
(3) Compute the conversion cost charged to Work in Process. (AICPA adapted)

P4-4 Income Statement Relationships. The following data are available for three companies at the end of their fiscal years:

Company A:	
Finished goods, January 1	$ 600,000
Cost of goods manufactured	3,800,000
Sales	4,000,000
Gross profit on sales	20%
Finished goods inventory, December 31	?
Company B:	
Freight in	$ 20,000
Purchases returns and allowances	80,000
Marketing expense	200,000
Finished goods, December 31	190,000
Cost of goods sold	1,300,000
Cost of goods available for sale	?
Company C:	
Gross profit	$ 96,000
Cost of goods manufactured	340,000
Finished goods, January 1	45,000
Finished goods, December 31	52,000
Work in process, January 1	28,000
Work in process, December 31	38,000
Sales	?

Required: Determine the amounts indicated by the question marks. (AICPA adapted)

P4-5 Cost accounting Cycle Entries in T Accounts. Dekker-Lopez Company charges its total actual factory overhead to Work in Process. Selected account balances for September are as follows:

	September 1	September 30
Finished Goods	$34,000	$ 30,000
Work in Process	7,000	?
Materials and Supplies	20,000	15,000
Accrued Payroll	13,000	9,000
Accounts Receivable	54,000	22,000
Accounts Payable	18,000	6,000
Sales		500,000

Additional information:

(a) All sales are on account.
(b) The accounts payable account is used for the purchase of materials and supplies only.
(c) Dekker's markup is 30% of sales.
(d) At the end of September, the work in process account had $2,000 of materials, $6,000 of direct labor, and $3,000 of factory overhead charged to it.
(e) Actual factory overhead costs for September were:

Supplies	$20,000
Indirect labor	55,000
Depreciation	10,000
Insurance	2,000
Miscellaneous	13,000

(f) Materials and supplies purchased on account were $65,000.

Required: Using T accounts, determine:
(1) Materials issued to production
(2) Direct labor
(3) Total factory overhead
(4) Cost of goods manufactured
(5) Cost of goods sold
(6) Payment of accounts payable
(7) Collection of accounts receivable
(8) Payment of payroll

CGA-Canada (adapted). Reprint with permission.

P4-6 Journal Entries for the Cost Accounting Cycle. Jaedicke-Shenkir Company incurred $40,000 direct labor cost in 19A and had the following selected account balances at the beginning and end of 19A:

	January 1	December 31
Finished Goods	$28,000	$ 45,000
Work in Process	12,000	14,000
Materials	17,000	24,000
Cost of Goods Sold		140,000
Factory Overhead Control		35,000

Required: Reconstruct the journal entries that recorded this information in 19A.

CGA-Canada (adapted). Reprint with permission.

P4-7 The Cost Accounting Cycle. The Hopkins & White Company's January 1 account balances are:

Debit		Credit	
Cash	$20,000	Accounts Payable	$15,500
Accounts Receivable	25,000	Accrued Payroll	2,250
Finished Goods	9,500	Accumulated Depreciation	10,000
Work in Process	4,500	Common Stock	60,000
Materials	10,000	Retained Earnings	21,250
Machinery	40,000		

During January, the following transactions were completed:

(a) Materials purchased on account cost $92,000.
(b) Miscellaneous factory overhead incurred on account was $26,530.
(c) Labor, accumulated and distributed using a payroll account, was consumed as follows: for direct production, $60,500; indirect labor, $12,500; sales salaries, $8,000; administrative salaries, $5,000. The total accrued payroll, including the January 1 balance, was then paid.
(d) Materials were consumed as follows: direct materials, $82,500; indirect materials, $8,300.
(e) Factory overhead charged to production was $47,330.
(f) Work finished and placed in stock cost $188,000.
(g) All but $12,000 of the finished goods were sold, terms 2/10, n/60. The markup was 30% above production cost. The sale and the receivable are recorded in the gross amount.
(h) Of the total accounts receivable, 80% was collected, less 2% discount. (Round to the nearest dollar.)
(i) A liability was recorded for various marketing and administrative expenses totaling $30,000. Of this amount, 60% was marketing and 40% was administrative.
(j) The check register showed payments of $104,000 for liabilities other than payrolls.

Required:

(1) Prepare T accounts with January 1 balances.
(2) Prepare journal entries and post January transactions into the ledger accounts. Open new accounts as needed.
(3) Prepare a trial balance as of January 31.

CHAPTER 5

Job Order Costing

Learning Objectives

After studying this chapter, you will be able to:

1. Perform job order cost accumulation.
2. Identify and prepare the eight basic cost accounting entries involved in job order costing.
3. Prepare a job order cost sheet.
4. Use a predetermined overhead rate in job order costing.
5. Recognize job order cost sheets in a variety of forms, for both manufacturing and service businesses.

Chapter 4 illustrated cost accumulation in general, briefly described the job order and process methods, and gave examples of businesses that use each. This chapter illustrates job order costing in detail. It also elaborates on some parts of the previous chapter's general discussion of cost accumulation.

Overview of Job Order Costing

In **job order costing**, or **job costing**, production costs are accumulated for each separate **job**; a job is the output identified to fill a certain customer order or to replenish an item of stock on hand. This differs from process costing, in which costs are accumulated for an operation or a subdivision of the company, such as a department.

In order for job costing to be effective, jobs must be separately identifiable. For the detail of job costing to be worth the effort, there must be important differences in unit costs from one job to another. For example, if a printing plant simultaneously prepares orders for foil labels, printed paper wrappers, and adhesive paper stickers, the orders are easily distinguished by their physical appearance and the unit costs of the orders differ, so job costing is used.

Details about a job are recorded on a **job order cost sheet**, or simply **cost sheet**, which can be in paper or electronic form. Although many jobs may be worked on simultaneously, each cost sheet collects details for one specific job. The contents and arrangement of cost sheets differ from one business to another. Figure 5-1 is an example of a cost sheet. The upper section provides space for the job number, customer name, quantity and description of the items to be produced, and dates started and completed. The next sections detail the direct material, direct labor, and overhead costs charged to the job.[1] Some cost sheets have an

[1] In the cost sheet for a departmentalized operation, the direct materials, direct labor, and factory overhead added by each department or cost center are separately identified.

additional section, like the lower section of the cost sheet shown in Figure 5-1, that summarizes the production costs, shows marketing and administrative expenses and profit, and compares estimated and actual costs.

FIGURE 5-1 ***Cost Sheet for a Nondepartmentalized Plant***

Rayburn Company
1101 Maple Street, Cincinnati, OH 45227

Job Order No. **5574**

FOR: Lawrenceville Construction Co.	DATE ORDERED: 1/10
PRODUCT: #14 Maple Drain Boards	DATE STARTED: 1/14
SPECIFICATION: 12'x 20"x 1" Clear Finishes	DATE WANTED: 1/22
QUANTITY: 10	DATE COMPLETED: 1/18

DIRECT MATERIALS

DATE	REQ. NO.	AMOUNT	TOTAL
1/14	516	$1,420.00	
1/17	531	780.00	
1/18	544	310.00	
			$2,510.00

DIRECT LABOR

DATE	HOURS	COST	
1/14	40	$ 320.00	
1/15	32	256.00	
1/16	36	288.00	
1/17	40	320.00	
1/18	48	384.00	
	196		$1,568.00

FACTORY OVERHEAD APPLIED

DATE	MACHINE HOURS	COST	
1/14	16.2	$ 684.00	
1/16	10.0	400.00	
1/17	3.2	128.00	
	29.4 x $40		$1,176.00

Direct Materials	$2,510.00	Selling Price		$7,860.00
Direct Labor	1,568.00	Factory Cost	$5,254.00	
Factory Overhead Applied	1,176.00	Marketing Expense	776.00	
		Admin. Expense	420.00	
Total Factory Cost	$5,254.00	Cost to Make and Sell		6,450.00
		Profit		$1,410.00

Job order costing accumulates the costs of direct material, direct labor, and overhead charged to each job. As a result, job costing can be viewed in three related parts. Materials accounting maintains materials inventory records, charges direct material to jobs, and charges indirect material to overhead. Labor accounting maintains payroll-related accounts, charges direct labor to jobs, and charges indirect labor to overhead. Overhead accounting accumulates overhead costs, maintains overhead detail records, and charges a share of overhead to each job. The basics of job order costing involve only eight types of accounting entries, one for each of the following:

1. Materials purchased
2. Factory labor costs incurred
3. Factory overhead costs incurred
4. Materials used
5. Factory labor costs distributed
6. Estimated factory overhead applied
7. Jobs completed
8. Products sold

Types 1 through 3 are common to both job order and process costing. They are presented in this chapter to provide a more complete illustration and to build upon the general discussion of cost accumulation in Chapter 4. Types 1, 2, and 8 generally are recorded during an accounting period on dates when certain transactions occur. Types 4 through 7 are often recorded only in summary form at the end of a period. Type 3 entries are recorded both during and at the end of a period. This chapter illustrates the eight types of entries and describes job costing for Rayburn Company. Figure 5-2 summarizes the flow of costs through Rayburn's work in process, finished goods, and cost of goods sold accounts during January. The rest of this chapter will explain and elaborate on each part shown in Figure 5-2.

FIGURE 5-2 ***Work In Process, Finished Goods, and Cost of Goods Sold Accounts of Rayburn Company***

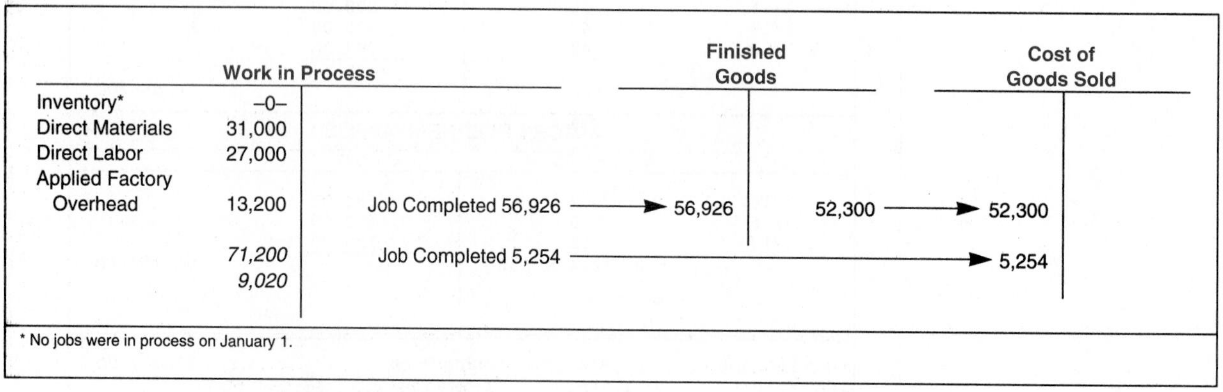
Work in Process
Inventory* –0–
Direct Materials 31,000
Direct Labor 27,000
Applied Factory Overhead 13,200
71,200
9,020
Job Completed 56,926
Job Completed 5,254
Finished Goods
56,926
52,300
Cost of Goods Sold
52,300
5,254
* No jobs were in process on January 1.

Accounting for Materials

Inventory accounts for supplies and direct and indirect materials can be separate, but common practice is to use a single general ledger account entitled Materials, as illustrated in Figure 5-3.

Materials Purchased

Cost accounting for purchased materials is the same as it is for any perpetual inventory system. As materials are received, the account Materials is debited (rather than Purchases, in a periodic inventory system). Rayburn Company received a shipment of $25,000 of purchased materials on January 5. The journal entry is:

Materials	25,000	
Accounts Payable		25,000

The quantity and unit cost of each purchase are entered on materials record cards. One card is maintained for each kind of material. These cards function as perpetual inventory records and constitute a subsidiary ledger supporting the account Materials. These and related documents can exist in paper or electronic form. Materials accounting is discussed in detail in Chapter 9.

Materials Used

Direct materials for a job are issued to the factory on the basis of **materials requisitions**, which are documents prepared by production schedulers or other personnel specifying the job number and type and quantity of materials required. A copy of each requisition is sent to the storekeeper, who gathers the materials specified. The quantity and cost of each item are entered on the requisition and posted to materials record cards.

The flow of direct materials from storeroom to factory is accounted for as a transfer of cost from Materials to Work in Process. Often this is done in summary form at the end of a month or other period. A total of $31,000 of direct materials were requisitioned in January at Rayburn Company, consisting of $2,510 for Job 5574,[2] $24,070 for Job 5575, and $4,420 for Job 5576. The summary entry is:

Work in Process	31,000	
Materials		31,000

A copy of each requisition is sent to the cost department, where the requisitions are sorted by job number and entered, daily or weekly, in the materials sections of the job cost sheets. In this way, the quantity and cost of materials used in each job are accumulated in a timely fashion, even if general journal entries are recorded less frequently. If materials for a job are returned to the storeroom unused, Materials is debited, Work in Process is credited, and the materials record cards and job cost sheets are adjusted.

Requisitions also are used in issuing indirect materials or supplies. If not used in the factory, supplies are charged to marketing or administrative expense accounts. If used in the factory, they are charged to Factory Overhead Control. Factory supplies totaling $6,000 were requisitioned during January at Rayburn Company. Rayburn Company records these requisitions by a monthly summary entry:

Factory Overhead Control	6,000	
Materials		6,000

The details of overhead costs are also posted to an overhead subsidiary record, which can be a worksheet called a **factory overhead analysis sheet**. Overhead accounting is discussed in detail in Chapters 12 and 13.

Because more timely information is needed for the purposes of product costing and customer billing, requisitions are entered into job cost sheets at intervals of a week or less, as stated previously. Because updated general ledger accounts are needed only at month-end when financial statements are prepared, the general journal entries can be made monthly in summary form, as shown. In a highly automated accounting system, individual requisitions can be

[2] These subsidiary details, permit comparison with the completed cost sheet of Job 5574, shown in Figure 5-1. Similar cost sheets would exist for the other two jobs, but for brevity they are not illustrated.

recorded electronically, with job cost sheets and the subsidiary records for overhead and materials becoming updated instantly. Figure 5-3 summarizes the accounting for materials.

FIGURE 5-3 ***Materials Purchased and Used***

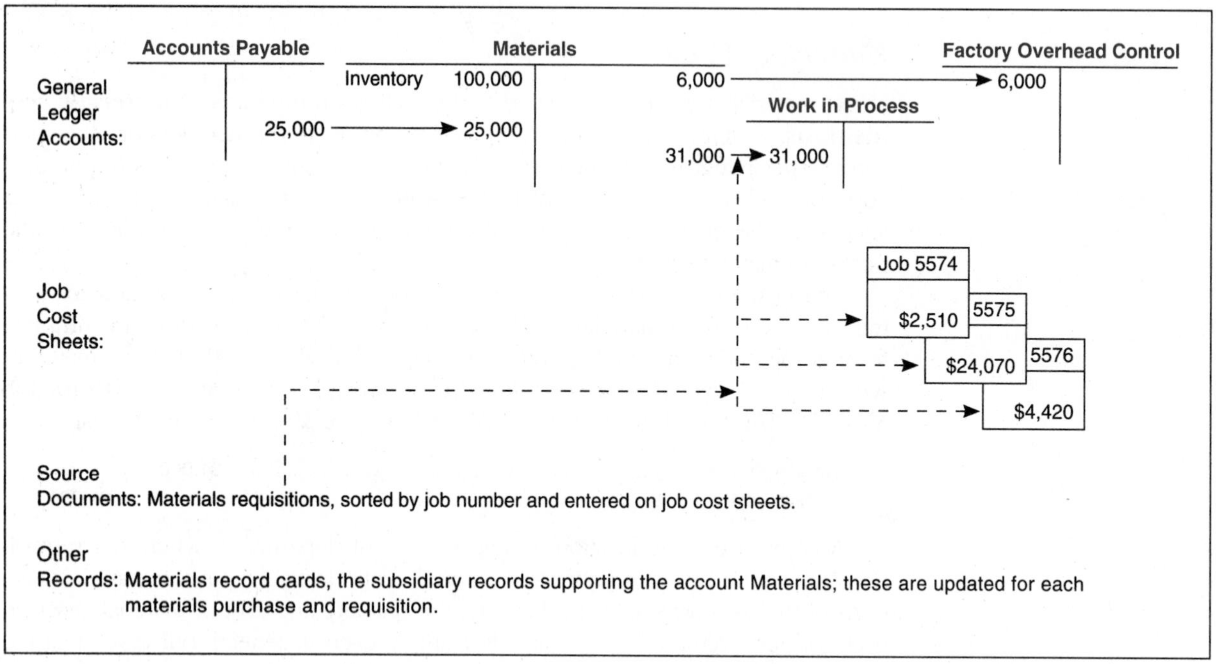

Accounting for Labor

In most companies, a time clock registers each employee on an individual clock card when the employee enters and leaves the facility. Clock cards thus show the amount of time worked and are used to compute earnings of hourly wage earners.

To identify direct and indirect labor cost, each worker prepares one or more **labor time tickets** each day. Each labor time ticket is a document showing the time spent by one worker on a job order (direct labor) or any other task (indirect labor).[3] Time tickets are costed and summarized, and time ticket hours for each employee are reconciled periodically with clock card hours.

Factory Labor Cost Incurred

For each pay period, the liabilities for wages and other payments due are journalized and posted to the general ledger. (As in Chapter 4, Accrued

[3] If the labor was not used in manufacturing, it is charged to marketing or administrative expense accounts.

Payroll is the only liability that will be illustrated here, so the entire payroll will be credited to Accrued Payroll.) Regardless of the number of liabilities recorded, the offsetting debit will be made to Payroll, where labor cost is accumulated temporarily until it is distributed to the cost accounts, usually at month-end.

It is common to pay some employees monthly and others more frequently, which entails the recording of several payrolls in each month in addition to month-end accruals. Because these details of payroll accounting are voluminous and are not unique to job costing, a discussion of them is deferred to Chapter 11. For brevity, suppose Rayburn Company pays factory workers only once each month. Factory payroll of $31,000 is calculated and recorded on January 31 (and will be paid in early February). The general journal entry is:

Payroll	31,000	
Accrued Payroll		31,000

Factory Labor Costs Distributed

Most companies distribute labor costs monthly: labor time tickets are sorted by job, entered on job cost sheets, and recorded by summary general journal entries. Rayburn's direct labor time tickets from January total $1,568 for Job 5574, $22,832 for Job 5575, and $2,600 for Job 5576. Indirect labor totals $4,000.[4] Rayburn Company records both direct and indirect labor by monthly summary entries:

Work in Process	27,000	
Payroll		27,000
Factory Overhead Control	4,000	
Payroll		4,000

These entries produce a zero balance in Payroll and charge the direct and indirect factory labor to the appropriate cost accounts. The accounting for labor is summarized in Figure 5-4.

Time tickets are sorted and entered on job cost sheets weekly, or even daily, to cost products and bill customers more promptly. On the other hand, because updated general ledger balances are needed only at month-end when financial statements are prepared, the general journal entries are made in month-end summary form as shown. In some highly automated systems, employees' encoded identification cards are scanned at the beginning and end of their work on each job or other task, and all records are updated instantly. If the time clock also can scan the cards, both clock cards and time tickets may exist only in electronic form.

[4] In an automated factory with very little direct labor and a single conversion cost classification, all factory labor can be treated the way indirect labor is treated here. No direct labor is charged to any job, and cost sheets contain sections for direct materials and conversion cost only.

FIGURE 5-4 *Labor Cost*

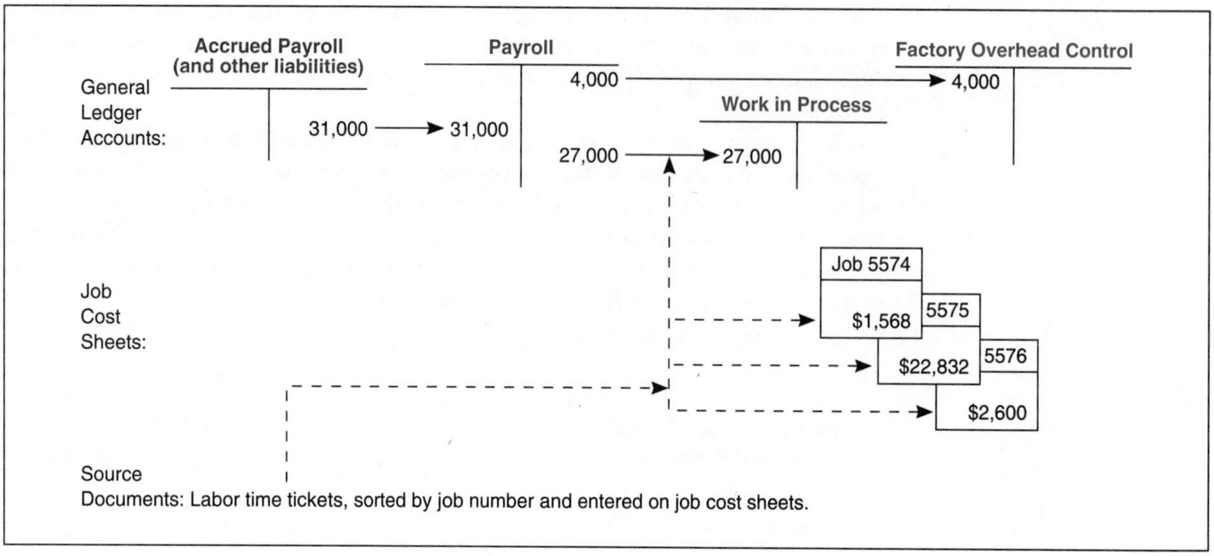

Accounting for Factory Overhead

Factory overhead consists of all the costs that are incurred in production (not marketing and administration) and not traced directly to jobs. The lack of direct tracing makes the accounting very different; specifically, the roles played by direct materials requisitions and direct labor time tickets have no counterpart in overhead accounting. Instead, overhead costs are broadly accumulated without distinction as to job; and then total overhead costs are allocated among all jobs.

Actual Factory Overhead Incurred

Some actual overhead costs, such as indirect materials and indirect labor, are recorded when they are incurred or by periodic summary entries, as illustrated previously. Others, such as depreciation and expired insurance, are recorded only by adjusting entries made at the end of a period. Rayburn Company calculates factory depreciation of $4,929 and expired factory insurance of $516 for the month. The entries for these costs are:

Factory Overhead Control	4,929	
Accumulated Depreciation—Machinery		4,929
Factory Overhead Control	516	
Prepaid Insurance		516

Only four overhead costs have been illustrated: indirect materials, indirect labor, machinery depreciation, and insurance. A category such as indirect labor can be divided into many parts (material handling, cleaning, and so on), each with a separate subsidiary record. There are many other overhead costs, such as property taxes, rent, building depreciation, pension cost, medical insurance, vacation pay, utilities, and purchased services such as security and repairs. No additional concepts are involved in accounting for these overhead costs, however. In every case, Factory Overhead Control is debited with subsidiary detail also recorded, and the offsetting credit is made to the appropriate asset account (e.g., Prepaid Rent), liability account (e.g., Property Taxes Payable), or other account (e.g., Payroll).

Estimated Factory Overhead Applied

A job's prime costs are determined from materials requisitions and time tickets. Determining the amount of overhead to be charged is more difficult. Some overhead costs, such as rent and insurance, are fixed regardless of the amount of production. Others, such as power and lubricants, will vary with the quantity of production. Overhead costs such as major cleaning and remodeling efforts are intermittent or seasonal; they benefit all production but may be incurred when some jobs are in production and not incurred at all at other times.

To overcome the difficulties of overhead accounting, all overhead costs are distributed over all jobs. The amount charged is in proportion to an activity—such as direct labor usage, machine usage, processing time, material usage, or a combination of two or more of these. As automation increases and the use of direct labor decreases, the activity chosen is more likely to be not direct labor hours or direct labor cost, but rather machine hours, processing time, material cost, or material weight.

The activity chosen is called the **overhead allocation base** or simply the **base**. The base chosen should be the one most closely related to the costs being allocated; that is, the one that appears to drive most of the factory overhead. Total overhead is divided by the total of the base, and the resulting ratio is called the overhead rate. This rate is multiplied by the amount of the base that a job uses, and the result is the overhead charge for that job. For example, if the rate is $5 per direct labor hour and a certain job uses 100 direct labor hours, then $500 of overhead cost will be applied to that job.

Some overhead costs are not measured until year-end, long after many jobs are completed. For that reason (and other reasons discussed in Chapter 12), actual overhead cannot be charged to jobs in a timely fashion; estimates are needed. To permit timely application of overhead, a **predetermined overhead rate** is used, the ratio of estimated total overhead to the estimated total of the overhead allocation base.[5]

Rayburn Company has determined that the strongest relationship is between machine hours[6] and factory overhead, and that those two measures are expected to total 7,500 and $300,000, respectively, for the year. These estimates produce a predetermined overhead rate of $40 per machine hour ($300,000 divided by 7,500). The amount of overhead charged to a job, called **applied overhead**, is determined by multiplying $40 by the number of machine hours used on that job. Because Rayburn's machine logs show a total of 29.4 machine hours for Job 5574, applied factory overhead of $1,176 (29.4 × $40) is entered on the cost sheet in Figure 5-1. Applied overhead is calculated similarly for all jobs and is entered on the respective cost sheets.

The factory overhead applied to all jobs worked on during a period is debited to Work in Process at the end of the period. In addition to the 29.4 machine hours

---

[5] Some manufacturing operations use job order costing but do not account for direct labor as a separate cost element; instead, all factory labor is treated as an overhead cost. In these situations, the predetermined rate is for total conversion costs, and its use parallels the use of the predetermined overhead rate illustrated here.

[6] For discussion of why machine hours might be selected as the base, see Robin Cooper, "When Should You Use Machine-Hour Costing?" *Journal of Cost Management*, Vol. 2, No.1, pp. 33-39.

for Job 5574, Rayburn Company's machine logs show 250.6 hours for Job 5575 and 50 hours for Job 5576, for a total of 330 hours used in January. Therefore, applied overhead of $13,200 ($40 × 330) is charged to Work in Process. The offsetting credit can be made directly to Factory Overhead Control, or a separate account, Applied Factory Overhead, can be used, as in the following entry:

Work in Process	13,200	
Applied Factory Overhead		13,200

Applied Factory Overhead usually is closed to Factory Overhead Control at year-end, but for illustrative purposes assume Rayburn Company closes Applied Factory Overhead monthly. If the preceding $13,200 journal entry is the only application of overhead for the month, the closing entry is:

Applied Factory Overhead	13,200	
Factory Overhead Control		13,200

An account for applied factory overhead has the advantage of separating the records of applied and actual overhead. Separate records make it easier for managers to evaluate the overhead rate by comparing actual and applied totals with the amounts budgeted. Companies that do not use an applied factory overhead account will credit Factory Overhead Control when debiting Work in Process. This eliminates the need for the closing entry and has the same net effect on Factory Overhead Control as the entries illustrated.

The accounting for overhead in job order costing is summarized in Figure 5-5. The entries for $6,000 of indirect materials and $4,000 of indirect labor appeared in Figures 5-3 and 5-4, respectively. Because those two entries are also part of overhead accounting, they appear again in Figure 5-5, but they would be journalized and posted only once.

FIGURE 5-5 ***Actual Overhead Incurred and Estimated Overhead Applied***

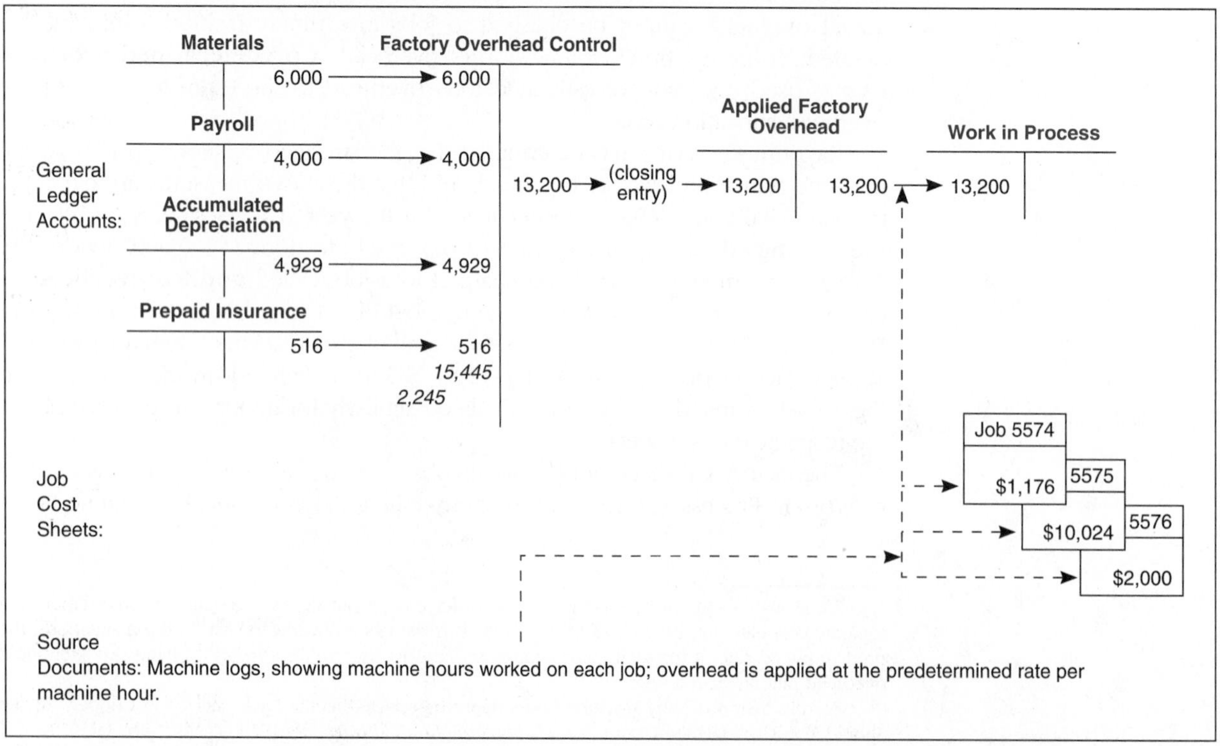

The $2,245 debit balance in Factory Overhead Control indicates that the actual overhead incurred exceeded the amount applied; that is, overhead was underapplied by $2,245. Underapplied overhead is interpreted as an unfavorable cost variance. The significance of an underapplied or overapplied balance, and the disposition of it, are discussed in Chapter 12. If the balance at year-end is small, it typically is transferred to Cost of Goods Sold at year-end.

Accounting for Jobs Completed and Products Sold

As jobs are completed, their cost sheets are moved from the in-process category to a finished work file. When a completed job is intended to replenish stock on hand, the quantity and cost are recorded on finished goods record cards, which serve as a subsidiary ledger supporting the finished goods account. Rayburn Company completed Jobs 5574 and 5575 during January at costs of $5,254 (shown in Figure 5-1) and $56,926,[7] respectively.

A job for a specific customer can be shipped when completed and never enter finished goods inventory; Sales and Cost of Goods Sold are recorded when the job is transferred from Work in Process. Because Job 5574 was shipped immediately to Lawrenceville Construction Company on January 18, it is not included in the entry transferring completed work to Finished Goods. Only Job 5575 is transferred to Finished Goods, and the completion of Job 5574 is recorded by the following entries:

Accounts Receivable	7,860	
Sales		7,860
Cost of Goods Sold	5,254	
Work in Process		5,254

Job 5575 was transferred to Finished Goods[8] to replenish stock, and the entry recording the transfer was made at month-end as follows:

Finished Goods	56,926	
Work In Process		56,926

When stock on hand is shipped to customers, the finished goods record cards are updated, sales invoices prepared, and sales and the cost of goods sold recorded, just as in any perpetual inventory system. On January 27, Rayburn Company shipped finished goods costing $52,300, consisting of a portion of Job 5575 and portions of various jobs that were completed in the preceding year. The sales price was $70,000, and the entries are:

Accounts Receivable	70,000	
Sales		70,000
Cost of Goods Sold	52,300	
Finished Goods		52,300

[7] A cost sheet for Job 5575 would show this total, which is the sum of the $24,070 of material, $22,832 of labor, and $10,024 of overhead charged to Job 5575 in the journal entries illustrated in Figures 5-3, 5-4, and 5-5.

[8] When the purpose of a completed job is to replenish the stock of a component used in making other products, the cost of the completed job is charged to Materials rather than Finished Goods.

The preceding Work in Process, Finished Goods, and Cost of Goods Sold entries are summarized in Figure 5-2. The ending balance of Work in Process in Figure 5-2, $9,020, represents the cost of Job 5576, the only job still in process at the end of January.

Job Order Costing in Service Businesses

In service businesses where jobs differ from each other and cost information is desired for individual jobs, several varieties of job order costing are used. These service businesses include laundries, tailors, lawn service companies, temporary-help companies, repair shops, and professional services such as legal, architectural, engineering, accounting, and consulting. In these businesses, direct labor and labor-related costs are usually larger than any other cost, often by a wide margin, so the predetermined overhead rate typically is based on direct labor cost. It is also common to combine labor cost with the predetermined overhead rate, so the amount charged to a job for each hour of direct labor represents both labor and overhead.

The only remaining items to be charged to each job are the directly traceable costs other than labor. In a repair shop, this category usually includes only the cost of parts, which corresponds to direct material cost in manufacturing. But in a professional service business, there are many directly traceable costs other than labor. Examples are travel, meals, entertainment, long-distance telephone charges, photocopying, and subcontracted services. In tracing these costs to jobs, a crucial link in the accounting system is the fact that many of these costs are incurred by personnel who are later reimbursed in cash.

For example, an employee who incurs reimbursable expenses such as meals, travel, or entertainment typically is required to report the date of the expenditure, the client's name or job number, the nature of the cost, and an original receipt for large amounts. Of course, this information establishes the legitimacy of the reimbursement, but it also enables the costs to be traced directly to jobs. To trace photocopying costs directly to jobs, all photocopying is entered in a log kept near the copier. To trace long distance telephone charges, each employee is required to log each call.

Weekly or monthly summaries of all costs are prepared and entered on job cost sheets, which may be called by any of several names, depending on the type of business. A partially completed job cost sheet for a law firm is shown in Figure 5-6. Notice that there is no separate category for overhead, because the predetermined overhead cost rate is included in the hourly charges for labor.

Summary

When customer orders or other segments of output are not all alike, job order costing is used to trace some costs directly to each segment of output. Each identified segment of output is called a job; details of jobs' costs are collected on job cost sheets, which also serve as subsidiary records for Work in Process. Indirect costs are also charged to jobs, usually by means of predetermined overhead rates. A predetermined rate is calculated by dividing an estimate of total indirect costs by an estimate of the total of a selected allocation base. Job order costing is used in both manufacturing and service businesses.

FIGURE 5-6 *Job Cost Sheet for a Service Business*

Vise, Freud, & Graff, Attorneys at Law

Summary of Engagement Account

Client Name: Charles Harmed Date Contracted: 5/9/19A
Engagement Type: Civil Date Terminated: ______
Engagement Number: 1057 Supervising Partner: Vise

PARTNERS' TIME:

Period Ending	Hours	Rate	Amount	
5/31/19A	30	$150*	$4,500.00	
6/30/19A				
Subtotals:				$

ASSOCIATES' TIME:

Period Ending	Hours	Rate	Amount	
5/31/19A	200	$60*	$12,000.00	
6/30/19A				
Subtotals:				$
Total time:				$

OTHER:

Period Ending	5/31/19A	6/30/19A		
Travel	$ 391.00			
Meals	206.00			
Photocopies	52.60			
Telephone	143.49			
Detective	300.00			
Witnesses	900.00			
Total other:	$1,993.09			$
Total for engagement:				$

* Represents the sum of direct labor cost and the predetermined overhead rate based on direct labor.

Key Terms

job order costing, job costing *(96)*
job *(96)*
job order cost sheet, cost sheet *(96)*
materials requisitions *(99)*
factory overhead analysis sheet *(99)*
labor time tickets *(100)*
overhead allocation base, base *(103)*
predetermined overhead rate *(103)*
applied overhead *(103)*

Discussion Questions

Q5-1 It has been said that an actual product cost does not exist, in the sense of absolute authenticity and verifiability. Why?

Q5-2 What is the primary objective in job order costing?

Q5-3 What is the rationale supporting the use of process costing instead of job order costing for product costing purposes?

Q5-4 Describe the uses of a job order cost sheet.

Q5-5 What is the function of the work in process account in job order costing?

Q5-6 How is control over prime costs achieved in job order costing?

Q5-7 Distinguish between actual and applied factory overhead.

Q5-8 Some service businesses use job order costing. What characteristic of a service business makes it likely that job order costing will be used?

Exercises

E5-1 Simple Job Order Cost Sheet. Review this chapter's journal entries, which record the January activity of Rayburn Company.

Required: Prepare a brief cost sheet for the completed Job 5575.

E5-2 Simple Job Order Cost Sheet. Review this chapter's journal entries, which record the January activity of Rayburn Company.

Required: Prepare a brief cost sheet showing the costs incurred to date on the incomplete Job 5576.

E5-3 Manufacturing Costs. The work in process account of Bamersmith Company showed:

Work in Process			
Materials	$15,500	Finished goods	$37,500
Direct labor	14,750		
Factory overhead	11,800		

Materials charged to the one job still in process amounted to $3,200. Factory overhead is applied as a predetermined percentage of direct labor cost.

Required: Compute the following:
(1) The amount of direct labor cost in finished goods.
(2) The amount of factory overhead in finished goods.

E5-4 Manufacturing Costs. Information concerning Westmack Company's manufacturing activities for December follows:

	Inventories	
	December 1	December 31
Finished goods	$12,000	
Direct materials		$5,000
Direct labor		$3,000
Machine time		60 hours
Work in process	3,000 units	2,000 units
Direct materials, $2.40 per unit		
Direct labor, $.80 per unit		
Machine time	48 hours	32 hours
Materials	$ 9,000	$4,500

Total December manufacturing cost was $180,000, of which $30,000 was direct labor cost. A total of 600 machine hours were used in the month. Westmack uses a predetermined overhead rate of $100 per machine hour to assign factory overhead to work in process and finished goods inventories. Materials purchased in December were $84,000 and freight-in on these purchases totaled $1,500.

Required: Compute the following:
(1) Materials used in December
(2) Work in process at December 31
(3) December cost of goods manufactured
(4) Finished goods at December 31
(5) December cost of goods sold

CGA-Canada (adapted). Reprint with permission.

E5-5 Manufacturing Costs. Selected data concerning last year's operations of Multicom Company are as follows (in thousands of dollars):

	Inventories	
	Beginning	**Ending**
Finished Goods	$90	$110
Work in Process	80	30
Materials	75	85

Other data:
(a) Materials used, $326
(b) Total manufacturing costs charged to jobs during the year (includes materials, direct labor, and factory overhead applied at a rate of 60% of direct labor cost), $686
(c) Cost of goods available for sale, $826
(d) Marketing and administrative expenses, $25

Required: Compute the following:
(1) Cost of materials purchased
(2) Direct labor cost charged to production
(3) Cost of goods manufactured
(4) Cost of goods sold

(ICMA adapted)

E5-6 Manufacturing Costs. Hutto Company is to submit a bid on the production of 11,250 ceramic plates. It is estimated that the cost of materials will be $13,000 and the cost of direct labor will be $15,000. Factory overhead is applied at $2.70 per direct labor hour in the Molding Department and at 35% of the direct labor cost in the Decorating Department. It is estimated that 1,000 direct labor hours, at a cost of $9,000, will be required in Molding. The company wants a markup of 45% of its total production cost.

Required: Determine the following:
(1) Estimated cost to produce
(2) Estimated prime cost
(3) Estimated conversion cost
(4) Bid price

E5-7 Job Order Cost Sheet. Wadsworth Machine Works collects its cost data by job order cost accumulation. For Job 909, the following data are available:

Direct Materials	Direct Labor
9/14 Issued, $600	Week of Sept. 20, 90 hrs. @ $6.20/hr.
9/20 Issued, 331	Week of Sept. 26, 70 hrs. @ $7.30/hr.
9/22 Issued, 200	

Factory overhead is applied at the rate of $80 per machine hour. Ten machine hours were used on Job 909 on September 20.

Required:
(1) Enter the appropriate information on a job order cost sheet.
(2) Determine the sales price of the job, assuming that it was contracted with a markup of 50% of cost.

E5-8 Journal Entries for Job Order Costing. The following job order cost detail pertains to the three jobs that were in process at the Equinaut Company during January.

	Job 66	Job 67	Job 68
Cost charged in prior period	$40,000	$15,000	$ —
Costs added in January:			
Direct materials	35,000	45,000	55,000
Direct labor	45,000	40,000	35,000
Factory overhead ($50 per machine hour)	?	?	?
January machine hours used	720	640	560

Required: Prepare the appropriate journal entry to record each of the following January transactions:
(1) Direct materials were issued from the materials storeroom to work in process.
(2) The payroll was distributed to work in process.
(3) Factory overhead was applied to production for the period.
(4) Job orders 66 and 67 were completed and transferred to the finished goods storeroom.

E5-9 Journal Entries for Job Order Costing. Angelina Company's July transactions included the following:
(a) Purchased materials on account cost $35,000.
(b) Requisitions for $8,000 of direct materials and $2,000 of indirect materials were filled from the storeroom.
(c) Factory payroll totaling $9,400 consisted of $7,600 direct labor and $1,800 indirect labor.
(d) Depreciation of $1,200 on factory equipment was recorded.
(e) A job order was completed with $1,830 of direct labor and $1,450 of materials previously charged to the order. Factory overhead is to be applied at 66⅔% of direct labor cost.
(f) Miscellaneous factory overhead of $1,250 was accrued.
(g) The job order referred to in transaction (e) was shipped to Dixon Associates, who were billed for $5,400.

Required: Prepare journal entries to record the transactions.

E5-10 Flow of Costs Through T Accounts. The Emerson Company had the following inventories at the beginning and end of January:

	January 1	January 31
Materials	$10,000	$ 38,000
Work in Process	?	110,000
Finished Goods	50,000	150,000

During January, the cost of materials purchased was $138,000 and factory overhead of $90,000 was applied at a rate of 50% of direct labor cost. January cost of goods sold was $200,000.

Required: Prepare completed T accounts showing the flow of the cost of goods manufactured and sold.

CGA-Canada (adapted). Reprint with permission.

E5-11 Brief Job Costing Journal Entries. Micro Solutions Incorporated produced Job 121 using $11,250 of direct materials and $3,945 of direct labor. Overhead is applied at a predetermined rate of 150% of direct labor cost.

Required: Prepare general journal entries, omitting subsidiary detail, to record the following:
(1) The costs of Job 121
(2) The transfer of Job 121 to the finished goods stockroom

Problems

P5-1 Manufacturing Costs. Last month, Georgetown Company put $60,000 of materials into production. The Grinding Department used 8,000 labor hours at $5.60 per hour, and the Machining Department used 4,600 hours at a cost of $6 per hour. Factory overhead is applied at a rate of $6 per labor hour in the Grinding Department and $8 per labor hour in the Machining Department. Inventory accounts had the following beginning and ending balances:

	Beginning	Ending
Finished Goods	$22,000	$17,000
Work in Process	15,000	17,600
Materials	20,000	18,000

Required: Without preparing a formal income statement, compute the following:
(1) Total cost of work put into process
(2) Cost of completed jobs
(3) Cost of jobs sold
(4) Conversion cost
(5) Cost of materials purchased

P5-2 Manufacturing Costs. Langston Tool uses job order cost accumulation and applies overhead based on direct labor hours. Any underapplied or overapplied overhead is adjusted directly to Cost of Goods Sold at the end of each month. On April 1, job cost sheets indicated the following:

	Job 201	Job 202	Job 203	Job 204
Direct materials	$3,590	$2,000	$1,480	$2,000
Direct labor	2,700	1,500	1,000	1,200
Applied overhead	2,160	1,200	800	960
Total cost	$8,450	$4,700	$3,280	$4,160
Job status	Finished	In process	In process	In process

On April 30, Finished Goods contained only Jobs 204 and 207, which had the following total costs:

	Job 204	Job 207
Direct materials	$2,970	$2,450
Direct labor	2,200	1,900
Applied overhead	1,760	1,520
Total cost	$6,930	$5,870

Besides working on Jobs 204 and 207 in April, Langston continued work on Jobs 202 and 203 and started work on Jobs 205 and 206. A summary of direct materials used and direct labor hours worked on Jobs 202, 203, 205, and 206 during April showed the following:

	Job 202	Job 203	Job 205	Job 206
Direct materials	$1,250	$ 555	$2,500	$1,980
Direct labor hours	100	75	105	50

Other information:
(a) On April 30, the only jobs still in process were 203 and 206.
(b) All workers are paid $20 per hour. Wage rates have been stable throughout the year.
(c) Langston maintains only one raw materials account (Materials Control) from which it issues both direct and indirect materials. The balance in this account was $2,750 on April 1.
(d) All sales are billed on account at 150% of total cost.
(e) Other items in April:

Depreciation, factory equipment	$ 1,375
Raw materials purchased	11,500
Indirect labor	2,500
Factory rent and utilities	2,700
Indirect materials used	2,790

Required:

(1) Determine the April 30 balances for Materials Control and for Work in Process.
(2) Prepare all journal entries required for Job 202 in April.
(3) Calculate the cost of goods manufactured in April. (A complete statement of cost of goods manufactured is not required.)
(4) Calculate the over- or underapplied overhead for April.
(5) Calculate gross profit for April.

(SMAC adapted)

P5-3 Manufacturing Cost Computations with T Accounts. The following information pertains to the Cloverdale Company:

	Account Balances	
	Beginning	**Ending**
Finished Goods	$80,000	$?
Work in Process	20,000	?
Materials	15,000	23,000
Accounts Payable	7,000	5,000
Accrued Payroll	11,000	14,000
Accounts Receivable	45,000	65,000

(a) All sales were on account, with a markup equal to 28% of the sales price.
(b) The accounts payable account was used for materials purchases only.
(c) Factory overhead was applied at 150% of direct labor cost.
(d) Miscellaneous factory overhead cost totaled $60,000.
(e) Direct materials issued to production cost $80,000.
(f) Payment of accounts payable totaled $102,000.
(g) There was only one job in process at the end of the period, with charges to date of materials costing $10,000 and direct labor of $8,000.
(h) Collection of accounts receivable totaled $480,000.
(i) Cost of goods manufactured was $320,000.
(j) Payrolls totaling $172,000 were paid in cash.

Required: Using T accounts, compute:

(1) Materials purchased
(2) Cost of goods sold
(3) Finished goods ending inventory
(4) Work in process ending inventory
(5) Direct labor cost
(6) Applied factory overhead
(7) Over- or underapplied factory overhead
(8) Assuming the over- or underapplied overhead is relatively small, what is its disposition?

CGA-Canada (adapted). Reprint with permission.

P5-4 Income Statement; Cost of Goods Sold Statement; Factory Overhead Analysis. On October 1, the accountant of Columbus Company prepared a trial balance from which the following accounts were extracted:

	Dr.	Cr.
Finished Goods (2,800 units)	$ 9,800	
Work in Process (1,200 units)	4,070	
Materials and Supplies	40,700	
Buildings	48,000	
Accumulated Depreciation—Buildings		$ 6,000
Machinery and Equipment	96,000	
Accumulated Depreciation—Machinery and Equipment		37,500
Office Equipment	3,200	
Accumulated Depreciation—Office Equipment		1,000
Accrued Payroll		650

The following transactions and other data have been made available for October:

(a) Purchased materials and supplies costing $24,800.
(b) Paid factory overhead of $20,100.
(c) Paid marketing expenses of $25,050.
(d) Paid administrative expenses were $19,700.
(e) Requisitions for direct materials were $29,800 and indirect materials were $3,950.
(f) Annual depreciation for building was 5% (75% to manufacturing, 15% to marketing, and 10% to administrative expenses); for machinery and equipment, 10%; and for office equipment, 15% (40% to marketing and 60% to administrative expenses).
(g) Sales (20,700 units) totaled $144,900.
(h) Sales returns and allowances totaled $1,300.
(i) Cash payments for accounts payable were $75,000 and for payroll were $21,800.
(j) Distribution of payroll earned was $18,600 for direct labor and $4,400 for indirect labor.
(k) Cash collected from customers totaled $116,900.
(l) Applied factory overhead based on machine hours used was $27,450.
(m) 20,400 units were transferred to finished goods.
(n) Cost of goods sold is calculated on the fifo basis.
(o) Work in process inventory on October 31 totaled $4,440.

Required:

(1) Prepare in detail the cost of goods sold section of the income statement for October, assuming that over- or underapplied factory overhead is deferred until the end of the calendar year.
(2) Prepare the income statement for October.
(3) Calculate the amount of over- or underapplied factory overhead for October.

P5-5 Balance Sheet; Income Statement. On December 31, 19A, Morrisville Canning Company, with outstanding common stock of $30,000, had the following assets and liabilities:

Cash	$ 5,000
Accounts receivable	10,000
Finished goods	6,000
Work in process	2,000
Materials	4,000
Prepaid expenses	500
Property, plant, and equipment (net)	30,000
Current liabilities	17,500

During 19B, the retained earnings balance increased 50% as a result of the year's business. No dividends were paid during the year. Balances of accounts receivable, prepaid expenses, current liabilities, and common stock were the same on December 31, 19B, as they had been on December 31, 19A. Inventories were reduced by exactly 50%, except finished goods, which was reduced by 33⅓%. Plant assets (net) were reduced by depreciation of $4,000, charged three-fourths to factory overhead and one-fourth to administrative expense. Sales of $60,000 were made on account, costing $38,000. Direct labor cost was $9,000. Factory overhead was applied at a rate of 100% of direct labor cost, leaving $2,000 underapplied, which was closed into the cost of goods sold account. Total marketing and administrative expenses (including depreciation) amounted to 10% and 15%, respectively, of the gross sales.

Required:

(1) Prepare a balance sheet as of December 31, 19B.
(2) Prepare an income statement for the year 19B, with details of the cost of goods manufactured and sold.

(AICPA adapted)

P5-6 Job Order Costing. Tropez Inc. had the following inventories on March 1:

Finished Goods	$15,000
Work in Process	19,070
Materials	14,000

The work in process account controls three jobs:

	Job 621	Job 622	Job 623
Materials	$2,800	$3,400	$1,800
Labor	2,100	2,700	1,350
Applied Factory Overhead	1,680	2,160	1,080
Total	$6,580	$8,260	$4,230

The following information pertains to March operations:

(a) Materials purchased and received cost $22,000 at terms n/30.

(b) Materials requisitioned for production cost $21,000. Of this amount, $2,400 was for indirect materials; the difference was distributed: $5,300 to Job 621; $7,400 to Job 622; and $5,900 to Job 623.

(c) Materials returned to the storeroom from the factory totaled $600, of which $200 was for indirect materials, the balance from Job 622.

(d) Materials returned to vendors totaled $800.

(e) Payroll of $38,000 was accrued in March.

(f) Of the payroll, direct labor represented 55%; indirect labor, 20%; sales salaries, 15%; and administrative salaries, 10%. The direct labor cost was distributed: $6,420 to Job 621; $8,160 to Job 622; and $6,320 to Job 623.

(g) Factory overhead, other than any previously mentioned, amounted to $9,404.50. Included in this figure were $2,000 for depreciation of factory building and equipment and $250 for expired insurance on the factory. The remaining overhead, $7,154.50, was unpaid at the end of March.

(h) Factory overhead was applied to production at a rate of 80% of the direct labor cost to be charged to the three jobs, based on the labor cost for March.

(i) Jobs 621 and 622 were completed and transferred to the finished goods warehouse.

(j) Both Jobs 621 and 622 were shipped and billed at a gross profit of 40% of the cost of goods sold.

(k) Cash collections from accounts receivable during March were $69,450.

Required:

(1) Prepare job order cost sheets to post beginning inventory data.

(2) Journalize the March transactions with current postings to general ledger inventory accounts and to job order cost sheets.

(3) Prepare a schedule of inventories on March 31.

P5-7 Ledger Accounts Covering Cost Accounting Cycle and Job Order Cost Accumulation. The books of Rio Grande Products Company show the following account balances as of March 1:

Finished Goods	$ 78,830
Work in Process	292,621
Materials	65,000
Over- or Underapplied Factory Overhead	12,300 (Cr.)

The work in process account is supported by the following job order cost sheets:

Job	Item	Direct Materials	Direct Labor	Factory Overhead	Total
204	80,000 Balloons	$ 15,230	$ 21,430	$ 13,800	$ 50,460
205	5,000 Life rafts	40,450	55,240	22,370	118,060
206	10,000 Life belts	60,875	43,860	19,366	124,101
		$116,555	$120,530	$ 55,536	$292,621

During March, the following transactions occurred:

(a) Purchase of materials, $42,300.

(b) Purchase of special materials was $5,800 for new Job 207, which calls for 4,000 life jackets.

(c) Indirect labor cost was $12,480. Direct labor was as follows:

Job	Amount	Hours
204	$26,844	3,355.5
205	22,750	3,250.0
206	28,920	3,615.0
207	20,370	2,910.0

(d) Materials issued:

Job 204	$ 9,480
Job 205	11,320
Job 206	10,490
Job 207	16,640*

* Excluding $5,800 of special materials, which are also issued at this time.

(e) Other factory overhead incurred or accrued (for brevity, credit the entire amount to Various Credits):

Insurance on factory	$ 830.00
Tax on real estate	845.00
Depreciation—machinery	780.00
Depreciation—factory building	840.00
Light	560.00
Coal used	1,810.00
Power	3,390.00
Repairs and maintenance	2,240.00
Indirect supplies	1,910.00
Miscellaneous	15,256.87

(f) Factory overhead is applied at the rate of $2.30 per direct labor hour. An applied factory overhead account is used and is then closed to the overhead control account.
(g) Job 204 was shipped and billed at a contract price of $117,500.

Required:
(1) Construct ledger accounts, inserting beginning balances and entering transactions for March. (Factory overhead is to be posted to the control account only.)
(2) In itemized form, compute the total cost of each job at the end of March.
(3) Determine the amount of over- or underapplied factory overhead remaining in the overhead control account.

P5-8 Job Order Cost Cycle; General and Subsidiary Ledgers; Cost of Goods Sold Statement. On January 1, the general ledger of Mid-State Company contained the following accounts and balances:

Cash	$ 47,000
Accounts Receivable	50,000
Finished Goods	32,500
Work in Process	7,500
Materials	22,000
Machinery	45,300
Accumulated Depreciation—Machinery	10,000
Accounts Payable	59,375
Common Stock	100,000
Retained Earnings	34,925

Details of inventories are:

Finished goods inventory: $32,500

	Job 101	Job 102
Work in process inventory:		
Direct materials: 500 units of A @ $5	$2,500	
200 units of B @ $3		$ 600
Direct labor: 500 hours @ $4	2,000	
200 hours @ $5		1,000
Factory overhead applied at the rate of $2 per direct labor hour	1,000	400
Total	$5,500	$2,000

Materials inventory: $22,000

During January, the following transactions were completed:

(a) Materials were purchased on account for $114,520.

(b) Payroll totaling $110,000 was accrued.

(c) Payroll was distributed as follows: Job 101, 2,500 direct labor hours @ $8; Job 102, 4,000 direct labor hours @ $10; Job 103, 3,000 direct labor hours @ $6; indirect labor, $12,000; marketing and administrative salaries, $20,000.

(d) Materials were issued as follows: $51,600 to Job 101; $42,000 to Job 102; $14,575 to Job 103. Indirect materials costing $7,520 were issued.

(e) Factory overhead was applied to Jobs 101, 102, and 103 at a rate of $4.50 per direct labor hour.

(f) Jobs 101 and 102 were completed and immediately sold on account for $120,000 and $135,000, respectively.

(g) After allowing a 5% cash discount, a net amount of $247,000 was collected on accounts receivable.

(h) Marketing and administrative expenses (other than salaries) paid during the month amounted to $15,000. Miscellaneous factory overhead of $22,680 was paid in cash. Depreciation on factory machinery was $2,000.

(i) Payments on account, other than payrolls paid, amounted to $85,000.

(j) Applied Factory Overhead is closed to Factory Overhead Control. The over- or underapplied overhead is then closed to Cost of Goods Sold.

Required:

(1) Open general ledger accounts and record January 1 balances.

(2) Journalize the January transactions.

(3) Post January transactions to the general ledger and to a subsidiary ledger for work in process. In the subsidiary ledger, use a T account for each job rather than a job cost sheet, and enter the January 1 balances for each job.

(4) Prepare a trial balance of the general ledger as of January 31; Work in Process must reconcile to its subsidiary ledger.

(5) Prepare a cost of goods sold statement for January.

CHAPTER 6

Process Costing

Learning Objectives

After studying this chapter, you will be able to:

1. Cite examples of businesses in which process costing is used.
2. Explain three common patterns of manufacturing production flow.
3. Determine if a process cost system can be used, based on an examination of the manufacturing environment.
4. Calculate equivalent production and departmental unit costs.
5. Prepare a departmental cost of production report based on average costing.
6. Prepare general journal entries to record manufacturing costs in a process cost system.
7. (Appendix) Prepare a departmental cost of production report based on fifo costing.

In most manufacturing businesses, production costs are accounted for using one of two types of cost accumulation systems: a job order cost system, which was discussed in Chapter 5, or a process cost system, which is discussed in this chapter. This chapter begins with a discussion of the process cost accumulation concept and the environment in which a process cost system is appropriate. In the next section, the process cost accumulation concepts are illustrated by examples of cost of production reports along with the general journal entries required to record the charges to producing departments for costs incurred during the period and for transfers of products from one department to another and finally to Finished Goods Inventory.

Process Cost Accumulation

The primary objective of any costing system is to determine the cost of the products manufactured or the services provided by the company. The costing system should be economical to operate and should be one that can be used to assign an amount of cost to each product that reasonably reflects the cost of the resources required to manufacture the product. Because each company's manufacturing technologies, production organization, and product mixes differ, costing systems should be expected to differ as well. The costing system should be tailored to meet the needs of the company's particular form of manufacturing system.

In job order costing, products are accounted for in batches. Each batch is treated as a separate job, and the job is the cost object. All costs incurred in manufacturing the job are charged to the job cost sheet. If work is performed on a job in more than one department, the costs incurred in each is accumulated on the job cost sheet. When the job is completed, the cost per unit of product is determined by dividing the total cost charged to the job cost sheet by the number of units produced on the job. When products manufactured during the accounting period within a department or cost center are heterogeneous (that is, different quantities and combinations of resources are required to manufacture different products), job order costing is a logical choice because the cost to manufacture different products is not the same. In job order costing, different products can be produced on different jobs and their costs can be separately determined.

In contrast, when all units of product manufactured within a cost center are homogeneous (that is, essentially all alike), keeping track of the cost of separate batches of product is not necessary. Instead of job order costing, process costing can be used. In a **process cost system**, materials, labor and factory overhead are charged to cost centers. The cost assigned to each unit is determined by dividing the total cost charged to the cost center by the number of units produced. Cost centers are usually departments but may be processing centers within departments. The primary requirement is that all the products manufactured within the cost center during the period must be the same, otherwise process costing will result in a distortion of product cost.

Costing by Departments

In manufacturing firms, production can take place in several departments. Each department performs a specific operation or process leading to the completion of the product. For example, the first department typically performs the starting phase of work on the product, such as cutting, stamping, molding, or shaping the product or component parts. When the work in the first department is completed, the units are transferred to a second department. The second department then performs its work, such as assembling, sanding, painting, or packaging, and transfers the units on to the next department, which performs its work, and so forth, until the units are finally completed and transferred to the finished goods storeroom.

In a process cost system, materials, labor, and factory overhead are generally charged to the producing departments; however, if a department is organized into two or more cost centers, process costing can still be used, as long as the units of product manufactured within the cost center during the period are homogeneous. For example, a producing department that has four different assembly lines, each producing a different product, can use process costing. Each assembly line can be treated as a separate cost center. This requires keeping a separate record of the costs incurred on each assembly line. Although process costing is discussed and illustrated in the context of a department in this chapter, the concepts apply equally well to other forms of manufacturing organization. The primary criterion for using process costing is that a business unit be identified that produces only one kind of product during each period.

Process costing, when practical, is preferable to job order costing because it generally requires less record keeping, and less record keeping means that it costs less to operate. In job order costing, a separate work in process subsidiary record (a job cost sheet) must be kept for each batch of products manufactured. In process costing, since all units of product manufactured within a department are homogeneous, costs are charged to the producing departments. In companies that use job order costing, it is not uncommon for several hundred jobs to be worked on during a single accounting period, requiring a separate record for each job. In contrast, companies that use process costing rarely have more than five to ten producing departments in a single manufacturing facility, requiring a separate record for each department. The amount of time (and therefore cost) required to keep track of five to ten departmental cost records is substantially less than the amount of time required to keep track of several hundred job cost records.

Process costing is used when products are manufactured under conditions of continuous processing or under mass production methods where the products manufactured within a department (or cost center) are homogeneous. These conditions often exist in industries that produce such commodities as paper, lumber, pipe, plastics, petroleum, textiles, steel, wire, bricks, cement, flour, and sugar. Process costing is also used by firms that manufacture simpie machined parts and small electrical parts (nails, nuts and bolts, light bulbs, semiconductor chips, and floppy disks), and by assembly-type industries (automobiles, engines, tape recorders, personal computers, and household appliances). Some utilities (gas, water, and electricity) cost their products using process costing.

Physical Production Flow

A product can move through a factory in a variety of ways. Three different physical production flow formats associated with process costing—sequential, parallel, and selective—are presented here to illustrate that process costing can be applied to all types of product-flow situations.

Sequential Product Flow. In sequential product flow, each product is processed in the same series of steps. In a company with three departments, cutting, assembly, and packaging, such a flow can be illustrated shown in Figure 6-1.

FIGURE 6-1 *Sequential Product Flow*

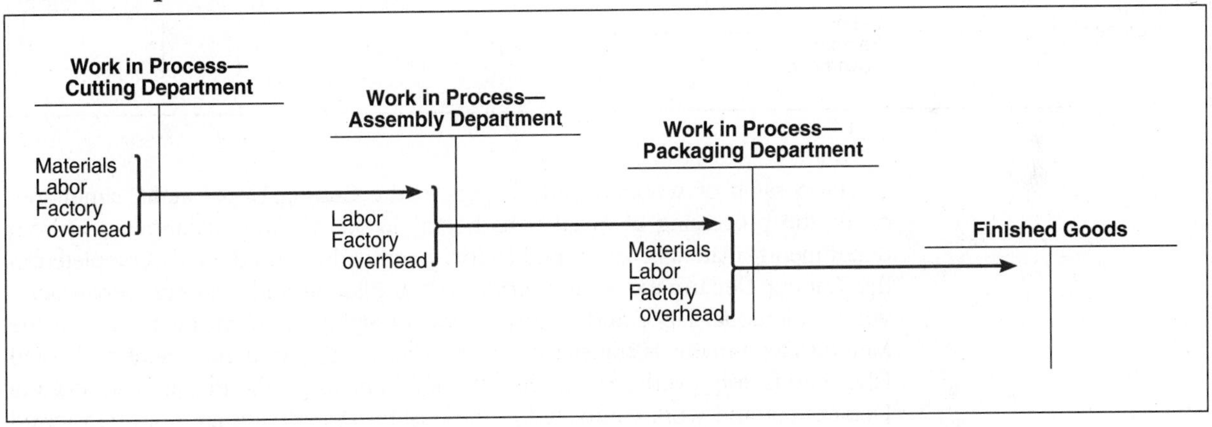

Processing begins in the Cutting Department where raw materials are combined and direct labor and factory overhead costs are added. When work is finished in the Cutting Department, the work moves to the Assembly Department, in which additional direct labor and overhead costs are incurred. Each department after the first may add more materials or, as in this example, may simply work on the partially completed input from the preceding process, adding only labor and factory overhead. After the product has been processed by the Assembly Department, it is transferred to the Packaging Department where more materials, direct labor, and factory overhead are used. After completion in the Packaging

Department, the unit is complete and is transferred to finished goods inventory for storage until it is purchased by a customer.

Parallel Product Flow. In parallel product flow, certain portions of the work are done simultaneously and then brought together in a final process or processes for completion and transfer to finished goods. The accounts shown in Figure 6-2 illustrate a parallel flow for a production process in which materials are added in subsequent departments.

FIGURE 6-2 ***Parallel Product Flow***

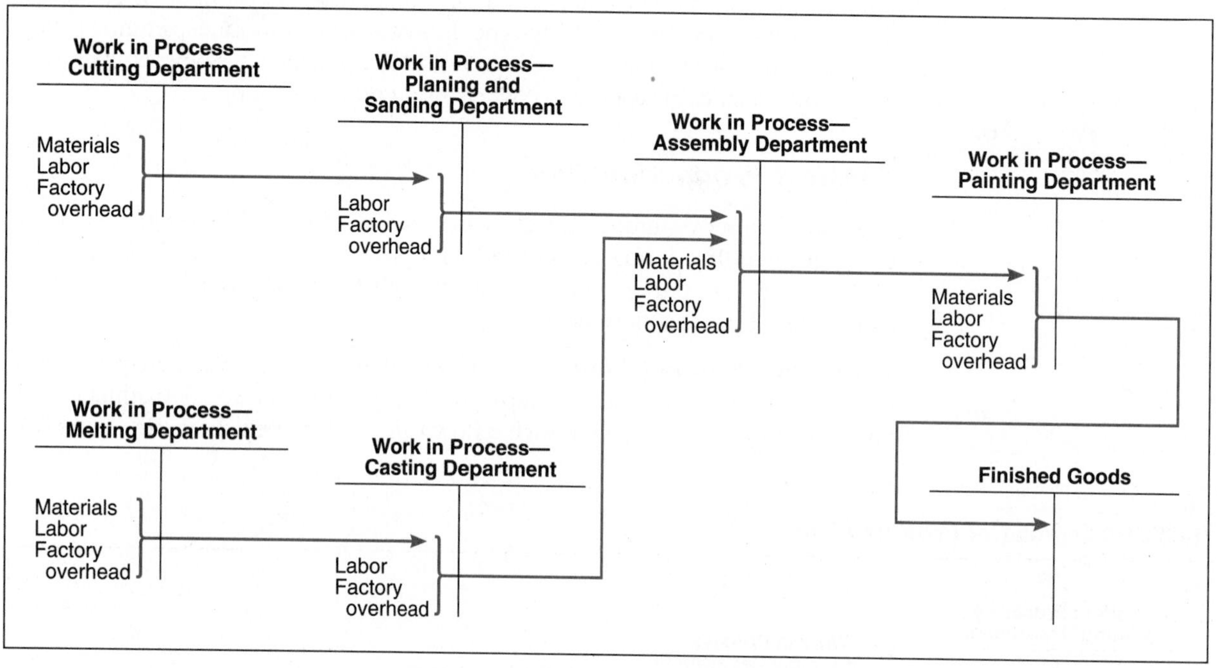

Processing of wooden parts begins in the Cutting Department; simultaneously, the processing of metal parts begins in the Melting Department; in both departments, materials, labor, and factory overhead are used. Work completed in the Cutting Department is transferred to the planing and Sanding Department, where additional labor and factory overhead are used. Work completed in the Melting Department is transferred to the Casting Department, where additional labor and factory overhead are used. Work completed in the Planing and Sanding Department and work completed in the Casting Department are both transferred to the Assembly Department, where additional materials, labor, and factory overhead are used. From there the work moves to the Painting Department, where additional materials, labor, and factory overhead are used; finally the product moves to the finished goods warehouse.

Selective Product Flow. In selective product flow, the product moves to different departments within the plant, depending on what final product is to be produced. The accounts shown in Figure 6-3 illustrate a selective flow in a meat processing plant. After the initial butchering process is completed, some of the product goes directly to the Packaging Department and then to finished goods; some goes to the Smoking Department, then to the Packaging Department, and finally to finished goods; some goes to the Grinding Department, then to the Packaging Department, and finally to finished goods.

FIGURE 6-3 *Selective Product Flow*

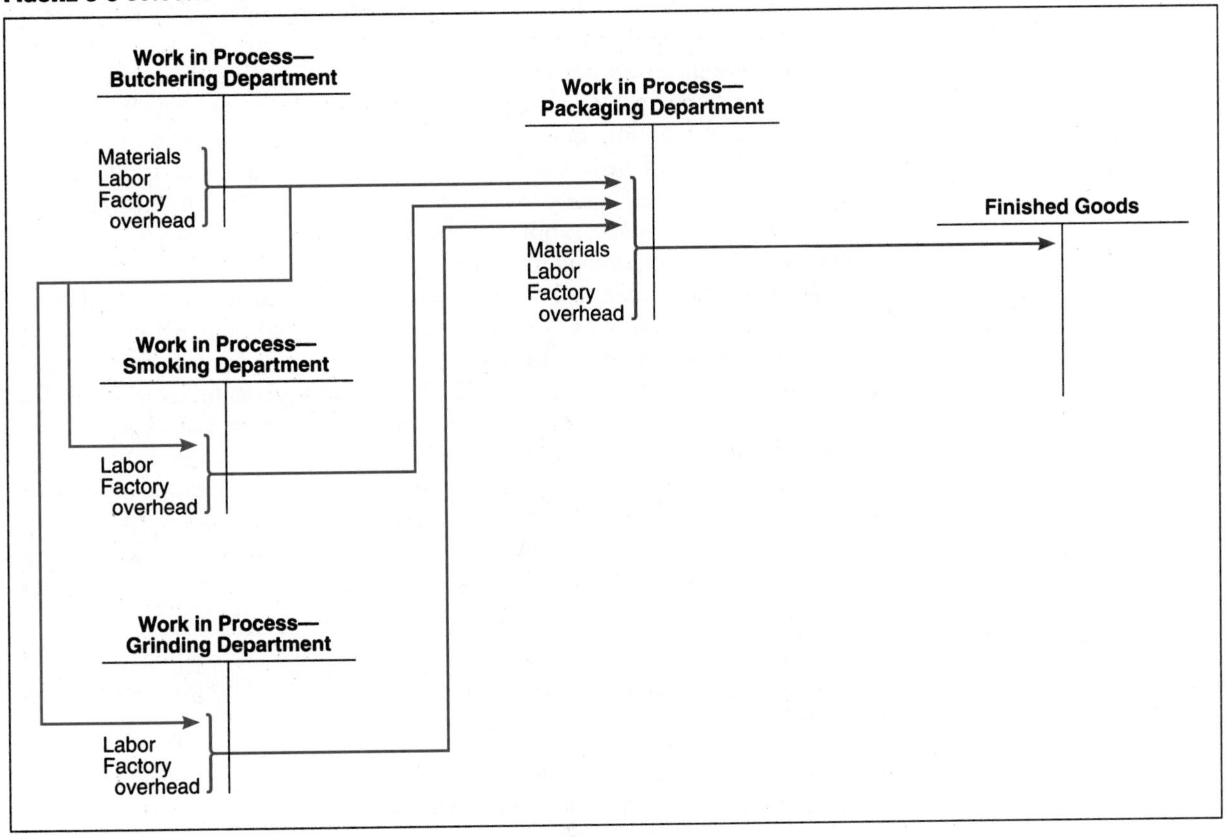

Accounting for Materials, Labor, and Factory Overhead Costs

Although the amount of record keeping detail involved in process costing is less than that required in job order costing, the basic concepts used in job order costing to accumulate materials, labor, and factory overhead costs also apply to process costing. The primary differences are that in process costing, costs are charged to departments (or cost centers) rather than to jobs, and if more than one department is required to manufacture the product, costs are transferred from one department to the next and eventually to Finished Goods.

In job order costing, a single work in process inventory account is used rather than a separate one for each job. Keeping a separate general ledger account for each job is not practical because there are too many jobs and because a separate account would have to be removed from the accounting system when the job is completed. In contrast, in a process costing situation, a separate general ledger account may be used for the work in process inventory of each department, because the number of departments is usually small and because departments continue to exist over long periods of time. For example, if there are two producing departments, there may be two separate work in process accounts in the general ledger. Although a single general ledger controlling account for work in process may be used in a process cost system, a separate account will be used for each producing department in this text in order to emphasize the flow of costs in a process cost system.

Materials Costs. In job order costing, materials requisitions are the basis for charging direct materials to specific jobs. In process costing, the details are reduced because materials are charged to departments rather than to jobs, and there are fewer departments using materials in process costing than the number of jobs handled at one time in job order costing. Materials requisition forms may be useful for control of materials. If the requisitions are not priced individually, the cost of materials used can be determined at the end of the production period through a periodic inventory approach—that is, adding purchases to beginning inventory and deducting ending inventory.

To illustrate the accounting for materials in a process cost system, assume the American Chair Company uses a process cost system and maintains separate work in process accounts in the general ledger for each of its two processing departments, Cutting and Assembly. The company manufactures a single style of chair. In the first department, the chair frame is cut out of wood, and the wooden parts are sanded and finished. The frame is transferred to the second department, where the chair frames are assembled and padding and covering are added. During the month of January, direct materials costing \$13,608 and \$7,296 were used in the Cutting Department and the Assembly Department, respectively. The journal entry to record the issue of materials to the two departments is:

Work in Process—Cutting Department	13,608	
Work in Process—Assembly Department	7,296	
Materials Inventory		20,904

Labor Costs. The detailed clerical work of accumulating labor costs by jobs is eliminated in process costing because labor costs are traced only to departments. Daily time tickets or clock cards are used instead of job time tickets. A summary entry distributes the direct manufacturing payroll to departments for the period. To illustrate the entries for labor, assume that, during January, 500 direct labor hours were worked in the Cutting Department, and 921 direct labor hours were worked in the Assembly Department. The wage rate is \$10 per hour in both departments, so the January charge to production for direct labor is \$5,000 and \$9,210 for Cutting and Assembly, respectively. The appropriate general journal entry to record the charge for labor is:

Work in Process—Cutting Department	5,000	
Work in Process—Assembly Department	9,210	
Payroll		14,210

Factory Overhead Costs. In both job order and process costing, the actual cost of factory overhead is accumulated in a general ledger control account and the details of factory overhead costs are accumulated in subsidiary records. In the subsidiary records, each overhead cost item, such as indirect materials or indirect labor, is broken down into amounts for each department. This detailed information is used as a basis for planning future costs and for controlling current costs. As overhead costs are incurred, they are recorded in a factory overhead general ledger account and are posted to the departmental subsidiary records for overhead. The following entry illustrates how actual factory overhead incurred during January would be recorded in the general ledger of American Chair Company.

Factory Overhead Control	20,900	
Accounts Payable (taxes, utilities, etc.)		7,400
Accumulated Depreciation—Machinery		5,700
Prepaid Insurance		500
Materials (for indirect materials)		1,700
Payroll (for indirect labor)		5,600

Because the actual cost of factory overhead incurred differs each month and is not perfectly variable with respect to production activity, a predetermined factory overhead rate is often used to smooth factory overhead costs to production activity throughout the year. Factory overhead is charged to the producing departments at the end of each month in order to determine the cost of the units of product manufactured during the month. If predetermined rates are used to apply overhead, the rates are multiplied by the actual amount of the activity base used in each producing department. For American Chair Company, factory overhead is charged to the producing departments using predetermined rates of \$7.60 per machine hour in the Cutting Department and \$12 per direct labor hour in the Assembly Department. During January, 1,040 machine hours were used in Cutting and 921 direct labor hours were worked in Assembly. Overhead charged to production for the month is \$7,904 in Cutting (1,040 machine hours × \$7.60 factory overhead rate) and \$11,052 in Assembly (921 direct labor hours × \$12 factory overhead rate).

The following entry illustrates the charge for factory overhead to the two producing departments of American Chair Company in January, assuming that the amount of overhead charged to production is kept in a separate account from the actual cost accumulated in the factory overhead control account.

Work in Process—Cutting Department	7,904	
Work in Process—Assembly Department	11,052	
Applied Factory Overhead		18,956

The \$1,944 difference between the actual factory overhead of \$20,900 incurred during January and the applied amount of \$18,956 represents underapplied factory overhead. If the amount of underapplied or overapplied overhead at the end of the year is small relative to other production cost, it would be charged to Cost of Goods Sold. If the amount is large, it must be allocated between ending inventories and Cost of Goods Sold for external reporting purposes. The significance and disposition of underapplied and overapplied overhead are discussed in detail in Chapter 12.

Combining Labor and Factory Overhead Costs. The preceding illustration shows direct labor being charged separately to each department by means of a general journal entry. Increasing levels of automation cause direct labor to be a decreasing proportion of total manufacturing cost. Furthermore, in highly automated factories the distinction between the tasks performed by direct and indirect labor is often blurred. Concomitantly, factory overhead costs, such as equipment depreciation, power, and maintenance, tend to increase with automation. As a result, some manufacturers combine the labor and factory overhead cost elements and refer to them as conversion cost or simply as factory overhead. Direct labor is then not charged separately to departments; instead, a single amount of applied conversion cost is charged to each department.

The Cost of Production Report

In process costing, all costs chargeable to a department are summarized in a departmental cost of production report. The **cost of production report** is a device for presenting the amount of costs accumulated and assigned to production during a month. It is also the source of information for preparing summary journal entries to record the cost of units of product transferred from one producing department to another and finally to finished goods inventory.

A cost of production report for a department can take many forms, but it should show (1) total and unit costs of work received from one or more other departments; (2) total and unit costs of materials, labor, and factory overhead added by the department; (3) the cost of the beginning and ending work in process inventories; and (4) the cost transferred to a succeeding department or to finished goods. The cost section of the report is usually divided into two parts: one showing total costs for which the department is accountable, and the other showing the disposition of these costs. The total cost reported in each of these two sections must be equal. The cost of production report also can include a quantity schedule, which shows the total number of units of product for which a department is accountable and the disposition of these units. Information in the quantity schedule is used to determine the number of equivalent units of production for each element of cost, which in turn is used in determining the departmental unit costs.

Determining the cost of the units transferred out of a department and those remaining in ending inventory is essentially an allocation process. Since costs can change over time, a cost flow assumption must be adopted. The most common cost flow assumption used for work in process inventory is average costing; therefore, average costing will be used here for illustrative purposes. (The preparation of a cost of production report when a fifo cost flow assumption is used is illustrated in the appendix to this chapter.) Next, since units of product in ending inventories usually are not fully completed, the number of equivalent units must be computed for each cost element. An **equivalent unit** is the amount of a resource (such as, materials, labor, or overhead) that is required to complete one unit of the product with respect to the cost element being considered. For example, if three units of the product in ending inventory each had one-third of the materials required to complete the product, the total amount of materials used for the three units would be equal to the amount of materials required to complete one unit of product (3 physical units × ⅓ complete each = 1 equivalent unit of materials). Because these units are hypothetical units rather than physical units, they are referred to as equivalent units.

To illustrate the cost of production report, assume that American Chair Company uses a process cost system with an average cost flow assumption to cost the production of its only product. The following production data are available for January:

	Cutting	Assembly
Units in Work in Process, beginning inventory..........	100	180
Units started in process in Cutting Department.........	600	
Units transferred to Assembly Department	500	
Units received from Cutting Department..................		500
Units transferred to Finished Goods Inventory..........		580
Units in Work in Process, ending inventory..............	200	100

Departmental supervisors report that ending work in process inventory is 60 percent complete with respect to materials in the Cutting Department and 100 percent complete in the Assembly Department. Ending inventory is 20 percent complete with respect to labor in the Cutting Department and 70 percent complete in the Assembly Department. With respect to factory overhead, ending inventory is 40 percent complete in the Cutting Department and 70 percent complete in the Assembly Department.[1] Cost data for January are:

	Cutting	Assembly
Work in Process, beginning inventory:		
Cost from preceding department	—	$ 8,320
Materials	$ 1,892	830
Labor	400	475
Factory overhead	796	518
Cost added to process during the current period:		
Materials	13,608	7,296
Labor	5,000	9,210
Factory overhead	7,904	11,052

The first step in assigning costs is to determine the number of equivalent units for each element of cost and then the cost of each equivalent unit. Since average costing is used by American Chair Company, the cost of each equivalent unit contains a portion of the cost in beginning inventory and a portion of the cost added during the current period. The average cost per equivalent unit for each element of cost is determined by dividing the total cost for each cost element (the amount in beginning inventory plus the amount added during the current period) by the number of equivalent units required to allocate that cost between the units transferred out of the department and units in ending inventory.

The units transferred from Cutting to Assembly are 100 percent complete with respect to all elements of cost added in the Cutting Department (500 equivalent units of materials, labor, and overhead). Ending inventory in the Cutting Department is 60 percent complete as to materials (200 units × 60% complete = 120 equivalent units of materials), 20 percent complete as to labor (200 units × 20% complete = 40 equivalent units of labor), and 40 percent complete as to factory overhead (200 units × 40% complete = 80 equivalent units of factory overhead). Equivalent units for each cost element in the Cutting Department are computed by adding the number of equivalent units transferred out of the department to those in ending inventory as follows:

	Materials	Labor	Overhead
Equivalent units transferred out	500	500	500
Equivalent units in ending inventory	120	40	80
Total equivalent units	620	540	580

The average cost per equivalent unit in the Cutting Department is determined as follows:

	Materials	Labor	Overhead
Cost in beginning inventory	$ 1,892	$ 400	$ 796
Cost added during the current period	13,608	5,000	7,904
Total cost to be accounted for	$15,500	$5,400	$8,700
Divided by total equivalent units	620	540	580
Cost per equivalent unit	$ 25	$ 10	$ 15

Based on these data, the January cost of production report for the Cutting Department is presented in Exhibit 6-1.

[1] The stage of completion of beginning inventory is not needed when the average cost method is used to prepare a cost of production report.

EXHIBIT 6-1

American Chair Company
Cutting Department
Cost of Production Report
For January, 19A

Quantity Schedule	Materials	Labor	Overhead	Quantity
Beginning inventory				100
Started in process this period				600
				700
Transferred to Assembly Department				500
Ending inventory	60%	20%	40%	200
				700

Cost Charged to Department	Total Cost	Equivalent Units*	Unit Cost**
Beginning inventory:			
Materials	$ 1,892		
Labor	400		
Factory overhead	796		
Total cost in beginning inventory	$ 3,088		
Cost added during the current period:			
Materials	$13,608	620	$25
Labor	5,000	540	10
Factory overhead	7,904	580	15
Total cost added during the current period	$ 26,512		
Total cost charged to the department	$ 29,600		$50

Cost Accounted for as Follows	Units	Percent Complete	Equivalent Units	Unit Cost		Total Cost
Transferred to Assembly Department	500	100	500	$50		$25,000
Work in Process, ending inventory:						
Materials	200	60	120	$25	$3,000	
Labor	200	20	40	10	400	
Factory overhead	200	40	80	15	1,200	4,600
Total cost accounted for						$29,600

* Total number of equivalent units required in the cost-accounted-for section (i.e., the sum of the equivalent units for the cost element listed in the cost-accounted-for section of the cost of production report).

** Total cost (i.e., the cost in beginning inventory plus the cost added during the current period) divided by the total number of equivalent units required in the cost-accounted-for section.

The journal entry to record the transfer of cost from the cutting department to the assembly department is:

Work in Process—Assembly Department	25,000	
Work in Process—Cutting Department		25,000

Once the cost of the units transferred from the Cutting Department to the Assembly Department has been determined, the cost of production report for the Assembly Department can be prepared. The units transferred from Assembly to Finished Goods are 100 percent complete with respect to all elements of cost (580 equivalent units of preceding department cost, materials, labor and overhead). Ending inventory is complete as to prior department cost[2]

[2] Units in ending inventory are always complete as to prior department costs. The preceding department would not have transferred units to the next department unless the units transferred were complete with respect to all costs added by the transferring department.

and materials (100 equivalent units of prior department cost and materials) but only 70 percent complete as to conversion cost (100 units × 70% complete = 70 equivalent units of labor and overhead). Equivalent units for each cost element in the Assembly Department are computed by adding the number of equivalent units transferred out of the department to those in ending inventory, as follows:

	From Preceding Department	Materials	Labor	Overhead
Equivalent units transferred out	580	580	580	580
Equivalent units in ending inventory.........	100	100	70	70
Total equivalent units	680	680	650	650

The average cost per equivalent unit in the Assembly Department is determined as follows:[3]

	From Preceding Department	Materials	Labor	Overhead
Cost in beginning inventory.....................	$ 8,320	$ 830	$ 475	$ 518
Cost added during the current period.......	25,000	7,296	9,210	11,052
Total cost to be accounted for.................	$33,320	$8,126	$9,685	$11,570
Divided by total equivalent units..............	680	680	650	650
Cost per equivalent unit	$ 49.00	$11.95	$14.90	$ 17.80

Based on these data, the January cost of production report for the Assembly Department is presented in Exhibit 6-2.

The journal entry to record the transfer of cost from the Assembly Department to the Finished Goods Inventory is:

Finished Goods Inventory	54,317	
Work in Process—Assembly Department		54,317

Increase in Quantity of Production When Materials Are Added

In some production processes, the addition of materials results in an increase in the total volume or number of units of the product. For example, in the manufacture of soft drinks, the syrup is often produced in one department and carbonated water added in a subsequent process. The addition of carbonated water increases the total volume of liquid product to be accounted for. Increasing the quantity of liquid dilutes the amount of syrup in each gallon, which in turn reduces the amount of prior department cost in each gallon of product produced in the second department. The increased quantity of liquid product absorbs the same total cost transferred from the preceding department.

To illustrate the preparation of a cost of production report for a department that adds materials that increase the total quantity of product to be accounted for,

[3] In this illustration, the Assembly Department's cost per unit received from the Cutting Department is less than the cost per unit transferred out of the Cutting Department. This occurred because the cost per unit received from the Cutting Department this period is greater than the cost per unit received from the Cutting Department in beginning inventory, and the two different unit costs are averaged in the Assembly Department.

EXHIBIT 6-2

American Chair Company
Assembly Department
Cost of Production Report
For January, 19A

Quantity Schedule	**Materials**	**Labor**	**Overhead**	**Quantity**
Beginning inventory				180
Received from Cutting Department				500
				680
Transferred to Finished Goods				580
Ending inventory	100%	70%	70%	100
				680

Cost Charged to Department	**Total Cost**	**Equivalent Units***	**Unit Cost****
Beginning inventory:			
Cost from preceding department	$ 8,320		
Materials	830		
Labor	475		
Factory overhead	518		
Total cost in beginning inventory	$10,143		
Cost added during the current period:			
Cost from preceding department	$25,000	680	$49.00
Materials	7,296	680	11.95
Labor	9,210	650	14.90
Factory overhead	11,052	650	17.80
Total cost added during the current period	$52,558		
Total cost charged to the department	$62,701		$93.65

Cost Accounted for as Follows	**Units**	**Percent Complete**	**Equivalent Units**	**Unit Cost**		**Total Cost**
Transferred to Finished Goods	580	100	580	$93.65		$54,317
Work in Process, ending inventory:						
Cost from preceding department	100	100	100	$49.00	$4,900	
Materials	100	100	100	11.95	1,195	
Labor	100	70	70	14.90	1,043	
Factory overhead	100	70	70	17.80	1,246	8,384
Total cost accounted for						$62,701

* Total number of equivalent units required in the cost-accounted-for section (i.e., the sum of the equivalent units for the cost element listed in the cost-accounted-for section of the cost of production report).

** Total cost (i.e., the cost in beginning inventory plus the cost added during the current period) divided by the total number of equivalent units required in the cost-accounted-for section.

assume that, in the Mixing Department of Tiger Paint Company, paint dye received from the Pigment Department is diluted and mixed with a liquid latex base to form paint. The following production data are available for the Mixing Department for April.

Gallons in Work in Process, beginning inventory	800
Gallons received from Pigment Department	2,000
Gallons of latex base added in Mixing Department	4,000
Gallons transferred to Canning Department	5,800
Gallons in Work in Process, ending inventory	1,000

The departmental supervisor reports that ending work in process inventory is complete as to materials and 50 percent complete as to conversion cost. Cost data for April are:

Work in Process, beginning inventory:	
Cost from preceding department	$ 1,532
Materials	1,692
Labor	57
Factory overhead	114
Cost added to process during the current period:	
Cost from preceding department	12,000
Materials	16,940
Labor	3,660
Factory overhead	7,320

Average costing is used in the Mixing Department, and overhead is allocated to production on the basis of labor cost. The units transferred from Mixing to Canning are 100 percent complete with respect to all elements of cost added in the Mixing Department (5,800 equivalent units of prior department cost, materials, labor and overhead), and ending inventory is complete as to prior department cost and materials (1,000 equivalent units of prior department cost and materials) but only 50 percent complete as to conversion cost (1,000 units × 50% complete = 500 equivalent units of labor and overhead). Equivalent units for each cost element in the Mixing Department are:

	From Preceding Department	Materials	Labor	Overhead
Equivalent units transferred out	5,800	5,800	5,800	5,800
Equivalent units in ending inventory	1,000	1,000	500	500
Total equivalent units	6,800	6,800	6,300	6,300

The average cost per equivalent unit in the Mixing Department is determined as follows:

	From Preceding Department	Materials	Labor	Overhead
Cost in beginning inventory	$ 1,532	$ 1,692	$ 57	$ 114
Cost added during the current period	12,000	16,940	3,660	7,320
Total cost to be accounted for	$13,532	$18,632	$3,717	$ 7,434
Divided by total equivalent units	6,800	6,800	6,300	6,300
Cost per equivalent unit	$ 1.99	$ 2.74	$ .59	$ 1.18

Based on these data, the April cost of production report for the Mixing Department is presented in Exhibit 6-3.

Assuming the company keeps a separate general ledger account for each of its production departments, the journal entry to record the transfer of cost from the Mixing Department to the Canning Department is:

Work in Process—Canning Department	37,700	
Work in Process—Mixing Department		37,700

EXHIBIT 6-3

Tiger Paint Company
Mixing Department
Cost of Production Report
For April, 19A

Quantity Schedule	**Materials**	**Labor**	**Overhead**	**Quantity**
Beginning inventory				800
Received from the Pigment Department				2,000
Added to process in Mixing Department				4,000
				6,800
Transferred to Canning Department				5,800
Ending inventory	100%	50%	50%	1,000
				6,800

Cost Charged to Department	**Total Cost**	**Equivalent Units***	**Unit Cost****
Beginning inventory:			
Cost from preceding department	$ 1,532		
Materials	1,692		
Labor	57		
Factory overhead	114		
Total cost in beginning inventory	$ 3,395		
Cost added during the current period:			
Cost from preceding department	$12,000	6,800	$1.99
Materials	16,940	6,800	2.74
Labor	3,660	6,300	.59
Factory overhead	7,320	6,300	1.18
Total cost added during the current period	$39,920		
Total cost charged to the department	$43,315		$6.50

Cost Accounted for as Follows	**Units**	**Percent Complete**	**Equivalent Units**	**Unit Cost**		**Total Cost**
Transferred to Canning Department	5,800	100	5,800	$6.50		$37,700
Work in Process, ending inventory:						
Cost from preceding department	1,000	100	1,000	$1.99	$1,990	
Materials	1,000	100	1,000	2.74	2,740	
Labor	1,000	50	500	.59	295	
Factory overhead	1,000	50	500	1.18	590	5,615
Total cost accounted for						$43,315

* Total number of equivalent units required in the cost-accounted-for section (i.e., the sum of the equivalent units for the cost element listed in the cost-accounted-for section of the cost of production report).

** Total cost (i.e., the cost in beginning inventory plus the cost added during the current period) divided by the total number of equivalent units required in the cost-accounted-for section.

Summary

In most manufacturing businesses, production costs are accounted for using one of two types of cost accumulation systems: a job order cost system, which was discussed in Chapter 5, or a process cost system, which was discussed in this chapter. This chapter began by comparing process costing with job order costing. Generally, process costing is a more economical product costing system than job order costing; however, process costing can be used only when homogeneous products are manufactured within the department or cost center. The process cost accumulation concepts were then illustrated by presenting examples of cost of production reports along with the general journal entries required to record the charges to producing departments for costs incurred during the period and for transfers of products from one department to another and finally to Finished Goods Inventory.

Appendix Process Costing with a Fifo Cost Flow Assumption

The preparation of a cost of production report with a fifo (first in, first out) cost flow assumption is demonstrated using the American Chair Company data used in the average cost illustration in this chapter. Recall from that illustration that the following production data are available for January.

	Cutting	Assembly
Units in Work in Process, beginning inventory..........	100	180
Units started in process in Cutting Department.........	600	
Units transferred to Assembly Department..............	500	
Units received from Cutting Department..................		500
Units transferred to Finished Goods Inventory..........		580
Units in Work in Process, ending inventory..............	200	100

Departmental supervisors report that ending work in process inventory is 60 percent complete with respect to materials in the Cutting Department and 100 percent complete in the Assembly Department. Ending inventory is 20 percent complete with respect to labor in the Cutting Department and 70 percent complete in the Assembly Department. With respect to factory overhead, ending inventory is 40 percent complete in the Cutting Department and 70 percent complete in the Assembly Department.

Under the fifo cost flow assumption, the cost of the first units transferred out of the department are deemed to come from beginning inventory. If the units in inventory are not complete at the beginning of the period, they must be completed with current period costs before they can be transferred out of the department. The balance of the units to be accounted for contain only current period costs. As a consequence of this inventory layering procedure, equivalent units are computed for current period costs *only*. Total current period equivalent units equal the sum of the number of equivalent units of current period cost added to complete the units in beginning inventory, plus the number of units started and completed during the current period, plus the number of equivalent units in ending inventory. In order to compute the number of equivalent units of current period cost required to complete the units in beginning inventory, the stage of completion of the units in beginning inventory must be known.

Assume that the cost of production reports from December (the preceding month) indicate that ending inventory in December (which is beginning inventory for January) was 80 percent complete with respect to materials in the Cutting Department and 40 percent complete in the Assembly Department. Inventory was 40 percent complete with respect to labor in the Cutting Department and 20 percent complete in the Assembly Department. With respect to factory overhead, inventory was 60 percent complete in the Cutting Department and 20 percent complete in the Assembly Department.

Cost data for January are:

	Cutting	Assembly
Work in Process, beginning inventory:		
Cost from preceding department	—	$ 8,320
Materials	$ 1,892	830
Labor	400	475
Factory overhead	796	518
Cost added to process during the current period:		
Materials	13,608	7,296
Labor	5,000	9,210
Factory overhead	7,904	11,052

The cost per equivalent unit for each element of current period cost is determined by dividing the cost added during the current period for each cost element by the number of equivalent units of that cost element added in the current period. The number of equivalent units of a cost element added in the current period is the sum of the number required to complete beginning inventory, the number in the units started and completed during the period, and the number in ending inventory.

The units of product transferred from Cutting to Assembly are 100 percent complete with respect to all elements of cost added in the Cutting Department. Of the 500 units transferred, 100 were in beginning inventory. Because beginning inventory was 80 percent complete as to materials, 40 percent complete as to labor, and 60 percent complete as to overhead, the units in beginning inventory require the addition of only 20 percent of their materials, 60 percent of their labor, and 40 percent of their overhead to be completed all from current period cost (100 units × 20% to complete = 20 equivalent units of materials; 100 units × 60% to complete = 60 equivalent units of labor; and 100 units × 40% to complete = 40 equivalent units of overhead). The remaining units transferred to Assembly this period contain only current period costs (500 total units transferred – 100 from beginning inventory = 400 started and completed this period, each of which contains one equivalent unit of materials, labor, and overhead). Ending inventory is 60 percent complete as to materials (200 units × 60% complete = 120 equivalent units of materials), 20 percent complete as to labor (200 units × 20% complete = 40 equivalent units of labor), and 40 percent complete as to overhead (200 units × 40% complete = 80 equivalent units of overhead). The equivalent units of current period cost for each of the elements of cost in the Cutting Department are determined as follows:[4]

	Materials	Labor	Overhead
Cost added in the current period:			
Equivalent units in beginning inventory	20	60	40
Equivalent units started and completed during the current period	400	400	400
Equivalent units in ending inventory	120	40	80
Equivalent units of current period cost	540	500	520

[4] Note that the number of current period equivalent units can also be computed by subtracting the number of equivalent units in beginning inventory from the total number of equivalent units that would have been computed if average costing were used. This equivalence is demonstrated using the same data as follows:

The cost per equivalent unit added during the current period in the Cutting Department is determined as follows:

	Materials	Labor	Overhead
Cost added during the current period.......	$13,608	$5,000	$7,904
Divided by equivalent units	540	500	520
Cost per equivalent unit	$ 25.20	$10.00	$15.20

Based on these data, the January cost of production report for the Cutting Department, determined on a fifo basis, is presented in Exhibit 6-4.

Assuming that the company keeps a separate general ledger account for each of the production departments, the journal entry to record the transfer of cost from the Cutting Department to the Assembly Department is:

Work in Process—Assembly Department....................................	24,960	
Work in Process—Cutting Department..................................		24,960

Once the cost transferred from Cutting to Assembly has been determined, the cost of production report for the Assembly Department can be prepared. Of the 580 units transferred from Assembly to Finished Goods during January, 180 were from beginning inventory. The units in beginning inventory were complete as to prior department cost[5], but only 40 percent complete as to materials and only 20 percent complete as to conversion cost. The units in beginning inventory required the addition of 60 percent of current period materials (180 units × 60% to complete = 108 equivalent units of materials) and 80 percent of current period conversion cost (180 units × 80% to complete = 144 equivalent units of labor and overhead). The remaining units transferred to finished goods this period contain only current period costs (580 total units transferred – 180 from beginning inventory = 400 started and completed this period, each of which contains one full equivalent unit of prior department cost, materials, labor, and overhead). Ending inventory is complete as to prior department cost and materials (100 equivalent units of prior department cost and materials) but only 70 percent complete as to conversion cost (100 units × 70% complete = 70 equivalent units of labor and overhead). The equivalent units for current period costs in the Assembly Department are determined as follows:

	From Preceding Department	Materials	Labor	Overhead
Costs added in the current period:				
Equivalent units in beginning inventory..	0	108	144	144
Equivalent units started and completed during the current period....................	400	400	400	400
Equivalent units in ending inventory	100	100	70	70
Equivalent units of current period cost...	500	608	614	614

[4] Continued

	Materials	Labor	Overhead
Equivalent units transferred out........................	500	500	500
Plus equivalent units in ending inventory	120	40	80
Total equivalent units..	620	540	580
Less equivalent units in beginning inventory...	80	40	60
Equivalent units of current period cost	540	500	520

[5] The units received from the preceding department in a prior period were complete with respect to the preceding department's cost when received in the prior period. As a consequence, current period prior department costs would never need to be added to complete beginning inventory.

EXHIBIT 6-4

American Chair Company
Cutting Department
Cost of Production Report
For January, 19A

Quantity Schedule	Materials	Labor	Overhead	Quantity
Beginning inventory	80%	40%	60%	100
Started in process this period				600
				700
Transferred to Assembly Department				500
Ending inventory	60%	20%	40%	200
				700

Cost Charged to Department	Total Cost	Equivalent Units*	Unit Cost**
Beginning inventory:			
Materials	$ 1,892		
Labor	400		
Factory overhead	796		
Total cost in beginning inventory	$ 3,088		
Cost added during the current period:			
Materials	$ 13,608	540	$25.20
Labor	5,000	500	10.00
Factory overhead	7,904	520	15.20
Total cost added during the current period	$ 26,512		
Total cost charged to the department	$ 29,600		$50.40

Cost Accounted for as Follows	Units	Current Percent	Equivalent Units	Unit Cost		Total Cost
Transferred to Assembly Department:						
From beginning inventory					$3,088	
Cost to complete this period:						
Materials	100	20	20	$25.20	504	
Labor	100	60	60	10.00	600	
Factory overhead	100	40	40	15.20	608	$ 4,800
Started and completed this period	400	100	400	50.40		20,160
Total cost transferred to Assembly Department						$24,960
Work in Process, ending inventory:						
Materials	200	60	120	$25.20	$3,024	
Labor	200	20	40	10.00	400	
Factory overhead	200	40	80	15.20	1,216	4,640
Total cost accounted for						$29,600

* Number of equivalent units of cost added during the current period (i.e., the sum of the equivalent units listed in the cost-accounted-for section of the cost of production report).

** Cost added during the current period divided by the number of equivalent units of cost added during the current period.

The cost per equivalent unit added during the current period in the Assembly Department is determined as follows:

	From Preceding Department	Materials	Labor	Overhead
Cost added during the current period	$24,960	$7,296	$9,210	$11,052
Divided by equivalent units	500	608	614	614
Cost per equivalent unit	$ 49.92	$12.00	$15.00	$ 18.00

Based on these data, the January cost of production report for the Assembly Department, prepared on a fifo basis, is presented in Exhibit 6-5.

EXHIBIT 6-5

American Chair Company
Assembly Department
Cost of Production Report
For January, 19A

Quantity Schedule	**Materials**	**Labor**	**Overhead**	**Quantity**
Beginning inventory	40%	20%	20%	180
Received from the Cutting Department				500
				680
Transferred to Finished Goods				580
Ending inventory	100%	70%	70%	100
				680

Cost Charged to Department	**Total Cost**	**Equivalent Units***	**Unit Cost****
Beginning inventory:			
Cost from preceding department	$ 8,320		
Materials	830		
Labor	475		
Factory overhead	518		
Total cost in beginning inventory	$ 10,143		
Cost added during the current period:			
Cost from preceding department	$24,960	500	$49.92
Materials	7,296	608	12.00
Labor	9,210	614	15.00
Factory overhead	11,052	614	18.00
Total cost added during the current period	$ 52,518		
Total cost charged to the department	$ 62,661		$94.92

Cost Accounted for as Follows	**Units**	**Current Percent**	**Equivalent Units**	**Unit Cost**		**Total Cost**
Transferred to Finished Goods Inventory:						
From beginning inventory					$10,143	
Cost to complete this period:						
Materials	180	60	108	$12.00	1,296	
Labor	180	80	144	15.00	2,160	
Factory overhead	180	80	144	18.00	2,592	$16,191
Started and completed this period	400	100	400	94.92		37,968
Total cost transferred to Finished Goods						$54,159
Work in Process, ending inventory:						
Cost from preceding department	100	100	100	$49.92	$ 4,992	
Materials	100	100	100	12.00	1,200	
Labor	100	70	70	15.00	1,050	
Factory overhead	100	70	70	18.00	1,260	8,502
Total cost accounted for						$62,661

* Number of equivalent units of cost added during the current period (i.e., the sum of the equivalent units listed in the cost-accounted-for section of the cost of production report).

** Cost added during the current period divided by the number of equivalent units of cost added during the current period.

The journal entry to record the transfer of cost from the Assembly Department to Finished Goods Inventory is:

Finished Goods Inventory	54,159	
Work in Process—Assembly Department		54,159

Increase in Quantity of Production When Materials are Added.

To illustrate the preparation of a cost of production report for a department that adds materials that increase the total quantity of product to be accounted for, assume the data as given in the Tiger Paint Company illustration. Recall that the Mmixing Department receives paint dye from the Pigment Department; the dye is diluted and mixed with a liquid latex base to form paint in the Mixing Department. The production data for April are:

Gallons in Work in Process, beginning inventory	800
Gallons received from Pigment Department	2,000
Gallons of latex base added in Mixing Department	4,000
Gallons transferred to Canning Department	5,800
Gallons in Work in Process, ending inventory	1,000

Based on the cost of production report for the month of March, work in process beginning inventory for April was 80 percent complete as to materials but only 25 percent as to conversion costs. The departmental supervisor reported that work in process ending inventory is complete as to materials and 25 percent complete as to conversion costs. Cost data for April are:

Work in Process, beginning inventory:	
Cost from preceding department	$ 1,532
Materials	1,692
Labor	57
Factory overhead	114
Cost added to process during the current period:	
Cost from preceding department	12,000
Materials	16,940
Labor	3,660
Factory overhead	7,320

Of the 5,800 gallons transferred from Mixing to Canning, 800 gallons were in process at the beginning of the period. Beginning inventory was complete as to prior department cost, but only 80 percent complete as to materials and 25 percent complete as to conversion costs. As a consequence, 20 percent of the materials cost (800 gallons × 20% to complete = 160 equivalent units of materials) and 75 percent of the conversion cost (800 gallons × 75% to complete = 600 equivalent units of labor and overhead) were added to complete the units in beginning inventory. The remaining 5,000 gallons transferred to canning in this period contain only current period costs (5,000 equivalent units of prior department costs, materials, labor, and overhead). Ending inventory is complete as to materials (1,000 equivalent units of materials) but only 50 percent complete as to conversion cost (1,000 units × 50% complete = 500 equivalent units of labor and overhead). Equivalent units for each cost element in the Mixing Department are:

	From Preceding Department	Materials	Labor	Overhead
Costs added in the current period:				
Equivalent units in beginning inventory	0	160	600	600
Equivalent units in the units started and completed this period	5,000	5,000	5,000	5,000
Equivalent units in ending inventory	1,000	1,000	500	500
Total equivalent units	6,000	6,160	6,100	6,100

The cost per equivalent unit added to process during the current period in the Mixing Department is determined as follows:

	From Preceding Department	Materials	Labor	Overhead
Cost added during the current period	$12,000	$16,940	$3,660	$7,320
Divided by equivalent units	6,000	6,160	6,100	6,100
Cost per equivalent unit	$ 2.00	$ 2.75	$ .60	$ 1.20

The April cost of production report, based on fifo costing for the Mixing Department, is presented in Exhibit 6-6.

The journal entry to record the transfer of cost from the Mixing Department to the Canning Department is:

Work in Process—Canning Department	37,665	
Work in Process—Mixing Department		37,665

EXHIBIT 6-6

Tiger Paint Company
Mixing Department
Cost of Production Report
For April, 19A

Quantity Schedule	Materials	Labor	Overhead	Quantity
Beginning inventory	80%	25%	25%	800
Received from Pigment Department				2,000
Added to process in Mixing Department				4,000
				6,800
Transferred to Canning Department				5,800
Ending inventory	100%	50%	50%	1,000
				6,800

Cost Charged to Department	Total Cost	Equivalent Units*	Unit Cost**
Beginning inventory:			
Cost from preceding department	$ 1,532		
Materials	1,692		
Labor	57		
Factory overhead	114		
Total cost in beginning inventory	$ 3,395		
Cost added during the current period:			
Cost from preceding department	$12,000	6,000	$2.00
Materials	16,940	6,160	2.75
Labor	3,660	6,100	.60
Factory overhead	7,320	6,100	1.20
Total cost added during the current period	$39,920		
Total cost charged to the department	$43,315		$6.55

Cost Accounted for as Follows	Units	Current Percent	Equivalent Units	Unit Cost		Total Cost
Transferred to Canning Department:						
From beginning inventory					$3,395	
Cost to complete this period:						
Materials	800	20	160	$2.75	440	
Labor	800	75	600	.60	360	
Factory overhead	800	75	600	1.20	720	$ 4,915
Started and completed this period	5,000	100	5,000	$6.55		32,750
Total cost transferred to Canning Department						$37,665
Work in Process, ending inventory:						
Cost from preceding department	1,000	100	1,000	$2.00	$2,000	
Materials	1,000	100	1,000	2.75	2,750	
Labor	1,000	50	500	.60	300	
Factory overhead	1,000	50	500	1.20	600	5,650
Total cost accounted for						$43,315

* Number of equivalent units of cost added during the current period (i.e., the sum of the equivalent units listed in the cost-accounted-for section of the cost of production report).
** Cost added during the current period divided by the number of equivalent units of cost added during the current period.

Key Terms

process cost system ***(118)*** **cost of production report** ***(123)*** **equivalent unit** ***(124)***

Discussion Questions

Q6-1 What is the basic objective of process costing?

Q6-2 Job order costing and process costing should be used in different types of manufacturing environments. Contrast the manufacturing environments for the two different costing methods.

Q6-3 For the following products, indicate whether job order or process costing would be more likely to be appropriate.

(a) Gasoline
(b) Sewing machines
(c) Chocolate syrup
(d) Textbooks
(e) Dacron yarn
(f) Cigarettes
(g) Space capsules
(h) Men's and women's suits

Q6-4 Discuss three physical product flow formats.

Q6-5 Compare the cost accumulation and summarization of job order costing and process costing.

Q6-6 Can predetermined overhead rates be used in process costing? Explain.

Q6-7 What is the purpose of a cost of production report?

Q6-8 What are the various sections commonly found in a cost of production report?

Q6-9 Separate cost of production reports are prepared for each producing department. Why is this method used in preference to one report for the entire company?

Q6-10 What is an equivalent unit of production? How is it used?

Exercises

E6-1 Equivalent Production and Unit Costs. The Wilton Company uses process costing with an average cost flow assumption in its two producing departments. On April 1, Department B had no units in beginning inventory. During April, 25,000 units were transferred from Department A to Department B. On April 30, Department B had 5,000 units of work in process, 60% complete as to labor and 40% complete as to factory overhead. During the month, 20,000 units were transferred from Department B to Finished Goods Inventory. Materials are added in the beginning of the process in Department B. The following journal entries summarize April activity.

Work in Process—Department A	25,000	
Work in Process—Department B	15,000	
Materials		40,000
Work in Process—Department A	10,800	
Work in Process—Department B	9,200	
Payroll		26,500
Work in Process—Department A	14,600	
Work in Process—Department B	15,400	
Applied Factory Overhead		30,000
Work in Process—Department B	40,000	
Work in Process—Department A		40,000

Required:

(1) Compute the equivalent units for each element of cost in Department B.
(2) Calculate the cost per equivalent unit for each element of cost in Department B.

E6-2 Journal Entries for Process Cost System. Plucky Corporation uses process costing in its two production departments. A separate work in process account is kept in the general ledger for each production department. The following data relate to operations for the month of May.

	Beginning Inventory	Added During May
Direct materials cost:		
Department X	$10,000	$50,000
Department Y	6,000	40,000
Direct labor cost:		
Department X	12,000	80,000
Department Y	9,000	70,000
Applied overhead:		
Department X	24,000	180,000
Department Y	9,000	70,000

During May, 31,000 units with a cost of $10 each were transferred from Department X to Department Y, and 28,000 units with a cost of $17 each were transferred from Department Y to Finished Goods Inventory.

Required: Prepare the appropriate general journal entries to record the cost charged to the producing departments during May and the cost of units transferred from Department X to Department Y and Department Y to Finished Goods Inventory.

E6-3 Cost of Production Report; Originating Department; Average Costing. Tyndol Fabricators Inc. manufactures a product in two departments. The product is cut out of sheet metal and bent to shape in the Cutting and Forming Department and then transferred to the Assembling Department, where parts purchased from outside vendors are added to the base unit. Since only one product is manufactured by the company, a process cost system is used. The company uses the average cost flow assumption to account for its work in process inventories. Data related to November operations in the Cutting and Forming Department are:

Units in beginning inventory..	800
Units started in process this period..	3,200
Units transferred to Assembling Department this period	3,400
Units in ending inventory (75% materials, 40% labor, 25% overhead)..........	600

	Beginning Inventory	Added This Period
Costs charged to the department:		
Materials..	$17,923	$68,625
Direct labor...	2,352	14,756
Factory overhead	3,800	29,996

Required: Prepare a November cost of production report for the Cutting and Forming Department.

E6-4 Cost of Production Report; Originating Department; Average Costing. Sonora Manufacturing Company produces a product in two manufacturing departments, Molding and Finishing. The product is molded out of plastic in the Molding Department and then transferred to the Finishing Department, where parts are added to the molded plastic unit. Since only one product is manufactured by the company, a process cost system is used with an average cost flow assumption.

Data related to August operations in the Molding Department are:

	Beginning Inventory	Added This Period
Costs charged to the department:		
Materials..	$4,120	$44,880
Direct labor...	522	12,638
Factory overhead	961	18,779

During the period, 9,200 units were transferred from the Molding Department to the Finishing Department. The Molding Department had 1,000 units still in process at the end of July (100% complete as to materials and 40% complete as to conversion cost) and 800 units still in process at the end of August (75% complete as to materials and 25% complete as to conversion cost).

Required: Prepare an August cost of production report for the Molding Department.

E6-5 Cost of Production Report; Second Department; Average Costing. Hypertec Corporation manufactures a product in three departments. The product is cut out of sheet metal in the Cutting Department, then transferred to the Forming Department where it is bent to shape and certain parts purchased from outside vendors are added to the unit. The product is finally transferred to the Painting Department, where it is primed, painted, and packaged. Since only one product is manufactured by the company, a process cost system is used. The company uses the average cost flow assumption to account for its work in process inventories. Data related to September operations in the Forming Department are:

Units in beginning inventory	1,400
Units received from the Cutting Department this period	4,600
Units transferred to Painting Department this period	5,000
Units in ending inventory (60% materials, 30% labor and overhead)	1,000

	Beginning Inventory	Added This Period
Costs charged to the department:		
Costs from the preceding department	$21,120	$70,380
Materials	5,880	20,440
Direct labor	2,614	17,526
Factory overhead	5,228	35,052

Required: Prepare a September cost of production report for the Forming Department.

E6-6 Cost of Production Report; Second Department; Average Costing. Ramirez Corporation manufactures a product in two departments, Cutting and Assembly. The product is cut out of wood in the Cutting Department and then transferred to the Assembly Department, where it is assembled along with component parts purchased from outside vendors. Since only one product is manufactured by the company, a process cost system is used. The company uses the average cost flow assumption to account for its work in process inventories. During February, 2,100 units were received from the Cutting Department, and 2,000 units were transferred out of the Assembly Department to Finished Goods. At the end of the last business day in February, there were 500 units in ending inventory in the Assembly Department, 80% complete as to materials and 60% complete as to conversion cost. Cost data related to February operations in the Assembly Department are:

	Beginning Inventory	Added This Period
Costs charged to the department:		
Costs from the preceding department	$12,590	$67,410
Materials	4,000	21,200
Direct labor	1,200	17,660
Factory overhead	2,400	35,320

Required: Prepare a February cost of production report for the Assembly Department.

E6-7 Cost of Production Report; Materials Added at Two Different Stages; Average Costing. Zupton Manufacturing Corporation produces a product in three departments. The product is cut out of sheet metal in the Cutting Department, then transferred to the Forming Department, where it is bent to shape and certain parts purchased from outside vendors are added to the unit. Finally, the product is transferred to the Finishing Department where it is painted and packaged. The company uses a process cost system with an average cost flow assumption to account for its work in process inventories. Materials are added at two different stages in the Forming Department. Material A is added at the beginning of the process, and material B is added at the end of the process. At the end of May, there were 600 units in process in the Forming Department, 50% complete as to labor and overhead. During June, 3,900 units were received from the Cutting Department, and 4,100 units were completed and transferred to the Finishing Department. At the end of June, there were 400 units still in process in the Forming Department, 30% complete as to labor and overhead. Cost data related to June operations in the Forming Department are:

	Beginning Inventory	Added This Period
Costs charged to the department:		
Costs from the preceding department	$4,422	$29,328
Material A	2,805	19,695
Material B	2,030	12,320
Direct labor	1,250	15,630
Factory overhead	1,875	23,445

Required: Prepare a cost of production report for the Forming Department for the month of June.

E6-8 Cost of Production Report; Increase in Quantity with Added Materials; Average Costing. Pop Cola Company produces a soft drink in three departments, Syrup, Carbonation, and Bottling. Syrup, which gives the drink its flavor, is produced in the first department. The syrup is then transferred to the second department, where carbonated water is added to give the drink its fizz. After carbonated water has been added, the liquid drink is bottled for storage and transport to customers. A process cost system with an average cost flow assumption is used to account for work in process inventories. Data related to operations in the Carbonation Department during the month of October are:

Units in beginning inventory	1,000
Units received from the Syrup Department this period	2,000
Units added to process in the Carbonation Department this period	6,000
Units transferred to Bottling Department this period	7,800
Units in ending inventory (100% materials, 25% labor and overhead)	1,200

	Beginning Inventory	Added This Period
Costs charged to the department:		
Costs from the preceding department	$1,120	$9,680
Materials	190	1,610
Direct labor	60	1,560
Factory overhead	120	3,120

Required: Prepare a cost of production report for the Carbonation Department.

E6-9 Cost of Production Report; Increase in Quantity with Added Materials; Average Costing. Donegal Chemical Company produces a chemical cleaning solvent in three departments, Refining, Blending, and Finishing. The process begins in the Refining Department, where the base solvent is removed from a petroleum derivative purchased from a large oil refinery. The base solvent is then transferred to the Blending Department, where cleaning compounds are added to the solvent, increasing the total quantity of the product. The blended product is then transferred to the Finishing Department, where it is filtered one last time and bottled for storage and shipment to customers. Since only one product is manufactured by the company, a process cost system is used. The company uses the average cost flow assumption to account for its work in process inventories. Data related to March operations in the Blending Department are:

Units in beginning inventory	5,000
Units received from the Refining Department this period	20,000
Units added to process in the Blending Department this period	5,000
Units transferred to Finishing Department this period	26,000
Units in ending inventory (100% materials, 80% labor, and 90% overhead)	4,000

	Beginning Inventory	Added This Period
Costs charged to the department:		
Costs from the preceding department	$4,750	$25,250
Materials	2,375	12,625
Direct labor	180	2,740
Factory overhead	767	8,113

Required: Prepare a March cost of production report for the Blending Department.

E6-10 (Appendix) Cost of Production Report; Originating Department; Fifo Costing. Brimhall Manufacturing Company produces a product that is manufactured in two departments. The product is cut out of wood in the Cutting Department and then transferred to the Assembly Department, where parts purchased from outside vendors are added to the base unit. Since only one product is manufactured by the company, a process cost system is used. The company uses the fifo cost flow assumption to account for its work in process inventories. Data related to July operations in the Cutting Department are:

	Beginning Inventory	Added This Period
Costs charged to the department:		
Materials	$2,940	$46,530
Direct labor	390	18,100
Factory overhead	585	27,150

At the end of June, there were 100 units in process in the Cutting Department, 60% complete as to materials and 20% complete as to conversion cost. During July, 850 units were transferred from the Cutting Department to the Assembly Department. At the end of July, there were 150 units still in process in the Cutting Department, 100% complete as to materials and 50% complete as to conversion cost.

Required: Prepare a July cost of production report on a fifo basis for the Cutting Department.

E6-11 (Appendix) Cost of Production Report; Second Department; Fifo Costing. Kandu Tool Company manufactures a product in two departments, Cutting and Assembly. The product is cut out of sheet metal, bent to shape, and painted in the Cutting Department. Then, it is transferred to the Assembly Department where component parts purchased from outside vendors are added to the unit. A process cost system with a fifo cost flow assumption is used to account for work in process inventories. Data related to November operations in the Assembly Department are:

Units in beginning inventory (50% materials, 40% labor and overhead)	1,200
Units received from the Cutting Department this period	2,800
Units transferred to Finished Goods Inventory this period	3,000
Units in ending inventory (90% materials, 80% labor and overhead)	1,000

	Beginning Inventory	Added This Period
Costs charged to the department:		
Costs from the preceding department	$17,280	$40,600
Materials	5,550	30,690
Direct labor	2,400	16,932
Factory overhead	3,600	25,398

Required: Prepare a November cost of production report on a fifo basis for the Assembly Department.

E6-12 (Appendix) Cost of Production Report; Increase in Quantity with Added Materials; Fifo Costing. Northeastern Chemical Company produces a chemical preservative in two departments, Refining and Blending. The process begins in the Refining Department, where the liquid chemical base is removed from a crude chemical stock purchased from a large domestic chemical company. The liquid base is then transferred to the Blending Department, where other chemicals are added, which increase the total quantity of the product. The blended product is then transferred to Finished Goods to await sale and shipment to customers. Materials are added at the beginning of the process in the Blending Department. At the end of April, there were 2,000 units in process in the Blending Department, 20% complete as to labor and 40% complete as to overhead. During May, 5,000 units were received from the Refining Department, and a sufficient quantity of materials was added in the Blending Department to double the quantity of units in process. At the end of May, there were 1,500 units still in process, 60% complete as to labor and 80% complete as to overhead. Cost data related to May operations in the Blending Department are:

	Beginning Inventory	Added This Period
Costs charged to the department:		
Costs from the preceding department	$2,460	$12,500
Materials	500	2,500
Direct labor	150	3,300
Factory overhead	600	7,630

Required: Assuming a process cost system with fifo cost flow is used to account for its work in process inventories, prepare a cost of production report for the Blending Department for the month of May.

Problems

P6-1 Cost of Production Report and Journal Entries; Average Costing. Modern Cabinet Company manufactures a single model of a commercial prefabricated wooden cabinet. The company uses a process cost system with an average cost flow assumption. It maintains a separate work in process account for each of its two producing departments, Cutting and Assembly. The basic cabinet components are cut out of wood in the Cutting Department and then transferred to the Assembly Department, where they are put together with the addition of hinges and handles purchased from outside vendors. Data related to manufacturing operations in August are:

	Cutting	Assembly
Units in beginning inventory	200	250
Units started in process in Cutting Department this period	600	
Units transferred from Cutting to Assembly this period	650	650
Units transferred from Assembly to Finished Goods this period		800
Units in ending inventory:		
Cutting Department (90% materials and 60% conversion cost)	150	
Assembly Department (40% materials and 20% conversion cost)		100

	Cutting	Assembly
Cost in beginning inventory:		
Cost from preceding department		$17,410
Materials	$5,365	3,451
Labor	530	3,611
Factory overhead	795	3,611
Cost added during the current period:		
Materials	26,035	13,433
Labor	8,350	20,989
Factory overhead	12,525	20,989

Required:

(1) Prepare a cost of production report for each department for August.

(2) Prepare the appropriate general journal entries to record the charge to the producing departments for the costs incurred during August and to record the transfer of units from Cutting to Assembly and from Assembly to Finished Goods Inventory.

P6-2 Cost of Production Report and Journal Entries; Average Costing. Rathbone Tool Corporation manufactures a single model of a commercial cutting tool. The product is cast from molten steel in the Casting Department, and then it is transferred to the Finishing Department, where it is ground and polished. Data related to December operations are:

	Casting	Finishing
Units in beginning inventory	1,000	1,500
Units started in process in Casting Department this period	8,000	
Units transferred from Casting to Finishing this period	7,500	7,500
Units transferred from Finishing to Finished Goods this period		7,000
Units in ending inventory:		
Casting Department (100% materials and 80% conversion cost)	1,500	
Finishing Department (40% labor and 50% overhead)		2,000

	Casting	Finishing
Cost in beginning inventory:		
Cost from preceding department		$4,785
Materials	$915	
Labor	60	201
Factory overhead	90	555

	Casting	Finishing
Cost added during the current period:		
Materials	$17,085	
Labor	4,290	$2,139
Factory overhead	6,435	3,125

Required:

(1) Assuming the company uses a process cost system with an average cost flow assumption, prepare a cost of production report for each department for the month of December.

(2) Assuming the company maintains a separate work in process account for each of its two producing departments, prepare the appropriate general journal entries to record the charge to the producing departments for the costs incurred during December and to record the transfer of units from Casting to Finishing and from Finishing to Finished Goods Inventory.

P6-3 Cost of Production Report and Journal Entries; Average Costing. Jetter Engine Corporation manufactures a single model of gasoline engine used in lawn mowers, portable generators, and pumps. The basic engine block is cast from steel and machined in the Casting Department. Then, it is transferred to the Assembly Department, where the crank shaft, valves, pistons, and other component parts are added. After Assembly, it is transferred to the Finishing Department where the engine is tested. The company uses a process cost system, with an average cost flow assumption. Data related to February operations are:

	Casting	Assembly	Finishing
Units in beginning inventory	500	1,000	300
Units started in process this period	3,000		
Units received from preceding department		2,700	2,900
Units transferred out of department this period	2,700	2,900	2,800
Units in ending inventory	800	800	400
Stage of completion with respect to materials	100%	70%	
Stage of completion with respect to labor	80%	30%	50%
Stage of completion with respect to overhead	90%	30%	50%

	Casting	Assembly	Finishing
Cost in beginning inventory:			
Cost from preceding department		$63,150	$42,840
Materials	$10,925	40,258	
Labor	338	12,426	2,760
Factory overhead	2,839	12,426	4,140
Cost added during the current period:			
Materials	146,575	116,480	
Labor	16,362	44,408	12,240
Factory overhead	48,461	44,408	18,360

Required:

(1) Prepare a cost of production report for each department for February.

(2) Assuming a separate work in process account is maintained for each producing department, prepare the appropriate general journal entries to record the charge to the producing departments for the costs incurred during February and to record the transfer of units from Casting to Assembly, from Assembly to Finishing, and from Finishing to Finished Goods Inventory.

P6-4 Cost of Production Report and Journal Entries; Materials Added in Second Department Increases Production Quantity; Average Costing. Persona Cologne Company produces cologne in a two-step process. A base fragrance is created by mixing several chemicals in the Blending Department. The liquid output of the Blending Department is transferred to the Finishing Department, where another chemical is added to thin the mixture. The diluted mixture is then bottled and transferred to Finished Goods Inventory to await sale. The company uses a process cost system, with an average cost flow assumption, and it maintains a separate work in process account for each of its two producing departments. Data related to June operations are:

	Blending	Finishing
Units in beginning inventory	1,000	1,400
Units started in process in Blending Department this period	6,000	
Units transferred from Blending to Finishing this period	6,400	6,400
Units added to process in Finishing Department this period		19,200
Units transferred from Finishing to Finished Goods this period		26,000
Units in ending inventory:		
Blending (60% materials, 20% labor, and 25% overhead)	600	
Finishing (100% materials, 70% labor, and 70% overhead)		1,000

	Blending	Finishing
Cost in beginning inventory:		
Cost from preceding department		$8,450
Materials	$19,620	1,395
Labor	944	106
Factory overhead	2,375	659
Cost added during the current period:		
Materials	129,100	25,605
Labor	6,880	19,919
Factory overhead	29,065	60,751

Required:

(1) Prepare a June cost of production report for each department.

(2) Prepare the appropriate general journal entries to record the charge to the producing departments for the costs incurred during June and to record the transfer of units from Blending to Finishing and from Finishing to Finished Goods Inventory.

P6-5 Cost of Production Report and Journal Entries; Materials Added in Second Department Increases Production Quantity; Average Costing. Hytest Chemical Corporation produces aircraft fuel in a two-step process. Unrefined gasoline is purchased from a major oil company and refined in the Refining Department. The refined gasoline is then transferred to the Blending Department, where cleansers and other additives are mixed with the refined gasoline. The chemicals added in the Blending Department increase the total volume of fuel. The company uses a process cost system, with an average cost flow assumption, and it maintains a separate work in process account for each of its two producing departments. Data related to operations for the month of March are:

	Refining	Blending
Units in beginning inventory	800	1,400
Units started in process in Refining Department this period	7,200	
Units transferred from Refining to Blending this period	7,000	7,000
Units added to process in Blending Department this period		1,800
Units transferred from Blending to Finished Goods this period		9,200
Units in ending inventory:		
Refining (100% materials, 75% labor, and 50% overhead)	1,000	
Blending (80% materials, 40% labor, and 40% overhead)		1,000

	Refining	Blending
Cost in beginning inventory:		
Cost from preceding department		$1,754
Materials	$ 728	620
Labor	30	68
Factory overhead	60	160
Cost added during the current period:		
Materials	7,272	4,380
Labor	1,520	3,100
Factory overhead	2,940	5,600

Required:

(1) Prepare a cost of production report for each department for March.

(2) Prepare the appropriate general journal entries to record the charge to the producing departments for the costs incurred during March and to record the transfer of units from Refining to Blending and from Blending to Finished Goods Inventory.

P6-6 (Appendix) Cost of Production Report and Journal Entries; Fifo Costing. Upton Manufacturing Company manufactures a single model of a portable work bench. The company uses a process cost system, with a fifo cost flow assumption, and it maintains a separate work in process account for each of its two producing departments, Cutting and Assembly. The work bench components are cut out of wood and metal in the Cutting Department and then transferred to the Assembly Department, where they are put together with the addition of springs, hinges, and handles purchased from outside vendors. Data related to operations in October are:

	Cutting	Assembly
Units in beginning inventory:		
Cutting (90% materials, 40% labor, and 20% overhead)	1,000	
Assembly (75% materials, 60% labor, and 60% overhead)		2,000
Units started in process in Cutting Department this period	9,000	
Units transferred from Cutting to Assembly this period	8,500	8,500
Units transferred from Assembly to Finished Goods this period		9,500
Units in ending inventory:		
Cutting (100% materials, 80% labor, and 100% overhead)	1,500	
Assembly (60% materials, 40% labor, and 40% overhead)		1,000

	Cutting	Assembly
Cost in beginning inventory:		
Cost from preceding department		$4,000
Materials	$8,010	400
Labor	1,750	800
Factory overhead	790	1,600
Cost added during the current period:		
Materials	81,900	30,100
Labor	18,600	21,315
Factory overhead	39,200	30,015

Required:

(1) Prepare an October cost of production report for each department.

(2) Prepare the appropriate general journal entries to record the charge to the producing departments for the costs incurred during October and to record the transfer of units from Cutting to Assembly and from Assembly to Finished Goods Inventory.

P6-7 (Appendix) Cost of Production Report and Journal Entries; Fifo Costing. Marston Manufacturing Company sells a single model of an auxiliary fuel tank which is manufactured in two producing departments, Fabricating and Finishing. Each fuel tank is cut from steel, shaped, and welded to its basic form in the Fabricating Department. Then the tanks are transferred to the Finishing Department, where they are coated with a sealant and painted. Data related to August operations are:

	Fabricating	Finishing
Units in beginning inventory:		
Fabricating (100% materials, 40% labor, and 80% overhead)	400	
Finishing (40% materials, 20% labor, and 20% overhead)		600
Units started in process in Fabricating Department this period	1,200	
Units transferred from Fabricating to Finishing this period	1,100	1,100
Units transferred from Finishing to Finished Goods this period		1,300
Units in ending inventory:		
Fabricating (100% materials, 80% labor, and 90% overhead)	500	
Finishing (100% materials, 60% labor, and 60% overhead)		400

	Fabricating	Finishing
Cost in beginning inventory:		
Cost from preceding department		$74,000
Materials	$29,280	230
Labor	1,900	1,600
Factory overhead	11,800	2,520
Cost added during the current period:		
Materials	90,000	2,920
Labor	16,080	19,880
Factory overhead	46,740	29,820

Required:

(1) Assuming the company uses a process cost system with a fifo cost flow assumption, prepare a cost of production report for each department for August.

(2) Assuming the company maintains a separate work in process account for each of its two producing departments, prepare the appropriate general journal entries to record the charge to the producing departments for the costs incurred during August and to record the transfer of units from Fabricating to Finishing and from Finishing to Finished Goods Inventory.

P6-8 (Appendix) Cost of Production Report and Journal Entries; Materials Added in Second Department Increases Quantity; Fifo Costing. Twonka Beverage Company produces a soft drink with a fruit juice base. Fruit is mashed into a juice in the Mashing Department. The juice is then transferred to the Blending Department, where it is mixed with carbonated water. The company uses a process cost system, with a fifo cost flow assumption, and it maintains a separate work in process account for each of its two producing departments, Mashing and Blending. Data related to September operations are:

	Mashing	Blending
Units in beginning inventory:		
Mashing (90% materials, 60% labor, and 30% overhead)	600	
Blending (50% materials, 20% labor, and 20% overhead)		1,000
Units started in process in Mashing Department this period	3,000	
Units transferred from Mashing to Blending this period	3,100	3,100
Units added to process in Blending Department this period		3,100
Units transferred from Blending to Finished Goods this period		6,400
Units in ending inventory:		
Mashing (60% materials, 40% labor, and 20% overhead)	500	
Blending (100% materials, 60% labor, and 60% overhead)		800

	Mashing	Blending
Cost in beginning inventory:		
Cost from preceding department		$1,770
Materials	$1,088	100
Labor	172	55
Factory overhead	172	74
Cost added during the current period:		
Materials	6,006	1,407
Labor	1,470	2,004
Factory overhead	3,020	2,672

Required:

(1) Prepare a September cost of production report for each department.

(2) Prepare the appropriate general journal entries to record the charge to the producing departments for the costs incurred during September and to record the transfer of units from Mashing to Blending and from Blending to Finished Goods Inventory.

CHAPTER 7

The Cost of Quality and Accounting for Production Losses

Learning Objectives

After studying this chapter, you will be able to:

1. Identify and differentiate among the three different kinds of quality costs.
2. Explain the concept of total quality management and the need for continuous improvement.
3. Compute the cost of scrap, spoilage, and rework in a job order cost system.
4. Prepare the appropriate journal entries required to account for scrap, spoilage, and rework in a job order cost system.
5. Compute the cost of spoilage in a process cost system with average costing and prepare a cost of production report when spoilage occurs.
6. Prepare the appropriate journal entries required to account for spoilage in a process cost system.
7. (Appendix) Compute the cost of spoilage and prepare a cost of production report when spoilage occurs in a process cost system with a fifo cost flow assumption.

Many companies today are concerned about the quality of their products. To a great extent, the current concern is the result of increased competition, particularly from abroad. During the 1970s, Japanese manufacturers gained a worldwide reputation for manufacturing high quality products at low cost. Throughout the 1980s, most American companies experienced declines in their market share, primarily because they did not effectively compete with foreign manufacturers.[1] Today many American manufacturers are reorganizing their manufacturing systems to improve efficiency and reduce costs, emphasizing product quality, and successfully competing with the highest quality manufacturers in the world. Such companies are frequently referred to as "world-class manufacturers." Although manufacturing companies have received most of the attention in the press, the adjective of world-class can be also applied to the service sector of the economy, to nonprofit organizations, and to all levels of government. Such organizations provide services, and services are the end result of processes and activities that are not substantially different from those required to manufacture tangible products.[2]

The purpose of this chapter is to explain the concept of quality costs and how quality costs relate to production losses. The chapter begins with a discus-

[1] William R. Pasewark, "The Evolution of Quality Control Costs in U.S. Manufacturing," *The Journal of Cost Management,* Vol. 5, No. 1, p. 49.

[2] Joseph M. Juran, "World-Class Quality—It's a Lot of Work," *Total Quality Management—A View from the Real World,* Washington, D.C.: Juran Institute, Inc. and George Washington University, GW National Satellite Network, March 31, 1992, p. B1.

sion of the cost of quality. This discussion includes defining and classifying quality costs, the concept of total quality management, explaining the need for continuous improvement, and reporting and measuring quality costs. The next section discusses the measurement of one type of quality cost, production losses, and illustrates the treatment of these losses in job order and process cost systems.

The Cost of Quality

The cost of quality is to some extent a misnomer. The cost of quality is not only the cost of obtaining quality but also the cost incurred from a lack of quality. In order to understand and minimize the cost of quality, the types of quality costs must be identified and distinguished.

Types of Quality Costs

Quality costs can be grouped into three broad classifications: prevention costs, appraisal costs, and failure costs.[3]

1. **Prevention costs** are the costs incurred to prevent product failure. Prevention is the cost of designing high-quality products and production systems, including the costs of implementing and maintaining such systems. Preventing product failures begins by designing quality into the product and the production processes. High-quality parts and equipment must be used. Preventive maintenance must be performed frequently on the equipment and machinery to maintain the high quality. Personnel must be well trained and highly motivated, and all personnel from top management to each worker in the factory must constantly seek ways to improve product quality.
2. **Appraisal costs** are the costs incurred to detect product failure. Appraisal cost is the cost of inspecting and testing materials, inspecting products during and after production, and obtaining information from customers about product satisfaction (or lack of satisfaction).
3. **Failure costs** are the costs incurred when a product fails; they can occur internally or externally. **Internal failure costs** are those that occur during the manufacturing or production process, such as the cost of scrap, spoilage (lost units), rework, and downtime due to machine failures or materials shortages. **External failure costs** are those that occur after the product has been sold, such as the cost of warranty repairs and replacements, the cost of handling customer complaints, and the cost of lost sales resulting from customer dissatisfaction with the product.[4]

Total Quality Management

In order to survive in a competitive business environment, a company must provide a quality product at a reasonable price. Companies such as Ford, Hewlett-Packard, Harley Davidson, and Celanese recognized in the early 1980s that they

---

[3] Thomas P. Edmonds, Bor-Yi Tsay, and Wen-Wei Lin, "Analyzing Quality Costs," *Management Accounting*, Vol. 71, No. 5, p. 26.

[4] Wayne Morse, Harold Roth, and Kay Poston, *Measuring, Planning, and Controlling Quality Costs* (Montvale, N.J.: Institute of Management Accountants (formerly National Association of Accountants), 1987).

could not continue to be competitive unless their products could compete with the highest quality products of their competitors.[5] In order to eliminate poor quality, world-class producers adopt a total quality management philosophy. **Total quality management (TQM)** is a companywide approach to quality improvement that seeks to improve quality in all processes and activities. It has evolved into more than just an objective of well-managed businesses. TQM has become a pervasive philosophy and way of doing business that applies to all functional areas of the company and to all personnel.

Because products and production processes differ among companies, approaches to TQM differ widely; however, the following characteristics are common to all.

1. *The company's objective for all business activity is to serve its customers.* The term *product* is extended beyond tangible goods to include services, and the term *customer* includes not only those who purchase the company's products but also those inside the company who use or benefit from the output of an internal operating activity. Employees are required to identify their customers and to determine their customers' needs and priorities through a process of interaction with the customers. Internally, this process translates into producers of products (or services) meeting with users. Externally, it requires market research and feedback from consumers. Producers cannot assume that they know what is best for the customer.
2. *Top management provides an active leadership role in quality improvement.* At successful companies, such as Westinghouse Electric[6] and Ford,[7] the chief executive officer assumes an active leadership role in the quality improvement program. Top management commitment and involvement is necessary in order to provide direction and to motivate employees at all levels to work together to improve product quality. Employees become actively involved only when they understand the importance of quality improvement to the company, and the active participation of top management demonstrates that importance.
3. *All employees are actively involved in quality improvement.* Improving quality is a way of doing business that extends to every part and every level of a company. All employees produce a product, most for internal consumption. Therefore, permitting poor quality to continue in any part of the company can result in an infectious spread of poor quality to other parts of the company. TQM requires the active involvement of all employees at all levels constantly seeking ways to improve the quality of the processes they individually control.
4. *The company has a system of identifying quality problems, developing solutions, and setting quality-improvement objectives.* A number of different systems are employed by different companies. Generally, these systems involve organizing employee groups into quality teams or quality circles, which meet frequently to discuss quality problems. These employee groups typically include a cross section of employees from

[5] Robert A. Howell and Stephen R. Soucy, "Operating Controls in the New Manufacturing Environment," *Management Accounting*, Vol. 69, No. 4, p. 26, and John Clark, "Costing for Quality at Celanese," *Management Accounting*, Vol. 66, No. 9, p. 42.

[6] Thomas E. Steimer, "Activity-Based Accounting for Total Quality," *Management Accounting*, Vol. 72, No. 4, p. 40.

[7] Lloyd Dobyns, "Ed Deming Wants Big Changes, and He Wants Them Fast," *The Smithsonian*, Vol. 21, No. 5, p 77.

different functional areas, including those who use the product as well as those who produce it. These groups not only include managers and laborers from the processes involved, but they also include at least one manager from a level higher than the operating level. These meetings are characterized by open and frank discussions about problems, and they often utilize brainstorming sessions to identify possible solutions. Initially, top management may identify quality problems that need immediate attention. As the system develops and matures, the team members begin to identify problems and opportunities for improvement.

5. *The company places a high value on its employees and provides continuous training as well as recognition for achievement.* Even in the most highly automated companies, people are still the company's most valuable assets. People plan, design, and organize; machines do not. Companies that strive to improve quality recognize that well trained and highly motivated employees are essential. Successful companies provide job-specific training that is designed to improve performance. This kind of training is especially important for highly technical jobs. Some companies also provide support for continuing education of a more general nature. Such education creates opportunities for self improvement and advancement that have a positive effect on employee morale. It is also important to recognize employees who make significant contributions to quality improvement and who achieve extraordinary levels of performance. Westinghouse Electric has two awards for levels of quality performance, one for best performance and one for most improved performance.[8] Recognizing achievement in quality performance instills a sense of pride among the work force and provides role models for employees.

Continuous Quality Improvement

The best way to reduce total quality costs is to reduce the lack of quality. Historically, companies attacked the quality problem through high volume production and inspection strategies. The idea was to produce a large enough volume of products so that, regardless of the number of units rejected at the end of the process, enough good units would survive to satisfy demand. This approach to insuring quality has several deficiencies. First, the approach waits too late to detect production losses. If a defect occurs early in the production process, costs that are added to the defective product are ultimately lost. This approach depends on large costly inventories to insure that sufficient good units survive. It results in inefficient use of manufacturing resources and wasted materials and labor. While some of this inefficiency and waste can be eliminated by adding more frequent inspections, inspections are costly and do not add value to the product. Second, the magnitude of the cost of these production losses is rarely measured. The cost of scrap, spoilage, and rework in this type of quality system is generally viewed as part of the normal cost of the surviving good units. As a consequence, these costs are generally ignored, thereby encouraging (or at least not discouraging) waste and inefficiency.

A better approach to quality improvement is to concentrate on prevention,—to seek out the causes of waste and inefficiency and then develop systematic plans to eliminate those causes. This approach to quality is founded on the belief that, by increasing prevention costs, fewer defects will occur and total quality costs will decline. This approach begins at the point of product design and proceeds through the entire production process. The product must meet the

[8] Steimer, "Activity-Based Accounting for Total Quality."

functional needs of the customer, and it should be reliable and durable. In addition, the product should be designed for efficient production.

The number of parts required to manufacture a product should be minimized. Readily available standardized parts should be used, if possible, in order to reduce the cost of fabricating new designs and inventorying a large variety of nonstandard parts. The materials should be error free, and the quantity required should be available when needed. The number of retoolings should be minimized, and the production processes required should be well understood before production begins.

The production facility should be organized to promote efficiency. The different processes required to produce the product should be physically located in a way that minimizes distances. This minimizes materials handling and promotes coordination of the production activity between processes. Machinery should be upgraded, if necessary, and preventive maintenance should be performed religiously on machinery and equipment to minimize breakdowns and stoppages. Employees should be trained not only to do their jobs more efficiently, but also encouraged to find ways of improving product and process quality.

While prevention is important in building quality, performance appraisal is also important. Inspecting production for defects is still important, but a more dynamic control approach is needed. One such approach is the use of statistical process control to monitor production quality and reduce product variability. Statistical process control is a method of measuring and monitoring the variability in the output during a production process. The output of a production process is viewed as a random variable with a mean and standard deviation. The characteristic of interest must be defined (for example, its length, width, weight, specific gravity, tensile strength, smoothness, shape, uniformity, percent of impurities) and the production tolerance level determined. The tolerance level may be expressed as a range of acceptable output, with an upper and lower limit around some predetermined specification. The objective of statistical process control is to determine when a process needs to be corrected. Output from the production process is sampled at periodic intervals during the production process. The means of these samples are then plotted. If the means begin to drift away from the predetermined specification in one direction or fall outside the predetermined control limits, an investigation into the cause is made and corrective action is taken. Corrective action may simply involve resetting a machine, but it can require retooling or repairing a machine, or redesigning the product or production process.

Quality improvement efforts also must be extended to marketing activities. Packaging, advertising effectiveness, sales methods, product image, and product distribution and delivery must be evaluated with an eye toward improving quality and service to the customer. Performance appraisals should include surveying recent customers to determine the level of their satisfaction with the product, recording the number of customer complaints and warranty repairs, determining the number of late deliveries (or percentage of on-time deliveries), and tracking repeat sales and new business.[9]

There is no one quick way to achieve quality. Corporate executives often seek a simple formula that will provide a quick fix to the quality problem. According to W. Edwards Deming, one of the pioneering leaders in the quality movement, lasting improvements in quality cannot be obtained in one large step.[10] Instead, he maintains that quality improvement must be a continuous process of a little

---

[9] Michael R. Sellenheim, "J. I. Case Company Performance Measurement," *Management Accounting*, Vol. 73, No. 3, p. 51.

[10] Dobyns, "Ed Deming Wants Big Changes, and He wants Them Fast", p. 82.

improvement here and a little there. He argues that **continuous quality improvement** requires the constant effort of everyone in the company, management and labor alike, working together, and that while quality will improve over time, the process of continual improvement never ends and never gets any easier.

The concept of continuous quality improvement differs substantially from the concept of optimization commonly employed by most American companies.[11] Optimization is a static approach to finding the best solution (greatest profit or smallest cost) given a set of fixed constraints. In contrast, the concept of continuous quality improvement is a dynamic approach to problem solving. Continuous quality improvement presumes that constraints change over time as techniques, practices, and customers' needs change. At the heart of the concept is the notion that the ideal is not an absolute that can be known, but that it evolves as a result of the continual efforts of individuals working together to improve the product.

Measuring and Reporting the Cost of Quality

In order to monitor successfully the cost of quality and evaluate improvements in quality, management accountants must be able to measure the cost of quality. For many companies the cost of quality is quite high. A study at Sola Optical of Petaluma, California, conducted by outside consultants in 1989, determined that the company's cost of quality was about 20 percent of its revenue.[12] Measuring and reporting costs of such magnitude will get the attention of top management and provide an incentive to improve. Reporting quality costs also provides direction by indicating opportunities for substantial improvement.[13]

Most of the various kinds of product failure costs can be measured and reported on a periodic basis. The volume of scrap, spoilage, rework, warranty repairs and replacements, and the handling of customer complaints can be monitored, costed, and reported to management monthly, or more often if it is viewed as desirable by top management. These failure costs can be tracked and reported for each department or cost center; however, top management should not attempt to use such detailed cost information to assign responsibility for these failures. Failure costs may be caused by poor-quality parts from vendors, worn-out machinery, poor-quality product design, or other factors outside of the control of a department or cost center manager. Nevertheless, detailed reports can provide a way of identifying quality problems that should be addressed by quality teams made up of personnel from the functional areas affected. If the costs involved are significant, top management should actively participate in the quality team to provide leadership and direction.

Accounting for Production Losses in a Job Order Cost System

Production losses in a job order cost system include the cost of materials scrap, spoiled goods (spoilage), and reworking defective goods. For the most part, these losses result from a lack of quality and should be eliminated if possible. One way to call attention to the need for reducing these types of quality failures

---

[11] James R. Martin, Wendi K. Schelb, Richard C. Snyder, and Jeffrey S. Sparling, "Comparing U.S. and Japanese Companies: Implications for Management Accounting," *Journal of Cost Management*, Vol. 6, No. 1, p. 9.

[12] Richard K. Youde, "Cost-of-Quality Reporting: How We See It," *Management Accounting*, Vol. 73, No. 7, p. 35.

[13] Clark, "Costing for Quality at Celanese," p. 43.

is to determine their costs and then report these costs to top management. Large costs signal an opportunity to improve quality substantially, which should be interpreted by management as an opportunity to improve profits.

Accounting for Scrap

Scrap includes (1) the filings or trimmings remaining after processing materials, (2) defective materials that cannot be used or returned to the vendor, and (3) broken parts resulting from employee or machine failures. If scrap has a value, it should be collected and placed in storage for sale to scrap dealers. If scrap is the result of trimmings, filings, or materials residue, it may not be possible to determine its cost. Nevertheless, a record of the quantity of scrap should be kept despite the fact that it cannot be assigned any cost. Although this sort of scrap cannot be eliminated, it should not be ignored. The quantities of scrap should be tracked over time and should be analyzed to determine if some of the waste is due to inefficient use of the materials and if the ineffiency can be eliminated, at least in part.

The full amount realized from the sale of scrap and waste can be accounted for in any one of several ways, as long as the alternative chosen is used consistently each period. To illustrate the various alternatives, assume that Woodco Manufacturing Company accumulates wood trimmings from the shop floor and sells it periodically to a nearby paper mill. Scrap sales this period total $500. The accounting alternatives are as follows:

1. The amount accumulated in Scrap Sales can be closed directly to Income Summary and shown on the income statement under Scrap Sales or Other Income. At the time of sale, the following journal entry is made:

Cash (or Accounts Receivable)	500	
Scrap Sales (or Other Income)		500

2. The amount accumulated can be credited to Cost of Goods Sold, thereby reducing the total costs charged against sales revenue for the period. Reducing Cost of Goods Sold results in an increase in income for the period that is the same as reporting the proceeds as Scrap Sales or Other Income. The entry at the time of sale is as follows:

Cash (or Accounts Receivable)	500	
Cost of Goods Sold		500

3. The amount accumulated can be credited to Factory Overhead Control, thereby reducing the cost of factory overhead for the period. If scrap is credited to Factory Overhead Control and if predetermined overhead rates are used to charge overhead to jobs, the net realizable value of scrap expected for the period should be estimated and deducted from total estimated factory overhead before the overhead rate is computed. Otherwise, the overhead rate will be overstated, which will result in more factory overhead being charged to jobs than is actually incurred during the period. The entry to record the sale of scrap is as follows:

Cash (or Accounts Receivable)	500	
Factory Overhead Control		500

4. When scrap is directly traceable to an individual job, the amount realized from the sale of scrap can be treated as a reduction in the materials cost charged to that job. The materials cost on the job cost sheet is reduced by

the value of the scrap, and the entry in the general journal to record the sale is as follows:

Cash (or Accounts Receivable)	500	
Work in Process		500

If scrap results from defective materials or broken parts, it should be considered an internal failure cost which can be reduced or eliminated. The cost of this kind of scrap should be determined and periodically reported to management. If the amount reported is large, it should get management's attention because it indicates a substantial opportunity for cost reduction through quality improvement. Management should take steps to identify the cause and then eliminate it.

If poor-quality materials are detected before they are issued, the defective materials should be returned to the vendor. If materials quality is unreliable, inspection may be necessary. If defective materials are issued to the factory, other costly factory resources—such as labor time, machine processing time, and good component parts—may be wasted in an attempt to convert the defective materials into a product. In most cases, the cost of inspecting materials and culling the defects before they are used is less expensive than issuing defective materials and incurring production failures later. Nevertheless, inspecting materials should be viewed as a cost of quality and targeted for elimination. To eliminate the need for inspection, management must identify suppliers of defective materials and either find alternative sources of high-quality materials or work with the suppliers to improve the quality of their materials.

Accounting for Spoiled Goods

Spoiled goods (spoilage) differ from scrap in that they are partially or fully completed units that are defective in some way. Spoiled goods are not correctable either because technically it is not possible to correct them or because it is not economical to correct them. A plastic product created in a misshapen or scarred mold or molded with the wrong color dye would not be correctable. On the other hand, a product that has bubbles in a painted surface can be corrected by resanding and repainting it. Resanding and repainting would not be economical, however, if the increase in revenue that could be obtained from selling the product at the regular price rather than selling it as is at a reduced price is less than the additional cost of sanding and repainting.

Spoilage can be caused by some action taken by the customer (such as an alteration after the job was begun or an imposition of abnormally close production tolerances by the customer) or because of an internal failure (such as an employee error or worn-out machinery). The accounting treatment for spoiled goods depends on the event causing the spoilage.

Spoilage Caused by the Customer. If spoilage occurrs because of some action taken by the customer, it should not be regarded as a cost of quality. The customer should pay for this kind of spoilage. The unrecoverable cost of the spoiled goods should be charged to the job (that is, the salvage value of the spoiled goods should be removed from the job, but all costs in excess of the salvage value should remain on the job and be charged to the customer). To illustrate, assume that Plastico Inc. manufactures 1,000 custom-designed plastic chairs for Pizza King Inc. on Job 876. After the first 100 chairs are completed, the customer changes the design specification. These 100 chairs are not usable by the customer and not correctable to an acceptable condition. Nevertheless, Plastico can sell the 100 unusable chairs as seconds for $10 each, or a total of $1,000. An additional 100 chairs are manufactured to meet the customer's order requirement, resulting in a total of 1,100 chairs (100 spoiled plus 1,000 acceptable to the customer). Total costs charged to job 876 follow:

Materials	$22,000
Direct labor	5,500
Factory overhead	11,000
Total job cost	$38,500

The entry to record the completion of the job and the shipment to the customer is:

Spoiled Goods Inventory	1,000	
Cost of Goods Sold	37,500	
Work in Process		38,500

Plastico normally sells its work for 150 percent of cost. Therefore, Job 876 is billed to Pizza King Inc. for $56,250 ($37,500 cost × 150%). The journal entry to record invoicing Job 876 is:

Accounts Receivable (or Cash)	56,250	
Sales		56,250

When the spoiled goods are subsequently sold, the entry would be:

Cash (or Accounts Receivable)	1,000	
Spoiled Goods Inventory		1,000

Spoilage Caused by an Internal Failure. If spoilage occurs because of an internal failure, such as an employee error or worn-out machinery, the unrecovered cost of the spoiled goods should be charged to Factory Overhead Control and reported periodically to management. If the cost of the spoilage is of a magnitude large enough to distort reported production costs, it should be reported separately as a loss on the income statement. All production costs expended on spoiled goods should be determined and removed from jobs and the work in process ledger account. If the spoiled goods have a salvage value, they should be inventoried at the salvage value, and the unrecoverable cost of the spoiled goods (that is, the cost incurred to produce the spoiled goods in excess of the salvage value) should be charged to Factory Overhead Control. A factory overhead subsidiary record of the unrecovered cost of spoilage should be maintained to provide a basis for preparing periodic reports for management.

To the extent that spoilage can be predicted but not eliminated, the predetermined factory overhead rate should be adjusted to reflect the increased cost of overhead. Before the predetermined rate is computed, the unrecoverable cost of the spoiled goods should be estimated and included in total budgeted factory overhead for the period. This approach increases the predetermined rate for the period, which in turn increases the factory overhead charged to each product.

To illustrate the accounting treatment when spoiled goods result from an internal failure, assume the same facts of the Plastico illustration above except that the 100 spoiled chairs result from a defect in the plastic mold. In this case, each chair costs $35 to manufacture ($38,500 total job cost divided by 1,100 total chairs); therefore, the total cost of the spoiled units is $3,500 ($35 per chair times 100 spoiled chairs). Because the spoiled chairs can be sold for $1,000 ($10 each times 100 chairs), the unrecovered spoilage cost is $2,500

[($35 each – $10 salvage) × 100 chairs]. The cost of the 1,000 good chairs shipped to Pizza King is $35,000 ($35 each × 1,000 units), and the sales price for the job is $52,500 ($35,000 job cost × 150%). Because the spoilage is the result of an internal failure, sales revenue and profits are less than when the spoilage results from a customer requirement. The entries to record the completion and shipment of the job are:

Spoiled Goods Inventory	1,000	
Factory Overhead Control	2,500	
Cost of Goods Sold	35,000	
Work in Process		38,500
Accounts Receivable	52,500	
Sales		52,500

Accounting for Rework

Rework is the process of correcting defective goods. As with spoilage, rework can result from either an action taken by the customer (which should not be regarded as a cost of quality) or from internal quality failures. And as with spoilage, the accounting treatment depends on the cause of the rework.

Rework Caused by the Customer. If the rework is caused by the customer, the cost of the rework is charged to the job and recovered through an increase in the sales price of the job. To illustrate, assume that Heavy Load Fabricators Inc. manufactures 200 custom-designed trailers on job number 901 to meet design requirements specified by the customer, Haul-It Rentals Corporation. Costs charged to Job 901 are:

Materials	$100,000
Labor ($10 per hour × 2,000 hours)	20,000
Applied factory overhead ($40 per direct labor hour)	80,000
Total cost charged to Job 901	$200,000

Before the trailers are shipped, the customer decides that suspension springs that are heavier than those specified in the original order are needed because some renters are expected to use the trailers to haul heavy loads over rough terrain. The springs cost $40 for each trailer and take ½ hour per trailer to install. As a consequence, the following rework costs are added to Job 901:

Materials ($40 each set of springs × 200 trailers)	$ 8,000
Labor (½ hour per trailer × 200 trailers × $10 per hour)	1,000
Applied factory overhead ($40 per hour × 100 hours)	4,000
Total rework cost added to Job 901	$13,000

The journal entry to record the cost of the rework on Job 901 is:

Work in Process	13,000	
Materials		8,000
Payroll		1,000
Applied Factory Overhead		4,000

The total costs on Job 901 are now $213,000 ($200,000 before the rework plus $13,000 of rework cost). Assuming that Heavy Load Fabricators bills its jobs to customers at a 50 percent markup on cost, job 901 will sell for $319,500 (150% × $213,000 job cost). When Job 901 is shipped to the customer, the following journal entries are recorded:

Cost of Goods Sold	213,000	
Work in Process		213,000
Accounts Receivable	319,500	
Sales		319,500

Rework Caused by an Internal Failure. If the rework is the result of an internal failure, the cost should be charged to Factory Overhead Control and periodically reported to management. Defective goods should be corrected if the cost of the rework is less than the increase in the net realizable value that will result from the rework. Otherwise, the defective goods should be sold as spoiled goods. In most cases, the increase in net realizable value used in deciding whether or not to rework the defective goods is the increase in the expected sales price that will result from the rework. However, for companies concerned about the quality image of their product, the potential effect of selling substandard products on the image of the company's quality products may be viewed as an unacceptably high cost of not correcting the defective units, in which case the decision will almost always be to correct the defects. To the extent that rework can be predicted but not eliminated, the estimated cost of the rework should be built into the predetermined factory overhead rate in the same way as is done for scrap and spoilage.

To illustrate the accounting treatment, assume the same facts of the Heavy Load Fabricators example except that replacement of suspension springs is required because a manufacturing employee incorrectly requisitioned the wrong springs when the trailers were initially assembled. Assuming the rework costs are the same as those in the preceding example, the appropriate journal entry to record the rework is as follows:

Factory Overhead Control	13,000	
Materials		8,000
Payroll		1,000
Applied Factory Overhead		4,000

Because the cost of rework was charged to factory overhead, the total cost of job 901 does not increase (it is still \$200,000) and the sales price is \$300,000 (\$200,000 cost × 150%). At the date the job is shipped to the customer, the following entries are made:

Cost of Goods Sold	200,000	
Work in Process		200,000
Accounts Receivable	300,000	
Sales		300,000

Accounting for Production Losses in a Process Cost System

As they do in a job order cost system, production losses in a process cost system include scrap, spoilage, and rework. Accounting for scrap and rework in a process cost system is essentially the same as in a job order cost system. Scrap Sales, Other Income, Cost of Goods Sold, Factory Overhead Control, or Work in Process should be credited for the revenue generated from the sale of scrap. Normally, the cost of rework should be charged to Factory Overhead Control rather than to Work in Process because rework in a process cost system is normally the result of an internal failure rather than a customer requirement.

On the other hand, while the treatment of spoiled goods is conceptually the same in both systems, the accounting process differs. As explained in Chapter 6, the cost of materials, labor, and overhead charged to a department or cost center (including the cost of beginning inventory) is allocated between the units of product completed and transferred out of the department and those that remain in the department's ending inventory. If average costing is used, the cost in beginning inventory is added to the cost charged to the department during the period. The number of equivalent units for each element of cost is determined next and then the cost of each equivalent unit. The cost transferred out of the department is then determined by multiplying the cost per equivalent unit times the number of units transferred out. The balance of the department's cost for the period remains in ending inventory. If some units of the product are spoiled or lost, they must be accounted for in some way.

Spoilage Attributable to Internal Failures

If the spoilage is the result of an internal failure, the cost should be measured and charged to Factory Overhead Control, as described for a job order cost system. In a process cost system, this cost is determined on the basis of equivalent units. As a consequence, the total number of equivalent units would include not only the number transferred out and the number in ending inventory but also the number in the spoiled units. If spoilage is detected by an inspection which takes place at some consistent point in the production process or if the spoilage occurs as the result of some critical event in the production process, the equivalent unit for each cost element is the portion of that element completed before the inspection or event occurs. If the spoilage can occur at different points in the production process, the department supervisor or someone from quality control must determine at what stage of completion the spoilage occurred and report it to cost accounting.

To illustrate the accounting for spoilage resulting from an internal failure, assume Deco Pottery Company manufactures ceramic coffee mugs in one of its plants in two production departments, Molding and Glazing. Although the mugs vary somewhat in appearance as a result of different colors and designs in the glaze, they are essentially alike in all other respects. As a consequence of this product homogeneity, the company uses a process cost system with an average cost flow assumption to cost its production. Since the production activity is essentially labor driven, factory overhead is allocated to production on the basis of labor.

In Molding, the first department, the mugs are molded of clay and fired in a kiln. As a result of the intense heat applied in the kiln and imperfections in the molded clay, some of the mugs break during firing. Spoiled mugs at this stage contain all their materials and 80 percent of their conversion cost. The broken mugs have no salvage value. The good mugs are cooled, deburred and polished, and then transferred to Glazing, the second department, where a ceramic glaze with a decorative design is applied and the mugs are fired in a kiln for a second time. Not as much heat is required in the Glazing Department's kiln, so mugs rarely break during this second firing; however, defects in the ceramic glaze, such as bubbles, hairline surface cracks, and design distortions, often occur. In order to detect these defects, the mugs are inspected at the end of the process in this department. The good mugs are transferred to Finished Goods Inventory, and the defective mugs are transferred to a separate Spoiled Goods Inventory. Good mugs sell for $2.50 each and spoiled mugs sell as seconds for $.50 each.

Spoilage in both departments is viewed by management as an internal quality failure, which can be avoided or at least significantly reduced with additional personnel training, improved production techniques, and employee diligence. The spoiled units detected at the end of the process in the Glazing Department are inventoried at their sales value, $.50 each. In order to facilitate quality cost control, the cost of the spoilage in both departments is determined each period, and the unrecoverable cost of the spoiled units is charged to Factory Overhead Control. The predetermined factory overhead rate includes an estimate of spoilage cost, and production reports to management include a comparison of actual spoilage cost with that expected for the period.

The following production data are available for the month of November:

	Molding	Glazing
Units in beginning Work in Process inventory	4,000	3,000
Units started in process in Molding Department	21,000	
Units transferred to Glazing Department	19,000	
Units received from Molding Department		19,000
Units transferred to Finished Goods Inventory		15,000
Units in ending Work in Process inventory	3,600	4,000
Units spoiled during the period	2,400	3,000

Departmental supervisors report that ending work in process inventory is complete as to materials in both departments, 30 percent complete as to conversion cost in Molding, and 25 percent complete as to conversion cost in Glazing. Cost data for November are:

	Molding	Glazing
Work in Process, beginning inventory:		
Cost from preceding department		$ 1,396.00
Materials	$ 615.00	196.00
Labor	366.40	310.00
Factory overhead	549.60	310.00
Cost added to process during the current period:		
Materials	3,885.00	1,520.00
Labor	2,273.60	3,718.00
Factory overhead	3,410.40	3,718.00

The first step in assigning costs is determining the number of equivalent units for each element of cost and then the cost of each equivalent unit. Because Deco Pottery Company uses average costing, the cost of each equivalent unit contains a portion of the cost in beginning inventory and a portion of the cost added during the current period. As explained in Chapter 6, the average equivalent unit cost for each element of cost is determined by dividing the total cost for each cost element (the amount in beginning inventory plus the amount added during the current period) by the number of equivalent units required to allocate that cost between the units transferred out of the department and units in ending inventory. In order to assign some cost to spoilage, the number of equivalent units for each element of cost in the spoiled units must be determined and added to the denominator before the cost per equivalent unit is computed. (The treatment of spoilage under a fifo cost flow assumption is essentially the same as treatment of spoilage under an average cost assumption; however, in a fifo system, the cost in beginning inventory is kept separate and not commingled with costs added during the period. The treatment of spoilage in a fifo system is illustrated in the appendix to this chapter.)

The units transferred from Molding to Glazing are 100 percent complete with respect to all elements of cost added in the Molding Department (19,000 equivalent units of materials, labor, and overhead). Ending inventory is complete as to materials (3,600 equivalent units of materials) but only 30 percent complete as to conversion cost (3,600 units × 30% complete = 1,080 equivalent units of labor and overhead). Since materials are added before firing in the Molding Department and spoilage occurs as a result of firing at the 80-percent stage of conversion, each spoiled unit in Molding contains one equivalent unit of material (2,400 equivalent units) and 80 percent of an equivalent unit of conversion cost (2,400 units × 80% complete = 1,920 equivalent units). Equivalent units for each cost element in the Molding Department are:

	Materials	Labor	Overhead
Equivalent units transferred out	19,000	19,000	19,000
Equivalent units in ending inventory	3,600	1,080	1,080
Equivalent units of spoilage	2,400	1,920	1,920
Total equivalent units	25,000	22,000	22,000

The average cost per equivalent unit in the Molding Department is determined as follows:

	Materials	Labor	Overhead
Cost in beginning inventory	$ 615.00	$ 366.40	$ 549.60
Cost added during the current period	3,885.00	2,273.60	3,410.40
Total cost to be accounted for	$4,500.00	$2,640.00	$3,960.00
Divided by total equivalent units	25,000	22,000	22,000
Cost per equivalent unit	$ .18	$ .12	$ .18

The cost of production report for the Molding Department based on these data is illustrated in Exhibit 7-1.

Assuming that the company keeps a separate general ledger work in process account for each of its production departments, the journal entry to record the transfer of cost from the Molding Department to the Glazing Department and Factory Overhead Control is:

Work in Process—Glazing Department	9,120	
Factory Overhead Control	1,008	
Work in Process—Molding Department		10,128

Once the disposition of cost is determined for the Molding Department, the cost of production report for the Glazing Department can be prepared. The units transferred from Glazing to Finished Goods are 100 percent complete with respect to all elements (15,000 equivalent units of prior department cost, materials, labor, and overhead). Ending inventory is complete as to prior department cost and materials (4,000 equivalent units of prior department cost and materials) but only 25 percent complete as to conversion cost (4,000 units × 25% complete = 1,000 equivalent units of labor and overhead). Because the spoiled units are detected at the end of the production process as the result of an inspection, the spoiled units are 100 percent complete as to all elements of cost (3,000 equivalent units of prior department cost, materials,

EXHIBIT 7-1

Deco Pottery Company
Molding Department
Cost of Production Report
For November, 19A

Quantity Schedule	**Materials**	**Labor**	**Overhead**	**Quantity**
Beginning inventory				4,000
Started in process this period				21,000
				25,000
Transferred to Glazing Department				19,000
Ending inventory	100%	30%	30%	3,600
Lost in the process	100%	80%	80%	2,400
				25,000

Cost Charged to Department	**Total Cost**	**Equivalent Units***	**Unit Cost****
Beginning inventory:			
Materials	$ 615.00		
Labor	366.40		
Factory overhead	549.60		
Total cost in beginning inventory	$ 1,531.00		
Cost added during the current period:			
Materials	$ 3,885.00	25,000	$ .18
Labor	2,273.60	22,000	.12
Factory overhead	3,410.40	22,000	.18
Total cost added during the current period	$ 9,569.00		
Total cost charged to the department	$11,100.00		$ .48

Cost Accounted for as Follows	**Units**	**Percent Complete**	**Equivalent Units**	**Unit Cost**		**Total Cost**
Transferred to Glazing Department	19,000	100	19,000	$.48		$ 9,120.00
Spoilage charged to factory overhead:						
Materials	2,400	100	2,400	$.18	$432.00	
Labor	2,400	80	1,920	.12	230.40	
Factory overhead	2,400	80	1,920	.18	345.60	1,008.00
Work in Process, ending inventory:						
Materials	3,600	100	3,600	$.18	$648.00	
Labor	3,600	30	1,080	.12	129.60	
Factory overhead	3,600	30	1,080	.18	194.40	972.00
Total cost accounted for						$11,100.00

* Total number of equivalent units required in the cost-accounted-for section (i.e., the sum of the equivalent units for the cost element listed in the cost-accounted-for section of the cost of production report).

** Total cost (i.e., the cost in beginning inventory plus the cost added during the current period) divided by the total number of equivalent units required in the cost-accounted-for section.

labor, and overhead). Equivalent units for each cost element in the Glazing Department are:

	From Preceding Department	**Materials**	**Labor**	**Overhead**
Equivalent units transferred out	15,000	15,000	15,000	15,000
Equivalent units in ending inventory	4,000	4,000	1,000	1,000
Equivalent units of spoilage	3,000	3,000	3,000	3,000
Total equivalent units	22,000	22,000	19,000	19,000

The average cost per equivalent unit in the Glazing Department is determined as follows:

	From Preceding Department	Materials	Labor	Overhead
Cost in beginning inventory	$ 1,396	$ 196	$ 310	$ 310
Cost added during the current period	9,120	1,520	3,718	3,718
Total cost to be accounted for	$10,516	$ 1,716	$ 4,028	$ 4,028
Divided by total equivalent units	22,000	22,000	19,000	19,000
Cost per equivalent unit	$ .478	$ .078	$ .212	$ .212

The November cost of production report for the Glazing Department based on these data is illustrated in Exhibit 7-2.

EXHIBIT 7-2

Deco Pottery Company
Glazing Department
Cost of Production Report
For November, 19A

Quantity Schedule	**Materials**	**Labor**	**Overhead**	**Quantity**
Beginning inventory				3,000
Received from Molding Department				19,000
				22,000
Transferred to Finished Goods Inventory				15,000
Ending inventory	100%	25%	25%	4,000
Lost in the process	100%	100%	100%	3,000
				22,000

Cost Charged to Department	**Total Cost**	**Equivalent Units***	**Unit Cost****
Beginning inventory:			
Cost from preceding department	$ 1,396		
Materials	196		
Labor	310		
Factory overhead	310		
Total cost in beginning inventory	$ 2,212		
Cost added during the current period:			
Cost from preceding department	$ 9,120	22,000	$ .478
Materials	1,520	22,000	.078
Labor	3,718	19,000	.212
Factory overhead	3,718	19,000	.212
Total cost added during the current period	$ 18,076		
Total cost charged to the department	$ 20,288		$ .980

Cost Accounted for as Follows	**Units**	**Percent Complete**	**Equivalent Units**	**Unit Cost**		**Total Cost**
Transferred to Finished Goods Inventory	15,000	100	15,000	$ .98		$14,700
Transferred to Spoiled Goods Inventory	3,000			$ .50		1,500
Spoilage charged to Factory Overhead:						
Cost of spoiled units	3,000	100	3,000	$ .98	$2,940	
Less salvage value of spoiled units	3,000			.50	1,500	1,440
Work in Process, ending inventory:						
Cost from preceding department	4,000	100	4,000	$.478	$1,912	
Materials	4,000	100	4,000	.078	312	
Labor	4,000	25	1,000	.212	212	
Factory overhead	4,000	25	1,000	.212	212	2,648
Total cost accounted for						$20,288

* Total number of equivalent units required in the cost-accounted-for section (i.e., the sum of the equivalent units for the cost element listed in the cost-accounted-for section of the cost of production report).

** Total cost (i.e., the cost in beginning inventory plus the cost added during the current period) divided by the total number of equivalent units required in the cost-accounted-for section.

The journal entry to record the transfer of cost from the Glazing Department to the Finished Goods and Spoiled Goods Inventories and to Factory Overhead Control for the unrecoverable cost of spoilage is:

Finished Goods Inventory	14,700	
Spoiled Goods Inventory	1,500	
Factory Overhead Control	1,440	
Work in Process—Glazing Department		17,640

When the spoiled goods are sold, the entry is:

Cash (or Accounts Receivable)	1,500	
Spoiled Goods Inventory		1,500

Normal Production Shrinkage

In some production processes, units are lost through evaporation or some other natural process that does not result from an internal quality failure. In such cases, the total cost is absorbed directly by the good units that remain. The loss or shrinkage in such cases should be monitored in order to insure that in the event an internal failure does occur, it will be detected and, if possible, corrected. Nevertheless, such losses are not usually assigned cost on the grounds that such cost assignment is not practical. To illustrate the effect of shrinkage on the cost allocation in a process cost system, assume that Sweet-Stuff Company produces waffle syrup in the Cooking Department. The waffle syrup is then transferred to the Bottling Department, where it is put into bottles for sale to customers. Ingredients are added at the beginning of the process in the Cooking Department, mixed, and then cooked in large vats. During the cooking process, some of the ingredients turn to liquid and some of the liquids evaporate. The following production data are available for the Cooking Department for the month of February:

Gallons in beginning Work in Process inventory	4,000
Gallons started in process in Cooking Department	26,000
Gallons transferred to Bottling Department	20,000
Gallons in ending Work in Process inventory	5,000
Gallons lost in process during the period	5,000

The departmental supervisor reports that ending work in process inventory is complete as to materials and 25 percent complete as to conversion cost. Cost data for February are:

Work in Process, beginning inventory:	
Materials	$ 5,450
Labor	535
Factory overhead	1,070
Cost added to process during the current period:	
Materials	32,550
Labor	7,540
Factory overhead	15,080

Average costing is used in the Cooking Department, and overhead is allocated to production on the basis of labor cost. The units transferred from Cooking to Bottling are fully complete with respect to all elements of cost added in the Cooking Department (20,000 equivalent units of materials, labor, and overhead), and ending inventory is fully complete as to materials (5,000 equivalent units of materials) but only 25 percent complete as to conversion cost (5,000 units × 25% complete = 1,250 equivalent units of labor and overhead). Because the loss of production volume is not related to an internal quality failure, the total cost of the lost units is absorbed by the remaining good units. This is accomplished by adding only surviving units in the equivalent unit computation. (By omitting the lost units, the remaining units absorb all the cost.) Equivalent units for each cost element in the Cooking Department are:

	Materials	Labor	Overhead
Equivalent units transferred out	20,000	20,000	20,000
Equivalent units in ending inventory	5,000	1,250	1,250
Total equivalent units	25,000	21,250	21,250

The average cost per equivalent unit in the Cooking Department is determined as follows:

	Materials	Labor	Overhead
Cost in beginning inventory	$ 5,450	$ 535	$ 1,070
Cost added during the current period	32,550	7,540	15,080
Total cost to be accounted for	$38,000	$ 8,075	$16,150
Divided by total equivalent units	25,000	21,250	21,250
Cost per equivalent unit	$ 1.52	$ .38	$ .76

The cost of production report for the Cooking Department based on these data is illustrated in Exhibit 7-3.

Assuming the company keeps a separate general ledger work in process account for each of its production departments, the journal entry to record the transfer of cost from the Cooking Department to the Bottling Department is:

Work in Process—Bottling Department	53,200	
Work in Process—Cooking Department		53,200

Summary

Many companies today are concerned about the quality of their products. To a great extent the current concern is the result of increased competition, particularly competition from abroad. Many manufacturers, recognizing the need to improve efficiency and reduce costs, have changed the emphasis of their businesses to continuous product quality improvement, and as a consequence are becoming world-class manufacturers.

The concept of quality costs and how quality costs relate to production losses were discussed in this chapter. The chapter began with a discussion of the cost of quality, which included defining and classifying quality costs, defining the concept of total quality management, pointing out that quality improvement is a continuous process, and explaining the need for reporting and measuring quality costs. The last sections discussed the measurement of one type of quality cost, production losses, and illustrated the treatment of these losses in job order and process cost systems.

EXHIBIT 7-3

Sweet-Stuff Company
Cooking Department
Cost of Production Report
For February, 19A

Quantity Schedule	Materials	Labor	Overhead	Quantity
Beginning inventory				4,000
Started in process during the period				26,000
				30,000
Transferred to Bottling Department				20,000
Units in ending inventory	100%	25%	25%	5,000
Units lost in the process				5,000
				30,000

Cost Charged to Department	Total Cost	Equivalent Units*	Unit Cost**
Beginning inventory:			
Materials	$ 5,450		
Labor	535		
Factory overhead	1,070		
Total cost in beginning inventory	$ 7,055		
Cost added during the current period:			
Materials	$32,550	25,000	$1.52
Labor	7,540	21,250	.38
Factory overhead	15,080	21,250	.76
Total cost added during the current period	$55,170		
Total cost charged to the department	$62,225		$2.66

Cost Accounted for as Follows	Units	Percent Complete	Equivalent Units	Unit Cost		Total Cost
Transferred to Bottling Department	20,000	100	20,000	$2.66		$53,200
Work in Process, ending inventory:						
Materials	5,000	100	5,000	$1.52	$7,600	
Labor	5,000	25	1,250	.38	475	
Factory overhead	5,000	25	1,250	.76	950	9,025
Total cost accounted for						$62,225

* Total number of equivalent units required in the cost-accounted-for section (i.e., the sum of the equivalent units for the cost element listed in the cost-accounted-for section of the cost of production report).

** Total cost (i.e., the cost in beginning inventory plus the cost added during the current period) divided by the total number of equivalent units required in the cost-accounted-for section.

Appendix Process Costing with a Fifo Cost Flow Assumption

Spoilage Attributable to Internal Failures

The accounting for spoilage resulting from an internal failure can be illustrated using the data from the Deco Pottery Company example. Assume, however, that the company uses the fifo cost flow assumption rather than average cost. Recall that the company manufactures ceramic coffee mugs in one of its plants in two production processes, Molding and Glazing. In addition, overhead is applied to production on the basis of labor. In the first department, Molding, materials are added at the beginning of the process and spoilage occurs at the 80-percent stage of conversion. The broken mugs have no salvage value. Mugs rarely break in the second department, Glazing; however, defects in the ceramic glaze, such as bubbles, hairline surface cracks, and design distortions, often occur. After the mugs are inspected at the end of the glazing process, good mugs are transferred to Finished Goods Inventory and defective mugs are transferred to a separate Spoiled Goods Inventory at a selling price of $.50 each. The following production data are available for November:

	Molding	Glazing
Units in beginning Work in Process inventory	4,000	3,000
Units started in process in Molding Department	21,000	
Units transferred to Glazing Department	19,000	
Units received from Molding Department		19,000
Units transferred to Finished Goods Inventory		15,000
Units in ending Work in Process inventory	3,600	4,000
Units spoiled during the period	2,400	3,000

Based on information in the departmental cost of production reports from October, beginning inventory for November (that is, ending inventory from the prior period) is complete as to materials in both departments but only 60 percent and 70 percent complete as to conversion cost in Molding and Glazing, respectively. Departmental supervisors report that units still in process at the end of November are complete as to materials in both departments, but only 30 percent and 25 percent complete as to conversion cost in Molding and Glazing, respectively. Cost data for November are:

	Molding	Glazing
Work in Process, beginning inventory:		
Cost from preceding department	—	$ 1,396.00
Materials	$ 615.00	196.00
Labor	366.40	310.00
Factory overhead	549.60	310.00
Cost added to process during the current period:		
Materials	3,885.00	1,520.00
Labor	2,273.60	3,718.00
Factory overhead	3,410.40	3,718.00

The first step in assigning costs is to determine the number of equivalent units for each element of cost and then to determine the cost of each equivalent unit. Since fifo costing is being used, the cost in beginning inventory is assigned to the first units transferred out, and the cost of each equivalent unit contains only cost added during the current period. As explained in Chapter 6, the cost per equivalent unit for each element of cost is determined by dividing the cost added during the current period for each cost element by the number of equivalent units of that cost element added in the current period. The equivalent units of a cost element added in the current period is the sum of the number required to complete beginning inventory, the number in the units started and completed during the period, and the number in ending inventory (which is the same as, the total number of equivalent units that would have been computed if average costing were used, reduced by the number of equivalent units in beginning inventory). In order to assign some cost to spoilage, the number of equivalent units for each element of cost in the spoiled units must be determined and added to the denominator before the cost per equivalent unit is computed. This approach assigns only current period cost to spoilage. Although some of the spoiled units actually may have been among those that were in beginning inventory, which technically contain cost added in a prior period, only cost added during the current period is typically assigned to the spoiled goods, rather than a portion from beginning inventory and a portion from the current period. This simplification is acceptable if it is applied consistently each period and if the difference in cost is not material.

The units of product transferred from Molding to Glazing are fully complete with respect to all elements of cost added in the Molding Department. Of the 19,000 units transferred, 4,000 were from beginning inventory. Because beginning inventory is complete as to materials but only 60 percent complete as to conversion cost, the units in beginning inventory require the addition of only 40 percent of current period conversion cost to complete them (4,000 units × 40% to complete = 1,600 equivalent units of labor and overhead). The remaining units transferred to Glazing this period contain only current period costs (19,000 total units transferred − 4,000 from beginning inventory = 15,000 started and completed this period, each of which contains one full equivalent unit of materials, labor, and overhead). Ending inventory is complete as to materials (3,600 equivalent units of materials) but only 30 percent complete as to conversion cost (3,600 units × 30% complete = 1,080 equivalent units of labor and overhead). Because materials are added at the beginning of the process in the Molding Department and spoilage occurs at the 80-percent stage of conversion, each spoiled unit in Molding contains one equivalent unit of material (2,400 equivalent units) and 80 percent of an equivalent unit of conversion cost (2,400 units × 80% complete = 1,920 equivalent units of labor and overhead). The equivalent units of current period cost for each element of cost in the Molding Department are determined as follows:

	Materials	Labor	Overhead
Cost added in the current period:			
Equivalent units in beginning inventory	0	1,600	1,600
Equivalent units started and completed during the current period	15,000	15,000	15,000
Equivalent units in ending inventory	3,600	1,080	1,080
Equivalent units of spoilage	2,400	1,920	1,920
Total equivalent units	21,000	19,600	19,600

The cost per equivalent unit added during the current period in the Molding Department is determined as follows:

	Materials	Labor	Overhead
Cost added during the current period	$3,885.00	$2,273.60	$3,410.40
Divided by equivalent units	21,000	19,600	19,600
Cost per equivalent unit	$ .185	$ .116	$ .174

The cost of production report for the Molding Department determined on a fifo basis and based on these data is illustrated in Exhibit 7-4.

Assuming that the company keeps a separate general ledger work in process account for each of its production departments, the journal entry to record the transfer of cost from the Molding Department to the Glazing Department and Factory Overhead Control is:

Work in Process—Glazing Department	9,120.00	
Factory Overhead Control	1,000.80	
Work in Process—Molding Department		10,120.80

EXHIBIT 7-4

Deco Pottery Company
Molding Department
Cost of Production Report
For November, 19A

Quantity Schedule	Materials	Labor	Overhead	Quantity
Beginning inventory	100%	60%	60%	4,000
Started in process during the period				21,000
				25,000
Transferred to Glazing Department				19,000
Ending inventory	100%	30%	30%	3,600
Lost in the process	100%	80%	80%	2,400
				25,000

Cost Charged to Department	Total Cost	Equivalent Units*	Unit Cost**
Beginning inventory:			
Materials	$ 615.00		
Labor	366.40		
Factory overhead	549.60		
Total cost in beginning inventory	$ 1,531.00		
Cost added during the current period:			
Materials	$ 3,885.00	21,000	$ .185
Labor	2,273.60	19,600	.116
Factory overhead	3,410.40	19,600	.174
Total cost added during the current period	$ 9,569.00		
Total cost charged to the department	$11,100.00		$ .475

Cost Accounted for as Follows	Units	Current Percent	Equivalent Units	Unit Cost		Total Cost
Transferred to Glazing Department:						
From beginning inventory					$1,531.00	
Cost to complete this period:						
Labor	4,000	40	1,600	$.116	185.60	
Factory overhead	4,000	40	1,600	.174	278.40	$ 1,995.00
Started and completed this period	15,000	100	15,000	$.475		7,125.00
Total cost transferred to Glazing Department						$ 9,120.00
Spoilage charged to Factory Overhead Control:						
Materials	2,400	100	2,400	$.185	$ 444.00	
Labor	2,400	80	1,920	.116	222.72	
Factory overhead	2,400	80	1,920	.174	334.08	1,000.80
Work in Process, ending inventory:						
Materials	3,600	100	3,600	$.185	$ 666.00	
Labor	3,600	30	1,080	.116	125.28	
Factory overhead	3,600	30	1,080	.174	187.92	979.20
Total cost accounted for						$11,100.00

* Number of equivalent units of cost added during the current period (i.e., the sum of the equivalent units listed in the cost-accounted-for section of the cost of production report).

** Cost added during the current period divided by the number of equivalent units of cost added during the current period.

Once the cost transferred from Molding to Glazing has been determined, the cost of production report for the Glazing Department can be prepared. Of the 15,000 units transferred from Glazing to Finished Goods during November, 3,000 were from beginning inventory. Since beginning inventory is complete as to prior department cost and materials but only 70 percent complete as to conversion cost, the units in beginning inventory require the addition of only 30 percent of current period conversion cost to complete them (3,000 units × 30% to complete = 900 equivalent units of labor and overhead). The remaining units transferred to finished goods this period contain only current period costs (15,000 total units transferred −3,000 from beginning inventory = 12,000 started and completed this period, each of which contains one full equivalent unit of prior department cost, materials, labor, and overhead). Ending inventory is complete as to prior department cost and materials (4,000 equivalent units of prior department cost and materials) but only 25 percent complete as to conversion cost (4,000 units × 25% complete = 1,000 equivalent units of labor and overhead). Because the spoiled units are detected by inspection at the end of the production process, the spoiled units are fully complete as to all elements of cost (3,000 equivalent units of prior department cost, materials, labor, and overhead). The equivalent units of current period cost for each of the elements of cost in the Glazing Department are determined as follows:

	From Preceding Department	Materials	Labor	Overhead
Costs added in the current period:				
Equivalent units in beginning inventory	0	0	900	900
Equivalent units started and completed during the current period	12,000	12,000	12,000	12,000
Equivalent units in ending inventory	4,000	4,000	1,000	1,000
Equivalent units of spoilage	3,000	3,000	3,000	3,000
Total equivalent units	19,000	19,000	16,900	16,900

The cost per equivalent unit added during November in the Glazing Department is determined as follows:

	From Preceding Department	Materials	Labor	Overhead
Cost added during the current period	$ 9,120	$ 1,520	$ 3,718	$ 3,718
Divided by equivalent units	19,000	19,000	16,900	16,900
Cost per equivalent unit	$ .48	$ .08	$ .22	$ .22

The November cost of production report for the Glazing Department based on these data is illustrated in Exhibit 7-5.

The journal entry to record the transfer of cost from the Glazing Department to the Finished Goods and Spoiled Goods Inventories and to Factory Overhead Control for the unrecoverable cost of spoilage is:

Finished Goods Inventory	14,608	
Spoiled Goods Inventory	1,500	
Factory Overhead Control	1,500	
Work in Process—Glazing Department		17,608

Normal Production Shrinkage

If the cost in the lost units is absorbed directly by the good units that remain, as in the case of losses resulting from evaporation or some other natural shrinkage, the loss is normally treated as if it occurs only from current production. This is, of course, a simplification, but it is acceptable if the same procedure is used each period and the difference in the cost distortion is not material.

EXHIBIT 7-5

Deco Pottery Company
Glazing Department
Cost of Production Report
For November, 19A

Quantity Schedule	Labor	Materials	Overhead	Quantity
Beginning inventory	100%	70%	70%	3,000
Received from Molding Department				19,000
				22,000
Transferred to Finished Goods Inventory				15,000
Ending inventory	100%	25%	25%	4,000
Lost in the process	100%	100%	100%	3,000
				22,000

Cost Charged to Department	Total Cost	Equivalent Units*	Unit Cost**
Beginning inventory:			
Cost from preceding department	$ 1,396		
Materials	196		
Labor	310		
Factory overhead	310		
Total cost in beginning inventory	$ 2,212		
Cost added during the current period:			
Cost from preceding department	$ 9,120	19,000	$ .48
Materials	1,520	19,000	.08
Labor	3,718	16,900	.22
Factory overhead	3,718	16,900	.22
Total cost added during the current period	$18,076		
Total cost charged to the department	$20,288		$ 1.00

Cost Accounted for as Follows	Units	Current Percent	Equivalent Units	Unit Cost		Total Cost
Transferred to Finished Goods Inventory:						
From beginning inventory					$2,212	
Cost to complete this period:						
Labor	3,000	30	900	$ .22	198	
Factory overhead	3,000	30	900	.22	198	$ 2,608
Started and completed this period	12,000	100	12,000	1.00		12,000
Total cost transferred to Finished Goods						$14,608
Transferred to Spoiled Goods Inventory	3,000			$ .50		1,500
Spoilage charged to factory overhead:						
Cost of spoiled units	3,000	100	3,000	$1.00	$3,000	
Less salvage value of spoiled units	3,000			.50	1,500	1,500
Work in Process, ending inventory:						
Cost from preceding department	4,000	100	4,000	$ .48	$1,920	
Materials	4,000	100	4,000	.08	320	
Labor	4,000	25	1,000	.22	220	
Factory overhead	4,000	25	1,000	.22	220	2,680
Total cost accounted for						$20,288

* Number of equivalent units of cost added during the current period (i.e., the sum of the equivalent units listed in the cost-accounted-for section of the cost of production report).

** Cost added during the current period divided by the number of equivalent units of cost added during the current period.

The use of fifo costing in such a process cost system can be illustrated with the data from the Sweet-Stuff Company example. Recall that Sweet-Stuff produces waffle syrup in the Cooking Department. The syrup is transferred to the Bottling Department when complete. Ingredients are added at the beginning of the process in the Cooking Department, mixed, and then cooked in large vats. During the cooking process, some of the ingredients turn to liquid and some of the liquids evaporate. The following production data are available for the Cooking Department for February:

Gallons in beginning Work in Process inventory	4,000
Gallons started in process in Cooking Department	26,000
Gallons transferred to Bottling Department	20,000
Gallons in ending Work in Process inventory	5,000
Gallons lost in process during the period	5,000

Based on the cost of production report from January, beginning work in process inventory for February is complete as to materials but only 60 percent as to conversion cost. The departmental supervisor reports that units still in process at the end of February are complete as to materials and 25 percent complete as to conversion cost. The cost data for February are:

Work in Process, beginning inventory:	
Materials	$ 5,450
Labor	535
Factory overhead	1,070
Cost added to process during the current period:	
Materials	32,550
Labor	7,540
Factory overhead	15,080

Of the 20,000 gallons transferred from Cooking to Bottling, 4,000 gallons are in process at the beginning of the period. Because beginning inventory is complete as to materials but only 60 percent complete as to conversion cost, the syrup in beginning inventory requires the addition of only 40 percent of current period conversion cost to complete it (4,000 units × 40% to complete = 1,600 equivalent units of labor and overhead). The remaining 16,000 gallons transferred to bottling this period contain only current period costs (16,000 equivalent units of materials, labor, and overhead). Ending inventory is complete as to materials (5,000 equivalent units of materials) but only 25 percent complete as to conversion cost (5,000 units × 25% complete = 1,250 equivalent units of labor and overhead). Since the loss of production volume is not related to an internal quality failure, the cost of the lost units is absorbed by the remaining good units. This is accomplished by adding only surviving units in the equivalent unit computation (that is by omitting the lost units, the remaining units absorb all the cost). Equivalent units for each cost element in the Cooking Department are:

	Materials	Labor	Overhead
Cost added in the current period:			
Equivalent units in beginning inventory	0	1,600	1,600
Equivalent units in the units started and completed this period	16,000	16,000	16,000
Equivalent units in ending inventory	5,000	1,250	1,250
Total equivalent units	21,000	18,850	18,850

The cost per equivalent unit added to process during February in the Cooking Department is determined as follows:

	Materials	Labor	Overhead
Cost added during the current period	$32,550	$ 7,540	$15,080
Divided by equivalent units	21,000	18,850	18,850
Cost per equivalent unit	$ 1.55	$ .40	$ .80

The February cost of production report based on fifo costing for the Cooking Department is illustrated in Exhibit 7-6.

The journal entry to record the transfer of cost from the Cooking Department to the Bottling Department is:

Work in Process—Bottling Department	52,975	
Work in Process—Cooking Department		52,975

EXHIBIT 7-6

Sweet-Stuff Company
Cooking Department
Cost of Production Report
For February, 19A

Quantity Schedule	Materials	Labor	Overhead	Quantity
Beginning inventory	100%	60%	60%	4,000
Started in process during the period				26,000
				30,000
Transferred to Bottling Department				20,000
Ending inventory	100%	25%	25%	5,000
Lost in the process				5,000
				30,000

Cost Charged to Department	Total Cost	Equivalent Units*	Unit Cost**
Beginning inventory:			
Materials	$ 5,450		
Labor	535		
Factory overhead	1,070		
Total cost in beginning inventory	$ 7,055		
Cost added during the current period:			
Materials	$32,550	21,000	$1.55
Labor	7,540	18,850	.40
Factory overhead	15,080	18,850	.80
Total cost added during the current period	$55,170		
Total cost charged to the department	$62,225		$2.75

Cost Accounted for as Follows	Units	Current Percent	Equivalent Units	Unit Cost		Total Cost
Transferred to Bottling Department:						
From beginning inventory					$7,055	
Cost to complete this period:						
Labor	4,000	40	1,600	$ .40	640	
Factory overhead	4,000	40	1,600	.80	1,280	$ 8,975
Started and completed this period	16,000	100	16,000	$2.75		44,000
Total cost transferred to Bottling Department						$52,975
Work in Process, ending inventory:						
Materials	5,000	100	5,000	$1.55	$7,750	
Labor	5,000	25	1,250	.40	500	
Factory overhead	5,000	25	1,250	.80	1,000	9,250
Total cost accounted for						$62,225

* Number of equivalent units of cost added during the current period (i.e., the sum of the equivalent units listed in the cost-accounted-for section of the cost of production report).

** Cost added during the current period divided by the number of equivalent units of cost added during the current period.

Key Terms

prevention costs *(149)*
appraisal costs *(149)*
failure costs *(149)*
internal failure costs *(149)*
external failure costs *(149)*
total quality management (TQM) *(150)*
continuous quality improvement *(153)*
scrap *(154)*
spoiled goods or spoilage *(155)*
rework *(157)*

Discussion Questions

Q7-1 List and define the three classifications of quality costs.

Q7-2 What is TQM?

Q7-3 What are five characteristics of TQM systems that can be found in most world-class manufacturing settings?

Q7-4 How does the concept of continuous quality improvement differ from the concept of quality optimization?

Q7-5 Some companies have attempted to obtain quality by inspecting it into the product. What is wrong with this approach?

Q7-6 Advocates of TQM argue that companies should concentrate their efforts on preventing poor quality rather than by trying to inspect it into the process. Why?

Q7-7 Why should quality costs be measured and reported to management?

Q7-8 What is the difference between scrap, spoiled goods, and rework?

Q7-9 Historically, many companies have ignored the cost of scrap, spoiled goods, and rework, theorizing that such costs are normal and unavoidable. Why is this a poor practice?

Q7-10 Spoilage and rework can be caused by customer requirements or by internal failure. Why is it important to determine the cause of the spoilage and rework?

Exercises

E7-1 Recording Scrap. Campton Metal Fabricators Inc. accumulates fairly large quantities of metal shavings and trimmings from the products it manufactures. At least once a month, the scrap metal is sold to a local smelter for reprocessing. This month's scrap sales on account total $1,800.

Required: Give the appropriate general journal entry to record the sale of the scrap for each of the following alternatives:
(1) The scrap sales are viewed as additional revenue.
(2) The scrap sales are viewed as a reduction of the cost of goods sold during the period.
(3) The scrap sales are viewed as a reduction of factory overhead.
(4) The scrap sales are traceable to individual jobs and are viewed as a reduction in the cost of materials used on the jobs.

E7-2 Recording Spoilage Attributable to an Internal Failure. Miller Wood Products Company manufactures custom wooden cabinets and furniture. During the current period, 80 table legs were incorrectly shaped on job number 5587 in the Lathe Department and had to be replaced. Although the defective table legs cannot be used on the job, they can be sold to a local lumber company for $1 each. The cost of the 80 defective table legs is:

Materials (80 legs × $2.50 each)	$200
Labor (2 hours × $12.00 per hour)	24
Factory overhead (2 hours × $24.00 per hour)	48
Total cost of spoilage on job number 5587	$272

Required: Give the appropriate general journal entry to record spoilage cost and the transfer of the spoiled goods to a separate inventory account.

E7-3 Spoilage in a Job Order Cost System Attributable to an Internal Failure. Valdeze Plastics Company uses a job order cost system to account for its production costs. During the current period, 1,000 chairs were molded and assembled on job number 9823. The total cost incurred on the job is:

Materials	$12,000
Labor (500 hours × $10 per hour)	5,000
Factory overhead ($20 per labor hour)	10,000
Total cost charged to job number 9823	$27,000

Before being transferred to Finished Goods Inventory, the chairs were inspected and 100 were found to be spoiled. The spoiled chairs cannot be reworked because the defects are embedded in the plastic; however, they can be salvaged for $10 each. The company maintains a separate Spoiled Goods Inventory for defective products and charges the unrecoverable cost of spoilage to Factory Overhead Control.

Required: Determine the cost of job number 9823 to be transferred to Finished Goods Inventory and to Spoiled Goods Inventory, and then give the appropriate general journal entry to record the spoilage and the transfers.

E7-4 Spoilage in a Job Order Cost System Attributable to Customer Change Order. Hargrove Sheet Metal Works manufactures custom sheet metal products ranging from cabinets and storage containers to portable buildings and custom trailers. During the current period, an order for 500 custom storage containers was begun on job number 308 for Wilmington Air Freight. After 100 units had been completed, the customer decided to change the design specifications for the containers. The design change was successfully implemented on the 400 units that were not complete at the date of the change order; however, the 100 completed units could not be reworked to meet the customer's new design requirements. As a consequence, an additional 100 units had to be manufactured (bringing the total number to 600, 500 that met the customers specifications and 100 that did not). The customer does not want the 100 units that do not meet its specifications; however, management of Hargrove Sheet Metal Works believes that the spoiled units can be sold in the seconds market for $100 each. Spoiled goods are kept in an inventory account that is separate from Finished Goods. Total costs charged to job number 308 for Wilmington Air Freight are:

Materials	$ 50,000
Labor (1,200 hours × $15 per hour)	18,000
Factory overhead ($30 per labor hour)	36,000
Total cost charged to job number 308	$104,000

Required: Determine the cost to be transferred to Spoiled Goods Inventory and the cost of the job shipped to the customer, and then prepare the appropriate general journal entry to record the transfer.

E7-5 Rework Attributable to Internal Failure. Lindle Sunshine Furniture Inc. manufactures several different designs of outdoor furniture. Production costs are accounted for using a job order cost system. During the current period, 100 metal tables were manufactured on job number 275. Costs charged to the job before inspection are:

Materials	$3,500
Labor (150 hours × $10 per hour)	1,500
Factory overhead ($12 per labor hour)	1,800
Total cost charged to job number 275	$6,800

On inspection, it was discovered that an umbrella ring had not been attached to the tables. To correct the oversight, a small part was welded to the table leg brace and the brace was repainted. The small part cost $.50 for each table, and the primer and paint cost $1.00 for each table. Each table required ¼ hour of labor.

Required: Prepare the appropriate general journal entry to record the rework and the transfer of the completed tables to Finished Goods Inventory.

E7-6 Rework Attributable to Customer Change Order. Wilson Electronics Inc. manufactures gauges and instruments for aircraft. During the current year, an order for 1,000 units of a custom-designed gauge was begun for the Tombstone Aircraft Corporation. The costs incurred on the job are:

Materials	$20,000
Labor (1,000 hours × $15 per hour)	15,000
Factory overhead ($30 per direct labor hour)	30,000
Total cost charged to Tombstone Aircraft Corporation job	$65,000

Before taking delivery of the gauges, engineers at Tombstone Aircraft changed the design specifications for the gauge. The change required the replacement of a part. The replacement part cost $1 and required 10 minutes for installation in each gauge. The change affected all 1,000 gauges manufactured on the job.

Required: Prepare the appropriate general journal entry to record the rework and the shipment of the completed job to the customer, assuming the company bills its jobs to customers at 150 percent of cost.

E7-7 Spoilage in a Process Cost System Using an Average Cost Flow Assumption. Manx Company uses a process cost system with average costing to account for the production of its only product. The product is manufactured in two departments. Units of product are started in the Forming Department and then transferred to the Finishing Department, where they are completed. Units are inspected at the end of the production process in the Forming Department, and the cost of spoilage is charged to Factory Overhead Control. Data related to August operations in the Forming Department are:

Units in beginning inventory (60% materials, 35% labor, 25% overhead)	1,000
Units started in process this period	9,000
Units transferred to the Finishing Department this period	8,000
Units in ending inventory (100% materials, 75% labor, 50% overhead)	1,500

	Beginning Inventory	Added This Period
Costs charged to the department:		
Materials	$1,260	$36,240
Labor	770	10,780
Factory overhead	1,400	21,725

Required:

(1) Prepare a cost of production report for the Forming Department based on the data presented for August.

(2) Prepare the appropriate general journal entry to record the transfer of cost out of the Forming Department this period.

E7-8 Spoilage with a Salvage Value in a Process Cost System Using an Average Cost Flow Assumption. Juniper Company manufactures a single product in two departments, Cutting and Finishing. Units of product are started in the Cutting Department and then transferred to the Finishing Department, where they are completed. Units are inspected at the end of the production process in the Finishing Department. Good units are transferred to Finished Goods Inventory, and spoiled units are transferred to Spoiled Goods Inventory. Spoiled units are inventoried at their salvage value of $15 each, and the unrecoverable cost of spoilage is charged to Factory Overhead Control.

At the end of June, 500 units were still in process in the Finishing Department, 80% complete as to materials and 60% complete as to conversion costs. During July, 4,500 units were transferred from the Cutting Department to the Finishing Department and 3,800 were transferred from the Finishing Department to Finished Goods Inventory. At the end of July, the Finishing Department still had 800 units in process, 40% complete as to materials and 20% complete as to conversion costs. Cost data related to July operations in the Finishing Department are:

	Beginning Inventory	Added This Period
Costs charged to the department:		
Cost from preceding department	$5,500	$54,500
Materials	1,950	20,650
Labor	1,180	16,260
Factory overhead	1,770	24,390

Required:

(1) Assuming the company uses a process cost system with average costing to account for its production, prepare a cost of production report for the Finishing Department based on the data presented for July.

(2) Prepare the appropriate general journal entry to record the transfer of cost out of the Finishing Department this period.

E7-9 Production Shrinkage in a Process Cost System Using an Average Cost Flow Assumption. Coastal Petroleum Inc. uses a process cost system with an average cost flow assumption to account for the production of its only product. The product is manufactured in two departments. Units of product are started in the Cracking Department and then transferred to the Refining Department, where they are completed. Because of the intense heat applied in the Cracking Department, some of the production volume is lost to evaporation. Since the department is capital intensive, the cost of direct labor is small relative to overhead. Consequently, labor and overhead are treated as one element of cost in the Cracking Department (that is, conversion cost). Data related to May operations in the Cracking Department are:

Units in beginning inventory	5,000
Units started in process this period	55,000
Units transferred to the Refining Department this period	49,000
Units in ending inventory (100% materials, 70% conversion cost)	6,000

	Beginning Inventory	Added This Period
Costs charged to the department:		
Materials	$1,900	$20,100
Conversion cost	360	7,620

Required:

(1) Prepare a cost of production report for the Cracking Department based on the data presented for May.

(2) Prepare the appropriate general journal entry to record the transfer of cost out of the Cracking Department this month.

E7-10 (Appendix) Spoilage in a Process Cost System with a Fifo Cost Flow Assumption. Sun Valve Company sells a single product that is manufactured in two departments, Tooling and Finishing. Units of product are started in the Tooling Department, where they are cut and shaped. The units are then transferred to the Finishing Department where they are ground and polished. Materials are added at the beginning of the process in the Tooling Department. Units are inspected at the 90-percent stage of completion in the Tooling Department. The cost of spoilage is charged to Factory Overhead Control. Cost data related to March operations in the Tooling Department are:

	Beginning Inventory	Added This Period
Costs charged to the department:		
Materials	$1,600	$9,750
Labor	290	2,320
Factory overhead	950	9,200

At the end of February, the Tooling Department had 2,000 units still in process, 70% complete as to labor and 60% complete as to overhead. At the end of March, 3,000 units were still in process in the Tooling Department, 50% complete as to labor and 40% complete as to overhead. During March, 13,000 units were started in the Tooling Department, and 7,000 units were completed and transferred to the Finishing Department.

Required:

(1) Assuming the company uses a process cost system with fifo costing to account for its production, prepare a cost of production report for the Tooling Department based on the data presented for March.

(2) Prepare the appropriate general journal entry to record the transfer of cost out of the Tooling Department this period.

E7-11 (Appendix) Spoilage with a Salvage Value in a Process Cost System with a Fifo Cost Flow Assumption. Plastico Furniture Company uses a process cost system with a fifo cost flow assumption to account for the production of plastic chairs, which are manufactured in two departments. Units of product are started in the Fabricating Department and then transferred to the Finishing Department, where they are completed. Units are inspected at the end of the production process in the Finishing Department. Good units are transferred to Finished Goods Inventory, and spoiled units are transferred to Spoiled Goods Inventory. Spoiled units are inventoried at their salvage value of $12 each, and the unrecoverable cost of spoilage is charged to Factory Overhead Control. Data related to September operations in the Finishing Department are:

Units in beginning inventory (80% materials, 40% labor, 40% overhead)	1,200
Units received from Cutting Department this period	6,000
Units transferred to the Finished Goods inventory this period	5,000
Units transferred to Spoiled Goods Inventory this period	700
Units in ending inventory (100% materials, 60% labor, 60% overhead)	1,500

	Beginning Inventory	Added This Period
Costs charged to the department:		
Cost from preceding department	$14,160	$72,000
Materials	1,210	6,240
Labor	1,300	12,240
Factory overhead	3,250	30,600

Required:

(1) Prepare a cost of production report for the Finishing Department based on the data presented for September.

(2) Prepare the appropriate general journal entry to record the transfer of cost out of the Finishing Department this period.

E7-12 (Appendix) Production Shrinkage in a Process Cost System with a Fifo Cost Flow Assumption. Local Pop Inc. uses a process cost system with fifo cost flow assumption to account for the production of its only product. The product is manufactured in three departments. Most of the required ingredients for flavoring are added and mixed in the Mixing Department. Next, the mixture is transferred to the Cooking Department, where more ingredients are added at various stages of the cooking process. Finally, the syrup is transferred to the Bottling Department, where the product is completed. Because of the heat applied in the Cooking Department, some of the production volume is lost to evaporation.

During December, 40,000 units were transferred from Mixing to Cooking, and 37,000 units were transferred from Cooking to Bottling. The Cooking Department had 10,000 units still in process (75% complete as to materials and 25% complete as to conversion cost) at the end of November and 8,000 units still in process at the end of December (complete as to materials but only 75% complete as to conversion cost). Cost data related to December operations in the Cooking Department are:

	Beginning Inventory	Added This Period
Cost from preceding department	$2,920	$10,850
Materials	305	1,500
Labor	140	2,430
Factory overhead	210	3,645

Required:

(1) Prepare a cost of production report for the Cooking Department based on the data presented for December.

(2) Prepare the appropriate general journal entry to record the transfer of cost out of the Cooking Department this period.

Problems

P7-1 Recording Scrap and Spoilage. Foxx Metal Works Inc. is a special order manufacturer of metal products. Each period the company accumulates fairly large quantities of metal shavings and trimmings from the products it manufactures. At least once a month, the scrap metal is sold to a local scrap-metals dealer. This month scrap sales for shavings and trimmings not traceable to any particular jobs total $550. In addition, during the current period 200 metal door facings were cut to an incorrect size on job number 492 and had to be replaced. Although the defective facings cannot be used on job 492, they can be sold as salvage for $2.25 each. The cost of cutting the 200 defective facings is:

Materials (1,200 square feet of sheet metal × $1 each)	$1,200
Labor (10 hours × $15.00 per hour)	150
Factory overhead (10 hours × $45.00 per hour)	450
Total cost of scrap on job number 492	$1,800

Required:

(1) Prepare the appropriate general journal entry to credit job number 492 for the cost of the spoiled door facings and to record the transfer of the spoiled door facings to Spoiled Goods Inventory at their salvage value.

(2) Prepare the appropriate general journal entry to record the sale on account of all the scrap accumulated during the period (i.e., the shavings and trimmings accumulated during the period) and the spoiled goods in inventory (i.e., the spoiled door facings inventoried in requirement 1).

P7-2 Spoilage in a Job Order Cost System. Purelli Foundry Inc. manufactures custom metal products that require casting, such as engine blocks, pistons, and engine housings. During the current period, an order for 5,000 custom housings was begun on job number 3387 for Raton Pump Company. After the job was completed, the housings were inspected and 200 units were determined to be defective. The customer has agreed to accept the order with only 4,800 units instead of the quantity originally ordered. The spoiled units can be sold as seconds for $15 each. Spoiled goods are kept in an inventory account separate from Finished Goods. Total costs charged to job number 3387 are:

Materials	$46,000
Labor (1,000 hours × $14 per hour)	14,000
Factory overhead ($30 per labor hour)	30,000
Total cost charged to job number 3387	$90,000

Custom jobs are priced at 140 percent of cost. The unrecoverable cost of spoilage is charged to Factory Overhead Control when it is the result of an internal failure.

Required:

(1) Assuming that the defective units are the result of an internal failure (that is, an employee error or a machine failure), prepare the appropriate general journal entry to record the transfer of the defective units to Spoiled Goods Inventory and the shipment of job number 3387 to the customer.

(2) Assuming that the defective units are the result of a change in design specified by the customer after the units are completed, prepare the appropriate general journal entry to record the transfer of the defective units to Spoiled Goods Inventory and the shipment of job number 3387 to the customer.

P7-3 Rework in a Job Order Cost System. Big Sky Cabinet Company manufactures custom cabinets for modular and prefabricated housing companies. During the current period, an order for 1,000 custom cabinets was begun on job number 8962 for Burrows Park Housing Corporation. Custom jobs are marked up 150 percent of cost. Total costs charged to job number 8962 are:

Materials	$ 92,000
Labor (3,000 hours × $12 per hour)	36,000
Factory overhead ($24 per labor hour)	72,000
Total cost charged to job number 8962	$200,000

On inspection, 100 of the cabinets were found to have defects. Materials costing $4 and ½ hour of labor are required to correct each defective unit. Factory overhead is charged to production on the basis of direct labor hours.

Required:

(1) Assuming that the defective units are the result of an internal failure (that is, an employee error or a machine failure), prepare the appropriate general journal entry to record the rework of the defective units and the shipment of completed job number 8962 to the customer.

(2) Assuming that the defective units are the result of a change in design specified by the customer after the units are completed, prepare the appropriate general journal entry to record the rework of the defective units and the shipment of completed job number 8962 to the customer.

P7-4 Spoilage Resulting from an Internal Failure in a Process Cost System Using an Average Cost Flow Assumption. Nimblerod Company sells a single product that is manufactured in two departments, Cutting and Assembling. Units of the product are started in the Cutting Department and then transferred to the Assembling Department, where they are completed. Units are inspected at the 90% stage of completion in the Cutting Department and at the end of the production process in the Assembling Department. Materials are added before inspection in both departments. Units of product that are spoiled in the Cutting Department have no salvage value; however, units found to be spoiled at the end of the Assembling Department process have a salvage value of $5 each. Good units are transferred from the Assembling Department to Finished Goods Inventory at cost, and spoiled units are transferred to Spoiled Goods Inventory at their salvage value. The unrecoverable cost of spoilage in both departments is viewed by management as an internal failure cost and charged to Factory Overhead Control. Data related to manufacturing operations during April are:

	Cutting	Assembling
Units in beginning inventory	5,000	4,000
Units started in process in Cutting Department this period	20,000	
Units transferred from Cutting Department to Assembling Department	18,000	18,000
Units transferred to Finished Goods Inventory this period		17,000
Units spoiled in process this period	3,000	1,000
Units in ending inventory:		
Cutting Department (100% materials, 60% labor and overhead)	4,000	
Assembling Department (80% materials, 20% labor and overhead)		4,000
Cost in beginning inventory:		
Cost from preceding department		$ 10,900
Materials	$ 1,260	38,028
Labor	789	3,356
Factory overhead	1,789	5,034
Cost added during the current period:		
Materials	36,240	164,432
Labor	10,761	15,444
Factory overhead	21,311	23,166

Required:

(1) Assuming the company uses a process cost system with average costing, prepare a cost of production report for each department for April.

(2) Assuming the company maintains a separate work in process account for each production department, prepare the appropriate general journal entries to record the transfer of cost out of each department during April.

P7-5 Spoilage and Shrinkage in a Process Cost System Using an Average Cost Flow Assumption. Hometown Brewery Company uses a process cost system with an average cost flow assumption to account for the production of its only product. Ingredients are mixed and then brewed in the first department (called the Mixing and Brewing Department), after which the product is transferred to the Canning Department, where the liquid brew is put in cans and cases for storage and transport. The brewing process requires the application of heat and results in some normal shrinkage of volume in the Mixing and Brewing Department. During processing in the Canning Department, some cans and some brew are spoiled. Spoilage in the Canning Department occurs at the 80-percent stage of conversion, and the lost units are complete as to materials. The production shrinkage in the Mixing and Brewing Department is viewed as part of the normal production process and is not measured; however, spoilage in the Canning Department is viewed as an internal failure cost and charged to Factory Overhead Control. Data related to January operations are:

	Mixing and Brewing	Canning
Units in beginning inventory	4,000	2,000
Units started in process in Mixing and Brewing Department this period	36,000	
Units transferred from Mixing and Brewing to Canning Department	28,000	28,000
Units transferred to Finished Goods Inventory this period		25,000
Units spoiled in process this period	6,000	4,000
Units in ending inventory:		
Mixing and Brewing (100% materials, 40% labor and overhead)	6,000	
Canning (100% materials, 50% labor and overhead)		1,000

	Mixing and Brewing	Canning
Cost in beginning inventory:		
Cost from preceding department		$ 550
Materials	$ 600	190
Labor	88	75
Factory overhead	128	150
Cost added during the current period:		
Materials	4,840	1,520
Labor	824	786
Factory overhead	1,088	1,572

Required:

(1) Prepare a January cost of production report for each department.

(2) Assuming the company uses a separate ledger account for each producing department, prepare the appropriate general journal entry to record the transfer of cost out of each department during January.

P7-6 (Appendix) Spoilage Resulting from an Internal Failure in a Process Cost System with a Fifo Cost Flow Assumption. Handy Tool Company uses a process cost system with a fifo cost flow assumption to account for the production of its only product, which is manufactured in two departments. Units of product are started in the Fabricating Department and then transferred to the Finishing Department, where they are completed. Units are inspected at the 60% stage of conversion in the Fabricating Department and at the end of the production process in the Finishing Department. Materials are added at the beginning of the process in both departments. Units of product that are spoiled in the Fabricating Department have no salvage value; however, units found to be spoiled at the end of the Finishing Department process have a salvage value of $1 each. Good units are transferred from the Finishing Department to Finished Goods Inventory at cost, and spoiled units are transferred to Spoiled Goods Inventory at their salvage value. The unrecoverable cost of spoilage in both departments is viewed by management as an internal failure cost and charged to Factory Overhead Control. Data related to April are:

	Fabricating	Finishing
Units in beginning inventory:		
Fabricating Department (100% materials, 70% labor and overhead)	2,000	
Finishing Department (100% materials, 40% labor and overhead)		3,000
Units started in process in Fabricating Department this period	9,000	
Units transferred from Fabricating Department to Finishing Department	9,000	9,000
Units transferred to Finished Goods Inventory this period		9,900
Units spoiled in process this period	500	100
Units in ending inventory:		
Fabricating Department (100% materials, 40% labor and overhead)	1,500	
Finishing Department (100% materials, 25% labor and overhead)		2,000
Cost in beginning inventory:		
Cost from preceding department		$ 6,100
Materials	$1,900	3,500
Labor	340	520
Factory overhead	1,020	780
Cost added during the current period:		
Materials	9,180	10,800
Labor	2,125	3,720
Factory overhead	6,375	5,580

Required:

(1) Prepare a cost of production report for each department based on the data presented for April.

(2) Prepare the appropriate general journal entry to record the transfer of cost out of each department during April. Assume the company maintains separate work in process accounts for each manufacturing department.

P7-7 (Appendix) Shrinkage in a Process Cost System with a Fifo Cost Flow Assumption. XXX Chemicals Company produces a single product in two departments, Distillation and Refining. Unrefined chemicals are mixed and then subjected to a heating process in the Distillation Department, after which the product is transferred to the

Refining Department, where the liquid mixture is filtered and put in drums for storage and transport. Because of the heat applied to the product in both departments, some production shrinkage occurs, which is viewed as part of the normal production process by management and not measured. Data related to operations during the month of June are:

	Distillation	Refining
Units in beginning inventory:		
Distillation Department (100% materials, 20% labor and overhead)	4,000	
Refining Department (100% materials, 50% labor and overhead)		2,000
Units started in process in Distillation Department this period	16,000	
Units transferred from Distillation Department to Refining Department	14,000	14,000
Units transferred to the Finished Goods Inventory this period		12,000
Units in ending inventory:		
Distillation Department (100% materials, 80% labor and overhead)	2,000	
Refining Department (100% materials, 30% labor and overhead)		2,000
Cost in beginning inventory:		
Cost from preceding department		$ 3,500
Materials	$ 3,624	240
Labor	96	160
Factory overhead	480	900
Cost added during the current period:		
Materials	10,800	1,440
Labor	1,480	1,740
Factory overhead	7,400	10,440

Required:

(1) Assuming the company uses a process cost system with a fifo cost flow assumption, prepare a June cost of production report for each department.

(2) Assuming the company uses separate ledger accounts for each production department, prepare the appropriate general journal entry to record the transfer of cost out of each department during June.

Cases

C7-1 Quality Improvement Program. Star Disk Corporation manufactures computer disk drives that it sells under its own brand name to computer manufacturers and to large retail outlets. Several years ago the company's sales volume and market share began to deteriorate. Top management became concerned and initiated an investigation to determine the causes of the decline. Based on a survey of customers, poor product quality was determined to be a major cause of the company's declining sales. Immediately, top management issued a statement to all company personnel that the company's most important mission is the manufacture of the world's highest quality disk drives. A campaign was initiated, the supervisor of the most productive manufacturing department was placed in charge of the quality improvement program and given a pay raise, and banners were posted throughout the company proclaiming Star disk drives to be the highest quality disk drives in the world. Inspection of the product was increased, and units that did not meet the quality standard were repaired or discarded if not repairable.

For the next few years sales continued to decline. Despite the fact that new advanced-technology products were introduced and top management continued to stress the importance of quality, promotions and bonuses appeared to be awarded to individuals who were high-volume producers. The supervisor of the quality program could not get the cooperation of the design engineers (who were primarily concerned with designing new technologies into the product) or the production department managers (who appeared to be primarily concerned with meeting production quotas). The number of units of product rejected continued to rise, and the amount of rework increased. Production cost per unit of product climbed to a point that exceeded the sales price of identical units sold by competitors, and product quality did not improve substantially. As a result of continuing declining sales, the company was forced to lay off 30% of its work force, and top management is now facing the possibility of bankruptcy.

Required: Explain why the quality improvement efforts at Star Disk Corporation failed and make suggestions for turning the problem around.

C7-2 Measuring Quality Costs. Hightone Electronics Corporation manufactures electronic appliances for home use. Recent market studies suggest that consumer perception of the quality of Hightone products is high; however, sales have declined in the past few years. Analysis of the market suggests that the decline in sales volume is the result of larger increases in sales prices for Hightone's products relative to increases by competitors for products of comparable quality. These price increases were viewed as necessary by Hightone's top management in order to cover increasing production costs.

Top management has always stressed the importance of quality, but for the most part rewards to operating managers have been based on objective criteria such as production volume. To guard against poor production quality, products are thoroughly inspected before they are transferred from one manufacturing department to another. Defective or broken parts that cannot be reworked are discarded, and defective products are reworked until they pass inspection. The cost of these activities is treated as part of normal departmental production cost, with the implication that such costs are not separately measured and reported to management.

Required: Criticize Hightone's treatment of scrap, spoilage, and rework, and explain why such costs should be measured and reported to management.

CHAPTER 8

Costing By-Products and Joint Products

Learning Objectives

After studying this chapter, you will be able to:

1. Distinguish by-products from joint products.
2. Define joint cost.
3. Assign cost to by-products by different methods.
4. Allocate joint production cost to joint products by different methods
5. Evaluate the relationship of joint costs to decision making and profitability analysis.

Many industrial concerns are confronted with the difficult problem of assigning costs to their by-products and/or joint products. Chemical companies, petroleum refineries, flour mills, coal mines, lumber mills, dairies, canners, meat packers, and many others produce in their manufacturing or conversion processes a multitude of products to which some costs must be assigned. Assignment of costs to these various products is required for inventory costing, for income determination, and for financial statement purposes. By-product and joint product costing also furnishes management with data that can be useful in planning maximum profit potentials and evaluating actual profit performance. However, management should recognize the limited usefulness of arbitrary joint cost allocations in the analysis of individual products.

By-Products and Joint Products Defined

The term **by-product** is generally used to denote a product of relatively small total value that is produced simultaneously with a product of greater total value. The product with the greater value, commonly called the **main product**, is usually produced in greater quantities than the by-products. Ordinarily, the manufacturer has only limited control over the quantity of by-product that is produced. However, the introduction of more advanced engineering methods, such as those used in the petroleum industry, has permitted greater control over the quantity of residual products. For example, one company, which formerly paid a trucker to haul away and dump certain waste materials, discovered that the waste was valuable as fertilizer. This by-product is now an additional source of income for the entire industry.

Joint products are produced simultaneously by a common process or series of processes, with each product possessing a more than nominal value in the form in which it is produced. The definition emphasizes the point that the manufacturing process creates products in a definite quantitative relationship. An increase in one product's output will bring about an increase in the quantity of the other product or products, or vice versa, but not necessarily in the same proportion. The **split-off point** is defined as the point at which these several products emerge as individual units. Before that point, the cost of the products forms a homogeneous whole.

Nature of By-Products and Joint Products

The accounting treatment of by-products necessitates a reasonably complete knowledge of the technological factors underlying their manufacture, since the origins of by-products can vary. By-products arising from the cleansing of the main product, such as gas and tar from coke manufacture, generally have a residual value. In some cases, the by-product is leftover scrap or waste, such as sawdust in lumber mills. In other cases, the by-product may not be the result of any manufacturing process but may arise from preparing raw materials before they are used in the manufacture of the main product. The separation of cotton seed from cotton, cores and seeds from apples, and shells from cocoa beans is an example of this type of by-product.

By-products can be classified into two groups according to their marketable condition at the split-off point: (1) those sold in their original form without need of further processing and (2) those that require further processing in order to be salable.

The classic example of joint products is found in the meat-packing industry. Various cuts of meat and numerous by-products are processed from one original carcass with one lump-sum cost. Another example of joint product manufacturing is the production of gasoline. The derivation of gasoline inevitably results in the production of such items as naphtha, kerosene, and distillate fuel oils. Other examples of joint product manufacturing are the simultaneous production of various grades of glue and the processing of soybeans into oil and meal. Joint product costing is also found in industries that must grade raw material before it is processed. Tobacco manufacturers (except in cases where graded tobacco is purchased) and virtually all fruit and vegetable canners face the problem of grading. In fact, such manufacturers have a dual problem of joint cost allocation: (1) materials cost is applicable to all grades and (2) subsequent manufacturing costs are incurred simultaneously for all the different grades.

Joint Costs

A **joint cost** can be defined as the cost that arises from the simultaneous processing or manufacturing of products produced from the same process. Whenever two or more different joint or by-products are created from a single cost factor, a joint cost results. A joint cost is incurred prior to the point at which separately identifiable products emerge from the same process.

The chief characteristic of a joint cost is the fact that the cost of several different products is incurred in an indivisible sum for all products, rather than in individual amounts for each product. The total production cost of multiple products involves both joint cost and separate, individual product costs. These **separable product costs** are identifiable with the individual product and, generally, need no allocation. However, a joint production cost requires allocation or assignment to the individual products.

Difficulties in Costing By-Products and Joint Products

By-products and joint products are difficult to cost because a true joint cost is indivisible. For example, an ore might contain both lead and zinc. In the raw state, these minerals are joint products, and until they are separated by reduction of the ore, the cost of finding, mining, and processing is a joint cost; neither lead nor zinc can be produced without the other prior to the split-off stage. The cost accumulated to the split-off stage must be borne by the difference between the sales price and the cost to complete and sell each mineral after the split-off point.

Because of the indivisibility of a joint cost, cost allocation and apportionment methods used for establishing the unit cost of a product are far from perfect and are, indeed, quite arbitrary. The costing of joint products and by-products highlights the problem of assigning costs to products whose origin, use of equipment, share of raw materials, share of labor costs, and share of other facilities cannot truly be determined. Regardless of the method of allocation employed, the total profit or loss figure is not affected—provided there are no beginning or ending inventories—by allocating costs to the joint products or by-products, since these costs are recombined in the final income statement. However, a joint cost is ordinarily allocated to the products on some acceptable basis to determine product costs needed for inventory carrying costs. For this reason, there is an effect on periodic income, because different amounts may be allocated to inventories of the numerous joint products or by-products under various allocation methods.

The allocation of costs to joint products may be required for such special purposes as justifying sales prices before governmental regulatory bodies. However, the validity of splitting a joint cost to determine fair, regulated prices for products has been questioned by both accountants and economists.

Methods of Costing By-Products

The accepted methods for costing by-products fall into two categories. In the first category, a joint production cost is not allocated to the by-product. In this category, two different methods are used. Any revenue resulting from sales of the by-product is credited either to income or to cost of the main product (recognition of gross revenue—method 1). In some cases, costs subsequent to split-off are offset against the by-product revenue (recognition of net revenue—method 2).

In method 1, recognition of gross revenue, revenue from sales of the by-product is listed on the income statement as:

a. Other income
b. Additional sales revenue
c. A deduction from the cost of goods sold of the main product
d. A deduction from the total production (manufacturing) cost of the main product

In method 2, recognition of net revenue, revenue from sales of the by-product less the costs of placing the by-product on the market (marketing and administrative expenses) and less any additional processing cost of the by-product, is shown on the income statement in any of the ways indicated for method 1.

In the second category of costing by-products, some portion of the joint production cost is allocated to the by-product. Inventory costs are based on this allocated cost plus any subsequent processing cost. In this category, two methods are used. Method 3 is the replacement cost method. Method 4 is the market value (reversal cost) method.

Method 1: Recognition of Gross Revenue

The recognition of gross revenue, called the **gross revenue method**, is a typical noncost procedure in which the final inventory cost of the main product is overstated to the extent that some of the cost belongs to the by-product. However, this shortcoming is somewhat removed in method 1d, although a sales value rather than a cost is deducted from the production cost of the main product.

Method 1a: By-Product Revenue as Other Income. The following income statement illustrates this method:

Sales (main product, 10,000 units @ $2)			$20,000
Cost of goods sold:			
Beginning inventory (1,000 units @ $1.50)		$ 1,500	
Total production cost (11,000 units @ $1.50)		16,500	
Cost of goods available for sale		$18,000	
Ending inventory (2,000 units @ $1.50)		3,000	15,000
Gross profit			$ 5,000
Marketing and administrative expenses			2,000
Operating income			$ 3,000
Other income: Revenue from sales of by-product			1,500
Income before income tax			$ 4,500

Method 1b: By-Product Revenue as Additional Sales Revenue. For this method, the preceding income statement would show the $1,500 revenue from sales of the by-product as an addition to sales of the main product. As a result, total sales revenue would be $21,500, and gross profit and operating income would increase accordingly. All other figures would remain the same.

Method 1c: By-Product Revenue as a Deduction from the Cost of Goods Sold. In this method, the $1,500 revenue from the by-product would be deducted from the $15,000 cost of goods sold figure, thereby reducing the cost and increasing the gross profit and operating income. The income before income tax remains at $4,500.

Method 1d: By-Product Revenue Deducted from Production Cost. In this method, the $1,500 revenue from by-product sales is deducted from the $16,500 total production cost, giving a net production cost of $15,000. This revised cost results in a new average unit cost of $1.3625 for the main product. The final inventory consequently is $2,725 instead of $3,000. Similarly, the beginning inventory of $1.35 per unit results from crediting revenue from by-product sales in the prior period to the main product's production costs incurred in that period. None of the three preceding treatments of by-product revenue affects the unit cost of the main product. This is an important distinction for product costing, although presumably the dollar amount of the difference is relatively small. The income statement would appear as follows:

Sales (main product, 10,000 units @ $2)			$20,000
Cost of goods sold:			
Beginning inventory (1,000 units @ $1.35)		$ 1,350	
Total production cost (11,000 units @ $1.50)	$16,500		
Revenue from sales of by-product	1,500		
Net production cost		15,000	
Cost of goods available for sale (12,000 units @ $1.3625 average cost)		$16,350	
Ending inventory (2,000 units @ $1.3625)		2,725	13,625
Gross profit			$ 6,375
Marketing and administrative expenses			2,000
Operating income			$ 4,375

The methods just described require no complicated journal entries. The revenue received from by-product sales is debited to Cash (or Accounts Receivable). In the first three cases, Income from Sales of By-Product is credited; in the fourth case, the production cost of the main product is credited.

Conceptual justification exists for subtracting by-product revenue from the cost of the main product in recognition that the main product is the principal reason for the production process. That is, the by-product is incidental to the main product. Also, such a procedure is expedient and cost-effective. However, there is a resulting reduction in the usefulness of the reporting system's information. The by-product can be neglected when by-product revenue or cost are absorbed in costing the main product. An approach is needed that provides and highlights relevant information, that encourages managerial attention to by-products, that promotes good decision making and control, and that identifies and rewards good performance.[1] These objectives are better met by recognizing and reporting the revenue and associated costs of each by-product separately. Such an approach would employ method 2, with separate reporting on the income statement as other income.

Method 2: Recognition of Net Revenue

The recognition of net revenue, called the **net revenue method**, recognizes the need for assigning traceable cost to the by-product. It does not attempt, however, to allocate any joint production cost to the by-product. Any costs involved in further processing or marketing the by-product are recorded in separate accounts. All figures are shown on the income statement, following one of the procedures described under method 1.

Journal entries in method 2 involve charges to by-product revenue for the additional work required and perhaps for factory overhead. The marketing and administrative expenses can be allocated to the by-product on some equitable predetermined basis. Some firms carry an account called By-Product, to which all additional expenses are debited and all income is credited. The balance of this account is presented in the income statement, following one of the procedures outlined under method 1. However, accumulated manufacturing costs applicable to by-product inventory should be reported on the balance sheet.

Method 3: Replacement Cost Method

The **replacement cost method** ordinarily is applied by firms whose by-products are used within the plant, thereby avoiding the necessity of purchasing certain materials and supplies from outside suppliers. The production cost of the main product is credited for such materials, and the offsetting debit is to the department that uses the by-product. The cost assigned to the by-product is the purchase or replacement cost existing in the market.

The costing of by-products that are used within a plant actually is a form of intracompany transfer pricing, which is discussed in Chapter 26. In this chapter,

[1] John P. Fertakis, "Responsibility Accounting for By-Products and Industrial Wastes," *Journal of Accountancy*, Vol. 161, No. 5, pp. 142, 144, 145.

alternatives to the use of a replacement cost or market price are discussed. For example, a price based on the cost to produce the by-product, a negotiated price, or an arbitrary price might be used. Whatever price is used, the credit is made to the production cost of the main product from which the by-product comes and the offsetting debit is made to the department that uses the by-product.

Method 4: Market Value (Reversal Cost) Method

The **market value method** (or reversal cost method) is basically similar to the technique illustrated in method 1(d). However, it reduces the manufacturing cost of the main product, not by the actual revenue received, but by an estimate of the by-product's value at the time of recovery. This estimate must be made prior to split-off from the main product. Dollar recognition depends on the stability of the market as to price and salability of the by-product; however, control over quantities is important as well. The by-product account is charged with this estimated amount, and the production (manufacturing) cost of the main product is credited. Any additional costs of materials, labor, or factory overhead incurred after the by-product is separated from the main product are charged to the by-product. Marketing and administrative expenses might be allocated to the by-product on some equitable basis. The proceeds from sales of the by-product are credited to the by-product account. The balance in this account can be presented on the income statement in one of the ways outlined for method 1, except that the manufacturing cost applicable to by-product inventory should be reported in the balance sheet.

The market value (reversal cost) method of ascertaining main product and by-product costs can be illustrated as follows:

Item	Main Product	By-Product	
Materials	$ 50,000		
Labor	70,000		
Factory overhead	40,000		
Total production cost (40,000 units)	$160,000		
Market value (5,000 units @ $1.80)			$9,000
Estimated gross profit consisting of:			
Assumed operating profit (20% of sales price)		$1,800	
Marketing and administrative expenses (5% of sales price)		450	2,250
			$6,750
Estimated production costs after split-off:			
Materials		$1,000	
Labor		1,200	
Factory overhead		300	2,500
Estimated value of by-product at split-off to be credited to main product	4,250		$4,250
Net cost of main product	$155,750		
Add back *actual* production cost after split-off			2,300
Total			$6,550
Total number of units	40,000		5,000
Unit cost	$ 3.894		$ 1.31

This illustration indicates that an estimated value of the by-product at the split-off point results when estimated gross profit and production cost after split-off are subtracted from the by-product's ultimate market value. Alternatively, if the by-product has a market value at the split-off point, the by-product account is charged with this market value, less its estimated gross profit, and the main product's production cost is credited. It is also possible to use the total market values of the main product and the by-product at the split-off point as a basis for assigning a share of the prior-to-split-off cost to the by-product, applying the offsetting credit to the production cost of the main product. In any event, subsequent-to-split-off cost related to the by-product is charged to the by-product.

Method 4 is based on the theory that the cost of a by-product is related to its sales value. It is a step toward the recognition of a by-product cost prior to its split-off from the main product. It is also the nearest approach to methods employed in joint product costing.

Underlying Accounting Theory

Because the total value of a by-product in relationship to a jointly produced main product is relatively small, the effect on periodic income of using one method versus another may be judged as immaterial. Furthermore, joint costs cannot be traced to a by-product. Nevertheless, preference for a particular by-product method is rightfully related to generally accepted concepts in accounting theory. If costs can be traced to a by-product, as would be the case with separate processing cost, they should be charged to the by-product.

The asset recognition concept argues for the recording of by-product inventory in the period of production at an amount approximating its cost to produce, provided there is a market for the by-product. And the matching concept requires expensing inventory in the period in which its sale is recorded. These concepts, balanced against the materiality concept, should be considered in selecting the by-product costing method. Whichever method is chosen, it should be applied consistently from period to period.

Methods of Allocating Joint Production Cost to Joint Products

Joint production cost, incurred up to the split-off point, can be allocated to joint products under one of the following methods.

1. The market value method, based on the relative market values of the individual products.
2. The average unit cost method.
3. The weighted-average method, based on predetermined weight factors.
4. The quantitative unit method, based on some physical measurement unit such as weight, linear measure, or volume.

Market Value Method

Proponents of the market value method often argue that the market value of any product is, to some extent, a manifestation of the cost incurred in its production. The contention is that if one product sells for more than another, it is because more cost was expended to produce it. In other words, were it not for such a cost, a sales value would not exist. Yet, by definition, the effort required to produce each of the joint products cannot be determined. If it could be determined, the allocation could be made on the basis of the relative amount of effort expended on each of the joint products. Furthermore, according to economic theory, prices in a competitive market economy are determined on the basis of the relative scarcity of goods demanded by consumers, not on the basis of the relative cost of producing those goods.

Another argument for using the market value method of allocating joint costs is that it is neutral. That is, it does not affect the relative profitability of the joint products. Decisions that must be based on an analysis of the relative profitability of the various joint products are not distorted by arbitrary cost allocations.

The choice between this and other methods tends to be arbitrary when the proportions of the joint products composing the output mix are fixed and cannot be changed. However, the choice is not arbitrary if the proportions can be varied and there is a relationship between the total joint cost and the total value of the output. This implies especially strong rational support for the market or sales value method if, for given inputs to the joint manufacturing process, two conditions hold: (1) the physical mix of output can be altered by incurring more (or less) total joint cost relative to other production costs and (2) this alteration produces more (or less) total market value.[2]

Joint Products Salable at Split-Off. The market value method prorates the joint cost on the basis of the relative market values of the items produced. The method is based on a weighted market value, using the total market or sales value of each product (quantity produced multiplied by the unit sales price). To illustrate, assume that joint products A, B, C, and D are produced at a total joint production cost of $120,000. Quantities produced are: A, 20,000 units; B, 15,000 units; C, 10,000 units; and D, 15,000 units. Product A sells for $.25; B, for $3; C, for $3.50; and D, for $5. These prices are market values for the products at the split-off point; that is, it is assumed that they can be sold at that point. Management can decide, however, that it is more profitable to process certain products further before they are sold. Nevertheless, this condition does not destroy the usefulness of the sales value at the split-off point for the allocation of the joint production cost. The proration of this joint cost is made in the following manner:

Product	Units Produced	Market Value per Unit at Split-Off	Total Market Value	Ratio of Product Value to Total Market Value	Apportionment of Joint Production Cost
A	20,000	$ .25	$ 5,000	3.125%	$ 3,750
B	15,000	3.00	45,000	28.125	33,750
C	10,000	3.50	35,000	21.875	26,250
D	15,000	5.00	75,000	46.875	56,250
Total			$160,000	100.000%	$120,000

The same results can be obtained if the total joint production cost ($120,000) is divided by the total market value of the four products ($160,000). The resulting 75 percent is the percentage of joint cost in each individual market value. By multiplying each market value by this percentage, the joint cost is apportioned as shown in the preceding table.

Under the market value method, each joint product yields the same unit gross profit percentage, assuming that the units are sold without further processing. This can be illustrated as follows, assuming no beginning inventories:

[2] William L. Cats-Baril, James F. Gatti, and D. Jacque Grinnell, "Joint Product Costing for the Semiconductor Industry," *Management Accounting*, Vol. 67, No. 8, p. 29.

	Total	A	B	C	D
Sales—units	52,000	18,000	12,000	8,000	14,000
Ending inventories	8,000	2,000	3,000	2,000	1,000
Sales—dollars	$138,500	$ 4,500	$36,000	$28,000	$70,000
Production cost	$120,000	$ 3,750	$33,750	$26,250	$56,250
Less ending inventory	16,125	375*	6,750	5,250	3,750
Cost of goods sold	$103,875	$ 3,375	$27,000	$21,000	$52,500
Gross profit	$ 34,625	$ 1,125	$ 9,000	$ 7,000	$17,500
Gross profit percentage	25%	25%	25%	25%	25%

* $3,750 production cost ÷ 20,000 units produced = $.1875; $.1875 × 2,000 units in ending inventory = $375.

Joint Products Not Salable at Split-Off. Products not salable in their stage of completion at the split-off point, and therefore without any market value, require additional processing to place them in marketable condition. In such cases, the basis for allocation of the joint production cost is a hypothetical market value at the split-off point. To illustrate the procedure, the following assumptions are added to the preceding example:

Product	Ultimate Market Value per Unit	Processing Cost after Split-Off
A	$ .50	$ 2,000
B	5.00	10,000
C	4.50	10,000
D	8.00	28,000

To arrive at the basis for the apportionment, it is necessary to use a working-back or reversal cost procedure, whereby the after-split-off processing cost is subtracted from the ultimate sales value to find a hypothetical market value. After-split-off marketing and administrative expenses traceable to specific products and an allowance for profit should also be considered if their amounts are proportionately different among the joint products, because the joint cost apportionment is affected. The following table indicates the steps to be taken:

Product	Ultimate Market Value per unit	Units Produced	Ultimate Market Value	Processing Cost after Split-Off	Hypothetical Market Value*	Apportionment of Joint Production Cost**	Total Production Cost	Total Production Cost Percentage***
A	$ .50	20,000	$ 10,000	$ 2,000	$ 8,000	$ 4,800	$ 6,800	68.0
B	5.00	15,000	75,000	10,000	65,000	39,000	49,000	65.3
C	4.50	10,000	45,000	10,000	35,000	21,000	31,000	68.8
D	8.00	15,000	120,000	28,000	92,000	55,200	83,200	69.3
Total			$250,000	$50,000	$200,000	$120,000	$170,000	68.0

* At the split-off point

** Percentage to allocate joint production cost:

$$\frac{\text{Total joint production cost}}{\text{Total hypothetical market value}} = \frac{\$120,000}{\$200,000} = .60 = 60\%;$$

60% × hypothetical market value = apportionment of joint production cost

*** The production cost percentage is calculated by dividing total production cost by the ultimate market value. For example:

$$\frac{\$49,000}{\$75,000} = .653 = 65.3\% \text{ for Product B, and } \frac{\$170,000}{\$250,000} = .68 = 68\% \text{ for all products combined.}$$

If in a given situation, certain of the joint products are salable at the split-off point while others are not, the market values at the split-off point are used for the former group. For the latter group, hypothetical market values are required.

The following gross profit statement uses the same number of units sold as was used in the preceding illustration, but the sales prices have been increased as a result of additional processing.

	Total	A	B	C	D
Sales—units	52,000	18,000	12,000	8,000	14,000
Ending inventories	8,000	2,000	3,000	2,000	1,000
Sales—dollars	$217,000	$ 9,000	$60,000	$36,000	$112,000
Cost of goods sold:					
Joint production cost	$120,000	$ 4,800	$39,000	$21,000	$ 55,200
Further processing cost	50,000	2,000	10,000	10,000	28,000
Total	$170,000	$ 6,800	$49,000	$31,000	$ 83,200
Less ending inventory	22,227	680*	9,800	6,200	5,547
Cost of goods sold	$147,773	$ 6,120	$39,200	$24,800	$ 77,653
Gross profit	$ 69,227	$ 2,880	$20,800	$11,200	$ 34,347
Gross profit percentage	32%	32%	35%	31%	31%

* $6,800 production cost ÷ 20,000 units produced = $.34; $.34 × 2,000 units in ending inventory = $680.

The statement has often been made that all joint products should be equally profitable. To accomplish this, the sales value technique can be modified by using the overall gross profit percentage to determine the gross profit for each product. In the following table, the gross profit (32 percent) is deducted from the sales value to find the total cost, which is reduced by each product's further processing cost to find the joint cost allocation for each product.

	Total	A	B	C	D
Ultimate sales value	$250,000	$10,000	$75,000	$45,000	$120,000
Less 32% gross profit	80,000	3,200	24,000	14,400	38,400
Total cost	$170,000	$ 6,800	$51,000	$30,600	$ 81,600
Further processing cost	50,000	2,000	10,000	10,000	28,000
Joint cost	$120,000	$ 4,800	$41,000	$20,600	$ 53,600

If sales value, gross profit percentage, or further processing costs are estimated, the balance labeled "Joint cost" serves as the basis for allocating the actual joint cost to the four products.

Average Unit Cost Method

The **average unit cost method** attempts to apportion the total joint production cost among the various products on the basis of an average unit cost. The average unit cost is obtained by dividing the total number of units produced into the total joint production cost. Companies using this method argue that all products turned out by the same process should receive a proportionate share of the total joint production cost based on the number of units produced. As long as all units produced are measured in terms of the same unit and do not differ greatly, this method can be used without too much misgiving. When the units produced are not measured in like terms or the units differ markedly, the method should not be applied.

Using figures from the market value example, the average unit cost method can be illustrated as follows:

$$\frac{\text{Total joint production cost}}{\text{Total number of units produced}} = \frac{\$120,000}{60,000} = \$2 \text{ per unit}$$

Product	Units Produced	Apportionment of Joint Production Cost
A	20,000	$ 40,000
B	15,000	30,000
C	10,000	20,000
D	15,000	30,000
	60,000	$120,000

Weighted-Average Method

In many industries, the average unit cost method does not give a satisfactory answer to the joint cost apportionment problem because individual units of the various joint products differ markedly. For this reason, predetermined weight factors often are assigned to each unit, based on such factors as size of the unit, difficulty of manufacture, time consumed in making the unit, difference in type of labor employed, and amount of materials used. Finished production of every kind is multiplied by weight factors to apportion the total joint cost to individual units.

Using figures from the previous example, weight factors assigned to the four products might be as follows:

Product A— 3 points
Product B—12 points
Product C—13.5 points
Product D—15 points

The joint production cost allocation results in the following values:

Product	Units Produced	×	Points	=	Weighted Units	×	Cost Per Unit*	=	Apportionment of Joint Production Cost
A	20,000		3		60,000		$.20		$ 12,000
B	15,000		12		180,000		.20		36,000
C	10,000		13.5		135,000		.20		27,000
D	15,000		15		225,000		.20		45,000
					600,000				$120,000

$$^{*}\ \frac{\text{Total joint production cost}}{\text{Total number of weighted units}} = \frac{\$120,000}{600,000} = \$.20 \text{ per unit}$$

Quantitative Unit Method

The **quantitative unit method** attempts to distribute the total joint cost on the basis of some common unit of measurement, such as pounds, gallons, tons, or board feet. If the joint products are not measurable by the basic measurement unit, the joint units must be converted to a denominator common to all units produced. For instance, in the manufacture of coke, products such as coke, coal tar, benzol, sulfate of ammonia, and gas are measured in different units. The yield of these recovered units is measured on the basis of quantity of product extracted per ton of coal.

The following table illustrates the quantitative unit method, using weight as the basis for joint cost allocation.

Product	Yield in Pounds of Recovered Product per Ton of Coal	Distribution of Waste to Recovered Products	Revised Weight of Recovered Products	Cost of Each Product per Ton of Coal
Coke	1,320.0 lbs.	69.474 lbs.*	1,389.474 lbs.	$27.790**
Coal tar	120.0	6.316	126.316	2.526
Benzol	21.9	1.153	23.053	.461
Sulfate of ammonia	26.0	1.368	27.368	.547
Gas	412.1	21.689	433.789	8.676
Waste (water)	100.0			
Total	2,000.0 lbs.	100.000 lbs.	2,000.000 lbs.	$40.000

* [1,320 ÷ (2,000 - 100)] = 69.474

** (1,389.474 ÷ 2,000) × $40 = $27.790

The average unit cost, weighted average, and quantitative unit methods can result in product cost for one (or more) of the joint products that exceeds that product's market value. In that case, the product appears unprofitable and the other joint products appear profitable. Since the choice of costing method affects product cost and is an arbitrary choice, it is argued that a chosen method should not result in an artificial loss—that is, a loss for one joint product and a profit for another. A family of joint products is either all profitable or all unprofitable at the point of separation. Avoidance of the problem of artificially creating different rates of profitability for joint products is the widely touted virtue of the market value method. In other words, if an arbitrary allocation must be made, it should at least be neutral.

Federal Income Tax Laws and the Costing of Joint Products and By-Products

Federal income tax laws concerning the costing of joint products and by-products are not numerous. Legislators recognize the impossibility of establishing a specific code of law for every conceivable situation involving this type of cost problem. Consequently, the written pronouncement of the law does not precisely establish the boundaries of acceptable procedures. A digest of legal viewpoint is given in the Federal Income Tax Regulations, which state the following:

> *Inventories of miners and manufacturers.* A taxpayer engaged in mining or manufacturing who by a single process or uniform series of processes derives a product of two or more kinds, sizes, or grades, the unit cost of which is substantially alike, and who in conformity to a recognized trade practice allocates an amount of cost to each kind, size, or grade of product which in the aggregate will absorb the total cost of production, may, with the consent of the Commissioner (of the Internal Revenue Service), use such allocated cost as a basis for pricing inventories, provided such allocation bears a reasonable relation to the respective selling values of the different kinds, sizes, or grades of product.[3]

The quotation does not fully and unequivocally authorize the utilization of the market value method of costing joint products and by-products. The words "in conformity to a recognized trade practice" and "with the consent of the

[3] *Regulations,* Section 1.471-7.

Commissioner" clearly imply that the multiplicity of conceivable situations is far too great to be covered by definite rules that allow or prohibit a particular costing procedure.

Clearly, tax laws have not solved the problem of costing joint products and by-products for the accountant and the manufacturer. Tax officials find themselves in exactly the same predicament as any coke producer, petroleum refiner, or chemical manufacturer, even though their immediate objective may be limited to collecting a proper tax. The necessity of defining and interpreting accepted practices in a given industry proves, at least partially, that if the present income tax law on joint product and by-product costing—with its implication that the market value method is desirable—is unfair or manifestly inaccurate and illogical, it can and will be changed if industry and the accounting profession can offer better reasons for the use of other procedures.

Joint Cost Analysis for Managerial Decisions and Profitability Analysis

Joint cost allocation methods indicate forcefully that the amount of the cost to be apportioned to the numerous products emerging at the point of split-off is difficult to establish for any purpose. Furthermore, the acceptance of an allocation method for the assignment of the joint production cost does not solve the problem. The idea has been advanced that no attempt should be made to determine the cost of individual products up to the split-off point; rather, it seems important to calculate the profit margin in terms of total combined units. Of course, costs incurred after the split-off point provide management with information needed for decisions relating to the desirability of further processing to maximize profits.

Using the example from pages 191-193, assume that Product B, which has an ultimate market value of $75,000, alternatively could be sold for $60,000 at the split-off point, without further processing. The same example specifies that processing cost after split-off and traceable to Product B is $10,000. The difference in revenue of $15,000 ($75,000 – $60,000) minus the $10,000 after split-off cost results in a $5,000 positive contribution. This makes further processing appear to be a desirable option in this case. Furthermore, in the short run, any portion of the $10,000 cost that is fixed rather than variable adds to the contribution from further processing. But, in the long run, the margin of contribution (revenue minus variable cost) must be sufficient to recover fixed cost and provide a reasonable profit. Also, consideration should be given to nonquantifiable factors, such as the impact on employment, if further processing of a product is not carried out. Observe that, in any case, the allocated joint cost is not relevant to the decision.

Production of joint products is greatly influenced by both the technological characteristics of the processes and by the markets available for the products. The establishment of a product mix that is in harmony with customer demands appears profitable but often is physically impossible. It is interesting to note that cost accounting in the meat-packing industry serves primarily as a guide to buying, since aggregate sales realization values of the various products that are obtained from cutting operations are considered in determining the price that a packer is willing to pay for livestock. Sales realization values are also considered when a packer decides to sell hams or other cuts in a particular stage or to process them further.

A joint cost is often incurred for products that are either interchangeable or not associated with each other at all. Increasing the output of one will, in most joint cost cases, unavoidably increase to some extent the output of the other. Evaluation of output in joint cost situations falls into the category of the cost-volume-profit relationship and differential cost analysis (discussed in Chapters 20 and 21). The many alternative combinations of output can lead to time consuming computations. Often such evaluations are carried out on a computer with sophisticated simulation techniques. Developments in operations research procedures have provided techniques helpful in solving such problems (Chapter 21 discusses linear programming).

For profit planning, and perhaps as the only reliable measure of profitability, management should consider a product's **contribution margin** after separable or individual costs are deducted from sales. This contribution margin allows management to predict the amount that a segment or product line will add to or subtract from company profits. This margin is not the product's net profit figure. It only indicates relative profitability in comparison with other products. Net profit determined by allocating to segments an equitable share of all costs, both separable and joint, associated with the group of segments is not a reliable guide to profit planning decisions because these data cannot be used for predicting the outcome of decisions in terms of the change in aggregate net profit. For these reasons, attempts to allocate joint marketing cost to products and customers by time studies of salespersons' activities, as well as attempts to allocate the joint production cost, often yield results that are unreliable for appraising segment profitability.

Ethical Considerations

Ethical considerations require use of the joint cost allocation methods that most fairly represent financial results. The methods employed should not intentionally distort inventory cost, resulting in the manipulation of reported income and current assets.

The *Standards of Ethical Conduct for Management Accountants* presented in Chapter 1 are pertinent, especially the following standards regarding integrity and objectivity:[4]

Integrity:
- Refrain from either actively or passively subverting the attainment of the organization's legitimate and ethical objectives.
- Communicate unfavorable as well as favorable information and professional judgments or opinions.
- Refrain from engaging in or supporting any activity that would discredit the profession.

Objectivity:
- Communicate information fairly and objectively.
- Disclose fully all relevant information that could reasonably be expected to influence an intended user's understanding of the reports, comments, and recommendations presented.

[4] "Standards of Ethical Conduct for Management Accountants" (New York: Institute of Management Accountants (formerly National Association of Accountants), 1989).

Summary

Joint product costs arise from the simultaneous processing or manufacturing of products from the same process. For inventory costing, these costs can be allocated to by-products, which have relatively small value. They must, however, be allocated to joint products that have more than a nominal value. For financial reporting, several methods are used for costing by-products and joint products; however, the Internal Revenue Service states a preference for a market value method for income-tax purposes. Management should recognize the limited usefulness of arbitrary joint cost allocations in the analysis of individual products.

Key Terms

by-product *(184)*
main product *(184)*
joint products *(184)*
split-off point *(185)*
joint cost *(185)*
separable product costs *(185)*
gross revenue method *(187)*
net revenue method *(188)*
replacement cost method *(188)*
market value method *(189)*
average unit cost method *(193)*
quantitative unit method *(194)*
contribution margin *(197)*

Discussion Questions

Q8-1 Distinguish between joint products and by-products.

Q8-2 How can the revenue from the sale of by-products be shown on the income statement?

Q8-3 Does the inclusion of revenue from by-products on the income statement influence the unit cost of the main product?

Q8-4 By what method can production cost be relieved of the value of a by-product that can be further utilized in production processes? Explain.

Q8-5 By-products that require no additional processing after the point of separation are often accounted for by assigning to them a cost of zero at the point of separation and crediting the cost of production of the main product as sales are made.

(a) Justify this method of treating by-products.

(b) Discuss the possible shortcomings of the treatment. (AICPA adapted)

Q8-6 Are by-products ever charged with any cost? Explain.

Q8-7 Describe methods for allocating the total joint production cost to joint products.

Q8-8 Discuss the advantages and disadvantages of the market value and average unit cost methods of joint cost allocation.

Q8-9 When is it necessary to allocate joint costs to joint products?

Q8-10 Does the Internal Revenue Service prescribe any definite joint product or by-product cost allocation methods for tax purposes? Explain.

Q8-11 A logging company obtains its cost information by dividing total cost by the number of board feet of lumber produced. The company's president states that money is lost on every foot of low-grade lumber sold but is made up on the high grades. Appraise the statement.

Q8-12 In a decision about the further processing of joint products, what costs are relevant?

Exercises

E8-1 By-Product Costing—Net Revenue and Market Value (Reversal Cost) Methods. In the manufacture of its main product, the Welsh Company produces a by-product. Joint production cost incurred to the point of separation totals $200,000. After separation, cost of $150,000 is incurred to complete the main product, and $5,000 is incurred to complete the by-product. The main product has a final market value of $400,000, and the by-product has a final market value of $20,000. There is no ending inventory.

Required:

(1) Assume that the net revenue method is used to account for the by-product as other income and that the by-product's marketing and administrative expenses are zero. How much other income should be reported on the income statement?

(2) Assume that management wants to allocate $2,000 of marketing and administrative expenses to the by-product and still have a profit of 10% of the sales price. Using the market value (reversal cost) method, calculate how much of the joint cost should be allocated to the by-product.

E8-2 By-Product Costing—Market Value (Reversal Cost) Method. Logan Company manufactures one main product and two by-products, A and B. For April, the following data are available:

	Main Product	By-Product A	By-Product B	Total
Sales	$75,000	$6,000	$3,500	$84,500
Manufacturing cost after separation	$11,500	$1,100	$ 900	$13,500
Marketing and administrative expenses	6,000	750	550	7,300
Manufacturing cost before separation				37,500

Profit allowed for A and B is 15% and 12%, respectively.

Required:

(1) Calculate manufacturing cost before separation for by-products A and B, using the market value (reversal cost) method.

(2) Prepare an income statement, detailing sales and costs for each product.

E8-3 Joint Product Cost Allocation—Market Value Method. Navarre Corporation manufactures products W, X, Y, and Z from a joint process. Additional information follows:

Product	Units Produced	Market Value at Split-Off	If Processed Further: Additional Cost	If Processed Further: Market Value
W	6,000	$ 80,000	$ 7,500	$ 90,000
X	5,000	60,000	6,000	70,000
Y	4,000	40,000	4,000	50,000
Z	3,000	20,000	2,500	30,000
Total	18,000	$200,000	$20,000	$240,000

Required: Assuming that the market value method is used, allocate a share of the total joint production cost of $160,000 to each product. (AICPA adapted)

E8-4 Joint Product Cost Allocation—Market Value Method; By-Product Cost Allocation—Market Value (Reversal Cost) Method. Alba Company manufactures joint products X and Y as well as by-product Z. Cumulative joint cost data for the period show $204,000, representing 20,000 completed units processed through the Refining Department at an average cost of $10.20. Costs are assigned to X and Y by the market value method, which considers further processing costs in subsequent operations. To determine the cost allocation to Z, the market value (reversal cost) method is used. Additional data:

	Z	X	Y
Quantity processed	2,000 units	8,000 units	10,000 units
Sales price per unit	$6	$20	$25
Further processing cost per unit	2	5	7
Marketing and administrative expenses per unit	1	—	—
Operating profit per unit	1	—	—

Required: Compute the joint cost allocated to Z, then the amount to X and Y.

E8-5 Joint Product Cost Allocation—Market Value Method. The Escambia Company produces three products, E, S, and C, as the result of joint processing, which costs $150,000.

	E	S	C
Units produced	30,000	15,000	13,000
Separable processing costs	$30,000	$24,000	$27,000
Unit sales price	$ 4.30	$ 6.60	$ 6.00

Required:

(1) Allocate the joint cost to the three products using the market value method.

(2) Suppose that product S could be sold at the split-off point for $5.25. Would that be a good idea? Show calculations.

CGA-Canada (adapted). Reprint with permission.

E8-6 Joint Product Cost Allocation—Market Value Method. Boyd Company manufactures three products—A, B, and C—as a result of a joint process. During October, joint processing costs totaled $288,000. Details regarding each of the three products show:

	Product		
	A	B	C
Units produced	1,000	3,000	5,000
Units sold	800	2,500	4,300
Further processing costs	$25,000	$60,000	$105,000
Sales price per unit	$ 100	$ 80	$ 50

Required:

(1) Compute the cost assigned to the ending inventory of each product and in total, using the market value method for joint product cost allocation. There were no units in finished goods on October 1.

(2) Customers have been found who would be willing to buy all of the output of each product at the split-off point for the following prices: A, $60; B, $65; and C, $25. Show which of the products should be sold at the split-off point.

(3) Would your answer to requirement 2 change if Product B's further processing cost of $60,000 included $18,000 of allocated fixed costs? Why or why not?

(4) Now suppose the $60,000 cost of B's further processing includes $18,000 of allocated fixed costs, and the facilities that would be used to further process B have an alternative use. If B is not processed further, the alternative use of these facilities will generate revenues of $6,000 and variable costs of $1,000. Should B be processed further?

CGA-Canada (adapted.) Reprint with permission.

E8-7 Joint Product Allocation—Average Unit Cost and Market Value Methods. Scott Company manufactures three products, A, B, and C, from a joint process. The joint costs for January total $100,000. Additional January information follows:

Product	Quantity	Processing Cost after Split-Off	Ultimate Market Value
A	3,000	$20,000	$ 60,000
B	4,000	30,000	110,000
C	3,000	50,000	90,000

Required:

(1) Compute the total production cost for each product, using the average unit cost method.

(2) Compute the total production cost for each product, using the market value method.

E8-8 Joint Product Cost Allocation. Jackson Inc. produces four joint products having a manufacturing cost of $70,000 at the split-off point. Data pertinent to these products follow:

Product	Units Produced	Ultimate Market Value per Unit	Processing Cost after Split-Off	Weight Factors
K	5,000	$5.50	$1,500	3.0 points
L	20,000	1.60	3,000	2.0 points
M	15,000	1.50	2,500	4.0 points
N	10,000	3.00	5,000	2.5 points

Required: Allocate joint products cost using:
(1) The average unit cost method.
(2) The weighted average method.
(3) The market value method.

E8-9 Joint Product Cost Allocation—Weighted-Average Method. A department's production schedule shows 10,000 units of X and 8,000 units of Y. Both articles are made from the same raw materials, but units of X and Y require estimated quantities of materials in the ratio of 3:2, respectively. Both articles pass through the same conversion process, but X and Y require estimated production times per unit in the ratio of 5:4, respectively.

Required: Compute the unit materials and conversion costs for each product if the total costs are: materials, $92,000; conversion cost, $123,000.

Problems

P8-1 Joint Product Cost Allocation—Average Unit Cost and Market Value Methods. Sage Products Company produces three products from a joint source. A single raw material is introduced into Process I from which products A, B, and C emerge. Product A is considered to be a by-product and is sold immediately after split-off. Products B and C are processed further in Process II and Process III, respectively, before they are sold as Butine and Cantol.

Production costs for February are as follows:

Process I (24 000 kg of raw materials)	$ 590,000
Process II	580,000
Process III	720,000
Total production cost	$1,890,000

The number of units (kg) of product produced and sold in February is as follows:

	Process I	Process II	Process III	Units Sold
Product A	4 000 kg	—	—	4 000 kg
Product B	10 000 kg	10 000 kg	—	9 000 kg (Butine)
Product C	10 000 kg	—	10 000 kg	9 500 kg (Cantol)

The average price per unit sold in February for each of the products is as follows:

Product A	$ 15 per kg
Butine	130
Cantol	120

There were no inventories of intermediate products B and C at the beginning or end of February and there was no waste or spoilage in any of the processes. The by-product is not accounted for separately; instead, revenue from sales of the by-product is treated as a deduction from joint cost.

Required:

(1) Calculate the cost of the finished goods inventories if the average unit cost method of joint cost allocation is used.

(2) Calculate the value of cost of goods sold if the market value method of joint cost allocation is used. Round allocated joint cost to the nearest one thousand dollars.

(3) The company controller argues that the market value method of allocation is the most accurate way to allocate joint cost. The president replies that the average unit cost method is simpler and easier to understand, especially if he has to make a decision about whether to drop a product or continue to process it. The controller claims that using the market value method to analyze a drop or continue decision would be better. Respond to both the president's and controller's comments, and briefly explain the reasons for allocating joint cost. (SMAC adapted)

P8-2 Joint Product Cost Allocation—Market Value Method. Hamilton Company produces three products jointly. During May, joint costs totaled $200,000. The following individual product information is available:

	Product C	Product L	Product T
Production	15,000	10,000	20,000
Sales units	13,000	9,000	16,000
Sales price	$ 20.00	$ 15.00	$ 9.50
Separable processing cost	$75,000	$25,000	$40,000

Required:

(1) Compute the May gross profit, for each product and in total, using the market value allocation method.

(2) A customer has offered to buy all of Product T output at the split-off point for $7 per unit. Advise the Hamilton management.

P8-3 Cost Allocation—Joint Products and By-Product. Brooks Corporation produces three products, Alpha, Beta, and Gamma. Alpha and Gamma are joint products; Beta is a by-product of Alpha. No joint cost is to be allocated to the by-product. The production processes for a given year are as follows:

(a) In Department 1, 110,000 pounds of material Rho are processed, at a total cost of $120,000. After processing, 60% of the units are transferred to Department 2, and 40% of the units (now Gamma) are transferred to Department 3.

(b) In Department 2, the material is further processed at a total additional cost of $38,000. Seventy percent of the units (now Alpha) are transferred to Department 4 and 30% emerge as Beta, the by-product, to be sold at $1.20 per pound. The marketing expense related to Beta is $8,100.

(c) In Department 4, Alpha is processed at a total additional cost of $23,660. After processing, Alpha is ready for sale at $5 per pound.

(d) In Department 3, Gamma is processed at a total additional cost of $165,000. In this department, a normal loss of units of Gamma occurs, which equals 10% of the good output of Gamma. The remaining good output is sold for $12 per pound.

Required:

(1) Prepare a schedule showing the allocation of the $120,000 joint cost between Alpha and Gamma, using the market value at split-off point and treating the net realizable value of Beta as an addition to the sales value of Alpha.

(2) Prepare a statement of gross profit for Alpha, independent of the answer to requirement 1, assuming that:
   (a) $102,000 of total joint cost is appropriately allocated to Alpha.
   (b) 48,000 pounds of Alpha and 20,000 pounds of Beta are available for sale.
   (c) During the year, sales of Alpha were 80% of the pounds available for sale. There was no beginning inventory.
   (d) The net realizable value of Beta available for sale is to be deducted from the cost of producing Alpha. The ending inventory of Alpha is to be based on the net cost of production.
   (e) All other costs, sales prices, and marketing expenses are those presented in the facts of the original problem. (AICPA adapted)

P8-4 Joint Product Cost Allocation—Same Gross Profit Percentage for Each Joint Product. Lond Company produces joint products Jana and Reta, together with by-product Bynd. Jana is sold at split-off, but Reta and Bynd undergo additional processing. Production data pertaining to these products for the year ended December 31, 19A are as follows:

	Jana	Reta	Bynd	Total
Joint costs:				
Variable				$ 88,000
Fixed				148,000
Separable costs:				
Variable		$120,000	$ 3,000	123,000
Fixed		90,000	2,000	92,000
Production in pounds	50,000	40,000	10,000	100,000
Sales price per pound	$ 4.00	$ 7.50	$ 1.10	

There are no beginning or ending inventories. No materials are spoiled in production. Variable costs change in direct proportion to production volume. Joint costs are allocated to joint products to achieve the same gross profit percentage for each joint product. Net revenue from by-product Bynd is deducted from production costs of the main products.

Required:

(1) Compute the total gross profit for the joint products.
(2) Allocate the joint costs to Jana and Reta.
(3) Compute the gross profit for Jana and for Reta. (AICPA adapted)

P8-5 Cost Allocation—Joint Products and By-Product. Alderon Industries is a manufacturer of chemicals for various purposes. One of the processes used by Alderon produces SPL-3, a chemical used in swimming pools; PST-4, a chemical used in pesticides; and RJ-5, a by-product that is sold to fertilizer manufacturers. Alderon uses the market value of its main products to allocate joint production costs, and the fifo inventory method to cost the main products. The by-product is inventoried at its market value less its disposal cost, and this value is used to reduce the joint production cost before allocation to the main products.

Data regarding Alderon's November operations are presented in the following table. During this month, Alderon incurred joint production cost of $1,702,000 in the manufacture of SPL-3, PST-4, and RJ-5.

	SPL-3	PST-4	RJ-5
Finished goods inventory in gallons (November 1)	18,000	52,000	3,000
November sales in gallons	650,000	325,000	150,000
November production in gallons	700,000	350,000	170,000
Sales value per gallon at split-off	—	—	$ .70*
Additional processing cost	$874,000	$816,000	—
Final sales value per gallon	$ 4.00	$ 6.00	—

* Disposal costs of $ .10 per gallon, which are incurred in order to sell the product, have not been deducted to arrive at this sales value.

Required:

(1) Determine Alderon Industries' allocation of joint production cost for November.
(2) Compute the cost assigned to the finished goods inventories for SPL-3, PST-4, and RJ-5 as of November 30.
(3) Alderon Industries has an opportunity to sell PST-4 at the split-off point for $3.80 per gallon. Prepare an analysis showing whether Alderon should sell PST-4 at the split-off point or continue to process this product further. (ICMA adapted)

P8-6 Cost of Production Report—Average and Fifo Process Costing Methods; Joint Products and By-Product. The following data appear in the records of Rodomontade Company for February:

	Process		
	1	2	3
Unit data:			
Beginning work in process inventory (⅓ complete in Processes 2 and 3)	—	3,000	3,000
Started or received	32,000	10,000	20,000
	32,000	13,000	23,000

	Process 1	Process 2	Process 3
Transferred to Process 2	10,000		
Transferred to Process 3	20,000		
Transferred to finished goods storeroom	—	9,000	20,000
Transferred out as by-product	2,000		
Normal loss	—	—	1,000
Ending work in process inventory (¼ complete in Process 2 and ½ complete in Process 3)	—	4,000	2,000
	32,000	13,000	23,000
Partial summary of costs:			
Beginning work in process inventory			
Transferred from process 1		$ 6,000	$11,500
Labor and factory overhead	—	2,000	3,000
Cost added by department:			
Materials	$58,000	—	—
Labor and factory overhead	30,000	18,000	60,000
	$88,000		
Less market value of by-product	4,000		
	$84,000		

Materials are issued in Process 1. At the end of processing in Process 1, the by-product appears. The balance of production is transferred out—some to Process 2 for additional processing of one main product and the rest to Process 3 for additional processing of the other main product.

The joint cost of Process 1, less the market value of the by-product, is apportioned to the main products using the market value method at the split-off point. Sales prices for the finished products of Processes 2 and 3 are $10 and $15, respectively. The by-product sells for $2.

Required:

(1) Prepare a departmental cost of production report for February, assuming that the company uses the average costing method. (Carry unit cost computations to four decimal places and round off multiplications to the nearest dollar.)

(2) Using computations from requirement 1, prepare journal entries transferring cost from each of the three processes.

(3) Repeat requirement 1, assuming that the company uses the fifo costing method and that the normal loss in Process 3 is from units transferred in during February.

(4) Using computations from requirement 3, prepare journal entries transferring cost from each of the three processes.

Cases

C8-1 Joint Cost Allocation—Market Value Method. Minimax Corporation is a chemical manufacturer that produces two main products, Pepco-1 and Repke-3, and a by-product, SE-5, from a joint process. If Minimax had the proper facilities, it could process SE-5 further into a main product. The ratio of output quantities to input quantity of direct material used in the joint process remains consistent with the processing conditions and activity level.

Minimax currently uses the quantitative method of allocating joint costs to the main products. The fifo inventory method is used to cost the main products. The by-product is inventoried at its net revenue, and this figure is used to reduce the joint production costs before the joint costs are allocated to the main products.

Jim Simpson, Minimax's controller, wants to implement the market value method of joint cost allocation. He believes that inventoriable cost should be based on each product's ability to contribute to the recovery of joint production cost. The market value of the by-product would be treated in the manner it is treated under the quantitative method.

Data regarding Minimax's operations for November follow. The joint cost of production amounts to $2,640,000 for November.

	Main Products		By-Product
	Pepco-1	Repke-3	SE-5
Finished goods inventory in gallons on November 1	20,000	40,000	10,000
November sales in gallons	800,000	700,000	200,000
November production in gallons	900,000	720,000	240,000
Sales value per gallon at split-off point	$ 2.00	$ 1.50	$ .55*
Additional processing cost after split-off	$1,800,000	$720,000	—
Final sales value per gallon	$ 5.00	$ 4.00	—

* Marketing costs of $.05 per gallon will be incurred in order to sell the by-product.

Required:

(1) Describe the market value method and explain how it accomplishes Jim Simpson's objective.

(2) Assuming Minimax Corporation adopts the market value method for internal reporting purposes:

(a) Calculate how the joint production cost for November is allocated.

(b) Determine the cost assigned to finished goods inventories for Pepco-1, Repke-3, and SE-5 as of November 30.

(3) Minimax Corporation plans to expand its production facilities to enable the further processing of SE-5 into a main product. Discuss how the allocation of the joint production cost under the market value method will change when SE-5 becomes a main product. (ICMA adapted)

C8-2 Costing Joint Products. Hayes Products Company produces three products, X, Y, and Z, from a single joint process. The company uses the average unit cost method for allocating the joint production cost. Some spoilage normally occurs in the joint process, but the company also has been experiencing some unexpected spoilage in the separable process to Product Y. In costing the three products for sale, all spoilage costs, together with joint and separable process costs, are included in product cost.

Over the past year, the company has been losing money on Product Z. Sentiments are mixed as to whether to drop Z or make modifications. The controller is convinced that the entire costing system needs to be revised and she has hired a consultant to present a proposal for a cost study.

Required: As the consultant, prepare a brief proposal for Hayes Products Company, outlining the aspects of its product costing that need to be reviewed. Explain why the areas cited need to be studied.

(SMAC adapted)

C8-3 Joint Cost Analysis for Managerial Decisions. Talor Chemical Company is a highly diversified chemical processing company. The company manufactures swimming pool chemicals, chemicals for metal processing companies, specialized chemical compounds for other companies, and a full line of pesticides and insecticides.

Currently, the Noorwood plant is producing two derivatives, RNA-1 and RNA-2, from the chemical compound VDB, developed by Talor's research labs. Each week 1,200,000 pounds of VDB are processed at a cost of $246,000 into 800,000 pounds of RNA-1 and 400,000 pounds of RNA-2. The proportion of these two outputs from this joint process is fixed and cannot be altered. RNA-1 has no market value until it is converted into a product with the trade name Fastkil. The cost to process RNA-1 into Fastkil is $240,000. Fastkil wholesales at $50 per 100 pounds.

RNA-2 is sold as is for $80 per hundred pounds. However, Talor has discovered that RNA-2 can be converted into two new products through further processing. The further processing requires the addition of 400,000 pounds of compound LST to the 400,000 pounds of RNA-2. This additional joint process yields 400,000 pounds each of DMZ-3 and Pestrol—the two new products. The additional raw materials and related processing costs are $120,000. DMZ-3 and Pestrol can each be sold for $57.50 per 100 pounds. Talor management has decided not to process RNA-2 further, based on the preceding analysis. Talor uses the average unit cost method to allocate costs arising from joint processing.

A new staff accountant, after reviewing the analysis, comments that it should be revised, stating: "Product costing of products such as these should be done on a market value basis, not an average unit cost basis."

Required:

(1) Discuss whether the use of the market value method provides data that are more relevant for the decision to market DMZ-3 and Pestrol.

(2) Critique Talor's analysis and make any revisions that are necessary. The critique and analysis should indicate:

(a) Whether Talor Chemical Company made the correct decision.

(b) What the gross savings (loss) per week will be as a result of Talor's decision not to process RNA-2 further, if different from the company-prepared analysis. (ICMA adapted)

	Sell as RNA-2	Process Further DMZ-3	Process Further Pestrol	Total
Production in pounds	400,000	400,000	400,000	
Revenue	$320,000	$230,000	$230,000	$460,000
Costs:				
VDB cost*	$ 82,000	$ 61,500	$ 61,500	$123,000
Additional raw materials (LST) and processing of RNA-2		60,000	60,000	120,000
Total cost	$ 82,000	$121,500	$121,500	$243,000
Weekly gross profit	$238,000	$108,500	$108,500	$217,000

* If RNA-2 is sold as is, the allocation basis is 1,200,000 pounds; if RNA-2 is processed further, the allocation basis is 1,600,000 pounds for VDB cost.

C8-4 Ethics. An internal auditor, George Vickery, has been assigned to test the pricing of the finished goods inventory for a subsidiary that manufactures a variety of digital watches in a common facility. Total manufacturing costs are allocated to the various finished goods stock items using the market value method. This method is supported by the notion that there should be some relationship between a product's cost and its sales price. Furthermore, IRS regulations permit this approach.

Vickery has found a wide sales price range for the watches. Yet, his observation of the manufacturing process indicates that all types of watches are almost identical except for the brand names by which they are sold and variations in the watch cases. The watch case variations do not represent cost differences.

Vickery also notes that the inventory contains an inordinate proportion of higher priced watches. These proportions do not match well with recent sales patterns or mix. He believes that allocation of joint cost based on an average unit cost method—that is assigning the same cost per unit to each watch—seems more reasonable than using the market value method.

This change would significantly lower inventory and profits for the audit year. He has proposed an adjusting entry to restate inventory, using the average unit cost method. He is opposed by the company controller, who supports using the market value method. As Vickery persists, he is informed that the struggling subsidiary has a bank loan stipulating a required current ratio and reported profit, which will be violated if the adjusting entry is made. The controller also points out that ownership will react unfavorably to a lower reported profit and, more personally, that the controller and other management personnel will not only lose their annual bonuses, but will face a threat to their jobs as well, if the internal auditors insist on making the adjusting entry.

Required:

(1) Which of the 15 responsibilities in the *Standards of Ethical Conduct for Management Accountants* apply to Vickery's situation?

(2) In addition to ethical responsibilities to his company, what other ethical responsibilities does Vickery have to consider?

PART 3

Planning and Control of Costs

CHAPTER 9

Materials: Controlling, Costing, and Planning

Learning Objectives

After studying this chapter, you will be able to:

1. Describe a system of materials procurement and use.
2. Identify the components of the cost of acquiring materials.
3. Define and calculate economic order quantity.
4. Define and calculate the order point.
5. Define and calculate safety stock.
6. Describe the ABC plan for inventory control.

Part 1 of this textbook presented cost concepts and objectives. Part 2 illustrated cost accumulation methods. Part 3 deals with the planning and control of costs, beginning with this chapter on materials.

Effective materials management is essential for providing the best service to customers, for producing efficiently, and for controlling the investment in inventories. Successful materials management requires the development of a system involving sales forecasting, purchasing, receiving, storage, production, and shipping. This chapter concerns environments in which the just-in-time philosophy has not been fully implemented; it discusses materials procurement and use and quantitative models for materials planning and control. Just-in-time inventory environments are the subject of Chapter 10.

Materials Procurement and Use

Although production processes and materials requirements vary according to a firm's size and industry, the procurement and use of materials usually involve the following steps:

1. For each product or product variation, engineering determines the **routing** for each product, which is the sequence of operations to be performed, and establishes the **bill of materials**, which is the list of materials requirements for each step in the sequence.
2. The **production budget** provides the master plan from which details concerning materials requirements are developed.
3. The **purchase requisition** informs the purchasing agent of the quantity and kind of materials needed.
4. The **purchase order** contracts for quantities to be delivered.

5. The **receiving report** certifies quantities received and may report results of inspection and quality testing.
6. The **materials requisition** (introduced in Chapter 5) authorizes the storeroom or warehouse to deliver specified types and quantities of materials to a given department at a specified time.
7. The **materials record cards** (also introduced in Chapter 5) record each receipt and issuance of each kind of material and serve as perpetual inventory records.

Materials procurement and use involve all the electronic or hard-copy records necessary for general financial accounting; for costing a job, process, or department; and for maintaining perpetual inventories. Some of these records are identified in Figure 9-1, which diagrams the procurement phase—purchasing, receiving, recording, and paying for materials.

FIGURE 9-1 ***Flowchart for Purchasing, Receiving, Recording, and Paying for Materials***

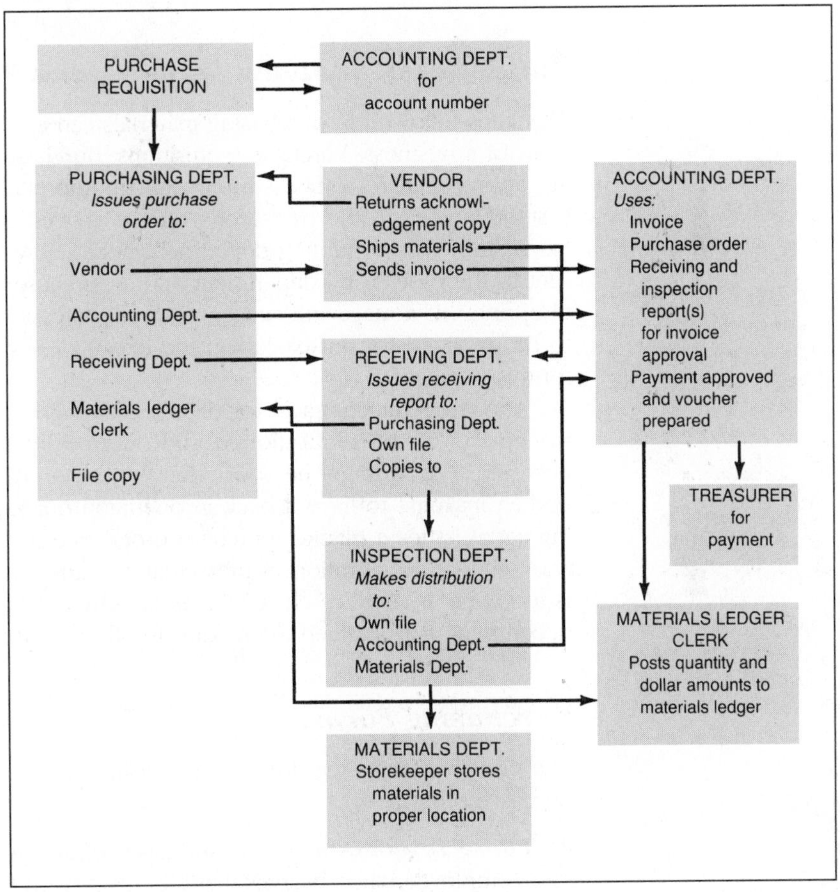

Purchase of Materials

Purchases of materials usually are made by the purchasing department, headed by a general purchasing agent. (In smaller companies and in settings described in Chapter 10, department heads or supervisors have authority to purchase materials as needed.) Purchasing procedures should be in writing, to fix responsibility and to provide information regarding the ultimate use of materials ordered.

The purchasing department (1) receives purchase requisitions for materials, supplies, and equipment; (2) keeps informed concerning sources of supply, prices, and shipping and delivery schedules; (3) prepares and places purchase orders; and (4) arranges for reporting among the purchasing, receiving, and accounting departments. An additional function of the purchasing department in some enterprises is to verify and approve for payment the invoices received from vendors; this has the advantage of centralizing the approval of invoices in the department that originates purchases and that has complete information concerning items and quantities ordered, prices, terms, shipping instructions, and other conditions. However, invoice approval by the purchasing department lessens internal control if the same individual prepares an order and later approves the invoice. Consequently, invoice audit and approval in many firms are functions of the accounting department; the purchase order then contains all necessary information regarding price, discounts agreement, and delivery terms, as well as the account number to be charged.

Purchases of Supplies, Services, and Repairs

The steps followed in purchasing materials can apply to all departments and divisions of a business. Purchase requisitions, purchase orders, and receiving reports are appropriate for office supplies and equipment, the company cafeteria, the first-aid unit, and the treasurer's office, as well as all other departments. For example, if the accounting department needs new forms printed, a requisition is sent to the purchasing department and a purchase order is prepared and sent to the printer. If a magazine subscription or professional association membership is to be provided for an executive, the executive's superior prepares a requisition for this purchase.

Annual repair contracts for data processing equipment and for some factory machinery can be requisitioned and ordered in the same manner. Sometimes, however, a department head or other employee may need to obtain service on a broken machine to have it back in operation quickly. In such cases, the purchasing agent issues a blanket purchase order, one that covers all costs of a specific type without specification of the actual amount that will be charged. When a bill is received, the invoice clerk verifies the amount of the bill with the head of the department that obtained the repairs and then approves the invoice for payment.

Purchasing Forms

The principal forms required in purchasing are the purchase requisition and the purchase order.

Purchase Requisition. The purchase requisition originates with (1) a storeroom employee who observes that the quantity on hand is at a set ordering point, (2) a materials record clerk responsible for notifying the purchasing agent when to buy, (3) a research, engineering, or other department employee or supervisor who needs materials of a special nature, or (4) a computer programmed to alert the purchasing department when replenishment is needed. One copy of each purchase requisition remains with the originator, and the original is sent to the purchasing department for execution of the request. The records can be electronic or hard copy. For standard materials, the requisition may indicate only the stock number of an item. It is then up to the purchasing agent to use judgment and established policy concerning sources and quantities. For nonstandard purchase requests, blueprints, catalog numbers, weights, standards, brand names, exact quantities, and suggested prices may need to be included with the purchase requisition.

Purchase Order. The purchase order, signed by the purchasing agent or other official, is authorization to a vendor to supply specified quantities of described goods at agreed terms and at a designated time and place. As a convenience, the vendor's order forms can be used. In typical practice, however, the order forms are prepared by the purchasing company, and the form is adapted to the particular needs of the purchaser. For accounting control, a purchase order can be issued for every purchase of materials, supplies, or equipment. When a purchase commitment is made by mail or telephone or through a sales representative, the purchase order serves as confirmation of the commitment.

The purchase order gives the vendor a description of the goods and services desired, as well as terms, prices, and shipping instructions. The description can refer to attached blueprints and specifications. The original and an acknowledgment copy are sent to the vendor, and other copies are distributed as shown in Figure 9-1. The vendor signs and returns the acknowledgment copy to indicate that the order is accepted.

Electronic Data Interchange. Electronic data interchange (EDI) is the exchange of transaction information between a computer in one company and the computer in another. It is a step toward achieving a paperless business environment by eliminating many hard-copy documents. Examples of information transferable by EDI are purchase orders, invoices, cash transfers to suppliers' banks, and updates on the status of an order or the location of a shipment. EDI is discussed in greater depth later in this chapter and in Chapter 10.

Receiving

The receiving department (1) unloads and unpacks incoming materials, (2) compares quantities received with the shipper's packing list, (3) matches materials received with descriptions on purchase orders, (4) prepares receiving reports, (5) notifies the purchasing department of discovered discrepancies, (6) arranges for inspection when necessary, (7) notifies the traffic department and the purchasing department of any damage in transit, and (8) routes accepted materials to the appropriate location.

The receiving report shows the purchase order number, the account number to be charged, the name of the vendor, details relating to transportation, and the quantity and type of goods received. It also provides a space for the inspection department to note either approval of the shipment or the quantity rejected and reason for rejection.

If materials are not inspected immediately on receipt, the receiving report is distributed as follows: (1) the receiving department keeps one copy and sends another to the purchasing department as notice of the materials' arrival, (2) all other copies go to the inspection department and are distributed after inspection. When inspection is completed, one copy is sent to the accounting department where it is matched with the purchase order and vendor's invoice, and the invoice is paid. Other copies are sent to appropriate departments, such as materials control and production planning. One copy is sent to the storeroom with the materials. Alternatively, receiving report data can be entered electronically, either at a keyboard or by an optical scanning device. The data then are automatically transferred to all appropriate recipients.

Invoice Approval and Data Processing

Invoice approval is important in materials control because it verifies that the goods have been received as ordered and that payment can be made. By the time materials reach the receiving department, the company usually will have received an invoice from the vendor. The invoice and a copy of the purchase order are filed in the accounting department. When the receiving report and inspection report arrive, the receiving report, purchase order, and invoice are compared as to kind of material, quantity, price, discounts, credit terms, shipping instructions, and other conditions. If the invoice is correct (or is corrected by a debit or credit memorandum for rejects, shortage, overage, and so on), the invoice clerk approves it and attaches it to the purchase order and receiving report for preparation of a voucher. Voucher data are journalized, posted to the subsidiary records, and entered in the cash payments journal according to the payment due date. Purchase transactions affect control accounts and subsidiary records, as shown in Exhibit 9-1.

EXHIBIT 9-1 ***Effects of Purchase Transactions on Accounts***

	General Ledger Control		
Transaction	**Debit**	**Credit**	**Subsidiary Records**
Materials purchased for stock	Materials	Accounts Payable	Entry in the Received section of the materials ledger record
Materials purchased for a particular job or department	Work in Process	Accounts Payable	Entry in the Direct Materials section of the production report or job order cost sheet
Materials and supplies purchased for factory overhead purposes	Materials	Accounts Payable	Entry in the Received section of the materials ledger record
Supplies purchased for marketing and administrative offices	Materials Marketing Expenses Control Administrative Expenses Control	Accounts Payable	Entry in the Received section of the materials ledger record or in the proper columns of the marketing or administrative expense analysis sheets
Purchases of services or repairs	Factory Overhead Marketing Expenses Control Administrative Expenses Control	Accounts Payable	Entry in the proper account columns of the expense analysis sheets
Purchases of equipment	Equipment	Accounts Payable	Entry on the equipment ledger record

The original voucher and two copies are sent to the treasurer for issuance of a check. The treasurer mails the check and original voucher to the vendor, files one copy of the voucher, and returns the other copy to the accounting department for the vendor's file.

When invoice data are received in an EDP system, an accounts payable clerk determines the account numbers to be charged and enters them at a terminal. If purchase orders include these account numbers, the system performs this step automatically by retrieving the account numbers from the computer file of purchase orders. The data are matched with purchase order and receiving report data; the common matching criterion on all documents is the purchase order number. Quantities, dollar amounts, due dates, terms, and unit prices are compared and reconciled. When in agreement, the cost data are entered into the accounts payable file (and listings in journal form are produced, as needed). Alternatively, payment can be made immediately by means of EDI or a computer-generated check. The receiving data are posted to materials subsidiary records; these postings and those for materials issuances are processed electronically to eliminate manual posting.

Cost of Acquiring Materials

The vendor's invoice price and transportation charges are the most visible costs of purchased goods. Less obvious are what may be called acquisition costs—the costs of performing the functions of purchasing, receiving, unpacking, inspecting, insuring, storing, and accounting. Practical limitations affect the treatment of these costs, because adjusting each invoice for all acquisition costs involves efforts that may outweigh the benefit of accurate cost measurement. Therefore, materials are commonly carried at the invoice price paid to the vendor, and acquisition costs and price adjustments are treated as factory overhead.

Purchases Discounts. Trade discounts and quantity discounts normally are not entered into any accounting records. Instead they are treated as price reductions. That is, the price paid to the vendor is originally recorded net of these discounts. Although the nature of a cash discount is similar, the amount charged to Materials often is determined before any deduction of cash discounts, and Cash Discounts is credited; this avoids the necessity of computing a cash discount on each materials item.

Freight-In. Freight-in is clearly a cost of materials, but practical difficulties can arise in accounting for it. Suppose a vendor's invoice for $600 shows 25 items, weighing 1,700 pounds, shipped in five crates, with a freight bill for $48. The delivered cost is $648. But how much of the freight is attributable to each of the invoice items, and what unit price should go on the materials record card? When the purchased units are few and have large unit costs, each item's actual amount of freight may be determinable from rates quoted by the carrier; otherwise, some expedient procedure is necessary.

If freight charges are included in the general ledger debit to Materials, then freight cost can be added proportionately to each materials record card. This can be done by assigning each dollar of materials cost an equal portion of the freight; in other words, by allocating freight cost on the basis of materials cost. For example, freight of $48 on materials costing $600 would add 8% ($48 ÷ $600) to the cost of each item. Alternatively, the weight of each item on the invoice might be determined and used as the basis for allocating freight cost. If an item weighs 300 pounds, then $8.47 of freight cost ((300 ÷ 1,700) × $48) would be added to its invoice cost.

A less cumbersome alternative is to charge all freight-in costs to an account entitled Freight-In and record only the invoice cost as the cost of materials. As materials are issued for production, an applied rate for freight charges is then added to the unit cost on the materials record cards; this amount is included in the debit to Work in Process (for direct materials) or Factory Overhead Control (for indirect materials), and Freight-In is credited. Any balance in Freight-In at the end of a period is closed to Cost of Goods Sold or prorated to Cost of Goods Sold and ending inventories.

A third approach is to include the total freight-in cost of the period in computing the factory overhead rate for the period. Freight-In then is one of the subsidiary accounts controlled by Factory Overhead Control. For materials or supplies used in marketing and administrative departments, freight is charged to Marketing Expenses or to Administrative Expenses.

Applied Acquisition Costs. If materials cost is to include acquisition costs, an applied rate can be added to each invoice and to each item, instead of charging these costs to factory overhead. A single rate for these costs can be used, or separate rates for each class of costs as follows:

$$\frac{\text{Estimated purchasing department cost for budget period}}{\text{Estimated number of purchases or estimated amount of purchases}} = \text{Rate per purchase or rate per dollar purchased}$$

$$\frac{\text{Estimated receiving department cost for budget period}}{\text{Estimated number of items to be received during period}} = \text{Rate per item}$$

$$\frac{\text{Estimated materials department cost for budget period}}{\text{Estimated number of items, feet of space, dollar value, etc.}} = \text{Rate per item, cubic foot, dollar value, etc.}$$

$$\frac{\text{Estimated applicable accounting department cost for budget period}}{\text{Estimated number of transactions}} = \text{Rate per transaction}$$

The logic of this approach is the same as that of activity costing, as discussed in Chapter 14. This procedure results in the following accounting treatment:

Materials (or Work In Process)	xxx	
Applied Purchasing Department Costs		xxx
Applied Receiving Department Costs		xxx
Applied Materials Department Costs		xxx
Applied Accounting Department Costs		xxx

For each department involved, actual costs incurred are debited to the applied account for that department. At the end of a period, the difference between costs incurred and amounts applied represents over- or underapplied costs; it is closed to Cost of Goods Sold or prorated to Cost of Goods Sold and ending inventories.

Inventory Costing for Income Tax Purposes. The Tax Reform Act of 1986 included new inventory costing requirements.[1] The uniform capitalization rules require inclusion in inventory of certain costs that previously could be expensed. Many categories of costs, such as rework labor, scrap and spoilage, materials procurement, warehousing and handling, factory administration, office salaries related to production services, and depreciation in excess of the amount calculated for financial reporting, now must be inventoried for tax purposes. Generally, these costs are capitalizable for financial reporting purposes as well, with the exceptions of excess depreciation and conditions where rework labor, scrap, and spoilage represent losses.

Storage and Use of Materials

Materials and a copy of the receiving report are forwarded to the storeroom from the receiving or inspection department. The storekeeper is responsible for safeguarding materials, placing them in bins or other spaces until needed, and seeing

[1] *Internal Revenue Code of 1986*, Section 263A.

that all materials taken from the storeroom are properly requisitioned. Admittance to the storeroom usually is tightly restricted, with materials being issued through cage windows.

Issuing and Costing Materials

In addition to effective purchasing, receiving, storing, and record keeping, the control of materials requires a system for issuing materials.

Materials Requisition. The materials requisition authorizes the storekeeper to issue materials. It is drawn by a production control clerk, department head, supervisor, group leader, or expediter. It is distinguished from the purchase requisition used to initiate an order to a vendor discussed earlier.

The materials requisition is used to withdraw materials from the storeroom. It is the source document for entries in the issued section of materials record cards, the direct-materials section of job order cost sheets (see Chapter 5) or departmental cost of production reports (see Chapter 6), and the departmental overhead analysis sheets. All withdrawals result in summary credits to Materials and summary debits to Work in Process, Factory Overhead Control, Marketing Expenses, or Administrative Expenses. A materials requisition is illustrated in Figure 9-2.

FIGURE 9-2 ***Materials Requisition***

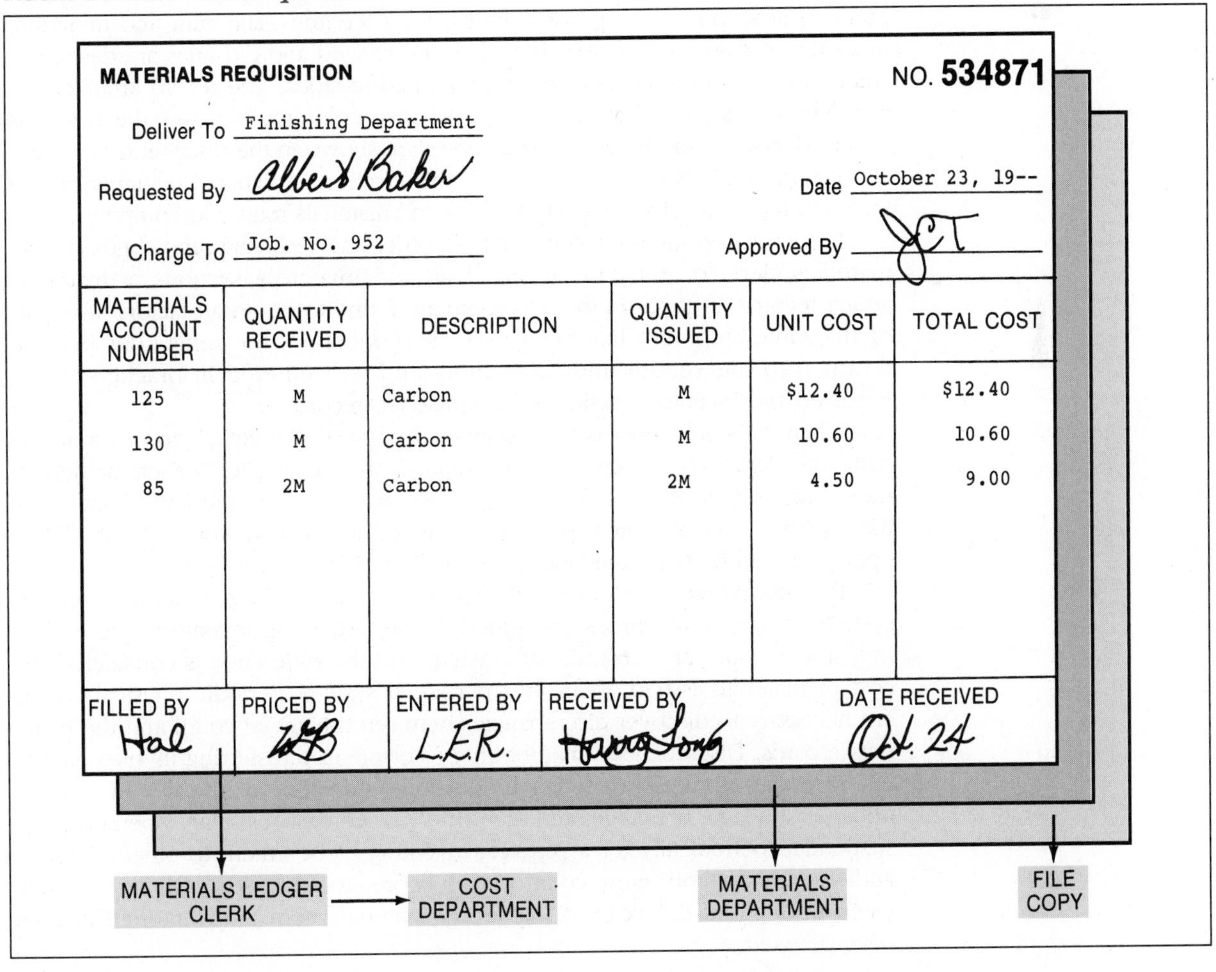
MATERIALS REQUISITION NO. 534871

Deliver To Finishing Department

Requested By Albert Baker Date October 23, 19--

Charge To Job. No. 952 Approved By JCT

MATERIALS ACCOUNT NUMBER	QUANTITY RECEIVED	DESCRIPTION	QUANTITY ISSUED	UNIT COST	TOTAL COST
125	M	Carbon	M	$12.40	$12.40
130	M	Carbon	M	10.60	10.60
85	2M	Carbon	2M	4.50	9.00

FILLED BY	PRICED BY	ENTERED BY	RECEIVED BY	DATE RECEIVED
Hal	WB	L.E.R.	Harry Long	Oct. 24

Electronic Data Processing for Materials Requisitions. When electronic data processing (EDP) is used for materials requisitions, the requisition information is entered and transmitted electronically rather than in written form. The system produces materials summaries as needed and updates subsidiary records and general ledger accounts automatically.

Bill of Materials. The bill of materials for a product is a list of all materials necessary for a typical job or production run. It can save time and reduce errors by serving as a master copy of materials requisitions for that product. When a job or production run is started, all materials listed on the bill of materials are sent to the factory or are issued on a prearranged time schedule. The bill of materials is a rather cumbersome medium for posting; EDP can greatly improve the procedure by providing printouts of the bill of materials, processing the information internally, and updating all accounting records automatically.

Materials Subsidiary Records

A perpetual inventory system enters each increase and each reduction of inventory to maintain up-to-date material records. These records, in either hard-copy or electronic form, constitute a subsidiary ledger controlled by the materials account in the general ledger. In addition to showing quantity and price for each kind of material received, issued, and on hand, the records commonly detail the account number, description or type of material, location, and maximum and minimum quantities to carry. New materials records are created and old ones are deleted as changes occur in the kinds of materials carried in stock. The record arrangement parallels the familiar debit, credit, and balance columns, but uses the headings Received, Issued, and Inventory. (Examples are shown in the discussion of materials costing methods in the appendix to this chapter.) Additional columns can be added to record receiving report numbers and materials requisition numbers.

The approved invoice (with purchase order and receiving report) goes to the materials clerk for entry in the Received and Inventory sections of materials ledger records. If goods in the storeroom are found to be unsatisfactory after part of the same shipment has been used in production, the remainder may be returned to the vendor and its quantity and cost entered in brackets in the Received and Inventory sections of the materials record.

When the storekeeper issues materials, a copy of the requisition is sent to the materials clerk, who enters the date, requisition number, lot (or job or department) number, quantity, and cost of the issued materials in the Issued section of the materials record; a new balance is entered in the Inventory column. These operations can be performed electronically in an EDP system.

The alternative to a perpetual inventory system is the periodic inventory system, in which purchases are added to the beginning inventory, the ending inventory's count and cost are subtracted, and the difference is considered the cost of materials issued. Even in a perpetual system, periodic physical counts are necessary to discover discrepancies between the actual count and the materials records. Discrepancies may be due to errors in transferring invoice data to the records, mistakes in costing requisitions, unrecorded invoices or requisitions, or spoilage, breakage, and theft. In some enterprises, plant operations are suspended periodically for a physical inventory to be taken. In others, internal auditors or inventory crew count one or more stock classes each day or each week throughout the year so that every materials item is inventoried at least once per year.

When the inventory count differs from the balance in the materials record, the record is adjusted to conform to the actual count. In addition to correction of materials records, the general ledger materials account is adjusted by a journal entry, such as the following entry to record a decrease:

Factory Overhead Control	XXXX	
Materials		XXXX

The one remaining step is to assign cost to the materials issued for use. This is done using a cost flow assumption such as average cost or first in, first out (fifo). These common cost flow assumptions are familiar to students of introductory accounting and are illustrated in the appendix to this chapter.

Quantitative Models

Inventories serve as a cushion between the production and consumption of goods. They exist in various forms: materials awaiting processing; partially completed products or components; and finished goods at the factory, in transit, at warehouse distribution points, and in retail outlets. At each of these stages, a sound economic justification for the inventory should exist, since each additional unit carried in inventory generates some additional costs.

Planning Materials Requirements

Materials planning deals with two fundamental factors—the quantity and the time to purchase. Determination of how much and when to buy involves two conflicting kinds of cost—the cost of carrying inventory and the cost of inadequate carrying. The nature of these conflicting costs is illustrated in the following comparison:

Cost of Carrying Inventory	Estimate	Cost of Inadequate Carrying
Interest on investment in working capital	10.00%	Extra purchasing, handling, and transportation costs
Property tax and insurance	1.25	Higher prices due to small order quantities
Warehousing or storage	1.80	Frequent stockouts resulting in disruptions of production schedules, overtime, and extra setup time
Handling	4.25	Additional clerical costs due to keeping customer back-order records
Deterioration and shrinkage of stocks	2.60	Inflation-oriented increases in prices when inventory purchases are deferred
Obsolescence of stocks	5.20	Lost sales and loss of customer goodwill
Total	25.10%	

Economic Order Quantity

The **economic order quantity (EOQ)** is the amount of inventory ordered at one time that minimizes annual inventory cost. If a company buys materials infrequently and in large quantities (the opposite of the just-in-time approach), the cost of carrying the inventory is high because of the sizable average investment in inventory. If purchases are made in small quantities, with frequent orders, correspondingly high ordering costs can result. Therefore, the optimum quantity to order at a given time is determined by balancing two factors: (1) the cost of possessing (carrying) materials and (2) the cost of acquiring (ordering) materials.

The costs of carrying inventory are often expressed as percentages of the average inventory investment, because the most common variable cost is interest or the cost of capital. Other factors can be estimated and measured; they should include only those costs that vary with the level of inventory. In the case of warehousing or storage, for example, only those costs that vary with changes in the number of units ordered should be included; in contrast, the cost of labor and equipment used in the storeroom is generally a fixed cost, which is not relevant to the decision.

It is difficult to determine the costs of not carrying enough inventory; yet they must be considered in determining order quantities and order points. These costs include ordering costs. (The fixed costs of ordering are not relevant; only the variable or out-of-pocket cost of procuring an order should be included). Ordering costs include preparing a purchase requisition, purchase order, and receiving report; handling the incoming shipment; communicating with the vendor; and accounting for the shipment and payment. Other costs of not carrying enough inventory relate to such matters as savings in freight and quantity discounts as well as to the question of when to order, including an appropriate allowance for safety stock.[2] Depending on many factors, it can cost from $10 to $100 or more to process an order. The annual cost of holding inventory can be from 10 to 35 percent of the average inventory investment.

Differential calculus makes it possible to use information about the quantity required, unit price, inventory carrying cost percentage, and cost per order, to compute EOQ by formula. One formula variation is as follows:

$$\text{Economic order quantity} = \sqrt{\frac{2 \times \text{Annual required units} \times \text{Cost per order}}{\text{Cost per unit of material} \times \text{Carrying cost percentage}}}$$

$$\textit{OR}\ \text{EOQ} = \sqrt{\frac{2 \times \text{RU} \times \text{CO}}{\text{CU} \times \text{CC}}}$$

Given the terms EOQ, RU, CO, CU, and CC as specified, the formula is based on the following relationships:

$$\frac{\text{RU}}{\text{EOQ}} = \text{Number of orders place annually}$$

$$\frac{\text{RU} \times \text{CO}}{\text{EOQ}} = \text{Annual ordering cost}$$

$$\frac{\text{EOQ}}{2} = \text{Average number of units in inventory at any point in time}$$

$$\frac{\text{CU} \times \text{CC} \times \text{EOQ}}{2} = \text{Annual carrying cost}$$

$$\frac{\text{RU} \times \text{CO}}{\text{EOQ}} + \frac{\text{CU} \times \text{CC} \times \text{EOQ}}{2} = \text{Total annual cost of ordering and carrying inventory, designated as AC}$$

The last equation is then solved, utilizing differential calculus to determine the minimum total annual cost of inventory:

$$\text{AC} = \frac{\text{RU} \times \text{CO}}{\text{EOQ}} + \frac{\text{CU} \times \text{CC} \times \text{EOQ}}{2}$$

$$\text{AC} = \text{RU} \times \text{CO} \times \text{EOQ}^{-1} + \frac{\text{CU} \times \text{CC} \times \text{EOQ}}{2}$$

[2] Although only variable costs are relevant in EOQ and order point computations, it is desirable to reduce both variable and fixed inventory costs. Fixed costs, such as inventory storage space cost, can be reduced by the just-in-time approach, as discussed in Chapter 10. Techniques for analyzing cost behavior, described and illustrated in Chapter 3, facilitate estimating the amount of carrying and ordering costs.

$$\frac{dAC}{dEOQ} = -RU \times CO \times EOQ^{-2} + \frac{CU \times CC}{2}$$

$$\frac{dAC}{dEOQ} = \frac{-RU \times CO}{EOQ^2} + \frac{CU \times CC}{2}$$

$$\text{Let } \frac{dAC}{dEOQ} = 0; \quad \frac{-RU \times CO}{EOQ^2} + \frac{CU \times CC}{2} = 0$$

$$\frac{CU \times CC}{2} = \frac{RU \times CO}{EOQ^2}$$

$$EOQ^2 \times CU \times CC = 2 \times RU \times CO$$

$$EOQ^2 = \frac{2 \times RU \times CO}{CU \times CC}$$

$$EOQ = \sqrt{\frac{2 \times RU \times CO}{CU \times CC}}$$

The EOQ is the square root of a fraction whose numerator is twice the product of annual unit demand and cost per order and whose denominator is the cost to carry a unit in inventory for one year (i.e., the product of unit price and the annual carrying cost percentage). The result is an order quantity that makes the total annual ordering cost exactly equal to the total annual carrying cost; within the constraints of the specified amounts of order cost and carrying cost, the EOQ lowers the total annual cost of inventory as much as possible. The formula assumes a uniform rate of materials usage.[3]

For example, assume an annual requirement of 2,400 units, a cost per unit of $.75, an ordering cost of $20 per order, and a carrying cost percentage of 20 percent. If the formula is applied to these data, the EOQ is:

$$EOQ = \sqrt{\frac{2 \times 2{,}400 \times \$20}{\$.75 \times 20\%}} = \sqrt{\frac{\$96{,}000}{\$.15}} = \sqrt{640{,}000} = 800 \text{ units}$$

Quantity Discounts. Some purchase prices are discounted if large quantities are ordered. Larger shipments also can generate freight savings. These changes result in a lower unit cost and thus can alter the EOQ calculation. Buying in larger quantities also alters the frequency of orders and thus changes the total ordering cost, and it involves a larger investment in inventories, all of which have an impact on the EOQ calculation.

Suppose the annual usage of an item is 3,600 units, costing $1 each, with no quantity discount available; the carrying cost is 20 percent of the average inventory investment; and the cost to place an order is $10. The EOQ is:

$$\sqrt{\frac{2 \times 3{,}600 \times \$10}{\$1 \times 20\%}} = \sqrt{\frac{\$72{,}000}{\$.20}} = \sqrt{360{,}000} = 600 \text{ units}$$

---

[3] The assumption of a uniform rate of usage is sometimes overlooked, and the EOQ formula is misused as a result. In deriving the EOQ formula, the assumption is made when the average number of units in inventory is expressed as EOQ/2, as shown on page 218. Only if the rate of usage is uniform can the average inventory be calculated as simply one-half of the order size.

Now assume the following quantity discounts become available:

Order Size	Quantity Discount
3,600 units	8.0%
1,800	6.0
1,200	5.0
900	5.0
720	4.5
600	4.0
450	4.0

The following table compares total costs, illustrating the effect of quantity discounts. Observe that the order quantity that minimizes total cost (900 units per order) differs from the EOQ computed when no quantity discount is available (600 units per order).

	Number of Orders per Year						
	1	2	3	4	5	6	8
List price per unit	$ 1	$ 1	$ 1	$ 1	$ 1	$ 1	$ 1
Quantity discount	8%	6%	5%	5%	4½%	4%	4%
Discouint price per unit	$ .92	$ .94	$ .95	$ .95	$ .955	$ .96	$ .96
Size of order in units	3,600	1,800	1,200	900	720	600	450
Average inventory in units*	1,800	900	600	450	360	300	225
Cost of average inventory	$1,656.00	$ 846.00	$ 570.00	$ 427.50	$ 343.80	$ 288.00	$ 216.00
Annual cost of materials...(a)	$3,312.00	$3,384.00	$3,420.00	$3,420.00	$3,438.00	$3,456.00	$3,456.00
Carrying cost (20% of average)...(b)	331.20	169.20	114.00	85.50	68.76	57.60	43.20
Cost to order...(c)	10.00	20.00	30.00	40.00	50.00	60.00	80.00
Total cost per year (a) + (b) + (c)	$3,653.20	$3,573.20	$3,564.00	$3,545.50	$3,556.76	$3,573.60	$3,579.20

* (Size of order in units + 0) ÷ 2

With quantity discounts, the cost of materials is not a constant because it is affected by the size of the discount. Therefore, the objective is to identify an order quantity that minimizes not just the sum of the ordering and carrying costs ((b) + (c) in the table), but the sum of these costs plus the cost of the materials ((a) + (b) + (c)). Because variable carrying cost in this example fluctuates directly with the average inventory investment, carrying cost is affected by the quantity discount.

The EOQ Formula and Production Runs

The EOQ formula also can be used to compute the optimum size of a production run, in which case CO represents an estimate of the setup cost, and CU represents the variable manufacturing cost per unit. To illustrate, assume that stock item A88 is manufactured rather than purchased; the setup cost (CO), such as the cost of labor to rearrange and adjust machines, is $62; variable manufacturing cost (CU) is $2 per unit; annual requirements are 6,000 units; and the carrying cost is 20 percent. The optimum size of a production run is computed as follows:

$$\sqrt{\frac{2 \times 6{,}000 \text{ units} \times \$62 \text{ setup cost}}{\$2 \text{ variable manufacturing cost per unit} \times 20\%}} = \sqrt{\frac{\$744{,}000}{\$.40}} = \sqrt{1{,}860{,}000} = 1{,}364 \text{ units}$$

Determining the Time to Order

The EOQ formula addresses the quantity problem of inventory planning, but the question of when to order is equally important. This question is controlled by three factors: (1) time needed for delivery, (2) rate of inventory usage, and (3) safety stock. Unlike the economic order quantity, the order point has no generally applicable and acceptable formula. Determining the order point would be relatively simple if precise predictions were available for both rate of usage and **lead time** (the interval between the time an order is placed and the time the materials are on the factory floor ready for production). For most stock items, there is a variation in either or both of these factors that almost always causes one of three results: (1) if lead time or usage is below expectation during an order period, the new materials arrive before the existing stock is consumed, thereby adding to the cost of carrying inventory; (2) if lead time or usage is greater than expected, a stockout will occur, with its many forms of costs, including lost customers; (3) if average or normal lead time and usage are used to determine an order point, a stockout can be expected on every other order.

Forecasting materials usage requires the expenditure of time and money. In materials management, forecasts are an expense as well as an aid to balancing the cost to acquire and the cost to carry inventory. Since perfect forecasts are rarely possible, an inventory cushion or safety stock is often the least costly device for protecting against a stockout. The basic problem is to determine the safety stock quantity. If the safety stock is greater than needed, the carrying cost will be unnecessarily high; if too small, frequent stockouts will occur and inconveniences, disruptions, and additional costs will result. The optimum safety stock is that quantity that results in the smallest total cost of stockouts plus safety stock carrying cost. This carrying cost is calculated in the same way as for EOQ. The annual cost of stockouts depends on the frequency of occurrence and the actual cost of each stockout.

To illustrate, assume a company uses an item for which it places 10 orders per year, the cost of a stockout is $30[4], the carrying cost is $.50 per year per unit, and the following probabilities of a stockout have been estimated for various levels of safety stock:

Safety Stock (in units)	Probability of Stockout
0	40%
50	20
100	10
200	5

The total carrying cost and stockout cost at each level of safety stock are determined as follows:

[4] If the action taken in the event of a stockout is to stop the job for which there is a materials shortage and start up a new job, the stockout cost equals the setup cost required for the change. On the other hand, if production cannot be shifted to another product, it may be necessary to shut down the facility until the materials resupply arrives, in which case the stockout cost depends on the length of time the facility is shut down. The shutdown period is likely to be longer, on average, (and stockout cost higher) for smaller quantities of safety stock than for larger quantities.

(A) Safety Stock (in Units)	(B) Expected Stockouts per Year	(C) Total Stockout Cost	(D) Total Carrying Cost	(E) Total Stockout and Carrying Cost
0	4.0	$120	-0-	$120
50	2.0	60	$ 25	85
100	1.0	30	50	80
200	.5	15	100	115

Notes: B = number of orders per year (i.e., 10) × probability of stockout

C = B × cost of one stockout (i.e., $30)

D = A × cost to carry one unit in inventory for one year (i.e., $.50)

E = C + D

In this illustration, the optimum level of safety stock is 100 units, since the total stockout and safety stock carrying cost is minimized at this level.

Order Point Formula

Order points are based on usage during the time necessary to requisition, order, and receive materials, plus an allowance for protection against stockout. The **order point** is reached when the available quantity is just equal to foreseeable needs; that is, when inventory on hand plus quantities due in equal the lead time usage quantity plus safety stock. In equation form, the order point can be expressed as:

$$I + QD = LTQ + SSQ$$

Where:

I = Inventory balance on hand
QD = Quantities due in from orders previously placed, materials transfers, and returns to stock
LTQ = Lead time quantity, which equals normal lead time in months, weeks, or days multiplied by a normal month's, week's, or day's use
SSQ = Safety stock quantity

If the weekly usage of a stock item is 175 units, and the lead time is normally four weeks but possibly as long as nine weeks, then the order point is 1,575 units: 700 units usage during normal lead time (175 units × 4 weeks) plus 875 units of safety stock (175 units × 5 weeks). If a beginning inventory of 2,800 units is assumed, with no orders outstanding, the usage, order schedule, and maximum inventory levels are:

Units in beginning inventory	2,800
Usage to order point (1,225 ÷ 175 weekly usage = 7 weeks)	1,225
Order point	1,575
Usage during normal lead time (700 ÷ 175 weekly usage = 4 weeks)	700
Maximum inventory or safety stock at date of delivery, assuming normal lead time and usage	875
Order quantity units received	2,090
Maximum inventory, assuming normal lead time and usage	2,965

Figure 9-3 depicts materials planning under the above assumptions and shows that a stockout will not occur unless lead time exceeds nine weeks, assuming normal usage.

FIGURE 9-3 ***Rate of Usage Known with Certainty and Lead Time Known but Variable***

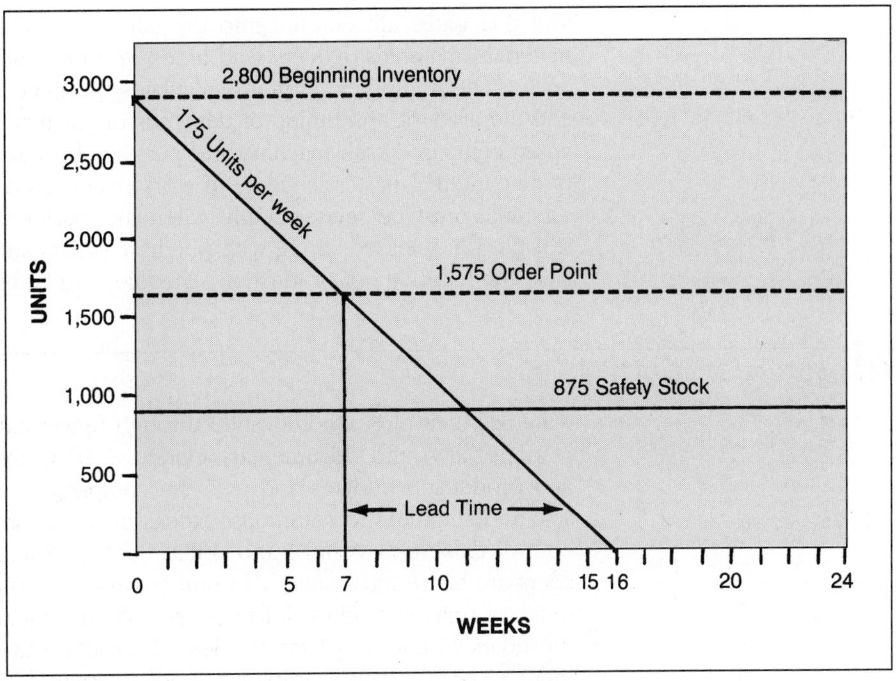

In most businesses, a constant normal usage is not likely to occur, because usage depends on production schedules, and production depends on sales. For instance, if the usage rate is as high as 210 units per week, with lead time normally four weeks but possibly as long as nine weeks, the safety stock is 1,190 units and the order point 1,890 units, calculated as follows:

Normal usage for normal lead time of four weeks (175 units × 4 weeks)		700 units
Safety stock:		
Normal usage for five weeks' delay (175 units × 5 weeks)	875	
Usage variation ((210 − 175) × 9 weeks)	315	1,190
Order point		1,890 units

If a beginning inventory of 2,800 units with no orders outstanding is assumed, the usage, order schedule, and maximum inventory levels would be:

Units in beginning inventory	2,800
Usage to order point (910 ÷ 210 maximum weekly usage = 4.3 weeks)	910
Order point	1,890
Normal usage for normal lead time (700 ÷ 175 normal weekly usage = 4 weeks)	700
Maximum inventory or safety stock at date of delivery, assuming normal lead time and usage	1,190
Order quantity units received	2,090
Maximum inventory, assuming normal lead time and usage	3,280

Computer Simulation for Materials Requirements Planning

Materials requirements planning (MRP) is a computer simulation for managing materials requirements based on each product's bill of materials, inventory status, and process of manufacture. A master schedule of items to be produced and due dates are entered into the computer, which then accesses the bill of materials, materials delivery lead times, and on-hand and on-order inventory balances. The computer program calculates the needed quantity for each material and the amount and timing of demands on each work location. These demands, when compared with machine and personnel capacities, determine the feasibility of meeting the master schedule. If work overloads cannot be resolved, the master schedule must be revised. Only when the master schedule is determined to be feasible is it released, along with purchase orders and operating schedules. In this way, the feasibility of production schedules can be tested prior to their release.[5]

Materials Control

Materials control is accomplished through functional organization, assignment of responsibility, and documentary evidence. It begins with the approval of sales and production budgets and with the completion of products that are ready for sale and shipment to warehouse stocks or to customers. Two levels of inventory control exist: unit control and dollar control. Purchasing and production managers are interested primarily in unit control; they think, order, and requisition in terms of units instead of dollars. Executive management is interested primarily in the financial control of inventories. These executives think in terms of an adequate return on capital employed—dollars invested in inventory must be utilized efficiently and effectively. Inventory control is operating successfully when increases or decreases in inventory follow a predetermined and predictable pattern closely linked to sales and production schedules.

The control of materials must meet two opposing needs: (1) maintenance of an inventory of sufficient size and diversity for efficient operations and (2) maintenance of a financially favorable inventory. A basic objective of materials control is the ability to place an order at the appropriate time with the best source to acquire the proper quantity at the right price and quality. Effective inventory control should:

1. Provide a supply of required materials for efficient, uninterrupted operations.
2. Provide ample stocks in periods of short supply (seasonal, cyclical, or strike) and anticipate price changes.
3. Store materials with a minimum of handling time and cost and protect them from loss by fire, theft, weather, and damage through handling.
4. Keep inactive, surplus, and obsolete items to a minimum by reporting product changes that affect materials.
5. Assure adequate inventory for prompt delivery to customers.
6. Maintain the amount of capital invested in inventories at a level consistent with operating requirements and management's plans.

Materials Control Methods

Materials control methods[6] differ primarily in the care and cost expended on the product. Critical items and items of high value require greater attention than do low-value items. For example, for low-cost items, large safety stocks and large

[5] Dale G. Sauers, "Analyzing Inventory Systems," *Management Accounting*, Vol. 67, No. 11, p. 31.
[6] Just-in-time is one type of materials control method; it is discussed in Chapter 10.

orders of materials to last three to six months are common, because carrying costs are usually low and the risk of obsolescence is often negligible. Two materials control methods are the order cycling method and the min-max method.

The **order cycling method** or **cycle review method** periodically examines the status of quantities of materials on hand for each item or class. Different companies use different time periods (e.g., 30, 60, or 90 days) between reviews and can use different cycles for different types of materials. High-value items and critical items (those that interrupt operations if the company runs out of stock) usually require a short review cycle. For noncritical items, a longer review cycle is common, because these materials are ordered in large quantities and a stockout is not as costly. At each review period in the order cycling system, orders are placed to bring quantities up to some desired level, expressed as a number of days' or weeks' supply.

The **min-max method** is based on the premise that the quantities of most stock items are subject to definable limits. A maximum quantity for each item is established. A minimum level provides the margin of safety necessary to prevent stockouts during a reorder cycle. The minimum level sets the order point, and the order quantity usually brings inventory up to the maximum level. Min-max can be based on physical observation, or it can be keyed in to the accounting system. Physical observation that an order point has been reached is illustrated by the **two-bin method**. Under this method, each stock item is stored in two bins, piles, or bundles. The first bin contains enough stock to satisfy usage that occurs between receipt of an order and the placing of the next order; the second bin contains the normal amount used from order date to delivery date plus the safety stock. When the first bin is empty and the second bin is tapped, a purchase requisition for a new supply is prepared. The min-max method can also be implemented through the accounting system. When a materials ledger record shows that the balance of stock on hand has dropped to the order point, it sets off the purchase sequence. This works especially well in an electronic data processing system.

Selective Control—The ABC Plan. Under **selective control**, called the **ABC plan**[7], the cost significance of each item is evaluated. Items are classified into three categories. High-value, critical items, called A items, are under the tightest control; B or middle-value items require moderate control; and C or noncritical items are under simple physical controls, such as the two-bin method.

The following table summarizes the handling of the three classes of inventory items:

	High-value A Items	Middle-value B Items	Low-value C Items
Quality of personnel	Best available	Average	Low
Records needed	Complete	Simple	Not essential
Order point and EOQ used	As guides, frequent review	Infrequent review	Strictly used
Number of orders per year	Generally high	Moderate	Low
Replacement time	As short as possible	Normal	Can be long
Amount of safety stock	Low	Moderate	High
Inventory turnover	High	Moderate	Low

[7] This use of the abbreviation ABC is not related to activity based costing, which is discussed in Chapter 14.

Control of Obsolete and Surplus Inventory

Almost every organization is faced at some time with the problem of surplus and obsolete inventory. Whatever the cause, some action is required to reduce or eliminate these items from inventory and free the related capital. To accomplish this, management should first make certain that the buildup is not continuing under present ordering policies; then it should take steps to dispose of stock. Accurate perpetual inventory records showing acquisition and issue quantities and dates, as well as periodic review of the records, are necessary to identify obsolete and surplus items. Obsolete inventory usually results when a product is redesigned or discontinued. Prompt sale of the inventory for the first reasonable offer is often the best policy.

Summary

Materials managers control a sizable portion of the total investment in many businesses. This fact makes the management of materials and other inventories a major concern. Effective management and control requires individuals who are vested with responsibility for, and authority over, the system for procuring, maintaining, and disposing of inventory. These persons must have the ability to obtain and evaluate the necessary data and the authority to take action when needed.

Appendix Inventory Costing Methods

When actual costs are recorded in a perpetual inventory system, each issuance of materials[8] is assigned a cost as it moves from storeroom to work in process as direct materials, to factory overhead as indirect materials, or to marketing and administrative accounts as supplies. The more common methods of costing are first in, first out (fifo); average; and last in, first out (lifo).[9] These methods represent different assumptions about the flow of costs; the cost flow assumption need not coincide with the actual physical flow of units.

As in the discussion of materials procurement and use, the following illustrations assume use of a perpetual inventory system. Any cost flow assumption other than fifo can result in unit costs that are affected by whether a perpetual or periodic inventory system is used. All methods illustrated are based on the following transactions:

Feb.	1	Beginning balance: 800 units @ $6 per unit.
	4	Received 200 units @ $7 per unit.

[8] Although this discussion refers to materials inventory, the same costing methods are applicable to finished goods.

[9] Other methods include market price, last purchase price, and standard cost. Materials traded on commodity exchanges, such as cotton, wheat, copper, and crude oil, are sometimes costed into production at the quoted price at date of issue or date of last purchase; this is essentially replacement cost accounting, and it is sometimes used for low-cost, relatively insignificant materials as well as for commodities. In standard costing, issued materials are costed at a predetermined or estimated cost, and the only data needed on materials record cards are the physical quantities; this greatly simplifies the work of posting receipts and issues.

10 Received 200 units @ $8 per unit.
11 Issued 800 units.
12 Received 400 units @ $8 per unit.
20 Issued 500 units.
25 Returned 100 excess units from the factory to the storeroom—to be recorded at the latest issued price (or at the actual issued price if physically identifiable).
28 Received 600 units @ $9 per unit.

First In, First Out (Fifo)

When materials are issued, the fifo method assigns them the cost of the oldest supply in stock. The fifo method is illustrated on the materials record card shown in Figure 9-4.

FIGURE 9-4 ***Materials Record Card Using Fifo Costing Method***

	Received			Issued			Inventory			
Date	Quantity	Unit Cost	Total Cost	Quantity	Unit Cost	Total Cost	Quantity	Unit Cost	Total Cost	Balance
Feb. 1							800	$6.00	$4,800	$4,800
4	200	$7.00	$1,400				800 200	6.00 7.00	4,800 1,400	6,200
10	200	8.00	1,600				800 200 200	6.00 7.00 8.00	4,800 1,400 1,600	7,800
11				800	$6.00	$4,800	200 200	7.00 8.00	1,400 1,600	3,000
12	400	8.00	3,200				200 600	7.00 8.00	1,400 4,800	6,200
20				200 300	7.00 8.00	1,400 2,400	300	8.00	2,400	2,400
25	100*	8.00	800				400	8.00	3,200	3,200
28	600	9.00	5,400				400 600	8.00 9.00	3,200 5,400	8,600

* Returns to storeroom.

The fifo method is convenient whenever only a few different receipts of the materials are on a materials record card at one time; it is cumbersome if frequent purchases are made at different prices and if units from several purchases are on hand at the same time.

Average Cost

The average cost method assumes that the cost of each issue of materials is a mix of the costs of all shipments that are in stock at the time the issue occurs. Often it is not feasible to mark or label each materials item with an invoice price in order to identify the used unit with its acquisition cost. The logic of average costing is that if all available materials of one kind are issued more or less at random, then an average cost of all units in stock at the time of issue is a satisfactory measure of materials cost. If materials tend to be made up of numerous small items that are low in unit cost, and especially if prices are subject to frequent change, average costing is appealing, because it is a practical and uncomplicated method. The averaging of costs minimizes the apparent effects of temporarily high or low purchase prices, thus providing more stable cost estimates for bids on future work.

The average cost method divides the total cost of all materials of a particular class by the number of units on hand to find the average cost. The cost of new invoices is added to the balance column of the inventory section of the materials card, the units are added to the existing quantity, and the total cost is divided by the total quantity to arrive at the new average cost. Materials are issued at this average cost until another purchase is recorded, at which time another average cost is calculated. The average cost method is illustrated on the materials record card shown in Figure 9-5, using the same transaction information as the previous example.

FIGURE 9-5 *Materials Record Card Using Average Costing Method*

	Received			Issued			Inventory			
Date	Quantity	Unit Cost	Total Cost	Quantity	Unit Cost	Total Cost	Quantity	Unit Cost	Total Cost	Balance
Feb. 1							800	$6.00		$4,800
4	200	$7.00	$1,400				1,000	6.20		6,200
10	200	8.00	1,600				1,200	6.50		7,800
11				800	$6.50	$5,200	400	6.50		2,600
12	400	8.00	3,200				800	7.25		5,800
20				500	7.25	3,625	300	7.25		2,175
25	100*	7.25	725				400	7.25		2,900
28	600	9.00	5,400				1,000	8.30		8,300

* Returns to storeroom.

Some companies establish an average cost for each kind of material at the end of each month and use this average cost for all issues in the next month. When a perpetual inventory system is not used, a variation of the average cost method can be applied. It entails waiting until the end of a period to compute the cost of materials consumed. The average cost is obtained by adding both quantities and costs of the period's total purchases to beginning inventory quantities and costs and using the resulting totals to calculate an average cost. The result can differ from that obtained when average costing is used in a perpetual inventory system.

Last In, First Out (Lifo)

The last in, first out (lifo) method assigns the cost of the most recent purchase in stock to each batch of materials issued to production. The logic of this method is that the most recent cost approximates the cost of replacing the consumed units and is therefore the most meaningful cost amount to be matched with revenue in calculating income.

Under lifo, the objective is to charge out the cost of current purchases and to leave the oldest costs in the inventory account. There are several ways to apply the lifo method. Because each variation yields different figures for the cost of materials issued, the cost of ending inventory, and profit, it is important to follow the chosen procedure consistently. The lifo method is illustrated on the materials record card shown in Figure 9-6.

FIGURE 9-6 *Materials Record Card Using Lifo Costing Method*

	Received			Issued			Inventory			
Date	Quantity	Unit Cost	Total Cost	Quantity	Unit Cost	Total Cost	Quantity	Unit Cost	Total Cost	Balance
Feb. 1							800	$6.00	$4,800	$4,800
4	200	$7.00	$1,400				800	6.00	4,800	
							200	7.00	1,400	6,200
10	200	8.00	1,600				800	6.00	4,800	
							200	7.00	1,400	
							200	8.00	1,600	7,800
11				200	$8.00	$1,600				
				200	7.00	1,400				
				400	6.00	2,400	400	6.00	2,400	2,400
12	400	8.00	3,200				400	6.00	2,400	
							400	8.00	3,200	5,600
20				400	8.00	3,200				
				100	6.00	600	300	6.00	1,800	1,800
25	100*	6.00	600				400	6.00	2,400	2,400
28	600	9.00	5,400				400	6.00	2,400	
							600	9.00	5,400	7,800

* Returns to storeroom.

In this illustration, a new inventory balance is computed after each issue of materials, with the ending inventory consisting of 1,000 units costed at $7,800. If a periodic rather than perpetual inventory system is used, the cost of materials issued is determined at the end of the period by ignoring day-to-day outflows and subtracting ending inventory from the total of the beginning balance and all receipts. The ending inventory would then consist of:

800 units @ $6, on hand in the beginning inventory..	$4,800
200 units @ $7, from the oldest purchase, on February, 4.............................	1,400
1,000 units, lifo inventory at the end of February (periodic system)	$6,200

Regardless of the cost flow assumption used, the periodic inventory system is convenient for process costing in situations where individual materials requisitions are seldom used and where materials move into process in bulk lots, as in flour mills, spinning mills, oil refineries, and sugar refineries. Periodic inventory systems also work well in companies that charge materials to work in process from month-end consumption sheets, which provide the cost department with information about quantities used.

Both variations of lifo are lumped together under the term **item-layer identification method**, although the two variations can produce different figures for the cost of materials issued and ending inventory.

Dollar-Value Lifo. The item-layer identification method is generally not practical for a company that maintains a wide variety of inventory items and that changes the mix of inventory frequently. Use of this method under such conditions virtually ensures frequent liquidation of lifo base layers of cost and a corresponding loss of the benefits of lifo. As a result, many companies employ the dollar-value lifo method for financial reporting and for income tax purposes.[10] This method reduces both the cost of administering lifo and the frequency with which lifo layers must be liquidated. Also, the income tax savings during periods of rising prices is greater if the dollar-value lifo method is used, instead of the item-layer identification method. Units issued are costed by average, fifo, or another cost flow assumption for internal purposes, and the figures for inventories and cost of goods sold are adjusted to dollar-value lifo figures for tax and financial reporting.[11]

Comparison of Costing Methods

In periods of rising prices, fifo measures issued items at lowest costs, lifo measures them at highest costs, and average costing yields a figure between the two. In a period of falling prices, fifo assigns the highest cost to issued materials, lifo assigns the lowest, and average cost again produces a result between these two.

For internal purposes, the average method is the most frequently used because of the advantages already described and because of the awkwardness of both the fifo and lifo methods. For external purposes, the lifo method is popular because of its income tax advantage in times of rising prices.[12] Lifo used for external reporting is usually dollar-value lifo. For inventory to be restated to lifo (from average or fifo), an end-of-period inventory adjustment is required, with the offsetting entry made to Cost of Goods Sold. The adjustment is then reversed at the beginning of the next accounting period.

Increasingly, companies minimize the inventory investment and employ just-in-time systems for production planning and control, as discussed in Chapter 10. Reduction of inventory also reduces the financial statement advantages of one costing method over another. In the extreme case of a mature just-in-time system applied to all inventories, the total cost of inventories and the differences among the costing methods are immaterial in the financial statements.

CASB Costing of Materials

Under Cost Accounting Standards Board regulations, materials can be charged directly to a contract if the contract is specifically identified at the time the materials are purchased or manufactured. Materials drawn from company-owned inventory can be priced using fifo, lifo, average, or standard cost. The method or methods selected must be used consistently for similar categories of materials, and the contractor must document the procedure for accumulating and allocating materials cost.[13]

---

[10] *Regulations,* Section 1.472-8.

[11] For a detailed discussion of dollar-value lifo, retail dollar-value lifo, and other approaches, see Jay M. Smith, Jr. and K. Fred Skousen, *Intermediate Accounting,* 11th ed. (Cincinnati: South-Western Publishing Co., 1992), Chapters 10 and 11.

[12] Because lifo is allowed under tax law only if it is also used for external financial reporting, its popular tax advantages make it common in external financial reporting.

[13] *Standards, Rules and Regulations, Part 411,* "Accounting for Acquisition Costs of Materials" (Washington, D. C.: Cost Accounting Standards Board, 1975), p. 226.

Lower of Cost or Market

U.S. financial accounting rules require that inventories be reported at the lower of their cost or market value. In the application of this rule, the word *cost* includes any of the common cost flow assumptions that have been discussed. The term *market value* means replacement cost, within certain limits. The limits on the use of replacement cost as market value, and other details of this area of external financial reporting, are discussed and illustrated in intermediate- and advanced-level financial accounting textbooks.

Interim Financial Reporting of Inventory

Companies are required to use the same inventory costing methods (and the same adjustments to the lower of cost or market) in interim reporting that they use in annual financial statements, with the following exceptions:[14]

1. Gross profit rates can be used to estimate ending inventory and cost of goods sold for interim periods.
2. If there is a liquidation of a lifo base of cost at an interim date but the base is expected to be replaced by the end of the year, then the inventory at the interim date should not give effect to the liquidation, and cost of goods sold for the interim period should include the expected cost of replacing the base.
3. If a market decline at an interim date can reasonably be expected to be restored by year-end, then the decline need not be recognized at the interim date.

Key Terms

routing *(208)*
bill of materials *(208)*
production budget *(208)*
purchase requisition *(208)*
purchase order *(208)*
receiving report *(209)*
materials requisition *(209)*
materials record card *(209)*
economic order quantity (EOQ) *(217)*
lead time *(221)*
order point *(222)*
materials requirements planning (MRP) *(223)*
order cycling method, cycle review method *(225)*
min-max method *(225)*
two-bin method *(225)*
selective control, ABC plan *(225)*
item-layer identification method *(230)*

Discussion Questions

Q9-1 List the documents most frequently used in the procurement and use of materials.

Q9-2 How is an invoice approved for payment?

Q9-3 For a retailer and wholesaler that purchases its inventories from various suppliers, what criteria should be used to determine which costs are inventoriable? (AICPA adapted)

Q9-4 Refer to question Q9-3. Are a retailer's administrative costs inventoriable? Explain. (AICPA adapted)

---

[14] *Opinion of the Accounting Principles Board, No. 28,* "Interim Financial Reporting" (New York: American Institute of Certified Public Accountants, 1973), par. 14.

Q9-5 When an inventory control system is designed, what are three key questions that must be answered?

Q9-6 How can a firm benefit from economic order quantity and order point techniques?

Q9-7 What is the purpose of the economic order quantity model?

Q9-8 What types of costs should be considered in deriving the economic order quantity?

Q9-9 What are the consequences of maintaining inadequate inventory levels? What are the difficulties of measuring precisely the costs associated with understocking?

Q9-10 In the computation of optimum production run size, what alterations to the EOQ formula's components are required?

Q9-11 Explain each of the following terms: (a) order point, (b) lead time, and (c) safety stock.

Q9-12 Define materials requirements planning (MRP).

Q9-13 Is general management concerned primarily with unit control or financial control of inventory?

Q9-14 The control of materials must meet two opposing needs. What are they?

Q9-15 In what situation are selective control and automatic control of materials effective?

Q9-16 (Appendix) Describe the fundamental cost flow assumptions of the average cost, fifo, and lifo inventory costing methods.

Q9-17 (Appendix) Discuss the reasons for using lifo in an inflationary economy.

Q9-18 (Appendix) During a period of oil price decline, oil companies were accused of making excess profits when the prices at the pump did not fall as quickly as the prices at the well head. In order to report a lower profit to offset the criticism, would lifo or fifo be used? Explain.
CGA-Canada (adapted). Reprint with permission.

Q9-19 (Appendix) Proponents of lifo and fifo procedures ascribe certain merits to each. Identify the inventory procedure, lifo or fifo, to which the following features are attributed:

(a) Matches actual physical flow of goods in most cases.

(b) Matches old costs with new prices.

(c) Costs inventory at approximate replacement cost.

(d) Matches new costs with new prices.

(e) Emphasizes the balance sheet.

(f) Emphasizes the income statement.

CGA-Canada (adapted). Reprint with permission.

Exercises

E9-1 Cost of Acquiring Materials—Freight-In. An invoice for Part A, Part B, and Part C is received from the Noble Company. Invoice totals are: Part A, $8,600; Part B, $5,060; and Part C, $3,840. The shipment weighs 1 400 kilograms and freight charges are $280. Weights for the respective materials are 630, 490, and 280 kilograms.

Required:

(1) Allocate freight to materials based on cost.
(2) Allocate freight to materials based on shipping weight.

E9-2 Quantity to Order. On September 1, a company wants to determine the number of units of Material X it should order for November delivery. The production schedule calls for 4,200 units of Material X for September operations, 4,400 units for October, and 4,700 units for November. On September 1, the inventory record shows 4,400 units on hand, 3,600 units on order for September delivery, and 4,500 units on order for October delivery. The inventory needed to begin December production is 3,600 units.

Required: Compute the quantity to be ordered for November delivery.

E9-3 Usage Forecast and Inventory Balances. On January 1, a materials analyst is asked to determine the number of units of Item AZ to be ordered for March delivery. The production schedule calls for 4,800 units of AZ for January operations, 5,000 units for February, and 5,600 units for March. On January 1, the AZ inventory is 6,000 units, 3,800 units are on order for January delivery, and 4,600 units are on order for February delivery. The desired inventory level to begin second-quarter production is 80% of the January 1 inventory.

Required:

(1) Compute the quantity to be ordered for March delivery.
(2) If the planned usage occurs and outstanding orders are received on expected delivery dates, what is the number of units on hand (a) on March 1 and (b) on March 31.

E9-4 EOQ. (Round all answers to the nearest whole number.)

(1) Franklin Inc. has an annual usage of 100 units of Item M, having a purchase price of $55 per unit. The following data are applicable to Item M:

Ordering cost	$5 per order
Carrying cost percentage	15%

Required: Compute the economic order quantity.

(2) Tyler Equipment Company estimates a need for 2,250 Ajets next year at a cost of $3 per unit. The estimated carrying cost is 20%, and the cost to place an order is $12.
Required: Compute the economic order quantity.

(3) Barter Corporation has been buying Product A in lots of 1,200 units, which represents a four-months supply. The cost per unit is $100; the order cost is $200 per order; and the annual inventory carrying cost for one unit is $25.
Required: Compute the economic order quantity. (AICPA adapted)

(4) Shubert Company estimates that it will need 25,000 cartons next year at a cost of $8 per carton. The estimated carrying cost is 25% of average inventory investment, and the cost to place an order is $20.
Required: Compute (a) the economic order quantity and (b) the frequency, in days, that orders should be placed, based on a 365-day year.

(5) The Alexander Company estimates that it will need 18,000 units of Material X next year, at a cost of $15 per unit. The estimated carrying cost is 20% of average inventory investment and the cost to place an order is calculated to be $15.
Required: Compute (a) the EOQ, (b) the frequency with which orders should be placed, in days, based on a 365-day year, and (c) the EOQ if Material X costs $6 per unit and other estimates remain unchanged.

(6) The Fairhaven Company estimates that it will need 18,000 Material Y units next year at a cost of $7.50 per unit. The estimated carrying cost is 20% of average inventory investment, and the cost to place an order is calculated to be $15.
Required: Compute (a) the most economical number of units to order, (b) the frequency, in days, for placing orders, based on a 365-day year, and (c) the most economical order quantity if Material Y costs $2.50 per unit and other estimates remain as originally stated.

(7) Zarba Sporting Goods Inc. buys baseballs at $20 per dozen from its wholesaler. Zarba sells 48,000 dozen balls evenly throughout the year. The firm incurs interest expense of 10% on its average inventory investment. In addition, rent, insurance, and property tax for each dozen baseballs in the average inventory is $.40. The cost involved in handling each purchase order is $10.
Required: Compute (a) the economic order quantity and (b) the total annual inventory expense to sell 48,000 dozen baseballs, if orders of 800 dozen each are placed evenly throughout the year.

(8) A customer has been ordering 5,000 specially designed metal columns at the rate of 1,000 per order during the past year. The variable production cost is $8 per unit: $6 for materials and labor, and $2 for factory overhead. It costs $1,000 to set up for one run of 1,000 columns, and the inventory carrying cost is 20%. Because this customer may buy at least 5,000 columns per year, the company would like to avoid making five different production runs.
Required: Compute the most economical production run.

(9) Fulton Company estimates that it will need 12,000 units of Material W next year, at a cost of $9 per unit. The estimated carrying cost is 20%, and the cost to place an order is calculated to be $16.
Required: Compute (a) the economic order quantity, (b) the frequency of order placement, and (c) the economic order quantity if forecast usage is changed to 8,000 and the carrying cost percentage is 22%.

(10) An item costs $10, has a yearly usage volume of 500 units, an ordering cost of $6, and a carrying cost of 25%.
Required: (a) Compute the economic order quantity and the total ordering and carrying cost per year. (b) Determine the effect on the total ordering and carrying cost if the order quantity is 10% above the EOQ. Comment on the magnitude of the effect.

(11) Bahner Inc. manufactures a line of walnut office products. Management estimates the annual demand for the double walnut letter tray at 6,000 units. The tray sells for $80. The costs relating to the letter tray are

(a) the variable manufacturing cost per tray, $50; (b) the cost to initiate a production run, $300; and (c) the annual cost of carrying the tray in inventory, 20%. In prior years, the production of the tray has been scheduled in two equal production runs.

Required: Find the expected annual cost savings the company could experience if it employs the economic order quantity model to determine the number of production runs that should be initiated during the year.

E9-5 EOQ and Quantity Discount. A particular material is purchased for $3 per unit. Monthly usage is 1,500 units, the ordering cost is $50 per order, and the annual carrying cost is 40%.

Required:

(1) Compute the economic order quantity.
(2) Determine the proper order size if the material can be purchased at a 5% discount in lots of 2,000 units.

E9-6 Ordering and Carrying Costs; Economic Order Quantity; Quantity Discount. George Company buys 500 boxes of Item X-100 every two months. Order costs are $380 per order; carrying costs are $1 per unit and vary directly with inventory investment. Currently the company purchases the item for $5 each.

Required:

(1) Determine total ordering and carrying costs under current policy.
(2) Determine the economic order quantity and the related ordering and carrying costs.
(3) What is the optimal order size if the supplier offers a 5% discount for orders of 3,000 units?

CGA-Canada (adapted). Reprint with permission.

E9-7 Safety Stock; Order Point. Eagle Company's usage of Material A is 9,600 units during 240 working days per year. Normal lead time and maximum lead time are 20 working days and 30 working days, respectively.

Required: Assuming Material A will be required evenly throughout the year, what is the safety stock and order point? (AICPA adapted)

E9-8 Order Point. Rider Company has obtained the following costs and other data pertaining to one of its materials:

Order quantity	1,500 units
Normal use per day	500 units
Maximum use per day	600 units
Minimum use per day	100 units
Lead time	5 days

Required: Compute the following:

(1) Safety stock (maximum)
(2) Order point
(3) Normal maximum inventory
(4) Absolute maximum inventory

CGA-Canada (adapted). Reprint with permission.

E9-9 Order Point Computations. The Pen Company is setting up an inventory control system. For one type of material, the following data have been assembled:

Order quantity	3,000 units
Minimum use per day	80 units
Normal use per day	120 units
Maximum use per day	200 units
Lead time	12 days

Required: Compute the following:

(1) Safety stock (maximum)
(2) Order point
(3) Normal maximum inventory
(4) Absolute maximum inventory

CGA-Canada (adapted). Reprint with permission.

E9-10 Safety Stock. Jackson & Sons Inc. would like to determine the safety stock it needs to maintain for a product, to incur the lowest combination of stockout cost and carrying cost. Each stockout costs $75; the carrying cost for each safety stock unit is $1; the product is ordered five times a year. The following probabilities of running out of stock during an order period are associated with various safety stock levels:

Safety Stock Level	Probability of Stockout
10 units	40%
20	20
40	8
80	4

Required: Determine the combined stockout and safety stock carrying cost associated with each level and the recommended level of safety stock. (AICPA adapted)

E9-11 (Appendix) Materials Costing Methods. Kenney Company made the following materials purchases and issues during January:

	Units	Price
Inventory: Jan. 1	500	$1.20
Receipts: Jan. 6	200	1.25
10	400	1.30
25	500	1.40
Issues: Jan. 15	560	
27	400	

Required: Compute the cost of materials consumed and the cost assigned to the inventory at the end of the month, using a perpetual inventory system combined with each of the following:
(1) Average costing, rounding unit costs to the nearest cent
(2) Fifo costing
(3) Lifo costing

Problems

P9-1 Applied Acquisition Costs. Benjamin Company Inc. records incoming materials at invoice price less cash discounts plus applied receiving and handling cost. For product Gamma, the following data are available:

	Budgeted for the Month	Actual Cost for the Month
Freight-in and cartage-in	$ 2,500	$ 2,580
Purchasing Department cost	4,800	4,500
Receiving Department cost	3,900	4,200
Storage and handling	4,200	3,800
Testing, spoilage, and rejects	2,600	3,120
Total	$18,000	$18,200

The purchasing budget shows estimated net purchases of $144,000 for the month. Actual invoices net of discounts total $148,500 for the month.

Required:
(1) Determine the applied acquisition costing rate for the month.
(2) Determine the amount of applied cost added to materials purchased during the month.
(3) Indicate the possible disposition of the variance.

P9-2 EOQ; Safety Stock. Maple Company sells a number of products to many restaurants in the area. One product is a special meat cutter with a disposable blade. Blades are sold in a package of 12 at $20 per package. It has been determined that the demand for the replacement blades is at a constant rate of 2,000 packages per month.

The packages cost the company $10 each from the manufacturer and require a three-day lead time from date of order to date of delivery. The ordering cost is $1.20 per order, and the carrying cost is 10% per year. The company uses the economic order quantity formula.

Required:
(1) Compute the economic order quantity.
(2) Compute the number of orders needed per year.
(3) Compute the cost of ordering and of carrying blades for the year.
(4) Determine the number of days until the next order should be placed, assuming that there is no safety stock and that the present inventory level is 400 packages. (360 days = 1 year.)
(5) Discuss the difficulties that most firms have in attempting to apply the EOQ formula to their inventory problems.
(ICMA adapted)

P9-3 Order Point; Inventory Levels. Cummings Company has developed the following figures to assist in controlling one of its inventory items:

Minimum daily use	150 units
Normal daily use	200 units
Maximum daily use	230 units
Working days per year	250
Lead time in working days	10
Safety stock	300 units
Cost of placing an order	$80
Order quantity	4,000 units

Required: Compute the following:
(1) Order point
(2) Normal maximum inventory
(3) Absolute maximum inventory
(4) Assuming demand is uniform and the EOQ formula is applicable, determine the cost of storing one unit for one year.

P9-4 Safety Stock. For Product 6E, ordered five times per year, stockout cost per occurrence is $80 and safety stock carrying cost is $3 per unit. Available options are:

Units of Safety Stock	Probability of Running out of Safety Stock
10	50%
20	40
30	30
40	20
50	10
55	3

Required: Compute the safety stock resulting in the lowest cost. (AICPA adapted)

P9-5 (Appendix) Inventory Costing Methods. Ewing Corporation had the following purchases and issues during March:

March 1	Beginning balance: 750 units @ $20 per unit
3	Purchased 400 units @ $19.50 per unit
5	Issued 600 units
12	Purchased 350 units @ $21.50 per unit
15	Issued 500 units
18	Purchased 500 units @ $22 per unit
22	Issued 400 units
26	Purchased 550 units @ $21 per unit
28	Issued 650 units
31	Purchased 200 units @ $20 per unit

Required: Compute the cost of units issued and the cost assigned to the March 31 inventory by each of these perpetual inventory costing methods:
(1) First in, first out
(2) Last in, first out
(3) Average, rounding unit cost to the nearest tenth of a cent

P9-6 (Appendix) Inventory Costing Methods. The records of the Blue Mercantile Company show the following data for Item A:

Balance, January 1 .... 200 units @ $10 per unit

	Purchases		
	Units	Price per Unit	Sales Units
January 12	100	$11	
February 1			200
April 16	200	12	
May 1			100
July 15	100	14	
November 10			100
December 5	100	17	
	500		400

The sales price for Item A was $15 per unit throughout the year.

Required:
(1) Compute the cost of the ending inventory under the fifo method when a periodic inventory system is used.
(2) Compute the cost of the ending inventory under the lifo method (a) when a periodic inventory system is used and (b) when a perpetual inventory system is used.

CGA-Canada (adapted). Reprint with permission.

P9-7 (Appendix) Inventory Costing. Token Company uses perpetual inventory costing for inventory Item 407, which it purchases for resale. The company began its operations on January 1 and is in the process of preparing its first financial statements.

The inventory ledger and other accounting records were examined, and the following information was gathered pertaining to the first four months of operations:

Purchases			Sales	
	Units	Cost per Unit		Units
January 2	2,000	$5	January 15	500
February 2	1,200	6	January 31	700
March 2	1,500	8	February 15	600
April 2	1,900	7	February 28	900
			March 15	600
			March 31	800
			April 15	700
			April 30	700

Management has not decided which of the following three inventory costing methods should be selected:
(a) Average method
(b) First in, first out method
(c) Last in, first out method

Required:

(1) Prepare an inventory record card for Item 407, using each of the methods mentioned. Carry all computations to three decimal places.

(2) Prepare a comparative statement showing the effect of each method on gross profit. The sales price is $10 per unit.

CGA-Canada (adapted). Reprint with permission.

Cases

C9-1 EOQ; Safety Stock Related to Production Runs. Thomas Peterson, general manager for Topp Desk Company, is exasperated because the company exhausted its finished goods inventory of Style 103—Modern Desk twice during the previous month. This led to customer complaints and disrupted the normal flow of operations.

"We ought to be able to plan better," declared Peterson during a presentation of his findings to management. "Our annual sales demand is 18,000 units for this model or an average of 75 desks per day based upon our 240-day work year. Unfortunately, the sales pattern is not this uniform. Our daily demand for that model varies considerably. If we do not have the units on hand when a customer places an order, 35% of the time we lose the sale, 40% of the time we pay an extra charge of $24 per unit to expedite shipping when the unit becomes available, and 25% of the time the customer accepts a back order at no out-of-pocket cost to us. A lost sale reduces the contribution to profit by $60."

Peterson displayed the following chart, showing the weighted average (sometimes called expected value) cost of a stockout on a given day.

75 desks per day × $60 × 35%	$1,575
75 desks per day × $24 × 40%	720
Back order (no out-of-pocket cost) × 25%	-0-
Stockout cost	$2,295

"When we run out of units", he continued, "we cannot convert the production line immediately, because we disrupt the production of our other products and cause cost increases. The setup process for this model on any stockout day results in the destruction of 12 finished desks, leaving no salvageable materials. Once we get the line up, we can produce 200 units per day. I would prefer to have several planned runs of a predetermined, uniform quantity rather than the short unplanned runs we have often used to meet unfilled customer orders."

The manager of the Cost Accounting Department suggested that they use an EOQ model to determine optimum production runs and then establish a safety stock to guard against stockouts. The cost data for the Modern Desk that sells for $110 are taken from the accounting records as follows:

Direct materials	$30.00
Direct labor (2 DLH @ $7.00)	14.00
Factory overhead:	
Variable (2 DLH @ $3.00)	6.00
Fixed (2 DLH @ $5.00)	10.00
Total manufacturing cost	$60.00

The Cost Accounting Department estimates that the company's carrying costs are 19.2% of the incremental out-of-pocket manufacturing costs. This percentage can be broken down into a 10.8% variable rate and an 8.4% fixed rate.

Required:

(1) Topp Desk Company believes that it can solve part of its production scheduling problems by adapting the EOQ model to determine the optimum production run.
   (a) Explain what costs the company will be attempting to minimize when it adapts the EOQ model to production runs.
   (b) Using the EOQ model, calculate the optimum quantity that Topp Desk Company should manufacture in each production run of Style 103—Modern Desk.
   (c) Calculate the number of production runs of Modern Desks that Topp Desk Company should schedule during the year based on the optimum quantity calculated in requirement 1b.

(2) Topp Desk Company should establish a safety stock level to guard against stockouts.
   (a) Explain the factors that affect the desired size of the safety stock for any inventory item.
   (b) Calculate the minimum safety stock level that Topp Desk Company could afford to maintain for Style 103—Modern Desk and not be worse off than it is when it is unable to fill orders equal to an average day's demand.

(ICMA adapted)

C9-2 Setup Cost. Pointer Furniture Company manufactures and sells office desks. For efficiency and quality control reasons, the desks are manufactured in batches. For example, 10 high quality desks might be manufactured during the first two weeks in October and 50 units of a lower quality desk during the last two weeks.

Because each model has its own unique manufacturing requirements, the change from one model to another requires the factory's equipment to be adjusted. Pointer management wants to determine the most economical production run for each of the items in its product line by adapting the economic order quantity inventory model.

One of the cost parameters that must be determined before the model can be employed is the setup cost incurred when there is a change to a different furniture model. As an example, the Accounting Department has been asked to determine the setup cost for Model JE 40 in its junior executive line.

The Equipment Maintenance Department is responsible for all changeover adjustments on production lines, in addition to the preventive and regular maintenance of all the production equipment. The equipment maintenance employees are paid $9 per hour, and employee benefits average 20% of wage costs. The other departmental costs, which include such items as supervision, depreciation, and insurance, total $50,000 per year. Two workers from the Equipment Maintenance Department are required to make the production change for Model JE 40. Each worker spends an estimated 5 hours in setting up the equipment as follows:

Machinery changes	3 hours
Testing	1 hour
Machinery readjustments	1 hour
Total	5 hours

The production line on which Model JE 40 is manufactured is operated by five workers. During the changeover, these workers assist the maintenance workers when needed and operate the line during the test run. However, they are idle for approximately 40% of the time required for the changeover and cannot be assigned to other jobs. The production workers are paid a basic wage of $7.50 per hour. Two factory overhead bases are used to apply the indirect costs, because some of the costs vary in proportion to direct labor hours, while others vary with machine hours. The factory overhead rates applicable for the current year are as follows:

	Based on Direct Labor Hours	Based on Machine Hours
Variable	$2.75	$ 5.00
Fixed	2.25	15.00
	$5.00	$20.00

These department overhead rates are based on an expected activity of 10,000 direct labor hours and 1,500 machine hours for the current year. This department is not scheduled to operate at full capacity because production capability currently exceeds sales potential.

The estimated cost of the direct materials used in the test run totals $200. Salvage materials from the test run should total $50.

Required:

(1) Estimate Pointer's setup cost for desk Model JE 40, for use in the economic production run model.

(2) Identify cost items to include in estimating Pointer's inventory carrying cost. (ICMA adapted)

C9-3 Cost of Carrying Inventory. Lacy Products is a regional firm that operates a manufacturing plant. The plant's operations are typical, involving raw materials, work in process, and finished goods inventories. Raw materials are purchased and stored until their introduction into the manufacturing process. On completion, the finished products are stored in the company's warehouse, awaiting final sale.

A recent study indicated that Lacy's annual cost of carrying inventory is more than 25% of the average inventory investment. Management believes that inventory carrying costs might be an excellent area in which to implement cost reductions and proposes two strategies: first, not requesting raw materials from suppliers until near the time needed in the manufacturing process, and second, transferring the finished goods to customers immediately following completion.

Required: Identify and discuss the circumstances necessary to make such a proposal feasible with respect to (1) raw materials inventory and (2) finished goods inventory. (ICMA adapted)

CHAPTER 10

Just-In-Time and Backflushing

Learning Objectives

After studying this chapter, you will be able to:

1. Describe a just-in-time (JIT) production system and contrast it with traditional production.
2. Define material velocity and state its relationship to inventory levels.
3. State the potential effect of JIT on production losses.
4. Describe JIT's effects on the purchasing function.
5. State the relationship between JIT and backflushing.
6. Prepare general journal entries and T accounts for backflush accounting.

The preceeding chapter illustrated materials accounting and control in settings characterized by large inventories. This chapter describes just-in-time and illustrates accounting for the flow of production costs in a mature just-in-time system.

Just-in-Time

Just-in-time (JIT) is a philosophy centered on the reduction of costs through elimination of inventory. All materials and components should arrive at a work station when they are needed—no earlier and no later. Products should be completed and available to customers when the customers want them—no earlier and no later. Elimination of inventories eliminates storage and carrying costs; however, it also eliminates the cushion against production errors and imbalances that inventories provide. As a result, high quality and balanced work loads are required in a JIT system to avoid costly shutdowns and customer ill will. Because of the need for quality and balanced production, JIT has come to be closely identified with efforts to eliminate waste in all its forms, and thus it is an important part of many total quality management (TQM) efforts.

JIT principles are applicable in improving routine housekeeping, such as the location and arrangement of the tools, dies, and fixtures used with production machinery. It is also useful in managing work in an office, a service business, or a service department of a factory; in reducing inventory requirements in a factory or a retail store; and in many other aspects of the operation of a business. The implementation of JIT among U.S. industries is a recent phenomenon, but JIT itself is not a new idea. Over sixty years ago, Henry Ford's book *Today and Tomorrow* described a JIT production system. Japanese auto companies developed JIT systems in the 1950s.

The most visible aspect of JIT is the effort to reduce inventories of work in process (WIP) and raw materials. Most writings on JIT concentrate on this one aspect, which is called **stockless production**, **lean production**, or **zero**

inventory production (**ZIP**). In JIT, authorization for a part to be made at a work station is generated by the need for that part at the next work station in the production line. As parts are used in final assembly, the production of their replacements is authorized. The process is repeated at all preceding work stations, thus "pulling" parts through the production system as they are needed and in turn pulling materials from suppliers. This differs from traditional systems, in which large stocks of WIP generally are kept at many work stations. The JIT ideal is to eliminate these stocks of WIP and produce parts only as needed. JIT is a special case of a very small economic order quantity (EOQ). The JIT ideal is a batch size of one. For JIT to operate properly, setup time must be short. Also, production flow through the various work stations must be uniform, a usual characteristic of repetitive manufacturing.

To avoid inventory buildup, the entire production line is stopped if parts are missing at any stage or if defects are found. Defects must be caught early before they can be built into a large number of units, so if a reasonable flow rate is to be achieved, the number of defects must be small. Workers must be highly involved in quality, because a defect at any station shuts down production.[1]

JIT seeks to reduce inventories because it views inventories as wasteful. Inventory represents resources not being used and is a form of slack or fat that covers up other forms of waste.[2] The objective of reducing inventory to zero, however, is possible only under the following conditions:

1. Low or insignificant setup (or order) times and costs.
2. Lot sizes equal to one.
3. Minimum and almost instantaneous lead times.
4. Balanced and level work loads.
5. No interruptions due to stockouts, poor quality, unscheduled equipment downtimes, engineering changes, or other unplanned changes.

Inventories are carried in virtually all systems because these idealized conditions do not exist. The concept of zero inventory connotes a level of perfection that is generally unattainable. However, JIT does stimulate constant improvement in the environmental conditions that cause inventory buildup. The continuing reduction of inventories is achieved by the following process:

1. Inventories are reduced until a problem (bump) is discovered and identified.
2. Once the problem is defined, the inventory level is increased to absorb the shock of this bump and to keep the system operating smoothly.
3. The problem is analyzed and practical ways are identified to reduce or remove the problem.
4. Once the problem is reduced or removed, the inventory level is reduced until another problem is discovered and identified.
5. Steps 2 through 4 are repeated until the minimum possible level of inventories is achieved.

In this way, reduction of inventory uncovers problems and stimulates the search for practical ways of solving them, so continuous improvement is made in eliminating wastes.[3] Reduction of inventory levels also affects processing speed, or the velocity at which a task or unit passes through the system.

---

[1] Larry Utzig, "Reconciling the Two Views of Quality," *Journal of Cost Management*, Vol. 1, No. 1, p. 68.

[2] Charles D. Mecimore and James K. Weeks, *Techniques in Inventory Management and Control* (Montvale, N.J.: Institute of Management Accountants (formerly the National Association of Accountants), 1987), pp. 6, 124.

[3] *Ibid.*, p. 125.

JIT and Velocity

There is an important and direct relationship between the size of WIP and the speed of production. If 1,000 units are produced per day, and 2,000 units are in process at any time, then a unit takes an average of two days (2,000 ÷ 1,000) to pass through the system. This is described as a **throughput time** of two days. If the speed of the system is then doubled so that throughput time is only one day, then the same output of 1,000 units per day is achieved with only 1,000 units in process. This relationship can be stated another way: if the rate of output is maintained while the number of units in process is cut in half, then the speed of the system has been doubled. As long as the rate of output is held constant, reducing the number of units in process and increasing the speed of the system are one and the same. The speed with which units or tasks are processed in a system is called the **velocity** and is inversely related to throughput time.

A strategic benefit of increased velocity is the reduced time needed to fill production orders. When velocity is increased tenfold, the average order is filled in one-tenth the time. Customers get faster service on routine orders as well as rush orders. In extreme cases, production speed is improved so much that finished goods inventory is no longer needed because all shipments can be made to order.

Velocity improvement can be extended forward to finished goods inventory and shipping. It can be extended backward through raw materials inventory, purchasing, product design, development, and research. In such a case, the result is a shorter total lead time for responding to any change in customer tastes or to any opportunity for a new product or product variation. For example, in the first five years of JIT implementation, one plant operated by Oregon Cutting Systems reported a reduction in lead time from 21 days to three days.[4] In high-technology industries characterized by continual innovation and short product life cycles, improvements in response time can make the difference between success and mere survival or between survival and failure.

Returning to WIP inventory as the example, refer to the concept of cycle time discussed in Chapter 2. The intent of JIT is to reduce total cycle time, because the only time that value can be added to a product is when it is being processed; moving time, waiting time, and inspection time do not add value. Only process time adds value; the rest solely add cost. Thus, reducing total cycle time means reducing cost and increasing competitiveness. And, of course, even process time should be at the lowest level consistent with quality production.

Because WIP is a costly asset that must be financed and maintained just as any other asset, the obvious benefit of a WIP reduction is that total investment is reduced, producing savings in inventory carrying costs. For example, suppose the annual carrying cost is 25% of variable production costs and the variable costs of average WIP is $200,000. Management plans to use JIT to double the velocity of WIP without changing total annual output. (This is achieved by cutting average batch size in half.) No change is planned in materials or finished goods inventory. Average WIP will be reduced by half,

[4] Jack C. Bailes and Ilene K. Kleinsorge, "Cutting Waste with JIT," *Management Accounting*, Vol. 63, No. 11, pp. 28–32.

producing a savings of \$25,000 (25% × ½ × \$200,000) in annual carrying costs.[5] In addition to the effect on inventory carrying costs, a more important result of a WIP reduction is its effect on production losses.

JIT and Production Losses

At individual work stations in a production line, the impact of WIP reduction is simple—fewer units will be waiting at, or moving to, each location. This can have an important impact on production losses, although the connection between losses and WIP levels is not obvious. Suppose step 5 in a production line processes each unit and sends it to await step 6, and suppose that 100 units are waiting between steps 5 and 6. If at some time step 5 begins producing units with a defect that will be discovered in step 6, then how many defectives might step 5 produce before the problem is discovered? The answer is 100; possibly less, if the problem at step 5 is discovered in some other way or if the defect enters only some of the units produced. The worst outcome is 100 defectives—the size of WIP at that work station. After 100 are produced, step 6 will have nothing but defective units to work on, and so the error will be discovered and presumably corrected. If 1,000 units are held waiting between steps 5 and 6, then a maximum 1,000 defectives can be produced. If only 10 units are held, the worst outcome is 10 defectives. If the inventory between steps is eliminated entirely, errors at step 5 will be discovered as soon as the first defective unit is produced.[6]

For example, suppose a production environment is described as follows:

Work stations where WIP is held	20
Average number of units in WIP per station	400
Annual inventory carrying cost	25%
Planned reduction in WIP levels	60%
Planned change in final output rate	none
Physical flow of units at each station	fifo
Average variable cost of a unit in WIP	\$100
Average dollar loss per defective unit	20

Further suppose that the total number of instances in which some work station goes out of its control limits and produces defects is expected to be 1,000 during the coming year. In half of such instances, the out-of-control condition is expected to be discovered immediately by the operator at the faulty work station. In the other half of these instances, a defect will enter 10% of the units produced; the defective units enter WIP between stations, where they are discovered by the next station's operator; and every out-of-control condition is corrected as soon as it is discovered.

[5] The EOQ discussion in Chapter 9 suggests the savings will be more than offset by the ordering (setup) costs of a larger number of smaller batches. The solution is to set EOQ at a fraction (half, using the above example) of its former level, and then find what reduction in ordering cost is needed to solve the EOQ equation. The implementation of the plan then consists of driving setup costs down to that lower level, making the smaller batch size become the EOQ. For this reason, much of JIT technology deals with reducing the duration and cost of setups.

[6] This phenomenon causes frequent shutdowns whenever WIP levels are significantly reduced. It is frustrating to shut down one step or another every few minutes, but the objective of manufacturing is not to maintain a steady stream of defective output. Further, one of JIT's objectives is to find problems and correct them.

If no unit contains more than one defect and no other changes are made in the system, then the 60% reduction in WIP levels is expected to provide annual savings of \$360,000, consisting of \$120,000 carrying costs savings and \$240,000 savings in the cost of defects, calculated as follows:

$$\begin{aligned}\text{Carrying cost savings} &= 25\% \times \text{Reduction in average variable cost of WIP}\\ &= 25\% \times 60\% \times \text{Past average variable cost of WIP}\\ &= .25 \times .6 \times (20 \times 400 \times \$100)\\ &= \$120{,}000\end{aligned}$$

$$\begin{aligned}\text{Savings in cost of defects} &= \$20 \times \text{Reduction in number of defective units}\\ &= \$20 \times \begin{array}{c}\text{Reduction in number}\\ \text{of defective units}\\ \text{produced per}\\ \text{undiscovered}\\ \text{out-of-control}\\ \text{condition}\end{array} \times \begin{array}{c}\text{Number of out-of-}\\ \text{control conditions}\\ \text{not discovered}\\ \text{immediately}\end{array}\\ &= \$20 \times (60\% \times 400 \times 10\%) \times (\tfrac{1}{2} \times 1{,}000)\\ &= \$20 \times 24 \times 500\\ &= \$240{,}000\end{aligned}$$

Many potential advantages of lower WIP levels are not included in these calculations because the description of the production environment provides no information about them. These potential advantages include the savings in setup costs that must be achieved to make the 60% smaller average batch size economical. The savings also include improvements in customer satisfaction from quicker response to orders and the possibility that the faster cycle time might permit all shipments to be made to order so that finished goods inventory is no longer needed. Of course, there are costs to be offset against the savings. These costs include (1) handling a larger number of smaller batches of WIP, including the cost of processing more production orders and material requisitions, if these documents continue to be used, and the cost of handling more loads of materials; (2) the higher probability of shutdowns due to the smaller safety stock at each work station; and (3) the possibility that setup costs cannot be reduced enough to offset the larger number of setups performed.

Because of the connection between losses and WIP levels, many successful JIT implementations dramatically reduce production losses and thus contribute to quality improvement. For example, in the first five years of JIT implementation, Oregon Cutting Systems reduced scrap and rework by 50% and defects by 80% with no increase in quality costs.[7]

Similar advantages come from reducing raw materials inventory. Not only is less storage space needed, but the risk of obsolescence, damage, and deterioration are reduced greatly if raw materials are held for an average of one or two days rather than three to six months. This aspect of JIT calls for very small and very frequent material receipts, close coordination and frequent communication with vendors and freight carriers, highly reliable material quality, and an error-free transportation system. These demanding conditions involve significant changes in the purchasing function.

[7] *Ibid.*

JIT and Purchasing

Because JIT pertains not only to WIP but also to raw materials inventory, the purchasing function is heavily involved in the adoption of JIT. The objective is that both raw materials and WIP inventories be held to absolute minimums.[8]

The JIT approach to purchasing emphasizes reducing the number of suppliers and improving the quality of both the materials and the procurement function. The objective is to move materials directly from the supplier to the plant floor with little or no inspection, and to eliminate storage except for brief periods directly on the plant floor.[9] A single vendor for each material is the ideal; in practice, a second vendor may be used to ensure sufficient supply in periods of unusually high demand. The goal is long-term vendor relationships, rather than short-run price breaks. Selecting and monitoring vendors requires a system of vendor performance appraisal that quantitatively rates each supplier on timely deliveries, quality of materials, and price competitiveness, rather than a subjective approach.[10]

Obstacles to JIT purchasing exist, such as the layout of the production process, frequency of schedule changes, attitudes of purchasing agents and suppliers, reliability of freight carriers, and distance from suppliers. When these problems can be overcome, the result usually is an impressive reduction in manufacturing costs.

Well-developed JIT purchasing uses **blanket purchase orders**, which are agreements with vendors stating the total quantities expected to be needed over a period of three or six months. The exact quantity and date of each shipment are established later by a telephone call or, with electronic data interchange (EDI), by a direct computer link between buyer and seller. The result is the elimination of the routine purchase requisitions, purchase orders, receiving reports, and materials requisitions discussed in Chapter 9.[11]

Received materials or their containers can have bar-coded[12] labels that are read by hand-held or built-in scanners on the buyer's assembly line, similar to the scanners at checkout counters of many retail stores. Scanned data can automatically update product cost records for the job or department involved, compare kinds and quantities of materials with recent EDI requests, and initiate a periodic electronic funds transfer to the vendor's bank account to pay for the materials. A later scanning of all items used or sold can initiate EDI requests to the appropriate vendors for small shipments of the kind and quantity needed.

---

[8] Sauers, "Analyzing Inventory Systems," pp. 31–32.

[9] A July 27, 1992 *Wall Street Journal* article described General Motors' factory in Eisenach, Germany: "It is clean and brightly lit, with nary a conveyor belt or storage bin. Delivery trucks will unload parts just a few meters from the assembly line; they will drive in one door and out another to eliminate the need for backing in and out of loading docks. Hundreds of such details add up to huge efficiencies."

[10] For an illustration of a formalized, objective vendor certification procedure, see Michael A. Robinson and John E. Timmerman, "How Vendor Analysis Supports JIT Manufacturing," *Management Accounting*, Vol. 69, No. 6, pp. 20–24.

[11] Invoices, cash transfers to payee banks, and updates on the location and status of shipments can also be provided via EDI. See Arjan T. Sadhurani and M. H. Sarhan, "Electronic Systems Enhance JIT Operations," *Management Accounting*, Vol. 69, No. 6, pp. 25–26.

[12] For an example of bar coding and EDI, see Lawrence Klein and Randy M. Jacques, "Pillow Talk for Productivity: Bar Coding and EDI Help Pillowtex Serve Its Customers Better," *Management Accounting*, Vol. 72, No. 8, pp. 47–49.

JIT and Factory Organization

One approach to JIT is to change from the traditional factory layout to **cells** or **work cells**. A cell is responsible for the entire production of one product or part, or a family of very similar ones. A traditionally organized factory may have a cutting department where all cutting is done and a drilling department where all drilling is done, but a cell arrangement places one cutting machine and one drilling machine in each cell. Every worker in the cell is trained to perform multiple tasks, so labor is easily shifted to the point in the cell where it is needed. The cell's workers can be evaluated and rewarded as a team rather than as individuals to promote cooperation and self-policing of problems. All workers are responsible for product quality, because the same workers do everything from initiating each delivery of materials from vendors to inspecting the cell's final output; every worker becomes an inspector.

In addition to inspection, other tasks that are normally considered indirect labor are assigned to cell workers. They stop production whenever their cell's output is not needed and resume production when it is needed; receive and move their materials; maintain, store, and replace the cell's tools, dies, and fixtures; and set up, maintain, and repair the cell's machines.[13] If an entire factory is organized into JIT cells, the result is the disappearance of not only the traditional producing departments (cutting and drilling in the previous example), but most of the service departments as well. Scheduling, receiving, materials handling, tool storage, setup, maintenance, repair, in-process inspection, and finished-goods inspection are all performed by cell labor rather than by separate service departments. Other traditional functions of service departments, including materials storage, WIP storage, finished goods storage, receiving inspection, and expediting, may not be needed at all. Because of the small size of a typical cell, the total distance a product is moved during production is reduced, with savings in materials handling and breakage; for example, one plant of Oregon Cutting Systems reduced its product-flow distance by 94%.[14]

The effects of this arrangement on product quality can be impressive. Recall that one ingredient of TQM is worker empowerment. A high degree of empowerment is possible when a cell team has autonomy over every production step from receiving to final inspection and performs most of its own support functions as well. Further, when things do go wrong, time is not wasted by placing blame on others. Workers know they cannot avoid responsibility for defective output by claiming the cause was bad material, careless handling, or a broken machine if part of their job is to eliminate those problems. They cannot avoid responsibility for a broken machine or a ruined tool by blaming it on an error in tool selection, tool installation, machine maintenance, or setup if part of their job is to perform those functions.

A final impact of JIT on factory organization is in floor space requirements. Many adopters of JIT have been surprised at how much of their floor space no longer is needed. Space savings have been large enough in some cases to permit

---

[13] As a result, it is impossible to measure direct and indirect labor separately, because a worker can shift from direct to indirect labor tasks every few minutes or seconds. Fortunately, there is no need to separate direct and indirect labor when the cell is devoted to one product or part or a family of very similar ones. This is because all cell labor and all other conversion costs in the cell are traceable to the cell and therefore to the cell's output. All units of output are processed similarly in the cell, so conversion costs are divided equally among all units.

[14] Bailes and Kleinsorge, "Cutting Waste with JIT."

consolidation of operations into fewer buildings, thus reducing facilities costs. For example, three plants of Oregon Cutting Systems reported savings in floor space from 30% to 40%.[15]

JIT–A Balanced View

In spite of the enormous advantages attributed to JIT, most of its adopters embrace it only partially. Many companies that are considered users of JIT purchasing handle only a small percentage of their materials requirements by JIT methods.[16] Among the reasons are (1) the time and effort required to convert many suppliers to a JIT shipping pattern, (2) the difficulty of obtaining shipping at a cost low enough to justify many small deliveries, (3) the likelihood of occasional shipping delays if suppliers are hundreds of miles away, and (4) the frustrating tendency for a low-cost, allegedly noncritical part to become critical when it does not arrive on time and an important customer's order cannot be finished because there is no safety stock. For these and other reasons, some companies claim to have adopted just in time but continue to keep safety stocks of many materials "just in case."

Among efforts to eliminate large WIP inventories, partial success is again the norm. The original WIP level may be cut to a half or a quarter, bringing big improvements in velocity, production losses, and space requirements, but typically the remaining WIP is still quite large. A common reason for this is the continual frustration of having one work station or another shut down because it is "starved" for work and there is no WIP safety stock at that station. If WIP velocity is improved so much that production need not be scheduled until a customer order is received, then finished goods inventory is no longer needed. This is a revolutionary change in the operation of a manufacturing company and its advantages are considerable. But what if WIP levels and production losses remain large (although only a fraction of their former levels)? What if a large materials inventory is maintained to avoid any delay in beginning work on an order (because every order is a rush order)? Then it can hardly be claimed that stockless production has been achieved. The concept of zero inventory simply cannot be taken literally;[17] what it really means is striving to reduce inventories.

Most adoptions of cell organization are also only partial. Some so-called JIT factories contain only one or a few JIT cells, representing a small fraction of total output. The reason may be a desire to experiment with JIT on a small scale, or a failure of most products to meet the conditions necessary for JIT implementation. Or the JIT cell may simply be a technology showcase proudly pointed out during plant tours.

JIT is limited in its applicability to different patterns of demand. Where demand is predictable and fairly level from period to period, JIT is the ideal system, and many factories and other settings can achieve such a demand pattern. Where demand fluctuates greatly from hour to hour and day to day, JIT is less practical. With no inventory to serve as a buffer between the rate of demand and rate of production, a facility must either turn away many customers or have

---

[15] *Ibid.*

[16] A. Ansari and B. Modarress, in *Just in Time Purchasing* (New York: The Free Press, 1990), report that the Nissan truck plant in Smyrna, Tennessee, has only one true JIT material—seats, delivered daily by a single supplier with no safety stock ever held. Some other materials are quasi-JIT, being delivered twice per week; but a sizable percentage of all parts are still supplied in large lots as in any traditional purchasing system.

[17] Sauers, "Analyzing Inventory Systems," p. 36.

enough personnel and equipment in place to handle peak demand. If average demand is a small fraction of the peak level, JIT results in either huge idle capacity or many missed sales, either of which can be prohibitively expensive. This problem can persist even if demand can be accurately predicted. For example, if the time interval from high to low demand is very short, it may not be practical to plan shutdowns and restarts at hourly or daily intervals. Large amounts of lost sales, idle capacity, and inventories cannot all be avoided under those conditions. For some businesses, the least of the three evils may be to maintain enough inventory to satisfy peak demand and replenish inventory when demand is low.

JIT implementation can create conflicts with performance measures. Measures of JIT performance include cycle time efficiency (defined in Chapter 2), inventory turnover, percentage of shipments on time, unscheduled machine downtime, number or percent of defects, and similar nonfinancial measures. Traditional performance measures, especially measures of capacity utilization,[18] encourage behavior contrary to the JIT approach. If a manager is evaluated in part on the basis of how fully capacity is utilized, then a rational response is to make certain that machines and workers are never idle. But whenever output is not needed at the next work station, being idle is exactly what JIT requires. Some JIT efforts have been derailed early, as managers and workers who clearly understood and implemented their new JIT instructions found themselves coming up short in the next performance evaluation because the old performance measures were still used. The shift to JIT, like TQM, requires a radical change in mindset and an overhaul of the system for motivating, measuring, and rewarding performance.[19]

Many JIT efforts can be criticized as quick fixes or cosmetic changes. Business folklore tells of JIT implementations that merely amount to forcing suppliers to carry larger inventory, make many small shipments, and charge much higher prices for it. Other JIT implementations create inventory management companies to buy in bulk and make the many frequent shipments needed. Both approaches merely shift large inventories to another point in the stream of production. Equally notorious are cases in which top management embraces the JIT idea, but does not change performance measures and rewards to be consistent with it.

Backflushing

Backflushing, also called **backflush costing** or **backflush accounting**, is an abbreviated approach to accounting for the flow of manufacturing costs. It is applicable to mature JIT systems in which velocity is so high that traditional accounting is impractical. Both job order and process costing, the common methods of cost accumulation, involve maintaining subsidiary records of the cost of WIP; these records are updated by many accounting entries. If the elapsed time between the receipt of raw materials and the completion of product is reduced to a few hours, then the usefulness of carefully tracking the cost of WIP is questionable for two reasons.

First, a total cycle time of a few hours means that an extremely small amount of work is in process at any time. As a result, accurate assignment of costs to the

[18] Examples are the volume and idle capacity variances discussed in Chapters 17, 18, and 19.

[19] See Robert D. McIlhattan, "The JIT Philosophy," *Management Accounting*, Vol. 69, No. 3, pp. 20–26.

very small WIP inventory is generally a trivial issue, both for financial reporting and for controlling work in process. For financial reporting, an end-of-period estimate of cost is sufficient if inventory is very small. For controlling a fast-moving WIP inventory, physical measures and visual observation are used. Second, even if a manager wants to track carefully the costs of WIP in these circumstances, there may to be no way to do it with available data processing technology.

The Essence of Backflush Costing

The purpose of backflush costing is to reduce the number of events that are measured and recorded in the accounting system. Compared to job order and process costing, backflush costing is notable for its lack of detailed tracking of the cost of WIP. Its keynote is simplicity. Concisely stated, inventory accounts are not adjusted throughout the accounting period to reflect all production costs—their balances are corrected instead by end-of-period journal entries—and there are no detailed subsidiary records maintained for units in process. Refer to Figure 4-2, which depicts the flow of manufacturing costs. Backflush costing eliminates some of the accounting steps shown there or combines them with other steps. Some of the general ledger accounts also can be combined.

The accounting for materials inventory, as well as for WIP, can be altered by backflush costing. This is because, in a successful JIT application where backflush costing is used, there may be no separate materials inventory. Instead, materials received are put immediately into production, so materials and work in process are combined in a single account. Different versions of backflush costing are possible, depending on whether a separate work in process account exists. If it does exist, some or all of the cost elements can be charged to it before the end of the accounting period. Similarly, the finished goods inventory account can be charged with some cost elements only by end-of-period entries.[20]

In job order and process cost accumulation, the cost of completed work is determined by assigning all cost elements—direct material, direct labor, and overhead—to the work in process inventory at various stages during production, as illustrated in Chapters 5 and 6. In contrast, backflush costing determines some or all elements of the cost of output only after production is complete. The cost of completed work is subtracted from the balance of the work in process account, or an equivalent combined account, in a step called **postdeduction** or **post-manufacturing deduction**.[21] In this terminology, *post* simply means after, and *deduction* refers to the subtraction of the amount of cost. In actual practice, there can be other items to be postdeducted, such as the estimated cost of scrapped materials, the cost of materials returned to vendors, shortages in material counts, and, in a standard cost system, the cost variances.[22]

The backflush calculation uses end-of-period estimates of the actual material and conversion cost components of all unfinished work, including any unprocessed raw material. (In a standard cost system, the standards eliminate the need for these estimates.) The cost estimates are made after a physical inventory

[20] There may be no finished goods inventory account at all, but that condition is not unique to backflush costing—any factory that produces only for customers' orders and ships completed work immediately has no finished goods inventory.

[21] Bruce R. Neumann and Pauline R. Jaouen, "Kanban, ZIPS and Cost Accounting: A Case Study", *Journal of Accountancy*, Vol. 162, No. 2, pp. 132–141.

[22] C. J. McNair, William Mosconi, and Thomas Norris, *Meeting the Technology Challenge: Cost Accounting in a JIT Environment*, (Montvale, N.J.: Institute of Management Accountants (formerly the National Association of Accountants), 1988), pp. 102–104.

count, which is usually done monthly or weekly. Estimates of the material cost components are derived from recent supplier invoices if actual costs are desired. Estimates of conversion cost amounts can be derived by first estimating the conversion cost of a finished unit, and then assigning a part of that per-unit conversion cost to the partly finished units on hand. The conversion cost of a finished unit can be estimated by dividing total conversion cost incurred in the period by the number of units started, or by the number of completed units, or by the total of completed units and unfinished units on hand, or any similar total for the period. In a mature JIT application, where backflush costing is likely to be used, all these will produce approximately the same result, because so few units are on hand at any time. Including the units on hand in the total count of units will affect the result by perhaps one percent or less.

Before backflush costing is illustrated, an analogy drawn from financial accounting will be used to demonstrate the logic of backflush costing and the differences between it and other methods.

A Basic Financial Accounting Analogy

Two different inventory methods are used by nonmanufacturing companies: perpetual and periodic. In the perpetual method, the merchandise inventory account is debited for each purchase of goods and is credited for the cost of each sale of goods. The objective is to record each increase or decrease in the merchandise inventory account, so that it provides a perpetual record of the cost of merchandise on hand. A significant amount of detailed accounting for merchandise inventory is done in this method, and it is analogous to the detailed tracking of work in process that job order and process costing entail for a manufacturer.

In contrast, the periodic inventory method leaves the beginning balance of the merchandise inventory account unchanged through the accounting period. An end-of-period adjustment is made to arrive at an ending balance equal to the physical inventory count. Cost of goods sold, which is the total outflow of merchandise for the accounting period, is calculated and recorded only at the end of the period. This is done by adding the beginning merchandise inventory cost to the total of purchases and subtracting the ending inventory cost. Journal entries adjust the merchandise inventory account to the correct ending balance and record cost of goods sold for the period. Just as no detailed accounting for merchandise inventory is done in the periodic method, no detailed tracking of WIP inventory is done by a manufacturer using backflush costing—both rely on end-of-period calculations and adjustments of inventory accounts.

Illustration of Backflush Costing

McIntire Company produces electronic equipment using purchased materials and components. Total time from receipt of raw material to completion of a unit is less than two days. McIntire maintains a small inventory of finished goods, but due to the mature JIT system that governs production, the raw materials and work in process inventories are minimal. The cost of raw materials on hand, including parts and other direct materials, is combined with work in process cost into a single inventory account entitled Raw and In Process (RIP), for which no detailed subsidiary records are maintained. A separate supplies account is maintained for indirect materials.

Like other manufacturers with minimal inventories, McIntire Company uses frequent physical counts for control. All inventories are physically counted at the end of each month, and estimates are then made of the amount of conversion cost that should be assigned to the finished goods inventory and to the small number of partially completed units in RIP. Because inventory levels change very little from month to month, these conversion cost estimates generally vary little from those of the preceding month.

Raw material cost is backflushed from RIP to Finished Goods and from Finished Goods to Cost of Goods Sold based on the monthly physical counts. (If standard costs were used, backflushing could be done daily or for each individual unit—the number of units would simply be multiplied by the standard per-unit material cost to arrive at the amount to be backflushed.) Direct labor and overhead costs are expensed to the cost of goods sold account. The estimated conversion cost components of the RIP and finished goods inventory account balances are adjusted at the end of each month, with the offsetting entry representing a correction of Cost of Goods Sold.[23]

General journal entries of McIntire Company can be compared with those of New Hope Manufacturing Company in Chapter 4. But first, two important observations can be made. One is that the most important difference between backflush costing and other cost accumulation methods does not become apparent by comparing general journal entries. It does, however, make for an enormous difference in actual practice: no subsidiary detailed records are maintained for units in production in the backflush system. Chapters 5 and 6 discussed the subsidiary records used in accounting for WIP in job order and process costing; backflush costing, in contrast, entails no such detailed tracking of these costs. The savings in clerical effort can be substantial.

The second observation is that the number of general journal entries to be demonstrated for McIntire Company will not be appreciably different from that shown in Chapter 4 for New Hope Manufacturing Company. This is because only two general ledger accounts are being eliminated. The first change to be noticed in the general journal entries is that any material cost that would be entered into the materials or WIP inventory accounts under job order or process cost accumulation (as illustrated by New Hope Manufacturing Company) will instead be entered into the RIP account in backflush costing. A second change is that, in backflushing, conversion costs are expensed, bypassing the inventory accounts entirely, with any necessary adjustments made at the end of the month.

Selected transactions and other information for McIntire for January are described and journalized as follows. For brevity, transactions that do not deal with manufacturing costs, such as sales and cash collections, are not listed; they would be handled in the usual manner. To facilitate comparison with the journal entries in Chapter 4 for New Hope Manufacturing Company, the portions of journal entries that differ due to backflush costing are in italics.

January 1 balances in inventory accounts:

Raw and In Process	$ 21,000
Finished Goods	170,000
Supplies	20,000

The RIP balance consisted of a $20,100 cost of materials, most of which were not yet in process, plus a $900 conversion cost estimate assigned to partially processed work. The Finished Goods balance consists of $84,000 material cost and an $86,000 estimate of conversion cost.

[23] Neumann and Jaouen, "Kanban, ZIPS and Cost Accounting: A Case Study."

January 31 inventories based on physical count:

Raw and In Process	$ 23,000
Finished Goods	174,000
Supplies	5,000

The RIP amount consisted of a $21,600 cost of materials, most of which were not yet in process, plus a $1,400 conversion cost estimate assigned to partially processed work. The Finished Goods amount consisted of $85,800 material cost and an $88,200 estimate of conversion cost.

McIntire Company

Transactions		Journal Entries		
(a) Direct material received from suppliers	$406,000	*Raw and in Process*	*406,000*	
		Accounts Payable		406,000
		A summary entry for all receipts of raw materials during the period. As direct materials are used, no entry is needed, because they remain a part of RIP.		
(b) Indirect materials used	$ 15,000	Factory Overhead Control	15,000	
		Supplies		15,000
		Indirect materials are recorded as used.		
(c) Gross payroll of $160,000 recorded; the payroll paid.		Payroll	160,000	
		Accrued Payroll		160,000
		Accrued Payroll	160,000	
		Cash		160,000
(d) The payroll distribution:		*Cost of Goods Sold*	*25,000*	
Direct labor	$ 25,000	Factory Overhead Control	45,000	
Indirect factory labor	45,000	Marketing Expenses Control	50,000	
Marketing salaries	50,000	Administrative Expenses		
Administrative salaries	40,000	Control	40,000	
(Due to the small amount of direct labor cost compared to total manufacturing costs, McIntire Company might use a single conversion cost account for direct labor and overhead. To facilitate comparison with New Hope Company, direct labor is accounted for separately in this illustration.)		Payroll		160,000
		Direct labor is expensed to the cost of goods sold account. (In job order or process cost accumulation, direct labor is charged to the work in process account.)		
(e) Factory overhead costs:		Factory Overhead Control	299,000	
Depreciation	$290,000	Accumulated Depreciation		290,000
Insurance	9,000	Prepaid Insurance		9,000
(f) Miscellaneous factory overhead costs:		Factory Overhead Control	21,000	
Paid in cash	$ 17,000	Cash		17,000
On account	4,000	Accounts Payable		4,000
(g) Factory overhead accumulated in the factory overhead control account expensed to Cost of Goods Sold.		*Cost of Goods Sold*	*380,000*	
		Factory Overhead Control		380,000
		Overhead is expensed to the cost of goods sold account. (In job order or process cost accumulation, the overhead is charged to the work in process account.)		
(h) The material cost component of completed work is backflushed from RIP.		*Finished Goods*	*404,500*	
		Raw and in Process		*404,500*
		To backflush material cost from RIP to Finished Goods. This is a postdeduction. The calculation is:		

Material in January 1 RIP balance	$ 20,100
Material received during January	406,000
	$426,100
Material in January 31 RIP, per physical count	21,600
Amount to be backflushed	$404,500

(i) The material cost component of work sold is backflushed from Finished Goods.	*Cost of Goods Sold*	*402,700*	
	Finished Goods		*402,700*
	To backflush material cost from Finished Goods to Cost of Goods Sold. The calculation is:		

Material in Jan. 1 finished goods,	84,000
Material cost transferred from RIP	404,500
	$488,500
Material in Jan. 31 finished goods, per physical count	85,800
Amount to be backflushed	$402,700

(j) Ending balances are established in inventory accounts by adjusting their conversion cost components.	*Raw and in Process*	*500*	
	Finished Goods	*2,200*	
	Cost of Goods Sold		*2,700*

Conversion costs in inventory accounts are adjusted to estimates made in the January 31 physical count. For RIP, the adjustment is from the $900 of January 1 to $1,400 on January 31; for Finished Goods, the adjustment is from the $86,000 of January 1 to $88,200 on January 31. The offsetting entry is made to the cost of goods sold account, where all conversion cost are charged during January. (If a conversion cost component had decreased during the month, an inventory account would be credited.)

Because this application of backflush costing expenses all conversion costs directly to the cost of goods sold account, the effects of the general journal entries can be more readily understood by examining the three McIntire Company accounts shown here:

Raw and In Process

1/1	21,000	(h)	404,500
(a)	406,000		
(j)	500		
	427,500		
23,000			

Finished Goods

1/1	170,000	(i)	402,700
(h)	404,500		
(j)	2,200		
	576,700		
174,000			

Cost of Goods Sold

1/1	-0-	(j)	2,700
(d)	25,000		
(g)	380,000		
(i)	402,700		
	807,700		
805,000			

To illustrate a second version of backflush costing, suppose Lightning Fast Company produces only for customer order, has an average elapsed time of less than two days between receipt of raw material and shipment of finished work, and keeps no finished goods on hand, but all other data are the same as those given above for McIntire Company. General journal entries are as follow.

Lightning Fast Company

General Journal Entries

(a) - (g) These entries are identical to entries (a) through (g) in the previous illustration of McIntire Company.

(h) *Cost of Goods Sold*	*404,500*	
Raw and In Process		*404,500*

To backflush material cost from RIP to Cost of Goods Sold. This is the postdeduction step.

(i) Not applicable, because there is no finished goods inventory.

(j) *Raw and In Process*	*500*	
Cost of Goods Sold		*500*

Conversion cost in the RIP account is adjusted from the $900 of January 1 to the $1,400 estimate made in the January 31 physical count. The offsetting entry is made to the cost of goods sold account, where all conversion costs were charged during January.

The effects of the general journal entries on two Lightning Fast Company general ledger accounts are as follows:

Raw and In Process

1/1	21,000	(h)	404,500
(a)	406,000		
(j)	500		
	427,500		
23,000			

Cost of Goods Sold

1/1	-0-	(j)	500
(d)	25,000		
(g)	380,000		
(h)	404,500		
	809,500		
809,000			

In the illustrations of McIntire and Lightning Fast, the basics of backflushing can be summarized by examining the journal entries that involve the RIP account. This is important for three reasons. First, there are only three such entries, (a), (h), and (j). This emphasizes a central point in backflushing—that there is a minimum of accounting for RIP. Second, the presence or absence of a finished goods inventory does not change the way those three entries affect RIP. As a result, focusing on the three entries to RIP provides an understanding of backflushing that applies regardless of whether or not finished goods are present. If there is no finished goods inventory, Cost of Goods Sold takes the place of Finished Goods in the entries. This can be seen by comparing entries (h) and (j) for McIntire and Lightning Fast. Third, other than the three entries involving RIP, there is only one difference between the journal entries of traditional cost accumulation (described in Chapter 4) and those of McIntire Company, namely, the practice of charging conversion costs directly to Cost of Goods Sold as illustrated for McIntire Company.

Backflush costing is used by a small but growing number of manufacturers. Except where the backflush costing method is specifically mentioned, the discussion throughout the remainder of this text is in the context of the job order and process costing methods, illustrated by New Hope Manufacturing Company in Chapter 4. A summary comparison of backflushing and other cost accumulation methods is provided in Exhibit 4-6.

Summary

JIT emphasizes minimizing inventory levels and improving integrated manufacturing processes rather than focusing on individual materials or operations. It complements the other materials planning and control tools, such as EOQ and safety stock calculations. A successful just-in-time system requires a change in manufacturing processes to accommodate this new inventory philosophy. What is involved is process management, not merely inventory management. The fundamental objective of JIT is to produce and deliver what is needed, when it is needed, at all stages of the production process—just in time to be fabricated, assembled, and shipped to the customer. Although in practice there are no such perfect plants, JIT is a worthy goal. Benefits include lower inventory needs, faster response time, higher output per employee, and minimum floor space requirements. An associated requirement of a successful JIT operation is the pursuit of quality, to eliminate the delays caused by defective units.

A mature JIT system calls for a change in the routine accounting entries for cost accumulation. Detailed subsidiary records for raw materials and WIP can be eliminated and many production costs can be expensed, with the balances of inventory accounts adjusted at the end of each period based on physical counts.

Key Terms

just-in-time (JIT) ***(240)***
stockless production lean production, or zero inventory production (ZIP) ***(240)***
throughput time ***(242)***
velocity ***(242)***
blanket purchase orders ***(245)***
cells ***(246)***
work cell ***(246)***
backflushing, backflush costing, or backflush accounting ***(248)***
postdeduction or postmanufacturing deduction ***(249)***

Discussion Questions

Q10-1 Regarding levels of raw materials and work in process inventories, what is the purpose of a JIT inventory system?

Q10-2 What is the relationship between JIT and TQM?

Q10-3 To achieve a good rate of flow through a JIT system, why is it necessary for the number of defects to be small?

Q10-4 Theoretically, what is the EOQ size in an ideal JIT system?

Q10-5 If a zero inventory level is unattainable, what improvement is actually achieved in JIT?

Q10-6 What is the relationship between velocity and WIP levels?

Q10-7 What is the strategic advantage of improving velocity throughout the company, from research and development to shipping?

Q10-8 Under what conditions does reducing the level of WIP also reduce the number of defectives produced?

Q10-9 What is a blanket purchase order?

Q10-10 Why do the distinction between direct and indirect labor and the distinction between producing departments and some service functions disappear in many JIT work cells?

Q10-11 In what ways does backflush costing alter the accounting for work in process inventory?

Q10-12 Why are the materials and work in process inventory accounts combined into a single account in backflush costing?

Q10-13 What is meant by postdeduction?

Q10-14 What basic inventory accounting method used by merchandising companies is analogous to backflush costing used by manufacturing companies?

Q10-15 If all conversion costs are expensed to the cost of goods sold account in a backflush costing system, how is the correct amount of conversion cost included in the inventory accounts when a balance sheet is prepared?

Exercises

E10-1 Cost Savings from Smaller Inventory. Circuitboard Assembly Company maintains a WIP inventory at each of 10 work stations, and the average size of the inventory is 300 units per station. The physical flow of units into and out of each WIP location is first in, first out. The total number of instances in which some work station goes out of its control limits is expected to be 600 during the coming year. In two-thirds of these instances, the out-of-control condition is expected to be discovered immediately by the operator at that station; in the other one-third of these instances, a defect enters 5% of the units produced. These defective units enter WIP between stations, where they are discovered by the next station's operator. Every out-of-control condition is corrected as soon as it is discovered. The average variable cost of a unit in WIP is $80, and the average loss from an out-of-control condition is $25 per defective unit produced. The annual cost of carrying WIP is 20% of the cost of the inventory.

Management plans to reduce the number of units held at every work station by 30%. The rate of final output will be unchanged and no other changes will be made in the system.

Required: Using only the information given, calculate the annual savings expected from the change planned by management, assuming no defective unit contains more than one defect.

E10-2 Inventory Size, Velocity, and Lead Time. Acrotemp Incorporated requires an average lead time of 37 days on customer orders that require parts not kept in stock. When such a customer order is received, the parts order is placed with a vendor immediately by telephone and the parts are received in an average of 18 days. The parts are inspected and put into production an average of two days after receipt. The average time spent in production is 12 days. After production is completed, the order goes through final inspection in two days and arrives at the customer's site after an additional three days, on average.

Management plans to leave the rate of final output unchanged, induce vendors to reduce their total lead time by one-sixth, and reduce the average size of WIP to one-third of its present level.

Required: Assuming management's plans are implemented successfully, calculate the average lead time on customer orders that require parts not kept in stock.

E10-3 Inventory Size, Velocity, and Lead Time. Tennessee Panel Company needs an average of eight weeks' lead time to produce and ship an order. Customers are willing to wait only five weeks for orders to be shipped, so presently all orders are filled from finished goods inventory. The annual carrying cost of inventory is 20% of the cost of the inventory. Average inventories are as follows:

Materials	$3,000,000
Work in process	5,000,000
Finished goods	7,000,000

Management is determined to double the velocities of all tasks from ordering materials to issuing materials to production and all tasks from the receipt of a customer order to shipment of the order. There will be no change in the total annual output of finished work, and because presently most flaws in processing are discovered promptly, no reduction in the cost of defects is expected.

Required: Using only the information given, calculate the annual savings expected.

E10-4 Comparison of Process Costing and Backflushing; Unit Cost Calculations. Quicker Company had 24 units in process, 50% converted, at the beginning of a recent, typical month; the conversion cost component of this beginning inventory was $740. There were 20 units in process, 50% converted, at the end of the month. During the month, 4,500 units were completed and transferred to finished goods, and conversion costs of $300,000 were incurred. No units were lost.

Required:

(1) Carrying calculations to three decimal places, find the conversion cost per unit for the month by each of the following methods:
   (a) The average cost method as used in process costing (described in Chapter 6).
   (b) Divide the total conversion cost incurred during the month by the number of units completed during the month (do not calculate equivalent units).

(Requirements continued.)

(c) Divide the total conversion cost incurred during the month by the number of units started during the month.

(2) Using the three unit costs calculated in requirement 1, calculate three amounts for the total conversion cost of the ending inventory of work in process, to the nearest dollar.

(3) In light of the results of requirement 2, which of the three methods of calculating unit conversion cost would you recommend for the purpose of inventory costing, 1a, 1b, or 1c?

(4) What one attribute of Quicker Company's production system is the most important in explaining the results of requirements 1, 2, and 3?

E10-5 Backflush Costing; Entries in RIP and Finished Goods. Charcola Manufacturing has a cycle time of less than a day, uses a raw and in process (RIP) account, and expenses all conversion costs to Cost of Goods Sold. At the end of each month, all inventories are counted, their conversion cost components are estimated, and inventory account balances are adjusted accordingly. Raw material cost is backflushed from RIP to Finished Goods. The following information is for the month of May:

Beginning balance of RIP account, including $2,300 of conversion cost	$ 21,300
Beginning balance of finished goods account, including $6,500 of conversion cost	22,500
Raw materials received on credit	456,000
Ending RIP inventory per physical count, including $2,100 conversion cost estimate	22,100
Ending finished goods inventory per physical count, including $5,000 conversion cost estimate	15,000

Required: Prepare all journal entries that involve the RIP account and/or the finished goods account.

E10-6 Backflush Costing; Entries in RIP and Finished Goods. The Sweetwater Manufacturing Company has a cycle time of 1.5 days, uses a raw and in process (RIP) account, and charges all conversion costs to Cost of Goods Sold. At the end of each month, all inventories are counted, their conversion cost components are estimated, and inventory account balances are adjusted. Raw material cost is backflushed from RIP to Finished Goods. The following information is for June:

Beginning balance of RIP account, including $1,200 of conversion cost	$ 11,700
Beginning balance of finished goods account, including $4,000 of conversion cost	12,000
Raw materials received on credit	222,000
Ending RIP inventory per physical count, including $1,800 conversion cost estimate	12,800
Ending finished goods inventory per physical count, including $3,500 conversion cost estimate	9,500

Required: Prepare all journal entries that involve the RIP account and/or the finished goods account.

E10-7 Backflush Costing; Entries in RIP Account. The Stillville Manufacturing Company uses a raw and in process (RIP) inventory account and expenses all conversion costs to the cost of goods sold account. At the end of each month, all inventories are counted, their conversion cost components are estimated, and inventory account balances are adjusted accordingly. Raw material cost is backflushed from RIP to Finished Goods. The following information is for March:

Beginning balance of RIP account, including $1,000 of conversion cost	$ 10,000
Raw materials received on credit	200,000
Ending RIP inventory per physical count, including $1,300 conversion cost estimate	10,500

Required: Prepare the three journal entries involving the RIP account.

E10-8 Backflush Costing; Entries in RIP Account. The Pensawater Manufacturing Company uses a raw and in process (RIP) inventory account and expenses all conversion costs to the cost of goods sold account. At the end of each month, all inventories are counted, their conversion cost components are estimated, and inventory account balances are adjusted accordingly. Raw material cost is backflushed from RIP to Finished Goods. The following information is for April:

Beginning balance of RIP account, including $1,400 of conversion cost	$ 31,000
Raw materials received on credit	367,000
Ending RIP inventory per physical count, including $1,800 conversion cost estimate	33,000

Required: Prepare the three journal entries involving the RIP account.

E10-9 Backflush Costing with No Finished Goods Account. The Highspeed Manufacturing Company produces only for customer order, and most work is shipped within 36 hours of receipt of an order. Highspeed uses a raw and in process (RIP) inventory account and expenses all conversion costs to the cost of goods sold account. Work is shipped immediately upon completion, so there is no finished goods account. At the end of each month, inventory is counted, its conversion cost component is estimated, and the RIP account balance is adjusted accordingly. Raw material cost is backflushed from RIP to Cost of Goods Sold. The following information is for May:

Beginning balance of RIP account, including $1,300 of conversion cost	$ 12,300
Raw materials received on credit	246,000
Ending RIP inventory per physical count, including $2,100 conversion cost estimate	12,100

Required: Prepare the three journal entries involving the RIP account.

E10-10 Calculation of Materials and Conversion Cost Components of Finished Goods in Backflushing. During the most recent month, Backflushers Inc. started 3,000 units, finished 3,100 units, and incurred conversion costs totaling $290,160. The finished goods ending inventory consisted of 50 units. The RIP ending inventory contained partially processed materials for 20 units, 50% converted, plus unprocessed raw materials sufficient to produce 200 units.

The last semimonthly EDI payment to the supplier covered materials shipments sufficient to produce 1,400 units of output, with a total cost of $420,000.

Required:

(1) Calculate the materials cost of the finished goods ending inventory, assuming fifo costing is used.

(2) Calculate three different amounts for conversion cost per unit by dividing the month's conversion costs by three different counts of physical units: (a) the number started; (b) the number finished; (c) the number finished plus the number of partially converted units in RIP ending inventory (use only physical units, not a calculation of equivalent units).

(3) Calculate the conversion cost component of the finished goods ending inventory. Provide three different answers using the three results from requirement 2.

(4) Using the results from requirements 1 and 3, calculate the lowest and highest of the three amounts that might be reported for the total cost of the finished goods ending inventory. Calculate the dollar amount of difference between the lowest and highest answers. Express the difference as a percent of the lowest answer, rounded to the nearest tenth of a percent.

E10-11 Calculation of Materials and Conversion Cost Components of RIP in Backflushing. Use the source data in the previous exercise.

(1) Calculate the materials cost of the RIP ending inventory.

(2) Calculate the conversion cost component of the RIP ending inventory. Provide three different answers using the three results from requirement 2 of the previous exercise.

(3) Using the results of requirements 1 and 2, calculate the lowest and highest of the three amounts that might be reported for the total cost of the RIP ending inventory. Calculate the dollar amount of the difference between the lowest and highest answers. Express the difference as a percent of the lowest answer, rounded to the nearest tenth of a percent.

Problems

P10-1 Effects of Smaller Inventory. (Expands on exercise E10-1.) Electronics Assembly Co. maintains WIP inventory at each of 40 work stations. The average size of inventory at each station is 200 units. The physical flow of all WIP is first in, first out. Based on recent experience, 1,400 processing flaws are expected to arise this year. Three-fourths of all flaws are discovered immediately by the operator at the faulty station; the other one-fourth of these flaws cause a defect to enter 20% of the units produced. Defective units enter WIP between stations and are discovered by the next station's operator. Every processing flaw is corrected as soon as it is discovered. The average variable cost of a unit in WIP is $400, and the average loss from a defect is $60 per unit per defect. The annual cost of carrying WIP is 30% of the cost of the inventory.

Management is committed to reducing the number of units held at every work station by 40%. The rate of final output will be unchanged and no other changes will be made in the system.

Required:

(1) Using only the information given, calculate the expected annual savings.

(2) In addition to the savings calculated in requirement 1, what other savings should be considered in evaluating the decision to reduce WIP levels?

(3) What costs and other negative factors should be compared with the savings in evaluating the decision to reduce WIP levels?

P10-2 Inventory Size, Velocity, and Lead Time. (Expands on exercise E10-2) On customer orders (excluding rush orders) that require special-ordered parts, Protech Company has achieved an average lead time of 78 days, the best in its industry. When such a customer order is received, Protech places the parts order with a vendor by telephone in 6 days and receives the parts after an additional 27 days, on average. The parts pass through receiving (including inspection) and into production in an average of two days. After production is complete, the order goes through final inspection in three days and arrives at the customer's site after an additional four days, on average. Protech's WIP inventory turnover rate is 10 times per year.

Management plans to leave the rate of final output unchanged, reduce the average size of WIP to one-fourth of its present level, and induce vendors to reduce their total lead time by one-third.

Required:

(1) Assuming one year equals 360 days, calculate the average lead time if management's plans are implemented successfully.

(2) What advantages can be expected from the shorter lead time?

(3) What costs and other negative factors should be compared with the advantages of the shorter lead time?

P10-3 Backflush Costing. The Fast Manufacturing Company produces finished product within two days of the receipt of raw materials. Inventory accounts consist of a supplies account for indirect factory materials, a finished goods account, and a combined raw and in process (RIP) inventory account. All conversion costs are charged to the cost of goods sold account. At the end of each month, all inventories are counted, their conversion cost components are estimated, and inventory account balances are adjusted. Raw material cost is backflushed from RIP to Finished Goods and from Finished Goods to Cost of Goods Sold. The following information is a summary of selected transactions and other information for the month of June:

Beginning balances in inventory accounts are:

Raw and In Process	$ 41,600
Finished Goods	370,000
Supplies	31,000

The June 1 RIP balance consisted of $40,000 cost of materials, most of which were not yet in process, plus a $1,600 conversion cost estimate assigned to partially processed work. The Finished Goods balance consisted of $190,000 material cost and a $180,000 estimate of conversion cost.

June 30 inventories based on physical count:

Raw and In Process	$ 47,900
Finished Goods	360,000
Supplies	17,000

The June 30 RIP amount consisted of a $46,000 cost of materials, most of which were not yet in process, plus a $1,900 conversion cost estimate assigned to partially processed work. The Finished Goods amount consisted of $182,000 material cost and a $178,000 estimate of conversion cost.

(a) Direct materials received on credit cost $850,000.

(b) Indirect materials used cost $13,000.

(c) Gross payroll of $400,000 is accrued; the payroll is paid.

(d) The payroll distribution was:

Direct labor	$ 60,000
Indirect factory labor	120,000
Marketing salaries	130,000
Administrative salaries	90,000

(e) Factory overhead costs:

Depreciation	$668,000
Insurance	13,000

(f) Miscellaneous factory overhead costs:

Paid in cash	$54,000
On account	29,000

(g) The factory overhead accumulated in the factory overhead control account was expensed to Cost of Goods Sold.
(h) The material cost component of completed work is backflushed from RIP.
(i) The material cost component of work sold is backflushed from Finished Goods.
(j) Ending balances are established in inventory accounts by adjusting their conversion cost components.

Required:
(1) Prepare journal entries based on the preceding information.
(2) Prepare completed T accounts for RIP, Finished Goods, and Cost of Goods Sold.

P10-4 Backflush Costing. The La Jolla Manufacturing Company has a mature JIT production system with average cycle time of less than one day. Total time from receipt of raw material to completion of finished product is less than three days. La Jolla uses a finished goods account and a combined raw and in process (RIP) inventory account; there is a separate account, entitled Supplies, for indirect factory materials. La Jolla expenses all conversion costs to the cost of goods sold account. At the end of each month, all inventories are counted, their conversion cost components are estimated, and inventory account balances are adjusted accordingly. Raw material cost is backflushed from RIP to Finished Goods and from Finished Goods to Cost of Goods Sold. The following information is a summary of selected transactions and other information for the month of May:

Beginning balances in inventory accounts:

Raw and In Process	$ 31,300
Finished Goods	280,000
Supplies	27,000

The May 1 RIP balance consisted of a $30,000 cost of materials, most of which were not yet in process, plus a $1,300 conversion cost estimate assigned to partially processed work. The Finished Goods balance consisted of $150,000 material cost and a $130,000 estimate of conversion cost.

May 31 inventories based on physical count:

Raw and In Process	$ 37,100
Finished Goods	294,000
Supplies	17,000

The May 31 RIP amount consisted of a $35,000 cost of materials, most of which were not yet in process, plus a $2,100 conversion cost estimate assigned to partially processed work. The Finished Goods amount consisted of $160,000 material cost and a $134,000 estimate of conversion cost.

(a) Direct materials received on credit cost $620,000.
(b) Indirect materials used cost $10,000.
(c) Gross payroll of $300,000 was recorded; the payroll was paid.
(d) The payroll distribution was:

Direct labor	$50,000
Indirect factory labor	90,000
Marketing salaries	90,000
Administrative salaries	70,000

(e) Factory overhead costs:

Depreciation	$514,000
Insurance	9,000

(f) Miscellaneous factory overhead costs:

Paid in cash	$26,000
On account	7,000

(g) The factory overhead accumulated in the factory overhead control account was expensed to Cost of Goods Sold.
(h) The material cost component of completed work is backflushed from RIP.
(i) The material cost component of work sold is backflushed from Finished Goods.
(j) Ending balances are established in inventory accounts by adjusting their conversion cost components.

Required:
(1) Prepare journal entries based on the preceding information.
(2) Prepare completed T accounts for RIP, Finished Goods, and Cost of Goods Sold.

P10-5 Cost Impact of Just-in-Time Inventory System. Margro Corporation is an automotive supplier that uses automatic machines to manufacture precision parts from steel bars. Margro's inventory of raw steel averages $600,000, with a turnover rate of four times per year.

John Oates, president of Margro, is concerned about the costs of carrying inventory. He is considering the adoption of the just-in-time inventory system in order to eliminate the need to carry any raw steel inventory. Oates has asked Helen Gorman, Margro's controller, to evaluate the feasibility of just-in-time for the corporation. Gorman identified the following effects of adopting just-in-time.

(a) Without scheduling any overtime, lost sales due to stockouts would increase by 35,000 units per year. However, by incurring overtime premiums of $40,000 per year, the increase in lost sales could be reduced to 20,000 units. This would be the maximum amount of overtime that would be feasible for Margro.
(b) Two warehouses presently used for steel bar storage would no longer be needed. Margro rents one warehouse from another company at an annual cost of $60,000. The other warehouse is owned by Margro and contains 12,000 square feet. Three-fourths of the space in the owned warehouse could be rented for $1.50 per square foot per year.
(c) Insurance and property tax costs totaling $14,000 per year would be eliminated.

Margro's projected operating results for the current calendar year are as follows:

Margro Corporation
Pro Forma Income Statement
for the Year Ending December 31
(in Thousands of Dollars)

Sales (900,000 units)		$10,800
Cost of goods sold:		
Variable	$4,050	
Fixed	1,450	5,500
Gross profit		$ 5,300
Marketing and administrative expenses:		
Variable	$ 900	
Fixed	1,500	2,400
Income before interest and income tax		$ 2,900
Interest		900
Income before income tax		$ 2,000
Income tax		800
Net income		$ 1,200

Long-term capital investments by Margro are expected to produce a rate of return of 12% after income tax. Margro is subject to an effective income tax rate of 40%.

Required:

(1) Calculate the estimated before-tax dollar savings (loss) for Margro Corporation that would result in the current year from the adoption of the just-in-time inventory system.

(2) Identify and explain the conditions that should exist in order for a company to successfully install just-in-time. (ICMA adapted)

CHAPTER 11

Labor: Controlling and Accounting for Costs

Learning Objectives

After studying this chapter, you will be able to:

1. Discuss the nature of productivity and its relationship to labor costs.
2. Explain the theory and application of incentive wage plans.
3. Explain and apply learning curve theory.
4. Discuss the necessary organization for labor cost accounting and control.
5. (Appendix) Account for nonwage benefits, payroll taxes, and other labor-related deductions.

Labor cost represents the human contribution to production, and in many accounting systems it is an important cost factor requiring constant measurement, control, and analysis. Labor cost consists of basic pay and fringe benefits. The basic pay for work performed is called the **base rate** or **job rate**. A base rate should be established for each operation in a plant or office and grouped by class of operation. An equitable wage rate or salary structure requires an analysis, description, and evaluation of each job within the plant or office. The value of all jobs must relate to wages and salaries paid for similar work in the community and in the industry or business as a whole. Maintaining competitive wage rates and salaries facilitates the acquisition and retention of quality personnel.

Fringe benefits also form a substantial element of labor cost. Fringe costs—such as the employer's share of FICA tax, unemployment taxes, holiday pay, vacation pay, overtime premium pay, insurance benefits, and pension costs—must be added to the base rate in order to arrive at the full labor cost. Although these fringe costs generally are included in overhead, they should not be overlooked in management's planning and control responsibilities, in decision-making analyses, or in labor–management wage negotiations. Workers' demands for a 50-cent-per-hour increase in pay can result in far greater expenditures by the company when related fringe costs are considered.

Wages and fringe benefits are only one element in employer–employee relations, however. Adequate records, easily understood and readily available, also are an important factor in harmonious relations between management, employees, labor unions, government agencies, and the general public.

Productivity and Labor Costs

All wage payments are directly or indirectly based on and limited by the productivity and skill of the worker. Therefore, proper planning, motivation, control, and accounting for this human cost factor is one of the most important problems in the management of an enterprise.

Labor productivity can be defined as the measurement of production performance using the expenditure of human effort as a yardstick. It is the amount of goods and services a worker produces. In a broader sense, productivity can be described as the efficiency with which resources are converted into commodities and/or services. Greater productivity can be achieved by more efficient production processes which eliminate non-value-added activities; by improved or modern equipment; or by any other factor that improves the utilization of resources. Changes in the utilization of a labor force often require changes in methods of compensating labor, followed by changes in accounting for labor costs.

Planning Productivity

A plan for improving productivity should assign to managers the responsibility for successfully implementing the plan. In addition, the plan should interface with other existing plans (for example, the operating budget, capital investment, research and technology, and human resource development).

Questions typically answered by the plan include the following:[1]

1. How does the organization define productivity and quality of work life?
2. What priority should be attached to productivity improvement? Who is responsible?
3. How will executive management's commitment be communicated?
4. How much uniformity of application is desired?
5. How much employee involvement in planning and implementation is appropriate?
6. How will progress be measured?

Measuring Productivity

Once plans have been formulated, productivity should be measured, analyzed, understood, and reported. The objective of productivity measurement is to provide management with a concise and accurate index for the comparison of actual results with a standard of performance. Productivity measurement should recognize the individual contribution of factors such as employees (including management), plant and equipment used in production, products and services utilized in production, capital invested, and government services utilized (as indicated by taxes). One such measure has been developed by American Standards for Productivity Measurement, of Houston, Texas. This measure considers use of capital, raw materials, energy, and labor, related to a plant's output. However, the most generally utilized measurement has been physical output per labor hour, which takes into account only one element of input—labor. Thus productivity measurement ratios are, at their best, crude statistical devices that often ignore such essential factors as capital and land.

[1] Carl G. Thor, "Planning Your Productivity Efforts," *Management Accounting*, Vol. 64, No. 12, pp. 28-29.

Setting a standard of labor performance is not easy, because it is often accompanied by serious disputes between management and unions. The pace at which the observed person is working is noted and referred to as a **rating** or **performance rating**. The rating factor is applied to the selected task to obtain a **normal time**; that is, the time it should take a person working at a normal pace to do the job. Allowances are added for personal time, rest periods, and possible delays. The final result is the **standard time** for the job, expressed in minutes per piece or in units to be produced per hour.

The **productivity–efficiency ratio** measures the output of an individual relative to the performance standard. This ratio can also be used to measure the relative operating achievement of a machine, an operation, a department, or an entire organization. To illustrate, if 4,000 hours are standard for a department and if 4,400 hours are used, then there is an unfavorable ratio of 90.9 percent (4,000 ÷ 4,400).

Economic Impact of Productivity

When productivity increases, business profits and the real earnings of workers also increase. Furthermore, increased productivity enables society to get more and better output from the basic resources of the economy. In recent years, productivity has generally been increasing, resulting in more available goods and services. However, the normal productivity gain has fallen below the average gain of earlier years. This slowdown has given rise to increased costs. When increases in output do not keep pace with rising costs, unit costs—and, therefore, selling prices—increase.

If prices are to be kept from rising, then wage increases should not exceed an amount that reflects the unit cost reduction resulting from increased productivity. In recent years, employment costs—wages, salaries, and fringe benefits—have risen more than output or production per labor hour, leading to inflationary higher prices to meet higher unit costs.

Increasing Productivity by Better Management of Human Resources

Production systems, such as automobile assembly lines, are technologically similar in Japan and in the West. But Japanese manufacturers make much better use of their work forces, which allows them to use fewer workers to do the same job. Workers need to learn many jobs, solve problems, and work in a flexible, dynamic business environment. Japanese levels of productivity can be achieved only by motivated workers, willing to participate on a large scale and with substantial responsibility.

Better management of human resources offers the prospect of increasing productivity as well as boosting product quality by enabling workers to participate more directly in the management of their work and the overall goals of their company. A continuous, long-term perspective rather than a sporadic, short-term perspective on the part of management is required, involving extensive training and a long-term view of results. Four fundamental assumptions characterize better human resource management:

1. People who do the work are best qualified to improve it.
2. Decision making should take place at the lowest level possible.
3. Worker participation increases both job satisfaction and commitment to company objectives.
4. There is a vast pool of ideas in the work force waiting to be tapped.

Coupled with the need for better management through broader participation is the necessity for investment in better trained workers. Many U.S. manufacturers employ advanced manufacturing technologies to enhance productivity and competitiveness. But few take the required steps to reconfigure their human resource needs to reap the full benefits of technological innovation. Technologically advanced manufacturing systems require high skill levels of all workers. Therefore, U.S. manufacturers must implement specific programs for recruiting, training, and retaining skilled workers if they are to compete successfully in global markets.

In summary, productivity and its related costs demand careful planning and measurement if the associated economic impact is to be controlled effectively. Better management of human resources is an essential requirement leading to increased productivity.

Incentive Wage Plans

A worker's wage is based on negotiated labor contracts, productivity studies, job evaluations, profit sharing, incentive wage plans, and guaranteed hourly wages. Because all wages are paid for work performed, an element of incentive is present in all wage plans. In contrast to pay by the hour, week, or month, an **incentive wage plan** should reward workers in direct proportion to their increased high quality output. A fair day's work standard should be established so that workers can meet and even exceed it with a reasonable effort, thereby receiving full benefit from the incentive wage plan.

The installation and operation of incentive wage plans require not only the combined efforts of the personnel department, labor unions, factory engineers, and accountants, but also the cooperation and willingness of each worker. To be successful, an incentive wage plan must: (1) be applicable to situations in which workers can increase output, (2) provide for proportionately more pay for output above standard, and (3) set fair standards so that extra effort will result in bonus pay. Along with these essentials, the plan needs to be reasonably simple and understandable to workers as well as to managers.

Purpose of an Incentive Wage Plan

The primary purpose of an incentive wage plan is to induce workers to produce more, to earn a higher wage, and at the same time to reduce unit costs. The plan seeks to insure greater output, to increase control over labor cost by insuring more uniform unit costs, and to change the basis for reward from hours served to work accomplished. Naturally, producing more in a given period of time should result in higher pay for workers. The greater number of units produced should also result in a lower cost per unit for factory overhead and labor cost combined.

To illustrate, assume that a factory operation takes place in a building that is rented for $2,400 per month ($80 per day or $10 per hour) and that depreciation, insurance, and property tax amount to $64 per day, or $8 per hour. Assume further that 10 workers on an 8-hour day are paid $6 per hour and that each worker produces 40 units of product per day (an individual production rate of 5 units per hour). Workers and management agree that a rate of $6.60 per hour will be paid if a worker produces 48 units per day, thereby increasing the hourly output from 5 to 6 units.

Exhibit 11-1 shows the cost per hour and cost per unit for the two systems, and indicates how a wage incentive can reduce unit costs and at the same time provide workers with higher income.

EXHIBIT 11-1

Effect of an Incentive Wage Plan on Unit Costs

	Original System, $6 per Hour (10 workers)			New System, $6.60 per Hour (10 workers)		
Cost Factor	Amount per Hour	Units per Hour	Unit Cost	Amount per Hour	Units per Hour	Unit Cost
Labor	$60	50	$1.20	$66	60	$1.1000
Rent	10	50	.20	10	60	.1667
Depreciation, insurance, and property tax	8	50	.16	8	60	.1333
Total	$78	50	$1.56	$84	60	$1.4000

Although the hourly labor cost of the work crew increases from $60 to $66, the cost of a complete unit of product is reduced from $1.56 to $1.40. The unit cost decrease is caused by two factors: (1) unit output per worker is increased 20 percent, with a 10 percent increase in wages, and (2) the same amount of factory overhead is spread over 60 instead of 50 units of production an hour. For greater precision, such an analysis should include labor-related costs, such as employer's payroll taxes, as well as any other relevant factory overhead that influences the unit cost. In this example, both labor and factory overhead unit costs were reduced. But even if the incentive wage causes the labor cost per unit to increase, the reduction of factory overhead cost per unit may be sufficient to result in a net reduction in unit cost, thus supporting the desirability of the incentive wage plan.

The lowering of conversion or manufacturing cost resulting from an incentive wage plan, illustrated here on a cost per unit basis, also should be analyzed in terms of differential cost, also called marginal or incremental cost (Chapter 21). The differential revenue associated with the additional output and the differential cost of an incentive wage plan should influence management's decision to install a plan.

Companies are striving to increase the efficiency and productivity of employees at every level. Just-in-time and similar productivity enhancement programs urge employees to perform well and to exercise individual and group initiative. Incentive wage plans can enhance the establishment of a working environment in which everyone must perform. However, there is an art to establishing appropriate wage levels and meaningful incentive plans. The danger over the long term is that base pay and incentives will lose their identity as employees begin to consider the incentive as part of the base. Therefore, standards should be clearly set and communicated to the workers, if the plan is to have its desired effect.

Types of Incentive Wage Plans

In actual practice, time wages and output wages are not clear-cut and distinct. Incentive plans typically involve wage rates based on various combinations of output and time. Many wage incentive systems retain the names of the industrial engineers and efficiency experts who originated the plans—the Taylor differential piece-rate plan, the Halsey premium plan, the Bedaux point system, the Gantt task and bonus plan, and the Emerson efficiency bonus plan. Most of these plans are no longer used, but many adaptations are still in use. To demonstrate the operation of incentive wage plans, the straight piecework plan and the 100-percent bonus plan for individual workers, and the group bonus plan are discussed as representative examples.

Straight Piecework Plan. The **straight piecework plan**, one of the simplest incentive wage plans, pays wages above the base rate for production above the standard. The production standard is computed in minutes per piece and then is translated into money per piece. If time studies determine that 2.5 minutes is to be the standard time required for producing one unit, the standard rate is 24 pieces per hour. If a worker's base pay rate is $7.44 per hour, the piece rate is $.31. Workers are generally guaranteed a base pay rate, even if they fail to earn that amount in terms of output. If a worker's production exceeds 24 pieces per hour, the $.31 per unit still applies. In Exhibit 11-2, the labor cost per unit of output declines until the standard is reached and then remains constant at any level of output above standard.

Although piece rates reflect an obvious cause–effect relationship between output and pay, the incentive is effective only when workers can control their individual rates of output. Piece rates are not effective when output is machine paced. Also, modification of production standards and labor rates becomes necessary when increases in output are the result of the installation of new and better machines. If the rate of output depends on a group effort, then a group rather than an individual incentive plan is appropriate.

EXHIBIT 11-2

Straight Piecework Plan

Units per Hour	Guaranteed Hourly Rate	Piece Rate	Earned per Hour	Labor Cost per Unit	Overhead per Hour	Overhead per Unit	Conversion Cost per Unit
20	$7.44	$ 0	$7.44	$.372	$4.80	$.240	$.612
22	7.44	0	7.44	.338	4.80	.218	.556
24	7.44	.31	7.44	.310	4.80	.200	.510
26	7.44	.31	8.06	.310	4.80	.185	.495
28	7.44	.31	8.68	.310	4.80	.171	.481
30	7.44	.31	9.30	.310	4.80	.160	.470
32	7.44	.31	9.92	.310	4.80	.150	.460

One-Hundred-Percent Bonus Plan. The **100-percent bonus plan** is a variation of the straight piecework plan. It differs in that standards are stated not in terms of money, but in time per unit of output. Instead of a price per piece, a standard time is allowed to complete a job or unit, and the worker is paid for the standard time at the hourly rate if the job or unit is completed in standard time or less. Thus if a worker produces 100 units in an 8-hour shift and the standard time is 80 units per shift (or 10 units per hour), the worker is paid the hourly rate for 10 hours. In other variations of the 100-percent bonus plan, savings are shared with the supervisor and/or the company.

Each payroll period, an efficiency ratio must be figured for every worker before earnings can be computed. Production standards in units of output per hour are set by industrial engineers. Hours of work and units produced are reported to the payroll department, where the reported hours worked are multiplied by the hourly production standard to determine the standard units. The worker's production is then divided by the standard quantity, resulting in the efficiency ratio. The efficiency ratio multiplied by the worker's base rate results in the hourly earnings for the period. Exhibit 11-3 illustrates how earnings are computed, assuming that standard production is 15 units per hour.

EXHIBIT 11-3

One-Hundred-Percent Bonus Plan

Worker	Hours Worked	Output Units	Standard Units	Efficiency Ratio	Base Rate	Base × Efficiency Ratio	Total Earned	Labor Cost per Unit	Overhead per Hour	Overhead per Unit	Conversion Cost per Unit
Abrams	40	540	600	.90	$7.50	—*	$300.00	$.5556	$5.40	$.4000	$.9556
Gordon	40	660	600	1.10	7.50	$ 8.250	330.00	.5000	5.40	.3273	.8273
Hanson	40	800	600	1.33	7.50	9.975	399.00	.4988	5.40	.2700	.7688
Jonson	38	650	570	1.14	7.60	8.664	329.23	.5065	5.40	.3157	.8222
Stowell	40	750	600	1.25	8.00	10.000	400.00	.5333	5.40	.2880	.8213
Wiebold	40	810	600	1.35	7.72	10.422	416.88	.5147	5.40	.2667	.7814

* When the efficiency ratio is less than 1.00, no bonus is earned.

The 100-percent bonus plan has gained in popularity because of the frequency of wage increases. The standards, stated in terms of time and output quantity, need no adjustment when wage rates change. Because the system emphasizes time rather than money, the plan lends itself to the development of controls and efficiency standards.

Group Bonus Plan. Industry uses a great variety of incentive wage plans, some of which depend on the superior productive performance of a whole department or an entire factory and can include support or indirect labor as well as direct labor. Factory operations using large machines often require employees to work in groups or crews. Although the work of each employee is essential to the machine operation, it is frequently impossible to separate the work of one member of a crew. A worker on an assembly line cannot increase output without the cooperation of the entire group. Also, the individual workers may be required to be flexible in work assignments, with the capability of performing a wide range of tasks or operations within a group's sphere of work. **Group bonus plans** have proved successful in such situations.

Group bonus plans, like those designed for individual incentive, are intended to encourage production at rates above a minimum standard. Each worker in the group receives an hourly rate for production up to the standard output. Units produced in excess of the standard are regarded as time saved by the group, and each worker is in effect paid a bonus for time saved as well as being paid for time worked. Usually, the bonus earned by the group is divided among the group members in accordance with their respective base rates.

Group plans reduce the amount of clerical work necessary to compute labor cost and payrolls and the amount of supervision necessary to operate the incentive system. Group plans may also contribute to better cooperation among workers, and good workers are likely to put pressure on poor workers who might jeopardize the group bonus. Group plans quite often lead to the reduction of accidents, spoilage, waste, and absenteeism. For example, a bonus may be paid to a crew or department that has not had an accident for a specified period of time, or that has a reject rate below a specified target.

Exhibit 11-4 illustrates the operation of a 100-percent group bonus plan. A crew of 10 workers uses costly equipment, and each is paid $10 an hour for a regular 8-hour shift. Standard production is 50 units per hour, or 400 units per shift; overhead is $320 per 8-hour shift, or $40 per hour. In this illustration, the bonus is computed for each day. In other group or individual incentive plans, it can be computed based on aggregate results for a week, a month, or some longer period.

EXHIBIT 11-4

One-Hundred-Percent Group Bonus Plan

Units Produced	Standard Hours for Units Produced	Actual Hours	Regular Group Wage	Bonus (Hours Saved @ $10)	Total Group Earnings	Labor Cost per Unit	Overhead Cost per Unit	Conversion Cost per Unit
350	70	80	$800	$ 0	$ 800	$2.286	$.914	$3.200
400	80	80	800	0	800	2.000	.800	2.800
425	85	80	800	50	850	2.000	.753	2.753
450	90	80	800	100	900	2.000	.711	2.711
475	95	80	800	150	950	2.000	.674	2.674
500	100	80	800	200	1,000	2.000	.640	2.640

Organizational Incentive (Gainsharing) Plans

Management should evaluate the pros and cons of both individual and group incentive plans in order to determine what best meets their organization's needs. In situations in which the productivity of the organization as a whole needs to be improved, an organizational or gainsharing plan may be the best answer.

Organizational incentive plans, otherwise known as **gainsharing plans**, have developed as an answer to the productivity problems that have plagued U.S. industries. These plans have been used with great success by the Japanese. The central characteristic of gainsharing plans is that all individuals have the capacity to make valuable contributions to an organization. Inherent to these plans is an employee-centered management style, which places great emphasis on the involvement and participation of all employees.

Gainsharing plans require a management style that is both participative and highly committed to making the incentive plan a success. Employee suggestions are the heart of a gainsharing plan. Finally, the gains that result from employee suggestions are shared between owners and employees throughout the organization.

Just like individual and group incentive plans, gainsharing plans have requirements for success that must occur in order for management and employees to realize the benefits that can be achieved. The keys to a successful implementation include measurable normal labor costs, a relatively stable ratio of sales value of production to labor costs, and, to all participants, fairness of the incentives and the policies that are established. These factors are important because the incentive equation usually is based on some ratio of labor costs to the value that is added to sales as a result of improved productivity.

One popular form of gainsharing is the Scanlon plan. In this plan, the company sets a predetermined formula comprising the factors described in this section. If improvement above a certain amount occurs, an employee incentive payment results. The payment is a stated fraction of the attributable savings. All employees, including management and labor, usually participate in the bonus.

Time Standards and Learning Curve Theory

Incentive wage plans assume that monetary bonuses motivate workers to achieve higher productivity rates. However, studies show that incentive wage plans based on fixed time standards—no matter how scientifically engineered—do not always appear to motivate workers.[2] Even so, incentive wage plans using fixed time

[2] A fixed time standard is best explained by the 100-percent bonus plan (page 268), in which the standard is fixed at 80 units per day (or 10 units per hour).

standards continue to be used. The deficiencies existing in wage incentive standards can be remedied by means of the learning curve theory.

The **learning curve theory** stipulates that every time the cumulative quantity of units produced is doubled, the cumulative average time per unit is reduced by a given percentage. If this reduction is 20 percent it means that producing two units requires 80 percent of the cumulative average time per unit required for the first unit; four units require 80 percent of the cumulative average time of the first two; and so on. Based on this theory, the following table of values for an 80 percent learning curve can be computed (assuming that 10 direct labor hours are required to produce the first unit):[3]

Units	×	Cumulative Average Required Labor Hours per Unit	=	Estimated Total Hours Needed to Perform the Task
1		10.0 hour		10.0 hours
2		8.0 (10.0 × 80%)		16.0
4		6.4 (8.0 × 80%)		25.6
8		5.1 (6.4 × 80%)		40.8
16		4.1 (5.1 × 80%)		65.6
32		3.3 (4.1 × 80%)		105.6
64		2.6 (3.3 × 80%)		166.4

The results indicate that the 80 percent rate is constant at each doubling of the accumulated number of times the task is performed. The figures in the third column are the cumulative average hours times the number of units. To estimate the total time needed to perform the task the first 32 times, the calculation is 32 × 3.3, or 105.6 hours.[4]

[3] James A. Broadston, "Learning Curve Wage Incentives," *Management Accounting*, Vol. 49, No. 12, pp. 15-23.

[4] The underlying learning curve formula is

$$y = ax^b$$

where

y = cumulative average required labor hours per unit
a = the first unit's time
x = number of units
b = the learning curve exponent, measured as follows:

$$b = \frac{\log (\%\ \text{learning})}{\log (2)}$$

For an 80 percent learning curve,

$$b = \frac{\log .80}{\log 2} = \frac{-.09691}{.301029} = -.3219$$

As an illustration, if x is 4 units and the first unit requires 10 labor hours, then

$$\begin{aligned} y &= (10)(4)^{-.3219} \\ \log y &= \log 10 + (-.3219) \log 4 \\ \log y &= 1 + (-.3219)\ .602059 \\ \log y &= .8061972 \\ y &= 6.4 \end{aligned}$$

This is the cumulative-average-time learning model, which is assumed in the illustrations, discussion, and end-of-chapter materials of this textbook. Instead, the incremental-unit-time learning model can be used, in which case y is redefined as the time taken to produce the last unit rather than as the cumulative average time per unit. This model requires the computation of each incremental unit's time in order to sum the resulting amounts to obtain cumulative total time. The total time for a given number of units is then divided by the corresponding number of units to obtain the cumulative average time per unit.

An advantage of the incremental unit model is that it provides an estimate of time for the last unit made, which may be the best basis for predicting future time requirements once a steady state is reached. The incremental-unit-time model predicts a higher cumulative total time required to produce two or more units than is the case when the cumulative-average-time model is used. The preferred model is the one most accurately approximating actual behavior. For further discussion of model preference, see Shu S. Liao, "The Learning Curve: Wright's Model vs. Crawford's Model," *Issues in Accounting Education*, Vol. 3, No. 2, pp. 302–315.

The 80 percent learning curve is used here for illustrative purposes. The 80 percent rate is frequent among industries, and typically the percentage is no lower than 60 nor higher than 85. The actual percentage depends on the particular situation. Generally, for more complicated tasks in terms of labor skill, there is more room for learning to occur and, therefore, a greater likelihood of a lower labor input percentage as production increases. For a lower learning curve percentage, i.e., for more rapid learning rates, more of the increase in efficiency occurs earlier as cumulative units are produced.

At the extremes, the actual percentage can range from 100 percent (if no learning occurs) to 50 percent. At the latter extreme, if the average accumulated time for the first unit is 100 minutes, then the time for the second unit must equal zero (i.e., 100 minutes × 50% = 50 minutes = accumulated average time per task unit at the 2-task-units level, or a total of 100 minutes for the 2 units). Thus the 50-percent rate is an upper limit of learning—one that can never be reached. If the production period is long or the labor operations routine, a point in production is reached when any improvement through repetition becomes imperceptible, and the learning curve levels out to a steady-state condition.

It must be observed that in some highly automated modern manufacturing processes, especially in those that are computer controlled and perhaps include robotics, there is no learning curve. The machine is as efficient producing one item as it is producing one thousand items. Learning curves still may be present, though, in areas where human effort is used, such as in programming computers.

After the learning curve percentage has been empirically determined for a specific operation, time requirements for successive increments in output can be estimated as long as conditions remain the same. Conditions which can cause deviations from times predicted by an established learning curve include changes in product design, changes in proportions of manufactured and purchased components, and changes in equipment. Of course, conditions also can change because of improvements in engineering design and in manufacturing techniques.

When production is not continuous and there are comparatively long lapses of time or changes in personnel, relearning is required. Furthermore, there may be a certain element of influence on learning curve behavior that is associated with individual worker variants over time, such as temporary productivity variations caused by health or emotional problems, or the Friday afternoon downturn of production as the weekend approaches. Worker group productivity attitudes can also have their impact.

By means of the learning curve, the time standard used for determining a worker's earnings has now changed to a variable time instead of the fixed time standard. The variable time standard meets the need of an incentive wage system more equitably because:

> *The improvement phenomenon, as well as its mathematical model, the learning curve, provides an insight into human capabilities that bears directly upon the ability of workers to do work and the time required for them to learn new skills. An actual learning curve may show small irregularities; yet it will eventually follow an underlying natural characteristic of group or individual human activity.*[5]

As soon as workers have passed the learning stage and begin to produce the expected number of units (i.e., reach the standard proficiency), they begin to draw bonus pay for doing the operation in less than standard time. They may

[5] *Ibid.*, p. 15.

even slow down a little and yet perform the operation in standard time or better, drawing the bonus pay but working less strenuously for it.

Government procurement agencies have used the learning curve as a tool for cost evaluation in negotiating prices for contracts. When a bid on a contract is entered, the unit labor cost is usually estimated. The learning curve permits the determination of lot costs for various stages of production. As production progresses, the cumulative average unit labor cost should decrease.

By comparing the budgeted cost with the experienced labor cost in the initial stages of production, the trend of the labor cost can be determined. If, for example, an average labor cost of $20 per unit is to be achieved, the following output and cost table with 80, 85, and 90 percent learning curves can be predetermined.[6]

Cumulative Quantity	Learning Curve 80%	85%	90%
25	$61.02	$45.06	$33.86
50	48.82	38.30	30.47
100	39.06	32.56	27.43
200	31.25	27.68	24.69
400	25.00	23.53	22.22
800	20.00	20.00	20.00

The learning curve allows projection of the cumulative average unit cost at any stage of production. It predicts labor hours with accuracy and reliability, establishes work load, and allows production control to take advantage of reducing time per unit by increasing lot sizes, thereby maintaining a level work force. It also provides a basis for standard cost variance calculations (Chapter 18), allows judgment of a manager's performance relative to the department's target, and provides a basis for cost control through analysis of undesirable shifts of the curve.

Organization for Labor Cost Accounting and Control

Labor costing involves the following:

1. The employment history of each worker—date hired, wage rate, initial assignment, promotions, tardiness, sickness, and vacations.
2. Adequate information for compliance with union contracts, social security laws, wage and hour legislation, income tax withholdings, and other federal, state, and local government requirements.
3. The establishment of labor time and cost standards for comparative purposes.
4. Productivity in relation to type of wage payment, creating the best system of compensation for each kind of work.
5. Each employee's time worked, wage rate, and total earnings for each payroll period.
6. The computation of deductions from gross wages for each employee.
7. The output or accomplishment of each employee.
8. The amount of direct labor cost and hours to be charged to each job, lot, process, or department, and the amount of indirect labor cost. Information on direct labor cost or hours can be used as a basis for factory overhead application.

[6] William H. Boren, "Some Applications of the Learning Curve to Government Contracts," *NAA Bulletin*, Vol. 46, No. 2, pp. 21–22.

9. Total labor cost in each department for each payroll period.
10. The compilation of cumulative earnings and deductions detail for each employee.

The accounting principles and objectives in labor costing are relatively simple. However, applying these principles can be difficult in the case of large numbers of workers or workers shifting from one type of work to another under various factory conditions. Basically, two sets of underlying detailed records are kept, one for financial accounting and the other for cost accounting. The procedures for labor accounting are outlined as follows. The journal entries associated with these procedures, as well as those pertaining to labor-related costs, are illustrated in the appendix to this chapter.

Financial Accounting

A record is kept of the total time worked and the total amount earned by each worker.

The daily or weekly amount earned by each worker is entered on the payroll record.

Each payroll period, the total amount of wages payable to workers results in the following entry:

	Dr.	Cr.
Payroll	XXX	
Employees Income Tax Payable		XXX
FICA Tax Payable		XXX
Accrued Payroll		XXX

Cost Accounting

A record is kept of the time worked on each job, process or department by each worker and the associated cost.

The direct labor hours and cost are entered on the respective job cost sheets or production reports; the indirect labor cost is entered on the departmental expense analysis sheets.

The weekly or month-end entry for labor distribution is:

	Subsidiary Record	Dr.	Cr.
Work in Process		XXX	
Factory Overhead Control		XXX	
Indirect Labor	XXX		
Payroll			XXX

Labor cost control begins with an adequate production planning schedule supported by labor-hour requirements and accompanying labor costs, determined well in advance of production runs. In most manufacturing plants, it is usually possible to establish a reasonably accurate ratio of direct labor hours and number of employees to dollar sales by product lines, and, by relating this ratio to the sales forecast, it is also possible to predict future labor requirements. The relationship between sales volume and personnel needs is perhaps more direct and predictable in wholesale, retail, financial, and service enterprises. The entire labor cost control process begins with the design of the product and continues until the product is sold. The departments that should cooperate in this process include the personnel, production planning, timekeeping, payroll, and cost departments.

Personnel Department

The chief function of a personnel department is to provide an efficient labor force. In a general way, this department is responsible for seeing that an entire organization follows good personnel policies. Personnel functions involve recruiting and employment procedures, training programs, job descriptions, job evaluations, and time and motion studies. Hiring of employees can be for replacement or for expansion. Replacement hiring starts with a labor requisition sent to the personnel department by a department head or supervisor. Expansion hiring requires authorization by executive management, in which case the authority to hire results from approval of the labor requirements of a production schedule rather than from separate requisitions to fill individual jobs. The personnel department, in conjunction with the department heads concerned, plans the expansion requirements and agrees on promotions and transfers to be made, the number and kinds of workers to be hired, and the dates at which new employees will report for work.

Employment practices must comply not only with regulations set forth at the federal level (i.e., the Equal Employment Opportunity Commission and the Department of Labor), but also with regulations of human rights commissions in the states.

Production Planning Department

A production planning department is responsible for scheduling work, releasing job orders to the producing departments, and dispatching of work in the factory. The release of orders is generally accompanied by materials requisitions and labor time tickets that indicate the operations to be performed on the product. A specific and understandable listing of detailed labor and machine operations is important if work is to be performed within the time allowed and with the materials provided. Delays caused by lack of materials, machine breakdowns, or need for additional instructions can cause complaints by workers and lead to additional labor costs. Production schedules prepared several weeks in advance, utilizing labor time standards for each producing department, lead to cost control through the use of departmental labor budgets similar to the one shown in Exhibit 11-5.

EXHIBIT 11-5

LABOR BUDGET

Department Cooler Assembly For October, 19--

Prepared September 10, 19--

Model No.	Units Scheduled	Budgeted Assembly Hours per Unit: Motor	Fan	Coolant	Total Budgeted Direct Labor Hours
625	2,000	1.5	.25	.5	4,500
748	1,000	1.5	.30	.6	2,400
500	3,000	1.5	.20	.4	6,300
600	1,500	1.3	.40	.5	3,300
	7,500				16,500

Variable and Fixed Costs	Total Cost	Cost per Unit	No. of Employees*
Variable costs:			
Direct labor -- 16,500 hrs. @ $6	$ 99,000	$13.200	94
Indirect labor -- 1,000 hrs. @ $4.80 ..	4,800	.640	6
Total variable labor budget	$103,800	$13.840	
Fixed costs:			
Supervision -- 700 hrs. @ $7	$ 4,900	$ .653	4
Clerical & Packing -- 350 hrs. @ $4.60	1,610	.215	2
Total fixed labor budget	$ 6,510	$ .868	
Total for October	$110,310	$14.708	106

*No. of hrs. ÷ 176 (22 days x 8 hrs.)

Timekeeping Department

Securing an accurate record of the time purchased from each employee is the first step in labor costing. To do so, it is necessary to provide the following:

1. A clock card (or time card) as unquestionable evidence of the employee's presence in the plant from the time of entry to departure.

2. A time ticket (or job ticket) to secure information as to the type of work performed.

Both documents are supervised, controlled, and collected by the timekeeping department. Because the earnings of the employee depend mainly on these two forms and the timekeeper processes them in the first step toward final payment, the timekeeping department forms a most valuable link in harmonious labor–management relationships. In fact, to many workers, the timekeeper is management. Frequently the timekeeper's performance is the basis for a worker's first opinion of the company.

Time Clock. The **time clock** (or **time recorder**) is a mechanical instrument for recording employee time in and out of the office and the factory. Under a typical procedure, each employee is assigned a clock number that identifies the department and the employee. The clock number is used for identification on the payroll and in charging labor time to departments and production orders.

A **clock card** provides space for the name and number of the employee and usually covers an entire payroll period. When completed, the clock card shows the time a worker started and stopped work each day or shift of the payroll period, with overtime and other premium hours clearly indicated.

Time clocks may be electronically on line as a part of the computerized system, making a hard-copy clock card unnecessary. Under such a procedure, each employee is provided a bar-coded identification card or badge. The employee passes the identification card through a slot in the time clock or uses a scanner, which automatically enters employee arrival and departure times directly into the computer data base.

Time Ticket or Report. In accounting for materials, the receiving report and the invoice are evidence that the goods have been received and payment is in order. In accounting for labor, the clock card is evidence that time has been purchased and is comparable to the receiving report. The **time ticket** shows the specific use that has been made of the time purchased and is comparable to the materials requisition. When an individual time ticket is used, a new ticket must be made out for each job worked on during the day. Since this procedure may lead to many tickets per employee, some plants use a **daily time report** on which the worker lists jobs worked on during the day. Increasingly, remote computer terminals, often augmented by bar coding, are used to report time distributions by direct entry to the computer, thus eliminating the hard-copy time ticket or daily time report.

The best procedure for filling in time tickets depends on many factors peculiar to shop operations. In some factories, the workers prepare their own time tickets, which are approved by the supervisor, or a supervisor prepares them. In other factories, timekeepers, dispatch clerks, and supervisors have desks near the work stations. When changing jobs, employees report to the timekeeper, get a new assignment from the dispatch clerk, secure instructions at the supervisor's desk, and get the required tools at the tool crib. A smooth shift from one job to another is thereby achieved, with time distributions entered by the timekeeper on approval by the supervisor.

The total time reported on each time ticket is compared with the total hours of each employee's clock card. If there is any difference, an adjustment is made. If the clock card correctly shows more hours than the time tickets, the difference is reported as idle time. If the time tickets show more hours than the clock card, the error is corrected in consultation with the supervisor and the worker.

The degree of accuracy in reporting time varies from plant to plant, but in most situations a report to the exact minute is neither necessary nor practical. Many companies find it advantageous to use a decimal system, which is fast and which measures the hour in 10 periods of 6 minutes each rather than the regular clock interval of 5-minute periods and 12 periods per hour. Under a decimal system, a job started at 9:23 a.m. and finished at 11:38 a.m. is reported as 9.4 and 11.6, with an elapsed time of 2.2 hours. The time distribution task is simplified if all of a worker's time is related to only one job or if a worker's time is charged to a single process or department.

Bar-Coding Technology. As previously mentioned, computerized on-site data entry for both clock cards and time tickets is enhanced by use of bar coding. **Bar codes** are symbols that can be processed electronically to identify numbers, letters, or special characters. In manufacturing and in service industries, perhaps no technical development has shown greater potential for improving efficiency and effectiveness than electronic identification using bar codes for computerized data entry. This technology helps internal accounting systems provide timely, accurate, and relevant information.

Bar-coded employee identification cards or badges replace clock cards and time tickets to collect payroll data and to measure the activity of workers and machines. The worker uses the card or badge to clock in and out at the beginning and end of the work day. And when beginning and ending a task, a worker scans information from her or his card or badge and from a bar-coded source that identifies the correct job, task or operation, and department.

To improve its attendance and time reporting system, Target Products, a manufacturer of concrete, masonry, and tile cutting equipment, introduced bar-coding technology into its manufacturing operations. To record attendance and time, employees are provided with bar-coded identification badges and task-identifying templates that are scanned using a light pen. The collected information is transmitted to the company's computer mainframe, where it is processed.

Prior to the implementation of bar coding, it was virtually impossible to account for labor costs at Target Products because of short cycle times. Time clocks were used but no attempt was made to keep track of labor costs by operation. Now, supervisors receive a labor report for employees within their departments for the previous day's transactions. This information is also used by the payroll and cost accounting departments.[7]

Payroll Department

Payroll data are processed in two steps: (1) computing and preparing the payroll and (2) distributing the payroll to jobs, processes, and departments. These steps can be performed by a payroll department, the size of which depends on the size and complexity of a company. The payroll department is responsible for the important task of recording the job classification, department, and wage rate for each employee. It records hours worked and wages earned, makes payroll deductions, determines the net amount due each employee, maintains a permanent earnings record for each employee, prepares the paychecks or provides the cashier's or treasurer's office with the necessary records to make the payments, and can also prepare the payroll distribution.

---

[7] Stanley F. Stec, "Manufacturing Control Through Bar Coding at Target Products," *Management Accounting*, Vol. 49, No. 10, p. 47.

Payroll Computation and Preparation. The company's payroll is prepared from the clock cards. The final computed payroll is recorded in a payroll journal or payroll record. The record must show total wages, deductions, and the net payroll. A record of individual employee earnings and deductions also must be maintained.

In most instances, employees are paid by check. Payroll checks are drawn against the regular checking account or a special payroll deposit. The special payroll bank account is especially advantageous in companies having large numbers of workers. When a payroll fund is deposited in the bank, the payroll department certifies the amount required for a particular payment date, a voucher is drawn for the specified amount, and a check is drawn against the regular deposit account and is deposited in the payroll fund. By utilizing this procedure, only one check, drawn on the general bank account, appears in the cash payments journal each payroll period. For each employee, the paymaster prepares a check drawn against the special payroll account. When computerized methods are used for payroll accounting, the payroll journal, the checks, the check register, and the employees' earnings records are commonly prepared in one simultaneous operation. An additional service provided by payroll can allow employees to authorize the direct electronic deposit of their net pay to their individual checking accounts.

Payroll Distribution. The individual time ticket or daily time report shows the use made of the time purchased from each factory employee. The tickets for each employee must agree with the employee's total earnings for the week. Time tickets are sorted by jobs, departments, and types of indirect labor to permit the distribution of the total payroll to Work in Process and to the departmental overhead analysis sheets controlled by Factory Overhead Control. Distribution of the payroll is speeded up when automated methods are used. If the payroll department does not prepare the distribution summary, the time tickets are sent to the cost department, which must perform this task. Labor costs distributed to jobs, processes, or departments must agree with the total amount recorded in the payroll account. The distribution summary can also show the labor hours when they are the basis for the application of factory overhead. In highly automated manufacturing, direct labor cost can be small relative to other production costs and/or not easily traced to jobs or production lines. In such cases, direct labor can be charged to Factory Overhead Control and included as part of the factory overhead rate rather than being charged directly to Work in Process.

If the labor cost to be assigned to ending work in process and finished goods inventories occurs in a just-in-time production environment, these costs can be charged directly to Cost of Goods Sold as incurred. An end-of-the-period adjustment is made, adjusting the inventory accounts for the portion of labor and other manufacturing costs appropriate to the units in inventory, with the offset to the cost of goods sold account, following the backflush costing approach covered in Chapter 10.

Cost Department

On the basis of the labor distribution summary or the time tickets, the cost department records the direct labor cost on the appropriate job cost sheets or production reports, and the indirect cost on the departmental overhead analysis sheets. In some factories, cost accounting activities are decentralized, and cost work becomes largely a matter of organization and direction in carrying out a system for recording payroll information and labor costs. In such a situation, cost clerks may be stationed in producing departments to assist in accumulating and classifying labor costs, using the time tickets to compute production costs and services by job orders, units of output, departmental operations, and product types. In other factories, the cost department may be highly centralized and may not direct and control any timekeeping or payroll preparation.

Departmental Interrelationships and Labor Cost Control and Accounting

The organization chart presented in Figure 11-1 summarizes the departmental interrelationships required for effective labor cost control and accounting.

The preceding labor costing discussion has emphasized manufacturing labor. Labor costing of nonmanufacturing labor, such as marketing and administrative employees, also requires the same detailed cost accumulation and distribution.

FIGURE 11-1 ***Organization Chart for Labor Cost Control and Accounting***

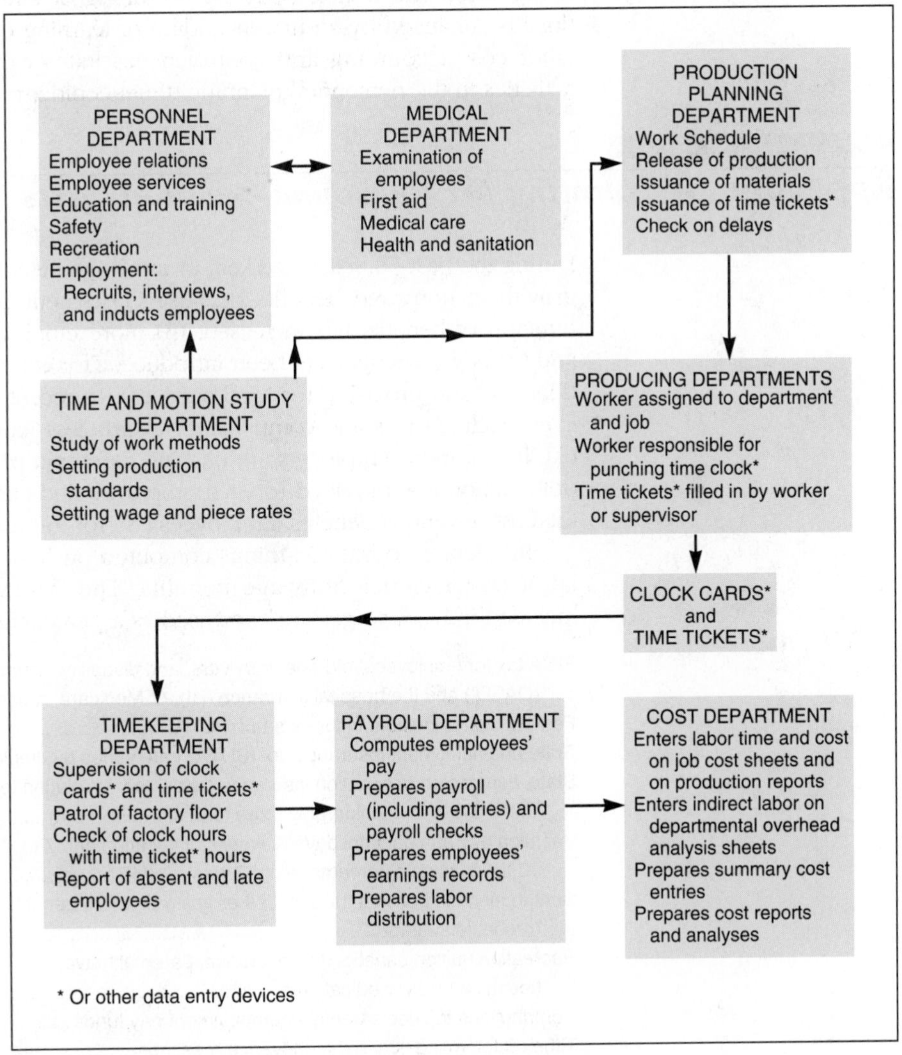

Ethical Considerations

Adhering to ethical standards is important in all aspects of human activity. In any organization, labor cost accounting and control is permeated with the need to abide by a code of ethics such as the *Standards of Ethical Conduct for Management Accountants* (discussed in Chapter 1).

These standards pertain to ethical conduct in a wide range of activities, including hiring practices, employee payment policies, budgeting and reporting of labor costs and time variances, administering productivity programs and incentive wage plans, and equity in employee benefits.

Summary

Labor costs, as the human contribution to production, have a direct impact on productivity. Productivity improvements require better management of human resources. Incentive wage plans represent tangible rewards for desired worker performance. Whether the plans are geared to individuals, groups, or the entire organization through a gainsharing plan, depends on the manner in which work is organized and accomplished. Fine tuning of employee performance expectations is enhanced by an understanding of learning curve theory. Organization for labor cost accounting and control necessitates careful coordination of related activities in the personnel, planning, timekeeping, payroll, and cost departments.

Appendix Accounting for Personnel-Related Costs

During the past 50 years, workers in the United States have enjoyed a spectacular growth in nonwage benefits because (1) benefit costs have increased, (2) the duration of benefits has increased, (3) more employees are covered by benefits, and (4) new benefits have been introduced (for example, insurance for vision and dentistry, and provision for legal services). In recent years, benefits stabilized and even declined in some companies. Nevertheless, employee benefits are substantial. Increasingly, employers are offering **cafeteria plans,** under which a specified dollar amount is provided to each employee and can be applied to part or all of the cost of various benefits. Employees pay for this amount with pretax dollars.

In addition to basic earnings computed on hours worked or units produced, labor cost includes nonwage benefits. The following labor-related costs not included in basic wages are expressed as a percentage of straight-time earnings.

FICA tax for employees' old-age, survivors, and disability insurance (OASDI) and the hospital insurance (HI), or Medicare, program	7.5%
Federal unemployment insurance tax (FUTA)	.8
State unemployment insurance tax (SUTA), rate varies by employer	4.0
State worker's compensation insurance (rates vary in relation to hazard—1% to 3%, and considerably more for hazardous work)	1.0
Vacation pay and paid holidays (2 weeks of vacation and 7 to 10 holidays as a percentage of 52 weeks of 40 hours)	8.0
Contributions to pension fund and other postretirement benefits (probable average)	8.0
Recreation, tuition benefits, life insurance, parental leave, health services, medical care	9.0
Contributions to supplemental unemployment pay funds	2.0
Time off for voting, jury duty, grievance meetings	1.3
Services related to parking lots, income tax, legal advice, meal money, uniforms	1.5
Total	43.1%

Some of the percentages, such as those for FICA, FUTA, and state unemployment insurance tax, apply to a base that may be less than total annual wages, which tends to lower the average annual percentage.

Labor cost also includes overtime earnings; premium pay for work on holidays, Saturdays, and Sundays; shift bonuses or differentials; bonuses for performance attendance, length of service, and no accidents; apprenticeship or trainee costs; and severance pay. This appendix discusses the accounting for many of these fringe benefits.

Overtime Earnings

The Fair Labor Standards Act of 1938, commonly referred to as the Federal Wage and Hour Law, established a minimum wage per hour with time and a half for hours worked in excess of 40 in one week. Subsequently, the act has been amended, broadening the coverage and raising the minimum wage. Some types of organizations and workers are exempt from the provisions of the act and its amendments or have lower minimums.

A number of payroll practices are mandatory to comply with the Federal Wage and Hour Law. For each employee, records must show the following:

1. Hours worked each working day and the total hours worked during each work week.
2. Basis on which wages are paid.
3. Total daily or weekly earnings at straight time.
4. Total extra pay for overtime worked each week.
5. Total wages paid during each pay period, the date of payment, and the work period covered by the payment.

Overtime earnings consist of two elements: (1) the regular pay rate and (2) the overtime premium, which is an additional amount for work done beyond the 40-hour work week or an 8-hour workday (as specified in some labor union contracts). For most workers, an employer must pay a minimum of one and one-half times the regular rate for overtime. For example, if an employee is paid $8 per hour for a regular work week of 40 hours, but works 45 hours, the gross earnings are as follows:

Regular work week	40 hours @ $8 =	$320
Overtime	5 hours @ 8 =	40
Overtime premium	5 hours @ 4 =	20
Gross earnings		$380

Charging the overtime premium to a specific job or product or to factory overhead primarily depends on the reason for the overtime work. The contract price of a particular job, taken as a rush order with the foreknowledge that overtime will be necessary, may include the overtime premium; if so, the premium should be charged to the specific job. But when regular orders cannot be completed in the regular working hours, the overtime premium should be charged to factory overhead control, because it is not caused by the work that happens to be done during overtime hours. If overtime is budgeted at the beginning of the year, it is included in the predetermined overhead rate.

Bonus Payments and Deferred Compensation Plans

Just as companies are attempting to stabilize or reduce fringe benefits, they are also seeking ways to reduce the basic wage structure. If an employee is given a raise, it becomes an entitlement, continues to be paid each year, and increases the worker's pension and other company-paid benefits. Employers can lower costs by keeping base salary increases to a minimum and by paying incentive bonuses.

A recent survey by Sibson & Company, reported in the *Wall Street Journal*, indicates that bonus plans for employees are popular. Of 412 companies surveyed, 48 percent had performance-based pay plans. A plan's structure can change under differing economic conditions. For example, Clark Johnson, chief executive officer for Pier 1 Imports, observed that "In good times, you reward sales gains. In bad times, you reward the ability to control expenses."

Bonus payments can be a fixed amount per employee or job classification, a percentage of profits, a fraction of one month's wages, or some other calculated amount. The amount of bonus for each employee can be a fixed and long-established tradition of a company, or the amount can vary from year to year. Bonus payments are a production cost, a marketing expense, or an administrative expense. If a direct labor employee's average weekly earnings are $250 and the company intends to pay 2 weeks' pay as a bonus at the end of the year, then earnings actually amount to $260 per week, but the additional $10 per week is paid in a lump sum of $500 ($10 × 50 weeks, assuming 2 weeks of vacation time) at the end of the year. The bonus cost is spread over production throughout the year through the predetermined factory overhead rate. The bonus is charged to factory overhead as follows:

	Subsidiary Record	Dr.	Cr.
Work in Process		250	
Factory Overhead Control		10	
Bonus Pay	10		
Payroll			250
Liability for Bonus			10

When the bonus is paid, the liability account is debited, and Cash and the withholding accounts are credited.

In theory, this and other costs related to direct labor are additional labor costs that are charged directly to Work in Process. In practice, such a procedure usually is impractical, so these costs generally are included in the predetermined factory overhead rate and charged to Work in Process indirectly through the overhead rate.

Long-term bonuses (related to periods longer than one year) and stock option plans are examples of **deferred compensation plans.** If a firm can accurately measure the liability and is legally committed to payment, then the present value of the future compensation payments is recognized as an expense in the period in which the benefit is earned. Cost Accounting Standards Board (CASB) regulations allow the same treatment in costing government contracts.[8] However, such benefits cannot be deducted for income tax purposes until actually paid or funded, depending on the nature of the plan.

---

[8] *Standards, Rules and Regulations, Part 415*, "Accounting for the Cost of Deferred Compensation" (Washington, D.C.: Cost Accounting Standards Board, 1977).

Vacation Pay

Vacation pay presents cost problems similar to those of bonus payments. When an employee is entitled to a paid vacation of 2 weeks, the vacation pay is accrued over the 50 weeks of productive labor. For example, assume that a direct labor employee has a base wage of $300 per week and is entitled to a paid vacation of 2 weeks. The cost of labor is $300, plus $12 per week. In 50 weeks at $12 per week, the deferred payment of $600 equals the expected vacation pay. The entry to record the weekly labor cost, including the provision for vacation pay, is:

	Subsidiary Record	Dr.	Cr.
Work in Process		300	
Factory Overhead Control		12	
Vacation Pay	12		
Payroll			300
Liability for Vacation Pay			12

When a vacation is taken, the liability account is debited and Cash and the withholding accounts are credited. Similarly, accrual should be made for employer liability pertaining to sick leave, holidays, military training, or other personal activities for which employees receive compensation. If it becomes necessary to use temporary replacements to perform the duties of personnel who are absent, this additional expense is charged to the department for which the replacement is made.

FASB Statement No. 43, "Accounting for Compensated Absences," requires an employer to accrue a liability for employees' rights to receive compensation for future absences when all the following conditions are met: (1) the rights are attributable to employees' services already rendered, (2) the rights vest or accumulate, (3) payment is probable, and (4) the amount can be reasonably estimated. Although the statement requires accrual of vacation benefits, it generally does not require a liability to be accrued for future sick pay benefits (unless the rights vest), holidays, and similar compensated absences until employees are actually absent.[9] In accounting for government contracts, CASB regulations require accrual of employer obligations for labor-related costs for personal absences.[10] Statement of Governmental Accounting Standards, No. 16[11] prescribes accrual by state and local governments. Conversely, vacation pay accruals are not allowed for income tax purposes.[12] The only exception is for vested plans, which can accrue amounts paid within two and one-half months after year-end.

Guaranteed Annual Wage Plans

Although a guaranteed annual wage plan for all industrial workers is far from realization, a step in that direction has been taken in labor contracts that provide for the company to pay employees who are laid off. The company pay is a supplement to the state unemployment insurance. For example, assume that an

[9] *Statement of Financial Accounting Standards, No. 43,* "Accounting for Compensated Absences" (Stamford, Conn.: Financial Accounting Standards Board, 1980).

[10] *Standards, Rules and Regulations, Part 408,* "Accounting for Costs of Compensated Personal Absence" (Washington, D.C.: Cost Accounting Standards Board, 1974).

[11] *Statement of Governmental Accounting Standards, No. 16,* "Accounting for Compensated Absences" (Norwalk, Conn.: Governmental Accounting Standards Board, 1992).

[12] The Tax Revenue Act of 1987 repealed Section 463 of the Internal Revenue Code.

unemployed worker is guaranteed 60 percent of normal take-home pay, beginning the second week of layoff and continuing for as long as 26 weeks. To recognize the liability for payments to be made during unemployment periods, a specified amount, such as 15 cents an hour for each worker, is accrued by the company.

In principle, if it is assumed that layoffs will eventually occur, it is clear that the working employee is earning 15 cents an hour that is not included in the paycheck at the end of the payroll period. This amount is held in reserve by the company in order to make payments during unemployment periods. For a direct labor employee whose base pay rate is $8 an hour, the cost effect of unemployment pay for a 40-hour week is illustrated by the following entry:

	Subsidiary Record	Dr.	Cr.
Work in Process		320	
Factory Overhead Control		6	
Unemployment Pay	6		
Payroll			320
Liability for Unemployment Pay			6

Pension Plans

A **pension plan** is an arrangement whereby a company provides retirement benefit payments for all employees in recognition of their work contribution to the company. A pension plan is probably the most important and most complicated factor associated with labor and labor costs. It influences personnel relations, company financing, income determination, income tax considerations, and general economic conditions. It also must comply with governmental regulations.

In the case of bonuses and paid vacations, part of an employee's total earnings is withheld or accrued for a period of months and then paid in a lump sum. In the case of pension payments, the wage is earned and the labor cost is incurred many years before the payment is made. As a matter of principle, if an employee is paid a base wage for a 40-hour week and if the employer's pension cost amounts to $1.50 an hour, the pension cost incurred is $60 per week and is chargeable to factory overhead, marketing expense, or administrative expense.[13]

Employee Retirement Income Security Act of 1974. The Employee Retirement Income Security Act of 1974 (more commonly known as ERISA) was enacted in order to make certain that promised pensions are actually paid at retirement. This act sets minimum government standards for vesting, participation, funding, management, and a variety of other matters. The act also covers a wide range of employee welfare plans for health, accident, and death benefits. In addition, it covers pension or retirement plans and establishes both labor standards (administered by the Secretary of Labor) and tax standards (administered by the Secretary of the Treasury). The labor and tax standards taken together form a common body of legislation pertaining to practically all employee benefit plans not specifically exempted from the act.

CASB Pension Cost Standards. In 1975, the Cost Accounting Standards Board promulgated CASB No. 412, "Cost Accounting Standards for Composition and Measurement of Pension Cost," establishing the components of pension cost, the bases for measuring such cost, and the criteria for assigning pension cost to cost

[13] For a detailed discussion of accounting for pension plans, see Jay M. Smith, Jr. and K. Fred Skousen, *Intermediate Accounting*, 11th ed., Chapter 21, Comprehensive Vol. (Cincinnati: South-Western Publishing Co., 1992.).

accounting periods. This standard is to be used in accounting for government contracts to which CASB regulations apply. This standard is compatible with the requirements of the Pension Reform Act of 1974, although certain of its provisions are more restrictive than the Pension Reform Act. Furthermore, the CASB standard, while attempting to stay within the constraints of generally accepted accounting principles (GAAP), specifies certain features of GAAP that are considered not appropriate for government contract costing purposes. In 1977, CASB No. 413, "Adjustment and Allocation of Pension Cost," declared that actuarial gains and losses should be calculated and gave criteria for assigning pension expense to accounting periods and to segments, as well as for valuing pension fund assets.

Postretirement Benefits Other Than Pensions. Employers are increasingly aware of a large and rapidly growing economic dilemma: providing other postretirement employee benefits (OPEBs), in addition to pensions. The costs are staggering. For example, the future cost of retiree medical benefits for all U.S. companies is estimated to be between $200 billion and $400 billion. Runaway medical inflation, an aging work force, early retirements, and significant Medicare cutbacks will escalate these costs even more.

In 1990, the Financial Accounting Standards Board issued Statement No. 106 entitled, "Employers' Accounting for Postretirement Benefits Other Than Pensions." The statement requires employers to use the accrual method of accounting for the cost of providing the promised benefits. The cash basis of accounting for benefits paid to retired employees is no longer permitted. While income tax laws have been favorable to early deduction of pension accruals, similar favorable treatment has not been granted to other postretirement benefits.

The FASB concluded that OPEBs are, in reality, similar to pension costs. Benefits are earned while employees provide service to the company, at least up to the eligibility date; thus, they are a form of deferred compensation. Because of this similarity, these costs must be accrued and the unfunded liability must be reported on the balance sheet. Because the accumulated liability is so large, the FASB statement makes possible a 20-year transition period to accrue fully all accumulated earned postretirement benefits rather than requiring immediate recognition of these liabilities.

The new standard will cause employers' reported retiree medical expenses to increase dramatically. A nationwide survey of 178 medium-sized and large employers found the following estimated changes in total annual retiree medical costs:[14]

	Estimated Annual Retiree Medical Costs	
	Before Implementing the FASB Standard	**After Implementing the FASB Standard**
Percent of active payroll	1.10%	6.25%
Percent of before-tax profit	2.00	7.50
Percent of equity	.50	2.00

The postretirement benefit costs accounting standards generally contain the same components as these defined for pension costs, including a requirement that costs be determined actuarially. However, the costs are attributed to the period of service from the date of hire to the full eligibility date rather than to the retirement date that is used for most pension plans. A disclosure policy similar to that for pensions is required, plus disclosures of changes in health care cost trends. Furthermore, trends in health care costs must be included in the actuarial computations.

[14] *Journal of Accountancy*, Vol. 171, No. 5, p. 15.

Although the FASB statement stresses health care costs, other postretirement benefits are included and must also be reported on an accrual basis. These costs include life insurance contracts, legal assistance benefits, and tuition assistance.[15]

The FASB in 1992 issued Statement 112, "Employers' Accounting for Postemployment Benefits," which requires employers to recognize a liability for postemployment benefits provided to former or inactive employees and their dependents and beneficiaries, before retirement. Here the liability is recognized in accordance with FASB Statement 43, "Accounting for Compensated Absences."

Additional Legislation Affecting Labor-Related Costs

Costing labor and keeping payroll records were relatively simple prior to the first social security act. This legislation made it necessary for many employers to initiate or redesign payroll accounting in order to account accurately for payroll deductions. Later, other state and federal legislation imposed additional requirements affecting the accounting for wages and salaries. For example, the Federal Insurance Contributions Act, federal and state unemployment tax laws, worker's compensation laws, and federal, state, and city income tax laws require periodic reports.[16]

Federal Insurance Contributions Act (FICA). This legislation is administered and operated entirely by the federal government. FICA includes a tax used to finance the federal old-age, survivors, and disability insurance program (OASDI) and a tax used to finance the hospital insurance (HI), or Medicare, program. Originally enacted in August of 1935, the Federal Insurance Contributions Act has been amended many times. The amendments have brought more employees under the act and have increased the benefits, the tax rate, and the wage base, including certain fringe benefits, upon which the tax is levied.[17] Under the 1965 FICA amendments, the Hospital Insurance Program (Medicare) was enacted.[18]

Employers are required to pay a tax equal to the amount paid by the employees. The employer is further required to collect the FICA tax from employees through payroll deductions. Federal income tax withheld and employee and employer FICA taxes must be periodically deposited with either an authorized commercial bank depository or a Federal Reserve Bank, and a quarterly report must be filed.

Federal Unemployment Tax Act (FUTA). Unlike FICA, which is strictly a federal program, FUTA provides for cooperation between state and federal governments in the establishment and administration of unemployment insurance.

Under the provisions of the Federal Unemployment Tax Act, an employer in covered employment pays an unemployment insurance tax of 6.2 percent. The

---

[15] For a detailed discussion of accounting for postretirement benefits, see Jay M. Smith, Jr. and K. Fred Skousen, *Intermediate Accounting*, 11th ed., Chapter 21, Comprehensive Vol. (Cincinnati: South-Western Publishing Co., 1992).

[16] These pages summarize the major provisions. U.S. Treasury Department Internal Revenue Service Circular E, entitled "Employer's Tax Guide," is an excellent source for a more comprehensive coverage of these regulations at the federal government level. A free copy of the current edition can be obtained by writing to the nearest District Director, Internal Revenue Service. State and local laws must be determined as they apply to specific employers.

[17] The Tax Reform Act of 1984 amended the *Internal Revenue Code*, Section 3121(a), to require the inclusion of fringe benefits (not specifically excluded by statute) in wages subject to FICA tax.

[18] A rate of 7.5 percent on an annual wage base of $55,000 per employee for FICA tax is used in the illustrations and in the end-of-chapter material but is not current. The actual rate and wage bases change from time to time. Also, the portion of the FICA tax that pertains to Medicare is applied to a higher base.

annual earnings base is $7,000 of each employee's wages paid, with .8 percent payable to the federal government and 5.4 percent to the state. States generally provide an experience rating plan under which an employer who has provided stable employment can pay less than 5.4 percent to the state agency, with zero as a possible payment. The laws of some states provide a higher rate or a larger annual earnings base for computing the state portion of the tax. While the federal act requires no employee contribution, some states also levy an unemployment insurance tax on the employee.[19]

The federal portion of the unemployment tax is payable quarterly. However, if the employer's tax liability (plus any accumulated tax liability for previous quarters) is $100 or less for the fiscal year, only one payment is required by January 31 of the following year. The related tax return is due annually on January 31.

Worker's Compensation Insurance. Worker's compensation insurance laws provide insurance benefits for workers or their survivors for losses caused by accidents and occupational diseases suffered in the course of employment. While the benefits, premium costs, and various other details vary from state to state, the total insurance cost is borne by the employer. The employer may have the option of insuring with an approved insurance company or through a state insurance fund. In some cases, if the size and the financial resources are sufficient, the enterprise can carry its own risk.

Withholding of Federal Income Tax, State Income Tax, and City Wage Tax. The employer is required to withhold federal income tax—and state income and city wage taxes if applicable—from employees' compensation, including certain fringe benefits, and to furnish information to the Internal Revenue Service and to state and city taxing authorities showing the amount of compensation paid each employee and the amount of income taxes withheld.[20] The collection of income taxes from employees and the remittance of these taxes affect payroll accounting.

Recordkeeping. Federal, state, and city taxing authorities require that employers keep payroll records for four years showing the following for each employee:

1. Name, address, social security number, and occupation.
2. Amounts and dates of remuneration payments and the period of service covered by each payment.
3. Amounts and dates of annuity and pension payments.
4. Amounts of payments that constitute taxable wages.
5. Amounts and dates of tax withheld.
6. Amounts of payments and dates covered for absence due to sickness or injury.
7. Copies of employees' withholding allowance certificate.

---

[19] The earnings base and rates are subject to change. To find the current levels, consult published government regulations. Also, the percentage payable to the federal government may be greater than .8 percent in certain states because those states failed to repay prior year advances that came from the federal government to the state unemployment compensation funds.

[20] The Tax Reform Act of 1984 amended the *Internal Revenue Code,* Section 61(a)(1), to require the inclusion of employee fringe benefits in the definition of gross income, i.e., income subject to taxation. Consequently, employers must include employee fringe benefits that are not specifically excluded by statute in income subject to withholding. To date, fringe benefits are generally excluded from income subject to taxation (1) if they are nondiscriminatory, i.e., if they are uniformly available to all employees, and (2) if they are not excessive. See the discussion of employer paid life insurance premiums for an example of a fringe benefit that is included in income subject to taxation.

8. A record of fringe benefits provided.
9. Amounts and dates of tax deposits made by the employer.
10. Amount of contributions paid into each state unemployment compensation fund, showing separately (a) payments made and not deducted from the remuneration of employees and (b) payments made and deducted from the remuneration of employees.
11. Copies of employer tax returns filed, as well as records of all information required to be shown on the prescribed tax returns.

Labor-Related Deductions

In addition to compulsory payroll deductions, a variety of other deductions can be withheld from take-home pay, with the consent of the employee. A few examples follow.

Insurance. Many companies provide various benefits for their employees, such as health, accident, hospital, and life insurance. It is common for the company and the employees to share the cost, with the employees' share being deducted from wages each payroll period or at regular intervals. If the company pays insurance premiums in advance, including the employees' share, an asset account such as Prepaid Health and Accident Insurance is debited when the payments are made. The employer's share subsequently is credited to the asset account and debited to overhead, marketing, and administrative expenses, and the asset account is credited for the employees' share of the premiums when the payroll deductions are made. In this payroll deduction, as in all similar cases, a subsidiary record showing the contributions of each employee is necessary, and one or more general ledger accounts are maintained.

A company's cost of group life insurance premiums for that portion of an employee's coverage exceeding $50,000 must be included as a part of the employee's gross income for income tax purposes; however, it is not subject to income tax withholding by the employer.[21] This cost also is deemed to be wages for FICA tax purposes, but not for unemployment tax. In addition, the Internal Revenue Code requires that employers must demonstrate that benefits to employees who are highly compensated are nondiscriminatory with respect to other employees. Specific nondiscrimination rules must be met. This requirement applies not only to insurance plans but to other employer-provided fringe benefits as well. Businesses that do not meet these rules must report the extra benefits paid as taxable income to their employees, and these employees must pay tax on it.[22]

Union Dues. Many enterprises employing union labor agree to a union shop and to a deduction of initiation fees and regular membership dues from the wages of each employee. To account for these deductions, a general ledger account entitled Union Dues Payable shows the liability for amounts withheld from the employees. At regular intervals, the company prepares a report and remits the dues collected to the union treasurer.

U.S. Savings Bonds. An employer and an employee frequently agree to some systematic plan of withholding from wages a fixed amount for the purpose of purchasing U.S. Savings Bonds. A general ledger account entitled U.S. Savings Bonds Payable is set up to show the liability for wages withheld. When the accu-

[21] *Internal Revenue Code of 1986,* Section 79(a)(1).
[22] *Internal Revenue Code of 1986,* Section 105(h).

mulated amount is sufficient to purchase a bond, an entry is made debiting U.S. Savings Bonds Payable and crediting Cash. Similar procedures may be used for other employee savings and investment plans.

Payroll Advances. For a variety of reasons, payroll advances can be made to employees. The advances can be in the form of cash, materials, or finished goods. To provide control, an advance authorization form is executed by a responsible official and sent to the payroll department. The asset account debited for all advances represents a receivable to the company and can be entitled Salary and Wage Advances.

At the regular payroll date, the employee's earnings are entered in the payroll journal as usual, and the advance is deducted from wages to be paid. The amount of the advance being deducted is credited to Salary and Wage Advances.

Recording Labor Costs

The basic principle of labor costing is simple and straightforward. A record of the labor time purchased is made through use of the clock card; a record of the performance received is made through the use of time tickets or the daily time report. These documents can exist in electronic or hard copy form. The accounting entries required are:

1. To record wage payments due employees and liabilities for all amounts withheld from wages.
2. To charge the total labor cost to appropriate jobs, processes, and departments.

On a weekly, semimonthly, or monthly basis, or as often as a payroll is met, the total amount earned by workers is debited to Payroll, with credits to Accrued Payroll and to the withholding accounts. The cost of labor purchased is summarized and recorded as debits to Work in Process, Factory Overhead Control, Marketing Expenses Control, and Administrative Expenses Control and as a credit to Payroll. Employer payroll taxes and other labor-related costs are recorded, and at appropriate times, payments are made to discharge payroll-related liabilities.

The accounting for labor costs and payroll liabilities is illustrated in general journal form beginning on page 290, based on the following assumptions:

1. The payroll period is for January, 19B.
2. The payroll is paid on January 9, 19B, and on January 23, 19B, covering wages earned through the preceding Saturday. Note that the wages of the last week of December, 19A, would be paid on January 9 and that the payment of January 23 would cover work done through January 19. Refer to the following calendar:

JANUARY, 19B

Sun	Mon	Tue	Wed	Thu	Fri	Sat
		1	2	3	4	5
6	7	8	9	10	11	12
13	14	15	16	17	18	19
20	21	22	23	24	25	26
27	28	29	30	31		

3. Payroll figures for wages earned during January are:

Direct factory labor	$38,500
Indirect factory labor	18,000
Sales salaries	20,000
Office and administrative salaries	12,000
Total payroll	$88,500

4. Wages paid during January, 19B: $50,000 on January 9, and $40,000 on January 23. Of the federal income tax withheld, $6,000 is on the payroll of January 9 and $5,500 on that of January 23.
5. Wages earned and unpaid on December 31, 19A, total $26,000. On January 31, the amount is $24,500.
6. The cost of the employer's payroll taxes is recorded at month-end, with separate liability accounts for federal and state agencies. In compliance with the regulations, employees' FICA taxes are recorded when they are withheld and determination of the payment of the total FICA tax (employer and employee portions) is based on the date the wages are paid.
7. Employees' income tax, employees' FICA tax, the employer's matching FICA tax payment, employees' union dues, and U.S. Savings Bonds payments are paid on the same dates that wages are paid to the employees. No other January payroll-related liabilities are paid in that month.

Added assumptions:

FICA tax: 7.5%.
Worker's compensation: 1% of payroll.
Unemployment insurance: .8% federal, 5.4% state.
Estimated pension cost: $4,000 per month (direct labor, $1,540; indirect labor, $900; sales salaries, $1,000; office and administrative salaries, $560).
Estimated postretirement benefits other than pensions, $2,000 (direct labor, $770; indirect labor, $450; sales salaries, $500; office and administrative salaries, $280).
Payroll advances: $2,200 (deducted on January 9 payroll).
Union dues collected: $1,000 each payroll period.
Savings bonds deductions: $1,200 on January 9; $900 on January 23.
Health and accident insurance: 8% of payroll, shared equally (employees' share as wages are paid; employer's share as wages are earned).
Cost for supplemental unemployment benefits: 2% of factory labor earned.

		Subsidiary Record	Dr.	Cr.
Jan. 2	Accrued Payroll		26,000.00	
	Payroll			26,000.00
	To reverse entry for wages payable as of December 31.			
9	Payroll		50,000.00	
	Accrued Payroll			33,850.00
	Employees Income Tax Payable			6,000.00
	FICA Tax Payable			3,750.00
	Salary and Wage Advances			2,200.00
	Union Dues Payable			1,000.00
	U.S. Savings Bonds Payable			1,200.00
	Health and Accident Insurance			2,000.00
	To record payroll liability.			
9	Accrued Payroll		33,850.00	
	Employees Income Tax Payable		6,000.00	
	FICA Tax Payable		7,500.00	
	Union Dues Payable		1,000.00	
	U.S. Savings Bonds Payable		1,200.00	
	Cash			49,550.00
	To record payroll payment.			

		Subsidiary Record	Dr.	Cr.
23	Payroll		40,000.00	
	Accrued Payroll			28,000.00
	Employees Income Tax Payable			5,500.00
	FICA Tax Payable			3,000.00
	Union Dues Payable			1,000.00
	U.S. Savings Bonds Payable			900.00
	Health and Accident Insurance Payable.			1,600.00
	To record payroll liability.			
23	Accrued Payroll		28,000.00	
	Employees Income Tax Payable		5,500.00	
	FICA Tax Payable		6,000.00	
	Union Dues Payable		1,000.00	
	U.S. Savings Bonds Payable		900.00	
	Cash			41,400.00
	To record payroll payment.			
31	Payroll		24,500.00	
	Accrued Payroll			24,500.00
	To record wages payable as of January 31.			
31	Work in Process		38,500.00	
	Factory Overhead Control		18,000.00	
	Indirect Labor	18,000.00		
	Marketing Expenses Control		20,000.00	
	Sales Salaries	20,000.00		
	Administrative Expenses Control		12,000.00	
	Office and Administrative Salaries	12,000.00		
	Payroll			88,500.00
	To distribute the payroll cost.			
31	Factory Overhead Control		10,279.50	
	FICA Tax	2,887.50		
	Unemployment Insurance Taxes	2,387.00		
	Workers' Compensation	385.00		
	Pensions	1,540.00		
	Other Postretirement Benefits	770.00		
	Health and Accident Insurance	1,540.00		
	Estimated Unemployment Tax	770.00		
	FICA Tax Payable			2,887.50
	Federal Unemployment Tax Payable			308.00
	State Unemployment Tax Payable			2,079.00
	Workers' Compensation Payable			385.00
	Liability for Pensions			1,540.00
	Liability for Other Postretirement Benefits			770.00
	Health and Accident Insurance Payable			1,540.00
	Liability for Unemployment Pay			770.00
	To record employer labor-related expenses for direct labor factory employees.			

		Subsidiary Record	Dr.	Cr.
31	Factory Overhead Control		5,076.00	
	FICA Tax	1,350.00		
	Unemployment Insurance Taxes	1,116.00		
	Workers' Compensation	180.00		
	Pensions	900.00		
	Other Postretirement Benefits	450.00		
	Health and Accident Insurance	720.00		
	Estimated Unemployment Tax	360.00		
	FICA Tax Payable			1,350.00
	Federal Unemployment Tax Payable			144.00
	State Unemployment Tax Payable			972.00
	Workers' Compensation Payable			180.00
	Liability for Pensions			900.00
	Liability for Other Postretirement Benefits			450.00
	Health and Accident Insurance Payable			720.00
	Liability for Unemployment Pay			360.00
	To record employer labor-related expenses for indirect labor factory employees.			
31	Marketing Expenses Control		5,240.00	
	FICA Tax	1,500.00		
	Unemployment Insurance Taxes	1,240.00		
	Workers' Compensation	200.00		
	Pensions	1,000.00		
	Other Postretirement Benefits	500.00		
	Health and Accident Insurance	800.00		
	FICA Tax Payable			1,500.00
	Federal Unemployment Tax Payable			160.00
	State Unemployment Tax Payable			1,080.00
	Workers' Compensation Payable			200.00
	Liability for Pensions			1,000.00
	Liability for Other Postretirement Benefits			500.00
	Health and Accident Insurance Payable			800.00
	To record employer labor-related expenses for marketing employees.			
31	Administrative Expenses Control		3,084.00	
	FICA Tax	900.00		
	Unemployment Insurance Taxes	744.00		
	Workers' Compensation	120.00		
	Pensions	560.00		
	Other Postretirement Benefits	280.00		
	Health and Accident Insurance	480.00		
	FICA Tax Payable			900.00
	Federal Unemployment Tax Payable			96.00
	State Unemployment Tax Payable			648.00
	Workers' Compensation Payable			120.00
	Liability for Pensions			560.00
	Liability for Other Postretirement Benefits			280.00
	Health and Accident Insurance Payable			480.00
	To record employer labor-related expenses for administrative employees.			

This illustration records the employer's payroll taxes as a liability when the wages are earned, which follows the accrual concept of accounting. As a practical matter, many employers do not accrue payroll taxes at the end of each fiscal period because the legal liability does not occur until the next period in which the wages are paid. This latter practice can be considered acceptable if it is consistently applied and if the amounts are not material. This latter practice is, however, required for tax purposes, and payments to the Internal Revenue Service must conform, as is done in this illustration. Conversely, accrual is prescribed by Governmental Accounting Standards Board Statement 16 in accounting for state and local governments.[23]

Key Terms

base rate, or job rate *(263)*
fringe benefits *(263)*
labor productivity *(264)*
rating, or performance rating *(265)*
normal time *(265)*
standard time *(265)*
productivity–efficiency ratio *(265)*
incentive wage plan *(266)*
straight piecework plan *(268)*
100-percent bonus plan *(268)*
group bonus plans *(269)*
organizational incentive plans, or gainsharing plans *(270)*
learning curve theory *(271)*
time clock, or time recorder *(276)*
clock card *(276)*
time ticket *(276)*
daily time report *(276)*
bar codes *(277)*
cafeteria plans *(280)*
deferred compensation plans *(282)*
pension plan *(284)*

Discussion Questions

Q11-1 Is it generally true that all wage payments are ultimately limited by and are usually based, directly or indirectly, on the productivity of the worker? Explain.

Q11-2 Define productivity.

Q11-3 Why is productivity important to the firm, to workers, and to society?

Q11-4 How can labor efficiency be determined or measured?

Q11-5 What is the purpose of an incentive wage plan?

Q11-6 In most incentive wage plans, does production above standard reduce the labor cost per unit of output? Discuss.

Q11-7 Wage incentive plans are successful in plants operating near full capacity.

(a) Discuss the desirability of using these plans during periods of curtailed production.

(b) Is it advisable to install an incentive wage plan in a plant operating at 60% of capacity? Discuss.

Q11-8 Describe the straight piecework plan, the 100-percent bonus plan, and the group bonus plan.

Q11-9 What is an organizational (gainsharing) incentive plan?

Q11-10 State the basic concept underlying the relationship involved in the cumulative-average-time learning curve model.

Q11-11 Name some situations in which the learning curve theory can be applied.

Q11-12 Accounting for labor has a twofold aspect: financial accounting and cost accounting. Differentiate between the two.

Q11-13 In what way are the creation and maintenance of an efficient labor force a cooperative effort?

Q11-14 What is the purpose of determining the labor hours (a) worked by each employee; (b) worked on each job, or in each department?

Q11-15 What purpose is served by (a) the clock card; (b) the time ticket?

Q11-16 If employees' clock cards show more time than their time tickets, how is the difference reconciled?

Q11-17 What are bar codes and how are they used in labor costing?

Q11-18 (Appendix) Give two costing methods of accounting for the premium costs of overtime direct labor. State circumstances in which each method is appropriate. (AICPA adapted)

Q11-19 (Appendix) For many years, a company has paid all employees 1 week's wages as a year-end

[23] *Statement of Governmental Accounting Standards, No. 16,* "Accounting for Compensated Absences." (Norwalk, Conn.: Governmental Accounting Standards Board, 1992).

bonus. It is also company policy to give 2-week paid vacations. What accounting should be followed with respect to the bonus and vacation pay?

Q11-20 (Appendix) The term *pension plan* has been referred to as a formal arrangement for employee retirement benefits, whether established unilaterally or through negotiation, by which specific or implied commitments have been made and used as the basis for estimating costs. Explain the preferable method for computing and accruing costs under a pension plan. (AICPA adapted)

Exercises

E11-1 One-Hundred-Percent Bonus Plan. Terry Pace, employed by the Orange City Canning Company, submitted the following labor data for the first week in June:

	Units	Hours
Monday	270	8
Tuesday	250	8
Wednesday	300	8
Thursday	240	8
Friday	260	8

Required: Prepare a schedule showing Pace's weekly earnings, the effective hourly rate, and the labor cost per unit, assuming a 100-percent bonus plan with a base wage of $9 per hour and a standard production rate of 30 units per hour. Assume the bonus is computed weekly, based on total production for the week. (Round the bonus percentage to two decimal places.)

E11-2 Incentive Wage Plans. Standard production for an employee in the Assembly Department is 20 units per hour in an 8-hour day. The hourly wage rate is $8.

Required: Compute an employee's earnings under each of the following conditions (carrying all computations to three decimal places):

(1) An incentive plan is used, with the worker receiving 80% of the time saved each day. Records indicate the following:

	Units	Hours
Monday	160	8
Tuesday	170	8
Wednesday	175	8

(2) The 100-percent bonus plan is used and 860 units are produced in a 40-hour week.

(3) An incentive plan is used, providing an hourly rate increase of 5% for all hours worked each day that quota production is achieved. Records indicate the following:

	Units	Hours
Monday	160	8
Tuesday	168	8
Wednesday	175	8

E11-3 One-Hundred-Percent Group Bonus Plan. The Forming Department of the Plastic-Powell Company employs six workers on an 8-hour shift at $12.50 per hour. Factory overhead is $120 per hour. Production for the second week of June shows: Monday, 460 units; Tuesday, 475 units; Wednesday, 492 units; Thursday, 500 units; and Friday, 510 units. The company has recently installed a group 100-percent bonus system with a standard production for the group of 60 units per hour. The bonus is computed for each day. The controller asks that an analysis of the week's production costs be made.

Required: Prepare a schedule showing earnings in the department, the unit labor cost, the unit overhead cost, and the total cost per unit. (Round unit costs to three decimal places.)

E11-4 Group Bonus Plan. Ten employees are working as a group in a particular manufacturing department. When the weekly production of the group exceeds the standard number of pieces per hour, each worker in the group is paid a bonus for the excess production in addition to wages at hourly rates. The amount of bonus is computed by first determining the percentage by which the group's production exceeds the standard; one-half of this percentage is then applied to a wage rate of $9 to determine an hourly bonus rate. The standard rate of production before a bonus can be earned is 200 pieces per hour for total hours worked.

	Production Record for the Week	
	Hours Worked	Production
Monday	80	17,824
Tuesday	74	16,206
Wednesday	80	18,048
Thursday	76	17,480
Friday	72	16,733

Required: On the basis of the production record, compute:
(1) The group's bonus for each day and for the week.
(2) The week's earnings of each employee.

E11-5 Organizational (Gainsharing) Incentive Plan. The Guyette Company employs an organizational incentive plan for its entire manufacturing facility. For the year 19B, 755 employees were eligible, and each participated equally.

The plan provides for a gainsharing pool totaling 50% of the value of wages saved. The saving is computed by determining the prior year's productivity ratio (standard hours for work done divided by total actual direct and indirect labor hours). This ratio (rounded to six decimal places) is then divided into the standard hours for the work done during the current year. The resulting figure is compared to current year actual direct and indirect labor hours.

	19B	19A
Standard hours for work done	558,510	643,823
Total actual direct and indirect labor hours	1,284,983	1,525,324

The 19B average hourly pay plus labor fringe benefits was $14.70.

Required: Compute the gainsharing incentive, in total and per employee.

E11-6 Learning Curve and Production Cost. A company's new process will be carried out in one department. The production process has an expected learning curve of 80%. The cost subject to the learning effect for the first batch produced by the process was $60,000.

Required: Compute the cumulative average cost per batch subject to the learning effect after the 16th batch has been produced, using the learning curve function.

E11-7 Learning Curve and Construction Time. A construction company has just completed a bridge over the Pearl River. This is the first bridge the company has built, and it required 100 weeks to complete. Now, having a bridge construction crew with some experience, the company would like to continue building bridges. Because of the investment in heavy machinery needed continuously by this crew, the company believes it would have to bring the average construction time to less than one year (52 weeks) per bridge in order to earn a sufficient return on investment. The average construction time will follow an 80% learning curve.

Required: Compute the number of additional bridges the crew must build to bring the average construction time (over all bridges constructed) below one year per bridge. (ICMA adapted)

E11-8 Learning Curve. Rutledge Company uses labor standards in manufacturing its products. Based on past experience, the company considers the effect of an 80% learning curve when developing standards for direct labor costs.

The company is planning the production of an automatic electrical timing device requiring the assembly of purchased components. Production is planned in lots of 5 units each. A steady-state production phase with no further increases in labor productivity is expected after the eighth lot. The first production lot of 5 units required 90 hours of direct labor time at a standard rate of $9 per hour.

Required:

(1) Compute the standard amount the company should establish for the total direct labor cost required for the production of the first 8 lots.

(2) Discuss the factors that should be considered in establishing the direct labor standards for each unit of output produced beyond the first 8 lots. (ICMA adapted)

E11-9 (Appendix) Overtime Earnings. A production employee in the Cutting Department is paid $9 per hour for a regular work week of 40 hours. During the week ended March 22, the employee worked 50 hours and earned time and a half for overtime hours.

Required:

(1) Prepare the journal entry to record the labor cost if the overtime premium is charged to production worked on during the overtime hours.

(2) Prepare the journal entry to record the labor cost if the overtime premium is not charged to production worked on during the overtime hours.

E11-10 (Appendix) Bonus and Vacation Pay Liability. Four factory workers and a supervisor make up a team in the Machining Department. The supervisor earns $10 per hour, and the combined hourly direct wages of the four workers is $32. Each employee is entitled to a 2-week paid vacation and a bonus equal to 4 weeks' wages each year. Vacation pay and bonuses are treated as an indirect cost and are accrued over the 50-week work year. A provision in the union contract does not allow these employees to work in excess of 40 hours per week.

Required: Prepare the journal entry to record the bonus and vacation pay liability applicable to one week's production.

E11-11 (Appendix) Employer's Labor-Related Expenses. Clarks Company has employees engaged in manufacturing, marketing, and administrative functions. The February payroll was:

Direct labor	$25,000
Indirect labor	10,000
Marketing	8,000
Administrative	7,000
	$50,000

The company incurs the following labor-related expenses as a percentage of the payroll:

Pension plan	7.8%
Other postretirement benefits	2.3
FICA tax	7.5
Federal unemployment insurance	.8
State unemployment insurance	4.6
Worker's compensation	1.0
Medical insurance	4.0

Required: Prepare the journal entry to record the employer's labor-related expenses.

CGA-Canada (adapted). Reprint with permission.

E11-12 (Appendix) Payroll Entries. For the second week in February, Wisconsin Products Company's records show direct labor, $18,000; indirect factory labor, $3,000; sales salaries, $4,200; and administrative office salaries, $1,500. The FICA tax rate is 7.5%; state and federal unemployment compensation insurance taxes are 3.2% and .7%, respectively; state and federal income taxes withheld are $500 and $2,500, respectively; and the city wage tax is 1% on employee gross earnings and is paid by the employee. The company treats employer payroll taxes on factory personnel as an indirect cost.

Required:

(1) Prepare the entry to record the payroll liability.

(2) Prepare the entry to distribute the payroll cost.

(3) Prepare the entry to record the employer's payroll taxes in one compound entry.

Problems

P11-1 Incentive Wage Plan Evaluation. Employees in the Assembly Department of the Bell Instruments Company are currently paid $10 per hour for an 8-hour shift. For the past several weeks, production has averaged 5 units per hour per worker. Factory overhead in this department is $12 per direct labor hour. Employees and management are considering the following piecework proposal:

Units Assembled per 8-Hour Day	Piecework Rate for All Units Produced for the Day
up to 44	$2.00
45 to 49	2.12
50 to 64	2.20
55 to 59	2.30
60 and above	2.40

Required:

(1) Prepare an analysis schedule for the proposal, assuming production of each of the following levels: 40, 45, 50, 55, and 60 units per 8-hour day. Compute unit costs to the nearest cent.

(2) Does the piecework proposal appear advantageous to employees and/or to management?

P11-2 Incentive Wage Plan Evaluation. Hughes Company, a relatively small supplier of computer parts, is currently engaged in producing a new component for the computer sensory unit. The company has been producing 150 units per week and factory overhead (all fixed) was estimated to be $1,200 per week. The following is a schedule of the pay rates of three workers assigned to the new component:

Employee	Hourly Rate
Clancy, D.	$6.00
Luken, T	8.00
Schott, J	7.00

Customers have been calling in for additional units, but management does not want work to exceed 40 hours per week. To motivate its workers to produce more, the company decided to institute an incentive wage plan. Under the plan, each worker would be paid a base rate per hour, as shown in the following schedule, and a premium of $1 per unit for all units when the total number exceeds 150.

Employee	Base Rate
Clancy, D.	$3.50
Luken, T	5.50
Schott, J	4.50

The first week the plan was put into operation, production increased to 165 units. The shop superintendent studied the results and considered the plan too costly. Production had increased 10%, but the labor cost had increased by approximately 23.2%. The superintendent requested permission to redesign the plan in order to make the labor cost increase proportionate to the productivity increase.

Required:

(1) Calculate the dollar amount of the 23.2% labor cost increase.

(2) Give an opinion, supported by figures, as to whether the shop superintendent was correct in assuming that the incentive wage plan was too costly, and discuss other factors to be considered.

P11-3 Incentive Wage Plans. Standard production for assembly operation A94 is 20 units per hour. For the first week in May a worker's record shows the following:

	Units	Hours
Monday	140	8
Tuesday	160	8
Wednesday	175	8
Thursday	180	8
Friday	200	8

Required: Compute the employee's earnings under each of the following conditions (carrying all computations to three decimal places):

(1) An incentive plan is used with a guaranteed rate of $9 per hour and a premium of 60% of the time saved on production in excess of standard for each day.

(2) A piecework plan with rates of $.40 per unit below standard, $.48 at standard and up to 20% above standard, and $.56 per unit for all production when output exceeds 20% above standard. Each day is computed independently.

(3) A 100-percent bonus plan is used with a base usage of $9 per hour. The bonus is computed based on total production for the week.

P11-4 Incentive Wage Plans. For the first week in March, the record of M. Roderick shows:

	Hours Worked	Units Produced
Monday	8	180
Tuesday	8	200
Wednesday	8	220
Thursday	8	224
Friday	8	192

Roderick's guaranteed hourly wage rate is $6 and standard production is 24 units per hour. Factory overhead per labor hour is $3.

Required:

(1) Assume Roderick receives 90% of the labor value of time saved during a day. Prepare a schedule to show Roderick's pay, using the following headings:

Day	Premium Wage
Units Produced	Total Pay
Daily Wage	Labor Cost per Unit (four decimal places)
Units above Standard	Overhead per Unit (four decimal places)
Hours Saved	Conversion Cost per Unit (four decimal places)

(2) Assume the 100-percent bonus plan is used (for each week's total production). Prepare a schedule to show Roderick's pay, using the following headings:

Hours Worked	Base × Efficiency Ratio
Units Produced	Week's Earnings
Standard Production	Labor Cost per Unit (four decimal places)
Efficiency Ratio (nearest %)	Conversion Cost per Unit (four decimal places)
Base Wage	

(3) Assume the daily quota is 192 units and the hourly rate increases 5% for each day the quota is achieved or exceeded. Prepare a schedule to show Roderick's pay, using the following headings:

Day	Amount Earned
Units Produced	Labor Cost per Unit (four decimal places)
Hourly Wage	Conversion Cost per Unit (four decimal places)

P11-5 Incentive Wage Plans. The company's union steward complained to the Payroll Department that several union members' wages had been miscalculated in the previous week. The following schedule indicates the incentive wage plan, hours worked, and gross wages calculated for each worker involved.

Worker	Incentive Wage Plan	Total Hours	Downtime Hours	Units Produced	Standard Units	Base Rate	Gross Wages per Books
Dodd	Straight piecework	40	5	400	—	$6.00	$284.00
Hare	Straight piecework	46	—	455*	—	6.00	277.20
Lowe	Straight piecework	44	4	420**	—	6.00	302.20
Ober	Percentage bonus plan	40	—	250	200	6.00	280.00
Rupp	Percentage bonus plan	40	—	180	200	5.00	171.00
Suggs	Emerson efficiency system	40	—	240	300	5.60	233.20
Ward	Emerson efficiency system	40	2	590	600***	5.60	280.00

* Includes 45 pieces produced during the 6 overtime hours.

** Includes 50 pieces produced during the 4 overtime hours. The overtime, brought about by the downtime, was necessary to meet a production deadline.

*** Standard units for 40 hours production.

The minimum wage for a worker is the base rate, which is also paid for any downtime when the worker's machine is under repair or there is no work. Workers are paid 150% of base rates for hours worked beyond the standard work week of 40 hours. The company's union contract contains the following description of each incentive wage plan:

(a) Straight piecework. The worker is paid at the rate of $.66 per piece produced.

(b) Percentage bonus plan. Standard quantities of production per hour are established by the Engineering Department. The worker's production is divided by the standard quantity of production to determine an efficiency ratio. The efficiency ratio is then applied to the base rate to determine the worker's hourly earnings for the period.

(c) Emerson efficiency system. A minimum wage is paid for total hours worked. A bonus, calculated from the following table of rates, is paid when the worker's production exceeds 66⅔% of standard output or efficiency. The bonus rate is applied only to wages earned during productive hours.

Efficiency	Bonus
Up to 66⅔%	0
66⅔ — 79%	10%
80 — 99%	20%
100 — 125%	45%

Required: Calculate the proper amount of gross wages for each worker in question. Present your results in a schedule comparing each individual's gross wages per books with the gross wages calculated.

(AICPA adapted)

P11-6 Group Bonus Plans. Employees of Dyson Enterprises work in groups of five, plus a group leader. Standard production for a group is 400 units for a 40-hour week. The workers are paid $6 an hour until production reaches 400 units; then a bonus of $1.20 per unit is paid for production over 400 units, with $1 being divided equally among the five workers and the remainder passing to the group leader (who is also paid a weekly salary of $300). Factory overhead is $7 per direct labor hour and includes the group leader's earnings.

The production record of a group for one week shows:

	Hours Worked	Units Produced
Monday	40	72
Tuesday	40	81
Wednesday	40	95
Thursday	40	102
Friday	40	102

Required:

(1) Compute the week's earnings of the group (excluding the leader), the labor cost per unit, the overhead cost per unit, and the conversion cost per unit, based upon the above data and bonus plan, and assuming the bonus is computed based on aggregate results for the week. (Calculate unit costs to four decimal places.)

(2) Prepare a schedule showing daily earnings of the group (excluding the leader), unit labor cost, unit overhead cost, and the conversion cost per unit, assuming that the company uses the group bonus plan, as described on page 269, and assuming the bonus is computed for (a) the day and (b) the week.

P11-7 Quarterly Bonus Allotment. Thomas Inc., manufacturers of standard pipe fittings for water and sewage lines, pays a bonus to employees based on production recorded each calendar quarter. Normal production is set at 240,000 units per quarter. A bonus of $.50 per unit is paid for any units in excess of the normal output for each quarter. Distribution of the bonus is made on the following point basis:

Employees Participating	Points Allowed for Each Employee
1 works manager	250
2 production engineers	200
5 shop supervisors	200
1 storekeeper	100
5 factory office clerks	10
150 factory workers	20

The employees' earnings are not penalized for any month in which the actual output falls below the monthly average of the normal quarterly production. When the output does fall below the monthly average, the deficiency is deducted from any excess in subsequent months before any bonus is earned by and paid to the employees.

At the end of March, cumulative actual production amounted to 270,000 units for the quarter.

Required:

(1) Calculate the amount of bonus payable to each group of employees. (Carry all calculations to three decimal places.)

(2) Prepare journal entries at the end of each month to record the bonus liability on the basis of the following production figures: January, 75,000 units; February, 94,000 units; March, 101,000 units. Assume that all of the bonus is charged to Factory Overhead Control.

P11-8 Learning Curve in Contract Price Negotiation. Catonic Inc. recently developed a new product that includes a rather complex printed circuit board as a component (Catonic's part number PCB-31). Although Catonic has the ability to manufacture PCB-31 internally, the circuit board is purchased from an independent supplier because the company's printed circuit line has been operating at capacity for some time.

The first contract for 50 units of PCB-31 was awarded to Rex Engineering Company in September, 19A, on the basis of a competitive bid. Rex's bid was significantly lower than those of other bidders. Additional orders for 50 units each were placed with Rex, as shown in the following purchase history schedule:

Date Ordered	Quantity	Unit Price	Total Price
September 15, 19A	50	$374	$18,700
November 15, 19A	50	374	18,700
January 1, 19B	50	374	18,700
February 1, 19B	50	374	18,700

Mark Polmik, a buyer for Catonic, has determined that the next order for PCB-31 should be for 600 units. He has contacted Kathy Wentz, a Rex salesperson. Polmik indicated that the next PCB-31 order would be for 600 units and that he believed that Catonic should receive a lower unit price because of the increased quantity. A few days later, Wentz provided a proposal of $355 per unit for the 600-unit contract.

Polmik has scheduled a meeting with Wentz for next week for the purpose of negotiating the 600-unit contract. He has asked Catonic's Cost Accounting Department for assistance in evaluating the $355 unit price.

The price bid on the original contract for 50 units was estimated to be based on full cost, because at that time Catonic was not sure if there would be future contracts for the PCB-31 board. The cost of materials included in PCB-31 is estimated to be $180 per unit. The Cost Accounting Department is fairly sure that Rex applies overhead at 100% of direct labor and employee benefit cost. Because Rex Engineering recently received a good deal of coverage by the local media when a strike was narrowly averted, the labor and fringe benefit costs at Rex are known to be approximately $20 per hour. The printed circuit line at Rex is similar to the one at Catonic, and Rex's overhead is believed to be approximately 50% variable and 50% fixed. Similar work at Catonic evidences a 90% learning curve effect. However, it is assumed that the learning curve effect on fixed overhead per unit is negligible.

Based on foregoing data, the price of a 50-unit order is estimated to comprise the following cost components:

Materials	$ 180
Labor and employee benefits (4 labor hours × $20)	80
Overhead (100% of labor and employee benefits)	80
Full cost of PCB-31 component	$ 340
Profit contribution (10% of full cost)	34
Unit price	$ 374
Units purchased	50
Total contract price	$18,700

Required:

(1) Prepare a schedule that can be used by Mark Polmik during his meeting with Kathy Wentz next week. This schedule should incorporate the learning curve effect that Rex would have experienced on the first 200 units already produced, which should be of use to Polmik in negotiating a contract with Rex Engineering. (Past production was, and future production will be, in lots of 50 units each.)

(2) What are the implications of an 80% learning curve as opposed to a 90% learning curve?

(3) Identify factors that could reduce the degree of learning that takes place in an industrial operation.

(ICMA adapted)

P11-9 (Appendix) Overtime Earnings. The pay stub of Olympic Manufacturing employee #1071, who works on the production line, showed the following for a 2-week pay period:

Gross earnings	$1,140.00
Income tax withheld	152.92
FICA tax	85.50
Company pension plan	83.54
Union dues	11.00
Net earnings	$ 807.04

The employee works a regular 40-hour week and is paid $12 per hour regular time and time and a half for overtime.

For this employee, the company paid an additional $273.20 in benefits for the 2-week pay period with regard to the employer's contribution to the company's pension plan and FICA tax.

Required:

(1) What was the amount charged to Work in Process for employee #1071 for the 2-week period, assuming that any overtime work is not traceable to a particular job order or product?

(2) How much would the department factory overhead control account have been charged for the 2-week period for employee #1071?

(3) Assume that in the second week of the pay period, the machine on which this employee worked was being repaired for 3 hours and the worker was unable to perform regular duties of production during that time. To which account should the cost of idle time be charged? (SMAC Adapted)

P11-10 (Appendix) Payroll Taxes, Vacation Pay, and Payroll. The normal workweek at Walfe City Publishing Inc. is Monday through Friday, with payday on the following Tuesday. On April 1, after the reversing entry was posted, the payroll account showed a $2,230 credit balance, representing labor purchased during the last 2 days of March. (See the following calendar.)

APRIL

Sun	Mon	Tue	Wed	Thu	Fri	Sat
			1	2	3	4
5	6	7	8	9	10	11
12	13	14	15	16	17	18
19	20	21	22	23	24	25
26	27	28	29	30		

Deductions of 7.5% for FICA tax and 9.5% for income tax are withheld from each payroll check.

The labor summary for April shows $16,400 of direct labor and $5,600 of indirect labor. Vacation pay is charged to current production at a rate of 8% of total payroll.

Payrolls were:

April 7	$5,890
14	4,920
21	5,900
28	4,880

Required:

(1) Prepare entries to record each payroll.

(2) Prepare entries on April 30 to distribute the payroll and to record the employer's payroll taxes for wages earned during April, treating the employer's payroll taxes and vacation pay as factory overhead. The state unemployment tax rate is 4%, and the federal unemployment tax rate is .8%. Include subsidiary record detail.

(3) Prepare T accounts for Payroll and Accrued Payroll and the entry to record accrued wages at the end of April.

Cases

C11-1 Setting Productivity Standards. Anvil Inc. intends to expand its Punch Press Department with the purchase of three new presses from Presco Inc. Mechanical studies indicate that for Anvil's intended use, the output rate for one press should be 1,000 pieces per hour. The company has similar presses now in operation that average 600 pieces per hour. This average is derived from the individual outputs as shown in the table that follows.

Worker	Hourly Output (In Pieces)
Allen, W	750
Miller, G	750
Salermo, J	600
Velasquez, E.	500
Underwood, P	550
Keppinger, J.	450
Total	3,600
Average hourly output	600

Anvil's management also plans to institute a standard cost accounting system in the very near future. The company's engineers are supporting a standard based on 1,000 pieces per hour; the Accounting Department, a standard based on 750 pieces per hour; and the Punch Press Department supervisor, a standard based on 600 pieces per hour.

Required:

(1) Specify arguments that could be used by each proponent.

(2) Decide which alternative best reconciles the needs of cost control and employee motivation. Explain.

(ICMA adapted)

C11-2 Incentive Wage Plan. Morac Industries is a rapidly growing 10-year-old company specializing in plumbing supplies. The company employs 100 persons. There are 25 salaried employees in office and management positions. The remaining 75 employees perform various production line functions and are paid on an hourly basis. Sales for 19A are forecasted at $3 million.

Management has been so preoccupied with its goals of growth and financial stability that employee relations have been virtually ignored. Many hourly employees do not believe their wage adjustments have kept pace either with industry standards or inflation. Additionally, these same employees do not believe they have been adequately rewarded for their contributions to the company's increase in productivity and performance.

Tien Li, president of Morac, believes wage incentive programs can be developed to deal with current discontent. Li, along with the company controller and manufacturing vice-president, developed a new wage incentive plan she hopes will meet the hourly employees' concerns. It would apply to workers once they have completed the company's 6-month training program. Currently, unskilled workers are hired at $5 per hour and immediately are put through the training program. At the end of the training program, the workers are assigned to specific jobs and awarded wage increases of about $2 per hour. Under the proposed plan, subsequent merit wage increases would be approved by fellow employees and would work as follows:

(a) Employees who believe they deserve merit wage increases would file a wage increase request form. This form would indicate the current wage rate, the amount of the requested pay increase, and the justification for the increase.

(b) Each employee's request would be posted for one week, giving the employee's peers ample time to study the request and observe performance. During this week, records of the employee's history, productivity, and job responsibilities would be available to the other employees.

(c) Fellow employees would vote on each individual's merit wage request by secret ballot. If the majority vote is favorable, the request for a merit wage increase would be approved.

Required: Discuss the advantages and disadvantages to Morac Industries of the new plan for approving merit wage increases. Specifically address the following issues:

(1) Employee motivation.
(2) Employee productivity.
(3) Goal congruence between employee and company.
(4) Administration of the plan. (ICMA adapted)

C11-3 Learning Curve. Kelly Company plans to manufacture a product called Electrocal, which requires a substantial amount of direct labor on each unit. Based on the company's experience with other products that required similar skills, management believes that there is a learning factor in the production process used to manufacture this product.

Each unit of Electrocal requires 50 square feet of raw materials at a cost of $30 per square foot for a total materials cost of $1,500. The standard direct labor rate is $25 per hour. Variable factory overhead is assigned to products at a rate of $40 per direct labor hour. The company adds a markup of 30% on variable manufacturing cost in determining an initial bid price for all products.

Data on the production of the first two lots (16 units) of Electrocal are as follows:

(a) The first lot of 8 units required a total of 3,200 direct labor hours.
(b) The second lot of 8 units required a total of 2,240 direct labor hours.

Based on prior production experience, Kelly anticipates that there will be no significant improvement in production time after the first 32 units. Therefore, a standard for direct labor hours will be established, based on the average hours per unit for units 17 through 32.

Required:

(1) What is the basic premise of the learning curve?
(2) Based on the data presented for the first 16 units, what learning rate appears to be applicable to the direct labor required to produce Electrocal?
(3) Calculate the standard for direct labor hours that Kelly Company should establish for each unit of Electrocal.
(4) After the first 32 units were manufactured, Kelly was asked to submit a bid on an additional 96 units. What price should Kelly bid on this order of 96 units?
(5) Knowledge of the learning curve phenomenon can be a valuable management tool. Explain how management can apply the learning curve in planning and controlling business operations.

(ICMA adapted)

C11-4 Payroll Procedures. A team of internal auditors was assigned to review the Galena Plant's Payroll Department, including the procedures used for payroll processing. Their findings are as follows:

(a) The payroll clerk receives the clock cards from the various department supervisors at the end of each pay period, compares the employee's hourly rate to information provided by the Personnel Department, and records the regular and overtime hours for each employee.
(b) The payroll clerk sends the clock cards to the plant's Data Processing Department for compilation and processing.
(c) The Data Processing Department returns the clock cards with the printed checks and payroll journal to the payroll clerk on completion of the processing.
(d) The payroll clerk verifies the hourly rate and hours worked for each employee by comparing the detail in the payroll journal to the clock cards.
(e) If errors are found, the payroll clerk voids the computer-generated check, prepares another check for the correct amount, and adjusts the payroll journal accordingly.
(f) The payroll clerk obtains the plant signature plate from the Accounting Department and signs the payroll checks.
(g) An employee of the Personnel Department picks up the checks and holds them until they are delivered to department supervisors for distribution to employees.

Required: Discuss the shortcomings in Payroll Department procedures and suggest corrective action.

(ICMA adapted)

C11-5 Ethical Considerations. Bert Osborne is currently assigned as an accountant in the Payroll Department of the Bay Bridge Company. One of his duties is the processing of engineering time reports, which are used to charge engineering time related overhead costs to maintenance jobs performed within the Bay Bridge plant. Each plant engineer is assigned a group of maintenance jobs for which she or he is responsible. Engineers are evaluated in part based on their ability to hold each maintenance job within budgeted limits. Furthermore, any job overrun in excess of 10% requires a time-consuming, detailed, written explanation to the plant manager.

Osborne's friend, Porter Wallace, is an engineer at Bay Bridge Company. Part of his duties involve the responsibility for several maintenance jobs, with several of these jobs in process at any given time.

Wallace is aware that one of his jobs is going to entail a substantial overrun. He has approached his Payroll Department friend, Bert Osborne, and asked that Bert shift sufficient charges from the overrun job to jobs that are well within the budget. These latter jobs are also Wallace's responsibility, so that no other engineer's maintenance job costs are affected.

Required: Which of the 15 responsibilities in the *Standards of Ethical Conduct for Management Accountants* presented in Chapter 1 apply to Osborne's situation?

CHAPTER 12

Factory Overhead: Planned, Actual, and Applied

Learning Objectives

After studying this chapter, you will be able to:

1. Define factory overhead and its components.
2. Define and calculate factory overhead rates.
3. Accumulate actual overhead costs.
4. Apply overhead using predetermined rates.
5. Dispose of over- or underapplied overhead.

The preceding chapters dealt with the planning and control of materials and labor costs. This chapter introduces the last of the three traditional cost elements, overhead.

The use of predetermined overhead rates for charging overhead to products was introduced briefly in Chapters 5 and 6. This chapter first discusses the methods and bases available for applying overhead, then describes the classification and accumulation of actual overhead costs, and finally shows the computation and disposition of over- or underapplied overhead.

The Nature of Factory Overhead

Factory overhead is generally defined as indirect materials, indirect labor, and all other factory costs that cannot be conveniently identified with or charged directly to specific jobs, products, or final cost objectives. Other terms used for factory overhead are **factory burden**, **manufacturing expense**, **manufacturing overhead**, **factory expense**, and **indirect manufacturing cost**.

Factory overhead has two characteristics that require consideration if products are to be charged with a reasonable share of this cost. These characteristics deal with the particular relationship of factory overhead to the product itself and the volume of production. Unlike direct materials and direct labor, factory overhead is an invisible part of the finished product. There is no materials requisition or labor time ticket to indicate the amount of overhead, such as factory supplies or indirect labor, that enters into a job or product. Yet factory overhead is as much a part of a product's manufacturing cost as direct materials and direct labor. Since automation has increased in modern manufacturing processes, factory overhead as a percentage of total product cost has increased, while the portion of direct labor has declined.

The second characteristic of factory overhead deals with the change in cost that many items of overhead undergo when there is a change in production volume. Overhead can be fixed, variable, or semivariable. As discussed in Chapter 3, fixed overhead remains relatively constant regardless of changes in the level of output, within the relevant range. This is equivalent to stating that fixed overhead per unit of output varies inversely with production volume. Variable overhead changes proportionately with production output, within the relevant range. That is, variable overhead per unit of output is constant. Semivariable overhead varies, but not in proportion to units produced. As production volume changes, the combined effect of these different overhead patterns causes unit manufacturing cost to fluctuate considerably, unless some method is provided to stabilize the overhead charged to the units produced.

Use of a Predetermined Overhead Rate

Overhead costs are charged to all work done during any period. The problem is how to make such a charge. It is possible to allocate actual overhead to all work completed during the month, using a base such as actual direct labor dollars, direct labor hours, or machine hours. As long as the volume of work completed each month is the same and costs are fairly constant and within control limits, this method results in a consistent charge to production each period. But as variations occur, work completed during different months receives a greater or smaller charge—an inequitable situation. For example, unreasonable product costs are calculated if actual costs incurred for repairs and maintenance are charged directly to a job or product when repairs are made. Ordinarily, repairs are necessary because of wear and tear over periods much longer and are made to permit continuous operation. Because overhead cost needs to be assigned promptly to production, factory overhead generally is charged at estimated amounts.

Because of the impossibility of tracing overhead to specific jobs or specific products, overhead cost is allocated to products. A **predetermined overhead rate** permits a consistent and logical allocation to each unit of output; in both job order and process cost accumulation, it provides the only feasible method of computing product overhead costs promptly enough to serve management needs, identify inefficiencies, and smooth out uncontrollable and somewhat illogical month-to-month fluctuations that would otherwise appear in reported unit costs.

In job order costing, actual costs of direct materials and direct labor used on a job are determined from materials requisitions and time cards and are entered on job order cost sheets. Overhead costs are estimated using a predetermined overhead rate. For example, factory overhead applicable to a job is calculated by multiplying actual machine hours used on the job by the predetermined overhead rate per machine hour. The result is entered on the job order cost sheet. The cost of a job is thus calculable at the time the job is completed, rather than being unavailable until month-end or year-end.

In process costing, unit costs are computed by dividing total weekly or monthly costs for each process by the output of that process. Product costs can be determined in process costing without the use of overhead rates, but predetermined overhead rates result in more uniform unit cost calculations each month despite monthly fluctuations in overhead or production levels. Overhead rates used in process costing are calculated the same way they are in job order costing.

Factors Considered in Selecting Overhead Rates

Types of overhead rates differ not only from one company to another, but also from one department, cost center, or cost pool to another within the same company. At least five factors influence the selection of overhead rates. The first three are discussed in this chapter; the last two are discussed in Chapter 13. The five factors are summarized in the following table:

1. Base to Be Used
   a. Physical output
   b. Direct materials cost
   c. Direct labor cost
   d. Direct labor hours
   e. Machine hours
   f. Transactions
2. Activity Level Selection
   a. Theoretical capacity
   b. Practical capacity
   c. Expected actual capacity
   d. Normal capacity
   e. Effect of capacity on overhead rates
   f. Idle capacity versus excess capacity
3. Including or Excluding Fixed Overhead
   a. Absorption costing
   b. Direct costing
4. Use of a Single Rate or Several Rates
   a. Plantwide or blanket rate
   b. Departmental rates
   c. Subdepartmental and activity rates
5. Use of Separate Rates for Service Activities

Base to Be Used

The factor included in the denominator of an overhead rate is called the **overhead rate base**, the **overhead allocation base,** or simply the **base**. Selection of the base is important if a cost system is to provide meaningful cost data. The primary objective in selecting a base is to ensure the application of factory overhead in a reasonable proportion to the indirect factory resources used or caused by the jobs, products, or work performed.

Ordinarily, the base selected should be closely correlated to functions represented by the overhead cost being applied. If, for example, factory overhead is predominantly labor oriented, including such costs as supervision and fringe benefits, the proper base is probably direct labor cost or direct labor hours. If overhead items are predominantly investment oriented, related to the ownership and operation of machinery, then a machine-hour base is probably most appropriate. If overhead is mainly materials oriented, including costs associated with the purchasing and handling of materials, for example, then materials cost may be suitable as the base. Correlation analysis tools discussed in Chapter 3 are especially useful in selecting the base to be used.

A secondary objective in selecting a base is minimization of clerical cost and effort relative to the benefits attained. When two or more bases provide approximately the same applied overhead cost for specific units of production, the simplest base should be used. Although the cost of administering the various methods differs from one company to another, the direct labor cost base and the direct materials cost base seem to cause the least clerical effort and cost, because the data they require are accumulated for other reasons and thus are readily available. The labor hour and machine hour bases generally entail additional clerical work because of the extra effort required to collect the data.

Physical Output. Physical output or units of production is the simplest and most direct base for applying factory overhead. Its use is illustrated as follows:

$$\frac{\text{Estimated factory overhead}}{\text{Estimated units of production}} = \text{Factory overhead per unit}$$

If estimated factory overhead is $300,000 and the company intends to produce 250,000 units during the next period, each completed unit is charged $1.20 ($300,000 ÷ 250,000 units) as its share of factory overhead. An order with 1,000 completed units is charged $1,200 (1,000 units × $1.20) of factory overhead.

The physical output base is satisfactory when a company manufactures only one product; otherwise, the method is generally unsatisfactory. If, however, a company's products are alike or closely related, their difference being merely one of weight or volume,[1] application of factory overhead can be made on a weight, volume, or point base. The weight base applies overhead according to the weight of each product and is illustrated as follows:

	Product		
	A	B	C
Estimated number of units manufactured	20,000	15,000	20,000
Unit weight of product	5 lbs.	2 lbs.	1 lb.
Estimated total weight produced	100,000 lbs.	30,000 lbs.	20,000 lbs.
Estimated factory overhead per pound ($300,000 ÷ 150,000)	$2	$2	$2
Estimated factory overhead for each product	$200,000	$60,000	$40,000
Estimated factory overhead per unit	$10	$4	$2

If the weight or volume base does not yield a reasonable apportionment of overhead, the method can be improved by assigning a certain number of points to each product to compensate for differences. For example, a company manufacturing Products L, S, M, and F computes an overhead rate per product as follows:

Product	Estimated Quantity	Points Assigned	Estimated Total Points	Estimated Factory Overhead per Point	Estimated Factory Overhead for Each Product	Estimated Factory Overhead Cost per Unit
L	2,000	5	10,000	$3	$ 30,000	$15
S	5,000	10	50,000	3	150,000	30
M	3,000	8	24,000	3	72,000	24
F	4,000	4	16,000	3	48,000	12
			100,000		$300,000	

If products differ in any respect not considered in the allocation base, such as processing time required, number and complexity of machinery setups, or method of production, a uniform charge based on physical output can result in inappropriate costing. In such instances, other methods must be adopted.

Direct Materials Cost Base. In some companies, a study of past costs reveals a correlation between direct materials cost and factory overhead. In such cases, a rate based on materials cost might be appropriate. The charge is computed by dividing total estimated factory overhead by total estimated direct materials cost, as follows:

[1] See Chapter 14 for additional problems to consider when the products differ in terms of volume.

$$\frac{\text{Estimated factory overhead}}{\text{Estimated materials cost}} \times 100 = \text{Factory overhead as a percentage of direct materials cost}$$

If the estimated overhead is $300,000 and the estimated materials cost is $250,000, each job or product completed is charged an additional 120 percent [($300,000 ÷ $250,000) × 100)] of its materials cost as its share of factory overhead. For example, if the materials cost of an order is $5,000, the order receives an additional charge of $6,000 ($5,000 × 120%) for factory overhead.

The materials cost base is of limited use, because in most cases no logical relationship exists between the direct materials cost of a product and the use or creation of factory overhead in its production. One product might be made from high-priced materials, another from less expensive materials; yet both products could require the same manufacturing process or even the same materials-related overhead costs, and thus use approximately the same amount of factory overhead. If the materials cost base is used to charge overhead, the product using expensive materials will be charged with more than its share. To overcome this discrepancy, two overhead rates can be calculated. One can be based on materials cost, weight, volume, number of different parts used, or some other measure of use, for materials-related costs such as purchasing, receiving, inspecting, handling, and storage costs. The second rate can be based on some other, more relevant activity for the remaining overhead costs. In this situation, the overhead cost of each job or process is calculated in two parts using the two rates.

Direct Labor Cost Base. The direct labor cost base method of applying overhead to jobs or products entails dividing estimated factory overhead by estimated direct labor cost to compute a percentage:

$$\frac{\text{Estimated factory overhead}}{\text{Estimated direct labor cost}} \times 100 = \text{Factory overhead as a percentage of direct labor cost}$$

If estimated factory overhead is $300,000 and total direct labor cost for the next period is estimated at $500,000, the overhead rate is 60 percent [($300,000 ÷ $500,000) × 100]. A job or product with a direct labor cost of $12,000 is charged $7,200 ($12,000 × 60%) for factory overhead.

The direct labor cost base is relatively easy to use, because the direct labor cost information needed is usually readily available. Its use is logical when a strong relationship between direct labor cost and factory overhead exists and when the rates of pay per hour for similar work are comparable. The weekly payroll provides the direct labor cost without any additional record keeping. If economy in obtaining underlying information is a main prerequisite, the direct labor cost base can be accepted as the quickest of the available methods of applying factory overhead in labor-intensive manufacturing.

This method is inappropriate when:

1. Factory overhead includes depreciation of high-cost machinery, which bears no relationship to the direct labor payroll.
2. Total direct labor cost represents the sum of wages paid to high- and low-wage production workers. By applying overhead on the basis of direct labor cost, a job or product is charged with more overhead when a high-wage operator performs work. Such a method can lead to an incorrect distribution of factory overhead, particularly when numerous operators with different hourly pay rates perform similar operations.

Direct Labor Hour Base. The direct labor hour base is designed to overcome the second disadvantage of using the direct labor cost base. The overhead rate based on direct labor hours is computed as follows:

$$\frac{\text{Estimated factory overhead}}{\text{Estimated direct labor hours}} = \text{Factory overhead per direct labor hour}$$

If estimated factory overhead is $300,000 and total direct labor hours are estimated to be 60,000, an overhead rate based on direct labor hours is $5.00 per hour of direct labor ($300,000 ÷ 60,000 hours). A job or product that requires 800 direct labor hours is charged $4,000 (800 hours × $5.00) for factory overhead.

The use of this method requires accumulation of direct labor hours by job or product. Timekeeping records must be organized to provide the additional data. The use of the direct labor hour base can be justified only if there is a strong relationship between direct labor hours and factory overhead. As long as labor operations are the chief factor in production, the direct labor hour method is acceptable as a base for applying overhead. However, if shop or factory departments use machines extensively, the direct labor hour base can lead to unreasonable costing.

Management goals in manufacturing in recent years have focused on decreasing the amount of direct labor as a component of total cost. The shift has been away from direct labor toward increasing levels of automation. As a result, the use of direct labor cost or direct labor hours for purposes of factory overhead application has become less appropriate, often giving way to the use of machine hours as the preferred base.

In highly automated manufacturing, direct labor may not only be an inappropriate base for factory overhead application, but it also may be a relatively small portion of total manufacturing cost. In this latter case, direct labor can be included with factory overhead in a single conversion cost classification and applied as a part of a conversion cost rate.

Machine Hour Base. When machines are used extensively, machine hours may be the most appropriate basis for applying overhead. This method is based on time required to perform identical operations by a machine or group of machines. Total machine hours expected to be used are estimated, and a machine hour rate is determined as follows:

$$\frac{\text{Estimated factory overhead}}{\text{Estimated machine hours}} = \text{Factory overhead per machine hour}$$

If factory overhead is estimated to be $300,000 and 20,000 machine hours are estimated, the rate is $15.00 per machine hour ($300,000 ÷ 20,000 machine hours). Work that requires 120 machine hours is charged $1,800 (120 hours × $15.00) for factory overhead.

If machines or groups of machines differ with respect to the overhead costs related to them, then a weighting procedure, such as that discussed for the physical output base, is required. An alternative is to use a separate rate for each machine or machine group. This requires segmentation of cost estimation, accumulation, and application, following the procedures discussed in the next chapter. A third alternative, increasingly popular in automated settings, is use of process time as the base. **Process time** is the total time that the manufacturing process requires to produce a unit of product.

The machine hour method entails additional clerical work, because a reporting system must be designed to assure correct accumulation of machine hour data. Unless the data are required for costing, shop personnel, supervisors, or timekeepers normally do not collect the machine hour data needed to charge overhead to jobs, products, or work performed. In computerized plants, this data collection effort can be entirely electronic. The machine-hour method is considered the most reasonable method for applying overhead if overhead cost comprises predominantly facility-related costs, such as depreciation, maintenance, and utilities. Indeed, with modern manufacturing technology, direct labor becomes an increasingly smaller portion of manufacturing costs, and facility costs become a greater portion. As a result, more and more situations require the use of a base other than direct labor. Machine hours or weighted machine hours are often chosen as the base.

Transactions Base. A group of costs may be associated with a particular activity in a manner not adequately represented by any of the bases previously discussed. For example, setup costs can be assigned more appropriately to products by a rate per setup. Each setup is thus viewed as a transaction, with costs assigned to a product or batch of products based on the number of transactions required. This transaction approach can also apply to such other activities as scheduling, inspections, materials movements, and changes in products and processes.

The greater the diversity and complexity in the product line, the greater the number of transactions. Such transactions often are responsible for a large percentage of overhead costs, and the key to managing overhead is controlling the transactions that drive it. This requires thinking carefully about which transactions are necessary and which are not, and about how to carry out the necessary ones most effectively. For example, adherence to a just-in-time philosophy of process design permits elimination or reduction of many transactions.[2]

The **transactions-base approach**[3] gives particular consideration to the fact that certain significant overhead costs may not be driven by volume of output. Rather, in modern multiproduct factories, overhead cost can be caused more by the complexity of the product line and by the handling required for special, low volume items than by the total volume of production. To the extent that overhead cost is driven by transactions that are not proportional to output volume, the use of a volume-of-output base tends to overcost the high-volume products and undercost the low-volume products. Use of the transactions base can correct this misallocation.[4]

The criteria of reasonable correlation and practicality, in both clerical efficiency and costing accuracy, should be foremost in the selection of an overhead costing base for a given situation. Different bases for different cost groups implies multiple departments with one or more rates for each, rather than a single plantwide factory overhead rate. This approach is discussed in detail in Chapters 13 and 14.

Selection of Activity Level

In calculating a predetermined overhead rate, a great deal depends on the activity level selected. The numerator used in calculating the rate is an estimate of overhead at whatever level of activity the denominator assumes. The greater the assumed activity, the lower the fixed portion of the overhead rate, because fixed

[2] Jeffrey G. Miller and Thomas E. Vollman, "The Hidden Factory," *Harvard Business Review*, Vol. 5, p. 146.

[3] The transactions-base approach to overhead allocation is popularly referred to as activity-based costing (ABC) and is discussed in detail in Chapter 14.

[4] John K. Shank and Vijay Govindarajan, "The Perils of Cost Allocation Based on Production Volumes," *Accounting Horizons*, Vol. 2, No. 4, p. 77. See Debbie Berlant, Reese Browning, and George Foster, "How Hewlett-Packard Gets Numbers It Can Trust," *Harvard Business Review*, Vol. 68, No. 1, pp. 178–183, for a description of Hewlett-Packard's experience with the transactions-base approach.

overhead is spread over a greater number of units of activity. The variable portion of the rate tends to remain constant at various activity levels within the relevant range of activity.

The following terms are used to describe different activity levels: theoretical capacity, practical capacity, expected actual capacity, and normal capacity. These descriptions are discussed in the following paragraphs. Current federal income tax regulations permit the use of expected actual capacity or normal capacity for assigning factory overhead costs to inventories.[5] The Internal Revenue Service does not permit the use of practical capacity nor theoretical capacity, arguing that it is an "exception to the general rules of 'full absorption' accounting that apply to the determination of inventoriable costs."[6]

Theoretical Capacity. The **theoretical capacity** of a department is its capacity to produce at full speed without interruptions. It is achieved if the plant or department produces at 100% of its rated capacity.

Practical Capacity. It is highly improbable that any company can operate at theoretical capacity. Allowances must be made for unavoidable interruptions, such as time lost for repairs, inefficiencies, breakdowns, setups, failures, unsatisfactory materials, delays in delivery of materials or supplies, labor shortages and absences, Sundays, holidays, vacations, inventory taking, and pattern and model changes. The number of work shifts must also be considered. These allowances reduce theoretical capacity to the **practical capacity** level. This reduction is caused by internal influences and does not consider the chief external influence—lack of customer orders. Reduction from theoretical to practical capacity typically ranges from 15% to 25%, which results in a practical capacity level of 75% to 85% of theoretical capacity.

Expected Actual Capacity. The short-range planning and control approach, the **expected actual capacity** concept, calculates an overhead rate by basing its numerator and denominator on the expected actual output for the period. This method usually results in the use of a different predetermined rate for each period, depending on increases or decreases in estimated factory overhead and production figures.

Normal Capacity. The long-range planning and control approach, the **normal capacity** concept, calculates an overhead rate by basing its numerator and denominator on average utilization of the physical plant over a time period long enough to level out the highs and lows. The normal capacity concept seeks to stabilize an overhead rate that otherwise would fluctuate because facilities are used to a greater or lesser degree in different periods. A job or product should not cost more to produce in any one accounting period just because production was lower and fixed charges were spread over fewer units. The rate is changed, however, when prices of certain overhead cost items change. Using normal rather than actual capacity usually means that applied overhead differs from actual overhead incurred.

Effect of Capacity on Overhead Rates. The effect of the various capacity levels on predetermined factory overhead rates is illustrated in Exhibit 12-1. If the 75% capacity level (normal capacity) is selected, the overhead rate is $2.40 per machine hour. At higher capacity levels, the rate is lower because the fixed overhead is spread over more machine hours.

[5] *Regulations,* Section 1.471-11.

[6] *Regulations,* Section 1.263A-1T(b)(2)(vii).

EXHIBIT 12-1

Effect of Various Capacity Levels on Predetermined Factory Overhead Rates

Item	Normal Capacity	Expected Actual Capacity	Practical Capacity	Theoretical Capacity
Percentage of theoretical capacity	75%	80%	85%	100%
Machine hours	7,500 hrs.	8,000 hrs.	8,500 hrs.	10,000 hrs.
Budgeted factory overhead:				
Fixed	$12,000	$12,000	$12,000	$12,000
Variable	6,000	6,400	6,800	8,000
Total	$18,000	$18,400	$18,800	$20,000
Fixed factory overhead rate per machine hour	$ 1.60	$ 1.50	$ 1.41	$ 1.20
Variable factory overhead rate per machine hour	.80	.80	.80	.80
Total factory overhead rate per machine hour	$ 2.40	$ 2.30	$ 2.21	$ 2.00

Idle Capacity Versus Excess Capacity. A distinction must be made between idle capacity and excess capacity. **Idle capacity** results from the idleness of production workers and facilities due to a temporary lack of sales. When sales demand increases, the idle production workers and facilities are restored to full use. When idle capacity is budgeted for the period, its cost is included in the factory overhead application rate only when expected actual capacity is used as the denominator. In that event, the cost of idle capacity becomes a part of the product cost. This is achieved by setting the denominator of the overhead rate at a lower level that reflects the idleness expected. If idle capacity exists but was not budgeted, there is a resulting factory overhead variance related to idle facilities. Overhead variances are discussed in Chapters 17 and 18.

Excess capacity, conversely, results either from greater productive capacity than a company can expect to use, or from an imbalance in equipment or machinery. This imbalance occurs when the capacity of one machine does not match the capacity of other machines with which it must be synchronized. Theoretically, any costs arising from excess capacity should be excluded from the factory overhead rate and from product cost and should be treated as an expense or loss in the income statement.

Including or Excluding Fixed Overhead

Ordinarily, cost accounting applies all factory costs to the output of a period. Under this approach, called **absorption costing**, **conventional costing**, or **full costing**, both fixed and variable costs are included in overhead rates. Another method of costing, termed **direct costing** or **variable costing**, is sometimes used, but only for internal management purposes. Under this method of costing, only variable overhead is included in overhead rates. The fixed portion of overhead cost does not become a product cost. It is instead treated as a period cost, meaning that it is charged off in total each period, as are marketing and administrative expenses. It is not included in either work in process or finished goods inventories. Direct costing is discussed in detail in Chapter 20.

Absorption costing and direct costing are the results of two entirely different cost concepts with respect to product cost, period cost, gross profit, and operating income. Although the two methods result in different inventory costs and different period profits, each of the various bases discussed for applying overhead can be used with absorption costing or direct costing. Overhead variances due to idle capacity do not arise under direct costing, however.

Calculation of an Overhead Rate

The first step in calculating the overhead rate is determining the activity level to be used for the base selected. Then each individual overhead cost item is estimated or budgeted at that activity level, arriving at the total estimated factory overhead. For example, assume that DeWitt Products has an expected capacity level of 20,000 machine hours. The total factory overhead is estimated to be $300,000. This overhead is classified into fixed or variable categories, as shown in Exhibit 12-2.

EXHIBIT 12-2

DeWitt Products
Estimated Factory Overhead for 19—

Expense	Fixed	Variable	Total
Supervisors	$ 70,000		$ 70,000
Indirect labor	9,000	$ 66,000	75,000
Overtime premium		9,000	9,000
Factory supplies	4,000	19,000	23,000
Repairs and maintenance	3,000	9,000	12,000
Electric power	2,000	18,000	20,000
Fuel	1,000	5,000	6,000
Water	500	500	1,000
Labor fringe benefits	10,500	48,500	59,000
Depreciation—building	5,000		5,000
Depreciation—equipment	13,000		13,000
Property tax	4,000		4,000
Insurance (fire)	3,000		3,000
Total estimated factory overhead	$125,000	$175,000	$300,000

The classification of costs according to changes in volume attempts to establish a variability pattern for each item. Once the classification has been determined, the item can remain in this category for a limited period of time. If underlying conditions change, the original classification is reviewed, and the cost items reclassified as necessary.

Total variable costs are a function of volume; that is, the amount of variable cost per unit is constant within the relevant range. Fixed costs have a constant total amount within the relevant range, so that their cost per unit is different for each production level. Increased production causes a decrease in fixed cost per unit. Knowledge of the effect of fixed and variable costs on unit cost is important in any study of overhead. A knowledge of the behavior of all costs is fundamental to planning, decision making, and cost control.

An examination of fixed and variable costs reveals the difficulty of categorizing all items as either fixed or variable. Some cost items are partly fixed and partly variable; some are fixed to a certain production level and then increase as production increases. Also, costs can change in step-like fashion at various production levels. Such items are called semivariable. Because costs must be classified as either fixed or variable, the fixed portion of any semivariable cost and the degree of change in the variable portion must be determined.

Chapter 3 presented the methods available for finding the constant portion and the degree of variability in the variable portion for determining cost behavior patterns. These methods determine the relationship between increases in production and increases in total and individual costs. For example, when production is expected to increase 10 percent, it is possible to determine the corresponding increase in total cost as well as the increase in individual cost items such as supplies, power, or indirect labor.

After the activity level and the factory overhead have been estimated, the overhead rates can be computed. Assuming that the machine hour base is used and machine hours for the coming year are expected to be 20,000 for DeWitt Products, the factory overhead rate at this selected activity level is:

$$\text{Factory overhead rate} = \frac{\text{Estimated factory overhead}}{\text{Estimated machine hours}} = \frac{\$300{,}000}{20{,}000} = \$15.00 \text{ per machine hour}$$

This rate is used to charge overhead to jobs, products, or work performed. Amounts applied are first entered in subsidiary ledgers such as job order cost sheets and cost of production reports. Machine hours actually used will determine the amount of overhead chargeable to each job, product, or department.

The factory overhead rate can be further broken down into its fixed and variable components as follows:

$$\frac{\$125{,}000 \text{ estimated fixed factory overhead}}{20{,}000 \text{ estimated machine hours}} = \$\ 6.25 \text{ fixed portion of the factory overhead rate}$$

$$\frac{\$175{,}000 \text{ estimated variable factory overhead}}{20{,}000 \text{ estimated machine hours}} = \underline{8.75} \text{ variable portion of the factory overhead rate}$$

$$\text{Total factory overhead rate} = \underline{\underline{\$15.00}} \text{ per machine hour}$$

Actual Factory Overhead

Determining the base and activity level, estimating the factory overhead, and calculating the overhead rate take place prior to incurring or recording actual costs. Factory overhead is applied as soon as the necessary data, such as actual machine hours, are available. Each day, however, actual overhead transactions are journalized and posted to general and subsidiary ledgers, independent of the application of factory overhead based on the predetermined rate.

A basic objective for accumulating factory overhead is the gathering of information for control. Control, in turn, requires first, reporting costs to the individual department heads responsible for them, and second, making comparisons with amounts budgeted for the level of operations achieved. The mechanics for collecting overhead cost data are based on the chart of accounts, which indicates the accounts to which various factory overhead items are to be charged.

The principal source documents used for recording overhead in the journals are purchase vouchers, materials requisitions, labor time tickets, and general journal vouchers. These documents provide a record of the overhead information that must be analyzed and accumulated in proper accounts. To obtain accurate and useful information, each transaction must be properly classified at its inception. Those responsible for this identification must be thoroughly familiar with the names and code numbers of cost accounts as well as with the purpose and function of each account.

Factory overhead includes numerous items that can be classified in many different ways. Every firm, because of its own manufacturing peculiarities, must devise its own particular accounts and methods of classifying them. Regardless of these possible variations, expenses are summarized in a factory overhead control account kept in the general ledger. Details of this general ledger account are kept in a subsidiary overhead ledger. This subsidiary ledger also can take many forms—it may be difficult to recognize, particularly when electronic data processing equipment is used. A subsidiary ledger groups various overhead cost items together under significant selective titles as to kinds of costs. The subsidiary ledger also can detail the costs chargeable to individual departments (Chapter 13), thereby permitting stricter control over factory overhead (Chapter 17).

The accumulation of factory overhead in accounting records presents several distinct problems. Due to the many varied potential requests and uses of factory overhead data for decision making, it is almost impossible to set up an all-purpose system for accumulating factory overhead.

Applied Overhead and the Over- or Underapplied Amount

At the end of the month or year, applied overhead and actual overhead are compared. **Actual overhead** is the amount of indirect cost incurred, while **applied overhead** is the amount of cost allocated to output. This section illustrates the mechanics of applying factory overhead and determining the over- or underapplied amount.

Applying Factory Overhead

During the period, job order cost sheets or departmental cost of production reports receive postings as soon as direct materials or direct labor data become available. Factory overhead is applied to the work done after the direct materials and the direct labor costs have been recorded. If machine hours or direct labor hours are the basis for overhead charges, these data must also be available to the cost department.

To continue the illustration for DeWitt Products, assume that actual machine hours totaled 18,900 and actual factory overhead totaled $292,000. The overhead applied during the period is $283,500 (18,900 machine hours × $15.00 per hour). The journal entry for summarizing factory overhead applied is:

Work in Process	283,500	
Applied Factory Overhead		283,500

Charges made to subsidiary records (the job order cost sheets or departmental cost of production reports) list in detail applied factory overhead charged to jobs or departments. The debit to the work in process control account brings into the general ledger the total applied overhead for the period, usually a month.

The applied factory overhead account subsequently is closed to the factory overhead control account at the end of the year by the following entry:

Applied Factory Overhead	283,500	
Factory Overhead Control		283,500

It is common practice to use an applied factory overhead account because it keeps applied costs and actual costs separate. This separation facilitates monthly comparison with budgeted overhead. These comparisons are necessary to evaluate the appropriateness of the predetermined overhead rate. If actual experience diverges substantially from the budget, the overhead rate should be adjusted to avoid misstating product costs during the year and to avoid large over- or underapplied overhead at year-end.

After the preceding entries are recorded, the factory overhead control account for DeWitt Products appears as follows:

Factory Overhead Control			
Dec. 31	292,000	Dec. 31 (18,900 × $15.00)	283,500
	Total Actual Overhead Incurred During Period		Overhead Applied During Period

Factory overhead costs are normally charged to Work in Process, but in a just-in-time production environment, the overhead costs can be charged directly to Cost of Goods Sold. An end-of-period entry is then made, adjusting the inventory accounts for the portion of factory overhead and other manufacturing costs appropriate to the units in inventory. The offsetting entry is made to the cost of goods sold account, using backflush costing as discussed in Chapter 10.

Over- or Underapplied Factory Overhead

Debits to the factory overhead control account reflect actual overhead costs incurred during the period, while credits reflect applied amounts. There may also be credit adjustments (e.g., for the return of supplies to the storeroom) that reduce the total actual factory overhead. Because the debits and credits are seldom equal, there is usually a debit or credit balance in the account. A debit balance indicates that overhead has been **underapplied**; a credit balance means that overhead has been **overapplied**. These over- or underapplied balances are analyzed carefully, because they can be the source of much information needed by management for controlling and judging the efficiency of operations and the use of available capacity during a particular period.

For DeWitt Products, applied factory overhead for the period is $8,500 less than actual factory overhead incurred, so factory overhead for the period is $8,500 underapplied. This difference can be analyzed to determine the reasons for the underapplied overhead, as discussed in Chapters 17 and 18.

Disposition of Over- or Underapplied Amount

Disposition of the over- or underapplied factory overhead is usually quite simple. At the end of the accounting period, it can be either treated as a period cost or allocated between inventories and the cost of goods sold.

If the amount of over- or underapplied overhead is insignificant,[7] it should be closed directly to Income Summary or to Cost of Goods Sold as a period cost. The entry to record underapplied factory overhead on the books of DeWitt Products is:

Income Summary	8,500	
Factory Overhead Control		8,500

[7] Insignificance in this sense refers to an amount so small that the effect on income of expensing all of it, rather than allocating part to inventories, is immaterial; that is, it is so small that the difference is not expected to affect the decisions of a reader of the financial statements.

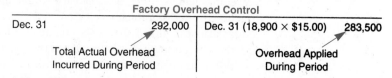

or

Cost of Goods Sold	8,500	
Factory Overhead Control		8,500

In the second case, the $8,500 becomes a part of the cost of goods sold account balance, which subsequently is closed into the income summary account. In either event, the over- or underapplied overhead amount can be reported as an adjustment in the income statement as shown in Exhibit 12-3.

EXHIBIT 12-3

DeWitt Products
Income Statement
for Year Ended December 31, 19—

Sales		$1,600,000
Less: Cost of goods sold	$1,193,500	
Underapplied factory overhead	8,500	1,202,000
Gross profit		$ 398,000
Less: Marketing expense	$ 150,000	
Administrative expense	100,000	250,000
Operating income		$ 148,000

Alternatively, over- or underapplied overhead can be reported as an adjustment in the cost of goods sold statement.[8] This statement and the income statement then appear as shown in Exhibit 12-4.

EXHIBIT 12-4

DeWitt Products
Cost of Goods Sold Statement
for Year Ended December 31, 19—

Direct materials used	$ 400,000	
Direct labor used	500,000	
Applied factory overhead	283,500	
Total manufacturing cost	$1,183,500	
Less increase in work in process inventory	20,000	
Cost of goods manufactured	$1,163,500	
Plus decrease in finished goods inventory	30,000	
Cost of goods sold	$1,193,500	
Plus underapplied factory overhead	8,500	
Adjusted Cost of goods sold	$1,202,000	

DeWitt Products
Income Statement
for Year Ended December 31, 19—

Sales		$1,600,000
Less cost of goods sold at actual		1,202,000
Gross profit		$ 398,000
Less: Marketing expense	$ 150,000	
Administrative expense	100,000	250,000
Operating income		$ 148,000

[8] This treatment may be based on management responsibility for the over- or underapplied overhead: if a responsibility of manufacturing managers, it is reported as an adjustment in the cost of goods sold statement; if a responsibility of general management, it is reported as an adjustment in the income statement as illustrated previously.

Rather than treat the over- or underapplied overhead as an adjustment to income or expense, instead it can be allocated to inventories and the cost of goods sold. This procedure has the effect of restating all applied overhead at amounts approximating actual overhead. It is required for financial reporting purposes if the variances are large, because to do otherwise would materially misstate financial results. Expensing a large underapplied overhead balance overstates expense, understates income, and understates inventory on the balance sheet.

To illustrate the allocation of over- or underapplied overhead between inventories and cost of goods sold, suppose Spander Company in all previous years had treated over- or underapplied overhead as an adjustment to income or expense. At the end of the current year the company had $4,000 of underapplied overhead, and the balances in inventories and cost of goods sold were:

	Work in Process	Finished Goods	Cost of Goods Sold
Direct material	$15,000	$ 7,000	$ 28,000
Direct labor	5,000	19,000	76,000
Applied overhead	5,000	19,000	76,000
Year-end balance	$25,000	$45,000	$180,000

The purpose of allocating the underapplied overhead is to revise all the amounts of overhead that were applied during the year. The revision is achieved by adjusting the three accounts shown, because all applied overhead amounts are contained in the year-end balances of those three accounts.[9].

The over- or underapplied overhead usually is allocated to the three accounts in proportion to their balances. The calculation and the journal entry to dispose of Spander Company's underapplied overhead are as follows:

	Account Balance	Percentage of Total
Work in process	$ 25,000	10%
Finished goods	45,000	18
Cost of goods sold	180,000	72
Total	$250,000	100%

Work in Process (10% of $4,000)	400	
Finished Goods (18% of $4,000)	720	
Cost of Goods Sold (72% of $4,000)	2,880	
Factory Overhead Control		4,000

If overhead had been overapplied, the inventories and cost of goods sold would be credited and Factory Overhead Control would be debited.

Often work in process consists mostly of direct material cost and relatively little overhead, so the approach just illustrated attributes too much of the adjustment to Work in Process. Technically, because only the overhead components of the three accounts need to be restated, the allocation should be in proportion to the amounts of applied overhead contained in the three accounts. Using this approach, the calculation and the journal entry to dispose of the underapplied overhead are as follows:

[9] The materials inventory account is not involved, because it contains no applied overhead. Also, this illustration assumes that the beginning balances of Work in Process and Finished Goods were very small compared to Cost of Goods Sold. When beginning inventories are significant, the appropriate disposition of over- or underapplied overhead parallels the disposition of overhead standard cost variances, as discussed in Chapter 19.

	Applied Overhead	Percentage of Total
Work in process	$ 5,000	5%
Finished goods	19,000	19%
Cost of goods sold	76,000	76%
Total	$100,000	100%

Work in Process (5% of $4,000)	200	
Finished Goods (19% of $4,000)	760	
Cost of Goods Sold (76% of $4,000)	3,040	
Factory Overhead Control		4,000

Under either approach, the inventories are reported on the balance sheet at their adjusted amounts, and Cost of Goods Sold is adjusted on either the Cost of Goods Sold Statement or the Income Statement, as illustrated previously.[10]

Internal Revenue Service regulations require that inventories include an allocated portion of significant annual overhead variances. When the amount involved is not significant in relation to total actual factory overhead, an allocation is not required unless such allocation is made for financial reporting purposes. Also, the taxpayer must treat both over- and underapplied overhead consistently. Further discussion of the analysis and disposition of under- or overapplied overhead is reserved for Chapter 19.

Changing Overhead Rates

Overhead rates usually are reviewed periodically. This approach helps level out costing through the year and links overhead control to budget control. Changes in production methods, prices, efficiencies, and sales expectancy make review, and possibly revision, of overhead rates necessary at least annually. Revisions should be based on a complete review of all factors involved. The extent to which a company revises its overhead rates depends on the frequency of changes, on factors that affect overhead rates, and on management's need and desire for current costs.

An overhead rate can be incorrect because of misjudgments regarding estimated overhead or anticipated activity. A large over- or underapplied overhead figure does not necessarily mean that the overhead rate was wrong. When the overhead rate is based on expected actual conditions, seasonal variations can result in a large amount of over- or underabsorbed overhead that will tend to even itself out during a full year. The best way to detect an incorrect overhead rate is to analyze the factors used in its determination. Because a rate is an estimate, small errors should be expected, and the rate need not be changed for such errors.

Summary

All production costs not traced directly to output are collectively referred to as factory overhead and generally are allocated to output through the use of predetermined rates. The denominator of the predetermined rate calculation can be set at the level of theoretical, practical, expected actual, or normal capacity;

[10] At the beginning of the next year, the portions of the journal entry that involve inventories are reversed.

capacity can be measured in machine hours, labor hours, material cost, or a variety of other measures. The numerator of the predetermined rate calculation is the amount of overhead estimated for whatever level of activity is used in the denominator.

This chapter's discussion of estimating and accounting for factory overhead is diagrammed in Figure 12-1.

FIGURE 12-1 *Factory Overhead*

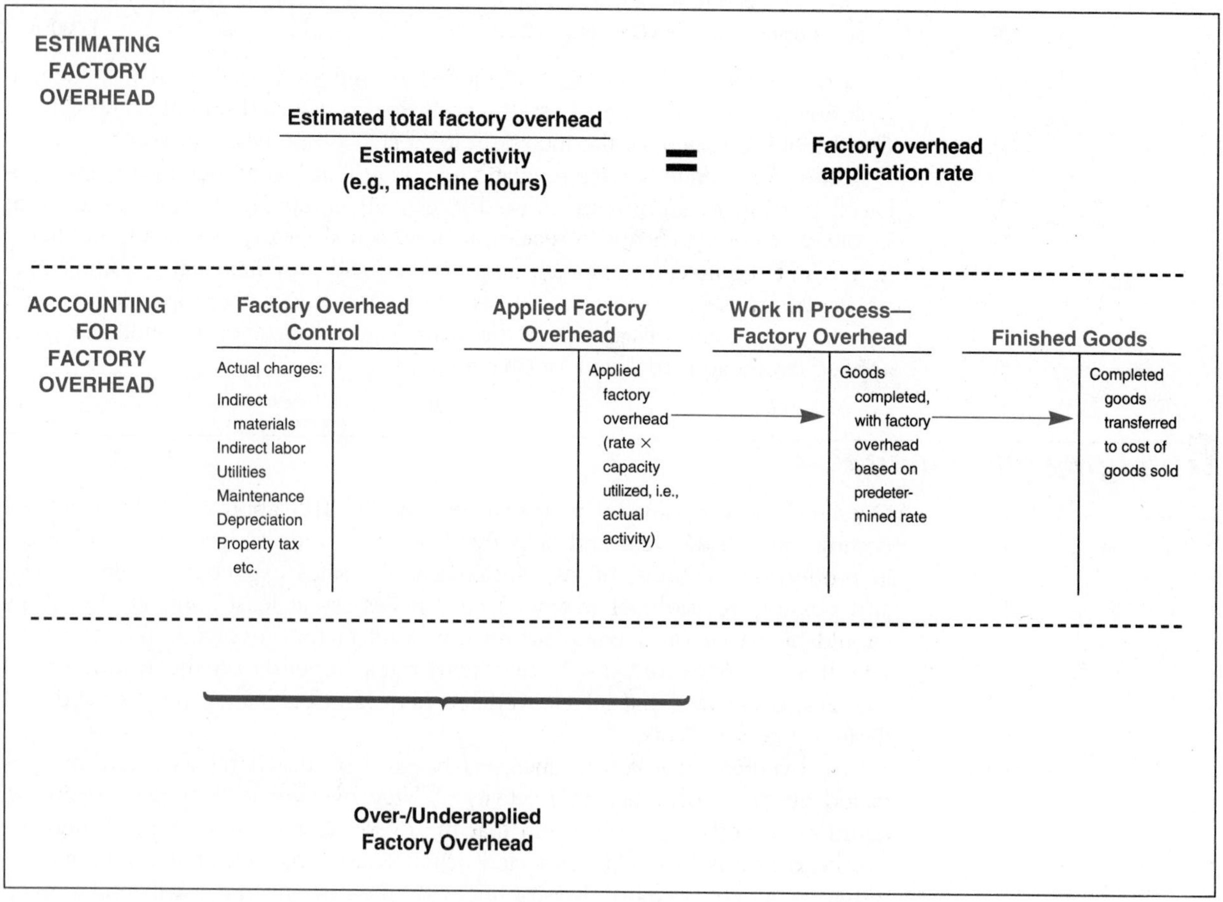

Key Terms

factory overhead, factory burden, manufacturing expense, manufacturing overhead, factory expense, or indirect manufacturing cost *(304)*
predetermined overhead rate *(305)*
overhead rate base, overhead allocation base, or base *(306)*
process time *(309)*
transactions-base approach *(310)*
theoretical capacity *(311)*
practical capacity *(311)*
expected actual capacity *(311)*
normal capacity *(311)*
idle capacity *(312)*
excess capacity *(312)*
absorption costing, conventional costing, or full costing *(312)*
direct costing or variable costing *(312)*
actual overhead *(315)*
applied overhead *(315)*
overapplied overhead *(316)*
underapplied overhead *(316)*

Discussion Questions

Q12-1 List some of the costs included in factory overhead.

Q12-2 Why does factory overhead vary from month to month?

Q12-3 When and why must predetermined factory overhead rates be used? Indicate the impracticalities and inaccuracies of charging actual overhead to jobs and products. (AICPA adapted)

Q12-4 Name six bases used for applying overhead. What factors must be considered in the selection of a particular base?

Q12-5 Why is the selection of a proper predetermined rate essential to reasonable costing? Explain.

Q12-6 Discuss the objectives and criteria that should be used in deciding whether to use direct labor hours or machine hours as the overhead allocation base. (AICPA adapted)

Q12-7 Differentiate among (a) theoretical capacity, (b) practical capacity, (c) expected actual capacity, and (d) normal capacity.

Q12-8 How does the selection of normal or maximum capacity affect operating profit in setting the overhead rate?

Q12-9 (a) What situations give rise to idle capacity costs?
(b) How and why are such costs accounted for?
(c) What is excess capacity cost?

Q12-10 What are the steps involved in accounting for actual overhead?

Q12-11 The factory overhead control account has a credit balance at the end of the period. Was overhead over- or underapplied?

Q12-12 A company applies overhead to production on the basis of direct labor dollars. At the end of the year, overhead has been overapplied to the extent of $60,000. What factors can cause this situation?

Q12-13 Describe two methods for disposing of over- or underapplied overhead and explain how the decision to use one of these methods rather than the other affects net income.

Q12-14 Comment on the following statement: If large amounts of underapplied overhead occur month after month, the overhead rate should be revised to make unit costs more accurate.

Exercises

E12-1 Predetermined Overhead Rates; Activity Levels. Parts Manufacturers (PM) is a maker of small steel machine parts. PM's total factory overhead costs are a linear function of the number of tons of steel processed. PM's theoretical capacity is 15,000 tons per year, practical capacity is 8,000 tons per year, normal capacity is 6,000 tons per year; 5,000 tons was the budgeted amount to be processed in the year just ended.

At the beginning of each year, PM budgets the expected actual factory overhead costs for the coming year and divides by the budgeted (expected actual) activity for the coming year. The result is the predetermined overhead rate.

Actual activity in the year just ended was 5,500 tons, and budgeted factory overhead costs were $5,350,000. The factory overhead budget would be $6,070,000 at normal capacity. Actual factory overhead costs in the year just ended were $5,340,500.

Required:

(1) Use the high and low points method (Chapter 3) to calculate the budgeted fixed overhead and the budgeted variable overhead rate per ton for the year just ended, assuming the practical capacity level of activity is within the relevant range.

(2) If PM had used practical capacity as the activity level in its predetermined overhead rate calculation for the year just ended, what would have been the predetermined factory overhead rate per ton? (Calculate to two decimal places.)

E12-2 Factory Overhead Application. The work in process account of Yorktown Inc. showed the following at the end of September:

Work in Process			
Materials	24,800	Finished goods	48,600
Direct labor	20,160		
Factory overhead	15,840		

Materials charged to the work still in process amounted to $5,560. Factory overhead is applied as a percentage of direct labor cost.

Required: Compute the individual amounts of factory overhead and direct labor charged to work still in process. (Round all amounts to four decimal places.)

E12-3 Calculation of Estimated Labor Base. The direct labor work force of Austin Inc. consists of 150 employees working full time, 8 hours, 5 days a week. Normal capacity assumes that the equivalent of 48 weeks of work can be expected from a full-time employee.

Required: Calculate the following:

(1) The number of direct labor hours to be used in setting up the firm's factory overhead rate based on normal capacity
(2) The number of direct labor hours if management and workers agree on a 10-hour, 4-day workweek

E12-4 Various Factory Overhead Rates. Vicksburg Company estimates factory overhead of $225,000 for the next year. An estimated 25,000 units will be produced, with materials cost of $500,000. Conversion will require an estimated 56,250 direct labor hours at a cost of $8 per hour, and an estimated 75,000 machine hours.

Required: Compute the predetermined factory overhead rate to be used in applying factory overhead to production on each of the following bases:

(1) Units of production
(2) Materials cost
(3) Direct labor hours
(4) Direct labor cost
(5) Machine hours

E12-5 Normal and Expected Actual Capacity. Theoretical capacity for Madison Tool Company is 80,000 direct labor hours, and normal capacity is 50,000 direct labor hours. The actual capacity attained for the fiscal year ended June 30, 19A, was 43,000 hours. It is estimated that 40,000 hours will be worked in 19B. Fixed factory overhead is $400,000, and variable factory overhead is $6.69 per direct labor hour.

Required:

(1) Using normal capacity, compute (a) the factory overhead rate, and (b) the fixed part of the factory overhead rate.
(2) Using expected actual capacity for 19B, compute (a) the factory overhead rate, and (b) the fixed part of the factory overhead rate.

E12-6 Over- or Underapplied Overhead. Sunny Inc. budgeted factory overhead at $255,000 for the period for Department A, based on a budgeted volume of 50,000 machine hours. At the end of the period, the actual factory overhead was $281,000 and actual machine hours were 52,500.

Required: Calculate the applied overhead and the over- or underapplied amount for the period.

E12-7 Entries for Factory Overhead. Black Inc. assembles and sells hand drills. All parts are purchased, and the cost of the parts per drill totals $50. Labor is paid on the basis of $32 per drill assembled. Because the company handles only this one product, the unit cost base is used for applying factory overhead at a predetermined rate. Estimated factory overhead for the coming period, based on a production of 30,000 drills, is as follows:

Indirect materials	$220,000
Indirect labor	240,000
Light and power	30,000
Depreciation	25,000
Miscellaneous	55,000

During the period, actual factory overhead was $561,600 and 29,000 drills were assembled. These units were completed but not yet transferred to the finished goods storeroom.

Required:
(1) Prepare the journal entries to record the preceding information.
(2) Determine the amount of over- or underapplied factory overhead.

E12-8 Over- or Underapplied Overhead. Normal annual capacity for Greencroft Company is 48,000 units, with production rates being level throughout the year. The October budget shows fixed factory overhead of $1,440 and an estimated variable factory overhead rate of $2.10 per unit. During October, actual output was 4,100 units, with a total factory overhead of $9,000.

Required: Calculate the over- or underapplied overhead for October.

E12-9 Applied Overhead; Over- or Underapplied Amount. Normal annual capacity for Daswan Company is 36,000 machine hours, with fixed factory overhead budgeted as $16,920 and an estimated variable factory overhead rate of $2.10 per hour. During October, actual production required 2,700 machine hours, with a total overhead of $7,800.

Required: Compute (1) the applied factory overhead and (2) the over- or underapplied amount for October.

E12-10 Over- or Underapplied Overhead. Quitman Company made the following data available from its accounting records and reports:

(a) $\frac{\$800{,}000 \text{ estimated factory overhead}}{200{,}000 \text{ estimated machine hours}} = \$4 \text{ predetermined factory overhead rate}$

(b) During the year, the company utilized 210,000 machine hours. Actual factory overhead was $832,000.

Required: Compute the over- or underapplied overhead amount for the year.

E12-11 Fixed and Variable Factory Overhead Rates; Over- or Underapplied Amount. Normal operating capacity of Baco Inc. is 100,000 machine hours per month, the level used to compute the predetermined factory overhead application rate. At this level of activity, fixed factory overhead is estimated to be $150,000, and variable factory overhead is estimated to be $250,000. During March, actual production required 105,000 machine hours and actual factory overhead totaled $415,000.

Required:
(1) Determine the fixed portion of the factory overhead application rate.
(2) Determine the variable portion of the factory overhead application rate.
(3) Is factory overhead for March over- or underapplied, and by how much?

E12-12 Over- or Underapplied Overhead. Granville Company was totally destroyed by fire during June. However, the following cost data were recovered: actual direct labor cost, $8,117; actual direct material cost, $16,550; actual overhead cost, $14,534; predetermined overhead rate, 200% of direct labor cost.

Required: Calculate the amount of over- or underapplied overhead.

E12-13 Disposition of Over- or Underapplied Overhead. The following information is available concerning the inventory and cost of goods sold accounts of Magnolia Company at the end of the most recent year:

	Work in Process	Finished Goods	Cost of Goods Sold
Direct material	$2,000	$ 6,000	$12,000
Direct labor	2,000	16,000	32,000
Applied overhead	2,000	16,000	32,000
Year-end balance	$6,000	$38,000	$76,000

Applied Overhead has already been closed to Factory Overhead Control. In all previous years, over- or underapplied overhead was treated as an adjustment to income or expense. Beginning inventories of the most recent year were insignificant.

Required: Give the journal entry to close Factory Overhead Control, assuming:

(1) Underapplied overhead of $6,000 is to be allocated to inventories and cost of goods sold in proportion to the balances in those accounts.
(2) Overapplied overhead of $6,000 is to be allocated to inventories and cost of goods sold in proportion to the balances in those accounts.
(3) Underapplied overhead of $6,000 is to be allocated to inventories and cost of goods sold in proportion to the amounts of applied overhead contained in those accounts.

Problems

P12-1 Over- or Underappplied Overhead; Predetermined Rates; Activity Levels; Disposition of Underapplied Amount. Amalgamated Manufacturing (AM) is a sheet-metal fabricator. AM's total factory overhead costs are a linear function of machine usage. AM's theoretical capacity is 25,000 machine hours (MH) per year, practical capacity is 15,000 MH per year, normal capacity is 8,000 MH per year; 10,000 MH were expected to be the actual activity for the year just ended.

At the beginning of each year, AM budgets the expected actual factory overhead costs for the coming year and divides it by the budgeted (expected actual) MH for the coming year. The result is the predetermined overhead rate.

Actual activity in the year just ended was 9,500 MH, and budgeted factory overhead costs were $3,500,000. The factory overhead budget would be $3,000,000 at normal capacity. Actual factory overhead costs for the year totaled $3,405,000.

Required:

(1) Calculate the amount of over- or underapplied overhead for the year just ended.
(2) If AM had used practical capacity as the activity level in its predetermined overhead rate calculation for the year just ended, what would the predetermined factory overhead rate have been per MH? (Calculate to two decimal places, and assume the practical capacity level of activity is within the relevant range.)
(3) Without being influenced by your answer to requirement 1, assume overhead was underapplied by $10,000. Give the end-of-period entries to close Applied Overhead to Factory Overhead Control and to close Factory Overhead Control to Cost of Goods Sold.
(4) Without prejudice to your answers to the preceding requirements, assume overhead was underapplied by $10,000 and Applied Overhead has already been closed to Factory Overhead Control. The underapplied amount is to be allocated to inventories and cost of goods sold in proportion to the balances in those accounts. The balances in Work in Process, Finished Goods, and Cost of Goods Sold are $200,000, $400,000, and $7,400,000, respectively. In all previous years, the over- or underapplied overhead was treated as an adjustment to income or expense. Beginning inventories were insignificant. Give the end-of-period entry to close Factory Overhead Control.

P12-2 Determining Variable and Fixed Factory Overhead Cost Behavior. Toms Company had the following budgeted amounts for production, sales, and costs in April and August, 19A, which are considered to be typical months:

	April	August
Production in units	10,000	15,000
Sales in units	12,000	16,000
Costs:		
Depreciation on factory building and equipment	$14,500	$ 14,500
Heat, light, and power (factory)	6,000	8,000
Supplies used (factory)	7,000	10,500
Direct materials used	50,000	75,000
Taxes on factory building	1,500	1,500
Bad debt expense	1,000	1,500
Indirect labor (factory)	60,000	70,000
Advertising expense	6,000	8,000
Maintenance (factory)	12,000	18,000
Direct labor	70,000	105,000

Required:

(1) Compute the variable overhead per unit for each factory overhead cost.
(2) Compute the fixed overhead for each factory overhead cost. CGA-Canada (adapted). Reprint with permission.

P12-3 Factory Overhead; Job Order Costing. Lamb Company uses job order cost accumulation. Manufacturing costs for December were:

Work in process, December 1 (Job 50)	$ 54,000
Materials and supplies requisitioned for:	
Job 50	$ 45,000
Job 51	37,500
Job 52	25,500
Supplies	3,500
Factory direct labor hours:	
Job 50	3,500
Job 51	3,000
Job 52	2,000
Labor costs:	
Direct labor wages	$102,000
Indirect labor wages	15,000
Supervisory salaries	6,000
Building occupancy costs	3,500
Factory equipment costs	6,000
Other factory costs	5,000

Jobs 50 and 51 were completed during December. The predetermined factory overhead rate is $4.50 per direct labor hour.

Required:

(1) Compute the total cost of Job 50.
(2) Determine the factory overhead costs applied to Job 52 during December.
(3) Compute the total factory overhead costs applied during December.
(4) Determine the actual December factory overhead incurred.
(5) How should Lamb dispose of any over- or underapplied factory overhead, assuming that the amount is not significant in relation to total factory overhead?
(6) Calculate the amount of over- or underapplied overhead for December. (ICMA adapted)

P12-4 Factory Overhead; Job Order Costing. Amalgamators Incorporated has made the following manufacturing cost data available for the most recent period:

Work in process–beginning of period:

Job No.	Materials	Labor	Factory Overhead	Total
1376	$17,500	$22,000	$33,000	$72,500

Costs for the period:

	Materials	Labor	Other	Total
Incurred by Jobs				
1376	$ 1,000	$ 7,000	—	$ 8,000
1377	26,000	53,000	—	79,000
1378	12,000	9,000	—	21,000
1379	4,000	1,000	—	5,000
Not Incurred by Jobs				
Indirect materials	17,000	—	—	17,000
Indirect labor	—	53,000	—	53,000
Employee benefits	—	—	$23,000	23,000
Depreciation	—	—	12,000	12,000
Supervision	—	20,000	—	20,000
Total	$60,000	$143,000	$35,000	$238,000

	Total
Factory overhead rate for 19-:	
Budgeted overhead:	
Variable—Indirect materials	$ 16,000
Indirect labor	56,000
Employee benefits	24,000
Fixed—Depreciation	12,000
Supervision	20,000
Total	$128,000
Budgeted direct labor cost	$ 80,000
Overhead rate per direct labor dollar ($128,000 ÷ $80,000)	160%

Required:

(1) Compute the actual factory overhead.
(2) Determine the over- or underapplied factory overhead.
(3) Calculate the amount included in cost of goods sold for Job 1376, which was the only job completed and sold in the period.
(4) Determine the cost assigned to the work in process account at the end of the period, unadjusted for any over- or underapplied factory overhead. (ICMA adapted)

P12-5 Predetermined Rates; Applied Overhead. Dagnut Company set normal capacity at 60,000 machine hours. The expected operating level for the period just ended was 45,000 hours. At this expected actual capacity, variable expenses were estimated to be $29,250 and fixed expenses, $18,000. Actual results show that 47,000 machine hours were used and that actual factory overhead totaled $48,000 during the period.

Required:

(1) Compute the predetermined factory overhead rate based on normal capacity.
(2) Compute the predetermined factory overhead rate based on expected actual capacity.
(3) Compute the amount of factory overhead charged to production if the company used the normal capacity rate.
(4) Compute the amount of factory overhead charged to production if the company used the expected actual capacity rate.
(5) Compute the amount of over- or underapplied overhead if the company used the normal capacity rate.
(6) Compute the amount of over- or underapplied overhead if the company used the expected actual capacity rate.

P12-6 Inventory Costing; Overhead Analysis; Statement of Cost of Goods Sold. The Cost Department of Columbus Company received the following monthly data, pertaining solely to manufacturing activities, from the general ledger clerk:

Work in process inventory, January 1	$ 32,500
Materials inventory, January 1	21,000
Direct labor	256,000
Materials purchased	108,000
Materials returned to suppliers	5,050
Supervision	17,500
Indirect labor	29,050
Heat, light, and power	23,800
Depreciation—factory buildings	7,500
Property tax—factory facilities	4,000
Insurance on factory buildings	3,000
Transportation in (factory overhead)	6,500
Repairs and maintenance—factory equipment	8,250
Depreciation—factory equipment	7,500
Miscellaneous factory overhead	9,900
Finished goods inventory, January 1	18,000
Applied factory overhead	115,200

Additional data:

(a) Physical inventory taken January 31 shows $9,000 of materials on hand.

(b) The January 31 work in process and finished goods inventories show the following direct materials and direct labor contents:

	Direct Materials	Direct Labor
Work in process....................	$ 9,000	$16,000 (2,000 hrs.)
Finished goods.....................	10,000	40,000 (5,000 hrs.)

(c) Factory overhead is applied to these two ending inventories on the basis of a predetermined factory overhead rate of $3.60 per direct labor hour.

Required:

(1) Determine the cost assigned to the ending work in process and finished goods inventories, including factory overhead.

(2) Prepare a schedule of the total actual factory overhead for the month.

(3) Calculate the over- or underapplied factory overhead.

(4) Prepare a detailed cost of goods sold statement, assuming that over- or underapplied overhead is closed to the cost of goods sold account.

Case

C12-1 Cost Behavior Analysis; Utility of Cost Behavior Information. Lawson Incorporated assigns factory overhead by a predetermined rate on the basis of direct labor hours. Factory overhead costs for two recent years, adjusted for changes using current prices and wage rates, are as follows:

	Year 1	Year 2
Direct labor hours worked..........	2,760,000	2,160,000
Factory overhead costs:		
Indirect labor........................	$11,040,000	$ 8,640,000
Employee benefits................	4,140,000	3,240,000
Supplies..............................	2,760,000	2,160,000
Power..................................	2,208,000	1,728,000
Heat and light......................	552,000	552,000
Supervision..........................	2,865,000	2,625,000
Depreciation........................	7,930,000	7,930,000
Property taxes and insurance............................	3,005,000	3,005,000
Total factory overhead cost	$34,500,000	$29,880,000

Required:

(1) The company expects to operate at a level of activity of 2,300,000 direct labor hours next year. Using the data from the two recent years, calculate the estimated total factory overhead for next year.

(2) Explain how the company can use the computed cost behavior information for:

(a) Evaluation of product pricing decisions

(b) Cost control evaluation

(c) Development of budgets (ICMA adapted)

CHAPTER 13

Factory Overhead: Departmentalization

Learning Objectives

After studying this chapter, you will be able to:

1. Describe the concept of departmentalization.
2. Distinguish between service and producing departments.
3. Define direct and indirect departmental costs and give examples of each.
4. Compute and use departmental overhead rates.
5. Accumulate actual departmental overhead costs.
6. Describe departmentalization in nonmanufacturing and not-for-profit organizations.

The preceding chapter discussed the establishment and use of a factorywide overhead rate, the accumulation of actual factory overhead, and the disposition of over- or underapplied factory overhead. This chapter expands these steps through the use of predetermined departmental factory overhead rates, which improve the charging of overhead to products and help control costs by means of responsibility accounting.

The computation of departmental overhead rates requires a series of departmental allocations. These allocations are necessary for computing predetermined overhead rates prior to the beginning of the fiscal period, and again at the end of the period in determining actual departmental overhead.

Departmentalization

Departmentalization of factory overhead means dividing the plant into segments, called departments, to which overhead costs are charged. For accounting purposes, dividing a plant into separate departments provides improved product costing and promotes responsible control of overhead costs.

Improved product costing is possible because departmentalization allows different departments to have different overhead rates. A job or product going through a department is charged with factory overhead for work done in that department, using the department's predetermined overhead rate. Depending on the type and number of departments through which they pass, jobs or products are charged with varying amounts of factory overhead, rather than with a single plantwide overhead amount. A single plantwide rate charges all jobs with a plantwide average amount of overhead cost per unit of the base; this plantwide average may be too high or too low for a particular product that involves primarily one or a few departments.

Responsible control of overhead costs is facilitated because departmentalization makes the costs a responsibility of a supervisor or manager. Costs that originate within a department are identified with the individual responsible for that department.

The process of departmentalizing factory overhead is an extension of methods previously discussed. Estimating or budgeting costs and selecting a proper base for applying them is still necessary, but in addition, departmentalizing overhead requires separate estimates or budgets for each department. Actual costs of a period still are recorded in a factory overhead control account and a factory overhead subsidiary ledger, but they are detailed by department as well as by the nature of the cost. This permits comparison of actual costs with applied amounts for each department.

Producing and Service Departments

Departments are classified as either producing or service departments. A **producing department** manufactures the product by changing the form or nature of material or by assembling parts. A **service department** renders a service that contributes in an indirect way to the manufacture of the product but does not change the form, assembly, or nature of the material. Examples of producing and service departments follow:

Producing		Service	
Cutting	Mill Room	Utilities	Shipping
Planing	Plating	Receiving	Medical
Assembly	Knitting	Inspection	Production Control
Upholstery	Mixing	Storage	Personnel
Finishing	Refining	Security	Maintenance
Machining	Bottling	Purchasing	Cafeteria
Cooking	Canning	Materials Handling	General Factory Cost Pool
Brewing	Glazing		
Distilling	Fabricating		

Selection of Producing Departments

A manufacturing company is usually organized along departmental lines for production purposes. Each department performs a different kind of work, as suggested by the names in the preceding list. Manufacturing processes dictate the type of organization needed to handle the different operations efficiently, to obtain the best production flow, and to establish responsibility for physical control of production.

The cost information system is designed to reflect the departmentalization. The system accumulates manufacturing costs by department, whether operations are of the job type or the continuous process type. Factors to be considered in deciding the kinds of departments required for establishing accurate departmental overhead rates are as follows:

1. Similarity of operations and machinery in each department.
2. Location of operations and machinery.
3. Responsibilities for production and costs.
4. Relationship of operations to flow of product.
5. Number of departments.

The establishment of producing departments for product costing and cost control is a problem for the management of every company. Although no hard and fast rules can be given, the most common approach divides the factory along lines of functional activities, with each activity or group of activities constituting a department. An emerging alternative is the work-cell arrangement, discussed in Chapters 10 and 14.

The number of producing departments used depends on the emphasis the cost system puts on cost control and the development of overhead rates. If the emphasis is on cost control, separate departments might be established for the plant manager and for each superintendent or supervisor. When the development of departmental overhead rates emphasizes costing, fewer or more departments might be used. Sometimes the number of departments needed for cost control is larger than that needed for product costing. In such cases, the cost control system can be adapted by combining departments for product cost calculations, thus reducing the number of rates used without sacrificing control of costs.

In certain instances, departments are further subdivided for cost control and overhead rate purposes, particularly when the product line is diverse, the cost structure is complex, or different types of machines are used. For example, different rates can be applied to reflect the cost of more expensive or less expensive machinery employed for one job, or for the processing of one product in a diverse product line.

Selection of Service Departments

Services that benefit both producing departments and other service departments can be organized by (1) establishing a separate service department for each function, (2) combining several functions into one department, or (3) placing service costs in a department called *general factory cost pool.* The specific service is not identified if service costs applicable to producing and service functions are accumulated in a general factory cost pool.

The kinds and numbers of service departments depend on the number of employees needed for each service function, the cost of providing the service, the importance of the service, and the assignment of supervisory responsibility. Establishing a separate department for every service function is rare, even in large companies. When relatively few employees are involved and activities are closely related, service functions are often combined, depending on individual circumstances in each company.[1] Because overhead rates for product costing generally are calculated for producing departments only, service department costs are transferred ultimately to producing departments for setting overhead rates.

Direct Departmental Costs

The majority of direct departmental overhead costs can be divided into the following categories: (1) supervision, indirect labor, and overtime, (2) labor fringe benefits, (3) indirect materials and factory supplies, (4) repairs and maintenance, and (5) equipment depreciation and rent. These categories generally are readily identified with the originating department, whether it is a producing or service department.

[1] CAS 418, "Allocation of Direct and Indirect Costs," states that a department should be homogeneous and specifies that this criterion is met "if each significant activity whose costs are included therein has the same or a similar beneficial or causal relationship . . . as the other activities whose costs are included in the [department]."

Supervision, Indirect Labor, and Overtime

Labor control and accounting, discussed in Chapter 11, are relevant to the first two categories—supervision, indirect labor, overtime, and the related fringe benefits. Any factory labor not classified as direct labor is automatically a part of overhead. Because overhead is allocated to all products, a lax or incorrect classification causes direct labor that applies to only one product to be allocated (as overhead) to other products, understating the one product's cost and overstating the cost of the others. Deciding how to classify costs can have an important effect on overhead rates, especially if direct labor is used as the base for determining overhead rates.

The premium portion of paid overtime generally should be charged as overhead to the departments in which the overtime occurs. This method should be followed for all labor except in special cases in which overtime is incurred for rush orders, as discussed in Chapter 11. However, the straight-time portion of all amounts paid to direct laborers is direct labor cost, not overhead.

Labor Fringe Benefits

Labor fringe benefits include such costs as vacation and holiday pay, FICA tax, state and federal unemployment taxes, worker's compensation insurance, pension costs, hospitalization benefits, and group insurance. In theory, these fringe benefits are additional labor costs and, when they pertain to direct labor employees, they should be added to the direct labor cost. In practice, this approach is often not practical; therefore, these costs that pertain to direct laborers and all other production workers are generally included in overhead and become part of the overhead rate.

Indirect Materials and Factory Supplies

The materials control, costing, and quantitative models discussed in Chapter 9 are equally appropriate in dealing with indirect materials and factory supplies. Incorrectly distinguishing between direct and indirect materials has the same adverse effect on product costing as failure to distinguish properly between direct and indirect labor. However, distinguishing between direct and indirect materials is usually not as difficult. In a manufacturing operation, direct materials are those that are significant in amount, are changed in form through processing, and become an integral part of the end product. Indirect materials, often referred to as factory supplies, are auxiliary to the processing operations and do not become an essential part of the end product. Even if insignificant amounts of direct materials are distinguishable, they can be charged to overhead as an expedient.

Repairs and Maintenance

It is essential to establish control over the total cost incurred by the repairs and maintenance department and to devise effective means for charging maintenance costs to departments receiving the service. Most repairs and maintenance costs generally are traceable to benefiting departments and often are classified as direct departmental costs, even though they may originate in a maintenance department. If practical, all actual maintenance costs should be charged to a maintenance department, so that the total cost controllable by the department supervisor is kept within the maintenance department budget. However, because maintenance is a service function, its costs ultimately must be distributed to departments that receive the service.

Equipment Depreciation

Depreciation is usually not controllable by department supervisors. However, their use of equipment influences maintenance and depreciation costs. This is true with respect to all types of depreciable assets—machinery and equipment, buildings, vehicles, and furniture and fixtures. For effective product costing and control, depreciation is usually identified with the department that uses the assets, so the cost is charged directly to departments. The recommended method is to compute depreciation based on the cost of each department's equipment, as recorded in detailed plant asset records. When no records are available or equipment is used by more than one department, depreciation is frequently accumulated in the general factory cost pool. Equipment rent is handled similarly.

Indirect Departmental Costs

Costs such as power, light, rent, and depreciation of factory buildings, when shared by all departments, are not charged directly to a department. These costs do not originate with any specific department. They are incurred for the benefit of all departments, so their cost is prorated among all departments.

Selecting appropriate bases for the distribution of most indirect departmental costs is difficult and arbitrary. At best, allocations will be intuitively reasonable. To charge every department with its share of a cost, a base common to all departments must be found.[2] For example, square footage can be used for prorating such expenses as building rent. In plants with departments occupying parts of the factory with ceilings of unequal height, cubic measurement rather than square footage can be used. Areas occupied by stairways, elevators, escalators, corridors, and aisles must also be considered. Some of the indirect departmental expenses that require prorating, together with the bases most commonly used, include the following:

Indirect Departmental Costs	Distribution Bases
Building rent	Square footage
Property tax	Square footage
Depreciation—buildings	Square footage
Fire insurance	Square footage
Building repairs	Square footage
Gas utility	Square footage
Superintendence	Number of employees
Telephone and telegraph	Number of employees or number of telephones
Worker's compensation insurance	Department payroll
Fixed portion of electricity	Square footage
Variable portion of electricity	Kilowatt hours

[2] While required only for costing large government contracts, CAS 418 also affords guidance for more general uses. It deals with accumulating and allocating indirect costs and requires federal government contractors to identify and describe allocation bases for all factory overhead, service center, and general and administrative cost pools. (See *Standards, Rules and Regulations, Part 418*, "Allocation of Direct and Indirect Costs," Washington, D.C.: Cost Accounting Standards Board, 1980). The allocation must be based on one of the following, listed in order of preference: (1) a resource consumption measure, (2) an output measure, or (3) a surrogate that is representative of resources consumed.

At times, a service that could be obtained separately by each of several departments can be obtained centrally at a lower aggregate cost. In such cases, the cost of having each department obtain the service separately, called the stand-alone cost, may be the most equitable base for distributing the centralized cost.[3] For example, assume that individual departments can obtain necessary rental space separately as follows:

Department	Cost of Rental Space Obtained Separately
A	$ 500,000
B	500,000
C	250,000
D	50,000
	$1,300,000

Assume further that the rental space can be provided under a consolidated rental agreement for a total cost of $1,030,000. Proration of the aggregate cost on a stand-alone basis yields the following result:

Department	Aggregate Cost		Allocation Base		Allocated Aggregate Cost
A	$1,030,000	×	$500,000/$1,300,000	=	$ 396,154
B	1,030,000	×	500,000/1,300,000	=	396,154
C	1,030,000	×	250,000/1,300,000	=	198,077
D	1,030,000	×	50,000/1,300,000	=	39,615
					$1,030,000

Establishing Departmental Overhead Rates

For convenience, factory overhead usually is applied on the basis of machine hours or direct labor hours or cost when only one factory overhead rate is used for the entire plant. However, the use of departmental rates requires a distinct consideration of each producing department's overhead, which often results in different bases for different departments (e.g., a direct labor hour rate for one department and a machine hour rate for another). A further refinement can lead to multiple bases and rates within a single producing department, as discussed in Chapter 14.

This can necessitate the establishment of subdepartments corresponding to physical subdivisions of the department. An example is a department that is physically divided into one segment that is heavily automated, using machine hours as the overhead allocation base, and another segment that is labor intensive, using labor hours as the allocation base. Multiple cost pools within a department, in contrast, can be based on kinds of costs and the activity base that drives them, even if the department is not physically segmented. An example is a workcenter that has a pool of machine-related overhead costs (repair and maintenance, setup, lubricants, and energy) and a pool of labor-related overhead costs (fringe benefits, small tools, and supplies). The result is two overhead rate bases within the same department (one for each cost pool), but without the physical segregation of subdepartments.

[3] Richard B. Troxel, "Corporate Cost Allocation Can Be Peaceful . . . Is Sharing the Key?" *Management Focus*, Vol. 28, No. 1, pp. 3–5.

The logic of such multiple cost pools is seen in the example of a machine shop producing two different kinds of products. One product comprises small rush orders produced on semiautomatic machines that require very little setup but only make one part per minute and require the machinist to remain present. The other product comprises larger routine orders produced on more automated machines that require the same machinist to spend half a day setting up and then run essentially untended at a rate of 10 parts per minute. If setup costs are considered part of overhead, a part made in a rush order may have little machine-related overhead—utilizing a small inexpensive machine with little setup time required—and a considerable portion of labor-related overhead. Conversely, a part made in a routine order may have just the opposite mix. Neither a single overhead pool based on labor nor a single pool based on machine type and machine time accurately costs both kinds of jobs. But if the same machinist's skills are required for both, it is logical to have a single department in which a machinist who has just set up a long automatic run can be assigned to produce a rush order rather than being idle until the next long run needs to be set up. A labor overhead rate and a machine overhead rate in the same department address these kinds of manufacturing settings.

The same need for multiple cost pools can occur in a service industry. An automobile dealership, for example, may have a parts-related overhead pool in which the assigned cost is based on the price of each part and a service-related overhead pool in which the assigned cost is based on an hourly service labor rate.

Because all factory overhead, whether from producing departments or service departments, is ultimately allocated to producing departments, the establishment of departmental factory overhead rates involves the following steps:

1. Estimate total departmental overhead of producing and service departments at the expected activity levels; determine, if possible, the fixed and variable nature of each cost category.
2. Prepare a survey (with measurements of all allocation bases) for the purpose of distributing indirect factory overhead and service department costs.
3. Estimate total indirect departmental overhead (such as electric power, fuel, water, building depreciation, property tax, and fire insurance) at the selected activity levels and allocate these costs among departments.
4. Distribute service department costs to benefiting departments.
5. Calculate departmental factory overhead rates.

These steps are illustrated in the total estimated factory overhead for DeWitt Products (Exhibit 12-2), which has now been departmentalized (Exhibit 13-1). The figures have been modified for ease in calculating departmental rates, but the fixed–variable cost classification has been retained. The illustration uses four producing departments: Cutting, Planing, Assembly, and Upholstery; and four service departments: Materials Handling, Inspection, Utilities, and General Factory.

Materials handling involves the operation of equipment such as cranes, trucks, forklifts, and loaders. Because many departments are served by this function, the preferred method of organization establishes a separate service department for materials handling activities, with a supervisor responsible for their control. All handling costs are charged to this department. Costs charged to this service department are the same as those charged to any department, including wages and labor benefit costs of the department's employees; supplies, such as batteries and gasoline; and repairs and maintenance of the equipment. In addition to centralizing responsibility for materials handling operations, departmentalization has the advantage of collecting all materials handling costs in one place.

For cost control, inspection costs are treated in the same manner as other service department costs. However, in certain instances, a special work order can require additional inspection or testing. This type of inspection cost is chargeable to the order and must be so identified. To accumulate these specific charges, separate cost centers can be established for the purpose of charging time and materials for special inspections.

Power and fuel are consumed for two major purposes: for operating manufacturing facilities such as machines, electric welders, and cranes, and for what might be termed working condition purposes, such as lighting, cooling, and heating. Although a single billing is common for electric power or natural gas, a direct departmental charge is possible, if separate meters to measure power or fuel are installed. In other instances, separate power sources (diesel fuel, gasoline, natural gas, coal, or electricity) can be used for different facilities or equipment. If utility costs are not directly traceable to specific departments, allocation is based on studies that determine information that includes such factors as each department's machine horsepower, number of machines, and expected operating time.

For departmental and product costing, two methods of accounting for costs of utilities are recommended:

1. Charge all power and fuel costs to a separate utilities department, then allocate to the benefiting departments.
2. Charge specific departments with power or fuel cost if separate meters are provided, and charge the remaining power and fuel costs to a separate utilities department or to a general factory account; this remainder is then allocated to the benefiting departments.

Costs other than those already discussed are classified as general factory costs, because they represent a variety of miscellaneous factory services. A separate general factory cost pool is established to accumulate and control these costs. Such an organizational unit can be the responsibility of the plant superintendent. Salaries of management personnel assigned to production are charged to this cost pool if they cannot be charged directly to specific departments. Janitor labor and supplies can be charged to general factory unless charged to maintenance or to building occupancy. Unless separate service departments for plant security and yard operation are established, these costs are also charged to general factory.

Estimating Direct Departmental Costs

Estimating or budgeting the direct costs of producing and service departments, as shown in Exhibit 13-1, is a joint undertaking of department heads, supervisors, and the budget or cost department. Labor fringe benefits costs are calculated by office personnel because the individual supervisor has little influence or knowledge in this area. Costs of indirect labor and indirect materials are of greater interest to the supervisor. Repairs and maintenance costs often are disputed items unless a definite maintenance program has been established. Although it is not illustrated here, they first may be charged to the maintenance department and then assigned to the benefiting departments. Departmental depreciation charges are based on management's decision regarding depreciation methods and rates. In the illustration, depreciation of equipment is charged directly to the departments on the basis of asset values and rates set by the controller. The plant manager, working with budget personnel, estimates and supervises the general factory costs.

DeWitt Products
Estimated Departmental Factory Overhead
for the Year 19—

Cost Account	F or V	Total	Producing Departments: Cutting	Planing	Assembly	Upholstery	Service Departments: Materials Handling	Inspection	Utilities	General Factory
Direct departmental costs:										
Supervisors	F	$ 70,000	$ 9,000	$ 8,000	$ 8,000	$ 8,000	$10,000	$ 6,000	$ 9,000	$12,000
Indirect labor	F	9,000	1,000	2,000	1,000	1,500	1,000	500	1,000	1,000
	V	66,000	9,000	3,000	5,000	5,500	11,000	8,500	10,000	14,000
Labor fringe benefits	F	10,000	1,500	1,000	1,000	1,000	2,000	1,000	1,500	1,000
	V	47,000	10,500	11,800	9,400	8,200	1,800	1,400	1,900	2,000
Indirect materials	F	4,000	500	500	800	1,200	300	200	200	300
	V	19,000	2,500	2,500	3,200	4,800	1,700	800	1,800	1,700
Repairs and maintenance	F	3,000	600	500	700	600			300	300
	V	9,000	1,400	1,500	1,300	1,800	500	200	1,700	600
Depreciation—equipment	F	13,000	1,500	3,500	1,000	3,000				4,000
Total direct departmental cost		$250,000	$37,500	$34,300	$31,400	$35,600	$28,300	$18,600	$27,400	$36,900
Indirect departmental costs:										
Electric power	F	$ 2,000							$ 2,000	
	V	20,000							20,000	
Fuel	F	1,000							1,000	
	V	10,000							10,000	
Water	F	1,000							1,000	
	V	4,000							4,000	
Depreciation—buildings	F	5,000	$ 1,250	$ 1,000	$ 1,500	$ 1,250				
Property tax	F	4,000	1,000	800	1,200	1,000				
Insurance (fire)	F	3,000	750	600	900	750				
Total indirect departmental cost		$ 50,000	$ 3,000	$ 2,400	$ 3,600	$ 3,000			$38,000	
Total departmental factory overhead		$300,000	$40,500	$36,700	$35,000	$38,600	$28,300	$18,600	$65,400	$36,900
Total fixed factory overhead		$125,000	$17,100	$17,900	$16,100	$18,300	$13,300	$ 7,700	$16,000	$18,600
Total variable factory overhead		$175,000	$23,400	$18,800	$18,900	$20,300	$15,000	$10,900	$49,400	$18,300

EXHIBIT 13-1

Factory Survey

To prorate indirect departmental costs and service department costs to the benefiting departments, the necessary data are obtained from a survey of factory facilities and records. The survey data include rated horsepower of equipment in each department, estimated kilowatt-hour consumption, number of employees in each department, estimated payroll costs, square footage, estimated materials consumption, asset values, and any other measures that serve as bases for distributing costs among departments. Functions performed by each service department are studied carefully to determine the most reasonable basis for distributing their costs. The factory survey for DeWitt Products appears in Exhibit 13-2.

EXHIBIT 13-2

DeWitt Products
Factory Survey at Beginning of Year

Producing Department	Number of Employees*	%	Kilo-watt-Hours	%	Horse-power-Hours	%	Floor Area (in square feet)	%	Cost of Materials Requisi-tioned	%
Cutting	8.0	20	12,800	20	200,000	40	5,250	25	$180,000	45
Planing.........	6.8	17	6,400	10	120,000	24	4,200	20	40,000	10
Assembly	12.0	30	19,200	30	80,000	16	6,300	30	40,000	10
Upholstery....	13.2	33	25,600	40	100,000	20	5,250	25	140,000	35
Total.............	40.0	100	64,000	100	500,000	100	21,000	100	$400,000	100

* Average based on portion of year employed.

Estimating and Allocating Indirect Costs

Indirect departmental costs, such as heat, electric power, fuel, water, and building depreciation, must be estimated and then allocated to producing departments and perhaps service departments; the method depends on management's decision. In Exhibit 13-1, indirect departmental costs are prorated in two ways: (1) Electric power, fuel, and water are charged to Utilities, from which a distribution is made to producing departments only, (2) Depreciation of building, property tax, and fire insurance are prorated only to producing departments on the basis of floor area as shown in the Factory Survey (Exhibit 13-2). For example, 25% of $5,000, or $1,250, is charged to the Cutting Department for building depreciation. Alternatively, these costs can be allocated to service departments as well as to producing departments to measure more completely the total cost of individual service departments as well as to provide information needed for cost planning and control.

Distributing Service Department Costs

The number and types of service departments in a company depend on the company's operations and the degree of cost control desired. As shown in Exhibit 13-1, each service department of DeWitt Products is charged with its direct costs. Service department costs should be allocated either to producing departments and service departments, or just to producing departments, on the basis of a common unit of measure that correlates closely with the causes of service department costs. The allocation can be based on number of employees, kilowatt-hour consumption, horsepower-hour consumption, floor space, asset value, or cost of materials to be requisitioned. The costs of service departments ultimately are allocated to producing departments to establish predetermined factory overhead rates. The common methods for allocating service department overhead to benefiting departments are the direct method, the step method, and the simultaneous method.

Direct Method. In some companies service department costs are allocated only to producing departments. This approach, called the **direct method**, minimizes clerical work, but fails to measure the total costs of individual service departments when such information is needed for cost planning and control. The direct method can be justified for product costing if the final costs of a producing department differ only immaterially, depending on whether the costs of a service department are or are not prorated to other service departments.

The direct method is illustrated for DeWitt Products in Exhibit 13-3. The distribution begins with Materials Handling. (In the direct method, the order in which the service departments are distributed does not matter.) The overhead of this department is distributed on the basis of estimated cost of materials requisitioned, as shown in the factory survey (Exhibit 13-2). For example, 45 percent of $28,300, or $12,735, is transferred to the Cutting Department. The Inspection cost is transferred to the Assembly and Upholstery producing departments on a fifty-fifty basis, because these two departments are the only ones receiving this type of service, and they receive it in equal amounts.

The Utilities cost is transferred in three parts: 20 percent of the cost based on kilowatt-hours; 50 percent, on horsepower-hours; and 30 percent, on floor area. The amount of $13,080 represents 20 percent of the total cost of the Utilities Department, $65,400. According to Exhibit 13-2, 20 percent of $13,080, or $2,616, is distributed to the Cutting Department. The same method is followed for the other costs and departments. General Factory is distributed on the basis of number of employees. For example, 20 percent of $36,900, or $7,380, is distributed to the Cutting Department.

The distribution of the service department costs in this illustration is based on percentages in the factory survey (Exhibit 13-2). Alternatively, the survey data can be used to calculate a rate per square foot, per kilowatt-hour, or per employee. For example, the amount of General Factory cost allocated to the Cutting Department is determined as follows:

$$\frac{\$36{,}900 \text{ General Factory Cost}}{40 \text{ employees}} = \$922.50 \text{ per employee}$$

$$\$922.50 \times 8 \text{ employees in the Cutting Department} = \$7{,}380$$

A more concise illustration of the direct method and other methods is based on the following data for Nickleby Company:

Department	Factory Overhead Before Distribution of Service Departments	Services Provided	
		Department Y	Department Z
Producing—A	$ 60,000	40%	20%
Producing—B	80,000	40	50
Service—Y	36,300	—	30
Service—Z	20,000	20	—
Total factory overhead	$196,300	100%	100%

DeWitt Products
Distribution of Estimated Service Department Costs
and
Calculation of Departmental Overhead Rates
for the Year 19—

		Producing Departments				Service Departments			
Cost Account	**Total**	**Cutting**	**Planing**	**Assembly**	**Upholstery**	**Materials Handling**	**Inspection**	**Utilities**	**General Factory**
Total departmental factory overhead before distribution of service departments	$300,000	$40,500	$36,700	$ 35,000	$ 38,600	$28,300	$18,600	$65,400	$36,900
Distribution of service department costs:									
Materials handling (Base: estimated cost of materials requisitioned)		$12,735	$ 2,830	$ 2,830	$ 9,905	(28,300)			
Inspection (Base: equally to assembly and upholstery departments)				9,300	9,300		(18,600)		
Utilities:									
(Bases: 20% on kwh		2,616	1,308	3,924	5,232			(13,080)	
50% on hph		13,080	7,848	5,232	6,540			(32,700)	
30% on floor area)		4,905	3,924	5,886	4,905			(19,620)	
General factory (Base: number of employees)		7,380	6,273	11,070	12,177				(36,900)
Total service department cost distributed		$40,716	$22,183	$ 38,242	$ 48,059				
Total departmental factory overhead after distribution of service departments	$300,000	$81,216	$58,883	$ 73,242	$ 86,659				
Bases: Direct labor hours		20,304			24,070				
Machine hours			9,200						
Direct labor cost				$122,000					
Rates		$ 4.00 per direct labor hour	$ 6.40 per machine hour	60% of direct labor cost	$ 3.60 per direct labor hour				

EXHIBIT 13-3

Recall that all services provided to other service departments are ignored by the direct procedure because this method allocates service department overhead only to producing departments. Thus, the order of distribution does not matter. For Nickleby Company, the distribution is as presented in Exhibit 13-4.

Exhibit 13-4

Distribution of Service Department Overhead Using the Direct Method

		Producing Departments		Service Departments	
	Total	A	B	Y	Z
Factory overhead before distribution of service departments	$196,300	$60,000	$ 80,000	$36,300	$20,000
Distribution of:					
Department Y		18,150	18,150	(36,300)*	
Department Z		5,714	14,286		(20,000)**
Total factory overhead	$196,300	$83,864	$112,436		

* 40/80 to A, 40/80 to B
** 20/70 to A, 50/70 to B

Step Method. An alternative method, the **step method**, transfers the costs of service departments by a sequence of steps; that is, in a prescribed order by department. The step method is also called the **sequential method** because costs are allocated from service departments in a predetermined sequence. Once cost is allocated from a service department, no other service department's cost is allocated back to it in a subsequent step. To use this method, a particular order must be decided on for allocating the service departments' costs because the order of departments does make a difference in the calculation. A partial recognition of interrelated benefits among service departments is achieved with this method. In the direct method, no such interrelationships are recognized. However, the step method is still only a partial consideration of the service departments' mutual benefits, because after distribution of a service department's costs, no further distributions are made to that department.

Service departments usually are distributed in order of the amount of service rendered and received. One approach is to start with the department serving the greatest number of other departments and receiving service from the smallest number of other service departments. Alternatively, the costs of the service department that provides the largest dollar value of services to other service departments can be distributed first.

The Nickleby Company data are used to demonstrate the step method in Exhibit 13-5. Because the service departments provide service to each other, the order of allocation is based on the amount of service department cost. The allocation begins with Department Y because it provides $7,260 of service to Department Z (20% of $36,300), while Department Z provides only $6,000 of service to Department Y (30% of $20,000). If Department Z is distributed first, different results are obtained. (The greater the number of service departments, the greater is the number of different allocation results that can be obtained by distributing the departments in different sequences.)

Exhibit 13-5

Distribution of Service Department Overhead Using the Step Method

		Producing Departments		Service Departments	
	Total	A	B	Y	Z
Factory overhead before distribution of service departments............................	$196,300	$60,000	$ 80,000	$36,300	$20,000
Distribution of:					
Department Y.......................		14,520	14,520	(36,300)*	7,260
Department Z.......................		7,789	19,471		(27,260)**
Total factory overhead................	$196,300	$82,309	$113,991		

* 40/100 to A, 40/100 to B, 20/100 to Z
** 20/70 to A, 50/70 to B

Simultaneous Method. When service departments serve each other, the step method prorates incompletely because one department is distributed before another—therefore, before receiving any cost proration from the other. Although the resulting difference in the final costs of a producing department may or may not be significant, the direct method and the step method fail to measure the total cost of individual service departments. This total cost information can be useful for product costing and cost control.

The **simultaneous method**, also called the **algebraic method**, considers completely all interrelationships among all service departments. The Nickleby Company data again are used for illustration. The costs of the service departments are allocated simultaneously, using the following algebraic technique.[4] First, each service department's total cost is expressed in the form of an equation as in the following calculation. For example, the first equation states that the total cost of Department Y is not limited to its reported cost of $36,300, but also includes 30% of the total cost of Department Z, because Y uses 30% of Z's services.

$$\begin{aligned}
\text{Let:}\quad & Y = \$36{,}300 + .30Z \\
& Z = \$20{,}000 + .20Y \\
\text{Substituting:}\quad & Y = \$36{,}300 + .30\ (\$20{,}000 + .20Y) \\
\text{Solving:}\quad & Y = \$36{,}300 + \$6{,}000 + .06Y \\
& .94Y = \$42{,}300 \\
& Y = \$45{,}000 \\
\text{Substituting:}\quad & Z = \$20{,}000 + .20\ (\$45{,}000) \\
\text{Solving:}\quad & Z = \$20{,}000 + \$9{,}000 = \$29{,}000
\end{aligned}$$

The distribution is then accomplished as shown in Exhibit 13-6.

Calculating Departmental Overhead Rates

After service department costs have been distributed, producing department overhead rates can be calculated by dividing each producing department's final total overhead by a selected allocation base. In Exhibit 13-3, three different bases are used: direct labor hours, machine hours, and direct labor cost.

[4] Matrix algebra is useful when there is a large number of service departments and the allocation is done by computer. See Thomas H. Williams and Charles H. Griffin, "Matrix Theory and Cost Allocation," *The Accounting Review*, Vol. 39, No. 3, pp. 671–678, and John L. Livingstone, "Matrix Algebra and Cost Allocation," *The Accounting Review*, Vol. 43, No. 3, pp. 503–508.

Exhibit 13-6

Distribution of Service Department Overhead Using the Simultaneous Method

		Producing Departments		Service Departments	
	Total	**A**	**B**	**Y**	**Z**
Factory overhead before distribution of service departments	$196,300	$60,000	$ 80,000	$36,300	$20,000
Distribution of:					
Department Y		18,000	18,000	(45,000)*	9,000
Department Z		5,800	14,500	8,700	(29,000)**
Total factory overhead	$196,300	$83,800	$ 112,500		

* 40/100 to A, 40/100 to B, 20/100 to Z
** 20/100 to A, 50/100 to B, 30/100 to Y

This discussion has described methods by which all factory overhead costs, for both producing and service departments, are assigned to work in process by accumulating factory overhead in producing departments and using overhead rates in the producing departments only. However, it is possible to assign certain service department costs directly from the service department to work in process. For example, materials handling costs can be accumulated in a materials handling department and a materials-cost-oriented rate used for assigning these costs directly to work in process. Such an approach can employ a transactions base, as discussed in Chapter 12 and in Chapter 14.

Using Departmental Overhead Rates

During the fiscal year, as information becomes available at the end of each week or month, factory overhead is applied to a job or process by inserting the applied overhead figure into the overhead section of a job cost sheet (in job order costing) or a departmental cost of production report (in process costing). Amounts applied are summarized periodically for entry into the general journal. The summary entry applicable to DeWitt Products is illustrated as follows:

Work in Process	285,000	
Applied Overhead—Cutting Department (21,005 actual direct labor hours × $4)		84,020
Applied Overhead—Planing Department (8,500 actual machine hours × $6.40)		54,400
Applied Overhead—Assembly Department ($111,700 actual direct labor cost × 60%)		67,020
Applied Overhead—Upholstery Department (22,100 actual direct labor hours × $3.60)		79,560

A separate work in process account can be used for each producing department, instead of the single work in process account illustrated here. In such a case, debits are made to departmental work in process accounts in the same amounts as the corresponding credits in the preceding journal entry.

Actual Overhead—Departmentalized

Actual overhead is summarized in the overhead control account in the general ledger. Details are entered into the factory overhead subsidiary ledger. Departmentalization of overhead requires that each cost be charged to a department as well as to a specific cost account. These charges are collected on departmental cost analysis sheets, which serve as the overhead subsidiary ledger. A portion of the form used for both producing and service departments is shown here.

DEPARTMENTAL COST ANALYSIS SHEET

Department No. 1–Cutting For March, 19–

Explanation	Date	411	412	413	421	433	451	453	Summary

In this form, each column represents a certain class of factory overhead that will be charged to the department. For example, the column coded 411 represents supervisors, and 412 represents indirect labor. The sum of all departmental entries equals the amount of a general journal debit to Factory Overhead Control.

Entries to departmental cost analysis sheets, whether computerized or manual, are facilitated by combining department numbers and cost codes. A code such as 1412 indicates that Department 1 (Cutting) is charged with indirect labor (Code 412). The chart of accounts establishes the codes. The subsidiary ledger also includes a sheet for each indirect factory cost not originally charged to a department, so that the total of the subsidiary overhead ledger equals the total in the factory overhead control account.

Steps at End of Fiscal Period

At the end of the fiscal period, actual overhead costs are assembled in the same manner as estimated costs at the beginning of the period. When actual indirect departmental overhead is distributed among all departments, and service departments' costs are redistributed to the producing departments, then it is possible to compare actual and applied overhead and calculate the over- or underapplied factory overhead for each producing department. The following steps are performed.

1. The actual direct departmental overhead of producing departments and service departments and indirect departmental overhead are summarized (Exhibit 13-7).
2. A second survey of the actual levels of allocation bases experienced during the year is prepared (Exhibit 13-8).
3. Actual indirect departmental overhead is allocated based on the results of the end-of-year survey (Exhibits 13-7 and 13-8).
4. Actual service department costs are allocated to benefiting departments based on the end-of-year survey (Exhibits 13-8 and 13-9).
5. Actual overhead is compared with applied overhead, both for the facility as a whole and for each producing department, and the over- or underapplied factory overhead is calculated (Exhibit 13-9).

DeWitt Products
Actual Departmental Factory Overhead
for the Year 19—

			Producing Departments				Service Departments			
Cost Account	F or V	Total	Cutting	Planing	Assembly	Upholstery	Materials Handling	Inspection	Utilities	General Factory
Direct departmental costs:										
Supervisors	F	$ 70,000	$ 9,000	$ 8,000	$ 8,000	$ 8,000	$10,000	$ 6,000	$ 9,000	$12,000
Indirect labor	F	9,000	1,000	2,000	1,000	1,500	1,000	500	1,000	1,000
	V	63,000	9,800	2,800	4,200	6,000	10,000	7,300	9,000	13,900
Labor fringe benefits	F	10,000	1,500	1,000	1,000	1,000	2,000	1,000	1,500	1,000
	V	45,000	10,000	11,400	9,700	8,000	1,700	1,300	1,600	1,300
Indirect materials	F	4,000	500	500	800	1,200	300	200	200	300
	V	23,000	4,300	3,600	2,900	5,400	1,800	1,200	2,100	1,700
Repairs and maintenance	F	3,000	600	500	700	600			300	300
	V	12,000	1,700	1,800	2,000	2,100	600	300	2,500	1,000
Depreciation—equipment	F	13,000	1,500	3,500	1,000	3,000				4,000
Total direct departmental cost		$252,000	$39,900	$35,100	$31,300	$36,800	$27,400	$17,800	$27,200	$36,500
Indirect departmental costs:										
Electric power	F	$ 2,000							$ 2,000	
	V	14,000							14,000	
Fuel	F	1,000							1,000	
	V	7,000							7,000	
Water	F	1,000							1,000	
	V	3,000							3,000	
Depreciation—buildings	F	5,000	$ 1,250	$ 1,000	$ 1,500	$ 1,250				
Property tax	F	4,000	1,000	800	1,200	1,000				
Insurance (fire)	F	3,000	750	600	900	750				
Total indirect departmental cost		$ 40,000	$ 3,000	$ 2,400	$ 3,600	$ 3,000			$28,000	
Total actual departmental factory overhead before distribution of service departments		$292,000	$42,900	$37,500	$34,900	$39,800	$27,400	$17,800	$55,200	$36,500

EXHIBIT 13-7

EXHIBIT 13-8

DeWitt Products
Factory Survey at End of Year

Producing Department	Number of Employees*	%	Kilo-watt-Hours	%	Horse-power-Hours	%	Floor Area (in square feet)	%	Cost of Materials Requisi-tioned	%
Cutting	9.1	24	16,978	26	210,000	42	5,250	25	$193,500	45
Planing.........	6.5	17	5,224	8	110,000	22	4,200	20	43,000	10
Assembly	10.6	28	16,325	25	90,000	18	6,300	30	47,300	11
Upholstery....	11.8	31	26,773	41	90,000	18	5,250	25	146,200	34
Total............	38.0	100	65,300	100	500,000	100	21,000	100	$430,000	100

* Average based on portion of year employed.

Chapters 17 and 18 discuss the analysis of the overhead cost variances that make up each over- or underapplied amount.

Multiple Overhead Rates

In a given company there may be a significant amount of labor-related overhead, machine-related overhead, materials-related overhead, or some combination of these. Any combination of two or more raises the possibility of using two or more overhead allocation bases. Further, some components of overhead cost may not be closely related to the usage of labor, machinery, materials, or any other measure of production volume. They may be related to activities or transactions such as the number of setups or the number of product design changes, neither of which is a measure of production volume. Costing systems that include one or more non-volume-related factors among the bases used for allocating overhead are called activity costing systems and are discussed in Chapter 14. The remainder of this section deals only with volume-related allocation bases.

Many plants have large overhead costs related to two or more bases, but this does not present costing problems if the product line is simple (one product, with minor variations, produced in large lots). Reasonable product costs can be calculated in these circumstances by using a single overhead allocation base.[5] Such a simple product line is more likely to be associated with process costing than with job order costing.

Many job order settings involve a diverse product line—a number of very different products, each of which can be produced in several sizes, grades, configurations, or types. For example, machine-tool manufacturers generally produce a variety of machine tools. One size of one metal-cutting tool can be fitted with manual, automatic, or computerized controls, digital or analog displays, and any combination of lubrication, noise-reduction, and safety devices. Some variations result in greater amounts of material-related overhead and others in greater amounts of machine-related overhead, so reliable product costs data cannot be obtained by using any single predetermined overhead rate.

[5] Typically the base is direct labor cost or direct labor hours, for which accurate measurements are available already. If direct labor is an insignificant part of total cost, or if it is not measured separately, machine hours or some other easily measured activity can be used.

DeWitt Products
Distribution of Actual Service Department Costs
and
Computation of Departmental Over- or Underapplied Factory Overhead
for the Year 19—

		Producing Departments				Service Departments			
Cost Account	**Total**	**Cutting**	**Planing**	**Assembly**	**Upholstery**	**Materials Handling**	**Inspection**	**Utilities**	**General Factory**
Total departmental factory overhead before distribution of service departments	$292,000	$42,900	$37,500	$ 34,900	$ 39,800	$27,400	$17,800	$55,200	$36,500
Distribution of service department costs:									
Materials handling (Base: estimated cost of materials requisitioned)		$12,330	$ 2,740	$ 3,014	$ 9,316	(27,400)			
Inspection (Base: equally to assembly and upholstery departments)				8,900	8,900		(17,800)		
Utilities:									
(Bases: 20% on kwh		2,870	883	2,760	4,527			(11,040)	
50% on hph		11,592	6,072	4,968	4,968			(27,600)	
30% on floor area)		4,140	3,312	4,968	4,140			(16,560)	
General factory (Base: number of employees)		8,760	6,205	10,220	11,315				(36,500)
Total service department cost distributed		$39,692	$19,212	$ 34,830	$ 43,166				
Total actual departmental factory overhead after distribution of service departments	$292,000	$82,592	$56,712	$ 69,730	$ 82,966				
Total applied factory overhead	285,000	84,020	54,400	67,020	79,560				
(Over-) or underapplied factory overhead	$ 7,000	$ (1,428)	$ 2,312	$ 2,710	$ 3,406				

EXHIBIT 13-9

One solution is to divide overhead into two or more categories, called **cost pools**, and calculate an overhead rate for each pool.[6] The allocation bases can include machine hours for a machine-related cost pool, direct labor hours or direct labor cost for a labor-related pool, and the number of parts or the cost or weight of direct material used for a material-related pool. The result is a multiple-part calculation of applied overhead. A job cost sheet in a nondepartmentalized plant still has three cost sections—direct material costs, direct labor costs, and applied factory overhead—but the section for overhead applied shows two or more calculations, each based on a different predetermined rate.

Do not confuse this approach to multiple overhead rates with the existence of multiple departments within a factory. If multiple departments exist, a job order cost sheet shows direct material, direct labor, and applied overhead for each department. A labor-driven department is likely to apply its overhead cost based on labor hours or labor cost, and a machine-driven department may apply its overhead cost based on machine hours. But within each department, there still may be only one overhead cost pool and one allocation base. In contrast, the use of multiple cost pools in one department or in a nondepartmentalized factory means that two or more forms of overhead application are carried out simultaneously, and their sum is the total overhead charged to jobs.

Refer to the completed job order cost sheet shown in Figure 5-1, and recall that separate departments do not exist within Rayburn Company. Suppose $100,000 of labor-related overhead, $200,000 of machine-related overhead, 25,000 direct labor hours, and 10,000 machine hours are the expected totals for the year. What if some of Rayburn Company's jobs require much machine time and little labor, while others require the opposite mix? A single overhead rate based on labor would assign too much cost to labor-intensive jobs and too little to machine-intensive jobs. A single rate based on machine hours would do just the opposite. Neither approach provides reliable job cost information. One solution is to calculate two rates: $4 per direct labor hour ($100,000 of expected labor-related overhead divided by 25,000 expected direct labor hours) and $20 per machine hour ($200,000 of expected machine-related overhead divided by 10,000 expected machine hours). The cost sheet shown in Figure 5-1 would then have a two-part calculation in its applied overhead section:

196 direct labor hours	× $4 =	$ 784
29.4 machine hours	× $20 =	588
Factory overhead applied	=	$1,372

Overhead Departmentalization in Nonmanufacturing Businesses and Not-for-Profit Organizations

Responsible control of departmental costs is equally essential in nonmanufacturing activities. The following large, complex entities should be divided into administrative and supervisory departments, sections, or service units for cost planning and control:

1. Nonmanufacturing segments of manufacturing concerns (e.g., marketing departments—see Chapter 25)

[6] For an example, see John W. Jonez and Michael A. Wright, "Material Burdening: Management Accounting *Can* Support Competitive Strategy," *Management Accounting*, Vol. 69, No. 2, pp. 27–31.

2. Retail stores
3. Banks and other financial institutions
4. Insurance companies
5. Educational institutions
6. Service organizations (hotels, motels, hospitals, nursing homes, law firms, accounting firms, medical or dental practices, and realtors)
7. Federal, state, and local governments and their agencies

Large retail stores have practiced departmentalization for many years by grouping their activities into the following typical categories: administration, occupancy, sales promotion and advertising, purchasing, selling, and delivery. These groups incur costs similar to those in manufacturing businesses. The occupancy category is almost identical to general factory and includes such expenses as building repairs, rent and property taxes, insurance on buildings and fixtures, light, heat, power, and depreciation on buildings and fixtures. In a parallel to factory allocations, group costs are prorated to revenue-producing sales departments by means of a charging or billing rate.

Financial institutions departmentalize their organizations to control expenses and establish a profitability rating of individual activities. The size of the institution and types of services offered determine the number of departments. The accumulation of departmental costs again parallels that in a factory. Direct costs, such as salaries, supplies, and depreciation of equipment, are charged directly. General costs, such as light, heat, and air conditioning, are prorated to the departments on appropriate bases. As income and costs are ascertained, it is possible to create a work cost unit that permits charging customer accounts for services rendered and analyzing account profitabilities.

The work of insurance companies is facilitated by dividing work among departments, some of which can have several hundred employees. This departmentalization can include actuarial, premium collection, group insurance, policyholders' service, registrar, medical, and legal information.

Educational institutions and service organizations find it increasingly necessary to budget their costs by departments to control costs and to calculate adequate fees for their services. Medicare makes knowledge of costs mandatory in hospitals and nursing homes. Departmentalization assists management in creating a costing or charging rate for short- or long-term care, for special services, for nurses' instruction, and for professional services such as surgical, medical, X-ray, laboratory examinations, and prescriptions.

Federal, state, and local governments employ a great number of people in a vast number of departments and agencies. Municipalities are good examples because their varied services are familiar. Some common services or departments are street cleaning, street repairing and paving, public works projects, police and fire departments, city hospitals, sewage disposal plants, and trash and garbage collection. These services should be budgeted and their costs controlled by responsibility accounting. Because the costs incurred generally are not linked to revenue but rather to services or benefits, an attempt should be made to measure the operating efficiency of an activity based on some unit of measurement such as per capita (police), per mile (street paving and cleaning), and per ton (trash and garbage collection). Increasing costs require additional revenue, which means additional taxes, and taxpayers expect efficient service in return.

Federal and state governments must be made equally aware of the need for responsible cost control, so that services are rendered at the lowest cost with greatest efficiency. With their many departments and agencies and huge sums budgeted, governments must ensure that these activities are being administered by cost-conscious and service-minded staff. The departmentalization process helps to assure the achievement of this goal.

Summary

Most production systems are divided into departments. Producing departments engage in the conversion of output, and service departments support the work of producing departments. Overhead rates can be established for each department, permitting improved product costing and cost control.

In calculating both budgeted and actual departmental overhead, some costs are identified directly with departments, such as supervisors' salaries; others, the indirect departmental costs such as building rent, are distributed among departments. Next, the total costs of service departments are redistributed to the producing departments by the direct, step, or simultaneous method so that all overhead is then identified with the producing departments. If predetermined overhead rates are calculated for each producing department, the amount of over- or underapplied overhead can be identified for each producing department as well as for the facility as a whole.

Key Terms

departmentalization *(328)*
producing department *(329)*
service department *(329)*
direct method *(338)*
step method *(340)*
sequential method *(340)*
simultaneous method or algebraic method *(341)*
cost pools *(347)*

Discussion Questions

Q13-1 State advantages of departmental overhead rates compared to a single plantwide rate.

Q13-2 The statement has been made that the entire process of departmentalizing factory overhead is an extension of methods used when a single overhead rate is used. Explain.

Q13-3 A company uses departmental factory overhead rates based on direct labor hours. Is the sum of departmental over- or underapplied overhead any different if a plantwide or blanket rate is used? Are the costs of goods sold and inventory different?

Q13-4 What is a producing department? A service department? Give illustrations of each.

Q13-5 What are some of the factors that must be considered in deciding the kinds and number of departments required to control costs and to establish accurate departmental overhead rates?

Q13-6 Why are overhead rates established for subdepartments or cost pools within departments?

Q13-7 Most companies keep plant asset records to identify equipment and its original cost by location or department. However, charges for depreciation, property tax, and fire insurance are often accumulated in general factory accounts and charged to departments on the basis of equipment values. Is this the best method for controlling such costs? If not, suggest possible improvements.

Q13-8 What are the important factors involved in selecting the rate to be used for applying the factory overhead of a producing department?

Q13-9 What are the steps followed in establishing departmental factory overhead rates?

Q13-10 What questions must be resolved in allocating service department costs to benefiting departments?

Q13-11 What methods can be used for allocating service department costs to producing departments? Which is recommended?

Q13-12 Procedures followed in computing departmental factory overhead rates determine the accounting for actual factory overhead. Explain.

Q13-13 How is departmental over- or underapplied overhead determined?

Q13-14 Within one department of a factory, or within a nondepartmentalized factory, the use of a single overhead rate does not necessarily give accurate product cost information if a complex product line is being produced. What is one approach to solving this product-costing problem?

Q13-15 Overhead control in a nonmanufacturing business can be achieved through departmentalization. Explain.

Q13-16 Federal, state, and local governments should practice cost control by means of responsibility accounting. Discuss.

Exercises

E13-1 Transfer Entries. The distribution of a company's actual factory overhead for the past year is given as follows. Budgeted factory overhead for the four producing departments (including apportioned service department costs) is also given for two levels of activity.

Actual Factory Overhead

	A	B	C	D	X	Y	Z	Total
Actual costs	$11,000	$16,000	$ 4,000	$7,000	$ 3,000	$ 5,000	$ 6,000	$52,000
Z's costs	1,500	750	1,250	500	1,000	1,000	(6,000)	
Y's costs	1,800	1,200	1,800	600	600	(6,000)		
X's costs	2,000	1,000	1,200	400	(4,600)			
Total	$16,300	$18,950	$ 8,250	$8,500				$52,000

Budgeted Factory Overhead

	20,000 Hours (Normal)	16,000 Hours
Department A	$17,800	$15,000
Department B	20,200	17,800
Department C	10,600	9,400
Department D	10,600	9,400
Total	$59,200	$51,600

The company uses a predetermined rate for each producing department, based on labor hours at the normal capacity level. Actual hours worked last year were 17,000 for Department A and 18,000 for Department B.

Required: Prepare entries to record the applied factory overhead for Department A and for Department B. (A single work in process account is used.)

E13-2 Entries with Overhead Subsidiary Ledger. The general ledger of Protech Company contains a factory overhead control account supported by a subsidiary ledger showing details by departments. The plant has one service department and three producing departments. The following table shows details with respect to these departments:

	Machining Department	Painting Department	Assembly Department	General Factory Cost Pool
Building space (square feet)	10,000	4,000	4,000	2,000
Cost of machinery	$300,000	$100,000	$60,000	$20,000
Horsepower rating	1,000	-0-	100	150
Worker's compensation insurance rate (per $100)	$1.50	$1.50	$1.00	$1.00

During January, certain assets expired and some liabilities accrued as follows:

(a) Depreciation on buildings, $3,000.
(b) Depreciation on machinery, $9,600.
(c) Property tax for the year ending December 31 is estimated to be $12,000 (60% on buildings and 40% on machinery).
(d) Worker's compensation insurance for January is based on the following earnings of factory employees; Machining Department, $30,000; Painting Department, $12,000; Assembly Department, $16,000; and General Factory Cost Pool, $6,000.
(e) The power meter reading at January 31 shows 12,500 kilowatt-hours consumed. The rate is $.06 per kilowatt-hour.
(f) The heat and light bill for January is $1,800.
(g) Supplies requisitions show $1,800 used in the Machining Department, $2,300 in the Assembly Department, and $410 in the General Factory Cost Pool.

Required: Prepare journal entries. Show details in four departmental overhead columns to support each general journal debit.

E13-3 Rate Calculation—Plantwide versus Departmental Direct Method. East Tennessee Company uses the direct method in allocating service department costs to producing departments. Costs of Department S1 are allocated on the basis of number of employees, while costs of Department S2 are allocated on the basis of machine hours. The allocation bases used in calculating predetermined overhead rates are machine hours in Department P1 and direct labor hours in Department P2.

	Producing Departments		Service Departments	
	P1	P2	S1	S2
Budgeted factory overhead	$410,000	$304,000	$100,000	$50,000
Number of employees	90	210	20	28
Machine hours	64,000	16,000		
Direct labor hours	35,000	100,000		

The following data pertain to Job 437:

	Department P1	Department P2
Materials cost	$90	$40
Direct labor hours	1	2
Machine hours	3	1

Required:

(1) Calculate predetermined factory overhead rates for the producing departments and compute the resulting overhead cost of Job 437.
(2) Calculate a plantwide predetermined factory overhead rate based on direct labor hours and compute the resulting overhead cost of Job 437.

CGA-Canada (adapted). Reprint with permission.

E13-4 Rate Calculation—Plantwide versus Departmental Step Method. Dell Company allocates some service department costs to other service departments. However, after a department's costs have been allocated, no costs are assigned back to it. Buildings and Grounds is allocated first, using square feet as a base. The number of employees is used as a base for allocating Factory Administration.

	Machining	Assembly	Buildings and Grounds	Factory Administration
Budgeted factory overhead	$360,000	$420,000	$40,000	$25,000
Square feet	9,000	10,000	1,500	1,000
Number of employees	440	460	50	30
Direct labor hours	452,000	567,250		
Machine hours	195,600	23,000		

Required:

(1) Compute a plantwide factory overhead rate, using direct labor hours as a base. Round answer to the nearest cent.

(2) Compute the factory overhead rate for Machining, using machine hours as a base, and for Assembly, using direct labor hours as a base. Round answers to the nearest cent.

CGA-Canada (adapted). Reprint with permission.

E13-5 Departmental Distribution of Estimated Overhead—Direct Method; Rate Calculation. Wiltonen Company's factory contains two producing departments, Cutting and Assembly, and two service departments, Maintenance and Administration. Maintenance Department cost is allocated based on square feet, and Administration Department cost is allocated based on number of employees. Service department costs are allocated to producing departments only. Producing department overhead rates are computed based on machine hours.

The estimated annual data are as follows:

	Cutting	Assembly	Maintenance	Administration
Number of employees	150	100	40	30
Square feet	21,000	9,000	4,000	3,000
Machine hours	25,000	20,000		
Overhead budget	$520,000	$400,000	$200,000	$150,000

Required: Prepare a factory overhead distribution and compute overhead rates.

CGA-Canada (adapted). Reprint with permission.

E13-6 Departmental Distribution of Estimated Overhead—Step Method; Rate Calculation. The Nettleville Mixing Company has two producing departments, Mixing and Finishing, and two service departments, Cafeteria and Product Design. The company assigns service department costs to other service departments; however, after a department's costs have been allocated, no costs are assigned back to it. Cafeteria is allocated first, based on the number of employees, and Product Design is allocated based on the number of product orders. In calculating predetermined factory overhead rates, machine hours are used as the basis in both producing departments.

The following estimated data are provided:

	Cafeteria	Product Design	Mixing	Finishing
Budget overhead	$10,000	$50,000	$100,000	$200,000
Number of employees	10	5	65	130
Number of product orders			100	200
Machine hours			40,000	60,000

Required: Develop predetermined factory overhead rates for the Mixing and Finishing departments.

CGA-Canada (adapted). Reprint with permission.

E13-7 Departmental Distribution of Estimated Overhead—Step Method; Rate Calculation. The Nickey Company uses the step method in allocating the costs of its two service departments, S1 and S2, to its two producing departments, P1 and P2. S1 is allocated first on the basis of number of employees. S2 is allocated on the basis of machine hours. Departmental overhead rates are based on machine hours in P1 and direct labor hours in P2. The following budget data are available:

	S1	S2	P1	P2
Budgeted overhead	$10,000	$34,750	$200,000	$300,000
Number of employees	15	10	180	210
Machine hours			4,000	3,000
Direct labor hours			5,000	10,000

Required:

(1) Develop predetermined overhead rates for the producing departments.

(2) If Nickey Company decides to change to a plantwide rate based on direct labor hours, what will that rate be?

(3) Why are separate departmental rates preferable to a single plantwide rate?

CGA-Canada (adapted). Reprint with permission.

E13-8 Departmental Distribution of Estimated Overhead—Step Method; Rate Calculation; Job Order Costing. Tenzell Company has two producing departments, Machining and Assembly, and two service departments, Maintenance and Personnel. The step method is used in allocating service department costs to producing departments, with Maintenance allocated first, based on square feet. In calculating predetermined factory overhead rates, machine hours are used as a base in Machining and direct labor hours are used as a base in Assembly.

Budgeted monthly cost and other operating data are as follows:

	Maintenance	Personnel	Machining	Assembly
Factory overhead	$30,000	$15,000	$150,000	$75,000
Square feet	2,000	4,000	19,000	17,000
Number of employees	5	3	40	80
Machine hours			22,700	
Direct labor hours			8,000	16,625

Cost and related data pertaining to Job No. 3752 are:

Machining:	Machine hours	10
	Materials	$60
	Direct labor ....4 hours @	$ 6
Assembly:	Materials	$ 7
	Direct labor ....11 hours @	$ 9

Required:

(1) Develop predetermined factory overhead rates for Machining and Assembly.

(2) Compute the total cost of Job No. 3752.

CGA-Canada (adapted). Reprint with permission.

E13-9 Departmental Distribution of Estimated Overhead—Simultaneous Method. The estimated departmental factory overhead for producing departments S and T and the estimated costs of service departments E, F, and G (before any service department allocations) are:

Producing Department		Service Department	
S	$60,000	E	$20,000
T	90,000	F	20,000
		G	10,000

The interdependence of the departments is as follows:

	Services Provided By		
Department	E	F	G
Producing—S	—	30%	40%
Producing—T	50%	40	30
Service—E	—	20	—
Service—F	20	—	—
Service—G	30	10	—
Marketing	—	—	20
General Office	—	—	10
	100%	100%	100%

Required:

(1) Compute the final amount of estimated overhead of each service department after reciprocal transfer costs have been calculated algebraically.

(2) Compute the total factory overhead of each producing department and the amount of Department G cost assigned to the Marketing Department and to General Office.

E13-10 Departmental Distribution of Actual Overhead—Step Method. The Minzell Mining Corporation has producing departments A and B, and service departments C, D, E, and F. Costs are distributed from F first, D second, C third, and E fourth. It is the company's policy that once a service department's costs have been allocated, no costs from other service departments are to be allocated to it. F distributes one half of its costs to A and the remainder to D and E on the basis of the number of employees. D distributes its costs on the basis of investment in equipment, C's are assigned to B, and E's are distributed on the basis of floor space. The following information pertains to the month just ended:

Department	Cost	Square Feet	Employees	Investment in Equipment
A	$15,000	2,000	40	$170,000
B	12,000	3,000	20	80,000
C	12,000	4,000	20	130,000
D	8,000	2,000	30	70,000
E	2,000	1,500	20	50,000
F	2,000	2,500	10	30,000
Total	$51,000	15,000	140	$530,000

Required: Distribute service department overhead.

E13-11 Departmental Distribution of Actual Overhead—Step Method. Todd Company has two producing departments, A and B, and four service departments, C, D, E, and F. Costs are distributed from Department F first, D second, C third, and E fourth. The company assigns some service department costs to other service departments; however, after a department's costs have been allocated, no costs are assigned back to it.

Department F distributes one-half of its costs to A and the remainder, on the basis of the number of employees, to Departments D and E. Department D distributes its costs on the basis of the investment in equipment. C's costs are assigned to B, and E's expenses are distributed on the basis of floor space.

The following information is available for March:

Department	Actual Costs	Square Feet	Employees	Investment in Equipment (in thousands)
A	$100,000	1,500	20	$12,500
B	80,000	2,500	10	6,000
C	120,000	3,000	10	10,000
D	56,000	1,500	15	5,000
E	15,000	1,000	10	4,000
F	30,000	1,200	5	2,000
Total	$401,000	10,700	70	$ 39,500

Required: Distribute service department costs, based on the data given.

E13-12 Departmental Distribution of Actual Overhead—Simultaneous Method. Potter Company has decided to distribute the costs of service departments by the simultaneous method. The producing departments are P1 and P2, the service departments are S1 and S2, and the monthly data are:

	Actual Factory Overhead Costs before Distribution	Services Provided By S1	Services Provided By S2
P1	$94,000	40%	50%
P2	85,000	50	30
S1	20,000	—	20
S2	17,600	10	—

Required: Compute the total factory overhead of producing department P1 after distribution of service department costs.

E13-13 Multiple Overhead Rates. Smith Tool Shop has a diverse product line, with some jobs requiring much labor and little machine use and others requiring the opposite mix. Because no single base for a predetermined overhead rate provides STS management with reliable product cost information, overhead is classified into two cost pools, and two predetermined overhead rates are used. For 19A, it is estimated that total overhead costs will consist of $200,000 of overhead related to the usage of direct labor hours and $300,000 of overhead related to machine usage. Total machine usage is expected to be 4,000 hours for the year, and total direct labor hours are expected to be 16,000.

Job 345, which was completed early in the year 19A, required $1,000 of direct material, 30 hours of labor at $10 per hour, and 10 hours of machine time.

Required:

(1) Calculate the predetermined overhead rates for 19A.
(2) Prepare a completed job cost sheet for Job 345.

E13-14 Multiple Overhead Rates. Noel's Bulk Fabricators (NBF) produces a varied product line in a highly automated facility without the use of direct labor. A large number of bulky materials are used, and weight-related material handling costs are high. Some jobs use much bulky material and little machine time, and others use the opposite mix. Because no single base for a predetermined overhead rate provides NBF with reliable product cost information, overhead is classified into two cost pools, and two predetermined overhead rates are used. For 19A, it is estimated that total overhead costs will consist of $525,000 of overhead related to materials and $900,000 of overhead related to machine usage. Total machine usage is expected to be 3,600 hours for the year, and the total weight of materials used is expected to be 300 tons.

Job 103, which was completed early in the year 19A, required 70 hours of machine time and four tons of materials with a direct material cost of $22,000.

Required:

(1) Calculate the predetermined overhead rates for 19A.
(2) Prepare a completed job cost sheet for Job 103.

Problems

P13-1 Departmental Distribution of Estimated Overhead; Direct Method and Rate Calculation; Parts of Step and Simultaneous Methods. Great Manufacturing has two producing departments, Grinding and Smoothing, and two service departments, Maintenance and General Factory. Departmental overhead costs for the coming year have been budgeted as follows, before the distribution of service department costs to producing departments: Grinding, $175,000; Smoothing, $230,000; Maintenance, $76,000; and General Factory, $200,000. Maintenance costs are allocated based on hours of maintenance services provided. General Factory costs are allocated based on the maximum number of employees during the year.

Overhead will be applied to products using predetermined departmental overhead rates. The predetermined rate in Grinding is based on machine hours, and the predetermined rate in Smoothing is based on direct labor hours. The factory survey for the coming year is summarized as follows:

	Grinding	Smoothing	Maintenance	General Factory
Direct labor hours used	7,500	30,000	0	0
Machine hours used	4,000	2,000	0	0
Hours of maintenance service used	180	900	200	720
Number of materials requisitions	200	10	30	10
Average number of employees	5	2	1	2
Maximum number of employees	6	3	1	2

Required:

(1) Calculate, to the nearest cent, the predetermined departmental overhead rates for the coming year, using the direct method to allocate service department costs.
(2) Calculate, to the nearest cent, the predetermined departmental overhead rates for the coming year, using the simultaneous method.
(3) Calculate, to the nearest cent, the predetermined departmental overhead rates for the coming year, using the step method. Use the following department allocation sequence: first Maintenance, then General Factory.

P13-2 Revision of Departmental Overhead Rates. Files Inc. manufactures metal office cabinets. The company's single manufacturing plant consists of the Cutting, Assembly, and Finishing Departments. Files Inc. uses departmental rates for applying factory overhead to production and maintains separate factory overhead control and applied factory overhead accounts for each of the three production departments.

The following predetermined departmental factory overhead rates were calculated for the fiscal year ending May 31, 19B.

Department	Rate
Cutting	$2.40 per machine hour
Assembly	5.00 per direct labor hour
Finishing	1.60 per direct labor dollar

Information regarding actual operations of the plant for the 6 months ended November 30, 19A is as follows:

	Department		
	Cutting	Assembly	Finishing
Factory overhead costs	$22,600	$56,800	$98,500
Machine hours	10,800	2,100	4,400
Direct labor hours	6,800	12,400	16,500
Direct labor dollars	$40,800	$62,000	$66,000

Based on this experience and updated projections for the last 6 months of the fiscal year, Files Inc. revised its operating budget. Projected data regarding factory overhead and operating activity for each department for the 6 months ending May 31, 19B, are as follows:

	Department		
	Cutting	Assembly	Finishing
Factory overhead costs	$23,400	$57,500	$96,500
Machine hours	9,200	2,000	4,200
Direct labor hours	6,000	13,000	16,000
Direct labor dollars	$36,000	$65,000	$64,000

Diane Potter, the controller, plans to develop revised departmental factory overhead rates that will be more representative of efficient operations for the current fiscal year ending May 31, 19B. She has decided to combine the actual results for the first 6 months of the fiscal year with the projections for the next 6 months to develop the revised departmental application rates. She then plans to adjust the applied factory overhead accounts for each department through November 19A to recognize the revised application rates. The analysis that follows was prepared by Potter from general ledger account balances as of November 30, 19A.

Account	Direct Material	Direct Labor	Factory Overhead	Account Balance
Work in Process Inventory	$ 53,000	$ 95,000	$ 12,000	$ 160,000
Finished Goods	96,000	176,000	48,000	320,000
Cost of Goods Sold	336,000	604,000	180,000	1,120,000
	$485,000	$875,000	$240,000	$1,600,000

Required:

(1) Determine the balance of the applied factory overhead accounts as of November 30, 19A, before any revision for the following departments:
   (a) Cutting
   (b) Assembly
   (c) Finishing

(2) Calculate the revised departmental factory overhead rates that Files Inc. should use for the remainder of the fiscal year ending May 31, 19B.

(3) Prepare an analysis that shows how the applied factory overhead account for each production department should be adjusted as of November 30, 19A, and prepare the adjusting entry to correct all general ledger accounts that are affected.
(ICMA adapted)

P13-3 Departmental Distribution of Estimated Overhead—Step Method; Rate Calculation. The president of Orange Products Company has been critical of the product costing methods by which factory overhead is charged to products by a plantwide overhead rate. The chief accountant suggested a departmentalization of the factory for the purpose of calculating departmental factory overhead rates. The following estimated direct departmental overhead data were accumulated on an annual basis:

	Producing Departments			Service Departments		
Overhead Items	**Department 10**	**Department 12**	**Department 14**	**Storeroom**	**Repairs and Maintenance**	**General Factory Cost Pool**
Supervision	$20,500	$16,000	$14,000	$ 7,200	$ 8,000	$24,000
Indirect labor	5,400	6,000	8,000	6,133	7,200	18,000
Indirect supplies	4,850	5,600	5,430	1,400	3,651	1,070
Labor fringe benefits	6,872	9,349	10,145	640	760	2,100
Equipment depreciation	6,000	8,000	10,000	560	1,740	1,100
Property tax, depreciation of buildings, etc						20,000
Total	$43,622	$44,949	$47,575	$15,933	$21,351	$66,270

The annual light and power bill is estimated at $9,300 and is allocated on the basis of electricity usage. The order and bases of distribution of service department costs (using the step method) are as follows:

(a) General Factory Cost Pool—area occupied
(b) Storeroom—estimated requisitions
(c) Repairs and Maintenance—estimated repairs and maintenance hours

The following departmental information is provided:

	Department 10	**Department 12**	**Department 14**	**Storeroom**	**Repairs and Maintenance**	**General Factory Cost Pool**
Percentage of usage of electricity	20%	25%	30%	3%	12%	10%
Area occupied (square feet)	21,000	25,200	29,400	3,360	5,040	2,000
Estimated number of requisitions	124,200	81,000	40,500	—	24,300	6,000
Estimated number of repairs and maintenance hours	4,800	4,200	6,000	3,000	—	1,000
Estimated machine hours	800	900	800	—	—	—

Required: Prepare a factory overhead distribution sheet, with calculation of overhead rates for the producing departments based on machine hours.

P13-4 Departmental Distribution of Estimated Overhead—Direct versus Simultaneous Method; Rate Calculation. Packers Corporation is developing departmental overhead rates based on direct labor hours for its two production departments—Molding and Assembly. The Molding Department employs 20 people, and the Assembly Department employs 80 people. Each person in these two departments works 2,000 hours per year. The production-related overhead costs for the Molding Department are budgeted at $200,000, and the Assembly Department costs are budgeted at $320,000. Two service departments, Repair and Power, support the two production departments and have budgeted costs of $48,000 and $250,000, respectively. The production departments' overhead rates cannot be determined until the service departments' costs are properly allocated. The following schedule reflects the use of the Repair Department's and Power Department's output by the various departments.

	Services Provided	
Department	**Repair Hours**	**KWH**
Molding	1,000	840,000
Assembly	8,000	120,000
Repair	—	240,000
Power	1,000	—
	10,000	1,200,000

Required:

(1) Calculate the overhead rates per direct labor hour for the two producing departments, allocating service department costs to producing departments only. (Round rates to the nearest cent.)

(2) Calculate the overhead rates per direct labor hour for the two producing departments, using the simultaneous method to distribute service department costs. (Round rates to the nearest cent.)

(3) Explain the difference between the methods and provide arguments to support the simultaneous method.

(ICMA adapted)

P13-5 Departmental Distribution of Actual Overhead—Direct, Step and Simultaneous Methods. Mooneys Company operates with two producing departments, P1 and P2, and two service departments, S1 and S2. Actual factory overhead before distribution of service department costs, together with the usage of service from the service departments, is as follows:

Department	Actual Factory Overhead Before Distribution of Service Department Costs	Services Provided By S1	Services Provided By S2
P1	$20,000	40%	20%
P2	23,800	50	40
S1	7,200	—	40
S2	9,000	10	—
	$60,000	100%	100%

Required:

(1) Determine the total factory overhead (including service department costs) for each producing department, allocating service department costs to producing departments only.

(2) Determine the total factory overhead (including service department costs) for each producing department, allocating service department costs stepwise, beginning with Department S2. After a department's expenses have been allocated, no expenses are assigned back to it.

(3) Determine the total factory overhead (including service department costs) for each producing department, using the simultaneous method.

P13-6 Departmental Distribution of Actual Overhead—Simultaneous Method. The controller of Planter Corporation instructs the cost supervisor to use an algebraic procedure for allocating service department costs to producing departments. The corporation's three producing departments are served by three service departments, each of which consumes part of the services of the other two. After primary but before reciprocal distribution, the account balances of the service departments and the interdependence of the departments were tabulated as follows:

Department	Departmental Overhead Before Distribution of Service Departments	Services Provided: Powerhouse	Services Provided: Personnel	Services Provided: General Factory
Mixing	$200,000	25%	35%	25%
Refining	90,000	25	30	20
Finishing	105,000	20	20	20
Powerhouse	16,000	—	10	20
Personnel	29,500	10	—	15
General Factory	42,000	20	5	—
	$482,500	100%	100%	100%

Required:

(1) Compute the final amount of overhead of each service department after reciprocal transfer costs have been calculated algebraically.

(2) Compute the total factory overhead of each producing department.

P13-7 Cost Center Rates. The Cost Department of Gainesville Company applies factory overhead to jobs and products on the basis of predetermined cost center overhead rates. In each of the two producing departments, two cost centers have been set up. For the coming year, the following estimates and other data have been made available:

	Estimated Annual Factory Overhead			Estimated Annual Hours
Department 10	**Fixed**	**Variable**	**Total**	
Cost Center 10-1	$14,040	$23,400	$37,440	15,600
Cost Center 10-2	26,910	43,290	70,200	23,400
Department 20				
Cost Center 20-1	$ 8,320	$21,580	$29,900	26,000
Cost Center 20-2	6,240	19,760	26,000	20,800

Required:

(1) Compute the annual normal cost center overhead rates, based on the estimated machine hours in Department 10 and the estimated direct labor hours in Department 20.

(2) Calculate applied overhead for the four cost centers and the two producing departments on the basis of the following actual machine or labor hours used or worked during February:

	Cost Centers			
	10-1	**10-2**	**20-1**	**20-2**
Machine hours	1,220	2,000		
Labor hours			2,250	1,650

(3) Compute the over- or underapplied overhead for the two producing departments. Actual factory overhead in Department 10 amounted to $9,430 and in Department 20 to $4,005.

P13-8 Multiple Overhead Rates. Machine Tools Inc. (MTI) has a diverse product line. Some jobs require much labor and little machine use, and others require the opposite mix. Because no single base for a predetermined overhead rate provides MTI management with reliable product cost information, overhead is classified into two cost pools, and two predetermined overhead rates are used. For 19A, it is estimated that total overhead costs will consist of $400,000 of overhead related to the usage of direct labor hours and $600,000 of overhead related to machine usage. Total machine usage is expected to be 20,000 hours for the year, and total direct labor hours are expected to be 16,000 hours.

Job 564, which was completed early in the year 19A, required $2,000 of direct materials, 30 hours of labor at $10 per hour, and 10 hours of machine time. Job 632 required $2,000 of direct material, 30 hours of labor at $10 per hour, and 60 hours of machine time.

Required:

(1) Calculate MTI's predetermined overhead rates for 19A.

(2) Determine the total cost of Job 564.

(3) Determine the total cost of Job 632.

(4) If MTI had used a single predetermined overhead rate based on direct labor hours to apply all overhead costs, then:

(a) What would the predetermined rate be?

(b) What would be reported as the total cost of Job 564?

(c) What would be reported as the total cost of Job 632?

(5) Compare the two total cost amounts for Job 564 calculated in requirement 2 and requirement 4b. Compare the two total cost amounts for Job 632 calculated in requirement 3 and requirement 4c. What are the competitive implications of using the single predetermined overhead rate and quoting prices at cost plus a small markup?

Cases

C13-1 Departmental Overhead Rates and Bases. Rose Bach has recently been hired as controller of Empco Inc., a sheet-metal manufacturer. Empco has been in the sheet-metal business for many years and is currently investigating ways to modernize its manufacturing process. At the first staff meeting Bach attended, Bob Kelley, chief engineer, presented a proposal for automating the Drilling Department. Kelley recommended that Empco purchase two robots that would have the capability of replacing eight direct laborers in the department. The cost savings outlined in Kelley's proposal included the elimination of direct labor cost in the Drilling Department, plus a reduction of manufacturing overhead cost in the department to zero, because Empco applies manufacturing overhead on the basis of direct labor dollars using a plantwide rate.

The president of Empco was puzzled by Kelley's explanation of cost savings, believing it made no sense. Bach agreed with the president, explaining that as firms become more automated, they should rethink their manufacturing overhead systems. The president then asked Bach to look into the matter and prepare a report for the next staff meeting.

To refresh her knowledge, Bach reviewed articles on manufacturing overhead allocation for an automated factory and discussed the matter with some of her peers. Bach also gathered the following historical data on the manufacturing overhead rates experienced by Empco over the years. Bach also wanted to have some departmental data to present at the meeting and, using Empco's accounting records, was able to estimate the following annual averages for each producing department in recent years.

Historical Data

Date	Average Annual Direct Labor Cost	Average Annual Manufacturing Overhead Cost	Average Manufacturing Overhead Application Rate
1940s	$1,000,000	$ 1,000,000	100%
1950s	1,200,000	3,000,000	250
1960s	2,000,000	7,000,000	350
1970s	3,000,000	12,000,000	400
1980s	4,000,000	20,000,000	500

Annual Averages

	Cutting Department	Grinding Department	Drilling Department
Direct labor	$ 2,000,000	$1,750,000	$ 250,000
Manufacturing overhead	11,000,000	7,000,000	2,000,000

Required:

(1) Disregarding the proposed use of robots in the Drilling Department, describe the shortcomings of the system for applying overhead that is currently used by Empco.

(2) Explain the misconceptions underlying Bob Kelley's statement that the manufacturing overhead cost in the Drilling Department would be reduced to zero if automation eliminated all direct labor in the department.

(3) Recommend ways to improve Empco's way of applying overhead by describing how it should revise its overhead accounting system:
   (a) in the Cutting and Grinding Departments.
   (b) to accommodate the automation of the Drilling Department. (ICMA adapted)

C13-2 Departmental Factory Overhead Rates. The Cheetah Company produces custom-made stuffed toy animals and competes in a highly competitive marketplace. The company's selling prices are calculated as the cost of production plus a 30% markup. The production process consists of two departments: the Skins Department where the outside liners (skins) are handmade for each toy animal from specially ordered materials, and the Stuffing Department where the skins are filled by machine with a standard stuffing material to complete the toys. The Skins and Stuffing Departments both receive services from the company's two service departments, the Purchasing Department and the Cleaning and Maintenance Department. A description of each service department's operations and the allocation of the costs of these two departments are as follow:

Purchasing:

(a) Purchases all materials and supplies required for all departments.

(b) Its fixed cost is allocated to the two production departments based on the number of square feet each department occupies.

(c) Its variable cost is allocated based on total volume of materials ordered by each department.

Cleaning and Maintenance:

(a) Cleans the entire building and maintains all equipment in the company.

(b) Both variable and fixed costs of the department are allocated to the two production departments on the basis of the number of square feet each department occupies.

Required:

(1) Should the company use a plantwide overhead rate or departmental overhead rates? Explain.

(2) Comment on the company's cost allocation methods, and, where necessary, suggest improvements. Fully justify any suggested improvements.

(SMAC adapted)

C13-3 Types of Factory Overhead Rates. Summerville Inc. engages the services of a CPA firm for the installation of a job order cost system. Preliminary investigation of manufacturing operations discloses the following facts:

(a) The company makes a line of light fixtures and lamps. The materials cost of any particular item ranges from 15% to 60% of total factory cost, depending on the kind of metal and fabric used.

(b) The business is subject to wide cyclical fluctuations, because the sales volume reflects new housing construction.

(c) About 60% of the manufacturing is normally finished during the first quarter of the year.

(d) For the whole plant, the direct labor wage rates range from $6.50 to $12 an hour. However, within each of the eight individual departments, the spread between the high and low wage rate is less than 5%.

(e) Each product requires the use of all eight of the manufacturing departments, but not proportionately.

(f) Within the individual manufacturing departments, factory overhead ranges from 30% to 80% of conversion cost.

Required: Prepare a letter to the president of Summerville Inc., explaining whether its cost system should use the following procedures. Include the reasons supporting each of these recommendations:

(1) A predetermined overhead rate or an actual overhead rate—departmental or plantwide.

(2) A method of factory overhead distribution based on direct labor hours, direct labor cost, or prime cost.

(AICPA adapted)

C13-4 Assigning Costs to Activity Centers in a Data Processing Department. Fitzgerald Associates recently reorganized its computer and data processing activities. In the past, small computer units were located in accounting departments at the firm's plants and subsidiaries. These units have been replaced with a single Electronic Data Processing Department at corporate headquarters. The new department has been in operation for two years, regularly producing reliable and timely data for the past 12 months.

Because the department has focused its activities on converting applications to the new system and producing reports for the plant and subsidiary managements, little attention has been devoted to data processing costs. Now that the department's activities are operating relatively smoothly, company management has requested that the department manager recommend a cost accumulation system to facilitate cost control and the development of suitable service charging rates.

For the past 2 years, the data processing costs have been recorded in one account. The costs have then been allocated to user departments on the basis of computer time used. Following are the costs and charging rate for the current year:

(a) Salaries and benefits	$ 622,600
(b) Supplies	40,000
(c) Equipment maintenance contract	15,000
(d) Insurance	25,000
(e) Heat and air conditioning	36,000
(f) Electricity	50,000
(g) Equipment and furniture depreciation	285,400
(h) Building improvement depreciation	10,000
(i) Building occupancy and security	39,300
(j) Corporate administrative charge	52,700
Total cost	$1,176,000
Computer hours for user processing*	2,750
Hourly rate ($1,176,000 ÷ 2,750)	$428

* Use of available computer hours:	
Testing and debugging programs	250
Setup of jobs	500
Processing jobs	2,750
Downtime for maintenance	750
Idle time	742
Total	4,992

The department manager recommends that the data processing costs be accumulated by five activity centers within the department: Systems Analysis, Programming, Data Preparation, Computer Operations (processing), and Administration. The Administration activity cost should be allocated to the other four activity centers before a separate rate for charging users is developed for each of the first four activities.

The manager notes that the subsidiary accounts within the department contain the following charges:

(a) Salaries and benefits—the salary and benefit costs of all employees in the department.
(b) Supplies—diskette cost, paper cost for printers, and a small amount for miscellaneous other costs.
(c) Equipment maintenance contracts—charges for maintenance contracts covering all equipment.
(d) Insurance—cost of insurance covering the equipment and the furniture.
(e) Heat and air conditioning—a charge from the corporate Heating and Air Conditioning Department estimated to be the differential costs that meet the special needs of the Electronic Data Processing Department.
(f) Electricity—the charge for electricity, based on a separate meter within the department.
(g) Equipment and furniture depreciation—the depreciation charges for all owned equipment and furniture within the department.
(h) Building improvement depreciation—the depreciation charges for the building changes that were required to provide proper environmental control and electrical service for the computer equipment.
(i) Building occupancy and security—the department's share of the depreciation, maintenance, heat, and security costs of the building; these costs are allocated to the department on the basis of square feet occupied.
(j) Corporate administrative charge—the department's share of the corporate administrative costs, which is allocated to the department on the basis of number of employees in the department.

Required:

(1) State whether each of the 10 cost items (a through j) should be allocated to the five activity centers. For each cost item that should be distributed, specify the basis on which the distribution should be made. Justify your answer in each case and indicate if the cost would be included in a rate designed to include only variable costs as opposed to a full cost rate.
(2) Calculate the total number of hours needed to determine the charging rate for Computer Operations. Use the analysis of computer utilization shown as a footnote to the department cost schedule, and assume that the Computer Operations activity cost will be charged to the user departments on the basis of computer hours. Explain. (ICMA adapted)

C13-5 Overhead Analysis. Lakeviews Company uses predetermined departmental overhead rates. The rate for the Fabricating Department is $4 per direct labor hour. Direct labor employees are paid $10.50 per hour. A total of 15,000 direct labor hours were worked in the department during the year. Total overhead charged to the department for supervisors' salaries, indirect labor, labor fringe benefit costs, indirect materials, and service department costs was $65,000.

Required:

(1) Determine the over- or underapplied factory overhead.
(2) Determine the effect on the amount of over- or underapplied factory overhead in each of the following situations. Discuss each item separately, disregarding the other items.
    (a) Direct laborers worked 100 overtime hours for which time and a half was paid. Overtime premium, the amount in excess of the regular rate, is charged as overhead to the department in which the overtime is worked.
    (b) A 35-cents-per-hour wage increase was granted November 1. Direct labor hours worked in November and December totaled 2,500.
    (c) The company cafeteria incurred a $1,500 loss, which was distributed to producing departments on the basis of number of employees. Nine of the 120 employees work in the Fabricating Department. No loss was anticipated when predetermined overhead rates were computed.

C13-6 Factory Overhead Rate Bases. Aqua Furnishings Company, a manufacturer of custom designed restaurant and kitchen furniture, uses job order costing. Actual factory overhead costs incurred during the month are applied to the products on the basis of actual direct labor hours required to produce the product. Overhead costs consist primarily of supervision, employee benefits, maintenance costs, property tax, and depreciation.

Aqua recently won a contract to manufacture the furniture for a new fast food chain that is expanding rapidly in the area. In general, this furniture is durable but of a lower quality than what Aqua normally manufactures. To produce this new line, Aqua must produce more molded plastic parts for furniture than it does for its current line. Through innovative industrial engineering, an efficient manufacturing process for this new furniture line has been developed, requiring only a minimum capital investment. Management is optimistic about the profit improvement the new product line will bring.

At the end of October, the start-up month for the new line, and again in November, the controller prepared a separate income statement for the new product line. On a consolidated basis, the gross profit percentage was normal; however, the profitability for the new line was smaller than expected. Management is concerned that knowledgeable stockholders will criticize the decision to add this lower-quality product line at a time when profitability appeared to be increasing with their standard product line. Gross profit results for the first 9 months, for October, and for November are as follows:

Aqua Furnishings Company
Statement of Gross Profit
(Thousands of Dollars)

	First 9 Months			October			November		
	Fast Food Furniture	Custom Furniture	Consolidated	Fast Food Furniture	Custom Furniture	Consolidated	Fast Food Furniture	Custom Furniture	Consolidated
Sales	—	$8,100	$8,100	$400	$900	$1,300	$800	$800	$1,600
Direct materials	—	$2,025	$2,025	$200	$225	$ 425	$400	$200	$ 600
Direct labor:									
Forming	—	758	758	17	82	99	31	72	103
Finishing	—	1,314	1,314	40	142	182	70	125	195
Assembly	—	558	558	33	60	93	58	53	111
Factory overhead	—	1,779	1,779	60	180	240	98	147	245
Cost of goods sold	—	$6,434	$6,434	$350	$689	$1,039	$657	$597	$1,254
Gross profit	—	$1,666	$1,666	$ 50	$211	$ 261	$143	$203	$ 346
Gross profit percentage	—	20.6%	20.6%	12.5%	23.4%	20.1%	17.9%	25.4%	21.6%

The controller contends that the factory overhead allocation based solely on direct labor hours is inappropriate and that only supervision and employee benefits should use this base, with the balance of factory overhead allocated on a machine hour basis. In the controller's judgment, the increase in custom design furniture profitability is partially a result of overhead misallocation.

The actual direct labor hours and machine hours for the past 2 months are as follows.

	Fast Food Furniture	Custom Furniture
Machine hours:		
October:		
Forming	660	10,700
Finishing	660	7,780
Assembly	—	—
	1,320	18,480
Direct labor hours:		
October:		
Forming	1,900	9,300
Finishing	3,350	12,000
Assembly	4,750	8,700
	10,000	30,000
Machine hours:		
November:		
Forming	1,280	9,640
Finishing	1,280	7,400
Assembly	—	—
	2,560	17,040
Direct labor hours:		
November:		
Forming	3,400	8,250
Finishing	5,800	10,400
Assembly	8,300	7,600
	17,500	26,250

The actual factory overhead costs for the past 2 months were:

	October	November
Supervision	$ 13,000	$ 13,000
Employee benefits	95,000	109,500
Maintenance	50,000	48,000
Depreciation	42,000	42,000
Property tax	8,000	8,000
All other	32,000	24,500
Total	$240,000	$245,000

Required:

(1) Reallocate actual factory overhead for October and November following the controller's preference. (Round allocated costs to the nearest $100.)

(2) Present support or criticism of the controller's contention, based on requirement 1 results, and include revised statements of gross profit for October and November. (ICMA adapted)

CHAPTER 14

Activity Accounting: Activity-Based Costing and Activity-Based Management

Learning Objectives

After studying this chapter, you will be able to:

1. Define activity-based costing and activity-based management and distinguish them from traditional analysis of costs.
2. Identify the circumstances in which activity-based costing gives more credible results than traditional product costing.
3. Identify the different levels of costs and cost drivers in activity-based costing and give examples of each.
4. Calculate product costs using activity-based costing and reconcile them with a traditional system's product costs.
5. Identify the strategic importance of activity-based costing in pricing and product-line decisions.
6. Identify ways in which activity-based management can achieve improvements in an organization.
7. State the link between activity accounting and total quality management.

Chapters 12 and 13 illustrated traditional accounting for indirect costs with emphasis on the analysis and control of manufacturing overhead. This chapter examines another way of using information about indirect costs, called activity accounting. In certain circumstances, activity accounting can provide important insights by generating product cost information that is different from and more credible than information provided by traditional accounting. This is the first phase of activity accounting, and it is called activity-based costing. In practically any circumstances, activity accounting can give insights into how to improve competitiveness by managing resources more efficiently. This is the second phase of activity accounting, called activity-based management, and it is an important tool for achieving continuous improvement.

Activity-Based Costing[1]

Activity-based costing (ABC) was introduced briefly in Chapter 12 and was defined as a costing system in which multiple overhead cost pools are allocated using bases that include one or more non-volume-related factors. Compared to traditional cost accounting, ABC represents a more thorough application of cost tracing. Traditional product costing traces only direct material and direct labor to each unit of output. In contrast, ABC recognizes that many other costs are in fact traceable—not to units of output, but to the activities required to produce output.

Levels of Costs and Drivers

In ABC, the bases used to allocate overhead costs are called **drivers**. A **resource driver** is a base used to allocate the cost of a resource to the different activities using that resource.[2] An **activity driver** is a base used to allocate the cost of an activity to products, customers, or other **final cost objects**.[3] (The word ***final*** refers to the last step in cost allocation.) The nature and variety of activity drivers is what distinguishes ABC from traditional costing.

ABC recognizes activities, activity costs, and activity drivers at different **levels of aggregation** within a production environment. The four levels are the unit, batch, product, and plant. Exhibit 14-1 provides examples of activities, costs, and activity drivers at each of the four levels. The different levels are simply different degrees of data aggregation. A batch is the sum, or aggregation, of the units that make it up. A product is an aggregation of many batches. A plant can be thought of as an aggregation of all its products.

Unit Level. **Unit-level costs** are the costs that inevitably increase whenever a unit is produced; they are the only costs that always can be assigned accurately to units in proportion to volume. Examples of unit-level costs include electricity cost if electric machinery is used in producing each unit, and inspection labor if each unit of product requires inspection. These costs are purely variable and theoretically can be treated as direct costs but usually are accounted for as indirect costs.[4] **Unit-level drivers** are measures of activities that vary with the number of units produced and sold. All unit-level drivers are proportional to the volume of output. (Drivers at all other levels are not proportional to volume.) Examples of unit-level drivers are direct labor hours, direct labor cost, machine hours, direct material weight, direct material cost, direct material pieces, total direct costs, and units produced.

---

[1] Much of the material in this section is based on the award-winning series of articles on "The Rise of Activity-Based Costing" by Robin Cooper in *Journal of Cost Management*: "Part One: What Is an Activity-Based Cost System?", Vol. 2, No. 2, pp. 45–54; "Part Two: When Do I Need an Activity-Based Cost System?" Vol. 2, No. 3, pp. 41–48; "Part Three: How Many Cost Drivers Do You Need, and How Do You Select Them?" Vol. 2, No. 4, pp. 34–46; and "Part Four: What Do Activity-Based Cost Systems Look Like?" Vol. 3, No. 1, pp. 38–49.

[2] The name *resource driver* is new, but the idea is not. For example, most traditional accounting systems allocate some plant-wide costs to departments based on each department's number of employees or square footage occupied. Square footage and number of employees are called allocation bases in that context. If an ABC system allocates the cost of a resource to several activities based on the square footage or number of employees devoted to each activity, then square footage and number of employees are called resource drivers.

[3] *See* Michael R. Ostrenga and Frank R. Probst, "Process Value Analysis: The Missing Link in Cost Management," *Journal of Cost Management*, Vol. 6, No. 3, pp. 4–13.

[4] Technically, direct material and direct labor fit the definition of unit-level costs, but because ABC is a system for assigning *indirect* costs, the assignment of direct material cost and direct labor cost is outside the subject matter of ABC. Apart from the question of unit-level costs, however, direct labor dollars and direct material dollars are perfect examples of unit-level drivers.

EXHIBIT 14-1

Levels and Examples of Activities, Costs, and Activity Drivers

	Level			
	Unit	**Batch**	**Product**	**Plant**
Examples of Activities				
	cutting soldering painting assembling packaging	scheduling setting up blending moving	designing developing prototyping advertising warehousing	heating lighting cooling providing security
Examples of Costs				
	portions of electricity and indirect materials	salaries of schedulers, setup personnel, or material handlers	salaries of designers and programmers advertising fees costs of patents	depreciation insurance taxes on buildings
Examples of Activity drivers				
	units or pounds of output direct labor hours machine hours	number of batches, setups, material moves, or production orders	number of products, design changes, or design hours	square footage occupied

Batch Level. The next higher level of aggregation is the batch. **Batch-level costs** are costs caused by the number of batches produced and sold.[5] Examples of batch-level costs include setup costs and most material handling costs. If materials are ordered from a supplier for a particular batch, then part of materials procurement, receiving, and inspection costs are batch-level costs. If the first unit produced in each batch is inspected, this inspection cost is a batch-level cost. Significant batch-level costs also exist outside the production function. For example, if a product is not kept in stock but instead a batch is produced for each customer order, then batch-level costs include some marketing and administrative costs. Examples of these costs are the marketing costs incurred in obtaining and processing orders and the administrative costs of accounting and billing.[6] **Batch-level drivers** are measures of activities that vary with the number of batches produced and sold. Examples of batch-level drivers are setups, setup hours, production orders, work orders, and material requisitions.

Product Level. The next level above the batch is the product. **Product-level costs** are costs incurred to support the number of different products produced. They are not necessarily influenced by the production and sale of one more

[5] The distinction between the batch and unit levels is not lost when a batch consists of one unit. Batch-level costs would not increase if one or more units were added to the batch. Batch-level costs are influenced by the number of batches, and producing another unit does not necessarily require another batch. Similar distinctions exist among all four levels of costs.

[6] For a detailed example of how marketing and administrative costs can be included in an ABC system, see "Kanthal (A)," Harvard Business School Case 190-002, by Robert Kaplan, 1989.

batch or one more unit. Some examples of product-level costs are the costs of product design, development, prototyping, and production engineering. If workers need additional training before producing a particular product, then the cost of this training is a product-level cost. If special tools are made or purchased for use in producing one particular product, or if some machinery is used exclusively for one product, then the costs of such tooling and machinery are product-level costs. If some materials are unique to one product and are not ordered separately for each batch produced, then the costs of procuring, receiving, and inspecting those materials are product-level costs. Significant product-level costs also can exist outside the factory. For example, the costs of patents, market research, and product promotions are product-level costs.[7] An example of product-level cost in a service business is a consulting firm's cost of acquiring new computer software to provide a new kind of service to clients. **Product-level drivers** are measures of activities that vary with the number of different products produced and sold. Examples of product-level drivers are design changes, design hours, and the number of different kinds of parts needed (called "number of part numbers").

Plant Level. Several levels of costs and drivers can exist above the product level. These include the product line level, process level, and plant level. Most applications of ABC recognize only one of these, the plant level. **Plant-level costs** are the costs of sustaining capacity at a production site. Examples of plant-level costs include rent, depreciation, property taxes, and insurance on the factory building. Floor space occupied is referred to often as the **plant-level driver** for assigning plant-level costs. However, this stretches the idea of a driver, because the assignment of plant-level costs to products, batches, or units is usually an arbitrary allocation.[8] Even in ABC systems, plant-level costs often are allocated to output using unit-level measures, despite the fact that plant-level costs are very different from unit-level costs.

Comparison of ABC and Traditional Costing

Regardless of the number of different departments, overhead cost pools, and allocation bases used, traditional costing systems are characterized by their exclusive use of unit-level measures as bases for allocating overhead to output. For this reason, traditional systems are also called **unit-based systems**.

Notice that any ABC system necessarily uses multiple overhead cost pools, but not every multiple-pool system is an ABC system. For example, a florist shop might cost its floral arrangements by separately calculating the per-minute costs of cutting, arranging, and decorating. But if every individual floral arrangement (unit) requires some cutting, some arranging, and some decorating, the costing system is a volume-based system, not ABC.

Other distinctions usually exist between traditional and ABC systems. The number of overhead cost pools and allocation bases tends to be higher in ABC

[7] For a detailed example of the insights ABC can provide when applied to marketing costs, see "Winchell Lighting, Inc. (A)", Harvard Business School Case 187-074, by Robin Cooper and Robert Kaplan, 1987.

[8] An exception exists in factories that are subdivided into work cells or subplants, sometimes called a flotilla arrangement or factories within a factory. If a work cell is devoted entirely to a single product, then the fraction of the total plant floor space occupied by that cell can be assigned unambiguously to that product, along with the same fraction of total plant-level costs.

systems, but this is largely because many traditional systems use a single cost pool or a single base for all cost pools. This distinction is not universal. Theoretically, a system can use very large numbers of overhead cost pools and allocation bases, but if all the bases are at the unit level, the system is a traditional system.

A general distinction between ABC and traditional systems is in the homogeneity of costs within a cost pool. ABC requires calculating an activity cost pool and identifying an activity driver for each significant, costly activity. As a result, more care often is taken in forming at least some cost pools in ABC than in traditional costing. The usual result is that all the costs within an activity cost pool are very much alike in their logical relationship to the activity driver, while the same cannot be said of most traditional systems.

Another distinction between ABC and traditional systems is that all ABC systems are two-stage costing systems, while traditional systems may be one- or two-stage. In the first stage of ABC, activity cost pools are formed when resource costs are allocated to activities based on resource drivers. In the second stage, costs of activities are allocated from the activity cost pools to products or other final cost objects. In contrast, a traditional system uses two stages only if departments or other cost centers are created. Resource costs are allocated to cost centers in the first stage and are then allocated from the cost centers to products in the second stage. Some traditional systems are single-stage because they do not use separate cost centers, but there is no such thing as a single-stage ABC system.

ABC and Product Cost Distortion

The following example compares ABC with traditional costing and demonstrates the product cost distortion that can occur in traditional systems. The Dual Company produces two products, Common and Special, and has decided to implement ABC. Exhibit 14-2 shows costs and other information for Dual Company's most recent year of operations. The details about batch- and product-level overhead would not be available in a traditional costing system.

To implement ABC, activity cost pools usually are calculated by estimating what portion of the efforts of each cost center, team, or employee is devoted to each significant activity. Using these estimates, the costs of each cost center or other overhead cost category are divided into portions assigned to each activity.[9] This is the first stage of allocation in ABC.

In Dual Company, departments already exist and overhead costs are routinely accumulated for each department, as discussed in Chapter 13. For convenience, Dual Company formed activity cost pools by reallocating each department's overhead to activities. (This is often done in actual practice, rather than having activity cost pools formed by allocating each budget line item or each manufacturing asset.) Dual Company used estimates of employees' time spent on

[9] Many activity cost pools can result, and for each one an appropriate activity driver is selected. Two cost pools with the same activity driver can be combined. If a single activity driver cannot be identified for practically all the costs in a cost pool, the pool is divided into two or more smaller, more homogeneous cost pools, each with its own activity driver.

each activity as the resource driver for allocating each department's total overhead to activity cost pools.

For example, the Production Department manager estimated that his workers spend one-seventh of their time learning new skills required by improvements in product design. Based on that estimate, one-seventh of Production Department overhead, or $200,000, was identified as a cost of design changes (a product-level cost). Because all design changes require approximately equal amounts of this activity, the number of design changes was chosen as the activity driver. The $200,000 appears in the Production Department column in the lower portion of Exhibit 14-2. Similarly, the Engineering Department manager estimated that one-third of her staff's time is devoted to assisting with setups and another one-third is devoted to improvements in product design. Two resource cost allocations were made using these estimates. First, one-third of Engineering Department overhead, or $300,000, was identified as a cost of setups (a batch-level cost); because all setups require equal amounts of Engineering time and effort, the number of setups was selected as the activity driver. Second, another $300,000 was identified as a cost of design changes (a product-level cost) with the number of design changes as its activity driver. These $300,000 amounts are found in the Engineering Department column in the lower portion of Exhibit 14-2.

Dual Company obtained similar estimates from the managers of all departments. From those estimates, a total of $800,000 of batch-level costs were found to have the

EXHIBIT 14-2

Dual Company
Summary of Most Recent Year's Production

	Common	Special	Total
Units produced	98,000	200	
Direct material cost:			
Per unit	$ 10	$ 150	
Total	980,000	30,000	$1,010,000
Direct labor:			
Hours per unit	1	10	
Total hours	98,000	2,000	
Total cost ($10 per hour)	$980,000	$20,000	$1,000,000
Setups	40	40	
Design changes	12	8	
Overhead costs: Production Department			$1,400,000
Engineering Department			900,000
General Factory			700,000
Total overhead			$3,000,000
Total manufacturing cost			$5,010,000

Formation of activity cost pools:

	Production	Engineering	General Factory	Total
Total overhead	$1,400,000	$900,000	$700,000	$3,000,000
Less costs related to:				
Setups	$ 200,000	$300,000	$300,000	$ 800,000
Design changes	200,000	300,000	100,000	600,000
	$ 400,000	$600,000	$400,000	$1,400,000
Other overhead	$1,000,000	$300,000	$300,000	$1,600,000

number of setups as their activity driver. A total of $600,000 of product-level costs were found to have the number of design changes as their activity driver. These amounts are found in the last column in the lower portion of Exhibit 14-2.

In practice, ABC systems can use a large number of activity cost pools and many different activity drivers. For brevity in this example, Dual Company uses only two. All of Dual Company's remaining factory overhead is identified as other overhead in Exhibit 14-2. The "other" category includes all of Dual's unit-level and plant-level overhead. It also includes the costs of insignificant activities, the costs of activities for which no suitable activity driver was identified, and the costs of activities for which a reasonable estimate of cost was not available. Stated another way, Dual's other overhead category includes all overhead for which neither setups nor design changes is the appropriate activity driver. In designing the ABC system, Dual Company selected direct labor hours as the allocation base for the other over-head category.

In contrast, Dual's existing traditional costing system identified only the total of all overhead and allocated it based on direct labor hours.[10] The total and unit costs of each product as reported by the traditional costing system are shown in Exhibit 14-3, and by the ABC system, in Exhibit 14-4.[11]

A few points should be noted about the differences between the two systems' reported product costs. First, the direction of the cost difference is predictable: compared to ABC, the traditional system inevitably reports a higher unit cost for the high-volume product and a lower unit cost for the low-volume product. This is because the traditional system's entire overhead allocation is based on volume. In a volume-based (or unit-based) costing system, a higher-volume product inevitably is allocated a larger share of all overhead costs, including those costs that are not related to volume. This fact has important product pricing implications that will be explored later.

Second, the amount of cost difference between the two systems can be explained systematically. Common represents 98 percent of volume—as measured by direct labor hours—so the traditional system assigns Common 98 percent of all overhead, including batch- and product-level costs. The activity detail in Exhibit 14-2 suggests that Common is responsible for only 50 percent of batch-level activity (40 of the 80 setups) and only 60 percent of product-level activity (12 of the 20 design changes). As a result, the traditional system contains cost distortions equal to 48 percent (98% – 50%) of batch-level costs and 38 percent (98% – 60%) of product-level costs. The costs of Common from the two systems can be reconciled as follows:

		Total	Per Unit
Cost of Common from traditional system (Exhibit 14-3)		$4,900,000	$50.00
Adjustments for:			
Overstatement of batch-level costs, $800,000 × (98% – 50%)	$ (384,000)		
Overstatement of product-level costs, $600,000 × (98% – 60%)	(228,000)		
Total adjustments		(612,000)	(6.24)
Cost of Common from ABC system (Exhibit 14-4)		$4,288,000	$43.76

[10] Even if they are departmentalized, traditional systems do not approximate ABC, because departments generally do not correspond to activities. One department can perform many activities, and a single activity can involve many departments. The cost distortion illustrated in Dual Company also can occur within each department of a departmentalized plant.

[11] Overhead rates in ABC, like those in traditional volume-based costing, can be actual or predetermined. The exhibits use actual overhead costs of the past year; that is, the calculated ABC rates are actual overhead rates, not predetermined rates. To use ABC for routine product costing during the year, the rates generally are calculated from estimated amounts of overhead costs and estimated measures of the drivers; that is, predetermined rates are used.

EXHIBIT 14-3

Dual Company
Product Costs from Traditional Costing System

Overhead rate: $3,000,000 of overhead divided by 100,000 direct labor hours (DLH) = $30 per direct-labor hour

	Common	Special	Total
Direct material	$ 980,000	$ 30,000	$1,010,000
Direct labor	980,000	20,000	1,000,000
Overhead:			
$30 × 98,000 DLH	2,940,000		
$30 × 2,000 DLH		60,000	3,000,000
Total cost	$4,900,000	$110,000	$5,010,000
Units produced	98,000	200	
Cost per unit	$ 50	$ 550	

EXHIBIT 14-4

Dual Company
Product Costs from Activity-Based Costing System

Overhead rates:
$800,000 batch-level costs divided by 80 setups (40+40) = $10,000 per setup
$600,000 product-level costs divided by 20 design changes (12+8) = $30,000 per design change
$1,600,000 other overhead divided by 100,000 direct labor hours = $16 per direct labor hour

	Common	Special	Total
Direct Material	$ 980,000	$ 30,000	$1,010,000
Direct Labor	980,000	20,000	1,000,000
Overhead:			
$10,000 × 40 setups	400,000		
$10,000 × 40 setups		400,000	800,000
$30,000 × 12 design changes	360,000		
$30,000 × 8 design changes		240,000	600,000
$16 × 98,000 DLH	1,568,000		
$16 × 2,000 DLH		32,000	1,600,000
Total Cost	$4,288,000	$722,000	$5,010,000
Units produced	98,000	200	
Cost per unit	$ 43.76	$ 3,610	

There are only two products, so when the traditional system assigns 98 percent of all overhead to Common, it assigns the other 2 percent to Special. The data in Exhibit 14-2 show that Special actually accounts for 50 percent of batch-level activity (40 of 80 setups) and 40 percent of product-level activity (8 of the 20 design changes). The costs of Special reported by the two systems can then be reconciled as follows:[12]

[12] The $722,000 cost of Special in the ABC system is an increase of more than 500 percent over the $110,000 reported by the traditional system, although the two systems differ only in their treatment of the batch- and product-level costs, which are less than 50 percent of overhead and less than 30 percent of total manufacturing costs. There really is no limit on the percentage increase that can occur in the cost of a low-volume product when the costing system is changed. Suppose total manufacturing costs are $10,000, of which $5,000 are indirect costs, and the traditional costing system costs product X at $1 of direct cost plus 1 percent of a $100 indirect cost pool, for a total of $2. A new system assigns product X $1 of direct cost plus 21 percent of the $100 indirect cost pool, for a total of $22; the only cost amount handled differently by the two systems is the $100 indirect cost pool—just 2 percent of indirect costs and 1 percent of total manufacturing costs—but the new system increases the reported cost of product X from $2 to $22, which is a 1,000 percent increase.

		Total	Per Unit
Cost of Special from traditional system (Exhibit 14-3)		$110,000	$ 550
Adjustments for:			
Understatement of batch-level costs, $800,000 × (50% – 2%)	$384,000		
Understatement of product-level costs, $600,000 × (40% – 2%)	228,000		
Total adjustments		612,000	3,060
Cost of Special from ABC system (Exhibit 14-4)		$722,000	$3,610

The reconciliations use direct labor hours (DLH) as the measure of product volume because DLH is the allocation base in Dual's traditional system. Whatever volume measure is the base in the traditional system is the critical measure for assessing cost distortion. If the traditional system uses multiple bases for allocating overhead, reconciliations are much more complex, although no new principle is involved.

A third point concerning the differences of the two systems is that the two circumstances causing a traditional system's cost distortion can be identified by linking the data in Exhibit 14-2 to the reconcilations. One circumstance necessary for product cost distortion to occur is a complex cost structure, one that entails significant amounts of non-volume-related costs. If non-volume-related costs are insignificant, the traditional system's distortions are insignificant, because they are percentages of insignificant amounts. In Dual Company, however, the amounts of batch-level and product-level costs are clearly significant.[13]

The other circumstance necessary for product cost distortion to occur is a diverse product line. A diverse product line is one in which different products consume different mixes of volume-related and non-volume-related costs. Common consumes 98 percent of volume-related costs, but only 50 percent of batch-related costs and 60 percent of product-related costs. In this mix, volume-related costs are very dominant. In contrast, Special represents 2 percent of volume-related costs, 50 percent of batch-related costs, and 40 percent of product-related costs. In that mix, volume-related costs are not dominant. If all products consume the same mix, traditional costing cannot distort product costs regardless of how large the non-volume-related costs may be, because the distortion is calculated as zero percent of some cost amount.

Strategic Advantage of ABC

The following example illustrates circumstances in which ABC is not needed. When compared with Dual Company, it demonstrates the strategic advantage of ABC for setting prices and making product-line decisions such as discontinuing a product.

The Vanilla Company produces two products, Common and Plain. Common's quantities and costs are identical to those found in the preceding Dual Company

[13] This condition is very realistic. Companies producing thousands of different products devote significant resources to batch-level tasks such as setting up, scheduling, moving, and expediting, and to product-level tasks such as updating product designs, designing new products, testing and correcting designs, and procuring materials and components.

illustration. Vanilla Company's other product, Plain, is produced with quantities and costs similar to those of Common.

Notice that while Dual Company produces one high- and one low-volume product, Vanilla Company produces two high-volume products. To facilitate comparisons, Vanilla Company's batch-level costs per setup, product-level costs per design change, and other-overhead costs per direct labor hour are identical to Dual Company's. In other words, the two firms are equally efficient. This point is crucial to the strategic analysis and will be emphasized later in this section.

Exhibit 14-5 shows costs and other information for Vanilla Company's most recent year of operations. The batch- and product-level information would not be available in a traditional costing system. For brevity, departmental overhead and the calculations of batch- and product-level activity cost pools are not shown.

EXHIBIT 14-5

Vanilla Company
Summary of Most Recent Year's Production

	Common	Plain	Total
Units produced	98,000	49,000	
Direct material cost:			
Per unit	$ 10	$ 15	
Total	980,000	735,000	$1,715,000
Direct labor:			
Hours per unit	1	2	
Total hours	98,000	98,000	
Total cost ($10/hour)	$980,000	$980,000	$1,960,000
Setups	40	40	
Design changes	12	12	
Overhead:			
Batch-level costs			$ 800,000
Product-level costs			720,000
All other overhead			3,136,000
Total overhead			$4,656,000
Total manufacturing cost			$8,331,000

Like Dual Company, Vanilla Company performed 40 setups for each product and incurred setup (batch-level) costs of $800,000 for an average of $10,000 per setup. Vanilla Company made 12 design changes for each product, for a total of 24 design changes, and incurred design change (product-level) costs of $720,000 for an average of $30,000 per design change, the same as in Dual Company. Vanilla Company used 196,000 direct labor hours and incurred other overhead (e.g., unit- and plant-level overhead) of $3,136,000 for an average of $16 per direct labor hour, the same as Dual's rate for other overhead.

For Vanilla Company's products, the total and unit costs from the traditional costing system are shown in Exhibit 14-6, and from the ABC system in Exhibit 14-7. Vanilla Company reports the same product costs under both the traditional and ABC systems. That is, Vanilla Company's traditional system does not distort product costs. This result is as expected, because Vanilla Company lacks a diverse product line—Common and Plain each consume the same mix of volume-related and non-volume-related costs.[14] This remains true even though a complex cost structure is present in Vanilla Company. This illustrates the specific meaning of a diverse product line in ABC. Even if products have very different uses, prices, costs, customers, and so on, the product line is not diverse in the sense the term is used in ABC, if all products consume the same mix of costs.

Compare the unit costs of Common in the two costing systems of the two companies: Vanilla Company reports a unit cost of $43.76 for Common regardless of the costing system used, while Dual Company reports $43.76 with ABC and $50 with traditional costing. If Dual uses only a traditional costing system, it will report negative gross profit on Common at any sales price below $50. But at a price of, say, $49.95, Vanilla Company will report a positive gross profit of $6.19 ($49.95 – $43.76) for each unit of Common, while Dual Company will identify Common as an unprofitable product and may make the strategic mistake of discontinuing Common.

It is important to understand why Dual's decision to discontinue Common can be considered a strategic mistake. The reason is that Dual Company is as efficient a producer of Common as Vanilla Company is. (Recall that the costs and other information in the Vanilla Company illustration were constructed to make the two companies equally efficient.) Vanilla Company knows the cost of a unit of Common is $43.76 regardless of what costing system Vanilla uses. Dual Company, because of its diverse product line, knows the cost of Common is $43.76 only if ABC is used. If Dual's managers rely on traditional costing and evaluate products by reported profit margins, they will conclude that Common is unprofitable and may decide to discontinue it.

To make matters worse, Dual Company's other product, Special, has a unit cost of $550 reported by traditional costing. Managers relying on a traditional system will view Special as a very profitable product if its sales price is, say, $1,000. But the ABC system reports a unit cost of $3,610 for Special. A cost of $3,610 means that Special is actually unprofitable at a sales price of $1,000, or even at $2,000 or $3,000. Depending on the levels of sales prices, the traditional costing system is thus capable of misstating the profitability of both Dual products. The misstatements are not just modest degrees of difference. They are enough to make the profitable product appear unprofitable and the unprofitable product appear profitable. The strategic importance of such misinformation is enormous.

It is important to understand the preceding discussion's realism concerning sales prices. Many high-volume products in a diverse product line tend to become standardized, commodity-type items. These products often face intense price competition that drives market prices down to a level at which efficient producers earn just enough profit to stay in the business. Low-volume products, in contrast, are often customized, specialty items that face little or no price competition because they are close to being one-of-a-kind products. As a result, the competitive situation illustrated for Dual Company is realistic. This is not to say that producers of

[14] To avoid cost distortion, it is *not* essential that all products share all activities equally, as in Vanilla Company. However, an individual product must consume the same share of every level of activity or its cost will be distorted. In the following example, product A's cost will not be distorted by traditional costing, B's will be distorted downward, C's will be distorted upward, and D's will not be distorted.

	Percentage of Each Level of Activity Consumed				
Level	**A**	**B**	**C**	**D**	**Total**
Unit	30%	10%	40%	20%	100%
Batch	30	30	20	20	100
Product	30	25	25	20	100

EXHIBIT 14-6

Vanilla Company
Product Costs from Traditional Costing System

Overhead rate: $4,656,000 total overhead divided by 196,000 direct labor hours
= $23.7551 per direct labor hour

	Common	Plain	Total
Direct material	$ 980,000	$ 735,000	$1,715,000
Direct labor	980,000	980,000	1,960,000
Overhead:			
$23.7551 × 98,000 DLH	2,328,000		
$23.7551 × 98,000 DLH		2,328,000	4,656,000
Total cost	$4,288,000	$4,043,000	$8,331,000
Units produced	98,000	49,000	
Cost per unit	$ 43.76	$ 82.51	

EXHIBIT 14-7

Vanilla Company
Product Costs from Activity-Based Costing System

Overhead rates:
$800,000 batch-level costs divided by 80 setups = $10,000 per setup
$720,000 product-level costs divided by 24 design changes = $30,000 per design change
$3,136,000 other overhead divided by 196,000 direct labor hours = $16 per direct labor hour

	Common	Plain	Total
Direct Material	$ 980,000	$ 735,000	$1,715,000
Direct Labor	980,000	980,000	1,960,000
Overhead:			
$10,000 × 40 setups	400,000		
$10,000 × 40 setups		400,000	800,000
$30,000 × 12 design changes	360,000		
$30,000 × 12 design changes		360,000	720,000
$16 × 98,000 DLH	1,568,000		
$16 × 98,000 DLH		1,568,000	3,136,000
Total Cost	$4,288,000	$4,043,000	$8,331,000
Units produced	98,000	49,000	
Cost per unit	$ 43.76	$ 82.51	

diverse product lines necessarily face the pricing decisions illustrated in Dual Company, but the underlying economic forces do make Dual's situation a realistic possibility. Important mistakes can be made if Dual relies on distorted product cost information to make a strategic realignment of its product line.

This simple example vividly illustrates an important role of cost accounting: the subtle choice of a system for calculating product costs can have important strategic implications. Using the wrong product costing system can lead to disaster.

The strategic advantage of ABC lies in its potential to save Dual Company from mistakenly discontinuing Common due to price competition from Vanilla Company. While Vanilla might rationally price Common at $49.95 or even slightly lower, Dual's traditional costing system will tell Dual's management that Common is an unprofitable product at that price. In contrast, ABC would show Dual's management that it can indeed compete with Vanilla in the long run. The focus on long-run competition is crucial to this argument. In the short run, cost-volume-profit analysis may show Dual's management that it can match Vanilla's price and still generate positive contribution margin, i.e., still cover all variable costs. But in the long run, *all* costs must be covered, and eventually Dual's management will seriously consider discontinuing Common. So while traditional costing with an analysis of contribution margin may lead Dual to the correct decision in the short run, in the long run the potential for serious error is still present.

Equally important, ABC can show Dual's management the high cost of a low-volume product like Special. This does not mean that Dual necessarily should discontinue Special, even if customers are unwilling to pay much more than $3,610 for it. (It may be essential to provide Special to satisfy customers who also buy large quantities of Common, or Special may involve a new technology that must be learned to maintain competitiveness.) Rather, it does mean that Dual's management is in a better position to set prices and to evaluate products and customers if it has better information about the cost of Special.

Examples of ABC Implementation

A well-documented example of ABC implementation is found in Schrader Bellows (SB),[15] a producer of pneumatic controls such as the flow control valves used in pressurized air equipment. SB made over 2,700 different products and used over 20,000 different manufactured and purchased parts. SB was one of several companies studied for insight into how traditional costing can systematically distort product costs.

> These companies had several significant common characteristics. They all produced a large number of distinct products in a single facility. The products formed several distinct product lines and were sold through diverse marketing channels. The range in demand volume for products within a product line was high, with sales of high-volume products between 100 and 1,000 times greater than sales of low-volume products. As a consequence, products were manufactured and shipped in highly varied lot sizes. . . .
>
> Product costs played an important role in the decisions that surrounded the introduction, pricing, and discontinuance of products. . . . Cost-plus pricing to achieve a desired level of gross margin predominantly was used for the special products, though substantial modifications to the resulting estimated prices occurred when direct competition existed. Such competition was common for high-volume products but rarely occurred for the low-volume items.[16]

SB used four unit-level drivers, including direct-labor cost and number of units; three batch-level drivers, including both setup hours and number of setups; and nine product-level drivers, including number of customer orders and number of shipments of parts received.[17] Compared with the old costing system, the ABC system increased the overhead cost assigned to low-volume products as much as 1,000 percent and increased their reported total manufacturing cost as much as 500 percent. Based on ABC results, most of SB's flow control valves were generating negative gross margins.

---

[15] Described in *"Schrader Bellows (B)"*, Harvard Business School Case 186-051, by Robin Cooper, 1985.

[16] Robin Cooper and Robert S. Kaplan, "How Cost Accounting Distorts Product Costs," *Management Accounting*, Vol. 69, No. 10, p. 21.

[17] A concise summary of the ABC implementations in Schrader Bellows and five other companies is given in "Cost Classification in Unit-Based and Activity-Based Manufacturing Cost Systems," by Robin Cooper, *Journal of Cost Management*, Vol. 4, No. 3, pp. 4–14.

An early example of a full-fledged ABC implementation occurred in John Deere Component Works (JDCW),[18] a producer of machined parts for the automotive industry and for other John Deere plants. In JDCW, the ABC system used three unit-level drivers, three batch-level drivers, and one product-level driver. The unit-level drivers included direct labor dollars, for labor-related overhead costs; and machine hours, for machine operation costs. The batch-level drivers included setup hours, for machine setup costs; and loads of material, for material handling costs. The product-level driver was the number of part numbers, for parts administration costs.

Under the ABC system, two of JDCW's products were assigned overhead costs more than 500 percent higher than in its previous costing system. Of the 10 products whose reported overhead costs increased the most under ABC, the average increase in overhead cost was more than 100 percent. These large increases occurred despite the ABC system's assigning only 41 percent of overhead using batch- and product-level drivers. A JDCW manager described the impact of ABC:

> Few things have generated more excitement. Even though it is still an allocation, it's such an improvement. Parts we suspected we were undercosting have turned out to be even more expensive than we had thought.[19]

Strengths and Weaknesses of ABC

As indicated in the preceding quotation, ABC produces more credible product cost information but is nonetheless a system of allocation. Particularly for plant-level costs, ABC has little or no advantage over traditional costing. All product costing systems arbitrarily allocate plant-level costs to products. In a year of low volume, both ABC and traditional costing report higher unit costs.

A partial solution to this problem is simply to allocate no plant-level costs to products, batches, or units, and instead to treat plant-level costs as period costs. Direct (variable) costing offers a similar solution, in which fixed costs are treated as period costs (see Chapter 20). However, the fixed costs in direct costing typically include much of the cost that ABC identifies at the batch and product levels. Examples are the payroll and equipment costs of performing batch- and product-level activities. Traditional absorption costing allocates these costs using unit-level allocation bases that can distort product costs. Direct costing treats them as period costs with the result that they are never identified with products (or units or batches) at all. ABC is conceptually superior to both systems, because management has the option of viewing ABC's plant-level costs as period costs but can still allocate to products their batch- and product-level costs.

ABC requires managers to make a radical change in their way of thinking about costs. For example, at first it is hard for many managers to understand how ABC can show a low-volume product to be a money-loser when contribution margin analysis shows that the sales price exceeds the variable cost of production. Although contribution margin analysis may be useful for short-run decision making, it can be disastrous when used as a basis for long-run decisions. If most product-level costs are classified as fixed, for example, they will be considered irrelevant in the decision to add or drop one product in a firm producing many products.

---

[18] Described in *"John Deere Component Works (A)"*, Harvard Business School Case 187-107, by Artemis March, 1987.

[19] *"John Deere Component Works (B)"*, Harvard Business School Case 187-108, by Artemis March, 1987, p. 1.

Over the long run, however, product-level costs certainly do increase if the number of products increases dramatically. Tasks such as scheduling production, procuring materials, and expediting rush orders inevitably become more burdensome. In the long run, almost all costs are variable. Even plant-level costs are variable in the long run because a plant of practically any size, or any number of different plants, can be purchased, constructed, or sold. A useful way of understanding the logic of ABC is to recognize that ABC treats all costs as variable. This treatment is appropriate because ABC is designed to be a long-run, strategic decision-making tool.

ABC does not show the costs that will be avoided by discontinuing a product or by producing fewer batches of it. (See the discussion of differential costs in Chapter 21). ABC shows how much batch-level and product-level activity is devoted to each product, not how much less money will be spent if fewer products or batches are produced. If ABC shows a low-volume product is a money-loser, the entire loss cannot be avoided by discontinuing the product because some costs assigned to the product may not be avoidable. For example, even if fewer setups are performed, the company may continue to employ all its setup personnel, pay them the same salaries, and retain all their equipment. If fewer design changes are made, the company may not terminate any design engineers and may not spend any less to maintain the computers and software they use. Especially if the numbers of setups and design changes show only small reductions, there may not be any resources on which the firm can begin spending less money. ABC attempts to show each products' long-run consumption of resources; it does not predict how spending will be affected by certain decisions.

Finally, ABC requires data-gathering efforts beyond those needed to satisfy external reporting requirements. Traditional costing systems are sufficient for financial and tax reporting, so new systems such as ABC must be justified by the benefits they generate. In companies with a long history of success in relying on traditional costing, it can be hard to convince management that a new costing system is needed. A competitor who takes away the firm's high-volume business by offering lower prices may finally convince management that the traditional system is distorting product costs. By then, unfortunately, it may be too late if the firm is left with only its low-volume products on which it must raise prices dramatically.

A solution to this final problem is to continue with the familiar traditional system and experiment with ABC separately, using it initially for only one product line, one facility, or one category of costs such as the costs of service departments. If important new insights are gained from the experiment, managers may become convinced that ABC deserves wide application. Note also that it is not necessary to replace the traditional system with ABC to get ABC's benefits. Both systems can be operated, the traditional system for financial and tax reporting and ABC for occasional special studies. Such special studies might be conducted when products are considered for addition or deletion from the product line, when production technology changes, or when a resource's cost has increased or decreased significantly. Many companies that have implemented ABC use it for decision making and planning but do not apply it to the routine, continuous costing of output. They continue to use simpler traditional systems for routine external reporting.

Activity-Based Management

Activity-based management (ABM) is the use of information obtained from ABC to make improvements in a firm.[20] One form of improvement follows

[20] Peter B. B. Turney, "Activity-Based Management: ABM Puts ABC Information to Work," *"Management Accounting"*, Vol. 63, No. 7, pp. 20–25.

directly from the revision of reported product costs as discussed in the section on the strategic advantage of ABC. This improvement occurs when revised product costs from an ABC system lead to strategic changes in prices. Such price changes can permit the firm to retain or regain high-volume business in spite of pricing pressure from competitors. Similarly, revised product costs can prompt management to re-examine the strategic importance of low-volume products that are found to be extremely costly to produce. When ABC is applied to marketing costs, it can lead management similarly to rethink the profitability of different classes of customers and different channels of distribution.

Over the long term, ABC information can help management position the firm to take better advantage of its strengths. For example, management may learn that for one product line, the costs of being a full-line producer are not justified by the benefits. In such a product line, the firm should produce only the high-volume products or drop the line altogether. Another product line may also show that substantial costs result from being a full-line producer. But buyers of the low-volume products in that line may be willing to pay prices high enough for the firm to continue the full line and perhaps even to reduce prices on the high-volume products.

Within a single facility, ABC information can show the inefficiency of producing special-order, customized products on equipment designed for long production runs. Managers may have known all along that it is not very efficient to produce a batch of two units in a plant designed for large batches. However, ABC can show just how expensive it is, and the result is often surprising. These are just a few examples of how ABC can help management position the firm strategically.

A second area for improvement in a firm is unrelated to cost distortion. It concerns ABC's revelations about the process used to produce goods and services. Implementing ABC requires information that traditional accounting neither needs nor provides. First, it is necessary to measure the total cost of each significant activity performed in delivering goods or services to the customer (the activity cost pools). Second, the best activity driver must be selected for allocating each activity cost pool. Finally, the driver rate for each activity must be calculated by dividing each pool's total cost by the total of its activity driver. Whether or not product costs are revised, this ABC information provides new insights about the efficiency of processes.

Many traditional systems report the costs of each manager's responsibility area for purposes of control and evaluation. These costs can be subdivided into accounts such as indirect labor, supplies, electricity, and so on. Traditional systems can also provide total costs of each cost center for use in product costing. Traditional systems, however, do not require careful study of how each task is done and just how expensive it is to do, but ABC systems require precisely that. When this information becomes available to management, it usually reveals opportunities for improvement. In general, there are four ways in which activities can be managed to achieve improvements in a process:[21]

1. Activity reduction: reducing the time or effort required to perform the activity.
2. Activity elimination: eliminating the activity entirely.
3. Activity selection: selecting the low-cost alternative from a set of design alternatives.
4. Activity sharing: making changes that permit the sharing of activities with other products to yield economies of scale.

---

[21] Peter B. B. Turney, "How Activity-Based Costing Helps Reduce Costs," *Journal of Cost Management*, Vol. 4, No. 4, pp. 29–35.

For example, it was explained in the discussion on batch-level costs how the impact of doing a setup can extend far beyond the setup department. The costs associated with a setup are likely to be much larger than managers would guess. How does this differ from the information given by a traditional costing system? Traditional costing systems do not measure the costs of activities; they measure the cost of each cost center or department. If there is a setup department, its total cost is calculated each period and it is easy to divide the total by the number of setups performed. However, the result can be a gross understatement of the total costs of setting up, because each setup may also require significant efforts in many other departments. Examples are a first-piece inspection performed by the inspection department and material movements required of the material-handling department.

When management learns the total cost of each significant activity in the plant (or in the entire firm, if ABC is extended to marketing and administrative functions), its attention is naturally focused on large amounts of resources devoted to some activities. Recall the total quality management (TQM) philosophy discussed in Chapter 7. One step in TQM is to identify every place in the organization in which resources are expended without adding value to the product—that is, without increasing customer satisfaction. Some of these activities, such as complying with laws and regulations, are necessary aspects of being in business. Others are not necessary; these are called **non-value-added activities**, or simply waste. One goal of TQM is to eliminate as many non-value-added activities as possible and to reduce those that cannot be eliminated. Activity cost information can make important contributions to a TQM effort, because ABC can reveal non-value-added activities with high costs. If these activities are reduced substantially or eliminated, the cost structure becomes simpler because some batch- or product-level costs shrink or disappear. The ABC system then becomes simpler, too, because one or more activity cost pools can be deleted from the design of the ABC system.

The cost of setups again provides a useful example. If ABC shows the cost of setups is much higher than previously assumed, the first reaction may be to perform fewer setups. It is tempting to use the economic order quantity model described in Chapter 9 to determine a longer optimal production run (batch size) to balance inventory carrying costs against the high setup costs. But larger batch sizes increase the amount of time each unit spends waiting at each step in the process, and waiting time does not add value. Larger batch sizes also increase the potential number of defects produced whenever one step in the process goes out of its control limits, and reworking defective units is a non-value-added activity. TQM forces management to recognize the futility of solving a problem if more non-value-added activity is the result.

Once management starts thinking in terms of avoiding non-value-added activity, the nature of setups becomes clearer: it is another non-value-added activity. Customers do not want the product more, nor are they willing to pay more for it, because of the huge amount of resources expended in setting up. (The same is true of the resources expended in moving materials, storing and retrieving materials, inspecting and reinspecting product, and many other tasks.) Once ABC shows the cost of setups, TQM directs management to find ways to reduce it to make the firm more efficient. At best, a flexible manufacturing system (FMS) eliminates the setup problem, the need to find optimal batch sizes, and the batch-level costs of setting up.

The contribution of ABC to this improvement process is subtle. TQM alone says that setting up does not add value, so management does not need ABC to know that the resources devoted to setups should be reduced. The contribution of ABC is that it measures the cost of setups and every other significant activity, making it clear where improvement efforts should be devoted first. The most costly activities represent the most urgent problems and biggest opportunities for improvement. In this sense, ABC provides information that prioritizes the possible improvements.

Behavioral Changes

The design of products is a third area in which activity cost information can be used. Traditional costing shows product costs as the sum of direct material, direct labor, and applied overhead based on labor or some other volume measure. If designers know the product must be sold for a certain price to be competitive, they will make design decisions that reduce reported unit cost below that price.

One such decision is to use more direct materials, such as purchased components and subassemblies, and less direct labor. In this way, the charges for both labor and overhead are reduced. Another such decision is to design the product to be produced on machinery that requires little direct labor. These motivations are especially strong if overhead is applied on the basis of direct-labor cost and overhead is high, producing an overhead rate of several hundred percent of labor, which heavily penalizes a product for using much direct labor. However, when designers design direct labor out of the product, total direct labor cost declines and the labor-based overhead rate becomes even higher.

Another problem with such design decisions is that traditional costing systems do not capture the cost of ordering, receiving, and inspecting complex components or subassemblies. These costs can be substantial. They are included in overhead and are allocated based on direct labor or some other volume measure, again making the overhead rate even higher in the next period.

Changing the overhead allocation base to machine hours does not solve the problem. It merely gives designers an incentive to redesign the machine time out of the product, again by using purchased components and subassemblies that do not need to be machined. Activity cost information, in contrast, can show the cost of each significant activity, including ordering, receiving, and inspecting purchased components. An ABC system can show whether it is more economical to set up and operate a machine to make a part rather than to purchase it. An ABC system can show whether it is more economical to use large amounts of direct labor or to use automated machinery requiring no direct labor but extensive setup. In short, an ABC system can provide information that will elicit the desired behavior because it permits designers to make cost-based design decisions accurately. The best a traditional system can do is accurately capture the costs of unit-level activities, but it then distorts them by allocating batch- and product-level costs using unit-level allocation bases.

Cost Control

A final area in which activity-based information is useful to management is in controlling costs. Activity cost reporting provides an alternative to traditional responsibility reporting and can help reduce dysfunctional behavior. This topic is discussed in Chapter 17.

Summary

Activity accounting recognizes that units of product are not the only important cost objects for which management needs reliable cost information. In complex organizations, relatively little cost may be directly traceable to units of output. Larger amounts of cost may be traceable to the activities needed to produce batches of product, or to activities that sustain the firm's ability to produce a number of different products. To understand and improve a product or a process, the cost of each significant activity must be determined and traced to the appropriate cost object. The results show that traditional costing systems, by assigning all costs to units of output based on one or more volume measures, can distort product costs and give misleading signals to decision makers.

When knowledge about activities is applied to managing the firm, it helps achieve improvements in processes, decision making, and cost control. By identifying the high costs of non-value-added activities, activity accounting plays an important role in total quality management.

Key Terms

activity-based costing (ABC) *(365)*
drivers *(365)*
resource driver *(365)*
activity driver *(365)*
final cost objects *(365)*
levels of aggregation *(365)*
unit-level costs *(366)*
unit-level drivers *(366)*
batch-level costs *(366)*
batch-level drivers *(367)*
product-level costs *(367)*
product-level drivers *(367)*
plant-level costs *(367)*
plant-level driver *(367)*
unit-based systems *(368)*
activity-based management (ABM) *(378)*
non-value-added activities *(380)*

Discussion Questions

Q14-1 In terms of the direct traceability of costs, how do traditional costing systems differ from ABC?

Q14-2 What role is played by activities in assigning costs to products using ABC? How does this differ from traditional costing?

Q14-3 Give some examples of significant, costly activities.

Q14-4 What two circumstances must be present for a traditional costing system to report distorted product costs?

Q14-5 What is meant by a complex cost structure in ABC?

Q14-6 What is meant by a diverse product line in ABC?

Q14-7 Name the four levels of costs and drivers in ABC.

Q14-8 State as briefly as possible how traditional costing distorts the reported cost of a product that consumes 10% of all unit-level activities and 30% of all batch-level activities.

Q14-9 When both low- and high-volume products are produced in a company using traditional costing, which kind of product is likely to have its cost distorted by the largest percentage? In which direction will its cost be distorted?

Q14-10 Of the four levels of costs in ABC, at which level does ABC offer little or no advantage over traditional costing?

Q14-11 Contribution margin (CM) analysis is a short-run decision-making technique that recognizes many of ABC's batch-level and product-level costs as fixed, while ABC treats these costs as being essentially variable. How is this difference between ABC and CM explained?

Q14-12 If ABC shows a product to be a money-loser and management discontinues that product, will the cost of the product reported by ABC necessarily be avoided? Why or why not?

Q14-13 What is the relationship between activity-based costing (ABC) and activity-based management (ABM)?

Q14-14 What aspect of ABM follows directly from ABC's revision of product costs?

Q14-15 What specific information from ABC sometimes leads management to focus on the need to improve a process?

Q14-16 In what way does ABC lead to improved decisions in designing a product?

Q14-17 What is the link between ABC and total quality management?

Exercises

E14-1 Levels of Cost Drivers Each of the following is a potential activity driver. Identify the most likely level of each driver with U for a unit-level driver, B for a batch-level driver, and P for a product-level driver.

(a) Loads of materials moved
(b) Materials cost
(c) Pounds of finished product produced
(d) Shipments to customers (where no finished goods inventory is maintained)
(e) Number of part numbers used
(f) Machine hours
(g) Purchase orders issued (where large materials inventories are maintained)
(h) Direct costs
(i) Pieces inspected (where output is 100% inspected)
(j) Pieces inspected (where only the first piece is inspected after each setup)

E14-2 Levels of Cost Drivers. Each of the following is a potential activity driver. Identify the most likely level of each driver with U for a unit-level driver, B for a batch-level driver, and P for a product-level driver.

(a) Pounds of materials used
(b) Work orders
(c) Direct labor hours
(d) Total value added
(e) Units produced
(f) Machine setups
(g) Design changes
(h) Marketing promotions

E14-3 Distortion of Batch-Level Costs. Cooper Company's existing cost system accumulates all overhead in a single cost pool and allocates it based on machine hours. Last year, overhead costs totaled $2,100,000 and Product 1 used 1,500 of the 30,000 total machine hours. An ABC study revealed that, of the total overhead cost of last year, $100,000 represented batch-level costs; these batch-level costs are driven by work orders; and a total of 1,000 work orders were issued, of which 30 were for Product 1.

Required: With respect to batch-level costs only, calculate the existing cost system's direction and amount of cost distortion for Product 1.

E14-4 Distortion of Batch-Level Costs. Brimson Company uses a traditional volume-based system for allocating overhead to products. Materials-related overhead costs are accumulated in a separate cost pool and allocated based on direct materials cost. Last year, materials-related overhead totaled $1,200,000 and direct materials costs totaled $3,000,000. Product AA used $15,000 of direct materials last year.

An ABC study has revealed that materials-related overhead costs are driven by materials requisitions. Last year, a total of 40,000 materials requisitions were processed, of which 40 were for Product AA.

Required: With respect to materials-related overhead only, calculate the traditional cost system's direction and amount of cost distortion for Product AA.

E14-5 Distortion of Product-Level Costs. Overhead costs in Kaplan Company totaled $8,100,000 last year, and Product RK used 50 direct labor hours out of the company's total of 50,000 direct labor hours used. All overhead costs are accumulated in a single cost pool and allocated based on direct labor hours.

A consulting firm has just completed an ABC study for the company. The ABC study showed that, of the last year's total overhead cost, $2,000,000 represented the costs of design changes. The activity driver selected for design change costs is the number of design hours. A total of 6,000 hours were spent on design changes last year, of which 120 hours were spent making a total of three changes in the design of Product RK.

Required: Considering only the costs of design changes, calculate the direction and amount of cost distortion for Product RK in the original cost system.

E14-6 Distortion of Product-Level Costs. An ABC study by Turney Company has revealed that, of the last year's total overhead cost, $50,000 represented the costs of maintaining supplies of purchased subassemblies. The activity driver chosen for these costs is the number of different subassemblies available from vendors. A total of 200 subassemblies were available last year, of which 2 are used exclusively in Product BB.

Turney Company's existing cost system accumulates all overhead in a single cost pool and allocates it based on direct labor cost. Last year, overhead totaled $800,000, direct labor totaled $200,000, and Product BB used $40,000 of direct labor.

Required: Considering only the costs of maintaining supplies of purchased subassemblies, calculate the existing cost system's direction and amount of distortion in the reported cost of Product BB.

E14-7 Overhead under ABC and Traditional Costing. Caldwell Company manufactures a variety of high- and low-volume products, including Product 456, in its Westchester Plant. The following information pertains to the most recent year:

	Total for Product 456	Total for Westchester
Unit-level overhead		$ 200,000
Batch-level overhead		300,000
Product-level overhead		500,000
Plant-level overhead		400,000
Total overhead		$1,400,000
Units produced	100	5,000
Direct labor hours	200	20,000
Machine hours	90	10,000
Setups	6	120
Setup hours	30	500
Design changes	4	40
Design hours	280	4,000

Required:

(1) If the Westchester Plant accumulates all overhead in a single cost pool and allocates it on the basis of machine hours, how much overhead cost will be allocated to a unit of Product 456?

(2) If the Westchester Plant uses ABC with setups as the driver for all batch-level overhead, design hours as the driver for all product-level overhead, and machine hours as the driver for all unit- and plant-level overhead, how much overhead cost will be allocated to a unit of Product 456?

E14-8 Reconciliation of ABC and Traditional Costing

Required: Using the data from exercise 7, prepare a reconciliation of the overhead costs reported for Product 456 by the two costing systems. Begin the reconciliation with the amount of overhead allocated by the traditional system. Use columns for total and per-unit costs.

E14-9 Overhead under ABC and Traditional Costing

Required: Using the data from exercise 7, calculate the following:

(1) If the Westchester plant accumulates all overhead in a single cost pool and allocates it on the basis of direct labor hours, how much overhead cost will be allocated to a unit of Product 456?

(2) If the Westchester plant uses ABC with setup hours as the driver for all batch-level overhead, design changes as the driver for all product-level overhead, and direct labor hours as the driver for all unit- and plant-level overhead, how much overhead cost will be allocated to a unit of Product 456?

E14-10 Reconciliation of ABC and Traditional Costing

Required: Using the data from exercise 7 and the results from exercise 9, prepare a reconciliation of the overhead costs reported for Product 456 by the two costing systems. Begin the reconciliation with the overhead allocated by the traditional system. Use columns for total and per-unit costs.

E14-11 Value-Added and Non-Value-Added Activities. Sequential Company's sole product, a piece of machine housing made from sheet metal, is produced in the following sequence of steps:

(a) Metal received and inspected at receiving dock
(b) Metal moved to stores inventory
(c) Metal placed into stores
(d) Metal retrieved from stores as needed
(e) Metal moved to Cutting Department
(f) Metal placed in queue to await cutting machine
(g) Pieces cut to size
(h) Placed on hand truck to await material handler
(i) Moved to Deburring Department
(j) Placed in queue to await deburring
(k) Sandblasted to remove burrs from cut edges
(l) Placed on hand truck to await material handler
(m) Moved to in-process storage area
(n) Moved to Inspection Department
(o) Placed in queue to await inspection
(p) Inspected
(q) Placed on hand truck to await material handler
(r) Moved to in-process storage area
(s) Moved to Drilling Department
(t) Placed in queue to await drilling machine
(u) Holes drilled to accomodate customer's fasteners
(v) Placed on hand truck to await material handler
(w) Moved to Deburring Department
(x) Placed in queue to await deburring machine
(y) Sandblasted to remove burrs from edges of holes
(z) Placed on hand truck to await material handler
(aa) Moved to in-process storage area
(bb) Moved to Painting Department
(cc) Placed in queue to await painting
(dd) Painted and oven-dried
(ee) Placed on hand truck to await material handler
(ff) Moved to in-process storage area
(gg) Moved to Inspection Department
(hh) Placed in queue to await inspection
(ii) Inspected
(jj) Placed on hand truck to await material handler
(kk) Moved to shipping dock

Required: Which of the steps add value to the product?

Problems

P14-1 Allocation Rates and Driver Rates. The Wilkes Division of Darling Company manufactures many high-volume products and many low-volume products. Wilkes's existing costing system allocates all machine-related overhead based on machine hours and all the remaining overhead based on direct labor hours. However, a recent study determined that machine setup costs and material handling costs are primarily related to the number of setups performed, and other materials-related costs are primarily related to the number of purchase orders issued. Wilkes does not keep significant materials inventories on hand. Selected information follows for Wilkes's most recent year of operations:

Indirect costs:	
Machine related:	
Machine operation	$ 65,000
Machine setup	15,000
Total machine overhead	$ 80,000
Materials related:	
Material handling	$ 30,000
Other materials related	35,000
Total materials overhead	$ 65,000
Other overhead	$215,000
Total overhead	$360,000
Machine hours	4,000
Pounds of materials	25,000
Setups	1,000
Purchase orders	700
Direct labor hours	20,000

Required:

(1) Calculate the two overhead rates in Wilkes' existing cost system for the most recent year.

(2) Create an ABC system for Wilkes, making only the changes suggested by the results of the recent study. Give your answer in the form of a list of cost pools. Beside the name of each pool, list the driver that is to be used to allocate that cost pool to products.

(3) Calculate the overhead (driver) rates that the ABC system should use for the most recent year.

P14-2 Allocation Rates and Driver Rates. Division 1 of Carlton Company manufactures a variety of both high- and low-volume products. The following information is for Division 1's most recent year of operations:

Direct material cost	$1,000,000
Direct labor cost	2,000,000
Total direct costs	$3,000,000
Overhead cost:	
Machine related:	
Machine operation	$ 500,000
Machine setup	200,000
Total machine overhead	$ 700,000
Materials related:	
Material handling	$ 300,000
Materials administration	350,000
Freight-in	150,000
Total materials overhead	$ 800,000
Other overhead	$2,500,000
Total overhead	$4,000,000
Machine hours	40,000
Pounds of materials	200,000
Setups	500
Purchase orders	10,000

Division 1's existing costing system allocates all machine-related overhead based on machine hours, all materials-related overhead based on direct material cost, and all remaining overhead based on direct labor cost. However, a recent study determined that machine setup costs and material handling costs are primarily related to the number of setups performed; materials administration cost is primarily related to the number of purchase orders issued; and freight-in is primarily related to pounds of materials. Division 1 does not keep significant materials inventories on hand.

Required:

(1) Calculate the three overhead rates in Division 1's existing costing system for the most recent year.

(2) Create an ABC system for Division 1, making only the changes suggested by the results of the recent study. Give your answer in the form of a list of cost pools. Beside the name of each pool, list the driver that is to be used to allocate that cost pool to products.

(3) Calculate the overhead (driver) rates that the ABC system should use for the most recent year.

P14-3 Comparison of ABC and Traditional Costing; Two Products. The Draper Company produces two products, Standard and Custom, and uses a costing system that accumulates all overhead in a single cost pool and allocates it based on direct labor cost. Draper's management has decided to implement ABC, having just finished a study that revealed significant amounts of overhead cost are related to setup activity and design activity. The number of setups and the number of design hours were selected as the activity drivers for the two new cost pools, and direct labor cost will continue as the base for allocating the remaining overhead. Information concerning Draper Company's most recent year of operations is as follows:

	Standard	Custom	Total
Units produced	73,500	125	73,625
Direct material cost:			
Per unit	$ 12	$ 100	
Total	$ 882,000	$12,500	$ 894,500
Direct labor cost	$2,910,000	$90,000	$3,000,000
Setups	30	30	60
Design hours	12,000	3,000	15,000
Overhead:			
Setup related			$ 300,000
Design related			900,000
Other			3,300,000
Total overhead			$4,500,000

Required:

(1) Calculate the total and per-unit costs reported for the two products by the existing costing system, using the format shown in Exhibit 14-3.

(2) Calculate the total and per-unit costs reported for the two products by the ABC system, using the format shown in Exhibit 14-4.

(3) Reconcile the costs reported for Custom by the two costing systems. Use columns for total and per-unit costs.

(4) What percentage of Draper's total overhead is treated differently by the two costing systems? By what percentage did the cost of Custom change as a result of the change in the system? Calculate each answer to the nearest whole percent.

P14-4 Comparison of ABC and Traditional Costing; Two Products. Shauton Company produces two products, Fancy and Plain, and uses a costing system in which all overhead is accumulated in a single cost pool and allocated based on direct labor hours. Shauton's management has decided to implement ABC, because a cost study has revealed significant amounts of overhead cost related to setup activity and design activity. The number of setups and the number of design hours will be the activity drivers for the two new cost pools, and direct labor hours will continue as the base for allocating all remaining overhead. Selected information for Shauton Company's most recent year of operations is as follows:

	Fancy	Plain	Total
Units produced	200	16,000	16,200
Direct material cost:			
Per unit	$ 300	$ 10	
Total	$60,000	$160,000	$ 220,000
Direct labor:			
Hours	2,800	27,200	30,000
Cost	$28,000	$272,000	$ 300,000
Setups	45	45	90
Design hours	3,000	5,000	8,000

	Total
Overhead:	
Setup related	$ 135,000
Design related	240,000
Other	825,000
Total overhead	$1,200,000

Required:

(1) Calculate the total and per-unit costs reported for the two products by the existing costing system, using the format shown in Exhibit 14-3.

(2) Calculate the total and per-unit costs reported for the two products by the ABC system, using the format shown in Exhibit 14-4.

(3) Reconcile the costs reported for Fancy by the two costing systems. Use columns for total and per-unit costs.

(4) What percentage of total overhead is treated differently by the two costing systems? By what percentage did the cost of Fancy change as a result of the change in the system? Calculate each answer to the nearest whole percent.

P14-5 Comparison of ABC and Traditional Costing; Three Products. The Tunney Company produces three products, Normal, Enhanced, and Super, and uses a costing system that accumulates all overhead in a single cost pool and allocates it based on direct labor hours. Tunney's management has decided to implement ABC, and has just finished a study that revealed significant amounts of batch-level overhead cost are incurred in requisitioning, retrieving, moving, and handling materials. The number of material requisitions was selected as the activity driver for this cost pool, and direct labor hours will still be used as the allocation base for the remaining overhead cost. Information concerning Tunney Company's most recent year of operations is as follows:

	Normal	Enhanced	Super	Total
Units produced	30,000	1,000	50	31,050
Direct material:				
Cost per unit	$ 2	$ 20	$ 100	
Total cost	$ 60,000	$20,000	$5,000	$ 85,000
Direct labor:				
Hours per unit	1.5	4.5	10	
Total hours	45,000	4,500	500	50,000
Total cost (average rates differ)	$300,000	$35,000	$5,000	$ 340,000
Setups	150	100	50	300
Design changes	12	10	10	32
Material pounds	26,900	4,100	1,800	32,800
Material requisitions	150	200	150	500
Overhead:				
Batch level				$ 400,000
Other				600,000
Total overhead				$1,000,000

Required:

(1) Calculate the total and per-unit costs reported for each product by the existing costing system, using the format shown in Exhibit 14-3.

(2) Calculate the total and per-unit costs reported for each product by the ABC system, using the format shown in Exhibit 14-4.

(3) Reconcile the costs reported for Super by the two costing systems. Use columns for total and per-unit costs.

(4) What percentage of Tunney's overhead is treated differently by the two costing systems? By what percentage did the cost of Super change as a result of the change in the system?

P14-6 ABC and Traditional Costing; Two Products with Equal Unit Volumes. The Teksize Company makes two products, Regular and Large, using the same equipment. Large is simply a bigger version of Regular. One production run of each product is scheduled approximately each week. Teksize uses a costing system that accumulates all overhead in a single cost pool and allocates it based on direct labor hours. Teksize's management has decided to implement ABC, and has just finished a study that revealed significant amounts of costs related to the number of setups. Direct labor hours will still be used as the allocation base for the remaining overhead cost. Information concerning Teksize Company's most recent year of operations is as follows:

	Regular	Large	Total
Units produced	10,000	10,000	20,000
Direct material cost:			
Per unit	$ 1	$ 4	
Total	$ 10,000	$ 40,000	$ 50,000
Direct labor:			
Hours per unit	1	4	
Total hours	10,000	40,000	50,000
Total cost	$120,000	$ 480,000	$ 600,000
Setups	51	52	103
Overhead:			
Setup related			$ 515,000
Other			985,000
Total overhead			$1,500,000

Required:

(1) Calculate the total and per-unit costs reported for the two products by the existing costing system, using the format shown in Exhibit 14-3.

(2) Calculate the total and per-unit costs reported for the two products by the ABC system, using the format shown in Exhibit 14-4.

(3) Reconcile the costs reported for Regular by the two costing systems. Use columns for total and per-unit costs.

(4) Does Teksize have a diverse product line, in the sense the term is used in ABC? Why or why not?

Cases

C14-1 ABC and Traditional Costing. Perkins Company manufactures a wide variety of products in its Dallas Division. The Dallas plant was created to be an efficient producer of standardized products made in long production runs, although both high- and low-volume products are now produced there. Annual volumes range from several thousand units for some products to fewer than 10 for others. In recent years, much of the Dallas plant's usual business in high-volume products has been lost to competitors who price aggressively and who do not produce a full product line. The general manager of Dallas Division states, "I know we're as skilled as anybody else in the industry, and our quality is second to none. In addition, we're the only major competitor that offers a full line of products, so our customers have the convenience of getting all their requirements from us and not having to deal with several vendors. What I don't understand is how a couple of our competitors can price as low as they do on some of our bread-and-butter products."

To better understand the costs of its products, the Dallas Division is considering changing its product costing system. The existing system accumulates all overhead in a single cost pool and allocates it based on direct labor hours. Because of the very large number of products, the general manager has decided to focus initially on just two products: Product 321, which is representative of most of Dallas' high-volume products; and Product 333, a representative low-volume product. The following information pertains to the most recent year's operations of the Dallas plant; for brevity, details for products other than Product 321 and Product 333 are not shown, but totals for the entire division are given in the last column.

	Total for Product 321	Total for Product 333	Total for Dallas
Direct material cost	$ 6,000	$150	$ 25,000
Direct labor cost	30,000	600	100,000
Total direct cost	$36,000	$750	$125,000
Unit-level overhead			$140,000
Batch-level overhead			240,000
Product-level overhead			200,000
Plant-level overhead			220,000
Total overhead			$800,000

	Total for Product 321	Total for Product 333	Total for Dallas
Units produced	2,400	6	6,000
Direct material pounds	36,000	200	100,000
Material requisitions	40	5	1,000
Direct labor hours	7,200	120	20,000
Machine hours	3,800	30	10,000
Setups	40	4	1,600
Setup hours	400	36	8,000
Design changes	1	4	40
Design hours	320	200	2,000
Usual selling price	$150	$1,500	
Competitor's price	$100	—	

Required:

(1) Using the existing costing system, calculate the total and unit product costs of the two products. Use the format shown in Exhibit 14-3, omitting the column for the total costs of the Dallas division.

(2) If the Dallas Division adopts an ABC system, with the number of setups as the activity driver for all batch-level overhead, design hours as the activity driver for all product-level overhead, and direct labor hours as the driver for all unit- and plant-level overhead, what will be reported as the total and per-unit costs of the two products? Use the format shown in Exhibit 14-4, omitting the column for the total costs of the Dallas Division. Calculate unit costs to the nearest cent.

(3) Using the usual selling prices and the product costs reported by the existing system, calculate the gross margin in dollars and as a percent of sales, to the nearest whole percent, on one unit of each product.

(4) Using the usual selling prices and the product costs reported by the ABC system, calculate the gross margin in dollars and as a percent of sales, to the nearest whole percent, on one unit of each product.

(5) Compare the information provided by the costing system described in requirement 1 to the ABC information. What new insight is revealed by the ABC system?

(6) Make pricing and product-line recommendations for Dallas Division's management based on the results of the ABC study. Include other options Dallas should consider, and suggest how each possible action could be implemented.

C14-2 Product Cost under ABC and Traditional Costing. Craig Company's Warrenton Division manufactures a variety of products, including Product 33 and Product 44. Recently, competitors have introduced new products competing with Product 44 and with other high-volume Warrenton products, at prices substantially lower than Warrenton's prices. To better understand its product costs, Warrenton Division changed its costing system at the beginning of the most recent year and is considering changing it again.

Until the beginning of the most recent year, the Warrenton Division used a costing system that accumulated all overhead in a single cost pool and allocated it based on direct labor hours; this system was called the one-pool indirect cost system, or OPICS. Over a period of many years, the OPICS overhead rate gradually had approached $100 per direct labor hour. Management came to believe that products were simply being penalized for using direct labor, because engineers seemed to be going to wasteful lengths to redesign the direct labor out of products. The results of these design efforts included further increases in the overhead rate.

In an attempt to remedy the situation, management implemented a three-pool indirect cost system, or TPICS, at the beginning of the most recent year. TPICS allocates all machine-related overhead based on machine hours, all material-related overhead based on direct material cost, and all remaining overhead based on direct labor hours.

Warrenton's controller states, "The logic of TPICS was a big improvement over OPICS, but it was really just a first step and we quickly realized it was not enough. We needed a careful study of cost pools and allocation bases to see if we could better capture the economics of producing both high- and low-volume products."

The ensuing study revealed substantial costs related to setup activity, plus some material handling costs primarily related to the number of loads of material handled, and materials administration cost primarily related to the number of orders placed with vendors. The study also revealed that engineers' troubleshooting efforts primarily consisted of assisting with setups. To eliminate the penalty for using direct labor, machine hours was selected as the base for allocating costs that have an unclear relationship with output. Based on these decisions, a new cost system was proposed, with the followng overhead cost pools and allocation bases:

Pool	Base
Machine setup and troubleshooting	Setup hours
Material handling	Loads handled
Materials administration	Vendor orders
Engineering design	Design hours
Machine operation and all remaining overhead	Machine hours

Because of the large number of products manufactured at Warrenton, management has decided to focus initially on just two products: 33, which is representative of most of Warrenton's low-volume products; and 44, a representative high-volume product. The following information pertains to the most recent year's operation of the Warrenton Division. For brevity, details for products other than 33 and 44 are not shown, but the division's totals are given in the last column.

	Total for Product 33	Total for Product 44	Total for Warrenton
Direct material	$15,000	$120,000	$1,320,000
Direct labor (average wage differs among products)	6,000	60,000	300,000
Total direct costs	$21,000	$180,000	$1,620,000
Overhead:			
Machine related:			
Machine operation			$ 200,000
Machine setup			140,000
Total			$ 340,000
Materials related:			
Material handling			$ 135,000
Materials administration			195,000
Total			$ 330,000
Engineering:			
Troubleshooting			$ 100,000
Design			260,000
Total			$ 360,000
Other overhead			$ 900,000
Total overhead			$1,930,000
Units	100	2,000	5,000
Loads of material handled	20	60	15,000
Vendor orders	90	150	10,000
Direct labor hours	450	6,000	25,000
Machine hours	300	3,000	20,000
Setup hours	300	400	3,000
Design hours	280	300	4,000
Usual selling price	$800	$450	
Competitor's price	—	300	

Required:

(1) If OPICS had been used in the most recent year, what would have been reported as the total and unit costs of the two products? Use the format shown in Exhibit 14-3, omitting the column for the total costs of the division.

(2) Using TPICS, what are the total and unit costs of the two products? Use the format shown in Exhibit 14-3, omitting the column for the total costs of the division.

(3) Does TPICS constitute an ABC system? Why or why not?

(4) Using the proposed new costing system, what are the total and unit costs of the two products? Use the format shown in Exhibit 14-3, omitting the column for the total costs of the division.

(5) Does the proposed new costing system constitute an ABC system? Why or why not?

(6) Compared to TPICS, what new insight is revealed by the proposed new system?

(7) Make recommendations for Warrenton Division's management based on the results of the recent cost study and the results of requirement 6. In addition to pricing and product-line recommendations, include other options Warrenton should consider, and suggest how each possible action might be implemented.

PART 4

Budgeting and Standard Costs

CHAPTER 15

Budgeting: Profits, Sales, Costs, and Expenses

Learning Objectives

After studying this chapter, you will be able to:

1. Define profit planning.
2. Distinguish between long-range and short-range planning.
3. List the advantages and disadvantages of profit planning.
4. List the fundamental principles of budget development and implementation.
5. Point out employee motivational hazards in the budgeting process and list budget system requirements to avoid such hazards.
6. Prepare a complete operating budget, including budget schedules for sales, production, commercial expenses, income statement, and balance sheet.

Management sets goals and objectives for a company and then formulates plans for achieving these goals and objectives. The expected financial impacts of management's plans are developed and evaluated through the budgeting process. Once the accepted plans are set in motion, effective control of operations then depends on cost accounting, which provides management with detailed statements of the actual cost of materials, labor, factory overhead, marketing expenses, and administrative expenses. Comparisons and analyses of actual costs with those budgeted enable management to identify deviations from its plans. This process in turn provides a basis for controlling operations. The reasons for significant deviations from the budget can then be determined and appropriate corrective action taken.

This chapter begins with a discussion of the concept of profit planning, including long-range and short-range budgets. Next, the principles of budgeting are discussed, after which a detailed illustration of an operating budget is presented. Budgets for capital expenditures, research and development, and cash, along with budgeting for nonmanufacturing business and not-for-profit organizations, zero-base budgeting, PERT and PERT/cost, and probabilistic budgets, are discussed in Chapter 16.

Profit Planning

The terms *profit planning* and *budgeting* are often viewed as synonymous. **Profit planning** is the process of consciously developing a well-thought-out operational plan that will achieve a company's goals and objectives. The word *profit* is part of the term because the overriding objective of a plan must be a satisfactory profit for the company. A budget is simply a plan expressed in financial and other quantitative terms. A company's profit plan consists of a detailed operating budget along with long- and short-range income statements, balance sheets, and cash budgets.

Budgets should be distinguished from forecasts. A profit plan or budget represents the expected profit level or target that management strives to achieve. A forecast, on the other hand, is a level of some activity that the organization predicts will occur. For example, if demand for a particular product is forecast, a sales budget detailing revenues and costs can be prepared on the basis of the forecast of demand for the product.

Sound profit planning is difficult to achieve, because external forces (such as changes in technology, the actions of competitors, the economy, demographics, consumer tastes and preferences, social attitudes, and political factors) exert strong influences on business. These forces generally are not controllable by the firm, and the magnitude and direction of changes are often difficult to predict.

Setting Profit Objectives

Fundamentally, three different approaches can be followed in setting profit objectives.[1]

1. In the **a priori method**, profit objectives take precedence over the planning process. At the outset, management specifies a given rate of return, which it seeks to realize in the long run by means of planning toward that end.
2. In the **a posteriori method**, the determination of profit objectives is subordinate to planning, and objectives emerge as the product of the planning itself.
3. In the **pragmatic method**, management uses a profit standard that has been tested empirically and sanctioned by experience. By using a target rate of profit derived from experience, expectations, or comparisons, management establishes a relative profit standard that is considered satisfactory for the company.

In setting profit objectives, management should consider the following factors:

1. Profit or loss resulting from a given volume of sales
2. Sales volume required to recover all consumed costs and produce a profit adequate to pay dividends to shareholders and provide sufficient retained earnings for future business needs
3. Break-even point
4. Sales volume that the present operating capacity can produce
5. Operating capacity necessary to attain the profit objectives
6. Return on capital employed

Public expectations and social responsibilities compel companies to consider the social consequences of profit objectives. Increasingly, important actions must be evaluated in a context that includes social as well as economic impacts. Potential social impacts specifically pertain to "environmental pollution, the consumption of nonrenewable resources, and other ecological factors; the rights of individuals and groups; the maintenance of public service; public safety; health and education; and many other social concerns."[2]

---

[1] *Research Report No. 42,* "Long-Range Profit Planning" (New York: Institute of Management Accounting (formerly National Association of Accountants), 1964), pp. 60–65.

[2] Robert K. Elliott, "Social Accounting and Corporate Decision-Making," *Management Controls,* Vol. 21, No. 1, p. 2.

Long-Range Profit Planning

Business has become increasingly aware of a need to develop long-range profit plans. **Long-range planning** has been defined as "the continuous process of making present decisions systematically and, with the best possible knowledge of their futurity, organizing systematically the efforts needed to carry out these decisions, and measuring the results of these decisions against the expectations through organized, systematic feedback."[3] Long-range plans are not stated in precise terms, nor are they expected to be completely coordinated future plans. They deal rather with specific areas such as sales, capital expenditures, extensive research and development activities, and financial requirements.

In long-range profit planning, management attempts to find the most probable course of events. Of greatest importance, however, is flexibility and adaptability to changing conditions. Long-range planning does not eliminate risk, for risk taking is the essence of economic activity. An end result of successful long-range profit planning is a capacity to take a greater risk, which is a fundamental way to improve entrepreneurial performance.

Market trends and economic factors, inflation, growth of population, personal consumption expenditures, and indexes of industrial production form the background for long-range planning. Quantitative and dollar sales estimates for a three- to five-year forecast can be developed from this information. A prospective income statement can then be prepared, showing anticipated sales, fixed and variable costs (factory, marketing, and administrative), contribution margin, and operating income by years. A balance sheet by years should indicate anticipated cash balances, inventory levels, accounts receivable balances, and liabilities. This financial long-range plan can also be supported by a cash flow statement.

The rate of return on capital (total assets) employed is an important statistic in long-range profit planning and in setting profit objectives. To measure the effectiveness with which management is likely to use the assets, rates of return are computed for each individual year covered in the long-range plan. These figures show whether planned increases in total net income keep pace with increases in assets at the corporate as well as divisional or operating levels. Though return on capital employed is the basic measure of profit performance (discussed in detail in Chapter 26), companies typically use several other measures, such as the ratio of net income to sales, the ratio of sales to shareholders' capital, and earnings per common share.[4]

Short-Range Budgets

Management's long-range plans can only be achieved through successful long-run profit performance, which requires growth and a reasonably high and stable level of profit. Long-range plans with their future expectancy of profits and growth, however, must be incorporated into a shorter-range budget for both planning and control of the contemplated course of action. Although one year is the usual planning period, **short-range budgets** can cover periods of 3, 6, or 12 months, depending on the nature of the business. For efficient planning, the annual operating budget should be expanded into an 18-month budget, allowing for a 3-month period at the end of the old year, 12 months for the regular budget period, and an additional 3 months into the third year. These overlapping months

---

[3] Peter F. Drucker, "Long-Range Planning," *Management Science*, Vol. 5, No. 3, p. 240.

[4] *Research Report No. 42.*

are needed to allow transition from year to year and to make adjustments based on prior months' experience. The budget period should:

1. Be divided into months.
2. Be long enough to complete production of the various products.
3. Cover at least one entire seasonal cycle for a business of a seasonal nature.
4. Be long enough to allow for the financing of production well in advance of actual needs.
5. Coincide with the financial accounting period to compare actual results with budget estimates.

Some organizations use a continuous budget, in which a month or quarter in the future is added as the month or quarter just ended is dropped, and the budget for the entire period is revised and updated as needed. This procedure forces management to think continually about its short-range plans.

Advantages of Profit Planning

Profit planning, or budgeting, has the following benefits and advantages:

1. Profit planning provides a disciplined approach to problem identification and problem solving. Management is obliged to study and evaluate systematically every aspect of the business in developing the periodic budget. This affords the opportunity to re-appraise every facet of operations periodically and re-examine the company's basic policies and programs.
2. Profit planning provides a sense of direction and purpose to all levels of management. It helps to develop an atmosphere of profit-mindedness throughout the organization and to encourage an attitude of cost-consciousness and efficient resource utilization.
3. Profit planning enhances coordination of business activity. It provides a way to coordinate the efforts of all segments of the business in achieving the goals and objectives of the firm. The budgeting process makes it possible to spot and eliminate bottlenecks before they occur and to channel capital and effort into the most profitable activities.
4. Profit planning provides a vehicle to enlist the ideas and cooperation of all levels of management. The skill and knowledge of all managers are needed to develop the most effective plan possible. Participation by personnel at all levels not only brings the best ideas to light, but it also provides a way to communicate objectives and gain support for the final plan. Managers who participate in the budget process learn what is expected of them and develop a sense of commitment to the budget goals they help establish.
5. The budget provides a yardstick that can be used to evaluate actual performance and gauge the managerial judgment and ability of individual executives. This in turn encourages managers to plan and perform efficiently, thereby increasing output and reducing cost.

Limitations of Profit Planning

While the advantages of profit planning are unquestionably impressive and far-reaching, the following limitations and pitfalls should be mentioned:

1. Forecasting is not an exact science; a certain amount of judgment is present in any estimate. Because a budget must be based on forecasts of

future events, a revision or modification of the budget should be made when variations from the estimates warrant a change of plans. Flexibility should be built into the budget wherever possible, and management should keep the effect of forecast error in mind when using the budget as an evaluation tool. If actual performance deviates substantially from the budget, the reason may simply be the result of a forecasting error.

2. The budget can focus a manager's attention on goals (such as high production or high credit sales) that are not necessarily in harmony with the organization's overall objectives. Thus, care must be used in setting goals in order to channel managers' efforts properly. To accomplish this task, managers must be motivated to strive for attainment of their personal objectives in congruence with the organization's objectives. A budgetary system is inadequate whenever it motivates an individual to take an action that is not in the best interest of the organization. Regardless of how sophisticated budgetary systems become, their effectiveness ultimately depends on how they influence human behavior and attitudes.[5]
3. A profit-planning program must have the commitment of top management and the cooperation and participation of all members of the management team in order to be successful. The basis for success is executive management's sustained adherence to and enthusiasm for the profit plan. Too often a profit plan fails because executive management has given it only token support. If top management does not consistently support the budget process, lower-level management quickly begins to view the budget process as a meaningless exercise, and as a result, the quality of the budget deteriorates. Also, involvement of all levels of management is needed to avoid the feeling at lower levels that the budget is being imposed on them without their participation.
4. Excessive use of the budget as an evaluation tool can result in dysfunctional behavior. Managers may attempt to build slack into the budget or engage in activities that are costly to the company in order to look good when they are evaluated. (Dysfunctional behavior is discussed in detail in Chapter 17.)
5. Profit planning does not eliminate or take over the role of administration. Executives should not feel restricted by the budget. Rather, the profit plan is designed to provide detailed information that allows executives to operate with strength and vision toward achievement of the organization's objectives.
6. Installation takes time. Management often becomes impatient and loses interest because it expects too much too soon. The budget first must be sold to the responsible people, and they, in turn, must then be guided, trained, and educated in the fundamental steps, methods, and purposes of a budgetary system.

Principles of Budgeting

A company's organization chart and its chart of accounts form the basic framework on which to build a coordinated and efficient system of managerial planning and budgetary control. The organization chart defines the functional responsibilities of executives and thereby justifies their budgets. Although final responsibility for the budget rests with executive management, all managers are

[5] Paul J. Carruth and Thurrell O. McClendon, "How Supervisors React to 'Meeting the Budget' Pressure," *Management Accounting*, Vol. 67, No. 5, p. 54.

responsible for the preparation and execution of their departmental budgets. If a budgetary control system is to be successful, these managers must fully cooperate and must understand their role in making the budget system successful. The budget must be the joint effort of many people—a working document that forms the basis for action.

The Budget Committee

The budgeting process usually is directed by a **budget committee**, which is composed of the sales manager, the production manager, the chief engineer, the treasurer, and the controller. The principal functions of the budget committee are to:

1. Decide on general policies.
2. Request, receive, and review individual budget estimates.
3. Suggest revisions in individual budget estimates.
4. Approve budgets and later revisions.
5. Receive and analyze budget reports.
6. Recommend actions designed to improve efficiency where necessary.

In performing these functions, the budget committee becomes a management committee. It is a powerful force in coordinating the various activities of the business and in controlling operations.

Budget Development and Implementation

The process of developing a budget can be as important as the budget's content and should incorporate the following fundamental principles:

1. Adequate guidance should be provided so that all management levels are working on the same assumptions, targeted objectives, and agenda. All managers should understand the limitations and constraints of their participation and the bounds of their decision making. Participants should be told, prior to the time the budget is established, how their activities will fit into the entire organization and what constraints will be placed on them and their activities by upper-level administrative decisions.
2. Participation in the budgeting process should be encouraged at each level within the organization. The activity of developing the budget must be structured to involve the individuals who will be responsible for implementing the budget and who will be rewarded according to its accomplishments. The participation of those who are responsible for implementation improves the quality of the budget by utilizing the widest possible base of expertise. In addition, managers who are responsible for implementation will gain understanding and commitment by participating in the development of the budget.
3. The climate of budget preparation should aim to eliminate anxiety and defensiveness. Individuals need to have the freedom and authority to influence and accept their own performance levels, and should assume the responsibility for accomplishment. When budget preparation is oriented to the problems and opportunities of the participants, their anxiety is reduced, and their desire to incorporate slack into the budget is thereby alleviated.
4. The preparation of the budget should be structured so that there is a reasonably high probability of successful attainment of objectives. When

challenging but attainable objectives are achieved, feelings of success, confidence, and satisfaction are produced and aspiration levels are raised. If objectives are not accomplished, the reasons for this failure should be clear. A careful distinction should be made between controllable factors for which individuals should be responsible and for uncontrollable factors for which they are not.

5. Numerous sets of assumptions should be evaluated in developing the budget. This iterative process is facilitated by the use of computers.

If the proper principles for developing a budget are followed, implementation difficulties are minimized. Proper budget implementation requires adherence to the following principles:

1. Rewards and reward contingencies should be established that will lead to achieving the organizational objectives. Too often, the budgeting process does not provide sufficient rewards to induce employees to accomplish organizational objectives.
2. The organization should focus on rewarding achievement rather than punishing failure. Feelings of success or failure largely determine attitudes toward the budget and the level of performance to which employees will aspire.
3. Rapid feedback should be provided on the performance of each work team or individual. This principle necessitates the use of reports and reporting procedures that are understandable to workers and supervisors at the department level, so that they can analyze their results and initiate corrective action.[6]

Budgeting and Human Behavior

Anyone who is charged with the task of creating a budget and establishing budget figures, particularly of department overhead, is aware of the irrational and often obstinate behavior of certain supervisors with respect to the contemplated budget program.[7] In some firms, budgeting is perhaps the most unpopular management and/or accounting device for planning and control.

Considerable attention has been given to the behavioral implications of providing managers with the data required for planning, coordinating, and controlling activities. Cost accounting and budgeting play an important role in influencing individual and group behavior at all the various stages of the management process including: (1) setting goals, (2) informing individuals what they must do to contribute to the accomplishment of these goals, (3) motivating desirable performance, (4) evaluating performance, and (5) suggesting when corrective action should be taken. In short, accountants cannot ignore the behavioral sciences (psychology, social psychology, and sociology) because the accounting function of providing information for decision making is essentially a behavioral function.[8]

---

[6] J. Owen Cherrington and David J. Cherrington, "Budget Games for Fun and Frustration," *Management Accounting*, Vol. 57, No. 7, p. 32.

[7] Chris Argyris, *The Impact of Budgets on People* (New York: Financial Executives Research Foundation (formerly Controllership Foundation, Inc.), 1952).

[8] For references explaining behavioral implications of accounting in some detail, see William J. Bruns, Jr., and Don T. DeCoster, *Accounting and Its Behavioral Implications* (New York: McGraw-Hill Book Company, 1969) and Edwin H. Caplan, *Management Accounting and Behavioral Science* (Reading, Mass.: Addison-Wesley Publishing Co., Inc., 1971).

For budget building, James L. Pierce advises top management to use the budget as a tool for directing activity and not as a club to be held over the heads of lower-level managers. He argues that the entire planning and control process should be used as a device for freeing employees to do their best work and not as a machine of destruction and condemnation.[9]

An individual manager's attitude toward the budget will depend greatly on the existing good relationship within the management group. If properly guided by the company plan, with an opportunity for increased compensation, greater satisfaction, and eventual promotion, the middle and lower management group can achieve remarkable results. On the other hand, a discordant management group, unwilling to accept the budget's underlying figures, can perform so poorly that top management will be compelled "to defer trying the planning and control idea until it has put its house in order."[10]

No budget can be successful as long as people are unwilling to accept it. The problem of motivating a company's personnel, however, is difficult to solve. As pointed out in Chapter 11, pay incentives for factory workers do not necessarily lead to greater productivity. Motivational requirements that have been suggested include the following:[11]

1. A compensation system that builds and maintains a clearly understood relationship between results and rewards.
2. A system for performance appraisal that employees understand with regard to their individual effectiveness and key results, their tasks and their responsibilities, their degree and span of influence in decision making, as well as the time allowed to judge their results.
3. A system of communication that allows employees to query their superiors with trust and honest communication.
4. A system of promotion that generates and sustains employee faith in its validity and judgment.
5. A system of employee support through coaching, counseling, and career planning.
6. A system that not only considers company objectives, but also employees' skills and capacities.
7. A system that will not settle for mediocrity, but that reaches for realistic and attainable standards, stressing improvement and providing an environment in which the concept of excellence can grow.

The Complete Periodic Budget

A complete set of budgets generally consists of the following elements:

1. A sales budget
2. Estimates of inventory and production requirements
3. Budgets of materials, labor, and factory overhead, combined into a cost of goods manufactured and sold schedule
4. Budgets for marketing and administrative expenses

[9] James L. Pierce, "The Budget Comes of Age," *Harvard Business Review*, Vol. 32, No. 3 pp. 58–66.
[10] *Ibid*, p. 60.
[11] Paul E. Sussman, "Motivating Financial Personnel," *Journal of Accountancy*, Vol. 141, No. 2, p. 80.

5. Estimates of other income and expense items and income tax
6. A budgeted income statement
7. A budget of capital expenditures and of research and development expenditures
8. A cash receipts and disbursements budget
9. A budgeted balance sheet showing the estimated financial position of the company at the end of the budget period

Items 1 through 5 form the basis for preparing the budgeted income statement. They, along with items 6 and 9, are discussed and illustrated in the remainder of this chapter. Items 7 and 8 are covered in Chapter 16.

The data for Franklin Company are used to illustrate the budget components that make up the income statement. As each budget component is discussed, the relevant data are used to illustrate the preparation of the related budget schedule. Subsequent schedules are cross-referenced to show the link between the various budget parts, building to the budgeted income statement. Assume that Franklin Company manufactures three products, A, B, and C, which are marketed in two territories, the East and the West. The production departments are designated Cutting, Assembling, and Finishing. Budget estimates for the coming year ending on December 31, 19A are presented in Exhibit 15-1.

To achieve a concise yet comprehensive illustration, only annual data are shown. As previously noted, however, monthly budget details are not only desirable but often necessary. Also, customer group classifications for sales are omitted, there is no beginning or ending work in process inventory, and marketing and administrative expenses are not shown in detail.

Sales Budget

One of the most important elements in a budgetary control system is a realistic sales estimate that is based on analyses of past sales and the present market. Yet the sales variable is often the budget component that is the most difficult to predict with reasonable precision. The demand for an entity's products or services normally depends on forces and factors largely beyond the scope of management's control. In most instances, this uncertainty makes expected sales the focal point of the planning process.[12]

The task of preparing the **sales budget** is usually approached from two different angles: (1) judging and evaluating external influences and (2) considering internal influences. These two influences are brought together in a workable sales budget. External influences include the general trend of industrial activity, actions of competitors, governmental policies, cyclical phases of the nation's economy, price-level expectations, purchasing power of the population, population shift, and changes in buying habits and modes of living. Internal influences are sales trends, factory capacities, new products, plant expansion, seasonal products, sales estimates, and establishment of quotas for salespeople and sales territories. The profit desired by the company is a highly significant consideration.

The annual sales budget in Exhibit 15-2 for Franklin Company, detailed by product and by territory, is prepared from the data in Exhibit 15-1.

---

[12] Eugene A. Imhoff, Jr., *Sales Forecasting Systems* (Montvale, N.J.: Institute of Management Accountants (formerly National Association of Accountants), 1986), pp. 5–6.

EXHIBIT 15-1

Sales

Product	East (units)	West (units)	Sales Price (per unit)
A	4,000	3,000	$200
B	6,000	5,000	150
C	9,000	6,000	100

Inventories

Materials:

Material	Units in Beginning Inventory	Units in Ending Inventory	Unit Cost
X	30,000	40,000	$ 1.00
Y	10,000	12,000	14.00
Z	2,000	2,500	2.50

Work in process: None at the beginning or end of the period.

Finished goods (fifo):

Product	Beginning Inventory Units	Beginning Inventory Unit Cost	Units in Ending Inventory
A	200	$140	250
B	400	95	200
C	500	75	400

Materials Quantity Requirements and Unit Costs

	Material X	Material Y	Material Z
Product A	12	5	2
Product B	8	3	1
Product C	6	2	1
Materials unit cost	$1.00	$14.00	$2.50

Labor Time Requirements and Departmental Labor Rates

	Cutting (hours)	Assembling (hours)	Finishing (hours)
Product A	.500	2.500	.800
Product B	.375	2.000	.500
Product C	.375	1.750	.500
Rate per labor hour	$8.00	$10.00	$9.00

Budgeted Factory Overhead

	Cutting Department		Assembling Department		Finishing Department	
	Fixed Cost Estimate	Variable Rate per Machine Hour	Fixed Cost Estimate	Variable Rate per Labor Hour	Fixed Cost Estimate	Variable Rate per Labor Hour
Indirect materials and supplies	$ 5,957	$ .35	$ 9,949	$ .50	$ 6,185	$ .20
Indirect labor	25,000	.50	25,000	.20	22,000	1.00
Payroll taxes	13,030	.05	67,800	.02	56,585	.10
Employee fringe benefits	14,333	—	74,580	—	62,244	—
Equipment depreciation	5,000	—	—	—	2,000	—
Small tools	—	—	2,500	.25	—	—
Repairs and maintenance	2,000	.10	1,500	.10	1,500	.10
Allocated building costs	1,000	—	1,000	—	1,000	—
Allocated general factory costs	6,000	—	9,000	—	7,500	—

Estimated Cutting Department Machine Time Required for Each Unit of Product

	Product A	Product B	Product C
Machine time in hours	.80	.60	.40

Commercial Expenses and Income Tax

Marketing expenses: $356,790
Administrative expenses: $290,000
Income tax rate: 40%

EXHIBIT 15-2

Franklin Company
Schedule 1
Sales Budget
For the Year Ending December 31, 19A

	Territories		
	East	West	Total
Product A			
Units	4,000	3,000	7,000
Unit price	$ 200	$ 200	$ 200
Total	$ 800,000	$ 600,000	$1,400,000
Product B			
Units	6,000	5,000	11,000
Unit price	$ 150	$ 150	$ 150
Total	$ 900,000	$ 750,000	$1,650,000
Product C			
Units	9,000	6,000	15,000
Unit price	$ 100	$ 100	$ 100
Total	$ 900,000	$ 600,000	$1,500,000
Total sales	$2,600,000	$1,950,000	$4,550,000

Estimating Sales. The preparation of sales estimates usually is the responsibility of the marketing manager, assisted by individual salespeople and market research personnel. Because of the many dissimilarities in the marketing of products, actual methods used to estimate sales vary widely. One method used by many companies is the preparation of sales estimates by individual salespeople. All salespeople supply their district managers with estimates of probable sales in their territories. These estimates are consolidated and adjusted by the district marketing manager and then forwarded to the general marketing manager, who makes further adjustments. These adjustments include allowances for expected economic conditions and competitive conditions of which salespeople are unaware, as well as allowances for expected canceled orders and sales returns that salespeople likely would disregard because their estimates are based on the orders they expect to procure. During the budget preparation process, it is not unusual for sales estimates to be revised a number of times. The ultimate sales estimates tend to be improved when forecasts from several sources, such as a group of managers, are averaged.

In estimating sales as well as expenditures, the tendency to over- or underestimate plans must be recognized. Individuals tend to be overly pessimistic or optimistic in setting goals and in making plans. Therefore, the budgeting system should be designed to monitor this tendency in order to keep goals and plans within reasonable bounds.

In most large organizations, the estimating procedure usually starts with known factors; namely, (1) the company's sales of past years broken down by product groups and profit margins, (2) industry or trade sales volume and perhaps profits, and (3) unusual factors influencing sales in the past. The company's past sales figures often require a restudy or reclassification due to changes in products, profit margins, competition, sales areas, distribution methods, or changes within the industry. Industry or trade sales and profits are secured from trade associations, trade publications, and various business magazines. For some industries, the U.S. Department of Commerce publishes information that is useful as background data. Unusual factors influencing past sales are inventory conditions, public economic sentiment, competition, and customer relations.

Charting a company's volume in units of various products for a three- to five-year period and comparing it with the industry's volume will disclose a company's sales trend and will pinpoint factors that affected past sales. However, a recent study indicated that, for most companies, the use of historical sales data is generally limited to the most recent two years. Thus, the amount of time-series data used is reduced. The study also finds that managers tend to use current and prospective information in preference to historical trends, even though there is research evidence that time-series models are often good predictors of future sales.[13]

Although it is all too often felt that a crystal ball is required to prepare a sales budget, a sound basis for estimating future sales often can be established by using time-series models and by applying probability analysis techniques to the consideration of general business conditions, the industry's prospects, the company's potential share of the total industry market, and the plans of competitive companies.

Seasonal Variations. When the annual sales estimate has been approved, it is divided into smaller operating periods, usually months. The monthly sales budget incorporates seasonal sales patterns based on historical experience tempered by expected changes in market demand. Trends and fluctuations in historical data should be considered and the causes identified. Factors that affect seasonal variations include local customs, consumer habits, fads, changes in climate, holidays, and the actions of competitors.

Incorporating seasonal variations into monthly sales budgets provides a reasonable basis for planning montly production and evaluating monthly sales performance. Using a budgeted average is not sufficient for these purposes because actual monthly sales are affected by seasonal variations and are not expected to equal the annual average.

Sales Budget on a Territory and Customer Basis. A sales budget not only should be divided into a monthly budget for each product, but it also should be classified by territories or districts and by types of customers. The customer classification should show sales to jobbers, wholesalers, retailers, institutions, governmental agencies, schools and colleges, foreign businesses, and so on. Such a breakdown indicates the contribution of each territory and customer class to total sales and profits. This form of analysis often reveals that certain territories or classes of customers are not given sufficient attention by sales managers and sales representatives. A detailed sales budget can be an effective means of analyzing possible new trade outlets. It assists in identifying reasons for a drop in sales, in investigating such a decrease, and in taking remedial steps.

Estimating Production and Inventory Requirements. Prior to the final acceptance of a sales budget, the factory's capacity to produce the estimated quantities must be determined. The production level should maintain inventories that are sufficient to fulfill periodic sales requirements.

If factory capacity is available, production should be planned at a level that will keep workers and equipment operating all year. Drastic fluctuations in employment are expensive and do not promote good labor relations. If a sales budget indicates that factory employment in certain months is likely to fall below

---

[13] *Ibid.*, pp. 20, 36.

a desirable level, it points up the necessity of attempting to increase sales volume or increase inventories. At the same time, the investment in inventories should be held to a level consistent with sound financial policy. If estimated sales are higher than available capacity, the purchase or rental of new machinery and factory space must be considered as a means of increasing plant capacity.

Sales Estimate Follow-Up. Follow-up review should occur at intervals influenced by the frequency of change in the company, its industry, and general economic conditions. The review should determine (1) the accuracy of past estimates, (2) the location of the major estimation errors, (3) the best method by which to update estimates, and (4) the steps needed for improvement of the making and monitoring of future estimates.

Past errors indicate the reliance that can be placed on sales estimates and provide insight into the company and the personal bias built into the estimate. When estimates are monitored, comparison with actual results should extend beyond financial results to include consideration of the underlying factors and key assumptions. Such comparisons might require the monitoring of unit sales volumes, prices, production rates, backlogs of sales orders, changes in capacity, and economic indicators.

Production Budget

The **production budget** deals with the scheduling of operations, the determination of volume, and the establishment of maximum and minimum quantities of finished goods inventories. It provides the basis for preparing the budgets for materials, labor, and factory overhead.

A production budget is stated in physical units. As shown in Exhibit 15-3, this budget is the budgeted sales quantity adjusted for any inventory changes.

EXHIBIT 15-3

Franklin Company
Schedule 2
Production Budget
For the Year Ending December 31, 19A

	Product A	Product B	Product C
Units required to meet sales budget (Schedule 1)	7,000	11,000	15,000
Add desired ending inventory	250	200	400
Total units required	7,250	11,200	15,400
Less beginning inventory	200	400	500
Planned production for the year	7,050	10,800	14,900

If there are work in process inventories, the equivalent number of such units in the ending inventory would be added to, and units in the beginning inventory would be subtracted from, the calculations in the example in order to determine the units to be produced. In a just-in-time system, work in process inventory may be so small that changes in the level of work in process inventory are ignored in preparing the production budget.

The production budget, like other budgets, can be detailed by months or quarters as well as annually. For comparison with actual production, the detailed budget should be broken down by work stations. The nature of this division will be determined by plant layout, type of production, and other factors.

For a company that does not manufacture standard products but produces only on order, a detailed production budget may not be possible. In special-order work, the primary problem is to be prepared for production when orders are received. Work must be routed and scheduled through the factory so that delays are prevented and production facilities are fully utilized.

No division of a manufacturing business has made so much progress in scientific management as the production department. Constant effort is directed toward devising new techniques that will lead to more efficient production and cost savings that will be reflected in earnings.

Manufacturing Budgets

With the forecast sales translated into physical units in the production budget, the estimated manufacturing costs essential to the sales and production program can be computed. Detailed **manufacturing budgets** are prepared for direct materials and direct labor in order to identify these costs with products and responsible managers. Factory overhead is budgeted in detail by responsibility centers or departments. This budget information becomes part of the master budget to be used as a standard or target against which the performance of the individual department is judged and evaluated.

Direct Materials Budget. The **direct materials budget** specifies the quantity and cost of materials required to produce the predetermined units of finished goods. It (1) leads to the determination of quantities of materials that must be on hand, (2) permits the purchasing department to set up a purchasing schedule that assures delivery of materials when needed, and (3) establishes a means by which the treasurer can include in the cash budget the necessary funds for periodic purchases as well as for all other cash payments. Although the materials budget usually deals only with direct materials, these budgeting procedures are also applicable to supplies and indirect materials that are included in the factory overhead budget and the commercial expenses budget.

The schedules for Franklin Company consist of (1) the direct materials budget expressed in units required for production (Exhibit 15-4), (2) **the purchases budget**, specifying inventory levels and units as well as the cost of purchases (Exhibit 15-5), and (3) the **budgeted cost of materials required for production** (Exhibit 15-6).

The production planning department determines the quantity and type of materials required for the various products manufactured by a company. Most companies have standard parts lists and bills of materials, which detail all materials requirements. These requirements are given to the purchasing department, which sets up a buying schedule. This schedule is based on the objective of providing sufficient materials without overstocking, and entails an increasing trend by manufacturers to minimize inventory by utilizing a just-in-time inventory stocking policy. In preparing a buying schedule, the purchasing department must consider changes in possible delivery promises by the supplier and changes in the rate of materials consumption because of unforeseen circumstances. In a just-in-time materials inventory system, materials inventory may be so small that inventory changes can be ignored in preparing the direct materials budget. In such a situation, there may be no separate accounting for a materials inventory; instead, Materials and Work in Process may be combined into a single asset account.

EXHIBIT 15-4

Franklin Company Schedule 3 Direct Materials Budget in Units For the Year Ending December 31, 19A	Material X	Material Y	Material Z
Product A			
Units of A to be manufactured (Schedule 2)	7,050	7,050	7,050
Materials quantity required per unit of A	12	5	2
Units of materials required	84,600	35,250	14,100
Product B			
Units of B to be manufactured (Schedule 2)	10,800	10,800	10,800
Materials quantity required per unit of B	8	3	1
Units of materials required	86,400	32,400	10,800
Product C			
Units of C to be manufactured (Schedule 2)	14,900	14,900	14,900
Materials quantity required per unit of C	6	2	1
Units of materials required	89,400	29,800	14,900
Total units of materials required	260,400	97,450	39,800

EXHIBIT 15-5

Franklin Company Schedule 4 Purchases Budget For the Year Ending December 31, 19A	Material X	Material Y	Material Z	Total
Units required for production (Schedule 3)	260,400	97,450	39,800	
Add desired ending inventory	40,000	12,000	2,500	
Quantity required	300,400	109,450	42,300	
Less beginning inventory	30,000	10,000	2,000	
Units to be purchased	270,400	99,450	40,300	
Unit cost	$ 1.00	$ 14.00	$ 2.50	
Total cost of purchases	$270,400	$1,392,300	$100,750	$1,763,450

Direct Labor Budget. The annual budget is the principal tool for the overall planning for human resources. When the budget is completed and approved, it should include a human resources plan that is coordinated with planned sales and production activities as well as the profit goal.

The **direct labor budget**, based on specifications drawn up by product engineers, guides the personnel department in determining the number and type of workers needed. If the labor force has been with the firm for several years and if the production schedule does not call for additional workers, the task of the personnel department is rather easy. If an increase in the labor force is required, the personnel department must make plans in advance to assure the availability of workers. Frequently, the personnel department must provide a training program that provides workers to the production department at the proper time. When workers are to be laid off, the personnel department must prepare a list of those affected, giving due recognition to skill and seniority rights. In many companies,

EXHIBIT 15-6

Franklin Company
Schedule 5
Cost of Materials Required for Production Budget
For the Year Ending December 31, 19A

	Material X	Material Y	Material Z	Total
Product A				
Units of materials required for production (Schedule 3)	84,600	35,250	14,100	
Unit cost	$ 1.00	$ 14.00	$ 2.50	
Total	$ 84,600	$ 493,500	$ 35,250	$ 613,350
Product B				
Units of materials required for production (Schedule 3)	86,400	32,400	10,800	
Unit cost	$ 1.00	$ 14.00	$ 2.50	
Total	$ 86,400	$ 453,600	$ 27,000	567,000
Product C				
Units of materials required for production (Schedule 3)	89,400	29,800	14,900	
Unit cost	$ 1.00	$ 14.00	$ 2.50	
Total	$ 89,400	$ 417,200	$ 37,250	543,850
Total cost of materials required for production	$260,400	$1,364,300	$ 99,500	$1,724,200

this schedule is prepared in collaboration with union representatives in order to protect employees from any injustice or hardship.

For each type of labor, the hours or the number of workers must be translated into dollar values. Normally, established labor rates are used; however, if conditions indicate that rates will change, the new rates should be used so that the financial budget will reflect realistic costs. The direct labor budget presented in Exhibit 15-7 for Franklin Company is prepared from the data in Exhibit 15-1.

Indirect labor is included in the factory overhead budget and consists of such employees as helpers in producing departments, maintenance workers, crane operators, materials clerks, and receiving clerks. In addition, if labor is not traceable to the products manufactured, as is often the case in fully automated manufacturing plants, no separate direct labor budget is prepared. Instead, the cost of paying employees who operate production machinery and equipment would be included in the factory overhead budget, along with indirect labor. In such a system, labor is charged to products through the factory overhead rate. Labor requirements for marketing and administrative activities must be budgeted as part of the commercial expenses budget.

Factory Overhead Budget. The detailed **factory overhead budget** follows the chart of accounts. As discussed and illustrated in Chapters 12 and 13, costs are grouped in accounts according to:

1. Natural cost classification, such as indirect materials and supplies, indirect labor, payroll taxes, employee fringe benefits, utilities, depreciation, repairs and maintenance, casualty insurance, and property taxes.
2. Departmental or cost center classification according to the organizational unit or functional area in which the cost originates.

EXHIBIT 15-7

Franklin Company
Schedule 6
Direct Labor Budget
For the Year Ending December 31, 19A

	Product A	Product B	Product C	Total
Cutting Department				
Units to be manufactured (Schedule 2)	7,050	10,800	14,900	
Hours required per unit	.500	.375	.375	
Total hours required	3,525	4,050	5,587.5	13,162.5
Departmental labor rate	$ 8	$ 8	$ 8	$ 8
Total departmental labor cost	$ 28,200	$ 32,400	$ 44,700	$105,300
Assembling Department				
Units to be manufactured (Schedule 2)	7,050	10,800	14,900	
Hours required per unit	2.500	2.000	1.750	
Total hours required	17,625	21,600	26,075	65,300
Departmental labor rate	$ 10	$ 10	$ 10	$ 10
Total departmental labor cost	$176,250	$216,000	$260,750	$653,000
Finishing Department				
Units to be manufactured (Schedule 2)	7,050	10,800	14,900	
Hours required per unit	.800	.500	.500	
Total hours required	5,640	5,400	7,450	18,490
Departmental labor rate	$ 9	$ 9	$ 9	$ 9
Total departmental labor cost	$ 50,760	$ 48,600	$ 67,050	$166,410
Total direct labor cost	$255,210	$297,000	$372,500	$924,710

The natural cost (primary account) classification alone is not useful for budget purposes, because costs usually are incurred in or for the benefit of different organizational units within the factory. By classifying costs according to individual departments or cost centers, budgetary control is enhanced. Preparation of any cost budget should be guided by the principle that every cost is chargeable to a department or cost center and that the supervisor of each unit should be held accountable and responsible for the costs incurred within that unit. Those costs for which the supervisor is directly responsible should be identified in the supervisor's budget. Allocated costs for which the supervisor has little or no responsibility also should be identified.

If department or cost center supervisors accept a budget, they are more likely to cooperate in its execution. Therefore, supervisors should be asked to prepare their own estimates of departmental costs, based on the department's projected activity for the budget period. The accuracy of cost estimates depends on a thorough understanding of the behavior of cost with respect to activity, as discussed in Chapter 3. The activities that drive cost must be identified, and fixed costs and variable rates must be estimated. The variable rates are then multiplied times the quantity of activity required to meet the production budget for the department or cost center. These estimates and any revisions should be reviewed and coordinated with other budgets before they are incorporated into the overall budget.

For Franklin Company, overhead is allocated to production on the basis of machine hours in the Cutting Department and on the basis of labor hours in the Assembling and Finishing Departments. Labor hour requirements are obtained from the Direct Labor Budget (Exhibit 15-7); however, because machine hours are used in the Cutting Department, they must be estimated for planned production as illustrated in Exhibit 15-8.

EXHIBIT 15-8

Franklin Company
Schedule 7
Cutting Department Budgeted Machine Hours
For the Year Ending December 31, 19A

	Product A	Product B	Product C	Total
Units to be manufactured (Schedule 2)	7,050	10,800	14,900	
Hours of machine time required for each unit	.80	.60	.40	
Total machine hours required in department	5,640	6,480	5,960	18,080

With the level of activities that drive cost in Franklin Company's producing departments determined, departmental factory overhead for the period can be budgeted, including service department cost allocations (as illustrated in Chapter 13). When factory overhead has been budgeted in the producing departments, predetermined factory overhead rates can be computed. In this illustration, the departmental overhead rates are computed on the basis of expected capacity, so there is no budgeted over- or underapplied fixed factory overhead. If normal capacity were used as the basis for computing departmental rates and normal capacity differed from expected capacity, a provision for over- or underapplied fixed factory overhead would be included in the budget. Budgeted factory overhead and the predetermined departmental overhead rates for Franklin Company are illustrated in Exhibit 15-9.

Beginning and Ending Inventories. Not only must inventory quantities be determined for materials, work in process, and finished goods, but the inventories must be costed in order to make available the necessary information leading to preparation of a **budgeted cost of goods manufactured and sold statement** and ultimately to an income statement and a balance sheet. Before the ending balance in Finished Goods can be determined, the budgeted unit cost for the products manufactured during the period must be computed. For Franklin Company, the computation of budgeted unit costs is presented in Exhibit 15-10. Observe that the unit costs for the products are the summation of estimates for direct materials, direct labor, and applied factory overhead.

Franklin Company uses a fifo cost flow assumption for all inventories. The beginning and ending quantities and costs for all inventories are summarized in Exhibit 15-11.

EXHIBIT 15-9

Franklin Company
Schedule 8
Budgeted Factory Overhead and Departmental Rates
For the Year Ending December 31, 19A

	Fixed Cost	Variable Cost Rate	Budgeted Activity	Variable Cost	Total
Cutting Department					
Indirect materials and supplies	$ 5,957	$ .35	18,080	$ 6,328	$ 12,285
Indirect labor	25,000	.50	18,080	9,040	34,040
Payroll taxes	13,030	.05	18,080	904	13,934
Employee fringe benefits	14,333	—	—	—	14,333
Equipment depreciation	5,000	—	—	—	5,000
Repairs and maintenance	2,000	.10	18,080	1,808	3,808
Allocated building cost	1,000	—	—	—	1,000
Allocated general factory cost	6,000	—	—	—	6,000
Total departmental overhead					$ 90,400
Budgeted overhead allocation base (machine hours from Schedule 7)					18,080
Departmental predetermined factory overhead rate					$ 5.00
Assembling Department					
Indirect materials and supplies	$ 9,949	$ .50	65,300	$32,650	$ 42,599
Indirect labor	25,000	.20	65,300	13,060	38,060
Payroll taxes	67,800	.02	65,300	1,306	69,106
Employee fringe benefits	74,580	—	—	—	74,580
Small tools	2,500	.25	65,300	16,325	18,825
Repairs and maintenance	1,500	.10	65,300	6,530	8,030
Allocated building cost	1,000	—	—	—	1,000
Allocated general factory cost	9,000	—	—	—	9,000
Total departmental overhead					$261,200
Budgeted overhead allocation base (labor hours from Schedule 6)					65,300
Departmental predetermined factory overhead rate					$ 4.00
Finishing Department					
Indirect materials and supplies	$ 6,185	$ .20	18,490	$ 3,698	$ 9,883
Indirect labor	22,000	1.00	18,490	18,490	40,490
Payroll taxes	56,585	.10	18,490	1,849	58,434
Employee fringe benefits	62,244	—	—	—	62,244
Equipment depreciation	2,000	—	—	—	2,000
Repairs and maintenance	1,500	.10	18,490	1,849	3,349
Allocated building cost	1,000	—	—	—	1,000
Allocated general factory cost	7,500	—	—	—	7,500
Total departmental overhead					$184,900
Budgeted overhead allocation base (labor hours from Schedule 6)					18,490
Departmental predetermined factory overhead rate					$ 10.00
Cutting Department Budgeted Factory Overhead					$ 90,400
Assembling Department Budgeted Factory Overhead					261,200
Finishing Department Budgeted Factory Overhead					184,900
Total Budgeted Factory Overhead					$536,500

EXHIBIT 15-10

Franklin Company
Schedule 9
Budgeted Unit Product Cost
For the Year Ending December 31, 19A

	Product A Input Quantity	Input Unit Cost	Cost per Unit of Product A	Product B Input Quantity	Input Unit Cost	Cost per Unit of Product B	Product C Input Quantity	Input Unit Cost	Cost per Unit of Product C
Materials:									
X	12	$ 1.00	$ 12.00	8	$ 1.00	$ 8.00	6	$ 1.00	$ 6.00
Y	5	14.00	70.00	3	14.00	42.00	2	14.00	28.00
Z	2	2.50	5.00	1	2.50	2.50	1	2.50	2.50
Total..........			$ 87.00			$52.50			$36.50
Direct labor:									
Cutting Dept.........	.50	$ 8.00	$ 4.00	.375	$ 8.00	$ 3.00	.375	$ 8.00	$ 3.00
Assembling Dept...	2.50	10.00	25.00	2.00	10.00	20.00	1.75	10.00	17.50
Finishing Dept......	.80	9.00	7.20	.50	9.00	4.50	.50	9.00	4.50
Total..........			$ 36.20			$27.50			$25.00
Applied overhead:									
Cutting Dept. (MH basis).........	.80	$ 5.00	$ 4.00	.60	$ 5.00	$ 3.00	.40	$ 5.00	$ 2.00
Assembling Dept... (DLH basis).......	2.50	4.00	10.00	2.00	4.00	8.00	1.75	4.00	7.00
Finishing Dept. (DLH basis).......	.80	10.00	8.00	.50	10.00	5.00	.50	10.00	5.00
Total..........			$ 22.00			$16.00			$14.00
Total cost per unit.....			$145.20			$96.00			$75.50

EXHIBIT 15-11

Franklin Company
Schedule 10
Beginning and Ending Inventories Budget
For the Year Ending December 31, 19A

	Beginning Inventory			Ending Inventory		
	Units	Cost	Total	Units	Cost	Total
Materials:						
X	30,000	$ 1.00	$ 30,000	40,000	$ 1.00	$ 40,000
Y	10,000	14.00	140,000	12,000	14.00	168,000
Z	2,000	2.50	5,000	2,500	2.50	6,250
Total			$175,000			$214,250
Work in process: None						
Finished goods:						
Product A..........	200	$140.00	$ 28,000	250	$145.20	$ 36,300
Product B..........	400	95.00	38,000	200	96.00	19,200
Product C..........	500	75.00	37,500	400	75.50	30,200
Total			$103,500			$ 85,700
Total inventories..........			$278,500			$299,950

Budgeted Cost of Goods Manufactured and Sold Statement. This statement requires no new estimates. Figures taken from various manufacturing schedules are arranged in the form of a cost of goods manufactured and sold statement, illustrated in Exhibit 15-12. Source schedules are referenced to indicate the link with the budget components previously discussed and illustrated.

EXHIBIT 15-12

Franklin Company
Schedule 11
Budgeted Cost of Goods Manufactured and Sold Statement
For the Year Ending December 31, 19A

Materials:	
Beginning inventory (Schedule 10)	$ 175,000
Add purchases (Schedule 4)	1,763,450
Total materials available for use	$1,938,450
Less ending inventory (Schedule 10)	214,250
Cost of materials used (Schedule 5)	$1,724,200
Direct labor (Schedule 6)	924,710
Factory overhead (Schedule 8)	536,500
Total manufacturing cost	$3,185,410
Add beginning finished goods inventory (Schedule 10)	103,500
Cost of goods available for sale	$3,288,910
Less ending finished goods inventory (Schedule 10)	85,700
Cost of goods sold	$3,203,210

Budgeting Commercial Expenses

The company's chart of accounts is the basis for budgetary control of commercial expenses, which include both marketing (selling and distribution) and administrative expenses. These expenses can be classified by primary accounts and by functions.

Budgeting and analyzing commercial expenses by primary accounts is the simplest method of classification. This method stresses the nature or the type of expenditure, such as salaries, commissions, repairs, light and heat, rent, telephone and telegraph, postage, advertising, travel expenses, sales promotion, entertainment, delivery expense, freight out, insurance, donations, depreciation, taxes, and interest. As expenses are incurred, they are recorded in primary expense accounts, posted to ledger accounts, and then taken directly to the income statement. No further allocation is made. At the end of an accounting period, actual expenses are compared with either budgeted expenses or expenses of the previous month or year.

To control commercial expenses effectively, it is necessary to group them by functional activities or operating units. Classification by function emphasizes departmental activities, such as selling, advertising, warehousing, billing, credit and collection, transportation, accounting, purchasing, engineering, and financing. Such a classification is consistent with the concept of responsibility accounting and can be compared to collecting factory overhead by departments or cost centers. A departmental classification adds to, rather than replaces, the process of classifying expenses by primary accounts, because primary account classifications are maintained within each department.

When a departmental classification system is used, it is important that each expense be charged to a department and that the classification conform to the company's organization chart at the corporate level as well as each marketing territory level. However, it is impossible to suggest exact classifications, because organizational structures vary so much in business organizations. Departments having the same name can perform widely differing functions in different companies.

Commercial expenses grouped by department can be subclassified as direct and indirect expenses. Direct expenses, such as salaries and supplies, are charged directly to a department. Indirect expenses are general or service department expenses that are prorated to benefiting departments. Expenses such as rent, insurance, and utilities, when shared by several departments, constitute this type of expense. Also, expenses should be estimated and identified as to their variable and fixed components, again utilizing the cost behavior analysis tools described in Chapter 3. Such identification will help highlight control responsibility.

To identify an outlay of cash or the incurrence of a liability with a function requires considerably more work than is required by the primary account method. However, the chart of accounts normally provides the initial breakdown of expenses. Usually the allocation of expenses to departments and the identification of the primary account classification within each department can be made when the voucher is prepared. This procedure requires coding the expenditure when it is requisitioned for purchase. Any increase in expenses caused by the use of this functional method is more than offset by the advantages of improved cost control. Furthermore, to the extent that the identifications are practical and meaningful, commercial expenses can be assigned to individual products or product groups and to individual marketing territories.

Commercial expenses are not detailed in the Franklin Company illustration, but rather are shown only in summary form in the budgeted income statement. Budget detail for primary accounts as well as for functional activities, products, and territories is shown in Chapter 25, using marketing expenses as the basis for illustration.

Marketing Expenses Budget. A company's marketing activities can be divided into two broad categories:

1. Obtaining the order, which involves the functions of selling and advertising.
2. Filling the order, which involves the functions of warehousing, packing and shipping, credit and collection, and general accounting (for marketing).

The supervisors of functions connected with marketing activities should prepare estimates of these costs to be included in the **marketing expenses budget**. Some estimates are based on individual judgment, while others are based on the costs experienced in previous years, modified by expected sales volume. Expenses such as depreciation and insurance depend upon the policy established by management.

Administrative Expenses Budget. The **administrative expenses budget** includes some costs that are peculiar to the administrative function, such as directors' fees, franchise taxes, capital stock taxes, and professional services of accountants, lawyers, and engineers. Other expenses that are included, such as purchasing, engineering, personnel, and research, are shared by the production and marketing as well as the administrative functions.

As a result of the problem of classifying certain expenses, the budgeting and control of administrative expenses often is quite difficult. The difficulty is increased because the persons responsible for the control of certain of these expenses may not be identifiable. However, an attempt should be made to place every item of expense under the jurisdiction and control of an executive, such as the chief executive, treasurer, controller, general accounting supervisor, or office manager. This person should be responsible for estimating the administrative expenses of a specific section or division, and should have authority to control the incurrence of the division's expenses. For example, the office manager should supervise filing clerks, mail clerks, librarians, stenographers, secretaries, and receptionists. This arrangement permits better control and more intense utilization of personnel in clerical jobs, where overlapping and overexpansion are common.

Budgeted Income Statement

A **budgeted income statement** contains summaries of the sales, manufacturing, and expense budgets. It projects net income, the goal toward which all efforts are directed, and it offers management the opportunity to judge the accuracy of the budget work and to investigate causes for variances. The budgeted income statement for Franklin Company is presented in Exhibit 15-13.

EXHIBIT 15-13

Franklin Company
Schedule 12
Budgeted Income Statement
For the Year Ending December 31, 19A

Sales (Schedule 1)		$4,550,000
Cost of goods sold (Schedule 11)		3,203,210
Gross profit		$1,346,790
Commercial expenses:		
Marketing expenses	$356,790	
Administrative expenses	290,000	646,790
Income before income tax		$ 700,000
Less provision for income tax		280,000
Net income		$ 420,000

The sales budget gives expected sales revenue, from which the budgeted cost of goods sold is deducted to give the estimated gross profit. Budgeted marketing and administrative expenses are subtracted from estimated gross profit to arrive at income from operations. Finally, the provision for income tax is deducted to determine net income.

The budgeted income statement and related supporting budgets can be shown by months or quarters. They also can be segmented by individual products or product groups and by individual marketing territories.

Budgeted Balance Sheet

A balance sheet for the beginning of the budget period is the starting point in preparing a **budgeted balance sheet** for the end of the budget period. The budgeted balance sheet for Franklin Company presented in Exhibit 15-14 incorporates changes in assets, liabilities, and stockholders' equity resulting from the budgets submitted by the various departments, functions, or segments.

EXHIBIT 15-14

Franklin Company
Schedule 13
Budgeted Balance Sheet
December 31, 19A

Assets		
Cash		$ 245,750
Accounts receivable	$ 370,260	
Less allowance for doubtful accounts	7,400	362,860
Inventories:		
Finished goods	$ 85,700	
Materials	214,250	299,950
Plant and equipment	$2,604,740	
Less accumulated depreciation	418,610	2,186,130
Other assets		105,310
Total assets		$3,200,000
Liabilities and Stockholders' Equity		
Current liabilities		$ 327,900
Long-term debt		850,000
Common stock		1,000,000
Retained earnings		1,022,100
Total liabilities and stockholders' equity		$3,200,000

The finished goods and materials inventory balances in the budgeted balance sheet agree with those shown in the company's beginning and ending inventory budget (Exhibit 15-11) and the budgeted cost of goods manufactured and sold statement (Exhibit 15-12). Although these inventory account changes are directly related to income statement transactions, other accounts can be affected in part by non-income statement transactions. For example, in the case of cash, proceeds from a bank loan or the payment of a cash dividend to stockholders are of the latter type of transaction.

Numerous advantages result from the preparation of a budgeted balance sheet. One advantage is that it discloses potentially unfavorable financial ratios before they occur. Unfavorable ratios can lower credit ratings or cause a drop in the value of the corporation's securities. A second advantage is that it provides a basis for computing the company's expected return on investment (budgeted income divided by budgeted capital employed). If projected financial ratios are unfavorable or the expected return on investment is inadequate, budgets should be revised to ensure that satisfactory results are achieved.

Summary

This chapter began with a discussion of the profit planning concept, including long-range and short-range budgets. The principles of developing and implementing the budget and its effects on human behavior were then discussed. A properly developed and implemented profit plan provides direction and facilitates coordination of all business activity. Central to implementation is the operating budget, which is composed of detailed budget schedules for sales, production, commercial expenses, income statement, and balance sheet. The budget process and the relationships among the various budget schedules were demonstrated with a detailed illustration of an annual operating budget. The capital expenditures budget, the research and development budget, and the cash budget are discussed in the next chapter.

Key Terms

profit planning *(394)*
a priori method *(395)*
a posteriori method *(395)*
pragmatic method *(395)*
long-range planning *(396)*
short-range budgets *(396)*
budget committee *(399)*
sales budget *(402)*
production budget *(406)*
manufacturing budgets *(407)*
direct materials budget *(407)*
purchases budget *(407)*
budgeted cost of materials required for production *(407)*
direct labor budget *(408)*
factory overhead budget *(409)*
budgeted cost of goods manufactured and sold statement *(411)*
marketing expenses budget *(415)*
administrative expenses budget *(415)*
budgeted income statement *(416)*
budgeted balance sheet *(416)*

Discussion Questions

Q15-1 Profit planning includes a complete financial and operational plan for all phases and facets of the business. Discuss.

Q15-2 Distinguish between a budget and a forecast.

Q15-3 Discuss the three different procedures that a company's management might follow to set profit objectives.

Q15-4 Differentiate between long-range profit planning and short-range budgeting.

Q15-5 What is a budget and how is it related to the control function?

Q15-6 The development of a budgetary control program requires specific systems and procedures needed in carrying out management's functions of planning, organizing, and control. Enumerate these steps.

Q15-7 Explain whether the periodic budget represents a formal or an informal communication channel within a company. (ICMA adapted)

Q15-8 "Budgets are meaningless in my business because I simply cannot estimate my sales for next year. Only if you can tell me which of my bids will be accepted can I prepare a meaningful budget," protested the president of a small custom manufacturer of die-cast parts for the automobile industry. Discuss, with respect to the preceding statement, the role of budgets and explain to the president how budgeting helps in bidding.
CGA-Canada (adapted). Reprint with permission.

Q15-9 The human factors in budget preparation are more important than its technical intricacies. Explain.

Q15-10 While the budget is usually thought to be an important and necessary tool for management, it has been subject to some criticism from managers and researchers studying organizations and human behavior.
(a) Describe and discuss the benefits of budgeting from the behavioral point of view.
(b) Describe and discuss the criticisms leveled at the budgeting processes from the behavioral point of view.
(c) What solutions are recommended to overcome the criticisms described in part b?
(ICMA adapted)

Q15-11 Commercial expenses are generally identified as marketing and administrative expenses. How should these expenses be grouped for budgetary purposes?

Q15-12 The budgeted income statement can be viewed as the apex of budgeting. Explain this statement.

Q15-13 The budgeted balance sheet can indicate an unsatisfactory financial condition. Discuss.

Exercises

E15-1 Sales Budget. Brown Brothers is a wholesaler for three chemical compounds, Rex-Z, Sip-X, and Tok-Y. The following information on these products relates to the year 19A:

Product	Sales (in pounds)	Average Sales Price per Pound	Gross Profit per Pound
Rex-Z	10,000	$30	$10
Sip-X	9,000	23	8
Tok-Y	7,500	18	5

Demand for Rex-Z has greatly increased and is expected to double in 19B. Sip-X will probably experience a 40% increase in demand, while demand for Tok-Y is expected to remain constant. In line with the overall economy, sales prices for Sip-X and Tok-Y will increase by 5%; the sales price for Rex-Z will increase by 15%. Unit costs of goods sold are expected to increase by the following amounts: Rex-Z, 25%; Sip-X, 20%; Tok-Y, 10%.

Required: Prepare a schedule presenting budgeted sales revenue and gross profit, by product, for 19B.

E15-2 Production Budget. Fineflex Corporation's sales forecast for its second quarter, ending June 30, indicates the following:

Product	Expected Sales
Flop	21,000 units
Olap	37,500
Ryke	54,000

Quantities in finished goods inventory at the beginning of the quarter and the desired quantities at the end of the quarter are as follows:

Product	March 31	June 30
Flop	5,500 units	6,000 units
Olap	11,000	10,500
Ryke	14,500	14,500

Required: Prepare a production budget for the second quarter.

E15-3 Production Budget. Magic Enterprises produces three perfumes. The sales department prepared the following tentative sales budget for the first quarter of the coming year:

Perfume	Units
Moon Glow	250,000
Enchanting	175,000
Day Dream	300,000

The following inventory levels have been established:

	Work in Process				Finished Goods	
	Beginning		Ending			
Perfume	Units	Percent Processed	Units	Percent Processed	Beginning Units	Ending Units
Moon Glow	4,000	50%	7,000	60%	16,000	15,000
Enchanting	6,000	30	5,000	40	12,000	10,000
Day Dream	8,000	80	8,000	75	25,000	20,000

Required: Prepare a production budget, by product.

E15-4 Production Budget and Raw Materials Purchases Requirements. Dakota Industries produces two-way radio antennas and has estimated sales for the next six-month period as follows:

Model	Units
Low band	200
Mid band	300
High band	400
Low and mid band	250
Mid and high band	350
Three band	200

Quantities of materials required for each model are:

Model Number	Metal Tubing (in feet)	Inductors	Feedline Connector
Low band	10	1	1
Mid band	7	1	1
High band	5	1	1
Low and mid band	17	2	1
Mid and high band	12	2	1
Three band	22	3	1

Quantities in beginning inventories and desired quantities in ending inventories follow:

	Beginning Inventory	Ending Inventory
Materials		
Metal tubing	5,000 feet	7,000 feet
Inductors	1,000 units	800 units
Feedline connectors	500	500
Finished Goods		
Low band	50 units	40 units
Mid band	30	30
High band	70	50
Low and mid band	20	50
Mid and high band	30	50
Three band	20	30

Required:

(1) Prepare a production budget detailing production requirements for each product.
(2) Compute the purchase requirement for each material.

E15-5 Sales Budget, Production Budget, and Materials Budget. The Maverick Company manufactures and sells three products: X, Y, and Z. In September, 19A, Maverick's budget department gathered the following forecast data related to its operations in the coming year.

Projected Sales for Fourth Quarter

Item	Quantity	Unit Price
Product X	4,500	$ 12
Product Y	2,000	25
Product Z	3,000	20

Inventories in Units

Item	Beginning	Desired Ending
Product X	600	900
Product Y	500	400
Product Z	400	500
Material A	2,000	2,500
Material B	1,500	2,000
Material C	2,500	2,000

Materials Production Requirements for Each Unit of Product

Item	Units of Material A	Units of Material B	Units of Material C
Product X	3	1	2
Product Y	2	2	4
Product Z	1	3	2

There is no beginning or ending inventory of work in process. Budgeted unit costs for materials A, B, and C are $.50, $2.00, and $1.50, respectively.

Required:
(1) Prepare a sales budget that includes quantities and revenues for each of the three products.
(2) Prepare a production budget for all three products.
(3) Prepare a materials usage budget.
(4) Prepare a materials purchases budget.

E15-6 Production Budget, Purchase Requirements, and Manufacturing Costs. Provence Company prepared the following figures as a basis for its annual budget:

Product	Units of Expected Sales	Estimated Sales Price per Unit	Required Material A per Unit (in kilograms)	Required Material B per Unit (in kilograms)
Tribolite	80,000	$1.50	1	2
Polycal	40,000	2.00	2	—
Powder X	100,000	.80	—	1

Estimated inventories at the beginning and desired quantities at the end of the year are:

Material	Beginning Inventory (in kilograms)	Ending Inventory (in kilograms)	Purchase Price per Kilogram
A	10 000	12 000	$ .20
B	12 000	15 000	.10

Product	Units in Beginning Inventory	Units in Ending Inventory	Direct Labor Hours per 1,000 Units
Tribolite	5,000	6,000	50.0
Polycal	4,000	2,000	125.0
Powder X	10,000	8,000	12.5

The direct labor cost is budgeted at $8 per hour and variable factory overhead at $6 per hour of direct labor. Fixed factory overhead, estimated to be $40,000, is a common cost and is not allocated to specific products in developing the manufacturing budget for internal management use.

Required:
(1) Prepare a production budget.
(2) Prepare a purchases budget for each material.
(3) Prepare a budget of manufacturing costs, by product and in total.

E15-7 Budgeted Cost of Goods Sold Statement. WKZ Inc., with $20,000,000 of par stock outstanding, plans to budget earnings of 6%, before income tax, on this stock. The Marketing Department budgets sales at $12,000,000. The budget director approves the sales budget and expenses as follows:

Marketing	15% of sales
Administrative	5%
Financial	1%

Labor is expected to be 50% of the total manufacturing cost; materials issued for the budgeted production will cost $2,500,000; therefore, any savings in manufacturing cost will have to be in factory overhead. Inventories are to be as follows:

	Beginning of Year	End of Year
Finished goods	$800,000	$1,000,000
Work in process	100,000	300,000
Materials	500,000	400,000

Required: Prepare the budgeted cost of goods manufactured and sold statement, showing the budgeted purchases of materials and the adjustments for inventories of materials, work in process, and finished goods.

E15-8 Budgeted Income Statement. Patz Company has just received a franchise to distribute air conditioners. The company began business on January 1 with the following assets:

Cash	$ 60,000
Inventory	90,000
Warehouse, office, and delivery facilities and equipment	800,000

All facilities and equipment have a useful life of 20 years and no residual value. First quarter sales are expected to be $500,000 and should be doubled in the second quarter. Third quarter sales are expected to be $1,200,000. Two percent of sales are considered to be uncollectible. The gross profit margin should be 40%. Variable marketing expenses (except uncollectible accounts) are budgeted at 10% of sales and fixed marketing expenses at $50,000 per quarter, exclusive of depreciation. Administrative expenses are all considered to be fixed expenses and should total $40,000 per quarter, exclusive of depreciation.

Required: Prepare a budgeted income statement for the second quarter.

CGA-Canada (adapted). Reprint with permission.

E15-9 Budgeted Income Statement. Mexia Inc. has been a wholesale distributor of automobile parts for domestic automakers for 20 years. Mexia has suffered through the recent slump in the domestic auto industry, and its performance has not rebounded to the levels of the industry as a whole. Mexia's income statement for the year ended December 31, 19A, is as follows:

Mexia Inc.
Income Statement
For the Year Ended December 31, 19A
(in thousands)

Net sales		$9,000
Less cost of goods sold		6,000
Gross profit		$3,000
Less commercial expenses:		
Marketing expenses	$780	
Administrative expenses	900	1,680
Income before interest and taxes		$1,320
Less interest expense		140
Income before income tax		$1,280
Less income tax		512
Net income		$ 768

Mexia's management team is considering the following actions for 19B, which they expect will improve profitability and result in a 5% increase in unit sales:

(a) Increase sales prices 10%.
(b) Increase advertising by $420,000 and hold all other marketing and administrative expenses at 19A levels.
(c) Improve customer service by increasing average current assets (inventory and accounts receivable) by a total of $300,000, and hold all other assets at 19A levels.
(d) Finance the additional assets at an annual interest rate of 10% and hold all other interest expense at 19A levels.
(e) Improve the quality of products carried; this will increase the unit cost of goods sold by 6%.

Mixia's 19B effective income tax rate is expected to be 40%—the same as in 19A.

Required: Prepare a budgeted income statement for Mexia Inc. for the year ending December 31, 19B, assuming that planned actions would be carried out and that the 5% increase in unit sales would be realized.

(ICMA adapted)

Problems

P15-1 Sales and Manufacturing Budgets. Scarborough Corporation manufactures and sells two products, Thingone and Thingtwo. In July, 19A, Scarborough's Budget Department gathered the following data in order to project sales and budget requirements for 19B:

Projected sales:

Product	Units	Price
Thingone	60,000	$ 70
Thingtwo	40,000	100

Inventories (in units):

Product	Expected January 1, 19B	Desired December 31, 19B
Thingone	20,000	25,000
Thingtwo	8,000	9,000

To produce one unit of Thingone and Thingtwo, the following raw materials are used:

	Amount Used per Unit	
Raw Material	Thingone	Thingtwo
A	4 lbs.	5 lbs.
B	2 lbs.	3 lbs.
C	—	1 unit

Projected data for 19B with respect to raw materials are as follows:

Raw Material	Anticipated Purchase Price	Expected Inventories January 1, 19B	Desired Inventories December 31, 19B
A	$8	32,000 lbs.	36,000 lbs.
B	5	29,000 lbs.	32,000 lbs.
C	3	6,000 units	7,000 units

Projected direct labor requirements and rates for 19B are as follows:

Product	Hours per Unit	Rate per Hour
Thingone	2	$8
Thingtwo	3	9

Factory overhead is applied at the rate of $2 per direct labor hour.

Required: Based on the projections and budget requirements for 19B for Thingone and Thingtwo, prepare the following 19B budgets:

(1) Sales budget
(2) Production budget
(3) Raw materials purchases budget
(4) Direct labor budget
(5) Budgeted finished goods inventory at December 31, 19B

(AICPA adapted)

P15-2 Production and Direct Labor Budget. Roletter Company makes and sells artistic frames for pictures of weddings, graduations, christenings, and other special events. Lynn Anderson, controller, is responsible for preparing Roletter's budget and has accumulated the following information for 19B:

	January	February	March	April	May
Estimated unit sales	10,000	12,000	8,000	9,000	9,000
Sales price per unit	$ 50.00	$ 47.50	$47.50	$47.50	$47.50
Direct labor hours per unit	2.0	2.0	1.5	1.5	1.5
Wage per direct labor hour	$ 8.00	$ 8.00	$ 8.00	$ 9.00	$ 9.00

Labor-related costs include pension contributions of 25 cents per hour, workers' compensation insurance of 10 cents per hour, employee medical insurance of 40 cents per hour, and social security and unemployment taxes of 10% of wages. The cost of employee benefits paid by Roletter on its employees is treated as a direct labor cost.

Roletter has a labor contract that calls for a wage increase to $9 per hour on April 1, 19B. New labor saving machinery has been installed and will be fully operational by March 1, 19B.

Roletter expects to have 16,000 frames on hand at December 31, 19A, and has a policy of carrying an end-of-month inventory of 100% of the following month's sales plus 50% of the second following month's sales.

Required:

(1) Prepare a production budget and a direct labor budget for Roletter Company by month and for the first quarter of 19B. Both budgets can be combined in one schedule. The direct labor budget should include direct labor hours and show the detail for each direct labor cost category.

(2) For each item used in Roletter's production budget and its direct labor budget, identify the other component(s) of the periodic budget that also use these data. (ICMA adapted)

P15-3 Production and Manufacturing Budgets. The following data are provided for Hanska Corporation:

(a) Sales: Sales through June 30, 19A, the first 6 months of the current year, are 24,000 units. Expected sales for the full year are 60,000 units. Actual sales in units for May and June and estimated unit sales for the next 4 months are as follows:

	Units
May	4,000
June	4,000
July	5,000
August	6,000
September	7,000
October	7,000

(b) Direct materials: At each month end, Hanska wants to have sufficient materials on hand to produce the next month's estimated sales. Data regarding materials are as follows:

Direct Material	Units of Material Required	Cost per Unit	Units in Inventory June 30, 19A
101	6	$2.40	35,000
211	4	3.60	30,000
242	2	1.20	14,000

(c) Direct labor:

Process	Hours per Unit	Hourly Labor Rate
Forming	.80	$8.00
Assembly	2.00	5.50
Finishing	.25	6.00

(d) Factory overhead: The company produced 27,000 units during the 6-month period through June 30,19A, and expects to produce 60,000 units during the year. The actual variable factory overhead costs incurred during this 6-month period are as follows. The controller believes that these costs will be incurred at the same rate during the remainder of 19A.

Supplies	$ 59,400
Electricity	27,000
Indirect labor	54,000
Other	21,600
Total variable factory overhead	$162,000

The fixed factory overhead costs incurred during the first 6 months of 19A amounted to $93,000. Fixed overhead costs are budgeted for the full year as follows:

Supervision	$ 60,000
Property tax	7,200
Depreciation	86,400
Other	32,400
Total fixed factory overhead	$186,000

(e) Finished goods inventory: The desired monthly ending finished goods inventory in units is 80% of the next month's estimated sales. There are 5,600 finished units in the June 30, 19A, inventory.

Required:

(1) Prepare the production budget for the third quarter ending September 30, 19A.
(2) Prepare the direct materials purchases budget for the third quarter.
(3) Prepare the direct labor budget for the third quarter.
(4) Prepare the factory overhead budget for the 6 months ending December 31, 19A, presenting two figures—for total variable and fixed overhead. (ICMA adapted)

P15-4 Sales Budget; Purchases and Materials Requirements. The management of Bannister Food Products decided to install a budgetary control system under the supervision of a budget director and a committee. Among its products, the company manufactures a patented breakfast food that is sold in packages of two sizes—1 pound and 2 pound. The cereal is made from two types of grain, called R (rye) and S (soy). There are two operations: (a) processing and blending and (b) packaging. The grains are purchased by the bushel measure, a bushel of R containing 70 pounds and a bushel of S containing 80 pounds. Three bushels of grain mixed in the proportion of 2R:1S produce 198 pounds of finished product. The entire loss occurs in the first department.

To prepare estimated sales figures for the first 6 months of the coming year, the budget committee first asked the sales staff to prepare sales estimates in units. The following data were submitted:

	Territory I	Territory II	Territory III	Other	6-Month Total
1-lb. package	10,000	15,000	12,000	613,000	650,000
2-lb. package	12,000	18,000	12,000	783,000	825,000
Total	22,000	33,000	24,000	1,396,000	1,475,000

The figures submitted are analyzed by the budget committee in light of general business conditions. The company uses the Federal Reserve Board Index, together with its own trade index, to calculate a trend percentage for the business. The trend percentage indicates that a .90 general index figure should be applied to the estimates in order to arrive at the final sales figures. The finished goods inventory is to be kept at zero, if possible. The work in process inventory is to be kept near the present level, which is about 160,000 pounds of blended material.

Factory facilities permit processing sales requirements as stated in the sales budget. The production manager accepted the monthly sales figures for the production budget.

Purchases of grains in bushels have been arranged as follows:

	Type R		Type S	
	Quantity (in bushels)	Price	Quantity (in bushels)	Price
January	5,000	$1.30	2,000	$1.20
February	2,000	1.40	1,000	1.20
March	0	0	3,000	1.25
April	8,000	1.50	3,000	1.00
May	3,000	1.50	0	0
June	4,000	1.60	4,000	1.00
Beginning inventory, January 1	10,000	1.20	3,000	1.00

Materials are charged into production on the fifo basis.

Required:

(1) Prepare a revised sales budget in units for the 6-month period, based on the index.
(2) Prepare a sales budget in dollars, assuming that the 1-pound package sells for 25 cents and the 2-pound package for 50 cents.

(Requirements continued.)

(3) Prepare a schedule of materials purchases.
(4) Prepare a computation of materials requirements for production. (Round to the nearest whole amount.)
(5) Prepare a schedule of the materials account (fifo basis), in units and dollars, indicating beginning inventory, purchases, usage, and ending inventory for the 6-month period taken as a whole.

P15-5 Budgeted Income Statement. The president of a hardware manufacturing company has asked the controller to prepare an income forecast for the next year, by quarters, with sales reported for each of the two major segments—commercial and government.

The Marketing Department provided the following sales estimates:

	1st Quarter	2d Quarter	3d Quarter	4th Quarter
Commercial sales	$250,000	$266,000	$275,000	$300,000
Government sales	100,000	120,000	110,000	115,000

The controller's office assembled the following figures:

(a) Cost of goods sold: 46% of total sales.
(b) Advertising expenditures: $6,000 each quarter.
(c) Selling expenses: 10% of total sales.
(d) Administrative expenses: 16.8% of gross profit.
(e) General office expenses: 12% of gross profit.
(f) Corporate income tax rate: 40%.

Required:

(1) Prepare a budgeted income statement, by quarters and in total. All figures should be shown in thousands of dollars and rounded to the nearest thousand. Add the four quarters across to obtain total figures.
(2) Prepare an analysis of the effect of a 5% increase in commercial sales revenue, using the same income statement format as for requirement 1.

P15-6 Time Budget, Billing Rates, and Budgeted Income Statement. In June, 19A, after 10 years with a large CPA firm, Anna B. Johnson, CPA, opened an office as a sole practitioner. In 19C, Walter L. Smith, CPA, joined Johnson as a senior accountant. The partnership of Johnson and Smith was organized July 1, 19H, and a fiscal year ending June 30 was adopted and approved by the Internal Revenue Service.

Continued growth of the firm has required additional personnel. The current complement, including approved salaries for the fiscal year ending June 30, 19N, is as follows:

Partners:	
Anna B. Johnson, CPA	$60,000
Walter L. Smith, CPA	40,000
Professional staff:	
Manager:	
Harold S. Vickers, CPA	31,200
Senior accountant:	
Duane Lowe, CPA	24,960
Staff accountants:	
James M. Kennedy	20,800
Viola O. Quinn	20,800
Secretaries:	
Livia A. Garcia	14,560
Johnnie L. Hammond	12,480
Mary Lyons	12,480

During a severe illness, which kept Johnson away from the office for over 4 months in late 19L, the firm suffered, mainly because other personnel lacked knowledge about the practice. After Johnson's return, a plan was developed for delegation of administrative authority and responsibility and for standardization of procedures. The goals of the plan included income objectives, standardized billing procedures (with flexibility for adjustments by the partners), and assignment schedules to eliminate overtime and to allow for nonchargeable time such as vacations and illness. The firm plans a 52-week year with 5-day, 40-hour weeks.

The partners would like to achieve an annual income target of at least $80,000 (after deducting partners' salaries). The budget for fiscal year 19N is 700 hours of chargeable time at $90 per hour for Johnson and 1,100 hours at $70 for Smith. Johnson and Smith are to devote all other available time, except as specified below, to administration. The billing rates for all other employees including secretaries are to be set at a level to recover their salaries plus the following overhead items: fringe benefits of $35,000, other operating expenses of $62,370, and a contribution to the targeted income of at least $50,000.

The partners agree that salary levels are fair bases for allocating overhead in setting billing rates, with the exception of salary costs of the nonchargeable secretarial time, which are to be added to overhead to arrive at total overhead to be allocated. Thus, the billing rates for each secretary will be based on the salary costs of chargeable time plus a share of the total overhead. No portion of total overhead is to be allocated to partners' salaries.

The following information is available for nonchargeable time:

(a) Because of the recent illness, Johnson expects to be away an additional week. Smith expects no loss of time from illness. All other employees are to be allowed one illness day per month.

(b) Allowable vacations are as follows:

Johnson	1 month (173 hours)
Smith	1 month (173 hours)
Vickers	3 weeks
Garcia	3 weeks
All other employees	2 weeks

(c) If any of the holidays observed (7 annually) fall on a weekend, the office is closed the preceding Friday or the following Monday.

(d) Kennedy and Quinn should each be allotted 3 days to sit for the November 19N CPA examination.

(e) Hours are budgeted for other miscellaneous activities of personnel as follows:

Name	Firm Projects	Professional Development	Professional Meetings	Community Activities	Miscellaneous Office Time	Total
Johnson	48	80	184	80	0	392
Smith	148	80	120	40	0	388
Vickers	88	56	40	40	84	308
Lowe	64	40	40	24	72	240
Kennedy	89	40	16	16	0	161
Quinn	39	50	16	16	0	121
Garcia	248	24	24	12	1,000	1,308
Hammond	8	16	8	0	716	748
Lyons	8	24	8	0	808	848

(f) Unassigned time should be budgeted for Lowe, Kennedy, and Quinn as 8, 38, and 78 hours, respectively.

Required:

(1) Prepare a time allocation budget for each partner and each employee that begins with maximum hours available (without incurring overtime) and ends with chargeable hours.

(2) Prepare a schedule computing the billing rates for each employee (excluding the partners) for the year ending June 30, 19N. The schedule should show the proper allocation of appropriate expenses and should target income contribution to salaries applicable to chargeable time in accordance with the objective established by the partners.

(3) Prepare a condensed budgeted income statement for the year ending June 30, 19N. (AICPA adapted)

P15-7 Operating Budget with Budgeted Income Statement. A1 Sound Systems manufactures speakers for component stereo systems. Three models are produced: Model 150, Model 100, and Model 50. The speakers are marketed in two regions, South and Southwest. The production departments are designated Cutting, Assembling, and Finishing. Lumber, speakers, and a finishing compound are the materials used in producing the speakers. The following estimates have been made for the coming year:

(a) Sales forecast by territory:

Product	South (in units)	Southwest (in units)	Sales Price per Unit
Model 150	3,000	4,000	$175
Model 100	5,000	7,000	120
Model 50	7,000	8,000	90

(b) Inventories:

	Units in Beginning Inventory	Cost per Unit in Beginning Inventory	Desired Units in Ending Inventory
Materials:			
Lumber (board feet)	40,000	$ .75	30,000
Speakers	10,000	15.00	8,000
Finish (pints)	1,500	2.00	2,000

Work in process: None at the beginning or end of the period.

	Units in Beginning Inventory	Cost per Unit in Beginning Inventory	Desired Units in Ending Inventory
Finished goods (fifo):			
Model 150	200	$98.00	200
Model 100	300	62.00	400
Model 50	400	47.00	300

(c) Materials requirements:

Product	Lumber (in board feet)	Speakers	Finish (in pints)
Model 150	12	5	2
Model 100	8	3	1
Model 50	6	2	1

(d) Estimated materials cost:

Lumber, $.75 per board foot
Speakers, $15 per speaker
Finish, $2 per pint

(e) Estimated labor cost:

	Cutting	Assembling	Finishing
Rate per hour	$6.00	$5.00	$4.00

Estimated labor time requirements in hours:

Model	Cutting	Assembling	Finishing
150	.375	2.0	.375
100	.375	1.5	.250
50	.375	1.5	.250

(f) Factory overhead budgets show the following unit overhead rates:

Model	Cutting	Assembling	Finishing
150	$1.00	$2.00	$ .75
100	1.00	1.50	.50
50	1.00	1.50	.50

(g) Budgeted commercial expenses:

Marketing: $500,000.
Administration: $300,000.

(h) Income tax rate is 50%.

Required: Prepare annual budget schedules utilizing the budget estimates provided. The schedules should be designed to provide essential data in a form that is easily understood and should include the following:
(1) Sales budget—by models and by sales regions
(2) Production budget—by models and by units
(Requirements continued.)

(3) Direct materials budget in units—by materials and by models
(4) Purchases budget—by materials and by cost
(5) Cost of materials required for production—by materials and by models
(6) Direct labor budget—by models and by departments
(7) Factory overhead budget (applied overhead)—by models and by departments
(8) Beginning and ending inventories—by materials and by models
(9) Budgeted cost of goods manufactured and sold statement
(10) Budgeted income statement

P15-8 Operating Budget with Budgeted Income Statement. Gilbert Electronics Inc. is an original equipment manufacturer of electric power supply units. The company manufactures three different models, called Economy, Standard, and Deluxe, which are sold in four different markets, Eastern United States, Western United States, Europe, and Asia. Each power supply unit converts electric current from AC to DC for use in various types of electronic equipment ranging from radios and televisions to computers. The three different units produce DC output at different wattage levels. The product is manufactured in two different producing departments: Assembly and Testing. Estimates for the coming year follow:

(a) Sales forecast by territory:

	Units				
Model	Eastern U.S.	Western U.S.	Europe	Asia	Sales Price per Unit
Economy	60,000	50,000	75,000	25,000	$50.00
Standard	40,000	45,000	60,000	35,000	70.00
Deluxe	20,000	25,000	35,000	30,000	90.00

(b) Inventories:

	Units in Beginning Inventory	Cost per Unit in Beginning Inventory	Desired Units in Ending Inventory
Materials:			
Boxes	10,000	$1.50	5,000
Transformers	15,000	4.50	10,000
Diode rectifiers	25,000	.70	25,000
Filters	25,000	1.75	20,000
Resistors	10,000	.20	50,000
Wire (in feet)	30,000	.50	40,000

Work in Process: None at beginning or end of period.

	Units in Beginning Inventory	Cost per Unit in Beginning Inventory	Desired Units in Ending Inventory
Finished Goods (fifo):			
Economy Model	15,000	$25.00	20,000
Standard Model	15,000	38.50	15,000
Deluxe Model	15,000	55.25	10,000

(c) Materials requirements for products and estimated materials costs:

Material	Economy Model	Standard Model	Deluxe Model	Estimated Cost per Unit of Material
Boxes	1	1	1	$1.50
Transformers	1	2	3	4.50
Diode rectifiers	2	4	5	.70
Filters	2	3	6	1.75
Resistors	5	8	10	.20
Wire (in feet)	5	6	8	.50

(d) Estimated labor time requirements and rates in hours:

Product	Assembly Department	Testing Department
Economy Model	.50	.05
Standard Model	.75	.05
Deluxe Model	1.00	.05
Direct labor rate per hour	$10	$12

(e) Estimated machine time in Testing Department:

Product	Hours Required
Economy Model	.15
Standard Model	.25
Deluxe Model	.35

(f) Budgeted factory overhead:

	Assembly Department		Testing Department	
	Fixed Cost Estimate	Variable Rate per Labor Hour	Fixed Cost Estimate	Variable Rate per Machine Hour
Indirect materials and supplies	$158,000	$1.50	$157,000	$ .35
Indirect labor	350,000	.50	250,000	1.00
Payroll taxes	382,500	.05	55,000	.10
Employee fringe benefits	347,500	—	114,000	—
Equipment depreciation	65,000	—	215,000	—
Repairs and maintenance	25,000	.40	35,000	1.50
Allocated building costs	12,000	—	9,000	—
Allocated general factory costs	241,125	—	82,700	—

Overhead is allocated to production on the basis of direct labor hours in the Assembly Department and on the basis of machine hours in the Testing Department.

(g) Budgeted commercial expenses:

Marketing: $6,145,000.
Administration: $2,330,500.

(h) Income tax rate is 40%.

Required: Prepare annual budget schedules utilizing the budget estimates provided. The schedules should be designed to provide essential data in a form that is easily understood and should include the following:

(1) Sales budget—by models and by sales territories
(2) Production budget—by models and by units
(3) Direct materials budget in units—by materials and by models
(4) Materials purchases budget—by materials and by cost
(5) Cost of materials required for production—by materials and by models
(6) Direct labor budget—by models and departments, with costs and hours
(7) Budgeted machine hours in the Testing Department
(8) Budgeted factory overhead and departmental rates
(9) Budgeted unit product costs
(10) Beginning and ending inventories
(11) Budgeted cost of goods manufactured and sold
(12) Budgeted income statement

P15-9 Budgeted Income Statement and Balance Sheet. CL Corporation appears to be experiencing a good year, with sales in the first quarter of 19B one third ahead of last year's sales and the Sales Department predicting continuation of this rate throughout the year. The controller has been asked to prepare a new forecast for the year and to analyze the differences from 19A results. The forecast is to be based on actual results obtained in the first quarter plus the expected costs of programs to be carried out in the remainder of the year. Various department heads (production, sales, etc.) have provided the necessary information, which is summarized and presented in the accompanying prospective trial balance.

CL Corporation
Prospective Trial Balance
December 31, 19B
(in thousands)

Cash	1,200	
Accounts Receivable	80,000	
Inventory (1/1/19B, 40,000 units)	48,000	
Plant and Equipment	130,000	
Accumulated Depreciation		41,000
Accounts Payable		45,000
Accrued Payables		23,250
Notes Payable (due within one year)		50,000
Common Stock		70,000
Retained Earnings		108,200
Sales		600,000
Other Income		9,000
Cost of Goods Sold	—	
Manufacturing costs:		
Materials	213,000	
Direct Labor	218,000	
Variable Factory Overhead	130,000	
Depreciation	5,000	
Other Fixed Factory Overhead	7,750	
Marketing:		
Salaries	16,000	
Commissions	20,000	
Promotion and Advertising	45,000	
General and administrative:		
Salaries	16,000	
Travel	2,500	
Office Costs	9,000	
Income Tax	—	
Dividends	5,000	
	946,450	946,450

Adjustments for the change in inventory and for income tax have not been made. The scheduled production for 19B is 450 million units; the sales volume will reach 400 million units. Sales and production volume in 19A was 300 million units. A full-cost, first in, first out inventory system is used. The company is subject to a 40% income tax rate. The actual financial statements for 19A follow on page 432.

Required:

(1) Prepare prospective financial statements (statement of income and retained earnings, and balance sheet) for 19B.

(2) Using the 19A information for comparison:

(a) Evaluate the 19B prospective profit performance.

(b) Specify areas of 19B operating performance to be investigated.

(c) Recommend programs for improved management performance.

(ICMA adapted)

CL Corporation
Balance Sheet
December 31, 19A
(in thousands)

Assets		
Current assets:		
Cash	$ 23,000	
Accounts receivable	50,000	
Inventory	48,000	$121,000
Plant and equipment	$130,000	
Less accumulated depreciation	36,000	94,000
Total assets		$215,000
Liabilities and Shareholders' Equity		
Current liabilities:		
Accounts payable	$ 13,000	
Accrued payables	12,800	
Notes payable	11,000	$ 36,800
Shareholders' equity:		
Common stock	$ 70,000	
Retained earnings	108,200	178,200
Total liabilities and shareholders' equity		$215,000

CL Corporation
Statement of Income and Retained Earnings
for Year Ended December 31, 19A
(in thousands)

Revenue:			
Sales		$450,000	
Other income		15,000	$465,000
Expenses:			
Cost of goods manufactured and sold:			
Materials	$132,000		
Direct labor	135,000		
Variable factory overhead	81,000		
Fixed factory overhead	12,000		
	$360,000		
Beginning inventory	48,000		
	$408,000		
Ending inventory	48,000	$360,000	
Marketing:			
Salaries	$ 13,500		
Commissions	15,000		
Promotion and advertising	31,500	60,000	
General and administrative:			
Salaries	$ 14,000		
Travel	2,000		
Office costs	8,000	24,000	
Income tax		8,400	452,400
Net income			$ 12,600
Beginning retained earnings			100,600
			$ 113,200
Less dividends			5,000
Ending retained earnings			$108,200

Cases

C15-1 Need for Profit Planning. George Mai invented a special valve for application in the paper manufacturing industry. At the time of its development, he could not find any company willing to manufacture the valve. As a result, he formed Maiton Company to manufacture and sell the valve.

Maiton Company grew quite slowly. George Mai found it difficult to persuade paper companies to try this new valve designed and manufactured by an unknown company. However, the company has prospered and now has a number of smaller paper companies as regular customers. In fact, there is increasing interest by a number of large paper companies because of the very good results experienced by the smaller paper companies.

The size of the potential new customers and their probable needs over the next several years will dramatically increase the sales of the valve. George Mai was an engineer for a large company prior to his invention. His business experience is limited to the activities of Maiton Company.

Required:

(1) Explain why it is important for George Mai to introduce business planning and budgeting activities into his company at this time.

(2) Identify major problems that likely would be disclosed as Maiton Company attempts to prepare a 5-year plan. Explain why the problems identified were selected. (ICMA adapted)

C15-2 Long-Range Planning; Periodic Sales Budget. Marval Products manufactures and wholesales several lines of luggage. Each luggage line consists of various pieces and sizes. One line is a complete set of luggage designed to be used by both men and women, but some lines are designed specifically for men or women. Some lines also have matching attaché cases. Luggage lines are discontinued and introduced as tastes change or as product improvements are developed.

Marval Products also manufactures luggage for large retail companies according to each company's specifications. This luggage is marketed under the retail companies' own private labels rather than the Marval label.

Marval has been manufacturing several lines of luggage under its own label and private lines for retail companies for the last 10 years.

Required:

(1) Identify the factors Marval Products needs to consider in its periodic review of long-range planning.

(2) Identify the factors Marval Products needs to consider when developing the sales component of its annual budget. (ICMA adapted)

C15-3 Budget preparation. RV Industries manufactures and sells recreation vehicles. The company has eight divisions strategically located near major markets. Each division has a sales force and two to four manufacturing plants. These divisions operate as autonomous profit centers responsible for purchasing, operations, and sales.

Dale Collins, the corporate controller, described the divisional performance measurement system as follows: "We allow the divisions to control the entire operation from the purchase of raw materials to the sale of the product. We, at corporate headquarters, get involved only in strategic decisions, such as developing new product lines. Each division is responsible for meeting its market needs by providing the right products at a low cost on a timely basis. Frankly, the divisions need to focus on cost control, delivery, and services to customers in order to become more profitable.

"While we give the divisions considerable autonomy, we watch their monthly income statements very closely. Each month's actual performance is compared with the budget in considerable detail. If the actual sales or contribution margin is more than 4% or 5% below the budget, we jump on the division people immediately. I might add that we don't have much trouble getting their attention. All of the management people at the plant and division level can add appreciably to their annual salaries with bonuses if their actual profit is considerably greater than budget."

The budgeting process begins in August when division sales managers, after consulting with their sales personnel, estimate sales for the next calendar year. These estimates are sent to plant managers, who use the sales forecasts to prepare production estimates. At the plants, production statistics, including raw material quantities, labor hours, production schedules, and output quantities, are developed by operating personnel. Using the statistics prepared by the operating personnel, the plant accounting staff determines costs and prepares the plant's budgeted variable cost of goods sold and other plant expenses for each month of the coming calendar year.

In October, each division's accounting staff combines plant budgets with sales estimates and adds additional division expenses. "After the divisional management is satisfied with the budget," said Collins, "I visit each division to go over its budget and make sure it is in line with corporate strategy and projections. I really emphasize the sales forecasts because of the volatility in the demand for our product. For many years, we lost sales to our competitors because we didn't project high enough production and sales, and we couldn't meet the market demand. More recently, we were caught with large excess inventory when the bottom dropped out of the market for recreational vehicles.

"I generally visit all eight divisions during the first two weeks in November. After that, the division budgets are combined and reconciled by my staff and they are ready for approval by the board of directors in early December. The board seldom questions the budget.

"One complaint we've had from plant and division management is that they are penalized for circumstances beyond their control. For example, they failed to predict the recent sales decline. As a result, they didn't make their budget and, of course, they received no bonuses. However, I point out that they are well rewarded when they exceed their budget. Furthermore, they provide most of the information for the budget, so it's their own fault if the budget is too optimistic."

Required: Discuss the following:

(1) Biases that corporate management should expect in the communication of budget estimates prepared by its division and plant personnel
(2) Sources of information that corporate management can use to monitor the budget estimates prepared by its divisions and plants
(3) Services that corporate management can offer the divisions to aid them in their budget development, without appearing to interfere with division budget decisions
(4) Factors that corporate management should consider in deciding whether or not it should become more involved in the budget process (ICMA adapted)

C15-4 Evaluation of Budget Procedures. Schaffer Company, a large multidivisional firm having several plants in each division, uses a comprehensive budgeting system for planning operations and measuring performance. The annual budgeting process begins in August, 5 months prior to the beginning of the fiscal year. At this time, the division managers submit proposed budgets for sales, production and inventory levels, and expenses. Capital expenditure requests also are formalized at this time. The expense budgets include direct labor and all factory overhead items, separated into fixed and variable components. Direct materials are budgeted separately when the production and inventory schedules are developed.

The expense budgets for each division are developed from each plant's results, as measured by the percent variation from an adjusted budget in the first 6 months of the current year, and a target expense reduction percentage established by the corporation.

To determine plant percentages, the plant budget for the half-year period just completed is revised to recognize changes in operating procedures and costs outside the control of plant management (such as labor wage rate changes and product style changes). The difference between this revised budget and the actual expenses is the controllable variance, expressed as a percentage of the actual expenses. If unfavorable, this percentage is added to the corporate target expense reduction percentage. A favorable plant variance percentage is subtracted from the corporate target. If a plant had a 2% unfavorable controllable variance and the corporate target reduction was 4%, the plant's budget for next year should reflect costs approximately 6% below this year's actual costs.

Next year's final budgets for the corporation, its divisions, and plants are adopted after corporate analysis of the proposed budgets and a careful review, with each division manager, of the changes made by corporate management.

Division profit budgets include allocated corporate costs, and plant profit budgets include allocated division and corporate costs.

Required: Evaluate the budget procedures of Schaffer Company with respect to its effectiveness for planning and controlling operations. (ICMA adapted)

C15-5 Setting Segment Profit Objectives. The Noton Company has operated a comprehensive budgeting system for many years. This system is a major component of the company's program to control operations and costs at its widely scattered plants. Periodically the plants' general managers gather to discuss the overall company control system with the top management.

At this year's meeting the budgetary system was severely criticized by one of the most senior plant managers. He said that the system discriminated unfairly against the older, well-run and established plants in favor of the newer plants. The impact was lower year-end bonuses and poor performance ratings. In addition, there were psychological consequences in the form of lower employee morale. In his judgment, revisions in the system were needed to make it more effective. The basic factors of Noton's budget include the following:

(a) Announcement of an annual improvement percentage target established by top management
(b) Plant submission of budgets implementing the annual improvement target
(c) Management review and revision of the proposed budget
(d) Establishment and distribution of the final budget

To support his arguments, he compared the budget revisions and performance results. The older plants were expected to achieve the improvement target but often were unable to meet it. On the other hand, the newer plants were often excused from meeting a portion of this target in their budgets. However, their performance was usually better than the final budget.

He further argued that the company did not recognize the operating differences that made attainment of the annual improvement factor difficult, if not impossible. His plant has been producing essentially the same product for its 20 years of existence. The machinery and equipment, which underwent many modifications in the first 5 years, have had no major changes in recent years. Because they are old, repair and maintenance costs have increased each year, and the machines are less reliable. The plant management team has been together for the last 10 years and works well together. The labor force is mature, with many of the employees having the highest seniority in the company. In his judgment, the significant improvements have been "wrung out" of the plant over the years and merely keeping even is difficult.

For comparison, he noted that one plant, opened within the past 4 years, would have an easier time meeting the company's expectations. The plant is new, containing modern equipment that is, in some cases, still experimental. Major modifications in equipment and operating systems have been made each year as the plant management has obtained a better understanding of the operations. The plant's management, although experienced, has been together only since its opening. The plant is located in a previously nonindustrial area and therefore has a relatively inexperienced work force.

Required:

(1) Evaluate the manufacturing manager's views.

(2) Equitable application of a budget system requires the ability of corporate management to remove "budgetary slack" in plant budgets. Discuss how each plant could conceal "slack" in its budget.

(ICMA adapted)

C15-6 The Budget and Human Behavior. Drake Inc. is a multiproduct firm with several manufacturing plants. Management generally has been pleased with the operation of all but the Swan Plant. Its poor operating performance has been traced to poor control over plant costs. Four plant managers have resigned or been terminated during the last 3 years.

David Green was appointed the new manager of the Swan Plant on February 1, 19B. Green is a young and aggressive individual who had progressed rapidly in Drake's management development program and had performed well in lower-level management positions.

Green had been recommended for the position by Susan Bradley, Green's immediate supervisor. Bradley was impressed by Green's technical ability and enthusiasm. Bradley explained to Green that the assignment as Swan Plant manager was approved despite the objections of some of the other members of the executive management team. Bradley told Green that she had complete confidence in him and his ability and was sure that Green wanted to prove that she had made a good decision. Therefore, Bradley expected Green to have the Swan Plant on budget by June 30.

As a result of Swan Plant's past difficulties, Susan Bradley has had responsibility for formulating the last four annual budgets for the plant. The 19B budget was prepared during the last 6 months of 19A, before Green had been appointed plant manager. The budget report covering the 3-month period ended March 31, 19B, showed that Swan's costs were slightly over budget. At a meeting with Bradley, Green described the changes he had instituted during the last month. Green was confident that the costs would be held in check with these changes and the situation would get no worse for the rest of the year.

Bradley repeated that she not only wanted the cost controlled but she expected Swan Plant to be on budget by June 30. Green pointed out that the Swan Plant had been in poor condition for 3 years. He further stated that, while he appreciated the confidence Bradley had in him, he had only been in charge 2 months.

Susan Bradley then replied, "I am expected to meet my figures. The only way that can occur is if my subordinates exercise control over their costs and achieve their budgets. Therefore, to assure that I achieve my goals, get the Swan Plant on budget by June 30 and keep it on budget for the rest of the year."

Required:

(1) Critically evaluate the budget practices described in the case.

(2) What are the likely immediate and long-term effects on David Green and Drake Inc. if the present method of budget administration is continued?

(ICMA adapted)

CHAPTER 16

Budgeting: Capital Expenditures, Research and Development Expenditures, and Cash; PERT/Cost

Learning Objectives

After studying this chapter, you will be able to:

1. Distinguish capital expenditures from revenue expenditures and state the role of the capital expenditure budget in the company's long- and short-range plans.
2. Name some purposes of a research and development program.
3. List common sources of cash receipts and cash disbursements.
4. Prepare a cash budget.
5. State reasons why budgeting is important in nonmanufacturing and not-for-profit organizations.
6. Define zero-base budgeting and contrast it with traditional budgeting.
7. Prepare a PERT network and determine the critical path of a planned project.
8. Prepare a PERT/cost network and state how the addition of cost is useful in controlling and analyzing projects.

Budgeting is an iterative process. Budgets are prepared, reviewed, and revised until executive management is satisfied that the results represent the best plans that can be devised under existing circumstances. As the budget period unfolds, events may not materialize as expected and conditions may change, necessitating further budget revisions. To facilitate revisions during the budget period, flexibility should be built into the budget where possible, and management should develop contingency plans for dealing with probable changes.

This chapter discusses specific budgets, such as capital expenditures and research and development budgets, that play a significant part in the long- and short-range plans of any management. Closely related to these budgets is the cash budget, which reveals excesses or shortages of funds. Budgeting for non-manufacturing businesses and not-for-profit organizations, zero-base budgeting, PERT and PERT/cost, and probabilistic budgets conclude the presentation.

Capital Expenditures Budget

Capital expenditures are long-term commitments of resources to realize future benefits. Budgeting capital expenditures is one of the most important managerial decision-making functions. Facility improvements and plant expansion programs must be geared to a limited supply of funds from internal operations and external sources. The magnitude of funds involved in each expenditure and the length of time required to recover the investment call for penetrating analysis and capable judgment. Decisions regarding current manufacturing operations can always be changed, but because substantial amounts are invested in a capital project, which can be recovered only over a fairly extended time, errors can be quite costly.

Evaluating Capital Expenditures

To minimize capital expenditure errors, many firms establish systems for evaluating the merits of a project before funds are released. Control of capital expenditures is exercised in advance by requiring that each request be based on evaluation analyses, described and illustrated in Chapters 22 and 23. Managerial control requires knowledge of engineering estimates, expected sales volumes, production costs, and marketing costs. Management usually has a firm conviction as to what is consistent with the long-range objectives of the business. It is fundamentally interested in making certain that the project will contribute to earnings.

Short- and Long-Range Capital Expenditures

Capital expenditure programs involve both short- and long-range projects. The economic value of each project must be determined and compared with other projects. Budgeting provides the only opportunity to examine projects side by side and to evaluate their contribution to future periods. For short-range capital expenditures, the current budget should include a detailed capital expenditures budget as well as a determination of the impact on budgeted depreciation expense, cash, fixed asset, and liability accounts.

Long-range projects that will not be implemented in the current budget period need only be stated in general terms. Long-range capital expenditures are management's responsibility and are translated into budget commitments for the period in which they are to be implemented. Timing is very important to the achievement of the most profitable results in planning and budgeting capital expenditures.

Research and Development Budget

Research and development (R & D) activities have been defined as follows:[1]

1. *Research* is planned search or critical investigation aimed at discovery of new knowledge with the hope that such knowledge will be useful in developing a new product or service (hereinafter "product") or a new process or technique (hereinafter "process") or in bringing about a significant improvement to an existing product or process.
2. *Development* is the translation of research findings or other knowledge into a plan or design for a new product or process or for a significant improvement to an existing product or process whether intended for sale or use. It includes the conceptual formulation, design, and testing of product alternatives, construction of prototypes, and operation of pilot plants. It does not include routine or periodic alterations to existing

[1] *Statement of Financial Accounting Standards, No. 2,* "Accounting for Research and Development Costs" (Stamford, Conn.: Financial Accounting Standards Board, 1974), par. 8.

products, production lines, manufacturing processes, and other ongoing operations even though those alterations may represent improvements, and it does not include market research or market testing activities.

The managements of many firms are acutely aware of the increased necessity and growth of R & D activities and of the need to consider their costs from both long- and short-range points of view. From the long-range viewpoint, management must assure itself that a program is in line with future market trends and company objectives and that the future cost of a program is not at odds with forecast economic and financial conditions. From the short-range viewpoint, management must be assured that experimental efforts are being expended on programs that promise a satisfactory rate of return.

R & D projects compete with other projects for available financial resources. The value of the R & D program must be shown as clearly as possible, so that management can compare it with similar programs and other investment opportunities. Therefore, the motivation and intent of experimental activities must be identified carefully.

R & D efforts can require significant resources and can involve considerable risk. One source suggests that the cost of the resources can be estimated by using the "rule of sevens." That is, if an incremental technology to be sold through existing channels costs $1 million for R & D, it will likely cost $7 million for design and $7 million more to produce the first commercial unit. To these costs must be added working capital requirements and consideration of lead time. Studies have shown that generally, if the time to complete the research is one year, the time to produce the first unit is another three years, with still another two years before significant profit occurs.[2]

As to risk, studies have also shown that average probabilities are .6, .6, and .7, respectively, of successfully completing the phases of, first, determining that the product is technologically sound, second, deciding that the product can be commercially successful, and third, actually achieving commercial success. Thus, one in four projects can be expected to succeed ($.6 \times .6 \times .7 = .25$). Therefore, while many businesses require R & D efforts, they should be planned with a realistic understanding of the associated resource commitment and risk.[3]

The research and development budget involves identifying program components and estimating their costs. Other planning devices are used at times, but the budget is considered best for (1) balancing the research and development program, (2) coordinating the program with the company's other projects, and (3) checking certain phases of nonfinancial planning. The budget forces management to think in advance about planned expenditures, both in total amounts and in sphere of effort. It helps achieve coordination, because it presents an overall picture of proposed R & D activities, which can be reviewed and criticized by other operating managers. Exchange of opinions and information at planning meetings is management's best control over the program.

Another important purpose of research and development budgeting is to coordinate these plans with the immediate and long-term financial plans of the company. The budget also forces the R & D director and staff to think in advance about major aspects of the program: personnel requirements, individual or group work loads, equipment requirements, special materials, and necessary facilities. These phases of the research and development program are often overlooked or duplicated.

[2] Francis W. Wolek, "The Business of Technology, Part 1: A Board Guide to Progress and Profits," *Directors & Boards*, Vol. 9, No. 4, p. 33.

[3] *Ibid.*

Form of a Research and Development Budget

Management expects the R & D staff to present ideas along with a complete and detailed budget that can be evaluated as part of the entire planning program. The controller's staff can assist in the preparation of budgets with clearly defined goals and properly evaluated cost data.

Submission of data takes many forms. Information regarding segmentation and allocation of time and effort to various phases of the program is of particular interest to executive management as well as to divisional managers. One example of a research and development budget is presented in Exhibit 16-1.

EXHIBIT 16-1

Planned Research and Development Budget Program by Product Line for 19A (Percentages of Total Effort by Area of Inquiry and by Phase)

	Cost Reduction			Improved Products			New Products			
Phase	A*	B	C	A	B	C	A	B	C	Total
Basic research	4%	3%	3%	2%	4%	4%	1%	1%	3%	25%
Applied research	5	12	3	4	1		2		3	30
Development	7	6	2	5			10		15	45
Total by product lines	16%	21%	8%	11%	5%	4%	13%	1%	21%	100%
Total by area of inquiry		45%			20%			35%		

* A, B, and C refer to different product lines.

The overall R & D program should be supported by a specific budget request that indicates the jobs or steps within each project, the necessary labor hours, the service department time required, and required direct departmental funds. Each active project should be reviewed monthly, comparing projected plans with results attained.

The Franklin Company illustration in Chapter 15 did not include budgeted research and development expenditures. Such a budget could be detailed in dollars, using a format similar to the one in Exhibit 16-1. The dollar amount would be included in the budgeted income statement, consistent with the accounting procedures described in the following paragraph.

Accounting for Research and Development Costs

Research and development costs generally should be expensed in the period in which they are incurred because of the uncertainty of the extent or length of future benefit to the company. An exception to the expensing requirement applies to costs of R & D expenditures that are (1) conducted for others, (2) unique to extractive industries, or (3) incurred by a government-regulated enterprise, such as a public utility, which often defers research and development costs because of the rate-regulated aspects of its business. Equipment and purchased intangibles having alternative future uses should be recorded as assets and expensed through depreciation or amortization. R & D costs, when expensed, should be reported as one item in the operating expense section of the income statement.[4]

[4] *Statement of Financial Accounting Standards, No. 2,* pp. 11–14.

For government contract costing, the Cost Accounting Standards Board promulgated a standard dealing with accounting for independent research and development costs and bid and proposal costs. It provides criteria for (1) accumulation of such costs, (2) their allocation among contractor divisions, and (3) allocation of these costs to contracts.[5]

Cash Budget

A **cash budget** involves detailed estimates of anticipated cash receipts and disbursements for the budget period or some other specific period. It has generally been recognized as an extremely useful and essential management tool. Planning and controlling cash is basic to good management.

Effective cash management entails having the right amounts of cash in the right places at the right times. It involves the management of flows of cash by looking at an organization's liquid funds as an income-producing asset rather than simply as currency for paying bills. Even if a company does not prepare extensive budgets for sales and production, it should set up a budget or estimate of cash receipts and disbursements as an aid to cash management.

Purpose and Nature of a Cash Budget

A cash budget does the following:

1. Indicates cash requirements needed for current operating activities.
2. Aids in focusing on cash usage priorities that are currently required and unavoidable versus those that are postponable or permanently avoidable.
3. Indicates the effect on the cash position of seasonal requirements, large inventories, unusual receipts, and slowness in collecting receivables.
4. Indicates the availability of cash for taking advantage of discounts.
5. Indicates the cash requirements for a plant or equipment expansion program.
6. Assists in planning the financial requirements of bond retirements, income tax installments, and payments to pension and retirement funds.
7. Shows the availability of excess funds for short-term or long-term investments.
8. Shows the need for additional funds from sources such as bank loans or sales of securities and the time factors involved. In this connection, it might also exert a cautionary influence on plans for plant expansion, leading to a modification of capital expenditure decisions.
9. Serves as a basis for evaluating the actual cash management performance of responsible individuals, using measurement criteria such as the target average daily balance as compared with the actual average daily balance in each cash account.

Cash budgets for different time spans have different uses and origins. A long-range cash projection, which can cover periods ranging from three to five years, is useful in planning business growth, investments in projects, and introduction of new products. It focuses primarily on significant changes in the firm's cash

[5] For specifics, see *Standards, Rules and Regulations, Part 420*, "Accounting for Independent Research and Development Costs and Bid and Proposal Costs" (Washington, D.C.: Cost Accounting Standards Board, 1980).

position. A medium-range cash budget is related to periodic (usually yearly) activity, detailed by quarters and months. Improved cash utilization within this time frame comes from control of accounts payable, control of inventory turnover, and review of credit, billing, and collection. The short-range cash budget details the daily availability of cash for current operations, usually 30 to 60 days, and indicates any need for short-term financing. This kind of projection generally is based on records of current transactions of the business.[6]

Preparation of a Periodic Cash Budget

Preparation of a periodic cash budget involves estimating cash receipts and disbursements by time periods. All anticipated cash receipts, such as cash sales, cash collections of accounts receivable, dividend income, interest income, proceeds from sales of assets, royalty income, borrowings from banks, bond issues, and stock sales, are carefully estimated. Likewise, cash requirements for materials purchases, supplies, payroll, interest payments, repayment of loans, dividend payments, taxes, and purchases of plant or equipment must be determined.

The primary sources of cash receipts are cash sales and collections of accounts receivable. Estimates of collections of accounts receivable are based on the sales budget and on the company's collection experience. A representative period is studied to determine how customers pay their accounts, how many take the discount offered, and how many pay within 10 days, 30 days, and so forth. These experiences are set up in a schedule of anticipated collections from credit sales. Collections during a month will be the result of this month's sales and the accounts receivable of prior months' sales. Seasonal variations also should be considered if they affect the collections pattern. To illustrate, assume that the PTX Corporation pattern of collecting credit sales is as follows:

	Percent
Portion of credit sales collected during the month of sale	10.8%
Portion of credit sales collected after the month of sale:	
First month following the month of sale	77.4
Second month following the month of sale	6.3
Third month following the month of sale	2.1
Fourth month following the month of sale	1.2
Cash discounts taken	1.2
Uncollectible accounts	1.0
	100.0

On the basis of these percentages, PTX Corporation collections for January, as an illustrative month, are computed as follows:

Month	Estimate of Credit Sales	Percent	Collections
January	$400,000	10.8%	$ 43,200
December	385,000	77.4	297,990
November	420,000	6.3	26,460
October	360,000	2.1	7,560
September	340,000	1.2	4,080
Total collections for January			$379,290

[6] Robert A. Leitch, John B. Barrack, and Sue H. McKinley, "Controlling Your Cash Resources," *Management Accounting*, Vol. 62, No. 4, p. 59.

Estimated cash disbursements are computed from:

1. The purchases budget, which shows planned purchases of materials and supplies.
2. The direct labor budget, which indicates direct labor wages to be paid.
3. Various types of expense budgets, both factory overhead and commercial, which indicate expenses expected to be incurred. Noncash expenses such as depreciation are excluded.
4. Plant and equipment budget, which details cash needed for the purchase of new equipment or replacements.
5. Treasurer's budget, which indicates requirements for items such as dividends, interest and payments on loans and bonds, donations, and income tax.

For each item, the estimated timing of the cash disbursements is required. If the amount and timing of borrowing does not occur uniformly, variations in the pattern should be considered in estimating the timing of cash disbursements.

A cash budget includes no accrual items. Using the PTX Corporation example, assume that the direct labor payroll accrued at the beginning and the end of January is $14,800 and $13,300, respectively, and the budget shows that $90,000 will be earned by direct labor employees. The treasurer computes the monthly cash requirement for the direct labor payroll as follows:

Accrued payroll at beginning of January	$ 14,800
Add payroll earned as per budget	90,000
	$104,800
Deduct accrued payroll at end of January	13,300
Amount of cash to be paid out during January	$ 91,500

A similar approach can be used to estimate the timing of other cash disbursements as well. Alternatively, a cash payment can be estimated in the following manner. Assume that direct materials purchases and other items, such as factory overhead and commercial expenses, occur fairly uniformly throughout each month and that approximately 10 days (⅓ month) normally elapse between the recording of an indebtedness and its payment. Assume further that cash discounts are always taken and that they average 2 percent. Using data that would be obtained from the direct materials budget, the PTX Corporation January cash disbursement for direct materials purchased is:

December purchases [($200,000 – 2% cash discount) × ⅓ paid in January]	$ 65,333
January purchases [($130,000 – 2% cash discount) × ⅔ paid in January]	84,933
January cash disbursement for direct materials purchased	$150,266

After all the cash receipts and cash disbursements have been estimated for each month of the budget year, the year-end cash balance can be determined for inclusion in the budgeted balance sheet. This amount is the beginning of the budget year's cash balance, plus the estimated total annual cash receipts from all sources, less the estimated total annual disbursements necessary to satisfy all cash demands. The cash budget for PTX Corporation for the month of January is presented in Exhibit 16-2.

EXHIBIT 16-2

PTX Corporation
Cash Budget
January, 19A

January 1, cash balance		$181,506
Budgeted cash receipts:		
Collections of accounts receivable	$379,290	
Dividend and interest income	9,000	
Issue of long-term debt	50,000	438,290
Cash available during January		$619,796
Budgeted cash disbursements:		
Payroll	$ 91,500	
Payment of accounts payable for materials purchases	150,266	
Pension plan payments	9,000	
Insurance, utilities, and miscellaneous expenses	11,000	
Repayment of bank loans	50,000	
Interest payment on bank loans	6,000	
Purchases of new machinery	60,000	377,766
January 31, cash balance		$242,030

Development of Daily Cash Budget Detail

Daily cash receipts and disbursements schedules are necessary for prudent and efficient cash management. Development of daily cash budget detail begins with identification of the timing of major cash flows for items such as taxes, dividends, lease payments, debt service, and wages. Most major cash flows are either easily forecast or, if not forecastable, are offset by a single financial transaction, such as the use of short-term borrowing to provide funds for a specific expenditure or short-term investing of a large cash inflow.

Numerous small receipts and payments may also occur. These minor flows are amenable to some combination of two basic approaches—distribution and scheduling. **Distribution** refers to using statistical estimation to spread a forecast of the total monthly minor flow components over the days of the month in order to reflect the known intramonth cash flow.[7] **Scheduling** refers to the construction of a forecast from information-system-based data, such as disbursement data from invoices, purchase authorizations, production schedules, and work plans.

Electronic Cash Management

The basic premise of cash management is that dollars in transit are not earning assets. They cannot be utilized until they are available as deposits. Similarly, cash lying idle in non-interest-bearing checking accounts contributes little to corporate profitability.

Organizations with multiple, geographically dispersed units, or firms with a widespread customer base making individual payments to dispersed collecting units, can especially benefit from electronic cash management systems. The system involves cash concentration by means of nationwide electronic transfers, which accelerate the collection of deposits from local banks into a central

[7] For an illustration of this procedure, see Bernell K. Stone and Robert A. Wood, "Daily Cash Forecasting: A Simple Method for Implementing the Distribution Approach," *Financial Management*, Vol. 6, No. 3, pp. 40–50.

account on a same-day basis. By drawing checks on its centrally located account, the firm has the additional advantage of **float** for the time it takes the check to be cleared back to the central bank account.

For whatever number of bank accounts a firm has, electronic balance reporting affords a valuable aid to efficient and effective cash management. This bank service provides accurate, up-to-date, and on-line daily information on amounts and locations of available cash. Depending on the level of service, the information furnished may be highly detailed, via a computer terminal, or abbreviated by means of a telephone-to-computer inquiry that results in each bank's computer "telling" the firm's balances. This information is especially useful in the short-term investment management of the day-to-day difference between the firm's book balance of cash and the bank's balance, that is, in the management of float.

Another and broader electronic cash management application is found in **electronic funds transfer systems (EFTS)**. These systems are designed to reduce the number of paper documents and to increase the use of electronic data in carrying out banking cash transfer functions, thus reducing bank transaction costs and expediting cash transfers. These developing cash payment systems include unstaffed customer banking facilities, automated clearinghouses for interbank cash transfers, point-of-sale facilities, pay-by-phone service, and corporate funds transfers.[8] For the manager, the potential for virtually instantaneous receipts and payments of cash requires consideration in the management of cash resources.

Planning and Budgeting for Nonmanufacturing Businesses and Not-for-Profit Organizations

Many industrial concerns still pay only lip service to budgeting. To an even greater extent, nonmanufacturing businesses—and especially not-for-profit organizations—lack effective planning and control mechanisms. However, examples of effective budgeting do exist.

Nonmanufacturing Businesses

Under the guidance of the National Retail Merchants Association, department stores have followed merchandise budget procedures that have a long and quite successful history. A budget for a retail store is a necessity, because the profit per dollar of sales is generally low, usually from 1 to 3 percent. Planning, budgeting, and control administration is strongly oriented toward profit control on the total store as well as on a departmental basis. The merchandise budget shows predetermined sales and profits, generally on a 6-month basis following the two merchandising seasons: spring–summer and fall–winter. The merchandise budget includes sales, purchases, expenses, capital expenditures, cash, and annual statements.

Although it is logical for a department store or a wholesaler to plan and budget its activities, banks, savings and loan associations, and insurance companies also should create long-range profit plans coordinating long-term goals and institutional objectives. In these businesses, forecasting deals with deposit size and mix, number of insured and mix of policies, capital requirements, types of earning assets, physical facilities, personnel requirements, operational changes, and

---

[8] Howard C. Johnson and Edward C. Arnold, "The Emerging Revolution in Electronic Payments," *Price Waterhouse Review*, Vol. 22, No. 3, pp. 26–31.

new, additional, or changed depositor or client services. The long-range goal should be translated into short-range budgets, starting at the lowest level of responsibility, building and combining the various organizational units into a whole. Similar needs exist for professional service organizations, such as law firms, accounting firms, medical and dental practices, and realtors.

Not-for-Profit Organizations

While business organizations are concerned with profits, the not-for-profit sector is concerned with programs. Yet neither can succeed without sound budgeting. Management in a not-for-profit organization, as in any entity, is a process that entails planning, resource allocation, execution, and evaluation. Budgeting is the common denominator that links these management activities.

Periodic budgets in any enterprise—not-for-profit or business—are usually begun at the bottom of the organizational hierarchy and then passed upward for refinement and approval. Department managers in not-for-profit organizations develop their program needs in the context of policies, priorities, and assumptions expressed in long-range plans and in accordance with periodic budget guidelines established by senior management. A comprehensive budget format is required—presented by program to indicate the purpose of expenditures and with adequate detail to establish control. Each program should emphasize the relationship between the input of resources and the output of services to be performed, including the measures necessary to evaluate achievement of program objectives.[9]

Measuring the benefits or outputs of programs poses difficulties. A private enterprise measures its benefits in terms of increased revenue or decreased cost. In the nonprofit sector, however, social problems complicate the measurement of benefits. Consequently, such endeavors often have resulted in relatively meaningless monetary outcome data. Problems encountered in monetary output measurements suggest that monetary inputs (costs) might be more meaningfully related to nonmonetary outcomes for specific programs.[10]

Annual budgets for governments at all levels in the United States are now well in excess of one trillion dollars—an enormous sum of money. Yet, in spite of the many decades in which governmental budgeting has been practiced, the general public is increasingly critical of services received for money spent. While the federal government might be under more obvious attack, state, county, and municipal governments are equally criticized not only for the lack of a satisfactory control system, but also for the ill-conceived procedure for planning the costs and revenues needed to govern. Therefore, budgets based on a managerial approach could go a long way toward responsibly meeting these criticisms.

An example of such an effort in government is found in the concept of a **planning, programming, budgeting system**, commonly referred to as **PPBS**. PPBS can be defined as an analytical tool to assist management in the analysis of alternatives as the basis for rational decision making and in the allocation of resources to accomplish stated goals and objectives over a designated time period. It had its origin in the Defense Department's attempt to quantify huge

---

[9] R. Schuyler Lesher, Jr., and Craig Becker, "Total Recall," *Management Focus*, Vol. 30, No. 5, pp. 13, 15.

[10] For additional discussion and illustration, see James E. Sorensen and Hugh D. Grove, "Cost-Outcome and Cost-Effectiveness Analysis: Emerging Nonprofit Performance Evaluation Techniques," *Accounting Review*, Vol. 52, No. 3, pp. 658–675.

expenditures in terms of benefits derived from activities and programs in the public sector. This analysis technique is closely related to cost-benefit analysis, focusing on the outputs or final results, rather than the inputs or the initial dollars expended. The outputs are directly relatable to the planned objectives through the use of performance budgets.

The idea that governmental programs should be undertaken in the light of final benefits has caused agencies in the field of health, education, and welfare services as well as other nonprofit organizations to apply PPBS to their activities and programs. However, PPBS has been criticized because its required specification of objectives cannot be transformed readily into operational outcome quantities or statistics. To be effective, PPBS needs a great deal of refinement and innovation, an understanding of its aims and methods, and active participation of executive and middle management.

In the same way that governmental units have become budget and cost conscious, not-for-profit organizations, such as hospitals, churches, school districts, colleges, universities, fraternal orders, libraries, and labor unions, are adopting strong measures of budgetary control. In the past, efforts to control costs were generally exercised through pressure to reduce budget increases rather than through method improvements or program changes. Long-range planning was seldom practiced.

Basically, the objectives of not-for-profit organizations are directed toward the economic, social, educational, or spiritual benefit of individuals or groups who have no vested interest in such organizations in the form of ownership or investment. The presidents, boards of directors, trustees, or administrative officers, like their counterparts in profit-seeking enterprises, are charged with the stewardship of economic resources, except that their job is primarily to use or spend these resources instead of trying to derive monetary gain. It is expressly for this not-for-profit objective that these organizations should install adequate and effective methods and procedures in planning, budgeting, and cost control.[11]

Zero-Base Budgeting

Customarily, those in charge of an established budgetary program are required to justify only the increase sought above last year's appropriation. What they are already spending is usually accepted as necessary, with little or no examination. **Zero-base budgeting**, however, is a budget-planning procedure for the reevaluation of an organization's existing program and expenditures. It requires each manager to justify the entire budget request in detail and places the burden of proof on the manager to justify why authorization to spend any money at all should be granted. It starts with the assumption that zero will be spent on each activity—thus, the term *zero-base.* What a manager is spending already is not accepted as a starting point.

Managers are asked to prepare for each activity or operation under their control a **decision package** that includes an analysis of cost, purpose, alternative courses of action, measures of performance, consequences of not performing the

[11] Budgeting for not-for-profit organizations other than governmental, health care, and higher education is discussed in considerable detail in *Financial Planning and Evaluation for the Nonprofit Organization,* by Anthony J. Gambino and Thomas J. Reardon (New York: Institute of Management Accountants (formerly National Association of Accountants), 1981).

activity, and benefits. The zero-base budgeting approach asserts that when managers build the budget from zero, two types of alternatives should be considered: (1) different ways of performing the same activity and (2) different levels of effort in performing the activity.

A decision package identifies an activity in a definitive manner for evaluation and comparison with other activities. Devising these decision packages, ranking them, and making funding decisions according to the rank order constitute the heart of the zero-base budgeting process.

Success in implementing zero-base budgeting requires the following:

1. Linkage of zero-base budgeting to the short- and long-range planning process.
2. Sustained support and commitment from executive management.
3. Innovation on the part of the managers who develop the budget decision packages.
4. Sale of the procedure to the persons who must perform the work necessary to keep the concept vigorous.

Computerized Budgeting[12]

The time required to assemble the periodic budget and to achieve a consensus of the managers involved is so great that the budgeting process often is inhibited. Time constraints can be handled more effectively, however, by converting the elements of the conventional budgeting process into a functional planning tool through the use of computer modeling techniques. Tedious arithmetic can be eliminated by converting budgeting procedures into a computerized set of straightforward algebraic formulas. The resulting computerized model entails the following primary components:

1. A line-by-line outline that describes the format of the desired output of budget schedules and statements.
2. A structure of algebraic logic or procedures that demonstrates the computational processes in simple formulas.
3. Elements of data that, when passed through the computational process, will generate the desired output.

The development of a computerized budgeting process can result in substantial benefits. These benefits include the following:

1. A shortened planning cycle time. A reduction in computational effort frequently allows the start of budget preparation to be delayed until more accurate inputs are available. Thus, the quality of sales and cost estimates can be improved.
2. Freedom to reconsider planning assumptions. Time savings make it feasible for managers to reconsider planning assumptions early in the budgeting process. Cost and profit implications of various assumptions can be estimated before any commitment is made.
3. Continuous budgeting. Plans can be updated continuously throughout the budget period, and in some cases, planning horizons can be extended beyond the current budget period.

---

[12] The following discussion is adapted from Richard C. Murphy, "A Computerized Model Approach to Budgeting," *Management Accounting*, Vol. 56, No. 12, pp. 34–36, 38.

4. Operating analysis capability. If procedures and data are maintained in current form, the computerized model is available to produce instant answers to what-if questions. More alternatives can be evaluated when such a model is used.
5. Discipline. Development of a model requires precise understanding and definition of the organization and its accounting system. Therefore, the discipline of developing the relationships inherent in a computerized budgeting model is itself a valuable learning experience.

Prospective Financial Information for External Users

Recent years have seen increasing recognition of the importance of prospective financial information for external users, because investors and potential investors seek to enhance the process of predicting the future. What has happened in the past, as reported in the financial statements, can be viewed as an indicator of the future. Often, however, past results are not indicative of future expectations and need to be tempered accordingly.

The question of including prospective information in external financial statements is controversial. Opponents point out that the uncertainty of such information and the potential dangers of undue reliance upon it can result in added legal liability, a drop in credibility, or both. These concerns and potentially advantageous disclosures to competitors have been cited as causes of widespread opposition by management. On the positive side, however, it has been argued that the inclusion of prospective information in external financial statements "should be provided when it will enhance the reliability of user's predictions."[13]

In 1985, the AICPA issued a statement that establishes detailed procedures and reporting standards for engagements to examine, compile, or apply agreed-upon procedures to prospective financial information. Included are financial forecasts and financial projections. **Financial forecasts** are defined as an entity's expected financial position, results of operations, and changes in cash flow, reflecting conditions expected to exist and the course of action expected to be taken. A financial forecast can be expressed in specific monetary amounts as a single point estimate of forecasted results or as a range.

Financial projections present an entity's financial statements based on one or more hypothetical assumptions. One or more hypothetical courses of action can be presented for evaluation—as in a response to a question such as "What would happen if . . . ?" The presentation reflects conditions expected to exist and the course of action expected to be taken, given the assumptions. A projection, like a forecast, can contain a range.

The AICPA statement includes minimum presentation guidelines. Generally, the prospective financial information should be in the format of historical financial statements and should include a description of what management intends to present, a statement that the assumptions are based on information existing at the time the prospective information was prepared, a caveat that the prospective results may not be achieved, and a summary of significant assumptions.[14]

Securities and Exchange Commission regulations presently encourage but do not require inclusion of prospective financial data in external financial reports.

[13] Report of the Study Group on the Objectives of Financial Statements, *Objectives of Financial Statements* (New York: American Institute of Certified Public Accountants, 1973), p. 46.

[14] *Statement on Standards for Accountants' Services on Prospective Financial Information*, "Financial Forecasts and Projections" (New York: American Institute of Certified Public Accountants, 1985).

Furthermore, a safe harbor rule gives SEC-regulated companies and their auditors protection from legal liability should public prospective information fail to materialize. For the rule to apply, forecasts and projections must be made on a reasonable basis, in good faith, with assumptions disclosed. The SEC requires that materially incorrect predictions be corrected in subsequent financial reports. SEC guidelines are in harmony with AICPA requirements.

PERT and PERT/Cost Systems for Planning and Control

The accountant's involvement in management planning and control has led to the use of network analysis for planning, measuring progress to schedule, evaluating changes to schedule, forecasting future progress, and predicting and controlling costs. These kinds of analyses are variously referred to as the **program evaluation and review technique (PERT)** or the **critical path method (CPM)**. The origin of PERT is military; it was introduced in connection with the Navy Polaris program. CPM's origin is industrial.

Many companies use these methods in planning, scheduling, and costing such diverse projects as constructing buildings, installing equipment, and research and development. There is also an opportunity for using PERT in business administration tasks, such as scheduling the closing of books, revising standard cost data, scheduling the preparation of the various budgets that make up the annual profit plan, and audit planning and control. In conjunction with PERT and critical path techniques, computer systems provide executive management with far better means for directing large-scale, complex projects. Integrated measures of cost, time, and technical performance can be furnished to management. Actual results can be compared with the network plan and revisions made as needed.

The PERT System

PERT is a probabilistic diagram of the interrelationships of a complex series of activities. Regardless of the type of task—military, industrial, or business administration—time is the fundamental element of any of these activities. The major burden of PERT is the determination of the longest time duration for the completion of an entire project. This calculation is based on the length of time required for the longest sequence of activities.

All the individual tasks that complete a given job or program must be visualized in a **network** of events and activities. An **event** represents a specified accomplishment at a particular instant in time, such as B or E in the network illustrated in Figure 16-1. An **activity** represents the time and resources necessary to move from one event to another, such as B → E in Figure 16-1. Activities can be in series; for example, market research cannot be performed before the research design is planned. Other activities can be parallel; for example, the engines for a ship can be built at the same time the hull is being constructed.

Three estimates are made for each activity: optimistic (t_o), most likely (t_m), and pessimistic (t_p). In the network presented in Figure 16-1, the three time estimates, expressed in units of one week, are indicated under each activity line. From these estimates, an expected time (t_e) is calculated for each activity. The expected time represents the average time an activity would require if it were repeated a large number of times. The calculation is generally based on the assumption that the distribution of activity times closely approximates a Beta probability distribution. Such distributions can be symmetrical or skewed. The following formula is used to compute the mean of the Beta probability distribution, which is the expected time:

FIGURE 16-1 *PERT Network with Time Estimates in Weeks*

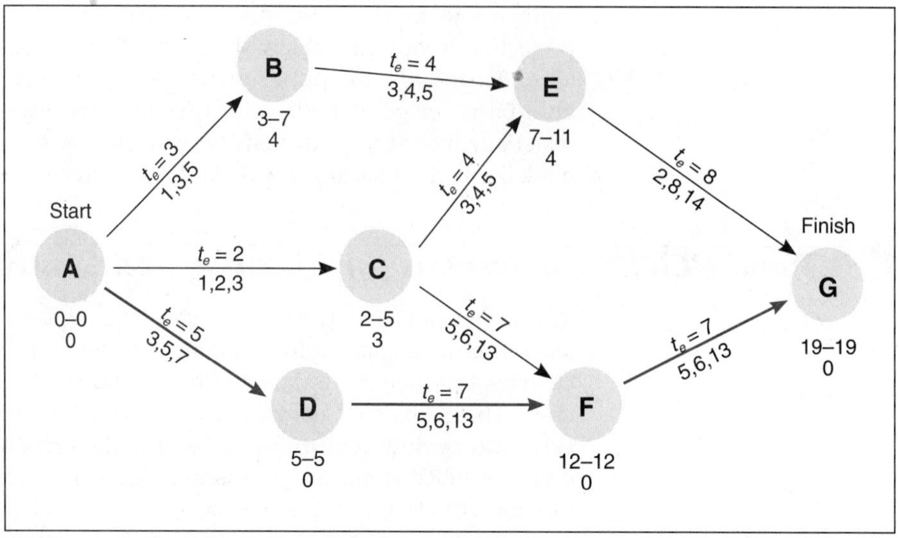

$$t_e = \frac{(t_o + 4t_m + t_p)}{6}$$

For example, the activity D–F in Figure 16-1 has a value of $t_e = 7$, determined as follows:

$$\begin{aligned} \text{If: } t_o &= 5 \\ t_m &= 6 \\ t_p &= 13 \\ \text{Then: } t_e &= \frac{[5 + 4(6) + 13]}{6} = \frac{42}{6} = 7 \end{aligned}$$

Below each event in the network are noted the earliest expected and latest allowable times, and below these two numbers, the slack time is shown. The **earliest expected time** is the earliest time that an activity can be expected to start, because of its relationship to pending activities. The **latest allowable time** is the latest time that an activity can begin and not delay completion of the project.

The Critical Path. The longest path through the network is known as the **critical path** and is denoted on the flow chart by the colored arrows connecting A–D–F–G in Figure 16-1. Shortening of total time can be accomplished only by shortening the critical path. However, if critical path A–D–F–G is shortened from 19 weeks to 15 weeks, A–C–F–G (assuming F–G remains unchanged) then becomes the critical path because it is now the longest.

Slack Time. **Slack time** is the amount of time that can be added to an activity without increasing the total time required on the critical path. Activities along the critical path (A–D–F–G) have a slack of zero. All noncritical activities have positive slack. The less the amount of slack time, the more critical an activity or path, and vice versa.

Slack is computed by subtracting the earliest expected time from the latest allowable time. It is determinable only in relation to an entire path through the network. When multiple activities lead to an event, the event's earliest expected starting time is always the largest sum of expected times of the preceding activities. When multiple activities lead from an event, the latest allowable time at that event is always the smallest figure found by subtracting from total project time the sum of expected times of subsequent network activities. In Figure 16-1, path A–C–E–G at event C has an earliest expected time of 2 weeks and a latest allowable time of 5 weeks [19 – (7 + 7)], for a slack time of 3 weeks. At event E, the earliest expected time is 7 weeks [3 (A–B) + 4 (B–E)] and the latest allowable time is 11 weeks (19 – 8), for a slack time of 4 weeks. However, if any slack time is used up, that is, if a noncritical activity utilizes more than the expected time, the slack times for subsequent activities must be recomputed. Recomputation also may be necessary when times shorter than the expected times are required.

Slack allows management some flexibility. If available slack time is not exceeded, noncritical activities can be delayed without delaying the project's completion date. Slack time information provides useful data for initial planning and continuous project monitoring when the project's status is compared with the plan.

The PERT/Cost System

PERT/cost is an integrated management information system designed to furnish management with timely information for planning and controlling schedules and costs of projects. The PERT/cost system is really an expansion of PERT. It assigns cost to time and activities, thereby providing total financial planning and control by functional responsibility. Each activity is defined at a level of detail necessary for individual job assignments and supervisory control. Control is on scheduled tasks, with time and cost as the common control factors.

PERT/cost estimates are activity- or project-oriented, and the addition of the cost component permits analyses involving time/cost tradeoffs. If the total time required to complete a project is greater than desired, management can evaluate each activity to determine if the normal completion time can be reduced and, if it can, to determine the required cost. The time saved in completing an activity that results from the incurrence of addition cost is referred to as **crash time**.

In the network presented in Figure 16-2, the activities noted by the dark circles, A, B, C, and D, represent completed events. The dollar figures in the white blocks represent estimated costs, for example, $30,000 for activity F–G. Figures in the shaded blocks to the right of the estimates are actual costs. Estimated times (t_e) and actual times (t_a) are shown below the activity lines.

Activities A–B, A–C, and A–D have been completed. A–B required ½ week more time than planned; however, it is not on the critical path and does not affect total project duration. If excess time were such that another path became long enough to be the critical path, then total time would be altered.

The actual activity cost of $10,000 for A–B compared to a budget of $12,000 indicates an underrun of $2,000. Activity A–C budget and actual figures coincide for time and cost. A–D had an overrun of $5,000 and a 2-week slippage. The slippage requires immediate attention because A–D is on the critical path. Immediate investigation and corrective action seem needed for B–E and C–E. According to the present status report, both activities have consumed the budgeted time and cost and one or both are not yet completed.

Although comparison of actual versus planned time and cost figures is essential, comparison alone is not enough to evaluate a project. Evaluation of performance is needed to complete the process. For example, a project is not necessarily in financial trouble when actual expenditures exceed those budgeted. Progress may be correspondingly ahead of schedule. Nor is a project necessarily meeting performance standards when it is within the budget. To evaluate a project's true status, management needs to study performance, cost, and timing.

FIGURE 16-2 *PERT/Cost Network with Time (in Weeks) and Cost (in Thousands of Dollars)*

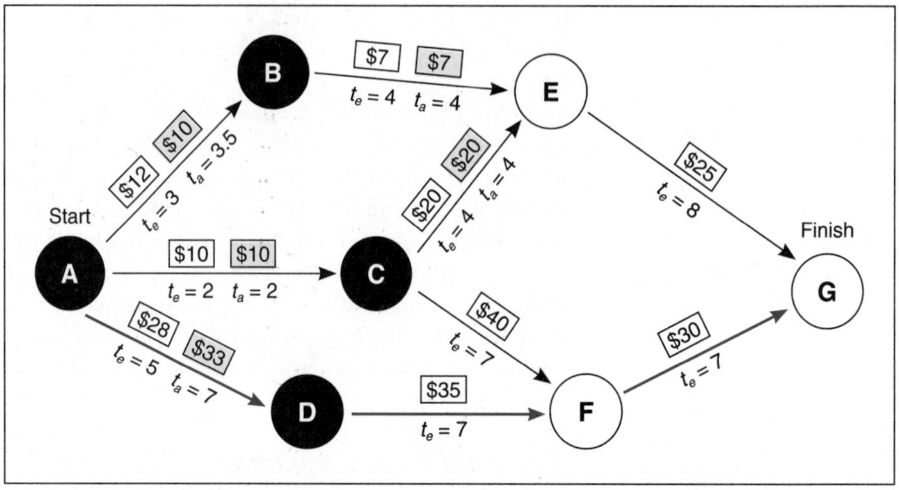

Computer Applications

Computer support provides distinct advantages to PERT and PERT/cost applications. PERT and PERT/cost procedures are mathematically oriented and therefore are ideally suited to the high-speed response of computers for deriving the critical path, slack times, and costs, and for storing and reporting results to management. Revisions to all schedule elements, whether during the initial estimating phase or during the active project phase, can be updated and the revised results promptly reported.

Probabilistic Budgets

A budget can be based on one set of assumptions as to the most likely performance in a forthcoming period. However, there is increasing evidence that several sets of assumptions are evaluated by management before a budget is finalized. One possibility is the PERT-like three-level estimates—optimistic, most likely, and pessimistic. This involves estimating each budget component assuming each of the three conditions. Probability trees can be used in which several variables can be considered in the analysis, such as number of units sold, sales price, and variable manufacturing and marketing costs.

To each discrete set of assumptions, a probability can be assigned, based on past experience and management's best judgment about the future, thus revealing to management not only a range of possible outcomes but also a probability associated with each. Further statistical techniques can then be applied, including an expected (weighted, composite) value, the range, and the standard deviation for the various budget elements, such as sales, manufacturing cost, and marketing cost. For example, an expected value for sales may be $960,000, with a range from a low of $780,000 to a high of $1,200,000 and a standard deviation of $114,600.

The computational capability of the computer facilitates the consideration of complex sets of assumptions and permits the use of simulation programs, making it possible to develop more objectively determined probabilities.[15]

[15] An exhaustive treatment of these techniques is beyond the scope of this discussion. For expanded discussion and illustrations, see: William L. Ferrara and Jack C. Hayya, "Toward Probabilistic Profit Budgets," *Management Accounting*, Vol. 52, No. 3, pp. 23–28; Belverd E. Needles, Jr., "Budgeting Techniques: Subjective to Probabilistic," *Management Accounting*, Vol. 53, No. 6, pp. 39–45; Edmund J. Hall and Richard J. Kolkmann, "A Vote for the Probabilistic Pro Forma Income Statement," *Management Accounting*, Vol. 57, No. 7, pp. 45–48; Davis L. S. Chang and Shu S. Liao, "Measuring and Disclosing Forecast Reliability," *Journal of Accountancy*, Vol. 143, No. 5, pp. 76–87 (Monte Carlo simulation).

Summary

This chapter discussed specific budgets, such as capital expenditures and research and development budgets, which play a significant role in management's long- and short-range plans for a company. Closely related thereto is the cash budget, which reveals expected excesses or shortages of funds during the budget period. The cash budget was illustrated with an example of some common sources of cash receipts and cash disbursements. Budgeting for nonmanufacturing businesses and not-for-profit organizations, zero-base budgeting, and PERT and PERT/cost were discussed. PERT and PERT/cost introduced the use of probabilities in the budgeting process, and the application in a PERT network was illustrated. The chapter concluded with a discussion of probabilistic budgets.

Key Terms

capital expenditures *(436)*
research and development (R&D) *(437)*
cash budget *(440)*
distribution *(443)*
scheduling *(443)*
float *(444)*
electronic funds transfer system (EFTS) *(444)*
planning, programming, budgeting system (PPBS) *(445)*
zero-base budgeting *(446)*
decision package *(446)*
financial forecasts *(448)*
financial projections *(448)*
program evaluation and review technique (PERT) or critical path method (CPM) *(449)*
network *(449)*
event *(449)*
activity *(449)*
earliest expected time *(450)*
latest allowable time *(450)*
critical path *(450)*
slack time *(450)*
PERT/cost *(451)*
crash time *(451)*

Discussion Questions

Q16-1 What is meant by a capital expenditure? How does it differ from a revenue expenditure?

Q16-2 Name some purposes of and some reasons for a research and development program.

Q16-3 Companies should establish budgetary procedures to provide control and accounting systems for research and development expenditures. What are such procedures specifically designed to achieve?

Q16-4 Managers consider a cash budget an extremely useful management tool. Why?

Q16-5 Discuss the need for planning and budgeting (a) in nonmanufacturing businesses and (b) in not-for-profit organizations.

Q16-6 What is the objective of the control concept generally referred to as PPBS?

Q16-7 Describe zero-base budgeting, and explain how zero-base budgeting differs from traditional budgeting.

Q16-8 What strengths and weaknesses might be associated with zero-base budgeting? (CICA adapted)

Q16-9 What governing criterion has been suggested for determining whether to include prospective information in external financial statements?

Q16-10 Discuss the conditions that determine when PERT is appropriate.

Q16-11 Explain the computation of slack in the PERT network.

Q16-12 State the relationship between PERT and PERT/cost systems.

Q16-13 What does computer support offer to PERT and PERT/cost users?

Q16-14 Discuss how PERT/costs could be used in planning the audit of a state government's highway construction and maintenance operation. (CIA adapted)

Q16-15 Contrast the probabilistic budget and the traditional budget in terms of information provided to management.

Exercises

E16-1 Budgeted Cash Collections and Accounts Receivable. A company's actual sales on account were as follows:

Month	Sales on Account
February	$160,000
March	100,000
April	180,000

Experience has shown that such sales are usually collected as follows:

	Percent
Month of sale	20%
Month after sale	50
Second month after sale	25
Never collected and written off in third month after sale	5
	100%

Required:

(1) Compute the budgeted cash collections for May, if May sales on account are budgeted at $150,000.
(2) Compute the balance of accounts receivable at April 30.
(3) Compute the balance of accounts receivable at May 31.
(4) What steps can the company take to reduce the balance in accounts receivable as of May 31st? Evaluate both the risks and advantages. (CIA adapted)

E16-2 Cash Budget. The management of LKM Corporation requested a cash budget for the coming quarter, January through March. The budget is to be prepared from the following data:

Item	November	December	January	February	March
Sales (on account)	$60,000	$70,000	$50,000	$60,000	$70,000
Payroll	20,000	22,000	21,000	22,000	23,000
Purchases (on account)	15,000	20,000	15,000	25,000	20,000
Depreciation expense	5,000	5,000	5,000	5,000	5,000
Miscellaneous cash operating expenses	5,000	6,000	6,000	7,000	6,000
Debt retirement	0	26,000	0	0	26,000

Collections of accounts receivable amount to 25% in the month of sale, 60% in the first month after sale, 10% in the second month after sale, and 5% written off as uncollectible. Purchases are paid off at the rate of 20% in the month of purchase and 80% in the first month following purchase. Cash on hand at January 1 is $6,000.

Required: Prepare a cash budget for January, February, and March.

E16-3 Budgeted Cash Disbursements. Olney Company is preparing its cash budget. The sales budget specifies the following budgeted monthly sales, in units:

April	9,000
May	10,000
June	12,000
July	11,000

The company's inventory policy is to budget for finished goods inventory equal to 20% of the following month's sales, and to budget for materials inventory equal to 40% of the following month's production requirements. Each unit of finished goods requires three pieces of material at a predicted price of $20 each. However, Olney intends to take advantage of a 2/10, n/30 discount.

Required: Compute the budgeted cash disbursements during May for payment of accounts payable for material purchases. Assume material purchases are made evenly throughout the month.

CGA-Canada (adapted). Reprint with permission.

E16-4 Cash Budget for Inventory Purchases. Partee Company manufactures a product called Par. Each unit of Par requires 3 pieces of a material called Tee, whose standard price per piece is $5. Budgeted inventory levels are as follows:

	Par	Tee
June 1	5,000	20,000
July 1	3,000	14,000
August 1	3,000	11,000

Budgeted sales of Par are 50,000 for June and 30,000 for July. The company intends to take advantage of a 2/10, n/30 discount. Assume one third of the purchases of any month due for discount are paid in the following month.

Required: Compute the cash required in July for purchases of Tee.

CGA-Canada (adapted). Reprint with permission.

E16-5 Cash Budget. Crockett Company is preparing a cash budget for July. The following estimates were made:

(a) Expected cash balance, July 1, $5,000.
(b) Income tax rate is 40%, based on accounting income for the month, payable in the following month.
(c) Crockett's customers pay for 50% of their purchases during the month of purchase and the balance during the following month. Bad debts are expected to be 2%.
(d) Merchandise is purchased on account for resale, with 25% of purchases paid for during the month of purchase and the balance paid during the following month.
(e) Marketing and administrative expenses are all paid in the current month.
(f) Dividends of $15,000 are expected to be declared and paid during July.
(g) Crockett's desire is to have a minimum month-end cash balance of $5,000.
(h) Other budgets include the following estimates:

	June	July
Sales (all on account)	$30,000	$40,000
Purchases	10,000	15,000
Depreciation expense for marketing and administration	5,000	6,000
Cost of goods sold	12,000	16,000
Other marketing and administrative expenses	9,000	10,000

Required:

(1) Prepare a cash budget for July.
(2) What financial action needs to be taken as a result of this cash budget?

CGA-Canada (adapted). Reprint with permission.

E16-6 PERT Network. Crespi Construction Company soon will begin work on a building for Echelon Savings Bank. Work on the building was started by another construction firm that has gone out of business. Crespi has agreed to complete the project. Crespi's schedule of activities and related expected completion times for the Echelon Savings Bank project are presented in the following table:

Activity Code	Activity Description	Estimated Time (in weeks)
1-2	Obtain on-site work permit	1
2-5	Repair damage done by vandals	4
2-3	Inspect construction materials left on site	1
3-5	Order and receive additional construction materials	2
3-4	Apply for waiver to add new materials	1
4-5	Obtain waiver to add new materials	1
5-6	Perform electrical work	4
6-7	Complete interior partitions	2

Required:

(1) Prepare the PERT network.
(2) Identify the critical path and determine the expected time in weeks for the project.
(3) Explain the effect on the critical path and expected time for the project if Crespi is not required to apply for and obtain the waiver to add new materials. (ICMA adapted)

E16-7 PERT Network. A company is faced with the following PERT network situation (time in days):

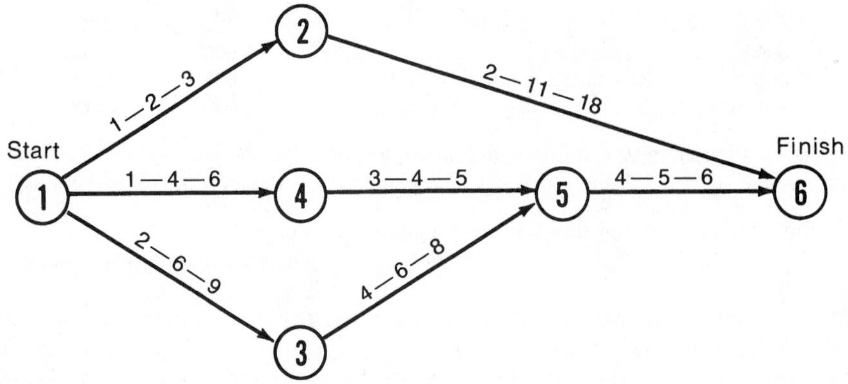

Required:

(1) Calculate t_e (expected time) for each activity, to two decimal places. For each activity, the estimates are t_o, t_m, and t_p, in that order.

(2) Calculate the total time for each path, and identify the critical path as well as total time for other paths.

CGA-Canada (adapted). Reprint with permission.

E16-8 PERT Network. The following PERT network has been prepared for a project, with expected time calculated in days, as shown.

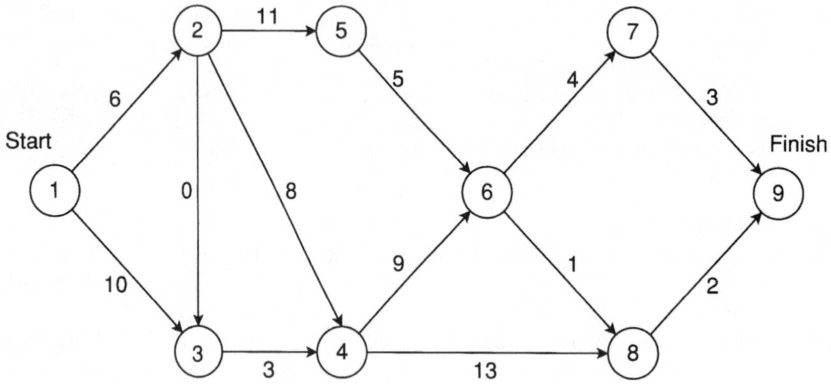

Required:

(1) Identify the critical path.

(2) Determine the slack time at each event.

CGA-Canada (adapted). Reprint with permission.

E16-9 PERT Network. The following time estimates, in days, have been obtained for each activity required for a certain construction project.

Activity	t_o	t_m	t_p	t_e
0-1				4
1-2				3
1-3				4
2-6				6
3-4	1	2	9	?
3-5				6
4-6				3
4-7				6
5-7				6
6-7				5

t_o = most optimistic time
t_m = most likely time
t_p = most pessimistic time
t_e = estimated completion time

Required:

(1) Compute the expected completion time for activity 3-4.
(2) Construct a PERT network of the activities and events necessary to complete the construction project.
(3) Determine the estimated time required to complete each path through the PERT network, and identify the critical path.
(4) What is the slack time for event 2?

Problems

P16-1 Cash and Purchases Budget for a Manufacturer. Huntsville Company seeks assistance in developing cash and other budget information for May, June, and July. On April 30, the company had cash of $5,500, accounts receivable of $437,000, inventories of $309,400, and accounts payable of $133,055. The budget is to be based on the following assumptions:

Sales:

(a) Each month's sales are billed on the last day of the month.
(b) Customers are allowed a 3% discount if payment is made within 10 days after the billing date. Receivables are recorded at the gross sales price.
(c) Sixty percent of the billings are collected within the discount period; 25% by the end of the month; 9% by the end of the second month; and 6% prove uncollectible.

Purchases:

(a) Fifty-four percent of all purchases of materials and a like percentage of marketing, general, and administrative expenses are paid in the month purchased, with the remainder paid in the following month.
(b) Each month's units of ending materials inventory are equal to 130% of next month's production requirement.
(c) The cost of each unit of inventory is $20.
(d) Wages and salaries earned each month by employees total $38,000.
(e) Marketing, general, and administrative expenses (of which $2,000 is depreciation) are equal to 15% of the current month's sales.

Actual and projected sales are as follows:

March	$354,000
April	363,000
May	357,000
June	342,000
July	360,000
August	366,000

Actual and projected materials needed for production:

	Units
March	11,800
April	12,100
May	11,900
June	11,400
July	12,000
August	12,200

Accrued payroll at the end of each month is as follows:

March	$3,100
April	2,900
May	3,300
June	3,400
July	3,000
August	2,800

Required: Compute the following:
(1) Budgeted cash disbursements during June.
(2) Budgeted cash collections during May.
(3) Budgeted units of inventory to be purchased during July. (AICPA adapted)

P16-2 Cash Budget. Crosley Corporation, a rapidly expanding distributor to retail outlets, is in the process of formulating plans for 19B. J. Caldwell, director of marketing, has completed the 19B sales forecast and is confident that sales estimates will be met or exceeded. The following sales figures show the growth expected and will provide the planning basis for other corporate departments.

Month	Gross Sales
January	$1,800,000
February	2,000,000
March	1,800,000
April	2,200,000
May	2,500,000
June	2,800,000
July	3,000,000
August	3,000,000
September	3,200,000
October	3,200,000
November	3,000,000
December	3,400,000

G. Brownell, assistant controller, has been given the responsibility of formulating the cash flow projection, a critical element during a period of rapid expansion. The following information will be used in the cash analysis preparation.

(a) Crosley Corporation has experienced an excellent record in accounts receivable collection and expects this trend to continue. Sixty percent of billings are collected in the month after the sale and 40% in the second month after sale. Uncollectible accounts are nominal and will not be considered in the analysis.
(b) The purchase of inventory is the company's largest expenditure; the cost of these items equals 50% of sales. Sixty percent of the inventory is received one month prior to sale and 40% is received in the month of sale.
(c) Prior experience shows that 80% of accounts payable is paid by the company one month after receipt of the purchased inventory, and the remaining 20% is paid in the second month after receipt.
(d) Hourly wages, including fringe benefits, are equal to 20% of the current month's sales. The wages are paid in the month incurred.
(e) General and administrative expenses are projected to be $2,640,000 for 19B. All these expenses are incurred uniformly throughout the year except the property taxes. Property taxes are paid in four equal installments in the last month of each quarter. The composition of the expenses is as follows:

Salaries	$ 480,000
Promotion	660,000
Property taxes	240,000
Insurance	360,000
Utilities	300,000
Depreciation	600,000
Total	$2,640,000

(f) Income tax payments are made by the company in the first month of each quarter based on the income for the previous quarter. The company's income tax rate is 40%. The company's income before taxes for the first quarter of 19B is projected to be $1,020,000.
(g) The company has a corporate policy of maintaining an end-of-month cash balance of $100,000. Cash is invested or borrowed monthly, as necessary, to maintain this balance.
(h) The company has a calendar-year reporting period.

Required: Prepare a schedule of cash receipts and disbursements for Crosley Corporation, by month, for the second quarter of 19B. Be sure that all receipts, disbursements, and borrowing/investing amounts are presented on a monthly basis. Ignore interest expense and interest income associated with borrowing and investing.

P16-3 Cash Budget. Mayne Manufacturing Co. has incurred substantial losses for several years and has become insolvent. On March 31, 19A, Mayne petitioned the court for protection from creditors and submitted the following balance sheet:

Mayne Manufacturing Co.
Balance Sheet
March 31, 19A

	Net Book Value	Liquidation Value
Assets		
Accounts receivable	$100,000	$ 50,000
Inventories	90,000	40,000
Plant and equipment	150,000	160,000
Total	$340,000	$250,000
Liabilities and Stockholders' Equity		
Accounts payable—general creditors	$600,000	
Common stock outstanding	60,000	
Deficit	(320,000)	
Total	$340,000	

Mayne's management informed the court that the company has developed a new product, and that a prospective customer is willing to sign a contract for the purchase of 10,000 units of this product during the year ending March 31,19B; 12,000 units during the year ending March 31, 19C; and 15,000 units during the year ending March 31, 19D, at a price of $90 per unit. This product can be manufactured using Mayne's present facilities. Monthly production with immediate delivery is expected to be uniform within each year. Receivables are expected to be collected during the calendar month following sales. Unit production costs of the new product are expected to be as follows:

Direct materials	$20
Direct labor	30
Variable overhead	10

Fixed costs (excluding depreciation) will amount to $130,000 per year. Purchases of direct materials will be paid during the calendar month following purchase. Fixed costs, direct labor, and variable overhead will be paid as incurred. Inventory of direct materials will be equal to 60 days' usage. After the first month of operations, 30 days' usage of direct materials will be ordered each month.

The general creditors have agreed to reduce their total claims to 60% of their March 31, 19A balances, under the following conditions:

(a) Existing accounts receivable and inventories are to be liquidated immediately, with the proceeds turned over to the general creditors.

(b) The balance of reduced accounts payable is to be paid as cash is generated from future operations, but in no event later than March 31, 19C. No interest will be paid on these obligations.

Under this proposed plan, the general creditors would receive $110,000 more than the current liquidation value of Mayne's assets.

Required: Ignoring any need to borrow and repay short-term funds for working capital purposes, prepare a cash budget for the years ending March 31, 19B and 19C, showing the cash expected to be available to pay the claims of the general creditors, payments to general creditors, and the cash remaining after payment of claims. (ICMA adapted)

P16-4 Cash Budget. J. Jones decided to start a business that would require the purchase of assets at a total cost of $200,000. He started his business with a cash investment of $50,000 and on January 1, 19A, took out a long-term loan from the bank in the amount of $150,000. The terms of the note stipulated that interest of 2% (monthly) would be paid at the end of each month, and a payment of $30,000, to be applied toward the principal, would be payable at the end of each quarterly period. The proceeds of the loan were used to purchase equipment. The company would produce a product with the following budgeted revenues and expenses, based on an expected monthly production volume of 5,000 units:

Selling price per unit		$ 150.00
Manufacturing costs per unit:		
Direct materials		$ 20.00
Direct labor		30.00
Variable factory overhead:		
Utilities	$ 5.00	
Supplies	6.00	
Indirect labor	4.00	15.00
Fixed factory overhead:		
Factory rent	$10.00	
Depreciation on machinery	15.00	25.00
Total manufacturing cost per unit		$ 90.00
Selling and administrative costs:		
Sales commissions per unit of product sold		$ 8.00
Bad debt expense per unit of product sold		3.00
Office equipment rentals per month		12,000.00
Equipment depreciation per month		5,000.00

Other information includes the following:

(a) Expected sales total $360,000 for January, $450,000 for February, $480,000 for March, and $600,000 for April.

(b) All sales are on credit, with terms 2/10, net 30 days. Collection of accounts receivable are expected to be in the following pattern:

30% collected in the month of the sale (of which 80% will take the discount)
30% collected in the month after the sale
38% collected two months after the sale
2% uncollected

(c) A direct materials inventory of $2,000 will have to be maintained at all times.

(d) In order to meet fluctuations in customer demand, a finished goods inventory equal to 100 units plus 10% of the expected demand for the following month (in units) will have to be maintained.

(e) All direct material purchases are expected to be incurred uniformly throughout the month with payments being made in the month of purchase.

(f) Wages payable at the end of each month are expected to average $7,500.

(g) A minimum cash balance of $10,000 is to be maintained at all times.

Required: Prepare a cash budget for the first quarterly period ending on March 31. Include any supporting schedules and/or budgets that are appropriate and indicate what financing (if any) may be required.

(SMAC adapted)

P16-5 Cash Budget for Not-for-Profit Organization. Triple-F Health Club (Family, Fitness, and Fun) is a not-for-profit family-oriented health club. The club's board of directors is developing plans to acquire more equipment and expand the club facilities. The board plans to purchase about $25,000 of new equipment each year and wants to begin a fund to purchase the adjoining property in four or five years. The adjoining property has a market value of about $300,000.

The club manager, Jane Crowe, is concerned that the board has unrealistic goals in light of its recent financial performance. She has sought the help of a club member with an accounting background to assist her in preparing for the board a report supporting her concerns.

The club member reviewed the club's records, including the following cash basis income statement. The review and discussions with Jane Crowe disclosed the additional information that follows the statement.

Triple-F Health Club
Statement of Income (Cash Basis)
For Years Ended October 31
(in thousands)

	19B	19A
Cash revenues:		
Annual membership fees	$355.0	$300.0
Lesson and class fees	234.0	180.0
Miscellaneous	2.0	1.5
Total cash received	$591.0	$481.5
Cash expenses:		
Manager's salary and benefits	$ 36.0	$ 36.0
Regular employees' wages and benefits	190.0	190.0
Lesson and class employee wages and benefits	195.0	150.0
Towels and supplies	16.0	15.5
Utilities (heat and light)	22.0	15.0
Mortgage interest	35.1	37.8
Miscellaneous	2.0	1.5
Total cash expenses	$496.1	$445.8
Cash income	$ 94.9	$ 35.7

Additional information:

(a) Other financial information as of October 31, 19B:

Cash in checking account, $7,000
Petty cash, $300
Outstanding mortgage balance, $360,000
Accounts payable arising from invoices for supplies and utilities that are unpaid as of October 31, 19B, $2,500

(b) No unpaid bills are expected to exist on October 31, 19C.

(c) The club purchased $25,000 worth of exercise equipment during the current year 19B. Cash of $10,000 was paid on delivery, and the balance was due on October 1 but was not paid as of October 31, 19B.

(d) The club began operations six years ago in rental quarters. Two years later it purchased its current property (land and building) for $600,000, paying $120,000 down and agreeing to pay $30,000 plus 9% interest annually on November 1 until the balance is paid off.

(e) Membership rose 3% during 19B. This is approximately the same annual rate the club has experienced since it opened.

(f) Membership fees were increased by 15% in 19B. The board has tentative plans to increase the fees by 10% in 19C.

(g) Lesson and class fees have not been increased for three years. The board policy is to encourage classes and lessons by keeping the fees low. The members have taken advantage of this policy and the number of classes and lessons have grown significantly each year. The club expects the percentage growth experienced in 19B to be repeated in 19C.

(h) Miscellaneous revenues are expected to grow at the same percentage as experienced in 19B.

(i) Operating expenses are expected to increase. Hourly wage rates and the manager's salary will need to be increased 15% because no increases were granted in 19B. Towels and supplies, utilities, and miscellaneous expenses are expected to increase 25%.

Required:

(1) Construct a cash budget for 19C for Triple-F Health Club.
(2) Identify and explain any operating problem(s) that this budget discloses for Triple-F Health Club.
(3) Is Jane Crowe's concern that the board's goals are unrealistic justified? Explain. (ICMA adapted)

P16-6 Budgeted Cash Receipts and Disbursements. Vincent Hospital provides a wide range of health services in its community. Vincent's board of directors has authorized the following capital expenditures:

Inter-aortic balloon pump	$1,100,000
CT scanner	700,000
X-ray equipment	600,000
Laboratory equipment	1,400,000
	$3,800,000

The expenditures are planned for October 1, 19A, and the board wishes to know the amount of borrowing, if any, necessary on that date. M. Kelly, the controller, has gathered the following information to be used in preparing an analysis of future cash flows.

(a) Billings, made in the month of service, for the first 6 months of 19A are listed below:

Month	Amount
January	$4,400,000
February	4,400,000
March	4,500,000
April	4,500,000
May	5,000,000
June	5,000,000

Of Vincent's billings, 90% are made to third parties, such as federal or state governments and private insurance companies. The remaining 10% of billings are made directly to patients. Historical patterns of billing collections are as follows:

	Percent of Third Party Billings	Percent of Direct Patient Billings
Month of service	20%	10%
Month following service	50	40
Second month following service	20	40
Uncollectible	10	10

Estimated billings for the last 6 months of 19A follow. The same billing and collection patterns that have been experienced during the first 6 months of 19A are expected to continue during the last 6 months of the year.

Month	Estimated Amount
July	$4,500,000
August	5,000,000
September	5,500,000
October	5,700,000
November	5,800,000
December	5,500,000

(b) The purchases that have been made during the past 3 months and the planned purchases for the last 6 months of 19A are presented in the following schedule:

Month	Amount
April	$1,100,000
May	1,200,000
June	1,200,000
July	1,250,000
August	1,500,000
September	1,850,000
October	1,950,000
November	2,250,000
December	1,750,000

All purchases are made on account, and accounts payable are remitted in the month following the purchase.

(c) Salaries for each month during the remainder of 19A are expected to be $1,500,000 per month plus 20% of that month's billings. Salaries are paid in the month of service.
(d) Vincent's monthly depreciation charges are $125,000.
(e) Vincent incurs interest expense of $150,000 per month and makes interest payments of $450,000 on the last day of each calendar quarter.
(f) Endowment fund income is expected to continue to total $175,000 per month.
(g) Vincent has a cash balance of $300,000 on July 1, 19A, and has a policy of maintaining a minimum end-of-month cash balance of 10% of the current month's purchases.
(h) Vincent Hospital employs a calendar year reporting period.

Required:
(1) Prepare a schedule of budgeted cash receipts by month for the third quarter of 19A.
(2) Prepare a schedule of budgeted cash disbursements by month for the third quarter of 19A.
(3) Determine the amount of borrowing, if any, necessary on October 1, 19A, to acquire the capital items totaling $3,800,000 and still maintain the minimum required cash balance. (ICMA adapted)

P16-7 PERT/Cost Network. The following network has been prepared for a project:

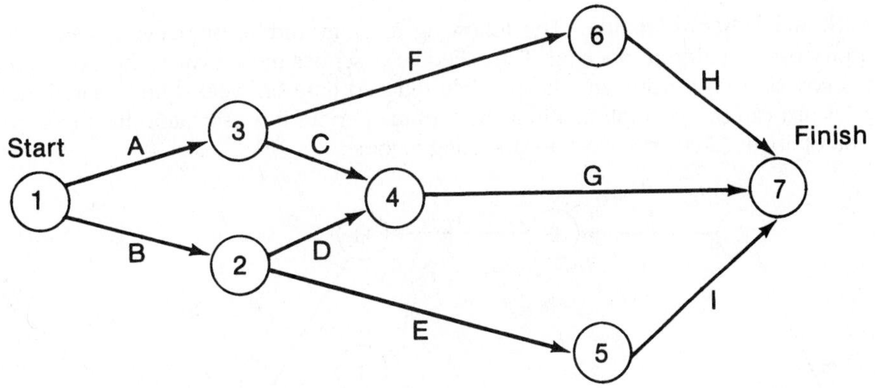

Expected time and cost estimates are:

Activity	Time (in days)	Cost
A	5	$ 4,000
B	5	4,000
C	10	15,000
D	7	3,500
E	5	10,000
F	7	14,000
G	5	5,000
H	10	20,000
I	10	30,000

Costs for each activity occur uniformly; for example, activity A requires $800 each day.

Required:
(1) Identify the critical path.
(2) Prepare a daily activity and cost schedule. CGA-Canada (adapted). Reprint with permission.

P16-8 PERT/Cost Network. The following data of activity times and costs have been prepared for a building construction project:

Activity	Normal Activity Time (in weeks)	Normal Activity Cost	Maximum Possible Crash Time (in weeks)	Cost to Reduce Activity Time by 1 Week
A–B	2	$1,000	1	$10,000
A–C	1	800	0	
B–D	2	1,500	0	
B–E	5	5,100	2	5,200
C–D	4	2,500	1	6,500
D–E	1	600	0	
E–F	4	1,700	1	3,700
E–G	3	1,200	1	4,600
F–H	3	1,400	1	2,800
G–H	3	1,300	1	2,300

Required:

(1) Prepare a PERT network diagram for the construction project showing the times and costs for each activity.
(2) Determine the critical path.
(3) Compute the total cost of the project as planned.
(4) Compute the minimum total cost of completing the project in 12 weeks. (ICMA adapted)

P16-9 PERT Network and Project Planning. The following diagram and accompanying schedule have been prepared for a proposed retail store opening. The schedule describes the activities, the expected time (in weeks), the expected cost of each activity, and the possible reduced time (in weeks) and related incremental cost for those activities that can be accomplished in a shorter time period. It is estimated that the store should produce a contribution of about $2,000 per week to operating income.

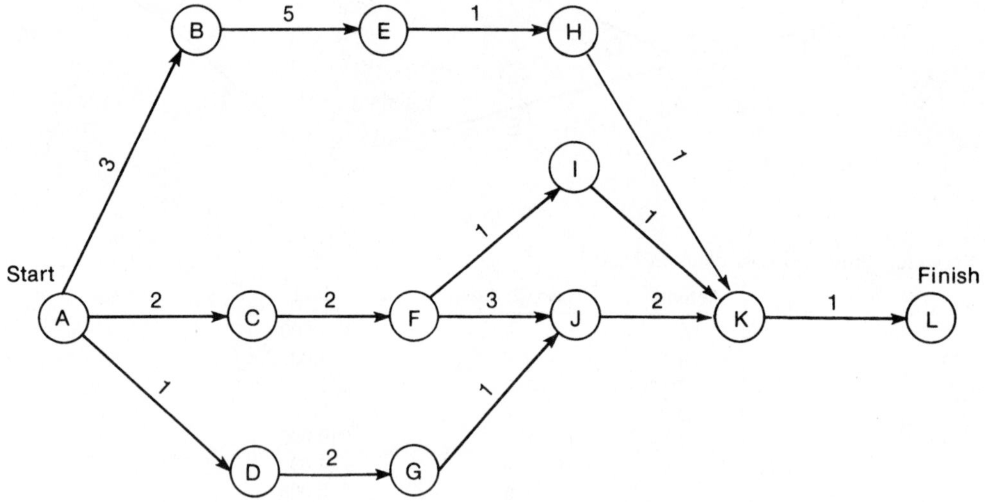

Activity	Description of Activity	Expected Time (in weeks)	Reduced Time (in weeks)	Possible Expected Cost	Incremental Cost to Achieve Reduced Time
A–B	Design exterior	3	1	$ 5,000	$4,500
A–C	Determine inventory needs	2	NC*	500	0
A–D	Develop staffing plan	1	NC	500	0
B–E	Do exterior structural work	5	3	27,000	3,500
E–H	Paint exterior	1	NC	4,000	0
H–K	Install exterior signs	1	NC	15,000	0
C–F	Order inventory	2	NC	1,500	0

Activity	Description of Activity	Expected Time (in weeks)	Reduced Time (in weeks)	Possible Expected Cost	Incremental Cost to Achieve Reduced Time
F–I	Develop special prices for opening	1	NC	2,000	0
I–K	Advertise opening and special prices	1	NC	8,000	0
F–J	Receive inventory	3	2	4,000	2,000
D–G	Acquire staff	2	1	3,000	1,000
G–J	Train staff	1	NC	5,000	0
J–K	Stock shelves	2	1	3,500	1,500
K–L	Final preparations for grand opening	1	NC	6,000	0

* NC denotes no change in time is possible.

Required:

(1) Determine the normal critical path, its length in weeks, and the normal cost to be incurred in opening the store.

(2) Compute the minimum time in which the store can be opened and the costs incurred to achieve the earlier opening.

(3) Explain whether the store should be opened following the normal schedule or the reduced program.

(ICMA adapted)

Case

C16-1 PERT Network Analysis. Caltron Inc. produces computer-controlled components for a wide variety of military hardware. As a defense contractor, the company is often under severe time and scheduling constraints. The development of a new component, Vector-12, is no exception. The project has the potential for generating future contracts that could bring in substantial revenue if development and testing can be accomplished in the allotted time.

The planning of the Vector-12 project has been assigned to Norm Robertson. This is Robertson's first assignment as a project director for Caltron, and he is eager to demonstrate his abilities.

This project, like many of Caltron's projects, cuts across departments. Therefore, scheduling and coordinating among departments are crucial. Caltron's management has long been an advocate of the Project Evaluation and Review Technique (PERT). Therefore, Robertson prepared the PERT diagram for the Vector-12 project that follows.

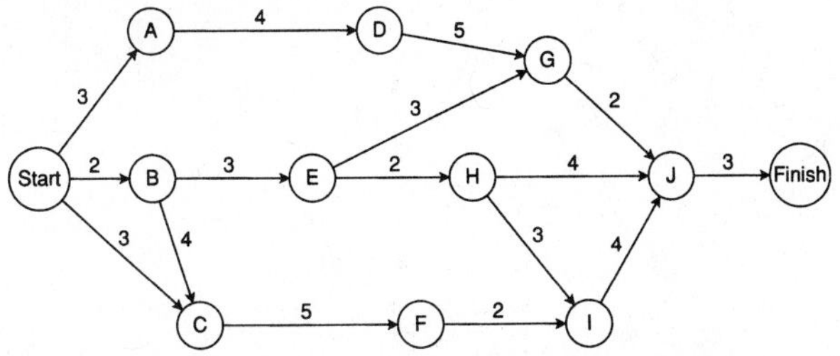

The circles containing letters correspond to the completion of significant activities; the arrows connecting the circles correspond to activities. The numbers by the activity arrows represent the expected time in weeks required to complete each activity. The responsibility for the critical path, Start–B–C–F–I–J–Finish, is shared by two departments, Electro-Mechanical Engineering (EME) and Fabrication (FAB). Resource Appropriation and Processing (RAP) is responsible for Start–A–D–G–J.

Robertson developed the PERT diagram with minimal input from the department directors affected. He reviewed the preliminary diagrams with the directors of EME and FAB. Robertson was unable to contact the director of RAP, Shiela Neill, and Robertson neglected to talk with Neill when she returned to the office. The directors of EME and FAB offered Robertson suggestions on how to revise the diagrams in terms of ordering activities and time estimates. They also indicated how Neill's activities would coordinate with their activities. However, none of the directors reviewed the final PERT diagram shown here.

As the Vector-12 project entered its fourth week, Robertson requested progress reports from the department directors. Neill told Robertson that activity A–D would take 10 to 12 weeks. When Robertson asked Neill to explain the delay, Neill replied, "I could have told you there would be a problem, but you never asked for my input. The time for activity A–D is understated as is, and I cannot even start until activity B–E is completed by FAB."

Required:

(1) Discuss the advantages and disadvantages of network analysis as a means of organizing and coordinating projects.
(2) Identify the specific reason that causes Norm Robertson to be concerned about the delay in activity A–D.
(3) Critique the way Norm Robertson developed the PERT diagram for the Vector-12 project.
(4) Discuss the behavioral problems that can arise within Caltron Inc. as a consequence of the planning of the Vector-12 project. (ICMA adapted)

CHAPTER 17

Responsibility Accounting and Reporting

Learning Objectives

After studying this chapter, you will be able to:

1. Define responsibility accounting and reporting.
2. Explain the organizational requirements necessary for the effective implementation of a responsibility accounting and reporting system.
3. Differentiate between controllable and noncontrollable costs and explain the problems that occur in trying to identify controllable costs.
4. List the objectives of responsibility reporting and explain the fundamental characteristics of a useful report.
5. Explain the concept behind flexible budgeting and prepare a flexible budget.
6. Compute and explain the meaning of spending and idle capacity variances.
7. Prepare a variance report.
8. List dysfunctional behaviors that can be caused by using responsibility reporting to evaluate the performance of managers.
9. Criticize the usefulness of information provided by responsibility reports to managers.

A well-designed accounting system not only should make it possible to determine product cost and periodic profit accurately, but it should also be a useful tool in helping management control cost and earn an acceptable profit. To be effective as a control mechanism, the accounting system should be designed so that the costs incurred as a result of each activity in the company can be recorded and reported to the individual manager who is responsible for that activity. If the activity is a revenue-producing activity, profitability should be measured as well and reported to the responsible manager. Such a system, often referred to as **responsibility accounting and reporting**, is the central subject of this chapter.

Although responsibility accounting and reporting is a widely applied tool in practice, it is often misunderstood and misused. Many firms use it as the primary basis for evaluating the performance of managers. Because of the need for continuous improvement and a shift in managerial philosophy from individual performance to teamwork, the value of responsibility accounting and reporting as a management tool has been seriously questioned. This chapter begins with a discussion of the traditional view of responsibility accounting and reporting, which includes an explanation of the basic concepts as well as practical illustrations. The first section is followed by an explanation of flexible budgeting and variance reporting, which are commonly used for responsibility reporting. The last section presents an alternative view of responsibility accounting and reporting, pointing out the current shift in management philosophy that has led to criticisms regarding the usefulness of responsibility accounting and reporting. Both problems and potential remedies are discussed.

Responsibility Accounting and Cost Control—the Traditional View

Business activities drive cost. The traditional view argues that in order to control costs, individuals in the company who have authority to control business activities must be held accountable for the resources consumed by those activities. The objective of responsibility accounting and reporting is to provide information that management can use to evaluate the efficiency with which the company's resources are utilized. In accordance with the traditional view, cost control follows from the evaluation process. If the evaluation discloses that resources were used inefficiently and the cost of the inefficiency is substantial, the cause should be identified and, if possible, steps should be taken to insure that the inefficiency does not recur.

To identify an inefficient use of resources, the analyst determines the cost actually incurred for each business activity during some period and compares it to the amount of cost that should have been incurred for that activity. Actual costs are usually compared to budgeted costs (preferably a flexible budget discussed later in this chapter) or to standard costs (discussed in Chapter 18), and the difference, referred to as a **variance**, is reported to the manager who has responsibility and control over the activity. The responsible manager then determines the cause of large unfavorable variances and, if possible, takes steps to prevent the recurrence of the inefficiency. Effort is directed toward eliminating systematic inefficiencies (for example, inefficiencies resulting from improper machine settings, poor quality materials, lack of supervision or training, inefficient organization of work resulting in duplication of effort, or wasted time). Random inefficiencies (such as inefficiencies resulting from a new employee's inexperience or a machine breakdown that has already been corrected) are ignored.

Organizational Structure

In order to have an effective responsibility accounting and reporting system in the traditional sense, a company must be organized in a manner that facilitates operational control. A responsibility accounting system must be designed around the company's organizational structure in order to capture the economic significance of the company's business activities. If the company's organizational structure lacks the essential characteristics necessary for operational control, a responsibility accounting system will not improve control.

Perhaps the most important organizational requirement for good control is to avoid overlapping lines of responsibility. No more than one manager should be responsible for the same task. If more than one manager is responsible for the same activity, confusion, conflict, and inefficiency can result. One responsible manager may ignore a task, assuming that the other responsible manager is taking care of it. If the other responsible manager makes the same assumption, the task does not get done or gets done inefficiently. When called to account for results, each of the responsible parties is likely to claim he or she thought the other person was taking care of the activity. This is often called "passing the buck." Even if buck passing is not a problem, the responsible managers may approach the task differently, in which case one may redo or undo what the other has done, thereby causing frustration, conflict, and wasted effort. To avoid these problems and to make it possible to determine who is responsible for the efficiency or inefficiency of an activity, only one person should have responsibility for each activity.

The principle that only one person should have responsibility for each activity does not mean that responsible individuals cannot delegate authority, nor does it preclude teamwork and cooperation among organizational units. An individual responsible for several activities can assign different activities to different subordinates and can coordinate the efforts of several individuals working toward a common goal. However, the primary responsibility for the successful operation of each activity always rests with the delegator. For example, the president of a corporation delegates authority to the vice-presidents of finance, marketing, and manufacturing, who in turn delegate some of their authority to the supervisors of the departments within their respective divisions. Despite the delegation of this authority, the company's vice-presidents are primarily responsible to the president for all activities of the departments under their control.

Another organizational requirement for good control is that each manager within the organization must have a clear understanding of her or his responsibilities. The company should have an organization chart in which the spheres of jurisdiction and lines of reporting are clearly depicted. In addition, each manager's responsibilities should be explained fully in a written job description that is made available to the individual at all times. This description may be subject to change, but changes must be communicated to the employee before responsibility can be assigned.

In order to achieve control, individuals who have been assigned responsibilities within a company must have sufficient authority to take the required actions necessary to meet those responsibilities. Holding a subordinate responsible for a task over which that person has no control is ineffective. Although this concept seems simple and straightforward, it is often difficult to apply in practice. Most managers are given limited amounts of general authority that are usually sufficient to accomplish most routine tasks. However, consciously or unconsciously, executive management often withholds or restricts authority needed by subordinates, making the efficient accomplishment of assigned tasks impossible. A common example is the executive management decision to assign or to acquire equipment that is not well suited to the job. Executive management may not be in a position to evaluate properly the quality of the equipment or to understand fully the operational demands that will be placed on the equipment. The equipment may simply be old and obsolete, or it may originally have been acquired for some other purpose. If the department manager is not permitted to alter or replace the equipment, inefficiencies result that cannot be controlled by the department manager. Another common example occurs as a result of the assignment or reassignment of personnel by executive management. If the most experienced and efficient personnel are transferred or promoted out of a department and replaced with inexperienced or less-capable personnel, department efficiency will decline. The inefficiency may be temporary or long term, depending on the availability of training and the quality of the replacement personnel, but in either case, the inefficiency is not controllable by the department manager. In both of these examples, the responsibility for the departmentally imposed inefficiency is attributable to executive management, not the department manager. When such situations cannot be avoided, the expected level of department performance should be adjusted to reflect the limitations.

Determining Who Controls Cost

An effective responsibility accounting and reporting system must segregate controllable costs from noncontrollable costs. According to the traditional view, the basic axiom of responsibility accounting and reporting is that individuals who have authority to control activities should be held accountable for the costs incurred as a result of those activities. In order to accomplish this purpose, the accounting system must facilitate the recording of costs incurred by each operating unit within the company and the identification of those costs that are controllable by the operating unit manager. Reports to responsible managers should segregate costs by activity and emphasize controllable costs so that managers can identify quickly those activities that require attention.

Although tracing costs to operating units within the company is fairly simple, it is often difficult to identify which of the traceable costs are controllable by the unit manager. The cost for any expenditure classification is composed of two elements: the unit price and the quantity of the items used. Because price is usually a function of market factors, it may not be controllable by anyone in the company, and if controllable to any extent, it is often controllable by a person other than the one who controls the quantity used. Price is often controlled by the purchasing department (in the case of materials and supplies) or the personnel department (in the case of employee wages), whereas the quantity used is often controlled by the department using the materials or supplies and employing the personnel.

Although separating price and quantity effects is possible, it is costly and may be unnecessary in situations in which prices are relatively stable. Even when the price and quantity of a cost can be separated, it is not always easy to determine controllability. For example, if the price of an item is a function of the quantity purchased, the individual responsible for purchasing and the individual responsible for the quantity used are jointly responsible for price. If the quantity of an item used is a function of the quality of the item purchased, the individual who places the order for the item and the individual who controls the use of the item are jointly responsible for the quantity used.

If a cost is traced to and charged directly to a department (or other organizational unit) and the amount of the cost is affected by changes in the department's activity, the cost is considered to be controllable by the department manager. Such costs are referred to as variable costs, because the total amount varies as activity varies. The activity that drives cost should be determined by deductive reasoning and supported by correlation analysis as described in Chapter 3. Theoretically, if the activity determined to be the cost driver is controlled by the unit manager, then the cost is controllable by the manager.

In contrast to the controllability of variable costs, variances in fixed costs are usually not controllable. Fixed costs do not change in response to changes in activity within the period. Differences in the amounts of fixed costs expected and the amounts actually incurred are usually the result of unexpected changes in prices, which are typically a result of external events that are not controllable by the manager of an operating unit. On the other hand, some fixed costs do change in response to substantial changes in volume, such as when activity extends above or below the relevant range (see Chapter 3). If the supervisor of the operating unit is responsible for changes in activity substantial enough to affect fixed cost, some of the difference between actual and expected fixed cost should be viewed as controllable. For example, if operating inefficiencies make it necessary for a production department to rent an additional piece of equipment in order to meet production requirements, the department supervisor is responsible for the incurrence of additional fixed cost. On the other hand, if the additional fixed costs are incurred as a result of the acquisition or assignment of inappropriate equipment for the job or the replacement or reassignment of personnel, executive management is responsible, not the production department supervisor.

Allocated costs, such as plantwide costs and service department costs, present a special problem. For the most part, such costs are not controllable by the departments receiving the allocation. Allocated costs generally controllable by the plant manager rather than department managers include property taxes, insurance, security, heating and air conditioning, building occupancy, dispensary, cafeteria, and employee parking. On the other hand, the amount of some allocated costs—such as the cost of power to operate machinery, repair and maintenance, and engineering—depends on activity that is controlled within the department that receives the allocation. To the extent that the allocation is a function of a controllable activity, the allocated cost is also controllable. However, the accountant and executive management should keep in mind that an allocated cost, like any cost, is composed of a unit price and a quantity of units. The cost of electric power depends not only on the number of kilowatt-hours used but also on the price of each kilowatt-hour. Similarly, the cost of equipment repair and maintenance depends not only on the quantity of replacement parts and maintenance hours used but also on the price of the parts and service department's billing rate per maintenance hour. Even if the quantity is controllable by the department receiving the allocation, the price may not be.

As a consequence of these numerous and often interdependent cost determination factors, costs must be assigned to individual managers on the basis of relative control rather than absolute control. Reported differences between actual costs and expected costs should be viewed as questions rather than answers. The exact cause of cost variances can be determined only by investigating and analyzing the events that occur during a period, and the responsibility for cost variances can be determined reliably only after the cause has been determined. Determining the cause of cost variances is costly. Managers have many important responsibilities other than investigating the causes of cost variances; therefore, the variance report should emphasize significant variances, so that management can concentrate on those inefficiencies that are correctable and that have the greatest effect on future profits.

Responsibility for Overhead Costs

As indicated in Chapter 13, many overhead items are directly chargeable to an individual department and become the direct responsibility of the departmental supervisor. Other overhead items must be allocated or distributed in order to calculate a departmental factory overhead rate that will be used to charge all the products manufactured during the period with a share of overhead. This allocation procedure, however, is not necessary or useful for cost control. For responsibility accounting purposes, costs should be allocated only when it has been determined that the recipient of the cost allocation has control over the allocated cost. However, the assignment of responsibility often depends a great deal on the methods of cost accumulation and allocation used by a firm.

In some firms, the cost system provides for the distribution of service department costs to benefiting departments on the basis of service hours, use hours, or some other measure of activity. The distribution can be regarded as a purchase by the department receiving the allocation and a sale by the service department.

The distribution to the recipient department is based on what is termed a **billing rate**, a **sold-hour rate**, a **charging rate**, or a **transfer rate**. The method is based on the idea that these departments purchase the services the same way they might purchase materials, supplies, and labor.

The comparison of actual and budgeted costs is made first in the service department to which the expenses are originally charged by comparing actual costs with the cost charged by the service department to benefiting departments; and second in the benefiting (recipient) departments, in which charges for service departments' services are compared with budget allowances. This step is the control phase of the service department's charging-out procedure. The supervisor of the service department is responsible for actual cost versus the cost for services charged out to benefiting departments. The benefiting department supervisor is responsible for the quantity of services purchased from the providing department and the resulting cost.

The billing rate of each service department is a function of the level of activity and the operating efficiency of the department. Because the benefiting department has no control over the operating efficiency of a service department, the billing rate should be predetermined. For the purposes of responsibility accounting, the benefiting department (the user or buyer of services) should know the cost of the services before the purchase so the user can weigh cost against expected benefit. To the extent that the user's actions result in cost incurrence, the user has control and should be held accountable. In addition, the provider of the service should be held accountable in some way for operating efficiency within the providing service department. The use of a predetermined rate makes it possible to evaluate efficiency by comparing total costs billed to user departments with costs actually incurred.

The following steps for determination of a service department's billing rate parallel those discussed in Chapter 13 for determining departmental factory overhead rates.

1. Estimate or budget costs directly traceable to the service department (supervision, indirect labor, payroll taxes, supplies, equipment depreciation, etc.).
2. Allocate a share of budgeted plantwide costs to the service department (plant superintendence, building depreciation, property taxes, insurance, utilities, etc.).
3. Allocate a share of the budgeted costs of other service departments to the service department.
4. Determine the billing rate by dividing total estimated service department cost by the number of hours (or other billing unit) of service the service department is expected to provide during the period.

Establishing the level of activity used in determining the billing rate is as important for billing rates as it is for factory overhead rates. The level of activity can be based either on normal capacity or on expected capacity as expressed in the budget. To the extent that a service department's cost is fixed, the level of activity chosen in determining the billing rate will affect the amount of fixed cost charged to users. This amount, when compared with the amount of fixed cost actually incurred, will affect the size of the reported variance for the providing service department. If the providing service department can control the level of capacity utilization, expected capacity should be used as the basis for determining the billing rate.

To illustrate the use of predetermined service department billing rates, assume that the Maintenance Department of Paloma Corporation provides maintenance services for two producing departments, Fabricating and Assembly, and one service department, Power. For the month, budgeted fixed cost was $150,000 and the budgeted variable cost was $20.00 for each hour of maintenance service provided. At the end of the month, actual maintenance costs totaled $245,000. Budgeted and actual activity for the month were as follow:

	Fabricating	Assembly	Power	Total
Budgeted maintenance hours	2,500	1,000	1,500	5,000
Actual maintenance hours	2,600	800	1,200	4,600

Based on budgeted data, the Maintenance Department's predetermined billing rate is $50 per maintenance hour, which comprises a fixed rate of $30 ($150,000 budgeted fixed cost / 5,000 budgeted hours) plus a $20 variable rate (the $20 budgeted variable cost per maintenance hour). Cost billed out during the month was as follows:

	Fabricating	Assembly	Power	Total
Actual hours of maintenance provided	2,600	800	1,200	4,600
Billing rate per maintenance hour	$ 50	$ 50	$ 50	$ 50
Cost billed to user departments	$130,000	$40,000	$60,000	$230,000

In this example, actual Maintenance Department cost exceeded the amount billed to user departments by $15,000 ($245,000 actual cost – $230,000 total billed cost). The manager of the Maintenance Department would be charged with this cost variance. In this case, $12,000 of the total $15,000 variance is attributable to underapplied (or undercharged) budgeted fixed cost [$150,000 budgeted fixed cost - ($30 fixed rate × 4,600 actual maintenance hours)]. This $12,000 portion of the total variance is a measure of capacity utilization; it is called the idle capacity variance (see discussion below). The remaining $3,000 of the total $15,000 variance can be attributable to one or more of the following:

1. Inefficient activities in the Maintenance Department
2. Changes in the unit prices of one or more overhead items
3. Errors in the budgeted quantities and/or prices of the various items of overhead for the month

This $3,000 portion of the total variance is a measure of differences between the actual and budgeted prices and quantities of the various items of overhead; it is called the spending variance (see discussion below). The cause of these variances may be known by the departmental manager or may need to be determined by investigation.

If user departments are responsible for the level of fixed cost required by the providing service department and users control the amount of services actually utilized, the allocation can be improved for responsibility accounting purposes by charging fixed cost to user departments on the basis of the service department's readiness-to-serve capacity (that is, its ability to provide services). In such a case, the variable cost should be charged to users by means of a predetermined rate on the basis of the actual usage of the provider's service. For example, the size of a power department's generators might be determined by the user departments' maximum capacity requirements. Because users are responsible for the size of the generators acquired and the consequent incurrence of fixed cost, all of the budgeted fixed costs should be charged to the users, based on the relative amount of power required by each at maximum capacity. On the other hand, because total variable cost increases (or decreases) in response to increases (or decreases) in activity, the amount of variable cost charged to each user should be determined by the user's actual usage—by multiplying a predetermined variable rate times the actual power used.[1]

To illustrate the use of multiple service department billing rates, assume that the Power Department of Paloma Corporation provides electricity for two producing departments, Fabricating and Assembly, and one service department, Maintenance. For the month, budgeted fixed costs were $50,000 and the budgeted variable cost was 10 cents per kilowatt-hour of electricity provided. Actual costs for the month totaled $75,000. Maximum planned and actual electricity usage for the month were as follow:

	Fabricating	Assembly	Maintenance	Total
Maximum kilowatt-hours available	150,000	80,000	20,000	250,000
Actual kilowatt-hours used	145,000	70,000	15,000	230,000

Because the amount of electricity used is controllable by the user departments, the Power Department uses a two-rate billing structure. Fixed cost is charged to users on the basis of the Power Department capacity to provide services (that is, the quantity of kilowatt-hours available at maximum capacity), and variable cost is charged to users on the basis of actual usage using a predetermined rate. The fixed billing rate is 20 cents per kilowatt-hour available at maximum capacity ($50,000 fixed cost/250,000 kilowatt-hours at maximum capacity), and the variable billing rate is 10 cents per actual kilowatt-hour. Cost billed out during the month was as follows:

	Fabricating	Assembly	Maintenance	Total
Maximum kilowatt-hours available	150,000	80,000	20,000	250,000
Fixed billing rate	$ .20	$ .20	$ .20	$ .20
Fixed cost charged to users	$ 30,000	$16,000	$ 4,000	$ 50,000
Actual kilowatt-hours used	145,000	70,000	15,000	230,000
Variable billing rate	$ .10	$ .10	$ .10	$ .10
Variable cost charged to users	$ 14,500	$ 7,000	$ 1,500	$ 23,000
Total cost charged to users	$ 44,500	$23,000	$ 5,500	$ 73,000

In this case, actual Power Department cost exceeded the amount billed to user departments by $2,000 ($75,000 actual cost - $73,000 total billed cost). The manager of the Power Department would be charged with this cost variance. Because all fixed cost was billed to user departments on the basis of maximum available capacity (which did not change during the period), there is no idle capacity variance for the Power Department. None of the $2,000 total variance is attributable to underapplied (or undercharged) budgeted fixed cost [$50,000 budgeted fixed cost – ($.20 fixed rate × 250,000 maximum available kilowatt-hours) = 0]. Therefore, the entire $2,000 total variance is a spending variance, which occurred because of differences between actual and budgeted prices and quantities for the various items of overhead.

[1] An example of more sophisticated allocation procedures is found in Daniel L. Jensen's "A Class of Mutually Satisfactory Allocations," *The Accounting Review*, Vol. 52, No. 4, pp. 842–856.

Responsibility Reporting

Responsibility accounting is a program encompassing all operating management for which the accounting, cost, or budget divisions provide technical assistance in the form of daily, weekly, or monthly control reports. **Responsibility reporting** is the reporting phase of responsibility accounting.

According to the traditional view of responsibility accounting and reporting, responsibility reports have two primary purposes:

1. To motivate individuals to achieve a high level of performance by reporting efficiencies and inefficiencies to responsible managers and their superiors.
2. To provide information that will help responsible managers identify inefficiencies so they can control costs more efficiently.

Responsibility reports are accountability reports. Managers who have authority to control activity know they will be held accountable for their actions. A responsibility report is prepared periodically and provided not only to the responsible manager but also to that manager's supervisor. In one form or another, these reports are used to evaluate performance. If the system is well designed, accountability provides a powerful motivation to be efficient.

Because they are being evaluated and held accountable for the efficient use of company resources, responsible managers tend to monitor closely the activities within their control. This makes it possible to detect inefficiencies when they occur and to take corrective action, if possible, close to the time of discovery. As a consequence, a responsibility report prepared and made available at regular periodic intervals does not necessarily disclose new information to the responsible manager. It may simply confirm what the manager already knows. On the other hand, close supervision does not always result in the detection of all inefficiencies. Furthermore, in the absence of a responsibility report, the economic significance of detected inefficiencies may not be fully understood. A manager who is aware of an inefficiency may not take corrective action because the inefficiency is not thought to be very costly. Responsibility reports not only disclose the existence of inefficiency but also reveal its cost. To this extent, responsibility reports provide information to responsible management that is useful in controlling cost.

Fundamental Characteristics of Responsibility Reports

In order to enhance their effectiveness, responsibility reports should have the following fundamental characteristics:

1. Reports should fit the organization chart; that is, they should be addressed primarily to the individuals responsible for controlling the activities covered by the reports.
2. Reports should be consistent in form and content each time they are issued. Changes should be made only for good reasons and with clear explanations to users. Frequent changes confuse users and make interperiod comparisons difficult.
3. Reports should be timely. Although many inefficiencies disclosed in reports are known by managers before the report is issued, some are not. Inefficiencies cannot be corrected until they are detected. If inefficiencies are systematic (that is, recurring and not temporary), the longer they go uncorrected, the greater the cost. For this reason, reports should be made available to responsible management as quickly as possible after a

systematic inefficiency occurs. On the other hand, frequent reporting is costly. Therefore, the cost of reporting at various intervals should be weighed against the expected cost of undetected systematic inefficiencies.

4. Reports should be issued with regularity. Reporting regularity enhances the usefulness of reports. Managers should know when the reports will be prepared and made available so they can plan effectively and control their activities.
5. Reports should be easy to understand. Often they contain accounting terminology that managers with little or no accounting training find difficult to understand. As a consequence, vital information can be misinterpreted or may not be communicated at all. Therefore, accounting terms should be explained or modified to fit the user. Management should have some knowledge of the kind of items chargeable to an account as well as the methods used to compute overhead rates, to allocate costs, and to analyze variances.
6. Reports should convey sufficient but not excessive detail. The amount and nature of the detail depend largely on the management level receiving the report. Generally, reports to executive-level managers should provide less detail than reports to operating-level managers. Executive managers should not be inundated with so much detail that they cannot readily evaluate overall results. In contrast, reports to operating managers should provide sufficient detail to make it possible for them to identify specific inefficiencies.
7. Reports should provide comparative data (comparing actual with budgeted costs or predetermined standards with actual results). Significant variances should be highlighted so that responsible management can quickly identify the problems that require attention.
8. Reports should be analytical. The accountant must understand the nature of the business activities of each organizational unit in order to provide responsible managers with useful data. Analysis of underlying papers, such as time tickets, scrap tickets, work orders, and materials requisitions, provides reasons for poor performance that might have been due to power failure, machine breakdown, an inefficient operator, poor quality of materials, or other similar factors.
9. Reports for operating management should be stated in physical units as well as in dollars, because dollar information may be irrelevant to a supervisor. Also, dollars may be more difficult to compare over time because of changes in prices.

To be of value, information must be used; to be used, it must be effectively communicated. Both the form and the method of the reporting techniques are critical, whether written or oral.

The written report should include tabular presentation as well as the use of charts and graphs.[2] Narrative comments are useful for conveying qualitative information and for analyzing and interpreting quantitative data. Oral presentations are especially effective in offering opportunities to convey information, raise questions, and voice opinions.

Responsibility-Reporting Systems Illustrated

The first step in a responsibility-reporting system is the establishment of lines of responsibility and responsibility areas. Each block in a company's organization

[2] For discussion and illustrations of these communication aids, see Anker V. Andersen, *Graphing Financial Information—How Accountants Can Use Graphs to Communicate,* New York. Copyright 1983 by Institute of Management Accountants (formerly National Association of Accountants). All rights reserved. Reprinted by permission.

chart represents a segment (cost center, division, department, and so on) that is reported upon and that receives reports on the functions responsible to it. Any report prepared according to this concept easily fits into one of the blocks of the organization chart illustrated in Figure 17-1.

FIGURE 17-1 ***Organization Chart for a Manufacturing Concern***

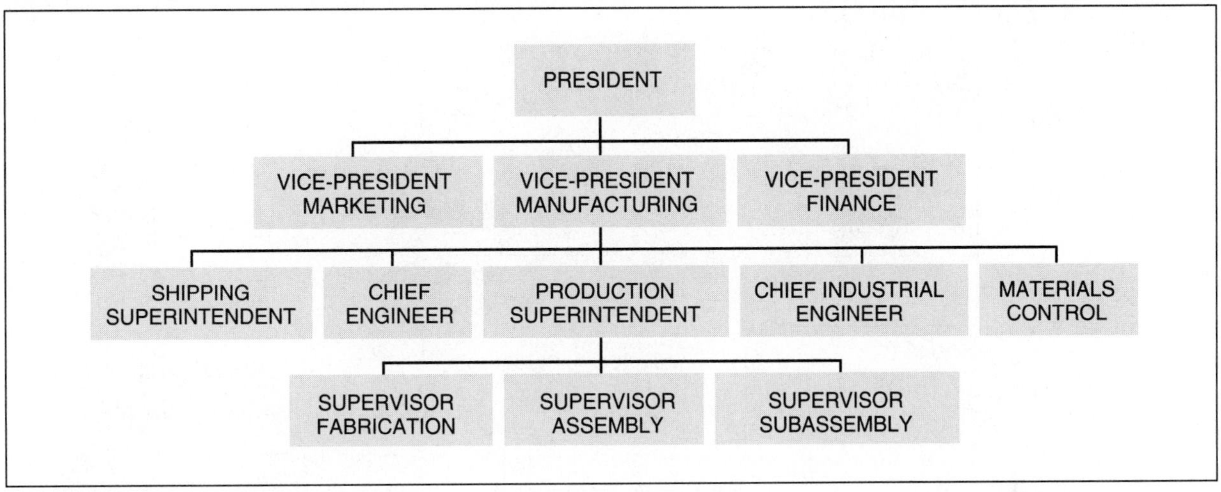

Figure 17-2 illustrates the factory overhead reporting structure for each level of responsibility and the relationship of each report to the next higher echelon of responsibility.[3] Starting with Report D, the Subassembly Department supervisor is provided with the factory overhead costs for the department. The supervisors for the Fabrication and Assembly Departments also receive similar reports. The supervisors of these three departments are responsible to the production superintendent. Report C summarizes the overhead costs for the production superintendent and the three departments for which the production superintendent is accountable. Report B provides the vice-president of manufacturing with performance figures for this office and for the five responsibility areas within this division. Finally, the president receives a summary, Report A, indicating overhead costs not only for the president's own area but also for the three divisions (Marketing, Manufacturing, and Finance) reporting to that office.

Reviewing the Reporting Structure

To provide all levels of management with all the facts when needed, the reporting system should be geared to the requirements of all managerial personnel. Each report should be so arranged that exceptions are highlighted and brought to the attention of the responsible manager without demanding too much searching and extensive reading. The number of reports issued and sent to a manager also needs constant examination. Too often, a reporting system becomes cluttered with old, detailed, and voluminous reports, with no regard for the cost of their preparation or their justification. No reporting system is ever perfect. It requires continuous examination in the light of changes in the nature of the business and the needs of management.

[3] James D. Wilson, "Human Relations and More Effective Reporting," *NAA Bulletin*, Vol. 42, No. 9, pp. 13–24. Copyright May, 1961, by the Institute of Management Accountants (formerly National Association of Accountants). All rights reserved. Reprinted by permission.

FIGURE 17-2 *Flow of Responsibility Reports in a Manufacturing Concern*

A — SUMMARY OF COMPANY OVERHEAD ($000s)

TO: The President

Division	Month: Amount	Month: Over (Under) Budget	Year-to-Date: Amount	Year-to-Date: Over (Under) Budget
President..........	$ 80	$(2)	$820	$ 3
VP, Marketing......	430	8		
VP, Manufacturing..	870	14		
VP, Finance........	120	1		
Total...........	$1,500	$21		

B — MANUFACTURING DIVISION OVERHEAD ($000s)

TO: Vice-President, Manufacturing

Department	Month: Amount	Month: Over (Under) Budget	Year-to-Date: Amount	Year-to-Date: Over (Under) Budget
VP, Manufacturing.	$ 30	$ (6)	$ 310	$ 15
Production........	590	40	5,700	322
Engineering.......	70	(5)		
Shipping..........	60	2		
Indus. Eng.	60	(18)		
Mtls. Control.....	60	1		
Total..........	$870	$ 14		

C — PRODUCTION DEPARTMENTS OVERHEAD ($000s)

TO: Production Superintendent

Department	Month: Amount	Month: Over (Under) Budget	Year-to-Date: Amount	Year-to-Date: Over (Under) Budget
Prod. Supt.	$ 20	$ 2	$ 180	$ (7)
Fabrication.....	130	5	1,180	(5)
Assembly........	250	43		
Subassembly.....	190	(10)		
Total........	$590	$ 40		

D — SUBASSEMBLY DEPARTMENT OVERHEAD ($000s)

TO: Supervisor, Subassembly Department

Item	Month: Amount	Month: Over (Under) Budget	Year-to-Date: Amount	Year-to-Date: Over (Under) Budget
Indirect Labor...	$ 90	$(12)	$ 847	$(46)
Fringe Benefits..	7	(1)	80	(4)
Maintenance......	44	6	420	(18)
Supplies.........	15	(3)	143	22
Power............	24	(4)	212	2
All Other........	10	4	100	4
Total.........	$190	$(10)	$1,802	$(40)

The Flexible Budget and Variance Analysis

The primary objective of responsibility accounting and reporting is the control of cost. Cost control is predicated on the idea that actual costs are compared with budgeted costs, relating what did happen with what should have happened. Budgets are based on certain definite assumed conditions and results. The budgets discussed and illustrated in Chapters 15 and 16 are known as **static budgets**; the budgets discussed in this section are known as **flexible budgets**.

Both static budgets and flexible budgets provide management with information necessary to attain the major objectives of budgetary control, which include:

1. An organized procedure for planning.
2. A means for coordinating the activities of the various divisions of a business.
3. A basis for cost control.

When a company's activities can be estimated within close limits, the static budget can be satisfactorily compared to actual cost for the purpose of cost control. However, completely predictable situations are rare. If actual volume differs from that planned, a comparison of actual results with a static budget may be misleading. For example, suppose that the Assembly Department of Plaxton Company budgets $10,000 of overhead for the production of 1,000 units of product, but 1,100 units are actually produced and actual overhead is

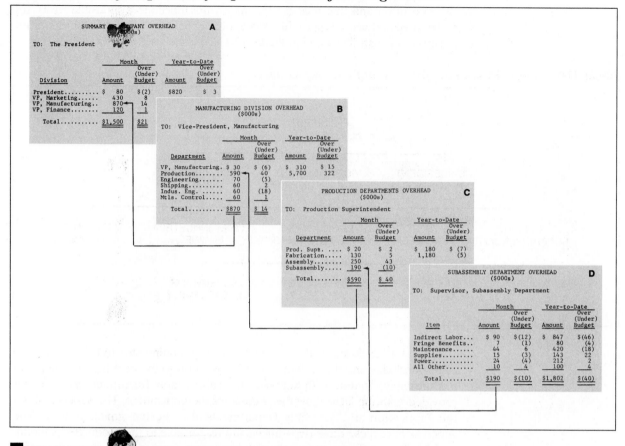

$10,500. A simple comparison of budgeted overhead with actual overhead indicates actual costs are $500 more than they should be. However, further examination reveals that actual production exceeds that planned by 100 units. Because budgeted and actual overhead contain both fixed and variable components, it is not clear from a comparison of actual results with the budget whether the $500 difference results from an efficient or inefficient use of company resources. Cost efficiency can be determined only by comparing actual cost with a budget based on actual volume. A flexible budget provides a measure of what costs should be under any given set of conditions—that is, a budget adjusted to actual volume.

Preparing a Flexible Budget

Before a flexible budget can be prepared, a formula must be developed for each account within each department or cost center using one of the techniques described in Chapter 3. Each formula indicates the fixed cost and/or the variable cost rate for the account. The variable portion of the formula is a rate of cost in relation to some measure of activity, such as labor hours, machine hours, or units of production. The fixed amount and the variable rate remain constant within the relevant range of activity.

Once the actual level of activity for a period is known (that is, at the end of the period), these formulas are used to compute allowable budget expenditures for the volume of activity actually attained for the period. A budget adjusted to reflect the actual level of activity experienced is called an **allowable budget** or a **budget allowance**. The allowable budget can be used to compute the spending and idle capacity variances, which when added together equal the over- or underapplied overhead for the department or cost center. These variances are useful in evaluating the performance of each department or cost center.

1. **Spending variance** is the difference between actual cost and the budget allowance (a budget adjusted to reflect the actual level of activity). If the budget allowance is a reasonable estimate of what should have been spent for the actual level of activity experienced, the spending variance can be viewed as a measure of efficiency. The spending variance is driven by differences in the budgeted and actual prices and quantities of the various items of cost. To the extent that the manager has control over either price or quantity, the manager should have some control over the spending variance.
2. **Idle capacity variance** is the difference between the budget allowance for actual activity and the amount of cost charged to products manufactured during the period (or to user departments for services rendered during the period). The idle capacity variance is the amount of over- or underapplied budgeted fixed factory overhead. It is viewed as a measure of capacity utilization because it is driven by the difference between the level of activity used in computing the predetermined overhead rate (or billing rate) and the level of activity actually experienced during the period. If the level of capacity used in computing the rate is an accurate estimate of the capacity that should have been utilized, the idle capacity variance is a measure of efficient utilization of the facility. To the extent that a manager has control over the

level of capacity utilized, the manager should have some control over the idle capacity variance.

For an illustration of computing spending and idle capacity variances, assume that the $10,000 of budgeted factory overhead for the Assembly Department of Plaxton Company (in the preceding example) is composed of $6,000 of fixed cost and $4,000 of variable cost. The variable cost is determined by multiplying the $4-per-unit variable rate times the 1,000 units of planned production. The overhead rate for the period is $10 per unit ($10,000 budgeted overhead ÷ 1,000 budgeted units), and $11,000 of factory overhead is charged to production for the period ($10 rate × 1,100 units actually produced). Because actual costs are $10,500, overhead is overapplied in the amount of $500 ($10,500 actual overhead – $11,000 of applied overhead). The overapplied overhead can be decomposed into spending and idle capacity variances as follows:

Actual factory overhead		$10,500	
Budget allowance for actual units produced:			
Variable costs ($4 rate × 1,100 actual units)	$4,400		
Fixed costs	6,000	10,400	
Spending variance		$ 100	unfavorable
Budget allowance for actual units produced (from above)		$10,400	
Applied factory overhead ($10 rate × 1,100 actual units)		11,000	
Idle capacity variance		$ (600)	favorable
Spending variance		$ 100	unfavorable
Idle capacity variance		(600)	favorable
Overapplied factory overhead		$ (500)	

The budget allowance is the amount of factory overhead that would have been budgeted to produce the actual output (1,100 in this example). The budget allowance differs from the original budget by $400 ($10,000 originally budgeted – $10,400 budget allowance), which is attributable to additional variable cost required to produce 100 units more than originally planned [(1,000 units originally planned – 1,100 units actually produced) × $4 predetermined variable overhead rate]. The difference between the actual amount of overhead incurred and the amount of overhead budgeted for actual activity (the spending variance) is not influenced by differences in planned and actual activity, but is instead attributable to differences in the actual and budgeted prices and quantities of the various items that constitute factory overhead. The spending variance in this example is unfavorable because actual cost exceeded the budget allowance by $100.

Notice that the amount of variable cost included in the budget allowance ($4 variable rate × 1,100 units actually produced) and the amount of variable cost applied to production (i.e., the $4 variable portion of the overhead rate × 1,100 units actually produced) are the same. When applied overhead is subtracted from the budget allowance, variable cost is eliminated. The $600 idle capacity variance is the difference between the fixed cost in the budget allowance and the amount of fixed cost in applied overhead—budgeted fixed cost ($6,000) less the amount of fixed cost applied to production [($10 overhead rate – $4 variable portion) × 1,100 units = $6,600]. Because capacity utilization exceeds that planned, the variance is referred to as favorable. If capacity utilization had been less than that planned, the idle capacity variance would be referred to as unfavorable.[4] Because the idle capacity variance is a measure of capacity utilization, it can be computed by multiplying the $6 fixed overhead rate ($6,000 budgeted fixed cost ÷ 1,000 budgeted units) times the difference between budgeted and actual activity [(1,000 budgeted units – 1,100 actual units) × $6 fixed rate = $600 overapplied or favorable variance].

Historically the flexible budget was applied principally to the control of departmental factory overhead. Now, however, the idea is applied to the entire budget, so that marketing and administrative budgets as well as manufacturing budgets are prepared on a flexible budget basis. The flexible budget is also a useful planning tool because it provides cost behavior information that can be used to evaluate the effects of different volumes of activity on profits and cash and to establish the approved periodic budget. Any increase or decrease in business activity must be reflected throughout the enterprise. In some activities or departments, changes will be greater or smaller than in others. Certain departments have the ability to increase production without much additional cost. In others, costs increase or decrease more or less in direct proportion to production increases or decreases. The flexible budget attempts to deal with this problem.

When the fixed dollar amount and the variable rate of an expense have been determined (employing cost behavior analysis as discussed in Chapter 3), budget allowances for any level within a relevant range of activity can be computed. For example, an overhead budget allowance schedule for the Machining Department of a manufacturing company, based on normal capacity, is presented in Exhibit 17-1.

The schedule of budget allowances is the basis for preparing a flexible budget. One approach to preparing a flexible budget is to compute the variable component of each item of cost at several different levels of activity and to prepare a flexible budget as illustrated in Exhibit 17-2.

The flexible budget in Exhibit 17-2 lists the Machining Department's budgeted factory overhead at capacity levels ranging from 70 percent to 100 percent in 10 percent increments. The items of variable cost are listed separately from the items of fixed cost. The variable cost for each item is determined by multiplying the variable rate for the item times the activity budgeted for each level of capacity utilization. For example, the variable cost of indirect labor at 70 percent of capacity ($437.50) is determined by multiplying the 50-cent variable rate for indirect labor (as indicated on the schedule of budget allowances shown in Exhibit 17-1) times 875 machine hours (or, 70% × 1,250 hours at 100% capacity level).

---

[4] A variance is referred to as favorable or unfavorable depending on whether it has a favorable or unfavorable effect on income and owners' equity (that is, whether it signals an increase or a decrease in income and owners' equity). Spending and idle capacity variances are usually not recorded in the accounting records; however, they are components of over- or underapplied factory overhead, which does appear in the accounting records. If actual factory overhead is less than the amount applied to products manufactured during the period, the overapplied amount is deducted from cost of goods sold, if not material, or ratably from cost of goods sold and ending inventories, if material (see Chapter 12). In either case, overapplied overhead decreases the cost of goods sold in the current period which in turn increases income and owners' equity. Because it has a positive effect on income and owners' equity, overapplied overhead is said to be favorable. In contrast, the excess of actual overhead over the amount applied to production (underapplied overhead) increases cost of goods sold and decreases income and owners' equity. Because it has a negative effect on income and owners' equity, underapplied overhead is said to be unfavorable. Because spending and idle capacity variances are parts of over- or underapplied overhead, they too affect income.

EXHIBIT 17-1

Overhead Budget Allowance for Machining Department

Activity Base: 1,000 machine hours per month at normal capacity, which is 80% of rated capacity.

Item of Overhead	Fixed Cost	Variable Rate per Machine Hour
Indirect labor	$ 5,000	$ .50
Supervision	3,000	
Factory supplies	1,500	.90
Power	900	1.10
Rework operations	500	.50
Payroll taxes	1,000	.15
Repair and maintenance	1,000	.75
Property insurance	800	
Property taxes	600	
Vacation pay	2,200	
Employee pension costs	1,400	
Employee health plan	600	
Machinery depreciation	3,400	
Water and heat	800	
Building occupancy (cost allocation)	1,300	
General factory (cost allocation)	2,000	.10
Total cost	$26,000	$4.00
Summary:		
Fixed cost	$26,000	
Variable cost (1,000 machine hours × $4 variable rate)	4,000	
Total cost at normal capacity	$30,000	
Factory overhead rate for Machining Department at normal capacity ($30,000/1,000 machine hours)	$ 30.00	per machine hour

Because fixed cost is not affected by changes in activity within the relevant range, the fixed cost for most items is the same as the fixed cost listed in the schedule of budget allowances. However, when activity increases beyond the relevant range, additional demands on capacity can necessitate an increase in one or more fixed costs. In this case, the fixed cost of supervision, payroll taxes, rework, and employee benefits related to increased supervision increases when activity increases from 90 to 100 percent of rated capacity. In other words, 1,250 machine hours lies outside the relevant range for these cost items, so fixed cost for these items is different at the 90 percent and 100 percent levels of activity.

In this budget, the factory overhead rate declines steadily as production moves to the 90 percent operating level. As production approaches maximum capacity, the overhead rate increases because some items of fixed cost increase. Although such cost increases are revealed through the flexible budget, one definite level must be agreed on and used for setting the predetermined factory overhead rate, both for applying overhead cost to production and for computing the spending and idle capacity variances.

Preparing a Variance Report

For an illustration of the determination of variances in a flexible budgeting system, assume that the Machining Department actually used 1,075 machine hours during the month and incurred the following actual costs:

EXHIBIT 17-2

One Month Flexible Overhead Budget for Machining Department

Operating level				
Machine hours	875	1,000	1,125	1,250
Percentage of capacity	70%	80%	90%	100%
Variable cost				
Indirect labor	$ 437.50	$ 500.00	$ 562.50	$ 625.00
Factory supplies	787.50	900.00	1,012.50	1,125.00
Power	962.50	1,100.00	1,237.50	1,375.00
Rework operations	437.50	500.00	562.50	625.00
Payroll taxes	131.25	150.00	168.75	187.50
Repair and maintenance	656.25	750.00	843.75	937.50
General factory	87.50	100.00	112.50	125.00
Total variable cost	$ 3,500.00	$ 4,000.00	$ 4,500.00	$ 5,000.00
Fixed cost				
Indirect labor	$ 5,000.00	$ 5,000.00	$ 5,000.00	$ 5,000.00
Supervision	3,000.00	3,000.00	3,000.00	5,700.00
Factory supplies	1,500.00	1,500.00	1,500.00	1,500.00
Power	900.00	900.00	900.00	900.00
Rework operations	500.00	500.00	500.00	975.00
Payroll taxes	1,000.00	1,000.00	1,000.00	1,300.00
Repair and maintenance	1,000.00	1,000.00	1,000.00	1,000.00
Property insurance	800.00	800.00	800.00	800.00
Property taxes	600.00	600.00	600.00	600.00
Vacation pay	2,200.00	2,200.00	2,200.00	2,500.00
Employee pension costs	1,400.00	1,400.00	1,400.00	1,600.00
Employee health plan	600.00	600.00	600.00	700.00
Machinery depreciation	3,400.00	3,400.00	3,400.00	3,400.00
Water and heat	800.00	800.00	800.00	800.00
Building occupancy	1,300.00	1,300.00	1,300.00	1,300.00
General factory	2,000.00	2,000.00	2,000.00	2,000.00
Total fixed cost	$26,000.00	$26,000.00	$26,000.00	$30,075.00
Total cost	$29,500.00	$30,000.00	$30,500.00	$35,075.00
Factory overhead rate per machine hour	$ 33.714	$ 30.000	$ 27.111	$ 28.060

Indirect labor	$ 5,750.00
Supervision	3,000.00
Factory supplies	2,625.50
Power	2,107.75
Rework operations	1,088.25
Payroll taxes	1,182.50
Repair and maintenance	1,525.75
Property insurance	830.00
Property taxes	625.00
Vacation pay	2,200.00
Employee pension costs	1,400.00
Employee health plan	600.00
Machinery depreciation	3,400.00
Water and heat	825.75
Building occupancy	1,300.00
General factory	2,315.25
Total actual cost	$30,775.75

A variance report can be prepared by comparing the budget allowance for actual activity (determined from flexible budget data) to actual overhead and applied overhead. In order to provide a detailed report to operating management, the spending variance is computed for each item of overhead by subtracting the flexible budget amount for each item of overhead from the item's actual cost. On the other hand, because the idle capacity variance is a measure of departmental capacity utilization, a single variance is computed by subtracting applied overhead from the total budget allowance. If the flexible budget shows variable and fixed costs separately, as in Exhibit 17-2, the variance report will be as illustrated in Exhibit 17-3.

EXHIBIT 17-3

Machining Department
Variance Report
For the Month Ended March, 19A

	Budget Allowance Expected Capacity	Budget Allowance Actual Activity	Actual Cost	Spending Variance (Favorable) Unfavorable
Based on machine hours	1,000	1,075		
Percentage of capacity	80%	86%		
Variable cost				
Indirect labor	$ 500.00	$ 537.50	$ 750.00	$212.50
Factory supplies	900.00	967.50	1,125.50	158.00
Power	1,100.00	1,182.50	1,207.75	25.25
Rework operations	500.00	537.50	588.25	50.75
Payroll taxes	150.00	161.25	182.50	21.25
Repair and maintenance	750.00	806.25	525.75	(280.50)
General factory	100.00	107.50	315.25	207.75
Total variable cost	$ 4,000.00	$ 4,300.00	$ 4,695.00	
Fixed cost				
Indirect labor	$ 5,000.00	$ 5,000.00	$ 5,000.00	0.00 *
Supervision	3,000.00	3,000.00	3,000.00	0.00
Factory supplies	1,500.00	1,500.00	1,500.00	0.00 *
Power	900.00	900.00	900.00	0.00 *
Rework operations	500.00	500.00	500.00	0.00 *
Payroll taxes	1,000.00	1,000.00	1,000.00	0.00 *
Repair and maintenance	1,000.00	1,000.00	1,000.00	0.00 *
Property insurance	800.00	800.00	830.00	30.00
Property taxes	600.00	600.00	625.00	25.00
Vacation pay	2,200.00	2,200.00	2,200.00	0.00
Employee pension costs	1,400.00	1,400.00	1,400.00	0.00
Employee health plan	600.00	600.00	600.00	0.00
Machinery depreciation	3,400.00	3,400.00	3,400.00	0.00
Water and heat	800.00	800.00	825.75	25.75
Building occupancy	1,300.00	1,300.00	1,300.00	0.00
General factory	2,000.00	2,000.00	2,000.00	0.00 *
Total fixed cost	$26,000.00	$26,000.00	$26,080.75	
Total cost	$30,000.00	$30,300.00	$30,775.75	$475.75
Applied factory overhead ($30 rate × 1,075 actual hours)		32,250.00		unfavorable
Idle capacity variance		$ (1,950.00)	favorable	

* These cost items contain both fixed and variable components. Any separation of the spending variance into fixed and variable components for these mixed costs is arbitrary. As a consequence, the spending variance for each item of cost is typically reported as variable. (That is, an amount equal to the budgeted fixed cost is reported as actual fixed cost, and the balance of actual cost for the item is reported as actual variable cost.)

The total spending variance plus the idle capacity variance equal the amount of over- or underapplied factory overhead for the period as follows:

Actual factory overhead cost	$30,775.75	
Applied factory overhead	32,250.00	
Overapplied factory overhead	$ (1,474.25)	
Spending variance	$ 475.75	unfavorable
Idle capacity variance	(1,950.00)	favorable
Overapplied factory overhead	$ (1,474.25)	

In the flexible budget for the Machining Department, the factory overhead rate based on machine hours means that variable expenses are more closely related to this activity base than to any other. Typically, some cost items within a department are closely related to one activity while other cost items are closely related to some other activity. For example, amount of factory supplies, power, rework, and repair and maintenance are driven by machine hours, while the amount of indirect labor and payroll taxes are driven by direct labor hours. Because the nature of the work performed in each department differs, the activity base used to allocate factory overhead in each department may differ.

In addition, some costs, such as indirect labor, can be closely related to several activities, some of which are not related to production volume at all (for example, retooling, machine setups, or moving inventory). In such cases, greater cost control and more meaningful product costing result when accountants use more than one factory overhead rate (for example, activity-based costing as discussed in Chapter 14). Because the use of multiple rates within a department is costly, the expected benefits to be derived from such added precision should be weighed against the costs of gathering and providing such information. However, if responsibility reports are to be used for performance evaluation and cost control, it is essential that the dollar cost for each item or group of items reported be highly correlated with the activity used in preparing the budget allowance. Otherwise, the budget allowance against which actual costs are compared will be unreliable, and the reported cost variances will be meaningless. A high correlation is obtainable in many cases only when multiple activities are used.

Responsibility Accounting and Reporting—an Alternative View

Responsibility accounting and reporting systems are a logical outgrowth of an autocratic style of management found in many businesses today. The philosophy of this style of management is that the job of a manager is to direct the workers. It follows that to direct the workers, the manager must have knowledge and skill and be the source of problem solutions. Therefore, the manager bears all responsibility for the success or failure of the business unit for which he or she has charge. With this kind of orientation, the use of responsibility accounting and reporting as an evaluation tool seemed logical.

During the 1980s, however, many U.S. companies began to question traditional management philosophy and the way they had been doing business. Declines in market share and increased competition from abroad led these companies to rethink what they were doing and to begin to experiment with alternative approaches. Given the complexities of modern manufacturing and the need for continuous improvement, companies began to promote cooperation and team effort. As a consequence, some companies began to shift away from an autocratic style of management toward a participative style of management. In a participative style of management, workers and management are viewed as equally responsible members of a team. A manager's job is viewed as that of facilitator and coach rather than director. The conduct of business is considered to be a team effort. This shift in emphasis from individual performance to team performance has led many to question the usefulness of responsibility accounting and reporting as a basis for evaluating managerial performance.

Criticisms about the usefulness of responsibility accounting and reporting can be grouped into two general classes: (1) those that relate to dysfunctional behavior by managers who are evaluated on the basis of performance reported by such a system and (2) those that relate to the usefulness to managers of the data produced by such a system.

Dysfunctional Behavior by Managers

The traditional view of responsibility accounting and reporting assigns responsibility for inefficiencies to individuals, and a variance from the budget (or standard) is the measure of inefficiency. Because managers presumably control the activities that drive cost, variances are blamed on managers rather than on the business system that allowed the variances to occur. Since individuals are evaluated rather than operating systems, the individuals tend to do whatever it takes to minimize or eliminate variances. This can have the following dysfunctional results:

1. Managers tend to take actions that are self-serving rather than beneficial to the company as a whole. Managers often engage in practices that will ensure that their individual evaluations will be good even when some of those practices are detrimental to the overall good of the company. Examples include increasing inventory to unnecessary levels to buffer potential work stoppages (machine breakdowns, employee illness, employee replacements, and so on) and decreasing the quality of output in order to cut overall costs or to produce larger quantities. Evaluating individuals on the basis of individual actions promotes self-serving behavior, not teamwork.[5]
2. Managers concentrate on meeting the budget rather than the best level of performance that can be achieved. The use of budgets as the basis for measuring performance tends to thwart continuous improvement, because measuring performance on the basis of variances from a budget conveys the message to operational managers that the budget is good enough. As a consequence, budget-based measures of performance tend to stifle initiative and promote suboptimization. "A world-class operation never accepts any cost level as 'good enough'; it continuously strives to reduce costs."[6]
3. Managers tend to focus their attention on short-run targets and ignore the long-term needs of the business. To eliminate variances and receive favorable evaluations, managers must concentrate their efforts on meeting the budget; however, the budget is based on current period expectations.

[5] Douglas L. Heerema and Richard L. Rogers, "Is Your Cost Accounting System Benching Your Team Players?" *Management Accounting*, Vol. 73, No. 3, p. 40.

[6] Germain B. Böer, "Making Accounting a Value-Added Activity," *Management Accounting*, Vol. 73, No. 2, p.39.

As a result, managers tend to ignore the long-term effects of actions taken to meet the current budget. Examples include: (a) deferring or abandoning preventive maintenance, which can lead to machine breakdown and premature replacement, (b) avoiding trying new methods that might improve productivity for fear that productivity might decline in the short-run, and (c) deferring or abandoning employee training and equipment upgrading in order to hold or to cut current costs.

4. Managers, who are unable to subvert the system sufficiently to get acceptable evaluations but who are otherwise competent and efficient, become frustrated, do not get promoted, and often leave the company. Those who remain tend to excel in manipulation and gamesmanship, because that is what got them promoted, rather than in productivity and technical expertise, which is what the company needs in order to succeed in the marketplace.

To overcome the problem of thwarting continuous improvement, two alternatives have been suggested as the basis for evaluating performance: the use of trends in actual performance over time[7] and budgets based on learning curve estimates.[8] These approaches may also be useful in reorienting the focus of managers from short-run to long-run performance. Although these alternatives offer improvement over the traditional approach that compares actual cost with a flexible budget, they do not cure the problem. They merely substitute one kind of expectation for another in the evaluation process. If managers are being evaluated on the basis of a prespecified level of performance, they still have a strong incentive to do whatever it takes to meet the expected level of performance. They have no incentive to exceed expectations nor to engage in cooperative activities that benefit the company.

Probably the most effective step in solving the problem of dysfunctional behavior is to discontinue the practice of using variance reports as a basis for evaluating individual managers. Variance reports should be used as a basis for evaluating the operating efficiency of business activities rather than individuals.[9] By shifting the focus of variance reporting to evaluating activities and business systems, individuals are not placed in the position of defending their actions. Managers are free to experiment and find new ways to improve the process. In addition, the responsibility for the efficient operation of each activity can be transferred from a single manager to all employees involved in the activity, thereby promoting cooperation and teamwork.

Usefulness of the Data to Managers

The traditional view of responsibility accounting and reporting is that the costs incurred in conducting a business activity should be reported to the manager who controls the business activity. Variances are reported for the following purposes: to hold responsible managers accountable for the incurrence of cost, and to provide information that can be used by responsible managers to control business activities efficiently. Some problems in determining who actually controls various items of cost have already been noted. Even if controllable cost can be segregated from noncontrollable cost effectively, however, responsibility reports are of limited use to responsible managers in helping them control costs. Problems include:

[7] *Ibid.*, p. 19.

[8] Joseph Fisher, "Use of Nonfinancial Performance Measures," *Journal of Cost Management*, Vol. 6, No. 1, pp. 35–36.

[9] C. J. McNair, "Interdependence and Control: Traditional vs. Activity-Based Responsibility Accounting," *Journal of Cost Management*, Vol. 4, No. 2, pp. 18–19.

1. Most responsibility accounting and reporting systems improperly base allowable budgets on volume-based measures of activity, which have little to do with cost incurrence. This can result in an improper segregation of controllable and noncontrollable costs. Even if a manager has control over cost, an allowable budget determined on the basis of the wrong activity (an activity that has a low correlation with cost) results in meaningless variances. Trying to make actual cost conform to a meaningless cost estimate is frustrating and potentially wasteful.
2. Control data available in a responsibility reporting system are too aggregated to be useful. A spending variance for a department does not provide enough information to help a manager pinpoint the cause, even when the variances are computed and reported for each item of cost. A spending variance is caused by differences between actual prices and quantities, and budgeted prices and quantities; the variance, however, does not signal whether a difference in price or a difference in quantity has the most impact. Even itemized variance reports aggregate more than one cost item in each classification (for example, several different kinds of supplies in indirect materials, several different activities in indirect labor, several different kinds of utility costs in utilities). Furthermore, costs incurred as the result of all the events that occurred during the reporting period are aggregated for each cost classification.
3. Control data available to managers are financial and not easily interpreted by all operating-level managers. Many operating-level managers who receive variance reports have little training in accounting and finance. For those individuals, financial reports may be difficult to understand. If they do not know how the cost variances were computed, they may not know how to use the reported data to determine the causes of the reported variances.
4. Control data available to managers are not timely enough to be useful. Even the most efficient accounting systems take a week or two to prepare reports. Furthermore, the accounting reports cover a period of time, usually a week to a month. A considerable amount of activity can occur within the reporting period. As a consequence, accounting reports are generally made available too late to be useful in controlling the activities that drive cost.

To a great extent, these problems stem from poorly designed responsibility accounting systems and from attempts to use responsibility reporting as the primary or exclusive cost control mechanism. The first of the problems listed in this section (determining the amount of budgeted cost with the wrong activity) can be effectively reduced by implementing an activity-based cost system and then designing the responsibility accounting and reporting system around the activity-based cost system. Activities should be carefully analyzed to determine if they are cost drivers, and if they are, which costs they drive. Correlation analysis should be used to determine the relationship between costs and activities. The implementation of activity-based costing not only improves product costing but also provides an improved basis for computing budgeted costs in a responsibility accounting and reporting system. Activity-based costing not only improves the quality of control data but also focuses attention on controlling business activities rather than individuals.[10]

The last three problems (control data too aggregated to be useful, financial data difficult to interpret, and control data not timely enough to be useful) are difficult to overcome with an accounting system. First, if the data reported to

[10] *Ibid.*, p. 18-19.

managers are made less aggregated, the volume of data reported can become unwieldy, and it is not clear that disaggregated financial information would improve control. Financial data are useful, but other kinds of data may be more useful, and there is a limit to the amount of data that can be used efficiently. The accountant should work with users of the system's reports to find out what users need and want.

Second, although accounting systems are designed to capture and summarize the economic significance of business activity, they can be designed to collect and report nonfinancial data, such as changes in inventory quantities, spoilage rates, and hours of machine utilization. These kinds of data are more understandable to some users and may be more relevant to their needs.[11] Financial results flow from operational activities. Business activity can be more effectively controlled by monitoring the activity rather than observing the costs that result from the activity. Examples of manufacturing activities that drive cost include: (1) the amount of time required to perform a task, (2) the number of engineering change orders, (3) the number of parts required for a product, (4) the spoilage rate, (5) the amount of rework, (6) the time required to get a product through the plant from start to finish, and (7) the amount of inventory on hand. Reductions in these activities reduce cost, but reductions are more easily measured by direct observation than by financial measures. Nevertheless, the tie between the reduction of an activity or the introduction of a new process and a subsequent change in income is crucial to the survival of a company.[12] Financial measures are still an important gauge of the effectiveness of controlling activity. The accountant should work with users to help them understand what the financial measures mean and to find out from users what kinds of nonfinancial data are needed.

Third, responsibility reports can be made available to users on a more frequent basis, but more frequent reporting is costly, and, at best, reports are still available several days after the occurrence of the activities that drive cost. Statistical control systems and other operational control systems are more effective for the day-to-day control of business activity. Accounting reports should be viewed as supplementary control data that provide a periodic economic assessment of the effectiveness of operational systems in controlling business activities. Accounting reports should not be used as the sole means of cost control.

Summary

Although responsibility accounting and reporting is a widely applied tool, in practice it is often misunderstood and misused. This chapter began with a discussion of the traditional view of responsibility accounting and reporting. That view holds that because activity drives cost, costs can be controlled by holding managers responsible for the costs generated by the activities over which they have control. This leads to attempts to isolate controllable costs and to the use of flexible budgets and variance reporting as cost control devices. However, as a result of poorly designed systems and overreliance on variance reporting, dysfunctional behavior and inefficiency frequently occur in practice. As a consequence, the value of responsibility accounting and reporting as a management tool has been seriously questioned, particularly as it relates to the need for cooperation among

---

[11] Robert A. Howell and Stephen R. Soucy, "Management Reporting in the New Manufacturing Environment," *Management Accounting*, Vol. 69, No. 8, p .24.

[12] Fisher, "Use of Nonfinancial Performance Measures," p. 38.

employees and continuous improvement, which are the foundations of world-class manufacturing. The last section presented an alternative view of responsibility accounting and reporting. The need to focus evaluation on activities rather than individuals and the use of responsibility reporting as supplementary rather than primary control data was stressed. Responsibility accounting and reporting is still a useful cost control tool, but it is not a substitute for good management.

Key Terms

variance ***(468)***
responsibility accounting and reporting ***(467)***
billing rate, sold-hour rate, charging rate, or transfer rate ***(472)***
responsibility accounting ***(475)***
responsibility reporting ***(475)***
static budgets ***(478)***
flexible budgets ***(478)***
allowable budget or budget allowance ***(479)***
spending variance ***(479)***
idle capacity variance ***(479)***

Discussion Questions

Q17-1 What is responsibility accounting?

Q17-2 How is the emphasis in responsibility accounting different from that in product costing?

Q17-3 Explain what is meant by controllable costs and how the idea of controllability is related to responsibility accounting.

Q17-4 What aspects of organizational structure are important to an effective responsibility accounting and reporting system?

Q17-5 How might a cost that is traceable to an activity not be controllable by the individual who controls the activity?

Q17-6 Overhead control reports received by department heads should include only those items over which they have control. Why?

Q17-7 Why are service department costs included in overhead rates? Why should actual service department costs be accumulated in service department accounts instead of being charged directly to production department accounts?

Q17-8 In a responsibility accounting and reporting system, service department costs should be charged to user departments using predetermined billing rates rather than simply waiting until the end of the period and allocating a share of actual cost. Why?

Q17-9 The following charges are found on the monthly report of a division that manufactures and sells products primarily to outside companies. State which, if any, of these charges are consistent with the responsibility accounting concept. Support each answer with a brief explanation.

(a) A charge for general corporate administration at 10% of division sales.
(b) A charge for the use of the corporate computer facility. The charge is determined by taking the actual annual Computer Department cost and allocating an amount to each user on the ratio of its use to total corporation use.
(c) A charge for goods purchased from another division. (The charge is based on the competitive market price for the goods.)

(ICMA adapted)

Q17-10 The cost of producing electric power at the Emmons Company increased from $50,000 to $70,000 between January and February. The full amount of Electric Power Department cost is allocated to the various user departments in the company on the basis of actual usage.

(a) What factors may have caused the increase?
(b) Is this an effective way of handling this cost? If not, suggest a better procedure.

Q17-11 An actual charging rate is frequently used to charge the Maintenance Department cost to departments using its services. The charge is determined by multiplying the number of hours of maintenance service actually provided times a billing rate. The billing rate is computed by dividing total actual Maintenance Department cost by total actual maintenance hours worked. The supervisor of the Stamping Department was upset by a $15,000 maintenance charge for work that involved approximately the same number of labor hours as work done in a previous month when the charge was $12,000.

(a) What factors may have caused the increased charge?

(b) What improvements can be made in the distribution of this company's Maintenance Department cost?

Q17-12 Name some relative advantages in the use of a flexible budget over a fixed budget as a basis for evaluating performance.

Q17-13 What is a spending variance, and how is it used in responsibility reporting?

Q17-14 A spending variance for each item or classification of cost should be reported to responsible management each period. Why?

Q17-15 What is an idle capacity variance, and how can it be used in responsibility reporting?

Q17-16 From a traditional point of view, what are the two primary purposes of responsibility reports?

Q17-17 The traditional view of responsibility accounting and reporting is that, because activities drive cost, cost can be controlled by holding individuals who control activities responsible for cost incurrence. This view has lead to the use of responsibility accounting and reporting as a basis for evaluating the performance of managers. What kinds of dysfunctional behavior can result from this practice?

Q17-18 If dysfunctional behavior can result from using reports generated by a responsibility accounting system as a basis for evaluating the performance of managers, should responsibility accounting and reporting be abandoned? Explain.

Q17-19 Assume for a moment that a responsibility accounting and reporting system can effectively segregate controllable costs from those that are not controllable. Criticize the usefulness of the control data reported by such a system to responsible managers.

Q17-20 If nonfinancial measures of operating performance are more easily interpreted and can be made available on a more timely basis than financial data, do financial reports generated by a responsibility accounting system still have value? Explain.

Exercises

E17-1 Billing Rates; Variance Analysis in Service Departments. Jadlow Company uses predetermined departmental overhead rates to apply factory overhead. In computing these rates, accounting makes every attempt to transfer service department costs to producing departments on the most equitable bases. Budgeted cost and other data for Jadlow's two service departments, Maintenance and General Factory, are as follows:

	Maintenance	General Factory
Monthly fixed cost	$7,500	$30,000
Variable cost	$8.50 per maintenance hour	$20 per producing department employee
Expected level of activity	15,000 maintenance hours per month	1,000 producing department employees
Actual November results:		
Total cost	$132,000	$51,000
Actual level of activity	14,000 maintenance hours	980 producing department employees

Required:

(1) Compute the predetermined billing rates to be used to transfer estimated maintenance and general factory costs to benefiting departments. Use a single billing rate for each department.

(2) Compute the spending and idle capacity variances for the two service departments.

E17-2 Billing Rates; Variance Analysis in Service Departments. A company's two service departments provide the following data:

Service Center	Monthly Budget	Service-Hours Available	Actual Monthly Expense
Carpenter Shop	$20,000	2,000	$19,800
Electricians	30,000	2,500	28,900

The two service departments serve three producing departments which show the following budgeted and actual cost and service-hours data:

Benefiting Department	Estimated Hours of Services Required		Actual Hours of Services Used	
	Carpenter Shop	Electricians	Carpenter Shop	Electricians
1	600	900	400	1,000
2	750	1,000	800	850
3	650	600	450	550

Required:

(1) Compute a predetermined billing rate for each service department.

(2) Compute the amounts charged to the producing departments for services rendered. Use the predetermined billing rates computed for requirement 1.

(3) Compute the spending and idle capacity variances for the two service departments, assuming that 70% of the budgeted expense is fixed for the Carpenter Shop and 80% for Electricians.

E17-3 Billing Rates; Variance Analysis in Service Departments. The management of Paley Company wishes to secure greater control over service departments and decides to create a billing rate for the Maintenance and Payroll Departments. For September, the following predetermined and actual operating and cost data have been made available:

Maintenance Department		
Predetermined data (beginning of the month):		
Normal level of maintenance hours per month		3,200
Average hourly rate for maintenance worker		$ 8.70
	Fixed Cost per Month	Variable Cost per Maintenance Hour
Other maintenance costs:		
Supervision	$ 9,800	$ .50
Tools and supplies	2,300	.75
Other miscellaneous items	700	.05
Actual data (end of the month):		
Maintenance hours worked		3,355
Maintenance workers' earnings		$29,610
Other costs (supervision, etc.)		$17,590

Payroll Department	
Predetermined data (beginning of the month):	
Average number of employees in factory and office	1,200
Budgeted cost for department	$12,000 plus $2 for each employee in factory and office
Actual data (end of the month):	
Number of employees in factory and office	1,165
Total cost in the Payroll Department	$13,875

Required:

(1) Compute the billing rate for the two departments.

(2) Compute the variances for the two departments for September.

E17-4 Readiness to Serve and Billing Rates for a Service Department. During November, the actual cost of operating a power plant was $12,800, of which $6,000 was considered a fixed cost. The schedule of horsepower-hours for the benefiting user departments is as follows:

	Producing Departments		Service Departments	
	Department A	Department B	Department X	Department Y
Needed at full capacity..............	10,000	20,000	12,000	8,000
Used during November..............	8,000	13,000	7,000	6,000

Required:

(1) Compute the dollar amounts of the power plant cost to be allocated to each producing and service department. The fixed cost is assigned on the basis of the power plant's readiness to serve.

(2) Criticize the method used here to allocate the power department's costs to user departments.

E17-5 Readiness to Serve and Billing Rates; Variance Analysis. Tyrex Company operates its own power-generating plant. Power cost is distributed to the benefiting departments by charging the fixed cost according to the standby capacity provided and by charging the variable cost on the basis of a predetermined rate multiplied by actual consumption. The rated standby capacity of the company's four departments, Cutting, Grinding, Polishing, and Stores is 35,000, 26,000, 30,000, and 9,000 kilowatt-hours, respectively, per quarter. Fixed cost is budgeted at $7,000 for each quarter. Variable cost for expected annual capacity of 300,000 kilowatt-hours is $30,000.

The following information relates to departmental consumption and actual power plant cost during the year:

	Actual Consumption in Kilowatt-Hours				Actual Power
Quarter	Cutting	Grinding	Polishing	Stores	Plant Cost
First	29,500	20,000	29,000	6,500	$15,450
Second	33,500	24,750	23,500	8,250	16,200
Third	32,750	21,250	25,500	6,500	15,900
Fourth	28,250	23,000	27,750	6,000	15,400

Required:

(1) Separately identify the fixed and variable power cost charged to each department for each quarter.

(2) Compute the spending variance for the power plant for each quarter.

E17-6 Flexible Budget for Performance Evaluation The University of Boyne offers an extensive continuing education program in many cities throughout the state. For the convenience of its faculty and administrative staff and to save costs, the university employs a supervisor to operate a motor pool. The motor pool operated with 20 vehicles until February, when an additional automobile was acquired. The motor pool furnishes gasoline, oil, and other supplies for its automobiles. A mechanic does routine maintenance and minor repairs. Major repairs are done at a nearby commercial garage.

Each year, the supervisor prepares an operating budget, which informs the university administration of the funds needed for operating the pool. Depreciation (straight-line) on the automobiles is recorded in the budget in order to determine the cost per mile.

The following schedule presents the annual budget approved by the university, with March's actual costs compared to one twelfth of the annual budget:

University Motor Pool
Budget Report for March

	Annual Budget	One-Month Budget	March Actual	(Over) Under
Gasoline..	$ 52,500	$ 4,375	$ 5,323	$(948)
Oil, minor repairs, parts, and supplies	3,600	300	380	(80)
Outside repairs..	2,700	225	50	175
Insurance	6,000	500	525	(25)
Salaries and benefits	30,000	2,500	2,500	0
Depreciation..	26,400	2,200	2,310	(110)
	$121,200	$10,100	$11,088	$(988)
Total miles..	600,000	50,000	63,000	
Cost per mile..	$ .2020	$ .2020	$ .1760	
Number of automobiles...........................	20	20	21	

The annual budget was based on the following assumptions:

(a) 20 automobiles in the pool
(b) 30,000 miles per year per automobile
(c) 16 miles per gallon of fuel usage for each automobile
(d) $1.40 cost per gallon of gasoline
(e) $.006 per mile for oil, minor repairs, parts, and supplies
(f) $135 per automobile for outside repairs

The supervisor is unhappy with the monthly report comparing budget and actual costs for March, claiming it presents an unfair picture of performance.

Required: Prepare a performance report showing budgeted amounts, actual costs, and monthly variations for March, using flexible budgeting. Include the cost per mile rounded to four decimal places.

(ICMA adapted)

E17-7 Flexible Budget. Clayton Company produces electrical appliances. Its Assembly Department operates under a flexible budget, with monthly allowances established at 20% intervals. The following information shows fixed and total expenses at the 80% and 100% levels:

		Total Cost	
	Fixed	80%	100%
Direct materials		$16,000	$20,000
Direct labor		9,000	11,250
Supervision	$ 500	500	500
Indirect materials	250	1,450	1,750
Property tax	300	300	300
Maintenance	600	1,400	1,600
Power	200	280	300
Insurance	175	175	175
Depreciation	1,600	1,600	1,600

Required: Prepare a flexible budget at the 90% level of activity.

E17-8 Flexible Budget. One-month budget allowances for the Finishing Department of Winston Corporation follow:

Activity Base: 900 direct labor hours per month at normal capacity,which is 90% of rated capacity

Category of Cost	Fixed Cost	Variable Rate per Labor Hour
Indirect labor	$ 4,000.00	$1.50
Supervision	2,500.00	
Factory supplies	900.00	2.35
Power	500.00	.75
Rework operations	200.00	.50
Payroll taxes	800.00	1.30
Repair and maintenance	600.00	.40
Property insurance	700.00	
Property taxes	300.00	
Vacation pay	2,200.00	
Employee pension costs	1,200.00	
Employee health plan	1,800.00	
Machinery depreciation	1,000.00	
Water and heat	600.00	
Building occupancy	1,000.00	
General factory	1,500.00	.20
Total cost	$19,800.00	$7.00

Summary:		
Fixed cost	$19,800.00	
Variable cost (900 direct labor hours × $7.00 variable rate)	6,300.00	
Total cost at normal capacity	$26,100.00	
Factory overhead rate for Finishing Department at normal capacity ($26,100/900 hours)	$ 29.00	per direct labor hour

Required: Prepare a flexible budget for the Finishing Department at the 80%, 90%, 100%, and 110% rated capacity levels. Assume that fixed costs are not expected to change between the 80% and 110% levels of capacity.

E17-9 Overhead Analysis; Report to Supervisor. The cost and operating data on December factory overhead for Department 12 are as follow:

	Budgeted Factory Overhead	Actual Factory Overhead
Variable departmental overhead:		
Supplies	$ 2,000	$ 2,300
Repairs and maintenance	800	900
Indirect labor	4,000	4,300
Power and light	1,200	1,400
Heat	400	500
Subtotal	$ 8,400	$ 9,400
Fixed departmental overhead:		
Building expense	$ 800	$ 840
Depreciation—machinery	2,400	2,400
Property tax and insurance	400	420
Subtotal	$ 3,600	$ 3,660
Total	$12,000	$13,060
Operating data:		
Normal capacity hours	8,000	
Factory overhead rate per hour	$ 1.50	
Actual hours		8,800

Required: Prepare a departmental report for the supervisor of Department 12 that shows the departmental spending variance for each item of factory overhead and includes a single idle capacity variance.

E17-10 Variance Report to Responsible Management. The controller of Flatbush Corporation has asked you to prepare a factory overhead variance report for the Finishing Department on an item by item of cost basis. You have been supplied with the following information:

	Budgeted Cost	Actual Cost
Variable costs:		
Indirect labor	$70,000	$70,000
Payroll taxes	61,500	60,000
Factory supplies	27,000	28,000
Electric utility	12,000	12,000
Gas utility	6,000	6,100
Water utility	1,500	1,500
Machinery repairs	10,000	10,000
Maintenance	21,000	15,000
Overtime premium	9,000	9,000

	Budgeted Cost	Actual Cost
Fixed costs:		
Supervision	$48,000	$48,000
Indirect labor	36,000	36,000
Vacation pay	40,000	40,500
Payroll taxes	8,000	8,000
Employee insurance	12,000	12,250
Factory supplies	19,000	19,000
Electric utility	15,000	15,000
Gas utility	9,000	9,000
Water utility	5,000	5,000
Maintenance	23,000	23,000
Machinery depreciation	50,000	50,000
Building rent	15,000	15,000
Property taxes	12,000	13,000
Property insurance	15,000	15,250

Factory overhead is charged to production in the Finishing Department on the basis of direct labor hours. Factory overhead for the period was budgeted at 10,000 hours, but 9,600 hours were actually worked.

Required: Prepare a variance report showing the spending variance for each item of factory overhead. Compute and include a single idle capacity variance in the report.

Problems

P17-1 Variance Analysis in Producing and Service Departments. Wright Products Inc. wants greater cost consciousness and cost responsibility among its departmental supervisors. Service department costs have been allocated to the producing departments using predetermined rates for some time. Now management asks the Cost Department, with the cooperation of the departmental supervisors, not only to prepare departmental budgets but also to give the supervisors monthly reports for cost control information.

The company operates three producing departments, A, B, and C, and two service departments, Repairs and Maintenance, and Utilities. For the year 19A, the Cost Department prepared the following departmental factory overhead budgets and determined the factory overhead rates based on direct labor hours:

	Producing Departments			Service Departments	
	A	B	C	Repairs and Maintenance	Utilities
Total budgeted expense	$52,000	$52,450	$41,900	$56,000	$49,000
Allocation of service department cost:					
Utilities (based on kilowatt-hours)	14,000	15,750	12,250	7,000	(49,000)
Repairs and maintenance (based on labor hours)	18,000	27,900	17,100	(63,000)	
Total	$84,000	$96,100	$71,250	0	0
Bases:					
Kilowatt-hours (KWH)	40,000	45,000	35,000	20,000	
Direct labor hours (DLH)	20,000	31,000	19,000		
Service department allocation rates				$ .90 per DLH	$ .35 per KWH
Departmental overhead rates	$ 4.20 per DLH	$ 3.10 per DLH	$ 3.75 per DLH		

Actual cost and operating data before allocation of service department costs at the end of the budget period are:

	Producing Departments			Service Departments	
	A	B	C	Repairs and Maintenance	Utilities
Total actual expense	$56,020	$52,850	$42,580	$56,320	$50,040
Operating data:					
Direct labor hours	20,480	29,850	20,100		
Kilowatt-hours	39,300	46,200	35,800	18,950	

Required:

(1) Compute the amount of factory overhead applied for each of the three producing departments.

(2) Compute the amount of over- or underapplied factory overhead for each of the three producing departments. To determine actual overhead in the producing departments, charge service department costs on the basis of actual kilowatt-hours and actual labor hours multiplied by the predetermined billing rate.

(3) Compute the total variance for each of the two service departments.

P17-2 Billing Rates; Variance Analysis in Producing and Service Departments. Perdido Tool Co. has two producing departments, Planers and Radial Drills, and two service departments, Maintenance and Utilities. Service department costs are allocated to producing departments by the direct method. The following data were collected:

	Producing Departments		Service Departments	
	Planers	Radial Drills	Maintenance	Utilities
Estimated data for 19A:				
Fixed overhead	$18,000	$15,000	$ 6,000	$ 4,800
Variable overhead	15,000	9,000	4,500	3,600
Total	$33,000	$24,000	$10,500	$ 8,400
Direct labor hours	12,000	7,500		
Maintenance hours	2,500	1,000	3,500	
Kilowatt-hours	45,000	25,000		70,000
Actual data for January 19A:				
Fixed overhead	$ 1,500	$ 1,250	$ 500	$ 400
Variable overhead	1,620	1,050	670	310
Total	$ 3,120	$ 2,300	$ 1,170	$ 710
Direct labor hours	1,020	680		
Maintenance hours	320	80	400	
Kilowatt-hours	4,000	2,000		6,000

Required:

(1) Compute the billing rate for each of the two service departments.

(2) Calculate the total predetermined factory overhead for each of the two producing departments and their departmental factory overhead rates based on direct labor hours. Service department costs are to be distributed on the basis of the billing rates calculated in requirement 1. (Carry all computations to three decimal places.)

(3) Prepare an analysis of the over- or underapplied factory overhead of each of the two producing departments for January, including the spending and idle capacity variances. Service department costs are to be charged on the basis of actual hours (maintenance or kilowatt) multiplied by the billing rate. This method treats these costs as being wholly variable.

(4) Prepare a calculation and analysis of the over- or underapplied factory overhead in each of the two service departments, including the spending and idle capacity variances. (Round off all amounts to four decimal places.)

(5) Prepare a reconciliation of the total variances.

P17-3 Budget Allowance; Variance Analysis in Producing and Service Departments. The controller of Cole Corporation prepared the following forecast income statement for the year:

		Amount	Unit
Sales (60,000 units)		$600,000	$10.00
Cost of goods sold (Schedule 1)		384,000	6.40
Gross profit		$216,000	$ 3.60
Commercial expenses:			
Marketing expense	$80,000		
Administrative expense	70,000	150,000	2.50
Income before income tax		$ 66,000	$ 1.10
Schedule 1—Estimated cost of goods sold:			
Direct materials		$102,000	$ 1.70
Direct labor		162,000	2.70
Factory overhead		120,000	2.00
Total		$384,000	$ 6.40

The product's manufacturing processes require two producing departments, which make use of the services of the Maintenance Department and the Janitorial Department. To charge the products moving through the two departments, the cost accountant has prepared an overhead distribution sheet and calculated predetermined factory overhead rates as follows:

	Producing Departments		Service Departments	
	Machining	Assembly	Maintenance	Janitorial
Production units	60,000	60,000		
Direct labor hours	15,000	12,000		
Direct labor cost	$90,000	$72,000		
Factory overhead:				
Variable overhead	$27,000	$22,800	$ 5,100	$2,700
Fixed overhead	17,520	34,230	8,400	7,200
			$13,500	$9,900
Share of Maintenance cost	7,500	6,000	(13,500)	
Share of Janitorial cost	1,980	2,970		(4,950)
Share of Janitorial cost charged to marketing and administrative expenses				(4,950)
Total factory overhead	$54,000	$66,000	0	0
Factory overhead rates (based on direct labor hours)	$ 3.60	$ 5.50		

Actual hours and costs at the end of the month are as follow:

	Producing Departments		Service Departments	
	Machining	Assembly	Maintenance	Janitorial
Hours worked	1,340	1,030		
Actual factory overhead:				
Variable overhead	$2,700	$2,240	$650	$440
Fixed overhead	1,500	3,000	700	600

Maintenance Department cost was allocated to the two producing departments on the basis of actual direct labor hours worked. Janitorial Department cost was prorated 50% to the factory producing departments and 50% to marketing and administrative expense. The Machining Department and the Assembly Department shared the factory allocation of Janitorial Department cost on a 40:60 basis, respectively. For January, the Planning Department scheduled 5,000 units of product to be completed. At the end of the month, sales and production achieved the following results:

Sales	4,900 units
Production—completed in both departments	5,200 units

Required:

(1) Compute the budget allowance for each of the two producing departments for January, based on (a) scheduled production hours and (b) actual production hours.

(2) Compute the spending and idle capacity variances for each of the two producing departments, based on actual production hours.

(3) Compute the spending variance for each of the two service departments. (Round all amounts to three decimal places.)

P17-4 Flexible Budget. The controller of Oakhill Corporation decided to prepare a flexible factory overhead budget ranging from 80% to 100% of capacity for the next year, with 50,000 hours as the 100% level. For costs of a semivariable nature, the fixed amount and the variable rate are determined by the high and low points method. The direct labor rate is $7.50 per hour. Additional data for factory overhead are as follow:

Annual fixed costs:	
Depreciation	$ 9,000
Insurance	1,500
Maintenance cost (including payroll taxes and fringe benefits)	24,000
Property tax	1,500
Supervisory staff (including payroll taxes and fringe benefits)	36,000
Variable costs:	
Shop supplies	$.10 per direct labor hour
Indirect labor (excluding inspection)	$.45 per direct labor hour
Payroll taxes and fringe benefits	18% of total labor cost, i.e., direct plus indirect

Semi-variable costs (from previous five years):

Year	Direct Labor Hours	Power and Light	Inspection (Including Payroll Taxes and Fringe Benefits)	Other Semivariable Expenses
19A	44,000	$1,500	$ 9,200	$8,000
19B	40,000	1,400	9,000	7,400
19C	45,000	1,600	9,200	8,200
19D	49,000	1,650	10,000	8,800
19E	50,000	1,700	10,200	8,900

Required: Prepare a flexible factory overhead budget ranging from 80% to 100% of capacity, in 10% intervals.

P17-5 Flexible Budget and Variance Analysis. A one-month budget allowance of factory overhead for the Fabrication Department of the El Toro Company is as follows:

Activity Base: 1,800 machine hours per month at normal capacity, which is 90% of rated capacity

Category of Cost	Fixed Cost	Variable Rate per Machine Hour
Indirect labor	$ 2,000.00	$2.15
Supervision	2,000.00	
Factory supplies	600.00	.75
Power	450.00	.50
Rework operations	.00	.30
Payroll taxes	1,000.00	.35
Repair and maintenance	1,400.00	.25
Property insurance	750.00	
Property taxes	500.00	
Vacation pay	1,700.00	
Employee pension costs	1,000.00	
Employee health plan	800.00	
Machinery depreciation	3,500.00	
Water and heat	400.00	
Building occupancy	900.00	
General factory	1,000.00	$ .20
Total cost	$18,000.00	$4.50

Summary:	
Fixed cost	$18,000.00
Variable cost (1,800 machine hours × $4.50 variable rate)	8,100.00
Total cost at normal capacity	$26,100.00
Factory overhead rate for Fabrication Department at normal capacity ($26,100/1,800 hours)	$14.50 per machine hour

Actual production for the month of February required 1,860 machine hours. Actual costs for February are as follow:

Indirect labor	$ 6,125.00
Supervision	2,000.00
Factory supplies	2,154.00
Power	1,420.50
Rework operations	1,088.25
Payroll taxes	1,675.50
Repair and maintenance	1,525.75
Property insurance	785.00
Property taxes	490.00
Vacation pay	1,700.00
Employee pension costs	1,000.00
Employee health plan	845.00
Machinery depreciation	3,500.00
Water and heat	465.00
Building occupancy	900.00
General factory	1,385.00
Total cost for August	$27,059.00

Required:

(1) Prepare a flexible budget for the Fabrication Department of the El Toro Company at the 80%, 90%, 100%, and 110% levels of the rated capacity. Assume that fixed costs are not expected to change between the 80% and 110% levels of capacity.

(2) Prepare a variance report for February, assuming that factory overhead was charged to production on the basis of the predetermined rate for normal capacity (90% of rated capacity). The variance report should show the spending variance for each item of departmental cost and a single figure for the department's idle capacity variance.

P17-6 Flexible Budget and Variance Analysis. A one-month budget allowance of factory overhead for the Assembly Department of the Rosebud Company is as follows:

Activity Base: 1,350 direct labor hours per month at normal capacity, which is 90% of rated capacity

Category of Cost	Fixed Cost	Variable Rate per Machine Hour
Indirect labor	$ 2,500.00	$2.25
Supervision	1,800.00	
Factory supplies	500.00	1.20
Power	150.00	.35
Rework operations	600.00	.50
Payroll taxes	1,000.00	.35
Repair and maintenance	350.00	.15
Property insurance	150.00	
Property taxes	200.00	
Vacation pay	1,800.00	
Employee pension costs	1,200.00	
Employee health plan	500.00	
Machinery depreciation	450.00	
Water and heat	400.00	
Building occupancy	900.00	
General factory	1,000.00	.20
Total cost	$13,500.00	$5.00

Summary:	
Fixed cost	$13,500.00
Variable cost (1,350 direct labor hours × $5.00 variable rate)	6,750.00
Total cost at normal capacity	$20,250.00
Factory overhead rate for Assembly Department at normal capacity ($20,250/1,350 hours)	$15.00 per direct labor hour

Actual production for the month of August required 1,290 direct labor hours. Actual costs for August are as follow:

Indirect labor	$ 5,750.00
Supervision	1,800.00
Factory supplies	2,154.00
Power	615.00
Rework operations	1,088.25
Payroll taxes	1,451.50
Repair and maintenance	1,525.75
Property insurance	165.00
Property taxes	210.50
Vacation pay	2,200.00
Employee pension costs	1,200.00
Employee health plan	500.00
Machinery depreciation	450.00
Water and heat	465.00
Building occupancy	900.00
General factory	1,385.00
Total cost for August	$21,860.00

Required:

(1) Prepare a flexible budget for the Assembly Department of the Rosebud Company at the 80%, 90%, 100%, and 110% levels of the rated capacity. Assume that fixed costs are not expected to change between the 80% and 110% levels of capacity.

(2) Prepare a variance report for August, assuming that factory overhead was charged to production on the basis of the predetermined rate for normal capacity (i.e., 90% of rated capacity). The variance report should show the spending variance for each item of departmental cost and a single figure for the department's idle capacity variance.

Cases

C17-1 Cost Responsibility and the Attitude of Managers. Declining profits compelled the management of the Wilmington Corporation to approach employees to work for production economy and increased productivity. Production managers were promised a monetary incentive based on cost reductions.

The production managers responded with (1) an increased rate of production; (2) a higher rejection rate for quantities of raw materials and parts received from the storeroom; (3) a postponement of repairs and maintenance work; and (4) a reliance on quick emergency repairs to avoid breakdowns.

The repair and maintenance policy is causing serious conflicts. The maintenance supervisor argues that the postponement of certain repairs in the short run and the use of emergency repair techniques will result in increased costs later and, in some instances, could reduce the life of machines as well as machine safety.

Even more serious is the growing bitterness caused by pressures placed on the maintenance managers by individual production managers to obtain service. Also, in several instances, some production departments, whose production has been halted due to machine breakdown, have had to wait while another production department, with an aggressive manager, has received repair service on machines not needed in the current production run. Furthermore, the demand for immediate service sometimes results in substandard repair work.

The production departments are charged with the actual cost of the repairs. A record of the repair work conducted in individual production departments is prepared by the maintenance managers. This record, when completed in the Accounting Department, shows the repair hours, the hourly rate of the maintenance worker, the maintenance overhead charge, and the cost of any parts. The record serves as the basis for the charges to production departments. Production managers have complained about the charging system, claiming that charges depend on which maintenance worker does the work (hourly rate and efficiency), when the work is done (the production department is charged for the overtime premium), and how careful the worker is in recording the time on the job.

Required:

(1) Identify and briefly explain the motivational factors that can cause friction between the production and maintenance managers.

(2) Develop a plan that revises the system employed to charge production departments for repair costs, so that the production departments' complaints are eliminated or reduced. (ICMA adapted)

C17-2 Performance Evaluation and Dysfunctional Behavior. The Marcheck Corporation, whose budget year-end is June 30, recently suffered a partial shutdown of operations. An investigation of the situation revealed the following chain of events:

- June 1—C. Valquez, the manager of the Fabricating Department, submitted a purchase requisition for 10,000 units of Part 88 at an expected cost of $18 per unit. The requisition was received three weeks prior to the expected usage date (company policy requires that all materials not kept in inventory be ordered at least two weeks in advance). H. Winston, the manager of the Purchasing Department, immediately placed a purchase order with the Albright Corporation for the units at the budget price. Albright Corporation promised delivery of the units ordered within 10 days. Although Winston had never used Albright Corporation as a supplier before, it was the only supplier offering the units at the budgeted price.
- June 10—The units had not yet arrived, so Winston contacted Albright Corporation and was informed that the goods were in transit and would be delivered within the next 3 days.
- June 13—The units had still not arrived, and Winston's inquiry resulted only in another promise of imminent delivery. Concerned with the delay, Winston contacted Valquez and explained the situation. Winston told Valquez that another supplier could provide the units with guaranteed delivery by June 21, but the units would cost $20 each and the Marcheck Corporation would have to pay $300 for air freight charges. Valquez replied that she would prefer not to reorder the part because the price was above her budgeted amount and any unfavorable variance would cause her to lose her annual bonus. Winston stated that, normally, his department would be able to cover the added cost of the air-freight, because the Purchasing Department had an annual allotment for additional freight costs. At this point, however, this amount had been used up and any additional charges would result in Winston losing his annual bonus.

  Valquez decided to continue to hope that the part would arrive on time and, if not, she had other work to occupy half of her employees; however, the other half would have to be laid off for at least two weeks. Valquez informed J. Dixon, manager of the Assembly Department, of this possible disruption. Dixon expressed concern over the possible slowdown because there was insufficient time to reschedule work and assemblers were too difficult to hire and train to justify a short-term layoff in his department.
- June 22—After repeated inquiries by Winston, the part had still not arrived. Valquez had to lay off half of her employees (thereby saving the company $1,000 in labor costs during this budget period) and put the others to work on another project that did not require Part 88.
- July 2—Winston resigned today as a result of not receiving his annual bonus. An examination of the actual results for the Purchasing Department showed the following charges:
  - $5,000 representing the cost of idle time in the Assembly Department ($6,000) because no work was available after the Machining Department had changed production over to units that did not require assembly. The $6,000 was reduced by the $1,000 savings resulting from the layoffs in the Machining Department.
  - $1,500 representing the cost that the Personnel Department will incur to hire and train machinists to replace those who were laid off in the Machining Department and did not return.
  - $20,000 representing the foregone profit on Marcheck Corporation sales lost due to the fact that the Assembly Department was unable to get the required units from the Machining Department.

Both Valquez and Dixon received their annual bonuses, as their departments had been able to keep their costs under the original budgeted costs for the period.

Required:

(1) Evaluate the company's methods of allocating the following costs, including your recommendations and justifications for any alternative allocations:

(a) The $6,000 cost of idle time in the Assembly Department.
(b) The $1,000 savings in costs due to layoffs in the Machining Department.
(c) The $1,500 cost of training in the Machining Department.
(d) The $20,000 lost profit on sales resulting from Assembly Department downtime.

(2) Evaluate the company's overall approach to the use of budgets and justify any recommended changes.

(SMAC adapted)

C17-3 Improving Reports. Denny Daniels is production manager of the Alumalloy Division of WRT Inc. Alumalloy has limited contact with outside customers and has no sales staff. Most of its customers are other divisions of WRT. All sales and purchases with outside customers are handled by other corporate divisions. Therefore, Alumalloy is treated as a cost center for reporting and evaluation purposes rather than as a revenue or profit center.

Daniels perceives the Accounting Department as a historical number-generating process that provides little useful information for conducting his job. Consequently, the entire accounting process is perceived as a negative motivational device that does not reflect how hard or how effectively he works as a production manager. Daniels tried to discuss these perceptions and concerns with Jana Scott, the controller for the Alumalloy Division. Daniels told Scott, "I think the cost report is misleading. I know I've had better production over a number of operating periods, but the cost report still says I have excessive costs. Look, I'm not an accountant. I'm a production manager. I know how to get a good-quality product out. Over a number of years, I've even cut the raw materials used to do it. But the cost report doesn't show any of this. Basically, it's always negative, no matter what I do. There's no way you can win with accounting or the people at corporate headquarters who use those reports."

Scott gave Daniels little consolation. Scott stated that the accounting system and the cost reports generated by headquarters are almost impossible for an individual to change. "Although these accounting reports are pretty much the basis for evaluating the efficiency of your division and they are the means corporate headquarters uses to determine whether you have done the job they want, you shouldn't worry too much. You haven't been fired yet! Besides, these cost reports have been used by WRT for the last 25 years."

Daniels perceived from talking to the production manager of the Zinc Division that most of what Scott said was probably true. However, some minor cost reporting changes for Zinc had been agreed to. He also knew from the trade grapevine that the turnover of production managers was considered high at WRT, even though relatively few were fired. Most seemed to end up quitting, usually in disgust, because of beliefs that they were not being evaluated fairly. Typical comments of production managers who have left WRT are:

(a) "Corporate headquarters doesn't really listen to us. All they consider are those misleading cost reports. They don't want them changed and they don't want any supplemental information."
(b) "The accountants may be quick with numbers but they don't know anything about production. As it was, I either had to ignore the cost reports entirely or pretend they were important even though they didn't tell how good a job I had done. No matter what they say about not firing people, negative reports mean negative evaluations. I'm better off working for another company."

A recent copy of the cost report prepared by corporate headquarters for the Alumalloy Division is as follows. Daniels does not like this report because he believes it fails to reflect the division's operations properly, thereby resulting in an unfair evaluation of performance.

Alumalloy Division
Cost Report for April, 19A
($000s omitted)

	Master Budget	Actual Cost	Excess Cost
Aluminum	$ 400	$ 437	$ 37
Labor	560	540	(20)
Overhead	100	134	34
Total	$1,060	$1,111	$ 51

Required:

(1) What are Daniel's perceptions of (a) Scott, the controller; (b) corporate headquarters; (c) the cost report; and (d) himself as a production manager.
(2) Discuss how Daniel's perceptions affect his behavior and probable performance as a production manager and employee of WRT.
(3) Identify and explain changes that could be made in the cost reports that would make the information more meaningful and less threatening to the production managers.

(ICMA adapted)

C17-4 Reviewing the Reporting Structure. McCumber Company employs a computer-based data processing system for maintaining all company records. The present system was developed in stages over the last five years and has been fully operational for the last 24 months.

When the system was being designed, all department heads were asked to specify the types of information and reports they would need for planning and controlling operations. The Systems Department attempted to meet the specifications of each department head. Company management specified that certain other reports be prepared for department heads. During the five years of systems development and operations, there have been changes in the department head positions due to attrition and promotions. New department heads have often requested additional reports according to their specifications; the Systems Department has complied with all these requests. Consequently, the data processing system generates a large quantity of reports each period. Occasionally a report has been discontinued at the request of a department head, but only if it was not a standard report required by executive management.

Company management became concerned about the quality of information being produced by the system, and the Internal Audit Department was asked to evaluate the effectiveness of these reports. The audit staff noted the following reactions to this information overload:

(a) Many department heads would not act on certain reports during periods of peak activity. The department head would let these reports accumulate with the hope of catching up during a subsequent lull.
(b) Some department heads had so many reports that they did not act at all on the information or made incorrect decisions because of misuse of the information.
(c) Frequently, action required by the nature of the report data was not taken until the department head was reminded by someone who needed the decision. These department heads did not appear to have developed a priority system for acting on the information produced by the data processing system.
(d) Department heads often would develop the information they needed from alternative, independent sources, rather than utilize the reports generated by the data processing system. This was often easier than trying to search among the reports for the needed data.

Required:

(1) Explain whether each of the observed reactions is a functional or dysfunctional behavioral response.
(2) Recommend procedures that the company could employ to eliminate any dysfunctional behavior and to prevent its recurrence. (ICMA adapted)

CHAPTER 18

Standard Costing: Setting Standards and Analyzing Variances

Learning Objectives

After studying this chapter, you will be able to:

1. Define standard cost and explain how standards are used.
2. Explain how standards are set.
3. Compute the standard cost of actual or equivalent units produced.
4. Compute standard cost variances for materials, labor, and factory overhead.
5. Define standard cost variances and state how their causes can be determined.
6. Explain how tolerance limits are set and used for variance control.
7. List problems that can result from overemphasizing variance reports for cost control and employee evaluation.

A **standard cost** is the predetermined cost of manufacturing a single unit or a specific quantity of product during a specific period. It is the planned cost of a product under current and/or anticipated operating conditions. A standard cost has two components: a physical standard (a standard quantity of inputs per unit of output) and a price standard (a standard cost or rate per unit of input).

A standard is like a norm. Whatever is considered normal can generally be accepted as standard. For example, if a score of 72 is the standard for a golf course, a golfer's score is judged on the basis of this standard. In industry, the standards for making a desk, assembling a microcomputer, refining crude oil, or manufacturing automobiles often are based on carefully determined quantitative and qualitative measurements and engineering methods. A standard should be thought of as a norm for production inputs, such as units of materials, hours of labor, and percentage of plant capacity used.

To provide a foundation for you to understand and effectively utilize a standard cost system, this chapter begins by discussing the usefulness of standard costs and the setting of standards. This foundation is followed by an explanation and illustration of the computation of standard cost variances. The chapter concludes with a discussion on the use of standard cost variances for cost control. Incorporating standards into the accounting records is discussed in Chapter 19.

Usefulness of Standard Costs

A standard cost system can be used in connection with either process or job order cost accumulation. Standard costing is most readily adaptable to manufacturing environments in which production technology is relatively stable and the products manufactured are homogeneous within the cost accumulation unit. The cost accumulation unit can be the department, cost center, or the job. It is difficult to establish standards if manufacturing technology changes rapidly or if each product manufactured is custom designed to meet a customer's unique specifications. Consequently, standard costing typically is found in firms that use process cost accumulation (for example, manufacturers of petroleum and chemical products, building supplies, steel, and soft drinks), and in firms that use job order cost accumulation in which homogeneous units are batch produced on each job (for example, manufacturers of radios and televisions, furniture, paper products, and processed foods).

Standard cost systems aid in planning and controlling operations and in providing insights into the probable impact of managerial decisions on costs and profits. Standard costs are used for:

1. Establishing budgets.
2. Controlling costs by motivating employees and measuring operating efficiencies.
3. Simplifying costing procedures and expediting cost reports.
4. Assigning costs to materials, work in process, and finished goods inventories.
5. Forming the basis for establishing contract bids and for setting sales prices.

Standards are quite useful in budget preparation. With standard costs, the preparation of budgets for any volume and mix of products is more reliably and speedily accomplished. Reliability is enhanced because the standards are based on detailed analyses of the production processes. The time required to prepare the operating budget is reduced because production requirements already are documented for each product.

The effectiveness of cost control depends on management's thorough understanding of both the processes that drive cost and the motivation of the personnel who control those processes. Typically, standards are used to provide performance goals for employees and as a basis for evaluating actual results much the same way as flexible budgets are used in responsibility accounting and reporting systems (Chapter 17). As results are made available through standard cost variance reports, executives and operating managers become more cost conscious. This cost consciousness tends to encourage economies in all phases of a business. Although more time and care are taken in developing standards than are taken to prepare budgets, excessive reliance on standards as a motivational tool and as a basis for evaluating actual performance can result in dysfunctional employee behavior the same way excessive reliance on variance reports generated in a responsibility accounting and reporting system causes problems (see the section on Dysfunctional Behavior by Managers in Chapter 17).

The use of standard costs simplifies costing by reducing clerical labor. A complete standard cost system usually is accompanied by standardization of productive operations. Production or manufacturing orders, which call for standard quantities of production and specific labor operations, and materials requisitions, labor time tickets, and operation schedules can be prepared in advance of production, and standard costs can be compiled. As orders for a part are placed into the shop, previously established standards are used to determine input quantities, production processes, and costs that will apply. As the production process becomes more standardized, clerical effort declines. Reports can be systematized to present complete information regarding standards, actual costs, and variances.

Although some companies that use standard costs for planning and control do not record inventories at standard cost, the incorporation of standard costs into the accounting records increases efficiency and accuracy in clerical work there, too. A complete standard cost file, detailed by parts and operations, simplifies assigning costs to materials, work in process, and finished goods inventories. Inventory costs are easily determined by multiplying the quantities of each product in inventory by the standard unit cost and then adding the total cost for each product. The use of standard costs also tends to stabilize the influence of fluctuating input prices and capacity utilization on product costs. Incorporating standard costs into accounting records is discussed and illustrated in Chapter 19.

Determining contract bids and establishing sales prices are greatly enhanced by a standard cost system. The computation of costs to be incurred on a contract is made simpler and more reliable by using standard costs for the products to be produced or, if a unique product is to be produced, by using standard costs for the production operations that will be required. Standards are useful in establishing sales prices by providing reliable, up-to-date product cost information. When the market price of a product is not readily observable, as would be the case for new products or products that are differentiated from those of competitors, product cost typically is used as the starting point in establishing the sales price.

Setting Standards

Calculation of a standard cost is based on physical standards, two types of which, basic and current, are discussed often in the literature. A **basic standard** is a yardstick against which both expected and actual performances are compared. It is similar to an index number against which all subsequent results are measured. **Current standards** comprise three types:

1. The **expected actual standard** is a standard set for an expected level of activity and efficiency. It is a reasonably close estimate of actual results.
2. The **normal standard** is a standard set for a normal level of activity and efficiency, intended to represent challenging yet attainable results.
3. The **theoretical standard** is a standard set for an ideal or maximum level of activity and efficiency. Such standards constitute goals to be aimed for rather than performances that can currently be achieved.

Materials and labor costs are generally based on normal, current operating conditions, allowing for expected changes in prices and rates and reflecting the desired efficiency level. Factory overhead usually is based on normal operating conditions and volume at the desired efficiency level.

The success of a standard cost system depends on the reliability, accuracy, and acceptance of the standards. Extreme care should be taken to make sure that all factors are considered when establishing standards. In some cases, standards are set on the basis of an average of the actual results of previous periods. In other cases, standards are set by industrial engineers on the basis of careful studies of product components and production operations, using appropriate sampling techniques and including participation by those individuals whose performance is to be measured by the standards.

Standards should be set in an atmosphere that gives full consideration to the behavioral characteristics of managers and workers. In the long run, workers and plant management will tend to react negatively if they feel threatened by imposed standards. If they participate in setting standards, they can more easily understand the basis on which the standards are determined and more readily identify with the standard cost system. In addition, because of their practical knowledge and experience, the employees who perform the work can contribute significantly to improving standards. Under ideal conditions, employees accept standards as personal production goals.

Standards that are too loose or too tight generally tend to have a negative impact on worker motivation. If standards are too loose, workers tend to set their goals at this low level, thereby reducing productivity to a level below what is attainable. If the standard is too tight, workers quickly realize the impossibility of attaining the standards. They become frustrated and soon begin to ignore the standard. A reasonable standard that can be attained under normal working conditions is likely to contribute to the workers' motivation to achieve the designated level of activity or production.

Historically many accountants believed that the most effective standards were those set by industrial engineers with the participation of the operating managers who were to be evaluated. Because of the need for continuous improvement in today's highly competitive global markets, this approach to setting standards has been challenged.[1] Some accountants argue that such standards are based on known levels of productivity and fail to provide sufficient incentive for employees to improve beyond the standard.

One approach to remedying this problem is to tighten the standard each period to reflect a targeted level of improvement. The problem with this approach is in determining how much improvement to incorporate each period. If the amount of improvement designed into the standard is less than can be achieved, the incentive to improve is not as effective as it could be. If the amount of improvement designed into the standard is more than can be achieved, employees can become discouraged and discontinue efforts to improve. An alternative approach is to base the standard on the most recent actual performance and then expect favorable variances as acceptable performance. The problem with this approach is that the amount of favorable variance considered acceptable is unspecified. As a consequence, managers are not motivated to improve to any meaningful extent.

This system can also encourage gamesmanship by those being evaluated. A manager who can make a substantial improvement in one period may decide instead to make a small improvement in each of the next several periods in order to guarantee favorable evaluations in the future.

A third approach to setting standards attempts to identify a cost standard that the market will support. In this approach, a sales price that the market will accept for the product is first estimated; then, marketing costs and an acceptable level of profit are subtracted from the sales price to arrive at a target cost. While this approach has the virtue of providing an incentive to manufacture a product that will be competitive in the marketplace, the standard that results may not be achievable, thereby discouraging employees rather than providing an incentive. If the standard is never achieved, it could result in the manufacture of a product that is unprofitable.

The problem with all these approaches is excessive reliance on a standard to provide motivation for performance. In many companies, executive management uses standard cost variance reports as the primary basis for evaluating managerial performance. When a manager knows he or she is to be evaluated on the basis of

[1] See C. J. McNair, Richard L. Lynch, and Kelvin F. Cross, "Do Financial and Nonfinancial Performance Measures Have to Agree?" *Management Accounting*, Vol. 72, No. 5, p. 29; and Toshiro Hiromoto, "Another Hidden Edge—Japanese Management Accounting," *Harvard Business Review*, July–August, 1988, pp. 24–25.

performance relative to a standard, the manager tends to do whatever is necessary to meet the standard. Unfortunately, hitting the standard is not always the best thing for the company. Standards are short-term in scope, and they tend to foster suboptimal performance because they are static in nature.[2] Although standards can provide guidance and direction, they should not be regarded as absolute mandates of performance. Standards are created by people, who, no matter how well trained and how smart, do not know all there is to be known. Humans function in a world of uncertainty with incomplete information. Even those who have the best intentions make mistakes. As a consequence, a significant variance from standard should be viewed by executive management as a basis for discussion and not a measure of the quality of a subordinate's performance. If continuous improvement is to be achieved, managers must be encouraged to experiment with different ways of doing things without fear of being punished for not meeting the standard.

Mature products are better candidates for standards than are new products, for which innovative behavior may be necessary. A new product is likely to begin in a somewhat fluid form, with process standards evolving over time from experimentation and experience. If standards are mandated for new products, "managers introducing new products, ...who are evaluated on the basis of cost minimization and productivity, may not be as responsive to customer needs, will freeze the design specifications of the products prematurely in an attempt to standardize production, and may not pay sufficient attention to producing consistently high-quality products."[3]

Standards usually are computed for a 6- or 12-month period, although a longer period sometimes is used. Standards should be changed when underlying conditions change or when they no longer reflect the original concept. On the other hand, changing physical standards frequently can weaken their effectiveness and increase clerical details. Frequent changes in the physical standards create confusion and uncertainty. Nevertheless, physical standards should be continuously monitored and frequently reviewed to determine their appropriateness. In order to compete effectively in global markets, continual improvement in the standard is necessary.

Events, rather than time, are the factors that determine when standards should be revised. These events can be classified as internal or external. Internal events, such as technological advances, design revisions, method changes, labor pay rate changes, and changes in physical facilities, are to some degree controllable by management. In contrast, external events, such as price changes (including the impact of inflation), market trends, specific customer requirements, and changes in the competitive situation, are generally not controllable by management. Consequently, price standards and product configuration standards can require frequent change as controlling external events occur.[4]

Once standards are set, a standard cost card should be prepared for each product. The card shows the itemized cost of each kind of material and

---

[2] John Lessner, "Performance Measurement in a Just-in-Time Environment: Can Traditional Performance Measurements Still Be Used?" *Journal of Cost Management,* Vol. 3, No. 3, p. 23.

[3] Robert S. Kaplan, "Measuring Manufacturing Performance: A New Challenge for Managerial Accounting Research," *The Accounting Review,* Vol. 58, No. 4, p. 695.

[4] Some firms facing technological change experiment with the use of standards that are essentially very recent actual costs, or a rolling average of past actual costs. Such standards may be redetermined as often as every month. For some examples, see C. J. McNair, William Mosconi, and Thomas Norris, *Meeting the Technology Challenge: Cost Accounting in a JIT Environment* (Montvale, NJ: Institute of Management Accountants (formerly the National Association of Accountants), 1988).

component part, labor operation, and overhead cost for the product. A master standard cost card, such as the one illustrated in Figure 18-1 for the Wilton Manufacturing Corporation, gives the standard cost for a single unit of one of the company's products. The product in this illustration is called Paxel and requires manufacturing in three different departments. Parts are cut out of metal in the Cutting Department and molded out of plastic in the Molding Department. Parts created in the Cutting and Molding Departments are transferred to the Assembly Department where they are assembled along with parts purchased from outside vendors.

FIGURE 18-1 *Standard Cost Card*

WILTON MANUFACTURING CORPORATION

DATE OF STANDARD July 1, 19A — STANDARD COST CARD FOR PRODUCT Paxel

DIRECT MATERIALS					DEPARTMENT		**TOTAL COST**
PART	STANDARD QUANTITY	STANDARD UNIT PRICE		CUTTING	MOLDING	ASSEMBLY	
1-34	4	$ 6.25		$25.00			
1-71	6	3.75		22.50			
2-05	10	2.45			$24.50		
3-89	2	7.50				$15.00	$ 87.00
DIRECT LABOR							
OPERATION	STANDARD HOURS	STANDARD RATE PER HOUR					
1-11	3/4	$13.00		$ 9.75			
1-19	1/4	13.00		3.25			
2-14	1/2	10.00			$ 5.00		
3-25	1/3	12.00				$ 4.00	22.00
FACTORY OVERHEAD							
OPERATION	ALLOCATION BASIS	STANDARD QUANTITY	RATE				
1-11	Machine hours	1 1/2	$15.60	$23.40			
1-19	Machine hours	2 1/2	15.60	39.00			
2-14	Processing time	1 1/2	18.50		$27.75		
3-25	Labor hours	1/3	15.00			$ 5.00	95.15
TOTAL MANUFACTURING COST PER UNIT							**$204.15**

A master standard cost card can be a paper document or an electronic record, depending on the company's system. In either case, the master standard cost card for each product should be supported by individual records that indicate how the standards were determined.

Determining Standard Production

The preceding discussion deals with the determination of the standards per unit of production. To determine the standard allowed for each cost component, the standard quantity allowed per unit of product is multiplied by the number of equivalent units of product produced during the period. This determination must include consideration of the stage of completion of work in process inventories. Because in standard cost variance analysis the emphasis is on control, the production standard is computed for the current period of production only. For example, assume that there were 864 units of Paxel in process in the Assembly Department of the Wilton Manufacturing Corporation at the beginning of the month, one-half complete as to materials and one-third complete as to conversion cost (i.e., labor and factory overhead). During the month, 4,200 units were completed and transferred to finished goods inventory. There were 900 units in process at the end of the month, complete as to materials and two-thirds complete as to labor and factory overhead. The equivalent units of product for each cost element are determined as follows:

	Materials	Conversion Cost
Units completed and transferred out this period	4,200	4,200
Less all units in beginning inventory	864	864
Equivalent units started and completed this period	3,336	3,336
Add equivalent units required to complete beginning inventory this period	432	576
Add equivalent units in ending inventory	900	600
Equivalent units of production this period	4,668	4,512

Often, standards include an allowance for normal spoilage. In such a case, equivalent unit computations for standard costing are based on good units only. By this procedure, the cost of excess or abnormal spoilage becomes a part of the computed variances. However, in accordance with the principles of total quality management and the need for continuous improvement (discussed in Chapter 7), all spoilage should be considered abnormal and targeted for elimination. If spoilage is to be eliminated, the standards should not contain any allowance for spoilage. The cost of spoilage either would be included in the variance or separately computed and reported as a cost of quality. If management wants to compute and report the cost of spoilage separately, equivalent production computations must include both good units and spoiled units.[5]

Determining Standard Cost Variances

For each item of direct material, for each labor operation, and for factory overhead attributable to each department (cost center or activity), actual costs are measured against standard costs, resulting in differences. These differences are analyzed and identified as specific types of standard cost variances. If the actual cost exceeds the standard cost, the variance is referred to as "unfavorable,"

[5] Once computed, the cost of the spoiled units can be reported as a quality variance. Reporting spoilage as an unfavorable variance draws attention to the cause of the variance and provides an incentive for improvement. See Carole Cheatham, "Updating Standard Cost Systems," *Journal of Accountancy*, Vol. 170, No. 6, pp. 57–60.

because the excess has an unfavorable effect on income. Conversely, if the standard cost exceeds the actual cost, the variance is referred to as "favorable," because it has a favorable effect on income.

The analysis does not end with such labeling, however. A standard cost variance is a question, not an answer. To control cost, managers should determine the reasons for each significant variance by investigating the circumstances that caused it. Effective action can be taken only when the causes of cost variances are known. The responsibility and control of variances is more fully discussed later in this chapter.

Materials Standards and Variances

Two standards are developed for direct materials costs, a materials price standard and a materials quantity standard (sometimes referred to as a materials usage standard). Price standards permit (1) monitoring the performance of the purchasing department and detecting the influence of internal and external factors on materials cost and (2) measuring the effect of materials price increases or decreases on the company's profits. Determining the price or cost to be used as the standard is often difficult because materials prices are controlled more by external factors than by a company's management. Prices selected should reflect current market prices, and the standards should be revised at inventory dates or whenever there is a major change in the market price of any of the principal materials or parts. Typically, prices are determined at the beginning of the accounting period and used throughout the period. However, during periods of rapidly changing prices, it may be necessary to change the price standard frequently, especially if inventory is recorded in the accounting records at standard.

If the actual price paid is more or less than the standard price, a price variance occurs. Materials price variances can be recorded at the time materials are purchased (referred to as a **materials purchase price variance**) or at the time materials are issued to the factory (referred to as a **materials price usage variance**). To hold the purchasing department fully accountable for price variances at the date they occur, the variances should be recorded at the time of purchase. Otherwise, materials used in the current period may include price variances related to materials purchased in an earlier period, or price variances applicable to current period purchases may be inventoried. In either case, the materials price usage variance would be difficult to interpret because of the compounding effects of inventory changes. On the other hand, in a just-in-time inventory system, there is little if any distinction between the two alternatives because there is practically no materials inventory. In such a case, the timing and quantity of purchases and uses differ only trivially.

To illustrate the computation of a materials purchase price variance, assume that 10,000 units of Part 3-89 on the standard cost card for Paxel (Figure 18-1) are purchased at a unit price of $7.44. The materials purchase price variance is computed as follows:

	Quantity	×	Unit Cost	=	Amount
Actual quantity purchased..............	10,000		$7.44 actual		$74,400
Actual quantity purchased..............	10,000		7.50 standard		75,000
Materials purchase price variance ...	10,000		$ (.06)		$ (600) favorable

The $600 materials purchase price variance is favorable because the actual price is less than the standard price (the actual cost is $.06 per unit less than the standard). Alternatively, the materials price usage variance can be computed. For example, if 9,500 units of Part 3-89 are issued and used by production, the materials price usage variance is computed as follows:

	Quantity	×	Unit Cost	=	Amount
Actual quantity used........................	9,500		$7.44 actual		$70,680
Actual quantity used........................	9,500		7.50 standard		71,250
Materials price usage variance	9,500		$ (.06)		$ (570) favorable

The $600 favorable materials purchase price variance is $30 greater than the $570 favorable materials price usage variance. The reason for this difference is that 500 units of Part 3-89 purchased this period at a favorable variance of $.06 per unit (500 × $.06 = $30) were added to inventory and not used this period.

Because carrying inventory is costly, inventory build up can be reported as an unfavorable variance and inventory reduction as a favorable variance.[6] The variance is called the **materials inventory variance**, which is defined as the standard cost of the increase (or decrease) in materials inventory. The materials inventory variance for Part 3-89 is computed as follows:

	Quantity	×	Unit Cost	=	Amount
Actual quantity purchased...............	10,000		$7.50 standard		$75,000
Actual quantity used........................	9,500		7.50 standard		71,250
Materials inventory variance	500		7.50 standard		$ 3,750 unfavorable

The $3,750 materials inventory variance is unfavorable because the quantity of Part 3-89 in materials inventory has increased, thereby increasing the materials inventory carrying costs. Although the actual cost of carrying excess inventory is not reported by the materials inventory variance, the variance nevertheless provides a signal to executive management that inventory is not being minimized. Such a signal is particularly important for companies concerned about inventory build up and for companies employing just-in-time inventory systems.

Quantity or usage standards generally are developed from materials specifications prepared by the departments of engineering (mechanical, electrical, or chemical) or product design. In a small or medium-sized company, the superintendent or the departmental supervisors provide basic specifications regarding type, quantity, and quality of materials needed and operations to be performed. Quantity standards should be set after analysis of the most economical size, shape, and quality of the product and the use of various kinds and grades of materials.

The **materials quantity (or usage) variance** is computed by a comparison of the actual quantity of materials used with the standard quantity allowed, both measured at standard cost. The standard quantity allowed is determined by multiplying the quantity of materials that should be required to produce one unit of product (the standard quantity allowed per unit) by the actual number of units produced during the period. The units produced are the equivalent units of production for materials.

The computation of the materials quantity (or usage) variance can be illustrated with the 4,668 equivalent units of Paxel produced in the Assembly Department of Wilton Manufacturing Corporation during the period with respect

[6] Horace W. Harrell, "Materials Variance Analysis and JIT: A New Approach," *Management Accounting,* Vol 73, No. 11, pp. 33–38. The author also suggests that the same kind of inventory variance be computed and reported for finished goods inventory.

to material Part 3-89. The standard cost card calls for two units of Part 3-89 per unit of Paxel produced (Figure 18-1), so the standard quantity of material Part 3-89 allowed is 9,336 units (4,668 × 2). The materials quantity (or usage) variance for material Part 3-89 is computed as follows:

	Quantity	×	Unit Cost	=	Amount
Actual quantity used	9,500		$7.50 standard		$71,250
Standard quantity allowed	9,336		7.50 standard		70,020
Materials quantity variance	164		7.50 standard		$ 1,230 unfavorable

The $1,230 materials quantity (or usage) variance is unfavorable because the actual quantity used exceeds the standard quantity allowed by 164 units at a standard cost of $7.50 each.

Labor Standards and Variances

Two standards are also developed for direct labor costs, a rate (wage or cost) standard, and an efficiency (time or usage) standard. In many plants, the standard is based on rates established in collective bargaining agreements that define hourly wages, piece rates, and bonus differentials. Without a union contract, rates are based on the earnings rate as determined by agreement between the employee and the personnel department. Because rates generally are based on definite agreements, labor rate variances are infrequent. If they occur, they usually are due to unusual short-term conditions existing in the factory.

To assure fairness in rates paid for each operation performed, job rating has become a recognized procedure in industry. When a rate is revised or a change is authorized temporarily, it must be reported promptly to the payroll department to avoid delays, incorrect pay, and faulty reporting. Any difference between the standard and actual rates results in a **labor rate (wage or cost) variance**.

To illustrate the computation of the labor rate variance for Operation 3-25 on the standard cost card for Paxel (FIgure 18-1), assume that 1,632 hours are actually worked at an actual rate of $12.50 per hour to produce 4,512 equivalent units of Paxel. The labor rate variance is computed as follows:

	Hours	×	Rate	=	Amount
Actual hours worked	1,632		$12.50 actual		$20,400
Actual hours worked	1,632		12.00 standard		19,584
Labor rate variance	1,632		$ .50		$ 816 unfavorable

The labor rate variance of $816 is unfavorable because the actual rate exceeds the standard rate by $.50 per hour. The actual labor hours worked exclude nonproductive time, which is charged to factory overhead. Idle labor cost, to the extent that it is not included as a budgeted overhead item, ultimately becomes part of the controllable variance in the two-variance method or the spending variance in the three-variance method, which are discussed later in this chapter.

Determination of labor efficiency standards is a specialized function. Therefore, such standards are best established by industrial engineers, using time and motion studies. Standards should be set in accordance with scientific methods and accepted practices. They are based on actual performance of a worker or group of workers possessing average skill and using average effort while performing manual operations or working on machines operating under normal conditions. Time factors for acceptable levels of fatigue, personal needs, and delays beyond the control of the worker are studied and included in the standard. Such allowances are an integral part of the labor standard, but time required for setting up machines, waiting, or a breakdown is included in the factory overhead standard.

The establishment of time standards requires a detailed study of manufacturing operations. Standards based on operations should be understood by supervisors and used to enhance labor efficiency. However, time standards are of limited use "where operating times are strongly influenced by factors which cannot be standardized and controlled by management or where output from highly mechanized work is a function of machine time and speed rather than of labor hours worked."[7]

When a new product or process is started, the labor efficiency standard for costing and budget development should be based on the learning curve phenomenon (Chapter 11). The learning curve may well be, at least in part, an explanation of the labor efficiency variance associated with employees assigned to existing tasks that are new to them. Labor-related factory overhead costs and materials usage also might be affected.

The **labor efficiency variance** is computed at the end of any reporting period (day, week, or month) by comparing actual hours worked with standard hours allowed, both measured at the standard labor rate. The standard hours allowed is determined by multiplying the number of direct labor hours established or predetermined to produce one unit (the standard labor hours per unit) times the actual number of units produced during the period for which the variances are being computed. The units produced are the equivalent units of production for the labor cost being analyzed. The standard hours allowed for the 4,512 equivalent units of Paxel produced in the Assembly Department of Wilton Manufacturing Corporation during the month is 1,504 (4,512 equivalent units × ⅓ standard hour per unit).

The labor efficiency variance for Operation 3-25 is computed as follows:

	Hours	×	Rate	=	Amount
Actual hours worked	1,632		$12.00 standard		$19,584
Standard hours allowed	1,504		12.00 standard		18,048
Labor efficiency variance	128		12.00 standard		$ 1,536 unfavorable

The unfavorable labor efficiency variance of $1,536 is due to the use of 128 hours in excess of standard hours allowed (128 × $12 = $1,536).

In highly automated production systems, labor is often a very small portion of total product cost, in which case it may be impractical (or impossible) to trace labor directly to individual products produced during the period. In such cases, labor is likely to be treated as part of overhead, and no separate labor variances are computed.[8]

Factory Overhead Standards and Variances

Methods for establishing and using standard factory overhead rates are similar to the methods discussed in Chapters 12 through 14 for calculating predetermined factory overhead rates and applying them to jobs and products. First, a factory

[7] Walter B. McFarland, *Manpower Cost and Performance Measurement* (New York: Institute of Management Accountants (formerly National Association of Accountants), 1977), p. 60.

[8] Labor is combined with overhead at one of Hewlett-Packard's highly automated manufacturing facilities, as reported by Pauline R. Jaouen and Bruce R. Neumann, "Variance Analysis, Kanban and JIT: A Further Study," *Journal of Accountancy*, Vol. 163, No. 6, pp. 164–173.

overhead budget is prepared. This process involves estimating each item of factory overhead expected to be incurred within each department, cost center, or activity at some predetermined level of activity, typically normal capacity or expected actual capacity. Next, budgeted service department costs are allocated to producing departments on the basis of services that are expected to be provided. If the producing department has multiple cost centers or if activity-based costing is being used, these allocated service department costs in turn are allocated to cost centers within the department or to activities. When all budgeted factory overhead costs have been allocated, the standard factory overhead rate is determined by totaling the budgeted direct and indirect factory overhead for the department, cost center, or activity, and dividing the total by the predetermined level of the allocation base to be used (for example, direct labor hours, direct labor dollars, machine hours, direct materials cost, units of product, machine setups, quantity of materials, or number of requisitions).

The activity measure used as an allocation base can vary from department to department, depending on the nature of the production process in each department. There are two important considerations in the selection of an appropriate allocation base. First, in order that overhead is assigned to products on a meaningful basis, the activity chosen should be the one that reflects the primary source of overhead cost incurrence within the department. For example, if the production process is labor intensive in one department and capital intensive in another, direct labor hours or direct labor cost should be used in the first department and machine hours or processing time in the second. However, if only one product is produced within the department, the equivalent units of product is a reasonable allocation base, regardless of the nature of the production process. If one activity within a department does not appear to be closely related to most of the overhead costs within that department and if different products are produced within the department, multiple rates can improve costing accuracy. In such a case, a different overhead rate, based on a different activity, is used for each different cost pool within the department. Of course, the cost of developing and administering a system with multiple rates is high and should be weighed against the potential usefulness of more accurate product costing.

The second consideration in selecting an allocation base is that the activity measure chosen must be one that is capable of being accurately monitored on a per-unit or per-job basis within the existing data-gathering system or with an inexpensive modification to that system. If machine hours are selected, a data gathering system that can accurately record the number of machine hours incurred in the production of each unit or job must be in place. Because such data normally are not collected and because the installation and operation of a system that accurately collects such data are costly, manufacturers traditionally have used readily available measures such as direct labor hours or direct labor cost to allocate factory overhead to production. However, with the increasing use of robotics in manufacturing, direct labor is becoming a less significant cost.[9] Consequently, many manufacturing companies are being forced to redesign their cost systems and find new ways of allocating factory overhead.

The monthly flexible budget for the Assembly Department of Wilton Manufacturing Corporation is presented in Exhibit 18-1. The Wilton data are used to illustrate the computation of the standard overhead rate and the overhead variances.

---

[9] Allen H. Seed, III, "Cost Accounting in the Age of Robotics," *Management Accounting*, Vol. 66, No. 4, pp. 39–43.

EXHIBIT 18-1

Wilton Manufacturing Corporation
Assembly Department
Monthly Flexible Budget

Capacity	80%	90%	100%		
Standard production	3,840	4,320	4,800		
Direct labor hours (DLH)	1,280	1,440	1,600		
Variable factory overhead:					
Indirect labor	$ 640	$ 720	$ 800	$ .50	per DLH
Supplies	1,600	1,800	2,000	1.25	
Payroll taxes	960	1,080	1,200	.75	
Repair and maintenance	320	360	400	.25	
Utilities	320	360	400	.25	
Total variable overhead	$ 3,840	$ 4,320	$ 4,800	$ 3.00	per DLH
Fixed factory overhead:					
Supervision	$ 1,800	$ 1,800	$ 1,800		
Indirect labor	3,000	3,000	3,000		
Payroll taxes	1,300	1,300	1,300		
Vacation cost	5,000	5,000	5,000		
Machinery depreciation	1,000	1,000	1,000		
Building rent	800	800	800		
Property taxes	600	600	600		
Property insurance	500	500	500		
Repair and maintenance	1,500	1,500	1,500		
Utilities	1,200	1,200	1,200		
General factory	2,500	2,500	2,500		
Total fixed overhead	$19,200	$19,200	$19,200	$19,200	per month
Total factory overhead	$23,040	$23,520	$24,000		plus $3.00 per DLH

Assuming the 100 percent column represents normal capacity, the standard factory overhead rate for the Assembly Department is computed as follows:

$$\frac{\$24{,}000 \text{ total factory overhead}}{1{,}600 \text{ direct labor hours}} = \$15.00 \text{ per standard direct labor hour}$$

At the 100 percent capacity level, the Assembly Department standard factory overhead rate consists of:

$$\frac{\$\ 4{,}800 \text{ total variable factory overhead}}{1{,}600 \text{ direct labor hours}} = \$\ 3.00 \text{ variable factory overhead rate}$$

$$\frac{\$19{,}200 \text{ total fixed factory overhead}}{1{,}600 \text{ direct labor hours}} = 12.00 \text{ fixed factory overhead rate}$$

Total factory overhead rate at normal capacity .... $15.00 per standard direct labor hour

The standard cost of factory overhead chargeable to each job or process is determined by multiplying the standard amount of the allocation base allowed (direct labor hours in this illustration) by the predetermined standard factory overhead rate. The standard amount of the allocation base allowed is determined by multiplying the standard amount of the allocation base allowed per unit of product by the actual number of equivalent units of product produced during the period. At the end of each period, usually a month, the factory overhead actually incurred is compared with the standard cost of factory overhead chargeable to work in process for the period. The difference between these two amounts is referred to as the **overall (or net) factory overhead variance**. If the standard cost system is fully integrated into the regular accounting records (that is, if inventories are recorded in the accounts at standard), the overall factory overhead variance is equal to over- or underapplied factory overhead (see Chapter 19).

For example, assume that Paxel is the only product produced in the Assembly Department of Wilton Manufacturing Corporation during March and that the following data are available at the end of the month:

Actual factory overhead	$24,422
Standard hours allowed for actual production	
(4,512 units × ⅓ standard labor hour per unit)	1,504
Actual direct labor hours used	1,632

The overall factory overhead variance is computed as follows:

Actual factory overhead	$24,422
Factory overhead chargeable to work in process at standard	
(1,504 standard hours allowed × $15 standard overhead rate)	22,560
Overall (or net) factory overhead variance	$ 1,862 unfavorable

The overall factory overhead variance should be further analyzed to reveal the sources of the variance to provide a guide to management in determining its causes. Causes must be known before effective remedial action can be taken. The overall variance can be broken down for analysis in many different ways; however, the most frequently used approaches are to compute two or three factory overhead variances. Regardless of the method used, the sum of the computed variances equals the overall factory overhead variance.

Two-Variance Method. The two-variance method is the most frequently used method in actual practice, perhaps because it is the easiest to compute. The two variances are the controllable variance and the volume variance.

The **controllable variance** is the difference between the actual factory overhead incurred and the budget allowance based on the standard amount of the allocation base allowed for actual production. The budget allowance can be thought of as the amount of factory overhead that would have been budgeted at standard if the actual quantity produced had been known in advance—that is, total budgeted variable overhead at standard for actual production plus total budgeted fixed factory overhead.

The controllable variance is the responsibility of department managers to the extent that they control the costs to which the variance relates. It is composed of two elements: (1) the difference between actual variable factory overhead and standard variable factory overhead allowed and (2) the difference between actual fixed factory overhead and budgeted fixed factory overhead. Based on the data presented for the Assembly Department, the controllable variance is computed as follows:

Actual factory overhead		$24,422
Budget allowance based on standard hours allowed:		
Variable factory overhead (1,504 standard		
hours × $3.00 variable overhead rate)	$ 4,512	
Budgeted fixed factory overhead	19,200	23,712
Controllable variance		$ 710 unfavorable

The **volume variance** is the difference between the budget allowance based on the standard amount of the allocation base allowed for actual production and the standard factory overhead chargeable to work in process. It indicates the cost of capacity available but not utilized or not utilized efficiently and, therefore, may be the responsibility of the department manager (to the extent caused by variances in production efficiencies) or of executive management (to the extent caused by unexpected changes in sales demand). The volume variance for the Assembly Department is computed as follows:

Budget allowance based on standard hours allowed (from previous computation)...	$23,712
Factory overhead chargeable to work in process at standard (1,504 standard hours allowed × $15 standard overhead rate)...	22,560
Volume variance	$ 1,152 unfavorable

When standard cost rather than actual cost is charged to production, the volume variance can be thought of as the amount of over- or underapplied budgeted fixed factory overhead. It is the difference between budgeted fixed factory overhead and the amount of fixed factory overhead chargeable to production, based on the standard amount of the allocation base allowed for actual production. Consequently, the volume variance for the Assembly Department can be computed as follows:

Budgeted fixed factory overhead	$19,200
Fixed factory overhead chargeable to production, based on the standard hours allowed for units produced (1,504 standard hours allowed × $12 fixed overhead rate)	18,048
Volume variance	$ 1,152 unfavorable

Alternatively, it also can be computed as follows:

Number of labor hours used to compute the overhead rate (normal or budgeted capacity)	1,600
Standard hours allowed for actual production	1,504
Capacity hours not utilized, or not used efficiently	96
Fixed factory overhead rate	× $12
Volume variance	$ 1,152 unfavorable

The controllable variance plus the volume variance equals the overall factory overhead variance for the Assembly Department, as follows:

Controllable variance	$ 710 unfavorable
Volume variance	1,152 unfavorable
Overall factory overhead variance	$1,862 unfavorable

Three-Variance Method. One problem of the two-variance method is that it conceals the over- or under utilization of the variable input used as the factory overhead allocation base (direct labor hours, in the Assembly Department illustration). The three-variance method attempts to remedy this problem. The three-variance method requires the computation of the spending variance, the variable efficiency variance, and the volume variance. The **spending variance** computed in the three-variance method is the same as the spending variance computed in Chapter 17. It is the difference between the actual factory overhead incurred and a budget allowance based on the actual number of units of the overhead allocation base used during the period. For the Assembly Department of Wilton Manufacturing Corporation, the spending variance is computed as follows:

Actual factory overhead incurred		$24,422
Budget allowance based on actual hours:		
Variable overhead (1,632 actual labor hours × $3.00 variable overhead rate)	$ 4,896	
Budgeted fixed overhead	19,200	24,096
Spending variance		$ 326 unfavorable

The **variable efficiency variance** is the difference between the actual amount of the allocation base used and the standard amount of the allocation base allowed for actual production, multiplied by the variable factory overhead rate. It is the portion of the efficiency variance that measures the effect of the efficient or inefficient use of the input used as an allocation base on the cost of variable factory overhead. The variable efficiency variance is computed as follows:

Budget allowance based on actual hours worked (previously computed for the spending variance)	$24,096	
Budget allowance based on standard hours allowed (previously computed for the two-variance method)	23,712	
Variable efficiency variance	$ 384	unfavorable

Alternatively, it can be computed as follows:

Actual hours worked	1,632	
Standard hours allowed for actual units produced	1,504	
Excess of actual hours over standard hours allowed	128	
Variable factory overhead rate	× $3	
Variable efficiency variance	$ 384	unfavorable

The unfavorable spending variance of $326 plus the unfavorable variable efficiency variance of $384 equals the unfavorable controllable variance of $710 computed under the two-variance method.

The third variance is the volume variance, which is the same as in the two-variance method (a $1,152 unfavorable volume variance, as previously computed). As in the two-variance method, the sum of the three variances equals the overall factory overhead variance as follows:

Spending variance	$ 326	unfavorable
Variable efficiency variance	384	unfavorable
Volume variance	1,152	unfavorable
Overall factory overhead variance	$1,862	unfavorable

Other Methods. There are numerous other methods of breaking down the overall factory overhead variance for analysis. For example, any portion of the spending or controllable variance attributable to the difference between budgeted and actual fixed factory overhead can be isolated separately and labeled as the fixed spending variance. The balance of the spending variance is then labeled as the variable spending variance. It also is possible to break down the spending variance into price and quantity variances for each item of factory overhead cost (illustrated in Exhibit 18-4). The variance system chosen by management should be the one it finds most useful in identifying the causes of the overall factory overhead variance. However, as a practical matter, management must weigh the costs of alternative data gathering and reporting systems against their expected benefits. An alternative three-variance method and a four-variance method of computing factory overhead variances are discussed and illustrated in the appendix to this chapter.

Mix and Yield Variances

Establishing a standard product cost requires determining price and quantity standards. In many industries, particularly of the process type, materials mix and materials yield play significant parts in the final product cost, in cost reduction, and in profit improvement.

Materials specification standards generally are set up for various grades and types of materials. In most cases, specifications are based on laboratory or engineering tests. Comparative costs of various grades of materials are used to arrive at a satisfactory materials mix, and changes often are made when it seems possible to use less costly grades of materials or substitute materials. In addition, a substantial cost reduction is sometimes achieved through the improvement of the yield of good product units in the factory. At times, trade-offs may occur. For example, a cost saving resulting from use of a less costly grade of materials may result in a poorer yield. A variance analysis program identifying and evaluating the nature, magnitude, and causes of mix and yield variances is an aid to operating management.

Mix Variance

After the standard specification has been established, a variance representing the difference between the standard cost of formula materials and the standard cost of the materials actually used can be calculated. This variance is generally recognized as a **mix (or blend) variance**, which is the result of mixing basic materials in a ratio that differs from standard materials specifications. In a woolen mill, for instance, the standard proportions of the grades of wool for each yarn number are reflected in the standard blend cost. Any difference between the actual wool used and the standard blend results in a blend or mix variance.

Industries such as textiles, rubber, and chemicals, whose products must possess certain chemical or physical qualities, sometimes find it economical to apply different combinations of basic materials and still achieve a perfect product. In cotton fabrics, a change in the mix of cotton from different parts of the world may reduce cost and improve profits. In many cases, a new mix is accompanied by either a favorable or an unfavorable yield of the final product, making it difficult to judge correctly the origin of the variances. A favorable mix variance, for instance, may be offset by an unfavorable yield variance, or vice versa.

Yield Variance

Yield can be defined as the amount of product manufactured from a given amount of materials. The **yield variance** is the result of obtaining a yield different from the one expected from actual input.

In sugar refining, a normal loss of yield develops because, on the average, it takes approximately 102.5 pounds of sucrose, in raw sugar form, to produce 100 pounds of sucrose in refined sugars. Part of this sucrose emerges as blackstrap molasses, but a small percentage is completely lost.

In the canning industry, it is customary to estimate the expected yield of grades per ton of fruit purchased or delivered to the plant. The actual yield is compared to the one expected and is evaluated in terms of cost. If the actual yield deviates from predetermined percentages, cost and profit will differ.

Illustration of Mix and Yield Variances

To illustrate the calculation of mix and yield variances, assume that the Springmint Company, a manufacturer of chewing gum, uses a standard cost system. Standard product and cost specifications for 1,000 pounds of chewing gum are as follow:

Material	Quantity (Pounds)	×	Unit Cost per Pound	=	Amount	
A	800		$ .25		$ 200	
B	200		.40		80	
C	200		.10		20	
Input	1,200				$ 300	($300 ÷ 1,200 lbs. = $.25 per lb.*)
Output	1,000				$ 300	($300 ÷ 1,000 lbs. = $.30 per lb.)

* Weighted average.

The production of 1,000 pounds of chewing gum requires 1,200 pounds of raw materials. Hence the expected yield is 1,000 pounds divided by 1,200 pounds, or five-sixths of input.

Materials records indicate:

Material	Beginning Inventory (pounds)	Purchases in January		Materials Available (pounds)	Ending Inventory (pounds)	Materials Used (pounds)
		Pounds	Unit Price			
A	10,000	162,000	$.24	172,000	15,000	157,000
B	12,000	30,000	.42	42,000	4,000	38,000
C	15,000	32,000	.11	47,000	11,000	36,000

Actual finished production for January is 200,000 lbs.

The materials variances for January consist of (1) price variances, (2) a mix variance, (3) a yield variance, and (4) quantity variances. The company computes the materials price variances as follows, and recognizes these variances when the materials are purchased.

Material	Actual Quantity	Actual Unit Cost	Standard Unit Cost	Cost Variation	Price Variance	
A	162,000	$.24	$.25	$(.01)	$(1,620)	favorable
B	30,000	.42	.40	.02	600	unfavorable
C	32,000	.11	.10	.01	320	unfavorable
Net materials purchase price variance					$ (700)	favorable

The materials mix variance results from combining materials in a ratio different from the standard materials specifications. It is computed as follows:

Actual quantities at individual standard materials costs:

Material	Actual Quantity in Pounds	Standard Unit Cost		Total Cost	
A	157,000	$.25	=	$39,250	
B	38,000	.40	=	15,200	
C	36,000	.10	=	3,600	$58,050
	231,000				
Actual quantity at weighted average of standard materials cost for input (231,000 lbs. × $.25)					57,750*
Materials mix variance					$ 300 unfavorable

* This figure can also be determined by multiplying the standard (expected) output from actual input (192,500 lbs., or 5/6 of 231,000 lbs.) by $.30 standard materials cost for output.

The influence of individual raw materials on the total materials mix variance can be computed in the following manner:

Material	Actual Total Quantity in Actual Mix (pounds)	Actual Total Quantity in Standard Mix (pounds)	Quantity Variation (pounds)	Standard Unit Cost	Materials Mix Variance	
A	157,000	154,000*	3,000	$.25	$750	unfavorable
B	38,000	38,500**	(500)	.40	(200)	favorable
C	36,000	38,500***	(2,500)	.10	(250)	favorable
	231,000	231,000	0		$300	unfavorable

* (800 lbs. of A/1,200 lbs. total on standard cost card) × 231,000 lbs.

** (200 lbs. of B/1,200 lbs. total on standard cost card) × 231,000 lbs.

*** (200 lbs. of C/1,200 lbs. total on standard cost card) × 231,000 lbs.

The yield variance is computed as follows:

Actual input quantity at weighted average of standard materials cost for input	$ 57,750
Actual output quantity at standard materials cost for output (200,000 lbs. × $.30)	60,000*
Materials yield variance	$ (2,250) favorable

* This figure can also be determined by multiplying the input needed to produce 200,000 lbs. (240,000 lbs.) by $.25.

The yield variance occurred because the actual production of 200,000 pounds exceeded the expected output of 192,500 pounds (5/6 of 231,000 pounds) by 7,500 pounds. The yield difference multiplied by the standard weighted materials cost of $.30 per output pound equals the favorable yield variance of $2,250.

The materials quantity variance can be computed for each item as follows.

Material	Quantity (in pounds)	×	Standard Unit Cost	=	Amount	Materials Quantity Variance
A: Actual quantity used	157,000		$.25		$39,250	
A: Standard quantity allowed	160,000*		.25		40,000	$ (750) favorable
B: Actual quantity used	38,000		.40		$15,200	
B: Standard quantity allowed	40,000**		.40		16,000	(800) favorable
C: Actual quantity used	36,000		.10		$ 3,600	
C: Standard quantity allowed	40,000***		.10		4,000	(400) favorable
Total materials quantity variance						$(1,950) favorable

* An output of 200,000 lbs. should require an input of 240,000 lbs., with a standard yield of 1,000 lbs. output for each 1,200 lbs. input. Then the 240,000 lbs. × (800 lbs./1,200 lbs.) Material A portion of the formula = 160,000 lbs.

** The 240,000 lbs. × (200 lbs./1,200 lbs.) Material B portion of the formula = 40,000 lbs.

*** The 240,000 lbs. × (200 lbs./1,200 lbs.) Material C portion of the formula = 40,000 lbs.

The total materials quantity variance can also be determined by comparing actual quantities of input at standard prices, $58,050 ($39,250 + $15,200 + $3,600), to actual output quantity at the standard materials cost for output, $60,000 (200,000 lbs. × $.30) for a total favorable variance of $1,950. The mix and yield variances separate the materials quantity variance into two parts:

Materials mix variance	$ 300 unfavorable
Materials yield variance	(2,250) favorable
Materials quantity variance	$(1,950) favorable

Responsibility and Control of Variances

Management scrutinizes variances in an attempt to determine why they occur and what corrective action can be taken, if any. There is no substitute for competent supervision, but variance reporting can be a valuable aid to the supervisor in carrying out control responsibilities. However, management should recognize that explanations for variances have limited usefulness in improving the future control of costs because the explanations seldom suggest the corrective action that should be taken. If cost control is to be effective, the results of corrective action taken must be measured and reported.

The extent of variance investigation should be based on the estimated cost of making the investigation versus the value of the anticipated benefits. If the costs to be saved from investigating a variance and taking corrective action are expected to exceed the cost of making the investigation, management should investigate to determine the cause of the variance. Variances should be identified and reported to management as frequently as economically feasible. The closer the detection and reporting is to the point of occurrence, the more effective is the remedial action and the larger is the amount of cost that can be saved. It may also be beneficial to report variances in physical units as well as in dollars of cost.

Causes of Variances

A variance is a signal. Large variances, whether favorable or unfavorable, should be investigated and critically analyzed. A variance can be caused by some random event that is not expected to recur, or it can be the result of some systematic problem that can be corrected. It is also possible that the standard is simply wrong or out-of-date. For example, if the manufacturing process changes, physical standards may change, or unexpected price changes may cause monetary standards to be out of date. In some cases, variances in different departments are related. Determination of such a relationship is particularly important when favorable variances in one area are more than offset by related unfavorable variances in another area. For example, a favorable materials price variance resulting from the purchase of inexpensive materials may be more than offset by unfavorable labor efficiency variances that result from increased labor time required to work with poor-quality materials.

The purchasing department carries the primary responsibility for materials price variances. To be useful, variance reports should list the variance for each item of materials purchased during the period. Control of prices is achieved by obtaining several quotations, buying in economical lots, taking advantage of cash discounts, and selecting the most economical means of delivery. However, economic conditions and unexpected price changes by suppliers may be outside the limits of the department's control and may be caused by unexpected inflation, an excess or shortage of the quantity available in the market, or a fortunate buy. Thus, a materials price variance can be more a measure of forecasting ability than a failure to buy at predetermined prices. Internal factors, such as costly rush orders requiring materials shipments on short notice or in small, uneconomical quantities, can have a negative impact on the materials price variance but are not the fault of the purchasing department.

Materials quantity variances result from many causes, which must be identified if the variances are to be controlled. Materials variance reports should be prepared on a departmental basis and should list the materials quantity variance for each item of material used during the period. If the materials are of substandard quality, the fault may be with the person who prepared the purchase requisition informing the purchasing department regarding the quality of materials needed. If the materials purchased vary from the purchase requisition specification, the fault may lie with the purchasing department. Or perhaps the faulty materials are not discovered during inspection when received. Other causes relate to the production activity and include inexperienced or inefficient labor, pilferage or theft, badly worn or new machinery, changes in production methods, faulty product planning, or lack of proper production supervision.

Labor rate variances tend to be fairly minor because labor rates usually are set by management for the period or by long-term union contract. Rate variances can occur, however, because of the use of a single average rate for a department, operation, or craft, while several different rates exist for the individual workers. In such cases, absenteeism or the assignment of workers to tasks that normally pay different rates can result in a rate variance. In these cases, the planning or scheduling of work assignments is the cause of the variance.

Labor efficiency variances can occur for a multitude of reasons. These reasons include a lack of materials, faulty materials, inexperienced workers and the related learning curve phenomenon (Chapter 11), badly worn or obsolete machinery, machinery breakdowns, new and unfamiliar machinery, changes in production methods, poor or incorrect production planning and scheduling, faulty blueprints or product design specifications, worker dissatisfaction, or work interruptions. From the point of view of department managers, the most useful labor efficiency report is one that reports an efficiency variance for each worker. However, because of the high cost of such reports, labor efficiency variances usually are reported on a departmental or production operation basis.

Factory overhead variances relate to the variable and the fixed portions of factory overhead. The variance computation methods discussed previously segregate controllable variances from capacity variances. The volume variance, which is a measure of capacity utilization, may result from production inefficiencies, or it may be the result of action taken by executive management. The decision regarding the utilization of plant capacity and the setting of predetermined factory overhead rates rests with the planning group. Within the range of fixed costs, however, changes occur due to changes in depreciation rates, increases in insurance premiums and taxes, and increases in salaries of top-level managers. Such changes generally become a part of the controllable variance or the spending variance.

Unless the portion of the controllable variance or spending variance attributable to each item of factory overhead is computed and reported to responsible management, large variances can go undetected. An itemized variance report can highlight a situation in which a large favorable variance for one item of cost is substantially offset by a large unfavorable variance for another item. An example of such a report for the Assembly Department of Wilton Manufacturing Corporation is illustrated in Exhibit 18-2, using the two-variance method. For this report, the budget allowance based on standard hours is determined for each item of overhead by multiplying the standard overhead rate per labor hour for each item of factory overhead (from the flexible budget in Exhibit 18-1) by the standard hours allowed for the work produced during the period. The controllable variance for each item shown in Exhibit 18-2 is computed by subtracting the actual cost of each item from its budget allowance (that is, the value in column 3 minus the value in column 2).

EXHIBIT 18-2

Wilton Manufacturing Corporation
Assembly Department
Factory Overhead Variance Report
For Month Ending March 31, 19A

	(1) Budget Allowance at Normal Capacity	(2) Budget Allowance at Standard Hours	(3) Actual Cost	(4) Controllable Variance Unfavorable (Favorable) (3) – (2)
Direct labor hours	1,600	1,504		
Capacity	100%	94%		
Variable factory overhead:				
Indirect labor	$ 800	$ 752	$ 792	$ 40
Supplies	2,000	1,880	2,220	340
Payroll taxes	1,200	1,128	1,250	122
Repair and maintenance	400	376	240	(136)
Utilities	400	376	570	194
Total variable cost	$ 4,800	$ 4,512	$ 5,072	
Fixed factory overhead:				
Supervision	$ 1,800	$ 1,800	$ 1,800	0
Indirect labor	3,000	3,000	3,000	0
Payroll taxes	1,300	1,300	1,300	0
Vacation costs	5,000	5,000	5,000	0
Machinery depreciation	1,000	1,000	1,000	0
Building rent	800	800	800	0
Property taxes	600	600	590	(10)
Property insurance	500	500	560	60
Repair and maintenance	1,500	1,500	1,500	0
Utilities	1,200	1,200	1,200	0
General factory cost	2,500	2,500	2,600	100
Total fixed cost	$19,200	$19,200	$19,350	
Total factory overhead	$24,000	$23,712	$24,422	$710 unfavorable
Standard overhead charged to work in process (1,504 standard hours allowed × $15 rate)		22,560		
Volume variance		$ 1,152 unfavorable		

Reconciliation of variances:	
Actual factory overhead	$24,422
Standard factory overhead charged to work in process	22,560
Overall factory overhead variance	$ 1,862 unfavorable
Controllable variance	$ 710 unfavorable
Volume variance	1,152 unfavorable
Overall factory overhead variance	$ 1,862 unfavorable

The controllable variance can be broken down into the spending variance and the variable efficiency variance. The variable efficiency variance is caused by the efficient or inefficient use of the input used to allocate factory overhead, and the spending variance results from the efficient or inefficient use of the various items of factory overhead. An example of such a report for the Assembly Department is illustrated in Exhibit 18-3, using the three-variance method. In addition to the budget allowance based on standard hours computed for the two-variance method, the budget allowance based on actual hours must be computed for each item by multiplying its standard overhead rate per labor hour (from the flexible budget in Exhibit 18-1) by the actual labor hours worked during the period. The variable efficiency variance for each item of cost shown in the report in Exhibit 18-3 is computed by subtracting its budget allowance based on standard hours from its budget allowance based on actual hours (that is, the value in column 3 minus the value in column 2), and the spending variance for each item is computed by subtracting the actual cost of each item from its budget allowance based on actual hours (that is, the value in column 4 minus the value in column 3).

EXHIBIT 18-3

Wilton Manufacturing Corporation
Assembly Department
Factory Overhead Variance Report
For Month Ending March 31, 19A

	(1) Budget Allowance at Normal Capacity	(2) Budget Allowance at Standard Hours	(3) Budget Allowance at Actual Hours	(4) Actual Cost	(5) Variable Efficiency Variance Unfavorable (Favorable) (3) – (2)	(6) Spending Variance Unfavorable (Favorable) (4) – (3)
Direct labor hours	1,600	1,504	1,632			
Capacity	100%	94%	102%			
Variable factory overhead:						
Indirect labor	$ 800	$ 752	$ 816	$ 792	$ 64	($24)
Supplies	2,000	1,880	2,040	2,220	160	180
Payroll taxes	1,200	1,128	1,224	1,250	96	26
Repair and maintenance	400	376	408	240	32	(168)
Utilities	400	376	408	570	32	162
Total variable cost	$ 4,800	$ 4,512	$ 4,896	$ 5,072		
Fixed factory overhead:						
Supervision	$ 1,800	$ 1,800	$ 1,800	$ 1,800	0	0
Indirect labor	3,000	3,000	3,000	3,000	0	0
Payroll taxes	1,300	1,300	1,300	1,300	0	0
Vacation costs	5,000	5,000	5,000	5,000	0	0
Machinery depreciation	1,000	1,000	1,000	1,000	0	0
Building rent	800	800	800	800	0	0
Property taxes	600	600	600	590	0	(10)
Property insurance	500	500	500	560	0	60
Repair and maintenance	1,500	1,500	1,500	1,500	0	0
Utilities	1,200	1,200	1,200	1,200	0	0
General factory cost	2,500	2,500	2,500	2,600	0	100
Total fixed cost	$19,200	$19,200	$19,200	$19,350		
Total factory overhead	$24,000	$23,712	$24,096	$24,422	$384 unfavorable	$326 unfavorable
Standard overhead charged to work in process (1,504 standard hours allowed × $15 rate)		22,560				
Volume variance		$ 1,152 unfavorable				

Reconciliation of variances:

Actual facatory overhead	$24,422
Standard factory overhead charged to work in process	22,560
Overall factory overhead variance	$ 1,862 unfavorable
Spending variance	$ 326 unfavorable
Variable efficiency variance	384 unfavorable
Volume variance	1,152 unfavorable
Overall factory overhead variance	$ 1,862 unfavorable

To further enhance the usefulness of the variance report, the spending variance can be broken down into price and quantity variances for each item of factory overhead cost. The computations are similar to those used in computing price and quantity variances for direct materials and direct labor. To break the spending variance down into price and quantity variances, more data are needed; specifically, the standard cost per unit, the actual cost per unit, and the actual quantity of each item of variable factory overhead. For example, assume the following additional data are available for the Assembly Department at the end of March:

Item of Variable Overhead	(1) Standard Cost per Unit	(2) Actual Cost per Unit	(3) Actual Quantity Used	(4) Actual Quantity Used at Standard Unit Cost (3) × (1)	(5) Actual Quantity Used at Actual Unit Cost (3) × (2)
Indirect labor	$ 8.00	$ 8.00	99 hours	$ 792	$ 792
Supplies	1.80	2.00	1,110 units	1,998	2,220
Payroll taxes	1.25	1.25	1,000 hours	1,250	1,250
Repair and maintenance	15.00	16.00	15 hours	225	240
Utilities	.90	.95	600 KWH	540	570

The spending quantity variance for each item of factory overhead is determined first by computing the actual quantity of input at the standard unit cost for each item. (That is, for each item of variable factory overhead, multiply its standard cost per unit by the actual quantity of the item used.) Then subtract that amount from the budget allowance based on actual hours. The spending price variance for each item is determined by subtracting the actual quantity of input used at the standard unit cost for each item from its actual cost. These variances are illustrated in the factory overhead variance report for the Assembly Department in Exhibit 18-4.

A variance report is an integral part of the cost control system. It provides a way for upper-level management to monitor the efficiency of departments or other activities, and it provides a way for responsible managers to identify problems that require attention. In its efficiency-monitoring capacity, upper-level management typically is not concerned about the variances for each item of overhead, except to make sure that subordinates do not cut desirable expenditures in one area to offset inefficiencies in another. For example, in the absence of a detailed variance report to upper-level management, a department supervisor who expects a large unfavorable supplies quantity variance during the period may be tempted to cut maintenance expenditures in order to mitigate or eliminate the overall unfavorable variance.

At the operating level, more detail may be desirable. Because executive management reviews operating-level variance reports and requires explanations of significant variances, departmental and other operating-level managers typically pay close attention to operating activities. As a consequence, they often are aware of inefficiencies and their causes before receiving a variance report at the end of the period. When this happens, a highly detailed variance report may not be necessary. On the other hand, even in situations in which managers closely monitor activity, surprises sometimes occur. Managers generally pay close attention to those activities that have been problems in the past and less attention to those areas that have not. As a consequence, inefficiencies may go undetected in the absence of a detailed variance report. In addition, a detailed variance report can be useful in that it identifies the magnitude of variances. Furthermore, if a

Wilton Manufacturing Corporation
Assembly Department
Factory Overhead Variance Report
For Month Ending March 31, 19A

	(1) Budget Allowance at Normal Capacity	(2) Budget Allowance at Standard Hours	(3) Budget Allowance at Actual Hours	(4) Actual Quantity Used at Standard Unit Cost	(5) Actual Cost	(6) Variable Efficiency Variance Unfavorable (Favorable) (3) – (2)	(7) Spending Variance Unfavorable (Favorable) (5) – (3)	(8) Spending Quantity Variance Unfavorable (Favorable) (4) – (3)	(9) Spending Price Variance Unfavorable (Favorable) (5) – (4)
Direct labor hours	1,600	1,504	1,632						
Capacity	100%	94%	102%						
Variable factory overhead:									
Indirect labor	$ 800	$ 752	$ 816	$ 792	$ 792	$ 64	($24)	($24)	$ 0
Supplies	2,000	1,880	2,040	1,998	2,220	160	180	(42)	222
Payroll taxes	1,200	1,128	1,224	1,250	1,250	96	26	26	0
Repair and maintenance	400	376	408	225	240	32	(168)	(183)	15
Utilities	400	376	408	540	570	32	162	132	30
Total variable cost	$ 4,800	$ 4,512	$ 4,896	$ 4,805	$ 5,072				
Fixed factory overhead:									
Supervision	$ 1,800	$ 1,800	$ 1,800	$ 1,800	$ 1,800	0	0	0	0
Indirect labor	3,000	3,000	3,000	3,000	3,000	0	0	0	0
Payroll taxes	1,300	1,300	1,300	1,300	1,300	0	0	0	0
Vacation costs	5,000	5,000	5,000	5,000	5,000	0	0	0	0
Machinery depreciation	1,000	1,000	1,000	1,000	1,000	0	0	0	0
Building rent	800	800	800	800	800	0	0	0	0
Property taxes	600	600	600	600	590	0	(10)	0	(10)
Property insurance	500	500	500	500	560	0	60	0	60
Repair and maintenance	1,500	1,500	1,500	1,500	1,500	0	0	0	0
Utilities	1,200	1,200	1,200	1,200	1,200	0	0	0	0
General factory cost	2,500	2,500	2,500	2,500	2,600	0	100	0	100
Total fixed cost	$19,200	$19,200	$19,200	$19,200	$19,350				
Total factory overhead	$24,000	$23,712	$24,096	$24,005	$24,422	$384 unfavorable	$326 unfavorable	($91) favorable	$417 unfavorable
Standard overhead charged to work in process (1,504 standard hours allowed × $15 rate)		22,560							
Volume variance		$ 1,152 unfavorable							

Reconciliation of variances:

Actual factory overhead		$24,422	
Standard factory overhead charged to work in process		22,560	
Overall factory overhead variance		$ 1,862	unfavorable
Spending variance:			
Spending quantity variance	($91) favorable		
Spending price variance	417 unfavorable	$ 326	unfavorable
Variable efficiency variance		384	unfavorable
Volume variance		1,152	unfavorable
Overall factory overhead variance		$ 1,862	unfavorable

EXHIBIT 18-4

manager is too busy to monitor operations closely, he or she may be unaware of inefficient activities. Even if a manager is aware of an inefficiency, it may be ignored on the grounds that the amount of cost involved is insignificant compared to the cost of correcting the problem.

In deciding the amount of detail to report to responsible managers, the accountant must weigh the cost of gathering and recording additional data against the expected benefit. If there is a high probability that significant controllable inefficiencies can occur and go undetected by operating-level managers, the potential cost savings may exceed the additional cost of providing detailed variance reports. This is more apt to be the case in situations in which inefficiencies are not easily observed or in which the responsible manager does not have sufficient time to monitor activities closely.

Tolerance Limits for Variance Control

Managers have many important time-consuming responsibilities other than variance investigation; therefore, their efforts should be concentrated on large variances, which have the greatest impact on cost and profit. Some variance in cost measurements can be expected as a result of imperfect measurement techniques. Typically, the activity measure used to estimate a cost does not explain all the variation in the cost. The question that should be asked is: How large a variance from standard should be tolerated before the variance should be investigated? In other words, some tolerance limit or range should be established, so that, if the cost variance falls within this range, it can be considered acceptable. If the variance is outside the range, an investigation should be made if the cost of doing so is reasonable.

Each reported variance should be highlighted, indicating if the variance is within the control limit. Such information enables responsible managers or supervisors to accept deviations from the standard as a valuable tool for the control of costs. The information also lessens the danger of their being more averse to risk than upper-level managers prefer. A manager who is unduly concerned about the penalty for even small variances will perform in a manner that hinders rather than enhances efficient operations.

Past data on established operations, tempered by estimated changes in the future, can furnish reliable bases for estimating expected costs and calculating control limits that serve to indicate good as well as poor operation and that can be weighed in the decision to investigate a variance. The limits can be expressed as minimum dollar amounts or as percentage differences. Their determination can be based on subjective judgments, hunches, guesses, and biases, or on careful analyses and estimates, including the use of statistical measures such as the standard error of the estimate (Chapter 3). In setting and applying tolerance limits, management must recognize that the relative magnitude of a variance is more significant than its absolute value. Furthermore, the cost versus benefit of tighter controls must be considered as tolerance reduction alternatives are explored.

To illustrate the use of tolerance limits, assume that maintenance cost is a semivariable cost that appears in the factory overhead budget for the period and that the method of least squares is used to estimate maintenance costs. The standard error of the estimate for maintenance cost, based on a statistical analysis of data gathered over the past 30 months, is $750. Company policy is to investigate any variance that exceeds the 95 percent confidence interval estimate, which in this case would be the estimated maintenance expense based on actual machine hours plus or minus $1,500 (the value of two standard errors).[10] The budget allowance based on actual machine hours for the current period indicates that maintenance costs should be \$12,500; however, actual maintenance costs are \$14,300. The current period spending variance for maintenance expense is unfavorable in the amount of \$1,800. The unfavorable spending variance exceeds two standard deviations, suggesting investigation of the causes of this excess.

If the actual maintenance cost is only \$13,800, the unfavorable spending variance is \$1,300. Because this variance is less than two standard deviations, investigation does not appear to be warranted. However, if the unfavorable variance persists in subsequent reporting periods, the causes should be examined because the variances will be significant in the long run.

Overemphasizing Variances

Although standard costs are not perfect measures of ideal performance, variance reports nevertheless provide valuable information to management. Large variances signal the existence of problems that may require attention or of opportunities for substantial improvement. However, executive management must keep in mind that, while standard cost variance reporting is a useful cost control tool, it is not a substitute for good supervision. Too much emphasis on meeting standards can result in costly inefficiencies and lost opportunities. Eliminating standard cost variances is not always the best thing for the company.

Overemphasis on price variances can result in a large number of low-cost vendors, high levels of inventory, and poor quality of materials and parts. In order to avoid unfavorable price variances, purchasing must have a large number of low-cost vendors available, which can be played one against the other to get the lowest possible prices. In order to keep prices down, purchasing can take advantage of purchase discounts available on large orders. Ordering in large quantities and keeping large inventories also reduces the need to place rush orders, which result in premium prices. As a consequence of these practices, inventory tends to become excessively large, which in turn translates into unnecessarily high carrying costs. When price is of primary importance, quality may be ignored, thereby resulting in poor product quality and/or excessive spoilage, scrap, and rework.

Overemphasis on efficiency variances can result in long production runs, large work in process inventories, and attempts to control quality through inspection alone. Long production runs require fewer machine setups. Inefficiencies resulting from learning required to change production from one product to another are minimized by changing less frequently and by spreading the cost of learning over a large number of units. Large work in process inventories result from long production runs, and large inventories are viewed by operating-level managers as buffers that can absorb machine breakdowns, employee absenteeism, and slack demand for the product. Although carrying large inventories is costly, the carrying costs do not affect the efficiency variance, which in turn encourages departmental managers to overproduce. Because efficiency variances measure the use of inputs in relation to output volume, efforts to control quality tend to be oriented to inspection alone. For example, stopping the process to experiment with alternative production methods to correct a problem permanently or improve quality can result in an unfavorable labor efficiency variance.

---

[10] In this situation the sample size is sufficiently large to treat maintenance cost as normally distributed, thereby making it possible to ignore the correction factor for small samples and Student's *t* distribution, discussed in Chapter 3.

In contrast, increasing the volume of production and reworking or discarding defects has a smaller impact on the efficiency variance. Although these actions may prevent or eliminate an unfavorable efficiency variance, they often cost the company more in inventory carrying cost and spoilage.

A standard cost variance says that actual performance is different from the standard. A variance does not automatically confirm that inefficiency has occurred. The circumstances under which the standard was developed may have changed, or the standard may not have been well thought out. At most, a variance from standard should be viewed as a basis for discussion. To achieve operating efficiency, executive management must be actively involved in coordinating and supervising subordinates. Executive management should provide the tools, the training, and the encouragement needed by subordinates to improve efficiency, not a straightjacket that limits and inhibits performance. This means that standards should be viewed as targets, not inflexible absolutes. Continual improvement is necessary in order for business to compete effectively in global markets, and continual improvement requires the efforts of everyone working together as a team. Standard costing is a useful tool in helping identify problems and opportunities for improvement, but it is not a substitute for good management.

Summary

This chapter began by discussing how standards are used in planning, controlling, and accounting for costs. The process of setting standards and the danger of overemphasizing the motivation and control aspects of standards were explained. This foundation was followed by explaination and illustration of the computation of standard cost variances for materials, labor, and factory overhead. The chapter concluded with a discussion about the use of standard cost variances for cost control and emphasized the importance of viewing variances as questions rather than answers.

Appendix Alternative Factory Overhead Variance Methods

There are many ways of dividing the overall factory overhead variance. Two common alternatives to the methods presented in this chapter are illustrated in this appendix. The Assembly Department data of Wilton Manufacturing Corporation are used for these illustrations.

Alternative Three-Variance Method.

There are two common alternative approaches for dividing the overall factory overhead variance into three variances. One of those is the three-variance method presented earlier in this chapter and is referred to in this text simply as the three-variance method. The other common three-variance method, referred to throughout the remainder of this text as the alternative three-variance method, requires the computation of the spending variance, the idle capacity variance, and the efficiency variance. The spending variance and the idle capacity variance are the same as those discussed in Chapter 17. In this alternative method, only the efficiency variance is unique to standard costing.

The spending variance is the difference between the actual factory overhead incurred and the budget allowance based on the actual number of units of the allocation base used in actual production. It is composed of (1) the difference between the actual variable factory overhead incurred and the amount that would have been budgeted at the actual level of activity and (2) the difference between the actual fixed factory overhead and the budgeted fixed factory overhead. With the data for the Assembly Department of the Wilton Manufacturing Corporation, the spending variance is computed as follows:

Actual factory overhead incurred		$24,422
Budget allowance based on actual hours:		
Variable factory overhead (1,632 actual hours × $3.00 variable overhead rate)	$ 4,896	
Budgeted fixed factory overhead	19,200	24,096
Spending variance		$ 326 unfavorable

The **idle capacity variance** is the difference between the budget allowance based on the actual number of units of the allocation base used in actual production and the amount of factory overhead chargeable to production in the absence of a standard cost system (that is, the actual number of units of the allocation base used multiplied by the factory overhead rate). It is a measure of the over- or under utilization of production capacity and is computed for the Assembly Department in the illustration as follows:

Budget allowance based on actual hours (computed above)	$24,096
Actual hours (1,632) × factory overhead rate ($15)	24,480
Idle capacity variance	$ (384) favorable

Conceptually, the idle capacity variance is the difference between the budgeted fixed factory overhead and the fixed factory overhead that would be charged to production on the basis of the actual capacity employed. Consequently, it can be computed as follows:

Budgeted fixed factory overhead	$19,200
Actual hours (1,632) × fixed overhead rate ($12)	19,584
Idle capacity variance	$ (384) favorable

Alternatively, it can also be computed as follows:

Number of labor hours used to compute the overhead rate (normal or budgeted capacity)	1,600
Actual labor hours	1,632
Capacity hours utilized in excess of budgeted capacity	(32)
Fixed factory overhead rate	× $12
Idle capacity variance	$ (384) favorable

The **efficiency variance** is the difference between the actual number of units of the allocation base used and the standard number of units of the allocation base allowed for actual production, multiplied by the standard factory overhead rate. It is largely the responsibility of department management because it reflects the efficient or inefficient use of the variable production input used as the allocation base. When labor hours are used as the basis for applying factory overhead, this variance reflects the efficient or inefficient use of labor, and when machine hours are used as the allocation base, this variance reflects the efficiency of machine usage. This variance is affected by inexperienced labor, fatigue, poor employee morale, changes in operating procedures, new or worn-out machinery, and poor quality of materials.

The efficiency variance for the Assembly Department is computed as follows:

Actual hours (1,632) × standard overhead rate ($15)	$24,480
Factory overhead chargeable to production at standard (1,504 standard hours × $15 overhead rate)	22,560
Efficiency variance	$ 1,920 unfavorable

Alternatively, it can be computed as follows:

Actual hours worked	1,632
Standard hours allowed for actual units produced	1,504
Excess of actual hours over standard hours allowed	128
Standard factory overhead rate	× $15
Efficiency variance	$ 1,920 unfavorable

The sum of the three variances computed under the alternative three-variance method equals the overall factory overhead variance for the Assembly Department, as follows:

Spending variance	$ 326 unfavorable
Idle capacity variance	(384) favorable
Efficiency variance	1,920 unfavorable
Overall factory overhead variance	$1,862 unfavorable

Four-Variance Method

The four-variance method is similar to the alternative three-variance method, except that the efficiency variance is divided into its fixed and variable components. The four variances are the spending variance, the variable efficiency variance, the fixed efficiency variance, and the idle capacity variance. The spending variance and the idle capacity variance are computed in the same manner as in the alternative three-variance method, and the variable efficiency variance is computed in the same manner as in the regular three-variance method. All three of these variances were illustrated previously. The fourth variance, the **fixed efficiency variance**, is the difference between the amount of fixed factory overhead that would be charged to production if based on the actual number of units of the allocation base used and the amount that would be charged to production based on the standard number of units of the allocation base allowed for actual production. Based on the information provided for the Assembly Department of the Wilton Manufacturing Corporation, the fixed efficiency variance is computed as follows:

Actual hours (1,632) × fixed overhead rate ($12)	$19,584
Standard hours allowed (1,504) × fixed overhead rate ($12)	18,048
Fixed efficiency variance	$ 1,536 unfavorable

Alternatively, it can be computed as follows:

Actual hours worked	1,632
Standard hours allowed for actual units produced	1,504
Excess of actual hours over standard hours allowed	128
Fixed factory overhead rate	× $12
Fixed efficiency variance	$ 1,536 unfavorable

8-2 Comparison of Alternative Factory Overhead Variance Methods

-VARIANCE IETHOD	THREE-VARIANCE METHOD	FOUR-VARIANCE METHOD	ALTERNATIVE THREE-VARIANCE METHOD
	Spending Variance $386 unfavorable	Spending Variance $386 unfavorable	Spending Variance $386 unfavorable
llable Variance unfavorable			
	Variable Efficiency Variance $384 unfavorable	Variable Efficiency Variance $384 unfavorable	
			Efficiency Variance $1,920 unfavorable
		Fixed Efficiency Variance $1,536 unfavorable	
me Variance 2 unfavorable	Volume Variance $1,152 unfavorable		
		Idle Capacity Variance $(384) favorable	Idle Capacity Variance $(384) favorable
erall Factory ıead Variance 2 unfavorable	Overall Factory Overhead Variance $1,862 unfavorable	Overall Factory Overhead Variance $1,862 unfavorable	Overall Factory Overhead Variance $1,862 unfavorable

erms

d cost *(505)*
andard *(507)*
standard *(507)*
d actual standard *(507)*
standard *(507)*
ical standard *(507)*
ls purchase price
nce *(512)*
ls price usage variance

materials inventory variance *(513)*
materials quantity (or usage) variance *(513)*
labor rate (wage or cost) variance *(514)*
labor efficiency variance *(515)*
overall (or net) factory overhead variance *(517)*
controllable variance *(518)*

volume variance *(518)*
spending variance *(519)*
variable efficiency variance *(520)*
mix (or blend) variance *(521)*
yield variance *(521)*
idle capacity variance *(533)*
efficiency variance *(533)*
fixed efficiency variance *(534)*

ssion Questions

Define standard costs.

What are some uses of standard costs?

The use of standard costs in pricing and budgeting is quite valuable, because decisions in the ields of pricing and budgetary planning are nade before the costs under consideration are ncurred. Discuss.

Q18-4 Explain how standards relate to job order and process cost accumulation.

Q18-5 Discuss the selection criteria for operational activities for which standards are to be set. (ICMA adapted)

Q18-6 Identify two uses of standards for which normal or currently attainable standards are preferable to theoretical or ideal standards. (SMAC adapted)

When all four variances for the Assembly Departmen
are added together, the total is equal to the overall factory
as follows:

Spending variance	$
Variable efficiency variance	
Fixed efficiency variance	
Idle capacity variance	
Overall factory overhead variance	$

The four different methods of computing factory overh
trated in this chapter are merely different combinations of e
basic variance computations.

The four-variance method reconciles to the two-variance
combining the spending variance and variable efficiency v
controllable variance, and then combining the fixed efficienc
idle capacity variance to get the volume variance. These re
Assembly Department of Wilton Manufacturing Corporation
as follows:

Spending variance	$
Variable efficiency variance	
Controllable variance	$
Fixed efficiency variance	$1
Idle capacity variance	
Volume variance	$1

The four-variance method reconciles to the alternative thre
by keeping the spending and idle capacity variances separat
the variable efficiency and the fixed efficiency variances to get
ance. These relationships for the Assembly Department illus
strated as follows:

Spending variance	$
Variable efficiency variance	$
Fixed efficiency variance	1,
Efficiency variance	$1,
Idle capacity variance	$ (

The four-variance method reconciles to the regular three-v
keeping the spending and variable efficiency variances separat
the fixed efficiency variance and the idle capacity variance to g
ance. These relationships for the Assembly Department illust
strated as follows:

Spending variance	$
Variable efficiency variance	$
Fixed efficiency variance	$1,
Idle capacity variance	(
Volume variance	$1,

The relationships among these four alternative methods of
overhead variances are illustrated graphically in Figure 18-2.

FIGUR

T
Co
$
V
$1
C
Ov
$1

Key
stand
basic
curre
expec
norm
theor
mater
var
mater
(51

Disc
Q18-1
Q18-2
Q18-3

Q18-7 Discuss the behavioral issues to be considered when the level of performance to be incorporated into a standard cost is selected. (ICMA adapted)

Q18-8 Discuss the role of the following departments in establishing standard costs:
(a) The accounting department
(b) The department having its performance measured
(c) The industrial engineering department. (ICMA adapted)

Q18-9 What is indicated by a factory overhead variable efficiency variance? (SMAC adapted)

Q18-10 What is indicated by a factory overhead spending variance?

Q18-11 What is indicated by a factory overhead volume variance? (SMAC adapted)

Q18-12 In a standard cost system, the computation of variances is a first step. What steps should follow?

Q18-13 (a) Describe the features of tolerance limits.
(b) Discuss potential benefits of tolerance limits to an organization.
(c) Identify and discuss potential behavioral problems that can occur when tolerance limits are used. (ICMA adapted)

Q18-14 Standard cost variance reporting is a useful management control tool; however, too much emphasis on meeting standards can result in inefficiencies and lost opportunities for improvement. Explain how this can occur.

Exercises

E18-1 Materials Variance Analysis. The standard cost per unit of material M-12 is $13.50 per pound. During the month, 4,500 pounds of M-12 were purchased at a total cost of $60,300. In addition, 4,000 pounds of M-12 were used during the month; however, the standard quantity allowed for actual production is 3,800 pounds.

Required: Compute the materials purchase price variance, price usage variance, and quantity variance, indicating whether the variances are favorable or unfavorable.

E18-2 Materials Variance Analysis. Because it is concerned about high inventory carrying costs, Putnam Corporation has adopted a just-in-time inventory philosophy. In line with this new orientation, the company treats increases in materials inventory as unfavorable variances and decreases as favorable variances. The company uses a standard cost system, and inventories its materials at standard cost. The standard cost per unit of part R-33 is $22.50. During the current month, 5,000 units of R-33 were purchased at a total cost of $110,000. In addition, 4,400 units of part R-33 were issued to production during the month; however, the standard quantity allowed for actual production is 4,300 units.

Required: Compute the materials purchase price variance, materials inventory variance, and materials quantity variance, indicating whether the variances are favorable or unfavorable.

E18-3 Materials Price Variance Analysis. The standard cost per unit of component part K-45 is $4. During the month, 6,000 units of K-45 were purchased at a total cost of $25,200. In addition, 7,100 units of K-45 were used during the month; however, the standard quantity allowed for actual production is 6,900 units.

Required:
(1) Compute the materials purchase price variance and the materials quantity variance and indicate whether the variances are favorable or unfavorable.
(2) Assume that materials are inventoried at actual cost and that the beginning inventory of K-45 contained 2,000 units at a total cost of $8,240. Compute the materials price usage variance assuming that the average cost method is used for materials inventory.
(3) Assume the facts from requirement 2 except that the company uses the fifo method for materials inventory. Compute the materials price usage variance.
(4) Assume the facts from requirement 2 except that the company uses the lifo method for materials inventory. Compute the materials price usage variance.

E18-4 Labor Variance Analysis. During the month, 1,200 units of Topo were produced. Actual direct labor required was 650 direct labor hours at an actual total cost of $6,435. According to the standard cost card for Topo, ½ hour of labor should be required per unit of Topo produced, at a standard cost of $10 per labor hour.

Required: Compute the labor rate and efficiency variances, indicating whether the variances are favorable or unfavorable.

E18-5 Materials and Labor Variance Analysis. The following data pertain to the first week of operations during June:

Materials:	
Actual purchases	1,500 units at $ 3.80 per unit
Actual usage	1,350 units
Standard usage	1,020 units at $ 4.00 per unit
Direct labor:	
Actual hours	310 hours at $12.10 per hour
Standard hours	340 hours at $12.00 per hour

Required: Compute the following variances, indicating whether the variances are favorable or unfavorable:
(1) Materials purchase price variance, price usage variance, and quantity variance.
(2) Labor rate and efficiency variances.

E18-6 Factory Overhead Variance Analysis, Two-Variance Method. The normal capacity of the Assembly Department is 12,000 machine hours per month. At normal capacity, the standard factory overhead rate is $12.50 per machine hour, based on $96,000 of budgeted fixed cost per month and a variable cost rate of $4.50 per machine hour. During April, the department operated at 12,500 machine hours, with actual factory overhead of $166,000. The number of standard machine hours allowed for the production actually attained is 11,000.

Required: Compute the overall factory overhead variance and then break the overall variance down into the controllable variance and the volume variance. Indicate whether the variances are favorable or unfavorable.

E18-7 Factory Overhead Variance Analysis, Two-Variance Method. The normal capacity of Department 3 is 6,000 direct labor hours per month. At normal capacity, the standard factory overhead rate is $22 per direct labor hour, based on $96,000 of budgeted fixed cost per month and a variable rate of $6 per direct labor hour. During November, the department operated at 5,600 direct labor hours, with actual factory overhead of $130,000. The number of standard direct labor hours allowed for the production actually attained is 5,700.

Required: Compute the overall factory overhead variance and the controllable and volume variances. Indicate whether the variances are favorable or unfavorable.

E18-8 Factory Overhead Variance Analysis, Three-Variance Method. The normal capacity of the Die Cutting Department is 4,500 machine hours per month. At normal capacity, the standard factory overhead rate is $24.80 per machine hour, based on budgeted fixed factory overhead of $85,500 per month and a variable overhead rate of $5.80 per machine hour. During July, the department operated at 4,600 machine hours, with actual factory overhead of $121,000. The number of standard machine hours allowed for the production actually attained is 4,200.

Required: Compute the overall factory overhead variance and the spending variance, variable efficiency variance, and the volume variance. Indicate whether the variances are favorable or unfavorable.

E18-9 Factory Overhead Variance Analysis, Three-Variance Method. Standard direct labor hours budgeted for February production were 2,000, with factory overhead at that level budgeted at $10,000, of which $3,000 is variable. Actual labor hours for the month were 1,900; however, the number of standard labor hours allowed for actual February production is 2,050. Actual factory overhead incurred during the month was $10,500.

Required: Compute the overall factory overhead variance and the spending variance, the variable efficiency variance, and the volume variance. Indicate whether the variances are favorable or unfavorable.

E18-10 Factory Overhead Variance Analysis. Montana Machine Company has developed the following standard factory overhead costs for each SX unit assembled in Department 6, based on a monthly capacity of 80,000 direct labor hours:

Variable overhead	2 hours at $6 per hour =	$12
Fixed overhead..	2 hours at $3 per hour =	6
Department 6 factory overhead per unit of SX..		$18

During August, 38,000 units of SX were actually produced. Actual direct labor hours totaled 77,500, and actual factory overhead totaled $700,000.

Required: Determine the overall factory overhead variance and analyze it with each of the following variance analysis methods, indicating whether the variances computed are favorable or unfavorable.
(1) Two-variance method, for controllable and volume variances.
(2) Three-variance method, for spending, variable efficiency, and volume variances.

E18-11 Price, Mix, and Yield Variances. Chocolate manufacturing operations require close control of daily production and cost data. The computer printout for a batch of one ton of cocoa powder indicates the following materials standards:

Ingredients	Standard Quantity (pounds)	Standard Unit Cost	Standard Batch Cost
Cocoa beans	800	$.60	$ 480
Milk....................................	3,700	.50	1,850
Sugar..................................	500	.40	200
Total batch	5,000		$2,530

On December 7, the company's Commodity Accounting and Analysis Section reported the following production and cost data for the December 6 operations:

Ingredients Put in Process	Actual Quantity (pounds)	×	Actual Unit Price	=	Actual Total Cost
Cocoa beans	325,000		$.62		$201,500
Milk..............................	1,425,000		.48		684,000
Sugar...........................	250,000		.39		97,500
Total........................	2,000,000				$983,000

Cocoa powder transferred to finished goods inventory totaled 387 tons. There was no work in process inventory.

Required: Compute the materials price, mix, and yield variances, and indicate whether each is favorable or unfavorable.

E18-12 Materials Price, Mix and Yield Variances. Energy Products Company produces a gasoline additive, Gas Gain. This product increases engine efficiency and improves gasoline mileage through more complete combustion.

Careful controls are required during the production process to ensure that the proper mix of input chemicals is achieved and that evaporation is controlled. If the controls are not effective, there can be loss of output and efficiency.

The standard material cost of producing a 500-liter batch of Gas Gain is $135. The standard materials mix and related standard cost of each chemical used in a 500-liter batch are as follow:

Chemical	Standard Input Quantity (liters)	Standard Cost per Liter	Total Cost
Echol	200	$.200	$ 40.00
Protex................................	100	.425	42.50
Benz	250	.150	37.50
CT-40	50	.300	15.00
	600		$135.00

The quantities of chemicals purchased and used during the current production period are shown in the following schedule. A total of 136 batches of Gas Gain were manufactured during the current production period. Energy Products determines its cost and chemical usage variations at the end of each production period.

Chemical	Quantity Purchased (liters)	Total Purchase Price	Quantity Used (liters)
Echol	25 000	$ 5,365	26 800
Protex	13 000	6,240	12 660
Benz	40 000	5,840	37 400
CT-40	7 500	2,220	7 140
	85 500	$19,665	84 000

Required:

(1) Calculate the purchase price variances by chemical for Energy Products Company.

(2) Compute the materials mix and yield variances. (ICMA adapted)

E18-13 Factory Overhead Variance Analysis Report. The Cost Department of Benjamin Products Company prepared the following flexible budget for Department 2 for June:

Production quantity based on standard	9,600	10,800	12,000
Direct labor hours at standard	4,800	5,400	6,000
Capacity utilization at standard	80%	90%	100%
Variable overhead:			
Indirect labor	$ 1,920	$ 2,160	$ 2,400
Manufacturing supplies	1,680	1,890	2,100
Repairs	640	720	800
Heat, power, and light	80	90	100
Total variable overhead	$ 4,320	$ 4,860	$ 5,400
Fixed overhead:			
Superintendence	$ 6,000	$ 6,000	$ 6,000
Indirect labor	5,400	5,400	5,400
Manufacturing supplies	1,020	1,020	1,020
Maintenance	960	960	960
Heat, power, and light	120	120	120
Machinery depreciation	540	540	540
Insurance and taxes	360	360	360
Total fixed overhead	$14,400	$14,400	$14,400
Total budgeted factory overhead	$18,720	$19,260	$19,800

Factory overhead is charged to production at the rate of $3.30 per direct labor hour. The overhead rate was determined on the basis of 100% capacity utilization, considered to be normal. At the end of the month, cost records showed 10,200 units of product were manufactured, 5,040 direct labor hours were used, and actual factory overhead was as follows:

Superintendence	$ 6,200
Indirect labor	7,500
Manufacturing supplies	2,825
Repairs	650
Maintenance	960
Heat, power, and light	225
Machinery depreciation	540
Insurance and taxes	372
Total actual factory overhead	$19,272

Required: Prepare a departmental factory overhead variance report that shows the controllable variance for each item of factory overhead and a single departmental volume variance. For each item of expense that contains both a fixed and a variable portion, assume that the actual fixed portion is equal to the budgeted fixed portion and that the balance of the actual expense is variable. Indicate whether the variances are favorable or unfavorable.

E18-14 (Appendix) Factory Overhead Variance Analysis, Alternative Three-Variance Method. Standard machine hours budgeted for December production were 2,500, with factory overhead at that level budgeted at $15,000, of which $5,000 is variable. Actual machine hours for the month were 2,700; however, the number of standard machine hours allowed for actual December production is 2,400. Actual factory overhead incurred during the month was $16,500.

Required: Compute the overall factory overhead variance and analyze it for spending, idle capacity, and efficiency variances, using the alternative three-variance method presented in the appendix to this chapter. Indicate whether the variances are favorable or unfavorable.

E18-15 (Appendix) Factory Overhead Variance Analysis, Four-Variance Method. Standard direct labor hours budgeted for April production were 1,200, with factory overhead at that level budgeted at $16,800, of which $4,800 is variable and $12,000 is fixed. Actual labor hours for the month were 1,120; however, the number of standard labor hours allowed for actual April production is 1,170. Actual factory overhead incurred during the month was $15,800.

Required: Compute the overall factory overhead variance and analyze it for spending, variable efficiency, fixed efficiency, and idle capacity variances, using the four-variance method presented in the appendix to this chapter. Indicate whether the variances are favorable or unfavorable.

Problems

P18-1 Variance Analysis: Materials, Labor, and Factory Overhead. Armando Corporation manufactures a product with the following standard costs:

Direct materials—20 yards at $1.35 per yard	$27
Direct labor—4 hours at $9 per hour	36
Factory overhead—4 direct labor hours at $7.50 per hour; ratio of variable to fixed factory overhead is 2:1	30
Total standard cost per unit of output	$93

Standards are based on normal monthly capacity of 2,400 direct labor hours. The following information pertains to July:

Units produced in July	500
Direct materials purchased—18,000 yards at $1.38 per yard	$24,840
Direct materials used—9,500 yards	
Direct labor—2,100 hours at $9.15 per hour	19,215
Actual factory overhead	16,650

Required:

(1) Compute the variable factory overhead rate per direct labor hour and the total fixed factory overhead based on normal monthly capacity.

(2) Compute the following variances and indicate whether they are favorable or unfavorable:

(a) Materials purchase price and quantity variances

(b) Labor rate and efficiency variances

(c) Factory overhead controllable and volume variances (AICPA adapted)

P18-2 Equivalent Units, Abnormal Spoilage, and Variance Analysis for Materials, Labor, and Factory Overhead. The Kryton Corporation uses a standard costing system in its process cost facility, which manufactures a product called Wikum. Material A is added at the beginning of the process and Material B is added only to good units immediately after they have been inspected. Inspection takes place at the end of machine conversion when 70% of labor has been incurred. All spoilage is considered abnormal. The standard cost card for one unit of Wikum follows:

Direct materials:	
A (3 units at $4.50 each)	$13.50
B (2 units at $2.00 each)	4.00
Direct labor (1/2 hour at $10.00 per hour)	5.00
Factory overhead:	
Variable (1 hour at $5.00 per machine hour)	5.00
Fixed (1 hour at $10.00 per machine hour)	10.00
	$37.50

The following additional information is available for the current period:

(a) 5,000 machine hours were budgeted for the period, and the factory overhead rate was based on budgeted capacity.

(b) Work in process beginning inventory had 500 units, 70% complete with respect to labor and 50% complete with respect to machining.

(c) Work in process ending inventory had 600 units, 90% complete with respect to labor and 100% complete with respect to machining.

(d) 4,600 units were transferred to finished goods and 200 units were spoiled.

(e) Materials inventory records indicate the following:

Material	Quantity Purchased	Actual Unit Cost	Quantity Used
A	16,000	$4.60	14,800
B	12,000	1.95	11,000

(f) 2,550 direct labor hours were worked at a total cost of $26,010.

(g) 5,300 actual machine hours were used, and actual factory overhead totaled $75,000.

Required:

(1) Compute the number of equivalent units and the standard quantity allowed for each element of cost.

(2) Compute two standard cost variances for each element of cost (that is, materials purchase price and quantity variances, labor rate and efficiency variances, and factory overhead controllable and volume variances). Indicate whether each variance is favorable or unfavorable.

(3) Determine the standard cost of the units transferred to finished goods, the spoilage charged to factory overhead control, and work in process ending inventory.

P18-3 Equivalent Production and Standard Cost Variance Analysis. Red Cloud Company uses a standard process costing system in its one production department. Material A is added at the beginning of the process, and Material B is added when the units are 90% complete. Inspection takes place at the end of the process, and all spoilage is expected to be abnormal. The standard cost of abnormal spoilage is charged to a current period expense account. Normal capacity is 7,800 direct labor hours per month.

The standard cost per unit is as follows:

Material A: 4 gallons at $1.20	$ 4.80
Material B: 2 square feet at $.70	1.40
Direct labor: 1 hour at $11.50	11.50
Variable factory overhead: 1 hour at $1.80	1.80
Fixed factory overhead: 1 hour at $5.00	5.00
Total	$24.50

Additional data for January are as follows:

(a) Beginning work in process inventory, 3,000 units (33-⅓% converted).

(b) Started in process during the month, 11,000 units

(c) Finished during the month, 8,000 units

(d) Ending work in process inventory, 5,000 units (40% converted)

(e) Actual costs incurred are as follow:

Material A used	50,000 gallons at $1.00
Material B used	18,000 sq. ft. at $.75
Direct labor	10,200 hours at $12.00
Factory overhead	$60,100

Required:

(1) Compute the January equivalent production for Material A, Material B, and for conversion costs.

(2) Compute the materials price usage and quantity variances for each kind of material, the labor rate and efficiency variances, and the factory overhead controllable and volume variances. Indicate whether the variances are favorable or unfavorable. CGA-Canada (adapted). Reprint with permission.

P18-4 Equivalent Units and Variance Analysis for Materials, Labor, and Three-Variance Method for Factory Overhead. Chaffey Corporation manufactures one product, Beta, for which it has developed the following standard cost per unit:

Direct materials (3 kg. at $4 per kg.)	$12.00
Direct labor (½ hr. at $11 per hour)	5.50
Variable overhead ($6 per direct labor hour)	3.00
Fixed overhead ($8 per direct labor hour)	4.00
Standard cost per unit of Beta produced	$24.50

Materials are added at the beginning of the process. Inspection takes place at the end of the process and spoilage is considered to be abnormal. Actual activity for November is as follows:

(a) Budgeted fixed factory overhead for the month was $80,000.

(b) There were 4,000 units in process on November 1 and they were 20% complete as to conversion costs.

(c) 60 000 kg. of materials were purchased at a unit cost of $3.95. The materials price variance is determined at the date the materials are purchased.

(d) 16,000 units of product were started during November.

(e) 50 000 kg. of materials were issued to production.

(f) The direct labor payroll was $108,000 for 9,000 hours.

(g) 17,000 units of product were transferred to finished goods inventory.

(h) There were 2,150 units in process on November 30 and they were 40% complete as to conversion costs.

(i) Actual factory overhead totaled $134,900.

Required:

(1) Compute equivalent units for materials and conversion costs.

(2) Compute the purchase price and quantity variances for materials, the rate and efficiency variances for labor, and reconcile the overall factory overhead variance using the three-variance method, (spending, variable efficiency, and volume variances). Indicate whether the variances are favorable or unfavorable. CGA-Canada (adapted). Reprint with permission.

P18-5 Process Costing; Equivalent Units; Variance Analysis for Materials, Labor, and the Three-Variance Method for Factory Overhead. LaFaver Company uses a standard process costing system in accounting for its one product, which is produced in one department. All materials are added at the beginning of the process. The standard cost card for one unit of product follows:

Materials: 3 units at $6.00 per unit	$18.00
Direct labor: ¼ hour at $10.00 per hour	2.50
Variable factory overhead: ¼ hour at $2.00 per labor hour	.50
Fixed factory overhead: ¼ hour at $8.00 per labor hour	2.00
Total	$23.00

Budgeted capacity is 8,500 direct labor hours for November. Actual data for November are as follow:

(a) Beginning work in process inventory was 5,000 units (40% converted).

(b) Ending work in process inventory was 2,000 units (80% converted).

(c) 32,000 units of product were transferred to finished goods during November.

(d) Actual costs incurred:

Materials purchased	100,000 units at \$6.54 (recorded at standard cost)
Materials used	92,000 units
Direct labor	8,000 hours at \$10.60
Factory overhead	\$75,000

Required:

(1) Compute the equivalent units and the standard quantity allowed for each element of cost for the month of November.

(2) Compute the materials purchase price, inventory, and quantity variances, the labor rate and efficiency variances, and the factory overhead spending, variable efficiency, and volume variances. Indicate whether the variances are favorable or unfavorable.

P18-6 Variance Analysis: Materials, Labor, and Factory Overhead; Job Order Costing. Fancy Fashions Inc. manufactures ladies' blouses of one quality, produced in lots to fill each special order from its customers, which are department stores located in various cities. Fancy sews the particular stores' labels in the blouses. The standard costs for a dozen blouses are:

Direct materials	24 yards at \$1.10 =	\$26.40
Direct labor	3 hours at \$4.90 =	14.70
Factory overhead	3 hours at \$4.00 =	12.00
Standard cost per dozen		\$53.10

During June, Fancy worked on three orders, for which the month's job cost records disclose the following:

Lot Number	Units in Lot (dozens)	Material Used (yards)	Hours Worked
22	1,000	24,100	2,980
23	1,700	40,440	5,130
24	1,200	28,825	2,890

The following information is also available:

(a) Fancy purchased 95,000 yards of material during June at a cost of \$106,400. The materials price variance is recorded when goods are purchased. All inventories are carried at standard cost.

(b) Direct labor during June amounted to \$55,000. According to payroll records, production employees were paid \$5 per hour.

(c) Factory overhead during June amounted to \$45,600.

(d) A total of \$576,000 was budgeted for factory overhead for 19A, based on estimated production at the plant's normal capacity of 48,000 dozen blouses annually. Factory overhead at this level of production is 40% fixed and 60% variable. Factory overhead is applied on the basis of direct labor hours.

(e) There was no work in process at June 1. During June, Lots 22 and 23 were completed. All material was issued for Lot 24, which was 80% completed as to direct labor.

Required:

(1) Prepare a schedule showing the computation of standard cost of Lots 22, 23, and 24 for June.

(2) Prepare a schedule showing the computation of the materials purchase price variance for June.

(3) Prepare a schedule showing, for each lot produced during June, computations of the following variances, indicating whether they are favorable or unfavorable:

(a) Materials quantity variance

(b) Labor efficiency variance

(c) Labor rate variance

(4) Prepare a schedule showing computations of the factory overhead controllable and volume variances for June. Indicate whether the variances are favorable or unfavorable. (AICPA adapted)

P18-7 Factory Overhead Variance Analysis Report. The Cost Department of Claffy Manufacturing Company prepared the following flexible budget for Department 2 for February:

Production quantity based on standard	6,400	7,200	8,000
Processing time in hours at standard	4,800	5,400	6,000
Capacity utilization at standard	80%	90%	100%
Variable overhead:			
Indirect labor	$ 1,600	$ 1,800	$ 2,000
Manufacturing supplies	1,920	2,160	2,400
Repairs	800	900	1,000
Heat, power, and light	240	270	300
Total variable overhead	$ 4,560	$ 5,130	$ 5,700
Fixed overhead:			
Superintendence	$ 4,000	$ 4,000	$ 4,000
Indirect labor	6,200	6,200	6,200
Manufacturing supplies	2,000	2,000	2,000
Maintenance	1,100	1,100	1,100
Heat, power, and light	1,400	1,400	1,400
Machinery depreciation	4,500	4,500	4,500
Insurance and taxes	900	900	900
Total fixed overhead	$20,100	$20,100	$20,100
Total budgeted factory overhead	$24,660	$25,230	$25,800

Factory overhead is charged to production at the rate of $4.30 per standard hour of processing time. The overhead rate was determined on the basis of 100% capacity utilization, considered to be normal. At the end of the month, cost records showed 7,600 units of product were manufactured during 5,840 processing hours, and actual factory overhead was as follows:

Superintendence	$ 4,000
Indirect labor	8,120
Manufacturing supplies	4,325
Repairs	1,050
Maintenance	1,080
Heat, power, and light	1,725
Machinery depreciation	4,500
Insurance and taxes	970
Total actual factory overhead	$25,770

Required: Prepare a departmental factory overhead variance report that shows the spending variance and the variable efficiency variance for each item of factory overhead, along with a single departmental volume variance. For each item of expense that contains both a fixed and a variable portion, assume that the actual fixed portion is equal to the budgeted fixed portion and that the balance of the actual expense is variable. Indicate whether the variances are favorable or unfavorable.

P18-8 Factory Overhead Variance Analysis Report. The Cost Department of Coffman Manufacturing Company prepared the following flexible budget for Department X for January:

Machine hours	4,000	4,500	5,000
Capacity utilized	80%	90%	100%
Variable factory overhead:			
Indirect labor	$ 2,800	$ 3,150	$ 3,500
Supplies	2,000	2,250	2,500
Machinery repairs	800	900	1,000
Electric power	4,000	4,500	5,000
Total variable overhead	$ 9,600	$10,800	$12,000
Fixed factory overhead:			
Supervision	$ 3,000	$ 3,000	$ 3,000
Supplies	1,700	1,700	1,700
Machinery maintenance	3,000	3,000	3,000
Depreciation of machinery	6,500	6,500	6,500
Insurance	1,800	1,800	1,800
Property tax	1,000	1,000	1,000
Gas heating	600	600	600
Electricity (lighting)	400	400	400
Total fixed overhead	$18,000	$18,000	$18,000
Total factory overhead	$27,600	$28,800	$30,000

Factory overhead is allocated to production on the basis of machine hours. The factory overhead rate is computed on the basis of normal capacity, which is 5,000 machine hours. During January, 4,650 machine hours were actually worked; however, based on the standard cost card, 4,800 machine hours were allowed for the actual quantity of production output. The following cost data have also been compiled by the cost department for January:

	Actual Quantity of Input at Standard Unit Costs	Actual Quantity of Input at Actual Unit Costs
Supervision	$ 3,000	$ 3,100
Indirect labor	3,300	3,400
Variable supplies	2,600	2,200
Fixed supplies	1,700	1,650
Machinery repairs	950	960
Machinery maintenance	3,200	3,200
Depreciation of machinery	6,500	6,500
Insurance	1,800	1,900
Property tax	1,000	1,100
Gas heating	700	845
Variable electricity	4,700	4,740
Fixed electricity	400	405
Total factory overhead	$29,850	$30,000

Required: Prepare a departmental factory overhead variance report that includes (1) a variable efficiency variance, a spending variance, a spending quantity variance, and a spending price variance for each item of factory overhead, and (2) a single departmental volume variance. Indicate whether the variances are favorable or unfavorable.

P18-9 (Appendix) Variance Analysis: Materials, Labor, and the Alternative Three-Variance Method for Factory Overhead. Trutch Company manufactures a product that is accounted for using a standard process costing system with the following standards:

Materials—2 pieces at $.48 each	$ .96
Labor—½ hour at $7.60 per hour	3.80
Variable factory overhead—½ hour at $1.40 per hour	.70
Fixed factory overhead—½ hour at $.40 per hour	.20
	$5.66

The company's standards include an allowance for normal spoilage. Equivalent production computations for standard costing are made for good units only. By this procedure, excess spoilage becomes a contributing factor to the computed variances. The following data are available for September:

Beginning inventory (all materials, 50% converted)	10,000 units
Started in process	40,000 units
Transferred to finished goods	42,000 units
Ending inventory (all materials, 90% converted)	5,000 units
Fixed factory overhead budgeted	$ 8,000
Materials used (76,000 pieces)	38,000
Labor (22,500 hours)	180,000
Variable factory overhead incurred	33,800
Fixed factory overhead incurred	8,200

Required: Compute two variances for materials and labor, and compute three variances for factory overhead, using the alternative three-variance method presented in the appendix to this chapter. Indicate whether the variances are favorable or unfavorable. CGA-Canada (adapted). Reprint with permission.

P18-10 (Appendix) Variance Analysis: Materials, Labor, and the Four-Variance Method for Factory Overhead

Terry Company manufactures a commercial solvent used for industrial maintenance. This solvent, which is sold by the drum, generally has a stable selling price. Terry produced and sold 60,000 drums in December.

The following information is available regarding Terry's operations for the month:

(a) Standard costs per drum of product manufactured were as follow:

Materials:	
10 gallons of raw material	$20
1 empty drum	1
Total materials	$21
Direct labor: 1 hour	$ 7
Fixed factory overhead per direct labor hour (normal capacity is 68,750 direct labor hours)	$ 4
Variable factory overhead per direct labor hour	6
Total factory overhead per direct labor hour	$10

(b) Costs incurred during December were:

Raw materials:	
600,000 gallons purchased at a cost of $1,150,000	
700,000 gallons used	
Empty drums:	
85,000 drums purchased at a cost of $85,000	
60,000 drums used	
Direct labor:	
65,000 hours worked at a cost of $470,000	
Factory overhead:	
Depreciation of building and machinery (fixed)	$230,000
Supervision and indirect labor (semivariable)	360,000
Other factory overhead (variable)	76,500
Total factory overhead	$666,500

Required: Compute two variances for each material and for labor and four variances for factory overhead. The materials price variance is determined at the time of purchase. Indicate whether the variances are favorable or unfavorable. (AICPA adapted)

Cases

C18-1 Motivation Using Standard Costing. Kelly Company manufactures and sells pottery items. All manufacturing takes place in one plant, having four departments, each department producing only one product. The four products are plaques, cups, vases, and plates. Sam Kelly, the president and founder, credits the company's success to well-designed, quality products and to an effective cost control system, which was installed early in the firm's existence to improve cost control and to serve as a basis for planning.

With the participation of plant management, the company establishes standard costs for materials and labor. Each year, the plant manager, the department heads, and the time-study engineers are invited by executive management to recommend changes in the standards for the next year. Executive management reviews these recommendations and the records of actual performance for the current year before setting the new standards. As a general rule, tight standards representing very efficient performance are established so that no inefficiency or slack will be included in cost goals. The plant manager and department heads are charged with control responsibility and the variances from standard costs are used to measure their performance in carrying out this charge.

No standards are set for factory overhead because management believes it is too difficult to predict and relate overhead to output. The actual factory overhead for the departments and the plant is accumulated in one pool. The actual overhead is then allocated to the departments on the basis of departmental output.

The company's executives are convinced that more effective cost control can be obtained than is currently being realized from the standard cost system. A review of cost performance for recent years disclosed several factors that led them to this conclusion:

(a) Unfavorable variances were the norm rather than the exception, although the size of the variances was quite uniform.

(b) Employee motivation, especially among first-line supervisors, appeared to be low.

Required:

(1) Identify the probable effects on motivation of plant managers and department heads resulting from:
   (a) The participative standard cost system.
   (b) The use of tight standards.

(2) State the effect on the motivation of department heads to control overhead costs when actual factory overhead costs are applied on the basis of actual units. (ICMA adapted)

C18-2 Motivation Using Standard Costing. Some executives believe that it is extremely important to manage "by the numbers." This form of management requires that all employees with departmental or divisional responsibilities spend time understanding the company's operations and how they are reflected by the company's financial reports. Because of the manager's increased comprehension of the financial reports and the activities that they represent, the manager's subordinates will become more attuned to the meaning of financial reports and the important signposts that can be detected in these reports. Companies utilize a variety of numerical measurement systems including standard cost variances, financial ratios, human resource forecasts, and operating budgets.

Required:

(1) (a) Discuss the characteristics that should be present in a standard cost system in order to encourage positive employee motivation.
   (b) Discuss how a standard cost system should be implemented to motivate employees positively.

(2) (a) Explain the meaning of management by exception.
   (b) Discuss the behavioral implications of management by exception.

(3) Explain how employee behavior can be adversely affected when standard cost variance reports are used as the sole basis for performance evaluation.

(ICMA adapted)

C18-3 Standard Setting. John Stevens, plant manager of the Fairlee Plant of Lockstead Corporation, called together the 25 employees of Department B and told them that production standards established several years previously were now too low in view of the recent installation of automated equipment. He gave the workers an opportunity to discuss the mitigating circumstances and to decide among themselves, as a group, what their standards should be. Stevens, on leaving the room, believed they would doubtlessly establish much higher standards than he himself would have dared propose.

After an hour of discussion, the group summoned Stevens and notified him that, contrary to his opinion, their group decision was that the standards were already too high, and since they had been given the authority to establish their own standards, they were making a reduction of 10%. These standards, Stevens knew, were far too low to provide a fair profit on the owner's investment. Yet it was clear that his refusal to accept the group decision would be disastrous.

Required:

(1) Identify the errors made by Stevens.

(2) Suggest a course of action to be taken by Stevens.

CGA-Canada (adapted). Reprint with permission.

C18-4 Developing Standards. ColdKing Company is a small producer of fruit-flavored frozen desserts. For many years, ColdKing's products have had strong regional sales on the basis of brand recognition; however, other companies have begun marketing similar products in the area, and price competition has become increasingly important. John Wakefield, the company's controller, is planning to implement a standard cost system for ColdKing and has gathered considerable information from his co-workers on production and material requirements for ColdKing's products. Wakefield believes that the use of standard costing will allow ColdKing to improve cost control and make better pricing decisions.

ColdKing's most popular product is raspberry sherbet. The sherbet is produced in batches. Each batch requires 6 quarts of good raspberries and 10 gallons of other ingredients to yield a net of 10 gallons of sherbet. The fresh raspberries are sorted by hand before entering the production process. Because of imperfections in the raspberries and normal spoilage, 1 quart of berries is discarded for every 4 quarts of acceptable berries. Three minutes is the standard direct labor time for sorting needed to obtain one quart of acceptable raspberries. The acceptable raspberries are then blended with the other ingredients; blending requires 12 minutes of direct labor time per batch. After blending, the sherbet is packaged in quart containers. Wakefield has gathered the following pricing information.

(a) ColdKing purchases raspberries at a cost of $.80 per quart. All other ingredients cost a total of $.45 per gallon.
(b) Direct labor is paid at the rate of $9.00 per hour.
(c) The total cost of material and labor required to package the sherbet is $.38 per quart.

Required:

(1) Develop the standard cost for the direct cost components of a 10 gallon batch of raspberry sherbet. The standard cost should identify the standard quantity, the standard rate, and the standard cost per batch for each direct cost component of a batch of raspberry sherbet.
(2) As part of the implementation of a standard cost system at ColdKing, Wakefield plans to train those responsible for maintaining the standards in the use of variance analysis. Wakefield is particularly interested in discovering the causes of unfavorable variances.
   (a) Discuss the possible causes of unfavorable material price variances and identify the individual(s) who may be responsible for these variances.
   (b) Discuss the possible causes of unfavorable labor efficiency variances and identify the individual(s) who may be responsible for these variances. (ICMA adapted)

C18-5 Implementing a Standard Cost System. Ogwood Company is a small manufacturer of wooden household items. A. Rivkin, corporate controller, plans to implement a standard cost system for Ogwood. Rivkin has information from several co-workers that will be useful in developing standards for Ogwood's products.

One of Ogwood's products is a wooden cutting board. Each cutting board requires 1.25 board feet of lumber and 12 minutes of direct labor time to prepare and cut the lumber. The cutting boards are inspected after they are cut. Because the cutting boards are made of natural material that has imperfections, one board is normally rejected for each five that are accepted. Four rubber foot pads are attached to each good cutting board. A total of 15 minutes of direct labor time is required to attach all four foot pads and finish each cutting board. The lumber for the cutting boards costs $3.00 per board foot, and each foot pad costs $.05. Direct labor is paid at the rate of $8.00 per hour.

Required:

(1) Develop the standard cost for the direct cost components of the cutting board. The standard cost should identify (a) the standard quantity, (b) the standard rate, and (c) the standard cost per board for each direct cost component.
(2) Identify the advantages of implementing a standard cost system.
(3) Explain the role of each of the following persons in developing standards:
   (a) Purchasing manager
   (b) Industrial engineer
   (c) Cost accountant (ICMA adapted)

C18-6 Price, Mix, and Yield Variances and Their Use. LAR Chemical Company manufactures a wide variety of chemical compounds and liquids for industrial uses. The standard mix for producing a single batch of 500 gallons of one liquid is as follows:

Liquid Chemical	Quantity in Gallons	Cost per Gallon	Total Cost
Maxan	100	$2.00	$200
Salex	300	.75	225
Cralyn	225	1.00	225
	625		$650

There is a 20% loss in liquid volume during processing due to evaporation. The finished liquid is put into 10-gallon bottles for sale. Thus, the standard materials cost for a 10-gallon bottle is $13.

A total of 4,000 bottles (40,000 gallons) were produced during November. The actual quantities and costs of the materials placed in production during November were as follows:

Liquid Chemical	Quantity in Gallons	Total Cost
Maxan	8,480	$17,384
Salex	25,200	17,640
Cralyn	18,540	16,686
	52,220	$51,710

Required:

(1) Compute the materials price, mix, and yield variances, including an analysis of the portion of the mix variance attributable to each material.

(2) Explain how LAR Chemical could use each of these variances to help control the cost to manufacture this liquid compound. (ICMA adapted)

C18-7 Variance Analysis; Variance Control Responsibility. Cappels Corporation manufactures and sells a single product, using a standard cost system. The standard cost per unit of product is:

Materials: 1 pound of plastic at $2	$ 2.00
Direct labor: 1.6 hours at $4	6.40
Variable factory overhead cost per unit	3.00
Fixed factory overhead cost per unit	1.45
	$12.85

The factory overhead cost per unit was calculated from the following annual overhead cost budget for a 60,000-unit volume:

Variable factory overhead cost:	
Indirect labor (30,000 hours at $4)	$120,000
Supplies (oil—60,000 gallons at $.50)	30,000
Allocated variable service department cost	30,000
Total variable factory overhead cost	$180,000
Fixed factory overhead cost:	
Supervision	$ 27,000
Depreciation	45,000
Other fixed costs	15,000
Total fixed factory overhead cost	$ 87,000
Total budgeted annual factory overhead cost for 60,000 units	$267,000

The charges to the Manufacturing Department for November, when 5,000 units were produced, were as follow:

Materials (5,300 pounds at $2)	$10,600
Direct labor (8,200 hours at $4.10)	33,620
Indirect labor (2,400 hours at $4.10)	9,840
Supplies (oil—6,000 gallons at $.55)	3,300
Allocated variable service department cost	3,200
Supervision	2,475
Depreciation	3,750
Other fixed costs	1,250
Total	$68,035

The Purchasing Department normally buys about the same quantity of plastic as is used in production during a month. In November, 5,200 pounds were purchased at a price of $2.10 per pound.

The company has divided its responsibilities so that the Purchasing Department is responsible for the price at which materials and supplies are purchased, while the Manufacturing Department is responsible for the quantities of materials used.

The Manufacturing Department manager performs the timekeeping function and, at various times, an analysis of factory overhead and direct labor variances has shown that the manager has deliberately misclassified labor hours (for example, direct labor hours might be classified as indirect labor hours and vice versa), so that only one of the two labor variances is unfavorable. It is not economically feasible to hire a separate timekeeper.

Required:

(1) Calculate these variances from standard costs for the data given: (a) materials purchase price variance; (b) materials quantity variance; (c) direct labor rate variance; (d) direct labor efficiency variance; (e) factory overhead controllable variance, analyzed for each expense classification.

(2) Explain whether the division of responsibilities should solve the conflict between price and quantity variances.

(3) Prepare a report that details the factory overhead budget variance. The report, which will be given to the Manufacturing Department manager, should display only that part of the variance that is the manager's responsibility and should highlight information useful to that manager in evaluating departmental performance and in considering corrective action.

(4) Suggest a solution to the company's problem involving the classification of labor hours.

(ICMA adapted)

C18-8 Revision of Standards. NuLathe Company produces a turbo engine component for jet aircraft manufacturers. A standard cost system has been used for years with good results. Unfortunately, NuLathe has recently experienced production problems. The source for its direct material went out of business. The new source produces a similar but higher quality material. The price per pound from the original source has averaged $7.00, while the price from the new source is $7.77. The use of the new material results in a reduction in scrap. This scrap reduction reduces the actual consumption of direct material from 1.25 to 1.00 pound per unit. In addition, the direct labor is reduced from 24 to 22 minutes per unit because there is less scrap labor and machine setup time.

The direct material changeover occurred at the same time that labor negotiations resulted in an increase of over 14% in hourly direct labor costs. The average rate rose from $12.60 per hour to $14.40 per hour. Production of the main product requires a high level of labor skill. Because of a continuing shortage in that skill area, an interim wage agreement had to be signed.

NuLathe started using the new direct material on April 1, the same date that the new labor agreement went into effect. NuLathe has been using standards that were set at the beginning of the calendar year. The direct material and direct labor standards for the turbo engine component are as follow:

Direct material—(1.2 lbs. at $6.80 per lb.)	$ 8.16
Direct labor—(20 min. at $12.30 per DLH)	4.10
Standard prime cost per unit of product	$12.26

H. Foster, cost accounting supervisor, had been examining the accompanying performance report that had been prepared at the close of business on April 30. When J. Keene, assistant controller, came into Foster's office, Foster said, "Look at this performance report. Direct material price increased 11% and the labor rate increased over 14% during April. I expected greater variances, yet prime costs decreased over 5% from the $13.79 we experienced during the first quarter of this year. The proper message just isn't coming through."

"This has been an unusual period," said Keene. "With all the unforeseen changes, perhaps we should revise our standards based on current conditions and start over."

NuLathe Company
Standard Prime Cost Variance Analysis
For April, 19A

	Standard	Price Variance		Quantity Variance		Actual
Direct materials	$ 8.16	($.97 × 1.0)	$.97 unfavorable	($6.80 × .2)	$1.36 favorable	$ 7.77
Direct labor	4.10	($2.10 × 22/60)	.77 unfavorable	($12.30 × 2/60)	.41 unfavorable	5.28
	$12.26					$13.05

NuLathe Company
Comparison of Actual Prime Costs
For April, 19A

	First Quarter Costs	April Costs	Percentage Increase (Decrease)
Direct materials	$ 8.75	$ 7.77	(11.2)%
Direct labor	5.04	5.28	4.8 %
	$13.79	$13.05	(5.4)%

Foster replied, "I think we can retain the current standards but expand the variance analysis. We could calculate variances for the specific changes that have occurred to direct material and direct labor before we calculate the normal price and quantity variances. What I really think would be useful to management right now is to determine the impact the changes in direct material and direct labor had in reducing our prime costs per unit from $13.79 in the first quarter to $13.05 in April—a reduction of $.74."

Required:

(1) Discuss the advantages of each of the following alternatives:
 (a) Revise the standards immediately.
 (b) Retain the current standards and expand the analysis of variances.

(2) Prepare an analysis that reflects the impact the new direct material and new labor contract had on reducing NuLathe's prime costs per unit from $13.79 in the first quarter to $13.05 in April. The analysis should show the changes in prime costs per unit that are due to (a) the use of new direct material, and (b) the new labor contract. This analysis should be in sufficient detail to identify the changes due to direct materials price, direct labor rate, the effect of direct material quality on direct material usage, and the effect of direct material quality on direct labor usage. (ICMA adapted)

CHAPTER 19

Standard Costing: Incorporating Standards into the Accounting Records

Learning Objectives

After studying this chapter, you will be able to:

1. Prepare general journal entries to record the elements of cost at standard, along with the standard cost variances.
2. Prepare general journal entries to account for completed products in a standard cost system.
3. Prepare the general journal entry to dispose of the standard cost variances in the accounting records.

Some companies prefer to use standard costs for planning, motivation, and evaluation purposes only. In such cases, standard costs do not enter into the company's journals and ledgers. However, the incorporation of standard costs into the regular accounting system permits the most efficient use of a standard cost system and leads to savings and increased accuracy in clerical work. In either case, variances can be analyzed for cost control, and standard costs can be used in developing budgets, bidding on contracts, and setting prices. The accumulation of standard costs in the company's accounts and the disposition of standard cost variances are presented in this chapter. The illustrative data and the resulting variance computations are the same as for Chapter 18.

Recording Standard Cost Variances in the Accounts

Standard costs should be viewed as costs that pass through the data processing system into financial statements. Because timely identification and reporting are major control features of standard cost systems, the accounting system should facilitate prompt identification and communication of standard costs and variances. Reported variances should reflect only activity that occurs during the reporting period. When standard costs are incorporated into the accounting records, timely identification and reporting is facilitated by charging Work in Process with the standard cost of inputs *only* and recording the variances at the same time.[1] Variance accounts are closed at the end of each period. In this way,

[1] Although the method described in this chapter is commonly used in practice, other approaches also exist. For example, the work in process account can be debited for the actual cost of materials, labor, and factory overhead and then credited at standard cost when goods are completed and transferred to finished goods inventory. In such an approach, any balance remaining in the work in process account consists of two elements: (1) the standard cost of work still in process and (2) the variances between actual and standard costs. To isolate these variances, additional analysis is needed.

the work in process account balance always reflects the standard cost of production; the units transferred to Finished Goods Inventory and Cost of Goods Sold are always at standard cost; and the variance accounts reflect only variances from standard that occurred during the reporting period. The journal entries are periodic summaries of standard costs, actual costs, and resulting variances. They are discussed in detail in the following sections and are used in the exercises and problems of this chapter.

Standard Cost Accounting for Materials

The purchase of materials can be recorded by the following three methods:

1. **The price variance is recorded when materials are received and placed in stores.** The general ledger control account, Materials, is debited at standard cost and the materials ledger records are kept in quantities only. A standard price is noted on the record when the standards are set. As purchases are made, no prices are recorded in these records. This approach results in clerical savings and speedier postings.
2. **The materials are recorded at actual cost when received; the price variance is determined when the materials are requisitioned for production.** The general ledger control account, Materials, is debited at actual cost and the materials ledger records show quantities and dollar values as in a historical cost system.
3. **A combination of methods 1 and 2.** Price variances are calculated when the materials are received, but are not charged to production until the materials actually are placed in process. At that time, only the price variance applicable to the quantity used will appear as a current charge, the balance remaining as a part of the materials inventory. This method results in two types of materials price variances: (1) a materials purchase price variance originating when materials purchases are first recorded, and (2) a materials price usage variance recorded when materials are used. The occurrence of the materials price usage variance recorded is a reduction of the materials purchase price variance.

For control purposes, the price variance should be determined when the materials are received. If it is not computed and reported until the materials are requisitioned for production, then remedial action is difficult because the time of reporting is far removed from the time of purchase. In addition, if the materials are charged to inventory at actual price rather than standard, the actual cost used in determining the price variance will depend on the cost flow assumption used to cost inventory (average, lifo, or fifo).[2]

The methods for recording materials purchased are illustrated using the following data for Item 3-89 used by the Wilton Manufacturing Corporation in its Assembly Department for the production of Paxel (from Figure 18-1).

Standard unit price as per standard cost record	$7.50
Purchased	10,000 pieces at $7.44
Requisitioned	9,500 pieces
Standard quantity allowed for actual production	9,336 pieces

[2] In a just-in-time inventory system, these differences are trivial because materials inventory is not significant. In such a system, the quantity of materials purchased essentially equals the quantity used.

Method 1

The journal entry when materials are purchased is as follows:

Materials*	75,000	
Accounts Payable**		74,400
Materials Purchase Price Variance***		600

* $7.50 standard price × 10,000 pieces purchased
** $7.44 actual price × 10,000 pieces purchased
*** $.06 favorable price variance per piece × 10,000 pieces purchased

When materials issued to the factory are recorded, the entry is as follows:

Work in Process*	70,020	
Materials Quantity Variance**	1,230	
Materials***		71,250

* $7.50 standard price × 9,336 pieces (standard quantity allowed)
** $7.50 standard price × 164 pieces unfavorable quantity variance
*** $7.50 standard price × 9,500 pieces actually used

Method 2

When materials are purchased, no variance is computed and the entry is as follows:

Materials*	74,400	
Accounts Payable		74,400

* $7.44 actual price × 10,000 pieces purchased

When materials issued to production are recorded, the entry is as follows:

Work in Process*	70,020	
Materials Quantity Variance**	1,230	
Materials***		70,680
Materials Price Usage Variance****		570

* $7.50 standard price × 9,336 pieces (standard quantity allowed)
** $7.50 standard price × 164 pieces unfavorable quantity variance
*** $7.44 actual price × 9,500 pieces used
**** $.06 favorable price variance per piece × 9,500 pieces used

For this computation, the actual cost used is $7.44 per piece. The assumption here is that there is no beginning materials inventory and that there are no other purchases during the period. In practice, the actual cost used would depend on the type of inventory costing methods employed, such as perpetual or periodic, and the inventory cost flow assumptions, such as fifo, lifo, or average costing.

In this method, the materials price usage variance account appears on the books after the materials are issued, and then only for the quantity issued—not for the entire purchase. The price variance occurred because the actual cost of the materials issued was $.06 less than the standard price; the quantity variance occurred because 164 pieces were used in excess of the standard quantity allowed. Notice that the cost charged to Work in Process and the amount recorded as the quantity variance are the same for method 1 and method 2. Only the price variance and the charge to the materials inventory are different.

Method 3

The following entry, identical to the first entry in method 1, is made when the materials are purchased:

Materials*	75,000	
Accounts Payable**		74,400
Materials Purchase Price Variance***		600

* $7.50 standard price × 10,000 pieces purchased

** $7.44 actual price × 10,000 pieces purchased

*** $.06 favorable price variance per piece × 10,000 pieces purchased

When the materials issued are recorded, two entries are made. The following entry, identical to the second entry in method 1, recognizes the 164 pieces of material used in excess of the standard quantity allowed.

Work in Process*	70,020	
Materials Quantity Variance**	1,230	
Materials***		71,250

* $7.50 standard price × 9,336 pieces (standard quantity allowed)

** $7.50 standard price × 164 pieces unfavorable quantity variance

*** $7.50 standard price × 9,500 pieces actually used

The next entry transfers $570 from the purchase price variance account to the price usage variance account.

Materials Purchase Price Variance	570	
Materials Price Usage Variance*		570

* $.06 favorable price variance per piece × 9,500 pieces actually used

In method 3, any balance remaining in the materials purchase price variance account at the end of the accounting period is used to adjust the inventory to actual cost. This balance is shown in the following partial balance sheet:

Materials purchased (at standard cost)		$75,000
Materials used during period (at standard cost)		71,250
Materials in ending inventory (at standard cost)		$ 3,750
Materials purchase price variance (favorable)	$(600)	
Less materials price usage variance (favorable)	(570)	(30)
Materials in ending inventory (adjusted to actual cost)		$ 3,720

Standard Cost Accounting for Labor

The payroll is computed on the basis of clock cards, job tickets, and other labor time information furnished to the payroll department. In a standard cost system, these records supply the data for computing labor variances.

The necessary journal entries are illustrated with the following data for Operation 3-25 in the Assembly Department of the Wilton Manufacturing Corporation:

Actual hours worked	1,632
Actual rate paid per hour	$12.50
Standard hours allowed for actual production	1,504
Standard rate per hour	$12.00

The following journal entry records the total actual direct labor payroll, assuming that there were no payroll deductions:

Payroll	20,400	
Accrued Payroll*		20,400

* $12.50 actual labor rate × 1,632 actual hours worked

To distribute the payroll and to set up the variance accounts, the journal entry is as follows:

Work in Process*	18,048	
Labor Rate Variance**	816	
Labor Efficiency Variance***	1,536	
Payroll		20,400

* $12.00 standard labor rate × 1,504 standard hours allowed

** $.50 unfavorable labor rate × 1,632 actual hours worked

*** $12.00 standard labor rate × 128 excess actual hours over standard

Standard Cost Accounting for Factory Overhead

The relationship between standard costs and budgetary control is particularly important for the analysis of factory overhead. Actual factory overhead is measured not only against the applied overhead cost, but also against a budget based on actual and standard activity allowed for actual production.

The following data for the Assembly Department of the Wilton Manufacturing Corporation are used to illustrate the general journal entries required for the factory overhead variances.

Normal capacity in direct labor hours (DLH)		1,600 DLH
Total factory overhead at normal capacity:		
Variable	$ 4,800	
Fixed	19,200	$24,000
Factory overhead rate per direct labor hour:		
Variable	$ 3.00	
Fixed	12.00	$ 15.00
Actual factory overhead		$24,442
Actual direct labor hours		1,632
Standard hours allowed for actual production		1,504

In actual practice, numerous entries are entered in the general journal during each month of the year to record the incurrence of actual factory overhead. A single entry is used as follows to illustrate the recording of actual factory overhead for the entire period:

Factory Overhead Control	24,422	
Various Credits*		24,422

* Accounts credited during the period typically include Payroll (for indirect labor and supervision), Materials (for indirect materials and supplies), Accumulated Depreciation, Prepaid Expenses, Accounts Payable, Accrued Vacation Pay, Pension Liability, Payroll Tax Liabilities, and Cash.

Typically, an entry to record the factory overhead charged to Work in Process is entered in the general journal at least once a month. Again, a single entry is used to illustrate the application of factory overhead to Work in Process:

Work in Process*	22,560	
Applied Factory Overhead		22,560

* $15.00 factory overhead rate × 1,504 standard hours allowed

At the end of the period, when Applied Factory Overhead is closed, the entry is:

Applied Factory Overhead	22,560	
Factory Overhead Control		22,560

The factory overhead control account now has a debit balance of $1,862. This balance represents underapplied overhead, which is also the net overhead variance; therefore, it will be closed to the appropriate factory overhead variance accounts. Methods of computing factory overhead variances are illustrated and discussed in detail in Chapter 18. The two-variance and three-variance methods discussed in Chapter 18 are illustrated here. The alternative three-variance and the four-variance methods are illustrated in the appendix to this chapter.

Two-Variance Method

In the two-variance method, the balance in the factory overhead control account is divided between the controllable variance and the volume variance. The entry to close the factory overhead control account and to record the controllable and volume variances is as follows:

Factory Overhead Volume Variance*	1,152	
Factory Overhead Controllable Variance**	710	
Factory Overhead Control***		1,862

* $12.00 fixed factory overhead rate × 96 hours (i.e., the difference between normal capacity (1,600 hours) and the standard hours allowed (1,504 hours))

** The amount required to balance the entry (see Chapter 18 for an illustration of the computation of the controllable variance)

*** The amount of underapplied factory overhead (i.e., the difference between actual factory overhead ($24,422) and applied factory overhead ($22,560))

Three-Variance Method

In the three-variance method, the amount of over- or underapplied factory overhead can be analyzed as spending, variable efficiency, and volume variances. The entry to close the factory overhead control account and to record these three variances is as follows:

Factory Overhead Volume Variance*	1,152	
Factory Overhead Variable Efficiency Variance**	384	
Factory Overhead Spending Variance***	326	
Factory Overhead Control****		1,862

* $12.00 fixed factory overhead rate × 96 hours (i.e., the difference between normal capacity (1,600 hours) and the standard hours allowed (1,504 hours))

** $3.00 variable factory overhead rate × 128 hours (i.e., the difference between the actual hours required (1,632 hours) and the standard hours allowed (1,504 hours))

*** The amount required to balance the entry (see Chapter 18 for an illustration of the computation of the spending variance)

**** The amount of underapplied factory overhead (i.e., the difference between actual factory overhead ($24,422) and applied factory overhead ($22,560))

Standard Cost Accounting for Completed Products

The completion of production requires the transfer of cost from the work in process account of one department to the work in process account of another department, or, in the case of the last department, to the finished goods inventory account. The cost transferred is the standard cost of the completed products.

Recall that in the Wilton Manufacturing Corporation illustration presented in Chapter 18, 4,200 units of Paxel were completed during the period and transferred to finished goods inventory. Assume that during the same period, 4,236 units of Paxel were transferred from the Cutting Department and from the Molding Department to the Assembly Department. The standard cost card for Paxel (Figure 18-1) indicates that the total standard cost of manufacturing a unit is $204.15, of which $122.90 was added in the Cutting Department, $57.25 in the Molding Department, and $24.00 in the Assembly Department. The general journal entry to record the transfer of 4,236 units from the Cutting Department and the Molding Department to the Assembly Department is as follows:

Work in Process, Assembly Department	763,115.40	
Work in Process, Cutting Department*		520,604.40
Work in Process, Molding Department**		242,511.00

* $122.90 standard cost per unit added in the Cutting Department × 4,236 units transferred to the Assembly Department

** $57.25 standard cost per unit added in the Molding Department × 4,236 units transferred to the Assembly Department

The units transferred from the Assembly Department to finished goods inventory contain the standard cost added in the Assembly Department plus the standard costs added by the two preceding departments (Cutting and Molding). The journal entry to record the transfer of the 4,200 finished units is as follows:

Finished Goods	857,430	
Work in Process*		857,430

* $204.15 standard cost per unit × 4,200 completed units

Usually the finished goods ledger card will show quantities only, because the standard cost of the units remains the same during a period unless substantial cost changes occur. The entry to record the sale of 4,000 units of Paxel during the year is:

Cost of Goods Sold	816,600	
Finished Goods*		816,600

* $204.15 standard cost per unit × 4,000 units sold

Disposition of Variances

Variances can be disposed of in one of two ways. They can be treated as period expenses (that is, closed to Cost of Goods Sold or directly to Income Summary) or treated as adjustments to Cost of Goods Sold and ending inventories.

Variances Treated as Period Expenses

Usually, standard cost variances are considered to be a manufacturing function responsibility. If the net amount of the variances is not material, the variances are closed to the cost of goods sold account. To illustrate, assume Radford Manufacturing Company has the following variances at the end of the year:

	Debit	Credit
Materials purchase price variance	$1,200	
Labor efficiency variance	1,800	
Factory overhead controllable variance		$ 600
Factory overhead volume variance	1,300	

The entry to close the variance accounts is as follows:

Cost of Goods Sold	3,700	
Factory Overhead Controllable Variance	600	
Materials Purchase Price Variance		1,200
Labor Efficiency Variance		1,800
Factory Overhead Volume Variance		1,300

The total amount in Cost of Goods Sold (the standard cost of units sold adjusted for the standard cost variances) is then closed to Income Summary along with other revenue and expense accounts. Financial statement presentation for Radford Manufacturing Company is illustrated Exhibit 19-1.

EXHIBIT 19-1

Radford Manufacturing Company
Income Statement
For Year Ending December 31, 19A

Sales		$78,000
Cost of goods sold (Schedule 1)		43,700
Gross profit		$34,300
Less commercial expenses:		
Marketing expenses	$16,000	
Administrative expenses	10,000	26,000
Operating income		$ 8,300

Schedule 1
Cost of Goods Sold
For Year Ending December 31, 19A

Materials (at standard)		$16,000
Direct labor (at standard)		10,000
Applied factory overhead (at standard)		18,000
Total cost added to work in process		$44,000
Add beginning work in process inventory		14,000
		$58,000
Deduct ending work in process inventory		16,000
Cost of goods manufactured		$42,000
Add beginning finished goods inventory		23,000
Cost of goods available for sale		$65,000
Deduct ending finished goods inventory		25,000
Cost of goods sold (at standard)		$40,000
Adjustments for standard cost variances:		
Materials purchase price variance	$ 1,200	
Labor efficiency variance	1,800	
Factory overhead controllable variance	(600)	
Factory overhead volume variance	1,300	3,700
Cost of goods sold		$43,700

As an alternative, variances can be closed to Income Summary rather than directly to Cost of Goods Sold. At the end of the period, the variance accounts for Radford Manufacturing Company are closed as follows:

Income Summary	3,700	
Factory Overhead Controllable Variance	600	
Materials Purchase Price Variance		1,200
Labor Efficiency Variance		1,800
Factory Overhead Volume Variance		1,300

This approach makes it possible to keep work in process, finished goods inventory, and cost of goods sold at standard costs, thereby facilitating comparison of sales revenue and standard cost by product class. Unfavorable (or debit) manufacturing cost variances are deducted from the gross profit calculated at standard cost. Favorable (or credit) variances are added to the gross profit computed at standard cost. The treatment of manufacturing cost variances using this method for Radford Manufacturing Company is depicted in the income statement in Exhibit 19-2.

EXHIBIT 19-2

Radford Manufacturing Company
Income Statement
For Year Ending December 31, 19A

Sales		$78,000
Cost of goods sold (at standard)—Schedule 1		40,000
Gross profit (at standard)		$38,000
Adjustments for standard cost variances:		
Materials purchase price variance	$ 1,200	
Labor efficiency variance	1,800	
Factory overhead controllable variance	(600)	
Factory overhead volume variance	1,300	3,700
Gross profit (adjusted)		$34,300
Less commercial expenses:		
Marketing expenses	$16,000	
Administrative expenses	10,000	26,000
Operating income		$ 8,300

Schedule 1
Cost of Goods Sold
For Year Ending December 31, 19A

Materials (at standard)	$16,000
Direct labor (at standard)	10,000
Applied factory overhead (at standard)	18,000
Total cost added to work in process	$44,000
Add beginning work in process inventory	14,000
	$58,000
Deduct ending work in process inventory	16,000
Cost of goods manufactured	$42,000
Add beginning finished goods inventory	23,000
Cost of goods available for sale	$65,000
Deduct ending finished goods inventory	25,000
Cost of goods sold (at standard)	$40,000

Accountants who use these approaches believe that only the standard costs should be considered the true costs. Variances are treated not as increases or decreases in manufacturing costs but as deviations from contemplated costs due to abnormal inactivity, extravagance, inefficiencies or efficiencies, or other changes of business conditions. This viewpoint suggests that all variances should be closed to the income summary account, which is an acceptable procedure as long as standards are reasonably representative of what costs ought to be. However, some proponents of this approach suggest that the unused portion of the materials purchase price variance should be linked with materials still on hand and shown on the balance sheet as part of the cost of the ending materials inventory.

If a part of the materials purchase price variance is allocated to the materials inventory, the following computation is made in the Radford Manufacturing Company example:

Balance in materials inventory: $4,000 or 20 percent of purchases made
Materials purchase price variance: $1,200
Variance transferred to the materials account: $240 (20% of $1,200)

Because the materials purchase price variance is unfavorable, the materials account is increased and the amount closed to Income Summary is decreased, thereby increasing the operating income from $8,300 to $8,540. The journal entry to close the variance accounts is as follows:

Income Summary	3,460	
Materials	240	
Factory Overhead Controllable Variance	600	
Materials Purchase Price Variance		1,200
Labor Efficiency Variance		1,800
Factory Overhead Volume Variance		1,300

Variances Allocated to Cost of Goods Sold and Ending Inventories

With respect to the cost of inventories, *Accounting Research Bulletin No. 43* implies that significant variances are to be allocated between cost of goods sold and inventories:

> Standard costs are acceptable if adjusted at reasonable intervals to reflect current conditions so that at the balance-sheet date standard costs reasonably approximate costs computed under one of the recognized bases. In such cases descriptive language should be used which will express this relationship, as, for instance, "approximate costs determined on the first-in, first-out basis," or, if it is desired to mention standard costs, "at standard costs, approximating average costs."[3]

CASB regulations require that significant standard cost variances be included in inventories. Current federal income tax regulations also require the inclusion of a portion of significant variances in inventories. With respect to factory overhead variances, when the amount involved is not significant in relation to total actual factory overhead for the year, an allocation is not required by the IRS unless such allocation is made for financial reporting purposes.[4] Also, the taxpayer must treat both favorable and unfavorable variances consistently.

[3] *Accounting Research Bulletin, No. 43,* "Inventory Pricing" (New York: American Institute of Certified Public Accountants, 1953), Chapter 4, par. 6.

[4] See *Code of Federal Regulations,* Section 1.471-11(d)(3) and Temporary Section 1.263A-1T(b)(3)(iii)(3)(D).

Although the tax law does not specifically mention the treatment of material and labor variances, they should be treated in the same manner as factory overhead variances. That is, when the amount involved is significant in relation to total cost, it should be allocated between ending inventories and cost of goods sold.

To illustrate the allocation of variances, the percentage of cost elements in the inventories and cost of goods sold of the previous example are as follows:

	Materials		Labor		Factory Overhead	
Account	**Amount**	**%**	**Amount**	**%**	**Amount**	**%**
Work in Process	$ 6,000	37.5	$ 2,000	20	$ 7,200	40
Finished Goods	2,000	12.5	2,000	20	1,800	10
Cost of Goods Sold	8,000	50.0	6,000	60	9,000	50
Total	$16,000	100.0	$10,000	100	$18,000	100

The allocation of the Radford Manufacturing Company variances for 19A is summarized in the table below. The materials purchase price variance of $960 ($1,200 – $240 allocated to Materials) is multiplied by the respective percentage of materials in the inventories and cost of goods sold accounts (37.5%, 12.5%, and 50.0%). The labor and factory overhead variances are allocated in a similar manner.

Account	Total Amount	Work in Process	Finished Goods	Cost of Goods Sold
Materials Purchase Price Variance	$ 960	$ 360	$120	$ 480
Labor Efficiency Variance	1,800	360	360	1,080
Factory Overhead Controllable Variance	(600)	(240)	(60)	(300)
Factory Overhead Volume Variance	1,300	520	130	650
Total	$3,460	$1,000	$550	$1,910

The entry to close the variance accounts is as follow:

Cost of Goods Sold	1,910	
Materials	240	
Work in process	1,000	
Finished goods	550	
Factory Overhead Controllable Variance	600	
Materials Purchase Price Variance		1,200
Labor Efficiency Variance		1,800
Factory Overhead Volume Variance		1,300

Assuming that variances in the preceding period were charged to period expense because they were not material, the proration of the current period variances to Work in Process, Finished Goods, and Cost of Goods Sold results in the income statement presented in Exhibit 19-3.

The $1,790 difference between the operating income of $10,090 reported in the income statement in Exhibit 19-3 and the operating income of $8,300 shown in the income statement in Exhibit 19-2 occurs as a result of charging a portion of the unfavorable variances of the period to ending inventories rather than period expense. The $1,790 difference is reconciled as follows:

Cost added to:	
Materials	$ 240
Work in process	1,000
Finished goods	550
Total	$1,790

EXHIBIT 19-3

Radford Manufacturing Company
Income Statement
For Year Ending December 31, 19A

Sales		$78,000
Cost of goods sold (standard adjusted to actual)—Schedule 1		41,910
Gross profit (actual)		$36,090
Less commercial expenses:		
Marketing expenses	$16,000	
Administrative expenses	10,000	26,000
Operating income		$10,090

Schedule 1
Cost of Goods Sold
For Year Ending December 31, 19A

	Standard	Variance	Actual
Materials	$16,000		
Materials purchase price variance		$ 960	$16,960
Direct labor	10,000		
Labor efficiency variance		1,800	11,800
Applied factory overhead	18,000		
Controllable variance		(600)	
Volume variance		1,300	18,700
Total cost added to work in process	$44,000	$ 3,460	$47,460
Add beginning work in process inventory	14,000	0	14,000
	$58,000	$ 3,460	$61,460
Deduct ending work in process inventory	16,000	1,000	17,000
Cost of goods manufactured	$42,000	$ 2,460	$44,460
Add beginning finished goods inventory	23,000	0	23,000
Cost of goods available for sale	$65,000	$ 2,460	$67,460
Deduct ending finished goods inventory	25,000	550	25,550
Cost of goods sold	$40,000	$ 1,910	$41,910

Entries transfer the prorated amounts to the respective accounts in the general ledger only. Subsidiary inventory accounts and records are not adjusted. The adjustments can be shown on the balance sheet as valuation or contra accounts against standard inventory values, or combined with them to form one amount. At the beginning of the next reporting period, the portion of these entries affecting inventory accounts is reversed in order to restore beginning inventories to standard costs. At the end of the new reporting period, new variances are allocated in the same manner as before, based on the elements of cost added to work in process that pertain to ending inventory and cost of goods sold account balances. The amount reversed from the previous period is either charged to cost of goods sold, if the units in beginning inventory have been sold, or allocated between cost of goods sold and ending inventories, if some of the units in beginning inventory are still in ending inventory.

The Logic of Disposing of Variances

The treatment of variances depends on the following factors: (1) type of variance (materials, labor, or factory overhead), (2) size of the variance, (3) experience with standard costs, (4) cause of the variance (for example, incorrect standards), and (5) timing of the variance (for example, a variance caused by seasonal fluctuations). Therefore, determining the most acceptable treatment requires consideration of more than the argument that only actual costs should be shown in the financial statements. Actual cost may be impossible to determine, and to argue that expensing variances distorts operating income reveals a misunderstanding of standard costs.

One view of the disposition of variances has been expressed as follows:[5]

1. When the standards are current and attainable, companies "state their inventories at standard cost and charge the variances against the income of the period in which the variances arise. They justify this practice on the grounds that variances represent inefficiencies, avoidable waste not recoverable in the selling price, and random fluctuations in actual cost."
2. Where standards are not current, "the general practice is to divide the variances between inventories and cost of goods sold or profit and loss, thereby converting both inventories and cost of sales to approximate actual costs."

Another view asserts the following:

1. Any variances that are caused by inactivity, waste, or extravagance (outside acceptable tolerance limits) should be written off, because they represent losses. They should not be deferred by capitalizing them in the inventory accounts. This includes quantity variances on materials and labor as well as idle time (capacity) and efficiency variances on overhead. Assigning a portion of such costs to inventory can cloud the product pricing decision. For example, "the inclusion of idle capacity costs in product costs has the effect of raising (inventory) costs when it is most difficult to raise prices (low volume periods) and lowering (inventory) costs when it is easiest to ask for higher prices (high volume periods)."[6]
2. An inventory reserve account should be established and charged with part of the price and quantity variances to an extent that the materials, work in process, and finished goods inventories are brought up to, but do not exceed, current market values. The rest of the variance amounts (as well as those variances described in the previous paragraph) should be written off, because they represent excess costs. In this way, the inventory accounts themselves are stated at standard cost while the inventories on the balance sheet are, as a whole, shown at reasonable costs through the use of the inventory reserve account. In addition, losses caused by excessive costs and inefficiencies are shown in the operating statement for the period in which they occur.[7]

Disposition of Variances for Interim Financial Reporting

The AICPA takes the following position concerning variance disposition for interim financial reporting in published financial statements.

[5] *NAA Research Report, Nos. 11-15,* "How Standard Costs Are Being Used Currently" (New York: Institute of Management Accountants (formerly National Association of Accountants), 1948), pp. 65–66.

[6] Edwin Bartenstein, "Different Costs for Different Purposes," *Management Accounting,* Vol. 60, No. 2, p. 46.

[7] W. Wesley Miller, "Standard Costs and Their Relation to Cost Control," *NA(C)A Bulletin,* Vol. 27, No. 15, p. 692.

> Companies that use standard cost accounting systems for determining inventory and product costs should generally follow the same procedures in reporting purchase price, wage rate, usage or efficiency variances from standard cost at the end of an interim period as followed at the end of a fiscal year. Purchase price variances or volume or capacity cost variances that are planned and expected to be absorbed by the end of the annual period, should ordinarily be deferred at interim reporting dates. The effect of unplanned or unanticipated purchase price or volume variances, however, should be reported at the end of an interim period following the same procedures used at the end of a fiscal year.[8]

Revision of Standard Costs

As discussed in Chapter 18, standards should be changed when underlying conditions change or when they no longer reflect the original concept. Changing standards more often than once a year can weaken their effectiveness and increase operational details. Nevertheless, standard costs require continuous review and should be changed when conditions dictate. In order to compete effectively in global markets, businesses must strive for continuous improvement, which implies continuous tightening of standards.

Events, rather than time, are the factors that determine when standards should be revised. These events can be classified as internal or external. Internal events, such as technological advances, design revisions, methodological changes, labor rate adjustments, and changes in physical facilities, are to some degree controllable by management. In contrast, external events, such as price changes (including the impact of inflation), market trends, specific customer requirements, and changes in the competitive situation, generally are not controllable by management. Consequently, price standards and product design standards may require frequent change as controlling external events occur.[9]

When standard costs are changed, any adjustment to inventory should be made with care so that inventories are not written up or down arbitrarily. The Institute of Management Accountants (formerly the National Association of Accountants) published the following comments concerning adjustments to ending inventory for such changes:

> 1. If the new standard costs reflect conditions which affected the actual cost of the goods in the ending inventory, most firms adjust inventory to the new standard cost and carry the contra side of the adjusting entry to cost of sales by way of the variance accounts. In effect, this procedure assumes that the standard costs used to cost goods in the inventory have been incorrect and that restatement of inventory cost is needed to bring inventories to a correct figure on the books. Since the use of incorrect standards has affected the variance accounts as well as the inventory, the adjustment is carried to the variance accounts.

---

[8] *Opinions of the Accounting Principles Board, No. 28*, "Interim Financial Reporting" (New York: American Institute of Certified Public Accountants, 1973), par. 14.

[9] Some firms, facing technological change, experiment with the use of standards that are essentially very recent actual costs, or a rolling average of past actual costs. Such standards can be redetermined as often as every month. For examples, see C.J. McNair, William Mosconi, and Thomas Norris, *Meeting the Technology Challenge: Cost Accounting in a JIT Environment* (Montvale, NJ: Institute of Management Accountants (formerly National Association of Accountants), 1988).

2. If the standard costs represent conditions which are expected to prevail in the coming period but which have not affected costs in the past period, ending inventories are costed at the old standards. It appears to be common practice to adjust the detailed inventory records to new standard costs.

   In order to maintain the control relationship which the inventory accounts have over subsidiary records, the same adjustment is entered in the inventory control accounts; and the contra entry is carried to an inventory valuation account. Thus, the net effect is to state the inventory in the closing balance sheet at old standard costs. In the next period the inventory valuation account is closed to cost of sales when the goods to which the reserve relates move out of inventories. By use of this technique, the detailed records can be adjusted to new standards before the beginning of the year while at the same time the net charge to cost of sales in the new period is for old standard cost since the latter cost was correct at the time the goods were acquired.[10]

Broad Applicability of Standard Costing

The use of standard costing is not limited to manufacturing. This powerful tool for planning and control can be used in other aspects of business organizations. For example, standards can be used for marketing activities, as discussed in Chapter 25, and for maintenance work.[11] The not-for-profit organization sector (hospitals, charitable organizations, governments, and so on) also affords many opportunities to utilize standard costing. Though standard costs may not be formally recorded in the accounts, many relatively small organizations, such as automotive repair shops and construction contractors, can utilize the comparison of actual to standard quantities, times, and costs for bidding, pricing of jobs or projects, and the planning and control of routine operating activities.

Summary

Incorporating standard costs into the accounting record permits the most efficient use of a standard cost system. Variances can be analyzed for cost control, and standard costs can be used in developing budgets, bidding on contracts, and setting prices just as in those cases in which standard costs are not entered into the records. However, incorporating standard costs into the accounting records leads to savings and increased accuracy in clerical work. The accumulation of standard costs in the company's accounts and the disposition of standard cost variances were presented in this chapter.

[10] *NAA Research Report, Nos. 11-15,* p. 64.

[11] See James H. Bullock, *Maintenance Planning and Control* (New York: Institute of Management Accountants (formerly National Association of Accountants), 1979), Chapter 6, "Maintenance Standards and Performance Measurement," pp. 99–111.

Appendix Alternative Factory Overhead Variance Methods

As mentioned in the appendix to Chapter 18, there are many ways of dividing the overall factory overhead variance. This appendix presents the general journal entries required for the two alternative methods presented in the appendix to Chapter 18. The data used to illustrate the computation of the variances are those used for the Assembly Department of the Wilton Manufacturing Corporation.

Alternative Three-Variance Method

In the alternative three-variance method, the amount of over- or underapplied factory overhead is analyzed as spending, idle capacity, and efficiency variances. The entry to close the factory overhead control account and to record these three variances is as follows:

Factory Overhead Efficiency Variance*	1,920	
Factory Overhead Spending Variance**	326	
Factory Overhead Idle Capacity Variance***		384
Factory Overhead Control****		1,862

* $15.00 factory overhead rate × 128 hours (i.e., the difference between the actual hours required (1,632 hours) and the standard hours allowed (1,504 hours))

** The amount required to balance the entry (see Chapter 18 for an illustration of the computation of the spending variance)

*** $12.00 fixed factory overhead rate × 32 hours (i.e., the difference between normal capacity (1,600 hours) and the actual hours required (1,632 hours))

**** The amount of underapplied factory overhead (i.e., the difference between actual factory overhead ($24,422) and applied factory overhead ($22,560))

Four-Variance Method

In the four-variance method, the amount of over- or underapplied factory overhead is divided into the spending, idle capacity, variable efficiency, and fixed efficiency variances. The entry to close the factory overhead control account and to record these four variances is as follows:

Factory Overhead Variable Efficiency Variance*	384	
Factory Overhead Fixed Efficiency Variance**	1,536	
Factory Overhead Spending Variance***	326	
Factory Overhead Idle Capacity Variance****		384
Factory Overhead Control*****		1,862

* $3.00 variable factory overhead rate × 128 hours (i.e., the difference between the actual hours required (1,632 hours) and the standard hours allowed (1,504 hours))

** $12.00 fixed factory overhead rate × 128 hours (i.e., the difference between the actual hours required (1,632 hours) and the standard hours allowed (1,504 hours))

*** The amount required to balance the entry (see Chapter 18 for an illustration of the computation of the spending variance)

**** $12.00 fixed factory overhead rate × 32 hours (i.e., the difference between normal capacity (1,600 hours) and the actual hours required (1,632 hours))

***** The amount of underapplied factory overhead (i.e., the difference between actual factory overhead ($24,422) and applied factory overhead ($22,560))

Discussion Questions

Q19-1 Some firms incorporate standard costs into their accounts; others maintain them only for statistical comparisons. Discuss these different uses of standard costs.

Q19-2 Compare the use of actual cost to standard cost for inventory costing.

Q19-3 Differences between actual costs and standard costs can be recorded in variance accounts. What considerations might determine the number of variance accounts?

Q19-4 Name several advantages of using standard costs for finished goods and cost of goods sold.

Q19-5 The determination of periodic income depends greatly on the cost assigned to materials, work in process, and finished goods inventories. What considerations determine whether inventories are costed at standard or approximate actual costs by companies using standard costs?

Q19-6 Present arguments in support of each of the following three methods of treating standard cost variances for purposes of financial reporting:

(a) As deferred charges or credits on the balance sheet

(b) As charges or credits on the income statement

(c) Allocated between inventories and cost of goods sold (AICPA adapted)

Exercises

E19-1 Journal Entries for Materials; Variance Analysis. Blackrock Electronics Company uses a standard costing system. The standard for one of its products, Tekal, is 2 units of component part F-25 at a cost of 42 cents per unit. During September, 8,200 units of Tekal were manufactured. During September, 20,000 units of component part F-25 were purchased on account for a total cost of $8,800, and 16,500 units were used in production.

Required: Prepare the journal entries for the purchase and issue of component part F-25 using the three methods for recording materials.

E19-2 Journal Entries for Materials; Variance Analysis. The standard cost per unit of component part G-34 is $8. During the month, 12,000 units of G-34 were purchased on account at a total cost of $96,960. In addition, there were 2,000 units in beginning materials inventory. Of the 14,000 units of G-34 available, 13,000 units were used during the month; however, the standard quantity allowed for actual production is 12,800 units.

Required:

(1) Assuming that the materials price variance is recorded at the date the materials are purchased, prepare the appropriate general journal entries to record the purchase of component part G-34 and the issue of component part G-34 to production.

(2) Assume that materials are inventoried at actual cost and that the beginning inventory of G-34 contained 2,000 units at a total cost of $15,880. The materials price variance is recorded at the date the materials are issued. Prepare the appropriate general journal entries to record the purchase and subsequent issue of component part G-34 assuming that the average cost method is used for materials inventory.

(3) Assume the same facts as for requirement 2 except that the company uses the fifo method for materials inventory. Prepare the appropriate general journal entry to record the issue of component part G-34 to production.

(4) Assume the same facts as for requirement 2 except that the company uses the lifo method for materials inventory. Prepare the appropriate general journal entry to record the issue of component part G-34 to production.

E19-3 Journal Entries for Labor; Variance Analysis. The processing of one unit of product Gaplock requires a standard of ¾ hours of direct labor at $9.50 per hour. During the month, 2,400 units of Gaplock were manufactured. Actual production required 1,920 direct labor hours at a total cost of $17,856.

Required: Prepare journal entries to record direct labor charged to production, including variances.

E19-4 Journal Entries for Materials and Labor; Variance Analysis. The standard cost card for one unit of Jellplug requires two quarts of Jelex at $2 a quart and ¼ hour of direct labor at $12 per hour. During the current month, 10,000 units of Jellplug were manufactured. Actual production required 21,000 quarts of Jelex at an actual cost of $2.10 per quart and 2,400 direct labor hours at an average rate of $12.25 per hour.

Required: Prepare general journal entries to record the issue of materials to production and the charge for direct labor, including variances. Assume the materials are inventoried at actual cost and the price variance is recorded when materials are issued.

E19-5 Journal Entries for Factory Overhead; Two-Variance Analysis. Factory overhead is charged to production in Department A on the basis of the standard machine hours allowed for actual production. The following data relate to the results of operations for May:

Normal capacity in machine hours	15,000
Standard machine hours allowed for actual production	12,000
Actual machine hours	13,000

The factory overhead rate based on normal capacity machine hours is as follows:

Variable overhead	$ 37,500	÷	15,000	hours	=	$2.50
Fixed overhead	67,500	÷	15,000	hours	=	4.50
Total factory overhead	$105,000	÷	15,000	hours	=	$7.00

Actual factory overhead incurred during May totaled $90,000. The company maintains two factory overhead accounts: Factory Overhead Control and Applied Factory Overhead.

Required: Prepare the journal entries necessary to record each of the following:
(1) The factory overhead applied to production during the period
(2) The closing of Applied Factory Overhead
(3) The closing of Factory Overhead Control into two factory overhead variance accounts

E19-6 Journal Entries for Factory Overhead: Two-Variance Method. Factory overhead is charged to production in the Assembly Department of Indiana Manufacturing Company on the basis of the standard direct labor hours allowed for actual production. The following data relate to the results of operations for December:

Normal capacity in direct labor hours	10,000
Standard labor hours allowed for actual production	11,000
Actual direct labor hours worked	10,500

The factory overhead rate based on normal capacity direct labor hours is as follows:

Variable overhead	$ 30,000	÷	10,000	hours	=	$3.00
Fixed overhead	20,000	÷	10,000	hours	=	2.00
Total factory overhead	$ 50,000	÷	10,000	hours	=	$5.00

Actual factory overhead incurred during December totaled $56,000.

Required: Prepare the journal entries necessary to record each of the following:
(1) The incurrence of actual factory overhead
(2) The factory overhead actually charged to production
(3) The closing of the applied factory overhead account
(4) The closing of the factory overhead control account into two factory overhead variance accounts.

E19-7 Journal Entries for Factory Overhead; Three-Variance Method. Factory overhead is charged to production in the Machining Department of Texas Tool Company on the basis of the standard machine hours allowed for actual production. The following data relate to the results of operations for November:

Normal capacity in machine hours	5,000
Standard machine hours allowed for actual production	4,800
Actual machine hours	5,200

The factory overhead rate based on normal capacity machine hours is as follows:

Variable overhead	$20,000	÷	5,000	hours	=	$ 4.00
Fixed overhead	60,000	÷	5,000	hours	=	12.00
Total factory overhead	$80,000	÷	5,000	hours	=	$16.00

Actual factory overhead incurred during November totaled $78,000.

Required: Prepare the journal entries necessary to record each of the following:
(1) The factory overhead actually charged to production
(2) The closing of the applied factory overhead account
(3) The closing of the factory overhead control account into three factory overhead variances

E19-8 Journal Entries for Factory Overhead; Three-Variance Method, Factory overhead is charged to production in the Finishing Department of Franklin Furniture Company on the basis of the standard direct labor hours allowed for actual production. The following data relate to the results of operations for February:

Normal capacity in direct labor hours	8,000
Standard labor hours allowed for actual production	7,000
Actual direct labor hours worked	7,600

The factory overhead rate based on normal capacity direct labor hours is as follows:

Variable overhead	$ 64,000	÷	8,000	hours	=	$ 8.00
Fixed overhead	24,000	÷	8,000	hours	=	3.00
Total factory overhead	$ 88,000	÷	8,000	hours	=	$11.00

Actual factory overhead incurred during February totaled $86,000. The company maintains two factory overhead accounts: Factory Overhead Control and Applied Factory Overhead.

Required: Prepare the journal entries necessary to record each of the following:
(1) The factory overhead charged to production during February
(2) The closing of Applied Factory Overhead
(3) The closing of Factory Overhead Control into three factory overhead variance accounts

E19-9 Disposition of Variances. Nanron Company uses a standard process cost system for all its products. All inventories are carried at standard. Inventories and cost of goods sold are adjusted for financial statement purposes for all variances considered material in amount at the end of the fiscal year. All products are considered to flow through the manufacturing process to finished goods and ultimate sale in a first in, first out pattern.

The standard cost of one of Nanron's products is as follows:

Materials	$2
Direct labor (.5 DLH at $8)	4
Factory overhead	3
Total standard cost	$9

There is no work in process inventory of this product due to the nature of the product and the manufacturing process.

The following schedule reports the sales and manufacturing activity measured at standard cost for the current fiscal year:

	Units	Dollars
Product manufactured	95,000	$855,000
Beginning finished goods inventory	15,000	135,000
Goods available for sale	110,000	$990,000
Ending finished goods inventory	19,000	171,000
Cost of goods sold	91,000	$819,000

The balance of the Finished Goods Inventory, $140,800, reported on the balance sheet at the beginning of the year included a $5,800 adjustment for variances from standard cost. The unfavorable standard cost variances for labor for the current fiscal year consisted of a wage rate variance of $32,000 and a labor efficiency variance of $20,000 (2,500 hours at $8). There were no other variances from standard cost for this year.

Required: Assuming the unfavorable labor variances totaling $52,000 are considered material in amount by management and are to be allocated to finished goods inventory and to cost of goods sold, compute the amount that will be shown on the year-end balance sheet for Finished Goods Inventory and the amount for Cost of Goods Sold on the income statement prepared for the fiscal year. (ICMA adapted)

E19-10 Disposition of Variances. Atlantic Manufacturing Corporation uses standard costing in accounting for manufacturing costs. Variances are allocated to the cost of goods sold and ending inventories. The following information was extracted from the corporation's books for March:

	Debit	Credit
Materials purchase price variance		$ 150
Materials quantity variance	$ 500	
Labor rate variance	600	
Labor efficiency variance	1,200	
Controllable variance	1,500	
Volume variance		1,800

The following inventories were on hand on March 31:

Finished goods	1,200 units
Work in process	1,500 units
Raw materials	none

The work in process inventory was fully complete as to materials and ⅓ complete as to direct labor and factory overhead. During January, 3,300 units were sold.

Required: Allocate the variances. Round distribution percentages to the nearest whole percent and allocations to the nearest cent.

E19-11 (Appendix) Journal Entries for Factory Overhead; Alternative Three-Variance Method. The practical capacity of Winslow Manufacturing Company is 5,000 units of product Dupto. At the normal capacity level (80% of practical), the following factory overhead amounts have been budgeted:

Fixed	$18,000
Variable	6,000

Standards were set as follows:

Processing time, 1.5 hours per unit of Dupto
Factory overhead, $4 per hour of processing

Actual data for November were:

Production, 3,450 units of Dupto
Processing time, 5,320 hours
Factory overhead, $21,230

Required: Assuming that actual and applied overhead are recorded in separate accounts, give the general journal entries to charge overhead to production, to close the two overhead accounts, and to record the overhead variances using the alternative three-variance method illustrated in the appendix to this chapter.

E19-12 (Appendix) Journal Entries for Factory Overhead; Four-Variance Method. Kipper Corporation charges factory overhead to production on the basis of the standard processing time allowed for actual production. The following data relate to the results of operations for December:

Normal capacity in processing hours	10,000
Standard processing hours allowed for actual production	9,400
Actual processing hours required during December	10,600

The factory overhead rate per hour of processing based on normal capacity is as follows:

Variable overhead	$ 45,000	÷	10,000	hours	=	$ 4.50
Fixed overhead	155,000	÷	10,000	hours	=	15.50
Total factory overhead	$200,000	÷	10,000	hours	=	$20.00

Actual factory overhead incurred during December totaled $196,000.

Required: Give the appropriate general journal entries to record the charge to production for overhead (assuming that actual and applied overhead are recorded in separate accounts) and the closing of the two overhead accounts along with the appropriate overhead variances (use the four-variance method illustrated in the appendix to this chapter).

Problems

P19-1 Journal Entries; Variance Analysis; Two Overhead Variances. Moore Manufacturing Company manufactures a product called Morestuff, which has the following standard costs:

Materials	6 units	at	$ 2 =	$12.00
Labor	¼ hr.	at	8 =	2.00
Variable factory overhead	¾ hr.	at	4 =	3.00
Fixed factory overhead (normal capacity is 4,000 hours of processing time)	¾ hr.	at	12 =	9.00
Total standard cost				$26.00

The following information pertains to actual production activity for August:

(a) 6,000 equivalent units of Morestuff were produced with respect to materials, 5,800 equivalent units with respect to labor, and 5,500 equivalent units with respect to factory overhead.
(b) 33,000 units of materials were purchased on account at a total cost of $64,350. The materials price variance is recorded when the materials are purchased.
(c) 40,000 units of materials were issued to production and used during the period.
(d) Direct labor cost was $12,300 for 1,500 actual hours. Assume that the liability has already been recorded, but not yet distributed.
(e) Actual processing required during August totaled 4,300 hours.
(f) Actual factory overhead was $65,000.
(g) 5,200 units were completed and transferred to finished goods inventory during the month.
(h) 5,500 units of Morestuff were sold during the month for $40 each.

Required: Prepare the journal entries to record the information provided, including two variances for each cost element.

P19-2 Journal Entries; Variance Analysis; Three Overhead Variances. Hytek Corporation manufactures a product called Tekothing, which has the following standard costs:

Materials	5 units	at	$ 6 =	$30.00
Labor	¾ hr.	at	12 =	9.00
Factory overhead (based on normal capacity of 5,000 machine hours)	2 hrs.	at	14 =	28.00
Total standard cost				$67.00

The following information pertains to actual production activity for July:

(a) Work in process, beginning inventory contained 300 units of Tekothing (complete as to materials but only ⅔ complete as to labor and ½ complete as to machining) and ending inventory contained 200 units (complete as to materials but only ½ complete as to labor and ¼ complete as to machining). 2,400 units of Tekothing were completed and transferred to finished goods inventory during July.

(b) 11,000 units of materials were purchased on account at a total cost of $67,650. The materials price variance is recorded when the materials are purchased.
(c) 12,000 units of materials were issued to production and used during the period.
(d) Direct labor cost totaled $20,570 for 1,700 actual hours worked. Assume that the liability has already been recorded.
(e) Actual machining required during July totaled 4,900 hours.
(f) Actual factory overhead was $69,000. Factory Overhead Control is closed at the end of each month.
(g) 20% of the factory overhead budgeted at 5,000 machine hours was variable cost and the balance was fixed cost.

Required: Prepare the journal entries to record the information provided, including two variances for materials and labor and three variances for factory overhead.

P19-3 Journal Entries; Variance Analysis; Two Overhead Variances. The following information pertains to production operations of Falcon Corporation for May:

(a) Inventories:

Work in process:	Beginning, 3,000 units, all materials, ⅓ converted; ending, 2,000 units, all materials, ¾ converted; no spoilage.
Finished goods:	200 units in beginning inventory and 100 units in ending inventory.

(b) Standard and actual costs:

Materials:	Standard quantity, 6 units of material per unit of product at $.50 per unit of material; 30,000 units of material were purchased on account for a total cost of $15,900 (the price variance is recorded at the date of purchase); 24,500 units of material were requisitioned from the storeroom.
Labor:	Standard per unit of product, ½ hour at $10 per hour; actual labor rate was $10.75 per hour for 2,600 hours.
Factory overhead:	Normal capacity, 2,500 labor hours; fixed factory overhead rate, $9 per labor hour; variable factory overhead rate, $3 per labor hour; actual factory overhead was $31,000.

Five thousand units of product were completed during the period, and 5,100 were sold on account for $22 each.

Required: Prepare the journal entries to record the cost accounting cycle transactions, using standard costing. Record two variances for each element of cost. CGA-Canada (adapted). Reprint with permission.

P19-4 Income Statement; Variance Analysis; Two Overhead Variances. Ensley Corporation manufactures Product G, which sells for $25 per unit. Material M is added before processing starts, and labor and overhead are added evenly during the manufacturing process. Production capacity is budgeted at 110,000 units of G annually. The standard costs per unit of G are as follows:

Direct materials: 2 pounds of material M at $1.50		$ 3.00
Direct labor: 1.5 hours at $8 per hour		12.00
Factory overhead:		
Variable	$1.50	
Fixed	1.10	2.60
Total standard cost per unit		$17.60

A process cost system is used. Inventories are costed at standard cost. All variances from standard costs are charged or credited to Cost of Goods Sold in the year incurred. Inventory data for 19A are as follow:

	January 1	December 31
Material M	50,000 pounds	60,000 pounds
Work in process:		
All materials, ⅖ processed	10,000 units	
All materials, ⅓ processed		15,000 units
Finished goods inventory	20,000 units	12,000 units

During 19A, 250,000 pounds of M were purchased at an average cost of $1.485 per pound, and 240,000 pounds were transferred to work in process inventory. Direct labor costs amounted to $1,313,760 at an average hourly labor rate of $8.16. Actual factory overhead for 19A was as follows:

Variable	$181,500
Fixed	114,000

A total of 110,000 units of G were completed and transferred to finished goods inventory. Marketing and administrative expenses were $681,000.

Required: Prepare an income statement for 19A, including all manufacturing cost variances and using the two-variance method for factory overhead. (AICPA adapted)

P19-5 Income Statement. The Kalman Company, a subsidiary of the Camper Corporation, submits interim financial statements. Camper combines these statements with similar statements from other subsidiaries to prepare its quarterly statements. The following data are taken from the records and accounts of the Kalman Company.

(a) Sales forecasts for the year are as follow:

Quarter	Stove Units	Percent
First	450,000	30%
Second	600,000	40
Third	150,000	10
Fourth	300,000	20
	1,500,000	100%

Sales have been achieved as forecasted in the first and second quarters of the current year.

(b) Management is considering increasing the selling price of a stove from $30 to $34. However, management is concerned that this price increase may reduce the already low sales volume forecasts for the third and fourth quarters.

(c) The production schedule calls for 1,500,000 stoves this year. The manufacturing facilities can produce 1,720,000 units per year or 430,000 units per quarter during regular hours. The following quarterly production schedule was developed to meet the seasonal sales demand and is being followed as planned.

Quarter	Scheduled Production (in units)	Percent
First	465,000	31%
Second	450,000	30
Third	225,000	15
Fourth	360,000	24
	1,500,000	100%

(d) The standard manufacturing cost of a stove unit, as established at the beginning of the current year, is as follows. This standard cost does not incorporate any charges for overtime.

Materials	$ 4.00
Labor	9.00
Variable factory overhead	2.00
Fixed factory overhead	3.00
Standard cost per stove	$18.00

(e) A significant and permanent price increase in the cost of raw materials resulted in a material price variance of $270,000 for the materials used in the second quarter. Unplanned variances that are significant and permanent in nature are prorated to the applicable accounts during the quarter in which they occur.

(f) There was a $36,000 unfavorable direct labor efficiency variance in the second quarter, which occurred as a result of unexpected inefficiencies. These inefficiencies are not regarded as significant, and they are not expected to recur.

(g) The second quarter unfavorable factory overhead spending variance of $126,000 was partially due to overtime paid during the second quarter and partially due to unexpected inefficiencies. Because overtime was incurred in order to produce enough product to meet the sales forecasts, the portion of the spending variance attributable to overtime is prorated between quarters on the basis of budgeted sales. Management does not expect to incur overtime in the last half of the year. The overtime premium is 50% of the standard labor rate.
(h) Total fixed factory overhead expected to be incurred and budgeted for the year is $4,500,000. Through the first two quarters, $2,745,000 of fixed factory overhead was applied to production. Of this amount, $1,350,000 was applied in the second quarter. The high production activity resulted in a total favorable fixed factory overhead volume variance of $495,000 for the first two quarters. However, because the fixed overhead rate is based on annual expected production of 1,500,000 units, a volume variance is reported on interim statements only if actual production differs from the planned production schedule.
(i) Selling expenses are 10% of sales and are expected to total $4,500,000 for the year.
(j) Administrative expenses are $6,000,000 annually and are incurred uniformly throughout the year.
(k) Inventory balances as of the end of the second quarter follow:

Materials (at actual cost)	$400,000
Work in Process (50% complete—at standard cost)	72,000
Finished Goods (at standard cost)	900,000

(l) The stove product line is expected to earn $7,500,000 before taxes this year. The estimated state and federal income tax expenses for the year are $4,050,000.

Required: Prepare the second quarter interim income statement for the Kalman subsidiary of Camper Corporation.

P19-6 Variance Analysis; Two Overhead Variances; Journal Entries; Income Statement The following information concerns Pacific Manufacturing Company, which manufactures a single product called Westco. The standard cost card for Westco follows:

Material A: 1 unit at $14	$14
Material B: 6 units at $2	12
Direct labor: ½ hour at $10	5
Variable factory overhead: ⅓ machine hour at $3	1
Fixed factory overhead: ⅓ machine hour at $24	8
	$40

Other information available for the year ending December 31, 19A, includes the following:
(a) Materials price variances are recorded when the materials are purchased. Transactions related to materials are as follow:

Material	Beginning Inventory	Purchased	Issued
A	1,200 units at $14	15,000 units at $13	14,200 units
B	6,300 units at $ 2	80,000 units at $ 3	82,300 units

(b) Beginning work in process contained 6,000 units of Westco, complete with respect to material A, ⅔ complete with respect to material B, ½ complete with respect to direct labor, and ⅔ complete with respect to machining.
(c) Ending work in process contains 5,000 units of Westco, complete with respect to material A, ½ complete with respect to material B, ¼ complete with respect to direct labor, and ½ complete with respect to machining.
(d) 15,000 units of Westco were completed and transferred to finished goods during the period. There were 4,000 units of Westco in finished goods at the beginning of the period and 3,600 units at the end of the period. Westco sells for $60 a unit.
(e) During the period, 6,500 direct labor hours were worked at a total cost of $71,500.
(f) Production machining time totaled 4,400 hours. The standard factory overhead rate is determined on the basis of a normal operating capacity of 5,000 machine hours.

(g) Actual factory overhead for the period totaled $122,000.
(h) Marketing and administrative expenses for the period totaled $120,000, and the effective income tax rate is 40%.

Required:
(1) Prepare journal entries to record the purchase and issue of materials, the production charge for labor and factory overhead, and the closing of the two factory overhead accounts (Factory Overhead Control and Applied Factory Overhead), along with the appropriate standard cost variances. Use the three-variance method for factory overhead.
(2) Prepare the journal entry to close the variance accounts into Income Summary.
(3) Prepare an income statement for the year ending December 31, 19A.

P19-7 Journal Entries; Variance Analysis; Three Overhead Variances; Income Statement. Grindle Corporation uses the following standard costs in accounting for its only product:

Materials: 3 liters × $4	$12.00
Direct labor: ½ hour × $7	3.50
Variable factory overhead: ½ hour x $6	3.00
Fixed factory overhead: ½ hour x $9	4.50
Total standard cost	$23.00

Fixed factory overhead budgeted was $49,500 per month. Actual activity for November was as follows:
(a) 40 000 liters of material were purchased on account for $159,200. The related price variance is recorded at the time of purchase.
(b) 10,000 units were produced.
(c) There was no work in process at the beginning or end of November.
(d) 31 000 liters of material were issued to production.
(e) The direct labor payroll to be distributed (credit the payroll account) is $35,616 for 4,800 hours.
(f) Actual factory overhead cost of $81,500 was incurred.
(g) 8,000 units were sold on account at $40 each.
(h) Marketing and administrative expenses of $60,000 were incurred.

Required:
(1) Prepare journal entries to record the November activity. (Ignore overhead variances.)
(2) Prepare a three-variance analysis of under- or overapplied factory overhead.
(3) Prepare an income statement, assuming that all variances are to be closed to Cost of Goods Sold.

CGA-Canada (adapted). Reprint with permission.

P19-8 Allocating Variances. Hamm Corporation commenced doing business on December 1. The corporation uses a standard cost system for the manufacturing costs of its only product, Hamex. The standard costs for a unit of Hamex are:

Materials: 10 kilograms at $.70	$ 7
Direct labor: 1 hour at $8	8
Factory overhead (applied on the basis of $2 per direct labor hour)	2
Total standard cost	$17

The following data were extracted from the corporation's books for December:

	Units	Debit	Credit
Budgeted production	3,000		
Units sold	1,500		
Sales			$45,000
Sales discounts		$ 500	
Materials price usage variance		1,500	
Materials quantity variance		660	
Direct labor rate variance		250	
Factory overhead spending variance			300
Discounts lost		120	

The company records purchases of materials net of discounts. The amounts shown for discounts lost and materials price usage variance are applicable to materials used in manufacturing operations during December.

Inventory data at December 31 indicate the following inventories were on hand:

	Units
Finished goods	900
Work in process	1,200
Materials	None

The work in process inventory was 100% complete as to materials and 50% as to direct labor and factory overhead. The corporation's policy is to allocate variances to the cost of goods sold and ending inventories; that is, work in process and finished goods.

Required: Prepare schedules to:

(1) Allocate the variances and discounts lost on purchases to the ending inventories and to cost of goods sold.

(2) Compute the cost of goods manufactured at standard cost and at actual cost for December. Show amounts for materials, labor, and factory overhead separately.

(3) Compute the actual cost of materials, labor, and factory overhead included in the work in process inventory and in the finished goods inventory at December 31. (AICPA adapted)

P19-9 (Appendix) Journal Entries; Variance Analysis with the Alternative Three-Variance Method for Overhead. Klingsted Manufacturing Company produces custom-made, tie-dyed sweat shirts for distribution on college campuses. The following standards have been established.

Materials:	
Cotton cloth: 2 yards at $1	$ 2.00
Dyes: 1 pint at $.50	.50
Labor: ½ hour at $6	3.00
Factory overhead: ½ hour at $10	5.00
Total standard cost	$10.50

The monthly production budget is based on normal plant operations of 1,600 hours, with fixed factory overhead of $11,200 (that is, a fixed overhead rate at normal capacity of $7 per direct labor hour). Inventories at January 1 were as follow:

Cotton Cloth (2,000 yards at $1)	$2,000
Dye (1,000 pints at $.50)	500
Work in Process (1,000 units; ¼ finished as to conversion; all materials issued)	4,500
Finished Goods (500 at $10.50)	5,250

Production for January:

3,000 units completed and transferred to finished goods

750 units ⅓ converted, all materials added, in work in process ending inventory

Transactions for January:

Cotton cloth purchased	5,000 yds. at $1.10
Dyes purchased	2,500 pints at $.49
Cotton cloth issued to factory	5,600 yards
Dyes issued to factory	2,700 pints
Direct labor payroll	1,550 hours at $5.90
Actual factory overhead	$16,100
Sales on account	3,100 sweatshirts at $14

Required: Prepare journal entries to record the January transactions, accounting for work in process at standard cost and recognizing variances in the proper accounts. Use the two-variance method in computing materials and labor, and the alternative three-variance method in computing factory overhead variances. Recognize the materials price variance at the time of purchase. Use separate inventory and variance accounts for each material. Close all variances to Cost of Goods Sold.

P19-10 (Appendix) Journal Entries; Variance Analysis with the Four-Variance Method for Overhead. Marfab Manufacturing Company uses a standard cost system in its accounting records. The standard costs for its one product are as follow:

Materials	9 kilograms	at $ 2.00 =	$18.00
Direct labor	2 hours	at 10.50 =	21.00
Variable overhead	2 hours	at 3.00 =	6.00
Fixed overhead	2 hours	at 10.00 =	20.00
Total standard cost			$65.00

Normal capacity is 2,000 direct labor hours per month. Materials, work in process, and finished goods are recorded in inventory at standard cost. The following information is taken from last month's records:

Production	900	units
Materials purchased	10 000	kilograms at $ 1.95
Materials used in production	8 600	kilograms
Direct labor payroll	1,740	hours at $11.55
Actual overhead	$24,000	

Required: Prepare journal entries to record the information provided. Use the two-variance method to compute materials and labor variances and the four-variance method to compute overhead variances.

CGA-Canada (adapted). Reprint with permission.

Cases

C19-1 Disposition of Variances. Jonesboro Company manufactures office equipment. The company historically has utilized standard costing to aid management decisions. Variances from standard usually have been minor and always have been expensed in the audited financial statements. However, two problems have been encountered this year. First, variances from standard are large because of rapid increases in labor and materials costs and because of a slowdown in production during the last quarter. Second, a considerable portion of manufactured inventory remains unsold. The company wishes to expense the variances from standard.

Required: Discuss the acceptability of the proposal insofar as external reporting is concerned.

(CICA adapted)

C19-2 Standard Costs in Inventory and Variance Disposition. Many advocates of standard costing take the position that these costs are a proper basis for inventory costing for external reporting purposes. *Accounting Research Bulletin No. 43*, however, reflects the widespread view that standard costs are not acceptable unless "adjusted at reasonable intervals to reflect current conditions so that at the balance-sheet date standard costs reasonably approximate costs computed under one of the recognized bases."

Required:

(1) Discuss the conceptual merits of using standard costs as the basis for inventory costing for external reporting purposes.
(2) Prepare general journal entries for three alternative dispositions of a $1,500 unfavorable variance, when all goods manufactured during the period are included in the ending finished goods inventory. Assume that a formal standard cost system is in operation, that $500 of the variance resulted from actual costs exceeding normal (attainable) standard cost, and that $1,000 of the variance resulted from the difference between the theoretical (ideal) standard and a normal standard.
(3) Discuss the conceptual merits of each of the three alternative methods of disposition used in requirement 2.

(AICPA adapted)

PART 5

Analysis of Costs and Profits

CHAPTER 20

Direct Costing and Cost-Volume-Profit Analysis

Learning Objectives

After studying this chapter, you will be able to:
1. Distinguish between direct costing and absorption costing.
2. Compute income on a direct costing basis and reconcile it with absorption costing income.
3. List uses of direct costing.
4. List the arguments for and against direct costing.
5. State the position of the accounting profession, the IRS, and the SEC on the nonacceptability of direct costing for external reporting purposes.
6. Compute the level of sales in dollars and units of product required to break even or to achieve a targeted level of profit.
7. Prepare a break-even chart.
8. Define and compute the margin of safety and the margin of safety ratio.

The chapters that cover factory overhead (Chapters 12, 13, and 14) presented the use of factory overhead rates for product costing. All budgeted factory overhead costs were combined into one or more composite, predetermined rates, which were then used to charge factory overhead to the products manufactured during the period. The construction of each rate requires that factory overhead for the accounting period be budgeted and the total be divided by the expected volume of the activity measure used to allocate factory overhead to production. The objective of this process is to assign a portion of each item of factory overhead incurred during the period to each unit of product produced during the period. This process results in the assignment of a share of both fixed and variable factory overhead to production and is referred to as **absorption, full,** or **conventional costing.**

When predetermined overhead rates are used, the amount of factory overhead assigned to production is a function of the predetermined rate and the actual volume of production activity. The use of predetemined rates typically results in a difference between actual factory overhead and the amount charged to production. This difference can be the result of differences in costs (when actual factory overhead for the period is not the same as budgeted factory overhead adjusted to the actual level of activity), differences in activity (when the actual volume of production activity is not the same as the budgeted level of activity used in computing the predetermined rate), or both. When actual and budgeted activity differ, fixed factory overhead is over- or underabsorbed. Whether this fixed cost variance is charged to period expense or ratably allocated between ending inventories and the cost of goods sold, fluctuations in the unit product cost occur as a result of differences in activity between periods.

A problem more serious than fluctuating unit costs occurs when absorption costing is used. A substantial amount of fixed overhead cannot be traced to individual products or activities, even when activity-based costing is used. As a consequence, a substantial portion of the fixed cost allocated to any particular product may have little relationship to actual costs incurred to manufacture that product. The allocation of fixed cost to products introduces an element of arbitrariness into product costs that limits its usefulness for internal decision making. Unreliable product costs lead to unreliable analyses of profitability, and planned changes in volume and product mix based on unreliable profitability estimates often have an unanticipated effect on profits.

In a competitive business environment, management needs information that will enable it to determine the effects of changes in volume and mix on profit. Direct costing was designed to enhance the usefulness of product costs in internal decision making by eliminating the arbitrary element of fixed cost. Cost–volume–profit analysis is a short-run planning tool that effectively utilizes direct costing data to analyze the relationships between costs, profits, product mix, and sales volume. Both are discussed in this chapter.

Direct Costing

Direct costing, also referred to as **variable costing** or **marginal costing**, charges units of product with only those manufacturing costs that vary directly with volume. Prime costs (direct materials and direct labor) plus variable factory overhead are assigned to inventories (both work in process and finished goods) and to the cost of goods sold. Thus, only variable manufacturing costs are charged to the product, while all fixed manufacturing costs are expensed in the period in which they are incurred. Fixed manufacturing costs, such as depreciation, insurance, taxes, supervisory salaries, and the salaries of janitors, guards, maintenance, and office personnel, are excluded from the cost of the product. Because the incurrence of fixed costs appears to be more closely associated with the passage of time than with production activity, such costs are often referred to as period costs and are charged to period expense rather than to inventories. In contrast, variable costs are often referred to as product costs and are assigned to inventories because they are more closely associated with production activity than with the passage of time.

Direct costing focuses attention on the product and the costs directly traceable to changes in production activity. This focus is directed in two ways: (1) to internal uses of the fixed–variable cost relationship and the contribution margin concept, and (2) to external uses involving the costing of inventories, income determination, and financial reporting. The internal uses deal with the application of direct costing in profit planning, product pricing, other phases of decision making, and in cost control. These facets of direct costing are presented in Figure 20-1.

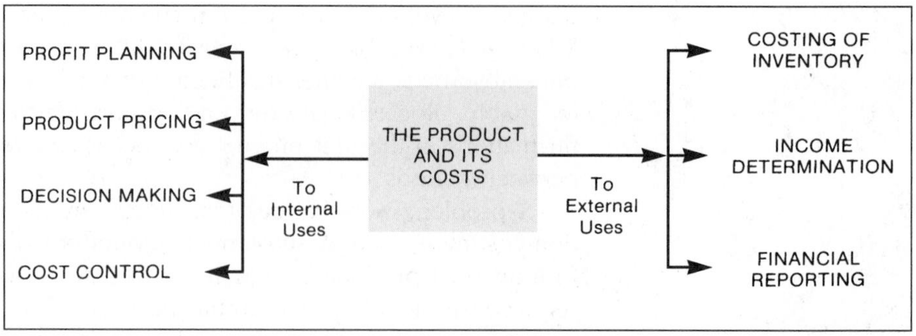

FIGURE 20-1 *Facets of Direct Costing*

Contribution Margin Defined

The **contribution margin**, sometimes referred to as **marginal income**, is the difference between sales revenue and variable costs. It is computed by subtracting all variable costs, both manufacturing and nonmanufacturing, from sales revenue. In direct costing, the contribution margin can be computed in total (for the entire firm or for each product line, sales territory, operating division, and so on) or on a per unit basis. However, income per unit is not computed. Total income is computed by subtracting total fixed costs from the total contribution margin, as shown in the following illustration. This illustration is based on the assumption that unit variable cost remains constant at $42 for all levels of activity, and that the fixed cost is fixed in total for all levels of activity.

	Per Unit	Total	Percentage of Sales
Sales (10,000 units)	$70	$700,000	100
Less variable cost	42	420,000	60
Contribution margin	$28	$280,000	40
Less fixed cost		175,000	25
Operating income		$105,000	15

Internal Uses of Direct Costing

Executive managers, including marketing executives, production managers, and cost analysts, frequently praise the planning, control, and analytical potential of direct costing. Fixed costs calculated on a unit cost basis under absorption costing vary for different volumes of production. Such variability in unit costs makes the use of absorption costing for many types of internal analysis difficult at best and misleading at worst. In contrast, variable unit costs and the contribution margin per unit tend to remain constant at all levels of activity (at least within the relevant range). Consequently, managers often find direct costing more understandable and more useful than absorption costing for most types of internal analysis.

The trend in manufacturing is toward increasing automation. In some cases, robotics technology has been used to replace direct labor, thereby significantly reducing variable manufacturing costs. In some fully automated plants, variable costs make up only a small portion of the total manufacturing cost. At first glance, one might assume that direct costing is of little value to decision makers when variable costs constitute such a small component of total cost. However, sometimes the opposite is true. Because fixed costs make up a larger share of total costs, the inclusion of fixed costs in the cost of the product results in larger changes in product costs as production volume fluctuates between periods.

Consequently, reliance on absorption costing figures can be even more misleading than when fixed costs are a small portion of total cost.

Direct Costing as a Profit-Planning Tool. As discussed in Chapter 15, a profit plan covers all phases of future operations to attain a stated profit goal. Direct costing is quite useful in short-term planning, in pricing special orders, and in making current operating decisions. With its separation of variable and fixed costs and its calculation of the contribution margin, direct costing facilitates analysis of the cost–volume–profit relationship. Direct costing aids in identifying the relevant analytical data for determining the break-even point, the rate of return on investment, the contribution margin by a segment of total sales, and the total profit from all operations based on a given volume. Direct costing also aids management in planning and evaluating the profit resulting from a change of volume, a change in the sales mix, make-or-buy situations, and the acquisition of new equipment. Knowledge of the variable or out-of-pocket costs, fixed costs, and contribution margin provides a basis for evaluating the profitability of products, customers, territories, and other segments of the entire business.

Direct Costing as a Guide to Product Pricing. In a highly competitive market, prices are determined through the interaction of supply and demand. The best or optimum price is the one that yields the maximum excess of total revenue over total cost. The volume at which the increase in total cost due to the addition of one more unit of volume is equal to the increase in total revenue (that is, the point at which marginal revenue is equal to marginal cost) is the profit-maximizing volume. The price at which this volume can be obtained is the optimum price. A higher price lowers the quantity demanded and decreases total profit. A lower price increases the quantity demanded but decreases total profit. Although management can control supply, demand is a function of such factors as the tastes and preferences of consumers and their financial capacity, over which management has little control. Direct costing provides the marginal cost of the product necessary to determine the profit-maximizing volume.

In multiproduct pricing, management needs to know whether each product can be priced competitively and still contribute sufficiently to the company's total contribution margin for fixed cost recovery and profit. Direct costing provides the data necessary to compute the contribution margin from each product line for different unit sales prices and different levels of sales. Although such information is useful in short-term pricing decisions, a long-run pricing policy should ensure that all fixed costs are fully recovered.

Direct Costing as a Basis for Evaluating the Profitability of Multiple Products. Direct costing is designed to improve the usefulness of the income statement prepared for management. With absorption costing, allocations of fixed manufacturing cost between inventories and cost of goods sold obscures the relationship between production costs and sales revenue. Such allocations do not occur in direct costing. When direct costing is adopted, management—marketing management in particular—finds the income statement furnished by the accountant to be more meaningful and understandable.

When an income statement is prepared on a direct costing and contribution margin basis, as shown in Exhibit 20-1, the variable manufacturing cost for each product is first subtracted from the sales of each product to arrive at a figure referred to as the gross contribution margin. Next, variable nonmanufacturing expenses are subtracted from the gross contribution margin of each product to compute the contribution margin for each product. The usefulness of the product-line income statement is improved when fixed costs that are traceable to individual products are subtracted from each product's contribution margin, yielding a figure known as the product contribution. Common costs are not allocated to individual products.[1] This type of statement makes the actual contribution of each product line to total profits and to the recovery of common costs readily apparent. When a product contributes nothing to the recovery of common costs, such as Product C in Exhibit 20-1, the cause should be determined and remedial steps taken, if possible. If the product cannot make a positive contribution toward the recovery of common costs, it should be eliminated unless there are compelling reasons to continue to lose money by continuing the product.

EXHIBIT 20-1

Product-Line Income Statement (Contribution Margin Approach)

	Total	Product A	Product B	Product C
Sales	$3,100,000	$1,540,000	$1,070,000	$490,000
Less variable cost of goods sold	1,927,000	925,000	590,000	412,000
Gross contribution margin	$1,173,000	$ 615,000	$ 480,000	$ 78,000
Less variable marketing expenses	507,000	255,000	168,000	84,000
Contribution margin	$ 666,000	$ 360,000	$ 312,000	$ (6,000)
Less traceable fixed costs:				
Manufacturing	$ 100,000	$ 30,000	$ 52,000	$ 18,000
Marketing	25,000	14,000	8,000	3,000
Total traceable fixed costs	$ 125,000	$ 44,000	$ 60,000	$ 21,000
Product contribution	$ 541,000	$ 316,000	$ 252,000	$ (27,000)
Less common fixed costs:				
Manufacturing	$ 45,000			
Marketing	80,000			
Administration	100,000			
Total common fixed costs	$ 225,000			
Operating income	$ 316,000			

Direct Costing for Managerial Decision Making. Installation of a direct costing system requires a study of cost behavior and a segregation of fixed and variable costs. In order for cost behavior to be understood, activities and the cost generated by each activity must be studied. Materials and labor are variable costs that are directly traceable to the product. On the other hand, overhead generally is not directly traceable. Traditionally, overhead is charged to products on the basis of some measure of production volume, such as labor hours or machine hours. As a consequence, traditional direct costing categorizes overhead as variable when it varies directly with some measure of production volume. However, companies having complex cost structures that manufacture multiple products may use activity-based costing, in which case both volume and nonvolume

[1] For the most part, common costs are fixed. However, costs and expenses can be variable with respect to some activity other than production output. In traditional direct costing, these nontraceable variable costs are not allocated to products but instead are included in common costs. Of course, there is no reason why variable costs cannot be allocated to products on the basis of both volume and nonvolume measures the same way they are in activity-based costing, in which case all value-added variable manufacturing costs are product costs.

production activities are used as bases to allocate overhead to products (see Chapter 14). Activity-based costing is an absorption costing concept, that is, both fixed and variable overhead are allocated to products. Nevertheless, direct costing can be adapted to an activity-based costing system by separating the variable and fixed costs in each activity cost pool, charging only the variable costs to products, and charging the fixed cost to expense. The analysis of all activities required for activity-based costing provides an opportunity to identify and eliminate unessential activities and to improve the efficiency of those activities that are essential. Separating variable and fixed costs for each activity enhances the usefulness of activity-based costing for short-term decision making.

The classification of costs as either fixed or variable, with semivariable costs properly subdivided into their fixed and variable components, provides a framework for the accumulation and analysis of costs. This also provides a basis for the study of contemplated changes in production levels or proposed actions concerning new markets, plant expansion or contraction, or special promotional activities. Of course, a study of cost behavior that identifies fixed and variable costs can be accomplished without the use of a formal direct costing system.

In *NAA Research Report No. 372,* findings on the usefulness of direct costing are summarized as follows:

> Companies participating in this study generally feel that direct costing's major field of usefulness is in forecasting and reporting income for internal management purposes. The distinctive feature of direct costing which makes it useful for this purpose is the manner in which costs are matched with revenues.
>
> The marginal income (contribution margin) figure which results from the first step in matching costs and revenues in the direct costing income statement is reported to be a particularly useful figure to management because it can be readily projected to measure increments in net income which accompany increments in sales. The theory underlying this observed usefulness of the marginal income figure in decision making rests upon the fact that within a limited volume range, period costs tend to remain constant in total when volume changes occur. Under such conditions, only the direct costs are relevant in costing increments in volume.
>
> The tendency of net income to fluctuate directly with sales volume was reported to be an important practical advantage possessed by the direct costing approach to income determination because it enables management to trace changes in sales to their consequence in net income. Another advantage attributed to the direct costing income statement was that management has a better understanding of the impact that period costs have on profits when such costs are brought together in a single group.[2]

Direct Costing for Cost Control. Direct costing is designed to improve the usefulness of the income statement prepared for management by eliminating arbitrary fixed cost allocations. As a consequence, direct costing focuses management attention on variable costs, which are more controllable than fixed costs in the short run. Variable costs must be computed and segregated in the accounting records in order to prepare periodic income statements on a direct costing basis. Identifying cost drivers and separating variable and fixed costs is the first step in determining who is responsible for incurring costs. Only when cost behavior and cost responsibility have been determined can variance reports be prepared and

[2] *NAA Research Report, No. 37,* "Applications of Direct Costing" (New York: Institute of Management Accountants (formerly National Association of Accountants), 1961), pp. 84–85.

distributed to responsible managers. Although direct costing is not required in order to have an effective responsibility accounting and reporting system, it provides the kind of information that is needed.

External Uses of Direct Costing

The proponents of direct costing believe that the separation of fixed and variable costs, and the accounting for each according to some direct costing plan, simplifies both the understanding of the income statement and the assignment of costs to inventories.

To keep fixed overhead out of the reported product costs, variable and fixed costs should be recorded in separate accounts. Therefore, the chart of accounts should be expanded so that each natural classification has two accounts, as needed—one for the variable and one for the fixed portion of the cost. Also, instead of one overhead control account, two should be used: Factory Overhead Control—Variable Costs, and Factory Overhead Control—Fixed Costs. When a predetermined overhead rate is used to charge variable costs to Work in Process, an applied overhead account entitled Applied Variable Factory Overhead is credited. The difference between actual and applied variable overhead is a spending variance, or, if a standard cost system is used, a controllable variance.[3] Because fixed costs are not charged to Work in Process, they are excluded from the predetermined overhead rate. The total fixed cost accumulated in the account, Factory Overhead Control—Fixed Costs, is charged directly to Income Summary.

The effects of direct costing on the income statement can be illustrated as follows. Assume that the QST Corporation, which produces only one kind of product, has a normal capacity of 20,000 units per quarter or 80,000 units per year. Variable standard costs per unit are: direct materials, $30; direct labor, $22; and variable factory overhead, $8. Fixed factory overhead is budgeted at $1,200,000 per year ($300,000 per quarter or $15 per unit under the absorption costing method at normal capacity). The units of production basis is used for applying factory overhead. Fixed marketing and administrative expenses are $200,000 per quarter during 19A or $800,000 for the year, and variable marketing expense is $5 per unit. The sales price per unit is $100.

Materials variances, labor variances, and the factory overhead controllable variance for 19A have net unfavorable totals of $15,000, $9,000, $14,000, and $17,000 for the first, second, third, and fourth quarters, respectively. These variances are not considered to be material and are closed to Cost of Goods Sold each quarter, whether absorption costing or direct costing is used, because they relate to variable costs that are included in the cost of the product under both methods. However, the factory overhead volume variance (that is, the over- or underapplied fixed factory overhead) is computed and closed to Cost of Goods Sold only for the absorption costing method, because fixed costs are not added to the cost of the product under direct costing.

For a simpler illustration, assume there is no work in process inventory at the beginning or end of 19A. Standard costs are assigned to finished goods, and the standard costs for the previous year are the same as the standard costs for the current year. If work in process inventories were present, they would also be assigned standard costs. If standard costs were not used or if standard costs in the current period

---

[3] The controllable variance can be broken down into two components, a spending variance and a variable efficiency variance. See Chapter 18.

were different from standard costs in the prior period, an assumption about the flow of costs (for example, average, fifo, or lifo) would be required to cost inventories.

There are 4,000 units in finished goods inventory at the beginning of the first quarter. Actual production, planned production, and sales for 19A in units are:

	First Quarter	Second Quarter	Third Quarter	Fourth Quarter
Planned production in units	20,000	20,000	20,000	20,000
Actual production in units	20,000	18,000	20,000	22,000
Actual sales in units	20,000	20,000	18,000	18,000

Quarterly income statements prepared on the absorption costing basis for the QST Corporation are presented in Exhibit 20-2. Notice that fixed factory overhead is included in the unit cost of the product and also in the costs assigned to inventory.

EXHIBIT 20-2

QST Corporation
Quarterly Income Statements
Absorption Costing Basis
For 19A

	First Quarter	Second Quarter	Third Quarter	Fourth Quarter
Sales	$2,000,000	$2,000,000	$1,800,000	$1,800,000
Standard cost of goods sold	$1,500,000	$1,500,000	$1,350,000	$1,350,000
Materials, labor, and controllable variances	15,000	9,000	14,000	17,000
Volume variance*	0	30,000	0	(30,000)
Adjusted cost of goods sold	$1,515,000	$1,539,000	$1,364,000	$1,337,000
Gross profit	$ 485,000	$ 461,000	$ 436,000	$ 463,000
Marketing and administrative expenses	300,000	300,000	290,000	290,000
Operating income	$ 185,000	$ 161,000	$ 146,000	$ 173,000

*The volume variance is determined as follows:

	First Quarter	Second Quarter	Third Quarter	Fourth Quarter
Budgeted fixed overhead	$ 300,000	$ 300,000	$ 300,000	$ 300,000
Actual production in units	20,000	18,000	20,000	22,000
Fixed factory overhead rate	× $15	× $15	× $15	× $15
Applied fixed overhead	$ 300,000	$ 270,000	$ 300,000	$ 330,000
Volume variance, unfavorable (favorable)	$ 0	$ 30,000	$ 0	$ (30,000)

Quarterly income statements for QST Corporation prepared on the basis of direct costing are presented in Exhibit 20-3. Notice that fixed factory overhead is not included in the unit cost of products. As a consequence, there is no volume variance,[4] and there is no fixed overhead in the units of product that are in inventory.

[4] The volume variance was defined in Chapter 18 as the amount of over- or underabsorbed budgeted fixed factory overhead in a standard cost system. Because fixed factory overhead is not charged to units of product produced during the period in direct costing but instead is charged entirely to period expense, there can be no over- or underabsorbed budgeted fixed factory overhead.

EXHIBIT 20-3

QST Corporation
Quarterly Income Statements
Direct Costing Basis
For 19A

	First Quarter	Second Quarter	Third Quarter	Fourth Quarter
Sales	$2,000,000	$2,000,000	$1,800,000	$1,800,000
Standard variable cost of goods sold	$1,200,000	$1,200,000	$1,080,000	$1,080,000
Materials, labor, and controllable variances	15,000	9,000	14,000	17,000
Adjusted variable cost of goods sold	$1,215,000	$1,209,000	$1,094,000	$1,097,000
Gross contribution margin	$ 785,000	$ 791,000	$ 706,000	$ 703,000
Variable marketing expenses	100,000	100,000	90,000	90,000
Contribution margin	$ 685,000	$ 691,000	$ 616,000	$ 613,000
Fixed factory overhead	$ 300,000	$ 300,000	$ 300,000	$ 300,000
Fixed marketing and administrative expenses	200,000	200,000	200,000	200,000
Total fixed expenses	$ 500,000	$ 500,000	$ 500,000	$ 500,000
Operating income	$ 185,000	$ 191,000	$ 116,000	$ 113,000

Costs Assigned to Inventory. To determine the costs assigned to ending finished goods inventory, the number of units in ending inventory must first be computed:

	First Quarter	Second Quarter	Third Quarter	Fourth Quarter
Units in beginning inventory	4,000	4,000	2,000	4,000
Units produced during period	20,000	18,000	20,000	22,000
Units available for sale	24,000	22,000	22,000	26,000
Less units sold	20,000	20,000	18,000	18,000
Units in ending inventory	4,000	2,000	4,000	8,000

Because standard costs are assigned to inventory and because QST Corporation's standard costs have not changed between periods, the cost assigned to the finished goods ending inventory under the absorption costing method and the direct costing method can be determined as follows:

	First Quarter	Second Quarter	Third Quarter	Fourth Quarter
Units in ending inventory	4,000	2,000	4,000	8,000
Standard full cost per unit	× $75	× $75	× $75	× $75
Cost of ending inventory under absorption costing	$300,000	$150,000	$300,000	$ 600,000
Units in ending inventory	4,000	2,000	4,000	8,000
Standard variable cost per unit	× $60	× $60	× $60	× $60
Cost of ending inventory under direct costing	$240,000	$120,000	$240,000	$480,000
Difference between absorption and direct costing inventory	$ 60,000	$ 30,000	$ 60,000	$120,000

The differences between absorption and direct costing income occur because fixed factory overhead is included in inventory in absorption costing but excluded in direct costing. In absorption costing, fixed factory overhead becomes a part of the predetermined factory overhead rate and, therefore, becomes a part of the product's cost. In direct costing, fixed factory overhead is charged to period expense and does not become a part of the product's cost.

Operating Profits. The inclusion or exclusion of fixed cost from inventories and the cost of goods sold causes the gross profit to vary considerably from the gross contribution margin. The gross contribution margin (sales less variable manufacturing cost) is greater than the gross profit in absorption costing. This difference is the cause of some criticism of direct costing. Some opponents argue that a greater gross contribution margin can mislead marketing personnel about product profitability and result in requests for lower product prices and demands for higher bonuses or benefits. In most cases, however, sales prices and bonuses are based not on gross profit but on operating income.

The income statements for the QST Corporation presented in Exhibits 20-2 and 20-3 also show differences in operating income. These differences are the result of charging fixed factory overhead to inventory under the absorption costing method but expensing it under direct costing. The differences in operating income between the two costing methods are summarized and reconciled as follows:

	First Quarter	Second Quarter	Third Quarter	Fourth Quarter
Operating income under absorption costing	$185,000	$ 161,000	$146,000	$173,000
Operating income under direct costing	185,000	191,000	116,000	113,000
Difference	$ 0	$ (30,000)	$ 30,000	$ 60,000
Inventory change under absorption costing:				
Ending inventory	$300,000	$ 150,000	$300,000	$600,000
Beginning inventory	300,000	300,000	150,000	300,000
Increase (decrease)	$ 0	$(150,000)	$150,000	$300,000
Inventory change under direct costing:				
Ending inventory	$240,000	$ 120,000	$240,000	$480,000
Beginning inventory	240,000	240,000	120,000	240,000
Increase (decrease)	$ 0	$(120,000)	$120,000	$240,000
Difference	$ 0	$ (30,000)	$ 30,000	$ 60,000

Because standard costing is used in this illustration, the differences in operating income determined under absorption costing and direct costing can be computed by multiplying the difference between the quantity produced and the quantity sold for each quarter by the fixed portion of the factory overhead rate used in absorption costing, as follows:

	First Quarter	Second Quarter	Third Quarter	Fourth Quarter
Units produced	20,000	18,000	20,000	22,000
Units sold	20,000	20,000	18,000	18,000
Unit change in inventories, increase (decrease)	0	(2,000)	2,000	4,000
Fixed factory overhead rate under absorption costing	× $15	× $15	× $15	× $15
Difference in operating income	$ 0	$(30,000)	$30,000	$60,000

The amount of fixed cost charged to inventory is affected not only by the quantities produced and sold but also by the inventory costing method employed—a fact that frequently is overlooked. In the illustrations presented, the operating profit is larger under absorption costing than under direct costing when the quantity produced exceeds the quantity sold (third and fourth quarters). Conversely, the operating profit is smaller under absorption costing than under direct costing when the quantity produced is less than the quantity sold (second quarter). These relationships hold only for the standard costing method when the standard cost does not change between periods (as in the illustration) and for the lifo inventory method. Under the fifo and the average costing methods, the results can differ from those demonstrated, depending on the magnitude and the direction of the changes in costs.[5]

The inventory change in this illustration is for finished goods only. If there were work in process inventories, they too would be included in the inventory change in order to reconcile the difference in operating income. Also, any volume variances (that is, over- or underapplied fixed factory overhead) deferred on the balance sheet, rather than being expensed currently, would be a reconciling item in explaining the difference in operating income.

The operating income is the same in each method when no inventories exist or, as demonstrated in the first quarter of the illustration, when no change in the total cost assigned to inventory occurs from the beginning to the end of the period. Although the illustrations of direct costing and absorption costing are prepared on a quarterly basis, they are equally representative of statements prepared on a monthly or an annual basis.

As previously explained, many managers favor direct costing because there is a direct correspondence between changes in sales and changes in costs. Variable cost of goods sold varies directly with sales volume, and the influence of production volume on profit is eliminated. The idea of charging overhead to inventories might sound plausible and appear pleasing at first; but when the prior period's inventories become this period's beginning inventories, the apparent advantages cancel out. The results of the third and fourth quarters under absorption costing offer good examples of the effects of large production with current period cost being deferred in inventories to be charged against income in a future period. The absorption costing income statement also demonstrates the effect of expensing the volume variance (that is, the over- or underapplied fixed factory overhead resulting from fluctuations in production volume).

External Reporting. The use of direct costing for financial reporting is not considered by the accounting profession to be consistent with generally accepted accounting principles. In addition, the Securities and Exchange Commission refuses to accept financial reports prepared on the basis of direct costing, and the Internal Revenue Service will not permit the computation of taxable income on the direct costing basis. The position of these groups is based on their opposition to excluding fixed costs from inventories.

The Position of the Accounting Profession. The basis for the accounting profession's position on direct costing is *Accounting Research Bulletin No. 43.* The chapter on Inventory Pricing begins by stressing that "a major objective of accounting for inventories is the proper determination of income through the process of matching appropriate costs against revenues."

[5] Yuri Ijiri, Robert K. Jaedicke, and John L. Livingstone, "The Effect of Inventory Costing Methods on Full and Direct Costing," *Journal of Accounting Research*, Vol. 3, No. 1, pp. 63–74.

The bulletin continues by stating that "the primary basis of accounting for inventories is cost, which has been defined generally as the price paid or consideration given to acquire an asset. As applied to inventories, cost means in principle the sum of the applicable expenditures and charges directly or indirectly incurred in bringing an article to its existing condition and location."

In discussing the second point, the bulletin states quite emphatically that "it should also be recognized that the exclusion of all overheads from inventory costs does not constitute an accepted accounting procedure." This last statement seems to apply to direct costing. Proponents of direct costing might argue, however, that while the exclusion of all overhead is not acceptable, by inference the exclusion of some is acceptable. This argument might sound true, but it does not seem to have any bearing on the accounting profession's acceptance of direct costing. In an earlier discussion of cost, the bulletin states that "under some circumstances, items such as idle facility expense, excessive spoilage, double freight, and rehandling costs may be so abnormal as to require treatment as current period charges rather than as a portion of the inventory cost." This appears to be the type of overhead that the bulletin recognizes as excludable from inventories.

The Position of the IRS. The Internal Revenue Service position is directed by Section 1.471-3(c) of the Regulations, which defines inventory cost in the case of merchandise produced to be: "(1) the cost of raw materials and supplies entering into or consumed in connection with the product, (2) expenditures for direct labor, and (3) indirect production costs incident to and necessary for the production of the particular article, including in such indirect production costs an appropriate portion of management expenses." Furthermore, Section 1.471-11(a) of the Regulations specifically requires the use of the full absorption method of inventory costing. As a result of the Tax Reform Act of 1986, Section 263A of the Internal Revenue Code requires the capitalization of indirect as well as direct costs incurred in the manufacture of products held for sale to customers.

The Position of the SEC. The SEC's refusal to accept annual financial reports prepared on the basis of direct costing generally is the result of two factors: its policy to favor consistency among reporting companies as far as possible and its attitude that direct costing is not generally accepted accounting procedure. In filing reports with the SEC, a firm that uses direct costing must adjust its inventories and reported income to what they would have been under absorption costing.

Adjustment of Direct Costing Figures for External Reporting Purposes. Companies using direct costing internally make adjustments when they prepare income tax returns and external financial reports. In actual practice, comparatively simple procedures are frequently used to determine the amount of periodic adjustment necessary to convert inventories recorded on the direct costing basis to the absorption costing basis required for external reporting. According to *NAA Research Report, No. 37,* one company reported that fixed factory overhead for the period is divided by actual production to create a costing rate that is applied to the units in the ending inventory. Another company expenses these fixed costs as a rate per dollar of variable costs at normal volume. The dollar amount of variable costs in the ending inventory is then multiplied by the foregoing rate to arrive at the fixed factory overhead component.[6] In both cases, the excess of the fixed factory overhead incurred during the period over the amount charged to the ending inventory is closed to the cost of goods sold, and the adjustment to the ending inventory is reversed at the beginning of the next accounting period.

Cost–Volume–Profit Analysis

Cost–volume–profit analysis is concerned with determining the sales volume and mix of products necessary to achieve a desired level of profit with available resources. It is an analytical tool that provides management with important information about the relationships among costs, profits, product mix, and sales volume. Cost–volume–profit analysis is based on the following assumptions: that all costs can be segregated into fixed and variable portions, that total fixed costs are constant over the range of the analysis, and that total variable costs change in proportion to changes in volume (that is, that variable cost per unit is constant over the range of activity being analyzed).

Break-even analysis is used to determine the level of sales and mix of products required to just recover all costs incurred during the period. The **break-even point** is the point at which cost and revenue are equal. There is neither a profit nor a loss at the break-even point. Because the objective of cost–volume–profit analysis is to determine the level of sales and the mix of products required to achieve a targeted level of profit, break-even analysis is a special case of cost–volume–profit analysis—it is the determination of the level of sales and the mix of products necessary to achieve a zero level of profit.

Although management typically plans for a profit each period, the break-even point is of concern. If sales fall below the break-even point, losses are incurred. Management must determine the break-even point in order to compute the **margin of safety**, which indicates how much sales can decrease from the targeted level before the company will incur losses. The margin of safety is a criterion used to evaluate the adequacy of planned sales.

Break-even and cost–volume–profit analysis can be based on historical data, past operations, or projected sales and costs. However, data for break-even and cost–volume–profit analysis cannot be taken directly from the absorption or full costing income statement, because the effect of activity on costs cannot be readily determined. Each item of expense must be analyzed to determine its fixed and variable components. In contrast to the absorption or full costing income statement, the direct or variable costing income statement segregates fixed costs from variable costs and, therefore, is quite useful in break-even and cost–volume–profit analysis. The flexible budget and standard cost cards are also good sources of data because they segregate fixed and variable costs. Consequently, the data available in each source can be used readily for break-even and cost–volume–profit analysis.

Break-even and cost–volume–profit analysis is based on the following accounting relationship:

$$\text{Profit} = \text{Total revenues} - (\text{Total variable costs} + \text{Total fixed costs})$$

which is equivalent to saying that:

$$\text{Total revenues} = \text{Total fixed costs} + \text{Total variable costs} + \text{Profit}$$

Because total fixed cost and the variable cost per unit are assumed to remain constant within the range of activity being analyzed, the basic accounting relationship can be expressed in the form of a linear equation, as follows:

[6] *NAA Research Report, No. 37*, pp. 94–95.

$$R = F + (V \times R) + \pi$$

where:
- R = Total sales revenue
- F = Total fixed cost
- V = Variable cost per dollar of sales revenue (i.e., total variable cost divided by total sales revenue)
- π = Total profit

The objective of break-even and cost–volume–profit analysis is to determine the volume of sales and the mix of products required to achieve a targeted level of profit (zero profit in the case of break-even analysis). If only one product is produced, as assumed initially, the only unknown of concern is the volume of sales. The volume of sales can be measured in terms of sales revenue or in terms of units of product. To determine the required level of sales revenue, the preceding equation can be solved for R, as follows:

$$\begin{aligned} R &= F + (V \times R) + \pi \\ R - (V \times R) &= F + \pi \\ R(1 - V) &= F + \pi \\ R &= \frac{F + \pi}{1 - V} = \frac{\text{Total fixed cost + Profit}}{\text{Contribution margin per sales dollar}} \end{aligned}$$

If profit is set equal to zero, the break-even point measured in sales revenue, R(BE), is computed as follows:

$$R(BE) = \frac{F}{1 - V} = \frac{\text{Total fixed cost}}{\text{Contribution margin per sales dollar}}$$

The contribution margin per sales dollar, also referred to as the **contribution margin ratio (C/M)**, is the portion of each sales dollar available to recover fixed costs and provide a profit. Below the break-even point, it is the portion of each sales dollar used to recover fixed cost. Above the break-even point, it is the portion of each sales dollar that provides an increase in profit. The computation of the break-even point is illustrated by assuming the following data taken from the flexible budget of Northstar Company:

Total sales revenue at normal capacity	$6,000,000
Total fixed costs	1,600,000
Total variable costs at normal capacity	3,600,000
Sales price per unit	400
Variable costs per unit	240

The break-even point is computed as follows:

$$\begin{aligned} R(BE) &= \frac{F}{1 - V} \\ &= \frac{\$1,600,000}{1 - (\$3,600,000 \div \$6,000,000)} \text{ or } \frac{\$1,600,000}{1 - (\$240 \div \$400)} \\ &= \frac{\$1,600,000}{.40} \\ &= \$4,000,000 \end{aligned}$$

Once fixed costs have been recovered, the contribution margin from each additional dollar of sales revenue provides a profit. Consequently, if the sales revenue required to break even has already been computed, the sales revenue required to achieve a targeted level of profit can be determined by simply dividing the targeted profit by the contribution margin per sales dollar and adding the quotient to the sales revenue required to break even. For example, based on Northstar Company data, a targeted profit of \$400,000 requires sales of \$1,000,000 beyond the break-even point (\$400,000 profit divided by \$.40 contribution margin per dollar of sales). Therefore, total sales of \$5,000,000 are required to yield a profit of \$400,000 (\$4,000,000 of sales to break even plus \$1,000,000 of sales beyond the break-even point). Alternatively, the required level of sales can be determined directly by adding the targeted level of profit to fixed costs and dividing the sum by the contribution margin per sales dollar, as indicated by the preceding formula derived and demonstrated as follows:

$$R = \frac{F + \pi}{1 - V}$$

$$= \frac{\$1,600,000 + \$400,000}{1 - (\$3,600,000 \div \$6,000,000)} \text{ or } \frac{\$1,600,000 + \$400,000}{1 - (\$240 \div \$400)}$$

$$= \frac{\$2,000,000}{.40}$$

$$= \$5,000,000$$

Because each unit sells for \$400, the total quantity of product to be sold to break even is 10,000 units (\$4,000,000 break-even sales divided by \$400 sales price per unit), and the total quantity to be sold to meet a targeted profit of \$400,000 is 12,500 units (\$5,000,000 of sales divided by \$400 sales price).

A units-of-product approach rather than the sales-revenue approach is sometimes taken in break-even and cost–volume–profit analyses. For some types of analyses, it is more expedient and convenient to work with units of product rather than sales revenue. Both approaches are conceptually the same. In the units-of-product approach, the basic equation is altered to include the quantity of product, the unit sales price, and the unit variable cost. Recall that the equation used in developing the sales-revenue approach to cost–volume–profit analysis is:

$$R = F + (V \times R) + \pi$$

Because sales revenue is equal to the unit sales price multiplied by the quantity of product sold, and because total variable cost is equal to the variable cost per unit multiplied by the quantity of product sold, the preceding equation can be restated as follows:

$$P \times Q = F + (C \times Q) + \pi$$

where: P = Sales price per unit
Q = Quantity of product sold
F = Total fixed cost
C = Variable cost per unit
π = Total profit

The unknown in the modified equation is the quantity of product, Q. Solving for Q yields:

$$P \times Q = F + (C \times Q) + \pi$$
$$(P \times Q) - (C \times Q) = F + \pi$$
$$Q \times (P - C) = F + \pi$$
$$Q = \frac{F + \pi}{P - C}$$

If profit is set equal to zero, then the break-even point in units of product, Q(BE), is as follows:

$$Q(BE) = \frac{F}{P - C}$$

Based on the data provided in the Northstar Company illustration, the break-even point in units of product is computed as follows:

$$Q(BE) = \frac{F}{P - C} = \frac{\$1{,}600{,}000}{\$400 - \$240} = \frac{\$1{,}600{,}000}{\$160} = 10{,}000 \text{ units}$$

A targeted profit of $400,000 requires sales of:

$$Q = \frac{F + \pi}{P - C}$$

$$= \frac{\$1{,}600{,}000 + \$400{,}000}{\$400 - \$240}$$

$$= \frac{\$2{,}000{,}000}{\$160}$$

$$= 12{,}500 \text{ units}$$

Constructing a Break-Even Chart

Break-even computations can be presented graphically on a break-even chart, in which the cost line and the sales line intersect at the break-even point. The data needed to construct this chart are forecast sales and fixed and variable costs. A conventional break-even chart for Northstar Company is illustrated in Figure 20-2.

FIGURE 20-2 ***Conventional Break-Even Chart***

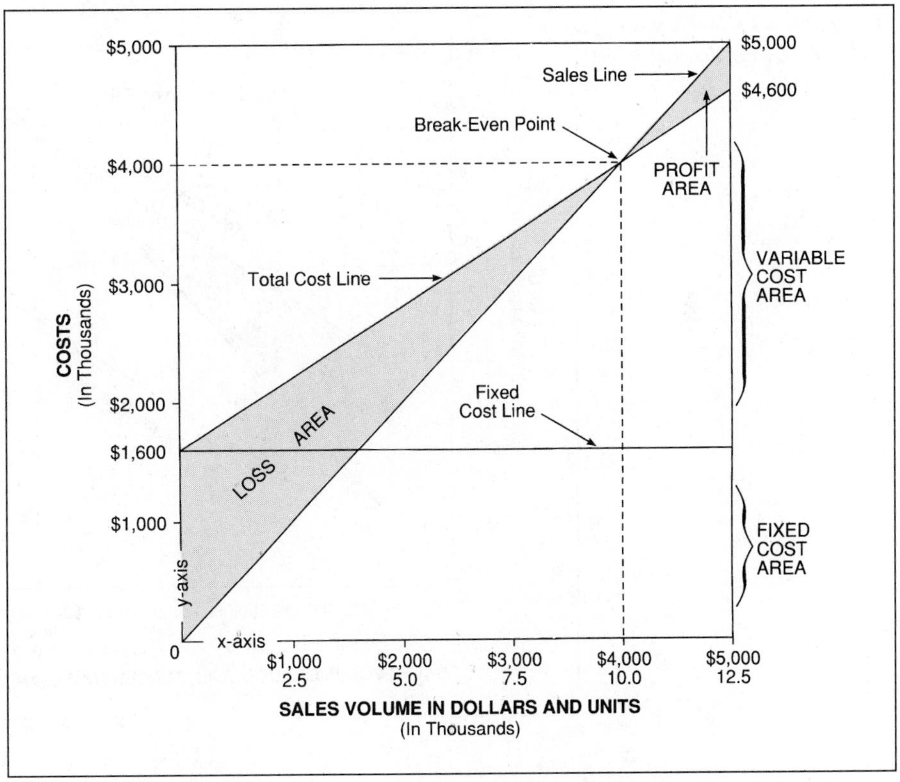

The conventional break-even chart is constructed as follows:

1. A horizontal base line, the x-axis, is drawn and spaced into equal distances to represent the sales volume in dollars or in number of units, or as a percentage of some specified volume.

2. A vertical line, the y-axis, is drawn at the extreme left and right sides of the chart. The y-axis at the left is spaced into equal parts and represents sales and costs in dollars.
3. A fixed cost line is drawn parallel to the x-axis at the $1,600,000 point of the y-axis.
4. A total cost line is drawn from the $1,600,000 fixed cost point on the left y-axis to the $4,600,000 cost point on the right y-axis.
5. The sales line is drawn from the 0 point on the left side of the graph (the intersection of the x-axis and y-axis) to the $5,000,000 point on the right y-axis.
6. The total cost line intersects the sales line at the break-even point, representing $4,000,000 sales or 10,000 units of sales.
7. The shaded area to the left of the break-even point is the loss area; the shaded area to the right is the profit area.

In the conventional break-even chart, the fixed cost line is parallel to the x-axis and variable cost is plotted above the fixed cost. Such a chart emphasizes fixed cost at a definite amount for various levels of activity. Many analysts, however, prefer an alternative form of chart, in which the variable cost is drawn first and fixed cost is plotted above the variable cost line. An example of the alternative type of chart, using Northstar Company data, is presented in Figure 20-3.

FIGURE 20-3 ***Break-Even Chart with Fixed Cost Plotted Above Variable Cost***

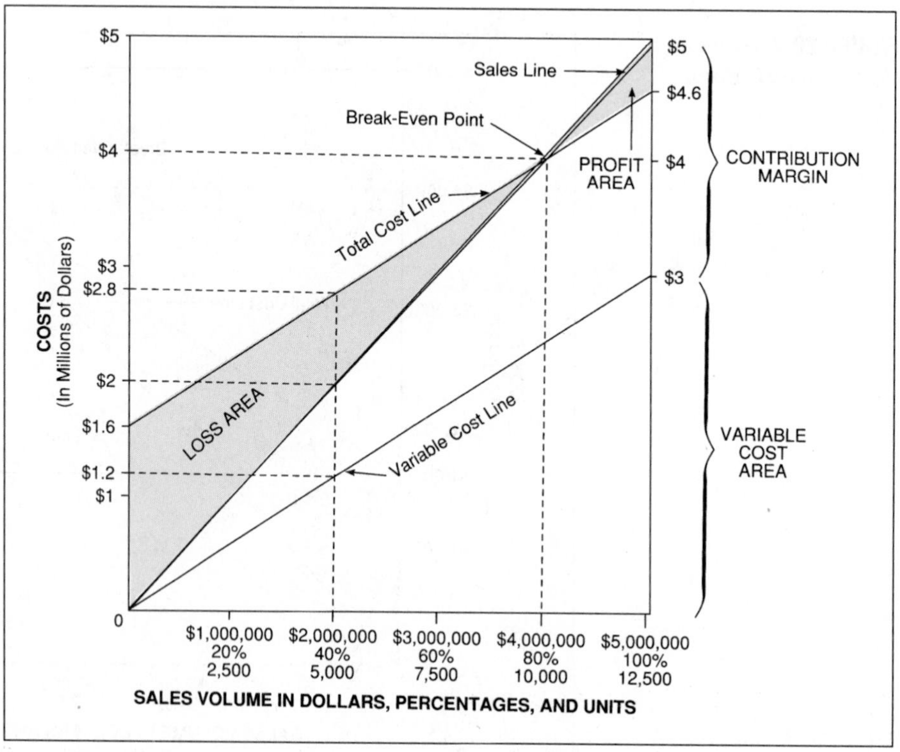

The space between the variable cost line and the sales line represents the contribution margin. Where the total cost line intersects the sales line, the break-even point has been reached. The space between the sales line and the total cost line beyond the break-even point represents the profit for the period at any volume. The space between the total cost line and the sales line to the left of the break-even point indicates the fixed costs not yet recovered by the contribution margin and is the loss for the period at any volume below the break-even point.

This alternative break-even chart indicates the recovery of fixed costs at various percentages of capacity and at various levels of dollar sales or unit sales. If sales, for example, drop to $2,000,000, variable costs are $1,200,000 (60% of $2,000,000) while fixed costs remain at $1,600,000. The loss at this point is $800,000 [($2,000,000 – ($1,200,000 + $1,600,000)]. The chart shows $2,000,000 on the sales line to be $800,000 below the total cost line. In columnar form, the analysis can be illustrated as follows:

(1) Number of Units	(2) Sales	(3) Variable Cost	(4) Contribution Margin (2) – (3)	(5) Fixed Cost	(6) Profit (Loss) (4) – (5)
2,500	$1,000,000	$ 600,000	$ 400,000	$1,600,000	$(1,200,000)
5,000	2,000,000	1,200,000	800,000	1,600,000	(800,000)
7,500	3,000,000	1,800,000	1,200,000	1,600,000	(400,000)
10,000	4,000,000	2,400,000	1,600,000	1,600,000	None
12,500	5,000,000	3,000,000	2,000,000	1,600,000	400,000

Break-Even and Cost–Volume–Profit Analysis for Decision Making

The accounting data involved, the assumptions made, the manner in which the information is obtained, and the way the data are expressed are limitations that must be considered in connection with the results of cost–volume–profit analysis. The break-even chart is fundamentally a static analysis. In most cases, changes can be shown only by drawing a new chart or a series of charts. The concept of relevant range as discussed in Chapter 3 is applicable. That is, the amount of fixed and variable costs, as well as the slope of the sales line, is meaningful only in a defined range of activity and must be redefined for activity outside the relevant range. Furthermore, costs and revenue are assumed to be linear with respect to activity.[7]

Despite its limitations, cost–volume–profit analysis offers wide application for testing proposed actions, for considering alternatives, or for other decision-making purposes. For example, the technique permits determination of the effect on profit of a shift in fixed and/or variable expenses when old machinery is replaced by new equipment. Firms having multiple plants, products, and sales territories can prepare charts to show the effects of shifts in sales quantities, sales prices, and sales efforts. With such information, management is able to direct the firm's operations into the most profitable channels. For a company having numerous divisions, the analysis is particularly valuable in determining the influence on profits of an increase in divisional fixed cost. If, for example, a company's overall contribution margin ratio is 25 percent, a division manager should realize that for every $1 of proposed increase in fixed cost, sales revenue must increase by no less than $4 if the existing profit position is to be maintained ($1 ÷ .25 = $4).

In using cost–volume–profit analysis, management should understand that:

1. A change in per unit variable cost changes the contribution margin ratio and the break-even point.

[7] Calculus can be employed in dealing with nonlinear functions. See Travis P. Goggans, "Break-Even Analysis with Curvilinear Functions," *The Accounting Review*, Vol. 40, No. 4, pp. 867–871.

2. A change in sales price changes the contribution margin ratio and the break-even point.
3. A change in fixed cost changes the break-even point but not the contribution margin ratio.
4. A combined change in fixed and variable costs in the same direction causes an extremely sharp change in the break-even point.

Changes in Fixed Cost. If Northstar Company management is able to reduce fixed expense to $1,450,000, the break-even point is $3,625,000 ($1,450,000 ÷ .40). If sales remain at $5,000,000, the profit increases from $400,000 to $550,000, and the break-even point is 72.5 percent of sales instead of 80 percent. The change in the break-even point resulting from a reduction in fixed cost is shown by the broken lines in the chart shown in Figure 20-4. The effects of changes in the per unit variable cost or in the unit sales price can also be charted, thereby adding a dynamic dimension to the analysis.

FIGURE 20-4 ***Break-Even Chart with a Reduction in Fixed Cost***

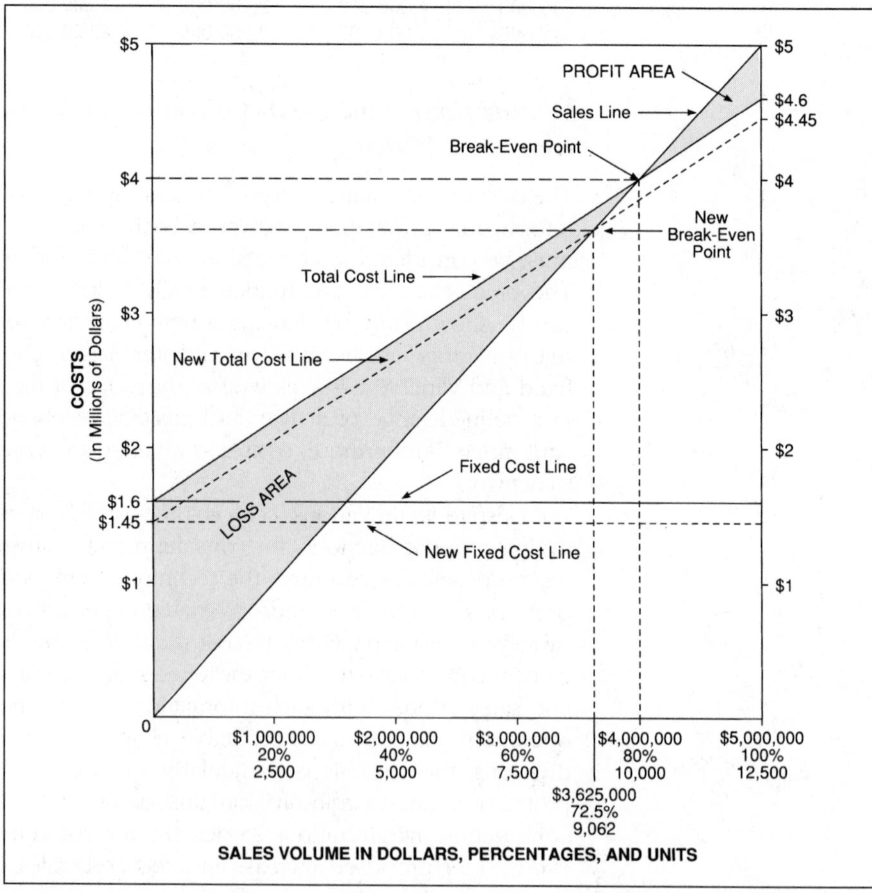

Multiple Products and Shifts in Sales Mix. When firms produce more than one product, the variable costs per dollar of sales revenue can be different for different products. In such cases, the contribution margin ratio is different for different sales mixes. As a consequence, the break-even point and the level of sales required to achieve targeted profit levels is different for different mixes of products. The mathematical computations in the multiple-product case are essentially the same as those in the single-product case, except that the analyst must remember that the results are valid only for the sales mix used in the analysis. If the sales mix is expected to change, the results should be recomputed for the new mix.

The computations in a multiple-product case can be illustrated as follows. Assume that Northstar Company expects the following product mix to be sold in the coming period:

Product	Unit Sales Price	Variable Cost per Unit	Expected Sales Mix
A....................................	$180	$100	1
B....................................	110	70	2

If the product mix is expected to remain constant at all levels of sales, the variable cost per dollar of sales revenue is determined as follows:

$$V = \frac{\text{Variable cost}}{\text{Sales revenue}} = \frac{\$100 + (2 \times \$\,70)}{\$180 + (2 \times \$110)} = \frac{\$240}{\$400} = .60$$

Once the variable cost per dollar of sales is computed, the break-even point and the sales revenue required to achieve a targeted level of profit are computed in the same manner as in the single-product case. Assume, for example, that fixed costs are still expected to be $1,600,000. The break-even point measured in sales revenue is:

$$R(BE) = \frac{F}{1 - V} = \frac{\$1{,}600{,}000}{1 - .60} = \frac{\$1{,}600{,}000}{.40} = \$4{,}000{,}000$$

For a profit of $400,000 to be achieved with this product mix, sales revenue must be $5,000,000, computed as follows:

$$R = \frac{F + \pi}{1 - V} = \frac{\$1{,}600{,}000 + \$400{,}000}{1 - .60} = \frac{\$2{,}000{,}000}{.40} = \$5{,}000{,}000$$

Once the break-even point has been determined, the quantity of each product to be sold can be determined by dividing the sales revenue required to break even by the sales revenue of a hypothetical package of the firm's products at the expected mix and multiplying the quotient by the number of units of each product in the package. If the expectation is that 1 unit of product A will be sold for every 2 units of product B sold, the hypothetical package of products contains one unit of product A and 2 units of product B. For Northstar Company, each package sells for $400 [(1 unit of A × $180 each) + (2 units of B × $110 each)]. As a result, the quantity of each product to be sold to break even with this sales mix can be determined as follows:

$$Q(BE) = \frac{R(BE)}{\$400} = \frac{\$4{,}000{,}000}{\$400} = 10{,}000 \text{ hypothetical packages}$$

$$10{,}000 \text{ packages} \times 1 \text{ unit of A per package} = 10{,}000 \text{ units of A}$$
$$10{,}000 \text{ packages} \times 2 \text{ units of B per package} = 20{,}000 \text{ units of B}$$

The quantity of each product to be sold at this mix to achieve sales revenue of $5,000,000 and a profit of $400,000 is determined as follows:

$$Q = \frac{R}{\$400} = \frac{\$5{,}000{,}000}{\$400} = 12{,}500 \text{ hypothetical packages}$$

$$12{,}500 \text{ packages} \times 1 \text{ unit of A per package} = 12{,}500 \text{ units of A}$$
$$12{,}500 \text{ packages} \times 2 \text{ units of B per package} = 25{,}000 \text{ units of B}$$

Alternatively, the quantity of hypothetical packages to be sold to break even or achieve a targeted level of profit can be computed directly using the units-of-product approach. In this case, the unit used in the formula presented on page 594 is the hypothetical package of the firm's products. For Northstar Company, the break-even point in hypothetical packages of product containing 1 unit of product A and 2 units of product B is determined as follows:

Sales revenue per package = (1 unit of A × \$180 each) + (2 units of B × \$110 each) = \$400
Variable cost per package = (1 unit of A × \$100 each) + (2 units of B × \$70 each) = \$240

$$Q(BE) = \frac{F}{P - C} = \frac{\$1{,}600{,}000}{\$400 - \$240} = \frac{\$1{,}600{,}000}{\$160} = 10{,}000 \text{ packages}$$

The number of units of each product required to break even is then computed by multiplying the number of hypothetical packages by the number of units of each product in the hypothetical package, as follows:

10,000 packages × 1 unit of A per package = 10,000 units of A
10,000 packages × 2 units of B per package = 20,000 units of B

The number of hypothetical packages required to achieve a targeted profit of \$400,000 is:

$$Q = \frac{F + \pi}{P - C} = \frac{\$1{,}600{,}000 + \$400{,}000}{\$400 - \$240} = \frac{\$2{,}000{,}000}{\$160} = 12{,}500 \text{ packages}$$

The number of units of each product is:

12,500 packages × 1 unit of A per package = 12,500 units of A
12,500 packages × 2 units of B per package = 25,000 units of B

In this multiple-product case, the break-even point and the sales revenue required to achieve a targeted level of profit are different for a different product mix because the variable cost and the contribution margin per dollar of sales are different. For example, if the expected sales mix is 1 unit of product A for every 3 units of product B, the variable cost per dollar of sales changes from \$.60 to \$.607843, determined as follows:

$$V = \frac{\text{Variable cost}}{\text{Sales revenue}} = \frac{\$100 + (3 \times \$\,70)}{\$180 + (3 \times \$110)} = \frac{\$310}{\$510} = \$.607843$$

The increase in variable cost per dollar of sales revenue results in a decline in contribution margin per dollar of sales revenue and an increase in the sales revenue required to break even. The sales revenue required to break even increases from \$4,000,000 to \$4,080,000, determined as follows:

$$R(BE) = \frac{F}{1 - V} = \frac{\$1{,}600{,}000}{1 - .607843} = \frac{\$1{,}600{,}000}{.392157} = \$4{,}080{,}000$$

As a result of this change in sales mix, the quantity of each product that must be sold to break even also changes. The number of hypothetical packages required to break even is determined as follows:

$$Q(BE) = \frac{R(BE)}{\$510} = \frac{\$4{,}080{,}000}{\$510} = 8{,}000 \text{ hypothetical packages}$$

or equivalently:

$$Q(BE) = \frac{F}{P - C} = \frac{\$1{,}600{,}000}{\$510 - \$310} = \frac{\$1{,}600{,}000}{\$200} = 8{,}000 \text{ hypothetical packages}$$

The number of units of each product that must be sold to break even with this mix is:

8,000 packages × 1 unit of A per package = 8,000 units of A
8,000 packages × 3 units of B per package = 24,000 units of B

A change in the mix of products sold can have a material effect not only on the break-even point but also on profitability. Based on a sales mix of 1 unit of product A to 2 units of product B, Northstar Company will have a $400,000 profit if it can generate sales revenue of $5,000,000. However, if the actual sales mix is 1 unit of product A to 3 units of product B, sales revenue of approximately $5,000,000 will result in only $360,800 of profit, determined as follows:

Sales:		
Product A (9,804* units at $180)	$1,764,720	
Product B (29,412** units at $110)	3,235,320	$5,000,040
Less variable cost of goods sold:		
Product A (9,804 units at $100)	$ 980,400	
Product B (29,412 units at $70)	2,058,840	3,039,240
Contribution margin		$1,960,800
Less fixed costs		1,600,000
Operating income		$ 360,800

* $5,000,000 sales ÷ [$180 + (3 × $110)] = 9,804 packages × 1 unit = 9,804 units of A

** 9,804 packages × 3 = 29,412 units of B

Because of uncertainty in the marketplace, this type of situation is not uncommon. It illustrates the desirability of considering alternative sales mixes in break-even and cost–volume–profit analysis. One way to overcome this difficulty is to prepare a separate analysis for each product. However, if arbitrarily allocated common or joint costs are included in the analysis, the results are of limited value. Another approach is to evaluate the sensitivity of the results of the targeted, or most probable, sales mix by preparing a separate analysis for each of several possible alternative sales mixes and comparing the results. This approach makes it possible for management to identify an acceptable range of profit.

Margin of Safety. Information developed from a break-even and cost–volume–profit analysis offers additional useful control data such as the margin of safety, which indicates how much sales can decrease from a selected sales figure before the company breaks even—that is, before the company begins to suffer a loss. In the Northstar Company illustration, sales are $5,000,000 and the margin of safety is $1,000,000 ($5,000,000 – $4,000,000). The margin of safety expressed as a percentage of sales is called the **margin of safety ratio (M/S)** and is computed for Northstar as follows:

$$\text{Margin of safety ratio (M/S)} = \frac{\text{Selected sales figure} - \text{Break-even sales}}{\text{Selected sales figure}}$$

$$= \frac{\$5{,}000{,}000 - \$4{,}000{,}000}{\$5{,}000{,}000}$$

$$= 20\%$$

Observe that the margin of safety and the margin of safety ratio are negative if the break-even sales exceed the selected sales figure.

The margin of safety is directly related to profit. Using the same illustration, with a contribution margin ratio of 40 percent and a margin of safety ratio of 20 percent, then:

$$\text{Profit ratio} = \text{Contribution margin ratio} \times \text{Margin of safety ratio}$$

$$PR = C/M \times M/S$$

$$= 40\% \times 20\%$$

$$= 8\%$$

This computation indicates that of the margin of safety dollars (the sales above the break-even point), the contribution margin ratio portion is available for profit. Thus, 8 percent (40 percent of 20 percent) is the profit ratio; that is, the percentage of the total selected sales figure that is profit.

$$\begin{aligned}\text{Profit} &= \text{Margin of safety dollars} \times \text{Contribution margin ratio}\\ &= \$1{,}000{,}000 \times 40\%\\ &= \$400{,}000\end{aligned}$$

and

$$\begin{aligned}\text{Profit} &= \text{Selected sales figure} \times \text{Profit ratio}\\ &= \$5{,}000{,}000 \times 8\%\\ &= \$400{,}000\end{aligned}$$

If the contribution margin ratio and the profit ratio are known, the margin of safety ratio is:

$$\text{M/S} = \frac{\text{PR}}{\text{C/M}} = \frac{8\%}{40\%} = 20\%$$

Summary

Because product cost determined on the absorption costing basis contains an arbitrarily allocated element of fixed cost that is based on budgeted production capacity and product mix, such cost is of limited usefulness for internal decision making. Direct costing was designed to enhance the usefulness of product costs in internal decision making by eliminating the fixed cost element in product cost. In direct costing, only variable costs are assigned to products. Cost–volume–profit analysis is a useful short-run planning tool that effectively utilizes direct costing data to analyze the relationships between costs, profits, product mix, and sales volume. The sales required to achieve a targeted level of profit can be determined, and the effects of changes in fixed and variable costs on profitability can be evaluated.

Key Terms

absorption costing, full costing, or conventional costing ***(580)***
direct costing, variable costing, or marginal costing ***(581)***
contribution margin or marginal income ***(582)***
cost–volume–profit analysis ***(592)***
break-even analysis ***(592)***
break-even point ***(592)***
margin of safety ***(592)***
contribution margin ratio (C/M) ***(593)***
margin of safety ratio (M/S) ***(601)***

Discussion Questions

Q20-1 Differentiate between direct costs and direct costing.

Q20-2 Distinguish between product and period costs and relate this distinction to direct costing.

Q20-3 Describe the difference between direct costing and absorption costing.

Q20-4 What is the theoretical justification for excluding fixed manufacturing costs from inventories in direct costing?

Q20-5 What is the rationale for using the direct costing method for internal reporting?
(AICPA adapted)

Q20-6 List the arguments for the use of direct costing.

Q20-7 List the arguments against the use of direct costing.

Q20-8 Assume that the quantity of ending inventory is larger than the quantity of beginning inventory and that the lifo method is being used. Would operating income using direct costing be different from operating income using absorption costing? If so, specify whether operating income would be larger or smaller and explain the rationale for your answer.
(AICPA adapted)

Q20-9 What is the break-even point?

Q20-10 What is the contribution margin?

Q20-11 Give the formulas commonly used by firms manufacturing a single product to determine the break-even point (a) in dollars of sales revenue and (b) in units of product.

Q20-12 Identify the numbered components in the following break-even chart:

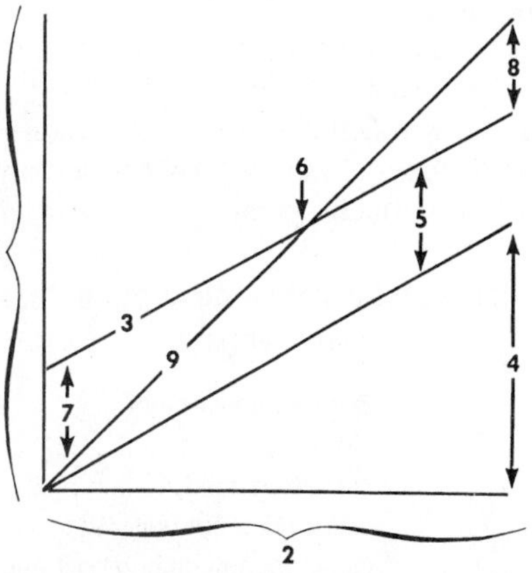

Q20-13 Discuss the significance that the concept of the relevant range has to break-even analysis.

Q20-14 Discuss weaknesses inherent in the preparation and uses of break-even analysis.

Q20-15 How does the break-even point move when changes occur in (a) variable cost? (b) fixed cost?

Q20-16 What is the margin of safety?

Q20-17 What is meant by the term *cost–volume–profit relationship?* Why is this relationship important in business management?

Exercises

E20-1 Operating Income Using Direct Costing. Dayton Manufacturing Company began its operations on January 1, 19A, and produces a single product that sells for $12 per unit. During 19A, 100,000 units of the product were produced, 90,000 of which were sold. There was no work in process inventory at the end of the year.

Manufacturing costs and marketing and administrative expenses for 19A were as follows:

	Fixed	Variable
Materials	—	$2.00 per unit produced
Direct labor	—	1.50 per unit produced
Factory overhead	$200,000	.50 per unit produced
Marketing and administrative	100,000	.20 per unit sold

Required: Prepare an operating income statement for 19A using direct costing. (AICPA adapted)

E20-2 Absorption Costing versus Direct Costing. Murphy Products began operations on January 3 of the current year. Standard costs were established in early January assuming a normal production volume of 160,000 units. However, Murphy Products produced only 140,000 units of product and sold only 100,000 units at a selling price of $180 per unit during the current year. Variable costs totaled $7,000,000, of which 60% were manufacturing and 40% were selling. Fixed costs totaled $11,200,000, of which 50% were manufacturing and 50% were selling. Murphy had no raw materials or work in process inventories at the end of the year. Actual input prices per unit of product and actual input quantities per unit of product were equal to standard.

Required:
(1) Determine Murphy Products' cost of goods sold at standard cost, using full absorption costing (excluding standard cost variances).
(2) How much cost would be assigned to Murphy Products' ending inventory using direct costing?
(3) Compute Murphy Products' factory overhead volume variance for the year.
(4) How much operating income would Murphy Products have using direct costing? (ICMA adapted)

E20-3 Income Statements—Absorption Costing versus Direct Costing. The following data pertain to April operations for Klinger Company:

Beginning inventory	3,000
Units sold	9,000
Units produced	8,000
Sales price per unit	$ 30
Direct manufacturing cost per unit	$ 10
Fixed factory overhead—total	$40,000
Fixed factory overhead—per unit	$ 5
Commercial expense (all fixed)	$30,000

Required:
(1) Prepare an income statement using absorption costing.
(2) Prepare an income statement using direct costing.
(3) Provide computations explaining the difference in operating income between the two methods.

E20-4 Break-Even Analysis. Woliver Company plans to market a new product. Based on its market studies, Woliver estimates that it can sell 5,500 units during the first year. The sales price will be $2 per unit. Variable cost is estimated to be 40% of the sales price. Fixed cost is estimated to be $6,000.

Required: Compute the break-even point in dollars and in units.

E20-5 Break-Even and Cost–Volume–Profit Analysis. Kenton Company produces only one product. Normal capacity is 20,000 units per year, and the unit sales price is $5. Relevant costs are:

	Unit Variable Cost	Total Fixed Cost
Materials	$1.00	
Direct labor	1.20	
Factory overhead	.50	$15,000
Marketing expenses	.30	5,000
Administrative expenses		6,000

Required: Compute the following:
(1) The break-even point in units of product
(2) The break-even point in dollars of sales
(3) The number of units of product that must be produced and sold to achieve a profit of $10,000
(4) The sales revenue required to achieve a profit of $10,000

E20-6 Margin of Safety. Marvel Corporation plans sales of $2,000,000 for the coming period, which top management expects will result in a profit of $200,000. The break-even point has been determined to be $1,500,000 of sales.

Required: Compute the margin of safety and the margin of safety ratio.

E20-7 Break-Even Analysis and Profit Formula. A month's operations of Sureflite Company show fixed cost of $9,300, an M/S ratio of 25%, and a C/M ratio of 62%.

Required: Compute the following:
(1) Break-even sales
(2) Actual sales
(3) Profit for the month

E20-8 Break-Even Analysis and Profit Formula. Operations of Gilley Company for the year disclosed an M/S ratio of 20% and a C/M ratio of 60%. Fixed cost amounted to $30,000.

Required: Compute the following:
(1) Break-even sales
(2) The amount of profit
(3) The contribution margin

E20-9 Cost–Volume–Profit Analysis. Hytech Semiconductor Company is planning to produce and sell 100,000 units of Chip A at $8 a unit and 200,000 units of Chip B at $6 a unit. Variable costs are 30% of sales for Chip A and 25% of sales for Chip B.

Required: If total planned operating profit is $250,000, what must the total fixed cost be? (AICPA adapted)

E20-10 Break-Even Analysis with Multiple Products. Anti-Que Furniture Company manufactures two products, tables and chairs. Tables sell for $110 each and chairs for $35 each. Four times as many chairs are sold each year as tables. Variable costs per unit are $50 and $20 for tables and chairs, respectively. Total fixed cost is $720,000.

Required: Compute the break-even point in sales dollars and in units of product.

E20-11 Break-Even and Cost–Volume–Profit Analysis. Puma Company manufactures two products, L and M. L sells for $20 and M for $15. Variable costs per unit are $12 and $10 for L and M, respectively. Total fixed cost is $372,000. Puma management has targeted profit for the coming period at $93,000. Two units of L are expected to sell for every three units of M sold during the period.

Required: Compute the following:
(1) The break-even point in units of product and in sales dollars
(2) The level of sales in units of product and dollars necessary to achieve Puma's profit goal

E20-12 Cost–Volume–Profit Analysis. Citation Company expects to incur the following costs to produce and sell 70,000 units of its product:

Variable manufacturing cost	$210,000
Fixed manufacturing cost	80,000
Variable marketing expense	105,000
Fixed marketing and administrative expenses	60,000

Required:
(1) What price does Citation have to charge for the product in order just to break even if all 70,000 units produced are sold?
(2) If Citation decides on a price of $8 and has a profit objective of 10% of sales, what sales volume is required?
(3) Citation plans to expand capacity next year to 100,000 units. The increased capacity will increase fixed manufacturing costs to $100,000. If the sales price of each unit of product remains at $8, how many units must Citation sell in order to produce a profit of 15% of sales?

CGA-Canada (adapted). Reprint with permission.

E20-13 Break-Even Chart. Groff Company expects annual sales of 10,000 units of its product at $20 per unit. Variable cost is $10 per unit, and fixed cost is expected to total $70,000.

Required: Prepare a break-even chart for Groff Company.

Problems

P20-1 Product-Line Income Statement Using Contribution Margin Approach. Masterpiece Tool Corporation produces and sells three different product lines: electric tools, pneumatic tools, and hand tools. Last year the company conducted an aggressive advertising campaign to boost sales of its products; however, this year's income was disappointing. The following absorption costing income statement was presented to management:

Sales		$3,000,000
Less cost of goods sold		1,950,000
Gross profit		$1,050,000
Less commercial expenses:		
Marketing	$800,000	
Administration	100,000	900,000
Operating income		$ 150,000

Management is concerned about the unexpected low level of profits and the effectiveness of the advertising campaign. To evaluate these concerns, management has requested a product-line income statement prepared on a contribution margin basis. Data related to last year's activities follow.

(a) Advertising expenditures for the year were:

Electric tools	$200,000
Pneumatic tools	200,000
Hand tools	50,000

(b) Variable marketing expenses related to packing and shipping the products sold to customers were:

Electric tools	$100,000
Pneumatic tools	100,000
Hand tools	50,000

(c) Analysis of manufacturing costs revealed the following:

	Electric Tools	Pneumatic Tools	Hand Tools
Materials	$400,000	$350,000	$150,000
Labor	200,000	100,000	30,000
Variable overhead	100,000	50,000	20,000
Fixed overhead traceable to products	100,000	100,000	50,000

(d) Half the sales revenue came from sales of electric tools, one third from sales of pneumatic tools, and the balance from sales of hand tools.

(e) All other costs and expenses incurred during the period were common fixed costs.

Required: Prepare a product-line income statement for Masterpiece Tool Corporation on a contribution margin basis.

P20-2 Absorption Costing versus Direct Costing. Roberts Corporation developed the following standard unit costs at 100% of its normal production capacity, which is 50,000 units per year:

Direct materials	$ 6
Direct labor	3
Variable factory overhead	1
Fixed factory overhead	5
	$15

The selling price of each unit of product is $25. Variable commercial expenses are $1 per unit sold, and fixed commercial expenses total $200,000 for the period. During the year, 49,000 units were produced and 52,000 units were sold. There are no work in process beginning or ending inventories, and finished goods inventory is maintained at standard cost, which has not changed from the preceding year. For the current year, there is a net unfavorable variable cost variance in the amount of $2,000. All standard cost variances are charged to cost of goods sold at the end of the period.

Required:

(1) Prepare an income statement on the absorption costing basis.
(2) Prepare an income statement on the direct costing basis.
(3) Compute and reconcile the difference in operating income for the current year under absorption costing and direct costing.

P20-3 Absorption Costing versus Direct Costing. Placid Corporation developed the following standard unit costs at 100% of its normal production capacity, which is 50,000 units per year:

Direct materials	$2
Direct labor	3
Variable factory overhead	1
Fixed factory overhead	3
	9

The selling price of each unit of product is $16. Variable commercial expenses are $1 per unit sold, and fixed commercial expenses total $100,000 for the period. During the year, 51,000 units were produced and 48,000 units were sold. There are no work in process beginning or ending inventories, and finished goods inventory is maintained at standard cost, which has not changed from the preceding year. For the current year, there is a net unfavorable variable cost variance in the amount of $1,000. All standard cost variances are charged to cost of goods sold at the end of the period.

Required:

(1) Prepare an income statement on the absorption costing basis.
(2) Prepare an income statement on the direct costing basis.
(3) Compute and reconcile the difference in operating income for the current year under absorption costing and direct costing.

P20-4 Income Statements—Absorption Costing versus Direct Costing On January 2, Commerce Reel Company began production of a new model. First quarter sales were 20,000 units and second quarter sales were 26,000 units at a unit price of $10. Unit production costs each quarter were: direct materials, $1; direct labor, $2; and variable factory overhead, $1.50. Fixed factory overhead was $62,400 each quarter and, for absorption costing, is assigned to inventory based on actual units produced.

Each quarter, marketing and administrative expenses consisted of a $15,000 fixed portion and a variable portion equal to 5% of sales. Units produced in the first and second quarters totaled 30,000 and 20,000, respectively. The fifo inventory costing method is used.

Required:

(1) Prepare comparative income statements for the first and second quarters under the absorption costing method.
(2) Prepare comparative income statements for the first and second quarters under the direct costing method.
(3) Compute and reconcile the differences in operating income under the two methods for each quarter.

P20-5 Break-Even Analysis Kimbrell Company has decided to introduce a new product. The new product can be manufactured by either a capital-intensive method or a labor-intensive method. The manufacturing method will not affect the quality of the product. The estimated unit manufacturing costs by the two methods follow:

	Capital Intensive	Labor Intensive
Materials	$5.00	$5.60
Direct labor	6.00	7.20
Variable factory overhead	3.00	4.80

Directly traceable incremental fixed factory overhead is expected to be $2,440,000 if the capital-intensive method is chosen and $1,320,000 if the labor-intensive method is chosen. Kimbrell's Market Research Department has recommended an introductory unit sales price of $30. Regardless of the manufacturing method chosen, the incremental marketing expenses are estimated to be $500,000 per year plus $2 for each unit sold.

Required:

(1) Calculate the estimated break-even point for the new product in annual units of sales, if Kimbrell Company uses the:
   (a) Capital-intensive manufacturing method.
   (b) Labor-intensive manufacturing method.

(2) Determine the annual unit sales volume at which the choice between the two manufacturing methods would not make a difference. (ICMA adapted)

P20-6 Break-Even and Cost–Volume–Profit Analysis. Castleton Company has analyzed the costs of producing and selling 5,000 units of its only product to be as follows:

Direct materials	$60,000
Direct labor	40,000
Variable factory overhead	20,000
Fixed factory overhead	30,000
Variable marketing and administrative expenses	10,000
Fixed marketing and administrative expenses	15,000

Required:

(1) Compute the number of units needed to break even at a per unit sales price of $38.50.

(2) Determine the number of units that must be sold to produce an $18,000 profit, at a $40 per unit sales price.

(3) Determine the price Castleton must charge at a 5,000-unit sales level, in order to produce a profit equal to 20% of sales. CGA-Canada (adapted). Reprint with permission.

P20-7 Cost–Volume–Profit Analysis The Desousa Company produces and sells two distinct products, B2 and B4. Available data for the year ending December 31, 19A, follow:

	B2	B4
Sales volume	20,000	40,000
Selling price per unit	$180	$160
Direct materials	$ 65	$ 40
Direct labor	40	40
Variable factory overhead	16	16
Fixed factory overhead	25	25
Full cost per unit	$146	$121
Gross profit per unit	$ 34	$ 39

Other information pertaining to operations during the year ending December 31, 19A, follow.

(a) Variable selling costs were 5% of sales.

(b) Fixed selling and administrative costs were $207,330 (with a capacity to handle volumes of up to twice those of 19A).

(c) The present plant facilities provide a capacity of 60,000 units; this can be increased to a capacity of 100,000 units at an additional cost of $80,000.

(d) The company is taxed at a rate of 40%.

Expected changes for the year ending December 31, 19B, include the following:

(a) The selling price of B4 is expected to increase by 10%, but no other changes are expected in costs or selling prices for either product.

(b) The sales mix for 19B is expected to be in the ratio of 2 units of B2 to 3 units of B4.

Required: Calculate the number of units of each product the company must sell in order to earn an aftertax net income of $135,000 for the year ending December 31, 19B. (SMAC adapted)

P20-8 Break-Even and Cost–Volume–Profit Analysis. Cabot Electronics produces and markets tape recorders and electronic calculators. Its 19A income statement is presented on page 609.

The tape recorder business has been fairly stable in recent years, and the company has no plans to change the tape recorder price. However, because of increasing competition and market saturation, management has decided to reduce its calculator price to $20, effective January 1, 19B, and to spend an additional $57,000 in 19B for advertising. As a result, Cabot estimates that 80% of its 19B revenue will be from electronic calculator sales. The sales units mix for tape recorders and calculators was 1:2 in 19A and is expected to be 1:3 in 19B at all volume levels. For 19B, materials costs are expected to drop 10% and 20% for the tape recorders and calculators, respectively; however, all direct labor costs are to increase 10%.

Cabot Electronics
Income Statement
For Year Ended December 31, 19A

	Tape Recorders		Electronic Calculators		
	Total (in thousands)	Per Unit	Total (in thousands)	Per Unit	Total (in thousands)
Sales	$1,050	$15.00	$3,150	$22.50	$4,200.00
Production costs:					
Materials	$ 280	$ 4.00	$ 630	$ 4.50	$ 910.00
Direct labor	140	2.00	420	3.00	560.00
Variable factory overhead	140	2.00	280	2.00	420.00
Fixed factory overhead	70	1.00	210	1.50	280.00
Total production cost	$ 630	$ 9.00	$1,540	$11.00	$2,170.00
Gross profit	$ 420	$ 6.00	$1,610	$11.50	$2,030.00
Fixed marketing and administrative expenses					1,040.00
Income before income tax					$ 990.00
Income tax (55%)					544.50
Net income					$ 445.50

Required:

(1) Compute the number of tape recorders and electronic calculators that must be sold to break even, using 19A data.

(2) Determine the sales dollars required to earn an aftertax profit of 9% on sales, using 19B estimates.

(3) Compute the number of tape recorders and electronic calculators that must be sold to break even, using 19B estimates. (ICMA adapted)

P20-9 Break-Even and Cost–Volume–Profit Analysis. Almo Company manufactures and sells adjustable canopies that attach to motor homes and trailers. The market includes both new unit purchasers and purchasers of replacement canopies. Almo developed its current business plan based on the assumption that canopies will sell at a price of $400 each. The variable costs for each canopy were projected at $200, and the annual fixed costs were budgeted at $100,000. Almo's aftertax profit objective was $240,000; the company's effective tax rate is 40%.

Although Almo's sales usually rise during the second quarter, the May financial statements reported that sales were not meeting expectations. For the first five months of the year, only 350 units had been sold at the established price, with variable costs as planned, and it was clear that the current year after tax profit projection would not be reached unless some actions were taken. Almo's president assigned a management committee to analyze the situation and develop several alternative courses of action. The following mutually exclusive alternatives were presented to the president.

(a) The sale price can be reduced by $40. The sales organization forecasts that, with the significantly reduced sales price, 2,700 units can be sold during the remainder of the year. Total fixed and variable costs will stay as budgeted.

(b) Variable costs per unit can be lowered by $25 through the use of less expensive materials and slightly modified manufacturing techniques. The sales price will also be reduced by $30, and the sales forecast is 2,200 units for the remainder of the year.

(c) Cut fixed costs by $10,000 and lower the sales price by 5%. Variable costs per unit will be unchanged. Sales of 2,000 units are expected for the remainder of the year.

Required:

(1) If no changes are made to the selling price or cost structure, what is the number of units that Almo Company must sell to achieve each of the following:
    (a) The break-even point
    (b) Its original aftertax profit objective of $240,000

(2) Determine which one of the three alternatives Almo Company should select. Support your selection with computations demonstrating the effect of each alternative on profit (ICMA adapted)

P20-10 Break-Even and Cost–Volume–Profit Analysis. Seco Corporation, a wholesale supply company, engages independent sales agents to market the company's lines. These agents currently receive a commission of 20% of sales, but they are demanding an increase to 25% of sales made during the year ending December 31, 19A. Seco had already prepared its 19A budget before learning of the agents' demand for an increase in commissions. The pro forma income statement below is based on this budget.

Seco Corporation
Pro Forma Income Statement
For the Year Ending December 31, 19A

Sales		$10,000,000
Cost of goods sold		6,000,000
Gross profit		$ 4,000,000
Selling and administrative expenses:		
Commissions	$2,000,000	
All other costs (fixed)	100,000	2,100,000
Income before income tax		$ 1,900,000
Income tax (30%)		570,000
Net income		$ 1,330,000

Seco is considering the possibility of employing its own salespersons. Three individuals would be required, at an estimated annual salary of $30,000 each, plus commissions of 5% of sales. In addition, a sales manager would be employed at a fixed annual salary of $160,000. All other fixed costs, as well as the variable cost percentages, would remain the same as the estimates in the 19A pro forma income statement.

Required:

(1) Compute Seco's estimated break-even point in sales dollars for the year ending December 31, 19A, based on the pro forma income statement prepared by the company.
(2) Compute Seco's estimated break-even point in sales dollars for the year ending December 31, 19A, if the company employs its own salespersons.
(3) For the year ending December 31, 19A, compute in sales dollars the estimated volume required to yield the same net income as projected in the pro forma income statement, if Seco continues to use the independent sales agents and agrees to their demand for a 25% sales commission.
(4) For the year ending December 31, 19A, compute the estimated volume in sales dollars that will generate net income that is identical whether Seco employs its own salespersons or continues to use the independent sales agents and pays them a 25% commission. (AICPA adapted)

Cases

C20-1 Sales and Production Volume Effects—Absorption Costing versus Direct Costing. Star Company, a wholly owned subsidiary of Orbit Inc., produces and sells three main product lines. The company employs a standard cost accounting system for record-keeping purposes.

At the beginning of the year, the president of Star Company presented the budget to the parent company and accepted a commitment to contribute $15,800 to Orbit's consolidated profit in 19A. The president has been confident that the year's profit would exceed the budget target, because the monthly sales reports have shown that sales for the year will exceed the budget by 10%. The president is both disturbed and confused when the controller presents an adjusted forecast as of November 30, indicating that profit will be 11% under budget. The two forecasts follow:

	Forecasts as of	
	January 1	November 30
Sales	$268,000	$294,800
Cost of goods sold at standard	212,000*	233,200
Gross profit at standard	$ 56,000	$ 61,600
Less underapplied factory overhead	—	6,000
Gross profit at actual	$ 56,000	$ 55,600
Marketing expense	$ 13,400	$ 14,740
Administrative expense	26,800	26,800
Total commercial expense	$ 40,200	$ 41,540
Income from operations	$ 15,800	$ 14,060

* Includes fixed factory overhead of $30,000.

There have been no sales price changes or product mix shifts since the January 1 forecast. The only cost variance on the income statement is underapplied factory overhead. This arose because the company used only 16,000 standard machine hours (budgeted machine hours were 20,000) during the year as a result of a shortage of raw materials. Fortunately, Star Company's finished goods inventory was large enough to fill all sales orders received.

Required:

(1) Analyze and explain the forecast profit decline, in spite of increased sales and good cost control.

(2) Explain and illustrate an alternative internal cost reporting procedure that would avoid the confusing effect of the procedure used presently. (ICMA adapted)

C20-2 Sales and Production Volume Effects—Absorption Costing versus Direct Costing. RGB Corporation is a manufacturer of a synthetic element. A. B. Meek, president of the company, has been eager to obtain the operating results for the fiscal year just completed. Meek was surprised when the income statement revealed that operating income dropped to $645,000 from $900,000, although sales volume had increased by 100,000 units. This drop in operating income occurred even though Meek had implemented the following changes during the past 12 months to improve the profitability of the company.

(1) In response to a 10% increase in production costs, the sales price of the company's product was increased by 12%. This action took place on December 1, 19A.

(2) The management of the Selling and Administrative Departments were given strict instructions to spend no more in fiscal 19B than they did in fiscal 19A.

RGB's Accounting Department prepared and distributed to top management the comparative income statements shown at the bottom of the page.

The accounting staff also prepared related financial information that is presented in the following schedule to assist management in its evaluation of the company's performance. RGB uses the fifo inventory method for finished goods.

RGB Corporation
Selected Operating and Financial Data
For 19A and 19B

	19A	19B
Sales price per unit	$10.00	$11.20
Materials cost per unit	1.50	1.65
Direct labor cost per unit	2.50	2.75
Variable factory overhead per unit	1.00	1.10
Fixed factory overhead per unit	3.00	3.30
Total fixed factory overhead	$3,000,000	$3,300,000
Total selling and administrative expenses	1,500,000	1,500,000
Quantity of units budgeted (normal capacity)	1,000,000	1,000,000
Quantity of units actually produced	1,200,000	850,000
Quantity of units sold	900,000	1,000,000
Quantity of units in beginning inventory	0	300,000
Quantity of units in ending inventory	300,000	150,000

Required:

(1) Explain to A. B. Meek why RGB Corporation's net income decreased in the current fiscal year, despite the sales price and sales volume increase.

(2) A member of RGB's Accounting Department has suggested that the company adopt direct costing for internal reporting purposes.

(a) Prepare an operating income statement for the fiscal years ended November 30, 19A and 19B, for RGB Corporation using the direct costing method.

(b) Present a numerical reconciliation of the difference in operating income between the absorption costing method currently in use and the direct costing method proposed.

(3) Identify and discuss some of the advantages and disadvantages of using the direct costing method for internal reporting purposes. (ICMA adapted)

C20-3 Break-Even and Cost-Volume-Profit Analysis. Daly Company has determined the number of units of

RGB Corporation
Statements of Operating Income
For the Years Ended November 30, 19A and 19B
(in thousands)

	19A		19B	
Sales revenue		$9,000		$11,200
Cost of goods sold	$7,200		$8,560	
Volume variance, (favorable) unfavorable	(600)	6,600	495	9,055
Gross profit		$2,400		$ 2,145
Selling and administrative expenses		1,500		1,500
Operating income		$ 900		$ 645

Product Y that Daly would have to sell in order to break even. However, Daly would like to attain a profit of 20% on sales of Product Y.

Required:

(1) Explain how cost–volume–profit analysis can be used to determine the number of units of Product Y that Daly would have to sell to attain a 20% profit on sales.

(2) If variable cost per unit increases as a percentage of the sales price, how will that affect the number of units of Product Y that Daly would have to sell in order to break even? Explain why.

(3) Identify the limitations of break-even and cost–volume–profit analysis in managerial decision making.

(AICPA adapted)

CHAPTER 21

Differential Cost Analysis

Learning Objectives

After studying this chapter, you will be able to:

1. Define the term *differential cost study* and relate it to short-term decision making.
2. Distinguish costs that are relevant to short-term decision making from those that are not.
3. List several examples of short-term decision problems for which differential cost can be computed.
4. Compute differential cost and use it to make short-run economic decisions.
5. (Appendix) Define linear programming and list its uses.
6. (Appendix) Formulate a linear programming problem and solve it using the graphic method.

To achieve company goals and objectives, management must make frequent decisions about the potential cost or profitability of alternative actions. The accountant facilitates this process by providing management information relevant to the decisions that must be made. Different kinds of decision problems require the use of different decision models, which in turn utilize different kinds of information. To provide relevant information, the accountant must understand the nature of the problem being evaluated and the decision model being used.

This chapter focuses on short-term decision making. The first section of the chapter defines differential cost studies and relevant costs. The second section illustrates its relevance in solving different types of short-term decision problems. Linear programming and its application to short-term decision problems are presented in the appendix to this chapter. Decisions that have long-term effects are discussed in Chapters 22 and 23, and techniques for dealing with the problem of uncertainty in both short-term and long-term decisions are presented in Chapter 24.

Differential Cost Studies

A **differential cost study** is an analysis undertaken to determine the desirability of a proposed project or activity that does not extend beyond one year. If expected differential benefits exceed expected differential cost, the action being evaluated should be undertaken. When alternatives that achieve the same goal are evaluated, differential cost studies show which alternative costs the least.

Usually the expected benefit of a business activity is revenue; however, it need not be. The benefit of a project can also be the avoidance of a fine or other legal action. Companies sometimes engage in nonprofit activities such as helping to clean up the environment, providing aid to the needy and underprivileged, and providing educational assistance. When the expected benefit of a differential cost study is revenue, it is referred to as **marginal revenue** or **incremental revenue** because it provides an increment or addition to the company's total revenue for the period.

Differential cost is the cost that must be incurred to complete a proposed project or to extend an activity already undertaken. It is often referred to as **marginal cost** by economists and as **incremental cost** by industrial engineers. Differential cost includes all cash expenditures required for the project or activity (fixed cost as well as variable cost). The required cash outlay is referred to as **out-of-pocket cost**. Similarly, differential cost can be thought of as the expenditure that can be avoided if an activity is abandoned or discontinued. In this sense, it is referred to as **avoidable cost**.

Differential cost does not include sunk costs or allocated fixed costs. **Sunk costs** are expenditures that have been made and cannot be recovered, such as the excess of the book value of an unneeded machine over its salvage value. Allocated fixed costs are costs that do not change as a result of accepting or rejecting the project or activity being evaluated and include such things as plant superintendence and building depreciation. Because sunk costs cannot be recovered and because allocated fixed costs are not affected by the decision, they are not relevant to short-run decisions.

Variable costs are relevant in differential cost studies because they are costs that must be incurred if the activity being evaluated is undertaken or extended but can be avoided if it is not. In contrast, fixed costs usually are not affected by short-run increases or decreases in activity. However, if additional fixed cost must be incurred in order to expand capacity to a level required to undertake or extend a project, the additional cost is a differential cost because it is an out-of-pocket expenditure that can be avoided. Any out-of-pocket expenditure required to provide sufficient capacity is relevant to the decision. For example, if a company currently operating at 95 percent of capacity must rent additional machinery in order to expand production to 110 percent of capacity, the cost of renting the additional machinery is a differential cost (even though it is also a fixed cost) because it is an out-of-pocket expenditure.

Opportunity costs should be considered in the evaluation of short-term decision problems. An **opportunity cost** is defined as the measurable value of the best forgone alternative, that is, the measurable value of an opportunity bypassed by rejecting the best alternative use of resources. For example, money can either be spent in producing and selling a product or it can be invested in an interest-earning asset, such as a bond. If money is spent producing and selling a product, the interest that could have been earned from the alternative (investment in the interest-earning asset) is an opportunity cost. Similarly, a machine can either be used in the manufacture of a product or it can be sold. The net realizable value[1] of the machine is an opportunity cost. Although opportunity costs are not routinely reported in financial statements, they should be considered in evaluating alternatives in order to determine the most profitable use of resources.

Imputed costs can also be relevant to differential cost studies. **Imputed costs** are hypothetical costs representing the cost of a resource measured by its use value. Imputed costs ordinarily do not appear in conventional accounting records and do not necessarily entail dollar outlays. An imputed cost is similar to an opportunity cost, except that an imputed cost may be an arbitrary measure. An example of an imputed cost is loss of public goodwill that might result from laying off employees when a project is abandoned. Another example is the fear of

[1] Net realizable value is defined as the excess of the proceeds received from selling the machine over the cost of selling it. The cost of selling a machine can include fix-up costs, advertising expenditures, shipping expenses, and sales commissions.

environmental pollution if certain projects are undertaken that might result in loss of goodwill.

Historical costs drawn from accounting records generally do not give management the differential cost information it needs to evaluate alternative courses of action. However, a flexible budget[2] with costs computed for different levels of capacity utilization can be useful in differential cost analyses. The flexible budget presented in Exhibit 21-1 for Gilbert Company shows costs at different levels of production capacity. It indicates that some costs increase proportionately with an increase in capacity, while other costs remain comparatively unchanged through various levels of activity.

EXHIBIT 21-1

Gilbert Company
Flexible Budget for Different Rates of Output
(100,000 Units = 100% Normal Capacity)

Capacity (as a percent of normal)	60%	80%	100%	120%
Variable costs:				
Direct manufacturing costs:				
Direct materials	$102,000	$136,000	$170,000	$204,000
Direct labor	93,000	124,000	155,000	186,000
Total	$195,000	$260,000	$325,000	$390,000
Indirect manufacturing costs:				
Heat	$ 720	$ 960	$ 1,200	$ 1,440
Light and power	1,440	1,920	2,400	2,880
Repairs and maintenance	2,460	3,280	4,100	4,920
Supplies	1,260	1,680	2,100	2,520
Indirect labor	9,120	12,160	15,200	18,240
Total	$ 15,000	$ 20,000	$ 25,000	$ 30,000
Commercial expenses:				
Clerical help	$ 11,580	$ 15,440	$ 19,300	$ 23,160
Wages, general	6,960	9,280	11,600	13,920
Supplies	1,260	1,680	2,100	2,520
Total	$ 19,800	$ 26,400	$ 33,000	$ 39,600
Fixed costs:				
Indirect manufacturing costs:				
Supervisors	$ 15,250	$ 20,500	$ 20,500	$ 25,750
Indirect Labor	15,000	15,000	15,000	17,750
Setup crew	5,000	7,500	7,500	8,500
Depreciation and rent	8,000	9,400	9,400	9,400
Property taxes and insurance	2,600	2,600	2,600	2,600
Total	$ 45,850	$ 55,000	$ 55,000	$ 64,000
Commercial expenses:				
Executives' salaries	$ 28,000	$ 35,000	$ 35,000	$ 40,000
Assistants' salaries	11,200	16,400	16,400	19,200
Property taxes	3,400	3,400	3,400	3,400
Advertising	6,000	7,200	7,200	8,600
Total	$ 48,600	$ 62,000	$ 62,000	$ 71,200
Total cost	$324,250	$423,400	$500,000	$594,800
Units of output	60,000	80,000	100,000	120,000
Average unit cost	$5.40	$5.29	$5.00	$4.96
Differential cost total		$99,150	$76,600	$94,800
Differential cost per unit		$4.96	$3.83	$4.74

[2] See Chapter 17 for a discussion of flexible budgets, including an illustration of the computations required to determine costs at various levels of activity.

In the flexible budget illustrated in Exhibit 21-1, the $5.40 average unit cost at 60 percent of normal capacity is computed by dividing the total cost at that capacity by the number of units produced ($324,250 ÷ 60,000 units). The total differential cost is determined by subtracting the total estimated cost for one level of activity from that of another level (for example, $423,400 – $324,250 = $99,150, which is the differential cost between the 80 percent and 60 percent levels). The differential unit cost is computed by first subtracting one level of output from the next higher level (80,000 units output at 80 percent of capacity minus 60,000 units output at 60 percent of capacity = 20,000 units). The total differential cost between these two levels of capacity is then divided by the difference in the number of units ($99,150 ÷ 20,000 units = $4.96).

Examples of Differential Cost Studies

Differential cost studies are short-term in orientation. They are not very useful for strategic planning because they ignore the long-term effects of decisions. In the long run, all costs must be recovered or the company will not be profitable, and if it is not profitable, it will not survive for long. For long-term product pricing and product mix decisions, activity-based costing provides useful cost information (see Chapter 14). If a proposed project extends beyond one year, one or more of the capital expenditure evaluation techniques discussed in Chapters 22 and 23 should be used. However, for projects or activities that do not extend beyond the current period, differential cost studies provide relevant information for decision making. Some examples of short-term decisions that may benefit from differential cost analysis include the following:

1. Accepting or refusing certain orders
2. Reducing the price of a single, special order
3. Making a price cut in a competitive market
4. Evaluating make-or-buy alternatives
5. Expanding, shutting down, or eliminating a facility
6. Increasing, curtailing, or stopping production of certain products
7. Determining whether to sell or to process further
8. Choosing among alternative routings in product manufacture
9. Determining the maximum price that can be paid for raw materials

Accepting Additional Orders

Differential cost is the cost that should be considered when a decision involves a change in output. The differential cost of added production is the difference between the cost of producing the present smaller output and that of the contemplated, larger output. If available capacity is not fully utilized, a differential cost analysis might indicate the possibility of selling additional output at a figure lower than the existing average unit cost. The additional business will be profitable as long as the revenue from the additional output exceeds the differential cost of manufacturing and selling the additional output.

For example, assume that a plant has a maximum production capacity of 100,000 units, but normal capacity is set at 80,000 units. The predetermined overhead rate is computed so that budgeted fixed overhead is fully absorbed when operations are at the 80,000-unit level. (That is, all the budgeted fixed overhead is applied to the 80,000 units produced during the period.) If fewer units are produced, fixed overhead is underapplied. If more units are produced, fixed overhead is overapplied. If this company makes only one unit, its total cost for the period and its unit cost are equal because the one unit produced must absorb all production cost incurred during the period. The total cost per unit is as follows:

Variable cost per unit	$ 5
Total fixed cost	100,000
Total cost per unit	$100,005

At normal capacity, the fixed cost per unit is reduced to \$1.25 (\$100,000 ÷ 80,000 units), and the total cost per unit is:

Variable cost per unit	$5.00
Share of fixed cost	1.25
Total cost per unit	$6.25

Notice that the differential cost of the additional 79,999 units is \$5 per unit (that is, the variable cost), because no additional fixed costs are incurred. If additional capacity can be utilized to produce an additional 1,000 units, the differential cost of these units would be only the \$5 variable cost per unit, unless the production of the additional 1,000 units incurs additional fixed cost. If the sales price is \$9 per unit, a differential cost analysis comparing present operating results with the total results after 1,000 additional units are produced and sold might appear as follows:

	Present Business	With Additional Business
Sales	$720,000	$729,000
Variable cost	400,000	405,000
Contribution margin	$320,000	$324,000
Fixed cost	100,000	100,000
Profit	$220,000	$224,000

The additional business requires additional variable cost only. Because adequate unused capacity is available to produce the additional 1,000 units, additional fixed cost will not be incurred. If the 1,000 units are sold at any price above the \$5 variable cost each, the sale will yield a positive contribution to short-run profit.

The preceding illustration can also be presented in the following manner to highlight the differential revenue of \$9,000 and cost of \$5,000.

	Present Business	Additional Business	Total
Sales	$720,000	$9,000	$729,000
Variable cost	400,000	5,000	405,000
Contribution margin	$320,000	$4,000	$324,000
Fixed cost	100,000	0	100,000
Profit	$220,000	$4,000	$224,000

Reducing the Price of a Special Order

Differential cost analysis is an aid to management in deciding at what price the firm can afford to sell additional goods. For example, assume that during 19A Walsenberg Company manufactures 450,000 units using 90 percent of its normal capacity. The fixed factory overhead is \$1,250,000, which is \$2.50 for each unit manufactured when operations are at 100 percent of normal capacity ($1,250,000 ÷ 500,000 units). The variable factory overhead rate is $.50 per unit. The direct materials cost is $1.80, and the direct labor cost is $1.40 per unit. Batch-level and product-level costs are zero, because only one product is produced by this company (see Chapter 14). Each unit sells for $10. Variable marketing expense (shipping expense and sales commission) is $.50 per unit. Fixed marketing and administrative expenses total $800,000. On the basis of these data, the accountant would prepare an income statement such as the one presented in Exhibit 21-2.

EXHIBIT 21-2

Walsenberg Company
Income Statement
For Year Ending December, 19A

Sales (450,000 units at $10)		$4,500,000
Cost of goods sold:		
Direct materials (450,000 units at $1.80)	$ 810,000	
Direct labor (450,000 units at $1.40)	630,000	
Variable factory overhead (450,000 units at $.50)	225,000	
Fixed factory overhead (450,000 units at $2.50)	1,125,000	2,790,000
Gross profit		$1,710,000
Underapplied fixed factory overhead [(500,000 units – 450,000 units) at $2.50]		125,000
Gross profit (adjusted)		$1,585,000
Less commercial expenses:		
Variable marketing expense (450,000 units at $.50)	$ 225,000	
Fixed marketing and administrative expenses	800,000	1,025,000
Income from operations		$ 560,000

The sales manager of Walsenberg Company reports that a customer has offered to pay $6 per unit for an additional 100,000 units. To make the additional units, an annual rental cost of $10,000 for additional equipment would be incurred. Using absorption cost data, the accountant might compute the gain or loss on this order as follows:

Sales (100,000 units at $6)		$600,000
Differential cost of goods sold:		
Direct materials (100,000 units at $1.80)	$180,000	
Direct labor (100,000 units at $1.40)	140,000	
Variable factory overhead (100,000 units at $.50)	50,000	
Fixed factory overhead (100,000 units at $2.50)	250,000	620,000
		$ (20,000)
Variable marketing expense (100,000 units at $.50)		50,000
Loss on this order		$ (70,000)

There are two problems with the preceding calculation. First, the $10,000 additional cost of equipment rental has been ignored, and second, fixed overhead, which is not affected by the decision, has been allocated to the additional business as if it were a differential cost. The use of absorption cost data in this case would cause management to reject the offer. In this computation, all cost elements are measured at the existing unit costs, and fixed overhead is allocated on the basis of the established rate ($2.50 per unit). A second look, however, reveals the following effect of the new order on total fixed factory overhead:

Fixed factory overhead (at present)	$1,250,000	
Fixed factory overhead (because of additional business)	10,000	
Total fixed factory overhead		$1,260,000
Fixed factory overhead charged into production:		
For 450,000 units (old business)	$1,125,000	
For 100,000 units (additional business)	250,000	1,375,000
Overapplied fixed factory overhead		$ 115,000

Instead of underapplied fixed factory overhead of $125,000, the additional business would result in overapplied factory overhead of $115,000, or an increase of $240,000 in applied factory overhead. The increase of $240,000 can also be computed by subtracting the additional fixed cost that must be incurred ($10,000 equipment rental) from the amount of fixed factory overhead allocated to the additional 100,000 units produced under the absorbtion costing method (100,000 units × $2.50 each = $250,000). This $240,000 minus the computed $70,000 loss on the order results in a gain of $170,000. This gain is shown more clearly in the following statement, which includes only the differential costs and revenue:

Sales (100,000 units at $6)		$600,000
Cost of goods sold:		
Direct materials (100,000 units at $1.80)	$180,000	
Direct labor (100,000 units at $1.40)	140,000	
Variable factory overhead (100,000 units at $.50)	50,000	
Additional fixed cost to produce this order	10,000	380,000
		$220,000
Variable marketing expense (100,000 at $.50)		50,000
Gain on this order		$170,000

The differential cost of manufacturing and selling each additional unit can be computed as follows:

$$\frac{\text{Differential cost of goods sold}}{\text{Additional units}} = \frac{\$380,000}{100,000} = \$3.80$$

Variable marketing expense per unit	.50
Total differential cost per unit	$4.30

Because the $4.30 differential cost is less than the $6 sales price, it is clear that the effect on profit will be favorable.

In practice, it is often difficult to determine whether an offer to buy additional output is really additional business.[3] An annual sales budget does not normally specify the quantities to be sold to each customer because the forecasts involved are generally based on historical trends in product sales and economic factors expected to affect demand during the forecast period. As a consequence, it is often difficult to evaluate whether or not a particular offer is incremental business or a component of the original budget. If the offer is actually an offer to purchase units included in the original sales forecast, the profits expected from the differential cost analysis will not materialize. If the price reduction and quantity of units involved in the order are large, total sales revenue might not even cover total fixed costs, in which case a loss would occur for the period.

[3] Bernard A. Coda and Barry G. King, "Manufacturing Decision-Making Tools," *Journal of Cost Management*, Vol. 3, No. 1, p. 34.

If management decides that an offer to purchase at a reduced price is indeed additional business, the long-run effect of the sale on other customers and the reaction of competitors should also be considered. If regular customers become aware that the product has been sold at a reduced price, they may demand similar cost concessions. If the concessions are not granted, a loss of business could result, and if the concessions are granted, a reduced profit margin could result. The firm must also be careful not to violate the Robinson-Patman Act (discussed in Chapter 25) and other governmental pricing restrictions. If the product sold at a reduced price affects the sales of competitors, they might retaliate by cutting their prices. Such actions can result in a price war and lost profits for all concerned.

Make-or-Buy Decisions

Another short-term decision that involves differential cost analysis is that of deciding whether to make or buy component parts for a finished product. The importance of the make-or-buy decision is evidenced by the fact that most manufacturing firms at some time during the course of their operations have to make such a decision. The choice of whether to manufacture an item internally or purchase it from outside the firm can be applied to a wide variety of decisions that are often major determinants of profitability and that can be significant to the company's financial health.

The objective of a make-or-buy decision should be optimal utilization of the firm's productive and financial resources. The decision must often be made in connection with the possible use of idle equipment, idle space, and even idle labor. In such situations, a manager is inclined to consider making the item instead of buying it in order to utilize existing facilities and to avoid laying off workers. Commitments of new resources may also be involved.

A make-or-buy analysis is illustrated as follows. Assume that Kiska Corporation plans to introduce a new product that requires a component part that can be purchased from an outside vendor at a cost of $5 per unit or manufactured in house. The corporation has sufficient excess capacity to manufacture 10,000 units of the component part, the quantity needed during the first year. The prime costs per unit for the component part are expected to be $1.80 for materials and $1.20 for direct labor. The factory overhead rate is 200 percent of direct labor cost ($1.20 direct labor cost per unit × 200% = $2.40 overhead per unit); however, only 25 percent of factory overhead budgeted for the year is variable. In order to manufacture the component part, specialized equipment must be rented at an annual cost of $7,200.

If the full absorption cost of the component part is compared to the vendor's price, management will decide to purchase the component part from the outside vendor, because the purchase price of $5 per unit is less than the full absorption cost of $5.40 per unit ($1.80 materials + $1.20 labor + $2.40 overhead). Such a decision is inappropriate, however, because the full absorption cost in this situation is not equal to the differential cost. The fixed portion of the overhead charged to each unit is not relevant to the decision ($2.40 overhead per unit × 75% fixed = $1.80 per unit). In addition, the $7,200 rental of specialized equipment, which is not included in the absorption cost computation, is an out-of-pocket fixed cost that is relevant to this decision. In the evaluation of the economic effect of the two alternatives, the differential costs of manufacturing the component part should be computed and compared to the cost of purchasing it from an outside vendor. Instead of purchasing the component part in this case, the company should manufacture it, as indicated by the following cost comparison:

Cost to purchase the part (10,000 units at $5)		$50,000
Differential cost to manufacture the part:		
Materials (10,000 units at $1.80)	$18,000	
Direct labor (10,000 units at $1.20)	12,000	
Variable factory overhead (10,000 units × $1.20 labor cost × 200% × 25% variable)	6,000	
Incremental fixed factory overhead	7,200	43,200
Savings from manufacturing the part		$ 6,800

Studies indicate that surprisingly few firms give adequate objective study to their make-or-buy problems despite their importance.[4] This important decision is also complicated by a host of factors, both financial (quantitative) and nonfinancial (qualitative), that must be considered. Faced with a make-or-buy decision, management should do the following:

1. Consider the quantity, quality, and dependability of supply of the items as well as the technical know-how required to produce them, weighing such requirements for both the short-run and long-run period.
2. Compare the cost of making the items with the cost of buying them.
3. Consider whether, if the items are purchased rather than made, there may be other, more profitable alternative uses for the firm's own facilities.
4. Consider differences in the required capital investment and the timing of cash flows (Chapters 22 through 24).
5. Adopt a course of action consistent with the firm's overall policies. Customers' and suppliers' reactions often play a part in these decisions. Retaliation or ill will can result from inconsistent treatment of customers and suppliers. Whether it is profitable to make or buy depends on the circumstances surrounding the individual situation.

The accountant should present a statement that compares the company's cost of making the items with the vendor's price. A cost study with only the differential costs and with no allocation of existing fixed overhead indicates possible short-run cost savings. However, if management is asked to sell the items at the differential cost, it might be unwilling to do so, because, in the long run, the full cost must be covered and a reasonable profit achieved. Furthermore, if there is only a slight advantage in favor of making, purchasing may be the most desirable alternative because more reliance can be put on a known cost to buy rather than an estimated cost to make.[5]

Decisions to Shut Down Facilities

Differential cost analysis also is used when a business is confronted with the possibility of a temporary shutdown of manufacturing and marketing facilities. In the short run, a firm may be better off operating than not operating, as long as the products or services sold recover the variable cost and make a contribution toward the recovery of the fixed cost. A shutdown of facilities does not eliminate all costs. Depreciation, interest, property tax, and insurance continue during complete inactivity.

Even if sales do not recover the variable cost and the avoidable portion of fixed cost, the firm still may be better off operating rather than temporarily

[4] Anthony J. Gambino, *The Make-or-Buy Decision* (New York: Institute of Management Accountants (formerly National Association of Accountants) and Hamilton, Ont.: The Society of Management Accountants of Canada, 1980), pp. 9–10.

[5] *Ibid.*, p. 21.

closing the facility. Closing a facility and subsequently reopening it is a costly process. The shutdown can entail certain maintenance procedures to preserve machinery and buildings during the period of inactivity (such as rust inhibitors, dust covers, and security equipment). The shutdown also can entail legal expenditures and employee maintenance pay. During the shutdown period, some employees will probably be lost (those who decide not to wait until the facility is reopened to go back to work), in which case the investment in training those employees will be lost. The morale of other employees, as well as community goodwill, may be adversely affected, and recruiting and training replacement workers when the facility is later reopened will add to costs. Although difficult to quantify, the loss of established market share is also a factor to be considered. When a company leaves a market for a while, its customers tend to forget about the company's product. As a consequence, reentering the market at a later time will probably require re-educating consumers about the company's product. These shutdown costs should be weighed against losses from continued operations.

An analysis of a possible temporary shutdown is illustrated as follows. Assume that Nigent Corporation has three production facilities that produce different kinds of products. The projected income statement on an absorption costing basis for the coming year, 19A, is presented in Exhibit 21-3.

EXHIBIT 21-3

Nigent Corporation
Prospective Income Statement
Absorption Costing Basis
For 19A

	Company Total	Plant 1	Plant 2	Plant 3
Sales	$200,000	$90,000	$70,000	$ 40,000
Less cost of goods sold	110,000	40,000	31,000	39,000
Gross profit	$ 90,000	$50,000	$39,000	$ 1,000
Less commercial expenses	50,000	20,000	16,000	14,000
Operating income (loss)	$ 40,000	$30,000	$23,000	$(13,000)

Plant 3 appears to be unprofitable; however, an evaluation of the relative profitability of the plants is obscured because some unavoidable common fixed costs have been allocated to each of the plants. Assuming that $32,000 of the commercial expenses is unavoidable common fixed cost allocated to the plants, a clearer picture of the expected operating efficiency of the various plants is obtained by preparing a contribution margin analysis (an income statement based on direct costing) as shown in Exhibit 21-4.

Based on the contribution margin analysis, Plant 3 still appears to be losing money. If Plant 3 is closed during the coming period, variable costs of $20,000 will be avoided ($19,000 of variable manufacturing costs and $1,000 of variable commercial costs); however, revenues of $40,000 also will be lost. This will result in a net reduction of the contribution margin in the amount of $20,000 ($40,000 revenue less $20,000 variable costs). If no more than $20,000 of Plant 3's traceable fixed cost can be avoided by closing, the plant should remain open. If unavoidable fixed cost such as depreciation, interest, insurance, and property taxes exceeds $3,000 at Plant 3, the avoidable fixed cost will be less than the $20,000 lost contribution margin. As a result, the most profitable short-run decision is to continue operations.

EXHIBIT 21-4

Nigent Corporation
Prospective Income Statement
Direct Costing Basis
For 19A

	Company Total	Plant 1	Plant 2	Plant 3
Sales	$200,000	$90,000	$70,000	$40,000
Less variable costs of goods sold	58,500	23,000	16,500	19,000
Gross contribution margin	$141,500	$67,000	$53,500	$21,000
Less variable commercial expenses	4,500	2,000	1,500	1,000
Contribution margin	$137,000	$65,000	$52,000	$20,000
Less traceable fixed costs:				
Manufacturing	$ 51,500	$17,000	$14,500	$20,000
Commercial	13,500	5,000	5,500	3,000
Total traceable fixed costs	$ 65,000	$22,000	$20,000	$23,000
Margin available to cover common expenses and provide a profit	$ 72,000	$43,000	$32,000	$ (3,000)
Common commercial fixed expenses	32,000			
Operating profit	$ 40,000			

Even if more than $20,000 of traceable fixed cost can be avoided by shutting down Plant 3, the shutdown costs (the costs of closing and reopening the plant, rehiring and retraining replacement employees, and reestablishing a market for the products manufactured by Plant 3) should be weighed against the potential savings before a decision is made to discontinue operations. Even if all $23,000 of traceable fixed costs can be avoided, Plant 3 should be shut down only if the shutdown costs are less than $3,000. If the shutdown costs exceed $3,000, the plant should continue operations unless the losses are expected to continue for more than one period, in which case the cost savings from a shutdown for several periods would have to be weighed against the shutdown costs.

Decisions to Discontinue Products[6]

Even if an entire facility is not closed or eliminated, management may decide to discontinue certain individual products because they produce no profit or inadequate profit. Decisions to discontinue products require careful analysis of relevant differential cost and revenue data through a structured and continuous product evaluation program. Several benefits can accrue from an effectively administered evaluation program that has as its objective the timely identification of products that should be eliminated or that can be made more profitable through appropriate corrective action. These benefits include the following:

1. Expanded sales
2. Increased profits
3. Reduced inventory levels
4. Executive time freed for more profitable activities

[6] This discussion is adapted from Stanley H. Kratchman, Richard T. Hise, and Thomas A. Ulrich, "Management's Decision to Discontinue a Product," *The Journal of Accountancy*, Vol. 139, No. 6, pp. 50–54.

5. Important and scarce resources, such as facilities, materials, and labor, made available for more promising projects
6. Greater management attention to why products get into difficulty or fail, thus enabling the institution of policies that will reduce the rate of product failure

Care must be taken not only to consider the profitability of the product being analyzed but also to evaluate the extent to which sales of other products will be adversely affected when one product is removed. Sometimes an unprofitable product is part of a line of products that must be complete in order to attract customers to the more profitable products. The unprofitable product may be a complement to more profitable products, in which case some customers may buy the more profitable products because the unprofitable product is also available from the same company. If the expected sales decrease of related products is severe enough, it probably is desirable to retain the product being scrutinized.

Management needs data that permit development of warning signals for products that may be in trouble. Such warning signals include the following:

1. Increasing number of customer complaints
2. Increasing number of shipments returned
3. Declining sales volume
4. Product sales volume decreasing as a percentage of the firm's total sales
5. Decreasing market share
6. Malfunctioning of the product or introduction of a superior competitive product
7. Past sales volume not up to projected amounts
8. Expected future sales and market potential not favorable
9. Return on investment below a minimum acceptable level
10. Variable cost approaching or exceeding revenue
11. Various costs consistently increasing as a percentage of sales
12. Increasing percentage of executive time required
13. Price that must be constantly lowered to maintain sales
14. Promotional budgets that constantly must be increased to maintain sales

Studies have shown that firms often do a poor job of identifying products that are in difficulty and that should be eliminated. Probably the major deficiency is the lack of timely, relevant data. To determine what data are required for a successful product monitoring program and its effective implementation and operation, management must draw on the accountant's experience and expertise.

The conditions that bring about the need to evaluate products or facilities are sometimes permanent or long-term in nature. If profitable alternative asset usage is not foreseen, asset divestment may be needed.[7]

A product abandonment decision is illustrated as follows. Assume that Plant 3 of Nigent Corporation produces three different products (tape cleaner, disk cleaner, and cleaning solvent) in three different production lines. Expected operations for the coming year, 19A, are presented in Exhibit 21-5.

The contribution margin from the expected sales of cleaning solvent is $3,300 compared to traceable fixed cost of $7,300. It therefore appears that the contribution margin available to cover company common costs will be improved by $4,000 if cleaning solvent is dropped from the product line. However, a portion

---

[7] For an expanded development of this topic, see Douglas M. Lambert, *The Product Abandonment Decision* (Montvale, N.J.: Institute of Management Accountants (formerly National Association of Accountants), and Hamilton, Ont.: The Society of Management Accountants of Canada, 1985).

of the $7,300 of fixed cost traceable to cleaning solvent may not be avoidable. If the unavoidable amount is less than $4,000, the profitability of operating Plant 3 will be improved by dropping cleaning solvent from the product line. On the other hand, if the unavoidable amount exceeds $4,000, dropping cleaning solvent from the product line will reduce profits even further. Even if the unavoidable cost is less than $4,000, before cleaning solvent is dropped from the product line, management should evaluate the potential effect on the sales of the other two products, tape cleaner and disk cleaner, as discussed previously.

EXHIBIT 21-5

Nigent Corporation
Prospective Income Statement
Direct Costing Basis
For 19A

	Plant 3 Total	Tape Cleaner	Disk Cleaner	Cleaning Solvent
Sales	$40,000	$16,000	$14,000	$10,000
Less variable costs of goods sold	19,000	7,000	5,500	6,500
Gross contribution margin	$21,000	$ 9,000	$ 8,500	$ 3,500
Less variable commercial expenses	1,000	400	400	200
Contribution margin	$20,000	$ 8,600	$ 8,100	$ 3,300
Less traceable fixed cost	15,000	4,000	3,700	7,300
Margin available to cover Plant 3 and company common cost	$ 5,000	$ 4,600	$ 4,400	$ (4,000)
Plant 3 common fixed cost	8,000			
Margin available to cover company common cost	$ (3,000)			

Additional Applications of Differential Cost Analysis

In the following pages, differential cost analysis is applied to alternatives that confront the management of an oil refinery. The hypothetical cases, which illustrate the methods that can be employed in solving such problems, demonstrate additional examples of differential cost analysis and can be generalized for other industry settings.[8]

The oil refining industry is characterized by processes that require management to choose between alternatives at various points during the processes. The basic function of oil refining is the separation, extraction, and chemical conversion of the crude oil's component elements, employing skillful utilization of heat, pressure, and catalytic principles. The basic petroleum products are obtained through a physical change caused by the application of heat through a wide temperature range. Within a temperature differential of 300 degrees (275°F to 575°F), the different liquid products (called fractions, ends, or cuts) pass off as vapors and are then condensed back into liquids. The initial application of heat drives off the lightest fractions—the naphthas and gasoline; the successively heavier fractions, such as kerosene and fuel oil, follow as the temperature rises. This process of vaporizing the crude oil and condensing the gaseous vapors to obtain the various cuts is commonly referred to as primary distillation.

[8] Adapted from a study prepared by John L. Fox, later published in *NA(C)A Bulletin*, Vol. 31, No. 4, pp. 403-413, under the title, "Cost Analysis Budget to Evaluate Operating Alternatives for Oil Refiners."

Certain cuts (such as gasoline) are marketable with little treating. Other products undergo further processing in order to make them more salable. Thus, heavier fractions, such as kerosene and fuel oil, can be subjected to cracking, which causes them to yield more valuable products, such as gasoline. Cracking is a process during which, by the use of high temperatures and pressures, sometimes in the presence of a catalyst, a heavy fraction is subjected to destructive distillation and converted to a lighter hydrocarbon possessing different chemical characteristics, one of which is a lower boiling point. The heaviest of the fractions resulting from primary distillation is known as residuum or heavy bottoms. This residuum, after further processing, treating, and blending, forms lubricating oils and ancillary wax or asphalt products.

The management of a refinery must decide what to do with each distillate or fraction and at what stage of refining each should be sold, whether additional fractions should be bought from other refineries and what price should be paid for the additional units, or whether the company should enlarge the plant in order to handle a greater volume. Managers must also determine what alternate courses should be taken in order to break into the most profitable market at the moment.

The accountant can help management by providing flexible budgets for the secondary operating departments in which further processing might take place. These departmental flexible budgets are called **cost analysis budgets**. They differ from the flexible budget used for control purposes in the following respects: all expenses (controllable as well as non-controllable costs) are included; budgeted expenses of service departments are allocated to operating departments at corresponding capacity levels; and their aim is to discover the departmental differential costs.

The amounts stated for each class of expense at each production level are computed on separate work sheets in which various individual expenses are separated into their fixed and variable elements. This separation is necessary to arrive at the estimated expenses for each level of production.

Cost analysis budgets for various activities for the following departments, which represent secondary processing or finishing operations of a refinery are prepared: Treating, Filters and Burners, Cracking, Solvent Dewaxing, Solvent Extraction, Wax Specialties, Canning, and Barrel House. The cost analysis budget for cracking fuel oil in the Cracking Department is shown in Exhibit 21-6.

EXHIBIT 21-6

Cracking Department
Cost Analysis Budget

Normal Capacity (100%) 100,000 gallons of throughput of fuel oil

	Shut-Down	60%	80%	100%	120%
Prime costs	$5,000	$12,000	$14,000	$16,000	$18,000
Traceable overhead	2,000	4,000	5,000	5,000	11,000
Total differential costs	$7,000	$16,000	$19,000	$21,000	$29,000
Throughput:					
Total gallons		60,000	80,000	100,000	120,000
Differential gallons		60,000	20,000	20,000	20,000
Total differential cost		$ 9,000	$ 3,000	$ 2,000	$ 8,000
Differential cost per unit		$ .1500	$ .1500	$ .1000	$ .4000
Average cost per unit		$ .2667	$ .2375	$ .2100	$ .2417

Cracking analysis budget:
Present operations, 80% of normal capacity
Differential cost (80% to 100%) = $.10 per gallon of input
Cracking yields: 75% gasoline; 15% residual fuel oil; 10% loss

Sell or Process Further. A refiner has on hand 20,000 gallons of fuel oil and must decide whether to sell it as fuel oil or crack it into gasoline and residual fuel oil. The following current prices per gallon are available:

Fuel oil	$1.40
Gasoline	1.68

The company is operating at 80 percent of capacity. Based on a cost analysis budget for the Cracking Department, processing an additional 20,000 gallons will result in a differential cost of 10 cents per gallon. Using this information, the following differential income computation can be prepared:

Net potential revenue—products from cracking:		
Gasoline (15,000 gallons at $1.68)	$25,200	
Fuel oil (3,000 gallons at $1.40)	4,200	
	$29,400	
Less differential cost (20,000 gallons at $.10)	2,000	$27,400
Net potential revenue—fuel oil (20,000 gallons at $1.40)		28,000
Loss from cracking of fuel oil		$ 600

Thus, judging from a quantitative standpoint, it would be more profitable to sell the 20,000 gallons of fuel oil as such rather than to process the oil further.

Choice of Alternate Routings. A refiner is trying to decide whether to treat and sell the kerosene fraction or to crack it for its gasoline content. The current decision involves 10,000 gallons of raw kerosene. Pertinent available information follows (from a cost analysis budget for cracking kerosene):

Current prices per gallon:		
Kerosene	$1.20	
Gasoline	1.68	
Fuel oil	1.40	
Cracking yields:		
Gasoline	85%	
Residual fuel oil	5%	
Loss	10%	
Differential costs associated with potential gallons throughput of kerosene:		
Cracking	$ .12	per gallon
Treating	.08	per gallon

Using these amounts, the refiner can prepare the following analysis:

Net potential revenue—products from cracking:		
Gasoline (8,500 gallons at $1.68)	$14,280	
Fuel oil (500 gallons at $1.40)	700	
	$14,980	
Less differential cost (10,000 gallons at $.12)	1,200	$13,780
Net potential revenue—kerosene:		
Total revenue (10,000 gallons at $1.20)	$12,000	
Less differential cost (10,000 gallons at $.08)	800	11,200
Gain from cracking rather than treating		$ 2,580

In this situation, the more profitable alternative is to crack the kerosene fraction.

Price to Pay for an Intermediate Stock. A refiner has been offered 10,000 gallons of cylinder stock. The usual bargaining process determines the final price. The refiner is interested in knowing how high a price it can pay and still make a profit. The stock will be processed into conventional bright stock and sold at that stage, because the blending unit for making finished motor oils is currently working at full capacity. Available information is as follows:

Cylinder stock is of such a quality and type that it will probably yield:
90% bright stock
5% petrolatum
5% loss
Current prices: bright stock, $1 per gallon; petrolatum—no market

Differential costs associated with processing 10,000 gallons of cylinder stock through several stages (from analysis budgets) are:

Solvent dewaxing	$.06 per gallon
Solvent extracting	.06
Filtering	.03
Total	$.15 per gallon

Using this information, the refiner's position can be analyzed and a bargaining margin can be determined:

Revenue—bright stock (9,000 gallons at $1)	$9,000
Differential cost (10,000 gallons at $.15)	1,500
Margin	$7,500
Margin per gallon of cylinder stock	$ .75

The refiner is now ready to bargain for the purchase of the cylinder stock, knowing that a purchase price of 75 cents a gallon represents a critical maximum point—to pay more will produce a loss, to pay less will result in a gain. Management can then decide how much profit is required to justify the purchase. Here the concept of opportunity costs also enters into the final decision. If the available capacity can be more profitably used for another purpose, then perhaps the proposed purchase should not be consummated.

Proposed Construction of Additional Capacity. A refiner discovers that the market for finished neutrals is such that present capacity will not satisfy the demand. The refiner feels certain that an addition to the solvent dewaxing and solvent extracting units would prove profitable. The additional wax distillate stock required can be purchased on the open market at the current rate. However, before going ahead with the construction, the chief accountant is consulted, who presents the following information.

Unit differential cost:
Capacity from 100% (normal) to 120% (increase of 10,000 gallons throughput)
Solvent Dewaxing Department—$.10 per gallon throughput
Solvent Extracting Department—$.10 per gallon throughput
Assumed yield from wax distillate:
90% Viscous neutral
1.5% Paraffin (8 pounds per gallon)
8.5% Loss
Current market prices:
Viscous neutrals—$1.50 per gallon
Paraffin—$.24 per pound
Wax distillate stock—$1.20 per gallon*

* Not a published market price, but the price management believes it will have to pay to acquire the stock.

This information is used to prepare the following analysis:

Differential revenue:		
9,000 gallons viscous neutrals at $1.50	$13,500	
1,200 pounds paraffin at $.24	288	
	$13,788	
Less cost of wax distillate stock (10,000 gallons at $1.20)	12,000	
Margin to apply against differential costs		$1,788
Differential costs:		
Solvent Dewaxing Department (10,000 gallons at $.10)	$ 1,000	
Solvent Extracting Department (10,000 gallons at $.10)	1,000	2,000
Potential loss from differential production		$ 212

The accountant's analysis indicates that the proposed increase in the productive capacity is not justified under the stated conditions.

Summary

This chapter focused on short-term decisions. The first section of the chapter defined differential cost as out-of-pocket or avoidable cost, and discussed the irrelevance of sunk costs and allocated common fixed costs in short-term decision making. To determine the desirability of any activity, the analyst must compare the expected differential cost to the expected benefit. If the expected benefit is revenue, the project should be undertaken only when incremental revenue exceeds differential cost. For problems not affecting revenue, differential cost should be minimized. The application of differential cost analysis was illustrated for problems involving the following kinds of decisions: accepting or refusing certain orders; reducing the price of a single, special order; making a price cut in a competitive market; evaluating make-or-buy alternatives; expanding, shutting down, or eliminating a facility; increasing, curtailing, or stopping production of certain products; determining whether to sell or process further; choosing among alternative routings in product manufacture; and determining the maximum price that can be paid for raw materials.

Appendix Linear Programming

A short-term resource allocation problem can become complex when several products are involved and numerous constraints are imposed. In one approach to solving the problem, the decision maker models the production process and makes an educated guess about the appropriate level of inputs and outputs. After modeling the production process, the decision maker can input different combinations of decision variables and select the combination that results in the best outcome from among the combinations evaluated. In contrast to this trial and error approach, **linear programming** is a quantitative decision tool that permits the decision maker to find the optimal solution to a short-term resource allocation problem without guessing.

Maximization of Contribution Margin

The contribution margin is a measure of business success that often is used as a measure of management performance. To maximize company profits, management must maximize the total contribution margin from the production and sale of products.

Linear programming is illustrated by applying it to the problem of maximizing the total contribution margin, as follows. Assume that a machine shop manufactures two models of a product, standard and deluxe. Each unit of the standard model requires 2 hours of grinding and 4 hours of polishing. Each unit of the deluxe model requires 5 hours of grinding and 2 hours of polishing. The manufacturer has three grinders and two polishers; therefore, in a 40-hour work week there are 120 hours of grinding capacity and 80 hours of polishing capacity available. A unit of the standard model sells for $9, and a unit of the deluxe model sells for $12. The variable costs of producing and selling one unit total $6 and $8 for the standard model and the deluxe model, respectively. Consequently, the contribution margins from the production and sale of a standard unit and a deluxe unit are $3 and $4, respectively. Market demand for both products is strong enough to absorb all units that the company can produce and sell with its present capacity. To maximize the total contribution margin, management must decide on (1) the allocation of the available production capacity between the standard and deluxe models and (2) the resulting number of units of each model to produce.

The relevant information required to solve the problem is summarized as follows:

	Grinding Time (in hours)	Polishing Time (in hours)	Sales Price	Variable Cost	Contribution Margin
Standard model...	2	4	$ 9	$6	$3
Deluxe model	5	2	12	8	4
Plant capacity......	120	80			

The problem can be expressed mathematically as follows:

1. First, the total contribution margin the manager can obtain from the production and sale of the two models of products (called the **objective function**) is written mathematically. Let x and y represent the quantities of the standard model and the deluxe model, respectively, to be produced and sold. Because a contribution margin of $3 is expected for each unit of the standard model and $4 for each unit of the deluxe model, the total contribution margin available is $3x + 4y$. Therefore, the objective function is:

$$\text{Maximize CM} = 3x + 4y$$

2. Next, the resource limitations in the problem (called **constraints**) are expressed in mathematical form. In the illustration, there are two constraints available, grinding time and polishing time. There are 120 hours of grinding time available. It takes 2 hours of grinding to produce one unit of the standard model (denoted x) and 5 hours of grinding to produce one unit of the deluxe model (denoted y). Therefore, the grinding constraint can be expressed mathematically as follows:

$$2x + 5y \leq 120$$

Because there are 80 hours of polishing time available and it takes 4 hours to produce a unit of the standard model and 2 hours to produce a unit of the deluxe model, the polishing constraint can be expressed mathematically as follows:

$$4x + 2y \leq 80$$

Both constraints in this example are less-than-or-equal-to constraints; that is, the amount of constraint used must be less than or equal to the amount of constraint available. Maximization problems can also include equal-to constraints (that is, all of the available constraint must be used) and greater-than-or-equal-to constraints (that is, the amount of resource used must be greater than or equal to the amount specified on the right-hand side of the constraint inequality). These two types of constraints are illustrated in the linear programming minimization problem in the next section.

When a linear programming problem involves only two variables, a two-dimensional graph can be used to determine the optimal solution. In this example, the maximum quantity of each model that can be produced, given the limited grinding and polishing capacity, is determined as follows:

	Production Quantity Maximization	
Production Operation	**Standard Model (x)**	**Deluxe Model (y)**
Grinding....................................	120 hrs. ÷ 2 = 60	120 hrs. ÷ 5 = 24
Polishing....................................	80 hrs. ÷ 4 = 20	80 hrs. ÷ 2 = 40

The smallest quantity in each of the two columns is the maximum quantity that can be produced with the limited capacity available. The company can produce no more than 20 units of the standard model, which results in a contribution margin (CM) of \$60 (20 units × \$3 CM per unit), or 24 units of the deluxe model, which would result in a contribution margin of \$96 (24 units × \$4 CM per unit). However, producing a combination of standard and deluxe models will result in a different, and perhaps better, solution.

The possible production combinations can be determined by plotting the constraints on a graph. Once they are graphically displayed, the production combinations can be evaluated to determine which alternative results in the maximum contribution margin. Because the relationship between the usage of each available constraint and the quantity of each model produced in this example is linear, the polishing and grinding constraints can be drawn by connecting the points, plotted on each axis, representing the maximum number of units of each model that can be produced with each constraint. These points are:

When $x = 0$: $y \leq 24$ for the grinding constraint
$y \leq 40$ for the polishing constraint

When $y = 0$: $x \leq 60$ for the grinding constraint
$x \leq 20$ for the polishing constraint

A graph of the constraints for the illustrated problem appears in Figure 21-1. The feasible solution space (referred to as the **feasible area**) is bounded by the lines AB, BC, CD, and DA. Any combination of standard and deluxe units that falls on or within the boundaries of the feasible area can be physically produced. Any combination that falls outside the feasible area cannot be produced because there is not enough constraint available.

The best feasible solution is found at one of the corner points, labeled A, B, C, and D in the graph. To determine which corner point is best, each must be evaluated as follows:

A ($x = 0, y = 0$) = (\$3)(0) + (\$4)(0) = \$ 0 CM
B ($x = 0, y = 24$) = (\$3)(0) + (\$4)(24) = \$ 96 CM
C ($x = 10, y = 20$) = (\$3)(10) + (\$4)(20) = \$110 CM
D ($x = 20, y = 0$) = (\$3)(20) + (\$4)(0) = \$ 60 CM

In this case, the total contribution margin is maximized when 10 standard models and 20 deluxe models are produced and sold—the combination indicated at corner point C.

FIGURE 21-1 ***Graph Depicting Feasible Area***

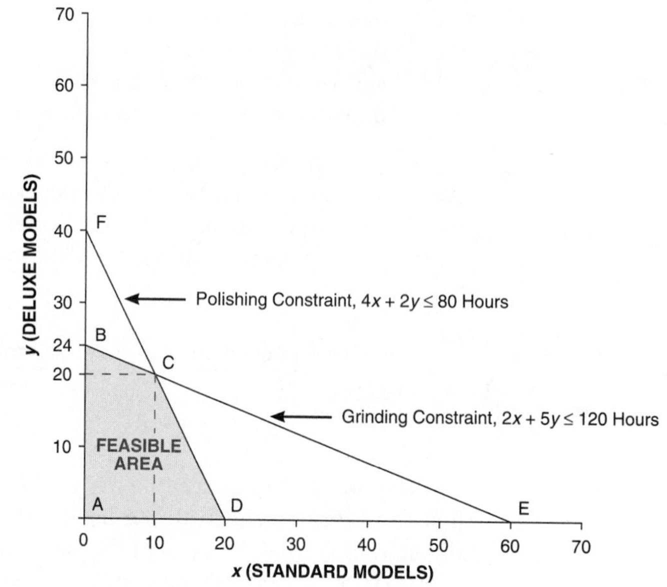

The fact that the optimal solution will be found at one of the corner points can be demonstrated graphically. Notice in the graph in Figure 21-1 that the largest quantities for each product combination occur at the farthest distances from point A (that is, the farthest away from 0 units of each product). Consequently, the production and sale of the product mix indicated at one of the points that lies on the line defining the outermost limit of the feasible area (that is, the line defined by points B, C, and D, which will be called line BCD) will result in the maximum contribution margin possible, given the constraints imposed on the problem. To determine which of those points is optimal, the analyst constructs a series of contribution margin lines (CM lines) (the colored lines on the graph illustrated in Figure 21-2). The production and sale of each combination of products represented by the points on a single CM line will result in the same total contribution margin. The total contribution margin will increase the farther the CM line is from point A.

The slope of a CM line is determined by multiplying –1 by the quotient of the contribution margin available from the sale of one unit of the product designated by the horizontal axis, divided by the contribution margin available from the sale of one unit of the product designated by the vertical axis. For products x and y in the illustration the slope is –¾. Because the total contribution margin in this example is $\$3x + \$4y$, a CM line can be constructed by drawing a line between a point plotted on the horizontal axis (indicating the quantity of x's required to yield the contribution margin represented by the line, given that y is zero) and a point plotted on the vertical axis (indicating the quantity of y's required to yield the *same* contribution margin, given that x is zero). The following points are computed for the CM lines on the graph in Figure 21-2:

CM	Quantity of x's Required when y = 0	Quantity of y's Required when x = 0
$ 48	$ 48 CM ÷ $3 = 16 units	$ 48 CM ÷ $ 4 = 12 units
60	60 CM ÷ 3 = 20 units	60 CM ÷ 4 = 15 units
84	84 CM ÷ 3 = 28 units	84 CM ÷ 4 = 21 units
96	96 CM ÷ 3 = 32 units	96 CM ÷ 4 = 24 units
110	110 CM ÷ 3 = 36⅔ units	110 CM ÷ 4 = 27½ units

FIGURE 21-2 ***Graph Depicting CM Lines and Optimal Solution***

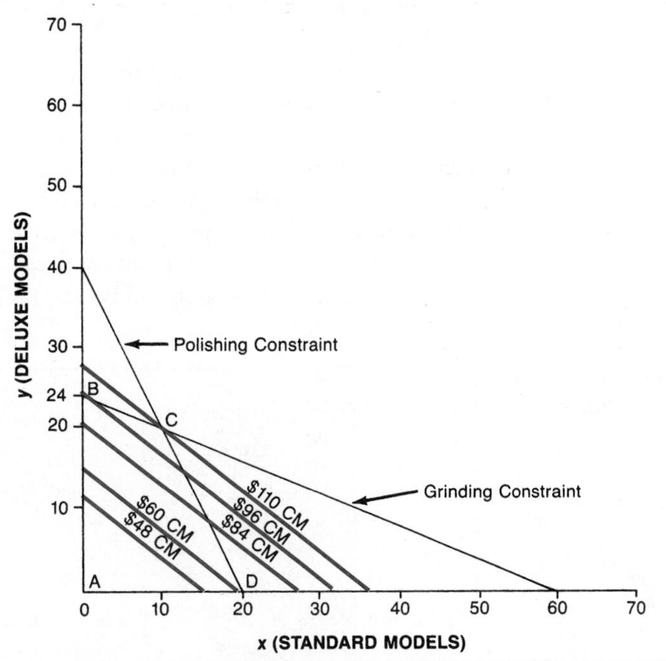

Notice in the graph in Figure 21-2 that the CM line is farthest from point A when it intersects point C.[9] Full utilization of all available resources occurs only at the point of common intersection of all of the constraint equations in the problem (point C in this example). However, utilization of all available resources does not necessarily result in an optimal solution. For example, if the contribution margin from the sale of a unit of x is $1 instead of $3, the optimal solution is found at point B instead of point C ($1(0) + $4(24) = $96 contribution margin at point B is greater than $1(10) + $4(20) = $90 contribution margin at point C). Therefore, the contribution margin available from the production and sale of the combination of products indicated at each corner point must be computed and compared.

Minimization of Cost

The previous problem deals with the maximization of the total contribution margin. Linear programming can also be used in problems whose objective is minimization of cost. The cost minimization problem can be illustrated as follows. Assume that a pharmaceutical firm is planning to produce exactly 40 gallons of a mixture in which the basic ingredients, x and y, cost $8 per gallon and $15 per gallon, respectively. No more than 12 gallons of x can be used, and to insure quality, at least 10 gallons of y must be used. The firm wants to minimize cost.

The objective function can be written as:

$$\text{Minimize cost} = 8x + 15y$$

subject to the following constraints:

$$x + y = 40$$
$$x \leq 12$$
$$y \geq 10$$

[9] If the contribution margin changes for either product or for both products, the slope of the CM line changes. If the change in slope is sufficiently large, the optimal solution shifts to a different corner point. If the slope of the CM line is equal to the slope of line BC, all points on line BC will be equally profitable; however, notice that it is never possible for a point on line BC between points B and C to be more profitable than points B and C.

The optimal solution in this case is obvious. Because x is cheaper than y, the maximum amount of x permitted by the constraint should be used first (12 gallons), and then the remaining required quantity (28 more gallons to meet the 40-gallon total requirement) should be filled with the more expensive y. However, in more complex problems, a solution may not be so obvious, especially if there are many ingredients, each having different constraints.

The graphic method can be applied to minimization problems in the same manner as for maximization problems. As with maximization problems, the constraints define the solution space for minimization problems when they are graphed. The constraints for this illustration can be graphed as shown in Figure 21-3.

FIGURE 21-3 ***Graph Depicting Feasible Solutions***

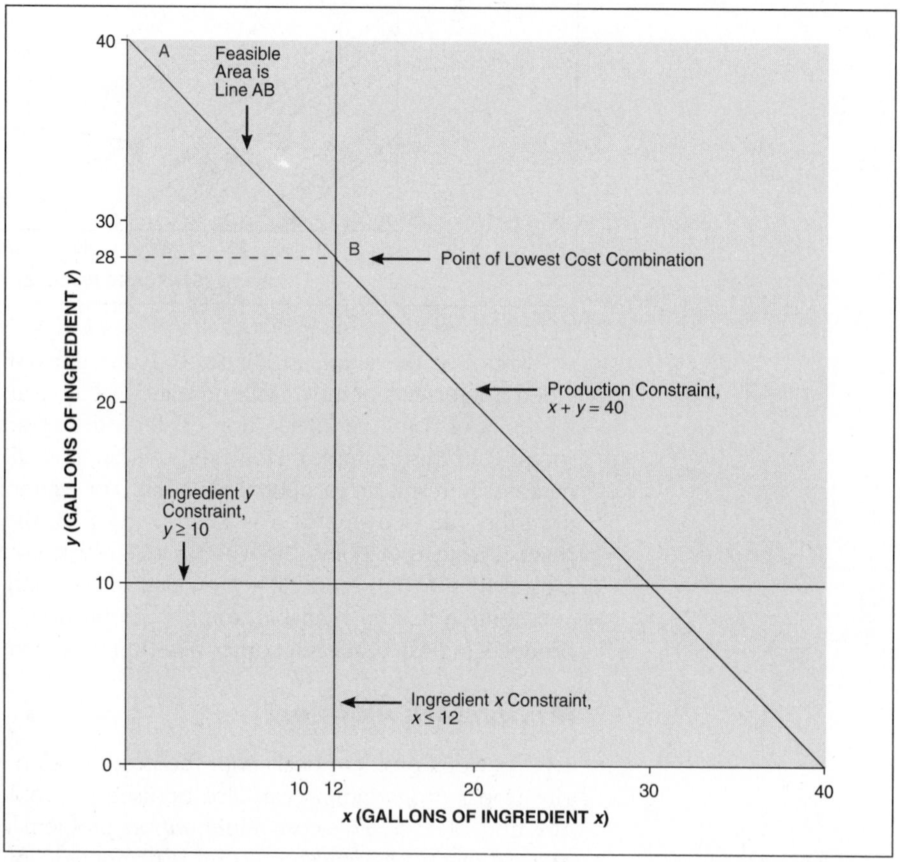

The feasible area in this example is confined to the points on line AB. Any combination of x and y that lies on line AB will result in a total production quantity of exactly 40 gallons, of which more than 10 gallons will be y and no more than 12 gallons will be x. As in the maximization problem, the optimal solution will be on one of the corner points of the feasible area, in this case point A or B. Consequently, the corner points must be evaluated to find the combination of inputs that minimizes the objective function (that is, cost). The values at each of the two corner points are:

$$A\ (x = 0,\ y = 40) = \$8(0) + \$15(40) = \$600 \text{ total cost}$$
$$B\ (x = 12,\ y = 28) = \$8(12) + \$15(28) = \$516 \text{ total cost}$$

To minimize total cost, the company should use 12 gallons of x and 28 gallons of y, which will result in a total cost of $516.

Simplex Method

Although linear programming problems with more than two constraints can be solved fairly easily with the graphic method, such an approach is not practical in solving problems having more than two variables in the objective function. A problem with three variables requires a three-dimensional graph, which, while not impossible, is certainly more difficult to handle than a two-dimensional graph. A problem with four or more variables would require a four- or more-dimensional graph, which is not physically tractable. Fortunately, linear programming problems with more than two variables can be solved algebraically with an iterative procedure referred to as the **simplex method**. Based on matrix (or linear) algebra, the simplex method provides a systematic way of algebraically evaluating each corner point in the feasible area. The process begins at the origin (point A in the maximization example) and systematically moves from one corner point to another until the optimal solution is found. Moves are selected that will provide the largest per unit improvement in the objective function. When the objective function can no longer be improved, the optimal solution has been found, and the iterative process stops.[10]

Key Terms

differential cost study *(613)*
marginal revenue or incremental revenue *(613)*
differential cost, marginal cost, or incremental cost *(614)*
out-of-pocket cost *(614)*
avoidable cost *(614)*
sunk cost *(614)*
opportunity cost *(614)*
imputed cost *(614)*
cost analysis budgets *(626)*
linear programming *(629)*
objective function *(630)*
constraints *(630)*
feasible area *(631)*
simplex method *(635)*

Discussion Questions

Q21-1 Give a broad definition of the term *differential cost*. What other terms are often used and by whom?

Q21-2 Distinguish between marginal cost and marginal (or direct) costing.

Q21-3 Differential costs are also called incremental costs. Why is the identification of incremental costs important in decision making?

Q21-4 Differential costs do not correspond to any possible accounting category. Explain.

Q21-5 In what way is a flexible budget useful in the preparation of differential cost analyses?

Q21-6 Why are historical costs usually irrelevant for decision making?

Q21-7 Why is variable cost so important in differential cost studies?

Q21-8 What are sunk costs?

Q21-9 Explain how a fixed cost can be relevant in a decision between alternative choices.

Q21-10 Define opportunity costs.

Q21-11 (Appendix) What is linear programming?

Q21-12 (Appendix) What kind of unit costs are used in linear programming?

Q21-13 (Appendix) Examine the graph in Figure 21-1 and answer the following questions:

(a) The area bounded by the lines AB, BC, CD, and AD is called the feasible area. Why?

(b) The triangles BCF and CDE are not part of the feasible area. Why?

(c) Which point in the feasible area designates the optimal solution? How can it be identified?

Q21-14 (Appendix) What is the simplex method?

[10] An illustration of the simplex method is beyond the scope of this text. For a detailed discussion of the simplex method, see Dennis Grawoig, *Decision Mathematics* (New York: McGraw-Hill, 1967),

Exercises

E21-1 Analysis of Proposed New Business. Saugus Insecticide Company is currently producing and selling 30 000 kilograms of Sta Ded monthly. This volume is 70% of capacity for Sta Ded. A wholesaler outside the Saugus marketing area offers to buy 5 000 kilograms of this product per month on a two-year contract at $1.80 per kilogram, provided the present pinkish color can be changed to green. The product will be marketed under the wholesaler's brand name.

To change the color Saugus must purchase a special mixing machine at a cost of $3,000. The machine will have no value at the end of the two-year contract period. Ingredients to change the color in the finished product will cost 1 cent per kilogram.

Marketing expense will not be increased if the new business is accepted, but additional administrative expense of $150 per month is estimated. No additional cost for supervision or property tax is contemplated. Additional payroll taxes will be $210.

A monthly income statement for the current operations is as follows:

Sales		$72,000
Cost to manufacture:		
Direct materials	$18,000	
Direct labor	15,000	
Factory overhead:		
Indirect labor	6,000	
Supervisory labor	4,000	
Power ($180 fixed)	780	
Supplies	600	
Maintenance and repair	810	
Depreciation	3,000	
Insurance	210	
Property tax	125	
Payroll taxes	1,250	
Cost of goods produced and sold		49,775
Gross profit		$22,225
Marketing expense	$11,000	
Administrative expense	4,500	15,500
Income before income tax		$ 6,725

Required: Prepare a differential cost analysis to show whether the company should accept the proposed new business.

E21-2 Differential Cost Analysis. The Budgeting Department of Jetco Manufacturing Corporation prepared the following schedule of factory overhead at various levels of production.

	40% of Capacity	60% of Capacity	80% of Capacity	100% of Capacity
Units of product	100,000	150,000	200,000	250,000
Variable factory overhead	$ 50,000	$ 75,000	$100,000	$125,000
Fixed factory overhead	90,000	100,000	115,000	125,000

Jetco manufactures gaskets for natural gas pipelines. In recent months, legislation unfavorable to gas transmission firms has been pending in Congress, and customer orders have been minimal. For example, in December only 150,000 gaskets were manufactured, representing 60% of capacity. At that level of production, direct materials and direct labor cost $150,000 and $112,500, respectively. Economic indicators point to rising production costs in the near future. Accordingly, management is considering stepping up January production to 100% of capacity (an additional 100,000 units) in order to build up an inventory of relatively low-cost product during this slack period.

Required:

(1) Determine the cost of the additional 100,000 units of product.
(2) Compute the total cost of producing 250,000 units in January.
(3) Determine the sales price required for January production in order to achieve a 20% markup on production cost.

E21-3 Acceptance of a Special Order. Over the past few months, Welburne Company produced and sold 10,000 units of Wartex each month. Monthly costs for Wartex are as follow:

Direct materials	$ 20,000
Direct labor	35,000
Variable factory overhead	10,000
Fixed factory overhead	45,000
Variable marketing expenses (shipping and sales commissions)	20,000
Allocated marketing and administrative expenses	30,000
Total costs	$160,000

The normal sales price is $25 per unit. One of the company's salespersons has been negotiating a contract with a prospective customer who has offered to purchase 15,000 units of Wartex for $12.50 per unit. The salesperson does not expect any repeat business from this customer after this sale and does not believe that this sale will affect the normal sales of Wartex. Welburne has a production capacity sufficient to produce only 15,000 units of Wartex. As a consequence, the company would have to rent additional equipment at a cost of $5,000 and pay overtime in the amount of $10,000 in order to manufacture the additional quantity of Wartex required.

Required: Prepare a differential cost analysis showing whether or not Welburne should accept this special order.

E21-4 Make-or-Buy Decision. Huntington Products manufactures 10,000 units of Part M-1 annually for use in its production. The following costs are reported:

Direct materials	$ 20,000
Direct labor	55,000
Variable factory overhead	45,000
Fixed factory overhead	70,000
	$190,000

Lufkin Company has offered to sell Huntington 10,000 units of Part M-1 annually for $18 per unit. If Huntington accepts the offer, some of the facilities presently used to manufacture Part M-1 could be rented to a third party at an annual rental of $15,000. Additionally, $4 per unit of the fixed factory overhead applied to Part M-1 would be totally eliminated.

Required: Should Huntington accept Lufkin's offer? Explain. (AICPA adapted)

E21-5 Make-or-Buy Decision. Creed Engine Corporation is considering manufacturing a new engine designated as model VX4. The engine will be a different size from any produced by Creed, and the company expects to sell 20,000 units a year. At the present time the company has the capacity to produce the projected quantity of all of the parts required for 20,000 units of VX4 except for the pistons. Each model VX4 engine requires 4 pistons, so 80,000 pistons will be required annually. Pistons are manufactured in the company's Tuscon plant, which is presently operating at full capacity. None of the company's other plants has the equipment or the expertise necessary to manufacture pistons. In order to manufacture the number of pistons required, the company can expand facilities at the Tuscon plant by renting additional machinery at an annual cost of $30,000 and hiring an additional supervisor at an annual cost of $40,000. Alternatively, the company can purchase the required number of pistons of equal quality from Wichita Machine Works, an outside supplier, at a contract price of $4.40 each. The projected cost of manufacturing 80,000 pistons at the Tuscon plant is as follows:

Direct materials	$160,000
Direct labor	80,000
Allocated factory overhead	240,000
Total cost of 80,000 pistons	$480,000

The Tuscon plant uses a predetermined factory overhead rate determined on the basis of absorption costing. Budgeted factory overhead used as the basis for determining the rate was composed of 80% fixed cost and 20% variable cost.

Required: Determine whether Creed Corporation should manufacture the pistons in its Tuscon plant or puchase them from Wichita Machine Works.

E21-6 Decision to Drop a Product. The Montreal Company manufactures and sells three products, Mift, Tift, and Lift. For the coming year, sales are expected to be as follows:

Product	Sales Price	Quantity	Total Sales
Mift	$10	5,000	$ 50,000
Tift	6	7,000	42,000
Lift	15	3,000	45,000
			$137,000

At the expected sales quantity and mix, the manufacturing cost per unit is as follows:

	Mift	Tift	Lift
Materials	$2	$2	$ 4
Direct labor	2	1	3
Factory overhead:			
Variable	1	1	2
Fixed	1	1	3
	$6	$5	$12

Variable marketing expense is $1 per unit for Mift and Tift and $2 per unit for Lift. Budgeted fixed marketing expenses for the coming year are $3,000, and budgeted fixed administrative expenses are $6,000.

The sales manager has recommended dropping Tift from the product line and using the production capacity currently committed to the production of Tift to produce more Mift. The production manager reports that 4,000 additional units of Mift can be produced with the production capacity now used in manufacturing Tift. In order to sell 4,000 additional units of Mift, the sales manager believes that the advertising budget will have to be increased by $5,000.

Required:

(1) Should the sales manager's proposal be accepted? Support your answer by computing the change in profitability that would result from this action.

(2) In addition to the factors mentioned by the production manager and the sales manager, what other factors should be considered?

CGA-Canada (adapted). Reprint with permission.

E21-7 Sell or Process Further. Enid Company produces a variety of cleaning compounds and solutions for both industrial and household use. One of its products, a coarse cleaning powder called Grit 337, has a variable manufacturing cost of $1.60 and sells for $2 per pound.

A small portion of this product's annual production is retained for further processing in the Mixing Department, where it is combined with several other ingredients to form a paste that is marketed as a silver polish selling for $4 per jar. The further processing requires one fourth of a pound of Grit 337 per jar; other ingredients, labor, and variable factory overhead associated with further processing cost $2.50 per jar, and unit variable marketing cost is $.30. If a decision is made to cease silver polish production, $5,600 of fixed Mixing Department costs will be avoided.

Required: Calculate the minimum number of jars of silver polish that must be sold to justify further processing Grit 337.

(ICMA adapted)

E21-8 Minimum Bid Price. Hall Company specializes in packaging bulk drugs in standard dosages for local hospitals. The company has been in business since 19A and has been profitable since its second year of operation. D. Greenway, director of cost accounting, installed a standard cost system after joining the company in 19E.

Wyant Memorial Hospital has asked Hall to bid on the packaging of one million doses of medication at full cost plus a return on full cost of no more than 9% after income taxes. Wyant defines cost as including all variable costs of performing the service, a reasonable amount of nonvariable overhead, and reasonable administrative costs. The hospital will supply all packaging materials and ingredients. Wyant has indicated that any bid over $.015 per dose will be rejected.

Greenway accumulated the following information prior to the preparation of the bid.

Direct labor	$ 5.00	per hour
Variable factory overhead	$ 2.00	per direct labor hour
Fixed factory overhead	$ 5.00	per direct labor hour
Administrative costs	$1,000	for the order
Production rate	1,000	doses per direct labor hour

Hall Company is subject to an effective income tax rate of 40%.

Required:

(1) Calculate the minimum bid price per dose that Hall Company can bid for the Wyant Memorial Hospital job and not reduce Hall's net income.

(2) Calculate the bid price per dose using the full cost criterion and the maximum allowable return specified by Wyant Memorial Hospital.

(3) Without prejudice to your answer to requirement 2, assume that the price per dose that Hall Company calculated using the cost-plus criterion specified by Wyant Memorial Hospital is greater than the maximum bid of $.015 per dose specified by Wyant. What factors should Hall Company consider before deciding whether or not to submit a bid at the maximum price of $.015 per dose?

(4) What factors should Wyant Memorial Hospital have considered before deciding whether or not to employ cost-plus pricing? (ICMA adapted)

E21-9 Alternative Cash Collection Procedures. Kleenvu Corporation is a franchisor of automatic car washes in the southeast. Kleenvu has 420 franchisees that operate 7 days per week. The average gross revenue for each location is $500 per day. Kleenvu collects 25% of the gross revenue as its franchise fee. The cash collection procedure requires each franchisee to mail one check, on a daily basis, to Kleenvu headquarters in Miami. The check is supposed to be mailed by noon each day. Many of the franchisees are lax, however, and payments are forwarded an average of 2 days late. Once mailed, the checks take an average of 1½ days in the mail and another 3 days to be processed in Kleenvu's receivables department.

Kleenvu's management is considering a change in the company's cash collection procedure. The two proposals it is considering follow. Kleenvu has a 15% before-tax opportunity cost and is subject to an income tax rate of 40%.

(a) The first proposal is to use local messenger services to collect and mail the checks. This will save the 2 days of late check forwarding. The cost of the messenger service is $20,000 per year.

(b) The second proposal is to combine the messenger service with a lock-box arrangement for a combined savings of 5 days. The cost of the second proposal is $20,000 per year for the messenger service plus $15,000 in a compensating balance required by the bank servicing the lock-box.

Required: Compute the annual change in Kleenvu's before-tax income that will result from the adoption of each of the two alternative proposals. (ICMA adapted)

E21-10 Choice of Production Method. Circutech Company is evaluating the use of AZ-17 Photo Resist for the manufacture of printed circuit boards. The major advantages of this process over the present silk-screen method include:

(a) Anticipated reduced manufacturing cycle time and cost due to elimination of the need for silk circuit screens and shorter operator time to produce circuit boards.

(b) Improved ease of registration between front and back patterns.

(c) The ability to achieve finer line widths and closer spacing between circuit paths.

The proposed AZ-17 process is as follows:

(a) Fabricate through the completion of the drilling and copper plating of inside holes.
(b) Pressure spray AZ-17 Photo Resist on one side, oven bake for 10 minutes, and repeat for other side.
(c) Use the photo negative and expose each side for seven minutes in a Nu-Arc Printer.
(d) Develop in AZ-17 Developer and proceed through normal operations for making printed circuit board.

Total direct labor time for the proposed AZ-17 process is 30 minutes. The original silk-screen method uses a wire mesh stencil film, screening ink, and frames. The direct labor time to prepare the screen for each circuit board is 1½ hours. The direct labor time to screen patterns on the printed wire board is 20 minutes. The hourly direct labor rate is $6.50. The monthly cost for materials and for equipment rental and operation needed for the proposed process is $4,000 greater than for the silk-screen method, excluding the direct labor. The company manufactures 20,000 circuit boards annually.

Required: Compute the annual savings or added cost from changing from the silk-screen method to the new AZ-17 process. (Round all computations to the nearest dollar.)

E21-11 (Appendix) Linear Programming Problem Formulation—Contribution Margin Maximization. Smythe Company manufactures two types of display boards that are sold to office supply stores. One board is hard-finished marking board that can be written on with a water-soluble felt-tip marking pen and then wiped clean with a cloth. The other is a conventional cork-type tack board.

Both boards pass through two manufacturing departments. All raw materials (board base, board covering, and aluminum frames) are cut to size in the Cutting Department. Both types of boards are the same size and use the same aluminum frame. The boards are assembled in one of Smythe Company's two assembly operations (the Automated Assembly Department or the Labor Assembly Department). The Automated Assembly Department is a capital intensive assembly operation. This department has been in operation for 18 months and was intended to replace the Labor Assembly Department. However, Smythe Company's business expanded so rapidly that both assembly operations are needed and used. The final results of the two assembly operations are identical. The only difference between the two is the proportion of machine time versus direct labor in each department and, thus, different costs. However, workers have been trained for both operations so that they can be switched between the two operations.

Smythe Company produced and sold 600,000 marking boards and 900,000 tack boards last year. Management estimates that the total unit sales volume for the coming year will increase 20% if the units can be produced. Smythe Company has contracts to produce and sell 30,000 units of each board each month. Sales, production, and cost incurrence are uniform throughout the year. Smythe Company has a monthly maximum labor capacity of 30,000 direct labor hours in the Cutting Department and 40,000 direct labor hours for the assembly operations (Automated Assembly and Labor Assembly Departments combined). It takes 12 minutes of labor in the Cutting Department for both kinds of boards. The Automated Assembly Department requires 3 minutes of labor for each board, regardless of type, and the Labor Assembly Department requires 15 minutes of labor per board.

Data regarding the two products and their manufacture follow:

	Marking Board	Tack Board
Sales price per unit	$60.00	$45.00
Variable marketing expenses	3.00	3.00
Materials:		
Base	6.00	6.00
Covering	14.50	7.75
Frame	8.25	8.25
Direct labor:		
Cutting Department	2.00	2.00
Automated Assembly Department	.60	.60
Labor Assembly Department	3.00	3.00
Variable factory overhead:		
Cutting Department	2.45	2.45
Automated Assembly Department	3.30	3.30
Labor Assembly Department	2.25	2.25

Machine Hour Data

	Cutting Department	Automated Assembly Department	Labor Assembly Department
Machine hours required per board	.15	.05	.02
Monthly machine hours available	25,000	5,000	1,500
Annual machine hours available	300,000	60,000	18,000

Required: Assuming that Smythe Company wants to maximize its profits, give the appropriate linear programming objective function and constraints for the production of the two boards. (ICMA adapted)

E21-12 (Appendix) Linear Programming Contribution Margin Maximization Problem—Graphic Method. An office supply company makes two types of paper pads, legal and regular. A box of legal pads requires 20 minutes to produce and a box of regular pads requires 10 minutes to produce. Two people work on the production line, which operates 7.5 hours per day, 5 days a week. The company can sell any combination of boxes of legal and regular pads up to a maximum of 300 boxes of pads per week. The legal pads have a contribution margin of $18 a box and the regular pads have a contribution margin of $12 a box.

Required: Using the graphic method, determine the quantity of legal and regular pads that should be produced daily in order to maximize total contribution margin.

CGA-Canada (adapted). Reprint with permission.

E21-13 (Appendix) Linear Programming Contribution Margin Maximization Problem—Graphic Method. Merz Inc. manufactures two kinds of leather belts—Belt A (a high-quality belt) and Belt B (of a lower quality). The respective contribution margins are $4 and $3 per belt. Production of Belt A requires twice as much time as Belt B. If all belts are of the Belt B type, Merz Inc. can produce 1,000 per day. The leather supply is sufficient for only 800 belts per day (both Belt A and Belt B combined). Belt A requires a fancy buckle, and only 400 buckles per day are available for this belt.

Required: Using the graphic method, determine the quantity of each type of belt to be produced to maximize the contribution margin.

E21-14 (Appendix) Linear Programming Cost Minimization Problem—Graphic Method. A company produces three products, A, B, and C, which use common materials, X and Y. Material X costs $3 per ton and Y $4 per ton. The amount of materials required per ton of product and the required weight per ton of product are as follow:

	Pounds of Product A	Pounds of Product B	Pounds of Product C
Material X	4	7	1.5
Material Y	8	2	5
Minimum weight required	32	14	15

Required: Using the graphic method, determine the number of tons of each material that is needed to meet the requirements at minimum cost.

E21-15 (Appendix) Linear Programming Cost Minimization Problem—Graphic Method. Deane Pulp Paper Company uses softwood and hardwood pulp as basic materials for producing converter-grade paper. Hardwood is 80% pulp fiber and 20% pulp binder, while softwood is 50% pulp fiber and 50% pulp binder. The cost per pound for hardwood and softwood is $.50 and $.40, respectively.

The company's quality control expert specifies that in order for the product to meet quality standards, each batch must contain at least 12,000 pounds of pulp fiber and at least 6,000 pounds of pulp binder. Because of equipment limitations, the size of a batch cannot exceed 24,000 pounds.

The Production Department recently received a new standard from the Cost Department, allowing $8,200 per batch. The production manager feels that this amount is too low, because such costs have never been less than $8,400.

Required: Using the graphic method, determine the hardwood and softwood mix necessary to minimize the cost per batch.

Problems

P21-1 Special Order Analysis. The Sommers Company, located in southern Wisconsin, manufactures several types of industrial valves and pipe fittings that are sold to customers in nearby states. Currently, the company is operating at about 70% of capacity and is earning a satisfactory return on investment.

Management has been approached by Glasgow Industries Ltd. of Scotland with an offer to buy 120,000 units of a pressure valve. Glasgow Industries manufactures a valve that is almost identical to Sommers' pressure valve; however, a fire in Glasgow's valve plant has shut down its manufacturing operations. Glasgow needs the 120,000 valves over the next four months to meet commitments to its regular customers; the company is prepared to pay $19 each for the valves, FOB destination.

Sommers' product cost for the pressure valve, based on currently attainable standards, is:

Direct materials	$ 5.00
Direct labor	6.00
Applied factory overhead	9.00
Total standard cost per unit	$20.00

Factory overhead is applied to production at the rate of $18 per standard direct labor hour. The overhead rate is comprised of the following components:

Variable factory overhead	$ 6.00
Fixed factory overhead:	
Directly traceable to the product	8.00
Allocated common cost	4.00
Applied factory overhead rate	$18.00

Additional costs incurred in connection with sales of the pressure valve include sales commissions of 5% and shipping expense of $1.00 per unit. However, the company will not pay sales commissions on the Glasgow special order because it came directly to the company and no salespersons were involved in obtaining the order.

To determine the sales prices of its products, Sommers adds a 40% markup on product cost. This results in a $28 suggested selling price for the pressure valve. The Marketing Department, however, has set the current selling price at $27 in order to maintain the company's market share.

Production management believes that it can handle the Glasgow order without disrupting its scheduled production. However, the order will require additional fixed factory overhead of $12,000 per month in the form of supervision and clerical costs.

If management accepts the order, 30,000 pressure valves will be manufactured and shipped to Glasgow each month for the next four months. Shipments will be made weekly, FOB destination.

Required:

(1) Prepare an differential cost analysis showing the impact of accepting the Glasgow Industries order.

(2) Calculate the minimum unit price that Sommers' management can accept for the Glasgow order without reducing net income.

(3) Identify factors other than price that Sommers' management should consider before accepting the Glasgow order. (ICMA adapted)

P21-2 Special Order Analysis. Framar Inc. manufactures automation machinery according to customer specifications. The company is relatively new and has grown each year. Framar operated at about 75% of practical capacity during its most recent fiscal year ended September 30, with the following operating results (000's omitted):

Sales		$25,000
Less sales commissions		2,500
Net sales		$22,500
Costs:		
Direct materials		$ 6,000
Direct labor		7,500
Factory overhead—variable:		
Supplies	$ 625	
Indirect labor	1,500	
Power	125	2,250
Factory overhead—fixed:		
Supervision	$ 500	
Depreciation	1,000	1,500
Corporation administration		750
Total expense		$18,000
Income before income tax		$ 4,500
Income tax (40%)		1,800
Net income		$ 2,700

Framar management has developed a pricing formula based on current operating costs, which are expected to prevail for the next year. This formula was used in developing the following bid for APA Inc.:

Direct materials cost	$ 29,200
Direct labor cost	56,000
Factory overhead calculated at 50% of direct labor	28,000
Corporate overhead calculated at 10% of direct labor	5,600
Total cost, excluding sales commission	$118,800
Add 25% for profit and tax	29,700
Suggested price (with profit) before sales commission	$148,500
Suggested total price (suggested price divided by .9 to adjust for 10% sales commission)	$165,000

Required:

(1) Compute the impact on net income if APA accepts the bid.
(2) Determine the suggested decision if APA is willing to pay only $127,000.
(3) Calculate the lowest price Framar can quote without reducing current net income.
(4) Determine the effect on the most recent fiscal year's profit if all work is done at prices similar to APA's $127,000 counteroffer. (ICMA adapted)

P21-3 Comparative Differential Costs. Valbec Company manufactures and distributes toy doll houses. Because the toy industry is a seasonal business, a large portion of Valbec's sales occur in the late summer and fall. The projected sales in units for 19A follow:

January	8,000
February	8,000
March	8,000
April	8,000
May	8,000
June	10,000
July	12,000
August	12,000
September	13,000
October	13,000
November	12,000
December	8,000

With a sales price of $10 per unit, sales revenue for 19A is projected to be $1,200,000. Valbec scheduled its production in the past so that finished goods inventory at the end of each month, exclusive of a safety stock of 4,000 units, would equal the next month's sales. One-half hour of direct labor is required to produce each unit under normal operating conditions. January, 19B sales are estimated to be 8,000 units.

The present labor force limits monthly production capacity to 8,000 units (4,000 direct labor hours). Although overtime is feasible, management wants to consider two other possible alternatives: (a) hire temporary help from an agency during the peak months, or (b) expand its labor force and adopt a level production schedule. Use of a second shift is not being considered.

Factory employees are paid $6 per hour for regular time, and fringe benefits average 20% of regular pay. For work in excess of 4,000 hours per month, employees receive time and a half; fringe benefits on these additional wages average only 10%. Past experience has shown that when overtime is required, labor inefficiencies occur during overtime work, which increases by 5% the overtime normally expected (the number of overtime hours required to accomplish a certain level of production increases by 5%). Temporary workers can be hired through an agency at the same labor rate of $6, but there are no fringe benefit costs. Management estimates that the temporary workers require 25% more time than regular employees to produce a unit of product. If Valbec goes to a level production schedule, the labor force will be expanded and no overtime would be required. The same labor rate ($6) and fringe benefit rate (20%) apply.

Manufacturing facilities have the capacity to produce 18,000 units per month and on-site storage facilities for completed units are adequate. The estimated annual cost of carrying inventory is $1 per unit. Valbec is subject to a 40% income tax rate.

Required:

(1) Compare the costs associated with each of the company's three alternatives: (a) schedule overtime hours, (b) hire temporary workers, and (c) expand the labor force and schedule level production of 10,000 units per month.

(2) What noncost factors should Valbec Company consider before making a final decision? (ICMA adapted)

P21-4 Comparative Cost Study to Make or Buy New Product Components. Meyers Surgical Products Company produces diverse lines of surgical instruments. It is considering a proposal, suggested by one of its sales managers, to produce dissection instrument sets for use by medical and premedical students. There is little competition in the market for the instrument sets, and the firm's present sales force can be used for effective distribution coverage. Moreover, the sales manager believes that the company can produce the instruments with the present facilities, except for the addition of certain minor auxiliary equipment.

Company management assigned two members of its Sales Department, two members from the Production Department, and an accounting staff representative to analyze the proposal. The team has assembled the following information.

(a) The proposed dissection instrument sets include the following:

	Quantity per Set
Dissection knives	3
Scissors	2
Tweezers	2
Scalpels	2
Clamps	4
Glass slides	100
Cover slips	400
Case	1

(b) The market price for such sets ranges from $55 to $65. An estimate of the total annual market demand ranges between 5,000 and 7,000 sets, and Meyers expects to sell 2,000 sets at $60.

(c) Set components can be purchased from suppliers at the following prices per unit:

Dissection knives	$3.20
Scissors	3.00
Tweezers	2.97
Scalpels	3.30
Clamps	3.28
Glass slides	.03
Cover slips	.01
Cases	6.00

(d) Meyers has the option of manufacturing all the components, except glass slides, cover slips, and the cases. The remaining components can be grouped into two categories for production and for product costing purposes: Group I—dissection knives and scalpels and Group II—scissors, tweezers, and clamps.

(e) Production costs were analyzed to be as follows:

	Group I	Group II
Materials	1 lb. of steel for 25 units at $3.27 per lb.	1 lb. of steel for 20 units at $3.60 per lb.
Labor	2.5 hrs for 25 units at $9.48 per hr.	2 hrs. for 20 units at $12.16 per hr.
Variable factory overhead	150% of labor cost	150% of labor cost

(f) Set assembly and packing costs will average $3 per set.

(g) Additional fixed factory overhead directly related to the sets will be $7,040 and $6,000 annually for Groups I and II, respectively.

(h) The new product will have the following amounts of presently existing annual fixed overhead allocated to it:

Group I manufacturing	$4,000
Group II manufacturing	6,000
All other dissection sets' production activity	7,000

(i) All sales are FOB Meyers' plant.

Required: Advise management on the desirability of the proposal, including supporting computations. Compute unit costs to one tenth of one cent.

P21-5 Minimum Bid Price. Chemco Inc. manufactures a combination fertilizer/weed-killer under the name Fertikil. It is the only product produced by Chemco at the present time. Fertikil is sold nationwide, through normal marketing channels, to retail nurseries and garden stores.

National Nursery Company plans to sell a similar fertilizer/weed-killer compound through its regional nursery chain under its own private label. National Nursery has asked Chemco to submit a bid for a 25,000-pound order of the private-brand compound. The chemical composition of the National Nursery compound differs from Fertikil, but the manufacturing process is similar.

The National Nursery compound would be produced in 1,000-pound lots. Each lot would require 60 direct labor hours and the following chemicals:

Chemicals	Quantity (in pounds)
CW-3	400
JX-6	300
MZ-8	200
BE-7	100

The first three chemicals (CW-3, JX-6, and MZ-8) are all used in the production of Fertikil. BE-7 was used in a compound that Chemco has discontinued. This chemical was not sold or discarded because it does not deteriorate, and there have been adequate storage facilities. Chemco can sell BE-7 at the prevailing market price less 10 cents per pound for selling and handling expenses.

Chemco also has on hand a chemical called CN-5, which was manufactured for use in another product that is no longer produced. CN-5, which cannot be used in Fertikil, can be substituted for CW-3 on a one-for-one basis without affecting the quality of the National Nursery compound. The quantity of CN-5 in inventory has a salvage value of $500.

Inventory and cost data for the chemicals that can be used to produce the National Nursery compound are as follow:

Chemical	Pounds in Inventory	Inventory Cost per Pound	Market Price per Pound
CW-3	22,000	$ .80	$ .90
JX-6	5,000	.55	.60
MZ-8	8,000	1.40	1.60
BE-7	4,000	.60	.65
CN-5	5,500	.75	salvage

The current direct labor rate is $7 per hour. The factory overhead rate is established at the beginning of the year and is applied consistently throughout the year, using direct labor hours (DLH) as the base. The predetermined overhead rate for the current year, based on a two-shift capacity of 400,000 total DLH with no overtime, is as follows:

Variable factory overhead	$2.25	per DLH
Fixed factory overhead	3.75	per DLH
Combined factory overhead rate	$6.00	per DLH

Chemco's production manager reports that the present equipment and facilities are adequate to manufacture the National Nursery compound. However, Chemco is within 800 hours of its two-shift capacity this month before it must schedule overtime. If need be, the National Nursery compound can be produced on regular time by shifting a portion of Fertikil production to overtime. Chemco's rate for overtime is one and one-half times the regular pay rate, or $10.50 per hour. There is no allowance for any overtime premium in the factory overhead rate.

Chemco's standard markup policy for new products is 25% of the full manufacturing cost.

Required:

(1) Calculate the lowest price Chemco can bid for the order and not reduce its net income. Assume that Chemco has decided to submit a bid for a 25,000-pound order of National Nursery compound. The order must be delivered by the end of the current month. It is presumed to be a one-time order (that is, it will probably not be repeated).

(2) Disregard your answer to requirement 1, and calculate the price Chemco should quote National Nursery for each 25,000-pound lot of the compound, assuming that National Nursery plans to place regular orders for 25,000-pound lots of the new compound during the coming year. Chemco expects the demand for Fertikil to remain strong again in the coming year. Therefore, the recurring orders from National Nursery will put Chemco over its two-shift capacity. However, production can be scheduled so that 60% of each National Nursery order can be completed during regular hours, or Fertikil production could be shifted temporarily to overtime, so that the National Nursery orders could be produced on regular time. Chemco's production manager has estimated that the prices of all chemicals will stabilize at the current market rates for the coming year, and that all other manufacturing costs are expected to be maintained at the same rates or amounts. (ICMA adapted)

P21-6 Proposed Construction of Additional Capacity. Westmore Company is considering expanding its production facilities with a building costing $260,000 and equipment costing $84,000. Building and equipment depreciable lives are 25 and 20 years, respectively, with straight-line depreciation and no salvage value. Of the additional depreciation cost, 5% is expected to be allocated to inventories.

The plant addition will increase volume by 50%; the product's sales price is expected to remain the same. The new union contract calls for a 5% increase in wage rates. Because of the increased plant capacity, quantity buying will yield an overall 6% decrease in materials cost. One additional supervisor must be hired at a salary of $15,000.

The following data pertain to last year:

Sales, 50,000 units at $10 per unit
Direct materials, $2 per unit
Direct labor, $4 per unit
Variable factory overhead, $1.30 per unit
Fixed factory overhead, $72,500
Variable marketing expense, $12,000
Fixed marketing expense, $7,000

With the volume increase, advertising, which is 10% of present fixed marketing expense, will be increased 25%.

Required: Prepare an analysis estimating the contribution margin and operating income for the present and the proposed plant capacities.

P21-7 Evaluating Production Alternatives. Marx Corporation has manufacturing plants in Boston and Chicago. Both plants produce the same product, Xoff, which sells for $20 per unit. Budgeted revenues and costs (in thousands) for the coming year are as follows:

	Total	Boston	Chicago
Sales	$6,200	$2,200	$4,000
Variable factory costs:			
Direct materials	$1,550	$ 550	$1,000
Direct labor	1,660	660	1,000
Variable factory overhead	1,140	440	700
Fixed factory overhead	1,600	700	900
Fixed regional promotional cost	200	100	100
Allocated home office cost	310	110	200
Total costs	$6,460	$2,560	$3,900
Operating income (loss)	$ (260)	$ (360)	$ 100

Home office costs are fixed and are allocated to manufacturing plants on the basis of relative sales levels. Fixed regional promotional costs are discretionary advertising costs needed to obtain budgeted sales levels. Because of the budgeted operating loss, Marx is considering the possibility of ceasing operations at its Boston plant. If Marx ceases operations at its Boston plant, proceeds from the sale of plant assets will exceed their book value and exactly cover all termination costs. Fixed factory overhead costs of $50,000 would not be eliminated. Marx is considering the following three alternative plans:

Plan A. Expand Boston's operations from the budgeted 110,000 units of Xoff to a budgeted 170,000 units. It is believed that this can be accomplished by increasing Boston's fixed regional promotional expenditures by $120,000.

Plan B. Close the Boston plant and expand Chicago's operations from the current budgeted 200,000 units of Xoff to 310,000 units in order to fill Boston's budgeted production of 110,000 units. The Boston region will continue to incur promotional costs in order to sell the 110,000 units. All sales and costs will be budgeted through the Chicago plant.

Plan C. Close the Boston plant and enter into a long-term contract with a competitor to serve the Boston region's customers. This competitor will pay Marx a royalty of $2.50 per unit of Xoff sold. Marx will continue to incur fixed regional promotional costs in order to maintain sales of 110,000 units in the Boston region.

Required:

(1) Without considering the effects of implementing Plans A, B, and C, compute the number of units of Xoff required by the Boston plant to cover its fixed factory overhead cost and fixed regional promotional cost.

(2) Prepare a schedule by plant and in total, computing Marx's budgeted contribution margin and operating income resulting from the implementation of each of the three alternative plans. (AICPA adapted)

P21-8 Evaluating New Purchasing Procedure.[11] The Lex Glass Company uses silica in the production of three different lines of glassware. The company plans to introduce a new line of glassware without expanding its present facilities. The company wants to purchase the required silica at a lower price in order to increase its profits. The present purchase price of silica is $2 per ton, and the company consumes approximately 120,000 tons per year. Silica is used at a fairly uniform rate throughout the year. The company's policy has been to place an order for materials once a month and to maintain a minimum inventory of 5,000 tons. This represents one half of one month's consumption and results in an average inventory of 10,000 tons (½ of the 10,000-ton monthly requirement + 5,000 ton minimum).

Other firms in the same industry and the same manufacturing area purchase the silica in small lots for $2.20 a ton. The purchasing manager contacted suppliers and determined that a price of $1.80 per ton can be obtained if the company purchases 400,000 tons of silica or more a year. The purchasing manager then contacted other manufacturers in the area and offered to sell silica to them for $2 a ton. Most of the manufacturers accepted the offer; however, they asked the purchasing manager to keep an inventory of at least one half of one month's consumption in storage at all times to be available for their use. The annual consumption of these manufacturers is expected to be 300,000 tons per year, and consumption is expected to be uniform each month. Lex Glass plans to continue its once-a-month ordering policy.

[11]Source: *Management Accounting Campus Report* (Montvale, N.J.: Institute of Management Accountants (formerly National Association of Accountants), 1987, pp. 4–5.

In order to handle the additional volume of silica required by these other manufacturers, Lex Glass will need to increase its labor force at an annual cost of $20,000 and incur $10,000 of additional administrative expenses annually. The company can borrow the additional funds necessary from the local bank at an interest rate of 5%. The additional materials can be stored in a company-owned warehouse, which is now being leased to another company for $10,000 a year.

Required: Determine whether or not the Lex Glass Company should take advantage of the quantity discount.

P21-9 Evaluation of Alternatives for a Charitable Foundation. J. Watson recently was appointed executive director of a charitable foundation. The foundation raises money for its activities in a variety of ways, but the most important source of funds is an annual mail campaign. Although large amounts of money are raised each year from this campaign, the year-to-year growth in the amount derived from this solicitation has been lower than expected by the foundation's board. In addition, the board wants the mail campaign to project the image of a well-run and fiscally responsible organization in order to build a base for future contributions. Consequently, the major focus of Watson's first-year efforts will be devoted to the mail campaign.

The campaign takes place in the spring of each year. The foundation staff makes every effort to secure newspaper, radio, and television coverage of the foundation's activities for several weeks before the mailing. In previous years, the foundation has mailed brochures that described its charitable activities to a large number of people and requested contributions from them. The addresses for the mailing are generated from the foundation's own file of past contributors and from mailing lists purchased from brokers.

The foundation staff is considering three alternative brochures for use in the upcoming campaign. All three will be 8½ by 11 inches in size. The simplest and the one most likely to be available on a timely basis for bulk mailing is a sheet of white paper with a printed explanation of the foundation's program and a request for funds. A more expensive brochure on colored stock contains pictures as well as printed copy. However, this brochure may not be ready in time to take advantage of bulk postal rates, but there is no doubt that it can be ready in time for mailing at first-class postal rates. The third alternative is an elegant, multicolored brochure printed on glossy paper with photographs as well as printed copy. The printer assures the staff that it will be ready on time to meet the first-class mailing schedule, but asks for a delivery date one week later just in case there are production problems.

The foundation staff has assembled the following cost and gross revenue information for mailing the three alternative brochures to 2,000,000 potential contributors:

	Brochure Costs				Gross Revenue Potential (in thousands)		
Type of Brochure	**Design**	**Typesetting**	**Unit Paper Cost**	**Unit Printing Cost**	**Bulk Mail**	**First Class**	**Late First Class**
Plain paper	$ 300	$ 100	$.005	$.003	$1,200	—	—
Colored paper	1,000	800	.008	.010	2,000	$2,200	—
Glossy paper	3,000	2,000	.018	.040	—	2,500	$2,200

The postal rates are 4 cents per item for bulk mail and 26 cents per item for presorted first-class mail. First-class mail is more likely to be delivered on a timely basis than bulk mail. Outside companies hired to handle the mailing will charge 1 cent per unit for the plain and colored paper brochures and 2 cents per unit for the glossy paper one.

Required:

(1) Calculate the net revenue potential for each brochure for each viable mailing alternative.

(2) The foundation must choose one of the three brochures for this year's campaign. The criteria established by the board—net revenue potential, image as a well-run organization, and image as a fiscally responsible organization—must be considered when the choice is made. Evaluate the three alternative brochures in terms of the three criteria. (ICMA adapted)

P21-10 Elimination of Market. Justa Corporation produces and sells three products, A, B, and C. The three products are sold in a local market and in a regional market. At the end of the first quarter of the current year, the following income statement was prepared:

	Total	Local	Regional
Sales	$1,300,000	$1,000,000	$300,000
Cost of goods sold	1,010,000	775,000	235,000
Gross profit	$ 290,000	$ 225,000	$ 65,000
Marketing expense	$ 105,000	$ 60,000	$ 45,000
Administrative expense	52,000	40,000	12,000
	$ 157,000	$ 100,000	$ 57,000
Operating income	$ 133,000	$ 125,000	$ 8,000

Management has expressed special concern with the regional market because of the extremely poor return on sales. This market was entered a year ago because of excess capacity. It was originally believed that the return on sales would improve with time, but after a year, no noticeable improvement can be seen from the results as reported in the quarterly statement.

In attempting to decide whether to eliminate the regional market, management gathered the following information:

	Product A	Product B	Product C
Sales	$500,000	$400,000	$400,000
Variable manufacturing cost as a percentage of sales	60%	70%	60%
Variable marketing cost as a percentage of sales	3%	2%	2%

	Sales by Markets	
Product	Local	Regional
A	$400,000	$100,000
B	300,000	100,000
C	300,000	100,000

All fixed cost is based on a prorated yearly amount. All administrative expense and fixed manufacturing expense are common to the three products and the two markets and are fixed for the period, whether or not a market is eliminated. Remaining marketing expense is fixed for the period and separable by market. All separable cost will be eliminated with the dropping of a market.

Required:

(1) Prepare the quarterly income statement, showing contribution margins by markets. Include a total column, combining the two markets.

(2) Assume there are no alternative uses for Justa Corporation's present capacity. Should the regional market be dropped? Why or why not?

(3) Prepare the quarterly income statement, showing contribution margins by products.

(4) It is believed that a new product to replace Product C can be ready for sale next year if Justa Corporation decides to go ahead with continued research. The new product can be produced by simply converting equipment presently used in producing Product C. This conversion will increase fixed costs by $10,000 per quarter. Calculate the minimum contribution margin per quarter for the new product if Justa Corporation is to be no worse off financially than at present. (ICMA adapted)

Cases

C21-1 Special Order Acceptance. Sportech Company manufactures and sells baseball spikes and ice skates. The baseball spikes are produced from January until the end of April. From May to December the company produces exclusively its three skate models, sold under brand names XL-100, XL-200, and XL-300.

At the beginning of April, 19A, the president analyzed the new budget for May through December, 19A, which had been revised by the controller on the basis of the new sales forecast prepared by the marketing manager. The budget included the following projections.

(a) Budgeted operating income:

	XL-100	XL-200	XL-300	Total
Sales:				
Number of pairs	20,000	18,000	10,000	
Prices per pair	× $14.00	× $15.00	× $25.00	
	$280,000	$270,000	$250,000	$800,000
Manufacturing costs	200,000	207,000	180,000	587,000
Gross profit	$ 80,000	$ 63,000	$ 70,000	$213,000
Commercial expenses:				
Delivery	$ 5,000	$ 4,500	$ 2,500	$ 12,000
Salaries and commissions	16,800	16,200	15,000	48,000
Salespersons' expenses	5,600	5,400	5,000	16,000
Advertising	15,000	15,000	15,000	45,000
Other fixed expenses	21,000	20,250	18,750	60,000
	$ 63,400	$ 61,350	$ 56,250	$181,000
Operating income	$ 16,600	$ 1,650	$ 13,750	$ 32,000
Underabsorbed fixed factory overhead				20,800
Adjusted operating income				$ 11,200

(b) Budgeted manufacturing costs (per unit):

	XL-100	XL-200	XL-300
Direct materials:			
Blades	$ 2.00	$ 2.00	$ 3.00
Other (leather, cap, etc.)	3.00	3.50	5.00
Direct labor*	2.00	2.40	4.00
Applied factory overhead (150% of direct labor)	3.00	3.60	6.00
	$10.00	$11.50	$18.00

* Direct labor was budgeted at $8 per hour.

(c) These budgeted figures were accompanied by the following explanatory notes:

- Fixed factory overhead costs ($144,000) are applied on the basis of the practical capacity of the plant (18,000 direct labor hours). Variable factory overhead costs are budgeted to be $.50 per direct labor dollar. Total factory overhead rate is determined as follows:

$$\text{Fixed rate} = \frac{\$144{,}000}{18{,}000 \text{ DLH} \times \$8} = \$1.00$$

Variable rate	.50
Rate per direct labor dollar	$1.50

- Budgeted direct labor hours:

XL-100 (20,000 units × .25 hour) =	5,000
XL-200 (18,000 units × .30 hour) =	5,400
XL-300 (10,000 units × .50 hour) =	5,000
	15,400

- Each of five salespersons receives a monthly salary of $400 and a commission of 4% of all sales to the customers visited regularly, even if customers order directly from the company.
- Variable salespersons' expenses, other marketing expenses (fixed), and administrative expenses are allocated as a percentage of sales.
- Advertisements in newspapers, on radio, and on television always mention the three models. Therefore, the expense is split evenly among the three models.

The president realizes that the plant is not operating at practical capacity for the first time in many years, and that idle capacity will be costly for the company.

A few days after receiving the revised budget, the president received a letter from the purchasing agent of Sunset Inc., which operates a large chain of department stores in the metropolitan area in which Sportech's plant is located. This letter stated that Sunset would buy 10,000 pairs of each model of skates before the end of the year on the following conditions:

(a) Sportech would deliver one fourth of the order on the last day of each of the last four months of the year at Sunset's central warehouse.
(b) Sunset would pay for the goods before the 10th of the month following the delivery.
(c) Cash and quantity discounts would amount to 15% of regular sales prices.

The president immediately called a meeting with the production manager, the sales manager, and the controller. The production manager saw an opportunity to wipe out the unabsorbed fixed factory overhead and mentioned that there would be no problem in hiring enough workers to operate at full capacity. The union contract provides for an overtime premium of 50% after a regular 8-hour day or 40-hour work week. Overtime is limited to 3 hours a day during the week, but employees can work 4 hours on Saturday mornings. The production manager estimated that of the additional direct labor hours needed to produce the order for Sunset, 7,900 would be overtime hours (all within the constraints specified in the union contract). Fixed manufacturing costs would increase by $3,000 a month; however, some of this cost could be offset because the blades manufacturer would agree to a price reduction of 10% on all blades, if the annual purchases totaled 60,000 pairs or more. The sales manager agreed to take care of all relations with Sunset but insisted that all regular orders be accepted. No sales commission would be paid on this special order.

After a brief discussion, the controller and the sales manager agreed to prepare an analysis of all the important factors, qualitative as well as quantitative, that might affect the decision.

Required:

(1) Compute the effect of this offer on operating income.

(2) What nonquantitative factors may have a bearing on the decision? (CICA adapted)

C21-2 Plant Closing Decision. Big-Auto Corporation manufactures automobiles, vans, and trucks. The Denver Cover Plant, one of Big-Auto's plants, produces coverings made primarily of vinyl and upholstery fabric that are sewn at Denver Cover and used to cover interior seating and other surfaces of Big-Auto products.

T. Vosilo is the plant manager for Denver Cover. The Denver Cover Plant was the first Big-Auto plant in the region. As other area plants were opened, Vosilo, in recognition of his management ability, was given responsibility for managing them. Vosilo functions as a regional manager although the budget for him and his staff is charged to the Denver Cover Plant.

Vosilo has just received a report indicating that Big-Auto could purchase the entire annual output of Denver Cover from outside suppliers for $30,000,000. Vosilo was astonished at the low outside price because the budget for Denver Cover's operating costs for the coming year was set at $52,000,000. Vosilo believes that Big-Auto will have to close down operations at Denver Cover in order to realize the $22,000,000 in annual cost savings.

The budget for Denver Cover's operating costs is as follows:

Denver Cover Plant
Budget for Operating Costs
For the Year ending December 31, 19A
(in thousands)

Materials		$12,000
Direct labor		13,000
Factory overhead:		
Supervision	$ 3,000	
Indirect labor	4,000	
Depreciation—equipment	5,000	
Depreciation—building	3,000	
Pension expense	4,000	
Plant manager and staff	2,000	
Corporate allocation	6,000	27,000
Total budgeted costs		$52,000

Additional facts regarding the plant's operations follow.

(a) Due to Denver Cover's commitment to use high-quality fabrics in all of its products, the Purchasing Department was instructed to place blanket purchase orders with major suppliers to ensure the receipt of sufficient materials for the coming year. If these orders are cancelled as a consequence of the plant closing, termination charges would amount to 15% of the cost of direct materials.

(b) Approximately 700 plant employees will lose their jobs if the plant is closed. This includes all the direct laborers and supervisors as well as the plumbers, electricians, and other skilled workers classified as indirect plant workers. Some will be able to find new jobs, but many others will have difficulty finding employment. All employees will have difficulty matching Denver Cover's base pay of $9.40 an hour, which is the highest in the area. A clause in Denver Cover's contract with the union will help some employees; the company must provide employment assistance to its former employees for 12 months after a plant closing. The estimated cost to administer this service is $1,000,000 for the year.

(c) Some employees will probably elect early retirement because Big-Auto has an excellent pension plan. In fact, $3,000,000 of the 19A pension expense will continue whether Denver Cover is open or not.

(d) Vosilo and his staff will not be affected by the closing of Denver Cover. They will still be responsible for administering three other area plants.

(e) Denver Cover considers equipment depreciation to be a variable cost and uses the units-of-production method to depreciate its equipment; Denver Cover is the only Big-Auto plant to use this depreciation method. However, Denver Cover uses the customary straight-line method to depreciate its building.

Required:

(1) Without regard to costs, identify the advantages to Big-Auto of continuing to obtain covers from its own Denver Cover Plant.

(2) Big-Auto plans to prepare a numerical analysis that will be used in its decision on whether or not to close the Denver Cover Plant.

   (a) Identify the recurring annual budgeted costs that can be avoided by closing the plant.

   (b) Identify the recurring annual budgeted costs that are not relevant to the plant-closing decision, and explain why they are not relevant.

   (c) Identify any nonrecurring costs that arise due to the closing of the plant, and explain how they affect the decision.

   (d) Identify any revenues or costs not specifically mentioned in the case that Big-Auto should consider before making its decision.

(ICMA adapted)

C21-3 New Product Proposal. Calco Corporation, a producer and distributor of plastic products for industrial use, is considering a proposal to produce a plastic storage unit designed especially for the consumer market. The product is well suited for Calco's manufacturing process, requiring no costly machinery modifications or Assembly Department changes. Adequate manufacturing capacity is available because of recent facility expansion and a leveling of sales growth in Calco's industrial product line.

Management is considering two alternatives for marketing the product. The first is to add this responsibility to Calco's current Marketing Department. The other alternative is to acquire a small, new company named Jasco Inc. at a nominal cost. This company was started by some former employees of a firm that specialized in marketing plastic products for the consumer market when they lost their jobs because of a merger. Jasco has not yet started operations.

The Product Engineering Department has prepared the following unit manufacturing cost estimate for the new storage unit at both the 100,000- and the 120,000-unit levels of production.

Direct materials	$14.00
Direct labor	3.50
Factory overhead (25% variable)*	10.00
Total	$27.50

* Total fixed factory overhead will be $750,000 at the 100,000-unit level and $900,000 at the 120,000-unit level.

Calco's Marketing Department has used its experience in the sale of industrial products to develop a proposal for the distribution of the new consumer product. The Marketing Department will be reorganized so that several positions that were scheduled for elimination now will be assigned to the new product. The Marketing Department's forecast of the annual financial results for its proposals to market the storage units is as follows:

Sales (100,000 units at $45)	$4,500,000
Costs:	
Cost of units sold (100,000 units at $27.50 each)	$2,750,000
Marketing costs:	
Positions that were to be eliminated	600,000
Sales commission (5% of sales)	225,000
Advertising program	400,000
Promotion program	200,000
Share of current Marketing Department's management costs	100,000
Total cost	$4,275,000
Income before income tax	$ 225,000

The Jasco founders also prepared a forecast of the annual financial results, based on their experience in marketing consumer products. The following forecast was based on the assumption that Jasco would become part of Calco and be responsible for marketing the storage unit:

Sales (120,000 units at $50)	$6,000,000
Costs:	
Cost of units sold (120,000 units at $27.50)	$3,300,000
Marketing costs:	
Personnel—sales	660,000
Personnel—sales management	200,000
Commission (10%)	600,000
Advertising program	800,000
Promotion program	200,000
Office rental (the annual rental of a long-term lease already signed by Jasco)	50,000
Total cost	$5,810,000
Income before income tax	$ 190,000

Required:

(1) List factors Calco should consider before it enters the consumer products market.

(2) Alter financial forecasts for use in deciding between the alternatives, if Calco decides to enter the consumer market.

(3) Compare the reliability of the two proposals.

(4) Identify the nonquantitative factors Calco should consider when choosing between the alternatives. Indicate whether or not any one of these factors is sufficiently important to warrant selection of one alternative over the other, regardless of the estimated financial effect on profit.

(ICMA adapted)

C21-4 Elimination of a Product. Precision Gauge Corporation produces three gauges. These gauges, which measure density, permeability, and thickness, are known as D-gauges, P-gauges, and T-gauges, respectively. For many years, the company has been profitable and has operated at capacity. In the last two years, however, prices on all gauges were reduced and selling expenses increased to meet competition and to keep the plant operating at full capacity. The following third quarter results are representative of recent experiences:

Precision Gauge Corporation
Income Statement
For Third Quarter, 19A
(in thousands)

	D-gauge	P-gauge	T-gauge	Total
Sales	$900	$1,600	$ 900	$3,400
Cost of goods sold	770	1,048	950	2,768
Gross profit	$130	$ 552	$ (50)	$ 632
Selling and administrative expenses	185	370	135	690
Income before income tax	$ (55)	$ 182	$(185)	$ (58)

Marvin Caplan, president of the company, is concerned about the results of the pricing, selling, and production policies. After reviewing the third quarter results, he announced that he would ask his management staff to consider a course of action that includes the following three suggestions:

(a) Discontinue the T-gauge line immediately. T-gauges will not be returned to the line of products unless the problems with the gauge are identified and resolved.
(b) Increase quarterly sales promotion by $100,000 on the P-gauge product line in order to increase sales volume 15%.
(c) Cut production on the D-gauge line by 50%, a quantity sufficient to meet the demand of customers who purchase P-gauges. In addition, the traceable advertising and promotion for this line will be cut to $20,000 each quarter.

Joan Garth, who is the controller, suggested that a more careful study of the financial relationships be made to determine the possible effect on the company's operating results as a consequence of the president's proposed course of action. The president agreed, and Tom Kirk, assistant controller, was assigned the analysis. To prepare the analysis, Tom gathered the following information:

(a) All three gauges are manufactured with common equipment and facilities.
(b) The quarterly general selling and administrative expenses of $170,000 are allocated to the three gauge lines in proportion to their dollar sales volume.
(c) Special selling expenses (primarily advertising, promotion, and shipping) are incurred for each gauge as follows:

	Quarterly Advertising and Promotion	Shipping Expense
D-gauge	$100,000	$ 4 per unit
P-gauge	210,000	10 per unit
T-gauge	40,000	10 per unit

(d) The unit manufacturing costs for the three products are as follows:

	D-gauge	P-gauge	T-gauge
Direct materials	$17	$ 31	$ 50
Direct labor	20	40	60
Variable factory overhead	30	45	60
Fixed factory overhead	10	15	20
	$77	$131	$190

(e) The unit sales prices for the three products are $90, $200, and $180 for the D-gauge, P-gauge, and T-gauge, respectively.
(f) The company is manufacturing at capacity and is selling all the gauges it produces.

Required:

(1) Tom Kirk has suggested that the Precision Gauge Corporation product-line income statement presented for the third quarter of 19A is not suitable for analyzing proposals and making decisions such as the ones suggested by Marvin Caplan.
 (a) Explain why the product-line income statement presented is not suitable for analysis and decision making.
 (b) Describe an alternative income statement format that is more suitable for analysis and decision making, and explain why it is better.
(2) Using the operating data presented for Precision Gauge Corporation and assuming that the president's proposed course of action had been implemented at the beginning of the third quarter of 19A, evaluate the president's proposed course of action by specifically responding to the following points:
 (a) Is each of the three suggestions cost effective? Support your discussion by a differential cost analysis that shows the net impact on income before tax for each of the three suggestions.
 (b) Was the president correct in eliminating the T-gauge line? Explain.
 (c) Was the president correct in promoting the P-gauge line rather than the D-gauge line? Explain.
 (d) Does the proposed course of action make effective use of Precision's capacity? Explain.
(3) Are there any nonquantitative factors that Precision Gauge Corporation should consider before it considers dropping the T-gauge line? Explain. (ICMA adapted)

C21-5 (Appendix) Linear Programming Problem Formulation—Contribution Margin Maximization. Leastan Company manufactures a line of carpeting that includes a commercial carpet and a residential carpet. Two grades of fiber—heavy duty and regular—are used in manufacturing both types of carpeting. The mix of the two grades differs in each type of carpeting, with the commercial grade using a greater amount of heavy duty fiber.

Leastan will introduce a new line of carpeting in two months to replace the current line. The fiber presently in stock will not be used in the new line; therefore, management wants to exhaust the present stock during the last month of production.

Data regarding the current line of commercial and residential carpeting are as follow:

	Commercial	Residential
Sales price per roll	$1,000	$800
Production specifications per roll of carpet:		
Heavy duty fiber	80 lbs.	40 lbs.
Regular fiber	20 lbs.	40 lbs.
Direct labor hours	15 hrs.	15 hrs.
Standard cost per roll of carpet:		
Heavy duty fiber ($3/lb.)	$ 240	$120
Regular fiber ($2/lb.)	40	80
Direct labor ($10/DLH)	150	150
Variable factory overhead	90	90
Fixed factory overhead	180	180
Total standard cost per roll	$ 700	$620

Leastan has 42,000 pounds of heavy duty fiber and 24,000 pounds of regular fiber in stock. All fiber not used in the manufacture of the present types of carpeting during the last month of production can be sold as scrap at 25 cents a pound.

There is a maximum of 10,500 direct labor hours available during the month. The labor force can work on either type of carpeting.

Sufficient demand exists for the present line of carpeting so that all quantities produced can be sold.

Required:

(1) Compute the number of rolls of commercial carpet and residential carpet that Leastan must manufacture during the last month of production in order to exhaust completely the heavy duty and regular fiber still in stock.

(2) Explain whether or not the solution quantities from requirement 1 can be manufactured during the last month of commercial and residential carpet production.

(3) Explain why linear programming would be useful in this application.

(4) Formulate the objective function and the constraints, so that this problem can be solved by linear programming. (ICMA adapted)

C21-6 (Appendix) Linear Programming—Application to Service Business. The firm of Miller, Lombardi, and York was recently formed by the merger of two companies providing accounting services. York's business was providing personal financial planning; Miller and Lombardi conducted audits of small governmental units and provided tax planning and preparation for several commercial firms. The combined firm has leased new offices and acquired several microcomputers that are used by the professional staff in each area of service. However, in the short run, the firm does not have the financial resources to acquire computers for all the professional staff.

The expertise of the professional staff can be divided into three distinct areas that match the services provided by the firm—tax planning and tax return preparation, insurance and investments, and auditing. Since the merger, the new firm has had to turn away business in all three areas of service. One of the problems is that although the total number of staff seems adequate, the staff members are not completely interchangeable. Limited financial resources do not permit hiring new staff in the near future, and therefore, the supply of staff is restricted in each area.

R. Oliva has been assigned the responsibility of allocating staff and computers to the various client engagements. Management wants Oliva to maximize revenues in a manner consistent with maintaining a high level of professional service in each of the areas of service. Management's time is billed at $100 per hour, and the staff's time is billed at $70 per hour for those with experience, and $50 per hour for inexperienced staff. P. Wren, a member of the staff, recently completed a course in quantitative methods at the local university. Wren suggested to Oliva that linear programming could be used to allocate appropriate staff and computers to the various assignments.

Required:

(1) Identify and discuss the primary assumption underlying the linear programming model.

(2) Explain why linear programming is appropriate for making staff assignments.

(3) Identify the data needed to develop a linear programming model for the company.

(4) List objectives other than revenue maximization that R. Oliva should consider before making staff allocations. (ICMA adapted)

CHAPTER 22

Planning for Capital Expenditures

Learning Objectives

After studying this chapter, you will be able to:

1. State the need for a structured framework for planning capital expenditures.
2. Cite examples of ethical problems in capital budgeting.
3. List different motivations and objectives for capital expenditures.
4. Classify capital expenditures.
5. Identify the amount and timing of cash flows.
6. Adjust cash flows to reflect anticipated inflation.
7. Adjust cash flows for the expected effect of income taxes.
8. Enumerate the steps in controlling capital expenditures.

Long-term investments (typically called **capital expenditures**) require commitment of resources for long periods of time. Because the size of capital expenditures is often large and the duration of the investment is long, the process of planning, evaluating, and controlling capital expenditures (sometimes called **capital budgeting**) has significant, long-term effects on the economic well-being of a company.

To survive in the long run, a firm must earn a reasonable return on invested funds. As a consequence, considerable attention has been devoted to techniques for evaluating capital expenditure proposals. Yet evaluation is only one essential requirement for the effective administration of a capital expenditure program. Effective planning and control is equally important for the following reasons. First, the long-term commitment increases financial risk; second, the magnitude of expenditures is substantial and the economic penalties for unwise decisions are usually severe; and third, decisions made in this area provide the structure for operation of the firm.

Planning for capital expenditures, evaluating proposals, estimating cash flows, and controlling capital expenditures are discussed in this chapter. Quantitative methods used to evaluate capital expenditures are discussed in Chapter 23.

Planning for Capital Expenditures

Planning for capital expenditures consists of relating plans to objectives, structuring a framework, searching for proposals, budgeting expenditures, and requesting authority for expenditures.

Relating Plans to Objectives

Individual capital projects must be consistent with company objectives and be capable of being incorporated into company operations. To achieve consistency, all management levels need to be conscious of company objectives and of the different roles played by each level. Ideally, executive management sets broad goals and objectives; managers of functional activities formulate specific policies and programs for action that, when approved, are executed by operating-level management. The lower the level at which a decision is authorized, the greater the need for detailed guidelines; capital expenditures not conducive to such detail require handling at a higher level.

Structuring the Framework

An organization's capital expenditure framework is the basis for implementing the capital expenditure program. Several factors influence the molding and revision of the framework: the company's organizational structure, philosophy, size, the nature of its operations, and the characteristics of individual capital projects.

A company manual can be used to detail policies and procedures and to illustrate forms required for administering the capital expenditure program. Such manuals should be stripped down to helpful levels to (1) encourage people to work on and submit ideas, (2) focus attention on useful analytical tasks, and (3) facilitate rapid project development and expeditious review.

Searching for Proposals

A capital expenditure program yields the best results only when the best available proposals are considered and all reasonable alternatives to each proposal have been evaluated and screened. Ideas should come from all segments of the enterprise. Everyone in the organization should participate in the search activity within the bounds of their technical knowledge and ability, their authority and responsibility, their awareness of operating problems, and existing management guidelines regarding desirable projects. Care must be taken to create and maintain an incentive to search out and bring good projects into the system. This incentive is strong when personnel trust that all proposals are reviewed fairly and objectively.

Budgeting Capital Expenditures

The capital expenditures budget is typically prepared for a one-year period. It presents management's investment plans at the time the budget is prepared for the coming period.

Some projects never materialize; others are added through amendments to the budget during the budget year. Thus, the budget must be adaptable to changing needs. The capital expenditures budget is not an authorization to commit funds; it merely affords an opportunity for decision makers to consolidate plans by looking at projects side by side. The capital expenditures budget should be reconciled with the other periodic budgeting activities of the firm, e.g., expense and cash budgets (as discussed in Chapters 15 and 16), and the annual capital budget should be reconciled with long-range capital investment and operating plans and objectives.

The capital expenditures budget passes through several management levels as it moves toward final approval at the executive management level. A clear explanation of the content of the approved budget should be transmitted to the various management levels to avoid misunderstandings.

Requesting Authority for Expenditures

The periodic budget is usually an approval of ideas and does not grant automatic approval to commit funds. Authority to commit funds for other than necessary preliminary administrative costs should be formally documented. A formally documented authorization process provides management a second look at budgeted projects, based on an up-to-date justification and description of the expenditure. Documentation and supporting detail should be originated at the level at which the expenditure will occur, with staff assistance if needed.

Approval of the expenditure proposal should be delegated to the organizational level having the necessary competence to make the decision. It should not be necessary to request executive management's approval for each project. The philosophies of companies vary as to decentralization of authority. The amount, type, and significance of an expenditure should be considered when the required level of approval is being determined.

During the budget year, periodic reports should be prepared by categories, comparing approved expenditures with budgeted expenditures. The reports should be prepared for use by the organization levels originating the requests for expenditures as well as those granting approval. Higher-level managers need summaries, with unusual items reported in detail.

Ethical Considerations

Ethics for management accountants were discussed in Chapter 1. In capital budgeting, accountants should be especially vigilant, because the capital budgeting process provides both opportunity and temptation for unethical behavior. Some common problems are described in the following paragraphs.

Pressure from Superiors or Associates to Circumvent the Approval Process. In most companies, only projects that require an expenditure in excess of a predesignated level must be evaluated and approved. One way of circumventing such a system is to break the capital project up into several small purchases, each of which falls below the designated level that requires approval. If detected by the accountant, the small purchases should be grouped into one project. Sometimes, pressure is put on the accountant to ignore the situation or to cooperate in subverting the system on the grounds that avoiding the evaluation and approval process saves time and that the project will be accepted anyway. In other cases, pressure is applied by simple threats. For example, an executive threatens to use his or her friendship or authority over the accountant's immediate supervisor to hinder the accountant's career advancement with the company.

Pressure to Write Off or Devalue Assets Below Their True Value in Order to Justify Replacement. Pressure is sometimes applied by well-meaning associates who believe that a project will benefit the company in some qualitative way that will not receive adequate consideration in the evaluation process. At times, pressure is applied by an executive who wants the project approved for personal prestige or comfort (such as new office furniture or a new automobile).

Exaggeration of Economic Benefits of Capital Projects to Increase the Likelihood of Approval. This is a particularly troublesome problem because predictions about the future necessarily contain some subjective judgements and are never perfectly accurate. The problem is compounded when the duration of a proposed capital project exceeds the period the proposing manager expects to remain in his or her current position. Promotions and job rotations among lower- and middle-level management typically occur at fairly short intervals. There is an incentive to exaggerate the expected benefits of a capital project to secure acceptance, if a subsequent failure of the project to live up to expectations can be blamed on a successor. Although accountants have access to a considerable amount of data, it is often difficult for them to determine whether predictions are realistic. Even if they believe predictions are unrealistic, providing convincing evidence is usually difficult.

The appropriate course of action in each of these situations (and any other, for that matter) depends to a great extent on the character of the individuals involved and the nature of the ethical violation. The accountant is obligated to make sure that legitimate policies and procedures are not circumvented and to make sure that the data used in evaluating capital projects are reliable and realistic. In most cases, the accountant should first discuss the perceived ethical problem with the accounting supervisor (to clarify the significance of the problem and identify possible courses of action) and then with the individual or individuals involved. If the problem cannot be resolved through discussion, the accountant is obligated to provide a full disclosure of all the details to the executives responsible for evaluating and approving the capital expenditure. If the individual involved is the accountant's immediate supervisor, the accountant should consult the next higher level of management.

Evaluating Capital Expenditures

Multiple evaluations of a single proposal may be necessary because (1) circumstances can change during the time span of the project, from its original idea to its completion, (2) alternative solutions may exist for the problem for which the project is designed, and (3) assumptions may vary as to the amount and timing of cash flows.

The economic evaluation of capital expenditure proposals has received considerable attention in the literature, with good reason. In order to survive in the long run, a firm must be profitable. Because capital investments require commitment of substantial resources for long periods of time, poor investments can have a material long-term effect on profitability and survival. Four commonly used techniques for evaluating capital expenditures are discussed in detail in Chapter 23. Although these techniques are useful in selecting projects that will maximize company profits, excessive reliance on quantitative answers is dangerous. Because the life of a capital project extends well into the future, the data used in its quantitative analysis are fraught with uncertainty. It is difficult to predict accurately what will happen next year, and even more difficult to predict what will happen several years in the future. Furthermore, because predictions of future costs and revenues unavoidably contain elements of subjectivity, such data can be easily manipulated by overzealous or misguided employees.

In evaluating capital expenditures, management must consider many imponderable factors. Strategic considerations and managerial intuition often drive investment decisions, rather than evaluations of the results of analytic techniques applied to quantitative data. In some cases, quantitative data are simply not available, or if available, are not reliable. In other cases, investment decisions are determined by the company's strategic plan or by past choices, in which case quantitative analysis may be unwarranted.[1] Other projects are so obviously necessary that economic evaluation is simply not needed. For example, a railway trestle washed out by a flood must be replaced if the line is to continue in use. If the line is profitable, a capital expenditure analysis of the track replacement would be a waste of time.

Some capital expenditures are made for qualitative or legal reasons, rather than for purely economic reasons. A manufacturer may be forced to invest in advanced manufacturing technologies, improve product quality, improve delivery and service, increase manufacturing flexibility, or produce a less-profitable product in response to competitive pressure.[2] A company may be forced into installing dining or recreation facilities for employee use in order to attract employees. Air and water pollution regulations may necessitate an expenditure for a waste disposal unit.

Because investments should be consistent with long-term goals, some potentially profitable projects may be rejected because they do not fit into the company's overall plan. Many firms, particularly small and medium-sized ones, are not diversified and invest only in activities related to their particular line of business. This may be simply a matter of choice, or it can be a matter of necessity. One firm may lack expertise while another lacks sufficient funds and is unwilling or unable to secure the necessary financing. The mechanics of various evaluation techniques are important, but of still greater importance is their relationship to the overall capital expenditure planning and control process and the need for creative and thoughtful management.

Classification of Capital Expenditures

Capital expenditure projects can be classified into three categories: replacement expenditures, expansion investments, and improvement expenditures. A proposal can, of course involve more than one classification. An example is a firm considering a proposal to replace an old printing press for which maintenance cost has become excessive (an equipment replacement expenditure), with a new press that will offer an expanded productive capacity (an expansion investment).

Some projects may not be independent of one another and therefore should be grouped together for evaluation as a compound project. The following quotation illustrates this point:

> Contingent or dependent projects can arise, for instance, when acceptance of one proposal is dependent on acceptance of one or more other proposals. One simple example would be the purchase of an extra-long boom for a crane which would be of little value unless the crane itself were also purchased; the latter, however, may be justified on its own. When contingent projects are combined with their independent prerequisites, the combination may be called a compound project. Thus, a compound project may be characterized by the algebraic sum of the payoffs and costs of the component projects plus, perhaps, an interaction term.[3]

---

[1] Bernard A. Coda and Barry G. King, "Manufacturing Decision-Making Tools," *Journal of Cost Management*, Vol. 3, No. 1, pp. 29–37.

[2] A sample of actual firms suggests that the use of qualitative justification for capital expenditures is common. See Robert A. Howell, James D. Brown, Stephen R. Soucy, and Alan H. Seed, *Management Accounting in the New Manufacturing Environment,* (Montvale, New Jersey: Institute of Management Accountants (formerly National Association of Accountants), 1987), p.88.

[3] H. Martin Weingartner, "Capital Budgeting of Interrelated Projects: Survey and Synthesis," *Management Science,* Vol. 12, No. 7, p. 492.

Replacement Expenditures. **Replacement expenditures** include the acquisition of new machinery and/or buildings to replace worn-out or obsolescent assets. Historically, the basis for such decision making has been the desire for prospective cost savings; that is, comparing future costs of the old assets with future costs of the replacement property. In addition to comparisons of operating costs, the analysis of future costs requires the determination of the prospective purchase price less any ultimate resale or salvage value. One of the most difficult problems is to estimate the probable economic life of the replacement assets. This is the core of any capital expenditure decision. For the present facility, the future decline in disposal value must be estimated. The original cost of the present facility is a sunk cost, not recoverable and totally irrelevant to the decision. Accumulated depreciation is also independent of the company's real future costs. Book values of existing assets are not relevant to the replacement decision, except for possible income tax consequences. For example, an increase or decrease in income tax liability can result from the recognition of a gain or loss, respectively, from the sale, exchange, or abandonment of an asset. On the other hand, in an exchange of like-kind assets, the income tax effect results from an adjustment to the tax basis of the new asset and the amount of depreciation available for tax purposes, which in turn affects the future income tax liability. An increase or decrease in income tax liability has a direct effect on cash flow and is, therefore, relevant to the capital expenditure decision.

Expansion Investments. **Expansion investments** involve plant enlargement for the purpose of expanding existing markets or invading new markets. In these cases, the expected results of expanding and not expanding are compared, and the basis for a decision shifts from cost savings to increased profits and cash inflows. The expected increase in profit is estimated by preparing a projected income statement showing additional revenue and expense over the life of the project. The degree of uncertainty in this type of investment can be great, but it is usually quantifiable.

Improvement Expenditures. Decisions to improve existing products or facilities, called **improvement expenditures**, are generally strategic. A firm may be forced to improve product quality or design in order to counter the actions of competitors. Failure to improve existing products can cause deterioration of market share. Improvement may require development of new processes, modernization of facilities, or both. Because no historical basis for making the capital expenditure decision exists and because the return on such an investment is based on maintaining profits in the face of competition, the benefits are often difficult to quantify. A high degree of sound judgment and business insight is required.

Decisions to add new products can involve the decision to drop existing products or to expand the product line. In either case, a capital expenditure may be necessary to alter or expand existing facilities. In such cases, the improvement expenditure is similar to the expansion expenditure in that the emphasis is generally on profit improvement rather than on reducing maintenance cost. The increase in profits over the life of the capital project must be estimated and compared with its cost in order for management to determine the value of adding the new product.

In the current business environment, there is considerable emphasis on modernizing manufacturing facilities by investing in advanced manufacturing technologies. Although it often produces cost savings, the movement toward computer integrated manufacturing (CIM), robotics, and flexible manufacturing systems (FMSs) is motivated primarily by strategic considerations. Such considerations include the need to improve product quality in the face of increasing competition and the desire to be able to adjust production output both in quantity and variety quickly to satisfy rapidly changing consumer demands. The cost of modernization is often very high, and the strategic benefit is generally difficult to quantify.[4] Nevertheless, in the face of increased competition, particularly from abroad, such investments may be necessary for the survival of a firm.

Estimating Cash Flows

In order to make an intelligent decision about a capital expenditure proposal, management must know the extent of the financial commitment required and the potential benefits to be derived from the expenditure. The amount and timing of cash inflows and outflows over the life of the project must be estimated. The extent and timing of financial commitments must be known in order for management to determine whether the company can make the expenditure. If sufficient resources are not available and are not expected to be generated from the project or from other operations when needed, external sources of funds must be sought to finance the project. The amount of accounting income to be generated from a capital expenditure is not relevant to this decision, because accounting income contains accruals of revenues and expenses that differ from the timing of cash flows. The amount and the timing of cash flows is also important as a basis for determining the economic value of a capital expenditure project. Methods used in determining the economic value of a capital expenditure project are discussed in detail in Chapter 23.

Cash Outflows. Most capital investments require an initial cash outflow before any cash inflows can be generated. The initial cash outflow usually consists of the purchase price of one or more assets (or a down payment) and the cost of installing the property and getting it ready for use. If the project requires the construction of a building or other large asset, interest and taxes during the construction period also may need to be paid before any cash inflows can be realized.

If the machinery being considered utilizes a more advanced technology than that currently in use, the initial startup cost may be significant. Startup costs include not only the cost of training personnel but also the cost of adjusting and testing the machinery. In addition, if a CIM system is being considered, substantial costs will be incurred initially to program the computer and to fine tune the system to produce the company's current products. Some of the computer software needed to link the machines with the computer can be purchased, but much of it must be written by programmers to meet the company's unique machinery configuration and product designs.[5]

If one or all of the assets being acquired in the project are leased, the initial cash outflow will include a lease payment. Unlike interest, lease payments are typically paid at the beginning of the lease period rather than at the end. Also, the

---

[4] Robert A. Howell and Stephen R. Soucy, "Capital Investment in the New Manufacturing Environment," *Management Accounting,* Vol. 69, No. 11, pp. 26–32; Joel C. Polakoff, "Computer Integrated Manufacturing: A New Look at Cost Justifications," *Journal of Accountancy,* Vol. 169, No. 3, pp. 24–29; and Michael Bromwich and Al Bhimani, "Strategic Investment Appraisal," *Management Accounting,* Vol. 72, No. 9, pp. 45–48.

[5] The initial cost of programming a CIM system to produce the first batch is high; however, the subsequent batch setup cost is very low. Once the software is fine tuned, it is stored and used again with no adjustment. When a new product is added to the line, new software, different machine tools, jigs, and fixtures, and more testing and debugging are required; however, changes are required only to the extent that the new product differs from the old. These new costs should be considered part of the cost of the new product. See Thornton Parker and Theodore Lettes, "Is Accounting Standing in the Way of Flexible Computer-Integrated Manufacturing?," *Management Accounting,* Vol. 72, No. 7, pp. 34–38.

additional business generated by a capital project may make it necessary for the company to increase its cash on hand, inventories, accounts receivable, and accounts payable. The expected increase in current assets in excess of the expected increase in current liabilities should be treated as a cash outflow when it occurs. Later, during the operating life of the project, additional cash outflows may be required to expand the project or to implement modifications or enhancements necessary to keep it going. In addition, operating cash outflows are incurred each period in the operation of the project, plus annual payments if assets are purchased on installment or leased.

Cash Inflows. Cash inflows received over the life of a project include revenues from the additional business generated by the project and/or cost savings. If the capital expenditure is for machinery that improves operating efficiency, a reduction in periodic operating costs may occur. Cost reductions that reduce cash outflows have the same effect on income and wealth as cash inflows. Consequently, reductions in cash outflows can be viewed as cash inflows.

Cost savings that often result from machinery replacements include reductions in scrap, rework, and spoilage (from the acquisition of newer, more efficient equipment) and reductions in repairs and maintenance expenditures (from replacing old, worn machinery with new machinery). If the capital expenditure involves acquisition of highly automated machinery, significant reductions in direct labor and manufacturing support costs (such as inspection and materials handling) can occur.

If the capital expenditure involves the acquisition of an FMS, work in process inventories should decline because the resulting shortened setup times reduce the need for large inventory buffers. Reductions in work in process inventories translate into cost savings from reduced inventory carrying cost. Such cost savings may extend to materials and finished goods, as well. In addition, a reduction in inventory quantities may result in sufficiently reduced floor space requirements that could translate into cash inflows from the rental of unused space or cost reductions from the reduced cost of a smaller facility.[6]

At the end of the life of a capital project, a cash inflow is sometimes generated from the sale of the property used in the project. The amount of cash inflow expected from the final sale of the property is referred to as **salvage value**, and while difficult to estimate, it can be considerable. For example, assume a building with an expected 40-year useful life is acquired to provide space to sell or manufacture a product that has an expected 10-year life cycle. At the end of 10 years, the building may well have a value in excess of its original purchase price. On the other hand, if the length of a project is determined by the useful life of the property used in the project, it usually will have a small salvage value, which for all practical purposes may be ignored.

Generally, cash flow estimates used to evaluate capital expenditures are based on incremental changes in the current level of cash inflows and outflows. This approach assumes that the current level of business will remain unchanged if the capital expenditure proposal is not accepted. However, this assumption does not apply in all cases. For example, if one company installs an advanced technology, such as a CIM system, when its principal competitor does not, the company with the advanced technology may gain a competitive advantage. In time, the company that rejected the advanced technology probably will experience a decline in sales and net cash inflows because it has greater product costs and/or poorer product quality or service than the company with the advanced

---

[6] Richard David, "Supplementing Cost Accounting Courses in Response to the Changing Business Environment," *Issues in Accounting Education,* Vol. 4, No. 1, p. 169.

technology. In such a scenario, rejecting the investment does not result in a continuation of business as usual. The actions of competitors should be considered. The estimated cash inflows from the acquisition of an advanced technology should include an estimate of the net cash inflows that are likely to be lost if the technology is not adopted.[7] Exhibit 22-1 summarizes typical cash outflows and inflows associated with capital expenditure projects.

EXHIBIT 22-1

Common Cash Flows Related to Capital Expenditure Proposals

Cash Outflows	Cash Inflows
Payments to purchase new assets	Additional revenues from increased sales
Payments to lease new assets	Reduction in maintenance and repairs
Equipment installation	Reduction in scrap, rework, and spoilage
Employee training	Reduction in labor, inspection, and handling
Computer programming and fine tuning	Reduction in inventory carrying costs
Increased working capital requirements	Salvage value at the end of the project
Periodic operating costs	

Cash Flow Illustration. Milski Corporation is considering the replacement of machinery used to manufacture one of its current products. The product, called Blixt, sells for $15 a unit. Variable manufacturing cost is $7 for each unit of Blixt manufactured, and variable marketing cost is $1 for each unit sold. The machine in current use has the capacity to manufacture 4,000 units of Blixt each year. The machine being considered for replacement could produce 6,000 units a year (2,000 units a year more than the machinery in current use), all of which would be sold at the current price of $15 a unit, according to Marketing Department forecasts. The replacement machine costs $110,000; however, the seller has offered a $40,000 trade-in allowance for the old machinery (which management believes is approximately equal to its fair market value). The machine in current use has a book value of $28,000 (an original cost of $60,000 less accumulated depreciation of $32,000). Although the machine in current use is 8 years old, management believes that it could be used for another 10 years. The useful life of the replacement machine is believed to be about the same as that of the currently used machine. This estimate is based in part on management's evaluation of the quality of materials used in constructing the replacement machine and in part on expected changes in production technology. The expected salvage value of the replacement machine at the end of its 10-year useful life is $5,000, whereas the expected salvage value of the currently used machine is zero. The variable manufacturing and marketing costs per unit of product are expected to be the same with the replacement machine as with the machine in current use; however, the Maintenance Department believes that the replacement machine will require less maintenance in the first 5 years of its use than will the currently used machine which should result in the following cost savings:

Year	Cost Savings from Reduced Maintenance
1	$1,000
2	800
3	600
4	400
5	200

[7] John Y. Lee, "Investing in New Technology to Stay Competitive," *Management Accounting*, Vol. 72, No. 12, p. 48; and Howell and Soucy, "Capital Investment in the New Manufacturing Environment," p. 30.

In this example, the cash flows relevant to the capital expenditure decision are those that would change as a result of the machine replacement. The three sources of these cash inflows are (1) the contribution margin (that is, the excess of revenue over variable costs from the manufacture and sale of the additional 2,000 units of Blixt, (2) the reduction of cash outflows for maintenance during the first 5 years the replacement machine is used, and (3) the salvage value of the replacement machine at the end of its economic life. The pretax net cash inflows from the additional sales of Blixt and reduced maintenance costs are computed in Exhibit 22-2.

EXHIBIT 22-2

Milski Corporation
Capital Expenditure Proposal for Machine Replacement
Pretax Net Cash Inflows

Year	(1) Estimated Demand	(2) Unit Sales Price	(3) Variable Production and Selling Cost per Unit	(4) Contribution Margin per Unit (2) – (3)	(5) Net Cash Inflows from Additional Sales (1) × (4)	(6) Cost Savings from Reduced Maintenance	(7) Cash Inflows from Sales and Cost Savings (5) + (6)
1	2,000	$15	$8	$7	$14,000	$1,000	$ 15,000
2	2,000	15	8	7	14,000	800	14,800
3	2,000	15	8	7	14,000	600	14,600
4	2,000	15	8	7	14,000	400	14,400
5	2,000	15	8	7	14,000	200	14,200
6	2,000	15	8	7	14,000	0	14,000
7	2,000	15	8	7	14,000	0	14,000
8	2,000	15	8	7	14,000	0	14,000
9	2,000	15	8	7	14,000	0	14,000
10	2,000	15	8	7	14,000	0	14,000
Total cash inflows from additional sales of Blixt and reduced maintenance							$143,000
Plus salvage value at end of economic life of machine							5,000
Total pretax net cash inflows from project							$148,000

The only cash outflow for this project occurs at the beginning of the first year to purchase the new machine. The amount will be $70,000 ($110,000 for the new machine less the $40,000 trade-in allowance). The vendor's price includes delivery and installation of the new machine and removal of the old machine. The book value of the old machine is not relevant to the investment decision because it does not affect cash flows.

Inflationary Considerations in the Estimation of Cash Flows

If inflation is expected to occur during the life of the project, the cash flows should be adjusted to reflect the anticipated effect of changing prices. For illustrative purposes, assume that the annual inflation rate expected during the 10-year life of the Milski Corporation capital project is 7 percent. Management believes that its costs will increase at the rate of inflation and that the sales price of the new product can be increased at the same rate. The cash flow adjustments required to reflect anticipated inflation is presented in Exhibit 22-3.

EXHIBIT 22-3

Milski Corporation
Capital Expenditure Proposal for Machine Replacement
Cash Flow Adjustment to Reflect Anticipated Inflation

Year	(1) Estimated Periodic Net Cash Inflows	(2) Price-Level Adjustment	(3) Adjusted Estimate of Net Cash Inflows (1) × (2)	(4) Difference (3) – (1)
1	$ 15,000	$(1+.07) = 1.070$	$ 16,050	$ 1,050
2	14,800	$(1+.07)^2 = 1.145$	16,946	2,146
3	14,600	$(1+.07)^3 = 1.225$	17,885	3,285
4	14,400	$(1+.07)^4 = 1.311$	18,878	4,478
5	14,200	$(1+.07)^5 = 1.403$	19,923	5,723
6	14,000	$(1+.07)^6 = 1.501$	21,014	7,014
7	14,000	$(1+.07)^7 = 1.606$	22,484	8,484
8	14,000	$(1+.07)^8 = 1.718$	24,052	10,052
9	14,000	$(1+.07)^9 = 1.838$	25,732	11,732
10	14,000	$(1+.07)^{10} = 1.967$	27,538	13,538
	$143,000		$210,502	$67,502
Salvage	5,000	$(1+.07)^{10} = 1.967$	9,835	4,835
	$148,000		$220,337	$72,337

If the machine's $5,000 estimated salvage value at the end of 10 years of use is based on current prices, it should be adjusted for the expected effects of inflation over the 10-year period. Unless the cash flows of the Milski Corporation capital expenditure proposal are adjusted for the expected effects of inflation, the cash inflows over the life of the project would be understated by $72,337. An understatement of this magnitude could result in an erroneous rejection of the project. If the impact of inflation is expected to be different for cash inflows and outflows, separate inflation adjustments must be made for each. Such a difference can occur, for example when either the sales price of output or the purchase price of input is set by a long-term contract.[8]

Income Tax Considerations in the Estimation of Cash Flows

The effect of income taxes on cash flows is an important consideration in planning and evaluating capital expenditures. The following paragraphs discuss the tax laws regarding depreciation, the investment tax credit, and construction period interest and taxes. Because the tax law changes frequently, this discussion should be regarded as illustrative only. It is presented to demonstrate the importance of considering the effect of taxes on capital expenditure analysis. Current income tax statutes and regulations should be consulted when actual capital expenditures are planned.

Depreciation. Depreciation is not a cash inflow or outflow. However, depreciation allowed for income tax purposes reduces taxable income and, consequently, tax liability, which directly affects cash flow.

[8] For an elaboration on the effect of inflation in capital budgeting, see Jon W. Bartley, "A NPV Model Modified for Inflation," *Management Accounting,* Vol. 62, No. 6, pp. 49–52; Debra D. Raiborn and Thomas A. Ratcliffe, "Are You Accounting for Inflation in Your Capital Budgeting Process?" *Management Accounting,* Vol. 61, No. 3, pp. 19–22; and Allen H. Seed, III, *The Impact of Inflation on Internal Planning and Control* (New York: Institute of Management Accountants (formerly National Association of Accountants), 1981), pp. 73–78, and 104–105.

The Economic Recovery Tax Act of 1981, with subsequent amendments, represented a substantial change in income tax accounting for capital expenditures. A new system for recovering the cost of capital expenditures, referred to as the **accelerated cost recovery system (ACRS)**, was required for tangible, depreciable property placed in service after 1980. Although the system was used for federal income tax purposes, some states did not allow businesses to use the ACRS rates in computing state income taxes. ACRS reduced the impact of inflation by accelerating the recovery of capital expenditures by (1) eliminating the useful-life concept and replacing it with a shorter recovery period, and (2) allowing more cost recovery in the earlier years of the recovery period, that is, accelerated depreciation rates.

The ACRS divided depreciable property into classes, each with a different recovery period. Under the Tax Reform Act of 1986, **modified ACRS (MACRS)** increased the number of property classes and lengthened the recovery periods of most kinds of depreciable property.[9] The 1986 act provides for the recovery of capital expenditures over periods of 3, 5, 7, 10, 15, 20, 27.5, or 31.5 years, depending on the type of property. Most of the common depreciable business assets other than buildings are classified as 5-year or 7-year property. For example, automobiles, light trucks, small aircraft, and technological equipment are classified as 5-year property, and railroad locomotives and cars, commercial aircraft, and most manufacturing machinery are classified as 7-year property. Buildings that qualify as residential rental property are depreciated over 27.5 years, and nonresidential buildings over 31.5 years.

The maximum depreciation rate allowable for 3-, 5-, 7-, and 10-year property is 200 percent of the declining balance, with an automatic switch to straight-line depreciation in the first year in which the straight-line deduction determined as of the beginning of the change year exceeds the declining balance deduction for the same year. The maximum depreciation rate allowable is reduced to 150 percent of the declining balance for 15-year and 20-year property and to straight-line for residential rental and nonresidential real property. For most tangible personal property, depreciation is computed as if the property were placed into service at the midpoint of the year (referred to as the half-year convention). Depreciation for real property is based on a midmonth convention (that is, property placed into service in any month is treated as being placed into service in the middle of the month). For all classes of property, salvage value is treated as zero. The IRS publishes tables of depreciation rates for the convenience of taxpayers, so calculating the depreciation rate is not necessary. Exhibit 22-4 provides an example of the cost recovery rates for 3-year, 5-year, and 7-year property classes.

The new machine being considered by the Milski Corporation is classified as 7-year property. For income tax purposes, gain is generally not recognized on the trade-in of used business property in exchange for replacement property. The tax basis of the replacement property is the same as the tax basis of the property traded in plus the value of boot given in the exchange (that is, cash paid to the vendor above the trade-in allowance).[10] For Milski Corporation the tax basis of the new machine will be $70,000 (zero tax basis for the machine traded in plus $70,000 cash). Tax depreciation available each year, based on the rates in Exhibit 22-4 for 7-year property, is determined as shown in Exhibit 22-5.

---

[9] *Internal Revenue Code,* Section 168. Generally, MACRS rules apply to property placed in service after December 31, 1986.

[10] *Internal Revenue Code,* Section 1031.

EXHIBIT 22-4

Sample of MACRS Depreciation Rates by Property Class (Half-Year Convention and 200-percent Declining Balance Method)			
Recovery Year	3-Year	5-Year	7-Year
1	.333	.200	.143
2	.444	.320	.245
3	.148	.192	.175
4	.075	.115	.125
5		.115	.089
6		.058	.089
7			.089
8			.045
	1.000	1.000	1.000

EXHIBIT 22-5

Milski Corporation Capital Expenditure Proposal for Machine Replacement Tax Depreciation			
Recovery Year	(1) Depreciable Basis of Machine	(2) 7-Year Property Recovery Percentage	(3) Tax Depreciation (1) × (2)
1	$70,000	0.143	$10,010
2	70,000	0.245	17,150
3	70,000	0.175	12,250
4	70,000	0.125	8,750
5	70,000	0.089	6,230
6	70,000	0.089	6,230
7	70,000	0.089	6,230
8	70,000	0.045	3,150
			$70,000

For the Milski Corporation capital expenditure proposal, the additional variable manufacturing and selling costs are deductible from the additional sales revenue when taxable income is computed, and the reduction in maintenance cost will reduce tax deductions and increase taxable income. As a consequence, additional periodic taxable income expected to occur as a result of the capital expenditure will be equal to the inflation-adjusted periodic cash inflows (from Exhibit 22-3) reduced by additional tax depreciation available on the replacement machine. Because the machine to be traded in is 8 years old, it has been fully depreciated for income tax purposes. As a consequence, all the tax depreciation available on the replacement machine will reduce the additional taxable income expected from the replacement machine. If the machine to be traded in is still depreciable, only the difference in the tax depreciation available from the two alternatives is relevant.

Gains on Disposals of Depreciable Property. For federal income tax purposes, gain recognized on the disposal of depreciable property other than buildings is treated as ordinary income to the extent of tax depreciation deducted prior to disposal.[11] Gain, if any, in excess of such depreciation is essentially treated as a capital gain.[12] The Tax Reform Act of 1986 repealed the preferential treatment accorded capital gains by removing the capital gain deduction previously available to individuals and by setting the capital gain tax rate for corporations equal to the ordinary income tax rate. However, the law still requires that capital gains be computed and reported separately from ordinary income. This requirement was presumably included in order to permit taxpayers to deduct unused capital loss carryovers. It may also have been included in order to keep in place a mechanism that would make it convenient for Congress to reenact some form of preferential tax treatment for capital gains at a later time.

For both financial accounting and income tax purposes, gain is generally not recognized on the trade-in of used business property in exchange for replacement property.[13] The book value and tax basis of the replacement property is the same as the book value and tax basis of the old property plus boot given in the exchange (that is, cash paid to the vendor above the trade-in allowance). On the other hand, if the asset being replaced is sold outright, any gain (or loss) realized on the sale must be recognized even though the proceeds of the sale are used to purchase replacement property. If a gain is recognized for income tax purposes on the sale of the old asset, a portion of the sales proceeds must be used to pay the tax, thereby reducing the amount of sales proceeds available to purchase the replacement property.

It is often difficult to determine whether the old asset should be sold outright or traded in. For example, in the Milski Corporation capital expenditure decision, the machine to be replaced, which has a tax basis of zero (that is, it is 7-year property that has been fully depreciated), could be sold for $40,000 or used as a trade in to reduce the $110,000 cost of the replacement machine by $40,000. If the old machine were sold, the after-tax cash inflow from the sale would be $24,000 {$40,000 sales proceeds – [40% tax rate × ($40,000 sales price – 0 basis)]}. The out-of-pocket cost of the replacement machine would be $86,000 ($110,000 cost – $24,000 after-tax cash inflow from sale of old machine), and the depreciable tax basis of the replacement machine would be $110,000 (its full cost). In contrast, if the old machine were traded in for the replacement, there would be no cash proceeds, no gain, and no tax liability to be paid. The out-of-pocket cost of the replacement machine would be $70,000 ($110,000 cost – $40,000 trade-in allowance), and the depreciable tax basis of the replacement machine would be $70,000 (0 basis of old machine + $70,000 cash paid). In this example, Milski Corporation would have to pay $16,000 more in the first year to purchase the replacement machine if the old machine were sold outright rather than traded in ($86,000 versus $70,000); however, because the depreciable tax basis of the replacement machine would be $40,000 greater if the old machine were sold

---

[11] *Internal Revenue Code,* Section 1245. *Internal Revenue Code,* Section 1250 generally provides that gain recognized on the disposition of buildings is to be treated as ordinary income to the extent that the depreciation allowed or allowable exceeds the depreciation that would have been allowed under the straight-line method. The remaining gain recognized, if any, is included in the Section 1231 pool. Because MACRS requires that buildings acquired after 1986 must be depreciated under the straight-line method on such buildings, there will be no excess of accelerated over straight-line depreciation to be recaptured as ordinary income under Section 1250.

[12] *Internal Revenue Code,* Section 1231 provides that all gains (those recognized in excess of the amount treated as ordinary income) and all losses recognized from the dispositions of trade or business properties during the tax year must be pooled. If the total is a net gain, it is added to the capital gain pool. If the total is a net loss, it is treated as an ordinary loss.

[13] See *Opinions of the Accounting Principles Board, No. 29,* "Accounting for Nonmonetary Transactions" (New York: American Institute of Certified Public Accountants, 1973), and *Internal Revenue Code,* Section 1031.

rather than traded in ($110,000 versus $70,000), cash inflows in future years will be $16,000 greater as a result of the additional tax depreciation deductions ($40,000 additional depreciable basis × 40% tax rate). Although the overall out-of-pocket cost is the same for both alternatives, Milski Corporation is better off trading in the old machine rather than selling it because of the time value of money (see discussion of time value of money in Chapter 23).

For the Milski Corporation capital expenditure proposal, the cash inflow from the salvage sale at the end of the project will be fully taxable because the tax basis of the machine will be zero (that is, the machine will be fully depreciated in 8 years). Because the tax rate is 40 percent, the tax on the cash inflow from salvage will be $3,934 ($9,835 salvage value × 40% tax rate). The total after-tax cash inflows from the project will be increased by the after-tax cash inflow from salvaging the machine. Exhibit 22-6 shows the periodic tax payments (or reductions) and the after-tax inflation-adjusted cash flows with an assumed income tax rate of 40 percent.

EXHIBIT 22-6

Milski Corporation
Capital Expenditure Proposal for Machine Replacement
Estimated Inflation-Adjusted Net After-Tax Cash Inflows

Year	(1) Estimated Inflation-Adjusted Net Cash Inflows	(2) Adjusted Tax Depre-ciation	(3) Taxable Income (Reduction) (1) – (2)	(4) Federal and State Income Tax Rate	(5) Income Tax Payment (Reduction) (3) × (4)	(6) Net After-Tax Cash Inflows (1) – (5)
1	$16,050	$10,010	$ 6,040	40%	$ 2,416	$ 13,634
2	16,946	17,150	(204)	40%	(82)	17,028
3	17,885	12,250	5,635	40%	2,254	15,631
4	18,878	8,750	10,128	40%	4,051	14,827
5	19,923	6,230	13,693	40%	5,477	14,446
6	21,014	6,230	14,784	40%	5,914	15,100
7	22,484	6,230	16,254	40%	6,502	15,982
8	24,052	3,150	20,902	40%	8,361	15,691
9	25,732	0	25,732	40%	10,293	15,439
10	27,538	0	27,538	40%	11,015	16,523
Total net after-tax cash inflows from additional sales and reduced costs						$154,301
After-tax cash inflow from salvage at end of economic life:						
Inflation adjusted cash inflow from salvage (Exhibit 22-3)					$ 9,835	
Tax payable on salvage sale (40% × 9,385)					(3,934)	5,901
Total inflation-adjusted after-tax cash inflows..						$160,202

Because tax depreciation exceeds cash inflows in the second year, taxable income from activities other than the capital project is reduced for the year. The corresponding reduction in the overall tax payment is a cost savings that effectively increases cash inflow for the year.

Investment Tax Credit. A tax credit differs from a deduction in one very important respect. A tax credit reduces the tax liability directly, whereas a deduction reduces taxable income, thereby indirectly reducing the tax liability. If an **investment tax credit** were available on the purchase of depreciable property (computed by multiplying the credit rate times the qualifying cost of the property), the purchaser's tax liability would be reduced directly by the investment tax credit and then again indirectly through depreciation deductions. The investment tax credit was originally enacted in 1962 for the stated purpose of stimulating the economy and generating additional employment by providing an incentive to business to invest and expand. Congress has repealed, reenacted, increased, and expanded the investment tax credit to meet varying economic conditions. The investment tax credit was repealed by the Tax Reform Act of 1986. Although the investment tax credit has not been a stable feature of the income tax law, it is an important capital expenditure consideration during periods when it is available, because it reduces income tax expense at the end of a project's first year.

When last a part of the law, the investment tax credit was available on the acquisition of most tangible property (other than buildings). The law has sometimes required that the property's depreciable basis be reduced by all or part of the credit claimed. When repealed in 1986, the most recent version of the investment tax credit required that the property's depreciable basis be reduced by 50 percent of the amount of the credit claimed. The regular credit rate was 10 percent. If new property was acquired in exchange for a trade-in of an old machine, the qualified cost for purposes of computing the investment tax credit was the tax basis of the old property plus the cash paid. On the other hand, when used property was acquired in a trade-in, the qualified cost was limited to the cash paid for the property.

Construction Period Interest and Taxes. *Statement of Financial Accounting Standards, No. 34,* "Capitalization of Interest Cost,"[14] prescribes the capitalization of interest costs incurred in the acquisition of assets that require a period of time to be made ready for their intended use, provided the effect on periodic income is material. The amount capitalized is recovered through depreciation over the economic life of the new asset. On the other hand, for federal income tax purposes, both construction period interest and taxes must be capitalized.[15] The tax law limits the capitalization of such costs to the acquisition or construction of property that meets any one of the following tests: (1) the property has a class life of 20 years or more, (2) the estimated construction period exceeds 2 years, or (3) the estimated construction period exceeds 1 year and the estimated construction costs exceed $1,000,000.[16] In addition, the tax law requires the capitalization not only of interest paid or accrued on funds specifically borrowed to construct the property but also of a portion of the interest paid or accrued on other liabilities if construction cost exceeds funds borrowed specifically to finance the project.[17]

In capital expenditure proposals that involve acquisition or construction of property over a period of time, the initial cash outflow is increased by both interest and taxes incurred during the construction period. Cash inflows in subsequent periods are increased by the reduction in income taxes that result from the amortization of the interest and taxes that had been capitalized during the construction period.

Economic Evaluation of Cash Flows

Ordinarily capital expenditures made for strategic or qualitative reasons are not subjected to economic evaluation.[18] In some cases, the data necessary to evaluate

---

[14] (Stamford, Conn.: Financial Accounting Standards Board, 1979).

[15] *Internal Revenue Code,* Section 263A(a)(2)(B) and Section 263A(f).

[16] *Internal Revenue Code,* Section 263A(f)(1)(B).

[17] *Internal Revenue Code,* Section 263A(f)(2)(A).

[18] See Ralph Pope, "Current Capital Budgeting Practices: A Comparison of Small and Large Firms," *Southwest Journal of Business and Economics,* Vol. 4, No. 2, pp. 16–24.

such projects are not available. In other cases, the strategic or qualitative importance of the expenditure may be considered more important than the cost.[19] If the primary motive for the investment is increasing company profits, however, the cash flows for the project should be estimated, and quantitative economic evaluation techniques should be used to determine the desirability of making the expenditure. Four different economic evaluation methods are frequently and widely used in practice: (1) the payback method, (2) the accounting rate of return method, (3) the net present value method, and (4) the internal rate of return method. Each of these techniques is discussed and illustrated in Chapter 23 using the cash flow data developed in the Milski Corporation example.

Controlling Capital Expenditures

The control of capital expenditures consists of control and review of a project in process and follow-up or postaudit of results.

Control While in Process

When a project or a series of projects has been approved, all project elements (costs, time, quality, and quantity) should be controlled and reviewed until construction or acquisition is completed. Control responsibility should be clearly designated; the need for assistance and coordination from many individuals, including those external to the company, should be recognized. Actual results should be compared with approved plans. Variations from plans should be reported promptly to responsible authorities to facilitate timely corrective action. Day-to-day, on-the-scene observation and up-to-date reports are good cost control vehicles.

PERT/cost (Chapter 16) is a network scheme showing the interrelationships among activities required to complete a project. Any project—the installation of a single large machine, a complex of machinery and equipment, or the construction of a new factory or office building—involves many diverse tasks. Some of them can be done simultaneously; others must await the completion of preceding activities. PERT/cost offers a clear and all-inclusive picture of the operation as a whole. This technique is particularly appropriate for cases in which more than one estimate is needed due to risk and uncertainty and when there is a desire to expedite and increase the reliability of difficult estimates.

The cost of administering the control phase should be commensurate with the value derived. Overcontrol is an inefficient use of administrative resources.

Follow-up of Project Results

A **follow-up** or **post audit** compares the actual results of a capital expenditure with the outcome that was expected when the investment project was approved. Follow-up provides the possibility of reinforcing successful projects, salvaging or terminating failing projects, and improving future investment proposals and decisions. In addition, the expectation of a postaudit can encourage managers to make more realistic estimates during the proposal stage.

---

[19] In cases in which neither the economic benefits nor the strategic benefits clearly outweigh the cost of the capital expenditure proposal, a decision support system that provides a way of quantifying both kinds of benefits may prove useful. See David E. Stout, Matthew J. Liberatore, and Thomas F. Monahan, "Decision Support Software for Capital Budgeting," *Management Accounting,* Vol. 73, No. 1, pp. 50–53.

After the construction and acquisition phase has been completed, the actual cash inflows from the project should be monitored and compared with those budgeted in each period. If actual cash inflows or outflows depart substantially from those budgeted, the cause should be determined and corrective action taken, if necessary. If corrective action requires an additional expenditure, an evaluation of future benefits and costs should be made. If the project cannot be put back on track, it should be abandoned and the property used in the project should be salvaged or converted to some other use.

Not only cash flows, but also qualitative benefits should be monitored and compared with those projected. Qualitative benefits—such as improved product quality, reduced setup times, shorter throughput times, and reduced manpower and inventory levels—are often the primary reasons for accepting a capital expenditure proposal. This is particularly important when the expected cost of a proposal exceeds its projected economic value.

Because qualitative benefits are often affected by more than one asset acquisition, strategic investments at Caterpillar Inc. are bundled into groups of assets that were acquired for a common purpose (for example, a new manufacturing process or a new product or product group). The qualitative benefits expected for each bundle are then monitored, and corrective action is taken for bundles not performing up to expectation.[20]

Although actual work in the area of follow-up lags behind advances made in other capital expenditure phases, there is a trend toward adopting follow-up procedures.[21] Common hindrances to follow-up include management's unwillingness to incur additional administrative costs, the difficulty of quantifying the results of certain types of investments, apparent failure of the accounting or cost system to produce needed information, lack of personnel qualified to perform the follow-up tasks, and resentment by those being audited.

The cost of obtaining follow-up information should be weighed against the expected value of the follow-up. For uniformity, efficiency, and independent review, management should designate a centralized group to prescribe procedures and audit the performance of the follow-up activity. The assembled data should be utilized as a control device and should be reported to the controlling levels of management. Out-of-line results should trigger corrective action, to achieve management by exception.

Summary

Because the size of capital expenditures is often large and the period over which the benefits are to be realized from the investment is long, the process of planning, evaluating, and controlling capital expenditures has significant, long-term effects. Because a firm must earn a reasonable return on invested funds in order to survive in the long run, considerable attention has been devoted to techniques for evaluating capital expenditure proposals. However, equally important is the effective planning and control of such expenditures. The processes of planning for capital expenditures, evaluating proposals, estimating cash flows, and controlling capital expenditures were discussed in this chapter.

[20] James A. Hendricks, Robert C. Bastian, and Thomas L. Sexton, "Bundle Monitoring of Strategic Projects," *Management Accounting,* Vol. 73, No. 8, pp. 31–35.

[21] Lawrence A. Gordon and Mary D. Meyers, "Postauditing Capital Projects," *Management Accounting,* Vol. 72, No. 7, pp. 39–42.

Key Terms

capital expenditures *(655)*
capital budgeting *(655)*
replacement expenditures *(660)*
expansion investments *(660)*
improvement expenditures *(660)*
salvage value *(662)*
accelerated cost recovery system (ACRS) *(666)*
modified ACRS (MACRS) *(666)*
investment tax credit *(669)*
follow-up or postaudit *(671)*

Discussion Questions

Q22-1 Why are effective planning and control of capital expenditures important?

Q22-2 The capital budgeting process provides both an opportunity and a temptation for unethical behavior. Give three examples.

Q22-3 What should the cost/managerial accountant do if faced with the ethical problems noted in question Q22-2?

Q22-4 Differentiate between the economic and physical life of a project.

Q22-5 List some cash outflows that might be expected for a capital expenditure.

Q22-6 List some sources of cash inflows that might be expected from a capital expenditure.

Q22-7 What are some nonquantifiable benefits of investing in such advanced manufacturing technologies as CIM, FMS, and robotics?

Q22-8 Is depreciation deducted for tax purposes likely to differ from book (or financial accounting) depreciation? Explain.

Q22-9 Should book depreciation be considered in the estimation of future cash flows of a proposed project? Explain.

Q22-10 Should tax depreciation be considered in the estimation of future cash flows of a proposed project? Explain.

Q22-11 Financial accounting data are not entirely suitable for use in evaluating capital expenditures. Explain. (AICPA adapted)

Q22-12 Discuss benefits to be derived from a follow-up of project results. (ICMA adapted)

Exercises

E22-1 Estimating Pretax Cash Inflows. Holland Corporation is considering purchasing a new machine to be used to manufacture a new product, called Dutchem, which will sell for $25 a unit. Variable manufacturing cost is expected to be $12 for each unit of Dutchem manufactured, and variable marketing cost is expected to be $3 for each unit sold. The machine being considered can produce 12,000 units a year, all of which the Marketing Department believes can be sold for $25 a unit. The proposed machine will cost $500,000. Although the machine will probably last 10 years, management believes that the product's life cycle will be only 5 years. The salvage value of the new machine at the end of the product's 5-year life cycle is expected to be $100,000. Management does not believe the machine can be used to manufacture any of the company's other products.

Required: Compute the pretax net cash inflow expected from the capital expenditure proposal for each year; and ignoring the effect of income taxes, determine the excess of cash inflows from all sources over the cost of the machine.

E22-2 Estimating Pretax Cash Inflows. Falcon Company is considering purchasing a new machine to be used to manufacture a new product, called Hyflier, which will sell for $12 a unit. Variable manufacturing cost is expected to be $8 for each unit of Hyflier manufactured, and variable marketing cost is expected to be $1 for each unit sold. The machine being considered will cost $150,000 and can produce a maximum of 10,000 units a year. Although the machine will probably last 15 years, management believes that the product's life cycle will be only 10 years. The salvage value of the new machine at the end of the product's 10-year life cycle is expected to be $15,000. Management does not believe the machine can be used to manufacture any of the company's other products. Sales expected during the products life cycle are as follow:

Year	Sales in Units of Product
1	6,000
2	8,000
3	10,000
4	10,000
5	10,000
6	10,000
7	10,000
8	8,000
9	6,000
10	4,000

Required: Compute the pretax adjusted net cash inflow expected from the capital expenditure proposal for each year; and ignoring the effects of income taxes on cash flows, determine the excess of cash inflows from all sources over the cost of the machine.

E22-3 Adjusting Estimated Cash Inflows for Anticipated Inflation. Jiffy Corporation is considering a capital expenditure proposal that will require an initial cash outlay of $75,000. The project life is expected to be 6 years. The estimated salvage value for the equipment (based on today's market price for similar used 6-year old equipment) is $5,000. Estimated annual net cash inflows from operations during the life of the project are as follow:

Year	Estimated Annual Cash Inflow
1	$15,000
2	20,000
3	20,000
4	20,000
5	15,000
6	10,000

Required: Compute the excess of cash inflows over cash outflows assuming management expects a constant 6% rate of inflation during the 6-year period. (Round the price level index to three decimal places.)

E22-4 Adjusting Estimated Cash Inflows for Anticipated Inflation. Wampum Company is considering a capital expenditure proposal that will require an initial cash outlay of $250,000. The project life is expected to be 10 years, after which the equipment will have an expected salvage value of $10,000 (not considering the effect of inflation). In addition, estimated annual net cash inflows from operations during the life of the project are as follow:

Year	Estimated Annual Cash Inflow
1	$20,000
2	30,000
3	40,000
4	60,000
5	60,000
6	60,000
7	60,000
8	60,000
9	40,000
10	20,000

Required: Compute the inflation-adjusted net cash inflows for each year and the excess of cash inflows over cash outflows assuming a constant 9% rate of inflation during the 10-year period. (Round your price level index to three decimal places.)

E22-5 Estimating After-Tax Cash Flows for CIM Project. Sparta Corporation is considering the various benefits that may result from the shortening of its production cycle by changing from the company's present manufacturing system to a computer integrated manufacturing (CIM) system. The proposed system can provide productive time equivalence close to the 20,000 hours available annually with the company's present system. The present system costs $20 per hour more to operate than the proposed CIM system. The company expects to operate the system at full capacity. The annual out-of-pocket costs of maintaining the proposed CIM system are $200,000 more than the company's present system. The proposed CIM system will require an initial investment of $600,000. The system is expected to have a useful life of 6 years with no expected salvage value. The company is in the 40% tax rate bracket.

Required: Compute the relevant annual after-tax cash flows expected from the CIM project. (Assume the equipment is 5-year class MACRS property, and use the rates provided in Exhibit 22-4 to compute tax depreciation.) (AICPA adapted)

E22-6 Computing After-Tax Cash Inflows. Nix Company is considering a capital expenditure with the following estimated net cash inflows:

Year	Estimated Pretax Inflation Adjusted Net Cash Inflow
1	$30,000
2	40,000
3	50,000
4	60,000
5	70,000
6	80,000
7	60,000

The equipment required for the project will have an initial cost of $200,000, and it is not expected to have any salvage value at the end of the life of the project. The equipment will be depreciated using the straight-line method over its economic life of 7 years for book purposes; however, it qualifies as 5-year property for tax purposes. The company's effective tax rate is 40%.

Required: Determine the estimated after-tax net cash inflow for each of the project's 7 years, and compute the total excess of cash inflows over cash outflows for the life of the project. (Use the MACRS rates provided in Exhibit 22-4 to compute tax depreciation.)

E22-7 Computing After-Tax Cash Inflows. Utex Corporation is considering a capital expenditure with the following estimated net cash inflows:

Year	Estimated Pretax Inflation-Adjusted Net Cash Inflow
1	$10,000
2	15,000
3	20,000
4	25,000
5	25,000
6	25,000
7	25,000
8	20,000
9	15,000
10	10,000

The equipment required for the project will have an initial cost of $100,000, and it is expected to have a salvage value at the end of the life of the project of $10,000. The equipment will be depreciated using the straight-line method over its economic life of 10 years for book purposes; however, it qualifies as 7-year property for tax purposes. The company's effective tax rate is 40%.

Required: Determine the estimated after-tax net cash inflow for each of the project's 10 years, and compute the excess of total cash inflows over the original cost of the equipment. (Use the MACRS rates provided in Exhibit 22-4 to compute tax depreciation.)

Problems

P22-1 Effect of Inflation and Taxes on Investment Decision. Fargonn Company is evaluating a capital expenditure proposal that will require an initial cash investment of $60,000. The project will have a 6-year life; however, the property will qualify as 5-year property for income tax depreciation purposes. The income tax rate is 40%. The annual cash inflows from the project, before any adjustment for the effects of inflation or income taxes, are expected to be as follow:

Year	Unadjusted Estimate of Cash Inflows
1	$20,000
2	22,000
3	24,000
4	18,000
5	15,000
6	10,000

The expected salvage value of the property is zero. Cash inflows are expected to increase at the anticipated inflation rate of 8% each year.

Required: Compute the inflation-adjusted after-tax cash inflow from the proposal for each year, and determine the excess of total net cash inflows over the initial cash outlay. (Use the MACRS depreciation rates provided in Exhibit 22-4 to compute tax depreciation, and round the price-level index to three decimal places.)

P22-2 Equipment Replacement Analysis. Kipling Company purchased a special machine 1 year ago for $10,000. At that time, the machine was estimated to have a useful life of 7 years with a $500 salvage value. A MACRS tax deduction of $2,000 was taken in the year of acquisition. The annual cash operating cost is $20,000.

A new machine that has just come on the market will do the same job but with an annual cash operating cost of only $16,000. This new machine costs $18,000 and has an estimated life of 6 years with no expected salvage value. The old machine can be used as a trade-in at an allowance of $9,000. The tax basis of the old machine is $8,000.

Both old and new machines qualify as 5-year property under MACRS, and the income tax rate is 40%.

Required: Compute the after-tax periodic cash inflows available from the purchase of the new machine, and determine the excess of periodic net cash inflows over the initial cash outlay. (Use the MACRS depreciation rates provided in Exhibit 22-4 to compute tax depreciation.)

P22-3 Make-or-Buy Decision Requiring Capital Expenditure Analysis. Lyons Company manufactures several lines of machine products. One unique part, a valve stem, requires specialized tools that need to be replaced. Management has decided that the only alternative to replacing these tools is to acquire the valve stem from an outside source. A supplier is willing to provide the valve stem at a unit sales price of $20 if at least 70,000 units are ordered annually.

Lyons' average usage of valve stems over the past 3 years has been 80,000 units each year. Expectations are that this volume will remain constant over the next 5 years. Cost records indicate that unit manufacturing costs for the last several years have been as follows:

Direct materials	$ 3.80
Direct labor	3.70
Variable overhead	1.70
Fixed overhead*	4.50
Total unit cost	$13.70

* Financial accounting depreciation accounts for two thirds of the fixed overhead. The balance is for other fixed overhead costs of the factory that require cash expenditures.

If the specialized tools are purchased, they will cost $2,500,000 and will have a disposal value of $100,000 after their expected economic life of 5 years. Straight-line depreciation is used for financial accounting purposes, but the most accelerated method available under MACRS is used for tax purposes. The specialized tools are considered 3-year property for MACRS purposes. The income tax rate is 40%.

The sales representative for the manufacturer of the new tools states: "The new tools will allow direct labor and variable overhead to be reduced by 80 cents per unit or $1.60 total reduction per unit." Another manufacturer, using identical tools and experiencing similar operating conditions, finds that annual production generally averages 110,000 units. This manufacturer confirms the direct labor and variable overhead savings. However, the manufacturer indicates that it did experience an increase in raw materials cost due to the higher quality of materials that had to be used with the new tools. The manufacturer indicated that its costs have been as follow:

Direct materials	$ 4.50
Direct labor	3.00
Variable overhead	.80
Fixed overhead	5.00
Total unit cost	$13.30

Required:

(1) Determine the annual net after-tax cash inflows available to Lyons Company if it purchases the new tools and manufactures the valve stem rather than purchasing the valve stems from the outside supplier. In this case the cash inflows will be from cost savings. (Use the MACRS rate provided in Exhibit 22-4 to compute tax depreciation.)

(2) By how much will the total after-tax cash inflows exceed the initial investment? (ICMA adapted)

P22-4 Feasibility Study. Winter-Sport Inc. is considering the installation of a ski lift facility in Hidden Valley, Colorado, which will require an investment of $200,000 for equipment. The equipment will have a 10-year economic life with no expected salvage value, and it will be 7-year property for income tax depreciation purposes. The income tax rate is 40%. The estimated annual revenues and expenses over the life of the project are as follow:

Year	Revenues	Operating Expenses	Lease Payments
1	$100,000	$40,000	$20,000
2	120,000	50,000	20,000
3	140,000	60,000	20,000
4	140,000	60,000	20,000
5	140,000	60,000	20,000
6	140,000	60,000	20,000
7	140,000	60,000	20,000
8	140,000	60,000	20,000
9	120,000	60,000	20,000
10	100,000	60,000	20,000

Winter-Sport management believes that the annual rate of inflation during the 10-year period will be 6%. Inflation is expected to affect both revenues and operating expenses equally; however, the lease payments to the government for use of the ski runs will not be affected because they are fixed by contract.

Required: Compute the annual inflation-adjusted after-tax cash inflows for the proposed capital expenditure, and compute the amount by which total after-tax cash inflows exceed the initial investment. (Use the

MACRS rate provided in Exhibit 22-4 to compute tax depreciation, and round the price level index to three decimal places.)

P22-5 Equipment Replacement Analysis. Plankitt Corporation is considering the purchase of a replacement machine. The new machine is priced at $54,000. However, the vendor has offered Plankitt a $14,000 trade-in allowance for its old machine. The old machine has a net book value of $10,000 and a tax basis of zero. The new machine will perform essentially the same function as the old machine, except that it will be able to produce 1,000 more units of product than the old machine each year. Each unit of product currently sells for $11. The variable cost of manufacturing the product is $4 a unit whether the new or the old machine is used, and variable marketing costs are $1 a unit. In addition to increased output, the new machine is expected to reduce maintenance costs by the following amounts:

Year	Cash Savings Related to Maintenance
1	$1,500
2	1,200
3	900
4	600
5	300

For financial accounting purposes, the new machine is to be depreciated on a straight-line basis over a period of 7 years, with an expected salvage value of $6,000 (based on current period prices). For tax purposes, however, the machine will be depreciated under MACRS as 5-year-class property. The tax rate is 40%. The anticipated inflation rate is 10%. All cash inflows and outflows are expected to be affected equally by inflation.

Required:

(1) Compute the inflation-adjusted after-tax cash flows that will be generated by the project for each year and in total. (Use the MACRS rates provided in Exhibit 22-4 to compute tax depreciation, and round the price-level index to three decimal places.)

(2) Compute the amount by which total after-tax cash inflows exceed the initial investment.

P22-6 Equipment Purchase Analysis; Inflation Adjustment. Morrison Company is considering the purchase of a large press costing $100,000. The estimated cash inflows before considering the effects of inflation and income taxes are considered follow:

Year	Unadjusted Cash Inflow
1	$15,000
2	20,000
3	25,000
4	25,000
5	25,000
6	25,000
7	25,000
8	20,000
9	15,000
10	10,000

For financial accounting purposes, the press is to be depreciated on a straight-line basis over a period of 10 years. Salvage value at the end of a 10-year life, based on current prices, will be about $2,000. For tax purposes, however, the press will be depreciated under MACRS, using the rates for 7-year property. The company's tax rate is 40%. The annual inflation rate is expected to be 10% for the planning period.

Required: Compute the inflation-adjusted after-tax cash inflow from the capital expenditure proposed for each year and the excess of total cash inflows over the initial cost of the capital project. (Use the MACRS rates provided in Exhibit 22-4, and round the price-level index to three decimal places.)

P22-7 Evaluating a Capital Expenditure Proposal for a CIM System; Inflation Adjustment. Largo Corporation is evaluating a capital expenditure proposal to acquire and install a computer integrated manufacturing system.

The proposed CIM system will have the same total productive capacity as the current manufacturing system. The computer equipment and machinery will require an initial cash investment of $1,000,000. The system has a projected life of 6 years; however, the equipment and machinery will qualify as 5-year property for income tax depreciation purposes. The income tax rate is 40%. In addition, installation and software development are expected to cost another $200,000 in the first year. Software costs are amortizable for tax purposes by the straight-line method over a 5-year period. Maintenance costs are expected to increase by $10,000 a year over the current system. The annual cash savings from the CIM system relative to the current manufacturing system (before any adjustment for inflation or income taxes) are expected to be as follows:

Year	Reduced Labor Cost	Reduced Machine Setup Time	Reduced Inventory Carrying Cost
1	$15,000	$25,000	$20,000
2	25,000	30,000	25,000
3	35,000	35,000	30,000
4	35,000	35,000	30,000
5	35,000	35,000	30,000
6	35,000	35,000	30,000

The salvage value expected at the end of the project is zero. An annual inflation rate of 6% is expected to affect all cash flows over the life of the project.

Required:

(1) Compute the inflation-adjusted after-tax cash inflow from savings for the CIM proposal for each year, and determine whether the total cash savings from the CIM system will exceed the system's cost. (Use the MACRS depreciation rates provided in Exhibit 22-4 for the equipment and machinery, and compute straight-line amortization for the software. Round the price-level index to three decimal places.)

(2) In addition to the facts already presented, assume management believes its principal competitor plans to acquire a CIM system. Unless Largo acquires a CIM system, it will not be able to compete effectively. Management estimates that without the CIM system, it will lose sales amounting to a loss in contribution margin of $200,000 each year (before the effects of inflation are considered). Based on this new information, recompute the after-tax cash inflow for each year, and determine whether the total cash savings from the CIM system will exceed the system's costs.

Cases

C22-1 Relevant Data for Investment Decision. Clewash Linen Supply Company provides laundered items to various commercial and service establishments in a large city. Clewash is scheduled to acquire some new cleaning equipment in mid-19A, which will enable the company to increase the volume of laundry it handles without any increase in labor costs. In addition, the estimated maintenance costs in terms of pounds of laundry processed will be reduced slightly.

The new equipment is justified not only on the basis of reduced cost but also on the basis of expected increase in demand starting in late 19A. However, since the original forecast was prepared, several potential new customers have either delayed or discontinued their own expansion plans in the market area serviced by Clewash, and the most recent forecast indicates that no great increase in demand can be expected until late 19B or early 19C.

Required: Identify and explain factors that tend to indicate whether the investment should be made as scheduled or delayed. (ICMA adapted)

C22-2 Decentralization and the Management of Capital Expenditures. Judy Knight founded the Neoglobe Company over 30 years ago. Although she has relied heavily on advice from other members of management, Knight has made all of the important decisions for the company. Neoglobe has been successful, experiencing steady growth in its early years and very rapid growth in recent years. During this period of rapid growth, Knight has had difficulty keeping up with the many decisions that need to be made. She feels that she is losing control of the company's progress.

Regular discussions regarding her concern have been held with George Armet, the company's executive vice-president. As a result of these discussions, Armet has studied possible alternative organizational structures that could replace the present highly centralized functional organization.

In a carefully prepared proposal, Armet recommended that the company reorganize according to its two product lines–plastic products and brass products—because their technology (both marketing skills and equipment) and marketing methods are quite different. The change can be accomplished easily because the products are manufactured in different plants. The marketing effort is also segregated along product lines within the sales function. The number of executive positions will not change, although the duties of the positions will change. There will no longer be the need for a vice-president for manufacturing or a vice-president for sales. Those positions will be replaced with the vice-president for each of the two product lines. Armet acknowledges that there may be personnel problems at the executive management level, because the current vice-presidents may not be competent to manage within the new structure.

Armet's proposal also contained the recommendation that some of the decision-making power, long held by Knight, be transferred to the new vice-presidents. Armet argued that this would be good for the company. The vice-presidents would be more aware of the problems and solution alternatives of their respective product lines because they are closer to the operations. Fewer decisions would be required of each new vice-president than are now required of Knight. This should reduce the time between problem recognition and implementation of the solution. Armet further argued that distributing the decision making power will improve the creativity and spirit of company management.

Knight is intrigued by the proposal and the prospect that it would make the company more manageable. However, the proposal did not spell out clearly which decisions should be transferred and which should remain with the president. Knight requested Armet to prepare a supplemental memorandum specifying the decisions to be delegated to the vice-presidents.

The supplemental memorandum presented the recommended decision areas, explaining in each case how the new vice-presidents would be closer to the situation and thereby be able to make prompt, sound decisions. The following list summarizes Armet's recommendations:

1. Sales
   a. Price policy
   b. Promotional strategy
   c. Credit policy
2. Operations
   a. Manufacturing procedures
   b. Labor negotiations
3. Development of existing product lines
4. Capital investment decision—up to amounts not exceeding the division depreciation flow plus 25% of its after-tax income (excluding ventures into new fields).

The corporate management (Knight and Armet) will be responsible for overall corporate development. Also, they will allocate the remaining available cash flow for dividends, for investment projects above the limits prescribed, and for investment into new ventures.

Required: Knight believes that the proposal, as presented, will not work. In Knight's judgment, the corporate-level management will be unable to control effectively the destiny of the firm because the proposal grants too much investment freedom to the new divisions. Do you agree with Knight that effective control over the future of the firm cannot be maintained at the corporate level if the capital rationing is shared in the manner specified in the proposal? Support your answer with appropriate discussion, including a recommended alternative procedure if you agree with Knight.

(ICMA adapted)

C22-3 Capital Expenditure Administration and Project Evaluation. The management of McAngus Inc. has never used formal planning techniques in the operation of its business. The president of McAngus has expressed interest in the recommendation of its accountants that the company investigate various techniques it could use to manage the business more effectively.

McAngus, a medium-sized manufacturer, has grown steadily. It recently acquired another company located approximately 1,000 miles away. The new company manufactures a line of products that complements the present product line. Both manufacturing plants have significant investments in land, buildings, machinery, and equipment. Each plant is to be operated as a separate division headed by a division manager. Each division manager is to have virtually complete authority for the management of her or his division—each will be primarily responsible for the profit contribution of her or his division. A complete set of financial statements is to be prepared for each division as well as for the company.

The president and the current management team intend to concentrate their efforts on coordinating the activities of the two divisions and investigating and evaluating such things as new markets, new product lines, and new business acquisition possibilities. Because of the cash required for the recent acquisition and the cash needs for desired future expansion, the president is particularly concerned about cash flow and the effective management of cash.

Required: Explain the objectives and describe the process that McAngus can use to plan for and evaluate the long-term commitment of its resources, including cash. (AICPA adapted)

C22-4 Ethical Considerations in Capital Budgeting. The Fore Corporation is an integrated food-processing company that has operations in over two dozen countries.

Fore's corporate headquarters is in Chicago, and the company's executives frequently travel to visit Fore's foreign and domestic facilities.

Fore has a fleet of aircraft comprising two business jets with international range and six smaller turbine aircraft, which are used on shorter flights. Company policy is to assign aircraft to trips on the basis of minimizing cost, but the practice is to assign the aircraft based on the organizational rank of the traveler. Fore offers other organizations its aircraft for short-term lease or for charter whenever Fore itself does not use the aircraft. Fore surveys the market often in order to keep its lease and charter rates competitive.

W. Earle, Fore's vice-president of finance, has claimed that a third business jet can be justified financially. However, some staff in the controller's office have surmised that the real reason for a third business jet is to upgrade the aircraft used by Earle. Presently, the people outranking Earle keep the two business jets busy, with the result that Earle usually flies in smaller turbine aircraft.

The third business jet will cost $11 million. A capital expenditure of this magnitude requires a formal proposal with projected cash flows and net present value computations using Fore's minimum required rate of return. If Fore's president and the finance committee of the board of directors approve the proposal, it will be submitted to the full board of directors. The board has final approval on capital expenditures exceeding $5 million, and has established a firm policy of rejecting any discretionary proposal that has projected cash outflows in excess of cash inflows.

Earle asked R. Arnett, assistant corporate controller, to prepare a proposal for a third business jet. Arnett gathered the following data:

(a) Acquisition cost of the aircraft, including instrumentation and interior furnishing.
(b) Operating cost of the aircraft for company use.
(c) Projected avoidable commercial airfare and other avoidable costs from company use of the plane.
(d) Projected value of executive time saved by using the third business jet.
(e) Projected contribution margin from incremental lease and charter activity.
(f) Estimated resale value of the aircraft.
(g) Estimated income tax effects of the proposal.

When Earle reviewed Arnett's completed proposal and observed that projected cash inflows were less than cash outflows, he returned the proposal to Arnett. With a glare, Earle commented, "You must have made an error. The proposal should look better than that."

Feeling some pressure, Arnett went back and checked the computations and found no errors. However, Earle's message was clear. Arnett discarded the realistic projections and estimates and replaced them with figures that had only a remote chance of actually occurring but that were more favorable to the proposal. For example, first class airfares were used to refigure the avoidable commercial airfare costs, even though company policy was to fly coach, and charter and lease time was increased to 100% of the expected time not used by Fore instead of the 50% actual experience rate. Arnett found revising the proposal to be distressing.

The revised proposal still had projected cash inflows less than cash outflows. Earle's anger was evident, and Arnett was directed to revise the proposal again, and to start with a $100,000 positive net cash inflow (that is, $100,000 of cash inflows in excess of cash outflows) and work backward to compute supporting estimates and projections.

Required:

(1) Explain whether Arnett's revision of the proposal was in violation of the Standards of Ethical Conduct for Management Accountants (see Chapter 1).
(2) Was Earle in violation of the Standards of Ethical Conduct for Management Accountants by telling Arnett how to revise the proposal? Explain.
(3) What elements of the projection and estimation process are compromised in preparing an analysis for which a preconceived result is sought?
(4) Identify specific internal controls that Fore Corporation could implement to prevent unethical behavior on the part of the vice-president of finance.

(ICMA adapted)

C22-5 Ethical Problems in Capital Budgeting. Evans Company must expand its manufacturing capabilities to meet the growing demand for its products and is considering two alternatives. The first alternative involves expanding its current manufacturing plant, which is located next to a vacant lot in the heart of the city. The second alternative is the conversion of a warehouse, already owned by Evans, that is located approximately 20 miles outside the city. Both alternatives involve large capital expenditures and will require approval by the company's board of directors. The board has final approval on capital expenditures exceeding $1,000,000, and has established a firm policy of rejecting any proposal that has a negative net present value.

Evans' controller, G. Watson, is responsible for the preparation of formal proposals for both alternatives; these proposals must include projected cash flows and net present value computations. Watson has assigned H. Dodge, assistant controller, to assist in the preparation of these proposals. Dodge has completed both proposals for Watson's review. The proposal for the expansion of the current manufacturing facility has a slightly positive net present value. However, the first draft of the proposal for the warehouse conversion has a large negative present value.

When Watson reviewed Dodge's first draft of the warehouse conversion proposal and saw the large negative net present value, he was displeased. He returned the proposal to Dodge with the comment, "You must have made an error. This proposal should look better."

Dodge suspected that Watson was anxious to have the warehouse proposal selected because the choice of this location would eliminate his long commute into the city. Feeling some pressure, Dodge rechecked the computations but found no errors. Dodge then reviewed the projections and estimates that had been used. Although the projections used seemed reasonable, Dodge discarded some of them and replaced them with more favorable estimates that seemed to Dodge to have a remote chance of occurring. Nevertheless, Dodge was comfortable with these revisions.

The revised proposal for the warehouse conversion still had a negative net present value. Watson's anger was evident as he told Dodge to prepare a second revision of the proposal. This time Watson told Dodge to start with a $250,000 positive cash flow and work backward to compute supporting estimates and projections. Dodge is distressed at being compelled to use this approach.

Required:

(1) Refer to the specific standards of competence, confidentiality, integrity, and objectivity in the Standards of Ethical Conduct for Management Accountants (discussed in Chapter 1). Explain the following:
  (a) Was H. Dodge's first revision of the proposal for the warehouse conversion unethical?
  (b) In what way was G. Watson's conduct unethical when he gave H. Dodge specific instructions to prepare the second revision of the proposal?

(2) Identify the steps recommended by the Standards of Ethical Conduct for Management Accountants that H. Dodge should follow in attempting to resolve this situation. (ICMA adapted)

C22-6 Ethical Concerns in Capital Budgeting. L. Forrest is a member of the planning and analysis staff for IDI Inc. Forrest has been asked by B. Rolland, chief financial offer of IDI, to prepare a capital expenditure analysis for a proposal to modernize the Western Plant. Because of the size of the proposed investment, this analysis will be given to the board of directors for expenditure approval.

Several years ago, as director of planning and analysis at IDI, Rolland was instrumental in convincing the board to open the Western Plant. However, recent competitive pressures have forced all of IDI's manufacturing divisions to consider alternatives to improve their market position. To Rolland's dismay, the Western Plant may be sold in the near future unless significant improvements in cost control and production efficiency are achieved.

Western's production manager, an old friend of Rolland, has submitted a proposal for the acquisition of an automated materials movement system. Rolland is anxious to have this proposal approved because it will ensure the continuance of the Western Plant and preserve her friend's position. The plan calls for the replacement of a number of forklift trucks and operators with a computer-controlled conveyer-belt system that feeds directly into refrigeration units. This automation would eliminate the need for a number of materials handlers and increase the output capacity of the plant.

Rolland gave this proposal to Forrest along with the data to be used in making the capital expenditure analysis. When Forrest completed his analysis, the proposed project appeared quite healthy. However, after investigating equipment similar to that proposed, Forrest discovered that the estimated residual value of $850,000 was very optimistic; information previously provided by several vendors estimates this value to be $100,000. Forrest also discovered that instead of 12 years industry trade publications considered 8 years to be the maximum life of similar conveyor-belt systems. As a result, Forrest prepared a second analysis based on this new information. When Rolland saw the second analysis, she told Forrest to discard this revised material, warned him not to discuss the new estimates with anyone at IDI, and ordered him not to present any of this information to the board of directors.

Required: Refer to the Standards of Ethical Conduct for Management Accountants (discussed in Chapter 1).

(1) Explain how L. Forrest, a management accountant, should evaluate B. Rolland's directives to repress the revised analysis. Take into consideration the specific standards of competence, confidentiality, integrity, and/or objectivity.

(2) Identify the specific steps L. Forrest should take to resolve this situation. (ICMA adapted)

CHAPTER 23

Economic Evaluation of Capital Expenditures

Learning Objectives

After studying this chapter, you will be able to:

1. Define the cost of capital and compute it.
2. Compute the payback period for a capital expenditure proposal.
3. Compute the accounting rate of return for a capital expenditure proposal.
4. Explain the concept of the time value of money.
5. Compute the net present value for a capital expenditure proposal.
6. Compute the internal rate of return for a capital expenditure proposal.

The economic evaluation of capital expenditure proposals has received considerable attention in the accounting literature, with good reason. To survive in the long run, a firm must be profitable. Capital investments require the commitment of substantial resources for relatively long periods of time. Poor investments can therefore have a material long-term effect on a firm's profitability and survival. Four commonly used project evaluation techniques are discussed in detail in this chapter. These techniques can be useful in the selection of projects that will maximize company profits, but excessive reliance on quantitative answers is dangerous. Because the life of a capital project extends well into the future, the data used in its quantitative analysis are fraught with uncertainty. It is difficult to predict accurately what will happen next year, and even more difficult to predict what will happen several years in the future. Furthermore, because predictions of future costs and revenues unavoidably contain elements of subjectivity, such data can be manipulated easily by overzealous or misguided employees.

The Cost of Capital

The **cost of capital** represents the expected return that investors demand for a given level of risk. Although this discussion is brief, the cost of capital as it relates to capital expenditures is a complex concept. The specific cost of financing a specific project often is called the **marginal cost of capital.** In this context the cost of capital directly links the financing decision with the investment decision. However, the usefulness of this concept for allocating capital has been challenged, because businesses rely on more than one source of funds to finance their activities. The funds available for one or all capital projects are usually considered to be a commingling of more than one source. In this context, the cost of capital is referred to as the **weighted-average cost of capital.** The weighted-average cost of capital varies over time and from firm to firm, depending on the mix and proportion of the sources of funds used to finance a business. Companies typically obtain funds from (1) bond issues, (2) preferred and common stock issues, (3) loans from banks, and (4) periodic earnings. The weighted-average cost of capital reflects the joint cost of all sources of funds. In the evaluation of future investments, the relative proportions and the cost of each source of funds used in computing the weighted-average cost of capital should be those expected over the investment horizon.[1] In practice, the relative proportions used are likely to be those desired by management in the long run, and the costs used are those currently applicable, adjusted for anticipated inflation. The computation of the weighted-average cost of capital can be illustrated as follows:

Source of Funds	(1) Proportion of Total Funds to Be Provided	(2) After-Tax Cost of Money Source	(3) Weighted-Average Cost (1) × (2)
Bonds	20%	5%	1%
Preferred stock	20	10	2
Common stock and retained earnings	60	15	9
Total	100%		12%

The cost of capital for each source is described as follows:

1. The cost of bonds is the after-tax rate of interest. Because interest expense is deductible for tax purposes, the after-tax rate of interest is the pretax rate of interest multiplied by one minus the tax rate. If bonds are sold at a premium or a discount, the premium or discount must be amortized for tax purposes; therefore, the rate used should be the after-tax market yield rate [market yield rate × (1 – tax rate)].
2. Because preferred dividends are not deductible for tax purposes, the cost of preferred stock is the dividend per share divided by the current market price per share.
3. The cost of common stock and retained earnings is the expected earnings per share, after income tax and after preferred dividends are paid, divided by the current market price per share.[2]

Economic Evaluation Techniques

Despite the fact that many capital expenditures are made for strategic or qualitative reasons (and therefore are not subjected to economic evaluation), quantitative economic evaluation techniques are widely used in practice.[3] The following four evaluation techniques are representative tools commonly found in current use: (1) the payback period method, (2) the accounting rate of return method, (3) the net present value method, and (4) the internal rate of return method. None of these methods serves every purpose or every firm. Circumstances determine the

[1] *Statement on Management Accounting, No. 4A,* "Cost of Capital" (Montvale, N.J.: Institute of Management Accountants (formerly the National Association of Accountants), 1984), pp. 3, 11.

[2] Conflicting opinions exist regarding the treatment of the investors' income tax effect on the cost of equity acquired through the retention of earnings.

[3] See Ralph Pope, "Current Capital Budgeting Practices: A Comparison of Small and Large Firms," *Southwest Journal of Business and Economics,* Vol. 4, No. 2, pp. 16-24.

appropriate choice of technique. Companies often use more than one technique (for example, payback period and internal rate of return) in evaluating projects, because different methods provide different insights. For example, the payback period is used to determine how quickly an initial investment will be recovered, whereas the accounting rate of return, the net present value, and the internal rate of return are measures of profitability. However, different projects cannot be compared unless the same methods are used uniformly for each project. The internal rate of return for one project is not comparable to the net present value of another. Comparing different projects that have not been evaluated with the same technique is like comparing apples and oranges.

These evaluation techniques, if thoroughly understood by the user, aid management in exercising judgment and making decisions. Certainly the cost of gathering data and applying the evaluation techniques should be justified in terms of the value of such activities to management. Moreover, inaccurate raw data used in the calculations or lack of uniform procedures can yield harmful or misleading conclusions.

For purposes of discussion and illustration of the four commonly used economic evaluation methods, the cash flow data developed in Chapter 22 for Milski Corporation will be used. In the example, Milski Corporation is considering replacing a machine in current use with a machine that will expand its production capacity. An initial cash outflow of $70,000 is required to purchase the replacement machine, which has an estimated useful life of 10 years. The after-tax cash inflows expected from the capital expenditure, adjusted for the anticipated effects of inflation, are summarized in Exhibit 23-1.

EXHIBIT 23-1

Milski Corporation
Capital Expenditure Proposal for Machine Replacement
Estimated Inflation-Adjusted Net After-Tax Cash Inflows

Year	(1) Inflation-Adjusted Estimated Net Cash Inflows*	(2) Tax Depreciation**	(3) Taxable Income (Reduction) (1) – (2)	(4) Federal and State Income Tax Rate	(5) Income Tax Payment (Reduction) (3) × (4)	(6) Net After-tax Cash Inflows (1) – (5)
1	$16,050	$10,010	$ 6,040	40%	$ 2,416	$ 13,634
2	16,946	17,150	(204)	40	(82)	17,028
3	17,885	12,250	5,635	40	2,254	15,631
4	18,878	8,750	10,128	40	4,051	14,827
5	19,923	6,230	13,693	40	5,477	14,446
6	21,014	6,230	14,784	40	5,914	15,100
7	22,484	6,230	16,254	40	6,502	15,982
8	24,052	3,150	20,902	40	8,361	15,691
9	25,732	0	25,732	40	10,293	15,439
10	27,538	0	27,538	40	11,015	16,523
Total after-tax cash inflows from sales and cost savings						$154,301
After-tax cash inflow from salvage at end of economic life:						
Cash inflow from salvage					$ 9,835	
Tax payable on salvage ($9,835 × 40% tax rate)					(3,934)	5,901
Total inflation-adjusted after-tax cash inflows						$160,202

* The inflation-adjusted estimated net cash inflows were computed in Exhibit 22-3 based on the cash flow estimate computed in Exhibit 22-2.

** Tax depreciation was computed in Exhibit 22-5 by multiplying the depreciable basis of $70,000 by the MACRS depreciation rates for 7-year property provided in Exhibit 22-4.

This example involves both a replacement investment and an expansion investment, in which the initial cash outlay is restricted to the cost of new machinery. Some projects require the commitment of working capital for inventories and receivables, etc., as well as expenditures that may not be capitalized. When such commitments and expenditures exist, they should be included as part of the initial investment and, to the extent that they are recoverable, should be shown as cash inflow in the recovery years.

The Payback Period Method

The **payback period method** (also called the **payout period method**) is widely used, either as an initial screening device or to complement more sophisticated methods. The technique measures the length of time required by the project to recover the initial cash outlay.[4] The calculated payback period is compared with the payback period acceptable to management for projects of the kind being evaluated. The computation for the Milski Corporation project is presented in Exhibit 23-2.

EXHIBIT 23-2

Milski Corporation
Capital Expenditure Proposal for Machine Replacement
Estimated Payback Period

Year	Net After-Tax Cash Flow	Recovery of Initial Outlay: Needed	Recovery of Initial Outlay: Balance	Payback Years Required
1	$13,634	$70,000	$56,366	1.0
2	17,028	56,366	39,338	1.0
3	15,631	39,338	23,707	1.0
4	14,827	23,707	8,880	1.0
5	14,446	8,880	0	0.6*
Total payback period in years				4.6

* $8,880 needed ÷ $14,446 recovered in 5th year

Because of the effects of variations in business activity, inflation, and accelerated methods of depreciation used for income tax purposes, it is highly unlikely that an actual project's estimated cash flows will be uniform for each year. However, professional examinations, such as the CPA and CMA examinations, may assume uniform cash flows for simplicity in problems requiring computation of the payback period. In such cases, the payback period can be computed by dividing the cash outflow in the initial period by the annual cash inflow. For example, if the cash inflow from the Milski Corporation capital project were $17,000 each year, the payback period would be 4.1 years ($70,000 initial cash investment divided by $17,000 annual cash inflow).

Advantages of using the payback method to evaluate capital expenditures include the following:

[4] The initial outlay used in calculating the payback period should exclude working capital to the extent that the working capital can be recovered through its own liquidation. Investment salvage value at the payback point will further reduce the payback period. Such adjustments result in what is referred to as the *bailout payback*.

1. It is simple to compute and easy to understand.
2. It can be used to select investments that will yield a quick return of cash, thus placing an emphasis on liquidity.
3. It permits a company to determine the length of time required to recapture its original investment, thus offering a possible indicator of the degree of risk of each investment. Such an indicator is especially useful when the danger of obsolescence is great.
4. It is a widely used method that is certainly an improvement over a hunch, rule of thumb, or intuitive method.

There are two disadvantages associated with the payback period method of evaluating capital expenditures.

First, the method ignores the time value of money. This disadvantage is illustrated as follows. Assume that the net after-tax cash inflow for Milski Corporation for year 1 is $30,000; for year 2, $16,000; for year 3, $10,000; for year 4, $9,000; and for year 5, $8,000—with the same 10-year total. The payback period is still 4.6 years, determined as follows:

Year	Net After-tax Cash Flow	Recovery of Initial Outlay Needed	Recovery of Initial Outlay Balance	Payback Years Required
1	$30,000	$70,000	$40,000	1.0
2	16,000	40,000	24,000	1.0
3	10,000	24,000	14,000	1.0
4	9,000	14,000	5,000	1.0
5	8,000	5,000	0	0.6
Total payback period in years				4.6

In both this example and the one in Exhibit 23-2, the payback period is 4.6 years. In this example, however, $16,366 more was received in the first year ($30,000 − $13,634). This situation is more desirable from an investment standpoint because money has a time value; that is, a dollar is worth more the earlier it is received because it can be reinvested.

The second disadvantage of the payback method is that it ignores cash flows that are expected to occur beyond the payback period. In the example in Exhibit 23-2, the payback period is 4.6 years, the economic life is 10 years, and the net after-tax cash inflow amount is $160,202. Assume that an alternative project with an economic life of 4 years has a net after-tax cash inflow of $70,000 in the first 3 years and a net after-tax cash inflow of $10,000 in the fourth year. Although the latter case has a shorter payback period, the original example of a 4.6-year payback and net cash inflow of $160,202 is more desirable when immediate cash problems are not of critical importance.

The Accounting Rate of Return Method

The **accounting rate of return method** is sometimes referred to as the **average annual return on investment method.** When this method is used to evaluate an investment proposal, the estimated accounting rate of return on the investment is compared with a target rate of return. If more than one project exceeds the target rate of return and funds are insufficient to finance all qualified projects, the acceptable projects are ranked and only the most profitable ones selected. The estimated rate of return for the Milski Corporation project is computed as follows:

Income before financial accounting depreciation is deducted (net after-tax cash inflow, excluding salvage value)	$154,301
Less financial accounting depreciation on additional investment ($70,000 acquisition cost less $9,835 salvage value)*	60,165
	$ 94,136
Less income tax on gain from sale of asset at the end of the economic life ($9,835 salvage value × 40%)	3,934
Net income over economic life of project	$ 90,202

* Depreciation is assumed to be the only noncash expense and is thus the only adjustment required in converting from cash flow to accrual basis income.

$$\begin{aligned}\text{Accounting rate of return on } \textit{original investment} &= \text{Average income} \div \text{Original investment}\\ &= \frac{\text{Net income}}{\text{Economic life}} \div \text{Original investment}\\ &= \frac{\$90{,}202}{10 \text{ years}} \div \$70{,}000\\ &= 12.89\%\end{aligned}$$

Another way to estimate a project's rate of return is to divide the average annual net income by the average investment rather than the original investment. If the straight-line depreciation method is to be used for the Milski Corporation project, the computation is as follows:

$$\begin{aligned}\text{Accounting rate of return on } \textit{average investment} &= \text{Average income} \div \text{Average investment}\\ &= \frac{\text{Net income}}{\text{Economic life}} \div \frac{(\text{Original investment} + \text{salvage value})}{2}\\ &= \frac{\$90{,}202}{10 \text{ years}} \div \frac{(\$70{,}000 + \$9{,}835)}{2}\\ &= \$9{,}020.20 \div \$39{,}917.50\\ &= 22.60\%\end{aligned}$$

There are two advantages of using the accounting rate of return method to evaluate capital expenditures. First, it facilitates expenditure follow-up because the data required are the same as those normally produced in accounting reports; that is, accrual accounting income and expenses rather than actual cash flows. Second, the method considers income over the entire life of the project.

A disadvantage of the accounting rate of return method of evaluating capital expenditures is that it ignores the time value of money. Two projects having the same rate of return can vary considerably in their pattern of cash flow. When this happens, the time value of money can be the deciding factor, pointing to the alternative yielding greater cash flow in the earlier periods of its life span.

Another disadvantage of this method is that it does not fully adjust for the effects of inflation. Cash flow estimates may be adjusted for inflation, but historical cost depreciation is not. The resulting expression of net income as a return on an investment can be quite misleading.

The Net Present Value Method

To understand the **net present value method,** one must first understand the concept of the time value of money.

Time Value of Money. A dollar received a year from now is not the equivalent of a dollar received today, because the use of money has a value. To illustrate, if \$500 can be invested at 20 percent, \$600 will be received a year later (\$500 + 20% of \$500). The \$600 to be received next year has a present value of \$500 if 20 percent can be earned [(\$600 ÷ (100% + 20%) = \$500)]. The difference of \$100 (\$600 – \$500) represents the time value of money. In line with this idea, the estimated future cash flows of an investment proposal can be stated at their **present value**, that is, as a cash equivalent at the present time.[5]

Compound interest tables facilitate the computation of present values. Table 23-1 on page 697 presents computations for the present value of \$1.00, calculated to three decimal places. It shows the present value of each dollar to be received or paid in the future for various rates of return and periods of time.[6] The present value of a future cash flow is determined by multiplying the future cash flow by the appropriate factor obtained from the table. The interest rate used in adjusting a future cash flow to present value is called the **discount rate**.

Table 23-2 on page 698 shows the **present value of an annuity,** the present value of a series of \$1 periodic receipts or payments for various rates and periods. This table is used when the cash flow is estimated to be the same for each period. The relationship between the values in the annuity table (Table 23-2) and those in the present value table (Table 23-1) is illustrated as follows:

Period	Present Value of \$1 at 12% (from Table 23-1)	Present Value of an Ordinary Annuity of \$1 at 12% (From Table 23-2)
1	.893	.893
2	.797	1.690 (.893 + .797)
3	.712	2.402 (1.690 + .712)
4	.636	3.037 (2.402 + .636)*
5	.567	3.605 (3.037 + .567)*
6	.507	4.111 (3.605 + .507)*
7	.452	4.564 (4.111 + .452)*
8	.404	4.968 (4.564 + .404)

* Difference of .001 results from rounding.

If the cash flow is uniform from period to period, the cash flow for one period can be multiplied by the cumulative factor to obtain approximately the same answer as is obtained by multiplying the individual factors by the flow for each period and totaling the products. For example, if a project costing \$20,000 is expected to yield a uniform annual after-tax cash inflow of \$5,000 for 7 years,

[5] The formula for present value is as follows:

$$PV = S\frac{1}{(1+i)^n} \text{ or } \frac{S}{(1+i)^n} \text{ or } S(1+i)^{-n}$$

where PV = present value of future sum of money
S = sum of money to be received in period n
i = earnings rate for each compounding period
n = number of periods

[6] Ordinary tables, such as those included in this chapter, assume that all cash flows occur at the end of each period and that interest is compounded at the end of each period. Either or both of these assumptions can be varied by the use of calculus so that, instead of cash flows occurring at the end of each period, they can occur continuously, and interest can be compounded continuously. Although the continuous assumptions often are more representative of actual conditions, the tables in this chapter are frequently used in practice. The differences between the two types are usually fairly small.

then the present value of the expected cash inflows discounted at 12 percent is $5,000 × 4.564, or $22,820, and the net present value is $2,820 ($22,820 present value of cash inflows – $20,000 initial cash outflow).[7]

Application of Present Value to Capital Budgeting. The present value concept can be applied to the Milski Corporation problem by discounting at the company's estimated cost of capital rate, assumed here to be 12 percent. For assets requiring a period of time to be made ready for use, the initial cash payment marks the project's origin, at which point the discount factor is 1.000. Subsequent cash payments, such as those for the project's acquisition or construction, are shown as outflows to be discounted back to the date of the initial cash outflow, along with periodic net cash inflows from the investment. The net present value of the Milski Corporation capital expenditure proposal is computed in Exhibit 23-3.

EXHIBIT 23-3

Milski Corporation
Capital Expenditure Proposal for Machine Replacement
Net Present Value of Estimated After-Tax Cash Flows

Year	(1) Net After-Tax Cash (Outflow) Inflow	(2) Present Value of $1 at 12%	(3) Present Value of Net Cash Flow (1) × (2)
0	$(70,000)	1.000	$(70,000)
1	13,634	.893	12,175
2	17,028	.797	13,571
3	15,631	.712	11,129
4	14,827	.636	9,430
5	14,446	.567	8,191
6	15,100	.507	7,656
7	15,982	.452	7,224
8	15,691	.404	6,339
9	15,439	.361	5,573
10	22,424*	.322	7,221
Net present value			$ 18,509

* $16,523 from sales and cost savings plus $5,901 from after-tax salvage.

Because the net present value of $18,509 is greater than zero, the project's rate of return is greater than the cost of capital rate. A net present value of zero indicates a project rate of return of exactly 12 percent. If investment funds are not rationed (if the company has sufficient funds available to finance all acceptable projects), all projects with a positive net present value should be accepted. On the other hand, if investment funds are being rationed (the typical case in practice), alternative projects are ranked according to their net present values.

Present Value Payback. A project's useful life is one of the uncertainties often associated with capital expenditure evaluations. Equipment obsolescence or shifts in market demands can occur. The conventional payback method determines the time necessary to recover the initial outlay, without regard to present value considerations. However, management may want to know what amount of time is required for the original investment of a project to be recovered and the

[7] As noted earlier, although uniform cash flow analysis is unusual in actual capital expenditure evaluation cases, it is included here because it is occasionally required on professional examinations such as the CPA and CMA examinations.

desired rate of return to be earned on the investment during the reviewing period. The present value payback calculation focuses on this question and is computed for Milski Corporation in Exhibit 23-4, using the present values of the net cash flows shown in Exhibit 23-3.

EXHIBIT 23-4

Milski Corporation
Capital Expenditure Proposal for Machine Replacement
Present Value Payback on Estimated After-Tax Cash Inflows

Year	Present Value of Net Cash Flow	Recovery of Initial Outlay: Needed	Recovery of Initial Outlay: Balance	Present Value Payback Years Required
1	$12,175	$70,000	$57,825	1.0
2	13,571	57,825	44,254	1.0
3	11,129	44,254	33,125	1.0
4	9,430	33,125	23,695	1.0
5	8,191	23,695	15,504	1.0
6	7,656	15,504	7,848	1.0
7	7,224	7,848	624	1.0
8	6,339	624	0	.1
Total present value payback in years				7.1

Based on the present value of estimated cash flows, it will take 7.1 years to recover the $70,000 original cash investment and earn a 12 percent rate of return on the annual unrecovered balance.

Advantages and Disadvantages of Net Present Value Analysis. Advantages of using the net present value method of evaluating capital expenditures include the following factors.

1. It considers the time value of money.
2. It considers cash flow over the entire life of the project.
3. It allows for different discount rates over the life of the project. That is, the discount rate used to discount the cash flows for each period can be altered to reflect anticipated changes in the cost of capital.

Disadvantages associated with the use of the present value method of evaluating capital expenditures include the argument that this method is difficult to compute and to understand. However, given the pervasive use of computers and sophisticated calculators in business today, computational difficulty is a weak argument against the present value method. Another disadvantage is that management must determine a discount rate to be used. A well-informed management should already be aware of the cost of its capital, which will represent the benchmark for discount rate purposes. However, some firms use a discount rate in excess of their cost of capital as a way of compensating for risk and uncertainty. These rates are sometimes referred to as **hurdle rates**, presumably because the padding built into the discount rate creates a hurdle to be overcome before the project is accepted. This approach is conceptually unsound. Cash received in early periods has more value than cash received in later periods only because early cash inflows can be reinvested. If the discount rate is inflated above the reinvestment rate, the value of the cash inflows is misstated.

The potential distortion caused by using hurdle rates to discount cashflows in the net present value method can be eliminated by using the reinvestment rate to compute the future **terminal value** of the cash inflows at the end of the life of the project. The terminal value is then discounted to the start of the project using a hurdle rate (for example, the cost of capital rate plus an additional component to compensate for risk).[8] The terminal value for the Milski Corporation illustration is computed in Exhibit 23-5 under the assumption that the cost of capital rate is a reasonable reinvestment rate.

EXHIBIT 23-5

Milski Corporation
Capital Expenditure Proposal for Machine Replacement
Terminal Value of Estimated After-Tax Cash Flows

Year	Net After-Tax Cash Inflow	Future Value of $1 at 12%	Terminal Value of Cash Inflows
1	$13,634	$(1.00 + .12)^9$ = 2.773	$ 37,807
2	17,028	$(1.00 + .12)^8$ = 2.476	42,161
3	15,631	$(1.00 + .12)^7$ = 2.211	34,560
4	14,827	$(1.00 + .12)^6$ = 1.974	29,268
5	14,446	$(1.00 + .12)^5$ = 1.762	25,454
6	15,100	$(1.00 + .12)^4$ = 1.574	23,767
7	15,982	$(1.00 + .12)^3$ = 1.405	22,455
8	15,691	$(1.00 + .12)^2$ = 1.254	19,677
9	15,439	$(1.00 + .12)$ = 1.120	17,292
10	22,424*	1.000	22,424
Total terminal value of after-tax cash inflows			$274,865

* $16,523 from sales and cost savings plus $5,901 from after-tax salvage.

If a risk premium of 3 percent is added to the 12 percent reinvestment rate, the net present value of the project is determined as follows:

Total terminal value of after-tax cash inflows	$274,865
Present value of $1 at 15% for 10 periods	.247
Present value of terminal after-tax cash inflows	$ 67,892
Initial cash outflow	70,000
Net present value of project	$ (2,108)

This project does not quite meet the 3 percent risk premium requirement, which indicates that it should be rejected. A better approach to compensating for the effects of risk and uncertainty is to incorporate explicit probabilities into the analysis.[9]

A third disadvantage of the present value method is that the profitability of different projects that do not require the same initial investment cannot be directly compared. The project having the largest net present value may not be the best project if it also requires a larger investment. For example, a net present value of $1,000 on an investment of $100,000 is not as profitable as a net present value of $900 on an investment of $10,000, provided the $90,000 difference in investments can be used to realize a net present value of at least $101 in other projects.

The problem of comparing projects that require different initial investments can be overcome by computing a **net present value index.** The index is used

[8] See Lester Barenbaum and Thomas Monahan, "Utilizing Terminal Values in Teaching Time Value Analysis'" *Journal of Accounting Education,* Vol. 1, No. 2, pp. 79-88.

[9] A more complete discussion of the problem of considering uncertainty in capital expenditure proposal evaluations is presented in Chapter 24.

as the basis of comparison in place of the net present value dollar figure. It places all competing projects on a comparable basis so they can be ranked. The highest index denotes the best project. For Milski Corporation, the computation is as follows:

$$\text{Net present value index} = \frac{\text{Net present value}}{\text{Required investment}} = \frac{\$18{,}509}{\$70{,}000} = .264$$

The net present value can also be a misleading measure of profitability when alternative projects have unequal lives. For example, assume a firm is faced with the problem of selecting between two alternative projects. Project A has an 18-year expected life, and project B has a 5-year expected life. There are three ways to deal with this problem.

1. Repeat the investment cycle for project B a sufficient number of times to cover the estimated life of project A; in this example, 3-3/5 times. An estimate of the salvage value of the fourth investment cycle for project B at the end of the life for project A is then made in order to reflect a common termination date.
2. The period considered can be that of the alternative having the shorter life, project B, coupled with an estimate of the salvage value of project A at the end of 5 years. The analysis then covers only the 5-year period, and the salvage value of project A is treated as a cash inflow at the end of the fifth year. A serious difficulty with this method rests in the need to estimate a value of the asset having the longer life at the end of 5 years. Such an intermediate recoverable value may not be an adequate measure of the service value of the property at that point in its useful life.
3. The net present value of each project can be annualized before the two are compared. To accomplish this, divide the net present value of each project by the present value of an ordinary annuity of $1 for that project's economic life. The alternative with the highest annualized net present value should be selected because it will provide the largest increase in the value of the firm.[10] For example, assume that projects A and B have net present values of $12,000 and $5,000, respectively, using a 10-percent discount rate. The annualized net present value is $1,463 for project A ($12,000 net present value ÷ 8.201, which is the present value of an ordinary annuity of $1 discounted at 10% for 18 periods) and $1,319 for project B ($5,000 net present value ÷ 3.791, which is the present value of an ordinary annuity of $1 discounted at 10% for 5 periods). Project A should be selected because its annualized net present value is greater than project B's.

The Internal Rate of Return Method

In the net present value method, the discount rate is known or at least predetermined. In the **internal rate of return method** (also called the **discounted cash flow rate of return method**, the discount rate is not known but is defined as the rate that results in a project net present value of zero. This discount rate is referred to as the internal rate of return of the project.

---

[10] Jack F. Truitt, "Capital Rationing: An Annualized Approach," *Journal of Cost Analysis,* Vol. 8, Summer 1988, pp. 63-75.

The internal rate of return for the Milski Corporation project can be determined by trial and error; that is, by computing the net present value at various discount rates to find the rate at which the net present value is zero. If a discount rate that results in a net present value of zero cannot be found in the present value table, the internal rate of return can be approximated by interpolation. The internal rate of return is between the discount rate that results in the smallest positive net present value and the one that results in the smallest negative net present value. This computation is illustrated as follows:

Year	(1) Net After-tax Cash (Outflow) Inflow	(2) Present Value of $1 at 16%	(3) Present Value of Cash Flows Discounted at 16% (1) × (2)	(4) Present Value of $1 at 18%	(5) Present Value of Cash Flows Discounted at 18% (1) × (4)
0	$(70,000)	1.000	$(70,000)	1.000	$(70,000)
1	13,634	.862	11,753	.847	11,548
2	17,028	.743	12,652	.718	12,226
3	15,631	.641	10,019	.609	9,519
4	14,827	.552	8,185	.516	7,651
5	14,446	.476	6,876	.437	6,313
6	15,100	.410	6,191	.370	5,587
7	15,982	.354	5,658	.314	5,018
8	15,691	.305	4,786	.266	4,174
9	15,439	.263	4,060	.225	3,474
10	22,424*	.227	5,090	.191	4,283
			$ 5,270		$ (207)

* $16,523 from sales and cost savings plus $5,901 from after-tax salvage.

Because the net present value of the cash flows is positive when a 16 percent discount rate is used and negative when an 18 percent discount rate is used, the internal rate of return is between 16 percent and 18 percent. An approximation of the internal rate of return can be obtained by interpolation, as follows:

$$16\% + \left[2\% \times \left(\frac{\$5,270}{\$5,270 + \$207}\right)\right] = 16\% + [(2\%)(.962)] = .1792 \text{ or } 17.92\%$$

The internal rate of return method permits management to maximize corporate profits by selecting proposals with the highest internal rates of return, as long as the rates are higher than the company's cost of capital plus management's allowance for risk and uncertainty and individual project characteristics. In many circumstances, the use of the internal rate of return method instead of the net present value method at a given interest rate will not seriously alter the ranking of projects.

Note that the rate of return resulting from either the internal rate of return method or the net present value method is computed on the basis of the unrecovered cash outflow from period to period, not on the original cash investment. In the illustration, the internal rate of return of 17.92 percent denotes that, over the 10 years, the after-tax cash inflow equals the recovery of the original cash investment plus a return of 17.92 percent on the unrecovered cash investment from period to period. The net present value of $18,509 (Exhibit 23-3) indicates that, $88,509 ($70,000 + $18,509) could have been spent on the machine, and the original cash investment, plus a return of 12 percent on the unrecovered cash investment from period to period, could still have been recovered.

Advantages of using the internal rate of return method of evaluating capital expenditures include the following factors.

1. It considers the time value of money.
2. It considers cash flow over the entire life of the project.
3. The internal rate of return is more easily interpreted than the net present value and the net present value index.
4. Alternative projects that require different initial cash outlays and have unequal lives can be ranked logically in accordance with their respective internal rate of return.

Disadvantages associated with the use of the internal rate of return method of evaluating capital expenditures include the argument that this method is too difficult to compute and to understand. Another problem is that, when cash flows change signs more than once (as in cash outflow in the first year, followed by cash inflow in the second year, followed by cash outflow in the third year, and so on), the project will have more than one rate of return. The number of rates of return will equal the number of sign changes. Multiple rates impede analysis because they are difficult to interpret and limit comparability with other projects.

Discounting at the project's internal rate of return implies that cash inflows can be reinvested to earn the rate earned by the investment being evaluated. In contrast, the present value method implies that cash inflows are reinvested at the discount rate being used, which is usually the weighted-average cost of capital. The latter assumption appears more reasonable, particularly when the internal rate of return for the project is high, because the weighted-average cost of capital is the company-wide expected earnings rate. Nevertheless, in many circumstances, the use of the internal rate of return method instead of the present value method does not seriously alter the ranking of alternative projects.

The Error Cushion

When a project's estimated desirability is near a cutoff point for the type of project being evaluated, there is little cushion for errors. For example, if the management of a chain of automotive muffler shops anticipates that a new location should yield a minimum internal rate of return of 12 percent, there is obviously a greater cushion for errors when the computed rate of return for a proposed new shop is 20 percent rather than 13 percent. Similarly, when one alternative is clearly superior to others for a particular project, there is a better cushion against errors than when two or more of the best alternatives indicate approximately the same expected results.

Reasonably accurate estimates enhance the evaluation of any project. However, a higher degree of sophistication and care, at a higher cost of obtaining the data, may be necessary to add confidence when an evaluation is close to a cutoff point or when two or more project alternatives yield approximately the same answer. Conversely, in many cases, the desirability of a project or the selection from alternatives for a particular project will be so obvious that the costs of making sophisticated data estimates and using economic evaluation techniques are not justified.

Purchasing versus Leasing

A lease arrangement is sometimes an alternative to investment in a capital asset. A lease arrangement can be evaluated by determining the incremental annual cost of leasing versus purchasing. This cost represents purchasing cost savings, which, on an after-tax basis, must be sufficient to yield the desired internal rate of return on the anticipated purchase price to warrant its adoption.

In the evaluation of the leasing and purchasing alternatives, the net present value method can be used as an alternative to the internal rate of return method in either of two ways.

1. The net present value of the purchase price and the associated after-tax savings are computed. The resulting net present value is used to evaluate the merits of purchasing versus leasing.
2. The net present values of the purchasing alternative and the leasing alternative cash flows are computed separately, each on an after-tax basis. The alternative having the more favorable net present value identifies the better choice.

Generally, the capital expenditure or investment decision is first justified, followed by the lease or financing decision. The rationale is that the acquisition must first be shown to be a sound investment. Only then can the financing strategy and the operating flexibility, obsolescence, and service and maintenance factors associated with leasing be weighed against those of purchasing. With a justified capital expenditure in hand, a lease-purchase decision can be made.[11]

Usually the lease is the more expensive alternative, because a lease avoids some ownership risks, for which a price must be paid. In such cases, a relevant question is whether or not the extra cost of leasing is worth paying to avoid risks of ownership. Management may prefer leasing to improve balance sheet position by avoiding a purchase liability. Also, the rate of return on capital employed is enhanced by a reduction in the investment in capital assets.[12]. However, generally accepted accounting principles prescribe rules that require capitalizing and recording liability for leases that are, in substance, purchases.[13]

Summary

Capital investments require commitment of substantial resources for relatively long periods of time. Because of the magnitude of the investments and the length of the commitments, poor investments can have a material long-term effect on the firm's profitability and, consequently, its ability to survive. As a consequence, the economic evaluation of capital expenditure proposals has received considerable attention in the literature. Four of the most commonly used economic evaluation techniques were discussed in detail in this chapter: the payback method, the accounting rate of return method, the net present value method, and the internal rate of return method. Although economic evaluation helps management select projects that will maximize company profits, excessive reliance on quantitative answers is dangerous. Because the life of a capital project extends well into the future, the data used in quantitative analysis are fraught with uncertainty. Some techniques for specifically incorporating uncertainty into the analysis are presented in the next chapter.

---

[11] William L. Ferrara, *The Lease-Purchase Decision: How Some Companies Make It* (New York: Institute of Management Accountants (formerly National Association of Accountants); Hamilton, Ont.: The Society of Management Accountants of Canada, 1978), p. 7. For a detailed discussion of the lease-purchase decision model, see William L. Ferrara, James B. Thies, and Mark W. Dirsmith, *The Lease-Purchase Decision* (New York: Institute of Management Accountants (formerly National Association of Accountants), 1980; Hamilton, Ont.: The Society of Management Accountants of Canada, 1979).

[12] Lawrence A. Gordon, Danny Miller, and Henry Mintzberg, *Normative Models in Managerial Decision-Making* (New York: Institute of Management Accountants (formerly National Association of Accountants); Hamilton, Ont.: The Society of Industrial Accountants of Canada, 1975), p. 67.

[13] *Statement of Financial Accounting Standards, No. 13,* "Accounting for Leases" (Stamford, Conn.: Financial Accounting Standards Board, 1976).

Future Years	1%	2%	4%	6%	8%	10%	12%	14%	15%	16%	18%	20%	22%	24%	25%	26%	28%	30%	35%	40%	45%	50%
1	.990	.980	.962	.943	.926	.909	.893	.877	.870	.862	.847	.833	.820	.806	.800	.794	.781	.769	.741	.714	.690	.667
2	.980	.961	.925	.890	.857	.826	.797	.769	.756	.743	.718	.694	.672	.650	.640	.630	.610	.592	.549	.510	.476	.444
3	.971	.942	.889	.840	.794	.751	.712	.675	.658	.641	.609	.579	.551	.524	.512	.500	.477	.455	.406	.364	.328	.296
4	.961	.924	.855	.792	.735	.683	.636	.592	.572	.552	.516	.482	.451	.423	.410	.397	.373	.350	.301	.260	.226	.198
5	.951	.906	.822	.747	.681	.621	.567	.519	.497	.476	.437	.402	.370	.341	.328	.315	.291	.269	.223	.186	.156	.132
6	.942	.888	.790	.705	.630	.564	.507	.456	.432	.410	.370	.335	.303	.275	.262	.250	.227	.207	.165	.133	.108	.088
7	.933	.871	.760	.665	.583	.513	.452	.400	.376	.354	.314	.279	.249	.222	.210	.198	.178	.159	.122	.095	.074	.059
8	.923	.853	.731	.627	.540	.467	.404	.351	.327	.305	.266	.233	.204	.179	.168	.157	.139	.123	.091	.068	.051	.039
9	.914	.837	.703	.592	.500	.424	.361	.308	.284	.263	.225	.194	.167	.144	.134	.125	.108	.094	.067	.048	.035	.026
10	.905	.820	.676	.558	.463	.386	.322	.270	.247	.227	.191	.162	.137	.116	.107	.099	.085	.073	.050	.035	.024	.017
11	.896	.804	.650	.527	.429	.350	.287	.237	.215	.195	.162	.135	.112	.094	.086	.079	.066	.056	.037	.025	.017	.012
12	.887	.788	.625	.497	.397	.319	.257	.208	.187	.168	.137	.112	.092	.076	.069	.062	.052	.043	.027	.018	.012	.008
13	.879	.773	.601	.469	.368	.290	.229	.182	.163	.145	.116	.093	.075	.061	.055	.050	.040	.033	.020	.013	.008	.005
14	.870	.758	.577	.442	.340	.263	.205	.160	.141	.125	.099	.078	.062	.049	.044	.039	.032	.025	.015	.009	.006	.003
15	.861	.743	.555	.417	.315	.239	.183	.140	.123	.108	.084	.065	.051	.040	.035	.031	.025	.020	.011	.006	.004	.002
16	.853	.728	.534	.394	.292	.218	.163	.123	.107	.093	.071	.054	.042	.032	.028	.025	.019	.015	.008	.005	.003	.002
17	.844	.714	.513	.371	.270	.198	.146	.108	.093	.080	.060	.045	.034	.026	.023	.020	.015	.012	.006	.003	.002	.001
18	.836	.700	.494	.350	.250	.180	.130	.095	.081	.069	.051	.038	.028	.021	.018	.016	.012	.009	.005	.002	.001	.001
19	.828	.686	.475	.331	.232	.164	.116	.083	.070	.060	.043	.031	.023	.017	.014	.012	.009	.007	.003	.002	.001	
20	.820	.673	.456	.312	.215	.149	.104	.073	.061	.051	.037	.026	.019	.014	.012	.010	.007	.005	.002	.001	.001	
21	.811	.660	.439	.294	.199	.135	.093	.064	.053	.044	.031	.022	.015	.011	.009	.008	.006	.004	.002	.001		
22	.803	.647	.422	.278	.184	.123	.083	.056	.046	.038	.026	.018	.013	.009	.007	.006	.004	.003	.001	.001		
23	.795	.634	.406	.262	.170	.112	.074	.049	.040	.033	.022	.015	.010	.007	.006	.005	.003	.002	.001			
24	.788	.622	.390	.247	.158	.102	.066	.043	.035	.028	.019	.013	.008	.006	.005	.004	.003	.002	.001			
25	.780	.610	.375	.233	.146	.092	.059	.038	.030	.024	.016	.010	.007	.005	.004	.003	.002	.001	.001			
26	.772	.598	.361	.220	.135	.084	.053	.033	.026	.021	.014	.009	.006	.004	.003	.002	.002	.001				
27	.764	.586	.347	.207	.125	.076	.047	.029	.023	.018	.011	.007	.005	.003	.002	.002	.001	.001				
28	.757	.574	.333	.196	.116	.069	.042	.026	.020	.016	.010	.006	.004	.002	.002	.002	.001	.001				
29	.749	.563	.321	.185	.107	.063	.037	.022	.017	.014	.008	.005	.003	.002	.002	.001	.001	.001				
30	.742	.552	.308	.174	.099	.057	.033	.020	.015	.012	.007	.004	.003	.002	.001	.001	.001					
40	.672	.453	.208	.097	.046	.022	.011	.005	.004	.003	.001	.001										
50	.608	.372	.141	.054	.021	.009	.003	.001	.001	.001												

TABLE 23-1 *Present Value $1*

Future Years	1%	2%	4%	6%	8%	10%	12%	14%	15%	16%	18%	20%	22%	24%	25%	26%	28%	30%	35%	40%	45%	50%
1	.990	.980	.962	.943	.926	.909	.893	.877	.870	.862	.847	.833	.820	.806	.800	.794	.781	.769	.741	.714	.690	.667
2	1.970	1.942	1.886	1.833	1.783	1.736	1.690	1.647	1.626	1.605	1.566	1.528	1.492	1.457	1.440	1.424	1.392	1.361	1.289	1.224	1.165	1.111
3	2.941	2.884	2.775	2.673	2.577	2.487	2.402	2.322	2.283	2.246	2.174	2.106	2.042	1.981	1.952	1.923	1.868	1.816	1.696	1.589	1.493	1.407
4	3.902	3.808	3.630	3.465	3.312	3.170	3.037	2.914	2.855	2.798	2.690	2.589	2.494	2.404	2.362	2.320	2.241	2.166	1.997	1.849	1.720	1.605
5	4.853	4.713	4.452	4.212	3.993	3.791	3.605	3.433	3.352	3.274	3.127	2.991	2.864	2.745	2.689	2.635	2.532	2.436	2.220	2.035	1.876	1.737
6	5.795	5.601	5.242	4.917	4.623	4.355	4.111	3.889	3.784	3.685	3.498	3.326	3.167	3.020	2.951	2.885	2.759	2.643	2.385	2.168	1.983	1.824
7	6.728	6.472	6.002	5.582	5.206	4.868	4.564	4.288	4.160	4.039	3.812	3.605	3.416	3.242	3.161	3.083	2.937	2.802	2.508	2.263	2.057	1.883
8	7.652	7.325	6.733	6.210	5.747	5.335	4.968	4.639	4.487	4.344	4.078	3.837	3.619	3.421	3.329	3.241	3.076	2.925	2.598	2.331	2.108	1.922
9	8.566	8.163	7.435	6.802	6.247	5.759	5.328	4.946	4.772	4.607	4.303	4.031	3.786	3.566	3.463	3.366	3.184	3.019	2.665	2.379	2.144	1.948
10	9.471	8.983	8.111	7.360	6.710	6.145	5.650	5.216	5.019	4.833	4.494	4.192	3.923	3.682	3.571	3.465	3.269	3.092	2.715	2.414	2.168	1.965
11	10.368	9.787	8.760	7.887	7.139	6.495	5.988	5.453	5.234	5.029	4.656	4.327	4.035	3.776	3.656	3.544	3.335	3.147	2.752	2.438	2.185	1.977
12	11.255	10.575	9.385	8.384	7.536	6.814	6.194	5.660	5.421	5.197	4.793	4.439	4.127	3.851	3.725	3.606	3.387	3.190	2.779	2.456	2.196	1.985
13	12.134	11.348	9.986	8.853	7.904	7.103	6.424	5.842	5.583	5.342	4.910	4.533	4.203	3.912	3.780	3.656	3.427	3.223	2.799	2.468	2.204	1.990
14	13.004	12.106	10.563	9.295	8.244	7.367	6.628	6.002	5.724	5.468	5.008	4.611	4.265	3.962	3.824	3.695	3.459	3.249	2.814	2.477	2.210	1.993
15	13.865	12.849	11.118	9.712	8.559	7.606	6.811	6.142	5.847	5.575	5.092	4.675	4.315	4.001	3.859	3.726	3.483	3.268	2.825	2.484	2.214	1.995
16	14.718	13.578	11.652	10.106	8.851	7.824	6.974	6.265	5.954	5.669	5.162	4.730	4.357	4.033	3.887	3.751	3.503	3.283	2.834	2.489	2.216	1.997
17	15.562	14.292	12.166	10.477	9.122	8.022	7.120	6.373	6.047	5.749	5.222	4.775	4.391	4.059	3.910	3.771	3.518	3.295	2.840	2.492	2.218	1.998
18	16.398	14.992	12.659	10.828	9.372	8.201	7.250	6.467	6.128	5.818	5.273	4.812	4.419	4.080	3.928	3.786	3.529	3.304	2.844	2.494	2.219	1.999
19	17.226	15.678	13.134	11.158	9.604	8.365	7.366	6.550	6.198	5.877	5.316	4.844	4.442	4.097	3.942	3.799	3.539	3.311	2.848	2.496	2.220	1.999
20	18.046	16.351	13.590	11.470	9.818	8.514	7.469	6.623	6.259	5.929	5.353	4.870	4.460	4.110	3.954	3.808	3.546	3.316	2.850	2.497	2.221	1.999
21	18.857	17.011	14.029	11.764	10.017	8.649	7.562	6.687	6.312	5.973	5.384	4.891	4.476	4.121	3.963	3.816	3.551	3.320	2.852	2.498	2.221	2.000
22	19.660	17.658	14.451	12.042	10.201	8.772	7.645	6.743	6.359	6.011	5.410	4.909	4.488	4.130	3.970	3.822	3.556	3.323	2.853	2.498	2.222	2.000
23	20.456	18.292	14.857	12.303	10.371	8.883	7.718	6.792	6.399	6.044	5.432	4.925	4.499	4.137	3.976	3.827	3.559	3.325	2.854	2.499	2.222	2.000
24	21.243	18.914	15.247	12.550	10.529	8.985	7.784	6.835	6.434	6.073	5.451	4.937	4.507	4.143	3.981	3.831	3.562	3.327	2.855	2.499	2.222	2.000
25	22.023	19.523	15.622	12.783	10.675	9.077	7.843	6.873	6.464	6.097	5.467	4.948	4.514	4.147	3.985	3.834	3.564	3.329	2.856	2.499	2.222	2.000
26	22.795	20.121	15.983	13.003	10.810	9.161	7.896	6.906	6.491	6.118	5.480	4.956	4.520	4.151	3.988	3.837	3.566	3.330	2.856	2.500	2.222	2.000
27	23.560	20.707	16.330	13.211	10.935	9.237	7.943	6.935	6.514	6.136	5.492	4.964	4.524	4.154	3.990	3.839	3.567	3.331	2.856	2.500	2.222	2.000
28	24.316	21.281	16.663	13.406	11.051	9.307	7.984	6.961	6.534	6.152	5.502	4.970	4.528	4.157	3.992	3.840	3.568	3.331	2.857	2.500	2.222	2.000
29	25.066	21.844	16.984	13.591	11.158	9.370	8.022	6.983	6.551	6.166	5.510	4.975	4.531	4.159	3.994	3.841	3.569	3.332	2.857	2.500	2.222	2.000
30	25.808	22.396	17.292	13.765	11.258	9.427	8.055	7.003	6.566	6.177	5.517	4.979	4.534	4.160	3.995	3.842	3.569	3.332	2.857	2.500	2.222	2.000
40	32.835	27.355	19.793	15.046	11.925	9.779	8.244	7.105	6.642	6.234	5.548	4.997	4.544	4.166	3.999	3.846	3.571	3.333	2.857	2.500	2.222	2.000
50	39.196	31.424	21.482	15.762	12.334	9.915	8.304	7.133	6.661	6.246	5.554	4.999	4.545	4.167	4.000	3.846	3.571	3.333	2.857	2.500	2.222	2.000

TABLE 23-2 ***Present Value of an Ordinary Annuity of $1***

Key Terms

cost of capital *(683)*
marginal cost of capital *(683)*
weighted-average cost of capital *(683)*
payback period method or payout period method *(686)*
accounting rate of return method or average annual return on investment method *(687)*
net present value method *(688)*
present value *(689)*
discount rate *(689)*
present value of an annuity *(689)*
hurdle rate *(691)*
terminal value *(691)*
net present value index *(692)*
internal rate of return method or discounted cash flow rate of return method *(693)*

Discussion Questions

Q23-1 Describe the procedure for computing the weighted-average cost of capital.
(ICMA adapted)

Q23-2 Why would a firm use its weighted-average cost of capital as the hurdle rate (minimum rate) for a project investment decision, rather than the specific marginal cost of funds?

Q23-3 Discuss the practical difficulties in estimating the firm's weighted-average cost of capital
CGA-Canada (adapted). Reprint with permission.

Q23-4 Define the payback (or payout) period method.

Q23-5 How do the two accounting rate of return methods differ?

Q23-6 What is the present value concept and why is it important in capital budgeting?

Q23-7 What is the basic difference between the payback method and the net present value method?
(AICPA adapted)

Q23-8 What is the difference between the net present value and the internal rate of return calculations?

Q23-9 Both the net present value method and the internal rate of return method assume that the earnings produced by a project are reinvested in the company. However, each approach assumes a different rate of return at which earnings are reinvested. Describe the rate of return assumed in each of the two approaches and discuss which of the assumed rates is more realistic.
CGA-Canada (adapted). Reprint with permission.

Q23-10 Some companies inflate the discount rate used in the net present value method in order to compensate for risk associated with the capital expenditure project. This approach is unsound. Explain why and suggest an alternative approach that is theoretically preferable.

Exercises

E23-1 Cost of Capital. Wiz Company wants to compute a weighted-average cost of capital for use in evaluating capital expenditure proposals. Earnings, capital structure, and current market prices of the company's securities are:

Earnings:	
Earnings before interest and income tax	$ 210,000
Interest expense on bonds	30,000
Pretax earnings	$ 180,000
Income tax (45% tax rate)	81,000
After-tax earnings	$ 99,000
Preferred stock dividends	24,000
Earnings available to common stockholders	$ 75,000
Common stock dividends	30,000
Increase in retained earnings	$ 45,000

Capital structure:	
Mortgage bonds, 10%, 10 years	$ 300,000
Preferred stock, 12%, $100 par value	200,000
Common stock, no par, 50,000 shares outstanding	350,000
Retained earnings (equity of common stockholders)	150,000
	$1,000,000
Market prices of the company's stocks:	
Preferred stock	$ 96
Common stock	10

Required: Assuming that the current cost and mix of sources of funds are expected to continue over the investment horizon, determine the weighted-average cost of capital.

E23-2 Cost of Capital. Magnum Tool Company is a manufacturer of diamond drilling, cutting, and grinding tools. $1,000,000 of its 8% bond issue will mature next month. To retire this debt, $1,000,000 in cash must be raised. One proposal under consideration is the sale and leaseback of the company's general office building.

The building would be sold to FHR Inc. for $1,000,000 and leased back on a 25-year lease, with annual payments of $110,168, permitting the lessor to recover its investment and earn 10% on the investment. Magnum Tool will pay all maintenance costs, property taxes, and insurance and will reacquire the building at the end of the lease period for a nominal payment.

The current capital structure is:

Capital Component	Pretax Amount	Pretax Cost of Component
Bonds (including amount to be retired next month)	$5,000,000	8.0%
Preferred stock (market value)	1,000,000	9.0%
Common stock and retained earnings (market value)	4,000,000	12.5%

Magnum Tool's income tax rate is 40%.

Required: Compute the weighted-average cost of capital before and after the bond retirement and the sale-leaseback transaction. (ICMA adapted)

E23-3 Payback and Accounting Rate of Return Methods. Watkins Company is considering the purchase of a $40,000 machine, which will be depreciated on the straight-line basis over an 8-year period with no salvage value for both book and tax purposes. The machine is expected to generate an annual pretax cash inflow of $15,000 a year. The income tax rate is 40%.

Required:
(1) Determine the payback period.
(2) Compute the accounting rate of return on the original investment. (AICPA adapted)

E23-4 Investment Analysis; Uniform Cash Flow. Dagwood Company is evaluating a capital budgeting proposal that will require an initial investment of $35,000. The project will have a 6-year life. The after-tax annual cash inflow expected from this investment is $10,000. The desired rate of return is 15%.

Required:
(1) What is the payback period?
(2) Compute the net present value of the project.
(3) What amount would Dagwood have had to invest 6 years ago, at 15% compounded annually, to have $35,000 now? (AICPA adapted)

E23-5 Equipment Investment Analysis; Net Present Value and Present Value Index. Tanglewood Printing Company is considering purchasing a new press, requiring an immediate $100,000 cash outlay. The new press is expected to increase annual net after-tax cash receipts by $20,000 in each of the next 10 years, after which it will be sold to yield $10,000 after taxes. The company desires a minimum return of 14% on invested capital.

Required:
(1) Compute the net present value of the project.
(2) Compute the net present value index.

E23-6 Effect of Depreciation Methods on Cash Flow. Kingsgate Corporation is planning to acquire a machine for one of its projects at a cost of $100,000. The machine has an economic life of 8 years, but it is classified as a 5-year property under MACRS. The company's cost of capital rate is 14%, and its income tax rate is 40%.

Required: Determine the present value of the income tax benefits that result from the use of the MACRS recovery percentages provided in Exhibit 22-4, and compare it to the straight-line depreciation alternative. In computing straight-line depreciation, use a 5-year life with one-half of a year's depreciation in the first year, a full year's depreciation in years 2 through 5, and one-half of a year's depreciation in the sixth year.

E23-7 Effect of Inflation on Investment Decision. Gilbert Company is evaluating a capital budgeting proposal that will require an initial cash investment of $60,000. The project will have a 5-year life. The net after-tax cash inflows from the project, before any adjustment for the effects of inflation, are expected to be as follow:

Year	Unadjusted Estimate of Cash Inflows
1	$20,000
2	18,000
3	16,000
4	10,000
5	10,000

No salvage is expected at the end of the project. Cash inflows are expected to increase at the anticipated inflation rate of 10% each year. The company's cost of capital rate is 15%.

Required:
(1) Compute the estimated cash inflow for each year, adjusted for the anticipated effects of inflation.
(2) Determine the net present value of the cash flows before and after the adjustment for the anticipated effects of inflation.

E23-8 Use of Net Present Value to Evaluate Asset Acquisition. Bald Eagle Air Transport Company is considering the acquisition of a new airplane at a cost of $500,000. The airplane has an estimated useful life of 10 years, but it qualifies as a 7-year property for tax purposes under MACRS. The annual pretax cash inflows from the new airplane, net of annual operating expenses, is expected to be $130,000 in each of the 10 years the airplane will be used. At the end of the 10-year period, company executives believe that the airplane can be sold for $100,000. The company is in a 40% income tax bracket, and its weighted-average cost of capital is 15%.

Required: Determine the net present value of the investment in the new airplane. (Use the MACRS rates provided in Exhibit 22-4.)

E23-9 Equipment Replacement Analysis. Del Norte Corporation purchased a special machine one year ago at a cost of $20,000. At that time, the machine was estimated to have a useful life of 7 years and a $1,000 disposal value. A MACRS tax deduction of $4,000 was taken in the year of acquisition. The annual cash operating cost is approximately $40,000.

A new machine that has just come on the market will do the same job but with an annual cash operating cost of only $34,000. This new machine costs $38,000 and has an estimated life of 6 years with no expected salvage value. The old machine can be used as a trade-in at an allowance of $18,000. The tax basis of the old machine is $16,000.

The new machine qualifies as 5-year property under MACRS. The company's income tax rate is 40%, and its cost of capital is 12%.

Required: Make a recommendation to management based on the capital expenditure proposal's expected internal rate of return. (Use the MACRS depreciation rates provided in Exhibit 22-4.)

E23-10 Comparing Net Present Value and Internal Rate of Return Reinvestment Assumptions. After-tax cash flows adjusted for the effects of inflation for two mutually exclusive projects (with economic lives of 5 years each) are as follow:

Year	Project A	Project B
0	$(15,000)	$(15,000)
1	5,000	0
2	5,000	0
3	5,000	0
4	5,000	0
5	5,000	35,000

The company's cost of capital is 15%.

Required:

(1) Determine the net present value for each project.
(2) Compute the internal rate of return for each project.
(3) Which project should be selected?

Problems

P23-1 Cost of Capital. Walcott Company is a retail grocery store chain of moderate size. Walcott was incorporated 15 years ago with a public offering of its stock. At that time, the company operated primarily in the Northeast. Five years ago the company acquired a small chain of grocery stores in the Southeast. The acquisition was financed by the private placement of a 20-year bond issue that originally sold with a market yield of 10%.

In the last 3 years, Walcott's primary competitor remodeled several of its stores and seems to have increased its market share substantially. At present Walcott management is considering a large-scale remodeling of all its stores to meet these competitive pressures. The following three financing alternatives have been proposed to provide the necessary funds for expansion.

(a) Pure debt financing alternative. This alternative consists of a public issue of bonds with a face value of $10,000,000. The bonds would have a 12% coupon rate and would net $10,000,000 after issue costs.
(b) Debt and preferred stock financing alternative. This alternative consists of (1) issuing bonds with a face value of $5,000,000 and a 12% coupon rate (to net $5,000,000 after issue costs), and (2) issuing preferred stock with a stated rate of 9% (to yield $5,000,000 after a 4% issue cost is deducted).
(c) Common stock financing alternative. This alternative consists of a public issue of common stock that would yield $10,000,000 after a 5% issue cost is deducted.

The current market value of Walcott's common stock is $20 per share. The after-tax earnings for common stock for the preceding year was $2.10 per share. Earnings for the current year are expected to be about the same. Walcott's present capital structure consists of $20,000,000 in long-term debt (which has an effective market yield rate of 10%), $10,000,000 in 9% preferred stock, and $45,000,000 in common stock equity (3,000,000 shares outstanding). The company is subject to a 40% effective income tax rate.

Required:

(1) Determine Walcott's marginal after-tax weighted-average cost of capital for each of the three financing alternatives. Round your answer to the nearest tenth of a percent.
(2) Determine Walcott's weighted-average cost of capital based on the current financing mix (that is, without considering additional financing needed for the proposed capital expenditure). Round your answer to the nearest tenth of a percent.
(3) Determine Walcott's overall after-tax weighted-average cost of capital (current plus additional financing required for the proposed capital expenditure) for each of the three financing alternatives. Round your answer to the nearest tenth of a percent.

P23-2 Use of Present Value to Determine Value of an Asset. The City of Grant has been contacted by a downtown bank about its desire to purchase land from the city. The land is adjacent to the bank, and the bank intends to use the property for a parking lot and possibly, at a later date, for expansion. The city is interested in working with the bank, because it wants to keep the bank located downtown. If the bank fails to obtain the adjacent property, it may have to close its downtown facility. Retention and perhaps expansion of the downtown bank is expected to enhance the overall health of the downtown business district and will increase the city's proceeds from property and sales taxes.

The appraised value of the city's property is $200,000 plus the loss of use of a water well and storage tank located on the property. The replacement cost of the storage tank is estimated to be $250,000. Loss of the water well means that water must be purchased from the neighboring City of Darnett in addition to what is already being purchased from that city.

The annual cost of producing from the existing well is $32,700 for electricity and $2,500 for labor service. The cost of pump repair and maintenance is estimated to be $20,000 per year for the years 19E through 19H. The annual cost of replacing this lost water supply by additional purchases from the City of Darnett is a fixed demand charge of $46,870 plus a charge of $.2585 per 1,000 gallons for the additional 100,000,000 gallons to be supplied. All costs except pump repair and maintenance are expected to increase at an annual rate of 8%. The City of Grant's cost of capital is estimated to be 10%, and it is estimated that the well has a remaining life of 8 years.

Required: Compute an estimated land value that includes the present value of the differential cost of water and identify other considerations that might affect the final price quoted to the bank.

P23-3 Comparison of Investment Alternatives. Winsburgh Corporation is considering investing in one of two alternative capital projects. Estimated cash flows relating to the two alternative projects follow:

	Project 1	Project 2
Initial cash investment	$120,000	$120,000
Estimated economic life of project	5 years	5 years
Annual after-tax cash inflows:		
Year 1	$10,000	$50,000
Year 2	20,000	45,000
Year 3	30,000	35,000
Year 4	60,000	25,000
Year 5	90,000	20,000

Required:
(1) Compute the net present value for each of the two alternative projects, assuming that the weighted-average cost of capital is 12%.
(2) Compute the internal rate of return for each of the two alternative projects.
(3) Considering the results of your computations in requirements 1 and 2, what would you recommend? Explain.

P23-4 Capital Expenditure Analysis. Walton Metal Company is considering a process computer for improved production control in its Tin Mill Department. This department receives coils of cold-rolled steel from another department of the company. It further reduces the gauge of this steel in its own five-stand tandem cold strip mill. The coils of steel, now much thinner in gauge, pass through a continuous annealing line, in which the strip is heated to 1300° and allowed to cool slowly in an atmosphere of inert gas. The strip is then cleaned in a pickling line before it moves to the electrolytic tinning line. This last process deposits a thin coating of tin on the continuously moving strip. The coiled tin plate is then shipped to customers in the canning industry.

The Tin Mill Department estimates that the proposed process computer will require an investment of $2,200,000. Resulting after-tax cash savings from reduced costs of labor, materials, utilities, and scrap losses over the useful life of the computer are estimated to be:

Year	Amount
1	$ 300,000
2	350,000
3	400,000
4	450,000
5	500,000
6	550,000
7	600,000
8	650,000
9	700,000
10	750,000
	$5,250,000

Required: With respect to the proposed capital expenditure, compute the following:
(1) The payback period
(2) The accounting rate of return on the original investment, rounded to the nearest tenth of a percent
(3) The accounting rate of return on the average investment, rounded to the nearest tenth of a percent
(4) The net present value at an assumed 14% cost of capital
(5) The internal rate of return

P23-5 Comparison of Equipment Alternatives. Two machines are being evaluated for possible acquisition by the Maxfield Corporation. Forecasts relating to the two machines are:

	Machine 1	Machine 2
Purchase price	$ 500,000	$ 600,000
Estimated economic life	8 years	8 years
Estimated salvage value	none	none
Annual after-tax cash benefit:		
Year 1	$ 125,000	$ 50,000
Year 2	125,000	75,000
Year 3	125,000	100,000
Year 4	125,000	125,000
Year 5	125,000	150,000
Year 6	125,000	200,000
Year 7	125,000	300,000
Year 8	125,000	400,000
Total cash benefit	$1,000,000	$1,400,000

Required: For each equipment alternative, compute the following:
(1) The payback period
(2) The accounting rate of return on the original investment, rounded to the nearest tenth of a percent
(3) The accounting rate of return on the average investment, rounded to the nearest tenth of a percent
(4) The net present value and the net present value index, rounded to three decimal places, using an assumed 15% cost of capital
(5) The internal rate of return

P23-6 Equipment Replacement Analysis. Kastlan Corporation is considering the purchase of a replacement machine. The new machine is priced at $64,000. However, the vendor has offered Kastlan a $10,000 trade-in allowance for the old machine. The old machine has a net book value of $4,000 and a tax basis of zero. The new machine will perform essentially the same function as the old machine, except that it will be able to operate at an increased capacity. The following cash flows (which have been adjusted for the anticipated effects of inflation) are predicted over the estimated useful life of the new machine:

Year	Cash Savings Related to Maintenance	Cash Flow from Additional Capacity	Total Increase in Cash Inflow
1	$1,500	$ 6,300	$ 7,800
2	1,200	7,280	8,480
3	900	17,188	18,088
4	600	25,260	25,860
5	300	25,560	25,860
6	0	22,912	22,912
7	0	22,500	22,500

For financial accounting purposes, the new machine is to be depreciated on a straight-line basis over a period of 7 years, with an expected salvage value of $6,000. For tax purposes, however, the machine will be depreciated under MACRS as 5-year property. The company's weighted-average cost of capital is 12%, and its tax rate is 40%.

Required: Using the MACRS rates provided in Exhibit 22-4, determine after-tax cash inflows and then compute each of the following:
(1) Payback period in years
(2) Accounting rate of return on the original investment and also on the average investment
(Requirements continued.)

(3) Net present value and the net present value index
(4) Internal rate of return

P23-7 Investment Analysis with Inflation Adjustment. Redcloud Company is considering the purchase of a die cutting machine costing $100,000. The estimated cash benefits before income taxes and the effects of inflation follow:

Year	Cash Benefit
1	$20,000
2	25,000
3	30,000
4	30,000
5	30,000
6	30,000
7	25,000
8	20,000
9	15,000
10	10,000

For financial accounting purposes, the die cutting machine is to be depreciated on a straight-line basis over a period of 10 years, with no expected salvage value. For income tax purposes, however, the press will be depreciated under MACRS, using the rates for 7-year property (see Exhibit 22-4 for MACRS rates). The company's tax rate is 40%. The annual inflation rate is expected to be 7% for the planning period.

Required: Adjust the cash flows for the expected effects of inflation (round the price-level index to three decimal places) and compute each of the following:
(1) Payback period in years
(2) Accounting rate of return on the original investment
(3) Accounting rate of return on the average investment
(4) Net present value and the net present value index at an assumed 15% cost of capital
(5) Present value payback in years
(6) Internal rate of return

P23-8 Evaluating a Capital Expenditure Proposal for a CIM System. RMX Manufacturing Corporation is evaluating a capital expenditure proposal to acquire and install a computer integrated manufacturing system. The proposed CIM system will have the same total productive capacity as the current manufacturing system. The computer equipment and machinery will require an initial cash investment of $2,000,000. The system has a projected life of 6 years; however, the equipment and machinery will qualify as 5-year property for income tax depreciation purposes. The income tax rate is 40%. In addition to machinery and equipment, software development is expected to cost another $200,000 in the first year. Software costs are amortizable for tax purposes by the straight-line method over a 5-year period. Maintenance costs are expected to increase by $25,000 a year over the current system. The annual cash savings from the CIM system relative to the current manufacturing system (before any adjustment for the effects of inflation or income taxes) are expected to be as follow:

Year	Reduced Labor Cost	Reduced Machine Setup Time	Reduced Inventory Carrying Cost	Lost Contribution Margin Avoided with CIM System
1	$15,000	$40,000	$25,000	$200,000
2	25,000	50,000	35,000	300,000
3	30,000	60,000	40,000	400,000
4	30,000	60,000	40,000	500,000
5	30,000	60,000	40,000	600,000
6	30,000	60,000	40,000	700,000

The expected salvage value for the equipment and machinery at the end of the project is $100,000 (based on current used equipment and machinery prices). Inflation is anticipated at an annual rate of 8%, and inflation is expected to affect all cash inflows and outflows.

Required:

(1) Compute the inflation-adjusted net after-tax cash inflow from savings for the CIM proposal for each year, and determine whether the total cash savings from the CIM system will exceed the system's cost. (Use the MACRS depreciation rates provided in Exhibit 22-4, and round the price-level index used to three decimal places.)

(2) Compute the payback period for the proposed investment in a CIM system.

(3) Assuming the company's cost of capital is 14%, compute the net present value of the proposed investment in a CIM system.

P23-9 Purchasing versus Leasing. Wheary Enterprises plans to operate a sightseeing boat along the Charles River in Boston. In negotiating the purchase of a new vessel from Yachts Dynamic Inc., Wheary learned that Yachts Dynamic would lease the boat to them as an alternative to selling it outright. Through such an arrangement, Wheary would not pay the $2,000,000 purchase price but would lease for $320,000 annually. Wheary expects the boat to last for 15 years and have a salvage value of $200,000. For tax purposes, however, the boat is 7-year property (that is, the cost of the boat would be recovered over a period of 8 years, using the MACRS rates for 7-year property provided in Exhibit 22-4.)

The annual net cash inflow, excluding any consideration of lease payments and income tax, is expected to be $600,000. The company's income tax rate is 40%, and its cost of capital is 14%.

Required: Make a recommendation to purchase or lease the boat, using the net present value method to evaluate each alternative.

P23-10 Make, Buy, or Lease. Egelston Corporation is a manufacturing concern that produces and sells a wide range of products. The company not only mass produces a number of products and equipment components, but is also capable of producing special-purpose manufacturing equipment to customer specifications.

The firm is considering adding a new product, with an estimated 6-year market life, to one of its product lines. More equipment will be required to produce the new product. There are three alternative ways to acquire the needed equipment: (1) purchase general-purpose equipment, (2) lease general-purpose equipment, or (3) build special-purpose equipment. A fourth alternative, purchase of the special-purpose equipment, has been ruled out because it would be prohibitively expensive.

The general-purpose equipment can be purchased for $125,000. The equipment has an estimated salvage of $15,000 at the end of its useful life of 10 years. After 6 years, the equipment can be used elsewhere in the plant or be sold for $40,000. Alternatively, the general-purpose equipment can be acquired by a 6-year lease for $40,000 annual rent. The lessor will assume all responsibility for property taxes, insurance, and maintenance.

Special-purpose equipment can be constructed by the Contract Equipment Department of Egelston Corporation. Although the department is operating at a level that is normal for the time of year, it is below full capacity. The department could produce the equipment without interfering with its regular revenue-producing activities.

For tax purposes, the company would depreciate both the general-purpose machine and the special-purpose machine over 6 years, using the MACRS rates for 5-year property (provided in Exhibit 22-4). The salvage value of the special-purpose equipment at the end of 6 years is estimated to be $30,000. The company uses an after-tax cost of capital of 14%. Its income tax rate is 40%.

The estimated departmental costs for the construction of the special-purpose equipment are:

Materials and parts	$ 75,000
Direct labor	60,000
Variable factory overhead (50% of direct labor)	30,000
Fixed factory overhead (25% of direct labor)	15,000
Total	$180,000

Corporation general and administrative costs average 20% of the labor cost.

Engineering and management studies provide the following revenue and cost estimates (excluding lease payments and depreciation) for producing the new product, depending on the equipment used:

	General-Purpose Equipment		Self-Constructed Equipment
	Leased	Purchased	
Unit selling price	$ 5.00	$ 5.00	$ 5.00
Unit production costs:			
Materials	$ 1.80	$ 1.80	$ 1.70
Variable conversion cost	1.65	1.65	1.40
Total unit production cost	$ 3.45	$ 3.45	$ 3.10
Unit contribution margin	$ 1.55	$ 1.55	$ 1.90
Estimated unit volume	× 40,000	× 40,000	× 40,000
Estimated total annual contribution margin	$ 62,000	$ 62,000	$ 76,000
Other costs:			
Supervision	$ 16,000	$ 16,000	$ 17,000
Property taxes and insurance	0	3,000	5,000
Maintenance	0	3,000	2,000
Total other costs	$ 16,000	$ 22,000	$ 24,000

Required:

(1) Calculate the net present value for each of the three alternatives that Egelston Corporation has at its disposal.

(2) Explain which, if any, of the three options Egelston Corporation should select. (ICMA adapted)

Cases

C23-1 Evaluating Alternative Projects. Quible Industries comprises four divisions, each operating in a different industry. The divisions are currently preparing their capital expenditure budgets for the coming year. The Caledonia Division, located in the northeastern United States, manufactures home appliances that it distributes nationally. The manufacturing and marketing departments of Caledonia have proposed six capital expenditure projects for next year. The division manager must now analyze these investment proposals and select those projects that will be included in the capital budget to be submitted to Quible Industries for approval. The proposed projects in the following list are considered to have the same degree of risk.

- Project A. Redesign and modification of an existing product that is currently scheduled to be dropped. The enhanced model would be sold for 6 more years.
- Project B. Expansion of a line of cookware that has been produced on an experimental basis for the past year. The expected life of the cookware line is 8 years.
- Project C. Reorganization of the plant's distribution center, including the installation of computerized equipment for tracking inventory. This project would benefit both administration and marketing.
- Project D. Addition of a new product, a combination bread and meat slicer. In addition to new manufacturing equipment, a significant amount of introductory advertising would be required. If this project is implemented, Project A would not be feasible due to limited capacity.
- Project E. Automation of the packaging department, which would result in cost savings over the next 6 years.
- Project F. Construction of a building wing to house offices presently located in an area that could be used for manufacturing. The change would not add capacity for new lines but would alleviate crowded conditions that currently exist, making it possible to improve the productivity of two existing product lines that have been unable to meet market demand.

Quible Industries has established a hurdle rate of 12% for capital expenditures for all four divisions. The hurdle rate is the company's long-term desired cost of capital. Additional information about each of Caledonia Division's six proposed projects follows:

	Project A	Project B	Project C	Project D	Project E	Project F
Initial investment	$106,000	$200,000	$140,000	$160,000	$144,000	$130,000
After-tax cash inflows:						
Year 1	$ 50,000	$ 20,000	$ 36,000	$ 20,000	$ 50,000	$ 40,000
Year 2	50,000	40,000	36,000	30,000	50,000	40,000
Year 3	40,000	50,000	36,000	40,000	50,000	40,000
Year 4	40,000	60,000	36,000	50,000	20,000	40,000
Year 5	30,000	60,000	36,000	60,000	20,000	40,000
Year 6	40,000	60,000		70,000	11,600	40,000
Year 7		40,000		80,000		40,000
Year 8		44,000		66,000		42,000
Total inflows	$250,000	$374,000	$180,000	$416,000	$201,600	$322,000
Payback period	2.2 yrs	4.5 yrs	3.9 yrs	4.3 yrs	2.9 yrs	3.3 yrs
Net present value	$ 69,683	$ 23,733	$ (10,228)	$ 74,374	$ 6,027	$ 69,513
Internal rate of return	35%	15%	9%	22%	14%	26%

Required:

(1) Explain how each of the following quantitative techniques is used in evaluating capital expenditure proposals and what it is designed to measure.
  (a) Payback method
  (b) Net present value method
  (c) Internal rate of return method

(2) If Caledonia Division has no budget restrictions for capital expenditures and has been told to maximize the value of the company, identify the capital investment projects that should be included in the Division's capital budget to be submitted to Quible Industries. Explain why the projects should be included or excluded.

(3) Assume that Quible Industries has specified that Caledonia Division will be restricted to a maximum of $450,000 for capital expenditures, and that Caledonia should select projects that maximize the value of the company. Further assume that any budget not spent on the identified projects will be invested at the hurdle rate of 12%. Identify the capital investment projects Caledonia should include in its capital expenditures budget to be submitted to Quible Industries in this situation, and explain the basis for their inclusion. (ICMA adapted)

C23-2 Follow-up of Project Results. Recap Corporation made a capital investment of $100,000 in new equipment 2 years ago. The analysis made at that time indicated that the equipment would save $36,400 in operating expenses per year over a 5-year period, or a 24% return on capital before taxes per year based on the internal rate of return analysis.

The department manager believed that the equipment was living up to expectations. However, the departmental report showing the overall return on investment (ROI) rate for the first year in which this equipment was used did not reflect as much improvement as had been expected. The department manager asked the accounting section to "break out" the figures related to this investment to find out why it did not contribute more to the department's ROI.

The accounting section was able to identify the equipment and its contribution to the department's operations. The report presented to the department manager at the end of the first year was as follows:

Reduced operating expenses due to new equipment	$ 36,400
Less depreciation (20% of cost)	20,000
Contribution before taxes	$ 16,400
Investment at beginning of year	$100,000
Investment at end of year	80,000
Average investment for the year	90,000
Return on investment ($16,400 ÷ $90,000)	18.2%

The department manager was surprised that the ROI was less than the 24% internal rate of return, because the new equipment was performing as expected.

Required:

(1) Discuss the reasons why the 18.2% return on investment for the new equipment as calculated in the department's report by the accounting section differs from the 24% internal rate of return calculated at the time the machine was approved for purchase.

(2) Explain how Recap Corporation might restructure the data from the internal rate of return analysis, so that the expected performance of the new equipment is consistent with the operating reports received by the department manager.

(ICMA adapted)

CHAPTER 24

Decision Making Under Uncertainty

Learning Objectives

After studying this chapter, you will be able to:

1. Define probability and conditional value.
2. Compute the expected value of an event given a probability distribution.
3. Compute the variance and the standard deviation of the expected value.
4. Define and compute the coefficient of variation.
5. Prepare a payoff table and determine the best strategy under conditions of uncertainty.
6. Compute the expected value of perfect information.
7. Revise probabilities on the basis of new information and construct a revised payoff table.
8. Construct and use decision trees to determine the best alternative course of action.
9. Compute the expected net present value and the standard deviation of the net present value for capital expenditure proposals.
10. Use multiattribute decision models that specifically consider both quantitative and nonquantitative factors in the decision.

In practice, most decisions are based on a single best guess about the future value of each decision variable relevant to the decision problem. Although decision makers recognize that the future is uncertain, formal attempts to incorporate uncertainty into the decision are rarely made. Instead, the problem of uncertainty is usually handled by tempering the decision with business judgment and a "feel" for the uncertainty inherent in the relevant data. As a result, many biased and naive decisions are made.

A better approach to dealing with the problem of uncertainty is to incorporate the likelihood of alternative outcomes into the decision model. This approach is sometimes referred to as probability analysis. **Probability analysis** is an application of statistical decision theory that, under conditions of uncertainty, leads to more consistent and reliable decisions than single best guesses. Probabilities, based on available information, are utilized to reduce the amount of uncertainty present in the decision problem and improve the quality of management decisions.

This chapter begins by defining probability and explaining how probabilities can be obtained and used in decision making. These concepts are extended in the following section, which illustrates the use of payoff tables and decision trees to determine the best strategy under uncertainty. The next section demonstrates the use of the normal distribution in evaluating the riskiness of short-term projects. It is followed by a brief explanation of Monte Carlo simulations. The last two sections of the chapter discuss and illustrate the use of the normal distribution to evaluate the riskiness of capital expenditure proposals and the use of the multiattribute decision model to incorporate both quantitative and nonquantitative factors into the analysis.

Using Probabilities in Descision Making

Technically, a **probability** is a number between 0 and 1 that represents the likelihood of the occurrence of a particular event. A probability may be thought of as the relative frequency of the occurrence of different recurring events. The probability is operational in the sense that historical events exhibit a frequency pattern, or conceptual in the sense that future events are expected to follow some frequency pattern. Alternatively, a probability can be thought of as the degree of belief about the outcome of a nonrecurring future event, such as the probability that the government will deregulate a particular industry before the end of the year. In either case, the probabilities are no more accurate than the data or subjective estimates on which they are based. Nevertheless, the incorporation of probabilities into the decision process provides a systematic way to evaluate the effect of alternative outcomes on complex decision problems.

In some decision settings, a wealth of reasonably reliable historical data permits the assignment of fairly objective probabilities. As long as the underlying process that generates the decision variable is not expected to change in the future, historical data can be used to model the probability distribution. For example, the actual historical demand for a particular product can be a good predictor of future demand as long as consumer tastes and preferences, the capacity of consumers to purchase the product, and the price and availability of competitive products do not change. If competitors introduce a new and better product, however, future demand for the old product is likely to decline, which in turn means that the frequency distribution of historic demand is not a very reliable model of the probability distribution of future demand.

The use of probabilities in decision making under uncertainty is illustrated as follows. Assume that Maxan Company's contribution margin is $10 per unit sold. A study of a 40-month period reveals that sales demand is random; that is, demand is irregular with no discernible trend or pattern. If no change is expected in the underlying process that generates demand for the product (that is, the action of competitors and the capacity and desire of consumers to purchase the product are not expected to change), experience is a reasonable basis for predicting the future. The relative frequency of the occurrence of each level of sales demand during the sample period can be used as a measure of the probability of the occurrence of each level of sales demand in the future (denoted as $P(x_i)$, where x_i is the ith event). The sum of the probabilities of all possible events must equal one, i.e., $\Sigma P(x_i) = 1$. If the sum of the probabilities of the events is less than one, some event other than those included in the distribution can occur.

Once the probability distribution for demand has been determined, the expected contribution margin from sales of the product, $E(x)$ (referred to as the **expected value**), is determined by adding the products of the contribution margin for each possible level of sales, x_i (referred to as the **conditional value**), multiplied by the relative probability of its occurrence, $P(x_i)$. That is, $E(x) = \Sigma\,[x_i\,P(x_i)]$. The computation is illustrated in Exhibit 24-1.

EXHIBIT 24-1

Maxan Company
Expected Value (Contribution Margin) of Monthly Sales

(1) Unit Sales each Month	(2) Historical Frequency in Months	(3) $P(x_i)$ Probability	(4) Contribution Margin per Unit	(5) x_i Conditional Value (1) × (4)	(6) $E(x)$ Expected Value (3) × (5)
4,000	8	8/40 = .20	$10	$40,000	$ 8,000
5,000	10	10/40 = .25	10	50,000	12,500
6,000	12	12/40 = .30	10	60,000	18,000
7,000	6	6/40 = .15	10	70,000	10,500
8,000	4	4/40 = .10	10	80,000	8,000
	40	40/40 = 1.00			$57,000

The expected value in this illustration can be thought of as the average contribution margin that the company can expect in the future, based on past experience. The expected value is the mean of the probability distribution. If several alternative projects are being evaluated, the alternative with the largest expected value has the largest expected average contribution margin and, consequently, the largest expected total contribution margin in the long run. However, management may be concerned not only about profitability but also about risk.

The variance and the standard deviation are measures of dispersion commonly used as measures of risk. The **variance** of a probability distribution is defined as $\sigma^2 = \Sigma P(x_i)[x_i - E(x)]^2$, and the **standard deviation** (denote as σ) is the square root of the variance. Each provides a numerical measure of the scatter of the possible conditional values around the expected value. The greater the dispersion, the greater the likelihood, and consequently the greater the risk, that the actual value (contribution margin in the illustration) will differ materially from the expected value. Computation of the standard deviation for Maxan Company monthly sales is illustrated in Exhibit 24-2.

EXHIBIT 24-2

Maxan Company
Standard Deviation of the Expected Value
(Contribution Margin) of Monthly Sales

(1) x_i Conditional Value	(2) $[x_i - E(x)]$ Difference from $57,000 Expected Value	(3) $[x_i - E(x)]^2$ (2) Squared	(4) $P(x_i)$ Probability	(5) $P(x_i)[x_i - E(x)]^2$ (3) × (4)
$40,000	$ (17,000)	$289,000,000	.20	$ 57,800,000
50,000	(7,000)	49,000,000	.25	12,250,000
60,000	3,000	9,000,000	.30	2,700,000
70,000	13,000	169,000,000	.15	25,350,000
80,000	23,000	529,000,000	.10	52,900,000
Variance (σ^2)				$151,000,000

Standard deviation (σ) = $\sqrt{\$151{,}000{,}000}$ = $12,288

If alternative expected values are being compared, such as the expected contribution margins for several different products, the relative riskiness of each alternative cannot be determined by simply comparing standard deviations. Because of the difference in the magnitudes of the expected values, an alternative with a large expected value is expected to have a larger standard deviation than an alternative with a small expected value. The problem of comparing the relative riskiness of alternatives can be resolved by computing and comparing the **coefficient of variation**, which is the ratio of the standard deviation of a probability distribution to its expected value. The coefficient of variation compensates for differences in the relative size of expected values involved.

For the Maxan Company illustration, the coefficient of variation is computed as follows:

$$\text{Coefficient of variation} = \frac{\text{Standard deviation } (\sigma)}{\text{Expected value (contribution margin) E}(x)} = \frac{\$12{,}288}{\$57{,}000} = .22$$

If another product has an expected contribution margin of $100,000 and a standard deviation of $18,000, the relative risk, as measured by the coefficient of variation, is less than for the product first illustrated ($18,000 ÷ $100,000 = .18, compared with .22) even though the standard deviation is larger ($18,000 compared with $12,288).

Determining the Best Strategy Under Uncertainty

Probabilities are especially useful in determining the best course of action under conditions of uncertainty. The course of action selected can be thought of as the decision maker's strategy for achieving some goal—maximizing profits, minimizing losses, or increasing market share. Payoff tables and decision trees are useful tools in determining the best strategy under uncertainty.

Payoff Tables

When several courses of action are being considered, a payoff table can be constructed to determine the best strategy. A **payoff table** is a table that presents both the conditional value of each event that can occur for each course of action being considered and the expected value of each alternative based on the probabilities of the events that can occur.

For illustrative purposes, assume that the manager of City Bakery must decide how many loaves of bread to bake each day. The normal sales price is $1 a loaf. However, the price of bread not sold on the day of delivery is reduced to $.30 a loaf. The variable cost of producing and distributing a loaf of bread is $.40. An additional cost of $.10 is incurred in distributing and selling each loaf at the reduced price. The unit contribution margin is computed as follows:

Regular sales price...............	$1.00	Reduced sales price		$.30
Less variable cost................	.40	Less: Variable cost.............	$.40	
Unit contribution margin .... at regular sales price.......	$ .60	Additional distribution cost......	.10	.50
		Unit loss at reduced price		$(.20)

Over the past 360 days, the company has experienced the following random sales demand (that is, there are no cycles or trends in sales demand):

Unit Sales per Day	Number of Days	Probability
10,000	72	.20
11,000	108	.30
12,000	144	.40
13,000	36	.10
	360	1.00

If sales demand in the future is expected to be the same as in the past, a payoff table can be constructed to determine the expected value of producing enough bread to satisfy each level of demand. The payoff table for City Bakery's bread production is presented in Exhibit 24-3. Each conditional value is the contribution margin expected when City Bakery produces the number of loaves listed in the left-hand column and customer demand is equal to the quantity shown at the head of the column. The expected value of producing bread in each of the four quantities is listed in the right-hand column. The expected value of each action is determined by multiplying each conditional value by the probability of its occurrence and then summing the products. The results for City Bakery indicate that the best strategy in the long run is to produce 12,000 loaves of bread each day, because such a strategy results in the largest average expected profit.

EXHIBIT 24-3

City Bakery
Payoff Table for Alternative Quantities of Bread Production

Possible Actions (Quantities to Be Produced)	Contribution Margin (Conditional Value) for Possible Sales Quantities				Contribution Margin (Expected Value of Each Strategy)
	10,000	11,000	12,000	13,000	
10,000	$6,000*	$6,000	$6,000	$6,000	$6,000
11,000	5,800**	6,600	6,600	6,600	6,440
12,000	5,600	6,400	7,200	7,200	6,640
13,000	5,400	6,200	7,000	7,800	6,520***
Probability	.20	.30	.40	.10	

* 10,000 units at the regular sales price × $.60 CM per unit = $6,000 conditional value.

** (10,000 units at the regular sales price × $.60 CM per unit) – (1,000 units at the reduced price × $.20 loss per unit) = $5,800 conditional value.

*** (.20 probability × $5,400 CM) + (.30 probability × $6,200 CM) + (.40 probability × $7,000 CM) + (.10 probability × $7,800 CM) = $6,520 expected value.

As in the previous illustration, the standard deviation and the coefficient of variation can be computed for each strategy. To illustrate the computations, the standard deviation and the coefficient of variation for the strategy with the largest expected value (the 12,000-loaf daily production level) is presented in Exhibit 24-4.

Expected Value of Perfect Information. Sometimes it is possible to acquire additional information that will be useful in selecting the best alternative. Information, however, like any good or service, is costly. For example, the baker in the City Bakery illustration could conduct a market survey, which would improve the prediction of consumer demand. However, a market survey costs money. Before such a decision is made, the cost of the additional information should be weighed against the increase in the expected value that can be obtained by using the information. If the increase in the expected value to be derived from the use of the additional information is greater than the cost, the cost should be incurred. Otherwise, it should not.

EXHIBIT 24-4

City Bakery
Standard Deviation and Coefficient of Variation
for 12,000-Loaf Daily Production Level

(1) x_i Conditional Value	(2) $[x_i - E(x)]$ Difference from \$6,640 Expected Value	(3) $[x_i - E(x)]^2$ (2) Squared	(4) $P(x_i)$ Probability	(5) $P(x_i)[x_i - E(x)]^2$ (3) × (4)
\$5,600	\$(1,040)	\$1,081,600	.20	\$216,320
6,400	(240)	57,600	.30	17,280
7,200	560	313,600	.40	125,440
7,200	560	313,600	.10	31,360
Variance				\$390,400

Standard deviation $\sigma = \sqrt{\$390{,}400} = \$625$

$$\text{Coefficient of Variation} = \frac{\text{Standard deviation } (\sigma)}{\text{Expected contribution margin } [E(x)]} = \frac{\$625}{\$6{,}640} = .09$$

In actual practice, it is difficult to determine the value of information about a future event until the event has occurred. A market survey would probably result in a better estimate of demand but not a perfectly accurate prediction. On the other hand, it is possible to compute the maximum expected value of additional information by computing the expected value under conditions of certainty and comparing it with the expected value of the best strategy under uncertainty. The expected value under conditions of certainty is the expected value when the probability distribution is an accurate representation of the relative frequency of future demand and the decision maker knows exactly when each possible event will occur. The maximum increase in the expected value that can be obtained from additional information is the expected value of perfect information and, consequently, the maximum amount one would be willing to pay for additional information.

In the City Bakery illustration, the expected value of perfect information is the difference between (1) the average contribution margin if the manager knows the sales demand for bread each day with certainty (and consequently produces exactly the amount demanded) and (2) the average expected contribution margin using the best strategy under uncertainty. The expected value of perfect information is computed in Exhibit 24-5. The results indicate that management can afford to pay up to \$200 per day for perfect information, because with perfect information the contribution margin is expected to increase an average of \$200 a day. While perfect information is generally not available, this analysis determines the upper limit of the value of additional information.

Revising Probabilities. Probabilities should be revised as new information becomes available. One approach to probability revision is an application of Bayes' theorem. However, before Bayes' theorem is presented, the following additional notation is needed:

1. Let P(A), P(B), and P(C) be the symbols for the probabilities of the occurrence of events A, B, and C, respectively.
2. Let P(AB) be the symbol for the probability of the occurrence of both event A and event B, and let P(BC) be the symbol for the probability of the occurrence of both event B and event C.

EXHIBIT 24-5

City Bakery
Expected Value of Perfect Information

(1) Unit Sales per Day	(2) Contribution Margin per Unit	(3) x_i Contribution Margin (Conditional Value)	(4) $P(x_i)$ Probability	(5) $E(x)$ Contribution Margin (Expected Value)
10,000	$.60	$6,000	.20	$1,200
11,000	.60	6,600	.30	1,980
12,000	.60	7,200	.40	2,880
13,000	.60	7,800	.10	780
Expected value (contribution margin) with perfect certainty				$6,840
Less the expected value (contribution margin) of the best strategy under uncertainty (production of 12,000 loaves per day)				6,640
Expected value of perfect information (on a per-day basis)				$ 200

3. Let P(A | B) be the symbol for the probability of the occurrence of event A given the occurrence of event B, P(B | A) be the symbol for the probability of the occurrence of event B given the occurrence of event A, and P(B | C) be the probability of the occurrence of event B given the occurrence of event C.

P(AB) and P(BC) are referred to as **joint probabilities**. P(A | B), P(B | A), and P(B | C) are referred to as **conditional probabilities**; that is, the events enclosed in parentheses are not independent, but instead are related in some way. If P(A | B) < 1.0 and P(B | A) < 1.0, then A can occur without the occurrence of event B, and B can occur without the occurrence of event A; however, assuming that P(A | B) > 0 and P(B | A) > 0, there is some possibility that both events will occur because there is some logical link between the two events. For example, a company can introduce a new product before the end of the year (event A) without hiring any new employees, and the same company can hire new employees (event B) without introducing a new product, but it is also quite possible that the company will hire new employees in order to have sufficient capacity to be able to produce a new product. In this case, because event A and event B are not independent events, P(AB) = P(B | A)P(A) = P(A | B)P(B). The joint probability of A and B is equal to the conditional probability of the occurrence of B, given the occurrence of A, multiplied by the probability of the occurrence of A, which is also equal to the conditional probability of the occurrence of A, given the occurrence of B, multiplied by the probability of the occurrence of B.

Now assume that event C is the event that will occur if event A does not occur; that is, event C is that the company in the example will not introduce a new product before the end of the year. In this case, event C and event A are mutually exclusive; the company either will or will not introduce a new product before the end of the year. However, both event C and event B can occur; the company can hire new employees but not introduce a new product. The Venn diagram in Figure 24-1 illustrates this relationship.

The rectangle labeled A and the rectangle labeled C represent events A and C, respectively, which in this case are of equal size and, therefore, have an equal chance of occurring. Because event A and event C together occupy all of the area in the Venn diagram and do not overlap, one or the other must occur, but not both. Therefore, P(A) + P(C) = .5 + .5 = 1. The circle in the Venn diagram represents P(B), which in this case is .4. The portion of B that overlaps A is the joint probability of the occurrence of both A and B; that is, P(AB), which is .3. Similarly, the portion of B that overlaps C is the joint probability of the occurrence of B and C; that is, P(BC), which is .1. Thus, P(B) = P(AB) + P(BC) = .3 + .1 = .4.

FIGURE 24-1 *Venn Diagram Illustrating Joint Probability*

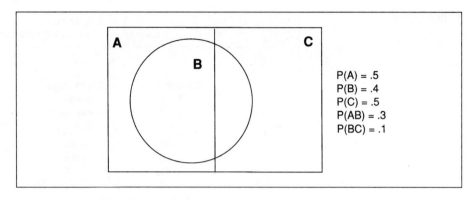

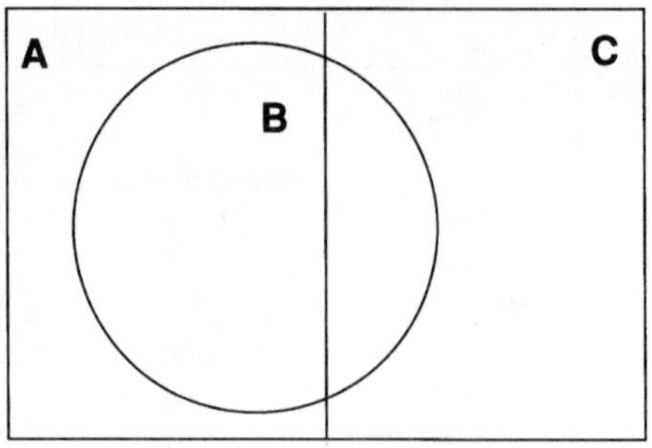

Recall from the preceding discussion that P(AB) = P(A | B)P(B). Because P(AB) and P(B) are both known in this situation, P(A | B), which is the conditional probability of the occurrence of event A given the occurrence of event B, can be determined by dividing both sides of the equation by P(B), as follows:

$$P(A|B) = \frac{P(AB)}{P(B)} = \frac{.3}{.4} = .75$$

In terms of the Venn diagram in Figure 24-1, this result means that 75 percent of the area occupied by B overlaps the area occupied by A; therefore, if B occurs, there is a 75 percent chance that A will also occur. Similarly, because P(AB) = P(B | A)P(A), P(BC) = P(C | B)P(B), and P(BC) = P(B | C)P(C), conditional probabilities P(B | A), P(C | B) and P(B | C) can be determined as follows:

$$P(B|A) = \frac{P(AB)}{P(A)} = \frac{.3}{.5} = .6$$

$$P(C|B) = \frac{P(BC)}{P(B)} = \frac{.1}{.4} = .25$$

$$P(B|C) = \frac{P(BC)}{P(C)} = \frac{.1}{.5} = .2$$

With these values determined, the fact that P(AB) = P(A | B)P(B) = P(B | A)P(A) and P(BC) = P(C | B)P(B) = P(B | C)P(C) can be demonstrated as follows:

P(AB) = .3	P(BC) = .1
P(A|B)P(B) = (.75)(.4) = .3	P(C|B)P(B) = (.25)(.4) = .1
P(B|A)P(A) = (.6)(.5) = .3	P(B|C)P(C) = (.2)(.5) = .1

Because P(AB) = P(A | B)P(B) = P(B | A)P(A), then P(B | A)P(A) can be substituted for P(AB), and because P(B) = P(AB) + P(BC) = P(B | A)P(A) + P(B | C)P(C), then P(B | A)P(A) + P(B | C)P(C) can be substituted for P(B). The following equation results:

$$P(A|B) = \frac{P(AB)}{P(B)} = \frac{P(B|A)P(A)}{P(B|A)P(A) + P(B|C)P(C)}$$

Similarly, because P(B | C)P(C) = P(C | B)P(B) = P(BC), the conditional probability of the occurrence of event C can be derived as follows:

$$P(C|B) = \frac{P(BC)}{P(B)} = \frac{P(B|C)P(C)}{P(B|A)P(A) + P(B|C)P(C)}$$

This formulation is Bayes' theorem expressed in its simplest form. Bayes' theorem can be used to revise the original probability estimates for events A and C when new information becomes available (in this case, the occurrence of event B). For this purpose, the term on the left-hand side of the equation (P(A | B) in the first equation or P(C | B) in the second equation) is the revised estimate of the probability of the occurrence of the event of concern (that is, the probability that event A will occur in the first equation or that event C will occur in the second equation now that event B has occurred). This revised probability estimate is referred to as a **posterior probability**. P(A) and P(C) are the probability estimates of the occurrences of events A and C, respectively, before event B occurred. Because these estimates were made before the new information became available, they are referred to as **prior probabilities**. P(B | A) and P(B | C) are conditional probabilities that express the expected relationship of the new information to events A and C (that is, the probability that event B will occur and be followed by event A or C). To revise the probabilities of the occurrence of events A and C using Bayes' theorem, multiply each prior probability by the conditional probability associated with the related event and then divide each product by the sum of all of the products. The sum of the posterior probabilities must equal the sum of the prior probabilities (P(A) + P(C) = P(A | B) + P(C | B) = 1.0). In the simple two-event world depicted by the foregoing equations, the numerator is P(B | A)P(A) for the revision of the probability of the occurrence of event A and P(B | C)P(C) for the revision of the probability of the occurrence of event C. Because A and C are the only two events that can occur, the denominator in both cases is the sum of these two products (P(B | A)P(A) + P(B | C)P(C)). As a result, the sum of the revised probabilities (P(A | B) + P(C | B) = 1.0) is equal to the sum of the prior probabilities (P(A) + P(C) = 1.0).

The use of Bayes' theorem in the revision of probabilities can be illustrated as follows. Assume that the top management of Kotts Company is planning to introduce a new version of Kotts' present product in order to expand its market share. Market surveys indicate that there is a sizable market for a less expensive version of the product and a smaller, but lucrative, market for a more expensive version. However, rumors are circulating that a competitor will introduce a new version of their product before the end of the year. The introduction of such a product by the competitor would have a material effect on the sales of Kotts Company's products. Based on familiarity with the competitor's previous actions, management assigns the following probabilities to each of the possible events:

Event	Description	Probability
A	No new product introduced	.5
B	Less expensive product introduced	.2
C	More expensive product introduced	.2
D	Both a less expensive and a more expensive product introduced	.1
		1.0

Based on available data, a payoff table such as the one presented in Exhibit 24-6 can be constructed for the Kotts Company decision problem.

EXHIBIT 24-6

Kotts Company
Payoff Table for Introduction of New Product

	Events (Actions of Competitor)				
Kotts Company Action	A No New Product	B Less Expensive Product	C More Expensive Product	D Both Kinds of Products	Expected Value
No new product	$1,000,000	$ 700,000	$ 700,000	$500,000	$ 830,000
Less expensive product	1,300,000	800,000	1,100,000	800,000	1,110,000
More expensive product	1,400,000	1,200,000	800,000	800,000	1,180,000
Both kinds of products	1,500,000	900,000	800,000	700,000	1,160,000
Probability	.50	.20	.20	.10	

The payoff table in Exhibit 24-6 indicates that the best course of action for Kotts Company is to introduce a more expensive product. However, before deciding on a course of action, management learns that the competitor is hiring engineers (event E). Management believes that there is a .80 probability that the hiring of engineers means that the competitor is planning to manufacture and introduce a more expensive product. This means that there is a .20 probability that the competitor would hire more engineers even if it had no intention of introducing a new product ($P(E|A) = .20$), a .20 probability that it would hire more engineers if it were planning to introduce a new less expensive product ($P(E|B) = .20$), a .80 probability that it would hire more engineers if it were planning to introduce a more expensive product ($P(E|C) = .80$), and a .80 probability that it would hire more engineers if it were planning to introduce both less and more expensive products ($P(E|D) = .80$). Based on these newly assessed conditional probabilities, the original probabilities can be revised as follows, using Bayes' theorem:

$$P(A|E) = \frac{P(E|A)P(A)}{P(E|A)P(A) + P(E|B)P(B) + P(E|C)P(C) + P(E|D)P(D)}$$

$$P(B|E) = \frac{P(E|B)P(B)}{P(E|A)P(A) + P(E|B)P(B) + P(E|C)P(C) + P(E|D)P(D)}$$

$$P(C|E) = \frac{P(E|C)P(C)}{P(E|A)P(A) + P(E|B)P(B) + P(E|C)P(C) + P(E|D)P(D)}$$

$$P(D|E) = \frac{P(E|D)P(D)}{P(E|A)P(A) + P(E|B)P(B) + P(E|C)P(C) + P(E|D)P(D)}$$

Event (Action of Competitor)	(1) Prior Probability	(2) Conditional Probability of Hiring Engineers	(3) Prior Probability Times Conditional Probability (1) × (2)	(4) Posterior Probability (3) line item ÷ (3) total
A (No new product)	.50	.20	.10	5/19
B (Less expensive product)	.20	.20	.04	2/19
C (More expensive product)	.20	.80	.16	8/19
D (Both kinds of products)	.10	.80	.08	4/19
	1.00		.38	19/19

Notice that the original values in column (3) correspond to the numerators in the equations that precede the table, and the column (3) total corresponds to the denominator in each equation. If more information becomes available before the decision is made, the posterior probabilities become prior probabilities, and the new conditional probabilities (the probabilities associated with the new information) would be used to compute new posterior probabilities. Also, notice that the conditional probabilities in column (2) are not totaled. Although each conditional probability must be less than 1, the sum of the conditional probabilities need not equal 1 because they do not represent a collectively exhaustive set of possibilities.

A revised payoff table based on the revised probabilities and the original conditional values for the alternative actions being considered by Kotts Company is presented in Exhibit 24-7. The expected values of the alternatives changed when the probabilities were revised. In addition, the best course of action for Kotts Company changed from the introduction of a more expensive product to the introduction of a less expensive product.

EXHIBIT 24-7

Kotts Company
Revised Payoff Table for Introduction of New Product

	Event (Action of Competitor)				
	A	B	C	D	
Kotts Company Action	**No New Product**	**Less Expensive Product**	**More Expensive Product**	**Both Kinds of Products**	**Expected Value**
No new product	$1,000,000	$ 700,000	$ 700,000	$500,000	$ 736,842
Less expensive product ..	1,300,000	800,000	1,100,000	800,000	1,057,895
More expensive product..	1,400,000	1,200,000	800,000	800,000	1,000,000
Both kinds of products ...	1,500,000	900,000	800,000	700,000	973,684
Probability.....................	5/19	2/19	8/19	4/19	

Decision Trees

Alternatives and their expected results can be portrayed graphically with a decision tree. A **decision tree** is a graphic representation of the decision points, the alternative actions available to the decision maker, the possible outcomes from each decision alternative along with their probabilities, and the expected values of each event. A decision tree expedites the evaluation of alternatives by giving the decision maker a visual map of the expected result of each alternative. This kind of analysis is especially useful when sequential decisions are involved.

The use of a decision tree in a sequential-decision problem is illustrated as follows. Assume that Wildcat Oil Company is faced with the problem of deciding whether or not to drill a well on a newly acquired lease. Based on historically available information, the probability of finding oil is .22, and the probability of finding no oil is .78. If oil is found, the company will gain a $1,000,000 profit; however, if oil is not found, the company will lose $300,000.

Before deciding whether or not to drill, Wildcat can pay a seismographic service company $50,000 to conduct a seismic test of the proposed site. There is a .2 probability that the seismic test result will be favorable, and a .8 probability that it will not. If the results are favorable, the probability of finding oil is .7 (with a .3 probability of finding no oil); and if the results are unfavorable, the probability of finding no oil is .9 (with a .1 probability of finding oil).

In this situation, Wildcat is faced with making two sequential decisions; first, whether or not to purchase a seismic test, and second, whether or not to drill. Based on the data provided, a decision tree can be constructed as shown in Figure 24-2.

The decision points—that is, the points at which the decision maker must choose some action—are denoted with squares. The chance points—the points at which some event related to the previous decision will occur—are denoted with circles. To determine the best choice of action, the analyst first determines the expected values for the last alternatives in the sequence. Then, the expected values for the next preceding alternatives are determined, based on the assumption that the best decision alternatives for the subsequent decisions are made. This process is sometimes referred to as *backward induction*. The expected value of each action is written above the related chance point, and the expected value of the best choice of action is written above the related decision point.

FIGURE 24-2 *Decision Tree*

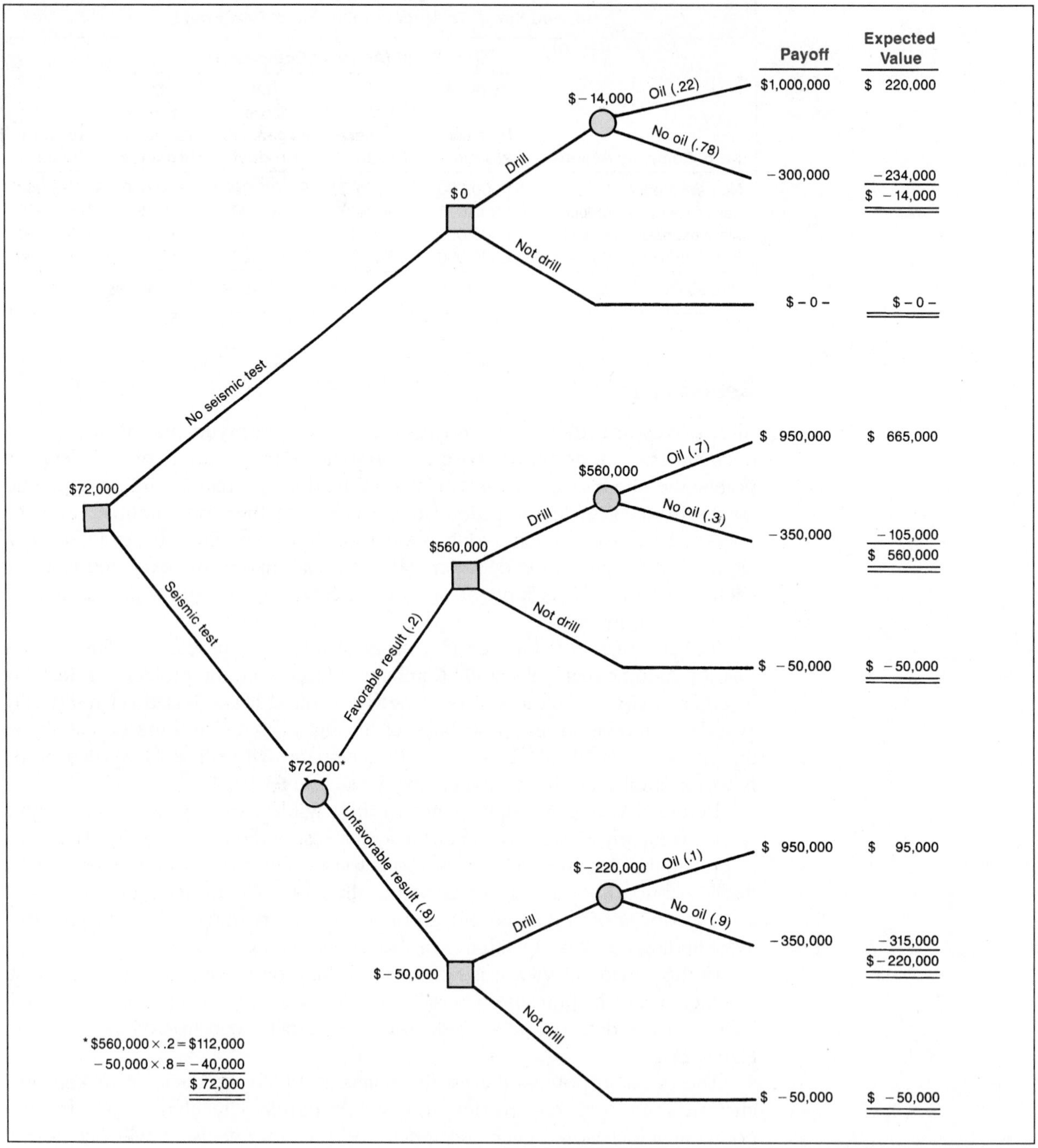

Notice in Wildcat's decision tree that if a seismic test is not purchased, the expected values of drilling and not drilling are a $14,000 loss and $0 profit or loss, respectively. The best course of action, given that a seismic test is not conducted, is not to drill. On the other hand, if a seismic test is conducted, two possible results can occur. If the test result is favorable, the expected values of drilling and not drilling are a $560,000 profit and a $50,000 loss (the cost of the seismic test), respectively. If the test result is unfavorable, the expected values of drilling and not drilling are a $220,000 loss and a $50,000 loss, respectively. If the test result is favorable, the best course of action is to drill. If the test result is unfavorable, the best course of action is not to drill. If the best courses of action are taken, the expected value of conducting a seismic test is a $72,000 profit. Because the expected value of conducting a seismic test exceeds the expected value of no test, the seismic test should be purchased.

More complex decision trees can be constructed to incorporate additional events and additional sequential decisions. For example, if several different quantities of oil can be found, several different payoffs are possible. In addition, further testing during the drilling process might decrease the uncertainty about the presence or absence of oil, thereby reducing the potential loss once drilling begins.

Continuous Probability Distributions

In the preceding illustrations, the number of possible outcomes was small and the probability distribution was discrete. However, when possible outcomes can take on any value within a defined range, a continuous probability distribution provides a better description of the nature of the variable and be a better basis for prediction.[1] As a practical matter, continuous probability distributions are usually assumed to have some familiar, well-behaved form such as a beta, gamma, or normal distribution, thereby making it convenient to calculate the distribution parameters of interest, such as the mean or expected value and the standard deviation.

The normal distribution is probably the most frequently applied continuous distribution. Although it appears to approximate closely many actual business processes, the normal distribution is not appropriate in all cases and should not be used indiscriminately. Its popularity probably stems from the fact that it has certain attractive mathematical properties. First, the normal distribution is symmetric (the area under the curve to the left of the median, or middle value, is a mirror image of the area to the right of the median). Second, it has only one mode (that is, there is only one most frequently occurring event[2]). Because the distribution is symmetric and unimodal, the mode is equal to the median and the mean (or weighted average). As a consequence, the value of the most likely event is the value in the middle between the two extremes, which is also the mean (and expected value) of the distribution.

Second, although the shape of the distribution can vary depending on the relative value of the standard deviation, the portion of the area under the curve for any given interval from the mean as measured in standard deviations is the same for all normal distributions. In this sense the standard deviation is not only a measure of dispersion of individual observations around the mean, but it is also a

[1] Technically, a variable is considered continuous if, over some interval, it can take any one of an infinite number of values. Examples of such variables include time, weight, volume, length, and economic value. Although these items are actually measured in units that are discrete, they are often viewed as continuous because, conceptually, they can be subdivided into infinitely small units of measure, and practically the number of different discrete values an item can have without such subdivision is large.

[2] Because a continuous variable can take any one of an infinite number of values, the probability of the occurrence of any individual event cannot actually be measured. As a consequence, it is necessary to think of the probability of the occurrence of an event as the probability that an event will have a value that lies within some interval, for example, the probability that sales will be between $20,000 and $21,000, or if a narrower interval is desired, the probability that sales will be between $20,000 and $20,001. This is the sense in which the "most frequently occurring event" is used here.

measure of distance. Notice in Figure 24-3 that the normal distribution is flatter when the standard deviation is large than when it is small.

FIGURE 24-3 ***Comparison of Normal Distributions with Different Standard Deviations***

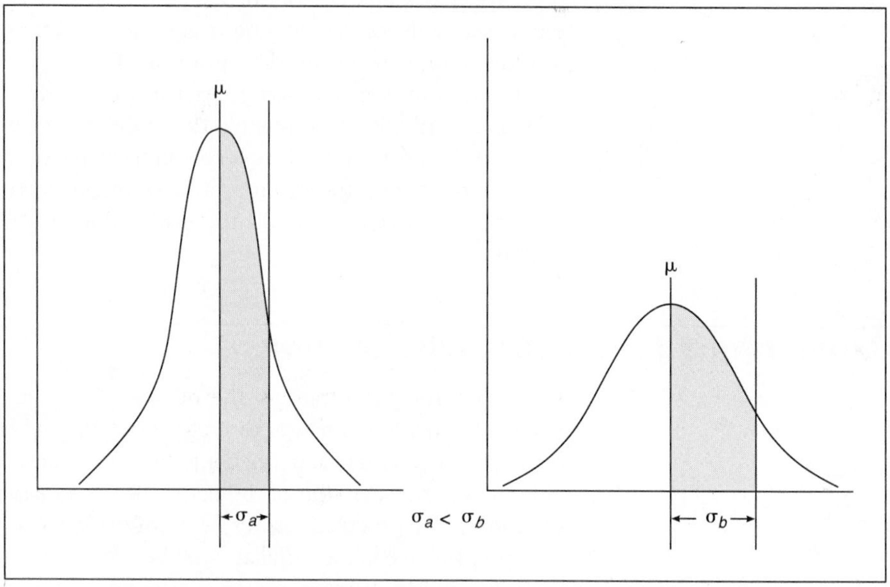

The total area under each of the two curves in Figure 24-3 is equal, and the area under each curve between the mean and a distance equal to one standard deviation above the mean is also equal. Because this relationship is the same for all normal curves, the portion of the total area under the curve between the mean of the distribution and any other possible value can be readily determined. First, divide the difference between the mean and the value of interest by the standard deviation to obtain a standardized measure (that is, a measure of the interval between the mean and the value in terms of standard deviations). Second, use a table of areas for a standard normal distribution to find the area under the curve for the standardized measure obtained. A partial table for selected areas under the normal curve is presented in Exhibit 24-8.

The use of the table of areas of the normal distribution can be illustrated as follows. Assume that Cliff Company is considering introducing a new product. Because the product is new, the mean and standard deviation cannot be computed on the basis of historical data. Nevertheless, assume that, based on experience, management believes that the distribution of sales is normal, and its best guess is that 20,000 units will be sold. Because sales are believed to be normally distributed, the most likely single event is the mean (and therefore the expected value) of the distribution, which in this case is 20,000 units. If the standard deviation cannot be estimated directly, an alternative approach is to have marketing personnel estimate a range of sales in which they have some quantifiable degree of confidence (for example, 50 percent or 90 percent), and then determine from the table the number of standard deviations required to include an area under the normal curve equal to that degree of confidence. In this case, assume that marketing is 90 percent confident that sales will be between 12,000 and 28,000 units, which means that the 90-percent interval is 16,000 units (28,000 – 12,000 units). Next, divide the confidence level by 2, and then from the table in Exhibit 24-8 find the number of standard deviations that must be added to or subtracted from the mean to include 45 percent of the area under the curve (.90 ÷ 2 = .45), which

EXHIBIT 24-8

Selected Areas Under the Normal Curve

$\frac{\mu - x}{\sigma}$	Area under Normal Curve between μ and x	$\frac{\mu - x}{\sigma}$	Area under Normal Curve between μ and x	$\frac{\mu - x}{\sigma}$	Area under Normal Curve between μ and x
.05	.01994	1.05	.35314	2.05	.47982
.10	.03983	1.10	.36433	2.10	.48214
.15	.05962	1.15	.37493	2.15	.48422
.20	.07926	1.20	.38493	2.20	.48610
.25	.09871	1.25	.39435	2.25	.48778
.30	.11791	1.30	.40320	2.30	.48928
.35	.13683	1.35	.41149	2.35	.49064
.40	.15542	1.40	.41924	2.40	.49180
.45	.17364	1.45	.42647	2.45	.49286
.50	.19146	1.50	.43319	2.50	.49379
.55	.20884	1.55	.43943	2.55	.49461
.60	.22575	1.60	.44520	2.60	.49534
.65	.24215	1.65	.45053	2.65	.49598
.70	.25804	1.70	.45543	2.70	.49653
.75	.27337	1.75	.45994	2.75	.49702
.80	.28814	1.80	.46407	2.80	.49744
.85	.30234	1.85	.46784	2.85	.49781
.90	.31594	1.90	.47128	2.90	.49813
.95	.32894	1.95	.47441	2.95	.49841
1.00	.34134	2.00	.47725	3.00	.49865

Definitions of symbols:
μ = mean of the distribution (which is also the expected value of a probability distribution).
x = a value drawn from the distribution.
σ = standard deviation of the distribution.

in this case is 1.65 standard deviations. Because 1.65 standard deviations must be added to or subtracted from the mean to include 45 percent of the area under the curve, the distance from one side of the 90 percent interval to the other is 3.3 standard deviations (1.65 × 2). Therefore, the standard deviation is determined by dividing the number of units in the 90 percent interval by the number of standard deviations required to include 90 percent of the area under the normal curve. The standard deviation in this case is approximately 4,848 units (16,000 units ÷ 3.3 standard deviations).

Assume further that the contribution margin from the sale of one unit of the new product is $2 and that specialized machinery must be rented at a cost of $30,000 in order to manufacture the product. Management would like to know the probability that the company will make a profit selling the new product. In this case, the company will break even if it sells 15,000 units ($30,000 fixed cost ÷ $2 contribution margin per unit) and incur a loss if it sells less than 15,000 units. Therefore, the probability of making a profit will be the area under the normal curve for sales greater than 15,000 units. The distance between the mean of 20,000 units and break-even sales of 15,000 units is 1.03 standard deviations [(20,000 – 15,000) ÷ 4,848], which means that the area under the curve between break-even sales and the mean is approximately .35. Because half the total area under the normal curve is above the mean, the probability that Cliff Company will make a profit from the new product is .85 (an area of .35 below the mean plus an area of .50 above the mean).

The reliability of the estimated probability of making a profit is highly dependent on the accuracy of the estimated mean and standard deviation and whether or not the normal curve reasonably approximates the actual distribution of the events of interest. If these estimates are based on historical data rather than subjective estimates, greater reliance can be placed on the results. If historical data are available, the estimated mean and standard deviation are computed from the sample data in the same manner as demonstrated in Chapter 3.

Monte Carlo Simulations

Many business problems contain variables over which decision makers have little or no control. Such variables can be treated as if they were generated by a stochastic process—a process that generates events that appear to the decision maker to occur at random. If the decision problem contains many stochastic variables, it becomes complex and difficult (and perhaps in some cases impossible) to evaluate with analytical techniques. In such cases, computer simulation can be a viable alternative. The primary requirement is that the decision problem be one that can be adequately modeled with one or more mathematical equations. Computer simulations that contain stochastic variables are often referred to as **Monte Carlo simulations**.

Monte Carlo simulation utilizes statistical sampling techniques in order to obtain a probabilistic approximation of the outcome of the business system being modeled. The probability distributions of the stochastic variables in the decision problem are simulated in the computer model, using a random number generator. The form of the stochastic processes simulated can be based on historical data or on estimates. The simulation is run numerous times in order to model the output of the business system. Based on the frequency distribution of the simulation results, the decision maker can determine the expected value (that is, the mean of the simulated probability distribution) and a measure of risk (that is, the variance and standard deviation) for the decision problem. Monte Carlo simulations are especially useful in planning and evaluating complex new business systems.

Considering Uncertainty in Capital Expenditure Evaluation

One way to evaluate systematically the potential effects of uncertainty on proposed capital expenditures is to incorporate probabilistic estimates in the evaluation. Probabilistic estimates are most frequently used with the present value method of capital expenditure evaluation. The net present value is computed as described in Chapter 23, except that the expected value of the net cash flow in each period, rather than the single most likely net cash flow in each period, is discounted to present value.

As was the case for the short-term decisions discussed earlier, the variance and the standard deviation are the commonly used measures of risk. For a capital expenditure proposal, the variance and the standard deviation are computed for the net present value of the investment. The relative riskiness of alternative proposals can be evaluated by computing and comparing each alternative's coefficient of variation, which for a capital expenditure proposal is determined by dividing the standard deviation of the net present value by the expected net present value. However, because capital expenditure problems encompass multiple periods, not a single period, the variance and the standard deviation of the expected net present value must be computed differently. In a multiperiod problem, cash flows from different periods must be treated as different random events; that is, the cash flow possibilities for each period form a separate distribution. As a consequence, the expected net present value for a capital expenditure proposal can be viewed as a random variable drawn from a multivariate distribution. The procedure for computing the variance and the standard deviation for the expected net present value varies, depending on whether the cash flows in each of the periods are assumed to be independent, perfectly correlated, or partially independent and partially correlated.

If the cash flows in each period are independent (that is, the magnitudes of the cash flows in subsequent periods are not affected in any way by the magnitude of cash flows that occur in earlier periods), the variance of the expected net present value is computed by adding the discounted variances of the cash flows in each period.[3] For a two-period project, the variance of the net present value under the assumption that periodic cash flows are independent is as follows:

$$\text{Variance of NPV} = \sigma_0^2 + \frac{\sigma_1^2}{(1+i)^2} + \frac{\sigma_2^2}{(1+i)^4}$$

where i is the discount rate (the weighted-average cost of capital in this case). The standard deviation is as follows:

$$\text{Standard deviation of NPV} = \sqrt{\sigma_0^2 + \frac{\sigma_1^2}{(1+i)^2} + \frac{\sigma_2^2}{(1+i)^4}}$$

Independent cash flows can occur in practice. For example, independent cash flows could occur when the capital expenditure relates to the production of an established product or service, and the demand for that product is expected to vary in response to temporary changes in consumers' tastes and preferences or their capacity to purchase, which are uncorrelated between periods.

If the cash flows are perfectly correlated (that is, the magnitude of cash flows in later periods are dependent on the magnitude of cash flows in early periods), the variance of the expected net present value is the square of the sum of the discounted periodic standard deviations.[4] For a two-period project, the variance of the expected net present value is as follows:

$$\text{Variance of NPV} = \left(\sigma_0 + \frac{\sigma_1}{(1+i)} + \frac{\sigma_2}{(1+i)^2}\right)^2$$

$$= \sigma_0^2 + \frac{\sigma_1^2}{(1+i)^2} + \frac{\sigma_2^2}{(1+i)^4} + \frac{2\sigma_0\sigma_1}{(1+i)} + \frac{2\sigma_0\sigma_2}{(1+i)^2} + \frac{2\sigma_1\sigma_2}{(1+i)^3}$$

The standard deviation is as follows:

$$\text{Standard deviation of NPV} = \sigma_0 + \frac{\sigma_1}{(1+i)} + \frac{\sigma_2}{(1+i)^2}$$

Notice that the variance of the expected net present value under the assumption that the cash flows are perfectly correlated contains interaction terms. As a result, the variance is larger when cash flows are dependent than when they are independent.

Perfectly correlated cash flows can occur if the capital expenditure relates to the production of a new product or the entrance into a new market. In such a

[3] See Frederick S. Hillier, "The Derivation of Probabilistic Information for the Evaluation of Risky Investments," *Management Science*, Vol. 9, No. 3, pp. 443-457.

[4] *Ibid.*, pp. 443-457

case, consumer acceptance of the product in one period might be expected to have a direct bearing on the level of sales in the following period.

If the cash flows are neither independent nor perfectly correlated, the cash flows can be treated as though they contain a mixture of independent and dependent periodic cash flows.[5] Mathematically, this procedure is fairly simple. In such a case, the expected periodic cash flows are divided into two components, the independent cash flows and the perfectly correlated cash flows. Separate periodic variances are then determined for the independent and the dependent cash flows. Once the periodic variances have been determined, a separate overall variance is computed for the independent and the dependent cash flows in the manner previously described. The standard deviation of the expected net present value is then determined by taking the square root of the sum of the overall variance of the independent cash flows and the overall variance of the dependent cash flows.

The difficult problem in practice is determining how much of each periodic cash flow is independent and how much is dependent. If the distribution of projected cash flows is based on a historical data set, it may be possible to determine statistically the degree of correlation in the cash flows over time. On the other hand, if the expected distribution is not based on historical data, the degree of correlation must be determined subjectively.

For illustrative purposes, assume that Tipton Company is considering the introduction of a new product called QM-30, which will require the acquisition of specialized equipment at a cost of $120,000. The new equipment will have an estimated useful life of 8 years with no expected salvage value. The machine qualifies as 7-year property, which means that the following tax depreciation will be available:

Year	Cost	Depreciation Rates	Annual Tax Depreciation
1	$120,000	.143	$ 17,160
2	120,000	.245	29,400
3	120,000	.175	21,000
4	120,000	.125	15,000
5	120,000	.089	10,680
6	120,000	.089	10,680
7	120,000	.089	10,680
8	120,000	.045	5,400
		1.000	$120,000

Management's best guess is that it will be able to produce and sell 2,400 units of QM-30 each year. The contribution margin from the sale of QM-30 will be $24 per unit. In order to produce and distribute the new product, the company must incur $15,000 in additional fixed production and marketing costs each year. Although management has no historical data on which to base its estimate, the after-tax net cash inflows for each year are expected to be normally distributed, which means that management's best guess estimates of the annual cash inflows are also the expected values of the annual cash inflows. The expected value of annual pretax cash inflows net of cash outflows is $42,600 [(2,400 units × $24 contribution margin) – $15,000 annual fixed cost]. Exhibit 24-9 illustrates the computation of the expected value of annual after-tax cash flows, based on an effective tax rate of 40 percent.

[5] *Ibid.*, pp. 443-457

EXHIBIT 24-9

Tipton Company
Capital Expenditure Proposal for New Equipment Acquisition
Estimated After-Tax Cash Flows

(1)	(2)	(3)	(4)	(5)	(6)
Year	Expected Value of Pretax Net Cash Flow	Tax Depreciation	Expected Value of Taxable Income (2) – (3)	Expected Value of Tax Liability (4) × 40%	Expected Value of After-Tax Net Cash Flow (2) – (5)
0	$(120,000)	—	—	—	$(120,000)
1	42,600	$17,160	$25,440	$10,176	32,424
2	42,600	29,400	13,200	5,280	37,320
3	42,600	21,000	21,600	8,640	33,960
4	42,600	15,000	27,600	11,040	31,560
5	42,600	10,680	31,920	12,768	29,832
6	42,600	10,680	31,920	12,768	29,832
7	42,600	10,680	31,920	12,768	29,832
8	42,600	5,400	37,200	14,880	27,720
					$ 132,480

In addition, management believes that the periodic standard deviation of sales will be about 800 units. As a consequence, the after-tax cash flow value of the periodic standard deviation is $11,520 [800 units × $24 contribution margin × (100% – 40% tax rate)].

If Tipton's weighted-average cost of capital is 12 percent, the expected net present value is determined as illustrated in Exhibit 24-10.

EXHIBIT 24-10

Tipton Company
Capital Expenditure Proposal for New Equipment Acquisition
Expected Net Present Value of After-Tax Cash Flows

(1)	(2)	(3)	(4)
Year	Expected Value of After-Tax Net Cash (Outflow) Inflow	Present Value of $1 at 12%	Present Value of Expected After-Tax Net Cash Flow (2) × (3)
0	$(120,000)	1.000	$(120,000)
1	32,424	.893	28,955
2	37,320	.797	29,744
3	33,960	.712	24,180
4	31,560	.636	20,072
5	29,832	.567	16,915
6	29,832	.507	15,125
7	29,832	.452	13,484
8	27,720	.404	11,199
Expected net present value			$ 39,674

Independent Cash Flows

If the cash flows in each period are independent, the standard deviation of the expected net present value of $39,674 is computed by taking the square root of the sum of the discounted periodic variances. For the proposed Tipton Company capital investment, the standard deviation under the independent cash flow assumption is computed as shown in Exhibit 24-11.

EXHIBIT 24-11

Tipton Company
Capital Expenditure Proposal for New Equipment Acquisition
Standard Deviation of Expected Net Present Value
Independent Cash Flow Assumption

(1) Year	(2) Periodic Standard Deviation	(3) Periodic Variance (2) Squared	(4) Present Value of $1 at 12%	(5) Present Value of $1 at 12% Squared (4) Squared	(6) Present Value of Variance (3) × (5)
0	0	0	1.000	1.000000	0
1	$11,520	$132,710,400	.893	.797449	$105,829,776
2	11,520	132,710,400	.797	.635209	84,298,840
3	11,520	132,710,400	.712	.506944	67,276,741
4	11,520	132,710,400	.636	.404496	53,680,826
5	11,520	132,710,400	.567	.321489	42,664,934
6	11,500	132,710,400	.507	.257049	34,113,076
7	11,500	132,710,400	.452	.204304	27,113,266
8	11,520	132,710,400	.404	.163216	21,660,461
Variance of net present value					$436,637,920

$$\text{Standard deviation of net present value} = \sqrt{\text{Variance of net present value}} = \sqrt{\$436{,}637{,}920} = \$20{,}896$$

Perfectly Correlated Cash Flows

If the cash flows in each of the periods are perfectly correlated with one another, the standard deviation of the expected net present value is determined by summing the discounted standard deviations for each period over the life of the project. For the proposed Tipton Company capital investment, the standard deviation of the expected net present value under the perfectly correlated cash flow assumption is illustrated in Exhibit 24-12.

EXHIBIT 24-12

Tipton Company
Capital Expenditure Proposal for New Equipment Acquisition
Standard Deviation of Expected Net Present Value
Perfectly Correlated Cash Flow Assumption

(1) Year	(2) Periodic Standard Deviation	(3) Present Value of $1 at 12%	(4) Present Value of Standard Deviation (2) × (3)
0	0	1.000	0
1	$11,520	.893	$10,287
2	11,520	.797	9,181
3	11,520	.712	8,202
4	11,520	.636	7,327
5	11,520	.567	6,532
6	11,520	.507	5,841
7	11,520	.452	5,207
8	11,520	.404	4,654
Standard deviation of net present value			$57,231

Notice that the standard deviation of the expected net present value when the cash flows are perfectly correlated ($57,231) is substantially larger than when the cash flows are independent ($20,896). This result is consistent with the intuitive notion that the introduction of established products is less risky than the introduction of new products.

Mixed Cash Flows

If the periodic cash flows are neither independent nor perfectly correlated, the cash flows can be treated as though they contain a mixture of independent and dependent periodic cash flows. The expected periodic cash flows are simply divided into two components, the independent cash flows and the perfectly correlated cash flows. A separate expected value and a separate variance are computed for the independent and the dependent cash flows in the usual way. The standard deviation of the expected net present value is then determined by taking the square root of the sum of the variance of the independent cash flows and the variance of the dependent cash flows. Assume that, of the expected annual after-tax net cash inflow for the proposed Tipton Company capital investment, 60 percent is determined to be independent and 40 percent is determined to be perfectly correlated. The expected net present value of the investment is presented in Exhibit 24-13.

EXHIBIT 24-13

Tipton Company
Capital Expenditure Proposal for New Equipment Acquisition
Expected Net Present Value of Cash Flows
Mixed Cash Flow Assumption

(1) Year	(2) Expected Independent After-Tax Net Cash Inflow	(3) Expected Dependent After-Tax Net Cash Inflow	(4) Total Expected After-Tax Net Cash Inflow (Outflow) (2) + (3)	(5) Present Value of $1 at 12%	(6) Present Value of Expected After-Tax Net Cash Flow (4) × (5)
0			$(120,000)	1.000	$(120,000)
1	$19,454	$12,970	32,424	.893	28,955
2	22,392	14,928	37,320	.797	29,744
3	20,376	13,584	33,960	.712	24,180
4	18,936	12,624	31,560	.636	20,072
5	17,899	11,933	29,832	.567	16,915
6	17,899	11,933	29,832	.507	15,125
7	17,899	11,933	29,832	.452	13,484
8	16,632	11,088	27,720	.404	11,199
Expected net present value					$ 39,674

For simplicity, also assume that 60 percent of the periodic standard deviation of 800 units is determined to be independent and 40 percent perfectly correlated. As a consequence, the periodic standard deviation for the independent cash flows is $6,912 [800 units × 60% × $24 contribution margin × (100% – 40% tax rate)], and the periodic standard deviation for the dependent cash flows is $4,608 [800 units × 40% × $24 contribution margin × (100% – 40% tax rate)]. Computation of the variance of the net present value of the independent cash flows is presented in Exhibit 24-14, and the variance of the net present value of the dependent cash flows is illustrated in Exhibit 24-15.

EXHIBIT 24-14

Tipton Company
Capital Expenditure Proposal for New Equipment Acquisition
Variance of Net Present Value for Independent Cash Flows
Mixed Cash Flow Assumption

(1) Year	(2) Independent Cash Flow Periodic Standard Deviation	(3) Independent Cash Flow Periodic Variance (2) Squared	(4) Present Value of \$1 at 12%	(5) Present Value of \$1 at 12% Squared (4) Squared	(6) Present Value of Variance (3) × (5)
0	0	0	1.000	1.000000	0
1	\$6,912	\$47,775,744	.893	.797449	\$38,098,719
2	6,912	47,775,744	.797	.635209	30,347,583
3	6,912	47,775,744	.712	.506944	24,219,627
4	6,912	47,775,744	.636	.404496	19,325,097
5	6,912	47,775,744	.567	.321489	15,359,376
6	6,912	47,775,744	.507	.257049	12,280,707
7	6,912	47,775,744	.452	.204304	9,760,776
8	6,912	47,775,744	.404	.163216	7,797,766
Variance of net present value for independent cash flows					\$157,189,651

EXHIBIT 24-15

Tipton Company
Capital Expenditure Proposal for New Equipment Acquisition
Variance of Net Present Value for Dependent Cash Flows
Mixed Cash Flow Assumption

(1) Year	(2) Dependent Cash Flow Periodic Standard Deviation	(3) Present Value of \$1 at 12%	(4) Present Value of Standard Deviation (2) × (3)
0	0	1.000	0
1	\$4,608	.893	\$ 4,115
2	4,608	.797	3,673
3	4,608	.712	3,281
4	4,608	.636	2,931
5	4,608	.567	2,613
6	4,608	.507	2,336
7	4,608	.452	2,083
8	4,608	.404	1,862
Standard deviation of net present value for dependent cash flows			\$22,894

$$\text{Variance of net present value for dependent cash flows} = \left(\text{Standard deviation of net present value for dependent cash flows}\right)^2 = (\$22{,}894)^2 = \$524{,}135{,}236$$

The standard deviation of the expected net present value of the investment is the square root of the sum of the variances of the independent and dependent cash flows. The standard deviation of the expected net present value for the Tipton Company investment is determined as follows:

Variance of net present value for dependent cash flows	\$524,135,236
Variance of net present value for independent cash flows	157,189,651
Variance of total net present value of investment	\$681,324,887

$$\text{Standard deviation of total net present value} = \sqrt{\text{Variance of total net present value}} = \sqrt{\$681{,}324{,}887} = \$26{,}102$$

Evaluating Investment Risk

Once the standard deviation of the expected net present value has been determined, it can be used to evaluate the riskiness of the proposed capital investment. The coefficient of variation, computed by dividing the standard deviation by the expected net present value (under the assumption of independent cash flows $20,896 ÷ $39,674 = .527 for the proposed Tipton Company project), can be compared to the coefficient of variation for similar projects. Alternatives with the smallest coefficients of variation are the least risky.

Management may also want to know the range of the return, measured in terms of net present value, that is likely to occur at some level of probability. As stated previously, one of the properties of the normal distribution is that areas of the normal distribution can be related to deviations from the mean expressed in terms of standard deviations. For example, the area under the normal curve from one standard deviation below the mean to one standard deviation above the mean is about 68 percent of the total area under the curve. The area bounded by two standard deviations above and below the mean is about 95 percent, and for three standard deviations, about 99 percent. Because the sum of more than one normally distributed random variable is itself a normally distributed random variable, the net present value of a multiperiod investment, for which the cash flows in each period are expected to be normally distributed, can be treated as a normally distributed random variable. Thus, for the proposed Tipton Company capital investment under the assumption of independent cash flows, there is about a 68 percent probability that the net present value will be between $18,778 ($39,674 – $20,896) and $60,570 ($39,674 + $20,896), and there is about a 95 percent probability that the net present value will be between –$2,118 [$39,674 – (2 × $20,896)] and $81,466 [$39,674 + (2 × $20,896)].

Management may also want to know the probability of achieving a net present value greater than zero. If the expected net present value is positive, the probability of actually achieving a net present value greater than zero is equal to the sum of (a) the portion of the area under the normal curve that is above the expected net present value (which is always 50 percent because the expected net present value is the mean, and the distribution is symmetrical) and (b) the portion of the area under the curve between the expected net present value and a net present value of zero. Area (b) can be measured in standard deviations (by dividing the expected net present value by the standard deviation) and then converted to the percentage of the area under the curve by using a table of Z values for the normal distribution, such as the one provided in Exhibit 24-8.

For the proposed Tipton Company capital investment under the assumption of independent normally distributed cash flows, the area under the curve between the expected net present value of $39,674 and a net present value of zero is 1.8986 standard deviations [($39,674 – 0) ÷ $20,896], which, according to the table of Z values (Exhibit 24-8), is about 47 percent of the total area under the curve. Consequently, the probability that the proposed investment will yield a positive net present value is 97 percent; that is, 47 percent (the area below the mean but above zero) plus 50 percent (the area above the mean). On the other hand, if the cash flows are expected to be perfectly correlated, the probability that the proposed investment will yield a positive net present value declines to about 76 percent, because the standard deviation of the expected net present value increases from \$20,896 to \$57,231. The area between the expected net present value of \$39,674 and a net present value of zero is .6932 standard deviations [(\$39,674 − 0) ÷ \$57,231], which, according to the table of Z values, is about 26 percent of the area below the mean. The 26 percent of the area below the mean plus the 50 percent above the mean is equal to 76 percent.

The reliability of the estimated range for the net present value and the probability of achieving a positive net present value are highly dependent on the accuracy of the estimates on which they are based; that is, the expected values of the annual cash flows and their estimated standard deviations. If these estimates are based on historical data rather than subjective estimates, greater reliance can be placed on the results.

Incorporating Nonquantitative Factors into the Analysis

Traditional economic evaluation tools are often criticized because they do not incorporate qualitative factors into the decision model. If the benefits to be derived from an expenditure do not result in an economically measurable value, they are ignored. Yet most of the benefits to be derived from investments in new technologies are strategic and difficult to quantify. The **multiattribute decision model (MADM)** is an expenditure evaluation tool that explicitly incorporates both quantitative and nonquantitative factors into the decision analysis.

In MADM, alternative courses of action are rated on how well each performs in achieving important quantitative and nonquantitative factors. The factors are the important benefits that management expects from the investment. Each factor is assigned a weight based on its importance relative to all other factors. Total factor weights must sum to 100. When the relative importance of the factors has been determined, each alternative is rated on the basis of how well management believes it will satisfy each factor. For example, a rating of 0 can be assigned for each factor that the alternative does not satisfy, 1 for each factor that it only minimally satisfies, and 2 for each factor that it more than adequately satisfies. These performance ratings are then weighted by management's estimate of the likelihood that the alternative will achieve the level of satisfaction expected. Each factor's relative importance weighting is multiplied by its performance rating and then again by the likelihood that it will achieve the performance expected. The results are weighted scores that are added together to arrive at a composite score for each alternative. The alternative with the highest composite score best satisfies the multiattribute objectives of management and is selected for implementation.

The use of MADM in a decision problem is illustrated as follows. Assume Nicady Corporation is considering replacing one of its production facilities. One choice is to replace the facility with one that utilizes the same technology. Alternatively, the facility can be replaced with a computer integrated manufacturing system (CIM). The net present value and the payback methods are used to evaluate the economic value of capital expenditure proposals. In a meeting, members of the management team identified additional nonfinancial benefits they would like to realize from the replacement. After considerable debate, the following seven factors and relative importance weightings were agreed on:

Factor	Relative Importance Weighting
Net present value	30
Payback period	10
Reduced customer response time	15
Reduced inventory levels	10
Improved product quality	15
Improved employee morale	10
Improved image to customers	10
Total	100

The net present value of an investment in CIM is negative. In contrast, the net present value of an investment in existing technology is positive and about 10 percent of the initial cash outflow. In addition, the payback period is considerably shorter for an investment in existing technology than for a CIM system. If the decision is based solely on quantifiable economic measures, the preferable choice is unambiguous: replace the present facility with a new one of the same technology. However, when nonfinancial factors are considered, the best decision is not clear. Customer response time and inventory levels are expected to be substantially reduced with an investment in CIM but not affected by an investment in existing technology. Both alternatives are expected to improve product quality, employee morale and the company's image to customers, but CIM is expected to provide a greater improvement in product quality and image to customers. Based on this analysis of the potential benefits and management's estimation of the likelihood that these benefits will be realized, a MADM worksheet such as the one presented in Exhibit 24-16 can be constructed.

EXHIBIT 24-16

Nicady Corporation
Capital Expenditure Proposal
MADM Worksheet

		Replace with Existing Technology			Replace with New Technology		
Factors	Relative Importance Weighting	Performance Rating	Likelihood	Weighted Score	Performance Rating	Likelihood	Weighted Score
Net present value	30	2	.8	48	0	.7	0
Payback period	10	2	.8	16	0	.6	0
Reduced customer response time	15	0	1.0	0	2	1.0	30
Reduce inventory levels	10	0	1.0	0	2	.9	18
Improved product quality	15	1	.4	6	2	.9	27
Improved employee morale	10	1	.6	6	1	.5	5
Improved image to customers	10	1	.5	5	2	.7	14
Total	100			81			94

The MADM worksheet in Exhibit 24-16 indicates that the company should replace its present production facility with a CIM system because the composite score for the CIM alternative (94) is greater than the composite score for the existing technology alternative (81). In this case, the importance of the nonfinancial benefits and expected likelihood that they will be achieved weights the decision in favor of the alternative that has the weakest measures of measurable economic value.

Summary

Probability analysis is an application of statistical decision theory that, under conditions of uncertainty, leads to more consistent and reliable decisions than single best guesses. Probability analysis improves the quality of decisions by incorporating the distribution of possible outcomes. Decisions are based on the expected value of an event rather than the single most likely outcome. In addition to the expected value of an event, the variance, standard deviation, and coefficient of variation can be computed and used to evaluate the relative riskiness of alternatives. Probability estimates can be used to construct payoff tables and decision trees, which help management select the best strategy under conditions of uncertainty. Furthermore, as new information becomes available, probability estimates can be revised and the quality of decisions improved. In addition to the use of discrete probabilities, the use of a continuous probability distribution was illustrated in the context of both short-term and long-term decision problems. The normal distribution was shown to be especially useful in evaluating risk. Finally, the multi-attribute decision model was presented as a workable approach to incorporating important nonquantitative factors into the decision model.

Key Terms

probability analysis *(709)*
probability *(710)*
expected value *(710)*
conditional value *(710)*
variance *(711)*
standard deviation *(711)*
coefficient of variation *(712)*
payoff table *(712)*
joint probabilities *(715)*
conditional probabilities *(715)*
posterior probability *(717)*
prior probabilities *(717)*
decision tree *(719)*
Monte Carlo simulations *(724)*
multi-attribute decision model (MADM) *(732)*

Discussion Questions

Q24-1 Why should a manager try to assess the probabilities associated with possible outcomes before making a decision under conditions of uncertainty?

Q24-2 Define expected value.

Q24-3 In what way is the standard deviation of the expected value useful?

Q24-4 What is the coefficient of variation, and how is it used in evaluating alternatives?

Q24-5 Contrast joint probability and conditional probability.

Q24-6 Why would management be interested in the revision of probabilities?

Q24-7 What is a decision tree and how is it used?

Q24-8 What is the difference between a discrete probability distribution and a continuous probability distribution?

Q24-9 What are the attractive properties of the normal distribution?

Q24-10 What is the purpose of Monte Carlo simulation?

Q24-11 Even if cash flows are normally distributed, it is desirable to incorporate probability analysis into capital expenditure evaluation. Why?

Q24-12 In what way does the computation of the variance of multiperiod cash flows differ from the variance of a single period cash flow?

Q24-13 In a capital budgeting context, what is meant by independent periodic cash flows and under what conditions might they be expected to occur?

Q24-14 In a capital budgeting context, what is meant by perfectly correlated periodic cash flows and under what conditions might they be expected to occur?

Q24-15 How might the variance of the net present value of a capital expenditure proposal be computed if the periodic cash flows are neither independent nor perfectly correlated?

Q24-16 What is MADM, and in what way is it useful?

Exercises

E24-1 Expected Value and Coefficient of Variation. Duguid Company is considering a proposal to introduce a new product, XPL. An outside marketing consultant prepared the following probability distribution describing the relative likelihood of monthly sales volume levels and related income (loss) for XPL:

Monthly Sales Volume	Probability	Income (Loss)
3,000	.05	$(35,000)
6,000	.15	5,000
9,000	.40	30,000
12,000	.30	50,000
15,000	.10	70,000

Required:
(1) Compute the expected income or loss (expected value).
(2) Compute the standard deviation and the coefficient of variation. (AICPA adapted)

E24-2 Expected Value and Coefficient of Variation. In planning its budget for the coming year, the controller of the Walsenberg Corporation obtained the following data concerning sales for one of the company's products for the most recent 60 months:

Monthly Sales Volume	Frequency
10,000	9
11,000	15
12,000	18
13,000	9
14,000	6
15,000	3

The contribution margin per unit for the coming month is expected to be $10.

Required:
(1) What is the expected value of the monthly contribution margin for the product?
(2) Compute the coefficient of variation of the contribution margin from the product.

E24-3 Make-or-Buy Decision Under Uncertainty. Unimat Company manufactures a thermostat designed for effective climatic control of large buildings. The thermostat requires a specialized thermocoupler, purchased from Cosmic Company at $15 each. For the past two years, an average of 10% of the purchased thermocouplers have not met quality requirements; however, the rejection rate is within the range agreed on in the purchase contract.

Unimat has most of the facilities and equipment needed to produce the components. Additional annual fixed cost of only $32,500 would be required. The Engineering Department has designed a manufacturing system that would hold the defective rate to 4%. At an annual demand level of 18,000 units, engineering estimates of the probabilities of several variable manufacturing unit costs, including allowance for defective units, are as follow:

Estimated Variable Cost per Unit	Probability
$10	.1
12	.3
14	.4
16	.2

Required: Prepare a make-or-buy decision analysis using the probability distribution estimates.
(ICMA adapted)

E24-4 Payoff Table. Jessica Company buys and resells a perishable product. A large purchase at the beginning of each month provides a lower per unit cost and assures that Jessica can purchase all the items it wishes. However, unsold units at the end of each month are worthless and must be discarded. If an inadequate quantity is purchased, additional units of acceptable quality are not available.

The units, which Jessica sells for $1.25 each, are purchased at a fixed fee of $50,000 per month plus $.50 each, if at least 100,000 units are ordered and if they are ordered at the beginning of the month.

The needs of Jessica's customers limit the possible sales volumes to only four quantities per month—100,000, 120,000, 140,000, or 180,000 units. However, the total quantity needed for a given month cannot be determined prior to the date Jessica must make its purchases. The sales managers are willing to place a probability estimate on each of the four possible sales volumes each month. They noted that the probabilities for the four sales volumes change from month to month because of the seasonal nature of the customers' businesses. Their probability estimates for December, 19A, sales quantities are 10% for 100,000, 30% for 120,000, 40% for 140,000, and 20% for 180,000.

Required: Prepare a payoff table showing the expected value of each of the four possible strategies of ordering units, assuming that only the four quantities specified are ever sold and that the occurrences are random events. Identify the best strategy.
(ICMA adapted)

E24-5 Payoff Table and the Expected Value of Perfect Information Wurst Inc. operates the concession stands at the State College football stadium. State College has had successful football teams for many years and, as a result, the stadium is virtually always filled. From time to time Wurst has found that its supply of hot dogs is inadequate, while at other times there has been a surplus. A review of Wurst's sales records for the past 10 seasons reveals the following frequency of hot dogs sold:

Quantity of Hot Dogs Sold	Number of Games
10,000	5
20,000	10
30,000	20
40,000	15
Total	50

Hot dogs that sell for $.50 each cost Wurst $.30 each. Unsold hot dogs are donated to the local orphanage.

Required:

(1) Prepare a payoff table depicting the expected value of each of the four possible strategies of ordering 10,000, 20,000, 30,000, or 40,000 hot dogs, assuming that the four quantities listed were the only quantities ever sold and that the occurrences were random events.

(2) Compute the dollar value of knowing in advance what the sales level would be at each game (that is, the expected value of perfect information).
(ICMA adapted)

E24-6 Revision of Probabilities. Victoria Manufacturing Company plans to introduce a new product known as Quintex. Based on experience and contacts with customers, the vice-president of marketing believes that the demand for Quintex will be between 30,000 and 60,000 units. The following probabilities have been assigned to each possible level of demand:

Demand	Probability
30,000	.10
40,000	.10
50,000	.50
60,000	.30

Before beginning production, the president of the company asked the vice-president of marketing to have the market demand analyzed by an expert system computer program available from a local marketing service company. The program is a market demand analysis model built on the basis of decisions made by several successful experts in the field of market demand analysis. Although the model may overlook some factors unique to the market for Quintex, it captures many important variables and has generally been found to be useful in forecasting product demand. The vice-president complied with the president's request, and the results of the expert system analysis follow:

Demand	Probability
30,000	.20
40,000	.50
50,000	.20
60,000	.10

Required: Using Bayes' theorem, compute the posterior probabilities for the various levels of demand for Quintex, assuming that the demand probabilities generated by the expert system provide new information (that is, assume the expert system probabilities are conditional probabilities).

E24-7 Decision Tree. The manager of Stereo-Fun is trying to decide whether to move his store to the new Market Shopping Mall or to keep it in its present location. Because of changing economic conditions, the market for stereo equipment may decline, remain the same, or increase during the coming year. The manager estimates the move to Market Shopping Mall will cost $10,000. In addition, the manager assesses market conditions and the associated net profits for the next year under both alternatives (excluding the cost of the move) to be as follows:

		Net Profits Expected	
State of Market	Probability	Move to Mall	Do not Move
Decline	.2	$(25,000)	$(10,000)
Remain the same	.5	50,000	40,000
Increase	.3	100,000	80,000

Required: Construct a decision tree for the manager's problem, and calculate the expected value for each alternative. Should the manager choose to move or not? CGA-Canada (adapted). Reprint with permission.

E24-8 Decision Tree. A firm producing stereo amplifiers can manufacture a subassembly or purchase it from another company. Anticipated profits for each alternative, make or buy, and for three different levels of demand for the stereo amplifier are as follow:

		Expected Net Profits	
State of Market	Probability	Make	Buy
High	.4	$50,000	$35,000
Medium	.3	30,000	30,000
Low	.3	(10,000)	5,000

Required: Construct a decision tree for the make-or-buy decision, and calculate the expected value for each alternative. Indicate whether the firm should make or buy. CGA-Canada (adapted). Reprint with permission.

E24-9 Decision Tree. A land developer needs to decide which of two parcels of land to bid on for development. The developer assesses the chance of success on bids to be 60% for parcel A and 80% for parcel B. Development of either parcel will take two years, after which time parcel A is expected to generate a profit of $200,000, and parcel B is expected to generate a profit of $100,000. However, if the area in which parcel B is located can be rezoned, this parcel could generate a $300,000 profit. Costs of $10,000 would be incurred in preparing and presenting the case for rezoning to the review board. The developer assesses the probability of a successful appeal for rezoning at 50%. An appeal for rezoning would not be undertaken unless parcel B were successfully acquired by bid.

Required: Construct the decision tree for the land developer's problem, and calculate the expected profits for each alternative. On which parcel should the developer place a bid? Should the developer apply for rezoning? CGA-Canada (adapted). Reprint with permission.

E24-10 Break-Even Analysis. Fargo Inc. is considering the introduction of a new product. Based on past experience, management believes that the distribution of sales demand is normal. Management's best guess is that the company will be able to sell 50,000 units of the new product in the first year, and management is 50% confident that first-year sales will be between 45,000 and 55,000 units. The contribution margin from the sale of each unit is $5. Special machinery must be rented at an annual cost of $193,750 in order to manufacture the new product.

Required:

(1) Determine the expected standard deviation. (The interval between the mean and x that includes 25% of the area under the normal curve is .667 standard deviations.)

(2) What is the probability that Fargo will make a profit on the sale of the new product? Round the answer to the nearest whole percent.

E24-11 Expected Net Present Value of Investment with Normally Distributed Cash Flows. Allset Enterprises is considering a capital expenditure proposal that will cost $20,000 and yield an expected after-tax cash inflow of $5,000 each year for 6 years. There is no expected salvage value at the end of the life of the project. The after-tax net cash inflows for each year are expected to be normally distributed with a standard deviation of $800. Allset's weighted-average cost of capital is 10%.

Required: Compute the expected net present value of the capital expenditure proposal.

E24-12 Standard Deviation of Expected Net Present Value when Periodic Cash Flows Are Normally Distributed and Independent. Purvis Company is considering a capital proposal that has an expected net present value of $3,000. The periodic cash inflows are normally distributed with a standard deviation of $500 each period. The initial cash outflow has a zero standard deviation. The company's weighted-average cost of capital is 12%, and the capital project has an expected life of 8 years. The periodic cash inflows are expected to be independent of one another.

Required: Compute the standard deviation of the expected net present value for the Purvis Company investment.

E24-13 Standard Deviation of Expected Net Present Value when Periodic Cash Flows Are Normally Distributed and Dependent. Ramos Company is considering a capital expenditure for which the periodic cash inflows are expected to be normally distributed and perfectly correlated. The expected net present value of the proposed project is $5,000, and the standard deviation of the cash inflows is $1,000 in each period. The initial cash outflow has a zero standard deviation. The company's weighted-average cost of capital is 10%, and the capital project is expected to have a life of 5 years.

Required: Compute the standard deviation of the expected net present value for the Ramos Company investment.

E24-14 Standard Deviation of Expected Net Present Value when Periodic Cash Flows Are Neither Independent nor Perfectly Correlated. Vincent Corporation is considering an investment in new machinery with a 7-year estimated useful life and an estimated net present value of $12,000. The cash inflows are expected to be normally distributed; however, 60% of each period's cash inflow is expected to be independent, and the remaining 40% is expected to be perfectly correlated. Cash inflows are expected to be $10,000 each period. The periodic independent cash inflows have a standard deviation of $1,000, and the periodic dependent cash inflows have a standard deviation of $1,500. The initial cash outflow has a standard deviation of zero. The corporation's weighted-average cost of capital is 12%.

Required: Compute the standard deviation of the expected net present value for Vincent Corporation.

E24-15 Evaluating Capital Project Risk. Oskervale Company is considering investing in a new plant that will produce a product for which there is an established market. Demand for the product historically has followed a random normal distribution and has been independent from one period to the next. Management has determined that the expected net present value of the investment is $30,000, and the standard deviation of the expected net present value is $25,000.

Required:

(1) Determine the 95% confidence interval for the net present value, that is, the range within which the net present value of the proposed investment will fall about 95% of the time.

(2) Using the table of selected areas under the normal curve in Exhibit 24-8, determine the probability that the net present value of the proposed investment will exceed zero.

Problems

P24-1 Introduction of New Product. Sofak Company is a manufacturer of precision sensing equipment. J. Adams, one of Sofak's project engineers, has developed a prototype of an automatic testing kit that continually evaluates water quality and chemical content in hot tubs. Adams believes that this kit will permit domestic tub owners to control water quality better at substantially reduced costs and with less time invested. The management of Sofak is convinced that the kit will have strong market acceptance. Furthermore, this new equipment uses the same technology that Sofak employs in the manufacture of some of its other equipment. Therefore, Sofak can use existing facilities to produce the product.

Adams, who is ready to proceed with developing cost and profit plans for the testing kit, asked the Marketing Department to develop a suggested selling price and estimate the sales volume. The Marketing Department contracted with Statico, a marketing research company, to develop price and volume estimates.

Based on an analysis of the market, Statico considered unit prices between $80 and $120. Within this price range, it recommended a price of $100 per kit. The frequency distribution of the unit sales volume that Sofak could expect at this selling price is as follows:

Annual Unit Sales Volume	Probability
50,000	.25
60,000	.45
70,000	.20
80,000	.10
	1.00

Sofak's Profit Planning Department accumulated cost data that Adams had requested. The new product will require direct materials costing $25 per unit and will require 2 hours of direct labor to manufacture. Sofak is currently in contract negotiations with its union, making projections of labor costs difficult. The current direct labor cost is $8 per hour. Representatives of management who are negotiating with the union have estimated the possible settlements and related probabilities that follow:

Direct Labor Cost per Hour	Probability
$8.50	.30
8.80	.50
9.00	.20
	1.00

Sofak applies factory overhead to its products using a plant-wide rate of $15 per direct labor hour. This rate is based on a planned activity level of 900,000 direct labor hours, which represents 75% of practical capacity. The budgeted factory overhead costs for the current year follow:

	Budgeted Cost	Cost per Direct Labor Hour
Variable overhead:		
Supplies	$ 360,000	$ .40
Materials handling	315,000	.35
Heat, light, and power	1,125,000	1.25
Fixed overhead:		
Supervisory salaries	1,440,000	1.60
Building depreciation	4,410,000	4.90
Machinery depreciation	3,420,000	3.80
Taxes and insurance	2,430,000	2.70
Total budgeted costs	$13,500,000	$15.00

The introduction of the new product will require some changes in the manufacturing plant. Although the plant is below capacity and current facilities can be used, a new production line requiring a new supervisor would need to be opened. The annual cost of a supervisor is $28,000. In addition, one piece of equipment that Sofak does not own would need to be obtained under an operating lease at an annual cost of $150,000.

Sofak has already paid Statico $132,000 for the marketing study that was mentioned previously. Statico has agreed to conduct the promotion and distribution of the new product for a fee of $6 per unit once Sofak introduces it.

Required:

(1) Determine the annual pretax advantage or disadvantage of introducing the new product using a deterministic approach (that is, use only the single most likely events in your analysis).

(2) Determine the annual pretax advantage or disadvantage of introducing the new product using an expected value approach (that is, incorporate the probability distributions in your analysis).

(3) Describe how Sofak can use the data presented to develop a simulation model that could be used for decision making. (ICMA adapted)

P24-2 Selecting Minimum Cost Alternative Under Uncertainty. Video Recreation Inc. (VRI) is a supplier of video games and video equipment such as large-screen televisions and video cassette recorders. The company recently concluded a major contract with Sunview Hotels to supply games for the hotel video lounges. Under this contract, a total of 4,000 games will be delivered to Sunview Hotels throughout the United States, and all games will have a warranty period of 1 year for both parts and labor. The number of service calls required to repair these games during the first year after installation is estimated as follows:

Number of Service Calls	Probability of Occurrence
400	.1
700	.3
900	.4
1,200	.2

VRI's Customer Service Department has developed the following three alternatives for providing the warranty service to Sunview:

(a) Under plan 1, VRI would contract with local firms to perform the repair services. It is estimated that six such vendors would be needed to cover the appropriate areas and that each of these vendors would charge an annual fee of $15,000 to have personnel available and to stock the appropriate parts. In addition to the annual fee, VRI would be billed $250 for each service call and would be billed for parts used at cost plus a 10% surcharge.

(b) Under plan 2, VRI would allow the management of each hotel to arrange for repair service when needed and then would reimburse the hotel for the expenses incurred. It is estimated that 60% of the service calls would be for hotels located in urban areas, where the charge for a service call would average $450. At the remaining hotels, the charge would be $350. In addition to these service charges, parts would be billed at cost.

(c) Under plan 3, VRI would hire its own personnel to perform repair services and to do preventive maintenance. Nine employees, located in the appropriate geographical areas, would be required to fulfill these responsibilities, and their average annual salary would be $24,000. The fringe benefit expense for these employees would amount to 35% of their wages. Each employee would be scheduled to make an average of 200 preventive maintenance calls during the year, and each of these calls would require an average of $15 worth of parts. Because of this preventive maintenance, it is estimated that the expected number of hotel calls for repair service would decline 30% and the cost of parts required for each repair service call would be reduced by 20%.

VRI's Accounting Department has reviewed the historical data on repair costs for equipment installations similar to those proposed for Sunview Hotels and found that the cost of parts required for each repair occurred with the following frequency:

Parts Cost per Repair	Frequency
$30	15%
40	15
60	45
90	25

Required: Which of the proposed plans should VRI adopt to minimize its warranty obligations to Sunview Hotels. Provide calculations that support your recommendation. (ICMA adapted)

P24-3 Differential Cost of Quality Control System Under Uncertainty. Home-Heaters Inc. manufactures gas-fired heaters together with circulator pumps and motors. The entire unit circulates hot water through baseboards in the house. Home-Heaters recently developed a compact unit, Model 390Z, that replaces the circulator pump and motor. The unit requires little maintenance and is warranted to operate trouble free for 3 years. Home-Heaters has established a reputation for high-quality products, and the company's management forecasts an annual demand of 1,000,000 units of Model 390Z.

The bill of materials for a unit of Model 390Z requires one precision ball bearing. The diameter of the bearing is 2.75 centimeters, and the engineering specifications do not allow tolerances beyond plus or minus 5%. If the actual bearing size is greater than the specification, the bearing will not fit in the casing. If the bearing is smaller than the specification, the unit will not function efficiently. The bearings used in the Model 390Z are not subjected to quality control inspection prior to assembly of the unit; however, the entire unit is performance tested after final assembly. Based on the pilot production runs, the following information has been gathered.

(a) Cost for a unit of Model 390Z:

Material (including the bearing at $5)	$ 30
Labor (5 hours at $8 per hour)	40
Variable overhead (150% of labor cost)	60
Total variable cost	$130

(b) The majority of the rejections experienced during the pilot run were related to the ball bearings.
(c) During assembly, bearings that are too big to fit in the casing are rejected, and new bearings are used. This change in bearings requires 6 minutes of additional direct labor for each affected unit.
(d) Units rejected during performance testing are reassembled with a new bearing. On average, one additional hour of labor is required for reassembly.
(e) The defective bearings are returned to the supplier for credit.

J. McGill, Home-Heaters' production manager, collected additional data on the rejections during the pilot production runs. McGill's estimate of the probability of rejections for a lot of 1,000 bearings is as follows:

Rejection During Assembly		Rejection During Performance Testing	
Quantity	Probability	Quantity	Probability
100	.50	20	.40
60	.25	15	.30
30	.15	10	.20
5	.10	5	.10

Required: Determine the maximum amount that Home-Heaters would be willing to spend annually to implement quality control inspection of the bearings before assembly begins. (ICMA adapted)

P24-4 Payoff Table and Coefficient of Variation. The owner of Kenton Clothiers must decide on the number of men's shirts to order for the coming season. One order must be placed for the entire season. The normal sales price is $30 per shirt; however, unsold shirts at season's end must be sold at half price. The following data are available:

Order Quantity	Unit Sales Price	Unit Cost	Unit Contribution Margin at Regular Price	Unit Loss at $15 Half Price
100	$30	$23	$ 7	$8
200	30	22	8	7
300	30	21	9	6
400	30	20	10	5

Over the past 25 seasons, Kenton Clothiers has experienced the following sales volume:

Quantity Sold	Frequency
100	3
200	12
300	9
400	1
	25

The historical sales have occurred at random; that is, they have exhibited no cycles or trends, and the future is expected to be similar to the past.

Required:

(1) Prepare a payoff table representing the expected contribution margin of each of the four possible strategies of ordering 100, 200, 300, or 400 shirts, assuming that only the four quantities listed are ever sold.
(2) Select the best of the four strategies in requirement 1, based on the expected contribution margin and compute the coefficient of variation for this strategy.
(3) Compute the expected value of perfect information in this problem.

P24-5 Probability Revision and Payoff Table. L. J. Gant is a builder who has recently acquired a tract of unimproved real estate on which new houses will be built. Gant feels that the local housing market is strong enough to absorb all houses built on the tract by the end of the year, provided the size of the houses meets the needs and preferences of the largest number of home buyers. Four different sizes of houses are being considered—1,600, 2,000, 2,400, and 2,800 square-foot houses. However, for economic and marketing reasons, only one size of house will be built on the tract. Based on past experience, Gant assigned the following subjective probabilities to the size of house most in demand in the local market:

House Size	Probability
1,600	.20
2,000	.50
2,400	.20
2,800	.10

Before beginning construction, Gant read in the paper that an electronics firm announced it was considering locating a research laboratory in the community not far from Gant's planned housing site. If the firm locates a research facility in town, it will significantly increase demand for the 2,400- and 2,800- square-foot houses. Gant believes there is a 75% probability that the electronics firm will locate its research facility in town and a 25% probability that it will not. The expected payoff for each alternative is as follows:

Action: House Size to Build (in square feet)	Event (House Size Most in Demand) 1,600	2,000	2,400	2,800
1,600	$200,000	$180,000	$160,000	$140,000
2,000	160,000	400,000	360,000	320,000
2,400	120,000	320,000	600,000	540,000
2,800	80,000	240,000	480,000	800,000

Required:

(1) Compute the posterior probabilities for each of the alternatives related to the proposed housing project.

(2) Compute the expected value of each alternative course of action, and make a recommendation to Gant about which course of action to take.

P24-6 Probability Revision. Tekno Institute is an accredited college that offers courses almost exclusively on a correspondence basis. Each student pays a tuition fee and receives a set of lesson materials by mail. These course materials are currently prepared and printed in-house by Tekno.

The following information is available from Tekno's financial records for the year just ended, in which Tekno had a total enrollment of 26,000 students:

	Printing Department	Shipping Department
Salaries	$160,000	$55,000
Employee benefits	18,200	7,700
Telephone and telegraph	4,000	700
Materials, supplies, and postage	165,100	16,000
Occupancy costs	10,800	3,400
Administration	7,300	700
Depreciation	25,700	2,500
Total	$391,100	$86,000

Recently, an outside printer presented Tekno with an offer to print Tekno's course lesson materials on a contract basis. The offer stipulated a flat fee of $325,000 for 25,000 sets of lesson materials plus a piecework fee of $15 per set for every set over 25,000. If Tekno decides to accept the offer, the following changes in Tekno's Printing Department would be necessary:

(a) All Printing Department employees would be laid off, except for one clerk who would work part-time to monitor communications between Tekno and the printer. The clerk currently works 5 days per week at a salary of $16,000 per year and has agreed to a part-time arrangement of 3 days per week at the same average daily salary rate plus benefits. Because the Printing Department would be eliminated, this clerk would become a member of the Shipping Department. All other Printing Department employees would receive an average of one month's salary as severance pay. In addition, all variable employee benefits of the Printing Department would be eliminated except for the relevant portion associated with the clerk. Variable benefits amount to 10% of salaries. Fixed benefit costs would continue to be incurred, but would be reallocated to other departments in the institute on some reasonable basis.

(b) Telephone and telegraph costs formerly charged to the Printing Department would be reduced to $80 per month.

(c) The Printing Department materials, supplies, and postage costs, which are fully variable, would be reduced to $1 per set of lesson materials. This amount would cover the cost of postage.

(d) Occupancy and administration costs of the Printing Department would be eliminated.

(e) The Printing Department's equipment and other fixed assets would be leased to a local business for $33,000 per year.

(f) One set of course lesson materials would be required for each student enrollment. The probability distribution for the anticipated number of student enrollments for next year is as follows:

Estimated Enrollment	Probability
25,000	.05
26,000	.15
27,000	.40
28,000	.25
29,000	.15

Required:

(1) On the basis of the information provided, determine whether or not Tekno Institute should accept the outside printer's offer (compare the fees that would be paid to the outside printer for one year with the savings available from closing the Printing Department for one year).

(2) Assume that, before the outside printer is notified, the local newspaper publishes a story indicating that a large manufacturing plant located in Tekno's market area may close. Tekno officials believe that the

(Requirements continued.)

probability that student enrollments will remain at 26,000 or decline to 25,000 will increase if the plant closes, and that the probability that the plant will close is 90% (a 10% probability that it will remain open). Compute the revised probabilities for student enrollments, and determine whether or not Tekno should accept the outside printer's offer in light of the new information. (SMAC adapted)

P24-7 Decision Tree. Global Credit Corporation (GCC) provides retail and banking institutions throughout the United States and Canada with credit histories of individuals who are seeking various types of financing, such as home mortgages, car loans, and retail store credit cards. GCC has branch offices in most major cities in order to provide rapid service to its customers. GCC employs a data-base system. The data base is maintained at the home office in Kansas City for security purposes. Each branch office is equipped with computer terminals that provide direct access to the data base for information retrieval. However, all data entry is completed in Kansas City.

GCC employs a staff of approximately 500 data entry clerks at the home office. The company hires inexperienced personnel and provides a training course as soon as new employees are hired. Hiring inexperienced personnel allows GCC to realize an average savings in annual salary and related employee benefits of $3,000 per employee. G. Webster, director of human resources, has just completed a review of the employment records of the data entry clerks and has discovered that only 50% of the trainees satisfactorily complete the training course and continue their employment with GCC. The remaining 50% are found lacking in aptitude for the job and are dismissed. While Webster is aware that the turnover rate for this type of position is typically high, this particular problem indicates a failure in the selection process.

Because the full training course for each data entry clerk costs GCC $600 and the retention rate is so poor, Webster is considering using a battery of tests to assist in determining which individuals should be hired and trained. The testing program would cost $200 per applicant to administer. Webster estimates that 75% of the applicants would achieve an acceptable score. Those applicants who achieve an acceptable score and are hired would be given an abbreviated training course at a cost of $300. Those applicants hired despite scoring below the cutoff point would still receive the full training course. In those cases there would be no saving in training costs.

After the results of the testing program are known, the Human Resource Department will consider other employee attributes before making a decision. As a result of this additional screening, Webster estimates that 90% of the high-scoring applicants would be hired and sent to the abbreviated training course, and 10% of the low-scoring applicants would be hired and sent to the full training course. The remaining applicants would not be hired.

To help her make a decision regarding the testing program, Webster has assigned probabilities to satisfactory and unsatisfactory training course completion under varying conditions. These probabilities follow:

	Training Course Completion	
	Satisfactory	Unsatisfactory
Test administered, result acceptable	.7	.3
Test administered, result unacceptable	.2	.8
Test not administered	.5	.5

Required: Prepare a decision tree representing GCC's decision problem, including all decision alternatives and possible outcomes with related expected values. (ICMA adapted)

P24-8 Decision Tree. Slick Inc. produces a product called Zap. T. Smoothy, marketing director of Slick Inc., is currently attempting to decide on an appropriate sales price for each unit of Zap for the coming year. Smoothy believes that a higher price would reduce demand for Zap, but that actual final demand would depend on whether the state of the economy next year is weak or strong.

Smoothy's situation is further complicated because next year's materials requirement must be purchased in a single lot of either 200,000 or 240,000 units, and the unit cost of the material will depend on the size of the lot ordered. The sole supplier of the material will accept no additional orders during the year. Therefore, if Slick Inc. does not purchase enough material to meet actual demand, some orders will be left unfilled. Furthermore, if more material is purchased than is required to fill demand, the excess material will spoil and be unusable at the end of the year. One unit of material is required for each unit of Zap. Material cost data follow:

Lot Size	Unit Cost
200,000 units	$3.00
240,000 units	2.90

Expected demand for Zap given different states of the economy and different sales prices follow:

	State of Economy	
Unit Sales Price	Weak	Strong
$5.25	180,000	200,000
5.00	200,000	240,000

Smoothy believes that there is a 60% probability that the economy will be weak and 40% that it will be strong.

Required: Prepare a decision tree representing Slick Inc.'s decision problem, including all decision alternatives and possible outcomes with related expected values. (SMAC adapted)

P24-9 Decision Tree. Strotz Brewery produces and sells nationally a popular premium beer and has enjoyed good profits for many years. In recent years, however, its sales volume has not grown with the general market. This lack of growth is due to the increasing popularity of light beer and the fact that Strotz has not entered this market.

Strotz is now developing its own light beer and is considering potential marketing strategies. Introducing the new light beer nationally will require a large commitment of resources for a full nationwide introduction because Strotz is a late entry into the light beer market. Strotz's advertising agency has helped assess the market risk and has convinced the Strotz management that there are only two reasonable alternative strategies to pursue.

(a) Strategy 1 is to perform a test advertising and sales campaign in a limited number of states for a 6-month period. Strotz would decide whether or not to introduce the light beer nationally and conduct a nationwide promotional campaign on the basis of the results of the test campaign.
(b) Strategy 2 is to conduct a nationwide promotion campaign and make the new light beer available in all 50 states immediately, without conducting any test campaign. The nationwide promotion and distribution campaign would be allowed to run for a full 2 years before a decision would be made to continue the light beer nationally.

Strotz management believes that if strategy 2 is selected, there is only a 50% chance of its being successful. The introduction of light beer nationally will be considered a success if $40 million of revenue is generated, while $30 million of variable cost is being incurred during the 2-year period in which the nationwide promotion and distribution campaign is in effect. If the 2-year nationwide campaign is unsuccessful, revenue is expected to be $16 million and variable cost will be $12 million. Total fixed cost for the 2-year period will amount to $6 million, regardless of the result.

The advertising agency consultants believe that if strategy 1 is selected, there is a 20% chance that the test will indicate that Strotz should conduct a nationwide promotion and distribution campaign when, in fact, a nationwide campaign would be unsuccessful. In addition, the consultants believe that there is a 20% chance that the test results will indicate Strotz should not conduct a nationwide promotion and distribution when, in fact, a nationwide campaign would be successful. The cost of the test campaign is estimated to be $500,000, and the probability of a successful test is 50%.

Required:
(1) Prepare a decision tree representing Strotz's decision problem, including all decision alternatives and possible outcomes with related expected values.
(2) Recommend the best strategy to Strotz management, based on the results indicated by the decision tree analysis.
(3) Criticize the expected value decision criterion. (ICMA adapted)

P24-10 Capital Expenditure Proposal with Normally Distributed, Independent Periodic Cash Flows. Ezell Corporation would like to expand the production of one of its product lines in order to enter into a new geographic market. To provide sufficient capacity, Ezell will need to purchase a new machine at a cost of $200,000. The new machine will have an estimated useful life of 10 years, with no expected salvage value;

however, for purposes of income tax depreciation, the machine qualifies as 7-year property. The historical demand for the product is normally distributed. Management believes that future demand will also be normally distributed and independent from one period to another. The expected value of the annual demand for the product produced by the new machine is 4,000 units with a standard deviation of 1,750 units. The contribution margin from the sale of the product is $14 per unit; however, in order to expand production, Ezell will need to incur additional fixed expenditures for marketing and production in the total amount of $8,100 per year. Ezell's weighted-average cost of capital is 12%, and the company is in the 40% income tax bracket.

Required:

(1) Determine the expected value of the periodic after-tax net cash flows and the after-tax cash flow value of the periodic standard deviation.
(2) Determine the expected net present value of the machine.
(3) Determine the variance and the standard deviation of the expected net present value of the machine.
(4) Compute the coefficient of variation for the capital expenditure proposal.
(5) Determine the probability that the net present value from this machine will be greater than zero.

P24-11 Capital Expenditure Proposal with Normally Distributed, Dependent Periodic Cash Flows. Jaffcon Manufacturing Company is considering purchasing a machine that will cost $180,000. The machine is expected to have a useful life of 8 years, with no expected salvage value; however, for purposes of determining income tax depreciation, the machine qualifies as 7-year property. Management's best guess is that it will be able to sell 5,000 units of the new product each year, with a periodic standard deviation of 2,000 units. Annual sales are believed to be normally distributed; however, because the product is new, sales from year to year are expected to be perfectly correlated. The contribution margin from the sale of one unit is $18. In order to manufacture and distribute the product, annual fixed costs of $10,000 must be incurred. Jaffcon's weighted-average cost of capital is 12%, and the company is in the 40% income tax bracket.

Required: With respect to the capital expenditure proposal, compute the following:

(1) The expected value of the periodic after-tax net cash flows and the after-tax cash flow value of the periodic standard deviation in monetary terms.
(2) The expected net present value of the capital expenditure proposal.
(3) The standard deviation of the expected net present value.
(4) The coefficient of variation.
(5) The probability that the net present value will exceed zero.

P24-12 Capital Expenditure Proposal with Normally Distributed Cash Flows that Are Neither Independent nor Perfectly Correlated. Winx Company is considering a capital expenditure proposal that will cost $30,000 but is expected to yield the following after-tax net cash inflows over its 5-year life:

Year	Expected After-Tax Cash Inflow
1	$ 8,000
2	11,000
3	10,000
4	9,000
5	7,000

The cash flows are expected to be normally distributed; however, the cash flows from year to year are not likely to be completely independent of one another. Management believes that for all practical purposes 70% of each year's cash inflows should be treated as independent and 30% as perfectly correlated. The best estimate of the periodic standard deviation of the independent portion of the cash inflows is $1,000, and the periodic standard deviation of the dependent portion is believed to be $500. The company's weighted-average cost of capital is 10%.

Required:

(1) Compute the expected net present value of the Winx Company proposal.
(2) Compute the variance and the standard deviation of the expected net present value.
(3) Compute the coefficient of variation for the capital expenditure proposal.
(4) Determine the probability that the net present value will exceed zero.

P24-13 Multi-attribute Decision Model. Glotyne Corporation is considering modernizing one of its manufacturing plants. Two choices are being considered:

(a) Replace all worn and obsolete machinery with modern machinery that utilizes essentially the same technology at a total cost of about $2,500,000.

(b) Replace all machinery with a fully computer integrated manufacturing (CIM) system at a total cost of about $4,000,000.

Corporate policy is to determine the economic value of all capital expenditure proposals using the net present value method. Analyses based on the most realistic data available result in a positive net present value of $500,000 for the existing technology alternative and a negative net present value of $50,000 for the CIM alternative. Concerned about the results of the economic analyses, top management called a meeting of marketing and manufacturing managers for the purpose of identifying nonfinancial benefits desired from plant modernization. The managers unanimously agreed that modernization should result in a more flexible manufacturing facility that will reduce setup time and decrease throughput time, thereby shortening production lead times and making the company more competitve. In addition, they agreed that modernization should improve product quality, reduce inventory levels, and improve the company's image to outsiders.

The corporate controller suggested use of a multi-attribute decision model, which would consider nonfinancial factors as well at the results of the economic analysis. The controller suggested that the management group assign a weight to each desired benefit that reflected its relative importance. Although the managers could agree on which factors were important, they did not unanimously agree on the relative importance of each factor. However, after considerable debate, a compromise was reached and the following relative factor weights were assigned:

Factor	Relative Importance Weighting
Net present value	30
Reduce setup time	20
Reduce throughput time	15
Improve product quality	15
Reduce inventory levels	10
Improve image to outsiders	10
Total	100

Next, the managers were directed to rate how well each modernization alternative would achieve the benefits desired and to determine the likelihood that the level of benefit expected would be achieved. For each alternative, each factor was assigned an achievement rating of 0, 1, or 2, depending on whether the alternative was expected to provide an unsatisfactory, a satisfactory, or a more than satisfactory benefit, respectively. A likelihood estimate for each factor was determined by averaging the managers' subjective probability estimates. The following averages resulted:

	Existing Technology		New Technology	
Factor	Achievement Rating	Likelihood Estimate	Achievement Rating	Likelihood Estimate
Net present value	2	.8	0	.5
Reduce setup time	0	.5	2	.9
Reduce throughput time	1	.5	2	.9
Improve product quality	1	.9	2	.5
Reduce inventory levels	0	.9	1	.6
Improve image to outsiders	1	.5	1	.6

Required: Using the multi-attribute decision model, determine which alternative approach to plant modernization Glotyne management should undertake.

CHAPTER 25

Marketing Expense and Profitability Analysis

Learning Objectives

After studying this chapter, you will be able to:

1. Compare marketing expenses with manufacturing costs.
2. List marketing functions and expense classifications.
3. Provide examples of the application of manufacturing cost control techniques to the control of marketing expenses.
4. Analyze profitability by territories, customers, products, and salespersons.
5. Define life-cycle costing and relate it to cost reduction and product pricing.
6. List six different product pricing approaches.

This chapter presents techniques that are useful in analyzing and controlling marketing expenses and in analyzing market profitability. **Marketing** is the matching of a company's products with markets for the satisfaction of customers at a reasonable profit for the firm. Marketing managers must decide the (1) product selection, design, color, size, and packaging, (2) prices to be charged, (3) advertising and promotion needed, and (4) physical distribution to be followed. These decisions require organization, planning, and control. Marketing is usually organized by functional activity, by product line, and by territory. The planning and control phases should be based on a well-structured marketing expense and profitability analysis system. The preparation of budgets and the need for planning the marketing effort are discussed in Chapter 15. Controlling marketing expenses and analyzing profitability are discussed in this chapter.

This chapter begins with a discussion of the scope of marketing activities and then provides a comparison of expenses incurred to market a product with those incurred to manufacture it. The next section discusses how manufacturing cost control techniques can be applied to control marketing expenses. This is followed by marketing profitability analysis (including gross profit analysis). The chapter concludes with a discussion of product pricing.

Scope of Marketing Activity

Marketing activities require substantial expenditures. One estimate of the magnitude of marketing expenses is that it makes up more than 50 percent of the total cost of many product lines and approximately 20 percent of the gross national product.[1] Although many firms spend considerable effort analyzing and controlling manufacturing costs, few attempt to analyze and control marketing expenditures. Nevertheless, the sheer magnitude of marketing expenditures suggests a potential for substantial cost savings.

Control and analysis of marketing expenses complement each other and involve the assignment of marketing expenses to various groupings such as territories, customers, and products. In order to control costs, management must know which activities drive cost and the cost of each activity. Normally at the end of each month, reports that compare actual results with some target are issued to responsible managers. However, the problems associated with marketing expenses do not end with these reporting procedures. Although the control of expenses at the departmental level is an important feature of any cost improvement program, unreasonable limitations on marketing expenditures can lead to a curtailment of sales activities, which in turn can result in the gradual deterioration or elimination of certain types of sales. On the other hand, indiscriminate and wasteful spending adversely affect a company's profits. Management needs meaningful marketing expense information in order to determine and analyze the profitability of (1) a territory or territories, (2) certain classes of customers, such as wholesalers, retailers, institutions, and governmental units, (3) products, product lines, or brands, and (4) promotional efforts by salespersons, telephone, mail, newspapers, magazines, television, or radio. Where possible, the revenue generating effect of each expenditure should be determined and those that have no value should be eliminated.

The scope of today's marketing activities includes not only fulfilling existing customer demand, but also creating and discovering new ways to meet future and unfulfilled customer needs. In a global competitive economy, businesses must concentrate on satisfying customers rather than on merely producing products or providing services. This outlook requires the best available information for management's use. In many organizations, the marketing activity has always received management's attention—in some cases, even more attention than that rendered to other business operations. In today's economy, the strategic importance and magnitude of marketing activity merit still greater attention.

Comparison of Marketing Expenses with Manufacturing Costs

The control and analysis of marketing expenses present certain complexities. First of all, logistic systems are many and varied. Manufacturers of certain products use basically the same materials and machinery. However, these companies may use vastly different channels of distribution, ranging from a simple, direct distribution to a complex marketing system, with promotional efforts directed to narrow or broad customer groups. Therefore, a meaningful comparison of the marketing expenses of one company with another is almost impossible.

Not only do distribution methods vary, but they are also extremely flexible. A company may find that a change in market conditions necessitates a change in its channels of distribution. The distribution expense budget must be revised with every change in the method of distribution, so tactics may change several times

[1] Ronald J. Lewis, "Activity-Based Costing for Marketing," *Management Accounting*, Vol. 73, No. 5, p. 33.

before the best method is found. In contrast, such sweeping changes are not as common in production. Once a factory is set up, management is not likely to make substantial changes in its manufacturing techniques until machinery is replaced or competition forces the company to adopt new production technologies. Therefore, standards set for a particular machine or production process seldom require significant revision.

The psychological factors present in selling a product are perhaps the main reasons for differences between marketing and manufacturing cost control. Management can control the cost of labor, hours of operation, and number of machines operated, but management cannot control what the customer will do. Different salespersons and different advertising appeals have different effects on customers. Customer resistance is the enigma in marketing expense analysis. The customer, whose wishes and peculiarities govern the method of doing business, is a controlling rather than a controllable factor.

The attitudes of marketing and manufacturing management also differ. Although factory managers often measure their accomplishments in terms of reduced cost per unit, most sales managers consider sales the yardstick for measuring their efficiency, even though increased sales do not necessarily mean greater profits.

Cause and effect, generally obvious in the factory, are not so readily discernible in the marketing processes. For example, many promotional expenditures are incurred for future results, creating a time lag between cause and effect. Conversely, the effects of manufacturing changes usually are quickly observable, and matching between effort and result can usually be achieved. Furthermore, manufacturing results are more readily quantified than are marketing results. For marketing, it is often not easy to identify quantities or units of activity with the expenditure incurred and results achieved.

Generally accepted accounting practice does not charge Cost of Goods Sold and ending inventories with marketing and administrative expenditures. Nonmanufacturing expenditures (other than acquisitions of long-lived assets such as buildings, furniture, vehicles and other depreciable assets) fall into the category of period expenses, which are charged against revenues in the period in which such expenditures are incurred. Although some marketing expenditures (such as advertising, market analysis, and product development) can contribute to the company's ability to earn revenue in future periods, the future value of such expenditures is not objectively measurable. As a consequence, such expenditures are charged to expense in the period in which they are incurred. In contrast, manufacturing expenditures are clearly incurred for the purpose of getting products into a condition to sell. Therefore, such costs are allocated to the products produced during the period and charged against revenue only when such products are sold.

In the field of marketing, marketing expenditures are commonly referred to as marketing costs, even though such expenditures would be defined as expenses by accountants. In addition, it is more common to speak of marketing cost analysis rather than of marketing cost accounting. A tie-in of marketing costing with the general accounts, although desirable, is often not necessary.

Marketing Expense Control

The control and analysis of marketing expenses should follow methods that are similar to those used for manufacturing costs. The first step in the control of marketing expenses is the classification of natural expenses according to marketing function. Each marketing function and its associated expenses should be made the responsibility of a manager or department head.

Marketing functions are of many types, depending on the nature of the business and its organization, size, and method of operation. Typically, each **marketing function** is a homogeneous unit, the principal activity of which is related to specific items of cost. A function can follow a particular pattern of natural expenses, but most functions have similar expenses, such as salaries, payroll taxes, employee benefits, insurance, equipment depreciation, property taxes, utilities, and supplies.

Functional classifications of marketing expenses might be structured in the following manner:

1. Selling
2. Advertising
3. Market research and forecasting
4. Product design and development
5. Warehousing
6. Packing and shipping
7. Credit and collection
8. General accounting (for marketing)

Most of these functional classifications are grouped into two broad categories: order-getting expenses and order-filling expenses. Order-getting expenses are the expenses of activities that bring in the sales orders and include selling and advertising. Order-filling expenses are the expenses of warehousing, packing and shipping, credit and collection, and general accounting. A third category of marketing expenses includes market research and forecasting and product design and development. Actual marketing expenses are recorded and charged to the appropriate departmental and natural expense classifications in a subsidiary ledger controlled by a marketing expense control account in the general ledger.

Fixed and Variable Expenses

Recognition of the fixed–variable expense classification is valuable in controlling marketing expenses and in making decisions dealing with the possible opening or closing of a territory, new methods of packaging goods, servicing different types of outlets, or adding or dropping a product line. Fixed marketing expenses include salaries of executive and administrative sales staffs; salaries of warehousing, advertising, shipping, billing, and collection departments; and rent and depreciation of associated permanent facilities. These fixed expenses are also called **capacity costs**.

Variable marketing expenses include the expenses of handling, warehousing, and shipping that tend to vary with sales volume. They can be referred to as **volume costs** or as expenses connected with the filling of an order. Another type of variable marketing expense originates in connection with promotional expenses such as salespersons' salaries, travel, entertainment, and some advertising expenses. Management should examine these expenses carefully in the planning stage, because sales volume may have little influence on their behavior. These expenses are variable because of management decisions. In fact, once agreed to by management, these expenses are fixed, at least for the budget period under consideration.

Direct and Indirect Expenses

Direct expenses are those expenses that can be traced directly to a function or department, such as the salary of a department manager or the depreciation of a delivery truck. Expenses that can be traced to a territory, customer, product, or sales outlet also can be considered direct expenses. Conversely, **indirect expenses** are incurred for more than one function or other classification. Marketing expenses can be considered direct, indirect, or a combination of both, depending on the purpose of the analysis. For example, marketing expenses may be directly identifiable with functional classifications while being only indirectly identifiable with regard to other marketing activities, such as sales territories, customers, or products.

Allocating Marketing Expenses

Where possible, marketing expenses should be directly traced to the marketing classification being analyzed, such as territory, customer group, or product. The allocation of indirect expenses introduces inaccuracies and arbitrariness into an analysis. Nevertheless, such allocation is necessary in some circumstances to present a more complete picture of the expenses created by or for the marketing classification being analyzed.

Allocating functional marketing expenses to territories, customer classes, or products poses two basic questions: What bases should be used for the allocation and how far should the allocations be carried out? As an answer to the first question, the base used should be the one most closely related to the incurrence of the expense being allocated. Functional marketing expenses can be allocated to territories, customer classes, or products for analysis by (1) use of a percentage based on actual sales, manufacturing cost, or some other appropriate basis, or (2) creation of a cost rate for each activity similar to activity-based costing for factory overhead described in (Chapter 14). The assignment of functional marketing expenses as percentages of actual sales or manufacturing costs is of dubious analytical value. Determining the cost rate for each marketing activity is a more useful approach.

Analyzing marketing expenses on the basis of the activities that drive expense is a logical extension of activity-based costing used in manufacturing and provides many of the same advantages. Analysis of expense drivers helps management identify those marketing activities that add value to the product or service provided to customers and those that do not. Detailed analysis of marketing activities and the expenses created by those activities provides a basis for controlling and improving efficiency. In marketing, this process is referred to as **activity-based management (ABM)**.

Managing value-added activities and eliminating or reducing non-value-added activities reduces expense and provides a focus for continuous improvement. The careful analysis required to determine the expense generated by each activity often reveals opportunities for improvement. For example, management may discover that the cost of processing an order is greater than the profit generated by small orders. Either the prices of small orders should be raised by adding an order processing charge, or more efficient ways of processing the orders should be found. Analysis sometimes reveals that certain procedures are not efficient. Restructuring the process or changing the organization of work can reduce the inefficiency and save money. Even in cases in which inefficiencies are not readily apparent, the magnitude of the expenses incurred by each activity is called to the attention of management. Those activities that are expensive should be carefully analyzed and monitored with the objective of finding a way to improve efficiency and reduce expense.

In addition to revealing opportunities for improving marketing activities, the availability of activity cost rates permits quick and accurate computation of expenses that lead to improved analysis and decisions. The selection of activity bases for allocating functional marketing expenses requires careful analysis, because the degree to which the activity cost rates correspond to actual expenses depends a great deal on the bases selected. The analyst must carefully examine each marketing function to determine the activity that most influences the incurrence of expense. If two or more activities drive significant amounts of expense, multiple rates should be used. Some examples of allocation bases for different marketing functions are included in the following table.

Function	Expense Allocation Bases
Selling	Gross sales dollar value of products sold or number of salespersons' calls on customers (based on salespersons' time reports)
Advertising	Quantity of product units sold, relative media circulation, or cost of space directly assignable
Warehousing	Size, weight, or number of products shipped or handled
Packing and shipping	Number of shipping units, weight, or size of units
Credit and collection	Number of customers' orders, transactions, or invoice lines
General accounting	Number of customers' orders, transactions, or invoice lines

The expense rate for an activity is calculated by dividing the total expense for the activity by the total amount of the activity base selected. A vast amount of information must be collected in order to establish an activity expense rate. The tedious assembly of such underlying information is often the reason for the lack of marketing expense control.

With respect to the question about how far allocations of functional expenses should be carried, the answer depends on the uses of the data. Despite the use of activity-based costing techniques, the allocation of functional expenses introduces some arbitrariness that can bias reports and mislead users. Functional classifications contain some fixed expenses that are not driven by any activity. When expenses are being allocated for analytical purposes, fixed expenses should be omitted. On the other hand, full marketing expense allocation is desirable in cost-plus pricing of contracts. With respect to government contracts, CAS 418 calls for the allocation of indirect costs to be based on one of the following, listed in order of preference: (1) a resource consumption measure, (2) an output measure, or (3) a surrogate that is representative of resources consumed.[2]

Flexible Budget and Standards for Marketing Functions

Sales estimates are the most important figures in any budget. The accuracy and usefulness of most other estimates depend on them. Methods used in determining sales estimates are discussed in Chapter 15. Ordinarily, the sales budget details the products to be sold, the monthly or weekly sales, and sales by salespersons, territories, classes of customers, and methods of distribution. For each organizational unit, quotas may be useful for management to determine the desirability of cultivating various outlets and to judge the efficiency of sales methods and policies.

Budgets are prepared to anticipate the amount of functional expenses for the coming period and to provide a basis for comparing and evaluating the actual expenses. Because some marketing expenses are variable, differences between actual and expected activity affect expense. For this reason, actual expenses should not be compared with a predetermined fixed budget for marketing expense control purposes. Instead, the use of flexible budgets should be considered.

The flexible budget for a distributive function, such as billing, might take the form shown in Exhibit 25-1. In this example, the primary functional expense

[2] *Standards, Rules and Regulations, Part 418,* "Allocation of Direct and Indirect Costs" (Washington, D.C.: Cost Accounting Standards Board, 1980).

driver is the number of invoice lines processed. All activity of the department is oriented toward generating invoices, and the number of lines on the invoice drives all variable expenses.

EXHIBIT 25-1

Flexible Budget for the Billing Department

Invoice lines	50,000	55,000	60,000	65,000
Variable Expenses:				
Supplies	$ 2,500	$ 2,750	$ 3,000	$ 3,250
Postage	1,250	1,375	1,500	1,625
Total variable expenses	$ 3,750	$ 4,125	$ 4,500	$ 4,875
Fixed Expenses:				
Clerical salaries	$ 4,000	$ 4,000	$ 4,000	$ 6,000
Supervision	3,000	3,000	3,000	3,000
Payroll taxes	1,000	1,000	1,000	1,500
Employee benefits	1,500	1,500	1,500	1,500
Utilities	800	800	800	800
Depreciation—building	750	750	750	750
Depreciation—equipment	900	900	900	900
Property taxes and insurance	350	350	350	350
Total fixed expenses	$12,300	$12,300	$12,300	$14,800
Total	$16,050	$16,425	$16,800	$19,675

A budgeted expense rate for each unit of activity is established for each marketing function on the basis of expected or normal capacity. These rates provide a basis for evaluating efficiency. Spending and idle capacity variances can be computed as an aid in identifying controllable expenditures. The Billing Department can be used as an example. Assuming that 60,000 invoice lines represent normal capacity, the targeted billing rate per invoice line can be computed as follows:

$$\frac{\$16{,}800}{60{,}000 \text{ invoice lines}} = \$.28 \text{ per invoice line}$$

Based on estimated variable expense of $4,500 in the flexible budget, the variable portion of the rate is as follows:

$$\frac{\$4{,}500}{60{,}000 \text{ invoice lines}} = \$.075 \text{ per invoice line}$$

The variances for billing expenses can be computed in a manner similar to that discussed in connection with factory overhead and consistent with the basic idea of flexible budgeting (Chapter 17). Assume that the Billing Department processed 58,000 invoice lines during March and actual expenses were as follows:

Supplies	$ 3,140
Postage	1,550
Clerical salaries	4,000
Supervision	3,000
Payroll taxes	1,000
Employee benefits	1,500
Utilities	900
Depreciation—building	750
Depreciation—equipment	900
Property taxes and insurance	360
Total billing department cost	$17,100

The Billing Department variances for March are determined as follows:

Actual expense		$17,100	
Budget allowance for actual activity:			
Variable expense ($.075 × 58,000 invoice lines)	$ 4,350		
Fixed expense budgeted	12,300	16,650	
Spending variance		$ 450	unfavorable
Budget allowance for actual activity (from above)		$16,650	
Chargeable expenses ($.28 × 58,000 invoice lines)		16,240	
Idle capacity variance		$ 410	unfavorable

The unfavorable idle capacity variance says that budgeted fixed costs were underabsorbed by $410 because actual activity was less than budgeted activity. The level of activity may be a function of sales and not controllable by the Billing Department supervisor. On the other hand, the unfavorable spending variance provides a signal that controllable expenditures were more than they should have been, by $450. A variance report detailing the spending variance for each item of expense, such as the one presented in Exhibit 25-2, enhances control by identifying which items cost too much. In this example, the costs of supplies and postage were responsible for more than 75 percent of the total spending variance and are probably the only controllable expenditures.

EXHIBIT 25-2

Billing Department
Variance Report
For period ended March 31, 19—

	Budget Allowance for Expected Capacity	Budget Allowance for Actual Capacity	Actual Expenses	Spending Variance (Favorable) Unfavorable
Invoice lines	60,000	58,000	58,000	
Variable Expenses:				
Supplies	$ 3,000	$ 2,900*	$ 3,140	$240
Postage	1,500	1,450**	1,550	100
Total variable expenses	$ 4,500	$ 4,350	$ 4,690	
Fixed Expenses:				
Clerical salaries	$ 4,000	$ 4,000	$ 4,000	0
Supervision	3,000	3,000	3,000	0
Payroll taxes	1,000	1,000	1,000	0
Employee benefits	1,500	1,500	1,500	0
Utilities	800	800	900	100
Depreciation—building	750	750	750	0
Depreciation—equipment	900	900	900	0
Property taxes and insurance	350	350	360	10
Total fixed expenses	$12,300	$12,300	$12,410	
Total	$16,800	$16,650	$17,100	$450 unfavorable
Chargeable expenses ($.28 × 58,000 invoice lines)		16,240		
Idle capacity variance		$ 410 unfavorable		

* $3,000 budgeted supplies ÷ 60,000 budgeted invoice lines × 58,000 actual invoice lines.

** $1,500 budgeted postage ÷ 60,000 budgeted invoice lines × 58,000 actual invoice lines.

Although variance analysis and reporting to managers of the various marketing functions is a commonly employed control mechanism, it can influence marketing managers to develop a myopic focus that often results in dysfunctional behavior. Although flexible budgets are useful in planning and coordinating activity, they send a message to employees that the budget or target levels of performance are acceptable. This thwarts continuous improvement, even when budgets are tightened each period. Variance analysis is often used as a basis for performance evaluation, which provides a strong incentive for managers to do whatever is necessary to improve performance in the short run whether it is good for the company or not. These are the same kinds of problems, discussed in Chapter 17, that arise when variance reports are used to evaluate managerial performance in a manufacturing setting.

Marketing Profitability Analysis

Activity expense rates for the various marketing functions are used to analyze expenses and determine the profitability of territories, customers, products, and salespersons. Analysis of many marketing activities and revenue sources is often required in order to explain completely the effectiveness of past decisions and to discover opportunities for future improvement. Marketing expense and profitability analysis has improved over the years with the increasing availability of high-speed computers capable of processing the great amount of quantitative detail so characteristic of these analyses.

Analysis by Territories

Perhaps the simplest analysis of marketing profitability is by territories. When marketing activities are organized on a territorial basis, each organizational unit or activity that can be identified in the geographical territory is charged directly with the expenses incurred by it. Proration of expenses is minimized because most marketing expenses are directly traceable to territories. Expenses that can be traced directly to a territory are: salespersons' salaries, commissions, and traveling expenses; transportation cost within the delivery area; packing and shipping costs; and advertising specifically identified with the territory.

The allocation of nontraceable expenses is of questionable value because for the most part they are not driven by activities at the territorial level. Examples of nontraceable expenses that can be allocated to the territory are: general management, general office, institutional advertising, product design and development, and general accounting. If nontraceable expenses are allocated to the territory, they should be shown separately, so that the territory's contribution to profit and the recovery of common expenses can be readily identified.

When expenses are identified by territories, a comparative income statement can be prepared. This statement, illustrated in Exhibit 25-3, permits control and analysis of expenses as well as the computation of profit margins. When sales or expenses seem to be out of line, management can take corrective action.

Analysis by Customers

Although most marketing expenses can be traced directly to territories, relatively few of these expenses can be traced directly to customers. Perhaps sales commissions, transportation expenses, and sales discounts can be considered direct expenses, but others can be allocated only on the basis of some arbitrary method.

EXHIBIT 25-3

Income Statement by Territories

	Territory		
	Number 1	**Number 2**	**Number 3**
Net sales	$210,000	$ 80,000	$175,000
Cost of goods sold	160,000	60,000	140,000
Gross profit	$ 50,000	$ 20,000	$ 35,000
Traceable marketing expenses:			
Selling	$ 15,000	$ 8,600	$ 23,900
Warehousing	3,600	1,400	3,100
Packing and shipping	1,500	400	1,900
Advertising	2,000	1,000	500
Credit and collection	800	250	1,200
Total traceable marketing expenses	$ 22,900	$ 11,650	$ 30,600
Contribution to profit and common costs	$ 27,100	$ 8,350	$ 4,400
Allocated indirect costs:			
Institutional advertising	$ 1,400	$ 1,400	$ 1,400
General administration	5,000	5,000	5,000
Total allocated indirect costs	$ 6,400	$ 6,400	$ 6,400
Operating income (loss) per territory	$ 20,700	$ 1,950	$ (2,000)

A large number of customers makes the allocation and analysis of marketing expenses by customers rather cumbersome if not impossible. For this reason, customers can be grouped according to certain characteristics to make the analysis meaningful. The grouping can be by (1) territory, (2) amount of average order, (3) customer-volume group, or (4) kind of customer.

Analysis of Customers by Territories. This type of analysis reflects territorial cost differences due to customers' proximity to warehouses, volume of purchases, service requirements, and the kinds of merchandise bought. These factors can make some sales profitable or unprofitable. The analysis proceeds in the same manner outlined for territories, except that the expenses are broken down by customers or kinds of customers within each territory.

Analysis of Customers by Amount of Average Order. The amount of a customer's order is closely related to profitability. An analysis can indicate that a considerable portion of orders comes from customers who cost the company more in selling to them than the orders are worth in terms of gross profit. In response to this information, a company can resort to setting minimum dollar values or minimum quantities for orders as well as price differentials, thereby reducing the number of transactions and increasing profits. Although selective selling has found much favor among many executives, it requires changes in habits and routines.

A quick view of the situation regarding the amount of the average order in relation to the number of customers, time spent, and total dollar sales, can be presented to management by means of a graphic, such as the chart presented in Figure 25-1.

Analysis by Customer-Volume Groups. An analysis of customers by customer-volume groups is similar to analysis of the amount of average order. Instead of customers being classified by an order's dollar value, however, the customer-volume group analysis is based on quantity or volume. This type of analysis yields information concerning the profitability of various customer-volume groups and the establishment of minimum orders and price differentials.

FIGURE 25-1 ***Analysis of Customers by Amount of Average Order***

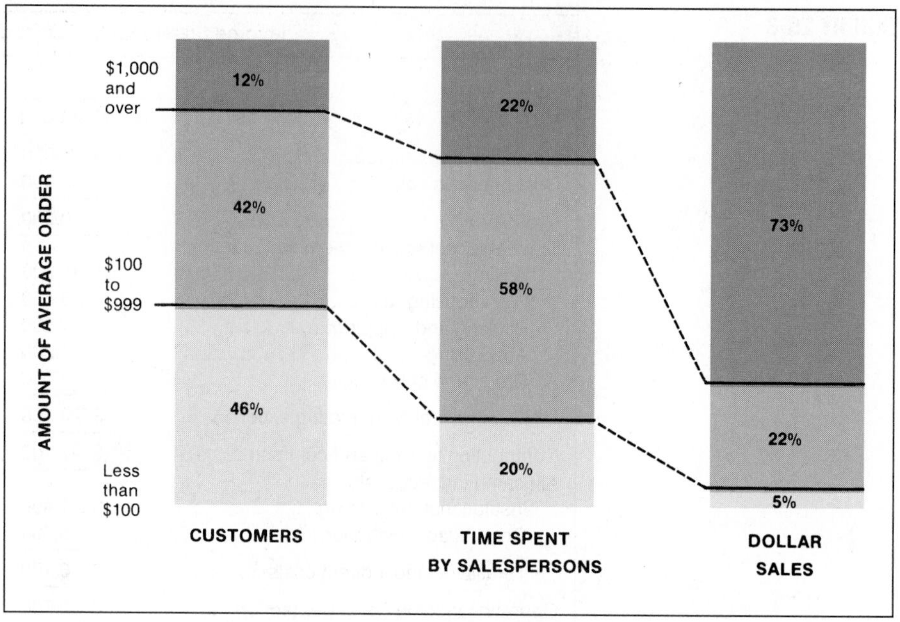

The analysis presented in Exhibit 25-4 indicates that only sales to customers who buy more than 150 units during a week result in a positive contribution margin.

EXHIBIT 25-4

Analysis by Customer-Volume Groups

Customer–Volume Group (Number of Units Purchased During Week)	Customers (% of Total)	Volume (% of Total)	Gross Contribution Margin per 100 Units	Variable Commercial Expenses per 100 Units	Contribution Margin per 100 Units
Customers unsuccessfully solicited	17.1%	—	—	—	—
1–25	7.6	0.2%	$1.66	$4.01	$(2.35)
26–50	8.3	0.7	1.38	2.55	(1.17)
51–100	12.0	1.9	1.25	1.78	(.53)
101–150	9.3	2.4	1.26	1.32	(.06)
151–200	7.8	2.9	1.14	1.13	.01
201–250	6.4	3.0	1.12	.95	.17
251–500	17.1	13.2	1.06	.75	.31
501–1,000	12.7	18.6	1.02	.49	.53
1,001–10,000	1.7	57.1	.81	.24	.57
Total	100.0%	100.0%			

The variable cost of goods sold is subtracted from sales to compute the gross contribution margin, from which the variable commercial (marketing and administrative) expenses are subtracted to compute the contribution margin. Although the customers buying more than 150 units weekly represent only about 46 percent of the customers, they purchase approximately 95 percent of the units sold and thus provide the profits. In spite of the higher gross contribution margin received from orders by customers who buy less than 150 units, it is not sufficient to cover variable commercial expenses. As a result, the sales to this group provide nothing for fixed expenses and profit.

Analysis by Kinds of Customers. This type of analysis makes a distinction between manufacturers, wholesalers, retailers, government (local, state, and federal), schools, colleges and universities, and hospitals. Prices that are uniform within each customer group might still vary between groups. Different salespersons are often employed for each category; hence their salaries and related expenses can be assigned directly to the group. Delivery to such groups can differ. For example, one delivery may be contracted with an outside trucker, and another may be made by the firm's own truck. For analytical purposes, revenue and expenses should be related to each kind of customer.

Analysis by Products

The effect of sales of each product or product line is of considerable importance in planning and controlling the marketing effort. The existence of a high sales volume and a company-wide profit does not necessarily mean that all is well. Profitable and unprofitable products should be identified so that profits can be planned and controlled effectively. Just as customers are grouped for purposes of analysis, products sold can be grouped according to product lines or brands possessing common characteristics.

Improving Product Cost Accuracy With Activity-Based Costing. Analysis of profitability by products can be misleading if product profit measures are based on inaccurate product costs. If manufacturing has a complex cost structure and a diverse product line, activity-based costing can improve the accuracy of product costs. A complex cost structure is present if a significant part of overhead cost is not related to output volume. A diverse product line is one in which different products consume different mixes of volume- and non-volume-related costs. This is likely to occur when some products are manufactured in large batches while others are produced in small batches. In such environments, traditional volume-based overhead rates tend to distort product costing. For example, the cost of setting up a production run for a small batch may be the same as for a large batch, yet overhead allocated on the basis of volume assigns more cost to the large batch than the small one. Other manufacturing costs, such as production engineering and production scheduling, are unrelated to batch size and similarly misallocated to products by volume-based measures. In contrast, activity-based costing allocates indirect costs to products on the basis of both volume- and non-volume-related activities. The cost rate is determined for each significant activity and then allocated to each job on the basis of the amount of each activity consumed in completing the job. (See Chapter 14 for a detailed discussion of activity-based costing.)

The use of activity-based costing generally results in substantially greater unit costs for low-volume products than is reported by traditional product costing. Although management may be aware that high-volume products are more profitable than low-volume products, the magnitude of the difference can be known only when products are costed on the basis of the resources they actually consume. Activity-based costing provides that information, thereby improving product profitability analysis.

Product-Line Income Statement Analysis. Although activity-based costing substantially improves the accuracy of product costing when complex cost structures and diverse product lines exist, some product cost distortion occurs. Many plant-wide or company-wide fixed costs often are included in overhead and allocated to products in one or more of the activity cost rates. No matter how carefully and how logically they are allocated, allocations of these common costs introduce some arbitrariness into product cost. One approach to eliminating the influence of arbitrary allocations is to assign only traceable variable costs to products. This approach to product costing, called direct costing or variable costing, was discussed in detail in Chapter 20.

In direct costing, fixed costs are viewed as expenses of the period. Arbitrary allocations of common costs are eliminated by first subtracting only traceable variable manufacturing cost from the sales of each product. This produces a figure referred to as the gross contribution margin. Next, traceable variable nonmanufacturing expenses are subtracted from the gross contribution margin of each product to compute the contribution margin for each product. Fixed costs are not allocated unless specifically traceable to a product. Nontraceable costs, which may include nontraceable variable costs[3] as well as common fixed costs, are shown separately. When a product contributes nothing to the recovery of nontraceable costs, the situation should be examined and remedial steps taken. The product-line income statement presented in Exhibit 25-5 illustrates this approach. This form of statement makes the actual contribution of each product line to total profits and to the recovery of nontraceable costs readily apparent.

EXHIBIT 25-5

Product-Line Income Statement
(Contribution Margin Approach)

		Product Line		
	Total	1	2	3
Net sales	$3,100,000	$1,540,000	$1,070,000	$490,000
Less variable cost of goods sold	1,927,000	925,000	590,000	412,000
Gross contribution margin	$1,173,000	$ 615,000	$ 480,000	$ 78,000
Less variable marketing expenses:				
Selling	$ 243,300	$ 112,300	$ 89,000	$ 42,000
Warehousing	87,100	48,000	27,500	11,600
Packing and shipping	66,000	39,000	17,800	9,200
Advertising	38,000	20,000	12,000	6,000
Credit and collection	19,700	12,300	4,200	3,200
General accounting	52,200	23,000	16,800	12,400
Total	$ 506,300	$ 254,600	$ 167,300	$ 84,400
Contribution margin	$ 666,700	$ 360,400	$ 312,700	$ (6,400)
Less traceable fixed expenses:				
Manufacturing	$ 100,000	$ 30,000	$ 52,200	$ 17,800
Marketing	15,000	8,000	6,000	1,000
Administration	5,000	2,000	1,800	1,200
Total	$ 120,000	$ 40,000	$ 60,000	$ 20,000
Margin available for common fixed expenses and operating income	$ 546,700	$ 320,400	$ 252,700	$ (26,400)
Less nontraceable costs	230,000			
Operating income	$ 316,700			

Gross Profit or Contribution Margin Analysis. If the cost per unit of product is entirely variable, as is the case for wholesalers and retailers, it is useful to

[3] Examples of nontraceable variable costs include expenditures for materials and labor in a joint production process and marketing expenditures that vary with some activity not directly traceable to individual products, such as travel and entertainment, billing, credit, and collection.

compare actual gross profit with planned gross profit and to analyze the sources of the observed difference. Because of the arbitrary nature of allocating fixed factory overhead, it is more useful for manufacturers to analyze the difference in actual and planned contribution margin.[4] The difference can be the result of one or a combination of the following:

1. Changes in sales prices of products, a **sales price variance**.
2. Changes in the volume sold, a **sales volume variance** plus a **cost volume variance**. (a) Changes in the number of physical units sold, a **final sales volume variance**. (b) Changes in the types of products sold, a **sales mix variance**.
3. Changes in elements of cost, a **cost price variance**.

The determination of the various causes for an increase or decrease in gross profit or contribution margin is similar to the computation of standard cost variances, although standard costs or budgets are not required. If standards or budgets are not used, prices and costs of the previous period, or any period selected as the basis for the comparison, serve as the basis for the computation of the variances.

To illustrate the analysis, the following gross profit sections of Spanton Wholesale Supply Company's operating statements are presented.

	Budgeted	Actual	Difference
Sales (net)	$120,000	$140,000	+ $20,000
Cost of goods sold	100,000	110,000	+ 10,000
Gross profit	$ 20,000	$ 30,000	+ $10,000 net increase

In comparison with the budget, actual sales increased $20,000 and costs increased $10,000, resulting in an increase in gross profit of $10,000.

Additional data taken from various records indicate that the sales and the cost of goods sold figures can be broken down as follow:

Product	Quantity (in units)	Budgeted Sales		Budgeted Cost of Goods Sold	
		Unit Price	Amount	Unit Cost	Amount
X	8,000	$5.00	$ 40,000	$4.000	$ 32,000
Y	7,000	4.00	28,000	3.500	24,500
Z	20,000	2.60	52,000	2.175	43,500
		Total sales	$120,000	Total cost	$100,000

Product	Quantity (in units)	Actual Sales		Actual Cost of Goods Sold	
		Unit Price	Amount	Unit Cost	Amount
X	10,000	$6.60	$ 66,000	$4.00	$ 40,000
Y	4,000	3.50	14,000	3.50	14,000
Z	20,000	3.00	60,000	2.80	56,000
		Total sales	$140,000	Total cost	$110,000

To analyze the gross profit data of Spanton Wholesale Supply Company, the budgeted sales and costs are used as the basis (or standard) for all comparisons. A sales price variance and a sales volume variance are computed first, followed

[4] A wholesaler or retailer may also want to analyze the contribution margin of products because the contribution margin includes not only the purchase price of the products but also the variable marketing and administrative expenses.

by the computation of a cost price variance and a cost volume variance. The sales volume variance and the cost volume variance are analyzed further as a third step, which results in the computation of a sales mix variance and a final sales volume variance.

The sales price and sales volume variances of Spanton Wholesale Supply Company are computed as follows:

Actual sales		$140,000
Actual sales at budgeted prices:		
X: 10,000 units at $5.00	$50,000	
Y: 4,000 units at $4.00	16,000	
Z: 20,000 units at $2.60	52,000	118,000
Sales price variance		$ 22,000 favorable
Actual sales at budgeted prices		$118,000
Total budgeted sales (used as standard)		120,000
Sales volume variance		$ 2,000 unfavorable

The cost price and cost volume variances are computed as follows:

Actual cost of goods sold		$110,000
Actual sales at budgeted costs:		
X: 10,000 units at $4.000	$40,000	
Y: 4,000 units at $3.500	14,000	
Z: 20,000 units at $2.175	43,500	97,500
Cost price variance		$ 12,500 unfavorable
Actual sales at budgeted costs		$ 97,500
Budgeted cost of goods sold (used as standard)		100,000
Cost volume variance		$ 2,500 favorable

The results of the preceding computations explain the reason for the $10,000 increase in gross profit.

Sales price variance		$22,000 favorable
Volume variances (net) consisting of:		
Cost volume variance	$2,500 favorable	
Less sales volume variance	2,000 unfavorable	
Net volume variance		500 favorable
		$22,500
Less cost price variance		12,500 unfavorable
Net increase in gross profit		$10,000

The net $500 favorable volume variance is a composite of the sales volume and cost volume variances. It should be further analyzed to determine the more significant sales mix and final sales volume variances. To accomplish this analysis, one additional figure must be determined—the budgeted average gross profit per unit. The computation is as follows:

$$\frac{\text{Total budgeted gross profit}}{\text{Total budgeted number of units sold}} = \frac{\$20{,}000}{35{,}000} = \$.5714 \text{ per unit}$$

The $.5714 average budgeted gross profit per unit sold is multiplied by the actual total number of units sold (34,000 units). The resulting $19,428 is the total gross profit that would have been achieved if all units had been sold at the budgeted average gross profit per unit.

The sales mix and the final sales volume variances can now be calculated:

Actual sales at budgeted prices		$118,000
Actual sales at budgeted costs		97,500
Difference		$ 20,500
Actual sales at budgeted average gross profit		19,428
Sales mix variance		$ 1,072 favorable
Actual sales at budgeted average gross profit		$ 19,428
Total budgeted sales (used as standard)	$120,000	
Budgeted cost of goods sold (used as standard)	100,000	
Difference		20,000
Final sales volume variance		$ 572 unfavorable
Check: Sales mix variance		$ 1,072 favorable
Final sales volume variance		572 unfavorable
Net volume variance		$ 500 favorable

The sales mix variance can be viewed in the following manner:

Product	(1) Actual Sales (in Units)	Budgeted Sales Units	Budgeted Sales %	(2) Actual Sales (in budgeted proportions)*	(3) (1) – (2)	(4) Budgeted Unit Gross Profit**	Sales Mix Variance (3) × (4)
X	10,000	8,000	22.86	7,772	2,228	$1.000	$2,228 favorable
Y	4,000	7,000	20.00	6,800	(2,800)	.500	(1,400) unfavorable
Z	20,000	20,000	57.14	19,428	572	.425	243 favorable
Total	34,000	35,000	100.00	34,000	0		$1,071 favorable
Rounding difference							1
Net sales mix variance							$1,072 favorable

* Total number of units actually sold × budgeted sales % for that product (e.g., 34,000 × 22.86% = 7,772).

** Budgeted sales price per unit – budgeted cost of goods sold per unit (e.g., $5 sales price – $4 cost of goods sold = $1).

With such an analysis, the influence of individual products on the total sales mix variance is specifically measured. The interactive effect of shifts in the mix is also revealed. This detailed information enables management to assess the effects of past as well as future sales mix variations.

The final sales volume variance is the difference in the number of units budgeted and sold, multiplied by the budgeted average gross profit per unit as follows:

Actual sales in units	34,000
Budgeted sales in units	35,000
Unit sales difference	1,000 unfavorable
Average budgeted gross profit per unit	× $.5714
	$ 571.40
Rounding difference	.60
Final sales volume variance	$ 572.00 unfavorable

Combining two or more products or product types having different cost or sales prices into a single product category should be avoided. Such aggregation will result in the price variances including a portion of what is actually the mix variance as the mix within such a combination changes.[5]

[5] Robert E. Malcolm, "The Effect of Product Aggregation in Determining Sales Variances," *The Accounting Review*, Vol. 53, No. 1, pp. 162–169.

The variances identified in the preceding computations are summarized as follow:

	Gains	Losses
Gain due to increased sales price	$22,000	
Loss due to increased cost		$12,500
Gain due to shift in sales mix	1,072	
Loss due to decrease in units sold		572
Total	$23,072	$13,072
	13,072	
Net increase in gross profit	$10,000	

The gross profit or contribution margin analysis based on budgets and standard costs depicts the weak spots in the period's performance. Management is now able to outline remedies that should correct the situation. Because the planned gross profit or contribution margin is the responsibility of the marketing as well as the manufacturing functions, this analysis brings together these two major functional areas of the firm and points to the need for further study by both of them. The marketing function must explain the changes in sales prices and marketing expenses, the shift in the sales mix, and the decrease in units sold, while the production function must account for the changes in manufacturing cost.

Analysis by Salespersons

The selling function includes expenses such as salaries, travel, and other expenses connected with the work of sales representatives. In many instances, salespersons' expenses form a substantial part of the total expense incurred in selling. The control and analysis of these expenses should, therefore, receive management's closest attention. To achieve this control, performance standards and standard costs should be established. These standards are used not only for the control of expenses but also for determining the profitability of sales made by salespersons.

Control of Expenses. Selling expenses can be allocated on the basis of the number of sales calls made. A call or visit by a salesperson usually is made for two reasons: to sell and to promote the merchandise or products. The problem is to determine the cost of doing each of these types of work and to compare the actual expense with the standard allowed for a call.

A salesperson's call often involves more than one kind of work—for example, not only calling on the customer, but also helping the merchant with a display in the store. This practice is common in cosmetic, pharmaceutical, and fast-food businesses. Because the salesperson's time is consumed by such activities, a standard time allowed per call is often difficult to establish. To obtain the necessary statistics for establishing such standards and to make comparisons, the sales representative is sometimes asked to prepare a report providing information regarding the types of calls made as well as the quantity, type, and dollar values of products sold. This information is the basis for much of the analysis discussed previously.

Profitability Analysis. It is possible to analyze sales in relation to profitability. Sales volume alone does not tell the complete story. High volume does not always ensure high profit, and the sales mix plays an important part in the final profit. Although a sales representative may choose to follow the line of least resistance, management must strive to sell the merchandise of all product groups, particularly those with the highest profit margins. Because sales territories are often planned for sales according to product groups, it is necessary that anticipated sales be followed up by analyzing the salespersons' efforts. The table presented in Exhibit 25-6 indicates how such an analysis can be made.

EXHIBIT 25-6

Sales, Costs, and Profits by Individual Salespersons
For April 19A

(1) Sales-person	(2) Ship-ments	(3) % of Quota	(4) Salary and Commis-sion	(5) Travel Expense	(6) Cost of Handling	(7) Total Cost (4) + (5) + (6)	(8) Gross Profit	(9) Profit (8) - (7)	(10) Profit, % of Sales (9) ÷ (2)	(11) Ship-ments, % of Total*	(12) Potential, % of Total*
A	$26,000	80%	$2,000	$3,000	$2,340	$ 7,340	$ 7,540	$ 200	.8%	6.7%	9.0%
B	26,000	122	1,900	1,800	2,340	6,040	7,800	1,760	6.8	6.7	5.5
C	39,000	100	2,800	2,100	3,500	8,400	11,700	3,300	8.5	10.1	10.5
D	22,000	108	1,800	2,000	1,980	5,780	7,050	1,270	5.8	5.8	5.5
E	21,000	110	1,700	1,700	1,890	5,290	6,720	1,430	6.8	5.4	5.0
F	54,000	125	3,500	3,100	5,700	12,300	14,600	2,300	4.3	14.0	10.0
G	21,000	98	1,600	1,200	1,700	4,500	6,720	2,220	10.6	5.5	5.5
H	46,000	101	3,400	1,000	4,100	8,500	13,800	5,300	11.5	12.0	12.0

* For 8 salespersons out of a total of 15 salespersons.

Product Pricing

Product pricing is a complex subject and is neither a one-person nor a one-activity job. Theorists and practitioners differ on the appropriateness of various pricing theories. In practice, the solution to a pricing problem becomes a research job that requires the cooperation and coordination of the economist, statistician, market specialist, industrial engineer, and accountant. Because the determination of a sales price requires consideration of many factors, some of which defy measurement or control, prudent and practical judgment is necessary. Accountants can provide executive management and marketing managers data they can use as guides when they travel the relatively uncharted road toward successful pricing.

Usually costs are considered to be the starting point in a pricing situation, even when a rigid relationship does not exist. Prices and pricing policy often depend on whether a long- or short-range view is taken and on market conditions. A long-range pricing policy considers changes in products, manufacturing technology, plant capacity, competition, and marketing and distribution methods. A normal or average product cost is usually the basis used for long-range pricing. Prices are set that will return all costs (developmental, production, and distribution) and provide an adequate return on the capital invested. Because all costs must be recovered, full absorption costing is used to cost products. If the company has a complex manufacturing environment and a diverse product line, activity-based costing should be used to improve costing accuracy.

A short-range pricing policy attempts to compensate for or take advantage of temporary fluctuations in sales demand. In the short run, the sales price should provide for the recovery of all differential costs and at least part of the company's capacity costs. In such cases, the differential cost of a product can serve as a guide for the determination of prices. Variable costs are the principal source of cost differentials that must be computed in such pricing problems. For both short- and long-range pricing, the data used should be current, which may require adjusting historical costs to reflect inflation.

Price setting is a field of business in which management truly becomes an art. A sales price, generally thought of as the rate of exchange between two commodities, is determined in many industries in a manner that gives individual companies some degree of control over the price. Even companies that experience a great deal of competition have some measure of control, because products, quality, and/or the services rendered may differ. Prices can be influenced not only by competition but also by what customers are willing to pay and by governmental regulations and controls.

Even if a firm exercises some control over sales prices, the costs incurred in order to do business are usually more within its control. When a company has little or no control over a sales price, it still faces the question of whether it can operate profitably at the price that can be charged. Costs must be known so the analyst can determine the minimum price required to justify entering or continuing in a given market, or costs must be reduced to make the product profitable.

Life Cycle Costing

Life cycle costing was developed by the Department of Defense in the early 1960s for the purpose of increasing the effectiveness of government procurements by encouraging vendors to adopt long-term planning horizons. **Life cycle costing** is a product costing approach that assigns a share of all costs that are incurred in connection with a product. The method is not used for financial or income tax reporting, but is instead used as a basis for cost planning and product pricing. Life cycle costs include *all* the costs the manufacturer will incur over the life of the product, including product design and development costs, manufacturing cost, selling and distribution expenses, and service expenses after the sale.

During the planning stage, a consideration of life cycle costs rather than manufacturing costs alone improves the effectiveness of cost planning and product pricing. It has been estimated that 80 to 85 percent of a product's total life cycle costs are committed by decisions made in the early stages of the product's life.[6] The greatest opportunities for cost reduction occur before manufacturing begins.[7] Manufacturers should carefully analyze demand for the product and then design the product to meet the needs of prospective customers before manufacturing begins. During the product design stage, total life cycle costs can be reduced in the following ways:

1. Quality can be designed into the product, thereby increasing the likelihood of customer acceptance and satisfaction and reducing the expenses associated with servicing the product after sale.
2. The product can be designed so that it can be efficiently and economically manufactured, thereby reducing the cost of retraining and retooling, altering existing machinery or acquiring new machinery, spoilage and scrap, and design changes after production has begun.
3. The product can be designed to use fewer parts and to use standardized parts where possible, thereby reducing the cost of carrying and handling materials and acquiring or making specialized parts.

---

[6] Michael D. Shields and S. Mark Young, "Managing Product Life Cycle Costs: An Organizational Model," *Journal of Cost Management*, Vol. 5, No. 3, p. 39.

[7] *Ibid.*, p.49.

Surveys indicate that the cost reduction strategies of major Japanese manufacturers focus on activities that occur before manufacturing begins.[8] Attempts to reduce costs after manufacturing has begun are considerably less effective than designing quality and manufacturability into the product initially.

Pricing based on life cycle costing has a long-run perspective. Because of expected changes in market demand, planned prices can vary during different stages of the product's life cycle: startup, growth, maturity, and decline. However, prices are set at each stage with a view toward recovering total life cycle costs and achieving an acceptable long-run profit.

Price-Setting Approaches

Setting prices is not an exact science. Pricing approaches commonly found in practice include (1) pricing to maximize profits, (2) pricing to achieve a desired return on capital employed, (3) pricing based on differential costs, (5) pricing based on standard costs, and (6) target pricing.

Pricing to Maximize Profits. The primary objective of most businesses is to obtain the largest amount of profit possible. Economic theorists describe this as **profit maximization.** The profit return on each unit sold is not as important as the total profit realized from all units sold. The price that yields the largest total profit is the price to be charged to a consumer.

Pricing to maximize profits is an approach that compares expected total revenue with expected total cost at different volumes of sales. According to economic theory, sales prices for most products should decline as output volume increases because, as a product becomes more readily available, consumers will not be willing to pay as much for it as when it is scarce. In addition, average unit cost should decline as output increases because fixed cost will be spread over more units. Profit is maximized at the level of sales at which total revenue exceeds total costs by the largest amount.

The schedule in Exhibit 25-7 shows the variable cost at $7 per unit, with fixed cost at $300,000 for all ranges of output. The most profitable sales price is $14 per unit, with a contribution margin of $560,000 and a profit of $260,000, after the fixed cost is deducted. In other situations, the unit variable cost and the total fixed cost can vary according to the total number of units to be sold, thus influencing the most profitable sales price.

EXHIBIT 25-7

Profitability at Different Unit Sales Prices

Sales Price per Unit	Number of Units to Be Sold	Total Sales Volume	Variable Cost ($7 per Unit)	Fixed Cost	Profit (Loss)
$20	20,000	$ 400,000	$140,000	$300,000	$ (40,000)
18	40,000	720,000	280,000	300,000	140,000
16	60,000	960,000	420,000	300,000	240,000
14	80,000	1,120,000	560,000	300,000	260,000
12	100,000	1,200,000	700,000	300,000	200,000
10	120,000	1,200,000	840,000	300,000	60,000
8	140,000	1,120,000	980,000	300,000	$(160,000)

[8] *Ibid.*, p. 42.

Profit maximization is not to be looked on as the immediate return expected, but rather as a goal to be realized over several months or years. During these months and years, however, sales policies, competition, customer practices, cost changes, and other economic influences can radically alter all previous assumptions. Profit maximization is not necessarily the single objective or even the dominant objective of all firms. One study found that most firms pursue multiple objectives in setting their prices. These include major objectives (such as profits, return on investment, market share, and total sales) and lesser objectives (such as price-earnings ratio, liquidity, employee job security, and industrial relations).[9]

Pricing to Achieve a Desired Return on Capital Employed. Some companies attempt to develop prices that will yield a predetermined or desired **return on capital employed**. For example, assume that a single-product company's total cost is $210,000, total capital employed is $200,000, sales volume is 50,000 units, and desired rate of return on capital employed is 20 percent. The formula used and the determination of the product's sales price are as follows:

$$\text{Price} = \frac{\text{Total cost} + (\text{Desired rate of return} \times \text{Total capital employed})}{\text{Sales volume in units}}$$

$$\text{Price} = \frac{\$210{,}000 + (20\% \times \$200{,}000)}{50{,}000 \text{ units}} = \frac{\$250{,}000}{50{,}000} = \$5$$

Proof:	Sales (50,000 units × $5)	$250,000
	Less total cost	210,000
	Profit (20% × $200,000)	$ 40,000

Pricing using capital employed as part of the pricing formula can be complex, however. The illustrations assume no change in capital employed. Actually, as prices and costs change, capital employed can be expected to change. With an increase in capital employed, more cash will be required to serve the business. With higher prices, accounts receivable will be higher, and inventory costs will increase in proportion to increases in factory costs. Decreases have the reverse effect.

If it is assumed that a firm is in business to maximize its value to the shareholders, then its pricing policy should be based largely on a target rate of return on capital employed. To be effective in its control and analysis, management's pricing decisions should be made after this rate, the standard cost, and the estimated plant capacity have been considered.

Pricing Based on Differential Costs. In direct costing, the contribution margin is the excess of a product's sales price over its variable costs. Classifying costs as fixed and variable makes it possible to compute and compare the contribution margin of each product. Management normally uses the contribution margin approach to evaluate the contribution of a firm's divisions, plants, products, product lines, customers, and territories toward the recovery of common fixed cost and the creation of a profit.

The differential cost of an order is all variable cost plus additional out-of-pocket fixed costs, if any, required to produce a product (or a batch of the product). In **differential cost pricing** the differential cost is accepted as a basis for pricing because any price over and above total differential cost will

[9] Lawrence A. Gordon, Robert Cooper, Haim Falk, and Danny Miller, *The Pricing Decision* (New York: Institute of Management Accountants (formerly National Association of Accountants), 1981; and Hamilton, Ont.: The Society of Management Accountants of Canada, 1980), pp. 9, 15–17.

yield a profit and be acceptable. This procedure is, of course, a short-run approach to pricing, and it is usually used only for pricing special orders. In order to survive in the long run, a company must recover all of its costs, non-traceable fixed costs as well as differential costs, and earn a reasonable return on its owners' equity.

Pricing Based on Standard Costs. In **standard cost pricing** cost estimates used for pricing purposes are prepared on the basis of the standard costs for materials, labor, and factory overhead. The tasks of preparing the estimate and using the data to set the price are simplified. The use of standard costs for pricing purposes makes cost figures more quickly available and reduces clerical detail. Because a standard cost represents the cost that should be attained in an efficiently operated plant at normal capacity, it is essential, once the sales price has been established, that the cost department furnish up-to-the-minute information to all parties to make certain that the cost stays within the rate set by the estimate. Any significant difference between actual and standard costs should come to light for quick action through the accounting system.

The Institute of Management Accountants (formerly the National Association of Accountants) divides companies into four groups with respect to the type of standard cost figures they supply to pricing executives. These groups are composed of the following types of companies:[10]

1. Those that supply executives with standard costs without the application of any adjustments to the standards.
2. Those in which the standard costs are adjusted by the ratio of actual costs to standard costs, as shown by the variance accounts.
3. Those that use current market prices for materials, and in a few cases for labor, with standard costs for other elements of product cost.
4. Those that adjust standard costs to reflect the actual costs anticipated during the period for which the prices are to be in effect, including inflation's impact on costs.

When standard costs are used for bid prices, they might be based on estimates previously submitted. However, although some materials, parts, or labor operations might be identical with those used for another product, executives need the most up-to-date information on all cost components in order to set a profitable price. Companies that must present bids adjust the costs developed from the detailed standards to approximate actual costs expected.

Target Pricing. **Target pricing** is a pricing strategy designed to create a competitive advantage. The product is priced as if its market share were larger than it actually is and as if its costs were less than they actually are. Pricing the product at a low level when it is first introduced increases market acceptance and accelerates initial sales. However, the thrust of this pricing strategy is to price the product to yield an acceptable profit at a targeted level of cost. Costs are targets for improvement. The strategy is successful if costs can be reduced sufficiently below the sales price to yield a satisfactory profit. This requires continuous improvement in manufacturing efficiency or reductions in the cost of inputs. Although a risky approach to product pricing, target pricing has been regularly employed with success by Japanese manufacturers.[11]

---

[10] *Research Series, No. 14,* "Standard Manufacturing Costs for Pricing and Budgeting," *NAA Bulletin*, Vol. 30, No. 3, pp. 165–166.

[11] Shields and Young, "Managing Product Life Cycle Costs," p. 42.

Effect of the Robinson-Patman Act on Pricing

The Robinson-Patman Act was enacted to ensure competitive equality of individual enterprises by precluding price discrimination that decreases competition. The seller has three acceptable defenses for price cuts:

1. The cuts resulted from changing conditions in the marketplace (discontinued products, distress sales, perishable goods, and so on).
2. Prices were temporarily lowered in a good-faith attempt to meet an equally low and lawful price of a competitor.
3. The cuts reflect lower costs that resulted from different methods or quantities of sale or delivery.

The act does not prohibit price differentials; however, the differentials granted must not exceed differences in the cost of serving different customers. The cost of serving includes the cost of manufacturing, selling, and delivering, which can differ according to methods of selling and quantities sold. The burden of proof is on both the buyer and the seller and requires a definite justification for the discounts granted and received.

A competitor who believes that discrimination exists must file a complaint substantiated by evidence acquired from published price lists or from other persuasive evidence. The complaint is valid if *all* of the following violations have been committed:

1. Price discrimination
2. Discrimination between competitors
3. Discrimination on products of like grades and quality
4. Discrimination in interstate commerce
5. Injurious effect on competition

The possibilities for legal differentials fall chiefly in the area of marketing expenses. Interesting problems have arisen because it is difficult to trace many marketing expenses to particular products. Therefore, it is important for concerns performing distribution functions to accumulate cost statistics regarding their marketing expenses, because the act makes allowances for differences in such costs. To avoid potential problems, the firm should first establish records showing that price differentials are extended only to the extent justified by maximum allowable cost savings, and second, keep the cost data current by conducting spot checks periodically to insure that the price differentials are in conformance with current cost conditions.

In judging the justification of price differentials, the government has consistently rejected the marginal cost approach to pricing. Only fully distributed or average total costs are acceptable for a cost justification defense under the Robinson-Patman Act. The government has held that only identifiable savings, whether manufacturing or marketing, resulting from specific methods or quantities connected with given orders can be properly passed in their entirety to specific customers. For example, if the price difference is related to special manufacturing runs, then cost factors that can be considered include the differences between customer runs, which can cause a difference in unit costs. Typical of such costs are setup costs, skill and number of direct laborers, tool-wear costs, machine downtime, scrap rates, order scheduling, and inspection.

The accountant must actively study and continuously track product prices and costs to help prevent violations of the law. Before any price differentials or discounts are granted, the accountant should prepare a cost justification study, clearly documenting actual differences in marketing expenses or manufacturing costs that justify the price differential. No firm should be placed in a situation of having to make a cost study after being cited for a violation of the law. Such belated cost justification studies are seldom successful as a defense.

Summary

The chapter began by defining marketing as the matching of a company's products with markets for the satisfaction of customers at a reasonable profit for the firm. To satisfy customers and make a profit, management must understand what drives marketing expenses and what marketing activities generate profits. Although marketing expenses are not as controllable as manufacturing costs, marketing activities can be departmentalized by function and responsibility assigned to managers in a manner similar to that employed in the factory. Once functional responsibilities have been assigned, cost control techniques like those used in manufacturing can be applied to control many marketing expenses. Activity-based management can be employed to identify opportunities for improving marketing activities and reducing expense. Marketing profitability analysis should be based on a thorough understanding of marketing expense drivers and manufacturing costs. The chapter concluded with a discussion of product pricing. Although several pricing methods were discussed, most firms base initial prices on some aspect of product cost. From a long-term perspective, the cost used in pricing decisions should include a share of all nonmanufacturing as well as manufacturing costs to be incurred over the life of the product.

Key Terms

marketing *(748)*
marketing function *(751)*
capacity costs *(751)*
volume costs *(751)*
direct expenses *(751)*
indirect expenses *(752)*
activity-based management (ABM) *(752)*
sales price variance *(761)*
sales volume variance *(761)*
cost volume variance *(761)*
final sales volume variance *(761)*
sales mix variance *(761)*
cost price variance *(761)*
life cycle costing *(766)*
profit maximization *(767)*
return on capital employed *(768)*
differential cost pricing *(768)*
standard cost pricing *(769)*
target pricing *(769)*

Discussion Questions

Q25-1 What general principles should be observed when a system of control for marketing expenses is being planned?

Q25-2 How should marketing expenses be classified so that control and analysis are facilitated?

Q25-3 What is activity-based management?

Q24-4 What are the objectives of profit analysis by sales territories?

Q25-5 What is activity-based costing, and how does it provide useful information for product profitability analyses?

Q25-6 How does the contribution margin approach improve product-line profitability analysis?

Q24-7 What causes changes in the gross profit or contribution margin?

Q25-8 Gross profit or contribution margin analysis compares actual sales and costs with some other value. What are the commonly used bases for comparison?

Q25-9 Discuss the following statement: Price setting is truly an art.

Q25-10 What is life cycle costing, and how does it relate to reducing costs and setting prices?

Q25-11 What are some common product pricing methods?

Q25-12 Explain the pricing approach that attempts to maximize profits.

Q25-13 How are standard costs helpful in setting prices?

Q25-14 What is target pricing?

Q25-15 The Robinson-Patman Act was enacted by Congress to prevent price discrimination among competitors. What three defenses for price cuts are available to the seller under the Act?

Exercises

E25-1 Controlling Functional Activity by Using a Flexible Budget. The flexible budget for the Warehousing Department of Jartec Supply Company is as follows:

	Functional Unit—Number of Transactions			
	1,000	2,000	3,000	4,000
Variable expense				
Employee wages	$ 300	$ 600	$ 900	$1,200
Supplies	100	200	300	400
Total	$ 400	$ 800	$1,200	$1,600
Fixed expense				
Supervision	$1,200	$1,200	$1,200	$1,200
Employee wages	1,000	1,000	1,000	1,000
Employee benefits	500	500	500	500
Depreciation	750	750	750	750
Insurance and taxes	250	250	250	250
Utilities	200	200	200	200
Total	$3,900	$3,900	$3,900	$3,900
Total expense	$4,300	$4,700	$5,100	$5,500

During April, the Warehousing Department handled 2,700 transactions. Actual expenses follow:

Supervision	$1,200
Employee wages	1,850
Employee benefits	500
Supplies	290
Depreciation	750
Insurance and taxes	260
Utilities	195

Required: Prepare a variance report for the Warehousing Department showing the spending variance for each item of expense and a single idle capacity variance, assuming that normal capacity is 3,000 transactions.

E25-2 Marketing Expense Analysis by Territories. Cimarron Hardware Company sells hardware items in Colorado, New Mexico, and Wyoming. Marketing expenses for the past quarter were as follows:

Sales salaries	$58,100
Sales commissions	8,460
Travel expense	2,240
Advertising expense	14,920
Warehousing expense	2,940
Collection expense	900

The company wants to know the cost of distributing its products in each of the three states. An analysis of marketing activities and related expenses revealed the following:

(a) Ten salespersons are employed (five in Colorado, three in New Mexico, and two in Wyoming). All are paid at the same base salary.
(b) Sales were as follows:

Salesperson	Colorado	New Mexico	Wyoming
1	$54,000	$11,000	$48,000
2	32,000	23,000	51,000
3	6,000	50,000	
4	49,000		
5	49,000		

(c) The following commission schedule has been established:

	Commission (% of Sales)
Sales less than $10,000	0%
Sales from $10,000 to $50,000	3
Sales over $50,000..............................	6

(d) Travel expense is allocated on the basis of the number of calls made, which is in the ratio of 4:3:1 for Colorado, New Mexico, and Wyoming, respectively.
(e) Advertising expense is allocated on the basis of sales.
(f) Warehousing expense is allocated on the basis of shipments to customers, which is 5:3:2 for Colorado, New Mexico, and Wyoming, respectively.
(g) Collection expense is allocated on the basis of remittances received from customers. 7,500, 3,000, and 4,500 remittances were received from Colorado, Wyoming, and New Mexico, respectively.

Required: Prepare a marketing expense analysis by territories, detailing each expense category.

E25-3 Income Statement by Customer Classes. Kiperton Manufacturing Company assembles a washing machine that is sold to three classes of customers. The data with respect to these customers follow:

Customer Class	Sales	Cost of Goods Sold	Number of Sales Calls	Number of Orders	Number of Invoice Lines
Department stores....................	$180,000	$158,000	240	120	2,100
Retail appliance stores.............	240,000	140,000	860	580	4,600
Wholesalers..............................	300,000	222,000	400	300	3,300
Total	$720,000	$520,000	1,500	1,000	10,000

Actual marketing costs for the year are:

Function	Costs	Measure of Activity
Selling	$75,000	Salespersons' calls
Packing and shipping	12,000	Customers' orders
Advertising	21,600	Dollar sales
Credit and collection.............	15,000	Invoice lines
General accounting..............	18,000	Customers' orders

Required: Prepare an income statement by customer classes, with functional distribution of marketing expenses. (When allocating the advertising expense, round to the nearest $100.)

E25-4 Contribution Margin Analysis. A cost analyst has prepared a monthly contribution margin analysis for Clifton Corporation, comparing actual to budgeted costs for the company's two products, Dee and Zee. August budget and actual data follow:

	Sales			Variable Costs		Contribution Margin	
	Units	Unit Price	Amount	Unit Cost	Amount	Per Unit	Amount
Budget:							
Dee	20,000	$9.00	$180,000	$5.00	$100,000	$4.00	$ 80,000
Zee	15,000	7.50	112,500	4.00	60,000	3.50	52,500
Total	35,000		$292,500		$160,000		$132,500
Actual:							
Dee	19,000	9.50	$180,500	5.40	$102,600	4.10	$ 77,900
Zee	17,000	7.30	124,100	4.20	71,400	3.10	52,700
Total	36,000		$304,600		$174,000		$130,600

Required: Compute the price and volume variances for sales and cost, and the sales mix and final sales volume variances.

E25-5 Gross Profit Analysis. Spiffy Sporting Goods Shop presents the following data for two types of racquetball gloves, leather and fabric, for 19A and 19B:

	19A			19B		
	Units	Per Unit	Amount	Units	Per Unit	Amount
Sales:						
Leather racquetball gloves	8,000	$8.00	$64,000	12,000	$10.00	$120,000
Fabric racquetball gloves	8,000	4.00	32,000	20,000	6.00	120,000
			$96,000			$240,000
Cost of goods sold:						
Leather racquetball gloves	8,000	$6.00	$48,000	12,000	$ 9.00	$108,000
Fabric racquetball gloves	8,000	3.00	24,000	20,000	5.00	100,000
			$72,000			$208,000
Gross profit	16,000	$1.50	$24,000	32,000	$ 1.00	$ 32,000

Required: Compute the price and volume variances for sales and cost, and the sales mix and final sales volume variances.

E25-6 Salespersons' Performance Reports. A corporate budget director designed a control scheme in order to compare and evaluate the efforts of the company's three salespersons and the results attained. Specifically, each salesperson is to make five calls per day; the budget provides for $40 per day per salesperson for travel and entertainment expenses; and each salesperson was assigned a sales quota of $400 a day. The Budget Department collects the data on actual performance from the daily sales reports and the weekly expense vouchers and then prepares a monthly report. This report includes variances from standard and performance indexes. For the performance index, standard performance equals 100.

The records for November, with 20 working days, show:

Salesperson	Sales Calls	Travel Expenses	Sales
Palmer, K.	70	$1,000	$14,000
Thompson, J.	100	800	8,400
Miller, O.	120	720	6,000

Required: Prepare a monthly report comparing the standard and actual performances of the salespersons, including the performance indexes for (1) sales calls, (2) travel expenses, (3) sales, and (4) sales revenue per call.

E25-7 Product-Line Income Statement—Contribution Margin Approach. Pralina Products Company has three major product lines—cereals, breakfast bars, and dog food. The following income statement for the year ended April 30, 19A, was prepared by product line, using full cost allocation.

Pralina Products Company
Income Statement
For the Year Ended April 30, 19A
(in thousands)

	Cereals	Breakfast Bars	Dog Food	Total
Sales (in pounds)	2,000	500	500	3,000
Revenue from sales	$1,000	$400	$200	$1,600
Cost of goods sold:				
Materials	$ 330	$160	$100	$ 590
Direct labor	90	40	20	150
Factory overhead	108	48	24	180
Total cost of goods sold	$ 528	$248	$144	$ 920
Gross profit	$ 472	$152	$ 56	$ 680
Commercial expenses:				
Marketing expenses:				
Advertising	$ 50	$ 30	$ 20	$ 100
Commissions	50	40	20	110
Sales salaries and related benefits	30	20	10	60
Total marketing expense	$ 130	$ 90	$ 50	$ 270
General and administrative expenses:				
Licenses	$ 50	$ 20	$ 15	$ 85
Salaries and related benefits	60	25	15	100
Total general and administrative expenses	$ 110	$ 45	$ 30	$ 185
Total commercial expense	$ 240	$135	$ 80	$ 455
Operating income	$ 232	$ 17	$ (24)	$ 225

Explanatory data are as follow:

(a) Cost of goods sold. The company's inventories of materials and finished products do not vary significantly from year to year. Factory overhead was applied to products at 120% of direct labor dollars. The factory overhead costs for the year were as follow:

Variable indirect labor and supplies	$ 15,000
Variable employee benefits on factory labor	30,000
Supervisory salaries and related benefits	35,000
Plant occupancy cost	100,000
	$180,000

There was no over- or underapplied factory overhead at year-end.

(b) Advertising. The company has been unable to determine any direct causal relationship between the level of sales volume and the level of advertising expenditures. However, because management believes advertising is necessary, an annual advertising program has been implemented for each product line, independent of the others.

(c) Commissions. Sales commissions are paid to the sales force at the rate of 5% on the cereals and 10% on the breakfast bars and dog food.

(d) Licenses. Various licenses are required for each product line, renewed annually for each product line at a fixed amount.

(e) Salaries and related benefits. Sales and general and administrative personnel devote time and effort to all product lines. Their salaries and wages are allocated on the basis of management's estimates of time spent on each product line.

(f) Fixed factory overhead, salaries and related benefits for sales and general and administrative personnel are not traceable to individual product lines on any objective basis.

Required: Prepare a product-line income statement, using the contribution margin approach. (ICMA adapted)

E25-8 Determining Advertising Costs. The Kirsty Company produces and sells three products—Economy, Standard, and Deluxe. The following actual results for the current year are based on absorption costing:

	Economy	Standard	Deluxe	Total
Sales in units	2,500	2,000	3,500	8,000
Sales revenue	$50,000	$80,000	$70,000	$200,000
Cost of goods sold	30,000	40,000	50,000	120,000
Gross profit	$20,000	$40,000	$20,000	$ 80,000
Operating expenses:				
Sales commissions	$ 5,000	$ 8,000	$ 7,000	$ 20,000
Allocated head office expenses	7,500	12,000	10,500	30,000
Total	$12,500	$20,000	$17,500	$ 50,000
Income from products	$ 7,500	$20,000	$ 2,500	$ 30,000
Unallocated head office expenses				20,000
Income before taxes				$ 10,000
Income tax expenses (45%)				4,500
Net income				$ 5,500

All head office expenses are fixed, and 60% of the manufacturing costs are fixed. The company is considering the implementation of an advertising campaign that is expected to increase the sales of Deluxe by 40% and the sales of Standard by 80%; however, the increased sales volume of these two products will cause a 20% decrease in the sales volume of Economy.

Required: Determine the maximum amount that the company can afford to spend on advertising if it wants to achieve a net income of $22,000. (SMAC adapted)

E25-9 Product Pricing. Mercado Company is considering changing the sales price of its product, Salien, which is presently $15. Increases and decreases of both 10% and 25%, as well as increases in advertising and promotion expenditures, are being considered, with the following estimated results for 19A and 19B:

	Estimated Unit Sales		Estimated Advertising and Promotion Expenditures	
Price	19A	19B	19A	19B
-25%	190,000	200,000	$200,000	$210,000
-10%	180,000	190,000	250,000	250,000
No change	160,000	170,000	300,000	300,000
+10%	140,000	150,000	400,000	450,000
+25%	130,000	140,000	450,000	550,000

The company has the necessary flexibility in its production capacity to meet these volume levels. The variable manufacturing cost per unit of Salien is estimated to be $7.25 in 19A and $7.80 in 19B.

Required: Determine the recommended sales price. (ICMA adapted)

E25-10 Contribution Margin Approach to Pricing The Gelotech Company is a large manufacturer of refrigeration units. The firm's product line includes refrigerators for homes, industry, and ships. The firm is composed of three divisions. The Motor Division is responsible for manufacturing the motors for all the various refrigeration units. In the Shell Division, the refrigerator shells are produced and the motors transferred from the Motor Division are installed. The Marketing Division is responsible for the sale and distribution of the final product.

Although a market exists outside the firm for both the motors and shells, the transfer price between divisions is set by executive management. This is done to avoid unnecessary friction, which management feels might impair efficiency and prove wasteful.

Recently the company was asked to submit a bid for 100 refrigeration units for a local shipbuilding firm. The following unit cost estimate has been prepared:

	Motor	Shell	Marketing
Manufacturing materials	$ 195	$ 180	—
Receiving and handling (60% fixed)	10	25	$ 20
Motor	—	600	—
Refrigeration units	—	—	1,240
Shipping materials	—	—	30
Direct labor	190	220	35
Factory overhead:			
Fixed	55	45	15
Variable	100	80	10
General administrative cost	28	57	67
Transfer price	600	1,240	—

Prior to submitting its bid, Gelotech has learned that its principal competitor has submitted a bid of $1,200 per unit.

Required: Prepare an analysis to determine whether or not Gelotech can match the competitor's bid.

Problems

P25-1 Marketing Cost Analysis by Territories. Starnes Company sells toiletries to retail stores throughout the United States. For planning and control purposes, the company is organized into 12 geographic regions, with two to six territories within each region. One salesperson is assigned to each territory and has exclusive rights to all sales made in that territory. Merchandise is shipped from the manufacturing plant to the 12 regional warehouses, from which the sales in each territory are shipped. National headquarters allocates a specific amount at the beginning of the year for regional advertising.

The net sales for Starnes Company for the 6 months ended September 30 total $10 million. Costs incurred by national headquarters are:

National administration	$250,000
National advertising	125,000
National warehousing	175,000
	$550,000

The results of operations for the South Atlantic Region for the 6 months ended September 30 are:

Starnes Company
Statement of Operations for South Atlantic Region
For the Six Months Ended September 30, 19A

Sales		$900,000
Costs and expenses:		
Advertising fees	$ 54,700	
Uncollectible accounts expense	3,600	
Cost of goods sold	460,000	
Freight out	22,600	
Insurance	10,000	
Salaries and employee benefits	81,600	
Sales commissions	36,000	
Supplies	12,000	
Travel and entertainment	14,100	
Wages and employee benefits	36,000	
Warehouse depreciation	8,000	
Warehouse operating cost	15,000	753,600
Territory contribution		$146,400

The South Atlantic Region consists of two territories—Green and Purple. The salaries and employee benefits consist of the following items:

Regional vice-president	$24,000
Regional marketing manager	15,000
Regional warehouse manager	13,400
Salespersons (one for each territory, with both receiving the same salary base)	15,600
Employee benefits (20%)	13,600
	$81,600

The salespersons receive a base salary plus a 4% commission on all items sold in their territory. Uncollectible accounts expense has averaged .4% of sales in the past. Travel and entertainment costs are incurred by the salespersons in calling on their customers and are based on a fixed authorized amount. Freight out is a function of the quantity of goods shipped and the distance shipped. Thirty percent of the insurance is expended for protection of the inventory while it is in the regional warehouse, and the remainder is incurred for the protection of the warehouse. Supplies are used in the warehouse for packing the merchandise to be shipped. Wages (a variable cost) relate to the hourly employees who fill orders in the warehouse. The warehouse operating cost account contains such costs as heat, light, and maintenance.

The following cost analyses and statistics by territory for the current period are representative of past experience and of expected future operations:

	Green	Purple	Total
Sales	$300,000	$600,000	$900,000
Cost of goods sold*	184,000	276,000	460,000
Advertising fees	21,800	32,900	54,700
Travel and entertainment	6,300	7,800	14,100
Freight out	9,000	13,600	22,600
Units sold	150,000	350,000	500,000
Pounds shipped**	210,000	390,000	600,000
Sales travel (miles)	21,600	38,400	60,000

* Use to allocate inventory insurance to territories.

** Use to allocate supplies and wages and employee benefits to territories.

The executive management of Starnes Company wants the regional vice-presidents to present their operating data in a more meaningful manner. Therefore, management has requested that the regions separate their operating costs into the fixed and variable components of order-getting, order-filling, and administrative. The data are to be presented in the following format:

	Territory Cost		Regional	Total
	Green	Purple	Cost	Cost
Order-getting				
Order-filling				
Administrative				

Required:

(1) Using management's suggested format, prepare a statement that presents the cost for the region by territory, with the costs separated into variable and fixed categories.

(2) Identify the data that are relevant to a decision for or against splitting the Purple Territory into two separate territories (Red and Blue). Specify other data needed to aid management in its decision.

(ICMA adapted)

P25-2 Income Statements by Products and Amount-of-Order Classes. The feasibility of allocating marketing expenses to products or amount-of-order classes for managerial purposes has been considered by Classen Company. It is apparent that some costs can be assigned equitably to these classifications, while others cannot. The company's cost analyst proposed the following bases for apportionment:

Expense	Type of Analysis: By Products	Type of Analysis: By Amount of Order
Sales salaries	Not allocated	Sales dollars times number of customers in class
Travel and entertainment	Not allocated	Number of customers in class
Sales office	Not allocated	Number of customers in class
Sales commissions	Direct	Direct
Credit management	Sales in dollars	Number of customers in class
Packing and shipping	Weight	Weight
Warehousing	Weight	Weight
Advertising	Not allocated	Not allocated
Bookkeeping and billing	Sales in dollars	Number of orders
General marketing administration	Not allocated	Not allocated

From books, records, and other sources, the following data have been compiled:

Amount of Order	Number of Customers	Number of Orders	Cost of Goods Sold	Total Sales	Product X Sales	Product Y Sales	Product Z Sales
Under $25	950	6,000	$ 58,500	$ 100,000	$ 35,000	$ 40,000	$ 25,000
$26-$100	250	4,000	175,500	300,000	105,000	120,000	75,000
$101-$200	100	4,000	351,000	600,000	210,000	240,000	150,000
Over $200	50	1,000	234,000	400,000	140,000	160,000	100,000
Total	1,350	15,000	$819,000	$1,400,000	$490,000	$560,000	$350,000

Other data follow:

Product	Weight (in pounds)	Cost of Goods Sold	Units Sold
X	1	$245,000	98,000
Y	3	294,000	70,000
Z	2	280,000	175,000

Marketing expenses for the year follow:

Sales salaries	$ 50,000
Travel and entertainment	27,000
Sales office	16,200
Sales commissions (5%)	70,000
Credit management	18,900
Packing and shipping	32,900
Warehousing	19,740
Advertising	150,000
Bookkeeping and billing	42,000
General marketing administration	53,260
Total	$480,000

Required: Carry all computations to four decimal places.

(1) Prepare a product income statement showing the allocation of marketing expenses to each product.

(2) Prepare an income statement showing the allocation of marketing expenses to each order class.

P25-3 Cost Allocations to Individual Stores; Sales Expansion Decision. Amar Supermarkets Corporation operates a chain of three retail stores in a state that permits municipalities to levy an income tax on businesses operating within their respective boundaries. The tax rate is uniform in all of the municipalities that levy the tax, and does not vary according to taxable income. Regulations provide that the tax is to be computed on income earned within the particular taxing municipality, after reasonable and consistent allocation of the corporation's overhead. Amar's overhead consists of expenses pertaining to the warehouse, central office, advertising, and delivery.

For the current year ending on December 31, operating results for each store before taxes and allocation of corporation overhead were as follow:

	Birch	Maple	Spruce	Total
Sales	$500,000	$400,000	$300,000	$1,200,000
Cost of goods sold	280,000	230,000	190,000	700,000
Gross profit	$220,000	$170,000	$110,000	$ 500,000
Local operating expenses:				
Fixed	$ 70,000	$ 60,000	$ 50,000	$ 180,000
Variable	66,000	73,000	31,000	170,000
Total	$136,000	$133,000	$ 81,000	$ 350,000
Income before corporation overhead and taxes	$ 84,000	$ 37,000	$ 29,000	$ 150,000

For the current year, corporate overhead was as follows:

Warehouse and delivery:		
Warehouse depreciation	$10,000	
Warehouse operations	15,000	
Delivery expenses	35,000	$ 60,000
Central office:		
Advertising	$ 8,000	
Salaries	30,000	
Other	2,000	40,000
Total corporation overhead		$100,000

Delivery expenses vary with distances from the warehouse and numbers of deliveries to stores. Delivery statistics for the current year follow:

Store	Miles from Warehouse	Number of Deliveries	Delivery Miles
Birch	100	150	15,000
Maple	200	50	10,000
Spruce	25	200	5,000

Management has engaged a CPA firm to evaluate two corporation overhead allocation plans that are being considered, so that operating results under both plans can be compared. In addition, management has decided to expand one of the stores in a plan to increase sales by $80,000. The contemplated expansion is expected to increase local fixed operating costs by $8,000 and to require 10 additional deliveries from the warehouse. The CPA firm has been requested to furnish management with a recommendation as to which store should be selected for the prospective expansion.

Required:

(1) For each store, compute the income that would be subject to municipal income tax under the following two plans:
   (a) All corporate overhead allocated on the basis of sales.
   (b) Central office salaries and other central office overhead allocated equally to warehouse operations and to each store first; the resulting warehouse operations costs, warehouse depreciation, and advertising allocated to each store on the basis of sales second; and delivery expenses allocated to each store on the basis of delivery miles last.

(2) Compute each store's increase in relevant expenses, including delivery expenses, before allocation of other corporation overhead and taxes as a result of the contemplated expansion. Determine which of the three stores should be selected for expansion to maximize corporation net income. (AICPA adapted)

P25-4 Statement of Product Line Contribution Margin. Stratford Corporation is a diversified company, marketing its products both domestically and internationally. The company's major product lines are pharmaceutical products, sports equipment, and household appliances. At the recent meeting of Stratford's board of directors, there was a lengthy discussion on ways to improve overall corporate profits without new acquisitions, because the company is already heavily leveraged. The members of the board decided that they required additional financial information about individual corporate operations in order to target areas for improvement.

D. Murphy, Stratford's controller, has been asked to provide additional data that would assist the board in its investigation. Stratford is not a public company and, therefore, has not prepared complete income statements by segment. Murphy regularly has prepared an income statement by product line through contribution margin. However, Murphy now believes that income statements prepared through operating income along both product lines and geographical areas would provide the directors with the required insight into corporate operations. The following data are available:

	Product Lines			
	Pharmaceutical	Sports Equipment	Appliances	Total
Production/sales in units	160,000	180,000	160,000	500,000
Average sales price per unit	$8.00	$20.00	$15.00	
Average variable manufacturing cost per unit	4.00	9.50	8.25	
Average variable marketing expense per unit	2.00	2.50	2.25	
Fixed factory overhead excluding depreciation				$ 500,000
Depreciation of plant and equipment				400,000
Administrative and marketing expenses				1,160,000

Murphy had several discussions with the division managers for each product line and compiled the following information from these meetings:

(a) The division managers concluded that Murphy should allocate fixed factory overhead on the basis of the ratio of variable costs expended per product line or per geographic area to total variable costs.

(b) Each of the division managers agreed that a reasonable basis for the allocation of depreciation on plant and equipment would be the ratio of units produced per product line or per geographical area to the total number of units produced.

(c) There was little agreement on the allocation of administrative and marketing expenses, so Murphy decided to allocate only those expenses that were directly traceable to the segment being delineated—manufacturing staff salaries to product lines and marketing staff salaries to geographic areas. Murphy used the following data for this allocation.

Manufacturing Staff		Marketing Staff	
Pharmaceutical	$120,000	U.S	$ 60,000
Sports equipment	140,000	Canada	100,000
Appliances	80,000	Europe	250,000

(d) The division managers were able to provide reliable sales percentages for their product lines by geographic area.

	Percentage of Unit Sales		
	United States	Canada	Europe
Pharmaceutical	40%	10%	50%
Sports equipment	40	40	20
Appliances	20	20	60

Murphy prepared the following product line income statement based on the preceding data.

Stratford Corporation
Statement of Income by Product Lines
For the Fiscal Year Ended April 30, 19A

	Product Lines				
	Pharmaceutical	Sports Equipment	Appliances	Unallocated	Total
Sales in units	160,000	180,000	160,000		
Sales revenue	$1,280,000	$3,600,000	$2,400,000	—	$7,280,000
Variable manufacturing and marketing costs	960,000	2,160,000	1,680,000	—	4,800,000
Contribution margin	$ 320,000	$1,440,000	$ 720,000	—	$2,480,000
Fixed costs:					
Factory overhead	$ 100,000	$ 225,000	$ 175,000	—	$ 500,000
Depreciation	128,000	144,000	128,000	—	400,000
Administrative and marketing expenses	120,000	140,000	80,000	$ 820,000	1,160,000
Total fixed costs	$ 348,000	$ 509,000	$ 383,000	$ 820,000	$2,060,000
Operating income	$ (28,000)	$ 931,000	$ 337,000	$(820,000)	$ 420,000

Required:

(1) Prepare a segmented income statement for Stratford Corporation based on the company's geographic areas of sales. The statement should show the operating income for each segment.

(2) Using the information disclosed by both segmented income statements (by product line and by geographical area), recommend areas on which Stratford Corporation should focus its attention in order to improve corporate profits. (ICMA adapted)

P25-5 Contribution Margin Analysis. Tribal Products Inc. was organized 10 years ago by James Littlebear for the purpose of making and selling souvenirs to tourists in Southwestern Arizona. After much experimentation, the product line has been limited to five products: moccasins, strings of beads, rawhide vests, leather belts, and feathered headdresses. All transactions take place in two small buildings located on tribal land.

In 19B, despite an increase in the total number of units sold, the contribution margin of the firm dropped. Littlebear tentatively blamed the drop in profit on a change in the sales mix.

The accountant has been given the task of analyzing the contribution margin of the past two years, shown as follows, in an attempt to pin down the cause of the loss in profits.

19A

Product	Quantity	Unit Variable Cost	Total Variable Cost	Unit Sales Price	Total Sales	Contribution Margin
Moccasins	1,000	$2.50	$ 2,500	$5.00	$ 5,000	$ 2,500
Beads	6,000	.20	1,200	.50	3,000	1,800
Vests	1,500	1.75	2,625	3.50	5,250	2,625
Belts	4,000	.45	1,800	1.00	4,000	2,200
Headdresses	500	4.00	2,000	7.50	3,750	1,750
Total	13,000		$10,125		$21,000	$10,875

19B

Product	Quantity	Unit Variable Cost	Total Variable Cost	Unit Sales Price	Total Sales	Contribution Margin
Moccasins	1,100	$2.60	$2,860	$5.00	$ 5,500	$ 2,640
Beads	6,800	.20	1,360	.50	3,400	2,040
Vests	1,200	1.80	2,160	3.50	4,200	2,040
Belts	4,200	.50	2,100	1.00	4,200	2,100
Headdresses	350	3.80	1,330	7.50	2,625	1,295
Total	13,650		$9,810		$19,925	$10,115

Required: Prepare an analysis of the decline in contribution margin from 19A to 19B. (Round the 19A average contribution margin per unit to four decimal places.)

P25-6 Gross Profit Analysis H. Pacer is the general manager for Ace Chemical Supply Company. The following is the company's gross profit data for November, in thousands of dollars:

	Actual	Budget
Sales	$14,005	$12,600
Cost of goods sold.......	11,323	9,850
Gross profit.................	$ 2,682	$ 2,750

Before receiving the statement, Pacer knew that sales were above budget for the month and that the effect of recent price increases on most products would be realized this month. Upset on finding that income results were below budget while sales were more than 10% above budget, Pacer asked the Accounting Department for an explanation. The Accounting Department looked at the detailed budget and found the following data:

Product	Sales in Pounds (in thousands)	Sales Price per Pound	Cost of Goods Sold per Pound	Gross Profit (in thousands)
1	2,000	$ .60	$ .60	
2	5,000	.80	.65	$ 750
3	7,000	.20	.12	560
4	4,000	1.50	1.14	1,440
	18,000			$2,750

$2,750 ÷ 18,000 = $.1528 budgeted gross profit per pound.

The following gross profit data pertain to November results:

Product	Sales in Pounds (in thousands)	Sales Price per Pound	Sales in Dollars (in thousands)	Cost of Goods Sold (in thousands)	Gross Profit (in thousands)
1	2,845	$ .735	$ 2,091	$ 1,692	$ 399
2	3,280	1.023	3,355	3,240	115
3	7,340	.195	1,431	991	440
4	4,320	1.650	7,128	5,400	1,728
	17,785		$14,005	$11,323	$2,682

Required: Compute the price and volume variances for sales and cost, and the sales mix and final sales volume variances. (Based on a problem in *Management Accounting Campus Report.*)

P25-7 Product Pricing. Brazos Corporation produces an electronic component. Product demand is highly elastic within a specified range. At present, 100,000 units are sold at $10 each, and the additional demand expected with price reductions is as follows:

Unit Price	Units of Estimated Demand
$9.75	120,000
9.50	150,000
9.25	190,000
9.00	240,000
8.75	300,000

Present capacity is 125,000 units. Further estimates are that the first capacity increase of 75,000 units will require a $500,000 capital expenditure and, including depreciation, will increase annual fixed costs by $100,000 from the present $250,000 level. Each subsequent addition of 75,000 units of capacity will require further capital investment of $450,000 and will increase annual fixed costs by $75,000. Commercial expenses included in the present $250,000 figure will not change at the higher volumes. The board of directors will not approve additional capital expenditures unless a minimum pretax return of 20% is anticipated. Average unit variable costs for total production at different levels follow:

	Less Than 150,000	150,000 to 200,000	More Than 200,000
Direct materials	$4.00	$3.80	$3.60
Direct labor	1.00	1.00	1.10
Variable factory overhead and commercial expenses	1.00	1.00	1.00

Required: Prepare a profitability statement at the various operating volumes, including the required 20% return on additional investment.

P25-8 Contribution Margin Approach to Pricing. J. Schifflein manufactures custom-made pleasure boats ranging in price from $10,000 to $250,000. For the past 30 years, Schifflein has determined each boat's sales price by estimating the costs of materials, labor, and a prorated portion of overhead and by adding 20% to these estimated costs. For example, a recent price quotation was determined as follows:

Direct materials	$ 5,000
Direct labor	8,000
Overhead	2,000
	$15,000
Plus 20%	3,000
Sales price	$18,000

The overhead figure was determined by estimating the total overhead cost for the year and allocating it at 25% of direct labor.

If a customer rejects the price and business is slack, Schifflein is often willing to reduce the markup to as little as 5% over estimated costs. Thus, average markup for the year is estimated at 15%.

Schifflein has just completed a pricing course and believes that the company could use some of the techniques taught in the course. The course emphasized the contribution margin approach to pricing, and Schifflein feels that such an approach would be helpful in determining the sales prices of custom-made pleasure boats.

Total overhead (including marketing and administrative expenses for the year) has been estimated at $150,000, of which $90,000 is fixed and the remainder is variable in direct proportion to direct labor.

Required:

(1) (a) Compute the difference in profit for the year if a customer's offer of $15,000, instead of the $18,000 quoted, is accepted.
(b) Determine the minimum sales price Schifflein could have quoted without reducing or increasing profit.

(2) State the advantages that the contribution margin approach to pricing has over the approach used by Schifflein.

(3) Identify the pitfalls, if any, in contribution margin pricing. (ICMA adapted)

Cases

C25-1 Marketing Profitability Analysis of Product Lines. Travil Corporation has been manufacturing high-quality wood furniture for over 50 years. Travil's five product lines are Mediterranean, Modern, Colonial, Victorian, and the recently introduced Country. Business has been very good for Travil recently.

Part of the reason for Travil's recent success has been the ability of S. Grant, chief executive officer. Grant has assembled a first-rate top management team that has now been together for the past four years. All major decisions are made by this centralized top management team after thorough study and review. Many members of top management were surprised by Grant's suggestion at a regular staff meeting that management should consider dropping the Victorian line—Travil's oldest furniture line.

Grant indicated that Victorian sales had dropped in total and as a percentage of Travil's total sales during the last three years. This conclusion was supported by the following schedule, which shows sales percentages by line for the last three years.

T. Mills, vice-president of sales, commented that the data did not reflect important regional differences in the market. Victorian total sales of $431,000 in 19C were almost entirely in New England and New York. In fact, Victorian sales constituted over one-half of all Travil sales in some of these locations. Mills indicated that more Victorian could be sold if Production could produce it, and that if the Victorian line is dropped, at least two top salespersons would likely be lost to competitors in New England.

Product-Line Sales Percentage

Year	Mediterranean	Modern	Colonial	Victorian	Country	Total
19A	31%	26%	21%	20%	2%	100%
19B	28	28	21	14	9	100
19C	24	26	23	10	17	100

However, Mills also conceded that many sales have been lost in other sales regions due to the long lead time on Country. Furthermore, Colonial had obviously benefited from the popularity of Country. In fact, sales in Colonial were dangerously ahead of supply.

B. Jamison, vice-president of production, pointed out that production of all lines was possible in existing facilities. However, Jamison also identified several problems with the Victorian line. The Victorian line is the least mechanized of Travil's lines, due in part to the high degree of detailed workmanship required. Furthermore, the equipment is old and outdated, requiring increased amounts of maintenance in recent years. The craftsmen needed to maintain the Victorian quality that had become Travil's greatest asset are just not available in the labor market anymore, making it difficult to support increased production. Several of Travil's craftsmen would need special training on their new production assignments if the Victorian line were eliminated. Jamison also indicated that margins on the Victorian line had dwindled due to the relative labor-intensity on that line and the high union wages of the skilled craftsmen. Dropping the Victorian line would also cause $80,000 worth of fabric in inventory to become totally obsolete.

Grant asked R. Turner, chief financial officer, to collect and assimilate data that would help the company evaluate whether to keep or drop the Victorian line. As the staff meeting closed, Grant stated, "Eventually we might consider expansion, but currently we must consider our present markets and resources."

Required:

(1) Discuss the type and nature of information that R. Turner should provide to Travil Corporation's top management team to assist in the decision to keep or drop the Victorian line. Give specific examples of information that Turner should prepare and present.

(2) If the management of Travil Corporation decides to drop the Victorian line for purposes of strengthening the remaining product lines, discuss:

(a) How Travil should communicate this decision to its employees.

(b) What steps should be taken to review the decision when operating results become available.

(ICMA adapted)

C25-2 Marketing Profitability Analysis by Products and by Salespersons. Caprice Company manufactures and sells two products, a small portable office file cabinet that it has made for over 15 years and a home-travel file introduced in 19A. The files are made in Caprice's only manufacturing plant. Budgeted variable production costs per unit of product are as follows:

	Office File	Home-Travel File
Sheet metal	$ 3.50	—
Plastic	—	$3.75
Direct labor (at $8 per DLH)	4.00	2.00
Variable factory overhead (at $9 per DLH)	4.50	2.25
	$12.00	$8.00

Variable factory overhead costs vary with direct labor hours. The annual fixed factory overhead costs are budgeted at $120,000. A total of 50% of these costs are directly traceable to the Office File Department, and 22% are traceable to the Home-Travel File Department. The remaining 28% of the costs are not traceable to either department.

Caprice employs two full-time salespersons, Pam Price and Robert Flint. Each salesperson receives an annual salary of $14,000 plus a sales commission of 10% of his or her total gross sales. Travel and entertainment expense is budgeted at $22,000 annually for each salesperson. Price is expected to sell 60% of the budgeted unit sales for each file and Flint the remaining 40%. Caprice's remaining marketing and administrative expenses include fixed administrative costs of $40,000 that cannot be traced to either file, plus the following traceable marketing expenses:

	Office File	Home-Travel File
Packaging expenses per unit	$ 2.00	$ 1.50
Promotion	30,000.00	40,000.00

Data regarding Caprice's budgeted and actual sales for the fiscal year ended May 31, 19D, are presented in the following schedule. There were no changes in the beginning and ending balances of either finished goods or work in process inventories.

	Office File	Home-Travel File
Budgeted sales volume in units	15,000	15,000
Budgeted and actual unit sales price	$ 29.50	$ 19.50
Actual unit sales:		
Pam Price	10,000	9,500
Robert Flint	5,000	10,500
Total units	15,000	20,000

Data regarding Caprice's operating expenses for the year ended May 31, 19D, are as follow:

(a) There were no increases or decreases in raw materials inventory for either sheet metal or plastic, and there were no usage variances. However, sheet metal prices were 6% above budget and plastic prices were 4% below budget.

(b) The actual direct labor hours worked and costs incurred were as follows:

	Hours	Amount
Office file	7,500	$ 57,000
Home-travel file	6,000	45,600
	13,500	$102,600

(c) Fixed factory overhead costs attributable to the Office File Department were $8,000 above the budget. All other fixed factory overhead costs were incurred at the same amounts as budgeted, and variable factory overhead costs were incurred at the budgeted hourly rates, except for a $9,000 unfavorable variance in the Home-Travel File Department.

(d) All marketing and administrative expenses were incurred at budgeted rates or amounts, except the following items:

Nontraceable administrative expenses		$ 34,000
Promotion:		
Office files	$32,000	
Home-travel files	58,000	90,000
Travel and entertainment:		
Pam Price	$24,000	
Robert Flint	28,000	52,000
		$176,000

Required:

(1) Prepare a segmented income statement of Caprice Company's actual operations for the fiscal year ended May 31, 19D. The report should be prepared in a contribution margin format by product and should reflect total operating income (loss) for the company.

(2) Identify and discuss any additional analyses that could be made from the data presented that would be of value to Caprice Company.

(3) Prepare a performance report for the year ended May 31, 19D, that management could use in evaluating the performance of Robert Flint. Include variable manufacturing costs at budgeted rates and compute Flint's contribution margin as well as his contribution net of traceable fixed costs. The only fixed costs traceable to individual salespersons are travel and entertainment and salary.

(4) Discuss the effects of Robert Flint's sales mix on Caprice Company's:
(a) Manufacturing operations.
(b) Profits.

(ICMA adapted)

C25-3 Compensation Program for Salespersons. Betterview Corporation manufactures a full line of windows and doors, including casement windows, bow windows, and patio doors. The bow windows and patio doors have a significantly higher profit margin per unit than casement windows, as shown in the following schedule:

	Casement Windows	Bow Windows	Patio Doors
Sales price	$130	$250	$260
Manufacturing costs:			
Direct materials	$ 25	$ 40	$ 50
Direct labor	20	35	30
Variable overhead	16	28	24
Fixed overhead	24	42	36
Total manufacturing cost	$ 85	$145	$140
Gross profit	$ 45	$105	$120

The company sells almost entirely to general contractors of residential housing. Most of these contractors complete and sell 15 to 50 houses per year. Each contractor builds tract houses that are similar, with some variations in exteriors and roof lines.

When contractors contact Betterview, they are likely to seek bids for all the windows in the houses they plan to build in the next year. At this point, the Betterview salespersons have an opportunity to influence the window configuration of these houses by suggesting patio doors or bow windows as variations for one or more casement windows for each of the several exteriors and roof lines built by the contractor.

The bow windows and patio doors are approximately twice as wide as the casement windows. A bow window or a patio door usually is substituted for two casement windows. Casement windows are usually ordered in pairs and placed side-by-side in those houses that can be modified to accept bow windows and patio doors.

Joseph Hite, president of Betterview Corporation, is perplexed by the company's profit performance. In a conversation with his sales manager, he declared, "Our total dollar sales volume is growing, but our net income has not increased as it should. Our unit sales of casement windows have increased proportionately more than the sale of bow windows or patio doors. Why aren't our sales representatives pushing our more profitable products?" The sales manager responded with a sense of frustration, "I don't know what else can be done. They have been told which type of windows we want sold, due to the greater profit margin. Furthermore, they have the best compensation plan in the industry. Their base monthly salaries are $1,000 and they receive commissions of 5% on sales dollars."

Required:

(1) Identify the needs of the salespersons that are being met by the current compensation program.

(Requirements continued.)

(2) Explain why Betterview's present compensation program for its salespersons does not support the president's objectives to sell the more profitable units.
(3) Specify alternative compensation programs that may be more appropriate for motivating the sales staff to sell the more profitable units.

(ICMA adapted)

C25-4 Sales Compensation Plans. Pre-Fab Housing Corporation, a relatively large company in the manufactured housing industry, is known for its aggressive sales promotion campaigns. Pre-Fab's innovative advertising and sales strategies have resulted in generally satisfactory performance in the last few years.

One of Pre-Fab's objectives is to increase sales revenue by at least 10% annually. This objective had been attained. Return on investment is considered good and had increased annually until last year, when net income decreased for the first time in nine years. The latest economic recession could be the cause of the change, but other factors, such as sales growth, discount this reason.

A significant portion of Pre-Fab's administrative expenses are fixed, but the majority of the manufacturing expenses are variable in nature. Increases in sales price have been consistent with the 12% increase in manufacturing expenses. Pre-Fab has consistently been able to maintain a company-wide manufacturing contribution margin of approximately 40%. However, the manufacturing contribution margin on individual product lines varies from 25 to 55%.

Sales commission expenses increased 30% over the past year. The prefabricated housing industry has always been sales oriented, and Pre-Fab's management believes in generously rewarding the efforts of its sales personnel. The sales force compensation plan consists of three segments:

(a) A guaranteed annual salary, which is increased annually at about a 6% rate. The salary is below industry average.
(b) A sales commission of 9% of total sales dollars. This is higher than the industry average.
(c) A year-end bonus of 5% of total sales dollars to each salesperson whose total sales dollars exceed the prior year's total by at least 12%.

The current compensation plan has resulted in an average annual income of $42,500 per sales employee, compared with an industry annual average of $30,000. However, the compensation plan has been effective in generating increased sales. Further, the Sales Department employees are satisfied with the plan. Management, however, is concerned about the financial implications of the current plan. Management believes that the plan has caused higher selling expenses and a lower net income relative to the sales revenue increase.

At a recent staff meeting, the controller suggested that the sales compensation plan be modified so that sales employees could earn an annual average income of $37,500. The controller believes that such a plan would still be attractive to its sales personnel and, at the same time, allow the company to earn a more satisfactory profit.

The vice-president for sales voiced strong objection to altering the current compensation plan because employee morale and incentive would drop significantly if there were any change. Nevertheless, most of the staff believes that the area of sales compensation merits a review. The president stated that all phases of a company operation can benefit from a periodic review, no matter how successful they have been in the past.

Several compensation plans known to be used by other companies in the manufactured housing industry follow:

(a) Straight commission as a percentage of sales
(b) Straight salary
(c) Salary plus compensation based on sales to new customers
(d) Salary plus compensation based on manufacturing contribution margin

Required:

(1) Discuss the advantages and disadvantages of Pre-Fab's current sales compensation plan with respect to:
 (a) The financial aspects of the company.
 (b) The behavioral aspects of the sales personnel.
(2) For each of the listed alternative compensation plans, discuss whether or not the plan would be an improvement over the current plan in terms of the financial performance of the company and the behavioral implications for the sales personnel.

(ICMA adapted)

C25-5 Gross Profit Variances. Handy Home Products Company distributes two home-use power tools to hardware stores, a heavy duty ½-inch hand drill and a table saw. The tools are purchased from a manufacturer that attaches the Handy Home Products label on the tools. The wholesale selling prices to the hardware stores are $60 each for the drill and $120 each for the table saw.

The budget for the current year and the actual results are presented in the following table. The budget was adopted late in the preceding year and was based on Handy Home Products' estimated share of the market for the two tools.

Handy Home Products Company
Income Statement
For the Year Ended December 31, 19A
(in thousands)

	Hand Drill		Table Saw		Total		
	Budget	Actual	Budget	Actual	Budget	Actual	Variance
Sales in units	120	86	80	74	200	160	40
Revenue	$7,200	$5,074	$9,600	$8,510	$16,800	$13,584	$3,216 unfavorable
Cost of goods sold	6,000	4,300	6,400	6,068	12,400	10,368	2,032 favorable
Gross profit	$1,200	$ 774	$3,200	$2,442	$ 4,400	$ 3,216	$1,184 unfavorable
Unallocated costs:							
Selling					$ 1,000	$ 1,000	$ 0
Advertising					1,000	1,060	60 unfavorable
Administration					400	406	6 unfavorable
Income tax (45%)					900	338	562 favorable
Total					$ 3,300	$ 2,804	$ 496 favorable
Net income					$ 1,100	$ 412	$ 688 unfavorable

During the first quarter of the current year, Handy Home Products' industry projections indicated that the total market for these tools would actually be 10% below original management estimates. In an attempt to prevent unit sales from declining as much as industry projections, management developed and implemented a marketing program. Included in the program were dealer discounts and increased direct advertising. The table-saw line was emphasized in this program.

Required:

(1) Analyze the unfavorable gross profit variance of $1,184,000 in terms of sales price variance, cost price variance, sales mix variance, and final sales volume variance.

(2) Discuss the apparent effect of the special marketing program (that is, dealer discounts and additional advertising) on actual operating results. Provide supporting numerical data where appropriate.

(ICMA adapted)

C25-6 Product Pricing. Kolesar Company manufactures office equipment for sale to retail stores. The vice-president of marketing has proposed that Kolesar introduce two new products to its line—an electric stapler and an electric pencil sharpener.

Kolesar's Profit Planning Department has been requested to develop preliminary sales prices for the two new products for review. The Profit Planning Department is to follow the company's standard policy for developing potential sales prices, using as much data as are available for each product. Data accumulated by the Profit Planning Department are shown in the following table.

	Electric Stapler	Electric Pencil Sharpener
Estimated annual demand in units	12,000	10,000
Estimated unit manufacturing costs	$10	$12
Estimated unit marketing and administrative expenses	$4	Not available
Assets employed in manufacturing	$180,000	Not available

Kolesar plans to employ an average of $2,400,000 in assets to support its operations in the current year. The condensed pro forma operating income statement represents Kolesar's planned goals with respect to cost relationships and return on capital employed for the entire company for all its products.

Kolesar Company
Pro Forma Operating Income Statement
For the Year Ending May 31, 19A
(in thousands)

Sales revenue	$4,800
Cost of goods sold	2,880
Gross profit	$1,920
Marketing and administrative expenses	1,440
Operating income	$ 480

Required:

(1) Calculate a potential sales price for the following:
 (a) The electric stapler, using return-on-capital-employed pricing
 (b) The electric sharpener, using gross-profit-margin pricing

(Requirements continued.)

(2) Can a sales price for the electric pencil sharpener be calculated using return-on-capital-employed pricing? Explain your answer.

(3) Which of the two pricing methods (return on capital employed or gross profit margin) is more appropriate for decision analysis? Explain your answer.

(4) The vice-president of marketing has received from the Profit Planning Department the potential sales prices for the two new products (as calculated in requirement 1). Discuss the additional steps that the vice-president is likely to take in order to set an actual sales price for each of the two products.

(ICMA adapted)

CHAPTER 26

Profit Performance Measurements and Intracompany Transfer Pricing

Learning Objectives

After studying this chapter, you will be able to:

1. Compute the percentage of profit to sales, the capital-employed turnover rate, and the rate of return on capital employed.
2. Distinguish between using the rate of return on capital employed to evaluate profitability and using it to evaluate the performance of divisional managers.
3. State the advantages and limitations of using the rate of return on capital employed.
4. Justify the use of residual income as a performance measure and the use of multiple performance measures.
5. List six different transfer pricing alternatives, and identify when they should be used.

As companies become larger, their geographic markets and the diversity of their products tend to expand. When this happens, the expertise needed and time required to plan and control the company's business also increase. Typically, companies first respond to these increasing needs by adding layers of management; however, at some point, central control of these widely different business operations becomes inefficient. When competitive pressures increase, companies then tend to decentralize the decision-making process in order to increase efficiency. **Decentralization** is a management philosophy that attempts to make each division of the business as autonomous as practical. The primary responsibility and the necessary authority to plan and control division operations are delegated to division management. Central management provides only general operating guidelines and profit goals for each division. The creation of decentralized, semiautonomous divisions within a company leads to the need for measuring and evaluating divisional performance. This chapter discusses the concept of return on capital employed, a measure used by management in appraising company-wide as well as divisional operating performance. It also discusses intracompany transfer pricing, which plays a significant role in measuring divisional results.

Rate of Return on Capital Employed

The **rate of return on capital employed** is the ratio of profit to capital employed in a business. It is used in this chapter as an internal measure. Because the capital employed in a business is frequently thought of as an investment, this ratio often is called **return on investment (ROI)**.

The Formula

The rate of return on capital employed can be expressed as the product of two factors: the percentage of profit to sales and the capital-employed turnover rate. The **percentage of profit to sales** is profit divided by sales. The **capital-employed turnover rate** is sales divided by capital employed. In equation form, the rate of return is developed as presented in Figure 26-1.

FIGURE 26-1 ***Rate of Return on Capital Employed***

$$\frac{\text{Profit}}{\text{Sales}} = \text{\% of Profit to Sales}$$

$$\frac{\text{Sales}}{\text{Capital Employed}} = \text{Capital-Employed Turnover Rate}$$

$$\times = \text{Rate of Return on Capital Employed}$$

Notice that sales cancels out in the two fractions to yield the measure called rate of return on capital employed. Although the final measure can be computed directly by dividing profit by capital employed, an evaluation of the full formula that includes profit on sales and turnover of capital employed can be informative. The profit percentage reflects a cost-price relationship affected by the sales level and mix, product prices, and cost control. The turnover rate reflects the rapidity with which committed assets are employed in the operations.

Because the rate of return on capital employed is the product of two factors, numerous combinations can lead to the same result, as illustrated in Exhibit 26-1 for a 20 percent rate of return.

EXHIBIT 26-1

Percentage of Profit to Sales	Capital-Employed Turnover Rate	Rate of Return on Capital Employed
10%	2.000	20%
8	2.500	20
6	3.333	20
4	5.000	20
2	10.000	20

There is no single rate of return on capital employed that is satisfactory for all companies. Manufacturing companies in various industries will have different rates, as will utilities, banking institutions, merchandising firms, and service companies. Management can establish an objective rate by using judgment and experience supported by comparisons with other companies. Every industry has companies with high, medium, and low rates of return. Structure and size of the firm influence the rate considerably. A diversified company might have only a fair return rate when the income and assets of all of its divisions are pooled in the analysis. In such cases, it may be advisable for management to establish separate objectives for each division as well as for the total company. Methods for divisional analyses are discussed later in this chapter.

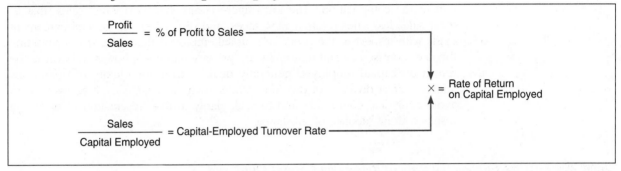

The Formula's Underlying Data

None of the factors or elements that produce the final rate can be disregarded, minimized, or overemphasized without impairing the quality of managerial decisions. Complete details of the relationships of the capital-employed ratio to the underlying ratios (percentage of profit to sales and capital-employed turnover rate) are presented in Figure 26-2.

A rate of return on capital employed is computed with data found in the balance sheet and income statement. Probability estimates can be incorporated as a part of the computation.[1] The sales figure commonly used is net sales (that is, gross sales less sales returns, allowances, and discounts). No general agreement exists with respect to the profit and capital-employed figures used in computing the rate. Consistency and uniformity are primary requisites, however, because the return on capital employed generally deals with a complexity of operations and/or a great diversity of divisions. Under such circumstances, it seems wise to avoid additional complexity and to seek clarity in the presentation of operating results without sacrifice of substance.

FIGURE 26-2 ***Factors Influencing Rate of Return on Capital Employed***

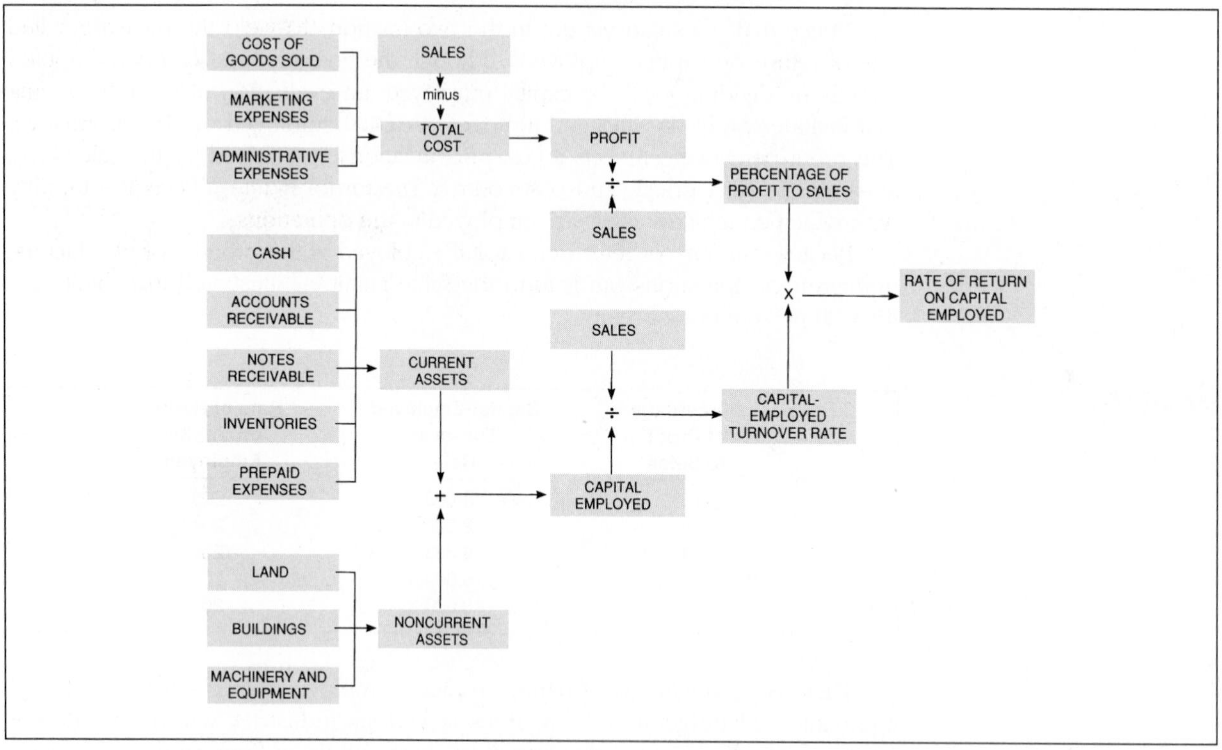

The income statement generally reports several different levels of profit, including (1) operating income, which is revenue less cost of goods sold and marketing and administrative expenses, (2) income before income tax, which is

[1] William L. Ferrara, "Probabilistic Approaches to Return on Investment and Residual Income," *The Accounting Review*, Vol. 52, No. 3, pp. 597-604.

operating income plus nonoperating income less nonoperating expenses, and (3) net income, which is the amount transferred to retained earnings after the income tax expense is deducted. Using operating income means that only transactions of an operating nature should be considered. This profit figure is preferred for divisional analyses, because nonoperating items are usually the responsibility of the entire company. The use of income before or after income tax is significant when the enterprise is judged as a whole; however, net income is more defensible because taxes deplete company resources, and firmwide performance should be judged only by the ultimate result. If capital employed is restated to give recognition to inflation, as discussed later in this chapter, then comparability calls for a similar recognition of the effect of inflation on profit.

Capital employed refers to total assets or the sum of current assets and noncurrent assets. Many accountants suggest that the amount of capital employed should be averaged over the fiscal period, if possible. Such a procedure tends to equalize unusually high or low year-end asset values or seasonal influences. Also, the sources of funds are not considered when the amount of capital employed is determined. Therefore, current and long-term liabilities, which provide the money used in the purchase of assets, are not deducted from the assets. However, some accountants believe that current liabilities should be deducted from current assets to obtain a working capital figure to be used in place of the current assets figure. This is considered theoretically appealing for the purpose of computing the rate of return of a division if division managers have control of current liabilities (that is, if current liabilities are incurred at the division level rather than at the corporate level).

Current Assets. The three most significant items classified as current assets are cash, receivables, and inventories. Problems of valuation are connected with each of these assets.

Cash. Ordinarily, the cash shown on the balance sheet is the amount required for total business operations. Cash funds set aside for pensions, taxes, or future expansion or development programs should be excluded. On the other hand, in computing a divisional rate of return, some managers do not accept the stated cash figure but prefer a predetermined percentage of cost of goods sold or annual operating expenses. The reasoning is that the routine transactions of a division require a certain minimum cash balance to be held. Amounts in excess of this minimum are a corporate-level responsibility, not an asset invested in the divisions.

Receivables. Values used for receivables should be either the gross amount or the net amount after the allowance for doubtful accounts is deducted.

Inventories. Different inventory costing methods, such as fifo, average, or lifo, give rise to some balance sheet and income statement differences. When return ratios of companies in the same industry are compared, an allowance for such differences should be made. Again, if an allowance account is used for lower of cost or market adjustments, the question arises as to whether the inventory figure used should be net of the allowance. Here, too, uniformity plays a significant role.

Some companies' inventories are costed on a standard cost or direct costing basis. The use of direct costing, as in the case of lifo, reduces inventory values on the balance sheet relative to absorption costing. Some accountants argue that, for internal comparison, the use of either method on a uniform basis should not influence results. However, the magnitude of the effects of any inventory method depends on the proportion of total capital tied up in inventory, and this proportion can vary widely among divisions. The same comparison problems apply to other accounting alternatives.

Noncurrent Assets. Three alternative valuation methods have been suggested for dealing with noncurrent assets: (1) original cost (original book value), (2) depreciated cost (original cost less the depreciation allowance—that is, net book value), and (3) inflation accounting.

Original Cost. Those accountants favoring the original cost basis argue as follows:

1. Assets of manufacturing companies, unlike those of mining companies, are on a continuing rather than on a depleted and abandoned basis.
2. Gross assets of one plant can be compared better with those of another plant, when depreciation practices or the age of the assets are different.
3. Accumulated depreciation should not be deducted from the gross asset value of property, because it represents retention of the funds required to keep the stockholders' original investment intact. Actually, noncurrent assets are used to produce a profit during their entire life. Therefore, full cost is considered an investment until the assets are retired from use.

Depreciated Cost. Those accountants who favor the use of the depreciated cost for noncurrent assets make the following two arguments. First, although noncurrent assets are conventionally understated at the present time, increasing the original cost should not be attempted, because this only adds to the confusion already existing in asset valuation. Second, an investment is something separate and distinct from the media through which it is made. The purchase price of a machine should be regarded as the prepaid cost for the number of years of production expected. Each year this number declines. One function of depreciation accounting is to maintain the aggregate capital by current provision of substitute assets to replace the aggregate asset consumption (depreciation) of the year.

The various acceptable depreciation methods, such as straight-line or accelerated methods, result in balance sheet and income statement differences. When return ratios of companies in the same industry are compared, such differences should be considered.

Inflation Accounting. Those accountants who maintain that noncurrent assets should be included at current cost or at historical cost adjusted to constant dollars argue that such values are more realistic. They believe that a company receiving a certain and apparently satisfactory return based on book values should recognize the situation as being out-of-step with actual conditions. They further assert that some equalization of facility values of different divisions or companies should be provided, especially between those with old plants that were built at relatively low cost and those with new plants that were built at high cost. This method, of course, poses the nontrivial problem of finding proper values.

Closely allied to any discussion of appropriate noncurrent asset values in an inflation accounting context are the effects on profits, sales, and capital employed. Sales, costs currently incurred, and current assets are measured in current dollar values, while the noncurrent assets and their expired cost lag years behind. When the noncurrent asset effects are translated into current costs or constant dollars, the rate of return on capital employed is more realistic.

Using the Rate of Return on Capital Employed

The rate of return on capital employed can be used as a measure of profitability for the total company, divisions, individual plants, and products. While a company's total analysis and comparison with the industry's ratios are significant for executive management, the real value of the rate of return on capital employed is for internal profit measurement and control. In this context, trends are more meaningful than single ratios. It is not a guide for shareholders or investors who measure profitability or earning power by relating profit to equity capital.

Executive managements of many companies have shown a growing interest in the concept of rate of return on capital employed as a tool for planning and measuring profitability. Information on return on capital employed is used by all levels of management because it is simple to understand. It provides a brief yet comprehensive picture of the success or failure of overall operations, of operations in each division, and of operations for plants and products. The performance of sales, earnings, and investments are captured in a single figure.

Budgeting is the principal planning and control technique employed by most companies. Of all the phases of budgeting, sales estimating is still considered the most difficult profit-planning task. If an acceptable sales budget has been established and production, manufacturing, and commercial expense budgets have been prepared, return on capital employed ratios are useful in the evaluation of the entire planning procedure.

Management's objectives with respect to the long-range return, as well as the immediate returns for each division, plant, or product, influence and guide budget-building activities. As sales, costs, and assets employed are placed in the perspective of the rate of return on capital employed as envisioned by management, there is a marked change in the attitude of the persons responsible for assembling the figures. Segment budgets are compared with predetermined goals. If they are too low, examination and action can be directed toward achieving the desired result. If an unusually excellent return is calculated, the reasons for it can be investigated. Management can either accept the situation as is or decide on a temporary modification of its planning goal. In any event, the return on capital employed offers a foundation for the construction of both annual and long-range planning budgets. When long-range plans are considered regarding addition of new products, dropping of old products, expansion of production facilities, or investing additional capital in research and development, application of the return on capital employed on any future projects has a sobering effect, if these projects have been conceived haphazardly or over optimistically.

A successful planning technique for improving profit includes the following steps: (1) define quantitatively (for sales, profits, and capital employed) the gap that exists between current performance and long-term objectives, (2) evaluate the problems precisely by examining each activity in detail, (3) formulate a specific program of action that will achieve the desired improvement, and (4) translate the planned results of each program into their effect on income and capital employed. The application of this technique for Warren Corporation is shown in Exhibit 26-2.

EXHIBIT 26-2

Warren Corporation
Effects of Planned Programs for Profit Improvement

	Present		Change by Volume	Change by Cost Reduction	Asset Curtailment	Future	
Assets							
Inventory	$ 500,000				–$100,000	$ 400,000	
Other current assets	200,000		+$ 20,000			220,000	
Noncurrent assets	300,000			+$ 80,000		380,000	
Total assets	$1,000,000		+$ 20,000	+$ 80,000	–$100,000	$1,000,000	
Profit:							
Sales billed	$1,000,000	100.0%	+$200,000			$1,200,000	100.0%
Manufacturing cost	$ 770,000	77.0%	+$140,000	–$ 88,000		$ 822,000	68.5%
Marketing and administrative expenses	130,000	13.0	+ 10,000	– 2,000		138,000	11.5
Total cost and expense	$ 900,000	90.0%	$150,000			$ 960,000	80.0%
Operating profit	$ 100,000	10.0%	+$ 50,000	+$ 90,000		$ 240,000	20.0%
Return on capital employed:							
Percent of profit to sales		10.0%					20.0%
Capital-employed turnover rate (times)		1.0					1.2
Return on capital employed (%)		10.0%					24.0%

Because return on capital employed is a financial measure of performance, it ignores nonfinancial performance. As a consequence, dysfunctional behavior can arise when return on capital employed is the sole criterion used to evaluate managerial performance. Managers who are evaluated tend to engage in activities that will result in short-term improvement or maintenance of the rate of return on capital employed even when such actions have unfavorable effects on long-term profitability. Actions that sometimes improve short-term return on capital employed at the expense of long-run profitability include the following:

1. Postponement or reduction of preventive maintenance, which reduces current expense but shortens the life of assets, thereby increasing future cost.
2. Reductions in research and development expenditures, which reduce current expense but make the company less competitive in the future.
3. Reduction or elimination of employee training and development, which reduces current expense but makes the company less competitive in the future.
4. Sale of needed assets, which are then rented. This gets the assets off the balance sheet but can cost the company more in the long-run than ownership does.
5. Deferment, reduction, or avoidance of modernization of facilities, especially substantial investments in automated manufacturing facilities,[2] which keeps asset cost on the balance sheet low but makes the company less competitive in the future.

[2] Gerald H. Lander and Mohamed E. Bayou, "Does ROI Apply to Robotic Factories?" *Management Accounting*, Vol. 73, No. 11, pp. 49- 53.

Divisional Rates of Return

The rate of return on capital employed is commonly used to evaluate divisional performance.[3] Although not always observed in practice, there are two distinctly different uses for the measure of rate of return on capital employed. It can be used to evaluate the profitability of the assets committed to a particular division, or it can be used to evaluate the performance of divisional management.[4] The components of income and the combination of assets used in the computation should depend on the use of the measure and should exclude arbitrarily allocated common costs.

If the rate of return on capital employed is used to evaluate the profitable use of the assets committed to the division, the measure should include only those items of income and only those assets directly traceable to use by or for the division. It should include only those items that can be avoided if the division is discontinued.[5] An allocation of common costs to divisions would be arbitrary and would consequently distort (and dilute) the economic value of the divisions to the company.

If the rate of return on capital employed is used to evaluate the performance of divisional managers, the measure should include only those items of income and only those assets that are controllable by divisional management.[6] Controllable costs may differ from separable costs. A cost that is avoidable if a division is eliminated is not necessarily controllable by the division's management. For example, the cost of corporate personnel services can be allocated to divisions on the basis of the number of personnel in each division. Clearly the number of personnel is a cost driver that is directly traceable to divisions (and therefore avoidable when divisions and personnel are eliminated); however, the efficiency of the personnel department (and therefore the cost per employee allocated to the divisions) is not controllable by divisional managers. On the other hand, the number of employees utilized at the divisional level typically is controllable by divisional management, in which case some cost should be allocated to the division. One solution to the problem is to allocate such costs on the basis of a predetermined rate and to compare actual divisional performance with budgeted performance. (See the discussion of responsibility accounting and reporting in Chapter 17.)

Whether the rate is being used to evaluate the economic value of a division or the performance of division managers, the rate logically can be compared to some target set by management (for example, the budgeted rate) or to the rate of return for the same division in preceding periods. However, comparing the rate of return on capital employed for one division with that of another division is unsound. Aside from the problem of determining divisional income and assets employed on comparable bases, each division produces different products and operates in different markets. As a consequence, market risk (that is, variability in demand) is likely to differ for each division, which in turn means that top management should expect divisional returns to differ as well. In order to compensate for risk, divisions operating in highly risky markets should be required to have

---

[3] Although this discussion refers to divisions, the rate of return on capital employed can be computed for other segments of a business, such as products or territories, following the steps described for divisions.

[4] Earl A. Spiller, Jr., "Return on Investment: A Need for Special Purpose Information," *Accounting Horizons*, Vol. 2, No. 2, pp. 2-4.

[5] *Ibid.*, p. 2.

[6] *Ibid.*, p. 3.

larger returns than those in less risky markets. If the rate of return for each division is adjusted for its respective market risk, comparison between or among the divisions is reasonable (assuming, of course, that income and assets employed are comparably measured).

On the other hand, comparing the rate of return on capital employed for one division with another for the purpose of evaluating division managers is almost always unsound. The economic environments of different divisions are generally too disparate to allow meaningful comparisons for this purpose.[7] One division may be in a highly competitive market, while another is in a protected or monopolistic market. One may be in a declining market, while another is in a growth market. It is one thing to evaluate divisional returns for the purpose of deciding whether to expand, contract, or discontinue operations, but it is quite another to attribute the differences in divisional rates to the performances of their respective managers. It is very possible that the manager of a division operating in a declining market is a far more efficient manager than one managing a division in a growth market, in spite of the fact that the former's divisional rate of return is lower. If rewards are based on the relative performance of the divisions, as measured exclusively by their rates of return, good managers may become discouraged and either diminish their efforts or quit, while the least efficient managers may be encouraged to continue inefficient behavior. The best managers often are assigned to the weakest divisions where their skills are most needed.

Divisional measures of return on capital employed have been criticized as a motivational tool because a division may seek to maximize its rate of return on capital employed rather than absolute profits. Assume that a division that is presently earning a 30 percent rate of return on capital employed is considering a project with a return of only 25 percent. The divisional management might decline the project because the return on total divisional capital would decrease. Yet, if the acceptance of the project would make the best use of these divisional resources from a total company point of view, then even with a lower rate of return for the division or for the total company, the project should be accepted.

Suboptimum behavior of this sort can be overcome by use of **residual income** (that is, a division's income less an amount representing the company's cost of capital employed by the division) to measure performance instead of or in addition to the rate of return on capital employed. This additional calculation emphasizes marginal profit dollars above the cost of capital, rather than the rate of return on capital employed. This motivates divisional management to maximize dollar profit rather than try to achieve a specified profit rate.

Residual income is a counterpart of the return on capital employed computation and is a dollar measure of profitability. The concept is analogous to the net present value obtained when cash flows are discounted (Chapter 23). A positive residual income indicates earnings in excess of the desired return, while a negative residual income indicates earnings less than the desired return.[8]

Graphs as Operating Guides

Sound planning and successful operation must point toward the optimum combination of profits, sales, and capital employed. As stated earlier, the combination will necessarily vary depending on the characteristics of the operation. An industry with products tailor-made to customers' specifications will not have the same

[7] *Ibid.*, p. 4.

[8] Ferrara, "Probabilistic Approaches," p. 599.

profit margins and turnover ratios as industries that mass produce highly competitive consumer goods.

In multiproduct companies, the three basic factors cannot be uniform, due to different types of operations. However, a special type of graph can be of assistance when the performance of segments or products need to be judged in their relationship to a desired overall return on capital employed. Such a graph has the advantage of flexibility in the appraisal of profit performance and offers an approach by which performance can be analyzed for improvement.

FIGURE 26-3 ***Relationship Between Percent of Profit to Sales and Capital-Employed Turnover Rate***

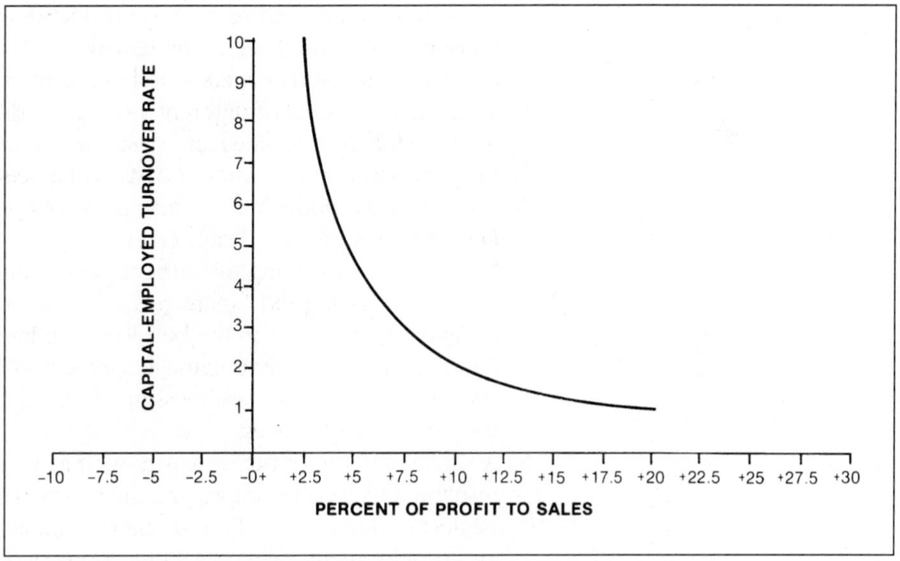

The graph in Figure 26-3 shows possible combinations of percentage of profit to sales and capital-employed turnover rate that yield a 20 percent return. When individual divisions or products are plotted on the graph, the segment's data point appears to the left or right of the basic curve. If the plotted data point falls on the left, the unit has a capital-employed-return performance below that expected for the company as a whole. A segment with a data point plotted on the right of the basic curve has a return in excess of that expected for the entire company. The same interpretation applies when the company's total return is plotted.

Advantages of Using the Return on Capital Employed

Use of the rate of return on capital employed has the following generally claimed advantages:

1. It focuses management's attention on earning the best profit possible on the capital (total assets) available.
2. It ties together the many phases of financial planning, sales objectives, cost control, and the profit goal.
3. It helps management detect the strengths and weaknesses of the use (or nonuse) of individual assets.
4. It serves as a yardstick for the measurement of performance and provides a basis for the evaluation of improvement over time and among divisions.
5. It develops a keener sense of responsibility and team effort among divisional managers by enabling them to measure and evaluate their own

activities in light of the budget and with respect to the results achieved by other divisional managers.

Limitations of Using the Return on Capital Employed

The return on capital employed ratio should be used with an awareness of the following limitations:

1. It may not be reasonable to expect the same return on capital employed from each division if the divisions sell their respective products in markets that differ widely with respect to product development, competition, and consumer demand. Lack of agreement on the optimum rate of return might discourage managers who believe the rate is set at an unfair level.
2. Valuations of assets of different vintages in different divisions can give rise to comparison difficulties and misunderstandings.
3. Proper allocation of common costs and assets requires detailed information about the budgeted and actual use of common facilities. The cost of keeping track of such details can be high.
4. For the sake of making the current period rate of return on capital employed "look good," managers are sometimes influenced to make decisions that are not in the best long-run interests of the firm. This problem is especially likely if managers expect to be in positions for only a short time before they are reassigned, thereby avoiding responsibility for long-run consequences.
5. A single measure of performance, such as return on capital employed, can result in a fixation on improving the components of the one measure to the neglect of needed attention to other desirable activities. Product research and development, managerial development, progressive personnel policies, good employee morale, and good customer and public relations are also important for increasing profit and assuring continuous growth.

Multiple Performance Measures

Many well-managed companies use multiple performance measures in order to overcome the limitations of a single measure. An evaluation and reward system should be based on nonfinancial measures of performance as well as financial measures. Multiple performance measures provide central management with a more comprehensive picture of divisional performance by considering a wider range of management responsibilities. The implementation of an evaluation and reward structure that includes multiple performance measures not only encourages managers to seek profitability, it also provides an incentive to divisional managers to engage in such desirable activities as basic research, new product development, quality improvement, production innovation, employee development, and new market development. In turn, such measures mitigate the problems inherent in evaluating divisional performance on the basis of a single profit measure that is computed on different bases in each division, and they provide managers with long-run as well as short-run incentives.

A multiple performance measurement system can be difficult to implement and administer. Because measurement criteria are not all equally quantifiable, it can be difficult to compare the overall performance of one division with another. In addition, central management may find it difficult to apply the multiple, nonquantifiable criteria on a consistent basis between periods and among divisions.

Uncertainty about the weight central management places on the various measures can lead to confusion for divisional managers, which in turn can result in diffusion of effort and instability in divisional performance.

One company that uses multiple measurements for rating divisional performance describes its method as a quantification of progress against agreed-on standards. Each year, common standards are adopted by agreement of divisional managers and corporate management. Points are assigned to standards reflecting those areas that require special attention in each division, as determined by management. Performance is measured as follows:

1. Profits for the current year are compared with the profits for the preceding year in absolute dollars, margins, and return on capital employed.
2. Profits are compared with the budget.
3. Cash and capital management measures are employed. Here, the emphasis is on effective management of inventory and receivables.

The company claims the advantages of this method are:

1. Performances of division managers are measured more fairly than they would be from the sole use of a return on capital employed figure.
2. Management can readily see which divisions are performing well and which are not.
3. Lost points serve as "red flags" and direct management to those areas requiring attention, to the reasons for the difficulty, and to the corrective actions taken or needed.
4. The system is flexible, allowing timely shifting of management emphasis when needed.

In this company, management concludes that it is not enough merely to tabulate performance statistics. The results must be effectively communicated, corrective action taken, and good performance rewarded. The system must have the interest and support of division and corporate management.[9]

Management Incentive Compensation Plans

Incentive compensation plans are used by top managements and boards of directors to encourage managers to pursue company goals. Managers in large corporations often receive a base salary plus some form of incentive compensation. Incentive compensation changes often in response to top management turnover and to changes in the company's environment.[10] Common forms of management incentive compensation include the following:[11]

1. Cash bonuses, which are usually paid in a lump sum at the end of a period and based on a combination of corporate performance, individual performance, and the management level.
2. Stock bonuses, which are determined in essentially the same way as cash bonuses.

---

[9] Frank J. Tanzola, "Performance Rating for Divisional Control," *Financial Executive*, Vol. 43, No. 3, pp. 20-24.

[10] Stephen A. Butler and Michael W. Maher, *Management Incentive Compensation Plans*, (Montvale, N.J.; Institute of Management Accounting (formerly National Association of Accountants), 1986), pp. 1–2.

[11] *Ibid.*, pp. 5-10.

3. Deferred compensation, which is paid in cash and/or stock that does not vest until a future period. In some cases, the manager is required to invest annually and the company matches the contribution.
4. Stock options, which give the manager a right to purchase stock at a set price within a set period. The incentive is to help the company increase the market price of its stock as much as possible within the option period.
5. Stock appreciation rights, which are similar to stock options except that the manager is not required to purchase stock but instead receives an amount equal to its appreciation at the end of a set period.
6. Performance shares, which are stock awards paid to the manager only after some long-run goal has been achieved.

The expectation of earning a stock or cash bonus provides an incentive for managers to achieve high levels of performance so long as the tasks to be performed are clearly understood and the performance levels required are achievable. However, each manager's incentive is to maximize the level of just those tasks tied to the expected reward regardless of the effect of those actions on the company's long-run profitability. As a consequence, the performance measure selected is crucial to the long-run success of the company. The performance incentive for each manager must be congruent with the overall best interest of the firm. Cash and stock bonuses that are based on the results of one period provide only short-run incentive. In contrast, stock options, stock appreciation rights, and performance shares are valuable only if the company improves in the long run.

Selecting Performance Measures

To be effective, the performance measures selected must be controllable by the managers who are to be evaluated. In addition, the measures must be clearly understood and accepted by all parties involved (the persons being evaluated and the persons doing the evaluating). Generally, performance measurements and related incentive compensation plans should (1) reward long-term performance; (2) tie incentive compensation to achieving strategic (nonfinancial) goals, such as target market share, productivity levels, improvement in product quality, product development, and personnel development; and (3) evaluate operating profits before gains from financial transactions; before deductions for approved expenditures on research and development, quality improvements, and preventive maintenance; and before deductions for the incremental amount of accelerated depreciation.[12]

Intracompany Transfer Pricing

The effectiveness of the rate of return on capital employed or residual income measures as devices for measuring divisional performance depends considerably on the accuracy of allocating the costs and assets associated with the division. In a decentralized multiplant or multiproduct organization, the divisional managers are expected to run their respective divisions as semiautonomous businesses. If the divisions are not entirely independent and separable, some centralized corporate services may be provided to the divisions and goods and services may be transferred from one division to another, a situation common to integrated corpo-

[12] Alfred Rappaport, "Executive Incentives vs. Corporate Growth," *Harvard Business Review*, Vol. 56, No. 4, pp. 85-86.

rations. The finished or semifinished product of one or more divisions frequently becomes the raw material of one or more other divisions. When transfers of goods or services are made, a portion of the revenue of one segment becomes a portion of cost of another, and the price at which transfers are made influences the earnings reported by each profit center. The value of these earnings as a measure of performance depends not only on a manager's executive abilities but also on the transfer prices used. The transfer pricing system used can distort any reported profit and make profit a poor guide for evaluation of divisional performance. In the end, the cost or price used for the transfer will be used in the calculation of the return on capital employed, due to the very nature of the formula.

At one time, transfer pricing played only a minor role in cost control. Today, many corporations have become large due to merger, acquisition, or internal growth and have turned to decentralization as a way of managing the increasing complexity and diversity of their business activities. As a result, the use of transfer pricing has expanded. The arbitrary nature of intracompany transfer pricing is one reason for criticism of proposals to report segment or product-line revenues and profits in published financial statements. For example, a steel company can operate a coal mine and sell some of its output on the open market but use the remainder in its own steel mills. The transfer price charged to its own steel mills can control whether the mining division shows a large or small profit or no profit.

Tax laws significantly influence transfer price determination. A company with an overseas plant, where tax rates are low, often tries to keep the transfer price high for materials sent to the domestic facility in order to retain profits abroad. A company with warehouses in a state with an inventory tax may keep transfer prices low on goods brought into the state in order to reduce its tax bill.

The existence of multiple management objectives makes it extremely difficult for a company to establish logical and sound intracompany transfer prices. A pricing method can be chosen only after the primary purposes for the use of the information from transfers have been identified. Therefore, a transfer pricing system must satisfy the following fundamental criteria:[13]

1. It must allow central management to judge as accurately as possible the performance of the divisional profit center in terms of its separate contribution to the total corporate profit.
2. It must motivate the divisional manager to pursue the division's own profit goal in a manner conducive to the success of the company as a whole.
3. It must stimulate the manager's efficiency without losing the division's autonomy as a profit center.

The system should also be easy to apply, meet legal and external reporting requirements, and permit each unit of a company to earn a profit commensurate with the functions it performs. As a practical matter, these criteria may be difficult to satisfy, because behavioral considerations are of paramount importance. Accordingly, a transfer price should be a fair price to both the selling and buying parties. An advantage gained by one is a disadvantage to the other and, in the end, may be detrimental to the corporate profit goal.

A profit center manager's interest must remain congruent with the firm's interest. For example, assume that Division X offers its Product A to Division Y at a transfer price of $14, which includes a $2 profit, a $9 variable cost, and a $3 fixed cost that presumably will remain unchanged in total as activity fluctuates. The

---

[13] Joshua Ronen and George McKinney III, "Transfer Pricing for Divisional Autonomy," *Journal of Accounting Research*, Vol. 8, No. 1, pp. 99-112.

same product is also available from an outside supplier at $11. Division Y, acting to minimize its costs, will prefer to purchase Product A at the lower external price of $11. However, assuming that from the total firm point of view, no more profitable use could be made of the Division X facilities used in supplying Product A to Division Y, such a decision would not be congruent with the best short-run interests of the total firm. This incongruence results because the $11 external price is greater than the $9 variable cost which, in this example, is the differential cost—that is, the incremental cost incurred to produce additional units. Additionally, it should be observed that, in the long run, full cost must be recovered and a reasonable profit achieved on the facilities that are to be employed.

Five basic methods of pricing intracompany transfers are: transfer pricing based on cost, market-based transfer pricing, cost-plus transfer pricing, negotiated transfer pricing, and arbitrary transfer pricing. No one method of transfer pricing can effectively satisfy all requirements in all circumstances, so the best transfer price can be defined only as it is best for a particular purpose in a particular circumstance. Regardless of the transfer price used, the differential cost of goods transferred from division to division should be determined and used for decision-making purposes.[14]

Historically, transfers are priced at cost when the transferring division is viewed as a cost center (meaning that its manager is responsible for cost but not revenue). However, if the transferor is a profit center (where the manager is responsible for cost and revenue), market value or cost-plus transfer prices are typically used.[15] A 1990 study of transfer pricing practices among the Fortune 500 companies found that 29.6 percent of respondent companies used cost-based transfer prices, 36.7 percent used market-based transfer prices, 16.6 percent used cost-plus transfer prices, 16.6 percent used negotiated transfer prices, and the rest used some other method.[16]

Transfer Pricing Based on Cost

In a totally centralized firm, executive management basically makes all operational decisions for the divisions. This responsibility makes cost control the basis for measuring a manager's performance. **Cost-based transfer pricing** is usually sufficient in this situation. A company with no integrated operations might have so little volume of intracompany transfers that it is too time consuming and costly to price the transfer at other than cost.

The cost figure can be the actual or standard cost, based on direct or absorption costing. The company's cost system should permit the computation of a product's unit cost, even at various stages of production. When service departments are involved in a company's operations, a service charging rate should be established in advance of the work performed, so that servicing and benefiting departments or plants know in advance the costs connected with services.

The cost method's primary advantage is simplicity. It avoids the necessity of eliminating intracompany profits from inventories in consolidated financial state-

[14] A further study of the nature and scope of several major transfer pricing models categorized as to (1) economic theory of the firm, (2) mathematical programming approaches, and (3) other analytical approaches, is covered in "Transfer Pricing—A Synthesis," by A. Rashad Abdel-khalik and Edward J. Lusk, *The Accounting Review*, Vol. 49, No. 1, pp. 8-23.

[15] Itzhak Sharav, "Transfer Pricing—Diversity of Goals and Practices," *The Journal of Accountancy*, Vol. 137, No. 4, p. 59.

[16] Roger Y. W. Tang, "Transfer Pricing in the 1990s," *Management Accounting*, Vol. 73, No. 8, p. 24.

ments and income tax returns. Also, the transferred cost can be used readily to measure production efficiency by allowing comparison of actual and budgeted costs. Finally, the method allows simple and adequate end-product costing for profit analysis by product lines.

On the other hand, a transfer price based on cost is not suited to decentralized companies that need to measure the profitability of autonomous units. Also, producing segments may not be sufficiently conscientious in controlling costs that are to be transferred, although the use of standard costs for transfer pricing can alleviate this problem. A transfer price based on cost lacks not only utility for divisional planning, motivating, and evaluating, but also the objectivity required of a good performance standard.

Another cost-based transfer price that has been advocated is standard variable cost plus the per unit contribution margin given up on the outside sale by the company when a segment sells internally. For profit centers, the result generally approximates market price, while for cost centers, the transfer price is standard variable cost plus the possibility of an assigned portion of fixed cost.[17]

Market-Based Transfer Pricing

In **market-based transfer pricing**, the price charged internally is usually identical with the one charged to outside customers, although some companies apply a discount to the market price to reflect the economies of intracompany trading. This method is the best profitability and performance measurement because it is objective. It reflects product profitability and division management performance, with divisions operating on a competitive basis. It also aids in the planning process and generally is required by foreign tariff laws and income tax regulations.

The most serious drawback to this method is the requirement of a well-developed outside competitive market. Unfortunately, a market price is not always determinable for intermediate or unique products. Also, the market-based price adds an element of profit or loss with each transfer of product. Consequently, the determination of the actual cost of the final product may be difficult, and intracompany profit must be eliminated from inventories in financial statements and consolidated income tax returns.

Statement of Financial Accounting Standards No. 14, "Financial Reporting for Segments of a Business Enterprise,"[18] does not specify the transfer pricing method to be used in segment reporting, but it does require disclosure of the method used. The SEC, however, requires disclosure of:

1. When and where intersegment transfers are made at prices substantially higher or lower than the prevailing market price or the price charged to unaffiliated parties for similar products or services.
2. The estimated or approximate amounts (or the percentage of increase or decrease in the amounts) of the revenue and operating profit or loss that the particular segments would have had if the intersegment transfers had been made at the prevailing market price.[19]

---

[17] Ralph L. Benke, Jr., and James Don Edwards, *Transfer Pricing: Techniques and Issues* (New York: Institute of Management Accountants (formerly National Association of Accountants), 1980).

[18] (Stamford, Conn.: Financial Accounting Standards Board, 1976).

[19] Robert Mednick, "Companies Slice and Serve Up Their Financial Results Under FASB 14," *Financial Executive*, Vol. 47, No. 3, p. 55.

Cost-Plus Transfer Pricing

Cost-plus transfer pricing includes the cost to manufacture plus a normal profit markup. It is often used when a market price is not available. In a sense, it is a surrogate for a market price. Although a cost-plus price has the virtue of being easy to compute, it is an imperfect price that can lead to distortions in the relative profitability of the selling and buying divisions. A cost-plus transfer price provides no incentive to the selling division to be efficient. On the contrary—because the profit markup is often a percentage of cost—there is an incentive to inflate cost through arbitrary allocation of common costs and through production inefficiency. In addition, cost-plus transfer pricing has the disadvantage of inflating inventories with intracompany profits that must be eliminated from the financial statements and consolidated income tax returns.

Negotiated Transfer Pricing

In **negotiated transfer pricing,** the transfer price is set by negotiation between buying and selling divisions. This allows unit managers the greatest degree of authority and control over the profit of their units. The managers should consider costs and market conditions and neither negotiating party should have an unfair bargaining position.

A serious problem encountered with this method is that negotiation can not only become time-consuming but can also require frequent reexamination and revision of prices. Negotiated transfer prices often divert the efforts of divisional managers away from productive activities that are in the best interests of the company to those that benefit the division. The divisional profit measures may be more of a reflection of the divisional manager's negotiating ability than the division's productive efficiency. As a result, evaluations of the relative operating performance of divisions can be distorted when negotiated transfer prices are used. In addition, because the transfer price includes a profit markup, the actual cost of the final products can be hard to determine, and intracompany profits must be eliminated from inventories for financial statements and consolidated income tax returns.

Arbitrary Transfer Pricing

In **arbitrary transfer pricing,** the price is simply set by central management. The price is generally chosen to achieve tax minimization or some other firmwide objective. Neither the buying division nor the selling division controls the transfer price. The advantage of this method is that a price can be set that will achieve the objectives deemed most important by central management. Because central management is responsible for the overall performance of the company, transfer prices set by central management should result in divisional actions that enhance firmwide performance. The method's disadvantages, however, far outweigh any advantage. It can defeat the most important purpose of decentralizing profit responsibility—making divisional personnel profit conscious. It also severely hampers the autonomy and profit incentive of division managers. Again, because arbitrary transfer prices generally include some markup for profit, determining the actual cost of the final products can be difficult, and intracompany profits must be eliminated from inventories for financial statement and consolidated income tax reporting.

Dual Transfer Pricing

The purpose a transfer price serves may differ in the consuming (buying) and producing (selling) divisions. For example, a consuming division may rely on a transfer price in make-or-buy decisions or in determining a final product's sales price based on an estimate of total differential cost. A producing division, on the other hand, may use a transfer price to measure its divisional performance and, accordingly, would argue against any price that does not provide a divisional profit. In such circumstances, a company may find it useful to adopt a **dual transfer pricing** approach in which:

1. The producing division uses a market-based, cost-plus, negotiated, or arbitrary transfer price in computing its revenue from intracompany sales.
2. The variable costs of the producing division are transferred to the purchasing division, together with an equitable portion of the fixed cost.
3. The total of the divisional profits is greater than for the company as a whole. The profit assigned to the producing division is eliminated when company-wide financial statements are prepared and income taxes are calculated.

This approach means that a producing division has a profit inducement to expand sales and production, both externally and internally. Yet, the consuming divisions are not misled. Their costs are the firm's actual costs and do not include an artificial profit. Variable costs, as well as fixed costs, should be associated with the purchase to ensure that the consuming division is aware of the total cost implications. Of course, the benefits from a dual transfer pricing approach can be achieved only if the underlying cost data are accurate and reliable.

Although the dual transfer pricing method appears to overcome many of the negative incentives inherent in the other transfer pricing methods, it is not commonly used in practice. This lack of use may be due in part to the record-keeping complexity of the method and in part to the difficulty inherent in evaluating the relative performance of the selling and buying divisions when their profits have been determined on different bases.

Summary

For decentralized, autonomous divisions of a company to be controlled, divisional operating and profit performance must be measured and evaluated. This chapter discussed the concept of rate of return on capital employed, a measure used by management in appraising company-wide as well as divisional operating performance. The discussion presented advantages and limitations of using return on capital employed to measure the profitability of committed assets and the performance of division managers. The advantages of using residual income and multiple performance measures were discussed. In the last section, intracompany transfer pricing, which plays a significant role in measuring divisional results, was presented. Various alternative approaches to transfer pricing were discussed: cost, market value, cost plus a normal markup for profit, a negotiated price, an arbitrary price set by central management, and a dual transfer price.

Key Terms

decentralization *(790)*
rate of return on capital employed *(790)*
return on investment (ROI) *(790)*
percentage of profit to sales *(791)*
capital-employed turnover rate *(791)*
residual income *(798)*
cost-based transfer pricing *(804)*
market-based transfer pricing *(805)*
cost-plus transfer pricing *(806)*
negotiated transfer pricing *(806)*
arbitrary transfer pricing *(806)*
dual transfer pricing *(807)*

Discussion Questions

Q26-1 What management activities are measured by percentage of profit to sales and by the capital-employed turnover rate?

Q26-2 What items are generally included in the term *capital employed?*

Q26-3 State two major objectives that management may have in mind when it sets up a system for measuring the return on divisional capital employed.

Q26-4 List five dysfunctional actions that managers can take to improve the short-term return on capital employed at the expense of long-term profitability.

Q26-5 List five frequently claimed advantages of using the rate of return on capital employed.

Q26-6 List five frequently encountered limitations of using the rate of return on capital employed.

Q26-7 What is the purpose of using multiple performance measures?

Q26-8 What types of management incentive compensation plans are commonly found, and which are likely to be the most effective in achieving long-term improvement?

Q26-9 Identify the basic methods of pricing intracompany transfers.

Q26-10 A cost-plus transfer price is often used as a surrogate for a market-based transfer price. Explain the primary disadvantage of a cost-plus transfer price relative to a market-based transfer price.

Q26-11 From an organizational point of view, two approaches to transfer pricing are (a) to let managers of profit centers bargain with one another and arrive at their own transfer prices (negotiated transfer pricing) and (b) to have the firm's executive management set transfer prices for transactions between the profit centers (arbitrary transfer pricing). State the fundamental advantage and disadvantage of each approach.
CGA-Canada (adapted). Reprint with permission.

Q26-12 Explain the dual transfer pricing approach in intracompany transfer pricing.

Exercises

E26-1 Rate of Return on Capital Employed. During the past year, Falcon Manufacturing Corporation had a net income of $200,000. Net sales were $800,000 and total capital employed was $2,000,000.

Required: Compute the following:
(1) Capital-employed turnover rate
(2) Percentage of profit to sales
(3) Rate of return on capital employed

E26-2 Rate of Return on Capital Employed for Corporate Divisions. Lindle Corporation has three operating divisions organized along product lines: the Recreational Products Division (RPD), the Household Products Division (HPD), and the Commercial Tools Division (CTD). The balance sheet at the beginning of the year showed total corporate assets of $66,000,000, and the year-end balance sheet showed total assets of $70,000,000, with $5,000,000 attributable to corporate headquarters at both the beginning and end of the year. The remainder of the corporation's assets were used by the three divisions in the following proportions: 25%, 40%, and 35% by RPD, HPD, and CTD, respectively. Corporate assets and expenses are not allocated to the divisions when their respective performances are evaluated, and average assets are used when divisional return on capital employed is computed. The condensed income statement for the current year is as follows:

Lindle Company
Income Statement
For the Year Ended December 31, 19A

	Corporate Products Divisions			
	Recreational	**Household**	**Commercial Tools**	**Total**
Sales	$15,750,000	$20,160,000	$15,435,000	$51,345,000
Cost of goods sold	9,750,000	13,160,000	10,435,000	33,345,000
Gross profit	$ 6,000,000	$ 7,000,000	$ 5,000,000	$18,000,000
Divisional marketing and administrative expenses	1,275,000	2,968,000	1,141,250	5,384,250
Divisional contribution	$ 4,725,000	$ 4,032,000	$ 3,858,750	$12,615,750
Corporate common costs				2,755,750
Net income before taxes				$ 9,860,000

Required: For each division and for the corporation as a whole, compute each of the following:
(1) Capital-employed turnover rate
(2) Percentage of profit to sales
(3) Rate of return on capital employed

E26-3 Transfer Pricing. Wallach Iron Mill produces high-grade pig iron in its single blast furnace in Bedford, Pennsylvania. Coal from nearby mines is converted into coke in company-owned ovens, and 80% of the coke produced is used in the blast furnace. The management of the mill is experimenting with divisional profit reporting and control and has established the blast furnace as well as the coke-producing activity as profit centers. Coke used by the blast furnace is charged to that profit center at $6 per ton, which approximates the current market price less costs of marketing (including substantial freight costs). The remaining 20% of the coke produced at a normal annual volume output of 80,000 tons is sold to other mills in the area at $7.50 per ton.

The cost of coal and other variable costs of coke production amount to $4.50 per ton. Fixed costs of the coke division amount to $40,000 a year.

The blast furnace manager, with authority to purchase outside, has found a reliable, independent coke producer who has offered to sell coke at a delivered price of $5 per ton on a long-term contract. The manager of Wallach Iron Mill's coke division claims the division cannot match that price and maintain profitable operations.

The manager of the coke division indicates that with an additional expenditure of $60,000 annually for fixed productive and delivery equipment, the division's entire annual normal output could be sold to outside firms at $6 per ton, FOB the Wallach Iron Mill plant. Other marketing expenses will be $.50 per ton. The increased fixed costs would reduce variable production costs by $1.50 per ton.

Required:
(1) Prepare calculations to guide the coke division manager in deciding whether to accept the outside offer, assuming that Wallach Iron Mill cannot increase its sales of coke to outsiders above 20% of normal production.
(2) Prepare calculations to aid executive management in deciding whether to make the additional investment and sell the entire coke division's output to outsiders.

E26-4 Transfer Pricing. Ace Division of Decker Corporation produces electric motors, 20% of which are sold to Deuce Division of Decker and the remainder to outside customers. Decker treats its divisions as profit centers and allows division managers to choose their sources of sale and supply. Corporate policy requires that all interdivisional sales and purchases be recorded at a transfer price equal to variable cost. Ace Division's estimated sales and standard cost data for the year, based on full capacity of 100,000 units, follow:

	Deuce	Outsiders
Sales	$ 900,000	$ 8,000,000
Variable cost	(900,000)	(3,600,000)
Fixed cost	(300,000)	(1,200,000)
Gross profit	$(300,000)	$ 3,200,000
Unit sales	20,000	80,000

Ace Division has an opportunity to sell to an outside customer the 20,000 units now committed to Deuce Division. The sale price would be $75 per unit during the current year. Deuce Division could purchase its requirements from an outside supplier at a price of $85 per unit.

Required:

(1) Assuming that Ace Division desires to maximize its gross profit, should it take on the new customer and discontinue its sales to Deuce Division? Support your answer by computing the increase or decrease in Ace Division's gross profit.

(2) Assume instead that Decker Corporation permits division managers to negotiate the transfer price. The managers agree on a tentative transfer price of $75 per unit, to be reduced based on an equal sharing of the additional gross profit to Ace Division resulting from the sale to Deuce of 20,000 motors at $75 per unit. What is the actual transfer price? (AICPA adapted)

E26-5 Transfer Pricing. The Blade Division of Dana Company produces hardened steel blades. One third of the Blade Division's output is sold to the Lawn Products Division of Dana; the remainder is sold to outside customers. The Blade Division's estimated sales and standard cost data for the year follow:

	Lawn Products	Outsiders
Sales	$ 15,000	$ 40,000
Variable cost	(10,000)	(20,000)
Fixed cost	(3,000)	(6,000)
Gross profit	$ 2,000	$ 14,000
Unit sales	10,000	20,000

The Lawn Products Division has an opportunity to purchase 10,000 identical quality blades from an outside supplier at a cost of $1.25 per unit on a continuing basis. Assume that the Blade Division cannot sell any additional products to outside customers, that the fixed costs cannot be reduced, and that no alternative use of facilities is available.

Required: Should Dana allow its Lawn Products Division to purchase the blades from the outside supplier? Support your answer by computing the increase or decrease in Dana Corporation operating costs. (AICPA adapted)

Problems

P26-1 Profit and Rate of Return on Capital Employed Using Various Proposals. Lauren Toy Company manufactures two specialty children's toys marketed under the trade names of Springy and Leapy. During the year, the costs, revenue, and capital employed by the company in the production of these two items were as follow:

	Springy	Leapy
Sales price per unit	$ 1.50	$ 1.95
Sales in units	280,000	150,000
Materials cost per unit	$ .20	$ .30
Labor cost per unit	.50	.75
Variable factory overhead per unit	.15	.20
Variable marketing cost per unit	.05	.10
Fixed factory overhead	100,000	30,000
Fixed marketing cost	30,000	15,000
Variable capital employed	10% of sales	20% of sales
Fixed capital employed	$148,000	$ 91,500

Fixed administrative and other nonallocable fixed costs amounted to $28,000, and nonallocable capital employed was $25,000.

Management, dissatisfied with the return on total capital employed, is considering a number of alternatives to improve this return.

The market for Springy appears to be underdeveloped, and the consensus is that with an increase of $9,500 in the fixed advertising cost sales can be increased to 325,000 units at the same price. An increase in the production of Springy will require use of some equipment previously utilized in the production of Leapy and a transfer of $10,000 of fixed capital and $5,000 of fixed factory overhead to the production of Springy.

For Leapy, it would mean limiting its production to 100,000 units, which could be marketed with the current sales effort at (a) an increase in price of $.15 per unit; (b) without a price increase and with a reduction in current fixed advertising cost of $9,000; or (c) with a $.05 per unit increase in price and a $7,500 reduction in the current fixed advertising cost.

Required:

(1) Compute the income before income tax and the return on capital employed for each product and in total for the year, to one tenth of 1%.

(2) Compute the income before income tax and the return on capital employed for each product and in total under each alternative, to one tenth of 1%.

P26-2 Product Pricing and Transfer Pricing. National Industries is a diversified corporation with separate and distinct operating divisions. Each division's performance is evaluated on the basis of total dollar profits and return on division investment.

The WindAir Division manufactures and sells air conditioner units. The coming year's budgeted income statement, based on a sales volume of 15,000 units, is as follows:

WindAir Division
Budgeted Income Statement
For 19A

	Per Unit	Total
Sales revenue	$400	$6,000,000
Manufacturing costs:		
Compressor	$ 70	$1,050,000
Other raw materials	37	555,000
Direct labor	30	450,000
Variable factory overhead	45	675,000
Fixed factory overhead	32	480,000
Total manufacturing cost	$214	$3,210,000
Gross profit	$186	$2,790,000
Commercial expenses:		
Variable marketing	$ 18	$ 270,000
Fixed marketing	19	285,000
Fixed administrative	38	570,000
Total commercial expense	$ 75	$1,125,000
Income before income tax	$111	$1,665,000

WindAir's division manager believes sales can be increased if the unit sales price is reduced. A market research study, conducted by an independent firm at the request of the manager, indicates that a 5% reduction in the sales price ($20) will increase sales volume 16%, or 2,400 units. WindAir has sufficient production capacity to manage this increased volume with no increase in fixed cost.

At the present time, WindAir uses a compressor in its units, which it purchases from an outside supplier at a cost of $70 each. The division manager of WindAir has approached the manager of the Compressor Division regarding the sale of compressor units to WindAir. The Compressor Division currently manufactures a unit that is similar to the unit used by WindAir and sells it exclusively to outside firms. Specifications for the WindAir compressor are slightly different. They would reduce the Compressor Division's raw materials cost by $1.50 per unit. In addition, the Compressor Division would not incur any variable marketing cost for the units sold to WindAir. The manager of WindAir wants all compressors it uses to come from one supplier and has offered to pay the Compressor Division $50 for each unit.

The Compressor Division has the capacity to produce 75,000 units. The coming year's budgeted income statement for the Compressor Division, shown below, is based on a sales volume of 64,000 units, without considering WindAir's proposal. It is as follows:

Compressor Division
Budgeted Income Statement
For 19A

	Per Unit	Total
Sales revenue	$100	$6,400,000
Manufacturing costs:		
Raw materials	$ 12	$ 768,000
Direct labor	8	512,000
Variable factory overhead	10	640,000
Fixed factory overhead	11	704,000
Total manufacturing cost	$ 41	$2,624,000
Gross profit	$ 59	$3,776,000
Commercial expenses:		
Variable marketing	$ 6	$ 384,000
Fixed marketing	4	256,000
Fixed administrative	7	448,000
Total commercial expense	$ 17	$1,088,000
Income before income tax	$ 42	$2,688,000

Required:

(1) Compute the estimated result if the WindAir Division reduces its sales price by 5%, even if it cannot acquire the compressors internally at $50 each.

(2) Compute the estimated effect on the Compressor Division, from its own viewpoint, if the 17,400 units are supplied to WindAir at $50 each.

(3) Determine if it is in the best interests of National Industries for the Compressor Division to supply the 17,400 units to Wind Air Division at $50 each.

(ICMA adapted)

P26-3 Transfer Pricing. Martin Corporation, a diversified company, recently implemented a decentralization policy under which divisional managers are expected to make their own operating decisions, including whether to do business with other divisions. The performances and year-end bonuses of divisional managers are measured by the return on capital employed of their divisions. Because most divisions operate at full capacity, it is company policy that all transfers between divisions are to be priced at 120% of standard manufacturing cost (to allow for a "normal" divisional profit margin). This transfer price is not negotiable.

The president of the company is currently faced with a dispute between the general managers of two divisions: the Consumer Products Division and the Engineering Division. The Consumer Products Division makes and sells several household articles, including a home appliance that, until recently, has been one of the company's steadiest sellers. Recently, this division has had marketing difficulties and has reduced its production of the appliance to 56,000 a year from its usual production at capacity. The unused capacity cannot be utilized for other products. The Engineering Division makes a wide variety of items, including a specialized part (Part TX), which is sold to the Consumer Products Division and to a few small outside companies. The latter buy a steady 12% of the Engineering Division's annual production capacity for the part.

The Consumer Products Division uses four of these parts in each home appliance unit and maintains no significant inventory of unused parts, but acquires them from the Engineering Division as needed to meet its production requirements. The parts are not available from any other source.

Because the Consumer Products Division recently has reduced its requirement for Part TX, the Engineering Division has been seeking new customers. A company has offered to buy 100,000 units of the part annually, at a price of $5 each, which is less than the $5.40 each paid by other small outside companies but more than the transfer price paid by the Consumer Products Division. The company making the offer is in a market unrelated to that of either the Consumer Products Division or the small outside companies.

The following data relate to Part TX and the home appliance involved in the dispute between the two managers:

	Part TX (Engineering Division)	Home Appliance (Consumer Products Division)
Annual production capacity	300,000 units	66,000 units
Unit sales price to outside customers	$ 5.40	$ 80.00
Standard manufacturing cost per unit (based on production at full capacity):		
Division's own costs:		
Variable	$ 2.00	$ 37.00
Fixed	1.75	13.00
Transfers from the Engineering Division		18.00
Standard manufacturing cost per unit	$ 3.75	$ 68.00

The manager of the Consumer Products Division has requested that the president instruct the manager of the Engineering Division to refuse the offer it has received, because (1) no other source for Part TX can be found, (2) the marketing problems with the home appliance are expected to be temporary, and (3) the Engineering Division cannot expand its production capacity for Part TX.

Required:

(1) Determine what action the manager of the Engineering Division should take in response to the offer, in order to maximize the results of that division. Include calculations of the offer's effect on the Engineering Division.
(2) Determine the overall effect on the company, under existing circumstances, if the Engineering Division's manager accepts the offer.
(3) Identify the factors that the president should consider in deciding whether to intervene in the dispute.
(4) Revise the transfer pricing policy to assist the divisional managers in making optimal decisions for the company. (CICA adapted)

P26-4 Transfer Pricing. Portco Products is a multidivision furniture manufacturer. The divisions are autonomous segments; each division is responsible for its own sales, costs of operations, working capital management, and equipment acquisition. Each division serves a different market in the furniture industry. Because the markets and products of the divisions are so different, there have never been any transfers between divisions.

The Commercial Division manufactures equipment and furniture that is purchased by the restaurant industry. The division plans to introduce a new line of counter and chair units that feature a cushioned seat for the counter chairs. J. Kline, the division manager, has discussed the manufacturing of the cushioned seat with R. Fiegel of the Office Division. They both believe a cushioned seat currently made by the Office Division for use on its deluxe office stool could be modified for use on the new counter chair. Consequently, Kline has asked Fiegel for a price for 100 unit lots of the cushioned seat. The following conversation took place about the price to be charged for the cushioned seats.

Fiegel: We can make the necessary modifications to the cushioned seat easily. The raw materials used in your seat are slightly different and should cost about 10% more than those used in our deluxe office stool. However, the labor time should be the same, because the seat fabrication operation basically is the same. I would price the seat at our regular rate—full cost plus 30% markup.

Kline: That's higher that I expected. I was thinking that a good price would be your variable manufacturing costs. After all, your capacity costs will be incurred regardless of this job.

Fiegel: I'm currently operating at capacity. By making the cushion seats for you, I'll have to cut my production of deluxe office stools. Of course, I can increase my production of economy office stools. The labor time freed by not having to fabricate the frame or assemble the deluxe stool can be shifted to the frame fabrication and assembly of the economy office stool. Fortunately, I can switch my labor force between these two models of stools without any loss of efficiency. As you know, overtime is not a feasible alternative in our company. I'd like to sell it to you at variable cost, but I have excess demand for both products. I don't mind changing my product mix to the economy model if I get a good return on the seats I make for you. My standard costs for the two stools and a schedule of my factory overhead are included in these statements (statements follow).

Office Division
Standard Costs and Prices

	Deluxe Office Stool	Economy Office Stool
Raw materials:		
Framing	$ 8.15	$ 9.76
Cushioned seat:		
Padding	2.40	
Vinyl	4.00	
Molded seat (purchased)		6.00
Direct labor:		
Frame fabrication (.5 × $7.50/DLH)	3.75	3.75
Cushion fabrication (.5 × $7.50/DLH)	3.75	
Assembly:		
(.5 × $7.50/DLH)	3.75	
(.3 × $7.50/DLH)		2.25
Factory overhead:		
(1.5 DLH × $12.80/DLH)	19.20	
(.8 DLH × $12.80/DLH)		10.24
Total standard cost per unit	$45.00	$32.00
Sales price per unit (30% markup)	$58.50	$41.60

Office Division
Factory Overhead Budget

Overhead Item	Nature of Item	Amount
Supplies	Variable—at current market prices	$ 420,000
Indirect labor	Variable	375,000
Supervision	Fixed	250,000
Power	Variable with activity—rate fixed	180,000
Heat and light	Fixed—light is fixed regardless of production while heat and air conditioning varies with fuel charges	140,000
Property taxes and insurance	Fixed—rate change is unrelated to production activity	200,000
Depreciation	Fixed	1,700,000
Employee benefits	20% of supervision, direct and indirect labor	575,000
	Total factory overhead	$3,840,000
	Capacity in DLH	300,000
	Factory overhead rate per DLH	$ 12.80

Kline: I guess I see your point, but I don't want to price myself out of the market. Maybe we should talk to corporate management to see if they can give us any guidance.

Required:

(1) Kline and Fiegel did ask Portco corporate management for guidance on an appropriate transfer price. Corporate management suggested they consider using a transfer price based on variable manufacturing cost plus opportunity cost. Calculate a transfer price for the cushioned seat based on variable manufacturing cost plus opportunity cost.

(2) Which alternative transfer price system, full cost, variable manufacturing cost, or variable manufacturing cost plus opportunity cost, is better as the underlying concept for Portco Products' intracompany transfer price policy? Explain your answer. (ICMA adapted)

P26-5 Transfer Pricing. Robert Products Inc. consists of three decentralized divisions, Bayside Division, Cole Division, and Diamond Division. The president of Robert Products has given the managers of the three divisions the authority to decide whether or not to sell outside the company, or among themselves at a transfer price determined by the division managers. Market conditions are such that sales made internally or externally do not affect market or transfer prices. Intermediate markets are available for Bayside, Cole, and Diamond to purchase all their manufacturing inputs and sell all their products. Each division manager attempts to maximize his or her contribution margin at the current level of operating assets for the division.

The manager of the Cole Division is currently considering the two alternative orders that follow.

(a) The Diamond Division is in need of 3,000 units of a motor that can be supplied by the Cole Division. To manufacture these motors, Cole must purchase components from the Bayside Division at a transfer price of \$600 per unit; Bayside's variable cost for these components is \$300 per unit. Cole Division will further process these components at a variable cost of \$500 per unit. If the Diamond Division cannot obtain the motors from Cole Division, it will purchase the motors from London Company, which has offered to supply the same motors to Diamond Division at a price of \$1,500 per unit. London Company would also purchase 3,000 components from Bayside Division at a price of \$400 for each of these motors; Bayside's variable cost for these components is \$200 per unit.

(b) The Wales Company wants to place an order with the Cole Division for 3,500 similar motors at a price of \$1,250 per unit. Cole Division would again purchase components from the Bayside Division at a transfer price of \$500 per unit; Bayside's variable cost for these components is \$250 per unit. Cole Division would further process these components at a variable cost of \$400 per unit.

The Cole Division's plant capacity is limited, and the company can accept the Wales contract or the Diamond Division order, but not both. The president of Robert Products and the manager of the Cole Division agree that it would not be beneficial in the short or long run to increase capacity.

Required:

(1) Assuming that the manager of the Cole Division wants to maximize the short-run contribution margin, determine whether the Cole Division should sell motors to the Diamond Division at the prevailing market price, or accept the Wales Company contract. Support your answer with appropriate calculations.

(2) Disregard your answer to requirement 1 and assume that the Cole Division decides to accept the Wales Company contract. Determine if this decision is in the best interest of Robert Products Inc. Support your answer with appropriate calculations. (ICMA adapted)

Cases

C26-1 Rate of Return on Capital Employed. Clarkson Company is a large, multidivision firm with several plants in each division. Rate of return on capital employed is used to measure the performance of divisions and plants. The asset base for a division consists of all assets assigned to the division, including its working capital, and an allocated share of corporate assets. The asset base for each plant includes the assets assigned to the plant plus an allocated portion of the division and corporate assets. Only limited control over plant assets is exercised at the plant level.

The plant managers exercise control only over the cost portion of the plant profit budget because the divisions are responsible for sales. Even with respect to costs, plant-level control is limited because of cost decisions made at higher levels, because the division profit budgets include allocated corporate costs, and because plant profit budgets include allocated division and corporate costs.

Recommendations for promotions and salary increases for the executives of the divisions and plants are influenced by how well the actual rate of return on capital employed compares with the budgeted rate.

The Dexter Plant is a major plant in the Huron Division of Clarkson. During 19A, the property adjacent to the Dexter Plant was purchased by Clarkson. This expenditure was not included in the 19A capital expenditure budget. Corporate management decided to divert funds from a project at another plant because the property appeared to be a better long-term investment. This expenditure was added to the Dexter Plant's capital employed.

Also, during 19A, Clarkson Company experienced depressed sales. In an attempt to achieve budgeted profit, corporate management announced in August that all plants were to cut their annual expenses by 6%. In order to accomplish this expense reduction, the Dexter Plant manager reduced preventive maintenance and postponed needed major repairs. Employees who quit were not replaced unless absolutely necessary. Employee training was postponed whenever possible. The raw materials, supplies, and finished goods inventory were reduced below normal levels.

Required:

(1) Is the Clarkson Company's use of rate of return on capital employed to evaluate the performance of the Dexter Plant appropriate? Explain.

(2) Analyze and explain the Dexter Plant Manager's behavior during 19A. (ICMA adapted)

C26-2 Rate of Return on Capital Employed as Measure of Division Performance. Torres Corporation is a large, multidivision manufacturing company. Each division is viewed as an investment center and has virtually complete autonomy for product development, marketing, and production.

Performance of division managers is evaluated periodically by senior corporate management. Divisional rate of return on capital employed is the sole criterion used in performance evaluation under current corporate policy. Corporate management believes that rate of return on capital employed is an adequate measure because it incorporates quantitative information from the divisional income statement and balance sheet in the analysis.

Some division managers complain that a single criterion for performance evaluation is insufficient and ineffective. These managers have compiled a list of criteria that they believe should be used in evaluating division managers' performance. The criteria include profitability, market position, productivity, product leadership, personnel development, employee attitudes, public responsibility, and balance between short-range and long-range goals.

Required:

(1) Discuss the shortcomings or possible inconsistencies of using rate of return on capital employed as the sole criterion to evaluate divisional management performance.

(2) Discuss the advantages of using multiple performance measures versus a single performance measure in the evaluation of divisional management performance.

(3) Describe the problems or disadvantages that can be associated with the implementation of a system of multiple performance measures as suggested to Torres Corporation by its division managers. (ICMA adapted)

C26-3 Rate of Return on Capital Employed Versus Residual Income. Lawton Industries has manufactured prefabricated houses for over 20 years. The houses are constructed in sections to be assembled on customers' lots.

Lawton expanded into the precut housing market in 19A when it acquired Presser Company, one of its suppliers. In this market, various types of lumber are precut into the appropriate lengths, banded into packages, and shipped to customers' lots for assembly. Lawton decided to maintain Presser's separate identity and, thus, established the Presser Division as a profit center of Lawton.

Lawton uses rate of return on capital employed as a performance measure. All investments in operating assets are expected to earn a minimum return of 15% before income tax. Presser's return has ranged from 19.3% to 22.1% since it was acquired in 19A. Presser had an investment opportunity in 19F that had an estimated return on assets of 16%. Presser's management decided against the investment because it believed the investment would decrease the division's overall rate of return on capital employed.

The 19F operating statement for Presser Division is presented below. The division's operating assets employed were $12,600,000 at the end of 19F, a 5% increase over the 19E year-end balance.

Presser Division
Lawton Industries
Operating Statement
For the Year Ended December 31, 19F
(in thousands)

Sales revenue		$24,000
Cost of goods sold		15,800
Gross profit		$ 8,200
Less commercial expenses:		
Administrative	$2,140	
Marketing	3,600	5,740
Income from operations before income tax		$ 2,460

Required:

(1) Calculate the following performance measures for 19F for the Presser Division of Lawton Industries:
   (a) Rate of return on capital employed
   (b) Residual income calculated on the basis of the average operating assets employed

(2) Would the management of Presser Division have been more likely to accept the investment opportunity it had in 19F if residual income were used as a performance measure instead of rate of return on capital employed? Explain.

(3) The Presser Division is a separate profit center within Lawton Industries. Identify the items Presser must control if it is to be evaluated fairly by either the rate of return on capital employed or residual income performance measures. (ICMA adapted)

C26-4 Divisional Performance Measures. Peregrine Enterprises is a large, diversified corporation with eight operating divisions. Each division is organized as a profit center. Each division manager's remuneration is augmented by a bonus based on the extent to which the divisional rate of return on capital employed exceeds 20% before taxes, with a ceiling set at 50% of the base salary. J. Black, president of Peregrine, is disturbed by the recent behavior of some of the company's division managers. The Marine Division operates salvage tugs very successfully, but it has come to Black's attention that the division manager recently turned down the opportunity to acquire a nuclear powered tug at a low price from an insolvent competitor. Similarly, the Airline Division manager has steadfastly refused to replace and update the division's fleet of aircraft despite increasing maintenance costs and pressure from federal safety officials. As the last straw, the Plastics Division manager recently ignored an opportunity to bid on a very attractive contract although the plant was operating well below capacity during December.

Black did not want to become involved in the internal decision making of the divisions, but in this instance, it appeared necessary. At a July planning meeting, Black emphasized to the division managers the need for Peregrine to increase its asset base and grow. Such capital additions served as a hedge against continuous inflation. Accordingly, Black instructed the corporate accountant to put together some of the relevant facts on these rejected investments and respective divisional operating performance. The data assembled follow:

Peregrine Enterprises
Division Operating Performance
For Year Ended December 31, 19A
(in thousands)

	Marine	Airline	Plastics
Sales revenue	$115,000	$ 35,000	$ 89,000
Cost of goods sold	105,300	32,370	78,880
Gross profit	$ 9,700	$ 2,630	$ 10,120
Less commercial expenses:			
Division selling and administration	$ 1,150	$ 395	$ 190
Corporate headquarters allocation	3,450	1,185	570
Total commercial expense	$ 4,600	$ 1,580	$ 760
Divisional profit (before income tax)	$ 5,100	$ 1,050	$ 9,360
Division current assets	$ 1,430	$ 2,748	$ 6,559
Division fixed assets	30,000	20,000	45,000
Less accumulated depreciation	(12,000)	(18,000)	(16,500)
Corporate headquarters allocation	970	252	941
Divisional capital employed	$ 20,400	$ 5,000	$ 36,000
Divisional return on capital employed	25%	21%	26%
Divisional managers' base salaries	$ 60,000	$ 50,000	$ 70,000
Bonus (10% of base salary for each 1% of return in excess of 20%, limited to 50% of base salary)	30,000	5,000	35,000
Total remuneration paid to division managers	$ 90,000	$ 55,000	$105,000

Financial Data on Recent Investments or Contracts
Turned Down by Divisions
(in thousands)

	Marine	Airline	Plastics
Capital investments:			
Nuclear powered tug	$10,000		
Fleet replacement		$25,000	
Incremental annual revenue	$10,500	$ 4,500	$10,000
Incremental operating cost	7,680	320	8,868
Incremental gross profit	$ 2,820	$ 4,180	$ 1,132
Less incremental commercial expenses:			
Division marketing and administration	$ 105	$ 45	$ 100
Corporate headquarters allocation	315	135	300
Total	$ 420	$ 180	$ 400
Incremental divisional profit	$ 2,400	$ 4,000	$ 732
Return on capital investment	24%	16%	N/A

Required:

(1) Make adjustments that improve the usefulness of the reported operating figures. Use your adjusted figures to recalculate the rate of return on capital employed. Also, calculate residual income for all three divisions.

(2) Evaluate the operating performance of each of the three divisions and explain the division managers' decisions to reject the investment and contract opportunities.

(3) Discuss whether or not the Airline Division should be sold. Support your conclusion with both quantitative and qualitative analysis.

(4) Discuss whether or not any changes should be made in the management bonus scheme.

(5) Discuss whether or not any changes should be made in the way the divisional performance measures are computed, that is, the items included in the measures.

CGA-Canada (adapted). Reprint with permission.

C26-5 Multiple Performance Measures. The Star Paper Division of Royal Industries is located outside Los Angeles. A major expansion of the division's only plant was completed in April of 19A. The expansion consisted of an addition to the existing building, additions to the production-line machinery, and the replacement of obsolete and fully depreciated equipment that was no longer efficient or cost effective.

On May 1, 19A, G. Harris became manager of Star Paper. Harris had a meeting with M. Fortner, vice-president of operations for Royal Industries, who explained to Harris that the company measured the performance of divisions and division managers on the basis of return on capital employed. When Harris asked if other measures were used in conjunction with return on capital employed, Fortner replied, "Royal Industries' top management prefers to use a single performance measure. There is no conflict when there is only one measure. Star Paper should do well this year now that it has expanded and replaced all its old equipment. You should have no problem exceeding the division's historical rate. I'll check with you at the end of each quarter to see how you are doing."

Fortner called Harris after the first quarter results were completed because Star Paper's return on capital employed was considerably below the historical rate for the division. Harris told Fortner that return on capital employed was not a valid measure for Star Paper. Fortner indicated that this opinion would be passed on to corporate headquarters and any feedback would be passed back down to Harris. However, there was no further discussion of the use of return on capital employed at the end of the second and third quarters. Now that the year has ended, Harris has received the following memorandum:

To: G. Harris, Star Paper Division
From: M. Fortner, Royal Industries
Subject: Divisional Performance

The operating results for the fourth quarter and for our fiscal year ended on April 30 are now complete. Your fourth quarter return on capital employed was only 9 percent, resulting in a return for the year of slightly under 11 percent. I recall discussing your low return after the first quarter and reminding you after the second and third quarters that this level of return is not considered adequate for the Star Paper Division.

The return on capital employed at Star Paper has ranged from 15 to 18 percent for the past five years. An 11 percent return may be acceptable at some of Royal Industries' other divisions, but not at a proven winner like Star Paper, especially in light of your recently improved facility. Please arrange to meet with me in the near future to discuss ways to restore Star Paper's return on capital employed to its former level.

Harris is looking forward to the meeting with Fortner to pursue the discussion about the appropriateness of return on capital employed as a performance measure for Star Paper. While the return on capital employed for Star Paper is below historical levels, the division's profits for the year are higher than at any previous time. Harris is going to recommend that return on capital employed be replaced with multiple criteria for evaluating performance, namely, dollar profit, receivable turnover, and inventory turnover.

Required:

(1) Identify general criteria that should be used in selecting performance measures to evaluate divisional managers.

(2) Describe the probable cause of the decline in the Star Paper Division's return on capital employed during the fiscal year ended April 30, 19B.

(3) On the basis of the relationship between M. Fortner and G. Harris, as well as the memorandum from Fortner, discuss apparent weaknesses in the performance evaluation process at Royal Industries.

(4) Discuss whether the multiple performance evaluation criteria suggested by G. Harris are appropriate for the evaluation of the Star Paper Division.

(ICMA adapted)

C26-6 Managerial Incentive Compensation Plans. Renslen Inc., a truck manufacturing conglomerate, has recently purchased two divisions, Meyers Service Company and Wellington Products Inc. Meyers Service provides maintenance service on large truck cabs for 18-wheel trucks, and Wellington Products manufactures air brakes for 18-wheel trucks.

The employees at Meyers Service take pride in their work, because Meyers Service proclaims to offer the best maintenance service in the trucking industry. The managers of Meyers Service have received additional compensation from a 10% bonus pool based on income before income tax and bonus. Renslen plans to continue to compensate Meyers Service management on this basis because it is the same incentive compensation plan used for all other Renslen divisions.

Wellington Products offers a high-quality product to the trucking industry and is the premium choice even when compared to foreign competition. The management team at Wellington Products strives for zero defects and minimal scrap costs. Current scrap levels are at 2%. The incentive compensation plan for Wellington Products management has been a 1% bonus based on gross profit margin. Renslen plans to continue to compensate Wellington Products management on this basis.

Condensed income statements for both divisions for the fiscal year ended May 31, 19B, follow:

Renslen Inc.
Divisional Income Statements
For the Year Ended May 31, 19B

	Meyers Service	Wellington Products
Revenues	$4,000,000	$10,000,000
Less costs and expenses:		
Cost of goods sold	$ 75,000	$ 4,950,000
Wages and salaries*	2,200,000	2,150,000
Fixed selling expenses	1,000,000	2,500,000
Interest expense	30,000	65,000
Other operating expenses	278,000	134,000
Total costs and expenses	$3,583,000	$ 9,799,000
Income before income tax and bonuses	$ 417,000	$ 201,000

* Each division has $1,000,000 of management salary expense that is eligible for the bonus pool.

Renslen has invited the management team from each of its divisions to an off-site management workshop in July, at which the bonus checks will be presented. Renslen top management is concerned that the different bonus plans at the two divisions may cause some heated discussion.

Required:

(1) Determine the 19B bonus pool available for the management team at each division.

(2) For each division, identify at least two advantages and at least two disadvantages to Renslen Inc. of the bonus pool incentive compensation plan.

(3) Having two different types of incentive compensation plans for two operating divisions in the same corporation can create problems.

(a) Discuss the behavioral problems that can arise from the use of different incentive compensation plans at the two divisions.

(b) Present arguments that Renslen Inc. can give to the management of each division that justify having two different incentive compensation plans. (ICMA adapted)

C26-7 Transfer Pricing. Defco Division of Gunnco Corporation requests of Omar Division a supply of Electrical Fitting 1726, which is not available from any other source. Omar Division, which is operating at capacity, sells this part to its regular customers for $7.50 each. Defco, operating at 50% capacity, is willing to pay $5 each for this fitting. Defco needs the fitting for a brake unit that it plans to manufacture on essentially a cost basis for an aircraft manufacturer.

Omar Division produces Electrical Fitting 1726 at a variable cost of $4.25. The cost (and sales price) of the brake unit to be built by the Defco Division is as follows:

Purchased parts (outside vendors)	$22.50
Omar Electrical Fitting 1726	5.00
Other variable costs	14.00
Fixed factory overhead and administrative expenses	8.00
Total	$49.50

Defco believes that the price concession is necessary to obtain the job from the aircraft manufacturer. Gunnco uses return on investment and dollar profits in measuring division and division manager performance.

Required:

(1) Recommend whether or not Omar Division should supply Electrical Fitting 1726 to Defco Division. (Ignore income tax.)

(2) Discuss whether or not it would be a short-run economic advantage to Gunnco Corporation for Omar Division to supply the Defco Division with Electrical Fitting 1726 at $5 each. (Ignore income tax.)

(3) Discuss the organizational and managerial behavior difficulties inherent in this situation and recommend to Gunnco's president how the problem should be handled. (ICMA adapted)

C26-8 Transfer Pricing. Lorax Electric Company manufactures a large variety of systems and individual components for the electronics industry. The firm is organized into several divisions, and division managers are given authority to make virtually all operating decisions. Management control over divisional operations is maintained by a system of divisional profit and return on investment measures that are reviewed regularly by executive management. The executive management of Lorax has been quite pleased with the effectiveness of the system it has been using, and believes the system is responsible for the company's improved profitability over the last few years.

The Devices Division manufactures solid-state devices and is operating at capacity. The Systems Division has asked the Devices Division to supply a large quantity of integrated circuit IC378. The Devices Division currently sells this component to its regular customers at $40 per hundred.

The Systems Division, which is operating at about 60% of capacity, wants this particular component for a digital clock system. It has an opportunity to supply large quantities of these digital clock systems to Centonic Electric, a major producer of clock radios and popular electronic home entertainment equipment. This opportunity represents the first time any Lorax division has been successful at tapping the potentially lucrative Centonic Electric market. Centonic Electric has offered to pay $7.50 per clock system.

The Systems Division prepared an analysis of the probable costs needed to produce the clock systems. The amount that could be paid to the Devices Division for the integrated circuits, five of which are required for each clock system, was determined by working backward from the sales price. The cost estimates employed by the division reflected the highest per unit cost the Systems Division could incur for each cost component and still leave a sufficient margin so that the division's income statement could show reasonable improvement. The cost estimates are summarized below as follow:

Proposed sales price		$7.50
Costs excluding required integrated circuits IC378:		
Components purchased from outside suppliers	$2.75	
Circuit-board etching—labor and variable factory overhead	.40	
Assembly, testing, packaging—labor and variable factory overhead	1.35	
Fixed factory overhead allocations	1.50	
Profit margin	.50	6.50
Amount that can be paid for integrated circuit IC378 (5 at $20 per hundred)		$1.00

As a result of this analysis, the Systems Division offered the Devices Division a price of $20 per hundred for the integrated circuit. This bid was refused because the manager of the Devices Division felt that the Systems Division should at least meet the price of $40 per hundred that regular customers pay. When the Systems Division found it could not obtain a comparable integrated circuit from outside vendors, the situation was brought to an arbitration committee that had been set up to review such problems.

The arbitration committee prepared an analysis showing that $.15 would cover the variable costs of producing the integrated circuit; $.28 would cover the full cost, including fixed factory overhead; and $.35 would provide a gross margin equal to the average gross margin on all of the products sold by the Devices Division. The manager of the Systems Division reacted by stating, "They could sell us that integrated circuit for $.20 and still earn a positive contribution toward profit. In fact, they should be required to sell at their variable cost ($.15) and not be allowed to take advantage of us."

The manager of Devices countered by arguing that, "It doesn't make sense to sell to the Systems Division at $20 per hundred when we can get $40 per hundred outside on all we can produce. In fact, Systems could pay us up to almost $60 per hundred, and they would still have a positive contribution to profit."

The committee recommended that the price be set at $.35 per unit ($35 per hundred) so that Devices could earn a "fair" gross margin. When this price was rejected by both division managers, the problem was brought to the attention of the vice-president of operations.

Required:

(1) What is the immediate economic effect on Lorax Electric Company as a whole if the Devices Division is required to supply IC378 to the Systems Division at $.35 per unit—the price recommended by the arbitration committee? Explain.

(2) Discuss the advisability of intervention by executive management as a solution to transfer pricing disputes between division managers, such as the one experienced by Lorax Electric Company.

(3) Suppose Lorax adopts a policy requiring that the price to be paid in all internal transfers be equal to the variable cost per unit of the selling division for that product and that the supplying division must sell if the buying division decides to buy the item. Discuss the consequences of adopting such a policy as a way of avoiding the need for the arbitration committee or for intervention by the vice-president.

(ICMA adapted)

Glossary

100-percent bonus plan Labor wage incentive plan that is a variation of the straight piecework plan based on time per unit of output.

A posteriori method An approach to setting profit objectives in which planning takes precedence over the determination of profit objectives, and objectives emerge as the product of the planning itself.

A priori method An approach to setting profit objectives in which management first specifies a given rate of return and then seeks to realize that rate in the long run.

ABC Activity-based costing.

ABC Plan (also called **selective control**) A materials control method which evaluates the cost significance of each item as high-value (**A** items), middle-value (**B** items), or low-value (**C** items). Not to be confused with activity-based costing.

Absorption costing (also called **conventional costing** or **full costing**) Matching some or all of the fixed manufacturing costs with units of product and then expensing these costs as part of the income statement's cost of goods sold figure when the related units are sold.

Accelerated cost recovery system (ACRS) A system for recovering the costs of capital expenditures which replaces the useful-life concept with a shorter recovery period and accelerates depreciation rates.

Accountability Reporting results to higher authority for the purpose of measuring the extent to which objectives are reached.

Accounting rate of return method (also called the **average annual return on investment method**) A technique for evaluating an investment proposal by comparing the estimated accounting rate of return with a target rate of return.

Activity In the PERT system, the time and resources necessary to move from one event to another.

Activity driver In ABC, a base used to allocate the cost of an activity to products, customers, or other final cost objects.

Activity-based costing (or **ABC**) A system in which multiple overhead cost pools are allocated using bases that include one or more nonvolume-related factors. Not to be confused with selective control, which is sometimes called ABC.

Activity based management (**ABM**) Detailed analysis of activities and the expenses created by those activities, used as a basis for controlling and improving efficiency, or the use of information obtained from activity-based costing to make improvements in a firm.

Actual cost system (also called **historical cost system**) A method of collecting cost information as cost is incurred. Presentation of results is delayed until the end of the accounting period.

Actual overhead Total indirect manufacturing cost.

Administrative expenses budget A list of the estimated costs of administrative functions.

Administrative expenses Expenses incurred in directing and controlling the organization.

Algebraic method (also called **simultaneous method**) A method of distributing service department costs which considers completely all interrelationships among all service departments.

Allowable budget (also called **budget allowance**) A budget adjusted to reflect the actual level of activity experienced during the reporting period.

Applied overhead The amount of overhead charged to products manufactured during the period.

Appraisal costs Costs incurred to detect product failure.

Arbitrary transfer pricing A method of pricing intracompany transfers in which the price is set by central management.

Authority The power to direct others to perform or not perform activities.

Autocorrelation (also called **serial correlation**) A pattern in which the observations around the regression line appear to be correlated with one another.

Average annual return on investment method Same as **accounting rate of return method**.

Average cost method An inventory costing method which assumes that the cost of each issue of materials is a mix of the costs of all shipments that are in stock at the time the issue occurs.

Average unit cost method A method of allocating joint production cost to joint products by apportioning the total production cost among the various products on the basis of an average unit cost.

Avoidable cost An expenditure that can be avoided if an activity is abandoned or discontinued.

Backflush costing (also called **backflushing** or **backflush accounting**) A method of cost accumulation which works backward through the available accounting information after production is completed. This is useful in settings in which processing speeds are extremely fast.

Balance sheet A financial statement showing financial position (assets, liabilities, and owners equity) at the end of the period. The balance sheet complements the income statement.

Bar codes Symbols that can be processed electronically to identify numbers, letters, or special characters.

Base (also called **overhead allocation base** or **overhead rate base**) The factor included as the denominator when computing an overhead rate, or, an activity to which costs are attributed for overhead accounting purposes.

Base rate (also called **job rate**) The basic pay for work performed.

Basic standard A yardstick against which expected and actual performances are compared.

Batch-level costs Costs caused by the number of batches produced and sold (example: setup costs).

Batch-level driver In ABC, a measure of an activity that varies with the number of batches produced (example: setup hours).

Bill of materials The list of materials requirements for each step in the production process.

Billing rate (also called **sold-hour rate**, **charging rate**, or **transfer rate**) A device for distributing overhead costs, based on the idea that departments purchase internal services the same way they purchase materials, supplies, and labor.

Blanket purchase orders Agreements with vendors stating the total quantities expected to be needed over a period of three or six months.

Break-even analysis A method of determining the level of sales and mix of products required to just recover all costs incurred during the period.

Break-even point The point at which cost and revenue are equal; at this point there is neither a profit nor a loss.

Budget The quantified, written expression of management's plans.

Budget allowance (also called **allowable budget**) A budget adjusted to reflect the actual level of activity experienced during the reporting period.

Budget committee The group which directs the budgeting process. Usually composed of the sales manager, the production manager, the chief engineer, the treasurer, and the controllers.

Budgeted balance sheet A balance sheet for the end of the budget period, incorporating changes in such factors as assets, liabilities, and stockholders' equity resulting from the budgets submitted by the various departments, functions, or segments.

Budgeted cost of goods manufactured and sold statement A list of manufacturing costs including estimates for direct materials, direct labor, and applied factory overhead required for the budget period.

Budgeted cost of materials required for production A manufacturing budget which specifies the quantity and cost of materials required to meet the budget production requirements.

Budgeted income statement A summary of sales, manufacturing, and expense budgets which projects net income.

By-product A product of relatively small total value that is produced simultaneously with a product of greater total value.

Cafeteria plan An employee benefit plan under which each employee can apply a specified dollar amount to part or all of the cost of various benefits.

Capacity costs Fixed costs that must be incurred in order to manufacture *and/or* market a given quantity of products.

Capital budgeting The process of planning, evaluating, and controlling capital expenditures.

Capital expenditure A cost which is intended to benefit future periods and is reported as an asset.

Capital-employed turnover rate Sales divided by capital employed.

Cash budget A detailed estimate of anticipated cash receipts and disbursements for a specific period.

Cell (also called **work cell**) An assemblage of workers and machines responsible for the entire production of one product or part, or a family of very similar ones.

Certified Management Accountant (CMA) The professional certification of a person engaged in cost accounting or other managerial accounting functions within an organization.

Charging rate (also called **billing rate**, **sold-hour**, or **transfer rate**) A device for distributing overhead costs, based on the idea that departments purchase internal services the same way they purchase materials, supplies, and labor.

Chart of accounts A list of all accounts used in an accounting system, designed to supply maximum information with a minimum of supplementary analysis.

Clock card A card which shows the time a worker started and stopped work each day or shift of the payroll period.

Coefficient of correlation A measure of the extent to which two variables are related linearly.

Coefficient of determination The square of the coefficient of correlation. It is the percentage of variance in the dependent variable explained by the independent variable.

Coefficient of variation The ratio of the standard deviation of a probability distribution to its expected value.

Commercial expenses Marketing expenses and administrative expenses.

Committed fixed costs Expenditures that require a series of payments over a long-term period of time.

Common costs Nontraceable costs incurred for the benefit of more than one functional classification or business unit.

Computer integrated manufacturing A fully automated, computer generated manufacturing system.

Conditional probabilities Probabilities of events which are in some way related to or conditional upon the occurrence of other events.

Conditional value The value of an event if it occurs (i.e., the profit, contribution margin, or cost) that will occur if the event occurs.

Constraints Resource limitations in linear programming problems.

Continuous quality improvement An ongoing, companywide effort to improve efficiency and quality, characterized by sensitivity to the customer's needs and dynamic, flexible interaction with changing conditions.

Contribution margin ratio (C/M) The portion of each sales dollar available to recover fixed costs and provide a profit.

Contribution margin (also called **marginal income**) The difference between sales revenue and variable costs.

Control Management's systematic effort to achieve objectives by comparing performance to plans and acting to correct differences between the two.

Controllable variance The difference between the actual factory overhead incurred and the budget allowance based on the standard amount of the allocation base allowed for actual production.

Controller The executive manager responsible for the accounting function.

Controlling account A general ledger account that summarizes financial data contained in subsidiary records.

Conventional costing (also called **absorption costing** or **full costing**) Matching some or all of the fixed manufacturing costs with units of product and then expensing these costs as part of the income statement's cost of goods sold figure when the related units are sold.

Conversion cost Direct labor cost plus factory overhead.

Correlation A measure of the covariation between two variables—the independent variable and the dependent variable.

Cost Accounting Standards Board (CASB) This board, established by congress in 1970, sets cost accounting standards for domestic companies that are awarded large federal contracts or subcontracts.

Cost accounting Calculation of costs for the purpose of planning and controlling activities, improving quality and efficiency, and making decisions. Also refers to management accounting.

Cost analysis budget A departmental flexible budget which includes all expenses and allocates budgeted expenses of service departments to operating departments at corresponding capacity levels. Its purpose is to discover the departmental differential costs.

Cost department This department, under the controller's direction, gathers and communicates information about a company's activities.

Cost object Any item or activity for which costs are accumulated and measured.

Cost of capital The expected return that investors demand for a given level of risk.

Cost of production report A process cost report presenting the amount of costs accumulated and assigned to production during a month.

Cost pools Categories into which overhead is divided for the purpose of calculating multiple overhead rates.

Cost price variance Changes in elements of cost.

Cost sheet (also called **job order cost sheet**) A list, on paper or in electronic form, of details about the cost of manufacturing a specific job.

Cost-volume variance Changes in cost caused by changes in the quantity of products.

Cost-based transfer pricing A method of pricing intracompany transfers based on cost (actual or standard cost, based on direct or absorption costing.)

Cost-plus transfer pricing A method of pricing intracompany transfers which includes the cost to manufacture plus a normal profit markup.

Cost-volume-profit analysis A method of determining the sales volume and mix of products necessary to achieve a desired level of profit with available resources.

CPM Critical path method.

Crash time In PERT/cost, the time saved in completing an activity that results from the incurrence of additional cost.

Critical path method (CPM) (also called **program evaluation and review technique** or **PERT**) A network analysis method for planning, measuring progress to schedule, evaluating changes to schedule, forecasting future progress, and predicting and controlling costs.

Critical path In the PERT system, the longest path through the network.

Current standards Performance guidelines for expected results, normal results, or ideal maximum results (see **expected actual standard**, **normal standard**, and **theoretical standard**).

Cycle review method (also called **order cycling method**) A materials control method which periodically examines the status of quantities on hand for each item or class of materials.

Daily time report A report which lists all jobs worked on by an employee during one day.

Data processing system The procedures, forms, and equipment used for data processing.

Data processing Collecting, classifying, analyzing, and reporting data.

Decentralization A management philosophy that attempts to make each division of the business as autonomous as practical.

Decision package In zero-base budgeting, a report for each activity or operation under a manager's control. The package includes analysis of cost, purpose, alternative courses of action, measures of performance, consequences of not performing the activity, and benefits.

Decision tree A graphic representation of the decision points, the alternative actions available to the decision maker, the possible outcomes from each decision alternative along with their probabilities, and the expected values of each event.

Deferred compensation plan A plan under which an employer agrees to pay benefits to an employee more than one year in the future.

Departmentalization Dividing a plant into functional segments called departments.

Differential cost pricing A pricing method which uses the differential cost as a basis for pricing.

Differential cost study An analysis undertaken to determine the desirability of a proposed project or activity that does not extend beyond one year.

Differential cost (also called **marginal cost** or **incremental cost**) The cost that must be incurred to complete a proposed project or to extend an activity already undertaken.

Direct costing (also called **variable costing**) A costing method in which costs allocated to units of production include only the variable manufacturing cost. Fixed overhead is expensed.

Direct departmental cost A cost which is traceable to the department in which it originates.

Direct expenses Expenses that can be traced directly to a function or department.

Direct labor Labor that converts direct materials into the finished product and can be assigned feasibly to a specific product.

Direct labor budget A manufacturing budget which estimates the labor costs required to meet the production budget.

Direct materials Materials that form an integral part of the finished product and that are included explicitly in calculating the cost of the product.

Direct materials budget A manufacturing budget which specifies the quantity and cost of materials required to meet the production budget.

Direct method A method of distributing service department costs by allocating costs only to producing departments.

Discretionary fixed costs (also called **programmed fixed costs**) Expenditures which are fixed as a result of management policy.

Discount rate The interest rate used in adjusting a future cash flow to present value.

Discounted cash flow rate of return method (also called **internal rate of return method**) A method of computing the present value of future cash flows when the discount rate is not known but is defined as the rate that results in a capital project net present value of zero.

Dollar value lifo method (see **lifo method** in this glossary) A lifo method variation which reduces the cost of administering lifo and reduces the frequency with which lifo layers must be liquidated.

Drivers In ABC, the bases used to allocate overhead costs.

Dual transfer pricing A method of pricing intracompany transfers in which 1) the producing division uses a market-based, cost-plus, negotiated, or arbitrary transfer price in computing its revenue from intracompany sales and 2) the variable costs of the producing division are transferred to the purchasing division, together with an equitable portion of the fixed cost.

Earliest expected time In the PERT system, the earliest time that an activity can be expected to start.

Economic order quantity The amount of inventory ordered at one time that minimizes annual inventory ordering and carrying cost.

Efficiency variance The difference between the actual number of units of the allocation base used and the standard number of units of the allocation base allowed for actual production, multiplied by the standard factory overhead rate.

Electronic data interchange (EDI) The exchange of transaction information between a computer in one company and a computer in another.

Electronic funds transfer system (EFTS) A computerized system for electronically carrying out banking cash transfer functions.

Equivalent unit In process costing, the amount of a resource that is required to complete one unit of a product with respect to the cost element being considered.

Event In the PERT system, a specified accomplishment at a particular instant in time.

Excess capacity Greater productive capacity than a company can expect to use; or, an imbalance in equipment caused by poor synchronization of interdependent machines.

Expansion investment Plant enlargement for the purpose of expanding existing markets or invading new markets.

Expected actual capacity A short-range production capacity concept which calculates an overhead rate by basing its numerator and denominator on the expected actual output for the period.

Expected actual standard A standard set for an expected level of activity and efficiency.

Expected value The mean (average) value of a probability distribution.

External failure costs Failure costs that occur after the product has been sold.

Factory burden (also called **factory expense**, **factory overhead**, **manufacturing overhead**, **manufacturing expense**, or **indirect manufacturing cost**) Indirect materials, indirect labor, and all other factory costs that cannot be conveniently identified with specific jobs, products, or final cost objectives.

Factory cost (also called **manufacturing cost** or **production cost**) Usually, the sum of three cost elements: direct materials, direct labor, and factory overhead.

Factory expense Same as **factory burden**.

Factory overhead analysis sheet An overhead subsidiary record listing details of overhead costs.

Factory overhead budget A manufacturing budget which follows the chart of accounts, grouping costs in accounts according to natural cost classification and departmental classification.

Factory overhead Same as **factory burden**.

Failure costs Costs incurred when a product fails.

Feasible area On a graph, the feasible solution space for a linear programming problem.

Fifo method (first in, first out) An inventory costing method which, when materials are issued, assigns them the cost of the oldest supply in stock.

Final cost object A product, customer, or other entity which represents the last step in cost allocation.

Final sales volume variance Changes in profit resulting from changes in the number of physical units sold.

Financial forecast An entity's expected financial position, results of operations, and changes in cash flow, reflecting conditions expected to exist and the course of action expected to be taken.

Financial projection An entity's financial statement based on one or more hypothetical assumptions.

Fixed cost A cost that does not change in total as business activity increases or decreases.

Fixed efficiency variance The difference between the amount of fixed factory overhead that would be charged to production if based on the actual number of units of the allocation base used and the amount that would be charged to production based on the standard number of units of the allocation base allowed for actual production.

Flexible budget A budget adjusted to actual volume, providing a measure of what costs should be under any given set of conditions.

Flexible manufacturing system (FMS) An integrated collection of automated production processes, automated materials movement, and computerized system controls to manufacture efficiently a highly flexible variety of products.

Float The time between the drawing of a check and the clearing of the check back to the bank account.

Follow-up (also called **post audit**) A comparison of the actual results of a capital expenditure with the outcome that was expected when the investment project was approved.

Fringe benefits Compensation to workers in addition to normal wages or salary. This can include unemployment taxes, holiday pay, vacation pay, overtime premium pay, insurance benefits, and pension costs.

Full costing (also called **conventional costing** or **absorption costing**) Matching some or all of the fixed manufacturing costs with units of product and then expensing these costs as part of the income statement's cost of goods sold figure when the related units are sold.

Gainsharing plan (also called **organizational incentive plan**) An incentive wage plan which encourages all employees to make suggestions and contributions and which awards incentive payments to all employees for improved overall productivity.

Gross revenue method A method of costing by-products in which the final inventory cost of the main product is overstated to the extent that some of the cost belongs to the by-product.

Group bonus plans An incentive wage plan which rewards groups of workers for units produced in excess of the standard.

Heteroscedastic Characterized by differing variance at different points on the regression line.

High and low points method A method of computing the fixed and variable elements of a cost from the periods of highest and lowest activity.

Historical cost system (also called **actual cost system**) A method of collecting cost information as cost is incurred. Presentation of results is delayed until the end of the accounting period.

Homoscedastic Characterized by uniform distribution of observations around the regression line for all values of the independent variable.

Hurdle rate A discount rate in excess of cost of capital, used to compensate for risk and uncertainty.

Idle capacity A production capacity concept which factors in the idleness of workers and facilities due to a temporary lack of sales. This approach sets the denominator of the overhead rate at a lower level that reflects the idleness expected.

Idle capacity variance The difference between the budget allowance based on the actual number of units of the allocation base used in actual production and the amount of factory overhead chargeable to production in the absence of a standard cost system. The amount of over- or underabsorbed budgeted fixed factory overhead in a non-standard cost system.

Improvement expenditure An investment made to improve existing products or facilities.

Imputed cost A hypothetical cost representing the cost of a resource measured by its use value (example: loss of public goodwill that might result from laying off employees when a project is abandoned).

Incentive wage plan A payment plan which rewards workers in direct proportion to their increased high quality output.

Incremental cost (also called **marginal cost** or **differential cost**) The cost that must be incurred to complete a proposed project or to extend an activity already undertaken.

Incremental revenue (also called **marginal revenue**) Revenue which provides an increment or addition to the company's total revenue for the period.

Indirect departmental cost A cost shared by several departments that benefit from its incurrence.

Indirect expenses Nontraceable expenses incurred for more than one function or department.

Indirect labor Labor not directly traceable to the construction or composition of the finished product.

Indirect manufacturing cost (also called **factory expense**, **factory overhead**, **factory burden**, **manufacturing overhead**, or **manufacturing expense**) Indirect materials, indirect labor, and all other factory costs that cannot be conveniently identified with specific jobs, products, or final cost objectives.

Indirect materials Materials needed for the completion of a product but not classified as direct materials because they do not become part of the product or are insignificant in amount.

Internal failure costs Failure costs that occur during the manufacturing or production process.

Internal rate of return method (also called **discounted cash flow rate of return method**) A method of computing the present value of future cash flows when the discount rate is not known but is defined as the rate that results in a capital project net present value of zero.

Investment tax credit A direct reduction of tax liability, linked to investment. This credit is an important but unstable feature of the income tax law.

Item-layer identification method An inventory costing method which assigns the cost of the most recent purchase in stock to each batch of materials issued to production.

Job The output identified to fill a certain customer order or to replenish an item of stock on hand.

Job order costing (also called **job costing**) A costing method in which costs are accumulated for each job (each batch, lot, or customer order).

Job order cost sheet (also called **cost sheet**) A list, on paper or in electronic form, of details about the cost of manufacturing a specific job.

Job rate (also called **base rate**) The basic hourly pay for work performed.

Joint cost The cost that arises from the simultaneous processing or manufacturing of products produced from the same process.

Joint probabilities The probability that two (or more) events will occur.

Joint products Products produced simultaneously by a common process or series of processes, with each product possessing a more than nominal value in the form in which it is produced.

Just-in-time (JIT) A philosophy centered on the reduction of costs through elimination of inventory.

Labor efficiency variance The difference between actual hours worked and standard hours allowed, both measured at the standard labor rate.

Labor productivity The measurement of production performance using the expenditure of human effort as a yardstick; the amount of goods or services a worker produces.

Labor rate (wage or cost) variance The difference between the standard and actual rates for direct labor multiplied times the actual hours worked.

Labor time ticket A document showing the time spent by one worker on a job order or any other task.

Latest allowable time In the PERT system, the latest time that an activity can begin and not delay completion of the project.

Lead time The interval between the time an order is placed and the time the materials are on the factory floor ready for production.

Lean production (also called **stockless production** or **zero inventory production—ZIP**) Production involving an effort to reduce inventories of work in process (WIP) and raw materials.

Learning curve theory A theory stipulating that every time the cumulative quantity of units produced is doubled, the cumulative average time per unit is reduced by a given percentage.

Levels of aggregation In ABC, the four common levels of activities, activity costs, and activity drivers. The levels are unit, batch, product, and plant.

Life-cycle costing A product costing approach that assigns a share of all costs that are incurred over the life of a product.

Lifo method (last in, first out) An item-layer identification costing method which assigns the cost of the most recent purchase in stock to each batch of materials issued to production.

Linear programming A quantitative decision tool that permits the decision maker to find the optimal solution to a short-term resource allocation problem without guessing.

Long-range plans (also called **long-range budgets**) Plans, typically extending three to five years into the future, which provide an intermediate step between short-range plans and strategic plans.

Main product A manufacturer's product of greatest value.

Manufacturing budget A list of estimated manufacturing costs used to identify direct materials and direct labor costs with products and responsible managers.

Manufacturing cost (also called **production cost** or **factory cost**) Usually, the sum of three cost elements: direct materials, direct labor, and factory overhead.

Manufacturing expense (also called **factory expense**, **factory overhead**, **factory burden**, **manufacturing overhead**, or **indirect manufacturing cost**) Indirect materials, indirect labor, and all other factory costs that cannot be conveniently identified with specific jobs, products, or final cost objectives.

Manufacturing overhead Same as **manufacturing expense**.

Margin of safety ratio (M/S) The margin of safety expressed as a percentage of sales.

Margin of safety The difference between the targeted level of sales and the break-even point.

Marginal cost of capital The specific cost of financing a specific project.

Marginal cost (also called **differential cost** or **incremental cost**) The cost that must be incurred to complete a proposed project or to extend an activity already undertaken.

Marginal costing (also called **direct costing** or **variable costing**) A costing method that assigns only variable manufacturing costs to products. Fixed overhead is expensed.

Marginal income (also called **contribution margin**) The difference between sales revenue and variable costs.

Marginal revenue (Also called **incremental revenue**) Revenue which provides an increment or addition to the company's total revenue for the period.

Market value method A method of allocating joint costs to joint products on the basis of their relative market value at the split-off point.

Market value (reversal cost) method A method of costing by-products which reduces the manufacturing cost of the main product(s) by the excess of the by-product's market value over its separately identifiable costs.

Market-based transfer pricing A method of pricing intracompany transfers based on the price charged to outside customers.

Marketing expenses budget A list of the estimated costs of marketing activities.

Marketing expenses Post-manufacturing expenses including promotion, selling, and delivery.

Marketing function A unit organized to control and analyze marketing expenses related to specific items of cost.

Materials inventory variance The standard cost of the increase or decrease in materials inventory.

Materials price usage variance A materials price variance recorded at the time materials are issued to the factory.

Materials purchase price variance A materials price variance recorded at the time materials are purchased.

Materials quantity (or **usage**) **variance** A variance computed by a comparison of the actual quantity of materials used with the standard quantity allowed, both measured at standard cost.

Materials record cards Cards which record each receipt and issuance of each kind of material and serve as perpetual inventory records.

Materials requirements planning (MRP) A computer simulation for managing materials requirements based on each product's bill of materials, inventory status, and process of manufacture.

Materials requisition Authorization for the storeroom or warehouse to deliver specified types and quantities of materials to a given department at a specified time.

Method of least squares (also called **regression analysis**) A cost behavior analysis method which determines mathematically a line of best fit or a linear regression line through a set of plotted points.

Min-max method A materials control method which establishes a maximum quantity for each item and also provides a minimum level to prevent stockouts during a reorder cycle.

Mix (or **blend**) **variance** The difference between the actual quantity of materials at the actual mix and the actual quantity at the standard mix, both priced at standard cost.

Modified accelerated cost recovery system (**MACRS**) ACRS modified to increase the number of property classes and lengthen the recovery periods of most kinds of depreciable property.

Monte Carlo simulations Computer simulations that contain stochastic variables.

Multiattribute decision model (**MADM**) An expenditure evaluation tool that explicitly incorporates both quantitative and non-quantitative factors into the decision analysis.

Multicollinearity A condition in which two or more independent variables in a multiple regression are correlated with one another.

Multiple regression analysis An application and expansion of the method of least squares, permitting consideration of more than one independent variable.

Negotiated transfer pricing A method of pricing intracompany transfers in which the transfer price is set by negotiation between buying and selling divisions.

Net present value index Net present value divided by required investment. Used to compare projects that require different initial investments.

Net present value method A method of computing the present value of future cash flows to assist in capital budgeting.

Net revenue method A method of costing by-products which recognizes the need for assigning traceable cost to the by-product.

Network In the PERT system, an organized overview of all the individual activities that complete a given job or program.

Non-value added activities Business activities which expend resources without adding value to the product, or general activities of the firm, not specific to the production of any particular good or service.

Nonfinancial performance measures Measurements of simple physical data, rather than accounting data, used to evaluate performance.

Normal capacity A long-range production capacity concept which calculates an overhead rate by basing its numerator and denominator on average utilization of the physical plant over a long time period.

Normal standard A standard set for a normal level of activity and efficiency.

Normal time The time it should take a person working at a normal pace to do a job.

Objective function In linear programming, the total contribution margin obtainable from the production and sale of one or more products in a maximization problem or the total cost in a minimization problem.

Opportunity cost The measurable value of an opportunity bypassed by rejecting the best alternative use of resources.

Order cycling method (also called **cycle review method**) A materials control method which periodically examines the status of quantities on hand for each item of class of materials.

Order point The point in the production process when the available quantity of materials is just equal to foreseeable needs.

Organization The systematization of interdependent parts into one unit.

Organization chart A chart showing an entity's principal management positions in order to define authority, responsibility and accountability.

Organizational incentive plans (also called **gainsharing plan**) An incentive wage plan which encourages all employees to make suggestions and contributions and which awards incentive payments to all employees for improved overall productivity.

Out-of-pocket cost The cash outlay required to complete a proposed project or to extend an activity already undertaken.

Overall (or **net**) **factory overhead variance** The difference between factory overhead actually incurred and the cost of factory overhead chargeable to work in process for the period.

Overapplied overhead Applied overhead in excess of actual overhead. This results in a credit balance in the factory overhead control account.

Overhead allocation base (also called **overhead rate base** or **base**) An activity to which costs are attributed for overhead accounting purposes, or the factor included in the denominator of an overhead rate.

Overhead rate base Same as **overhead allocation base**.

Parallel product flow A physical production flow format in which certain portions of the work are done simultaneously and then brought together in a final process or processes for completion and transfer to finished goods.

Payback period method (also called the **payout period method**) A technique for measuring the length of time required by a project to recover the initial cash outlay.

Payoff table A table that presents both the conditional value of each event that can occur for each course of action being considered and the expected value of each alternative based on the probabilities of the events that can occur.

Payout period method Same as **payback period method**.

Pension plan An arrangement whereby a company provides retirement benefit payments for all employees in recognition of their work contribution to the company.

Percentage of profit to sales Profit divided by sales.

Performance rating (also called **rating**) The pace at which an observed person is working. Ratings are used to set labor standards.

PERT/cost An expansion of PERT which assigns cost to time and activities, thereby providing total financial planning and control by functional responsibility.

PERT Program evaluation and review technique.

Planning The construction of a detailed operating program.

Planning, programming, budgeting system (PPBS) A method of analyzing alternatives which provides a basis for rational decision making. This system assists in the allocation of resources and helps accomplish stated goals and objectives over a designated time period.

Plant-level costs The costs of sustaining capacity at a production site (examples: rent and insurance).

Plant-level driver In ABC, a measure of plant-level costs.

Post audit (also called **follow-up**) A comparison of the actual results of a capital expenditure with the outcome that was expected when the investment project was approved.

Postdeduction (also called **postmanufacturing deduction**) A step of backflush costing in which the cost of completed work is subtracted from the balance of the work in process account or an equivalent combined raw and in process account.

Posterior probability The probability, estimated after the occurrence of a related event, that one or more events will occur as a result of the related event.

Practical capacity The production capacity of a department as influenced by internal factors such as breakdowns, unsatisfactory materials, labor shortages, and other inefficiencies.

Pragmatic method An approach to setting profit objectives in which management uses a profit standard that has been tested empirically and sanctioned by experience.

Predetermined overhead rate An estimated rate which allows factory overhead costs to be allocated to each unit of output.

Present value The present cash equivalent of an estimated future cash flow.

Present value of an annuity The present cash equivalent of the future value of an annuity.

Prevention costs Cost incurred to prevent product failure.

Prime cost Direct materials cost plus direct labor cost.

Prior probability The probability, estimated before the occurrence of a related event, that one or more events will occur.

Probability analysis an application of statistical decision theory that, under conditions of uncertainty, leads to more consistent and reliable decisions than single best guesses.

Probability Technically, a number between 0 and 1 that represents the likelihood of the occurrence of a particular event. Or, the relative frequency of the occurrence of different recurring events.

Process costing A method in which materials, labor, and factory overhead are charged to cost centers. The cost assigned to each unit of product manufactured is determined by dividing the total cost charged to the cost center by the number of units produced.

Process time The total time that the manufacturing process requires to produce a unit of product.

Producing department A department involved in manufacturing a product by changing the form or nature of material or by assembling parts.

Product-level costs Costs incurred to support the number of different products produced (examples: costs of product design and development).

Product-level driver In ABC, a measure of an activity that varies with the number of different products produced and sold (examples: design changes and design hours).

Production budget The master plan from which details concerning materials requirements are developed. Usually a list of units required to meet the sales budget, considering beginning inventory and desired ending inventory.

Production cost (also called **manufacturing cost** or **factory cost**) Usually, the sum of three cost elements: direct materials, direct labor, and factory overhead.

Productivity-efficiency ratio The measurement of the output of an individual relative to the performance standard.

Profit maximization A business approach whose primary objective is to obtain the largest amount of profit possible.

Profit planning The process of consciously developing a well-thought-out operational plan that will achieve a company's goals and objectives.

Program evaluation and review technique (**PERT**) (also called the **critical path method** (**CPM**)) A network analysis method for planning, measuring progress to schedule, evaluating changes to schedule, forecasting future progress, and predicting and controlling costs.

Programmed fixed costs (also called **discretionary fixed costs**) Expenditures which are fixed as a result of management policy.

Purchase order A contract for quantities of materials to be delivered.

Purchase requisition A list that informs the purchasing agent of the quantity and kind of materials needed.

Purchases budget A manufacturing budget which lists the quantity and cost of materials that must be purchased during the period to meet the budgeted production requirements.

Quantitative unit method A method of allocating joint production cost to joint products by distributing the total joint cost on the basis of some common unit of measurement.

Rate of return on capital employed (also called **return on investment**) The ratio of profit to capital employed in a business.

Rating (also called **performance rating**) The pace at which an observed person is working. Ratings are used to set labor standards.

Receiving report A report certifying quantities received, sometimes including results of inspection and quality testing.

Regression analysis (also called **method of least squares**) A cost behavior analysis method which determines mathematically a line of best fit or a linear regression line through a set of plotted points.

Relevant range A limited range of activity within which an expenditure can be accurately classified as fixed or variable.

Replacement cost method A method of costing by-products in which the production cost of the main product is credited for the replacement cost of the by-products used within the plant. The offsetting debit is to the department that uses the by-product.

Replacement expenditures Expenditures incurred by the replacement of worn-out or obsolescent assets.

Research and development (**R&D**) *Research* is planned effort to discover new knowledge which will be useful in developing a new product or service or a new process or technique. *Development* is the translation of knowledge into a plan or a design for a new product or process.

Residual income A division's income less an amount representing the company's cost of capital employed by the division.

Resource driver In ABC, a base used to allocate the cost of a resource to the different activities using that resource. (Examples: square feet occupied)

Responsibility accounting and reporting An accounting system which records and reports costs incurred as a result of each activity in the company to the individual manager who is responsible for that activity.

Responsibility The obligation to perform a duty and to be held accountable.

Return on capital employed A desired rate of return, used in price-setting formulas.

Return on investment (ROI) Same as **rate of return on capital employed**.

Revenue expenditure A cost which benefits the current period and is reported as an expense.

Rework The process of correcting defective goods.

Routing In a production process, the sequence of operations to be performed.

Sales budget A realistic sales estimate based on analyses of past sales and the present market.

Sales mix variance Changes in profit caused by changes in the mix of products sold.

Sales price variance The actual quantity of products sold times the changes in sales prices.

Sales volume variance Changes in the quantity of products sold priced at budgeted (or standard) prices.

Salvage value The amount of cash inflow expected from the final sale of a property used in a capital project at the end of the life of the capital project.

Scattergraph method A cost behavior analysis method in which the cost being analyzed (the dependent variable) is plotted on the y-axis and the associated activity (the independent variable) is plotted on the x-axis.

Scrap Filings or trimmings remaining after processing materials, defective materials that cannot be used or returned to the vendor, and broken parts resulting from employee or machine failures.

Selective control (also called the **ABC Plan**) A materials control method which evaluates the cost significance of each item as high-value (**A** items), middle-value (**B** items), or low-value (**C** items). Not to be confused with activity-based costing.

Selective product flow A physical production flow format in which the product moves to different departments within the plant, depending on what final product is to be produced.

Semivariable cost A cost that displays both fixed and variable characteristics.

Separable product costs Costs identifiable with an individual product.

Sequential method (also called **step method**) A method of distributing service department costs in a prescribed order by department.

Sequential product flow A physical production flow format in which each product is processed in the same series of steps.

Serial correlation (also called **autocorrelation**) A pattern in which the observations around the regression line appear to be correlated with one another.

Service department A department which contributes indirectly to the manufacture of a product but does not change the form, assembly, or nature of the material.

Short-range plans (often called **budgets**) Highly detailed plans, usually for a month, quarter, or year, focusing on the organization's internal operations.

Simplex method A method of algebraically solving linear programming problems with more than two variables.

Simultaneous method (also called **algebraic method**) A method of distributing service department costs which considers completely all interrelationships among all service departments.

Slack time In the PERT system, the amount of time that can be added to an activity without increasing the total time required on the critical path.

Sold-hour rate (also called **billing rate**, **charging rate**, or **transfer rate**) A device for distributing overhead costs, based on the idea that departments purchase internal services the same way they purchase materials, supplies, and labor.

Specification error The omission of important variables from the multiple-regression model.

Spending variance The difference between actual overhead and a budget adjusted to actual activity. Caused by price and quantity differences.

Split-off point The point in the manufacturing process at which joint products emerge as individual units.

Spoiled goods (also called **spoilage**) Partially or fully completed units that are defective and not correctible.

Standard cost pricing A pricing method which uses standard costs as a basis for pricing.

Standard cost system A system in which products, operations, and processes are costed based on predetermined quantities of resources to be used and predetermined prices of those resources.

Standard cost The cost that should be attained in an efficiently operated plant at normal capacity, or the predetermined cost of manufacturing a single unit or a specific quantity of product during a specific period.

Standard deviation The square root of the variance. Provides a numerical measure of the scatter of the possible conditional values around the expected value.

Standard error of the estimate The standard deviation about the regression line. It is used to determine whether a given level of cost variance requires management action.

Standard time The time it should take a person to do a job, including personal time, rest periods, and possible delays. Standard time is expressed in minutes per piece or units per hour.

Statement of cash flows A financial statement often accompanying the income statement and balance sheet.

Static budget A budget based on a single expected level of business activity.

Step method (also called **sequential method**) A method of distributing service department costs in a prescribed order by department. It considers some, but not all, interrelationships among service departments.

Stochastic process A process that generates events that appear to occur at random.

Stockless production (also called **lean production** or **zero inventory production—ZIP**) Production involving an effort to reduce inventories of work in process (WIP) and raw materials.

Straight piecework plan An incentive wage plan which pays a set wage for each unit produced.

Strategic plans Long-range plans, made at high management levels, concerned with a broad view of the firm, its products, its customers, and its environment.

Subsidiary accounts (also called **subsidiary records**) Highly specific accounts supporting a controlling account.

Subsidiary records Same as **subsidiary accounts**.

Sunk cost An expenditure that has already been made and cannot be recovered.

Super absorption (also called **super-full absorption**) A tax requirement that certain purchasing and storage costs be allocated to inventory in addition to full manufacturing costs.

Target pricing A pricing strategy, designed to create a competitive advantage, which prices the product as if its market share were larger than it actually is and as if its costs were less than they actually are.

Terminal value The value of all cash flows at the end of the life of a project based on the reinvestment rate.

Theoretical capacity The capacity of a department to produce at full speed without interruptions.

Theoretical standard A standard set for an ideal or maximum level of activity and efficiency.

Three-variance method A method of factory overhead cost accounting in which the amount of over- or underapplied factory overhead can be analyzed as spending, variable efficiency, and volume variances.

Throughput time In production, units in process divided by units produced per day.

Time clock (also called **time recorder**) A mechanical instrument for recording employee time in and out of the office and the factory.

Time recorder Same as **time clock**.

Time ticket A ticket which shows the specific use of an employee's work time.

Total quality management A companywide approach to quality improvement that seeks to improve quality in all processes and activities.

Traceability The accuracy with which costs can be attributed to a particular cost object.

Transactions-base approach An overhead costing method which allows for the fact that certain significant overhead costs are not driven by volume of output.

Transfer rate (also called **sold-hour rate**, **billing rate** or **charging rate**) A device for distributing overhead costs, based on the idea that departments purchase internal services the same way they purchase materials, supplies, and labor.

Two-bin method A materials control method in which each stock item is stored in two bins, piles, or bundles whose quantities are coordinated with planned order and delivery dates.

Two-variance method A method of factory overhead cost accounting which divides the balance in the factory overhead control account between the controllable variance and the volume variance.

Underapplied overhead Actual overhead which has not been allocated to products. This results in a debit balance in the factory overhead control account.

Unit-based system A costing system which exclusively uses unit-level measures as bases for allocating overhead to output.

Unit-level costs In ABC, costs that inevitably increase whenever a unit of product is produced (examples: electricity cost and inspection labor).

Unit-level driver In ABC, a measure of an activity that varies with the number of units produced and sold (examples: labor hours and machine hours).

Variable cost A cost that increases in total proportionately with an increase in activity and decreases proportionately with a decrease in activity.

Variable costing (also called **direct costing**) A costing method in which costs allocated to units of production include only the variable manufacturing costs. Total fixed costs are expensed.

Variable efficiency variance The difference between the actual amount of the allocation base used and the standard amount of the allocation base allowed for actual production, multiplied by the variable factory overhead rate.

Variance A statistical measure of the scatter of the possible conditional values around the expected value. Also, the difference between actual costs and budgeted costs, or the difference between actual costs and standard costs.

Velocity In production, the speed with which units or tasks are processed in a system.

Volume variance The difference between the budget allowance based on the standard amount of the allocation base allowed for actual production and the standard factory overhead chargeable to work in process. The amount of over- or underapplied budgeted fixed factory overhead in a standard cost system.

Weighted-average cost of capital Cost of capital which varies depending on the mix and proportion of the sources of funds used to finance a business.

Weighted-average method A method of allocating joint production cost to joint products by assigning predetermined weight factors to each unit.

Work cell (also called **cell**) An assemblage of workers and machines responsible for the entire production of one product or part, or a family of very similar ones.

Yield variance The cost of the difference between the yield expected from actual materials input and the yield obtained.

Zero inventory production (also called **stockless production** or **lean production**) Production involving an effort to reduce inventories of work in process (WIP) and raw materials.

Zero-base budgeting A budget-planning procedure which requires all managers to justify their entire budget requests in detail.

Index